Survey of Accounting

Thomas P. Edmonds
University of Alabama—Birmingham

Cindy D. Edmonds
University of Alabama—Birmingham

Frances M. McNair
Mississippi State University

Philip R. Olds
Virginia Commonwealth University

Bor-Yi Tsay
University of Alabama—Birmingham

Edward E. Milam
Mississippi State University

Boston Burr Ridge, IL Dubuque, IA Madison, WI New York
San Francisco St. Louis Bangkok Bogotá Caracas Kuala Lumpur
Lisbon London Madrid Mexico City Milan Montreal New Delhi
Santiago Seoul Singapore Sydney Taipei Toronto

SURVEY OF ACCOUNTING
Published by McGraw-Hill/Irwin, a business unit of The McGraw-Hill Companies, Inc., 1221 Avenue of the Americas, New York, NY, 10020.

This book is printed on acid-free paper.

1 2 3 4 5 6 7 8 9 0 WCK/WCK 0 9 8 7 6

ISBN-13: 978-0-07-110650-4
ISBN-10: 0-07-110650-2

www.mhhe.com

Brief Contents

Contents

Chapter 1 Elements of Financial Statements 2

Chapter 2 Understanding the Accounting Cycle 40

Chapter 4 Accounting for Inventories 124

Chapter 5 Accounting for Receivables 162

Chapter 7 Accounting for Liabilities 244

Chapter 8 Proprietorships, Partnerships, and Corporations 280

Chapter 9 Financial Statement Analysis 314

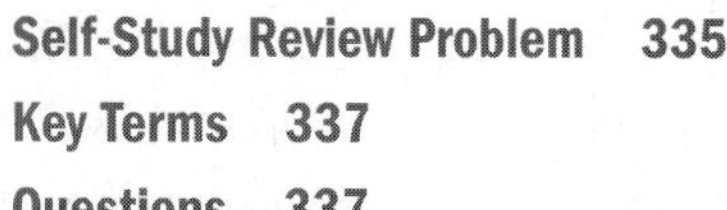

Chapter 10 Management Accounting: A Value-Added Discipline 354

Chapter 11 Cost Behavior, Operating Leverage, and Profitability Analysis 390

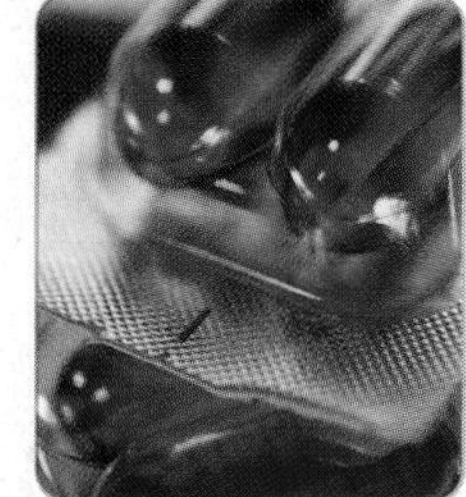

Chapter 13 Relevant Information for Special Decisions 452

Chapter 14 Planning for Profit and Cost Control 488

Chapter 15 Performance Evaluation 520

Chapter 16 Planning for Capital Investments 552

ABOUT THE AUTHORS

Thomas P. Edmonds

Thomas P. Edmonds, Ph.D., is the Friends and Alumni Professor of Accounting at the University of Alabama at Birmingham (UAB). Dr. Edmonds has taught in the introductory area throughout his career. He has coordinated the accounting principles courses at the University of Houston and UAB. He currently teaches introductory accounting in mass sections and in UAB's distance learning program. He is actively involved in the accounting education change movement. He has conducted more that 50 workshops related to teaching introductory accounting during the last decade. Dr. Edmonds has received numerous prestigious teaching awards including the 2005 Alabama Society of CPAs Outstanding Educator Award and the UAB President's Excellence in Teaching Award. Dr. Edmonds's current research is education based. He has written articles that have appeared in many publications including the *Accounting Review, Issues in Accounting, Journal of Accounting Education,* and *Advances in Accounting Education.* Dr. Edmonds has been a successful entrepreneur. He has worked as a management accountant for a transportation company and as a commercial lending officer for the Federal Home Loan Bank. Dr. Edmonds began his academic training at Young Harris Community College. His Ph.D. degree was awarded by Georgia State University. Dr. Edmonds's work experience and academic training have enabled him to bring a unique perspective to the classroom.

Cindy D. Edmonds

Cindy D. Edmonds, Ph.D., is an Associate Professor of Accounting at the University of Alabama at Birmingham. She serves as the coordinator of the introductory accounting courses at UAB. Dr. Edmonds has received five prestigious teaching awards. Dr. Edmonds's articles appear in numerous publications including *Advances in Accounting Education, Journal of Education for Business, Journal of Accounting Regulation, Advances in Accounting, Management Accounting, CMA Journal, Disclosures,* and *Business & Professional Ethics Journal.* Dr. Edmonds is heavily involved in service activities. She is a past president of the Birmingham Chapter of the American Society of Women Accountants. Dr. Edmonds has worked in the insurance industry, in a manufacturing company, and in a governmental agency. This work experience has enabled her to bring a real-world flavor to her writing. Dr. Edmonds holds a B.S. degree from Auburn University, an M.B.A degree from the University of Houston, and a Ph.D. degree from the University of Alabama.

Frances M. McNair

Frances M. McNair holds the KPMG Peat Marwick Professorship in Accounting at Mississippi State University (MSU). She has been involved in teaching principles of accounting for the past 12 years and currently serves as the coordinator for the principles of accounting courses at MSU. She joined the MSU faculty in 1987 after receiving her Ph.D. from the University of Mississippi. The author of various articles that have appeared in the *Journal of Accountancy, Management Accounting, Business and Professional Ethics Journal, The Practical Accountant, Taxes,* and other publications, she also coauthored the book *The Tax Practitioner* with Dr. Denzil Causey. Dr. McNair is currently serving on committees of the American Taxation Association, the American Accounting Association, and the Institute of Management Accountants as well as numerous School of Accountancy and MSU committees.

Philip R. Olds

Philip R. Olds is Associate Professor of Accounting at Virginia Commonwealth University (VCU). He serves as the coordinator of the introduction to accounting courses at VCU. Professor Olds received his A.S. degree from Brunswick Junior College in Brunswick, Georgia (now Costal Georgia Community College). He received a B.B.A. in Accounting from Georgia Southern College (now Georgia Southern University) and his M.P.A. and Ph.D. degrees from Georgia State University. After graduating from Georgia Southern, he worked as an auditor with the U.S. Department of Labor in Atlanta, Georgia. A CPA in Virginia, Professor Olds has published articles in various professional journals and presented papers at national and regional conferences. He also served as the faculty adviser to the VCU chapter of Beta Alpha Psi for five years. In 1989, he was recognized with an Outstanding Faculty Vice President Award by the national Beta Alpha Psi organization.

Bor-Yi Tsay

Bor-Yi Tsay, Ph.D., CPA, is Professor of Accounting at the University of Alabama at Birmingham (UAB) where he has taught since 1986. He has taught principles of accounting courses at the University of Houston and UAB. Dr. Tsay received the 1996 Loudell Ellis Robinson Excellence in Teaching Award. He has also received numerous awards for his writing and publications including the John L. Rhoads Manuscripts Award, the John Pugsley Manuscripts Award, the Van Pelt Manuscripts Award, and three certificates of merit from the Institute of Management Accountants. His articles have appeared in the *Journal of Accounting Education, Management Accounting, Journal of Managerial Issues, CPA Journal, CMA Magazine, Journal of Systems Management,* and *Journal of Medical Systems.* He currently serves as the treasurer of the Birmingham Chapter, Institute of Management Accountants. Dr. Tsay received a B.S. in Agricultural Economics from National Taiwan University, an M.B.A. from Eastern Washington University, and a Ph.D. in Accounting from the University of Houston.

Edward E. Milam

Edward E. Milam, Ph.D., CPA, is a Professor of Accounting at Mississippi State University (MSU). Dr. Milam has been the recipient of several prestigious teaching awards including the Federation of Schools of Accountancy Outstanding Educator Award, and the Mississippi Society of CPAs Educator of the Year Award. Dr. Milam is a past President of the Federation of Schools of Accountancy, and has served on various committees of the ATA, FSA, AICPA, American Accounting Association, and the Mississippi Society of Certified Public Accountants. He has authored numerous articles that have appeared in publications including *Journal of Accountancy, Taxes, Management Accounting, Financial Executive, Estate Planning, Trusts and Estates, CPA Journal,* and others. He has also coauthored seven books.

NOTE FROM AUTHORS

Over the past 15 years, major changes in accounting education have impacted the way most college and university professors teach introductory accounting. We are gratified that our concepts approach has been so effective that it has become a market leader in the change movement.

"I heartily applaud the authors' goal of providing students with a concepts-based approach rather than a strictly procedure-based approach to be an important contribution to improving accounting education, one that appeals to both users and preparers and that enables students to 'read between the lines.'"

MICHAEL R. DODGE, COASTAL CAROLINA COMMUNITY COLLEGE

HOW HAVE WE BECOME MARKET LEADERS?

We look at ourselves as innovative traditionalists. We don't aim to radically transform accounting education, but to make it more effective. With the concepts approach, students follow a different path toward the accomplishment of a conventional set of learning objectives. However, the path is easier to walk and students complete the journey with a far greater understanding of accounting.

In contrast to traditional textbooks, this is a **concepts-based approach** that **focuses on the big picture**. Details are presented after a conceptual foundation has been established. This approach enables students to understand rather than memorize. What do we mean by a concepts-based textbook? We mean the text stresses the relationships between business events and financial statements. The primary objective is to develop students who can explain how business events affect the income statement, balance sheet, and statement of cash flows. Do assets increase, decrease or remain unchanged? What effect does each event have on liabilities, equity, revenue, expense, gains, losses, net income, and dividends? Furthermore, how does the event affect cash flows? **The focus is on learning how business events affect financial statements.**

IMPLEMENTING THE CONCEPTS APPROACH IS SURPRISINGLY SIMPLE.

Instead of teaching students to record transactions in journals or T-accounts, teach them to record transactions directly into financial statements. While this shift is easy for instructors, it represents a dramatic improvement in how students have traditionally studied accounting. Making a direct connection between business events and financial statements encourages students to analyze conceptual relationships rather than memorize procedures.

This text helps teachers move from the traditional educational paradigm more easily than you might imagine. The content focuses on essential concepts, reducing the amount of material you must cover, and giving you more time to work on skill development. The Instructor's Resource Manual provides step-by-step instructions for implementing innovative teaching methods such as active learning and group dynamics. It offers enticing short discovery learning cases which provide class-opening experiences that effectively stimulate student interest and help develop critical thinking skills.

BUT DON'T TAKE OUR WORD FOR IT.

With over 200 colleges and universities successfully making the change to the concepts approach, we feel confident you will experience the same success as many of your colleagues. We would like to thank all of those who have been supportive of our teaching philosophy, and we highly encourage you to contact the author team or your local McGraw-Hill/Irwin representative to learn more about our texts.

Tom Edmonds+Cindy Edmonds+Frances McNair+Phil Olds +Bor-Yi Tsay

"Very clear, concise, yet sophisticated treatment of topics."

NICHOLAS P. MARUDAS, AUBURN UNIVERSITY AT MONTGOMERY

"I would say it is a positive, new approach to teaching an old subject."

FRANK BAGAN, COUNTY COLLEGE OF MORRIS

"I couldn't recommend this text too highly to any of my colleagues. It literally puts the 'sizzle' back into the teaching process!"

MICHAEL R. DODGE, COASTAL CAROLINA COMMUNITY COLLEGE

HOW DOES THIS BOOK HELP STUDENTS SEE THE BIG PICTURE?

"[The Horizontal Financial Statements Model is] well organized and a straightforward way to show the effects of transactions."

ANDY WILLIAMS, EDMONDS COMMUNITY COLLEGE

HORIZONTAL FINANCIAL STATEMENTS MODEL

A horizontal financial statements model replaces the accounting equation as the predominant teaching platform in this text. The model arranges the balance sheet, income statement, and statement of cash flows horizontally across a single line of text as shown below.

Assets	=	Liabilities	+	Stockholders' Equity	Revenue	−	Expense	=	Net Income	Cash Flow

The statements model approach enables students to see how accounting relates to real-world decision making. The traditional approach teaches students to journalize a series of events and to present summarized information in financial statements. They never see how individual transactions affect financial statements. In contrast, when students record transactions into a statements model, they see a direct connection between business events and financial statements. Most business people think "if I take this particular action, how will it affect my financials," not "if I do these fifteen things, how will they be journalized." Accordingly, the statements model approach provides a learning experience that is more intuitive and relevant than the one provided by traditional teaching methodology.

ESTABLISHING THE CONCEPTUAL FRAMEWORK

Chapter 1 introduces the key components of the conceptual framework for financial accounting. We expect students to master not only the definitions of financial statement elements but also the relationships between those elements. For example, the term "asset" is defined and then the term "revenue" is defined as an increase in assets. The definitions are expanded in a logical stepwise fashion. Once students have learned the elements, the text explains how to organize those elements into a set of financial statements. The financial statements model is introduced toward the end of the first chapter.

Accruals and deferrals are introduced in **Chapter 2** and it not only introduces new concepts but reinforces the core concepts introduced in Chapter 1. The basic conceptual components of the income statement are reinforced through repetition. By the time students have completed the first two chapters, they have a strong conceptual foundation.

THE EFFECTS OF CASH FLOWS ARE SHOWN THROUGH THE ENTIRE TEXT.

The statement of cash flows is introduced in the first chapter and included throughout the text. Students learn to prepare a statement of cash flows in the first chapter by learning to analyze each increase and decrease in the cash account. They can prepare a statement of cash flows by classifying each entry in the cash account as an operating, investing, or financing activity. This logical approach helps students understand the essential differences between cash flows and accrual-based income.

EFFECTS OF FINANCIAL STATEMENTS OVER MULTIPLE ACCOUNTING CYCLES

The text also uses a vertical statements model that shows financial statements from top to bottom on a single page. This model displays financial results for consecutive accounting cycles in adjacent columns, thereby enabling the instructor to show how related events are reported over multiple accounting cycles.

Exhibit 2
Elden Enterprises
Financial Statements Under Double-declining-balance

Income Statements	2003	2004	2005	2006	2007
Rent Revenue	$15,000	$ 9,000	$ 5,000	$ 3,000	$ -0-
Depreciation Expense	12,000	6,000	2,000	-0-	-0-
Operating Income	3,000	3,000	3,000	3,000	-0-
Gain on sale of Van	-0-	-0-	-0-	-0-	500
Net Income	$ 3,000	$ 3,000	$ 3,000	$ 3,000	$ 500
Balance Sheets					
Assets:					
Cash	$16,000	$25,000	$30,000	$33,000	$37,500
Van	24,000	24,000	24,000	24,000	-0-
Accumulated Depreciation	(12,000)	(18,000)	(20,000)	(20,000)	-0-
Total Assets	$28,000	$31,000	$34,000	$37,000	$37,500
Stockholders' Equity					
Common Stock	$25,000	$25,000	$25,000	$25,000	$25,000
Retained Earnings	3,000	6,000	9,000	12,000	12,500
Total Stockholders' Equity	$28,000	$31,000	$34,000	$37,000	$37,500
Statements of Cash Flows					
Operating Activities					
Inflow from Customers	15,000	9,000	5,000	3,000	-0-
Investing Activities					
Outflow to Purchase Van	(24,000)				
Inflow from Sale of Van					4,500
Financing Activities					
Inflow from Stock Issue	25,000				
Net Change in Cash	16,000	9,000	5,000	3,000	4,500
Beginning Cash Balance	0	16,000	25,000	30,000	33,000
Ending Cash Balance	$16,000	$25,000	$30,000	$33,000	$37,500

"I really like this approach of bringing the conceptual framework up front, helping students see the big picture before they find themselves bogged down in details. I find that students who have the clearest appreciation of the conceptual framework early have the greatest chance of mastering the details later on."

MICHAEL R. DODGE,
COASTAL CAROLINA
COMMUNITY COLLEGE

"I wish I had learned it (cash flows) this way. This helps our accounting students tremendously as they have a smoother transition into intermediate accounting. You make a difficult topic much easier to understand!"

SONDRA SMITH,
UNIVERSITY OF WEST GEORGIA

"I think the integration of the financial statements in the chapters is excellent. It reinforces the concepts."

RACHEL PERNIA, ESSEX COUNTY COLLEGE

MANAGERIAL ACCOUNTING CONCEPTS

Traditional texts have emphasized accounting practices for manufacturing companies, while the business environment has shifted toward service companies. This text recognizes this critical shift by emphasizing decision-making concepts applicable to both service and manufacturing companies. Topics such as cost behavior, operating leverage, and cost allocation are introduced early. Traditional topics such as manufacturing cost flow, job-order costing, and process costing are deemphasized.

A CONSISTENT POINT OF REFERENCE

Why do good students sometimes have so much trouble grasping the simplest concepts? A recent introductory accounting workshop participant supplied the answer. Most accounting events are described from the perspective of the business entity. For example, we say the business borrowed money, purchased assets, earned revenue, or incurred expenses. However, we usually shift the point of reference when describing equity transactions. We say the owners contributed capital, provided cash, or invested assets in the business. This reference shift confuses an entry-level accounting student. Your students will appreciate the fact that this text uses the business entity as a consistent point of reference in describing all accounting events. Accounting is a new language for most business students, so this text makes a conscious effort to minimize the road blocks that are frequently raised by the inconsistent use of technical terminology.

FOCUS ON CORPORATE FORM OF ORGANIZATION

We want students to learn that businesses acquire assets from three primary sources: from creditors, from investors, and from earnings. The corporate organization structure highlights these three asset sources by using separate account categories for liabilities, contributed capital, and retained earnings. We have found the corporate form to be pedagogically superior to the proprietorship form in the educational setting. While we cover accounting for proprietorships and partnerships in a separate chapter of the text, we use the corporate form as the primary teaching platform.

LESS IS MORE

Many educators recognize the detrimental effect of information overload. Research suggests that students resort to memorization when faced with too much content, and are unable to comprehend basic concepts. We make a conscious choice to reduce the breadth of content coverage in order to enhance student comprehension of concepts. For example, you don't need to teach both the net and gross methods to explain how cash discounts affect financial statements. Demonstrating just one method is sufficient to demonstrate the critical interrelationships.

By eliminating less critical details, this text is able to focus on developing a conceptual framework. This framework enables students to understand, rather than memorize, and less detail results in greater comprehension.

ANNUAL REPORT

The 2003 annual report for The Topps Company, Inc., is printed in Appendix B.

Business application problems related to the annual report are included at the end of each chapter.

In the Annual Report and Financial Statement Analysis Projects, located on the text website and the Instructor's Manual, projects for Topps Company are included, as well as a general purpose annual report project instructors can assign for any company's annual report.

"Very readable and understandable on the student level. Should be an easier approach for students to understand. Not too much material in any one chapter – smaller bites will be easier for students to digest."

LYNN A. SUBERLY,
VALDOSTA STATE UNIVERSITY

EXCEL SPREADSHEETS

Spreadsheet applications are essential to contemporary accounting practice. Students must recognize the power of spreadsheets and know how accounting data are presented in spreadsheets. We discuss Excel applications where appropriate throughout the text. In most instances, the text illustrates actual spreadsheets. End-of-chapter materials include problems students can complete using spreadsheet software.

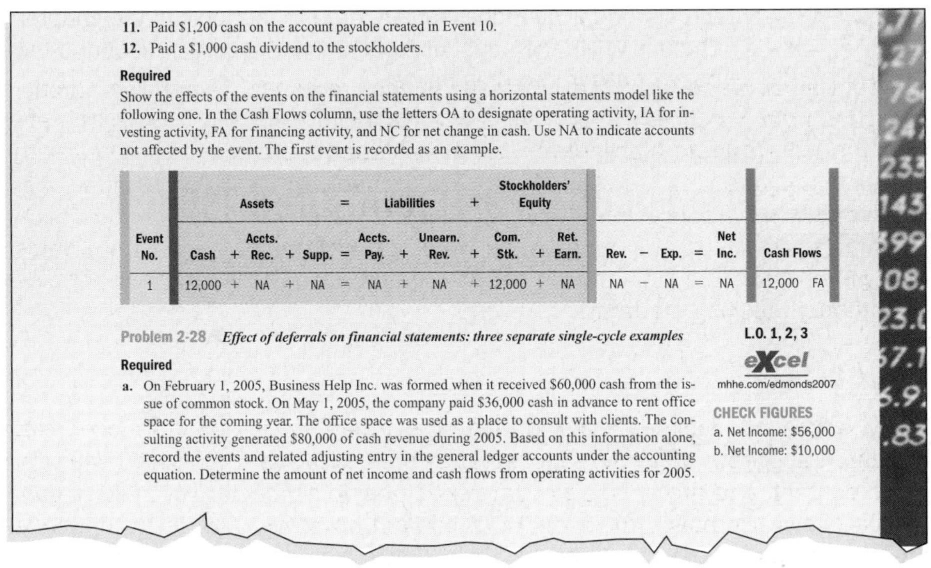

11. Paid $1,200 cash on the account payable created in Event 10.
12. Paid a $1,000 cash dividend to the stockholders.

Required

Show the effects of the events on the financial statements using a horizontal statements model like the following one. In the Cash Flows column, use the letters OA to designate operating activity, IA for investing activity, FA for financing activity, and NC for net change in cash. Use NA to indicate accounts not affected by the event. The first event is recorded as an example.

	Assets					=	Liabilities			+	Stockholders' Equity								
Event No.	Cash	+	Accts. Rec.	+	Supp.	=	Accts. Pay.	+	Unearn. Rev.	+	Com. Stk.	+	Ret. Earn.	Rev.	−	Exp.	=	Net Inc.	Cash Flows
1	12,000	+	NA	+	NA	=	NA	+	NA	+	12,000	+	NA	NA	−	NA	=	NA	12,000 FA

Problem 2-28 *Effect of deferrals on financial statements: three separate single-cycle examples*

L.O. 1, 2, 3

excel
mhhe.com/edmonds2007

Required

a. On February 1, 2005, Business Help Inc. was formed when it received $60,000 cash from the issue of common stock. On May 1, 2005, the company paid $36,000 cash in advance to rent office space for the coming year. The office space was used as a place to consult with clients. The consulting activity generated $80,000 of cash revenue during 2005. Based on this information alone, record the events and related adjusting entry in the general ledger accounts under the accounting equation. Determine the amount of net income and cash flows from operating activities for 2005.

CHECK FIGURES
a. Net Income: $56,000
b. Net Income: $10,000

"Excellent overall introduction to the whole subject, especially the role of accounting in society. The first text I have seen that distinguishes in a meaningful way between profit and nonprofit entities."

NICHOLAS P. MARUDAS,
AUBURN UNIVERSITY
AT MONTGOMERY

USER-FRIENDLY WRITING STYLE

Every chapter of the text has been designed to encourage students to read the book. Students will find the content easy to read and comprehend.

"The writing style is excellent. It is clear and concise."

MICHAEL J. FARINA,
CERRITOS COLLEGE

HOW DOES THE BOOK MOTIVATE STUDENTS?

The Curious Accountant

If a person wishes to subscribe to *Reader's Digest* for one year (12 issues), the subscriber must pay for the magazines before they are actually published. Suppose Paige Long sent $14 to the Reader's Digest Association in September 2007 for a one-year subscription; she will receive her first issue in October.

How should Reader's Digest account for the receipt of this cash? How would this event be reported on

The text provides a variety of thought-provoking, real-world examples of financial and managerial accounting as an essential part of the management process. There are descriptions of accounting practices from Coca-Cola, Enron, General Motors, JCPenney, and Amazon.com. These companies are highlighted in blue in the text.

Answers to The Curious Accountant

Because the Reader s Digest Association receives cash from customer s before actually sending any magazines to them, the company has not earned any revenue when it receives the cash. Reader s Digest has a liability called *unearned revenue*. If Reader s Digest closed its books on December 31, then $3.50 of Paige Long s subscription would be recognized as revenue in 2007. The remaining $10.50 would appear on the balance sheet as a liability.

Reader s Digest actually ends its accounting year on June 30 each year. A copy of the June 30, 2002, balance

zines to the subscriber s. However, Reader s Digest will need cash to pay for producing and distributing the magazines supplied to the customer s. Even so, the amount of cash required to provide magazines will probably differ significantly from the amount of unearned revenues. In most cases, subscription fees do not cover the cost of producing and distributing magazines. By collecting significant amounts of advertising revenue, publisher s can provide magazines to customer s at prices well below the cost of publication. The amount of unearned revenue is not likely to coincide with

THE CURIOUS ACCOUNTANT

Each chapter opens with a short vignette that sets the stage and helps pique student interest. These pose a question about a real-world accounting issue related to the topic of the chapter. The answer to the question appears in a separate sidebar a few pages further into the chapter.

FOCUS ON INTERNATIONAL ISSUES

IS THERE GLOBAL GAAP?

As explained in this chapter, financial reporting is a measurement and communication discipline based on generally accepted accounting principles (GAAP). The accounting rules described in this text represent the GAAP used in the United States. All economies in the world do not use the same accounting rules. Although there are similarities among the accounting principles used in different countries, there are also major differences. An independent body, the International Accounting Standards Board (IASB), has made an effort in recent years to create uniform international accounting standards. Individual countries, however, have retained the authority to establish their own accounting principles, so there is no single global GAAP, though the work of the IASB has reduced the extent of variation in accounting principles that exists among countries.

Accounting rules differ among countries for such reasons as the economic and legal environments in each country and the way in which a country establishes its accounting principles. In the United States, the Financial Accounting Standards Board (FASB), a nongovernmental rule-making body that the accounting profession established, has primary responsibility for establishing accounting rules. In some countries accounting principles are established by government

FOCUS ON INTERNATIONAL ISSUES

These boxed inserts expose students to international issues in accounting.

CHECK YOURSELF

These short question/answer features occur at the end of each main topic and ask students to stop and think about the material just covered. The answer follows to provide immediate feedback before students go on to a new topic.

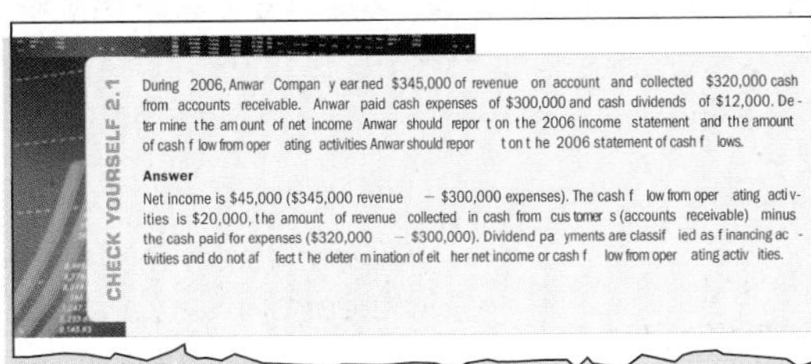
CHECK YOURSELF 2.1

During 2006, Anwar Company earned $345,000 of revenue on account and collected $320,000 cash from accounts receivable. Anwar paid cash expenses of $300,000 and cash dividends of $12,000. Determine the amount of net income Anwar should report on the 2006 income statement and the amount of cash flow from operating activities Anwar should report on the 2006 statement of cash flows.

Answer

Net income is $45,000 ($345,000 revenue − $300,000 expenses). The cash flow from operating activities is $20,000, the amount of revenue collected in cash from customers (accounts receivable) minus the cash paid for expenses ($320,000 − $300,000). Dividend payments are classified as financing activities and do not affect the determination of either net income or cash flow from operating activities.

REALITY BYTES

This feature provides examples or expansions of the topics presented by highlighting companies and showing how they use the accounting concepts discussed in the chapter to make business decisions.

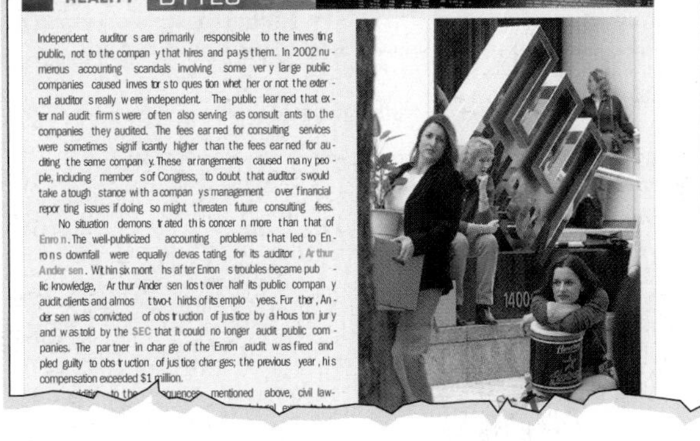
REALITY BYTES

Independent auditors are primarily responsible to the investing public, not to the company that hires and pays them. In 2002 numerous accounting scandals involving some very large public companies caused investors to question whether or not the external auditors really were independent. The public learned that external audit firms were often also serving as consultants to the companies they audited. The fees earned for consulting services were sometimes significantly higher than the fees earned for auditing the same company. These arrangements caused many people, including members of Congress, to doubt that auditors would take a tough stance with a company's management over financial reporting issues if doing so might threaten future consulting fees.

No situation demonstrated this concern more than that of Enron. The well-publicized accounting problems that led to Enron's downfall were equally devastating for its auditor, Arthur Andersen. Within six months after Enron's troubles became public knowledge, Arthur Andersen lost over half its public company audit clients and almost two-thirds of its employees. Further, Andersen was convicted of obstruction of justice by a Houston jury and was told by the SEC that it could no longer audit public companies. The partner in charge of the Enron audit was fired and pled guilty to obstruction of justice charges; the previous year, his compensation exceeded $1 million.

THE FINANCIAL ANALYST

Financial statement analysis is highlighted in each chapter under this heading.

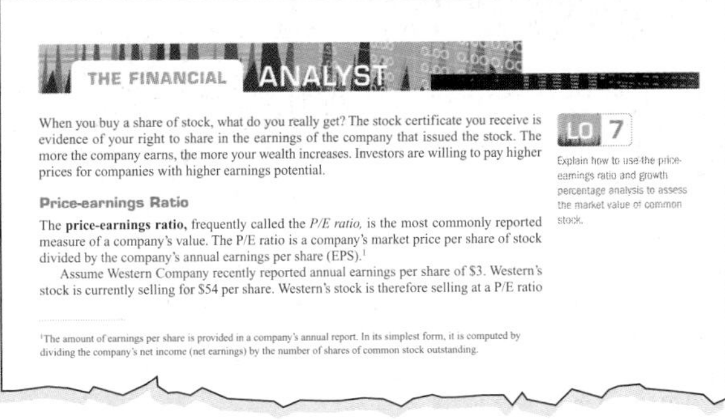
THE FINANCIAL ANALYST

When you buy a share of stock, what do you really get? The stock certificate you receive is evidence of your right to share in the earnings of the company that issued the stock. The more the company earns, the more your wealth increases. Investors are willing to pay higher prices for companies with higher earnings potential.

LO 7

Explain how to use the price-earnings ratio and growth percentage analysis to assess the market value of common stock.

Price-earnings Ratio

The **price-earnings ratio,** frequently called the *P/E ratio,* is the most commonly reported measure of a company's value. The P/E ratio is a company's market price per share of stock divided by the company's annual earnings per share (EPS).[1]

Assume Western Company recently reported annual earnings per share of $3. Western's stock is currently selling for $54 per share. Western's stock is therefore selling at a P/E ratio

[1]The amount of earnings per share is provided in a company's annual report. In its simplest form, it is computed by dividing the company's net income (net earnings) by the number of shares of common stock outstanding.

A LOOK BACK / A LOOK FORWARD

Students need a roadmap to make sense of where the chapter topics fit into the whole picture. A Look Back reviews the chapter material and a Look Forward introduces new material to come in the next chapter.

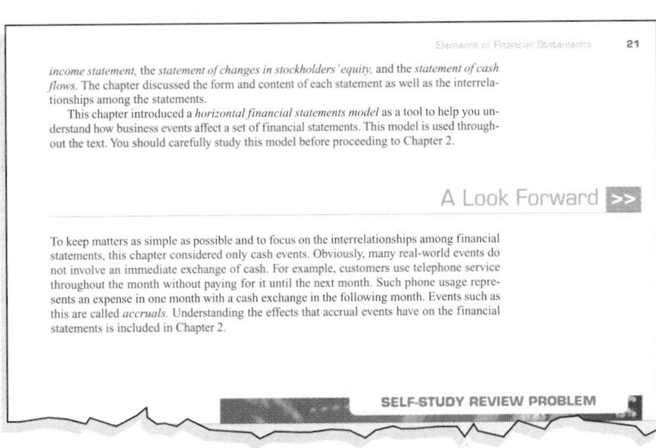
Elements of Financial Statements 21

income statement, the *statement of changes in stockholders' equity,* and the *statement of cash flows.* The chapter discussed the form and content of each statement as well as the interrelationships among the statements.

This chapter introduced a *horizontal financial statements model* as a tool to help you understand how business events affect a set of financial statements. This model is used throughout the text. You should carefully study this model before proceeding to Chapter 2.

A Look Forward >>

To keep matters as simple as possible and to focus on the interrelationships among financial statements, this chapter considered only cash events. Obviously, many real-world events do not involve an immediate exchange of cash. For example, customers use telephone service throughout the month without paying for it until the next month. Such phone usage represents an expense in one month with a cash exchange in the following month. Events such as this are called *accruals.* Understanding the effects that accrual events have on the financial statements is included in Chapter 2.

SELF-STUDY REVIEW PROBLEM

HOW ARE CHAPTER CONCEPTS REINFORCED?

Regardless of the instructional approach, there is no shortcut to learning accounting. Students must practice to master basic accounting concepts. The text includes a prodigious supply of practice materials and exercises and problems.

SELF-STUDY REVIEW PROBLEM

These sections offer problems and solutions of major chapter concepts.

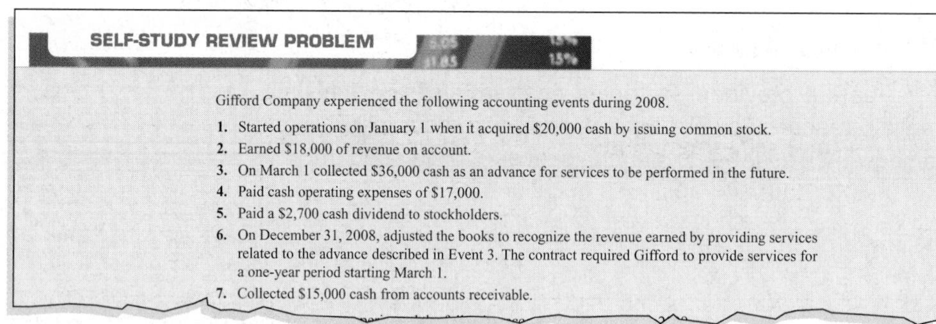

SELF-STUDY REVIEW PROBLEM

Gifford Company experienced the following accounting events during 2008.

1. Started operations on January 1 when it acquired $20,000 cash by issuing common stock.
2. Earned $18,000 of revenue on account.
3. On March 1 collected $36,000 cash as an advance for services to be performed in the future.
4. Paid cash operating expenses of $17,000.
5. Paid a $2,700 cash dividend to stockholders.
6. On December 31, 2008, adjusted the books to recognize the revenue earned by providing services related to the advance described in Event 3. The contract required Gifford to provide services for a one-year period starting March 1.
7. Collected $15,000 cash from accounts receivable.

EXERCISE AND PROBLEM SETS

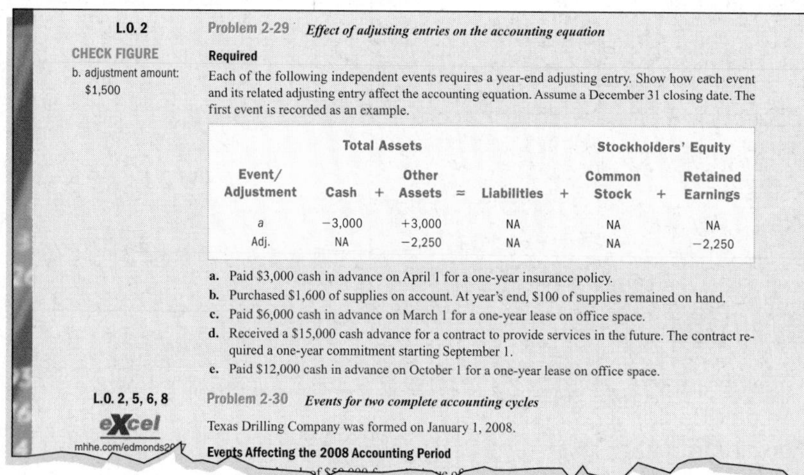

L.O. 2

CHECK FIGURE
b. adjustment amount: $1,500

Problem 2-29 *Effect of adjusting entries on the accounting equation*

Required

Each of the following independent events requires a year-end adjusting entry. Show how each event and its related adjusting entry affect the accounting equation. Assume a December 31 closing date. The first event is recorded as an example.

	Total Assets						Stockholders' Equity		
Event/ Adjustment	Cash	+	Other Assets	=	Liabilities	+	Common Stock	+	Retained Earnings
a	−3,000		+3,000		NA		NA		NA
Adj.	NA		−2,250		NA		NA		−2,250

a. Paid $3,000 cash in advance on April 1 for a one-year insurance policy.
b. Purchased $1,600 of supplies on account. At year's end, $100 of supplies remained on hand.
c. Paid $6,000 cash in advance on March 1 for a one-year lease on office space.
d. Received a $15,000 cash advance for a contract to provide services in the future. The contract required a one-year commitment starting September 1.
e. Paid $12,000 cash in advance on October 1 for a one-year lease on office space.

L.O. 2, 5, 6, 8

excel

mhhe.com/edmonds2007

Problem 2-30 *Events for two complete accounting cycles*

Texas Drilling Company was formed on January 1, 2008.

Events Affecting the 2008 Accounting Period

• Check figures

The figures provide a quick reference for students to check on their progress in solving the problem.

• Excel

Many exercises and problems can be solved using the Excel™ spreadsheet templates contained on the text's Online Learning Center. A logo appears in the margins next to these exercises and problems for easy identification.

ANALYZE, THINK, COMMUNICATE (ATC)

Each chapter includes an innovative section entitled Analyze, Think, Communicate (ATC). This section contains:

- Business application cases related to the annual report for Topps Company

- **Writing assignments**

- **Group exercises**

- **Ethics cases**

- **Internet assignments**

- **Excel spreadsheet applications**

- **Real company examples**

The Topps Company, Inc.

ANALYZE, THINK, COMMUNICATE

ATC 2-1 Business Applications Case *Understanding real-world annual reports*

Required—Part 1

Use the Topps Company annual report in Appendix B to answer the following questions.

a. Which accounts on Topps' balance sheet are accrual type accounts?

b. Which accounts on Topps' balance sheet are deferral type accounts?

c. Compare Topps' 2003 *net income* to its 2003 *cash provided by operating activities*. Which is larger?

d. First, compare Topps' 2002 net income to its 2003 net income. Next, compare Topps' 2002 cash provided by operating activities to its 2003 cash provided by operating activities. Which changed the most from 2002 to 2003, net income or cash provided by operating activities?

ATC 2-2 Group Assignment *Missing information*

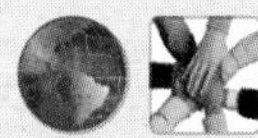

Verizon Communications Inc., is one of the world's largest providers of communication services. The following information, taken from the company's annual reports, is available for the years 2003, 2002, and 2001.

	2003	2002	2001
Revenue	$67,752	$67,304	$66,713
Operating Expenses	60,258	52,300	55,240

All dollar amounts are shown in millions.

HOW CAN TECHNOLOGY SUPPORT STUDENT SUCCESS?

Our technology resources help students and instructors focus on learning success. By using the Internet and multimedia, students get book-specific help at their convenience. Compare our technology to that of any other book and we're confident you'll agree that *Survey of Accounting* has the best in the market. Teaching aids make in-class presentations easy and stimulating. These aids give you more power than ever to teach your class the way you want.

McGRAW-HILL'S HOMEWORK MANAGER™

McGraw-Hill's Homework Manager is a Web-based homework management system that gives you unparalleled power and flexibility in creating homework assignments, tests, and quizzes. Homework Manager duplicates problem structures directly from the end-of-chapter material in your McGraw-Hill textbook, using algorithms to provide limitless variations of textbook problems. Use Homework Manager to supply online self-graded practice for students, or create assignments and tests with unique versions of every problem: Homework Manager can grade assignments automatically, provide instant feedback to students, and store all results in your private gradebook. Detailed results let you see at a glance how each student does and easily track the progress of every student in your course.

McGRAW-HILL'S HOMEWORK MANAGER PLUS™

McGraw-Hill's Homework Manager Plus combines the power of Homework Manager with the latest interactive learning technology to create a comprehensive, fully integrated online study package.

Students using Homework Manager Plus can access not only **Homework Manager** itself, but the **Interactive Online Textbook** as well. Far more than a textbook on a screen, this resource is completely integrated into Homework Manager, allowing students working on assignments to click a hotlink and instantly review the appropriate material in the textbook. **NetTutor** rounds out the package by offering live tutoring with a qualified expert in the course material, using our innovative virtual whiteboard to allow student and tutor to communicate in real time.

By including Homework Manager Plus with your textbook adoption, you're giving your students a vital edge as they progress through the course and ensuring that the help they need is never more than a mouse click away.

NETTUTOR™

Many students work or have other commitments outside of class, making it difficult for them to get help with their questions during regular school hours. NetTutor connects students with qualified tutors online. Students can work with an online tutor in real time, or post a question to be answered within 24 hours. Only available through Homework Manager Plus, adopters receive unlimited tutoring time on NetTutor.

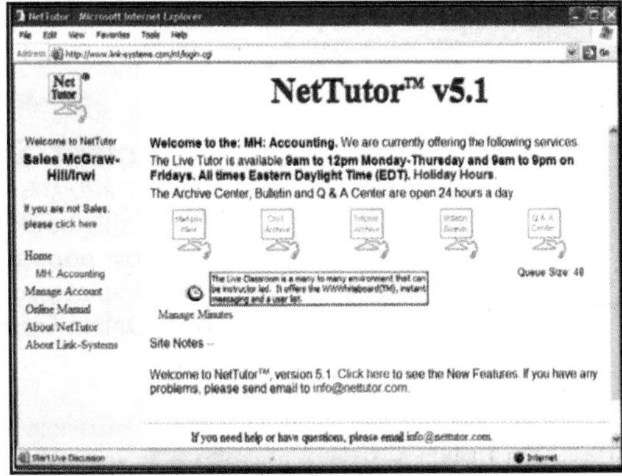

INTERACTIVE ONLINE VERSION OF THE TEXTBOOK

In addition to the textbook, students can rely on this online version of the text for a convenient way to study. While other publishers offer a simple PDF, this interactive Web-based textbook contains hotlinks to key definitions and is integrated with Homework Manager to give students quick access to relevant content as they work through problems, exercises, and practice quizzes.

ONLINE LEARNING CENTER (OLC)

www.mhhe.com/edmonds/survey

More and more students are studying online. That's why we offer an Online Learning Center (OLC) that follows *Survey of Accounting* chapter by chapter.

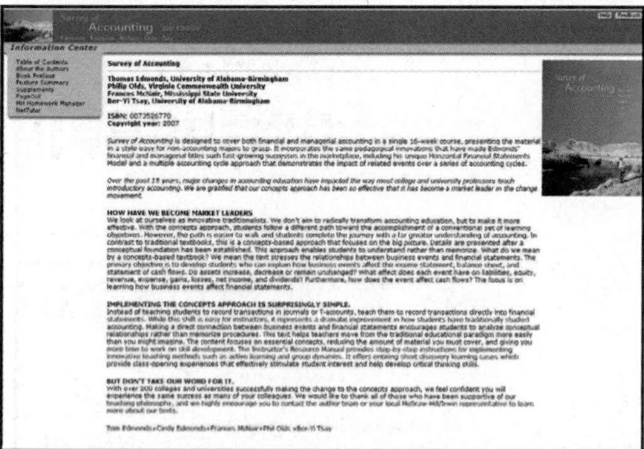

The OLC now includes the following:

- Excel Spreadsheets
- Spreadsheet Tips
- Text Updates
- Glossary
- Key Term Flashcards
- Chapter Learning Objectives
- Interactive Quizzes
- E Lectures (audio-narrated slide presentations)
- Additional Check Figures
- Mobile Resources

For instructors, the book's secured OLC contains essential course materials. You can pull all of this material into your PageOut course syllabus or use it as part of another online course management system. It doesn't require any building or maintenance on your part. It's ready to go the moment you type in the URL.

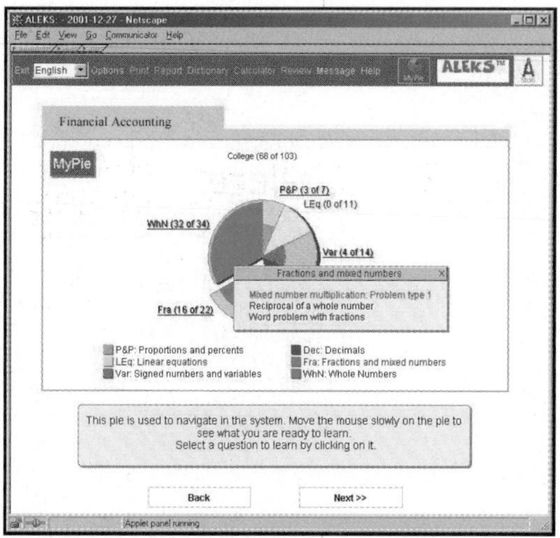

ALEKS

ALEKS for the Accounting Cycle and ALEKS for Financial Accounting ALEKS (Assessment and Learning in Knowledge Spaces) provides precise assessment and individualized instruction in the fundamental skills your students need to succeed in accounting. ALEKS motivates your students because it can tell what a student knows, doesn't know, and is most ready to learn next. ALEKS uses an artificial intelligence engine to exactly identify a student's knowledge of accounting. To learn more about adding ALEKS to your accounting course, visit **www.business.aleks.com.**

CPS CLASSROOM PERFORMANCE SYSTEM

This is a revolutionary system that brings ultimate interactivity to the classroom. CPS is a wireless response system that gives you immediate feedback from every student in the class. CPS units include easy-to-use software for creating and delivering questions and assessments to your class. With CPS you can ask subjective and objective questions. Then every student simply responds with their individual, wireless response pad, providing instant results. CPS is the perfect tool for engaging students while gathering important assessment data.

eInstruction®

PAGE OUT

McGraw-Hill's Course Management System PageOut is the easiest way to create a website for your accounting course. Just fill in a series of boxes with plain English and click on one of our professional designs. In no time your course is online with a website that contains your syllabus. If you need help, our team of specialists is ready to take your course materials and build a custom website to your specifications. To learn more visit **www.pageout.net.**

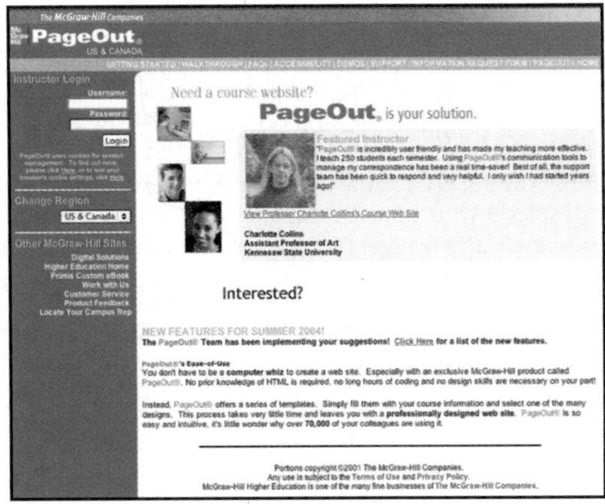

ONLINE COURSE MANAGEMENT WEBCT, ECOLLEGE, AND BLACKBOARD

We offer *Survey of Accounting* content for complete online courses. You can customize the Online Learning Center content and author your own course materials. No matter which online course solution you choose, you can count on the highest level of support. Our specialists offer free training and answer any question you have through the life of your adoption.

eCollege.com

SUPPLEMENTS FOR INSTRUCTORS

Instructor's Resource CD

ISBN-13: 978-0-07-321831-1 (ISBN-10: 0-07-321831-6) This CD includes electronic versions of the Instructor's Manual, Solutions Manual, Test Bank, and computerized Test Bank, as well as PowerPoint slides, all exhibits in the text in PowerPoint, and spreadsheet templates with solutions. This CD-ROM makes it easy for instructors to create multimedia presentations.

Instructor's Manual

(Available on the password-protected Instructor Online Learning Center (OLC) and Instructor's Resource CD.) This comprehensive manual includes step-by-step, explicit instructions on how the text can be used to implement alternative teaching methods. It also provides guidance for instructors who use the traditional lecture method. The guide includes lesson plans and demonstration problems with student work papers, as well as solutions. It was prepared by Tom Edmonds.

Solutions Manual

(Available on the password-protected Instructor Online Learning Center (OLC) and Instructor Resource CD.) Prepared by the authors, the manual contains complete solutions to all the text's end-of-chapter exercises, problems, and cases.

Test Bank

(Available on the Instructor's Resource CD.) This test bank in Word format contains multiple-choice questions, essay questions, and short problems. Each test item is coded for level of difficulty and learning objective. In addition to an expansive array of traditional test questions, the test bank includes new types of questions that focus exclusively on how business events affect financial statements.

Computerized Test Bank with Algorithmic Problem Generator (ISBN-13: 978-0-07-323051-1, ISBN-10: 0-07-323051-0)

(Available on the Instructor's Resource CD.) This computerized test bank is an algorithmic problem generator enabling instructors to create similarly structured problems with different values, allowing every student to be assigned a unique quiz or test. The user-friendly interface allows faculty to easily create different versions of the same test, change the answer order, edit or add questions, and even conduct online testing.

PowerPoint Presentation

(Available on the Online Learning Center and Instructor's Resource CD.) These slides can serve as interactive class discussions.

SUPPLEMENTS FOR STUDENTS

McGraw-Hill's Homework Manager Plus™

Homework Manager Plus integrates all of the text's multimedia resources. With just one access code, students can obtain state-of-the-art study aids, including Homework Manager, NetTutor and an online version of the text.

McGraw-Hill's Homework Manager™

This Web-based software duplicates problem structures directly from the end-of-chapter material in the textbook. It uses algorithms to provide a limitless supply of self-graded practice for students. It shows students where they made errors. All Exercises and Problems are available with Homework Manager.

Computerized Practice Sets

Wheels Exquisite, Level 1
Student ISBN 0072428457
Instructor ISBN 0072427531

Gold Run Snowmobile
Student ISBN 0072957883
Instructor ISBN 0072947683

Granite Bay Jet Ski, Level 2
Student ISBN 0072426950
Instructor ISBN 0072426209

Excel Templates

Available on the Online Learning Center (OLC), these templates allow students to develop spreadsheet skills to solve selected assignments identified by an icon in the end-of-chapter material.

E-Lectures

Available on the Online Learning Center (OLC), these slides cover key chapter topics in an **audio-narrated** presentation sure to help students learn.

ALEKS for Financial Accounting

ISBN 0072841966

ALEKS for the Accounting Cycle

ISBN 0072975326

Online Learning Center (OLC)

www.mhhe.com/edmonds/survey

ACKNOWLEDGMENTS

We would like to express our appreciation to the people who have provided assistance in the development of this textbook.

Special thanks to the talented people who prepared the supplements. These take a great deal of time and effort to write and we appreciate their efforts. Sue Cullers of Tarleton State University wrote the Test Bank questions. Kathleen Wilcox prepared the Electronic Slide presentations. Peggy Hussey of Northern Kentucky University prepared the Excel templates. We also thank our accuracy checker Beth Woods. A special thanks to Linda Bell of William Jewell College for her contribution to the Financial Statement Analysis material that appears in the Instructor's Manual and text website.

We are deeply indebted to our sponsoring editor, Steve Schuetz. His direction and guidance have added clarity and quality to the text. We especially appreciate the efforts of our developmental editor, Gail Korosa. Gail has coordinated the exchange of ideas among our class testers, reviewers, copy editor, and error checkers; she has done far more than simply pass along ideas. She has contributed numerous original suggestions that have enhanced the quality of the text. Our editors have certainly facilitated our efforts to prepare a book that will facilitate a meaningful understanding of accounting. Even so, their contributions are to no avail unless the text reaches its intended audience. We are most grateful to Rhonda Seelinger and Liz Farina and the sales staff for providing the informative advertising that has so accurately communicated the unique features of the concepts approach to accounting educators. Many others at McGraw-Hill/Irwin at a moment's notice redirected their attention to focus their efforts on the development of this text. We extend our sincere appreciation to Pat Frederickson, Elizabeth Mavetz, Debra Sylvester, Mary Kazak, Jeremy Cheshareck, and Matt Perry. We deeply appreciate the long hours that you committed to the formation of a high-quality text.

Thomas P. Edmonds
Cindy D. Edmonds
Frances M. McNair
Philip R. Olds
Bor-Yi Tsay

CHAPTER 1

Elements of Financial Statements

LEARNING OBJECTIVES

After you have mastered the material in this chapter you will be able to:

1. **Name and define the major elements of financial statements.**
2. **Describe the relationships expressed in the accounting equation.**
3. **Record business events in general ledger accounts organized under an accounting equation.**
4. **Distinguish among the different accounting entities involved in business events.**
5. **Explain how the historical cost and reliability concepts affect amounts reported in financial statements.**
6. **Classify business events as asset source, use, or exchange transactions.**
7. **Use general ledger account information to prepare four financial statements.**
8. **Record business events using a horizontal financial statements model.**
9. **Explain the importance of ethics to the accounting profession.**

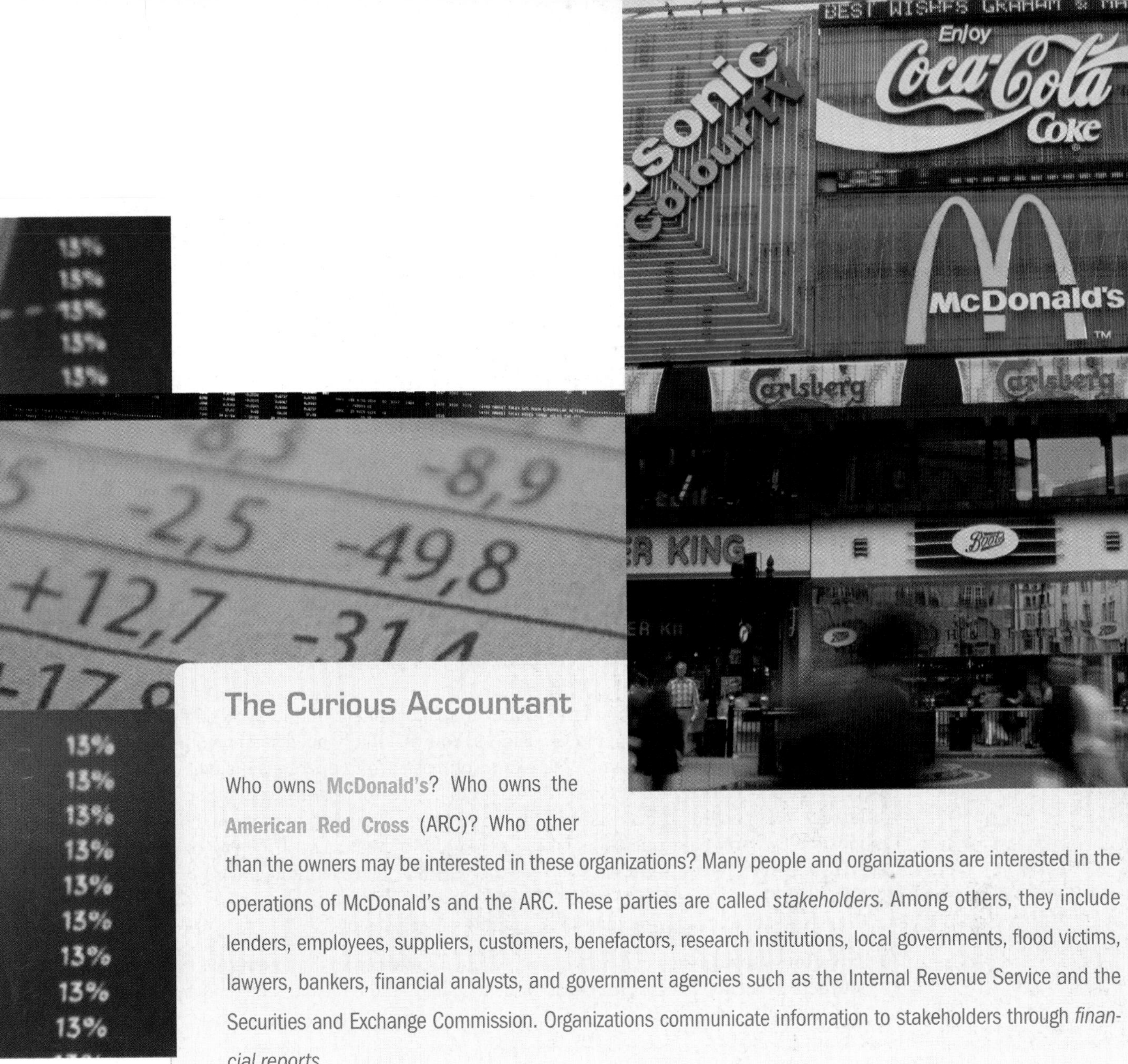

The Curious Accountant

Who owns **McDonald's**? Who owns the **American Red Cross** (ARC)? Who other than the owners may be interested in these organizations? Many people and organizations are interested in the operations of McDonald's and the ARC. These parties are called *stakeholders.* Among others, they include lenders, employees, suppliers, customers, benefactors, research institutions, local governments, flood victims, lawyers, bankers, financial analysts, and government agencies such as the Internal Revenue Service and the Securities and Exchange Commission. Organizations communicate information to stakeholders through *financial reports.*

How do you think the financial reports of McDonald's differ from those of the ARC? (Answer on page 5.)

CHAPTER OPENING

Why should you study accounting? You should study accounting because it can help you succeed in business. Businesses use accounting to keep score. Imagine trying to play football without knowing how many points a touchdown is worth. Like sports, business is competitive. If you do not know how to keep score, you are not likely to succeed.

Accounting *is an information system that reports on the economic activities and financial condition of a business or other organization. Do not underestimate the importance of accounting information. If you had information that enabled you to predict business success, you could become a very wealthy Wall Street investor. Communicating economic information is so important that accounting is frequently called the* language of business. ■

Elements of Financial Statements

Name and define the major elements of financial statements.

The individuals and organizations that need information about a business are called **stakeholders.** Stakeholders include owners, lenders, government agencies, employees, news reporters, and others. Businesses communicate information to stakeholders through four financial statements:[1] (1) an income statement, (2) a statement of changes in equity, (3) a balance sheet, and (4) a statement of cash flows.

The information reported in **financial statements** is organized into ten categories known as **elements.** Eight financial statement elements are discussed in this chapter: assets, liabilities, equity, contributed capital, revenue, expenses, distributions, and net income. The other two elements, gains and losses, are discussed in a later chapter. In practice, the business world uses various titles to identify several of the financial statement elements. For example, business people use net income, net **earnings,** and net profit interchangeably to describe the same element. Contributed capital may be called *common stock* and equity may be called *stockholders' equity, owner's capital,* and *partners' equity.* Furthermore, the transfer of assets from a business to its owners may be called *distributions, withdrawals,* or *dividends.* Think of accounting as a language. Different terms can describe the same business event. Detailed definitions of the elements and their placement on financial statements will be discussed in the following sections of the chapter.

Assets, Income, and Claims on Assets

You may have heard "you have to have money to make money." In fact, you will need more than just money to start and operate a business. You will likely need such resources as materials, equipment, buildings, and land. The resources used to operate a business are called **assets.** A business uses its assets in order to produce greater quantities of other assets. The difference between the assets used and the assets produced is called **income.** For example, suppose a law firm pays one of its employees $400 to create a will for one of its clients. The firm then charges its clients $700 for the will. In this case the law firm earned $300 ($700 − $400) of income.

The assets of a business belong to its creditors and investors.

- **Investors** provide financial resources in exchange for ownership interests in businesses. Owners expect businesses to return to them a share of the business income earned.
- **Creditors** lend financial resources to businesses. Instead of a share of business income, creditors expect businesses to repay borrowed resources at a future date.

If a business ceases to operate, its remaining assets are sold and the sale proceeds are returned to the investors and creditors through a process called business **liquidation.** Creditors have a priority claim on assets in business liquidations. After creditor claims are satisfied, any remaining assets are distributed to investors (owners).

To illustrate, suppose a business acquired $100 cash from investors and $200 cash from creditors. Assume the business lost $75 and returned the remaining $225 ($300 − $75) to the resource providers. The creditors would receive $200; the owners would receive only $25. If the business lost $120, the creditors would receive only $180 ($300 − $120); the investors would receive nothing.

As this illustration suggests, both creditors and investors can lose resources when businesses fail. Creditors, however, are in a more secure position because of their priority claim on resources. In exchange for their more secure position, creditors normally do not share business profits. Instead, they receive a fixed amount of money called **interest.**

[1]In practice these statements have alternate names. For example, the income statement may be called *results of operations* or *statement of earnings.* The balance sheet is sometimes called the *statement of financial position.* The statement of changes in equity might be called *statement of capital* or *statement of stockholders' equity.* Since the Financial Accounting Standards Board (FASB) called for the title *statement of cash flows,* companies do not use alternate names for that statement.

Answers to The Curious Accountant

Anyone who owns stock in **McDonald's** owns a part of the company. McDonald's has many owners. In contrast, nobody actually owns the **American Red Cross** (ARC). The ARC has a board of directors that is responsible for overseeing its operations, but the board is not its owner.

Ultimately, the purpose of a business entity is to increase the wealth of its owners. To this end, it "spends money to make money." The expense that McDonald's incurs for advertising is a cost incurred in the hope that it will generate revenues when it sells hamburgers. The financial statements of a business show, among other things, whether and how the company earned income during the current year.

The ARC is a not-for-profit entity. It operates to provide services to society at large, not to earn income. It cannot increase the wealth of its owners, because it has no owners. When the ARC spends money to assist flood victims, it does not spend this money in the expectation that it will generate revenues. The revenues of the ARC come from contributors who wish to support efforts related to assisting disaster victims. Because the ARC does not spend money to make money, it has no reason to prepare an *income statement* like that of McDonald's.

Not-for-profit entities do prepare financial statements that are similar in appearance to those of commercial enterprises. The financial statements of not-for-profit entities are called the *statement of financial position*, the *statement of activities*, and the *cash flow statement.*

The Accounting Equation

LO 2

Describe the relationships expressed in the accounting equation.

The assets of a business and the creditor and investor claims on those assets can be expressed though the **accounting equation:**

Assets = Claims

Creditor **claims** are called **liabilities** and investor claims are called **equity.** Substituting these terms into the accounting equation produces the following expanded form:

		Claims
Assets	=	Liabilities + Equity

Liabilities can also be viewed as future *obligations of the enterprise.* To settle the obligations, the business will probably either relinquish some of its assets (e.g., pay off its debts with cash), provide services to its creditors (e.g., work off its debts), or accept other obligations (e.g., trade short-term debt for long-term debt).

As indicated by the accounting equation, the amount of total assets is equal to the total of the liabilities plus the equity. To illustrate, assume that Hagan Company has assets of $500, liabilities of $200, and equity of $300. These amounts appear in the accounting equation as follows:

		Claims		
Assets	=	Liabilities	+	Equity
$500	=	$200	+	$300

The claims side of the accounting equation (liabilities plus equity) may also be viewed as listing the sources of the assets. For example, when a bank loans assets (money) to a business, it establishes a claim to have those assets returned at some future date. Liabilities can therefore be viewed as sources of assets.

Equity can also be viewed as a source of assets. In fact, equity represents two distinct sources of assets. First, businesses typically acquire assets from their owners (investors). Many businesses issue **common stock**[2] certificates as receipts to acknowledge assets received from owners. The owners of such businesses are often called **stockholders,** and the ownership interest in the business is called **stockholders' equity.**

Second, businesses usually obtain assets through their earnings activities (the business acquires assets by working for them). Assets a business has earned can either be distributed to the owners or kept in the business. The portion of the earned assets that is kept in the business is called **retained earnings.** Since stockholders own the business, they are entitled to assets acquired through its earnings activities. Retained earnings is therefore a component of stockholders' equity. Further expansion of the accounting equation can show the three sources of assets (liabilities, common stock, and retained earnings):

$$\text{Assets} = \text{Liabilities} + \overbrace{\text{Common stock} + \text{Retained earnings}}^{\text{Stockholders' equity}}$$

CHECK YOURSELF 1.1

Gupta Company has $250,000 of assets, $60,000 of liabilities, and $90,000 of common stock. What percentage of the assets was provided by retained earnings?

Answer

First, using algebra, determine the dollar amount of retained earnings:
Assets = Liabilities + Common stock + Retained earnings
Retained earnings = Assets − Liabilities − Common stock
Retained earnings = $250,000 − $60,000 − $90,000
Retained earnings = $100,000

Second, determine the percentage:
Percentage of assets provided by retained earnings = Retained earnings/Total assets
Percentage of assets provided by retained earnings = $100,000/$250,000 = 40%

Recording Business Events under the Accounting Equation

LO 3

Record business events in general ledger accounts organized under an accounting equation.

An **accounting event** is an economic occurrence that changes an enterprise's assets, liabilities, or stockholders' equity. A **transaction** is a particular kind of event that involves transferring something of value between two entities. Examples of transactions include acquiring assets from owners, borrowing money from creditors, and purchasing or selling goods and services. The following section of the text explains how several different types of accounting events affect a company's accounting equation.

[2]This presentation assumes the business is organized as a corporation. Other forms of business organization include proprietorships and partnerships. The treatment of equity for these types of businesses is slightly different from that of corporations. A detailed discussion of the differences is included in a later chapter of the text.

Asset Source Transactions

As previously mentioned, businesses obtain assets (resources) from three sources. They acquire assets from owners (stockholders); they borrow assets from creditors; and they earn assets through profitable operations. Asset source transactions increase total assets and total claims. A more detailed discussion of the effects of asset source transactions is provided below:

Event 1 **Rustic Camp Sites (RCS) was formed on January 1, 2004, when it acquired $120,000 cash from issuing common stock to investors.**

When RCS issued stock, it received cash and gave each investor (owner) a stock certificate as a receipt. Since this transaction provided $120,000 of assets (cash) to the business, it is an **asset source transaction.** It increases the business's assets (cash) and its stockholders' equity (common stock).

	Assets			=	Liab.	+	Stockholders' Equity		
	Cash	+	Land	=	N. Pay.	+	Com. Stk.	+	Ret. Earn.
Acquired cash through stock issue	120,000	+	NA	=	NA	+	120,000	+	NA

Notice the elements have been divided into subclassifications called **accounts.** For example, the element *assets* is divided into a Cash account and a Land account. Do not be concerned if some of these account titles are unfamiliar. They will be explained as new transactions are presented. The number of accounts a company uses depends on the nature of its business and the level of detail management needs to operate the business. For example, Sears would have an account called Cost of Goods Sold although GEICO Insurance would not. Why? Because Sears sells goods (merchandise) but GEICO does not.

Also, notice that a stock issue transaction affects the accounting equation in two places, under an asset (cash) and also under the source of that asset (common stock). All transactions affect the accounting equation in at least two places. It is from this practice that the **double-entry bookkeeping** system derives its name.

Entity Concept

Distinguish among the different accounting entities involved in business events.

Accounting reports are prepared for particular individuals or organizations called **reporting entities.** Each entity is a separate reporting unit. With respect to Event 1 described above, the business (RCS) and the investors are separate reporting entities. The information in the accounting equation for Event 1 applies to the business entity (RCS). The impact on the investors would be quite different. This text consistently describes accounting from the perspective of the business entity. To understand the effects of the subsequent transactions, ***focus on what happens to the business*** rather than to its investors, creditors, customers, employees, or other entities.

CHECK YOURSELF 1.2

In a recent business transaction, land was exchanged for cash. Did the amount of cash increase or decrease?

Answer

The answer depends on the reporting entity to which the question pertains. One entity sold land. The other entity bought land. For the entity that sold land, cash increased. For the entity that bought land, cash decreased.

Event 2 RCS acquired an additional $400,000 of cash by borrowing from a creditor.

This transaction is also an asset source transaction. It increases assets (cash) and liability claims (notes payable). The account title Notes Payable is used because the borrower (RCS) is required to issue a promissory note to the creditor (a bank). A promissory note describes, among other things, the amount of interest RCS will pay and for how long it will borrow the money.[3] The effect of the borrowing transaction on the accounting equation is indicated below.

	Assets			=	Liab.	+	Stockholders' Equity		
	Cash	+	Land	=	N. Pay.	+	Com. Stk.	+	Ret. Earn.
Beginning balances	120,000	+	NA	=	NA	+	120,000	+	NA
Acquired cash by issuing note	400,000	+	NA	=	400,000	+	NA	+	NA
Ending balances	520,000	+	NA	=	400,000	+	120,000	+	NA

The beginning balances above came from the ending balances produced by the prior transaction. This practice is followed throughout the illustration.

Asset Exchange Transactions

Businesses frequently trade one asset for another asset. In such cases, the amount of one asset decreases and the amount of the other asset increases. Total assets are unaffected by asset exchange transactions. Event 3 is an asset exchange transaction.

Event 3 RCS paid $500,000 cash to purchase land.

This asset exchange transaction reduces the asset account Cash and increases the asset account Land. The amount of total assets is not affected. An asset exchange transaction simply reflects changes in the composition of assets. In this case, the company traded cash for land. The amount of cash decreased by $500,000 and the amount of land increased by the same amount.

	Assets			=	Liab.	+	Stockholders' Equity		
	Cash	+	Land	=	N. Pay.	+	Com. Stk.	+	Ret. Earn.
Beginning balances	520,000	+	NA	=	400[illegible]	+	120,000	+	NA
Paid cash to buy land	(500,000)	+	500,000	=	[illegible]	+	NA	+	NA
Ending balances	20,000	+	500,000	=	400,000	+	120,000	+	NA

Another Asset Source Transaction

Event 4 RCS obtained $85,000 cash by leasing camp sites to customers.

Revenue represents an economic benefit a company obtains by providing customers with goods and services. In this example the economic benefit is an increase in the asset cash. Revenue transactions can therefore be viewed as *asset source transactions.* The asset increase is balanced by an increase in the retained earnings section of stockholders'

[3]For simplicity, the effects of interest are ignored in this chapter. We discuss accounting for interest in future chapters.

equity because producing revenue increases the amount of earnings retained in the business.

	Assets			=	Liab.	+	Stockholders' Equity		
	Cash	+	Land	=	N. Pay.	+	Com. Stk.	+	Ret. Earn.
Beginning balances	20,000	+	500,000	=	400,000	+	120,000	+	NA
Acquired cash by earning revenue	85,000	+	NA	=	NA	+	NA	+	85,000
Ending balances	105,000	+	500,000	=	400,000	+	120,000	+	85,000

Asset Use Transactions

Businesses use assets for a variety of purposes. For example, assets may be used to pay off liabilities or they may be transferred to owners. Assets may also be used in the process of generating earnings. All asset use transactions decrease the total amount of assets and the total amount of claims on assets (liabilities or stockholders' equity).

Event 5 **RCS paid $50,000 cash for operating expenses such as salaries, rent, and interest. (RCS could establish a separate account for each type of expense. However, the management team does not currently desire this level of detail. Remember, the number of accounts a business uses depends on the level of information managers need to make decisions.)**

In the normal course of generating revenue, a business consumes various assets and services. The assets and services consumed to generate revenue are called **expenses.** Revenue results from providing goods and services to customers. In exchange, the business acquires assets from its customers. Since the owners bear the ultimate risk and reap the rewards of operating the business, revenues increase stockholders' equity (retained earnings), and expenses decrease retained earnings. In this case, the asset account, Cash, decreased. This decrease is balanced by a decrease in the retained earnings section of stockholders' equity because expenses decrease the amount of earnings retained in the business.

	Assets			=	Liab.	+	Stockholders' Equity		
	Cash	+	Land	=	N. Pay.	+	Com. Stk.	+	Ret. Earn.
Beginning balances	105,000	+	500,000	=	400,000	+	120,000	+	85,000
Used cash to pay expenses	(50,000)	+	NA	=	NA	+	NA	+	(50,000)
Ending balances	55,000	+	500,000	=	400,000	+	120,000	+	35,000

Event 6 **RCS paid $4,000 in cash dividends to its owners.**

To this point the enterprise's total assets and equity have increased by $35,000 ($85,000 of revenue − $50,000 of expense) as a result of its earnings activities. RCS can keep the additional assets in the business or transfer them to the owners. If a business transfers some or all of its earned assets to owners, the transfer is frequently called a **dividend.** Since assets distributed to stockholders are not used for the purpose of generating revenue, *dividends are wealth transfers, not expenses.*

	Assets			=	Liab.	+	Stockholders' Equity		
	Cash	+	Land	=	N. Pay.	+	Com. Stk.	+	Ret. Earn.
Beginning balances	55,000	+	500,000	=	400,000	+	120,000	+	35,000
Used cash to pay dividends	(4,000)	+	NA	=	NA	+	NA	+	(4,000)
Ending balances	51,000	+	500,000	=	400,000	+	120,000	+	31,000

Historical Cost and Reliability Concepts

LO 5

Explain how the historical cost and reliability concepts affect amounts reported in financial statements.

Event 7 **The land that RCS paid $500,000 to purchase had an appraised market value of $525,000 on December 31, 2004.**

Although the appraised value of the land is higher than the original cost, RCS will not increase the amount recorded in its accounting records above the land's $500,000 historical cost. In general, accountants do not recognize changes in market value. The **historical cost concept** requires that most assets be reported at the amount paid for them (their historical cost) regardless of increases in market value.

Surely investors would rather know what an asset is worth instead of how much it originally cost. So why do accountants maintain records and report financial information based on historical cost? Accountants rely heavily on the **reliability concept.** Information is reliable if it can be independently verified. For example, two people looking at the legal documents associated with RCS's land purchase will both conclude that RCS paid $500,000 for the land. That historical cost is a verifiable fact. The appraised value, in contrast, is an opinion. Even two persons who are experienced appraisers are not likely to come up with the same amount for the land's market value. Accountants do not report market values in financial statements because such values are not reliable.

Measurement Rules

As indicated above accountants have decided to report historical cost instead of market value because historical cost is more reliable. Some stakeholders may argue that even though market value is less reliable, it should be used because it is more relevant. So, who decides which is more important, relevance or reliability? In the United States the **Financial Accounting Standards Board (FASB)**[4] is the primary authority for establishing accounting standards. The measurement rules established by the FASB are called **generally accepted accounting principles (GAAP).**

Recap: Types of Transactions

LO 6

Classify business events as asset source, use, or exchange transactions.

The transactions described above have each been classified into one of three categories: (1) asset source transactions; (2) asset exchange transactions; and (3) asset use transactions. A fourth category, claims exchange transactions, is introduced in a later chapter. In summary

- ***Asset source transactions*** increase the total amount of assets and increase the total amount of claims. In its first year of operation, RCS acquired assets from three sources: first, from owners (Event 1); next, by borrowing (Event 2); and finally, through earnings activities (Event 4).

[4]The FASB consists of seven full-time members appointed by the supporting organization, the Financial Accounting Foundation (FAF). The FAF membership is intended to represent the broad spectrum of individuals and institutions that have an interest in accounting and financial reporting. FAF members include representatives of the accounting profession, industry, financial institutions, the government, and the investing public.

- ***Asset exchange transactions*** decrease one asset and increase another asset. The total amount of assets is unchanged by asset exchange transactions. RCS experienced one asset exchange transaction; it used cash to purchase land (Event 3).
- ***Asset use transactions*** decrease the total amount of assets and the total amount of claims. RCS used assets to pay expenses (Event 5) and to pay dividends (Event 6).

As you proceed through this text, practice classifying transactions into one of the four categories. Businesses engage in thousands of transactions every day. It is far more effective to learn how to classify the transactions into meaningful categories than to attempt to memorize the effects of thousands of transactions.

Summary of Transactions

Record business events in general ledger accounts organized under an accounting equation.

The complete collection of a company's accounts is called the **general ledger.** The general ledger account information for RCS's 2004 accounting period is shown in Exhibit 1.1. The revenue, expense, and dividend account data appear in the retained earnings column. These account titles are shown immediately to the right of the dollar amounts listed in the retained earnings column. To help you review RCS's general ledger, the business events that the company experienced during 2004 are summarized below.

1. RCS issued common stock, acquiring $120,000 cash from its owners.
2. RCS borrowed $400,000 cash.
3. RCS paid $500,000 cash to purchase land.
4. RCS received $85,000 cash from earning revenue.
5. RCS paid $50,000 cash for expenses.
6. RCS paid dividends of $4,000 cash to the owners.
7. The land that RCS paid $500,000 to purchase had an appraised market value of $525,000 on December 31, 2004.

As indicated earlier, accounting information is normally presented to external users in four general-purpose financial statements. The information in the ledger accounts is used to prepare these financial statements. The data in the ledger accounts are color coded to help you understand the source of information in the financial statements. The numbers in *green* are used in the *statement of cash flows.* The numbers in *red* are used to prepare the *balance*

EXHIBIT 1.1

General Ledger Accounts Organized Under the Accounting Equation

	Assets			=	Liabilities	+	Stockholders' Equity			
Event No.	Cash	+	Land	=	Notes Payable	+	Common Stock	+	Retained Earnings	Other Account Titles
Beg. Bal.	0		0		0		0		0	
1.	120,000						120,000			
2.	400,000				400,000					
3.	(500,000)		500,000							
4.	85,000								85,000	Revenue
5.	(50,000)								(50,000)	Expense
6.	(4,000)								(4,000)	Dividend
7.	NA		NA		NA		NA		NA	
	51,000	+	500,000	=	400,000	+	120,000	+	31,000	

sheet. Finally, the numbers in *blue* are used to prepare the *income statement.* The numbers reported in the statement of changes in stockholders' equity have not been color coded because they appear in more than one statement. The next section explains how the information in the accounts is presented in financial statements.

Preparing Financial Statements

LO 7

Use general ledger account information to prepare four financial statements.

The financial statements for RCS are shown in Exhibit 1.2. The information used to prepare these statements was drawn from the ledger accounts. Information in one statement may relate to information in another statement. For example, the amount of net income reported on the income statement also appears on the statement of changes in stockholders' equity. Accountants use the term **articulation** to describe the interrelationships among the various elements of the financial statements. The key articulated relationships in RCS's financial statements are highlighted with arrows (Exhibit 1.2). A description of each statement follows.

Income Statement and the Matching Concept

Businesses consume assets and services in order to generate revenues, thereby creating greater quantities of other assets. For example, RCS may pay cash (asset use) to an employee who maintains the camp sites. Maintaining the sites is necessary in order to collect cash (obtain assets) from customers. The **income statement** *matches* asset increases from operating a business with asset decreases from operating the business.[5] Asset increases resulting from providing goods and services to customers in the course of normal operations are called **revenues.** Asset decreases resulting from consuming assets and services for the purpose of generating revenues are called **expenses.** If revenues are greater than expenses, the difference is called **net income.** If expenses exceed revenues, the difference is a **net loss.**

The income statement in Exhibit 1.2 indicates that RCS has earned more assets than it has used. The statement shows that RCS has increased its assets by $35,000 (net income) as a result of operating its business. Observe the phrase *For the Year Ended December 31, 2004,* in the heading of the income statement. Income is measured for a span of time called the **accounting period.** While accounting periods of one year are normal for external financial reporting, income can be measured weekly, monthly, quarterly, semiannually, or over any other desired time period. Notice that the cash RCS paid to its stockholders (dividends) is not reported as expense. The decrease in assets for dividend payments is not incurred for the purpose of generating revenue. Instead, dividends are transfers of wealth to the owners of the business. Dividend payments are not reported on the income statement.

CHECK YOURSELF 1.3

Mahoney Inc. was started when it issued common stock to its owners for $300,000. During its first year of operation Mahoney received $523,000 cash for services provided to customers. Mahoney paid employees $233,000 cash. Advertising costs paid in cash amounted to $102,000. Other cash operating expenses amounted to $124,000. Finally, Mahoney paid a $25,000 cash dividend to its stockholders. What amount of net income would Mahoney report on its earnings statement?

Answer

The amount of net income is $64,000 ($523,000 Revenue − $233,000 Salary Expense − $102,000 Advertising Expense − $124,000 Other Operating Expenses). The cash received from issuing stock is not revenue because it was not acquired from earnings activities. In other words, Mahoney did not work (perform services) for this money; it was contributed by owners of the business. The dividends are not expenses because the decrease in cash was not incurred for the purpose of generating revenue. Instead, the dividends represent a transfer of wealth to the owners.

[5]This description of the income statement is expanded in subsequent chapters as additional relationships among the elements of financial statements are introduced.

EXHIBIT 1.2 Financial Statements

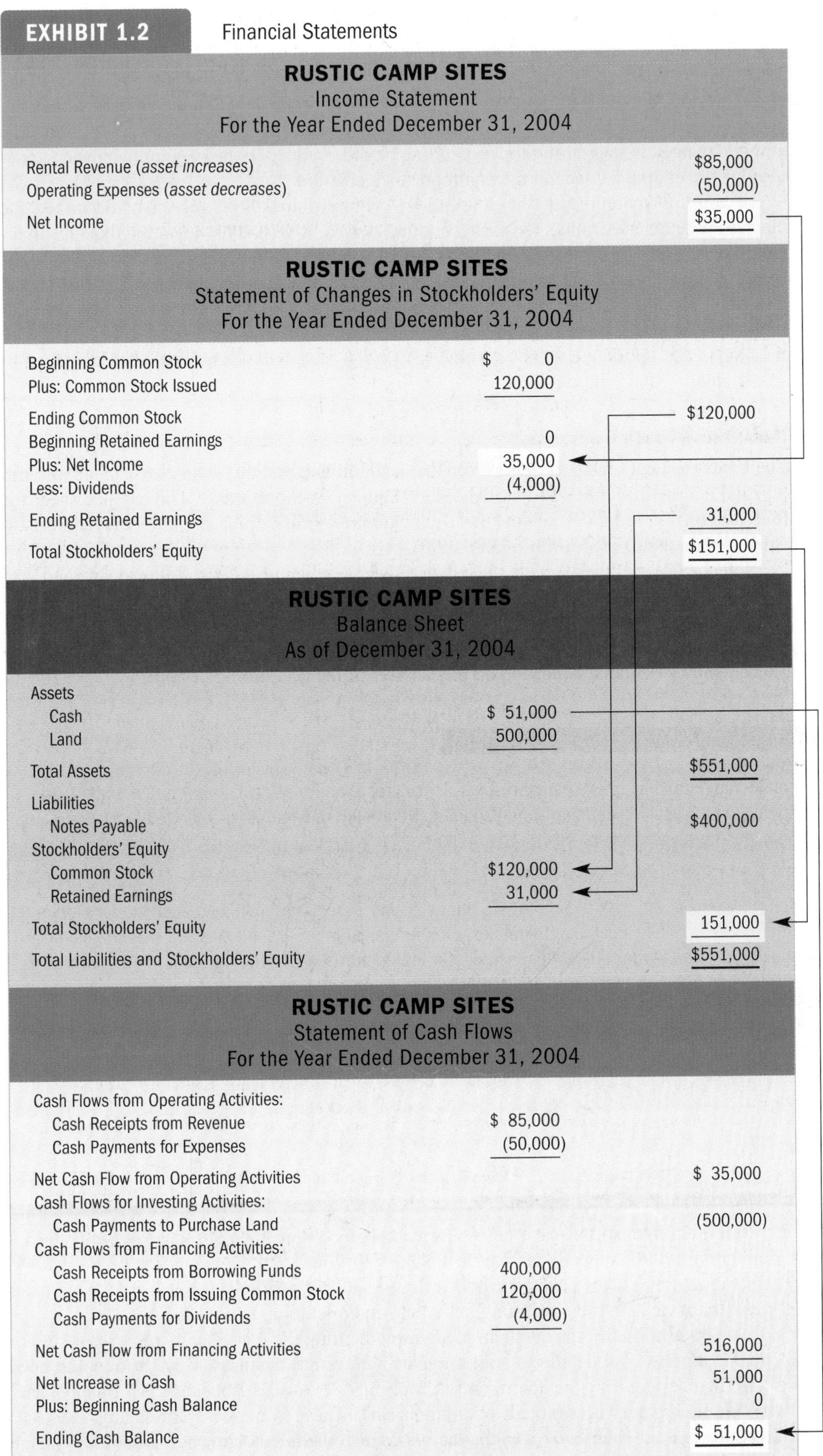

RUSTIC CAMP SITES
Income Statement
For the Year Ended December 31, 2004

Rental Revenue (*asset increases*)		$85,000
Operating Expenses (*asset decreases*)		(50,000)
Net Income		$35,000

RUSTIC CAMP SITES
Statement of Changes in Stockholders' Equity
For the Year Ended December 31, 2004

Beginning Common Stock	$ 0	
Plus: Common Stock Issued	120,000	
Ending Common Stock		$120,000
Beginning Retained Earnings	0	
Plus: Net Income	35,000	
Less: Dividends	(4,000)	
Ending Retained Earnings		31,000
Total Stockholders' Equity		$151,000

RUSTIC CAMP SITES
Balance Sheet
As of December 31, 2004

Assets		
Cash	$ 51,000	
Land	500,000	
Total Assets		$551,000
Liabilities		
Notes Payable		$400,000
Stockholders' Equity		
Common Stock	$120,000	
Retained Earnings	31,000	
Total Stockholders' Equity		151,000
Total Liabilities and Stockholders' Equity		$551,000

RUSTIC CAMP SITES
Statement of Cash Flows
For the Year Ended December 31, 2004

Cash Flows from Operating Activities:		
Cash Receipts from Revenue	$ 85,000	
Cash Payments for Expenses	(50,000)	
Net Cash Flow from Operating Activities		$ 35,000
Cash Flows for Investing Activities:		
Cash Payments to Purchase Land		(500,000)
Cash Flows from Financing Activities:		
Cash Receipts from Borrowing Funds	400,000	
Cash Receipts from Issuing Common Stock	120,000	
Cash Payments for Dividends	(4,000)	
Net Cash Flow from Financing Activities		516,000
Net Increase in Cash		51,000
Plus: Beginning Cash Balance		0
Ending Cash Balance		$ 51,000

Statement of Changes in Stockholders' Equity

The **statement of changes in stockholders' equity** explains the effects of transactions on stockholders' equity during the accounting period. It starts with the beginning balance in the common stock account. In the case of RCS, the beginning balance in the common stock account is zero because the company did not exist before the 2004 accounting period. The amount of stock issued during the accounting period is added to the beginning balance to determine the ending balance in the common stock account.

In addition to reporting the changes in common stock, the statement describes the changes in retained earnings for the accounting period. RCS had no beginning balance in retained earnings. During the period, the company earned $35,000 and paid $4,000 in dividends to the stockholders, producing an ending retained earning balance of $31,000 ($0 + $35,000 − $4,000). Since equity consists of common stock and retained earnings, the ending total equity balance is $151,000 ($120,000 + $31,000). This statement is also dated with the phrase *For the Year Ended December 31, 2004,* because it describes what happened to stockholders' equity during 2004.

Balance Sheet

The **balance sheet** draws its name from the accounting equation. Total assets balances with (equals) claims (liabilities and stockholders' equity) on those assets. The balance sheet for RCS is shown in Exhibit 1.2. Note that total claims (liabilities plus stockholders' equity) are equal to total assets ($551,000 = $551,000).

Note the order of the assets in the balance sheet. Cash appears first, followed by land. Assets are displayed in the balance sheet based on their level of **liquidity.** This means that assets are listed in order of how rapidly they will be converted to cash. Finally, note that the balance sheet is dated with the phrase *As of December 31, 2004,* indicating that it describes the company's financial condition on the last day of the accounting period.

CHECK YOURSELF 1.4

To gain a clear understanding of the balance sheet, try to create one that describes your personal financial condition. First list your assets, then your liabilities. Determine the amount of your equity by subtracting your liabilities from your assets.

Answer

Answers for this exercise will vary depending on the particular assets and liabilities each student identifies. Common student assets include automobiles, computers, stereos, TVs, phones, CD players, clothes, and textbooks. Common student liabilities include car loans, mortgages, student loans, and credit card debt. The difference between the assets and the liabilities is the equity.

Statement of Cash Flows

The **statement of cash flows** explains how a company obtained and used *cash* during the accounting period. Receipts of cash are called *cash inflows,* and payments are *cash outflows.* The statement classifies cash receipts (inflows) and payments (outflows) into three categories: financing activities, investing activities, and operating activities.

Businesses normally start with an idea. Implementing the idea usually requires cash. For example, suppose you decide to start an apartment rental business. First, you would need cash to finance acquiring the apartments. Acquiring cash to start a business is a financing activity. **Financing activities** include obtaining cash (inflow) from owners or paying cash (outflow) to owners (dividends). Financing activities also include borrowing cash (inflow) from creditors and repaying the principal (outflow) to creditors. Because interest on borrowed money is an expense, however, cash paid to creditors for interest is reported in the operating activities section of the statement of cash flows.

After obtaining cash from financing activities, you would invest the money by building or buying apartments. **Investing activities** involve paying cash (outflow) to purchase productive assets or receiving cash (inflow) from selling productive assets. **Productive assets** are sometimes called long-term assets because businesses normally use them for more than one year. Cash outflows to purchase land or cash inflows from selling a building are examples of investing activities.

After investing in the productive assets (apartments), you would engage in operating activities. **Operating activities** involve receiving cash (inflow) from revenue and paying cash (outflow) for expenses. Note that cash spent to purchase short-term assets such as office supplies is reported in the operating activities section because the office supplies would likely be used (expensed) within a single accounting period.

EXHIBIT 1.3

Classification Scheme for Statement of Cash Flows

Cash Flows from Operating Activities:
- Cash Receipts (Inflows) from Revenue (Including Interest)
- Cash Payments (Outflows) for Expenses (Including Interest)

Cash Flows from Investing Activities:
- Cash Receipts (Inflows) from the Sale of Long-Term Assets
- Cash Payments (Outflows) for the Purchase of Long-Term Assets

Cash Flows from Financing Activities:
- Cash Receipts (Inflows) from Borrowing Funds
- Cash Receipts (Inflows) from Issuing Common Stock
- Cash Payments (Outflows) to Repay Borrowed Funds
- Cash Payments (Outflows) for Dividends

The primary cash inflows and outflows related to the types of business activity introduced in this chapter are summarized in Exhibit 1.3. The exhibit will be expanded as additional types of events are introduced in subsequent chapters.

The statement of cash flows for Rustic Camp Sites in Exhibit 1.2 shows that the amount of cash increased by $51,000 during the year. The beginning balance in the Cash account was zero; adding the $51,000 increase to the beginning balance results in a $51,000 ending balance. Notice that the $51,000 ending cash balance on the statement of cash flows is the same as the amount of cash reported in the asset section on the December 31 year-end balance sheet. Also, note that the statement of cash flows is dated with the phrase *For the Year Ended December 31, 2004,* because it describes what happened to cash over the span of the year.

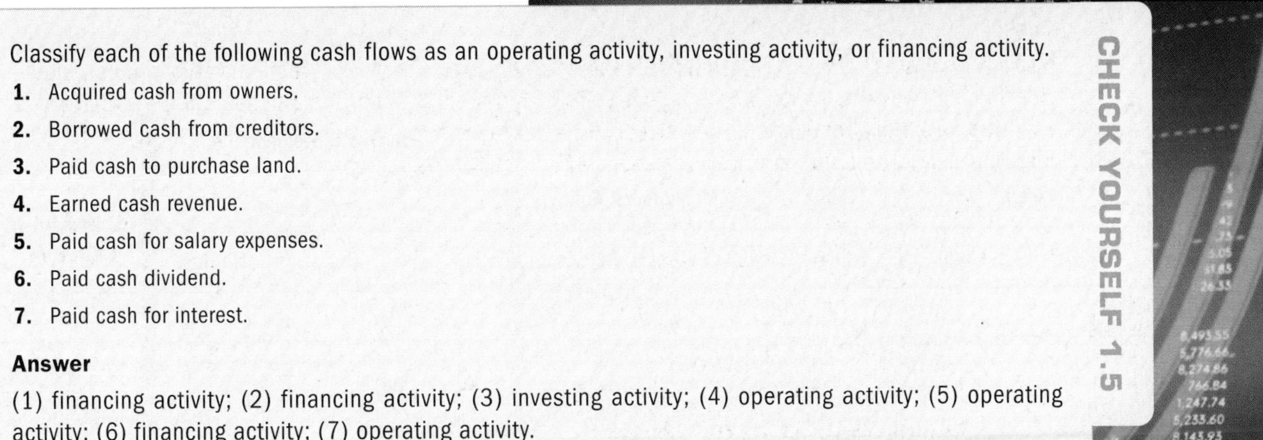

CHECK YOURSELF 1.5

Classify each of the following cash flows as an operating activity, investing activity, or financing activity.

1. Acquired cash from owners.
2. Borrowed cash from creditors.
3. Paid cash to purchase land.
4. Earned cash revenue.
5. Paid cash for salary expenses.
6. Paid cash dividend.
7. Paid cash for interest.

Answer

(1) financing activity; (2) financing activity; (3) investing activity; (4) operating activity; (5) operating activity; (6) financing activity; (7) operating activity.

Financial versus Managerial Accounting

The four financial statements described above are designed to meet the needs of stakeholders that exist outside of and separate from the business entity. These stakeholders include investors, creditors, lawyers, financial analysts, news reporters, and others. The branch of accounting that focuses on the needs of ***external stakeholders*** is called **financial accounting.**

In contrast, the accounting information designed to meet the needs of ***internal stakeholders*** such as managers and employees, is called **managerial accounting.** The first nine chapters of this text focus on financial accounting. The remainder of the text covers managerial accounting topics.

The Horizontal Financial Statements Model

LO 8

Record business events using a horizontal financial statements model.

Financial statements are the scorecard for business activity. If you want to succeed in business, you must know how your business decisions affect your company's financial statements. This text uses a **horizontal statements model** to help you understand how business events affect financial statements. This model shows a set of financial statements horizontally across a single page of paper. The balance sheet is displayed first, adjacent to the income statement, and then the statement of cash flows. Because the effects of equity transactions can be analyzed by referring to certain balance sheet columns, and because of limited space, the statement of changes in stockholders' equity is not shown in the horizontal statements model.

The model frequently uses abbreviations. For example, activity classifications in the statement of cash flows are identified using OA for operating activities, IA for investing activities, and FA for financing activities. NC designates the net change in cash. The statements model uses "NA" when an account is not affected by an event. The background of the *balance sheet* is red, the *income statement* is blue, and the *statement of cash flows* is green. To demonstrate the usefulness of the horizontal statements model, we use it to display the seven accounting events that RCS experienced during its first year of operation (2004).

1. RCS acquired $120,000 cash from the owners.
2. RCS borrowed $400,000 cash.
3. RCS paid $500,000 cash to purchase land.
4. RCS received $85,000 cash from earning revenue.
5. RCS paid $50,000 cash for expenses.
6. RCS paid $4,000 of cash dividends to the owners.
7. The market value of the land owned by RCS was appraised at $525,000 on December 31, 2004.

Event No.	Balance Sheet									Income Statement					Statement of Cash Flows
	Assets			=	Liab.	+	Stockholders' Equity								
	Cash	+	Land	=	N. Pay.	+	Com. Stk.	+	Ret. Earn.	Rev.	−	Exp.	=	Net Inc.	
Beg. bal.	0	+	0	=	0	+	0	+	0	0	−	0	=	0	NA
1.	120,000	+	NA	=	NA	+	120,000	+	NA	NA	−	NA	=	NA	120,000 FA
2.	400,000	+	NA	=	400,000	+	NA	+	NA	NA	−	NA	=	NA	400,000 FA
3.	(500,000)	+	500,000	=	NA	+	NA	+	NA	NA	−	NA	=	NA	(500,000) IA
4.	85,000	+	NA	=	NA	+	NA	+	85,000	85,000	−	NA	=	85,000	85,000 OA
5.	(50,000)	+	NA	=	NA	+	NA	+	(50,000)	NA	−	50,000	=	(50,000)	(50,000) OA
6.	(4,000)	+	NA	=	NA	+	NA	+	(4,000)	NA	−	NA	=	NA	(4,000) FA
7.	NA	+	NA	=	NA	+	NA	+	NA	NA	−	NA	=	NA	NA
Totals	51,000	+	500,000	=	400,000	+	120,000	+	31,000	85,000	−	50,000	=	35,000	51,000 NC

Recognize that statements models are learning tools. Because they are helpful in understanding how accounting events affect financial statements, they are used extensively in this book. However, the models omit many of the details used in published financial statements. For example, the horizontal model shows only a partial set of statements. Also, since the statements are presented in aggregate, the description of dates (i.e., "as of" versus "for the period ended") does not distinguish periodic from cumulative data.

This section of each chapter introduces topics related to analyzing real world financial reports. We focus first on the reliability of financial reporting. Accounting information is worthless if it cannot be trusted. Financial analysts must rely on accountants' integrity.

Importance of Ethics

Explain the importance of ethics to the accounting profession.

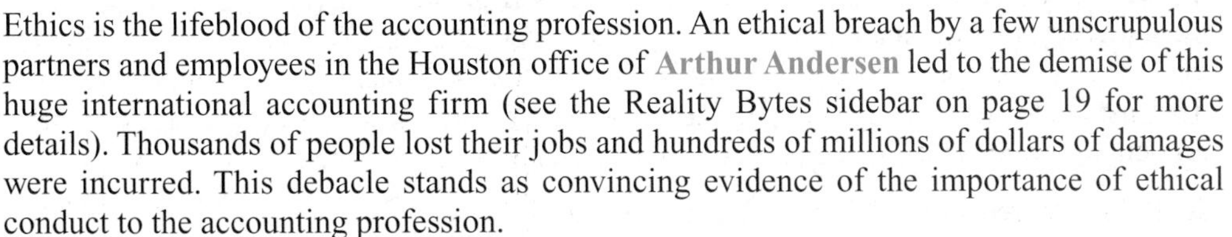

Ethics is the lifeblood of the accounting profession. An ethical breach by a few unscrupulous partners and employees in the Houston office of Arthur Andersen led to the demise of this huge international accounting firm (see the Reality Bytes sidebar on page 19 for more details). Thousands of people lost their jobs and hundreds of millions of dollars of damages were incurred. This debacle stands as convincing evidence of the importance of ethical conduct to the accounting profession.

The importance of ethical conduct is universally recognized by accountants. All the major professional accounting organizations require their members to follow formal codes of ethical conduct. The underlying principles of the **Code of Professional Conduct**[6] adopted by the American Institute of Certified Public Accountants are summarized in Exhibit 1.4. Other codes follow similar principles.

Sarbanes-Oxley Act of 2002

Codes of ethics cannot deter all unethical behavior. The massive surprise bankruptcies of Enron in late 2001 and WorldCom several months later suggested major audit failures on the part of the independent auditors. An audit failure means a company's auditor does not detect, or fails to report, that the company's financial reports are not in compliance with GAAP. The audit failures at Enron, WorldCom, and others prompted Congress to pass the Sarbanes-Oxley Act, which became effective on July 30, 2002. The provisions of this legislation are complex, and their full effects will not be known for some time. However, it is clear that the act has tightened the rules governing auditors' independence.

Prior to Sarbanes-Oxley, independent auditors often provided nonaudit services, such as installing computer systems, for their audit clients. The fees they earned for these services sometimes greatly exceeded the fees charged for the audit itself. This practice had been questioned prior to the audit failures at Enron and WorldCom. Critics felt the independent audit firm was subject to pressure from the company to conduct a less rigorous audit, or risk losing lucrative nonaudit work. The Sarbanes-Oxley Act prohibits auditors from providing most types of nonaudit services to companies they audit.

Another provision of Sarbanes-Oxley clarifies the legal responsibility that company management has for a company's financial reports. The company's chief executive officer (CEO) and chief financial officer (CFO) must certify in writing that they have reviewed the financial reports being issued, and that the reports present fairly the company's financial status.

[6]American Institute of Certified Public Accountants, Inc. (AICPA), *Code of Professional Conduct* (New York: AICPA, 1992).

EXHIBIT 1.4

Principles of AICPA Code of Professional Conduct

Article I Responsibilities
In carrying out their responsibilities as professionals, members should exercise sensitive professional and moral judgments in all their activities.

Article II The Public Interest
Members should accept the obligation to act in a way that will serve the public interest, honor the public trust, and demonstrate commitment to professionalism.

Article III Integrity
To maintain and broaden public confidence, members should perform all professional responsibilities with the highest sense of integrity.

Article IV Objectivity and Independence
A member should maintain objectivity and be free of conflicts of interest in discharging professional responsibilities. A member in public practice should be independent in fact and appearance when providing auditing and other attestation services.

Article V Due Care
A member should observe the profession's technical and ethical standards, strive continually to improve competence and the quality of services, and discharge professional responsibility to the best of the member's ability.

Article VI Scope and Nature of Services
A member in public practice should observe the principles of the Code of Professional Conduct in determining the scope and nature of services to be provided.

An executive who falsely certifies the company's financial reports is subject to significant fines and imprisonment.

Common Features of Ethical Misconduct

People who become involved in unethical or criminal behavior usually do so unexpectedly. They start with small indiscretions that evolve gradually into more serious violations of trust. To reduce the incidence of unethical or illegal conduct, business persons must be aware of conditions that lead to trust violations. To increase awareness, Donald Cressey studied hundreds of criminal cases to identify the primary factors behind ethical misconduct. Cressey found three factors common to all cases: (1) the existence of a nonsharable problem, (2) the presence of an opportunity, and (3) the capacity for rationalization.[7]

As the term implies, a *nonsharable problem* is one that must be kept secret. Individuals differ about what they keep to themselves. Consider two responses to the problem of an imminent business failure. One person may feel so ashamed that he or she cannot discuss the problem with anyone. Another person in the same situation may want to talk to anyone, even a stranger, in the hope of getting help. Other nonsharable problems include personal vices such as drug addiction, gambling, and promiscuity. Cressey's findings suggest that the person who is inclined toward secrecy is more likely to accept an unethical or illegal solution. In other words, the perceived need for secrecy increases vulnerability.

Accountants establish policies and procedures designed to reduce *opportunities* for fraud. These policies and procedures are commonly called **internal controls.** Specific internal control procedures are tailored to meet the individual needs of particular businesses. For example, banks use vaults to protect cash, but universities have little use for this type of equipment. Chapter 4 discusses internal control procedures in more detail. At this point, simply recognize that accountants are aware of the need to reduce opportunities for unethical and criminal activities.

[7]D. R. Cressey, *Other People's Money* (Montclair, NJ: Paterson Smith, 1973).

REALITY BYTES

Independent auditors are primarily responsible to the investing public, not to the company that hires and pays them. In 2002 numerous accounting scandals involving some very large public companies caused investors to question whether or not the external auditors really were independent. The public learned that external audit firms were often also serving as consultants to the companies they audited. The fees earned for consulting services were sometimes significantly higher than the fees earned for auditing the same company. These arrangements caused many people, including members of Congress, to doubt that auditors would take a tough stance with a company's management over financial reporting issues if doing so might threaten future consulting fees.

No situation demonstrated this concern more than that of **Enron**. The well-publicized accounting problems that led to Enron's downfall were equally devastating for its auditor, **Arthur Andersen**. Within six months after Enron's troubles became public knowledge, Arthur Andersen lost over half its public company audit clients and almost two-thirds of its employees. Further, Andersen was convicted of obstruction of justice by a Houston jury and was told by the **SEC** that it could no longer audit public companies. The partner in charge of the Enron audit was fired and pled guilty to obstruction of justice charges; the previous year, his compensation exceeded $1 million.

In addition to the consequences mentioned above, civil lawsuits were filed against Arthur Andersen, and legal experts believe its partners, even those not involved in the Enron audit, will likely be held personally liable for any damages resulting from inadequate audits. Congress has given CPAs a legal monopoly to provide independent audits for public companies. However, their protected status does not shelter them from the consequences of their actions. As the Enron case demonstrates, when CPAs fail, they are held to a high and costly standard.

Few individuals think of themselves as dishonest, so they develop *rationalizations* to justify their misconduct. Cressey found a significant number of embezzlers who contended they were only "borrowing the money," even after being convicted and sentenced to jail. Common rationalizations include peer pressure, loyalty to unscrupulous superiors, family needs, revenge, and a sense of entitlement. To avoid involvement in ethical misconduct, accountants must develop a strong sense of personal responsibility. They cannot allow themselves to blame other people or unfair circumstances for their problems. They must learn to hold themselves personally accountable for their actions.

Ethical misconduct is a serious offense in the accounting profession. A single mistake can destroy an accounting career. If you commit a white-collar crime, you normally lose the opportunity to hold a white-collar job. Second chances are rarely granted; it is extremely important that you learn how to recognize and avoid the common features of ethical misconduct. To help you prepare for the real-world situations you are likely to encounter, we include ethical dilemmas in the end-of-chapter materials. When working with these dilemmas, try to identify the (1) secret, (2) opportunity, and (3) rationalization associated with the particular ethical situation described. If you are not an ethical person, accounting is not the career for you.

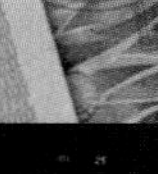

FOCUS ON INTERNATIONAL ISSUES

IS THERE GLOBAL GAAP?

As explained in this chapter, financial reporting is a measurement and communication discipline based on generally accepted accounting principles (GAAP). The accounting rules described in this text represent the GAAP used in the United States. All economies in the world do not use the same accounting rules. Although there are similarities among the accounting principles used in different countries, there are also major differences. An independent body, the International Accounting Standards Board (IASB), has made an effort in recent years to create uniform international accounting standards. Individual countries, however, have retained the authority to establish their own accounting principles, so there is no single "global GAAP," though the work of the IASB has reduced the extent of variation in accounting principles that exists among countries.

Accounting rules differ among countries for such reasons as the economic and legal environments in each country and the way in which a country establishes its accounting principles. In the United States, the Financial Accounting Standards Board (FASB), a nongovernmental rule-making body that the accounting profession established, has primary responsibility for establishing accounting rules. In some countries accounting principles are established by governmental bodies more like the way federal laws and regulations are established in the United States.

Finally, in the United States there is no direct connection between GAAP established by the FASB and the tax accounting rules established by Congress and the Internal Revenue Service (IRS). In some countries, government authorities require that companies use the same accounting rules for both financial and income tax reporting.

Annual Report for The Topps Company, Inc.

Organizations normally provide information, including financial statements, to *stakeholders* yearly in a document known as an **annual report.** The annual report for Topps is reproduced in Appendix B of this text. This report includes the company's financial statements (see pages 12–15 of the report). Immediately following the statements are footnotes that provide additional details about the items described in the statements (see pages 16–30). Annual reports also include written commentary describing management's assessment of significant events that affected the company during the reporting period. This commentary is called *management's discussion and analysis* (MD&A).

<< A Look Back

This chapter has discussed eight elements of financial statements: *assets, liabilities, equity, common stock (contributed capital), revenue, expenses, dividends (distributions),* and *net income.* The elements represent broad classifications reported on financial statements. Four basic financial statements appear in the reports of public companies: the *balance sheet,* the *income statement,* the *statement of changes in stockholders' equity,* and the *statement of cash flows.* The chapter discussed the form and content of each statement as well as the interrelationships among the statements.

This chapter introduced a *horizontal financial statements model* as a tool to help you understand how business events affect a set of financial statements. This model is used throughout the text. You should carefully study this model before proceeding to Chapter 2.

A Look Forward >>

To keep matters as simple as possible and to focus on the interrelationships among financial statements, this chapter considered only cash events. Obviously, many real-world events do not involve an immediate exchange of cash. For example, customers use telephone service throughout the month without paying for it until the next month. Such phone usage represents an expense in one month with a cash exchange in the following month. Events such as this are called *accruals.* Understanding the effects that accrual events have on the financial statements is included in Chapter 2.

SELF-STUDY REVIEW PROBLEM

During 2005 Rustic Camp Sites experienced the following transactions.

1. RCS acquired $32,000 cash by issuing common stock.
2. RCS received $116,000 cash for providing services to customers (leasing camp sites).
3. RCS paid $13,000 cash for salaries expense.
4. RCS paid a $9,000 cash dividend to the owners.
5. RCS sold land that had cost $100,000 for $100,000 cash.
6. RCS paid $47,000 cash for other operating expenses.

Required

a. Record the transaction data in a horizontal financial statements model like the following one. In the Cash Flow column, classify the cash flows as operating activities (OA), investing activities (IA), or financing activities (FA). The beginning balances have been recorded as an example. They are the ending balances shown on RCS's December 31, 2004, financial statements illustrated in the chapter. Note that the revenue and expense accounts have a zero beginning balance. Amounts in these accounts apply only to a single accounting period. Revenue and expense account balances are not carried forward from one accounting period to the next.

	Balance Sheet									Income Statement					
	Assets			=	Liab.	+	Stockholders' Equity								
Event No.	Cash	+	Land	=	N. Pay.	+	Com. Stk.	+	Ret. Earn.	Rev.	−	Exp.	=	Net Inc.	Statement of Cash Flows
Beg. bal.	51,000	+	500,000	=	400,000	+	120,000	+	31,000	NA	−	NA	=	NA	NA

b. Explain why there are no beginning balances in the Income Statement columns.

c. What amount of net income will RCS report on the 2005 income statement?

d. What amount of total assets will RCS report on the December 31, 2005, balance sheet?

e. What amount of retained earnings will RCS report on the December 31, 2005, balance sheet?

f. What amount of net cash flow from operating activities will RCS report on the 2005 statement of cash flows?

Solution

a.

Event No.	Balance Sheet: Assets: Cash	+	Land	=	Liab.: N. Pay.	+	Stockholders' Equity: Com. Stk.	+	Ret. Earn.	Income Statement: Rev.	−	Exp.	=	Net Inc.	Statement of Cash Flows
Beg. bal.	51,000	+	500,000	=	400,000	+	120,000	+	31,000	NA	−	NA	=	NA	NA
1.	32,000	+	NA	=	NA	+	32,000	+	NA	NA	−	NA	=	NA	32,000 FA
2.	116,000	+	NA	=	NA	+	NA	+	116,000	116,000	−	NA	=	116,000	116,000 OA
3.	(13,000)	+	NA	=	NA	+	NA	+	(13,000)	NA	−	13,000	=	(13,000)	(13,000) OA
4.	(9,000)	+	NA	=	NA	+	NA	+	(9,000)	NA	−	NA	=	NA	(9,000) FA
5.	100,000	+	(100,000)	=	NA	+	NA	+	NA	NA	−	NA	=	NA	100,000 IA
6.	(47,000)	+	NA	=	NA	+	NA	+	(47,000)	NA	−	47,000	=	(47,000)	(47,000) OA
Totals	230,000	+	400,000	=	400,000	+	152,000	+	78,000	116,000	−	60,000	=	56,000	179,000 NC*

*The letters NC on the last line of the column designate the net change in cash.

b. The revenue and expense accounts are temporary accounts used to capture data for a single accounting period. They are closed (amounts removed from the accounts) to retained earnings at the end of the accounting period and therefore always have zero balances at the beginning of the accounting cycle.

c. RCS will report net income of $56,000 on the 2005 income statement. Compute this amount by subtracting the expenses from the revenue ($116,000 Revenue − $13,000 Salaries expense − $47,000 Other operating expense).

d. RCS will report total assets of $630,000 on the December 31, 2005, balance sheet. Compute total assets by adding the cash amount to the land amount ($230,000 Cash + $400,000 Land).

e. RCS will report retained earnings of $78,000 on the December 31, 2005 balance sheet. Compute this amount using the following formula: Beginning retained earnings + Net income − Dividends = Ending retained earnings. In this case, $31,000 + $56,000 − $9,000 = $78,000.

f. Net cash flow from operating activities is the difference between the amount of cash collected from revenue and the amount of cash spent for expenses. In this case, $116,000 cash inflow from revenue − $13,000 cash outflow for salaries expense − $47,000 cash outflow for other operating expenses = $56,000 net cash inflow from operating activities.

KEY TERMS

general ledger 11
generally accepted accounting principles (GAAP) 10
historical cost concept 10
horizontal statements model 16
income 4
income statement 12
interest 4
internal controls 18
investing activities 15
investors 4
liabilities 5
liquidation 4
liquidity 14
managerial accounting 16
net income 12
net loss 12
operating activities 15
productive assets 15
reliability concept 10
reporting entities 7
retained earnings 6
revenue 8, 12
stakeholders 4
statement of cash flows 14
statement of changes in stockholders' equity 14
stockholders 6
stockholders' equity 6
transaction 6

QUESTIONS

1. Explain the term *stakeholder.*
2. Why is accounting called the *language of business?*
3. What type of compensation does an investor expect to receive in exchange for providing financial resources to a business? What type of compensation does a creditor expect from providing financial resources to an organization or business?
4. How do financial and managerial accounting differ?
5. What are the U.S. rules of accounting measurement called?
6. Is there a global GAAP (generally accepted accounting principles)? Explain your answer.
7. What body has the primary responsibility for establishing GAAP in the United States?
8. Distinguish between elements of financial statements and accounts.
9. What is the most basic form of the accounting equation?
10. What role do assets play in business profitability?
11. To whom do the assets of a business belong?
12. Explain the order of priority for asset distributions in a business liquidation.
13. Name the element used to describe the ownership interest in a business.
14. Name the element used to describe creditors' claims on the assets of a business.
15. What is the accounting equation? Describe each of its three components.
16. Who ultimately bears the risk and collects the rewards associated with operating a business?
17. What does *double-entry bookkeeping* mean?
18. Identify the three types of accounting transactions discussed in this chapter. Provide an example of each type of transaction, and explain how it affects the accounting equation.
19. How does acquiring resources from owners affect the accounting equation?
20. Name the two primary components of stockholders' equity.
21. How does earning revenue affect the accounting equation?
22. What are the three primary sources of assets?
23. What is included in retained earnings?
24. How does distributing assets (paying dividends) to owners affect the accounting equation?
25. What are the similarities and differences between dividends and expenses?
26. What four general-purpose financial statements do business enterprises use to communicate information to stakeholders?
27. Which of the general-purpose financial statements provides information about the enterprise at a specific designated date?
28. What causes a net loss?
29. What three categories of cash receipts and cash payments do businesses report on the statement of cash flows? Explain the types of cash flows reported in each category.
30. How are asset accounts usually arranged in the balance sheet?
31. What type of information does a business typically include in its annual report?
32. What are the six principles of ethical conduct set out under section I of the AICPA's Code of Professional Conduct?

EXERCISES

All Exercises are available with McGraw-Hill's Homework Manager

L.O. 4

Exercise 1-1 *Distributions in a business liquidation*

Assume that Mallory Company acquires $700 cash from creditors and $900 cash from investors (stockholders). The company then has an operating loss of $1,000 cash and goes out of business.

Required

a. Define the term *business liquidation.*

b. What amount of cash will Mallory's creditors receive?

c. What amount of cash will Mallory's investors (stockholders) receive?

L.O. 4

Exercise 1-2 *Identifying the reporting entities*

Reza Pierno recently started a business. During the first few days of operation, Mr. Pierno transferred $15,000 from his personal account into a business account for a company he named Pierno Enterprises. Pierno Enterprises borrowed $20,000 from the State Bank of Renu. Mr. Pierno's father-in-law, Edward Goebel, invested $32,000 into the business for which he received a 25 percent ownership interest. Pierno Enterprises purchased a building from Stokes Realty Company. The building cost $60,000 cash. Pierno Enterprises earned $28,000 in revenue from the company's customers and paid its employees $17,000 for salaries expense.

Required

Identify the entities that were mentioned in the scenario and explain what happened to the cash accounts of each entity that you identify.

L.O. 1

Exercise 1-3 *Financial statement elements and accounts*

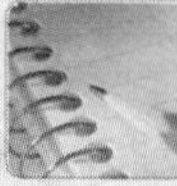

Required

Write a brief memo that distinguishes between the *elements* of financial statements and the *accounts* that appear on financial statements.

L.O. 1

Exercise 1-4 *Titles and accounts appearing on financial statements*

Annual reports normally include an income statement, a statement of changes in stockholders' equity, a balance sheet, and a statement of cash flows.

Required

Identify the financial statements on which each of the following titles or accounts would appear. If a title or an account appears on more than one statement, list all statements that would include it.

a. Common Stock

b. Land

c. Ending Cash Balance

d. Beginning Cash Balance

e. Notes Payable

f. Retained Earnings

g. Revenue

h. Dividends

i. Financing Activities

j. Salary Expense

L.O. 2

Exercise 1-5 *Components of the accounting equation*

Required

The following three requirements are independent of each other.

a. James Auto Parts has assets of $9,100 and equity of $6,500. What is the amount of liabilities? What is the amount of claims?

b. Best Candy Inc. has liabilities of $2,400 and equity of $5,400. What is the amount of assets?

c. Sam's Dive Shop has assets of $49,200 and liabilities of $21,600. What is the amount of its equity? What is the amount of the investors' claims on assets?

Exercise 1-6 *Effect of events on the accounting equation* L.O. 2

Sun Co. experienced the following events during 2006.

1. Acquired cash from the issue of common stock.
2. Provided services to clients for cash.
3. Borrowed cash.
4. Paid operating expenses with cash.
5. Paid a cash dividend to the stockholders.
6. Purchased land with cash.

Required

Explain how each of these events affects the accounting equation by writing the letter I for increase, the letter D for decrease, and NA for no effect under each of the components of the accounting equation. The first event is shown as an example.

			Stockholders' Equity	
Event Number	Assets =	Liabilities +	Common Stock +	Retained Earnings
1	I	NA	I	NA

Exercise 1-7 *Effects of issuing stock* L.O. 2, 3

Jeter Company was started in 2009 when it acquired $18,000 cash by issuing common stock. The cash acquisition was the only event that affected the business in 2009.

Required

a. Write an accounting equation, and record the effects of the stock issue under the appropriate general ledger account headings.

b. What is the amount of net income appearing on the income statement?

c. Where would the stock issue be reported on the statement of cash flows?

Exercise 1-8 *Effects of borrowing* L.O. 2, 3

South Pacific Company was started in 2007 when it issued a note to borrow $8,400 cash. Assume this is the only accounting event that occurred during 2007.

Required

a. Write an accounting equation, and record the effects of the borrowing transaction under the appropriate general ledger account headings.

b. What is the amount of net income reported on the income statement? (Ignore any effects of interest.)

c. Where would the note issue appear on the statement of cash flows?

Exercise 1-9 *Effects of revenue, expense, and dividend events* L.O. 1, 2, 3, 7

Epps Company was started on January 1, 2005. During 2005, the company experienced the following three accounting events: (1) earned cash revenues of $13,500, (2) paid cash expenses of $8,600, and (3) paid a $1,000 cash dividend to stockholders. These were the only events that affected the company during 2005.

Required

a. Write an accounting equation, and record the effects of each accounting event under the appropriate general ledger account headings.

b. Prepare an income statement for the 2005 accounting period and a balance sheet at the end of 2005 for Epps Company.

L.O. 1

Exercise 1-10 *Classifying items for the statement of cash flows*

Required

Indicate whether each of the following would be classified on the statement of cash flows as operating activities (OA), investing activities (IA), financing activities (FA), or not applicable (NA).

a. Paid $4,000 cash for salary expense.
b. Borrowed $8,000 cash from First State Bank.
c. Received $30,000 cash from the issue of common stock.
d. Purchased land for $8,000 cash.
e. Performed services for $14,000 cash.
f. Paid $4,200 cash for utilities expense.
g. Sold land for $7,000 cash.
h. Paid a cash dividend of $1,000 to the stockholders.
i. Hired an accountant to keep the books.
j. Paid $3,000 cash on the loan from First State Bank.

L.O. 1, 2, 3, 5

Exercise 1-11 *Effect of transactions on general ledger accounts*

At the beginning of 2004, Quick Service Company's accounting records had the following general ledger accounts and balances.

QUICK SERVICE COMPANY
Accounting Equation

Event	Assets		=	Liabilities	+	Stockholders' Equity		Acct. Titles for Ret. Earn.
	Cash	Land		Notes Payable		Common Stock	Retained Earnings	
Balance 1/1/2004	25,000	50,000		35,000		30,000	10,000	

Quick completed the following transactions during 2004:

1. Purchased additional land for $12,000 cash.
2. Acquired $20,000 cash from the issue of common stock.
3. Received $65,000 cash for providing services to customers.
4. Paid cash operating expenses of $42,000.
5. Paid $20,000 cash on notes payable.
6. Paid a $3,000 cash dividend to the stockholders.
7. Determined the market value of the land to be $72,000 at the end of the year.

Required

a. Record the transactions in the appropriate general ledger accounts. Record the amounts of revenue, expense, and dividends in the Retained Earnings column. Provide the appropriate titles for these accounts in the last column of the table.

b. Determine the amount of net income for the 2004 period.

c. What is the amount of total assets at the end of 2004? What is the amount of stockholders' equity at the end of 2004?

Exercise 1-12 ***Preparing financial statements*** **L.O. 1, 2, 3, 5, 7**

Dale Company experienced the following events during 2004.

1. Acquired $30,000 cash from the issue of common stock.
2. Paid $12,000 cash to purchase land.
3. Borrowed $8,000 cash.
4. Provided services for $20,000 cash.
5. Paid $1,000 cash for rent expense.
6. Paid $12,000 cash for other operating expenses.
7. Paid a $2,000 cash dividend to the stockholders.
8. Determined that the market value of the land purchased in Event 2 is now $12,700.

Required

a. The January 1, 2004, general ledger account balances are shown in the following accounting equation. Record the eight events in the appropriate general ledger accounts. Record the amounts of revenue, expense, and dividends in the Retained Earnings column. Provide the appropriate titles for these accounts in the last column of the table. The first event is shown as an example.

b. Prepare an income statement, statement of changes in stockholders' equity, year-end balance sheet, and statement of cash flows for the 2004 accounting period.

c. Determine the percentage of assets that was provided by retained earnings. How much cash is in the retained earnings account?

DALE COMPANY
Accounting Equation

Event	Assets		=	Liabilities	+	Stockholders' Equity		Acct. Titles for Ret. Earn.
	Cash	Land		Notes Payable		Common Stock	Retained Earnings	
Balance 1/1/2004	2,000	16,000		0		10,000	8,000	
1.	30,000					30,000		

Exercise 1-13 ***Classifying events as asset source, use, or exchange*** **L.O. 6**

Foster Company experienced the following events during its first year of operations.

1. Acquired $10,000 cash from the issue of common stock.
2. Borrowed $8,000 cash from First Bank.
3. Paid $4,000 cash to purchase land.
4. Received $5,000 cash for providing boarding services.
5. Acquired an additional $2,000 cash from the issue of common stock.
6. Purchased additional land for $3,500 cash.
7. Paid $2,500 cash for salary expense.
8. Signed a contract to provide additional services in the future.
9. Paid $1,000 cash for rent expense.
10. Paid a $1,000 cash dividend to the stockholders.
11. Determined the market value of the land to be $8,000 at the end of the accounting period.

Required

Classify each event as an asset source, use, or exchange transaction or as not applicable (NA).

L.O. 2

Exercise 1-14 *Relationship between assets and retained earnings*

Eastern Company was organized when it acquired $1,000 cash from the issue of common stock. During its first accounting period the company earned $800 of cash revenue and incurred $500 of cash expenses. Also, during the accounting period the company paid its owners a $100 cash dividend.

Required

a. Determine the ending amount of the retained earnings account.

b. As of the end of the accounting period, determine what percentage of total assets was provided by earnings.

L.O. 5

Exercise 1-15 *Historical cost versus market value*

Feloma Company purchased land in April 2001 at a cost of $520,000. The estimated market value of the land is $600,000 as of December 31, 2004. Feloma purchased marketable equity securities (bought the common stock of a company that is independent of Feloma) in May 2001 at a cost of $320,000. These securities have a market value of $360,000 as of December 31, 2004. Generally accepted accounting principles require that the land be shown on the December 31, 2004, balance sheet at $520,000, while the marketable equity securities are required to be reported at $360,000.

Required

Write a brief memo that explains the contradiction regarding why GAAP requires Feloma to report historical cost with respect to the land versus market value with respect to the marketable securities. This answer may require speculation on your part. Use your knowledge about the historical cost and reliability concepts to formulate a logical response.

L.O. 4, 6

Exercise 1-16 *Relating accounting events to entities*

Hanson Company was started in 2004 when it acquired $50,000 cash by issuing common stock to Michael Hanson.

Required

a. Was this event an asset source, use, or exchange transaction for Hanson Company?

b. Was this event an asset source, use, or exchange transaction for Michael Hanson?

c. Was the cash flow an operating, investing, or financing activity on Hanson Company's 2004 statement of cash flows?

d. Was the cash flow an operating, investing, or financing activity on Michael Hanson's 2004 statement of cash flows?

L.O. 2

Exercise 1-17 *Missing information in the accounting equation*

Required

Calculate the missing amounts in the following table:

					Stockholders' Equity		
Company	Assets	=	Liabilities	+	Common Stock	+	Retained Earnings
A	$?		$48,000		$52,000		$36,000
B	90,000		?		25,000		40,000
C	87,000		15,000		?		37,000
D	102,000		29,000		42,000		?

L.O. 1, 7

Exercise 1-18 *Missing information in the accounting equation*

As of December 31, 2006, Thomas Company had total assets of $156,000, total liabilities of $85,600, and common stock of $48,400. During 2007 Thomas earned $36,000 of cash revenue, paid $22,000 for cash expenses, and paid a $1,000 cash dividend to the stockholders.

Required

a. Determine the amount of retained earnings as of December 31, 2006.

b. Determine the amount of net income earned in 2007.

c. Determine the amount of retained earnings as of December 31, 2007.

d. Determine the amount of cash that is in the retained earnings account as of December 31, 2007.

Exercise 1-19 *Missing information for determining net income*

L.O. 5, 7

The December 31, 2006, balance sheet for Kerr Company showed total stockholders' equity of $62,500. Total stockholders' equity increased by $53,400 between December 31, 2006, and December 31, 2007. During 2007 Kerr Company acquired $11,000 cash from the issue of common stock. Kerr Company paid an $8,000 cash dividend to the stockholders during 2007.

Required

Determine the amount of net income or loss Kerr reported on its 2007 income statement. (*Hint:* Remember that stock issues, net income, and dividends all change total stockholders' equity.)

Exercise 1-20 *Effect of events on a horizontal financial statements model*

L.O. 5, 6, 8

Hayes Consulting Services experienced the following events during 2006.

1. Acquired cash by issuing common stock.
2. Collected cash for providing tutoring services to clients.
3. Borrowed cash from a local government small business foundation.
4. Purchased land for cash.
5. Paid cash for operating expenses.
6. Paid a cash dividend to the stockholders.
7. Determined the year-end market value of the land to be higher than its historical cost.

Required

Use a horizontal statements model to show how each event affects the balance sheet, income statement, and statement of cash flows. Indicate whether the event increases (I), decreases (D), or does not affect (NA) each element of the financial statements. Also, in the Cash Flows column, classify the cash flows as operating activities (OA), investing activities (IA), or financing activities (FA). The first transaction is shown as an example.

Event No.	Balance Sheet									Income Statement					Statement of Cash Flows	
	Cash	+	Land	=	N. Pay.	+	Com. Stk.	+	Ret. Earn.	Rev.	−	Exp.	=	Net Inc.		
1.	I	+	NA	=	NA	+	I	+	NA	NA	−	NA	=	NA	I	FA

Exercise 1-21 *Record events in the horizontal statements model*

L.O. 8

Marshall Co. was started in 2006. During 2006, the company (1) acquired $9,000 cash from the issue of common stock, (2) earned cash revenue of $18,000, (3) paid cash expenses of $12,500, and (4) paid a $1,000 cash dividend to the stockholders.

Required

a. Record these four events in a horizontal statements model. Also, in the Cash Flows column, classify the cash flows as operating activities (OA), investing activities (IA), or financing activities (FA). The first event is shown as an example.

Event No.	Balance Sheet							Income Statement					Statement of Cash Flows	
	Cash	=	N. Pay.	+	Com. Stk.	+	Ret. Earn.	Rev.	−	Exp.	=	Net Inc.		
1.	9,000	=	NA	+	9,000	+	NA	NA	−	NA	=	NA	9,000	FA

b. What does the income statement tell you about the assets of this business?

Exercise 1-22 *Effect of events on a horizontal statements model*

L.O. 8

Tax Help Inc. was started on January 1, 2006. The company experienced the following events during its first year of operation.

1. Acquired $30,000 cash from the issue of common stock.
2. Paid $12,000 cash to purchase land.

3. Received $30,000 cash for providing tax services to customers.
4. Paid $9,500 cash for salary expense.
5. Acquired $5,000 cash from the issue of additional common stock.
6. Borrowed $10,000 cash from the bank.
7. Purchased additional land for $5,000 cash.
8. Paid $6,000 cash for other operating expenses.
9. Paid a $2,800 cash dividend to the stockholders.
10. Determined the market value of the land to be $18,000.

Required

a. Record these events in a horizontal statements model. Also, in the Cash Flows column, classify the cash flows as operating activities (OA), investing activities (IA), or financing activities (FA). The first event is shown as an example.

Event No.	Balance Sheet									Income Statement					Statement of Cash Flows	
	Cash	+	Land	=	N. Pay.	+	Com. Stk.	+	Ret. Earn.	Rev.	−	Exp.	=	Net Inc.		
1.	30,000	+	NA	=	NA	+	30,000	+	NA	NA	−	NA	=	NA	30,000	FA

b. What is the net income earned in 2006?

c. What is the amount of total assets at the end of 2006?

d. What is the net cash flow from operating activities for 2006?

e. What is the net cash flow from investing activities for 2006?

f. What is the net cash flow from financing activities for 2006?

g. What is the cash balance at the end of 2006?

h. As of the end of the year 2006, what percentage of total assets was provided by creditors, investors, and earnings?

L.O. 5, 8

Exercise 1-23 *Types of transactions and the horizontal statements model*

The Shoe Shop experienced the following events during its first year of operations, 2008.

1. Acquired cash by issuing common stock.
2. Provided services and collected cash.
3. Borrowed cash from a bank.
4. Paid cash for operating expenses.
5. Purchased land with cash.
6. Paid a cash dividend to the stockholders.
7. Determined the market value of the land to be higher than the historical cost.

Required

a. Indicate whether each event is an asset source, use, or exchange transaction.

b. Use a horizontal statements model to show how each event affects the balance sheet, income statement, and statement of cash flows. Indicate whether the event increases (I), decreases (D), or does not affect (NA) each element of the financial statements. Also, in the Cash Flows column, classify the cash flows as operating activities (OA), investing activities (IA), or financing activities (FA). The first transaction is shown as an example.

Event No.	Balance Sheet									Income Statement					Statement of Cash Flows	
	Cash	+	Land	=	N. Pay.	+	Com. Stk.	+	Ret. Earn.	Rev.	−	Exp.	=	Net Inc.		
1.	I	+	NA	=	NA	+	I	+	NA	NA	−	NA	=	NA	I	FA

Exercise 1-24 ***Code of Professional Conduct*** **L.O. 9**

Jane Wong is a certified public accountant (CPA). She follows a code of professional conduct in the performance of her duties.

Required

a. Name the organization that established the code of conduct that Jane follows.
b. Name the six principles in the code of conduct that Jane follows.

PROBLEMS

All Problems are available with McGraw-Hill's Homework Manager

Problem 1-25 ***Accounting entities*** **L.O. 4**

CHECK FIGURE
Entities mentioned:
Tilly Jensen
Jensen Business

The following business scenarios are independent of one another.

1. Tilly Jensen starts a business by transferring $5,000 from her personal checking account into a checking account for the business.
2. A business that Bart Angle owns earns $2,300 of cash revenue.
3. Phil Culver borrows $20,000 from the National Bank and uses the money to purchase a car from Henderson Ford.
4. Lipka Company pays its five employees $2,000 each to cover their salaries.
5. Kevin Dow loans his son Brian $5,000 cash.
6. Asthana Inc. paid $150,000 cash to purchase land from Waterbury Inc.
7. Moshe Liu and Chao Porat form a partnership by contributing $30,000 each from their personal bank accounts to a partnership bank account.
8. Ken Stanga pays cash to purchase $2,000 of common stock that is issued by Krishnan Inc.
9. Omni Company pays a $42,000 cash dividend to each of its seven shareholders.
10. McCann Inc. borrowed $5,000,000 from the National Bank.

Required

a. For each scenario create a list of all of the entities that are mentioned in the description.
b. Describe what happens to the cash account of each entity that you identified in Requirement *a*.

Problem 1-26 ***Relating titles and accounts to financial statements*** **L.O. 1**

Required

Identify the financial statements on which each of the following items (titles, date descriptions, and accounts) appears by placing a check mark in the appropriate column. If an item appears on more than one statement, place a check mark in every applicable column.

Item	Income Statement	Statement of Changes in Stockholders' Equity	Balance Sheet	Statement of Cash Flows
Notes payable				
Beginning common stock				
Service revenue				
Utility expense				
Cash from stock issue				
Operating activities				
For the period ended (date)				

continued

Item	Income Statement	Statement of Changes in Stockholders' Equity	Balance Sheet	Statement of Cash Flows
Net income				
Investing activities				
Net loss				
Ending cash balance				
Salary expense				
Consulting revenue				
Dividends				
Financing activities				
Ending common stock				
Rent expense				
As of (date)				
Land				
Beginning cash balance				

L.O. 1, 2, 3, 5, 7

mhhe.com/edmonds2007

CHECK FIGURES

a. Net Income 2006: $23,000

b. Retained Earnings 2007: $40,500

Problem 1-27 *Preparing financial statements for two complete accounting cycles*

Keller Consulting experienced the following transactions for 2006, its first year of operations, and 2007. *Assume that all transactions involve the receipt or payment of cash.*

Transactions for 2006

1. Acquired $20,000 by issuing common stock.
2. Received $65,000 cash for providing services to customers.
3. Borrowed $25,000 cash from creditors.
4. Paid expenses amounting to $42,000.
5. Purchased land for $30,000 cash.

Transactions for 2007

Beginning account balances for 2007 are:

Cash	$38,000
Land	30,000
Notes Payable	25,000
Common Stock	20,000
Retained Earnings	23,000

1. Acquired an additional $24,000 from the issue of common stock.
2. Received $95,000 for providing services.
3. Paid $10,000 to creditors to reduce loan.
4. Paid expenses amounting to $71,500.
5. Paid a $6,000 dividend to the stockholders.
6. Determined the market value of the land to be $47,000.

Required

a. Write an accounting equation, and record the effects of each accounting event under the appropriate headings for each year. Record the amounts of revenue, expense, and dividends in the Retained Earnings column. Provide appropriate titles for these accounts in the last column of the table.

b. Prepare an income statement, statement of changes in stockholders' equity, year-end balance sheet, and statement of cash flows for each year.

c. Determine the amount of cash that is in the retained earnings account at the end of 2006 and 2007.

d. Compare the information provided by the income statement with the information provided by the statement of cash flows. Point out similarities and differences.

Problem 1-28 *Interrelationships among financial statements*

L.O. 1, 3, 7

CHECK FIGURES
a. Net Income: $16,000
b. Total Assets: $48,000

O'Shea Enterprises started the 2006 accounting period with $30,000 of assets (all cash), $18,000 of liabilities, and $4,000 of common stock. During the year, O'Shea earned cash revenues of $48,000, paid cash expenses of $32,000, and paid a cash dividend to stockholders of $2,000. O'Shea also acquired $10,000 of additional cash from the sale of common stock and paid $6,000 cash to reduce the liability owed to a bank.

Required

a. Prepare an income statement, statement of changes in stockholders' equity, period-end balance sheet, and statement of cash flows for the 2006 accounting period. (*Hint:* Determine the amount of beginning retained earnings before considering the effects of the current period events. Record all events under an accounting equation before preparing the statements.)

b. Determine the percentage of total assets that was provided by creditors, investors, and earnings.

Problem 1-29 *Classifying events as asset source, use, or exchange*

L.O. 2, 6

CHECK FIGURE
Event 2 Asset Exchange

The following unrelated events are typical of those experienced by business entities.

1. Acquire cash by issuing common stock.
2. Purchase land with cash.
3. Purchase equipment with cash.
4. Pay monthly rent on an office building.
5. Hire a new office manager.
6. Borrow cash from a bank.
7. Pay a cash dividend to stockholders.
8. Pay cash for operating expenses.
9. Pay an office manager's salary with cash.
10. Receive cash for services that have been performed.
11. Provide services for cash.
12. Acquire land by accepting a liability (financing the purchase).
13. Pay cash to purchase a new office building.
14. Discuss plans for a new office building with an architect.
15. Repay part of a bank loan.

Required

Identify each of the events as an asset source, use, or exchange transaction. If an event would not be recorded under generally accepted accounting principles, identify it as *not applicable* (NA). Also indicate for each event whether total assets would increase, decrease, or remain unchanged. Organize your answer according to the following table. The first event is shown in the table as an example.

Event No.	Type of Event	Effect on Total Assets
1	Asset source	Increase

Problem 1-30 *Recording the effect of events in a horizontal statements model*

L.O. 5, 8

Lighthouse Services experienced the following transactions during 2006.

1. Acquired cash by issuing common stock.
2. Received cash for performing services.
3. Paid cash expenses.
4. Borrowed cash from the local bank.
5. Purchased land for cash.
6. Paid cash to reduce the principal balance of the bank loan.

7. Paid a cash dividend to the stockholders.
8. Determined the market value of the land to be higher than its historical cost.

Required

Use a horizontal statements model to show how each event affects the balance sheet, income statement, and statement of cash flows. Indicate whether the event increases (I), decreases (D), or does not affect (NA) each element of the financial statements. Also, in the Cash Flows column, classify the cash flows as operating activities (OA), investing activities (IA), or financing activities (FA). The first transaction is shown as an example.

Event No.	Balance Sheet									Income Statement					Statement of Cash Flows	
	Cash	+	Land	=	N. Pay.	+	Com. Stk.	+	Ret. Earn.	Rev.	−	Exp.	=	Net Inc.		
1.	I	+	NA	=	NA	+	I	+	NA	NA	−	NA	=	NA	I	FA

L.O. 2, 5, 8

CHECK FIGURES
a. Net Income: $13,000
e. Net Cash Flow from Operating Activities: $13,000

Problem 1-31 *Recording events in a horizontal statements model*

Flick Company was started on January 1, 2007, and experienced the following events during its first year of operation.

1. Acquired $30,000 cash from the issue of common stock.
2. Borrowed $20,000 cash from State Bank.
3. Earned cash revenues of $48,000 for performing services.
4. Paid cash expenses of $35,000.
5. Paid a $4,000 cash dividend to the stockholders.
6. Acquired an additional $20,000 cash from the issue of common stock.
7. Paid $5,000 cash to reduce the principal balance of the bank note.
8. Paid $53,000 cash to purchase land.
9. Determined the market value of the land to be $60,000.

Required

a. Record the preceding transactions in the horizontal statements model. Also, in the Cash Flows column, classify the cash flows as operating activities (OA), investing activities (IA), or financing activities (FA). The first event is shown as an example.

Event No.	Balance Sheet									Income Statement					Statement of Cash Flows	
	Cash	+	Land	=	N. Pay.	+	Com. Stk.	+	Ret. Earn.	Rev.	−	Exp.	=	Net Inc.		
1.	30,000	+	NA	=	NA	+	30,000	+	NA	NA	−	NA	=	NA	30,000	FA

b. Determine the amount of total assets that Flick would report on the December 31, 2007, balance sheet.
c. Identify the sources of the assets that Flick would report on the December 31, 2007, balance sheet. Determine the amount of each of these sources.
d. Determine the net income that Flick would report on the 2007 income statement. Explain why dividends do not appear on the income statement.
e. Determine the net cash flows from operating activities, financing activities, and investing activities that Flick would report on the 2007 statement of cash flows.
f. Determine the percentage of assets that was provided by investors, creditors, and earnings.

L.O. 9

Problem 1-32 *Factors associated with white collar crime*

Clair Cubelic, a private accountant employed by a large corporation, holds the CMA professional designation. She is a trusted employee who is eager to help others whenever necessary. For example, Clair frequently orders merchandise when purchasing department personnel are overburdened. Clair's only problem is that she feels she is underpaid. Several men in her office make more money than she does and they are not even professionally certified accountants. Clair has significant debt that she acquired while she was a student and has trouble paying her monthly bills. A close friend of Clair's sells supplies to the company. When Clair complained to him about her pay situation, he joked that he could help her get even by sending the company less merchandise than was shown on the purchase orders. He laughed and suggested they could split the rewards of the rip-off between them. To his surprise she responded with a serious plan that would enable them to embezzle several thousand dollars per month from her company. She assured him that she could gain control of all phases of the purchasing system from ordering to payment. Unfortunately for Clair, what started as a joke ultimately ended with a jail sentence.

Required

Name the three factors that Donald Cressey found to be associated with white collar criminals. Identify these factors as they apply to Clair Cubelic's case.

ANALYZE, THINK, COMMUNICATE

ATC 1-1 Business Applications Case *Understanding real world annual reports*

Required

Use the Topps Company's annual report in Appendix B to answer the following questions.

a. What was Topps' net income for 2003?

b. Did Topps' net income increase or decrease from 2002 to 2003, and by how much?

c. What was Topps' accounting equation for 2003?

d. Which of the following had the largest percentage increase from 2002 to 2003: net sales, cost of sales, or selling, general, and administrative expenses? Show all computations.

ATC 1-2 Group Assignment *Missing information*

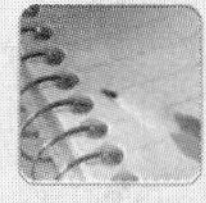

The following selected financial information is available for J&G Inc. Amounts are in millions of dollars.

Income Statements	2004	2003	2002	2001
Revenue	$ 661	$1,307	$ (a)	$ 894
Cost and Expenses	(a)	(a)	(1,859)	(769)
Income from Continuing Operations	(b)	174	71	(a)
Unusual Items	0	218	(b)	(b)
Net Income	$ 7	$ (b)	$ 47	$ 177

Balance Sheets	2004	2003	2002	2001
Assets				
Cash and Marketable Securities	$ 249	$1,247	$ (c)	$ 419
Other Assets	1,661	(c)	1,226	(c)
Total Assets	1,910	$2,904	$ (d)	$1,418
Liabilities	$ (c)	$ (d)	$ 907	$ (d)
Stockholders' Equity				
Common Stock	422	356	(e)	313
Retained Earnings	(d)	(e)	684	(e)
Total Stockholders' Equity	1,062	1,342	(f)	1,040
Total Liabilities and Stockholders' Equity	$1,910	$ (f)	$1,906	$1,418

Required

a. Divide the class into groups of four or five students each. Organize the groups into four sections. Assign Task 1 to the first section of groups, Task 2 to the second section, Task 3 to the third section, and Task 4 to the fourth section.

Group Tasks

(1) Fill in the missing information for 2001.
(2) Fill in the missing information for 2002.
(3) Fill in the missing information for 2003.
(4) Fill in the missing information for 2004.

b. Each section should select two representatives. One representative is to put the financial statements assigned to that section on the board, underlining the missing amounts. The second representative is to explain to the class how the missing amounts were determined.

c. Each section should list events that could have caused the unusual item category on the income statement.

ATC 1-3 Real-World Case *Classifying cash flow activities at five companies*

The following cash transactions occurred in five real world companies during 2004:

1. FedEx Corp., which is the holding company of Federal Express, purchased Kinko's, Inc., on February 12, 2004, for $2.4 billion.
2. Google Inc. issued 14.1 million shares of its stock on August 18, 2004, for $85 per share. On that same day, a few major shareholders of Google, including its founders, sold 5.5 million shares of its stock at the same price.
3. Payless ShoeSource, Inc., had cash sales of $2.8 billion during its fiscal year ending on January 31, 2004.
4. Red Hat, Inc., the leading provider of the open-source operating system Linux, issued $600 million of "convertible debentures" in January 2004. Convertible debentures are a form of long-term debt that is explained in more detail in Chapter 7.
5. Sears, Roebuck and Company completed the sale of its domestic Credit and Financial Products business to Citicorp on November 3, 2004, for $32 billion, $22 billion of which was received in cash.

Required

Determine if each of the above transactions should be classified as an *operating, investing,* or *financing* activity. Also, identify the amount of each cash flow and whether it was an *inflow* or an *outflow.*

ATC 1-4 Business Applications Case *Use of real-world numbers for forecasting*

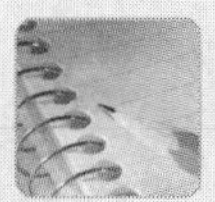

The following information was drawn from the annual report of Machine Import Company (MIC):

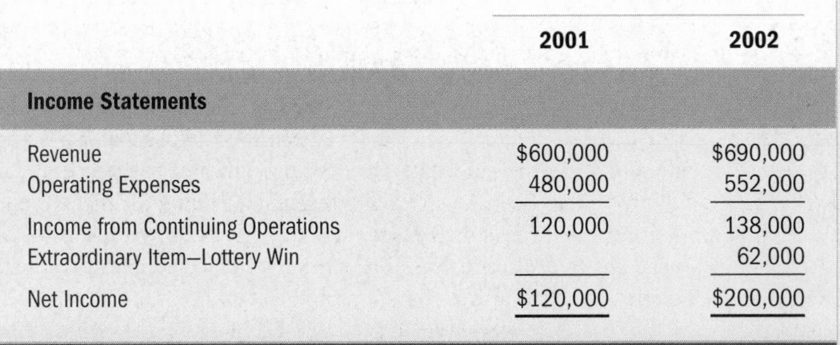

	For the Years	
	2001	**2002**
Income Statements		
Revenue	$600,000	$690,000
Operating Expenses	480,000	552,000
Income from Continuing Operations	120,000	138,000
Extraordinary Item—Lottery Win		62,000
Net Income	$120,000	$200,000
Balance Sheets		
Assets	$880,000	$880,000
Liabilities	$200,000	$ 0
Stockholders' Equity		
Common Stock	380,000	380,000
Retained Earnings	300,000	500,000
Total Liabilities and Stockholders' Equity	$880,000	$880,000

Required

a. Compute the percentage of growth in net income from 2001 to 2002. Can stockholders expect a similar increase between 2002 and 2003?

b. Assuming that MIC collected $200,000 cash from earnings (net income), explain how this money was spent in 2002.

c. Assuming that MIC experiences the same percentage of growth from 2002 to 2003 as it did from 2001 to 2002, determine the amount of income from continuing operations that the owners can expect to see on the 2003 income statement.

d. During 2003, MIC experienced a $40,000 loss due to storm damage (note that this would be shown as an extraordinary loss on the income statement). Liabilities and common stock were unchanged from 2002 to 2003. Use the information that you computed in Part *c* plus the additional information provided in the previous two sentences to prepare an income statement for 2003 and balance sheet as of December 31, 2003.

ATC 1-5 Writing Assignment *Elements of financial statements defined*

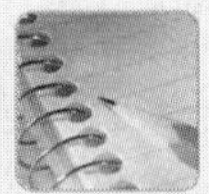

Bob and his sister Marsha both attend the state university. As a reward for their successful completion of the past year (Bob had a 3.2 GPA in business, and Marsha had a 3.7 GPA in art), their father gave each of them 100 shares of The Walt Disney Company stock. They have just received their first annual report. Marsha does not understand what the information means and has asked Bob to explain it to her. Bob is currently taking an accounting course, and she knows he will understand the financial statements.

Required

Assume that you are Bob. Write Marsha a memo explaining the following financial statement items to her. In your explanation, describe each of the two financial statements and explain the financial information each contains. Also define each of the elements listed for each financial statement and explain what it means.

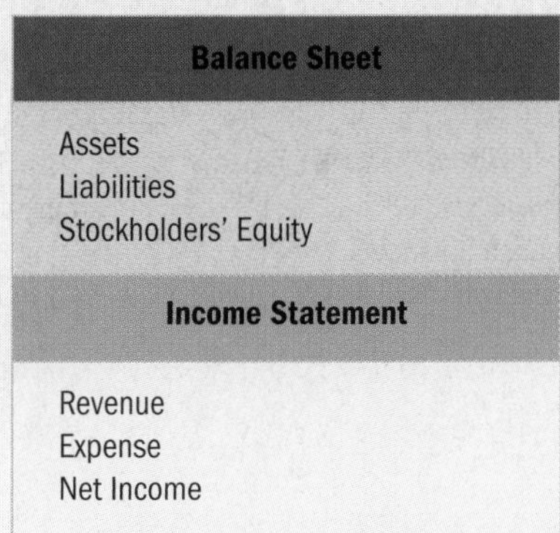

Balance Sheet
Assets
Liabilities
Stockholders' Equity
Income Statement
Revenue
Expense
Net Income

ATC 1-6 Ethical Dilemma *Loyalty versus the bottom line*

Assume that Jones has been working for you for five years. He has had an excellent work history and has received generous pay raises in response. The raises have been so generous that Jones is quite overpaid for the job he is required to perform. Unfortunately, he is not qualified to take on other, more responsible jobs available within the company. A recent job applicant is willing to accept a salary $5,000 per year less than the amount currently being paid to Jones. The applicant is well qualified to take over Jones's duties and has a very positive attitude. The following financial statements were reported by your company at the close of its most recent accounting period.

Financial Statements

Income Statement	
Revenue	$ 57,000
Expense	(45,000)
Net Income	$12,000

continued

Statement of Changes in Stockholders' Equity		
Beginning Common Stock	$20,000	
Plus: Stock Issued	5,000	
Ending Common Stock		$25,000
Beginning Retained Earnings	50,000	
Net Income	12,000	
Dividends	(2,000)	
Ending Retained Earnings		60,000
Total Stockholders' Equity		$85,000

Balance Sheet	
Assets	
Cash	$85,000
Stockholders' Equity	
Common Stock	$25,000
Retained Earnings	60,000
Total Stockholders' Equity	$85,000

Statement of Cash Flows		
Operating Activities		
Inflow from Customers	$57,000	
Outflow for Expenses	(45,000)	
Net Inflow from Operating Activities		$12,000
Investing Activities		0
Financing Activities		
Inflow from Stock Issue	5,000	
Outflow for Dividends	(2,000)	
Net Inflow from Financing Activities		3,000
Net Change in Cash		15,000
Plus: Beginning Cash Balance		70,000
Ending Cash Balance		$85,000

Required

a. Reconstruct the financial statements, assuming that Jones was replaced at the beginning of the most recent accounting period. Both Jones and his replacement are paid in cash. No other changes are to be considered.

b. Assume that you are a CPA. Would any of the principles of the AICPA Code of Professional Conduct prevent you from replacing Jones? Explain your answer.

ATC 1-7 Research Assignment *Finding real-world accounting information*

The Curious Accountant story at the beginning of this chapter referred to McDonald's Corporation and discussed who its stakeholders are. This chapter introduced the basic four financial statements companies use annually to keep their stakeholders informed of their accomplishments and financial situation. Complete the requirements below using the 2003 financial statements available on the McDonald's website. Obtain the statements on the Internet by following the steps below. (The formatting of the company's website may have changed since these instructions were written.)

1. Go to www.mcdonalds.com.
2. Click on the "Corporate" link at the bottom of the page. (Most companies have a link titled "investor relations" that leads to their financial statements; McDonald's uses "corporate" instead.)

3. Click on the "INVESTORS" link at the top of the page.
4. Click on *"Publications"* and then on *"Annual Report Archives."*
5. Click on *"McDonald's 2003 Annual Report"* and then on *"2003 Financial Report."*
6. Go to the company's financial statements on pages 17 through 20 of the annual report.

Required

a. What was the company's net income in 2003, 2002, and 2001?
b. What amount of total assets did the company have at the end of 2003?
c. How much retained earnings did the company have at the end of 2003?
d. For 2003, what was the company's cash flow from operating activities, cash flow from investing activities, and cash flow from financing activities?

CHAPTER 2

Understanding the Accounting Cycle

LEARNING OBJECTIVES

After you have mastered the material in this chapter you will be able to:

1. **Record basic accrual and deferral events in a horizontal financial statements model.**
2. **Organize general ledger accounts under an accounting equation.**
3. **Prepare financial statements based on accrual accounting.**
4. **Describe the closing process, the accounting cycle, and the matching concept.**
5. **Prepare a vertical financial statements model.**
6. **Explain how business events affect financial statements over multiple accounting cycles.**
7. **Explain how to use the price-earnings ratio and growth percentage analysis to assess the market value of common stock.**
8. **Classify accounting events into one of four categories:**
   a. **asset source transactions.**
   b. **asset use transactions.**
   c. **asset exchange transactions.**
   d. **claims exchange transactions.**

The Curious Accountant

If a person wishes to subscribe to *Reader's Digest* for one year (12 issues), the subscriber must pay for the magazines before they are actually published. Suppose Paige Long sent $14 to the Reader's Digest Association in September 2007 for a one-year subscription; she will receive her first issue in October.

How should Reader's Digest account for the receipt of this cash? How would this event be reported on Reader's Digest's December 31, 2007, financial statements? (Answers on page 56.)

CHAPTER OPENING

Users of financial statements must distinguish between the terms recognition *and* realization. **Recognition** *means formally* reporting *an economic item or event in the financial statements.* **Realization** *refers to collecting money, generally from the sale of products or services. Companies may recognize (report) revenue in the income statement in a different accounting period from the period in which they collect the cash related to the revenue. Furthermore, companies frequently make cash payments for expenses in accounting periods other than the periods in which the expenses are recognized in the income statement.*

To illustrate, assume Johnson Company provides services to customers in 2005 but collects cash for those services in 2006. In this case, realization occurs in 2006. When should Johnson recognize the services revenue?

Users of cash basis *accounting recognize (report) revenues and expenses in the period in which cash is collected or paid. Under cash basis accounting Johnson would recognize the revenue in 2006 when it collects the cash. In contrast, users of* **accrual accounting** *recognize revenues and expenses in the period in which they occur, regardless of when cash is collected or paid. Under accrual accounting Johnson would recognize the revenue in 2005 (the period in which it performed the services) even though it does not collect (realize) the cash until 2006.*

Accrual accounting is required by generally accepted accounting principles. Virtually all major companies operating in the United States use it. Its two distinguishing features are called accruals *and* deferrals.

- *The term* **accrual** *describes an earnings event that is recognized* **before** *cash is exchanged. Johnson's recognition of revenue in 2005 related to cash realized in 2006 is an example of an accrual.*
- *The term* **deferral** *describes an earnings event that is recognized* **after** *cash has been exchanged. Suppose Johnson pays cash in 2005 to purchase office supplies it uses in 2006. In this case the cash payment occurs in 2005 although supplies expense is recognized in 2006. This example is a deferral.* ■

Accrual Accounting

Record basic accrual and deferral events in a horizontal financial statements model.

The next section of the text describes seven events experienced by Cato Consultants, a training services company that uses accrual accounting.

Event 1 **Cato Consultants was started on January 1, 2008, when it acquired $5,000 cash by issuing common stock.**

The issue of stock for cash is an **asset source transaction.** It increases the company's assets (cash) and its equity (common stock). The transaction does not affect the income statement. The cash inflow is classified as a financing activity (acquisition from owners). These effects are shown in the following financial statements model:

Assets	=	Liab.	+	Stockholders' Equity								Cash Flow
Cash	=			Com. Stk.	+	Ret. Earn.	Rev.	−	Exp.	=	Net Inc.	
5,000	=	NA	+	5,000	+	NA	NA	−	NA	=	NA	5,000 FA

Accounting for Accounts Receivable

Event 2 **During 2008 Cato Consultants provided $84,000 of consulting services to its clients. The business has completed the work and sent bills to the clients, but not yet collected any cash. This type of transaction is frequently described as providing services *on account.***

Accrual accounting requires companies to recognize revenue in the period in which the work is done regardless of when cash is collected. In this case, revenue is recognized in 2008 even though cash has not been realized (collected). Recall that revenue represents the economic benefit that results in an increase in assets from providing goods and services to customers. The specific asset that increases is called **Accounts Receivable.** The balance in Accounts Receivable represents the amount of cash the company expects to collect in the future. Since the revenue recognition causes assets (accounts receivable) to increase, it is classified as an asset source transaction. Its effect on the financial statements follows:

Assets			=	Liab.	+	Stockholders' Equity								Cash Flow
Cash	+	Accts. Rec.	=			Com. Stk.	+	Ret. Earn.	Rev.	−	Exp.	=	Net Inc.	
NA	+	84,000	=	NA	+	NA	+	84,000	84,000	−	NA	=	84,000	NA

Notice that the event affects the income statement but not the statement of cash flows. The statement of cash flows will be affected in the future when cash is collected.

Event 3 **Cato collected $60,000 cash from customers in partial settlement of its accounts receivable.**

The collection of an account receivable is an **asset exchange transaction.** One asset account (Cash) increases and another asset account (Accounts Receivable) decreases. The amount of total assets is unchanged. The effect of the $60,000 collection of receivables on the financial statements is as follows:

Assets			=	Liab.	+	Stockholders' Equity								
Cash	+	Accts. Rec.	=			Com. Stk.	+	Ret. Earn.	Rev.	−	Exp.	=	Net Inc.	Cash Flow
60,000	+	(60,000)	=	NA	+	NA	+	NA	NA	−	NA	=	NA	60,000 OA

Notice that collecting the cash did not affect the income statement. The revenue was recognized when the work was done (see Event 2). Revenue would be double counted if it were recognized again when the cash is collected. The statement of cash flows reflects a cash inflow from operating activities.

Other Events

Event 4 Cato paid the instructor $10,000 for teaching training courses (salary expense).

Cash payment for salary expense is an **asset use transaction.** Both the asset account Cash and the equity account Retained Earnings decrease by $10,000. Recognizing the expense decreases net income on the income statement. Since Cato paid cash for the expense, the statement of cash flows reflects a cash outflow from operating activities. These effects on the financial statements follow:

Assets			=	Liab.	+	Stockholders' Equity								
Cash	+	Accts. Rec.	=			Com. Stk.	+	Ret. Earn.	Rev.	−	Exp.	=	Net Inc.	Cash Flow
(10,000)	+	NA	=	NA	+	NA	+	(10,000)	NA	−	10,000	=	(10,000)	(10,000) OA

Event 5 Cato paid $2,000 cash for advertising costs. The advertisements appeared in 2008.

Cash payments for advertising expenses are asset use transactions. Both the asset account Cash and the equity account Retained Earnings decrease by $2,000. Recognizing the expense decreases net income on the income statement. Since the expense was paid with cash, the statement of cash flows reflects a cash outflow from operating activities. These effects on the financial statements follow:

Assets			=	Liab.	+	Stockholders' Equity								
Cash	+	Accts. Rec.	=			Com. Stk.	+	Ret. Earn.	Rev.	−	Exp.	=	Net Inc.	Cash Flow
(2,000)	+	NA	=	NA	+	NA	+	(2,000)	NA	−	2,000	=	(2,000)	(2,000) OA

Event 6 Cato signed contracts for $42,000 of consulting services to be performed in 2009.

The $42,000 for consulting services to be performed in 2009 is not recognized in the 2008 financial statements. Revenue is recognized for work actually completed, *not* work expected to be completed. This event does not affect any of the financial statements.

Assets			=	Liab.	+	Stockholders' Equity								
Cash	+	Accts. Rec.	=			Com. Stk.	+	Ret. Earn.	Rev.	−	Exp.	=	Net Inc.	Cash Flow
NA	+	NA	=	NA	+	NA	+	NA	NA	−	NA	=	NA	NA

Accounting for Accrued Salary Expense (Adjusting Entry)

It is impractical to record many business events as they occur. For example, Cato incurs salary expense continually as the instructor teaches courses. Imagine the impossibility of trying to record salary expense second by second! Companies normally record transactions when it is most convenient. The most convenient time to record many expenses is when they are paid. Often, however, a single business transaction pertains to more than one accounting period. To provide accurate financial reports in such cases, companies may need to recognize some expenses before paying cash for them. Expenses that are recognized before cash is paid are called **accrued expenses.** The accounting for Event 7 illustrates the effect of recognizing accrued salary expense.

Event 7 **At the end of 2008 Cato recorded accrued salary expense of $6,000 (the salary expense is for courses the instructor taught in 2008 that Cato will pay him for in 2009).**

Accrual accounting requires that companies recognize expenses in the period in which they are incurred regardless of when cash is paid. Cato must recognize all salary expense in the period in which the instructor worked (2008) even though Cato will not pay the instructor again until 2009. Cato must also recognize the obligation (liability) it has to pay the instructor. To accurately report all 2008 salary expense and year-end obligations, Cato must record the unpaid salary expense and salary liability before preparing its financial statements. The entry to recognize the accrued salary expense is called an **adjusting entry.** Like all adjusting entries, it is only to update the accounting records; it does not affect cash.

This adjusting entry decreases stockholders' equity (retained earnings) and increases a liability account called **Salaries Payable.** The balance in the Salaries Payable account represents the amount of cash the company is obligated to pay the instructor in the future. The effect of the expense recognition on the financial statements follows:

Assets			=	Liab.	+	Stockholders' Equity								
Cash	+	Accts. Rec.	=	Sal. Pay.	+	Com. Stk.	+	Ret. Earn.	Rev.	−	Exp.	=	Net Inc.	Cash Flow
NA	+	NA	=	6,000	+	NA	+	(6,000)	NA	−	6,000	=	(6,000)	NA

This event is a **claims exchange transaction.** The claims of creditors (liabilities) increase and the claims of stockholders (retained earnings) decrease. Total claims remain unchanged. The salary expense is reported on the income statement. The statement of cash flows is not affected.

Be careful not to confuse liabilities with expenses. Although liabilities may increase when a company recognizes expenses, liabilities are not expenses. Liabilities are obligations. They can arise from acquiring assets as well as recognizing expenses. For example, when a business borrows money from a bank, it recognizes an increase in assets (cash) and liabilities (notes payable). The borrowing transaction does not affect expenses.

CHECK YOURSELF 2.1

During 2006, Anwar Company earned $345,000 of revenue on account and collected $320,000 cash from accounts receivable. Anwar paid cash expenses of $300,000 and cash dividends of $12,000. Determine the amount of net income Anwar should report on the 2006 income statement and the amount of cash flow from operating activities Anwar should report on the 2006 statement of cash flows.

Answer

Net income is $45,000 ($345,000 revenue − $300,000 expenses). The cash flow from operating activities is $20,000, the amount of revenue collected in cash from customers (accounts receivable) minus the cash paid for expenses ($320,000 − $300,000). Dividend payments are classified as financing activities and do not affect the determination of either net income or cash flow from operating activities.

Summary of Events

The previous section of this chapter described seven events Cato Consultants experienced during the 2008 accounting period. These events are summarized below for your convenience.

Event 1 Cato Consultants acquired $5,000 cash by issuing common stock.

Event 2 Cato provided $84,000 of consulting services on account.

Event 3 Cato collected $60,000 cash from customers in partial settlement of its accounts receivable.

Event 4 Cato paid $10,000 cash for salary expense.

Event 5 Cato paid $2,000 cash for 2008 advertising costs.

Event 6 Cato signed contracts for $42,000 of consulting services to be performed in 2009.

Event 7 Cato recognized $6,000 of accrued salary expense.

The General Ledger

Exhibit 2.1 shows the 2008 transaction data recorded in general ledger accounts. The information in these accounts is used to prepare the financial statements. The revenue and expense items appear in the Retained Earnings column with their account titles immediately to the right of the dollar amounts. The amounts are color coded to help you trace the data to the financial statements. Data in red appear on the balance sheet, data in blue on the income statement, and data in green on the statement of cash flows. Before reading further, trace each transaction in the summary of events into Exhibit 2.1.

Organize general ledger accounts under an accounting equation.

Vertical Statements Model

The financial statements for Cato Consultants' 2008 accounting period are represented in a vertical statements model in Exhibit 2.2. A vertical statements model arranges a set of financial statement information vertically on a single page. Like horizontal statements models, vertical statements models are learning tools. They illustrate interrelationships among financial statements. The models do not, however, portray the full, formal presentation formats companies use in published financial statements. For example, statements models may use summarized formats with abbreviated titles and dates. As you read the following explanations of each financial statement, trace the color coded financial data from Exhibit 2.1 to Exhibit 2.2.

Prepare financial statements based on accrual accounting.

Income Statement

The income statement reflects accrual accounting. Consulting revenue represents the price Cato charged for all the services it performed in 2008, even though Cato had not by the end

EXHIBIT 2.1 Transaction Data for 2008 Recorded in General Ledger Accounts

	Assets			=	Liabilities	+	Stockholders' Equity			
Event No.	**Cash**	**+**	**Accounts Receivable**	**=**	**Salaries Payable**	**+**	**Common Stock**	**+**	**Retained Earnings**	**Other Account Titles**
Beg. bal.	0		0		0		0		0	
1	5,000						5,000			
2			84,000						84,000	Consulting Revenue
3	60,000		(60,000)							
4	(10,000)								(10,000)	Salary Expense
5	(2,000)								(2,000)	Advertising Expense
6										
7					6,000				(6,000)	Salary Expense
End bal.	53,000	+	24,000	=	6,000	+	5,000	+	66,000	

Prepare a vertical financial statements model.

EXHIBIT 2.2 Vertical Statements Model

CATO CONSULTANTS
Financial Statements*
Income Statement
For the Year Ended December 31, 2008

Consulting Revenue		$84,000
Salary Expense		(16,000)
Advertising Expense		(2,000)
Net Income		$66,000

Statement of Changes in Stockholders' Equity
For the Year Ended December 31, 2008

Beginning Common Stock	$ 0	
Plus: Common Stock Issued	5,000	
Ending Common Stock		$ 5,000
Beginning Retained Earnings	0	
Plus: Net Income	66,000	
Less: Dividends	0	
Ending Retained Earnings		66,000
Total Stockholders' Equity		$71,000

Balance Sheet
As of December 31, 2008

Assets		
Cash	$53,000	
Accounts Receivable	24,000	
Total Assets		$77,000
Liabilities		
Salaries Payable		$ 6,000
Stockholders' Equity		
Common Stock	$ 5,000	
Retained Earnings	66,000	
Total Stockholders' Equity		71,000
Total Liabilities and Stockholders' Equity		$77,000

Statement of Cash Flows
For the Year Ended December 31, 2008

Cash Flows from Operating Activities		
Cash Receipts from Customers	$60,000	
Cash Payments for Salary Expense	(10,000)	
Cash Payments for Advertising Expenses	(2,000)	
Net Cash Flow from Operating Activities		$48,000
Cash Flow from Investing Activities		0
Cash Flows from Financing Activities		
Cash Receipt from Issuing Common Stock	5,000	
Net Cash Flow from Financing Activities		5,000
Net Change in Cash		53,000
Plus: Beginning Cash Balance		0
Ending Cash Balance		$53,000

*In real-world annual reports, financial statements are normally presented separately with appropriate descriptions of the date to indicate whether the statement applies to the entire accounting period or a specific point in time.

of the year received cash for some of the services performed. Expenses include all costs incurred to produce revenue, whether paid for by year-end or not. We can now expand the definition of expenses introduced in Chapter 1. Expenses were previously defined as assets consumed in the process of generating revenue. Cato's adjusting entry to recognize accrued salaries expense did not reflect consuming assets. Instead of a decrease in assets, Cato recorded an increase in liabilities (salaries payable). An **expense** can therefore be more precisely defined as *a decrease in assets or an increase in liabilities resulting from operating activities undertaken to generate revenue.*

Statement of Changes in Stockholders' Equity

The statement of changes in stockholders' equity reports the effects on equity of issuing common stock, earning net income, and paying dividends to stockholders. It identifies how an entity's equity increased and decreased during the period as a result of transactions with stockholders and operating the business. In the Cato case, the statement shows that equity increased when the business acquired $5,000 cash by issuing common stock. The statement also reports that equity increased by $66,000 from earning income and that none of the $66,000 of net earnings was distributed to owners (no dividends were paid). Equity at the end of the year is $71,000 ($5,000 + $66,000).

Balance Sheet

The balance sheet discloses an entity's assets, liabilities, and stockholders' equity at a particular point in time. Cato Consultants had two assets at the end of the 2008 accounting period: cash of $53,000 and accounts receivable of $24,000. These assets are listed on the balance sheet in order of liquidity. Of the $77,000 in total assets, creditors have a $6,000 claim, leaving stockholders with a $71,000 claim.

Statement of Cash Flows

The statement of cash flows explains the change in cash from the beginning to the end of the accounting period. It can be prepared by analyzing the Cash account. Since Cato Consultants was established in 2008, its beginning cash balance was zero. By the end of the year, the cash balance was $53,000. The statement of cash flows explains this increase. The Cash account increased because Cato collected $60,000 from customers and decreased because Cato paid $12,000 for expenses. As a result, Cato's net cash inflow from operating activities was $48,000. Also, the business acquired $5,000 cash through the financing activity of issuing common stock, for a cumulative cash increase of $53,000 ($48,000 + $5,000) during 2008.

Comparing Cash Flow from Operating Activities with Net Income

The amount of net income measured using accrual accounting differs from the amount of cash flow from operating activities. For Cato Consulting in 2008, the differences are summarized below:

	Accrual Accounting	Cash Flow
Consulting Revenue	$84,000	$60,000
Salary Expense	(16,000)	(10,000)
Advertising Expense	(2,000)	(2,000)
Net Income	$66,000	$48,000

Many students begin their first accounting class with the misconception that revenue and expense items are cash equivalents. The Cato illustration demonstrates that a company may recognize a revenue or expense without a corresponding cash collection or payment in the same accounting period.

The Closing Process

Describe the closing process, the accounting cycle, and the matching concept.

Much of the information disclosed in a company's financial statements summarizes business activity for a specified time period. The end of one time period marks the beginning of the next time period. Each time period, which typically lasts one year, represents an **accounting cycle.** Accounting cycles follow one after the other from the time a business is formed until it is dissolved.

The amounts in balance sheet accounts (assets, liabilities, common stock, and retained earnings) at the end of an accounting cycle carry forward to the beginning of the next accounting cycle. For example, a company will begin 2009 with the same amount of cash it had at the end of 2008. Because their balances carry forward, balance sheet accounts are sometimes called **permanent accounts.**

In contrast, revenue, expense, and dividend accounts are **temporary accounts,** used to capture accounting information for a single accounting cycle. After the financial statements have been prepared at the end of the accounting cycle, the amounts in the temporary accounts are moved to Retained Earnings, a permanent account. Accountants call the process of moving the revenue, expense, and dividend account balances to retained earnings **closing the books,** or simply **closing.** After closing, every temporary account has a zero balance and the retained earnings account is updated to reflect the earning activities and dividend distributions that took place during the accounting period.

Exhibit 2.3 shows the general ledger accounts for Cato Consultants after the revenue and expense accounts have been closed to retained earnings. The closing entry labeled Cl.1 transfers the balance in the Consulting Revenue account to the Retained Earnings account.

EXHIBIT 2.3

General Ledger Accounts for Cato Consultants

Assets = Liabilities + Stockholders' Equity

Assets

Cash	
(1)	5,000
(3)	60,000
(4)	(10,000)
(5)	(2,000)
Bal.	53,000

Accounts Receivable	
(2)	84,000
(3)	(60,000)
Bal.	24,000

Liabilities

Salaries Payable	
(7)	6,000
Bal.	6,000

Stockholders' Equity

Common Stock	
(1)	5,000

Retained Earnings	
Cl.1	84,000
Cl.2	(16,000)
Cl.3	(2,000)
Bal.	66,000

Consulting Revenue	
(2)	84,000
Cl.1	(84,000)
Bal.	0

Salary Expense	
(4)	(10,000)
(7)	(6,000)
Cl.2	16,000
Bal.	0

Advertising Expense	
(5)	(2,000)
Cl.3	2,000
Bal.	0

Closing entries Cl.2 and Cl.3 transfer the balances in the expense accounts to retained earnings.

Steps in an Accounting Cycle

A complete accounting cycle, which is represented graphically in Exhibit 2.4, involves several steps. The four steps identified to this point are (1) recording transactions; (2) adjusting the accounts; (3) preparing financial statements; and (4) closing the temporary accounts. The first step occurs continually throughout the accounting period. Steps 2, 3, and 4 normally occur at the end of the accounting period. Additional steps are described in coming chapters of the text.

EXHIBIT 2.4

The Accounting Cycle

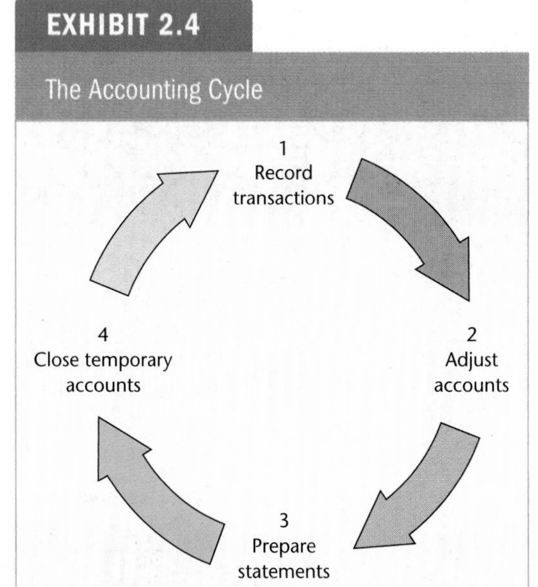

The Matching Concept

Cash basis accounting can distort reported net income because it sometimes fails to match expenses with the revenues they produce. To illustrate, consider the $6,000 of accrued salary expense that Cato Consultants recognized at the end of 2008. The instructor's teaching produced revenue in 2008. If Cato waited until 2009 (when it paid the instructor) to recognize $6,000 of the total $16,000 salary expense, then $6,000 of the expense would not be matched with the revenue it generated. By using accrual accounting, Cato recognized all the salary expense in the same accounting period in which the consulting revenue was recognized. A primary goal of accrual accounting is to appropriately match expenses with revenues, the **matching concept.**

Appropriately matching expenses with revenues can be difficult even when using accrual accounting. For example, consider Cato's advertising expense. Money spent on advertising may generate revenue in future accounting periods as well as in the current period. A prospective customer could save an advertising brochure for several years before calling Cato for training services. It is difficult to know when and to what extent advertising produces revenue. When the connection between an expense and the corresponding revenue is vague, accountants commonly match the expense with the period in which it is incurred. Cato matched (recognized) the entire $2,000 of advertising cost with the 2008 accounting period even though some of that cost might generate revenue in future accounting periods. Expenses that are matched with the period in which they are incurred are frequently called **period costs.**

Matching is not perfect. Although it would be more accurate to match expenses with revenues than with periods, there is sometimes no obvious direct connection between expenses and revenue. Accountants must exercise judgment to select the accounting period in which to recognize revenues and expenses. The concept of conservatism influences such judgment calls.

The Conservatism Principle

When faced with a recognition dilemma, **conservatism** guides accountants to select the alternative that produces the lowest amount of net income. In uncertain circumstances, accountants tend to delay revenue recognition and accelerate expense recognition. The conservatism principle holds that it is better to understate net income than to overstate it. If subsequent developments suggest that net income should have been higher, investors will respond more favorably than if they learn it was really lower. This practice explains why Cato recognized all of the advertising cost as expense in 2008 even though some of that cost may generate revenue in future accounting periods.

Second Accounting Cycle

LO 1

Record basic accrual and deferral events in a horizontal financial statements model.

The effects of Cato Consultants' 2009 events are as follows:

Event 1 **Cato paid $6,000 to the instructor to settle the salaries payable obligation.**

Cash payments to creditors are ***asset use transactions.*** When Cato pays the instructor, both the asset account Cash and the liability account Salaries Payable decrease. The cash payment does not affect the income statement. The salary expense was recognized in 2008 when the instructor taught the classes. The statement of cash flows reflects a cash outflow from operating activities. The effects of this transaction on the financial statements are shown here:

Assets	=	Liab.	+	Stk. Equity						
Cash	=	Sal. Pay.			Rev.	−	Exp.	=	Net Inc.	Cash Flow
(6,000)	=	(6,000)	+	NA	NA	−	NA	=	NA	(6,000) OA

Prepaid Items (Cost versus Expense)

Event 2 **On March 1, Cato signed a one-year lease agreement and paid $12,000 cash in advance to rent office space. The one-year lease term began on March 1.**

Accrual accounting draws a distinction between the terms *cost* and *expense. A* **cost** *might be either an asset or an expense.* If a company has already consumed a purchased resource in the process of earning revenue, the cost of the resource is an *expense.* For example, companies normally pay for electricity the month after using it. The cost of electric utilities is therefore usually recorded as an expense. In contrast, if a company purchases a resource it will use in the future to generate revenue, the cost of the resource represents an *asset.* Accountants record such a cost in an asset account and ***defer*** recognizing an expense until the resource is used to produce revenue. Deferring the expense recognition provides more accurate ***matching*** of revenues and expenses.

The cost of the office space Cato leased in Event 2 is an asset. It is recorded in the asset account *Prepaid Rent.* Cato expects to benefit from incurring this cost for the next twelve months. Expense recognition is deferred until Cato uses the office space to help generate revenue. Other common deferred expenses include *prepaid insurance* and *prepaid taxes.* As these titles imply, deferred expenses are frequently called **prepaid items.** Exhibit 2.5 illustrates the relationship between costs, assets, and expenses.

EXHIBIT 2.5

Relationship between Cost and Expense

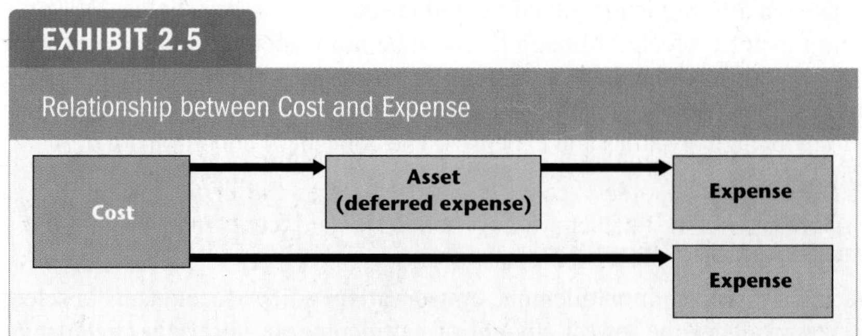

Purchasing prepaid rent is an asset exchange transaction. The asset account Cash decreases and the asset account Prepaid Rent increases. The amount of total assets is unaffected. The income statement is unaffected. Expense recognition is deferred until the office space is used. The statement of cash flows reflects a cash outflow from operating activities. The effects of this transaction on the financial statements are shown here:

Assets		=	Liab.	+	Stk. Equity						
Cash	+ Prep. Rent					Rev.	−	Exp.	=	Net Inc.	Cash Flow
(12,000)	+ 12,000	=	NA	+	NA	NA	−	NA	=	NA	(12,000) OA

Accounting for Receipt of Unearned Revenue

Event 3 **Cato received $18,000 cash in advance from Westberry Company for consulting services Cato agreed to perform over a one-year period beginning June 1.**

Cato must defer (delay) recognizing any revenue until it performs (does the work) the consulting services for Westberry. From Cato's point of view, the deferred revenue is a liability because Cato is obligated to perform services in the future. The liability is called **unearned revenue.** The cash receipt is an ***asset source transaction.*** The asset account Cash and the liability account Unearned Revenue both increase. Collecting the cash has no effect on the income statement. The revenue will be reported on the income statement after Cato performs the services. The statement of cash flows reflects a cash inflow from operating activities. The effects of this transaction on the financial statements are shown here:

Assets	=	Liab.	+	Stk. Equity						
Cash	=	Unearn. Rev.			Rev.	−	Exp.	=	Net Inc.	Cash Flow
18,000	=	18,000	+	NA	NA	−	NA	=	NA	18,000 OA

Accounting for Supplies Purchase

Event 4 **Cato purchased $800 of supplies on account.**

The purchase of supplies on account is an ***asset source transaction.*** The asset account Supplies and the liability account Accounts Payable increase. The income statement is unaffected. Expense recognition is deferred until the supplies are used. The statement of cash flows is not affected. The effects of this transaction on the financial statements are shown here:

Assets	=	Liab.	+	Stk. Equity						
Supplies	=	Accts. Pay.			Rev.	−	Exp.	=	Net Inc.	Cash Flow
800	=	800	+	NA	NA	−	NA	=	NA	NA

Other 2009 Events

Event 5 **Cato provided $96,400 of consulting services on account.**

Providing services on account is an ***asset source transaction.*** The asset account Accounts Receivable and the stockholders' equity account Retained Earnings increase. Revenue and net income increase. The statement of cash flows is not affected. The effects of this transaction on the financial statements are shown here:

Assets	=	Liab.	+	Stk. Equity						
Accts. Rec.	=			Ret. Earn.	Rev.	−	Exp.	=	Net Inc.	Cash Flow
96,400	=	NA	+	96,400	96,400	−	NA	=	96,400	NA

Event 6 Cato collected $105,000 cash from customers as partial settlement of accounts receivable.

Collecting money from customers who are paying accounts receivable is an ***asset exchange transaction.*** One asset account (Cash) increases and another asset account (Accounts Receivable) decreases. The amount of total assets is unchanged. The income statement is not affected. The statement of cash flows reports a cash inflow from operating activities. The effects of this transaction on the financial statements are shown here:

Assets			=	Liab.	+	Stk. Equity						Cash Flow
Cash	+	Accts. Rec.					Rev.	−	Exp.	=	Net Inc.	
105,000	+	(105,000)	=	NA	+	NA	NA	−	NA	=	NA	105,000 OA

Event 7 Cato paid $32,000 cash for salary expense.

Cash payments for salary expense are ***asset use transactions.*** Both the asset account Cash and the equity account Retained Earnings decrease by $32,000. Recognizing the expense decreases net income on the income statement. The statement of cash flows reflects a cash outflow from operating activities. The effects of this transaction on the financial statements are shown here:

Assets	=	Liab.	+	Stk. Equity						Cash Flow
Cash	=			Ret. Earn.	Rev.	−	Exp.	=	Net Inc.	
(32,000)	=	NA	+	(32,000)	NA	−	32,000	=	(32,000)	(32,000) OA

Event 8 Cato incurred $21,000 of other operating expenses on account.

Recognizing expenses incurred on account are ***claims exchange transactions.*** One claims account (Accounts Payable) increases and another claims account (Retained Earnings) decreases. The amount of total claims is not affected. Recognizing the expenses decreases net income. The statement of cash flows is not affected. The effects of this transaction on the financial statements are shown here:

Assets	=	Liab.	+	Stk. Equity						Cash Flow
		Accts. Pay.	+	Ret. Earn.	Rev.	−	Exp.	=	Net Inc.	
NA	=	21,000	+	(21,000)	NA	−	21,000	=	(21,000)	NA

Event 9 Cato paid $18,200 in partial settlement of accounts payable.

Paying accounts payable is an ***asset use transaction.*** The asset account Cash and the liability account Accounts Payable decrease. The statement of cash flows reports a cash outflow for operating activities. The income statement is not affected. The effects of this transaction on the financial statements are shown here:

Assets	=	Liab.	+	Stk. Equity						Cash Flow
Cash	=	Accts. Pay.			Rev.	−	Exp.	=	Net Inc.	
(18,200)	=	(18,200)	+	NA	NA	−	NA	=	NA	(18,200) OA

Event 10 Cato paid $79,500 to purchase land it planned to use in the future as a building site for its home office.

Purchasing land with cash is an ***asset exchange transaction.*** One asset account, Cash, decreases and another asset account, Land, increases. The amount of total assets is unchanged. The income statement is not affected. The statement of cash flows reports a cash outflow for investing activities. The effects of this transaction on the financial statements are shown here:

Assets			=	Liab.	+	Stk. Equity						
Cash	+	Land					Rev.	−	Exp.	=	Net Inc.	Cash Flow
(79,500)	+	79,500	=	NA	+	NA	NA	−	NA	=	NA	(79,500) IA

Event 11 **Cato paid $21,000 in cash dividends to its stockholders.**

Cash payments for dividends are ***asset use transactions.*** Both the asset account Cash and the equity account Retained Earnings decrease. Recall that dividends are wealth transfers from the business to the stockholders, not expenses. They are not incurred in the process of generating revenue. They do not affect the income statement. The statement of cash flows reflects a cash outflow from financing activities. The effects of this transaction on the financial statements are shown here:

Assets	=	Liab.	+	Stk. Equity						
Cash	=			Ret. Earn.	Rev.	−	Exp.	=	Net Inc.	Cash Flow
(21,000)	=	NA	+	(21,000)	NA	−	NA	=	NA	(21,000) FA

Event 12 **Cato acquired $2,000 cash from issuing additional shares of common stock.**

Issuing common stock is an ***asset source transaction.*** The asset account Cash and the stockholders' equity account Common Stock increase. The income statement is unaffected. The statement of cash flows reports a cash inflow from financing activities. The effects of this transaction on the financial statements are shown here:

Assets	=	Liab.	+	Stk. Equity						
Cash	=			Com. Stk.	Rev.	−	Exp.	=	Net Inc.	Cash Flow
2,000	=	NA	+	2,000	NA	−	NA	=	NA	2,000 FA

Adjusting Entries

Recall that companies make adjusting entries at the end of an accounting period to update the account balances before preparing the financial statements. Adjusting entries ensure that companies report revenues and expenses in the appropriate accounting period; adjusting entries never affect the Cash account.

Accounting for Supplies (Adjusting Entry)

Event 13 **After determining through a physical count that it had $150 of unused supplies on hand as of December 31, Cato recognized supplies expense.**

Companies would find the cost of recording supplies expense each time a pencil, piece of paper, envelope, or other supply item is used to far outweigh the benefit derived from such tedious recordkeeping. Instead, accountants transfer to expense the total cost of all supplies used during the entire accounting period in a single year-end adjusting entry. The cost of supplies used is determined as follows:

Beginning supplies balance + Supplies purchased = Supplies available for use − Ending supplies balance = Supplies used

Companies determine the ending supplies balance by physically counting the supplies on hand at the end of the period. Cato used $650 of supplies during the year (zero beginning balance + $800 supplies purchase = $800 available for use − $150 ending balance).

Recognizing Cato's supplies expense is an ***asset use transaction.*** The asset account Supplies and the stockholders' equity account Retained Earnings decrease. Recognizing supplies expense reduces net income. The statement of cash flows is not affected. The effects of this transaction on the financial statements are shown here:

Assets	=	Liab.	+	Stk. Equity						
Supplies	=			Ret. Earn.	Rev.	−	Exp.	=	Net Inc.	Cash Flow
(650)	=	NA	+	(650)	NA	−	650	=	(650)	NA

Accounting for Prepaid Rent (Adjusting Entry)

Event 14 **Cato recognized rent expense for the office space used during the accounting period.**

Recall that Cato paid $12,000 on March 1 to rent office space for one year (see Event 2). The portion of the lease cost that represents using office space from March 1 through December 31 is computed as follows:

Cost of annual lease ÷ 12 = Cost per month × Months used = Rent expense

$12,000 cost of policy ÷ 12 = $1,000 per month × 10 months = $10,000 Rent expense

Recognizing the rent expense decreases the asset account Prepaid Rent and the stockholders' equity account Retained Earnings. Recognizing rent expense reduces net income. The statement of cash flows is not affected. The cash flow effect was recorded in the March 1 event. These effects on the financial statements follow:

Assets	=	Liab.	+	Stk. Equity						
Prep. Rent	=			Ret. Earn.	Rev.	−	Exp.	=	Net Inc.	Cash Flow
(10,000)	=	NA	+	(10,000)	NA	−	10,000	=	(10,000)	NA

CHECK YOURSELF 2.2

Rujoub Inc. paid $18,000 cash for one year of insurance coverage that began on November 1, 2005. Based on this information alone, determine the cash flow from operating activities that Rujoub would report on the 2005 and 2006 statements of cash flows. Also, determine the amount of insurance expense Rujoub would report on the 2005 income statement and the amount of prepaid insurance (an asset) that Rujoub would report on the December 31, 2005, balance sheet.

Answer

Since Rujoub paid all of the cash in 2005, the 2005 statement of cash flows would report an $18,000 cash outflow from operating activities. The 2006 statement of cash flows would report zero cash flow from operating activities. The expense would be recognized in the periods in which the insurance is used. In this case, insurance expense is recognized at the rate of $1,500 per month ($18,000 ÷ 12 months). Rujoub used two months of insurance coverage in 2005 and therefore would report $3,000 (2 months × $1,500) of insurance expense on the 2005 income statement. Rujoub would report a $15,000 (10 months × $1,500) asset, prepaid insurance, on the December 31, 2005, balance sheet. The $15,000 of prepaid insurance would be recognized as insurance expense in 2006 when the insurance coverage is used.

Accounting for Unearned Revenue (Adjusting Entry)

Event 15 **Cato recognized the portion of the unearned revenue it earned during the accounting period.**

Recall that Cato received an $18,000 cash advance from Westberry Company to provide consulting services from June 1, 2009, to May 31, 2010 (see Event 3). By December 31,

Cato had earned 7 months (June 1 through December 31) of the revenue related to this contract. Rather than recording the revenue continuously as it performed the consulting services, Cato can simply recognize the amount earned in a single adjustment to the accounting records at the end of the accounting period. The amount of the adjustment is computed as follows:

$18,000 ÷ 12 months = $1,500 revenue earned per month

$1,500 × 7 months = $10,500 revenue to be recognized in 2009

The adjusting entry moves $10,500 from the Unearned Revenue account to the Consulting Revenue account. This entry is a ***claims exchange transaction.*** The liability account Unearned Revenue decreases and the equity account Retained Earnings increases. The effects of this transaction on the financial statements are shown here:

Assets	=	Liab.	+	Stk. Equity						
		Unearn. Rev.	+	Ret. Earn.	Rev.	−	Exp.	=	Net Inc.	Cash Flow
NA	=	(10,500)	+	10,500	10,500	−	NA	=	10,500	NA

Recall that revenue was previously defined as an economic benefit a company obtains by providing customers with goods and services. In this case the economic benefit is a decrease in the liability account Unearned Revenue. **Revenue** can therefore be more precisely defined as *an increase in assets or a decrease in liabilities that a company obtains by providing customers with goods or services.*

CHECK YOURSELF 2.3

Sanderson & Associates received a $24,000 cash advance as a retainer to provide legal services to a client. The contract called for Sanderson to render services during a one-year period beginning October 1, 2006. Based on this information alone, determine the cash flow from operating activities Sanderson would report on the 2006 and 2007 statements of cash flows. Also determine the amount of revenue Sanderson would report on the 2006 and 2007 income statements.

Answer

Since Sanderson collected all of the cash in 2006, the 2006 statement of cash flows would report a $24,000 cash inflow from operating activities. The 2007 statement of cash flows would report zero cash flow from operating activities. Revenue is recognized in the period in which it is earned. In this case revenue is earned at the rate of $2,000 per month ($24,000 ÷ 12 months = $2,000 per month). Sanderson rendered services for three months in 2006 and nine months in 2007. Sanderson would report $6,000 (3 months × $2,000) of revenue on the 2006 income statement and $18,000 (9 months × $2,000) of revenue on the 2007 income statement.

Accounting for Accrued Salary Expense (Adjusting Entry)

Event 16 **Cato recognized $4,000 of accrued salary expense.**

The adjusting entry to recognize the accrued salary expense is a ***claims exchange transaction.*** One claims account, Retained Earnings, decreases and another claims account, Salaries Payable, increases. The expense recognition reduces net income. The statement of cash flows is not affected. The effects of this transaction on the financial statements are shown here:

Assets	=	Liab.	+	Stk. Equity						
		Sal. Pay.	+	Ret. Earn.	Rev.	−	Exp.	=	Net Inc.	Cash Flow
NA	=	4,000	+	(4,000)	NA	−	4,000	=	(4,000)	NA

Answers to The Curious Accountant

Because the **Reader's Digest Association** receives cash from customers before actually sending any magazines to them, the company has not earned any revenue when it receives the cash. Reader's Digest has a liability called *unearned revenue.* If Reader's Digest closed its books on December 31, then $3.50 of Paige Long's subscription would be recognized as revenue in 2007. The remaining $10.50 would appear on the balance sheet as a liability.

Reader's Digest actually ends its accounting year on June 30 each year. A copy of the June 30, 2002, balance sheet for Reader's Digest is presented in Exhibit 2.6 on page 57. The liability for unearned revenue was $561.7 ($426.9 + $134.8) million—which represented about 25 percent of Reader's Digest's total liabilities!

Will Reader's Digest need cash to pay these subscription liabilities? Not exactly. The liabilities will not be paid directly with cash. Instead, they will be satisfied by providing magazines to the subscribers. However, Reader's Digest will need cash to pay for producing and distributing the magazines supplied to the customers. Even so, the amount of cash required to provide magazines will probably differ significantly from the amount of unearned revenues. In most cases, subscription fees do not cover the cost of producing and distributing magazines. By collecting significant amounts of advertising revenue, publishers can provide magazines to customers at prices well below the cost of publication. The amount of unearned revenue is not likely to coincide with the amount of cash needed to cover the cost of satisfying the company's obligation to produce and distribute magazines. Even though the association between unearned revenues and the cost of providing magazines to customers is not direct, a knowledgeable financial analyst can use the information to make estimates of future cash flows and revenue recognition.

Summary of Events

The previous section of this chapter described sixteen events Cato Consultants experienced the during the 2009 accounting period. These events are summarized below for your convenience.

Event 1 Cato paid $6,000 to the instructor to settle the salaries payable obligation.

Event 2 On March 1, Cato paid $12,000 cash to lease office space for one year.

Event 3 Cato received $18,000 cash in advance from Westberry Company for consulting services to be performed for one year beginning June 1.

Event 4 Cato purchased $800 of supplies on account.

Event 5 Cato provided $96,400 of consulting services on account.

Event 6 Cato collected $105,000 cash from customers as partial settlement of accounts receivable.

Event 7 Cato paid $32,000 cash for salary expense.

Event 8 Cato incurred $21,000 of other operating expenses on account.

Event 9 Cato paid $18,200 in partial settlement of accounts payable.

Event 10 Cato paid $79,500 to purchase land it planned to use in the future as a building site for its home office.

Event 11 Cato paid $21,000 in cash dividends to its stockholders.

Event 12 Cato acquired $2,000 cash from issuing additional shares of common stock.

The year-end adjustments are:

Event 13 After determining through a physical count that it had $150 of unused supplies on hand as of December 31, Cato recognized supplies expense.

Event 14 Cato recognized rent expense for the office space used during the accounting period.

Event 15 Cato recognized the portion of the unearned revenue it earned during the accounting period.

Event 16 Cato recognized $4,000 of accrued salary expense.

EXHIBIT 2.6 2002 Balance Sheet for Reader's Digest

THE READER'S DIGEST ASSOCIATION, INC., AND SUBSIDIARIES Consolidated Balance Sheets (in millions)		
	At June 30,	
	2002	2001 Restated
Assets		
Current Assets		
Cash and Cash Equivalents	$ 107.6	$ 35.4
Accounts Receivable, Net	306.0	274.8
Inventories	156.0	167.4
Prepaid and Deferred Promotion Costs	140.9	106.7
Prepaid Expenses and Other Current Assets	153.2	192.1
Total Current Assets	863.7	776.4
Property, Plant, and Equipment, Net	168.1	160.2
Goodwill and Other Intangible Assets, Net	1,244.6	409.8
Other Noncurrent Assets	426.3	334.5
Total Assets	$2,702.7	$1,680.9
Liabilities and Stockholders' Equity		
Current Liabilities		
Loans and Notes Payable	$ 132.7	$ 160.3
Accounts Payable	102.8	86.4
Accrued Expenses	283.2	251.1
Income Taxes Payable	28.4	41.2
Unearned Revenues	426.9	291.6
Other Current Liabilities	6.8	28.9
Total Current Liabilities	980.8	859.5
Postretirement and Postemployment Benefits Other than Pensions	128.1	138.7
Unearned Revenues	134.8	54.1
Long-Term Debt	818.0	9.8
Other Noncurrent Liabilities	169.1	159.0
Total Liabilities	2,230.8	1,221.1
Commitments and Contingencies (Notes 11 and 13)		
Stockholders' Equity		
Capital Stock	25.5	29.6
Paid-In Capital	224.6	226.1
Retained Earnings	1,261.2	1,191.3
Accumulated Other Comprehensive (Loss) Income	(89.7)	(84.6)
Treasury Stock, at Cost	(949.7)	(902.6)
Total Stockholders' Equity	471.9	459.8
Total Liabilities and Stockholders' Equity	$2,702.7	$1,680.9

The General Ledger

Exhibit 2.7 shows Cato Consultants' 2009 transaction data recorded in general ledger form. The account balances at the end of 2008, shown in Exhibit 2.3, become the beginning balances for the 2009 accounting period. The 2009 transaction data are referenced to the accounting events with numbers in parentheses. The information in the ledger accounts is the basis for the financial statements in Exhibit 2.8. Before reading further, trace each transaction in the summary of events into Exhibit 2.7.

Organize general ledger accounts under an accounting equation.

Vertical Statements Model

Financial statement users obtain helpful insights by analyzing company trends over multiple accounting cycles. Exhibit 2.8 presents for Cato Consultants a multicycle **vertical statements**

EXHIBIT 2.7

Ledger Accounts with 2009 Transaction Data

Assets = Liabilities + Stockholders' Equity

Assets

Cash	
Bal.	53,000
(1)	(6,000)
(2)	(12,000)
(3)	18,000
(6)	105,000
(7)	(32,000)
(9)	(18,200)
(10)	(79,500)
(11)	(21,000)
(12)	2,000
Bal.	9,300

Accounts Receivable	
Bal.	24,000
(5)	96,400
(6)	(105,000)
Bal.	15,400

Supplies	
Bal.	0
(4)	800
(13)	(650)
Bal.	150

Prepaid Rent	
Bal.	0
(2)	12,000
(14)	(10,000)
Bal.	2,000

Land	
Bal.	0
(10)	79,500
Bal.	79,500

Liabilities

Accounts Payable	
Bal.	0
(4)	800
(8)	21,000
(9)	(18,200)
Bal.	3,600

Unearned Revenue	
Bal.	0
(3)	18,000
(15)	(10,500)
Bal.	7,500

Salaries Payable	
Bal.	6,000
(1)	(6,000)
(16)	4,000
Bal.	4,000

Stockholders' Equity

Common Stock	
Bal.	5,000
(12)	2,000
Bal.	7,000

Retained Earnings	
Bal.	66,000

Dividends	
Bal.	0
(11)	(21,000)
Bal.	(21,000)

Consulting Revenue	
Bal.	0
(5)	96,400
(15)	10,500
Bal.	106,900

Other Operating Expenses	
Bal.	0
(8)	(21,000)
Bal.	(21,000)

Salary Expense	
Bal.	0
(7)	(32,000)
(16)	(4,000)
Bal.	(36,000)

Rent Expense	
Bal.	0
(14)	(10,000)
Bal.	(10,000)

Supplies Expense	
Bal.	0
(13)	(650)
Bal.	(650)

Explain how business events affect financial statements over multiple accounting cycles.

model of 2008 and 2009 accounting data. To conserve space, we have combined all the expenses for each year into single amounts labeled "Operating Expenses," determined as follows:

	2008	2009
Other Operating Expenses	$ 0	$21,000
Salary Expense	16,000	36,000
Rent Expense	0	10,000
Advertising Expense	2,000	0
Supplies Expense	0	650
Total Operating Expenses	$18,000	$67,650

Similarly, we combined the cash payments for operating expenses on the statement of cash flows as follows:

	2008	2009
Supplies and Other Operating Expenses	$ 0	$18,200*
Salary Expense	10,000	38,000
Rent Expense	0	12,000
Advertising Expense	2,000	0
Total Cash Payments for Operating Expenses	$12,000	$68,200

*Amount paid in partial settlement of accounts payable

Recall that the level of detail reported in financial statements depends on user information needs. Most real-world companies combine many account balances together to report highly summarized totals under each financial statement caption. Before reading further, trace the remaining financial statement items from the ledger accounts in Exhibit 2.7 to where they are reported in Exhibit 2.8.

The vertical statements model in Exhibit 2.8 shows significant interrelationships among the financial statements. For each year, trace the amount of net income from the income statement to the statement of changes in stockholders' equity. Next, trace the ending balances of common stock and retained earnings reported on the statement of changes in stockholders' equity to the stockholders' equity section of the balance sheet. Also, confirm that the amount of cash reported on the balance sheet equals the ending cash balance on the statement of cash flows.

Other relationships connect the two accounting periods. For example, trace the ending retained earnings balance from the 2008 statement of stockholders' equity to the beginning retained earnings balance on the 2009 statement of stockholders' equity. Also, trace the ending cash balance on the 2008 statement of cash flows to the beginning cash balance on the 2009 statement of cash flows. Finally, confirm that the change in cash between the 2008 and 2009 balance sheets ($53,000 − $9,300 = $43,700 decrease) agrees with the net change in cash reported on the 2009 statement of cash flows.

Explain how to use the price-earnings ratio and growth percentage analysis to assess the market value of common stock.

When you buy a share of stock, what do you really get? The stock certificate you receive is evidence of your right to share in the earnings of the company that issued the stock. The more the company earns, the more your wealth increases. Investors are willing to pay higher prices for companies with higher earnings potential.

Price-earnings Ratio

The **price-earnings ratio,** frequently called the *P/E ratio,* is the most commonly reported measure of a company's value. The P/E ratio is a company's market price per share of stock divided by the company's annual earnings per share (EPS).[1]

Assume Western Company recently reported annual earnings per share of $3. Western's stock is currently selling for $54 per share. Western's stock is therefore selling at a P/E ratio

[1]The amount of earnings per share is provided in a company's annual report. In its simplest form, it is computed by dividing the company's net income (net earnings) by the number of shares of common stock outstanding.

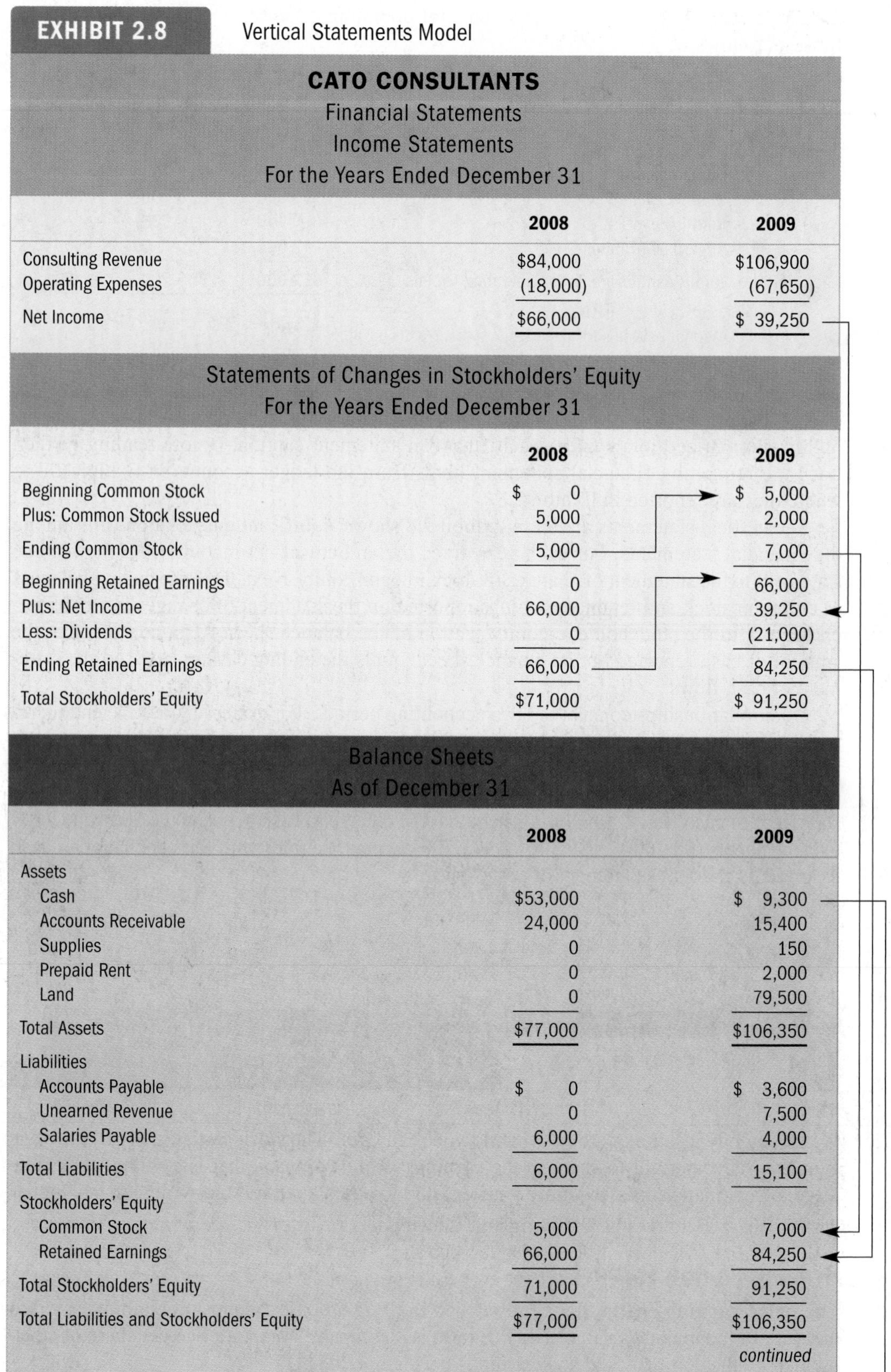

EXHIBIT 2.8 Vertical Statements Model

CATO CONSULTANTS
Financial Statements
Income Statements
For the Years Ended December 31

	2008	2009
Consulting Revenue	$84,000	$106,900
Operating Expenses	(18,000)	(67,650)
Net Income	$66,000	$ 39,250

Statements of Changes in Stockholders' Equity
For the Years Ended December 31

	2008	2009
Beginning Common Stock	$ 0	$ 5,000
Plus: Common Stock Issued	5,000	2,000
Ending Common Stock	5,000	7,000
Beginning Retained Earnings	0	66,000
Plus: Net Income	66,000	39,250
Less: Dividends	0	(21,000)
Ending Retained Earnings	66,000	84,250
Total Stockholders' Equity	$71,000	$ 91,250

Balance Sheets
As of December 31

	2008	2009
Assets		
Cash	$53,000	$ 9,300
Accounts Receivable	24,000	15,400
Supplies	0	150
Prepaid Rent	0	2,000
Land	0	79,500
Total Assets	$77,000	$106,350
Liabilities		
Accounts Payable	$ 0	$ 3,600
Unearned Revenue	0	7,500
Salaries Payable	6,000	4,000
Total Liabilities	6,000	15,100
Stockholders' Equity		
Common Stock	5,000	7,000
Retained Earnings	66,000	84,250
Total Stockholders' Equity	71,000	91,250
Total Liabilities and Stockholders' Equity	$77,000	$106,350

continued

of 18 ($54 market price ÷ $3 EPS). What does a P/E ratio of 18 mean? If Western continued earning $3 per share of stock each year and paid all its earnings out to stockholders in the form of cash dividends, it would take 18 years for an investor to recover the price paid for the stock.

EXHIBIT 2.8 *Concluded*

Statements of Cash Flows For the Years Ended December 31	2008	2009
Cash Flows from Operating Activities		
Cash Receipts from Customers	$60,000	$123,000
Cash Payments for Operating Expenses	(12,000)	(68,200)
Net Cash Flow from Operating Activities	48,000	54,800
Cash Flows from Investing Activities		
Cash Payment to Purchase Land	0	(79,500)
Cash Flows from Financing Activities		
Cash Receipts from Issuing Common Stock	5,000	2,000
Cash Payments for Dividends	0	(21,000)
Net Cash Flow from Financing Activities	5,000	(19,000)
Net Change in Cash	53,000	(43,700)
Plus: Beginning Cash Balance	0	53,000
Ending Cash Balance	$53,000	$ 9,300

In contrast, assume the stock of Eastern Company, which reported EPS of $4, is currently selling for $48 per share. Eastern's P/E ratio is 12 ($48 market price ÷ $4 EPS). Investors who buy Eastern Company stock would get their money back six years faster (18 − 12) than investors who buy Western Company stock.

Why would investors buy a stock with a P/E ratio of 18 when they could buy one with a P/E ratio of 12? If investors expect Western Company's earnings to grow faster than Eastern Company's earnings, the higher P/E ratio makes sense. For example, suppose Western Company's earnings were to double to $6 per share while Eastern's remained at $4 per share. Western's P/E ratio would drop to 9 ($54 market price ÷ $6 EPS) while Eastern's remains at 12. This explains why high-growth companies sell for higher P/E multiples than do low-growth companies.

Measuring Growth through Percentage Analysis

The income statements for Cammeron Inc. show that earnings increased by $4.2 million from 2005 to 2006. Comparable data for Diller Enterprises indicate earnings growth of $2.9 million. Is Cammeron a better-managed company than Diller? Not necessarily; perhaps Cammeron is simply a larger company than Diller. Investors frequently use percentage analysis to level the playing field when comparing companies of differing sizes. Consider the following actual earnings data for the two companies:

	2005*	2006*	Growth†
Cammeron	$42.4	$46.6	$4.2
Diller	9.9	12.8	2.9

*Earnings data shown in millions.

†Growth calculated by subtracting 2005 earnings from 2006 earnings.

EXHIBIT 2.9

Real-World Price-earnings Ratios and Growth Rates

Company	P/E Ratio	Average Annual Earnings Growth 1999–2001
High growth companies:		
Cisco Systems	90	35.3%
Microsoft	46	13.2
Medium growth companies:		
General Electric	20	6.2
General Mills	24	6.4
Low growth companies:		
DuPont	10	(4.2)
Sara Lee	10	1.4

Analysts can measure the percentage growth in earnings between 2005 and 2006 for each of the companies with the following formula:

$$\frac{\text{Alternative year earnings} - \text{Base year earnings}}{\text{Base year earnings}} = \text{Percentage growth rate}$$

Cammeron Inc.:

$$\frac{\$46.6 - \$42.4}{\$42.4} = 9.9\%$$

Diller Enterprises:

$$\frac{\$12.8 - \$9.9}{\$9.9} = 29.3\%$$

This analysis shows that Cammeron is the larger company, but Diller is growing much more rapidly. If this trend continues, Diller will eventually become the larger company and have higher earnings than Cammeron. This higher earnings potential is why investors value fast-growing companies. The P/E ratios of real-world companies are highly correlated with their growth rates, as demonstrated in the data reported in Exhibit 2.9. The data in this exhibit are based on the closing stock prices on June 25, 2002.

CHECK YOURSELF 2.4

Treadmore Company started the 2007 accounting period with $580 of supplies on hand. During 2007 the company paid cash to purchase $2,200 of supplies. A physical count of supplies indicated that there was $420 of supplies on hand at the end of 2007. Treadmore pays cash for supplies at the time they are purchased. Based on this information alone, determine the amount of supplies expense to be recognized on the income statement and the amount of cash flow to be shown in the operating activities section of the statement of cash flows.

Answer

The amount of supplies expense recognized on the income statement is the amount of supplies that were used during the accounting period. This amount is computed below.

Beginning balance	+	Supplies purchased	=	Supplies available	−	Ending balance	=	Supplies used
$580	+	$2,200	=	$2,780	−	$420	=	$2,360

The cash flow from operating activities is the amount of cash paid for supplies during the accounting period. In this case, Treadmore paid $2,200 cash to purchase supplies. This amount would be shown as a cash outflow.

REALITY BYTES

Under accrual accounting, revenue is recognized only after a company completes work. In contrast, investors focus on anticipated income when purchasing stock. This helps explain why the stock of some companies sells for more than the stock of other companies. For example, since the silicon-chip industry has a higher growth potential than the grocery-store industry, **Intel's** stock will likely sell for a higher earnings multiple than **Kroger's** stock. Indeed, on August 19, 2003, Intel's stock sold for 50 times earnings, while Kroger's sold for only 11 times earnings.

Significant differences in P/E ratios occur because investors base their stock purchases on a company's potential to earn future profits rather than its past earnings. Does this mean historically based financial statements are not useful in making investment decisions? No! Past earnings provide insight into future earnings. A company with a history of 20 percent per year earnings growth is more likely to experience rapid growth in the future than a company with a 5 percent historical growth rate. Financial statements based on accrual accounting can provide insight into the future even though they are historically based.

A Look Back

LO 8

Classify accounting events into one of four categories:

a. asset source transactions.
b. asset use transactions.
c. asset exchange transactions.
d. claims exchange transactions.

Chapters 1 and 2 introduced four types of transactions. Although businesses engage in an infinite number of different transactions, all transactions fall into one of four types. By learning to identify transactions by type, you can understand how unfamiliar events affect financial statements. The four types of transactions are:

1. *Asset source transactions:* An asset account increases, and a corresponding claims account increases.
2. *Asset use transactions:* An asset account decreases, and a corresponding claims account decreases.
3. *Asset exchange transactions:* One asset account increases, and another asset account decreases.
4. *Claims exchange transactions:* One claims account increases, and another claims account decreases.

Also, the definitions of revenue and expense have been expanded. The complete definitions of these two elements are as follows:

1. **Revenue:** Revenue is the *economic benefit* derived from operating the business. Its recognition is accompanied by an increase in assets or a decrease in liabilities resulting from providing products or services to customers.
2. **Expense:** An expense is an *economic sacrifice* incurred in the process of generating revenue. Its recognition is accompanied by a decrease in assets or an increase in liabilities resulting from consuming assets and services in an effort to produce revenue.

This chapter introduced accrual accounting. Accrual accounting distinguishes between *recognition* and *realization.* Recognition means reporting an economic item or event in the financial statements. In contrast, realization refers to collecting cash from the sale of assets or services. Recognition and realization can occur in different accounting periods. In addition, cash payments for expenses often occur in different accounting periods from when a company recognizes the expenses. Accrual accounting uses both *accruals* and *deferrals.*

- The term *accrual* applies to earnings events that are recognized before cash is exchanged. Recognizing revenue on account or accrued salaries expense are examples of accruals.
- The term *deferral* applies to earnings events that are recognized after cash has been exchanged. Supplies, prepaid items, and unearned revenue are examples of deferrals.

Virtually all major companies operating in the United States use accrual accounting.

>> A Look Forward

Chapters 1 and 2 focused on businesses that generate revenue by providing services to their customers. Examples of these types of businesses include consulting, real estate sales, medical services, and legal services. The next chapter introduces accounting practices for businesses that generate revenue by selling goods. Examples of these companies include **Wal-Mart, Circuit City, Office Depot,** and **Lowes**.

SELF-STUDY REVIEW PROBLEM

Gifford Company experienced the following accounting events during 2008.

1. Started operations on January 1 when it acquired $20,000 cash by issuing common stock.
2. Earned $18,000 of revenue on account.
3. On March 1 collected $36,000 cash as an advance for services to be performed in the future.
4. Paid cash operating expenses of $17,000.
5. Paid a $2,700 cash dividend to stockholders.
6. On December 31, 2008, adjusted the books to recognize the revenue earned by providing services related to the advance described in Event 3. The contract required Gifford to provide services for a one-year period starting March 1.
7. Collected $15,000 cash from accounts receivable.

Gifford Company experienced the following accounting events during 2009.

1. Recognized $38,000 of cash revenue.
2. On April 1 paid $12,000 cash for an insurance policy that provides coverage for one year beginning immediately.
3. Collected $2,000 cash from accounts receivable.
4. Paid cash operating expenses of $21,000.
5. Paid a $5,000 cash dividend to stockholders.
6. On December 31, 2009, adjusted the books to recognize the remaining revenue earned by providing services related to the advance described in Event 3 of 2008.
7. On December 31, 2009, Gifford adjusted the books to recognize the amount of the insurance policy used during 2009.

Required

a. Record the events in a financial statements model like the following one. The first event is recorded as an example.

	Assets					=	Liab.	+	Stockholders' Equity								
Event No.	Cash	+	Accts. Rec.	+	Prep. Ins.	=	Unearn. Rev.	+	Com. Stk.	+	Ret. Earn.	Rev.	−	Exp.	=	Net Inc.	Cash Flow
1	20,000	+	NA	+	NA	=	NA	+	20,000	+	NA	NA	−	NA	=	NA	20,000 FA

b. What amount of revenue would Gifford report on the 2008 income statement?

c. What amount of cash flow from customers would Gifford report on the 2008 statement of cash flows?

d. What amount of unearned revenue would Gifford report on the 2008 and 2009 year-end balance sheets?

e. What are the 2009 opening balances for the revenue and expense accounts?

f. What amount of total assets would Gifford report on the December 31, 2008, balance sheet?

g. What claims on assets would Gifford report on the December 31, 2009, balance sheet?

Solution to Requirement a

The financial statements model follows.

	Assets			= Liab.	+ Stockholders' Equity					
Event No.	**Cash**	**+ Accts. Rec.**	**+ Prep. Ins.**	**= Unearn. Rev.**	**+ Com. Stk.**	**+ Ret. Earn.**	**Rev.**	**− Exp.**	**= Net Inc.**	**Cash Flow**
2008										
1	20,000	NA	NA	NA	20,000	NA	NA	NA	NA	20,000 FA
2	NA	18,000	NA	NA	NA	18,000	18,000	NA	18,000	NA
3	36,000	NA	NA	36,000	NA	NA	NA	NA	NA	36,000 OA
4	(17,000)	NA	NA	NA	NA	(17,000)	NA	17,000	(17,000)	(17,000) OA
5	(2,700)	NA	NA	NA	NA	(2,700)	NA	NA	NA	(2,700) FA
6*	NA	NA	NA	(30,000)	NA	30,000	30,000	NA	30,000	NA
7	15,000	(15,000)	NA	NA	NA	NA	NA	NA	NA	15,000 OA
Bal.	51,300	3,000	NA	6,000	20,000	28,300	48,000	17,000	31,000	51,300 NC
	Asset, liability, and equity account balances carry forward						Rev. & exp. accts. are closed			
2009										
Bal.	51,300	3,000	NA	6,000	20,000	28,300	NA	NA	NA	NA
1	38,000	NA	NA	NA	NA	38,000	38,000	NA	38,000	38,000 OA
2	(12,000)	NA	12,000	NA	NA	NA	NA	NA	NA	(12,000) OA
3	2,000	(2,000)	NA	NA	NA	NA	NA	NA	NA	2,000 OA
4	(21,000)	NA	NA	NA	NA	(21,000)	NA	21,000	(21,000)	(21,000) OA
5	(5,000)	NA	NA	NA	NA	(5,000)	NA	NA	NA	(5,000) FA
6*	NA	NA	NA	(6,000)	NA	6,000	6,000	NA	6,000	NA
7†	NA	NA	(9,000)	NA	NA	(9,000)	NA	9,000	(9,000)	NA
Bal.	53,300	1,000	3,000	0	20,000	37,300	44,000	30,000	14,000	2,000 NC

*Revenue is earned at the rate of \$3,000 (\$36,000 ÷ 12 months) per month. Revenue recognized in 2008 is \$30,000 (\$3,000 × 10 months). Revenue recognized in 2009 is \$6,000 (\$3,000 × 2 months).

†Insurance expense is incurred at the rate of \$1,000 (\$12,000 ÷ 12 months) per month. Insurance expense recognized in 2009 is \$9,000 (\$1,000 × 9 months).

Solutions to Requirements b–g

b. Gifford would report \$48,000 of revenue in 2008 (\$18,000 revenue on account plus \$30,000 of the \$36,000 of unearned revenue).

c. The cash inflow from customers is \$51,000 (\$36,000 when the unearned revenue was received plus \$15,000 collection of accounts receivable).

d. The December 31, 2008, balance sheet will report \$6,000 of unearned revenue, which is the amount of the cash advance less the amount of revenue recognized in 2008 (\$36,000 − \$30,000). The December 31, 2009, unearned revenue balance is zero.

e. Since revenue and expense accounts are closed at the end of each accounting period, the beginning balances in these accounts are always zero.

f. Assets on the December 31, 2008, balance sheet are \$54,300 [Gifford's cash at year end plus the balance in accounts receivable (\$51,300 + \$3,000)].

g. Since all unearned revenue would be recognized before the financial statements were prepared at the end of 2009, there would be no liabilities on the 2009 balance sheet. Common stock and retained earnings would be the only claims as of December 31, 2009, for a claims total of \$57,300 (\$20,000 + \$37,300).

KEY TERMS

accounting cycle 48
accounts receivable 42
accrual 42
accrual accounting 41
accrued expenses 44
adjusting entry 44
asset exchange transaction 43
asset source transaction 42
asset use transaction 43
claims exchange transaction 44
closing 48
closing the books 48
conservatism 49
cost 50
deferral 42
expense 47, 63
matching concept 49
period costs 49
permanent accounts 48
prepaid items 50
price-earnings ratio 59
realization 41
recognition 41
revenue 55, 63
salaries payable 44
temporary accounts 48
unearned revenue 51
vertical statements model 57

QUESTIONS

1. What does accrual accounting attempt to accomplish?
2. Define *recognition.* How is it independent of collecting or paying cash?
3. What does the term *deferral* mean?
4. If cash is collected in advance of performing services, when is the associated revenue recognized?
5. What does the term *asset source transaction* mean?
6. What effect does the issue of common stock have on the accounting equation?
7. How does the recognition of revenue on account (accounts receivable) affect the income statement compared to its effect on the statement of cash flows?
8. Give an example of an asset source transaction. What is the effect of this transaction on the accounting equation?
9. When is revenue recognized under accrual accounting?
10. Give an example of an asset exchange transaction. What is the effect of this transaction on the accounting equation?
11. What is the effect on the claims side of the accounting equation when cash is collected in advance of performing services?
12. What does the term *unearned revenue* mean?
13. What effect does expense recognition have on the accounting equation?
14. What does the term *claims exchange transaction* mean?
15. What type of transaction is a cash payment to creditors? How does this type of transaction affect the accounting equation?
16. When are expenses recognized under accrual accounting?
17. Why may net cash flow from operating activities on the cash flow statement be different from the amount of net income reported on the income statement?
18. What is the relationship between the income statement and changes in assets and liabilities?
19. How does net income affect the stockholders' claims on the business's assets?
20. What is the difference between a cost and an expense?
21. When does a cost become an expense? Do all costs become expenses?
22. How and when is the cost of the *supplies used* recognized in an accounting period?
23. What does the term *expense* mean?
24. What does the term *revenue* mean?
25. What is the purpose of the statement of changes in stockholders' equity?
26. What is the main purpose of the balance sheet?
27. Why is the balance sheet dated *as of* a specific date when the income statement, statement of changes in stockholders' equity, and statement of cash flows are dated with the phrase *for the period ended?*
28. In what order are assets listed on the balance sheet?
29. What does the statement of cash flows explain?
30. What does the term *adjusting entry* mean? Give an example.

31. What types of accounts are closed at the end of the accounting period? Why is it necessary to close these accounts?
32. Give several examples of period costs.
33. Give an example of a cost that can be directly matched with the revenue produced by an accounting firm from preparing a tax return.
34. List and describe the four stages of the accounting cycle discussed in Chapter 2.
35. What does the P/E ratio measure?
36. Why might a high-growth company sell for a higher P/E multiple than a low-growth company?

EXERCISES

All Exercises are available with McGraw-Hill's Homework Manager

Where applicable in all exercises, round computations to the nearest dollar.

Exercise 2-1 *Effect of accruals on the financial statements*

L.O. 2, 3

Hamby Inc. experienced the following events in 2006, in its first year of operation.

1. Received $15,000 cash from the issue of common stock.
2. Performed services on account for $48,000.
3. Paid the utility expense of $1,250.
4. Collected $36,000 of the accounts receivable.
5. Recorded $8,000 of accrued salaries at the end of the year.
6. Paid a $1,000 cash dividend to the shareholders.

Required

a. Record the events in general ledger accounts under an accounting equation. In the last column of the table, provide appropriate account titles for the Retained Earnings amounts. The first transaction has been recorded as an example.

HAMBY INC.
General Ledger Accounts

Event	Assets		=	Liabilities	+	Stockholders' Equity		Acct. Titles for Ret. Earn.
	Cash	Accounts Receivable		Salaries Payable		Common Stock	Retained Earnings	
1.	15,000					15,000		

b. Prepare the income statement, statement of changes in stockholders' equity, balance sheet, and statement of cash flows for the 2006 accounting period.
c. Why is the amount of net income different from the amount of net cash flow from operating activities?

Exercise 2-2 *Effect of collecting accounts receivable on the accounting equation and financial statements*

L.O. 2, 3

Pilgram Company earned $6,000 of service revenue on account during 2008. The company collected $5,200 cash from accounts receivable during 2008.

Required

Based on this information alone, determine the following. (*Hint:* Record the events in general ledger accounts under an accounting equation before satisfying the requirements.)

a. The balance of the accounts receivable that Pilgram would report on the December 31, 2008, balance sheet.

b. The amount of net income that Pilgram would report on the 2008 income statement.
c. The amount of net cash flow from operating activities that Pilgram would report on the 2008 statement of cash flows.
d. The amount of retained earnings that Pilgram would report on the 2008 balance sheet.
e. Why are the answers to Requirements *b* and *c* different?

L.O. 2, 3

Exercise 2-3 *Effect of prepaid rent on the accounting equation and financial statements*

The following events apply to 2005, the first year of operations of ITS Consulting Services:

1. Acquired $20,000 cash from the issue of common stock.
2. Paid $12,000 cash in advance for a one-year rental contract for office space.
3. Provided services for $25,000 cash.
4. Adjusted the records to recognize the use of the office space. The one-year contract started on March 1, 2005. The adjustment was made as of December 31, 2005.

Required

a. Write an accounting equation and record the effects of each accounting event under the appropriate general ledger account headings.
b. Prepare an income statement and statement of cash flows for the 2005 accounting period.
c. Explain the difference between the amount of net income and amount of net cash flow from operating activities.

L.O. 1, 3

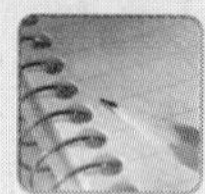

Exercise 2-4 *Effect of supplies on the financial statements*

The Copy Center Inc. started the 2005 accounting period with $8,000 cash, $6,000 of common stock, and $2,000 of retained earnings. The Copy Center was affected by the following accounting events during 2005:

1. Purchased $11,500 of paper and other supplies on account.
2. Earned and collected $27,000 of cash revenue.
3. Paid $10,000 cash on accounts payable.
4. Adjusted the records to reflect the use of supplies. A physical count indicated that $2,500 of supplies was still on hand on December 31, 2005.

Required

a. Show the effects of the events on the financial statements using a horizontal statements model like the following one. In the Cash Flows column, use OA to designate operating activity, IA for investing activity, FA for financing activity, and NC for net change in cash. Use NA to indicate accounts not affected by the event. The beginning balances are entered in the following example.

Event No.	Assets			=	Liab.	+	Stockholders' Equity									
	Cash	+	Supplies	=	Accts. Pay.	+	Com. Stk.	+	Ret. Earn.	Rev.	−	Exp.	=	Net Inc.	Cash Flows
Beg. bal.	8,000	+	0	=	0	+	6,000	+	2,000	0	−	0	=	0	0

b. Explain the difference between the amount of net income and amount of net cash flow from operating activities.

L.O. 1

Exercise 2-5 *Effect of unearned revenue on financial statements*

Meg Sanderfert started a personal financial planning business when she accepted $60,000 cash as advance payment for managing the financial assets of a large estate. Sanderfert agreed to manage the estate for a one-year period beginning April 1, 2007.

Required

a. Show the effects of the advance payment and revenue recognition on the 2007 financial statements using a horizontal statements model like the following one. In the Cash Flows column, use OA to designate operating activity, IA for investing activity, FA for financing activity, and NC for net change in cash. Use NA if the account is not affected.

Event	Assets	=	Liab.	+	Stockholders' Equity	Rev.	−	Exp.	=	Net Inc.	Cash Flows
	Cash	=	Unearn. Rev.	+	Ret. Earn.						

b. How much revenue would Meg recognize on the 2008 income statement?

c. What is the amount of cash flow from operating activities in 2008?

Exercise 2-6 *Unearned revenue defined as a liability*

L.O. 3

Steve Chang received $500 in advance for tutoring fees when he agreed to help Jon Seng with his introductory accounting course. Upon receiving the cash, Steve mentioned that he would have to record the transaction as a liability on his books. Seng asked, "Why a liability? You don't owe me any money, do you?"

Required

Respond to Seng's question regarding Chang's liability.

Exercise 2-7 *Distinguishing between an expense and a cost*

L.O. 3

Clair Seaton tells you that the accountants where she works are real hair splitters. For example, they make a big issue over the difference between a cost and an expense. She says the two terms mean the same thing to her.

Required

a. Explain to Clair the difference between a cost and an expense from an accountant's perspective.

b. Explain whether each of the following events produces an asset or an expense.

(1) Purchased a building for cash.
(2) Paid cash to purchase supplies.
(3) Used supplies on hand to produce revenue.
(4) Paid cash in advance for insurance.
(5) Recognized accrued salaries.

Exercise 2-8 *Revenue and expense recognition*

L.O. 3

Required

a. Describe an expense recognition event that results in an increase in liabilities.

b. Describe an expense recognition event that results in a decrease in assets.

c. Describe a revenue recognition event that results in a decrease in liabilities.

d. Describe a revenue recognition event that results in an increase in assets.

Exercise 2-9 *Transactions that affect the elements of financial statements*

L.O. 3

Required

Give an example of a transaction that will do the following:

a. Increase an asset and increase equity (asset source event).

b. Decrease an asset and decrease equity (asset use event).

c. Increase an asset and decrease another asset (asset exchange event).

d. Decrease a liability and increase equity (claims exchange event).

e. Increase a liability and decrease equity (claims exchange event).

f. Increase an asset and increase a liability (asset source event).

g. Decrease an asset and decrease a liability (asset use event).

Exercise 2-10 *Identifying deferral and accrual events*

L.O. 3

Required

Identify each of the following events as an accrual, a deferral, or neither.

a. Paid cash in advance for a one-year insurance policy.

b. Paid cash to settle an account payable.

c. Collected accounts receivable.
d. Paid cash for current salaries expense.
e. Paid cash to purchase supplies.
f. Provided services on account.
g. Provided services and collected cash.
h. Paid cash to purchase land.
i. Recognized accrued salaries at the end of the accounting period.
j. Paid a cash dividend to the stockholders.

L.O. 2

Exercise 2-11 *Prepaid and unearned rent*

On September 1, 2007, Ameriship paid West Coast Rentals $36,000 for a 12-month lease on warehouse space.

Required

a. Record the deferral and the related December 31, 2007, adjustment for Ameriship in the accounting equation.
b. Record the deferral and the related December 31, 2007, adjustment for West Coast Rentals in the accounting equation.

L.O. 3

Exercise 2-12 *Classifying events on the statement of cash flows*

The following transactions pertain to the operations of Stone Company for 2008:

1. Acquired $24,000 cash from the issue of common stock.
2. Provided $40,000 of services on account.
3. Incurred $25,000 of other operating expenses on account.
4. Collected $32,000 cash from accounts receivable.
5. Paid a $2,000 cash dividend to the stockholders.
6. Paid $18,000 cash on accounts payable.
7. Performed services for $8,000 cash.
8. Paid a $6,000 cash advance for a one year contract to rent equipment.
9. Recognized $9,000 of accrued salary expense.
10. Accepted an $18,000 cash advance for services to be performed in the future.

Required

a. Classify the cash flows from these transactions as operating activities (OA), investing activities (IA), or financing activities (FA). Use NA for transactions that do not affect the statement of cash flows.
b. Prepare a statement of cash flows. (There is no beginning cash balance.)

L.O. 3

Exercise 2-13 *Effect of accounting events on the income statement and statement of cash flows*

Required

Explain how each of the following events or series of events and the related adjusting entry will affect the amount of *net income* and the amount of *cash flow from operating activities* reported on the year-end financial statements. Identify the direction of change (increase, decrease, or NA) and the amount of the change. Organize your answers according to the following table. The first event is recorded as an example. If an event does not have a related adjusting entry, record only the effects of the event.

	Net Income		Cash Flows from Operating Activities	
Event No.	Direction of Change	Amount of Change	Direction of Change	Amount of Change
a	NA	NA	NA	NA

a. Acquired $50,000 cash from the issue of common stock.
b. Earned $12,000 of revenue on account. Collected $10,000 cash from accounts receivable.
c. Paid $2,400 cash on October 1 to purchase a one-year insurance policy.

d. Collected $9,600 in advance for services to be performed in the future. The contract called for services to start on August 1 and to continue for one year.

e. Accrued salaries amounting to $4,000.

f. Sold land that cost $15,000 for $15,000 cash.

g. Provided services for $7,500 cash.

h. Purchased $1,200 of supplies on account. Paid $1,000 cash on accounts payable. The ending balance in the Supplies account, after adjustment, was $300.

i. Paid cash for other operating expenses of $1,500.

Exercise 2-14 *Identifying transaction type and effect on the financial statements*

L.O. 1, 8

Required

Identify whether each of the following transactions is an asset source (AS), asset use (AU), asset exchange (AE), or claims exchange (CE). Also show the effects of the events on the financial statements using the horizontal statements model. Indicate whether the event increases (I), decreases (D), or does not affect (NA) each element of the financial statements. In the Cash Flows column, designate the cash flows as operating activities (OA), investing activities (IA), or financing activities (FA). The first two transactions have been recorded as examples.

					Stockholders' Equity										
Event No.	Type of Event	Assets	=	Liabilities	+	Common Stock	+	Retained Earnings	Rev.	−	Exp.	=	Net Inc.	Cash Flows
a	AS	I		NA		NA		I	I		NA		I	I OA
b	AS	I		I		NA		NA	NA		NA		NA	NA

a. Provided services and collected cash.

b. Purchased supplies on account to be used in the future.

c. Paid cash in advance for one year's rent.

d. Paid cash to purchase land.

e. Paid a cash dividend to the stockholders.

f. Received cash from the issue of common stock.

g. Paid cash on accounts payable.

h. Collected cash from accounts receivable.

i. Received cash advance for services to be provided in the future.

j. Incurred other operating expenses on account.

k. Performed services on account.

l. Adjusted books to reflect the amount of prepaid rent expired during the period.

m. Paid cash for operating expenses.

n. Adjusted the books to record the supplies used during the period.

o. Recorded accrued salaries.

p. Paid cash for salaries accrued at the end of a prior period.

Exercise 2-15 *Effect of accruals and deferrals on financial statements: the horizontal statements model*

L.O. 1

D. Downs, Attorney at Law, experienced the following transactions in 2007, the first year of operations:

1. Purchased $1,200 of office supplies on account.
2. Accepted $18,000 on February 1, 2007, as a retainer for services to be performed evenly over the next 12 months.
3. Performed legal services for cash of $66,000.
4. Paid cash for salaries expense of $20,500.
5. Paid a cash dividend to the stockholders of $5,000.
6. Paid $900 of the amount due on accounts payable.
7. Determined that at the end of the accounting period, $125 of office supplies remained on hand.

8. On December 31, 2007, recognized the revenue that had been earned for services performed in accordance with Transaction 2.

Required

Show the effects of the events on the financial statements using a horizontal statements model like the following one. In the Cash Flow column, use the initials OA to designate operating activity, IA for investing activity, FA for financing activity, and NC for net change in cash. Use NA to indicate accounts not affected by the event. The first event has been recorded as an example.

Event No.	Assets			=	Liabilities			+	Stk. Equity						
	Cash	+	Supplies	=	Accts. Pay.	+	Unearn. Rev.	+	Ret. Earn.	Rev.	−	Exp.	=	Net Inc.	Cash Flow
1	NA	+	1,200	=	1,200	+	NA	+	NA	NA	−	NA	=	NA	NA

L.O. 2, 3

Exercise 2-16 *Effect of an error on financial statements*

On May 1, 2007, Dobler Corporation paid $9,600 to purchase a 24-month insurance policy. Assume that Dobler records the purchase as an asset and that the books are closed on December 31.

Required

a. Show the purchase of the insurance policy and the related adjusting entry to recognize insurance expense in the accounting equation.

b. Assume that Dobler Corporation failed to record the adjusting entry to reflect the expiration of insurance. How would the error affect the company's 2007 income statement and balance sheet?

L.O. 2, 3

Exercise 2-17 *Net income versus changes in cash*

In 2008, Lott Inc. billed its customers $56,000 for services performed. The company collected $42,000 of the amount billed. Lott incurred $38,000 of other operating expenses on account. Lott paid $25,000 of the accounts payable. Lott acquired $30,000 cash from the issue of common stock. The company invested $12,000 cash in the purchase of land.

Required

Use the preceding information to answer the following questions. (*Hint:* Identify the six events described in the paragraph and record them in general ledger accounts under an accounting equation before attempting to answer the questions.)

a. What amount of revenue will Lott report on the 2008 income statement?

b. What amount of cash flow from revenue will Lott report on the statement of cash flows?

c. What is the net income for the period?

d. What is the net cash flow from operating activities for the period?

e. Why is the amount of net income different from the net cash flow from operating activities for the period?

f. What is the amount of net cash flow from investing activities?

g. What is the amount of net cash flow from financing activities?

h. What amounts of total assets, liabilities, and equity will Lott report on the year-end balance sheet?

L.O. 3

Exercise 2-18 *Adjusting the accounts*

Morgan Associates experienced the following accounting events during its 2006 accounting period.

1. Recognized revenue on account.
2. Issued common stock.
3. Paid cash to purchase supplies.
4. Collected a cash advance for services that will be provided during the coming year.
5. Paid a cash dividend to the stockholders.
6. Paid cash for an insurance policy that provides coverage during the next year.
7. Collected cash from accounts receivable.
8. Paid cash for operating expenses.

9. Paid cash to settle an account payable.
10. Paid cash to purchase land.

Required

a. Identify the events that would require a year-end adjusting entry.
b. Explain why adjusting entries are made at the end of the accounting period.

Exercise 2-19 ***Closing the accounts*** L.O. 4

The following information was drawn from the accounting records of Pearson Company as of December 31, 2007, before the temporary accounts had been closed. The Cash balance was $3,000, and Notes Payable amounted to $2,500. The company had revenues of $4,000 and expenses of $2,500. The company's Land account had a $5,000 balance. Dividends amounted to $500. There was $1,000 of common stock issued.

Required

a. Identify which accounts would be classified as permanent and which accounts would be classified as temporary.
b. Assuming that Pearson's beginning balance (as of January 1, 2007) in the Retained Earnings account was $3,500, determine its balance after the temporary accounts were closed at the end of 2007.
c. What amount of net income would Pearson Company report on its 2007 income statement?
d. Explain why the amount of net income differs from the amount of the ending Retained Earnings balance.
e. What are the balances in the revenue, expense, and dividend accounts on January 1, 2008?

Exercise 2-20 ***Closing accounts and the accounting cycle*** L.O. 4

Required

a. Identify which of the following accounts are temporary (will be closed to Retained Earnings at the end of the year) and which are permanent.
   (1) Cash
   (2) Salaries Expense
   (3) Prepaid Rent
   (4) Utilities Expense
   (5) Service Revenue
   (6) Dividends
   (7) Common Stock
   (8) Land
   (9) Salaries Payable
   (10) Retained Earnings
b. List and explain the four stages of the accounting cycle. Which stage must be first? Which stage is last?

Exercise 2-21 ***Closing entries*** L.O. 4

Required

Which of the following accounts are closed at the end of the accounting period?

a. Accounts Payable
b. Unearned Revenue
c. Cash
d. Accounts Receivable
e. Service Revenue
f. Advertising Expense
g. Dividends
h. Retained Earnings
i. Utilities Expense
j. Salaries Payable
k. Land
l. Operating Expenses

L.O. 3

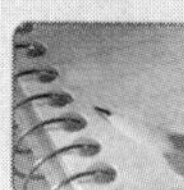

Exercise 2-22 *Matching concept*

Companies make sacrifices known as *expenses* to obtain benefits called *revenues*. The accurate measurement of net income requires that expenses be matched with revenues. In some circumstances matching a particular expense directly with revenue is difficult or impossible. In these circumstances, the expense is matched with the period in which it is incurred.

Required

a. Identify an expense that could be matched directly with revenue.
b. Identify a period expense that would be difficult to match with revenue. Explain why.

L.O. 8

Exercise 2-23 *Identifying source, use, and exchange transactions*

Required

Indicate whether each of the following transactions is an asset source (AS), asset use (AU), asset exchange (AE), or claims exchange (CE) transaction.

a. Acquired cash from the issue of stock.
b. Paid a cash dividend to the stockholders.
c. Paid cash on accounts payable.
d. Incurred other operating expenses on account.
e. Paid cash for rent expense.
f. Performed services for cash.
g. Performed services for clients on account.
h. Collected cash from accounts receivable.
i. Received cash for services to be performed in the future.
j. Purchased land with cash.

L.O. 8

Exercise 2-24 *Identifying asset source, use, and exchange transactions*

Required

a. Name an asset use transaction that will *not* affect the income statement.
b. Name an asset exchange transaction that will affect the statement of cash flows.
c. Name an asset source transaction that will *not* affect the income statement.
d. Name an asset source transaction that will *not* affect the statement of cash flows.
e. Name an asset source transaction that will affect the income statement.

L.O. 3

Exercise 2-25 *Relation of elements to financial statements*

Required

Identify whether each of the following items would appear on the income statement (IS), statement of changes in stockholders' equity (SE), balance sheet (BS), or statement of cash flows (CF). Some items may appear on more than one statement; if so, identify all applicable statements. If an item would not appear on any financial statement, label it NA.

a. Land
b. Consulting Revenue
c. Dividends
d. Salaries Expense
e. Net Income
f. Supplies
g. Ending Cash Balance
h. Cash Flow from Investing Activities
i. Prepaid Rent
j. Salaries Payable
k. Accounts Receivable
l. Retained Earnings
m. Accounts Payable
n. Utilities Payable
o. Unearned Revenue

Exercise 2-26 *Price-earnings ratio*

L.O. 7

The following information is available for two companies.

	Henry Company	Pager Company
Earnings per Share	$ 1.05	$ 4.50
Market Price per Share	38.50	108.00

Required

a. Compute the price-earnings ratio for each company.

b. Explain why one company would have a higher price-earnings ratio than the other.

PROBLEMS

All Problems are available with McGraw-Hill's Homework Manager

Problem 2-27 *Recording events in a horizontal statements model*

L.O. 1

CHECK FIGURES
Net Income: $10,000
Ending Cash Balance: $19,100

The following events pertain to The Plains Company:

1. Acquired $12,000 cash from the issue of common stock.
2. Provided services for $4,000 cash.
3. Provided $12,000 of services on account.
4. Collected $9,000 cash from the account receivable created in Event 3.
5. Paid $900 cash to purchase supplies.
6. Had $100 of supplies on hand at the end of the accounting period.
7. Received $1,800 cash in advance for services to be performed in the future.
8. Performed one-half of the services agreed to in Event 7.
9. Paid $4,600 for salaries expense.
10. Incurred $1,500 of other operating expenses on account.
11. Paid $1,200 cash on the account payable created in Event 10.
12. Paid a $1,000 cash dividend to the stockholders.

Required

Show the effects of the events on the financial statements using a horizontal statements model like the following one. In the Cash Flows column, use the letters OA to designate operating activity, IA for investing activity, FA for financing activity, and NC for net change in cash. Use NA to indicate accounts not affected by the event. The first event is recorded as an example.

	Assets						=	Liabilities			+	Stockholders' Equity								
Event No.	Cash	+	Accts. Rec.	+	Supp.	=	Accts. Pay.	+	Unearn. Rev.	+	Com. Stk.	+	Ret. Earn.	Rev.	−	Exp.	=	Net Inc.	Cash Flows
1	12,000	+	NA	+	NA	=	NA	+	NA	+	12,000	+	NA	NA	−	NA	=	NA	12,000 FA

Problem 2-28 *Effect of deferrals on financial statements: three separate single-cycle examples*

L.O. 1, 2, 3

mhhe.com/edmonds2007

CHECK FIGURES
a. Net Income: $56,000
b. Net Income: $10,000

Required

a. On February 1, 2005, Business Help Inc. was formed when it received $60,000 cash from the issue of common stock. On May 1, 2005, the company paid $36,000 cash in advance to rent office space for the coming year. The office space was used as a place to consult with clients. The consulting activity generated $80,000 of cash revenue during 2005. Based on this information alone, record the events and related adjusting entry in the general ledger accounts under the accounting equation. Determine the amount of net income and cash flows from operating activities for 2005.

b. On January 1, 2006, the accounting firm of Woo & Associates was formed. On August 1, 2006, the company received a retainer fee (was paid in advance) of $24,000 for services to be performed monthly during the coming year. Assuming that this was the only transaction completed in 2006, prepare an income statement, statement of changes in stockholders' equity, balance sheet, and statement of cash flows for 2006.

c. Sing Company had $350 of supplies on hand on January 1, 2007. Sing purchased $1,200 of supplies on account during 2007. A physical count of supplies revealed that $200 of supplies were on hand as of December 31, 2007. Determine the amount of supplies expense that should be recognized in the December 31, 2007, adjusting entry. Use a financial statements model to show how the adjusting entry would affect the balance sheet, income statement, and statement of cash flows.

L.O. 2

CHECK FIGURE

b. adjustment amount: $1,500

Problem 2-29 *Effect of adjusting entries on the accounting equation*

Required

Each of the following independent events requires a year-end adjusting entry. Show how each event and its related adjusting entry affect the accounting equation. Assume a December 31 closing date. The first event is recorded as an example.

	Total Assets						Stockholders' Equity		
Event/ Adjustment	Cash	+	Other Assets	=	Liabilities	+	Common Stock	+	Retained Earnings
a	−3,000		+3,000		NA		NA		NA
Adj.	NA		−2,250		NA		NA		−2,250

a. Paid $3,000 cash in advance on April 1 for a one-year insurance policy.

b. Purchased $1,600 of supplies on account. At year's end, $100 of supplies remained on hand.

c. Paid $6,000 cash in advance on March 1 for a one-year lease on office space.

d. Received a $15,000 cash advance for a contract to provide services in the future. The contract required a one-year commitment starting September 1.

e. Paid $12,000 cash in advance on October 1 for a one-year lease on office space.

L.O. 2, 5, 6, 8

mhhe.com/edmonds2007

CHECK FIGURES

a. Net Income, 2008: $21,200

b. Net Income, 2009: $21,500

Problem 2-30 *Events for two complete accounting cycles*

Texas Drilling Company was formed on January 1, 2008.

Events Affecting the 2008 Accounting Period

1. Acquired cash of $50,000 from the issue of common stock.
2. Purchased $800 of supplies on account.
3. Purchased land that cost $12,000 cash.
4. Paid $800 cash to settle accounts payable created in Event 2.
5. Recognized revenue on account of $38,000.
6. Paid $15,000 cash for other operating expenses.
7. Collected $22,000 cash from accounts receivable.

Information for 2008 Adjusting Entries

8. Recognized accrued salaries of $1,200 on December 31, 2008.
9. Had $200 of supplies on hand at the end of the accounting period.

Events Affecting the 2009 Accounting Period

1. Acquired an additional $10,000 cash from the issue of common stock.
2. Paid $1,200 cash to settle the salaries payable obligation.
3. Paid $3,600 cash in advance for a lease on office facilities.
4. Sold land that had cost $12,000 for $12,000 cash.
5. Received $5,400 cash in advance for services to be performed in the future.
6. Purchased $1,000 of supplies on account during the year.
7. Provided services on account of $26,000.
8. Collected $28,000 cash from accounts receivable.
9. Paid a cash dividend of $5,000 to the stockholders.

Information for 2009 Adjusting Entries

10. The advance payment for rental of the office facilities (see Event 3) was made on March 1 for a one-year lease term.
11. The cash advance for services to be provided in the future was collected on October 1 (see Event 5). The one-year contract started October 1.

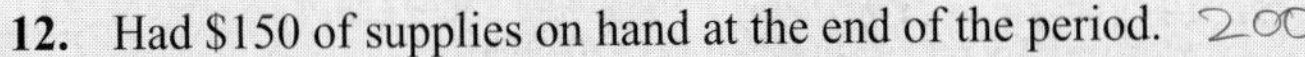

12. Had $150 of supplies on hand at the end of the period.
13. Recognized accrued salaries of $1,800 at the end of the accounting period.

Required

a. Identify each event affecting the 2008 and 2009 accounting periods as asset source (AS), asset use (AU), asset exchange (AE), or claims exchange (CE). Record the effects of each event under the appropriate general ledger account headings of the accounting equation.

b. Prepare an income statement, statement of changes in stockholders' equity, balance sheet, and statement of cash flows for 2008 and 2009, using the vertical statements model.

Problem 2-31 *Effect of events on financial statements*

L.O. 2, 3

CHECK FIGURES

b. $28,000

h. $(3,000)

Rios Company had the following balances in its accounting records as of December 31, 2006:

Assets		Claims	
Cash	$ 50,000	Accounts Payable	$ 25,000
Accounts Receivable	45,000	Common Stock	80,000
Land	25,000	Retained Earnings	15,000
Totals	$120,000		$120,000

The following accounting events apply to Rios's 2007 fiscal year:

Jan.	1	Acquired an additional $40,000 cash from the issue of common stock.
April	1	Paid $5,400 cash in advance for a one-year lease for office space.
June	1	Paid a $2,000 cash dividend to the stockholders.
July	1	Purchased additional land that cost $25,000 cash.
Aug.	1	Made a cash payment on accounts payable of $10,000.
Sept.	1	Received $7,200 cash in advance as a retainer for services to be performed monthly during the next eight months.
Sept.	30	Sold land for $22,000 cash that had originally cost $22,000.
Oct.	1	Purchased $900 of supplies on account.
Dec.	31	Earned $60,000 of service revenue on account during the year.
	31	Received $56,000 cash collections from accounts receivable.
	31	Incurred $12,000 other operating expenses on account during the year.
	31	Recognized accrued salaries expense of $5,000.
	31	Had $150 of supplies on hand at the end of the period.
	31	The land purchased on July 1 had a market value of $28,000.

Required

Based on the preceding information, answer the following questions. All questions pertain to the 2007 financial statements. (*Hint:* Record the events in general ledger accounts under an accounting equation before answering the questions.)

a. What two additional adjusting entries need to be made at the end of the year?
b. What amount would be reported for land on the balance sheet?
c. What amount of net cash flow from operating activities would Rios report on the statement of cash flows?
d. What amount of rent expense would Rios report in the income statement?
e. What amount of total liabilities would Rios report on the balance sheet?
f. What amount of supplies expense would Rios report on the income statement?
g. What amount of unearned revenue would Rios report on the balance sheet?
h. What amount of net cash flow from investing activities would Rios report on the statement of cash flows?

i. What amount of total expenses would Rios report on the income statement?
j. What total amount of service revenues would Rios report on the income statement?
k. What amount of cash flows from financing activities would Rios report on the statement of cash flows?
l. What amount of net income would Rios report on the income statement?
m. What amount of retained earnings would Rios report on the balance sheet?

L.O. 3

CHECK FIGURES
a. Total Assets $70,650
b. Net Income $34,150

Problem 2-32 *Identifying and arranging elements on financial statements*

The following accounts and balances were drawn from the records of Warren Company at December 31, 2005:

Cash	$11,400	Accounts Receivable	$19,000
Land	37,000	Cash Flow from Operating Act.	7,500
Insurance Expense	1,100	Beginning Retained Earnings	7,500
Dividends	5,000	Beginning Common Stock	1,000
Prepaid Insurance	2,500	Service Revenue	80,000
Accounts Payable	29,000	Cash Flow from Financing Act.	5,500
Supplies	750	Ending Common Stock	5,000
Supplies Expense	250	Cash Flow from Investing Act.	(7,000)
Rent Expense	2,500	Other Operating Expenses	42,000

Required

Use the accounts and balances from Warren Company to construct an income statement, statement of changes in stockholders' equity, balance sheet, and statement of cash flows (show only totals for each activity on the statement of cash flows).

L.O. 3

CHECK FIGURES
a. IS
z. BS/SE

Problem 2-33 *Relationship of accounts to financial statements*

Required

Identify whether each of the following items would appear on the income statement (IS), statement of changes in stockholders' equity (SE), balance sheet (BS), or statement of cash flows (CF). Some items may appear on more than one statement; if so, identify all applicable statements. If an item would not appear on any financial statement, label it NA.

a. Rent Expense
b. Salary Expense
c. Total Stockholders' Equity
d. Unearned Revenue
e. Cash Flow from Investing Activities
f. Insurance Expense
g. Ending Retained Earnings
h. Price-Earnings Ratio
i. Supplies
j. Beginning Retained Earnings
k. Utilities Payable
l. Cash Flow from Financing Activities
m. Accounts Receivable
n. Prepaid Insurance
o. Ending Cash Balance
p. Utilities Expense
q. Accounts Payable
r. Beginning Common Stock
s. Dividends
t. Total Assets
u. Consulting Revenue
v. Market Value of Land
w. Supplies Expense
x. Salaries Payable
y. Notes Payable
z. Ending Common Stock
aa. Beginning Cash Balance
bb. Prepaid Rent
cc. Net Change in Cash
dd. Land
ee. Operating Expenses
ff. Total Liabilities
gg. "As of" Date Notation
hh. Salaries Expense
ii. Net Income
jj. Service Revenue
kk. Cash Flow from Operating Activities
ll. Operating Income

ATC 2-3 Real-World Case *Classifying which company is the best investment*

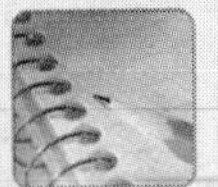

Following are the net earnings of four large companies for the fiscal years from 1999 to 2002. These amounts are in thousands of dollars.

		Net Earnings in $000			
Company	**Industry**	**2002**	**2001**	**2000**	**1999**
Autozone	Automobile parts retailer	$428,148	$175,526	$267,590	$244,783
Kohl's	Department store chain	643,381	495,676	372,148	258,142
Oshkosh B'Gosh	Children's clothing	32,045	32,808	32,217	32,448
Peoplesoft	Software development	182,589	191,554	145,691	(177,765)

Required

Based on this information alone, decide which of the companies you think would present the best investment opportunity for the future and which would be the worst. Write a brief memorandum supporting your choices, and show any computations that you used to reach your conclusions. As part of your analysis, compute the annual growth rates for each company's earnings. To do this, compute by what percentage each company's earnings increased or decreased from the year before. You will not be able to compute a growth rate for 1999 since the earnings for 1998 are not given. Perform whatever additional analysis you think is useful.

ATC 2-4 Business Applications Case *Calculating percentage growth rates at two companies*

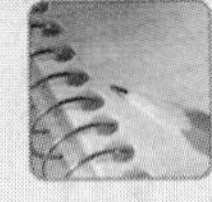

The following information relates to two companies in the same industry.

	Net Earnings by Year			
Company	**2007**	**2006**	**2005**	**2004**
Seven Grain	$2,000	$1,850	$1,660	$1,450
Whole Wheat	5,000	4,750	4,500	4,150

Required

a. Calculate the percentage growth rate of each company's net earnings from 2004 to 2007.

b. Based on this information alone, which company would you expect to have the higher price-earnings ratio? Explain your answer.

ATC 2-5 Business Applications Case *Calculating EPS and P/E ratios*

The following information was drawn from the financial statements of Last Minute Inc. and the Just-in-Time Co.

Statement Data	Last Minute Inc.	Just-in-Time Co.
Revenue	$15,000,000	$20,000,000
Net income	$ 1,150,000	$ 900,000
Number of shares of common stock outstanding	1,200,000	500,000
Market price per share	$ 17.25	$ 21.50

Required

a. Calculate the earnings per share (EPS) for each company.

b. Calculate the price-earnings (P/E) ratio for each company.

c. Which company does the market seem to be the most optimistic about?

ATC 2-6 Writing Assignment *Effect of stock options on real-world companies' P/E ratios*

Many companies grant certain members of management stock options that allow them to purchase designated amounts of stock for less than its market price. These arrangements are referred to as *stock compensation plans* and are intended to help the company retain high-quality management and to encourage management to increase the market value of the company's stock.

Deciding on the appropriate way to account for these plans is complex and controversial. Therefore, companies are allowed to *exclude* the estimated costs of the options they grant their management from net earnings provided that they disclose the estimated costs in the footnotes to the financial statements.

Listed here are data from four different companies that grant stock options to members of their management. The data are based on information provided in the companies' 10-K reports.

Costco Wholesale Corporation	
Basic EPS as reported on the fiscal year 2002 income statement	$ 1.48
Basic EPS if stock compensation is deducted	1.32
Selling price of the company's stock on July 1, 2003	36.51
Target Corporation	
Basic EPS as reported on the fiscal year 2003 income statement	$ 1.82
Basic EPS if stock compensation is deducted	1.79
Selling price of the company's stock on July 1, 2003	37.62
Cisco Systems, Inc.	
Basic EPS as reported on the fiscal year 2002 income statement	$ 0.26
Basic EPS if stock compensation is deducted	0.05
Selling price of the company's stock on July 1, 2003	17.24
Oracle Corporation	
Basic EPS as reported on the fiscal year 2003 income statement	$ 0.44
Basic EPS if stock compensation is deducted	0.37
Selling price of the company's stock on July 1, 2003	12.33

Required

a. Compute each company's P/E ratio on July 1, 2003, based on (1) EPS as reported and (2) EPS with stock compensation deducted. You will have eight P/E ratios.

b. Assuming these companies are representative of their respective industries (department stores and software companies), what conclusions can you draw from the data provided and from your P/E computations? Write a brief report presenting your conclusions and the reasons for them.

ATC 2-7 Ethical Dilemma *What is a little deceit among friends?*

Glenn's Cleaning Services Company is experiencing cash flow problems and needs a loan. Glenn has a friend who is willing to lend him the money he needs provided she can be convinced that he will be able to repay the debt. Glenn has assured his friend that his business is viable, but his friend has asked to see the company's financial statements. Glenn's accountant produced the following financial statements:

Income Statement		Balance Sheet	
Service Revenue	$ 38,000	Assets	$85,000
Operating Expenses	(70,000)	Liabilities	$35,000
Net Loss	$(32,000)	Stockholders' Equity	
		Common Stock	82,000
		Retained Earnings	(32,000)
		Total Liabilities and Stockholders' Equity	$85,000

Glenn made the following adjustments to these statements before showing them to his friend. He recorded $82,000 of revenue on account from Barrymore Manufacturing Company for a contract to clean its headquarters office building that was still being negotiated for the next month. Barrymore had scheduled a meeting to sign a contract the following week, so Glenn was sure that he would get the job. Barrymore was a reputable company, and Glenn was confident that he could ultimately collect the $82,000. Also, he subtracted $30,000 of accrued salaries expense and the corresponding liability. He reasoned that since he had not paid the employees, he had not incurred any expense.

Required

a. Reconstruct the income statement and balance sheet as they would appear after Glenn's adjustments. Comment on the accuracy of the adjusted financial statements.

b. Suppose you are Glenn and the $30,000 you owe your employees is due next week. If you are unable to pay them, they will quit and the business will go bankrupt. You are sure you will be able to repay your friend when your employees perform the $82,000 of services for Barrymore and you collect the cash. However, your friend is risk averse and is not likely to make the loan based on the financial statements your accountant prepared. Would you make the changes that Glenn made to get the loan and thereby save your company? Defend your position with a rational explanation.

c. Discuss Donald Cressey's features of ethical misconduct (described in Chapter 1) as they apply to Glenn's decision to change the financial statements to reflect more favorable results.

ATC 2-8 Research Assignment *Investigating nonfinancial information in Nike's annual report*

Although most of this course is concerned with the financial statements themselves, all sections of a company's annual report are important. A company must file various reports with the SEC, and one of these, Form 10-K, is essentially the company's annual report. The requirements below ask you to investigate sections of Nike's annual report that explain various nonfinancial aspects of its business operations.

To obtain the Form 10-K you can use either the EDGAR system following the instructions in Appendix A or the company's website.

Required

a. In what year did Nike begin operations?

b. Other than athletic shoes, what products does Nike sell?

c. Does Nike operate businesses under names other than Nike? If so, what are they?

d. How many employees does Nike have?

e. In how many countries other than the United States does Nike sell its products?

CHAPTER 3

Accounting for Merchandising Businesses

LEARNING OBJECTIVES

After you have mastered the material in this chapter you will be able to:

1. **Identify and explain the primary features of the perpetual inventory system.**
2. **Show the effects of inventory transactions on financial statements.**
3. **Explain the meaning of terms used to describe transportation costs, cash discounts, returns or allowances, and financing costs.**
4. **Compare and contrast single and multistep income statements.**
5. **Show the effect of lost, damaged, or stolen inventory on financial statements.**
6. **Use common size financial statements to evaluate managerial performance.**
7. **Use ratio analysis to evaluate managerial performance.**
8. **Identify the primary features of the periodic inventory system. (Appendix)**

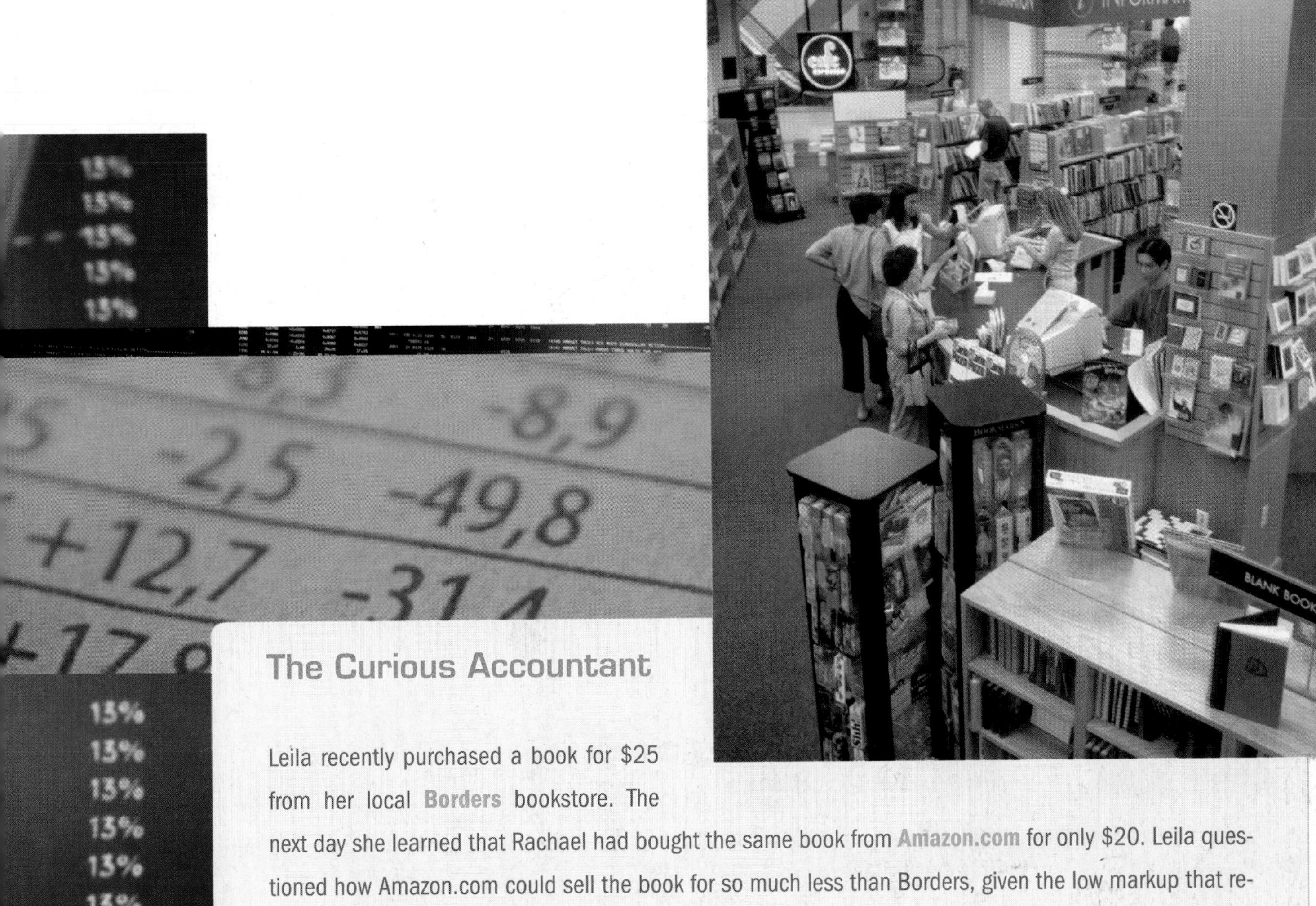

The Curious Accountant

Leila recently purchased a book for $25 from her local **Borders** bookstore. The next day she learned that Rachael had bought the same book from **Amazon.com** for only $20. Leila questioned how Amazon.com could sell the book for so much less than Borders, given the low markup that retail booksellers enjoy. Rachael suggested that although both booksellers purchase their books from the same publishers at about the same price, Amazon.com can charge lower prices because it does not have to operate expensive bricks-and-mortar stores, thus lowering its operating costs. Leila disagrees. She thinks the cost of operating huge distribution centers and Internet server centers would offset any cost savings Amazon.com enjoys from not owning retail bookstores.

Exhibit 3.1 presents the income statements for Amazon.com and Borders. Based on these income statements, do you think Leila or Rachael is correct? (Answer on page 88.)

CHAPTER OPENING

Previous chapters have discussed accounting for service businesses. These businesses obtain revenue by providing some kind of service such as medical or legal advice to their customers. Other examples of service companies include dry cleaning companies, maid service companies, and car washes. This chapter introduces accounting practices for merchandising businesses. **Merchandising businesses** *generate revenue by selling goods. They buy the merchandise they sell from companies called suppliers. The goods purchased for resale are called* **merchandise inventory.** *Merchandising businesses include* **retail companies** *(companies that sell goods to the final consumer) and* **wholesale companies** *(companies that sell to other businesses).* ***Sears***, ***JCPenney***, ***Target***, *and* ***SAM'S CLUB*** *are real-world merchandising businesses.* ■

Product Costs versus Selling and Administrative Costs

LO 1

Identify and explain the primary features of the perpetual inventory system.

Companies report inventory costs on the balance sheet in the asset account Merchandise Inventory. All costs incurred to acquire merchandise and ready it for sale are included in the inventory account. Examples of inventory costs include the price of goods purchased, shipping and handling costs, transit insurance, and storage costs. Since inventory items are referred to as products, inventory costs are frequently called **product costs.**

Costs that are not included in inventory are usually called **selling and administrative costs.** Examples of selling and administrative costs include advertising, administrative salaries, sales commissions, insurance, and interest. Since selling and administrative costs are usually recognized as expenses *in the period* in which they are incurred, they are sometimes called **period costs.** In contrast, product costs are expensed when inventory is sold regardless of when it was purchased. In other words, product costs are matched directly with sales revenue, while selling and administrative costs are matched with the period in which they are incurred.

Allocating Inventory Cost between Asset and Expense Accounts

The cost of inventory that is available for sale during a specific accounting period is determined as follows:

Beginning inventory balance	+	Inventory purchased during the period	=	Cost of goods available for sale

The **cost of goods available for sale** is allocated between the asset account Merchandise Inventory and an expense account called **Cost of Goods Sold.** The cost of inventory items that have not been sold (Merchandise Inventory) is reported as an asset on the balance sheet, and the cost of the items sold (Cost of Goods Sold) is expensed on the income statement. This allocation is depicted graphically as follows.

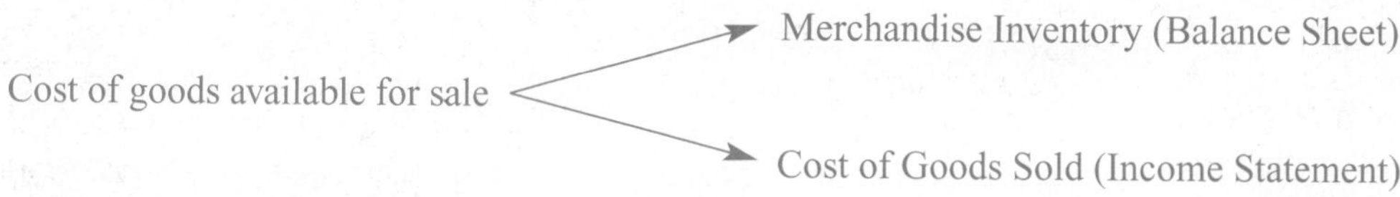

The difference between the sales revenue and the cost of goods sold is called **gross margin** or **gross profit.** The selling and administrative expenses (period costs) are subtracted from gross margin to obtain the net income.

Exhibit 3.1 displays income statements from the annual reports of **Amazon.com, Inc.**, and **Borders Group, Inc.** For each company, review the most current income statement and determine the amount of gross margin. You should find a gross profit of $992,618 (in thousands) for Amazon.com and a gross margin of $960.9 (in millions) for Borders.

EXHIBIT 3.1 Comparative Income Statements

AMAZON.COM, INC.
Consolidated Statements of Operations
(dollars in thousands)

	Years Ended December 31,		
	2002	2001	2000
Net Sales	$3,932,936	$3,122,433	$2,761,983
Cost of Sales	2,940,318	2,323,875	2,106,206
Gross Profit	992,618	798,558	655,777
Operating Expenses:			
Fulfillment	392,467	374,250	414,509
Marketing	125,383	138,283	179,980
Technology and Content	215,617	241,165	269,326
General and Administrative	79,049	89,862	108,962
Stock-Based Compensation	68,927	4,637	24,797
Amortization of Goodwill and Other Intangibles	5,478	181,033	321,772
Restructuring-Related and Other	41,573	181,585	200,311
Total Operating Expenses	928,494	1,210,815	1,519,657
Income (Loss) from Operations	64,124	(412,257)	(863,880)
Interest Income	23,687	29,103	40,821
Interest Expense	(142,925)	(139,232)	(130,921)
Other Income (Expense), Net	5,623	(1,900)	(10,058)
Other Gains (Losses), Net	(96,273)	(2,141)	(142,639)
Total Nonoperating Expenses, Net	(209,888)	(114,170)	(242,797)
Loss before Equity in Losses of Equity-Method Investees	(145,764)	(526,427)	(1,106,677)
Equity in Losses of Equity-Method Investees	(4,169)	(30,327)	(304,596)
Net Loss before Change in Accounting Principle	(149,933)	(556,754)	(1,411,273)
Cumulative Effect of Change in Accounting Principle	801	(10,523)	–
Net Loss	$ (149,132)	$ (567,277)	$(1,411,273)

BORDERS GROUP, INC.
Consolidated Statements of Operations
(dollars in millions)

	Fiscal Year Ended		
	January 26, 2003	January 27, 2002	January 28, 2001
Sales	$ 3,486.1	$ 3,387.9	$ 3,271.2
Other Revenue	26.9	25.3	25.9
Total Revenue	3,513.0	3,413.2	3,297.1
Cost of Merchandise Sold (Includes Occupancy)	2,550.3	2,464.5	2,380.4
Fulfillment Center and Other Inventory Writedowns	1.8	10.1	–
Gross Margin	960.9	938.6	916.7
Selling, General, and Administrative Expenses	745.2	744.8	736.2
Legal Settlement Expense	–	2.4	–
Preopening Expense	6.9	6.3	6.4
Asset Impairments and Other Writedowns	14.9	25.4	36.2
Goodwill Amortization	–	2.7	2.8
Operating Income	193.9	157.0	135.1
Interest Expense	12.6	14.4	13.1
Income from Continuing Operations before Income Tax	181.3	142.6	122.0
Income Tax Provision	69.6	55.2	48.2
Income from Continuing Operations	111.7	87.4	73.8
Discontinued Operations (Note 3)			
Loss from Operations of All Wound Up, Net of Income Tax Credits of $7.0 and $2.4	–	–	10.8
Loss on Disposition of All Wound Up, Net of Deferred Income Tax Credit of $8.9	–	–	19.4
Net Income	$ 111.7	$ 87.4	$ 43.6

Answers to The Curious Accountant

The income statement data show that **Amazon.com** had higher operating expenses than **Borders** although it does not operate traditional stores. As explained later in this chapter, the *gross margin percentage* indicates to some degree how much a company is charging in relation to what it pays to purchase the goods it is selling (its cost of goods sold). The *return on sales ratio* reveals how much profit, as a percentage of sales, a company is making after *all* of its expenses have been taken into account. For the calendar year 2002, the gross margin percentage for Borders was 27.4 percent and for Amazon.com was 25.2 percent, indicating that, on average, Amazon.com really does charge less for its books. The return on sales for Borders was 3.2 percent and for Amazon.com was −3.8 percent, suggesting that Borders is the one with the lower operating costs. In fact, Amazon.com's expenses were higher than those of Borders. Excluding cost of goods sold, the expenses at Borders were 24.4 percent of sales and at Amazon.com were 29.7 percent.

Perpetual Inventory System

LO 2

Show the effects of inventory transactions on financial statements.

Most modern companies maintain their inventory records using the **perpetual inventory system,** so-called because the inventory account is adjusted perpetually (continually) throughout the accounting period. Each time merchandise is purchased, the inventory account is increased; each time it is sold, the inventory account is decreased. The following illustration demonstrates the basic features of the perpetual inventory system.

June Gardener loved plants and grew them with such remarkable success that she decided to open a small retail plant store. She started June's Plant Shop (JPS) on January 1, 2006. The following discussion explains and illustrates the effects of the four events the company experienced during its first year of operation.

Effects of 2006 Events on Financial Statements

Event 1 ***JPS acquired $15,000 cash by issuing common stock.***

This event is an asset source transaction. It increases both assets (cash) and stockholders' equity (common stock). The income statement is not affected. The statement of cash flows reflects an inflow from financing activities. These effects are shown here:

Assets			=	Liab.	+	Stockholders' Equity			Rev.	−	Exp.	=	Net Inc.	Cash Flow
Cash	+	Inventory	=			Com. Stk.	+	Ret. Earn.						
15,000	+	NA	=	NA	+	15,000	+	NA	NA	−	NA	=	NA	15,000 FA

Event 2 ***JPS purchased merchandise inventory for $14,000 cash.***

This event is an asset exchange transaction. One asset, cash, decreases and another asset, merchandise inventory, increases; total assets remain unchanged. Because product costs are expensed when inventory is sold, not when it is purchased, the event does not affect the income statement. The cash outflow, however, is reported in the operating activities section of the statement of cash flows. These effects are illustrated below:

Assets			=	Liab.	+	Stockholders' Equity			Rev.	−	Exp.	=	Net Inc.	Cash Flow
Cash	+	Inventory	=			Com. Stk.	+	Ret. Earn.						
(14,000)	+	14,000	=	NA	+	NA	+	NA	NA	−	NA	=	NA	(14,000) OA

Event 3a ***JPS recognized sales revenue from selling inventory for $12,000 cash.***

The revenue recognition is the first part of a two-part transaction. The *sales part* represents a source of assets (cash increases from earning sales revenue). Both assets (cash) and stockholders' equity (retained earnings) increase. Sales revenue on the income statement increases. The $12,000 cash inflow is reported in the operating activities section of the statement of cash flows. These effects are shown in the following financial statements model:

Assets			=	Liab.	+	Stockholders' Equity			Rev.	−	Exp.	=	Net Inc.	Cash Flow
Cash	+	Inventory	=			Com. Stk.	+	Ret. Earn.						
12,000	+	NA	=	NA	+	NA	+	12,000	12,000	−	NA	=	12,000	12,000 OA

Event 3b ***JPS recognized $8,000 of cost of goods sold.***

The expense recognition is the second part of the two-part transaction. The *expense part* represents a use of assets. Both assets (merchandise inventory) and stockholders' equity (retained earnings) decrease. An expense account, Cost of Goods Sold, is reported on the income statement. This part of the transaction does not affect the statement of cash flows. A cash outflow occurred when the goods were bought, not when they were sold. These effects are shown here:

Assets			=	Liab.	+	Stockholders' Equity			Rev.	−	Exp.	=	Net Inc.	Cash Flow
Cash	+	Inventory	=			Com. Stk.	+	Ret. Earn.						
NA	+	(8,000)	=	NA	+	NA	+	(8,000)	NA	−	8,000	=	(8,000)	NA

Event 4 ***JPS paid $1,000 cash for selling and administrative expenses.***

This event is an asset use transaction. The payment decreases both assets (cash) and stockholders' equity (retained earnings). The increase in selling and administrative expenses decreases net income. The $1,000 cash payment is reported in the operating activities section of the statement of cash flows. These effects are illustrated below:

Assets			=	Liab.	+	Stockholders' Equity			Rev.	−	Exp.	=	Net Inc.	Cash Flow
Cash	+	Inventory	=			Com. Stk.	+	Ret. Earn.						
(1,000)	+	NA	=	NA	+	NA	+	(1,000)	NA	−	1,000	=	(1,000)	(1,000) OA

Financial Statements for 2006

The financial statements for JPS's 2006 accounting period are shown in Exhibit 3.2. JPS had no beginning inventory in its first year, so the cost of merchandise inventory available for sale was $14,000 (the amount of inventory purchased during the period). Recall that JPS must allocate the ***Cost of Goods (Inventory) Available for Sale*** between the ***Cost of Goods Sold*** ($8,000) and the ending balance ($6,000) in the ***Merchandise Inventory*** account. The cost of goods sold is reported as an expense on the income statement and the ending balance of merchandise inventory is reported as an asset on the balance sheet. The difference

EXHIBIT 3.2

Financial Statements

2006 Income Statement

Sales Revenue	$12,000
Cost of Goods Sold	(8,000)
Gross Margin	4,000
Less: Operating Exp.	
Selling and Admin. Exp.	(1,000)
Net Income	$ 3,000

12/31/06 Balance Sheet

Assets		
Cash	$12,000	
Merchandise Inventory	6,000	
Total Assets		$18,000
Liabilities		$ 0
Stockholders' Equity		
Common Stock	$15,000	
Retained Earnings	3,000	
Total Stockholders' Equity		18,000
Total Liab. and Stk. Equity		$18,000

2006 Statement of Cash Flows

Operating Activities		
Inflow from Customers	$12,000	
Outflow for Inventory	(14,000)	
Outflow for Selling & Admin. Exp.	(1,000)	
Net Cash Outflow for Operating Activities		$ (3,000)
Investing Activities		0
Financing Activities		
Inflow from Stock Issue		15,000
Net Change in Cash		12,000
Plus: Beginning Cash Balance		0
Ending Cash Balance		$12,000

between the sales revenue ($12,000) and the cost of goods sold ($8,000) is labeled ***gross margin*** ($4,000) on the income statement.

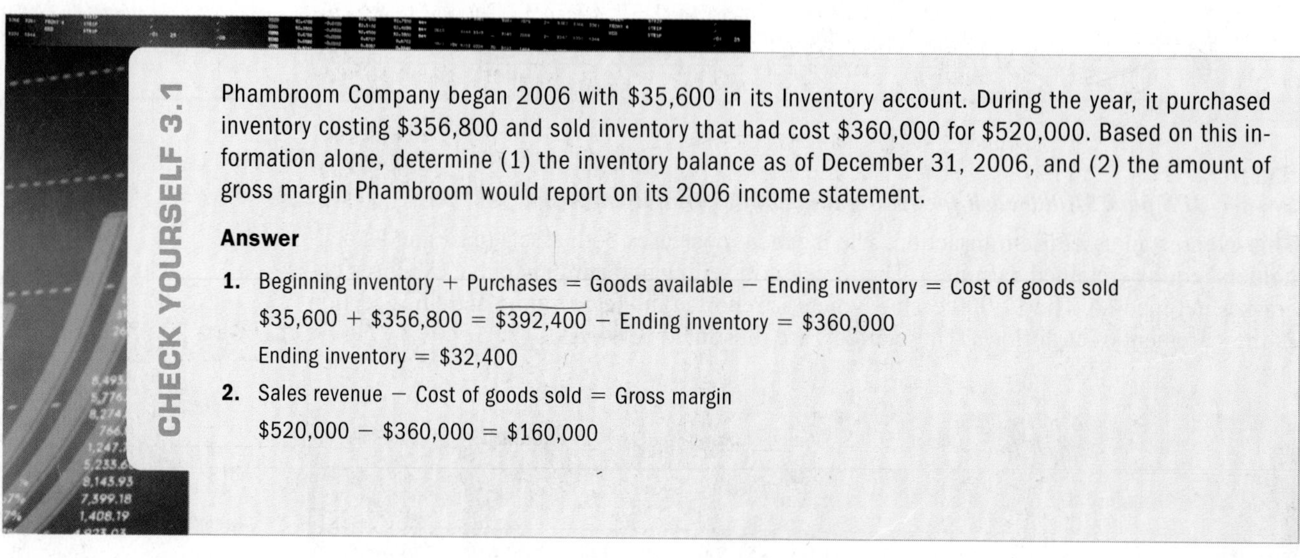

CHECK YOURSELF 3.1

Phambroom Company began 2006 with $35,600 in its Inventory account. During the year, it purchased inventory costing $356,800 and sold inventory that had cost $360,000 for $520,000. Based on this information alone, determine (1) the inventory balance as of December 31, 2006, and (2) the amount of gross margin Phambroom would report on its 2006 income statement.

Answer

1. Beginning inventory + Purchases = Goods available − Ending inventory = Cost of goods sold
   $35,600 + $356,800 = $392,400 − Ending inventory = $360,000
   Ending inventory = $32,400
2. Sales revenue − Cost of goods sold = Gross margin
   $520,000 − $360,000 = $160,000

Transportation Cost, Purchase Returns and Allowances, and Cash Discounts Related to Inventory Purchases

LO 3

Explain the meaning of terms used to describe transportation costs, cash discounts, returns or allowances, and financing costs.

Purchasing inventory often involves: (1) incurring transportation costs, (2) returning inventory or receiving purchase allowances (cost reductions), and (3) taking cash discounts (also cost reductions). During its second accounting cycle, JPS encountered these kinds of events. The final account balances at the end of the 2006 fiscal year become the beginning balances for 2007: Cash, $12,000; Merchandise Inventory, $6,000; Common Stock, $15,000; and Retained Earnings, $3,000.

Effects of 2007 Events on Financial Statements

JPS experienced the following events during its 2007 accounting period. The effects of each of these events are explained and illustrated in the following discussion.

Show the effects of inventory transactions on financial statements.

Event 1 ***JPS purchased merchandise inventory on account with a list price of $8,000. The payment terms were 2/10, n/30.***

The expression **2/10, n/30** (two-ten net thirty) means the seller will allow a 2 percent **cash discount** if the purchaser pays cash for the merchandise within 10 days from the date of purchase. If the purchaser pays later than 10 days from the purchase date, the full amount is due within 30 days. Based on these terms, the net (cash) cost of the inventory is computed as follows:

List price	$8,000
Purchase discount ($8,000 × .02)	160
Net price (Cash price $8,000 × .98)	$7,840

Since JPS could purchase the inventory for $7,840 cash, that is the cost JPS will record in the Merchandise Inventory account. The **purchase discount** is an additional charge JPS will incur if it chooses to delay payment. The real cost of the inventory is the net price. Although accounting practice permits recording the inventory cost at either the list price or the net price, the net price is theoretically preferable. This text uses the **net method** of accounting for inventory cost.

The inventory purchase increases both assets (merchandise inventory) and liabilities (accounts payable) on the balance sheet. The income statement is not affected until later, when inventory is sold. Since the inventory was purchased on account, there was no cash outflow. These effects are shown here:

Assets					=	Liab.	+	Stockholders' Equity			Rev.	−	Exp.	=	Net Inc.	Cash Flow
Cash	+	Accts. Rec.	+	Inventory	=	Accts. Pay.	+	Com. Stk.	+	Retained Earnings						
NA	+	NA	+	7,840	=	7,840	+	NA	+	NA	NA	−	NA	=	NA	NA

Event 2 ***JPS returned some of the inventory purchased in Event 1. The list price of the returned merchandise was $1,000.***

To promote customer satisfaction, many businesses allow customers to return goods for reasons such as wrong size, wrong color, wrong design, or even simply because the purchaser changed his mind. The effect of a purchase return is the *opposite* of the original purchase. For JPS the purchase return decreases both assets (merchandise inventory) and liabilities (accounts payable). There is no effect on either the income statement or the statement of cash flows. Since the inventory purchase was originally recorded at the net price (list price less purchase discount), the return is also recorded at the net price, $980 ($1,000 × .98). These effects are shown below:

Assets			=	Liab.	+	Stockholders' Equity		Rev. − Exp. = Net Inc.	Cash Flow
Cash +	Accts. Rec. +	Inventory	=	Accts. Pay.	+	Com. Stk.	+ Retained Earnings		
NA +	NA +	(980)	=	(980)	+	NA	+ NA	NA − NA = NA	NA

Sometimes dissatisfied buyers will agree to keep goods instead of returning them if the seller offers to reduce the price. Such reductions are called **allowances.** Purchase allowances affect the financial statements the same way purchase returns do.

Event 3 ***JPS paid cash to settle the account payable due on the inventory purchased in Event 1. The payment was made after the end of the discount period.***

Recall that JPS purchased merchandise inventory with a list price of $8,000 and returned merchandise with a list price of $1,000. JPS therefore has a liability for merchandise with a list price of $7,000. The net price of this merchandise is computed as follows:

List price	$7,000
Purchase discount ($7,000 × .02)	140
Net price (Cash price $7,000 × .98)	$6,860

Since JPS records inventory purchases at the net price, its account payable for this merchandise is recorded at $6,860. JPS must pay the list price ($7,000), however, because it failed to pay within the discount period. The purchase discount ($140) is incurred because JPS failed to pay the liability (accounts payable) in a timely manner. Since the $140 charge is due to carrying a liability, it is classified as interest expense.

The $7,000 cash payment results in a compound entry that reduces the asset account, Cash, reduces the liability account, Accounts Payable, and recognizes interest expense. The interest expense reduces net income. Since paying the account payable and paying interest expense are both operating activities, the statement of cash flows reflects a single outflow of $7,000. These effects are illustrated in the following financial statements model:

Assets			=	Liab.	+	Stockholders' Equity		Rev. − Exp. = Net Inc.	Cash Flow
Cash +	Accts. Rec. +	Inventory	=	Accts. Pay.	+	Com. Stk.	+ Retained Earnings		
(7,000) +	NA +	NA	=	(6,860)	+	NA	+ (140)	NA − 140 = (140)	(7,000) OA

Event 4 ***The shipping terms for the inventory purchased in Event 1 were FOB shipping point. JPS paid the freight company $300 cash for delivering the merchandise.***

The terms **FOB shipping point** and **FOB destination** identify whether the buyer or the seller is responsible for transportation costs. If goods are delivered FOB shipping point, the buyer is responsible for the freight cost. If goods are delivered FOB destination, the seller is responsible. When the buyer is responsible, the freight cost is called **transportation-in.** When the seller is responsible, the cost is called **transportation-out.** The following table summarizes freight cost terms.

Responsible Party	Buyer	Seller
Freight terms	FOB shipping point	FOB destination
Cost title	Transportation-in	Transportation-out

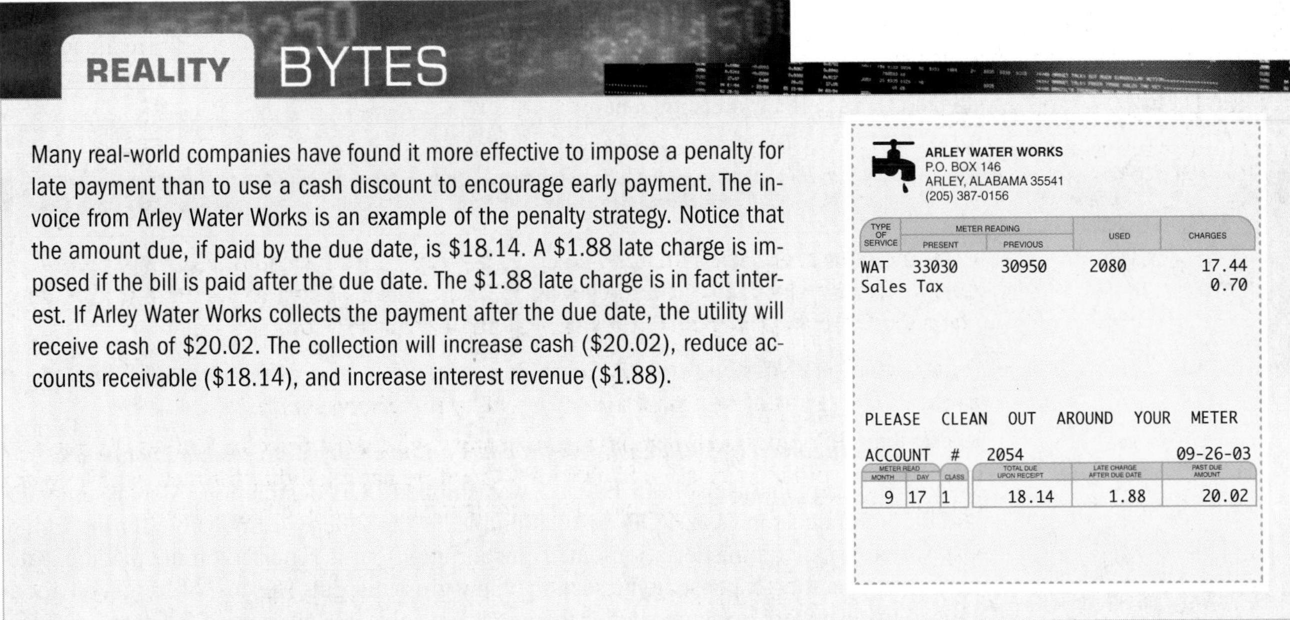

REALITY BYTES

Many real-world companies have found it more effective to impose a penalty for late payment than to use a cash discount to encourage early payment. The invoice from Arley Water Works is an example of the penalty strategy. Notice that the amount due, if paid by the due date, is $18.14. A $1.88 late charge is imposed if the bill is paid after the due date. The $1.88 late charge is in fact interest. If Arley Water Works collects the payment after the due date, the utility will receive cash of $20.02. The collection will increase cash ($20.02), reduce accounts receivable ($18.14), and increase interest revenue ($1.88).

Event 4 indicates the inventory was delivered FOB shipping point, so JPS (the buyer) is responsible for the $300 freight cost. Since incurring transportation-in costs is necessary to obtain inventory, these costs are added to the inventory account. The freight cost increases one asset account (Merchandise Inventory) and decreases another asset account (Cash). The income statement is not affected by this transaction because transportation-in costs are not expensed when they are incurred. Instead they are expensed as part of *cost of goods sold* when the inventory is sold. However, the cash paid for freight when inventory is delivered to customers is reported as an outflow in the operating activities section of the statement of cash flows. The effects of *transportation-in costs* are shown here:

Assets						=	Liab.	+	Stockholders' Equity			Rev.	−	Exp.	=	Net Inc.	Cash Flow
Cash	+	Accts. Rec.	+	Inventory		=	Accts. Pay.	+	Com. Stk.	+	Retained Earnings						
(300)	+	NA	+	300		=	NA	+	NA	+	NA	NA	−	NA	=	NA	(300) OA

Event 5a ***JPS recognized $24,750 of revenue on the cash sale of merchandise that cost $11,500.***

The sale increases assets (cash) and stockholders' equity (retained earnings). The revenue recognition increases net income. The $24,750 cash inflow from the sale is reported in the operating activities section of the statement of cash flows. These effects are shown below:

Assets						=	Liab.	+	Stockholders' Equity			Rev.	−	Exp.	=	Net Inc.	Cash Flow
Cash	+	Accts. Rec.	+	Inventory		=	Accts. Pay.	+	Com. Stk.	+	Retained Earnings						
24,750	+	NA	+	NA		=	NA	+	NA	+	24,750	24,750	−	NA	=	24,750	24,750 OA

Event 5b ***JPS recognized $11,500 of cost of goods sold.***

When goods are sold, the product cost—*including a proportionate share of transportation-in and adjustments for purchase returns and allowances*—is transferred from the Merchandise

Inventory account to the expense account, Cost of Goods Sold. Recognizing cost of goods sold decreases both assets (merchandise inventory) and stockholders' equity (retained earnings). The expense recognition for cost of goods sold decreases net income. Cash flow is not affected. These effects are shown here:

Assets					=	Liab.	+	Stockholders' Equity			Rev.	−	Exp.	=	Net Inc.	Cash Flow
Cash	+	Accts. Rec.	+	Inventory	=	Accts. Pay.	+	Com. Stk.	+	Retained Earnings						
NA	+	NA	+	(11,500)	=	NA	+	NA	+	(11,500)	NA	−	11,500	=	(11,500)	NA

Event 6 ***JPS incurred $450 of cash freight costs on inventory delivered to customers.***

Assume the merchandise sold in Event 5 was shipped FOB destination. Also assume JPS paid the freight cost in cash. FOB destination means the seller is responsible for the freight cost, which is called transportation-out. Transportation-out is reported on the income statement as an operating expense in the section below gross margin. The cost of freight on goods shipped to customers is incurred *after* the goods are sold. It is not part of the costs to obtain goods or ready them for sale. Recognizing the expense of transportation-out reduces assets (cash) and stockholders' equity (retained earnings). Operating expenses increase and net income decreases. The cash outflow is reported in the operating activities section of the statement of cash flows. These effects are shown below:

Assets					=	Liab.	+	Stockholders' Equity			Rev.	−	Exp.	=	Net Inc.	Cash Flow
Cash	+	Accts. Rec.	+	Inventory	=	Accts. Pay.	+	Com. Stk.	+	Retained Earnings						
(450)	+	NA	+	NA	=	NA	+	NA	+	(450)	NA	−	450	=	(450)	(450) OA

Event 7 ***JPS purchased $14,000 of merchandise inventory on account with credit terms of 1/10, n/30. The inventory was delivered FOB destination. The freight costs were $400.***

Merchandise inventory and accounts payable both increase by the net price of the merchandise, $13,860 ($14,000 × .99). Net income and cash flow are not affected. *The freight costs do not affect JPS since the freight terms are FOB destination and the seller is responsible for them.* These effects are shown here:

Assets					=	Liab.	+	Stockholders' Equity			Rev.	−	Exp.	=	Net Inc.	Cash Flow
Cash	+	Accts. Rec.	+	Inventory	=	Accts. Pay.	+	Com. Stk.	+	Retained Earnings						
NA	+	NA	+	13,860	=	13,860	+	NA	+	NA	NA	−	NA	=	NA	NA

Event 8a ***JPS recognized $16,800 of revenue from the sale on account of merchandise that cost $8,660. The freight terms were FOB shipping point. The party responsible paid freight costs of $275 in cash. JPS does not offer a cash discount to customers.***

The effect on the balance sheet of recognizing revenue is an increase in both assets (accounts receivable) and stockholders' equity (retained earnings). The event increases revenue and net income. Since JPS sold the inventory on account, cash flow is not currently affected. These effects are illustrated here:

Assets					=	Liab.	+	Stockholders' Equity			Rev.	−	Exp.	=	Net Inc.	Cash Flow
Cash	+	Accts. Rec.	+	Inventory	=	Accts. Pay.	+	Com. Stk.	+	Retained Earnings						
NA	+	16,800	+	NA	=	NA	+	NA	+	16,800	16,800	−	NA	=	16,800	NA

Event 8b ***JPS recognized $8,660 of cost of goods sold.***

As discussed previously, when inventory is sold, the product cost is transferred from the Merchandise Inventory account to the expense account, Cost of Goods Sold. Recognizing cost of goods sold decreases both assets (merchandise inventory) and stockholders' equity (retained earnings) by $8,660. The expense recognition for cost of goods sold decreases net income. Cash flow is not affected. *The freight costs do not affect JPS since the freight terms are FOB shipping point and the buyer is responsible for them.* These effects are shown here:

Assets					=	Liab.	+	Stockholders' Equity			Rev.	−	Exp.	=	Net Inc.	Cash Flow
Cash	+	Accts. Rec.	+	Inventory	=	Accts. Pay.	+	Com. Stk.	+	Retained Earnings						
NA	+	NA	+	(8,660)	=	NA	+	NA	+	(8,660)	NA	−	8,660	=	(8,660)	NA

Event 9 ***JPS paid $9,900 cash in partial settlement of the account payable that arose from purchasing inventory on account in Event 7. The partial payment was made within the discount period for merchandise with a list price of $10,000.***

Assume that JPS was not able to pay the entire account payable of $13,860 (recorded at the net amount) in time to receive the 1% purchase discount offered by the supplier, but JPS was able to pay part of the liability within the discount period. The effect of the event on the balance sheet is to decrease both assets (cash) and liabilities (accounts payable) by $9,900 ($10,000 × .99). The $9,900 cash outflow is included in the operating activities section of the statement of cash flows. These effects are shown below.

Assets					=	Liab.	+	Stockholders' Equity			Rev.	−	Exp.	=	Net Inc.	Cash Flow
Cash	+	Accts. Rec.	+	Inventory	=	Accts. Pay.	+	Com. Stk.	+	Retained Earnings						
(9,900)	+	NA	+	NA	=	(9,900)	+	NA	+	NA	NA	−	NA	=	NA	(9,900) OA

Event 10 ***JPS paid $8,000 cash for selling and administrative expenses.***

The effect on the balance sheet is to decrease both assets (cash) and stockholders' equity (retained earnings). Recognizing the selling and administrative expenses decreases net income. The $8,000 cash outflow is reported in the operating activities section of the statement of cash flows. These effects are shown below.

Assets					=	Liab.	+	Stockholders' Equity			Rev.	−	Exp.	=	Net Inc.	Cash Flow
Cash	+	Accts. Rec.	+	Inventory	=	Accts. Pay.	+	Com. Stk.	+	Retained Earnings						
(8,000)	+	NA	+	NA	=	NA	+	NA	+	(8,000)	NA	−	8,000	=	(8,000)	(8,000) OA

CHECK YOURSELF 3.2

Choi Company purchased $24,000 of inventory on account with payment terms of 2/10, n/30 and freight terms FOB shipping point. Freight costs were $1,200. Choi paid $18,000 of the accounts payable within the 10-day discount period and the remaining $6,000 after the discount period had expired. Choi sold all of the inventory for $32,000. Based on this information, determine the amount of gross margin and interest expense Choi would report on the income statement.

Answer

The cost of the inventory is determined as follows:

Net price ($24,000 × .98)	$23,520
Plus: Transportation-in	1,200
Total cost	$24,720

The gross margin is $7,280, the sales price less cost of goods sold ($32,000 − $24,720). The amount of interest expense is $120 ($6,000 × .02).

LO 4

Compare and contrast single and multistep income statements.

Financial Statements

The financial statements for JPS's 2007 accounting period are shown in Exhibit 3.3. The income statement displayed in the exhibit is more informative than one which simply subtracts expenses from revenues. By reporting gross margin, it shows the relationship between the cost of goods sold and the sales revenue earned from those particular goods. This income statement also separates routine operating results from nonoperating results, which enables analysts to distinguish between recurring revenues and expenses and those related to peripheral

EXHIBIT 3.3

Financial Statements

2007 Income Statement

Sales Revenue	$41,550
Cost of Goods Sold	(20,160)
Gross Margin	21,390
Less: Operating Expenses	
Selling and Admin. Exp.	(8,000)
Transportation-out	(450)
Operating Income	12,940
Nonoperating Items	
Interest Expense	(140)
Net Income	$12,800

12/31/07 Balance Sheet

Assets		
Cash	$11,100	
Accounts Receivable	16,800	
Merchandise Inventory	6,860	
Total Assets		$34,760
Liabilities		
Accounts Payable		$ 3,960
Stockholders' Equity		
Common Stock	$15,000	
Retained Earnings	15,800	
Total Stockholders' Equity		30,800
Total Liab. and Stk. Equity		$34,760

2007 Statement of Cash Flows

Operating Activities		
Inflow from Customers	$24,750	
Outflow for Inventory	(17,060)	
Outflow for Transportation-out	(450)	
Outflow for Selling and Admin. Exp.	(8,000)	
Outflow for Interest	(140)	
Net Cash Outflow for Operating Activities		$ (900)
Investing Activities		-0-
Financing Activities		-0-
Net Change in Cash		(900)
Plus: Beginning Cash Balance		12,000
Ending Cash Balance		$11,100

transactions, such as gains and losses, interest revenue, and interest expense. Income statements that show these additional relationships, including **operating income (or loss),** are called **multistep income statements.** Income statements that display a single comparison of total revenues and total expenses are called **single-step income statements.** Exhibit 3.4 shows the percentage of companies that use the multistep versus the single-step format.

On a multistep income statement, interest revenue and interest expense are classified as nonoperating items. In contrast, cash receipts of interest revenue and cash payments of interest expense are reported as operating activities on the statement of cash flows. When developing the statement of cash flows, the Financial Accounting Standards Board (FASB) faced two alternatives regarding how to classify interest, each of which had legitimate theoretical support. Even though interest is reported as a nonoperating item on the income statement, the FASB voted to require that interest be reported as an operating activity on the statement of cash flows. Awareness of this inconsistency is helpful in avoiding confusion when reading financial statements.

Whether using the single-step or multistep income statement format, companies are required to report revenues or expenses from discontinued operations or extraordinary items on separate lines just above net income.

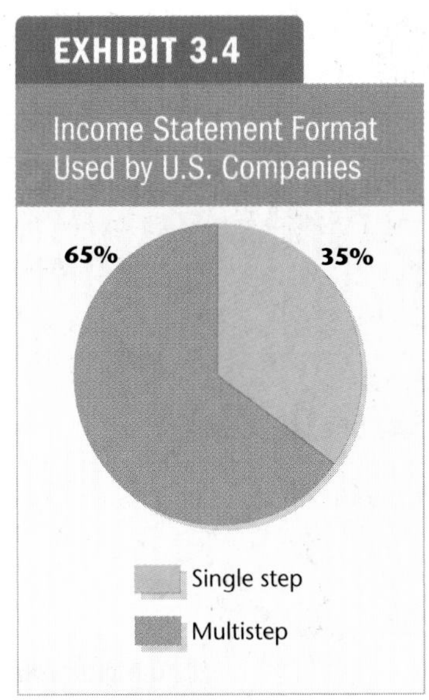

Data Source: AICPA, *Accounting Trends and Techniques*, 2002.

Events Affecting Sales

To this point we assumed JPS did not offer cash discounts to its customers. However, sales, as well as purchases, of inventory can be affected by returns, allowances, and discounts. **Sales discounts** are price reductions offered by sellers to encourage buyers to pay promptly. To illustrate, assume JPS engaged in the following selected events during January 2008.

Show the effects of inventory transactions on financial statements.

Event 1a ***JPS sold on account merchandise with a list price of $8,500. Payment terms were 1/10, n/30. The merchandise had cost JPS $5,100.***

The sale is recorded at the net price of $8,415 ($8,500 × .99). It increases both assets (accounts receivable) and shareholders' equity (retained earnings). Recognizing revenue increases net income. The statement of cash flows is not affected. The effects on the financial statements follow:

Assets					=	Liab.	+	Stockholders' Equity			Rev.	−	Exp.	=	Net Inc.	Cash Flow
Cash	+	Accts. Rec.	+	Inventory	=	Accts. Pay.	+	Com. Stk.	+	Retained Earnings						
NA	+	8,415	+	NA	=	NA	+	NA	+	8,415	8,415	−	NA	=	8,415	NA

Event 1b ***JPS recognized $5,100 of cost of goods sold.***

Recognizing the expense decreases assets (merchandise inventory) and stockholders' equity (retained earnings). Cost of goods sold increases and net income decreases. Cash flow is not affected. The effects on the financial statements follow:

Assets					=	Liab.	+	Stockholders' Equity			Rev.	−	Exp.	=	Net Inc.	Cash Flow
Cash	+	Accts. Rec.	+	Inventory	=	Accts. Pay.	+	Com. Stk.	+	Retained Earnings						
NA	+	NA	+	(5,100)	=	NA	+	NA	+	(5,100)	NA	−	5,100	=	(5,100)	NA

Event 2a ***The customer from Event 1a returned inventory with a $1,000 list price that JPS had sold with 1/10, n/30 payment terms. The merchandise had cost JPS $600.***

Since JPS originally recorded the sales revenue at the net price, it must also record the sales return at the net price, $990 ($1,000 × .99). The return decreases both assets (accounts receivable) and stockholders' equity (retained earnings) on the balance sheet. Sales and net income decrease. Cash flow is not affected. The effects on the financial statements follow:

Assets					=	Liab.	+	Stockholders' Equity			Rev.	−	Exp.	=	Net Inc.	Cash Flow
Cash	+	Accts. Rec.	+	Inventory	=	Accts. Pay.	+	Com. Stk.	+	Retained Earnings						
NA	+	(990)	+	NA	=	NA	+	NA	+	(990)	(990)	−	NA	=	(990)	NA

Event 2b ***The cost of the goods ($600) is returned to the inventory account.***

Since JPS got the inventory back, the sales return increases both assets (merchandise inventory) and stockholders' equity (retained earnings). The expense (cost of goods sold) decreases and net income increases. Cash flow is not affected. The effects on the financial statements follow:

Assets					=	Liab.	+	Stockholders' Equity			Rev.	−	Exp.	=	Net Inc.	Cash Flow
Cash	+	Accts. Rec.	+	Inventory	=	Accts. Pay.	+	Com. Stk.	+	Retained Earnings						
NA	+	NA	+	600	=	NA	+	NA	+	600	NA	−	(600)	=	600	NA

Event 3 ***JPS collected the balance of the account receivable from the customer that purchased the goods in Event 1a.***

If the customer paid within the discount period, JPS would receive the net amount, which equals the balance in the Accounts Receivable account. The cash collection would represent an asset exchange, with cash increasing and accounts receivable decreasing for the net amount of $7,425 ($7,500 × .99). The statement of cash flows would report an inflow of $7,425 from operating activities. The effects on the financial statements follow:

Assets					=	Liab.	+	Stockholders' Equity			Rev.	−	Exp.	=	Net Inc.	Cash Flow
Cash	+	Accts. Rec.	+	Inventory	=	Accts. Pay.	+	Com. Stk.	+	Retained Earnings						
7,425	+	(7,425)	+	NA	=	NA	+	NA	+	NA	NA	−	NA	=	NA	7,425 OA

Alternatively, if the customer paid after the discount period expired, JPS would receive the list price of $7,500. The $75 ($7,500 − $7,425) difference between the list price and the net price is interest revenue. The asset cash would increase, the asset accounts receivable would decrease, and revenue would increase. The statement of cash flows would report an inflow of $7,500 from operating activities. The effects on the financial statements follow:

Assets					=	Liab.	+	Stockholders' Equity			Rev.	−	Exp.	=	Net Inc.	Cash Flow
Cash	+	Accts. Rec.	+	Inventory	=	Accts. Pay.	+	Com. Stk.	+	Retained Earnings						
7,500	+	(7,425)	+	NA	=	NA	+	NA	+	75	75	−	NA	=	75	7,500 OA

Lost, Damaged, or Stolen Inventory

LO 5

Show the effect of lost, damaged, or stolen inventory on financial statements.

Most merchandising companies experience some level of inventory **shrinkage,** a term that reflects decreases in inventory for reasons other than sales to customers. Inventory may be stolen by shoplifters, damaged by customers or employees, or even simply lost or misplaced. Since the *perpetual* inventory system is designed to record purchases and sales of inventory as they occur, the balance in the Merchandise Inventory account represents the amount of inventory that *should* be on hand at any given time. By taking a physical count of the merchandise inventory at the end of the accounting period and comparing that amount with the book balance in the Merchandise Inventory account, managers can determine the amount of any inventory shrinkage. If goods have been lost, damaged, or stolen, the book balance will be higher than the actual amount of inventory on hand and an adjusting entry is required to reduce assets and equity. The Merchandise Inventory account is reduced, and an expense for the amount of the lost, damaged, or stolen inventory is recognized.

Adjustment for Lost, Damaged, or Stolen Inventory

To illustrate, assume that Midwest Merchandising Company maintains perpetual inventory records. Midwest determined, through a physical count, that it had $23,500 of merchandise inventory on hand at the end of the accounting period. The balance in the Inventory account was $24,000. Midwest must make an adjusting entry to write down the Inventory account so the amount reported on the financial statements agrees with the amount actually on hand at the end of the period. The write-down decreases both assets (inventory) and stockholders' equity (retained earnings). The write-down increases expenses and decreases net income. Cash flow is not affected. The effects on the financial statements follow:

Assets			=	Liab.	+	Stockholders' Equity			Rev.	−	Exp.	=	Net Inc.	Cash Flow
Cash	+	Inventory	=			Com. Stk.	+	Ret. Earn.						
NA	+	(500)	=	NA	+	NA	+	(500)	NA	−	500	=	(500)	NA

Theoretically, inventory losses are operating expenses. Because such losses are normally immaterial in amount, however, they are usually added to cost of goods sold for external reporting purposes.

Recognizing Gains and Losses

When Pepper Place, a retail merchandising company, sells *merchandise inventory* for more than cost, Pepper includes the profit from the transaction in the amount of *gross margin* on its income statement. In contrast, if Pepper sells *land* for more than cost, Pepper labels the profit from the transaction as a *gain* on the income statement. In both cases, Pepper subtracts the cost of the asset sold (inventory or land) from its sales price. What is the difference between gross margin and a gain? By using these labels, Pepper discloses the different nature of the underlying transactions.

Pepper's primary business is selling inventory, not land. The term **gain** indicates profit resulting from an incidental transaction not likely to regularly recur. Pepper may sell land (store sites) occasionally as a side effect of its ongoing inventory sales business. If Pepper had sold the land for less than cost the expense would have been labeled a **loss,** which also indicates it did not result from normal, recurring operating activities.

Gains and losses are so labeled in financial statements to communicate the expectation that they are nonrecurring. To illustrate, assume Pepper Place started the accounting period with the following balance sheet:

Assets	
Cash	$ 2,000
Merchandise Inventory	16,000
Land (future building sites)	68,000
Total Assets	$86,000
Stockholders' Equity	
Common Stock	$24,000
Retained Earnings	62,000
Total Stockholders' Equity	$86,000

The three events Pepper experienced during the accounting period follow. Each event is also presented in general journal format.

Event 1 ***Sold inventory that cost $12,000 for $19,000 cash.***

Event 2 ***Sold land that cost $31,000 for $47,000 cash.***

Event 3 ***Paid $5,000 cash for operating expenses.***

The effects of these three events on Pepper's financial statements are shown below:

Event No.	Balance Sheet									Income Statement					Statement of Cash Flows
	Assets					=	Stockholders' Equity								
	Cash	+	Inv.	+	Land	=	Com. Stk.	+	Ret. Ear.	Rev./Gain	−	Exp.	=	Net Inc.	
Beg. bal.	2,000	+	16,000	+	68,000	=	24,000	+	62,000	0	−	0	=	0	NA
1a.	19,000	+	NA	+	NA	=	NA	+	19,000	19,000	−	NA	=	19,000	19,000 OA
1b.	NA	+	(12,000)	+	NA	=	NA	+	(12,000)	NA	−	12,000	=	(12,000)	NA
2.	47,000	+	NA	+	(31,000)	=	NA	+	16,000	16,000	−	NA	=	16,000	47,000 IA
3.	(5,000)	+	NA	+	NA	=	NA	+	(5,000)	NA	−	5,000	=	(5,000)	(5,000) OA
Totals	63,000	+	4,000	+	37,000	=	24,000	+	80,000	35,000	−	17,000	=	18,000	61,000 NC

Pepper's financial statements at the end of the period appear in Exhibit 3.5:

EXHIBIT 3.5

Pepper Place

Income Statement

Net Sales	$19,000
Cost of Goods Sold	(12,000)
Gross Margin	7,000
Less: Operating Exp.	(5,000)
Operating Income	2,000
Nonoperating Items	
Gain on Sale of Land	16,000
Net Income	$18,000

Balance Sheet

Assets	
Cash	$ 63,000
Merchandise Inventory	4,000
Land	37,000
Total Assets	$104,000
Stockholders' Equity	
Common Stock	$ 24,000
Retained Earnings	80,000
Total Stockholders' Equity	$104,000

Statement of Cash Flows

Operating Activities		
Inflow from Customers	$19,000	
Outflow for Operating Exp.	(5,000)	
Net Cash Inflow from Operating Activities		$14,000
Investing Activities		
Infow from Sale of Land		47,000
Financing Activities		0
Net Change in Cash		61,000
Plus: Beginning Cash Balance		2,000
Ending Cash Balance		$63,000

On the multistep income statement, the gain on the sale of land is reported as a nonoperating item. The gain does not appear in the operating activities section of the statement of cash flows. The entire amount received from the land sale is reported as an inflow from the sale of land in the investing activities section of the statement of cash flows.

THE FINANCIAL ANALYST

Merchandising is a highly competitive business. In order to succeed, merchandisers develop different strategies to distinguish themselves in the marketplace. For example, companies like Wal-Mart, Kmart, and Target focus on price competition while others such as Neiman Marcus and Saks Fifth Avenue sell high price goods that offer superior quality, fashionable style, and strong guaranties. Financial analysts have developed specific tools that are useful in scrutinizing the success or failure of a company's sales strategy. The first step in the analysis is to develop common size statements so that comparisons can be made between companies.

LO 6

Use common size financial statements to evaluate managerial performance.

Common Size Financial Statements

Raw accounting numbers can be difficult to interpret. Suppose that Smith Company earns a 10 percent return on its assets while Jones Company earns only 8 percent on its assets. If Smith Company's total assets are $1,000,000 and Jones Company's are $2,000,000, Smith Company would report less income ($1,000,000 × 0.10 = $100,000) than Jones Company ($2,000,000 × 0.08 = $160,000) even though Smith Company was doing a better job of investing its assets.

Similar difficulties arise when comparing a single company's current period financial statements to those of prior periods. How good is a $1,000,000 increase in net income? The increase is certainly not as good if the company is IBM rather than a small computer store. To more easily compare between accounting periods or between companies, analysts prepare **common size financial statements** by converting absolute dollar amounts to percentages.

With respect to the income statement, we begin by defining net sales as the base figure, or 100%. **Net sales** is total sales minus sales returns, sales allowances, and sales discounts. The other amounts on the statement are then shown as a percentage of net sales. For example, the cost of goods sold percentage is the dollar amount of cost of goods sold divided by the dollar amount of net sales, and so on for the other items on the statement. Exhibit 3.6 displays a common size income statement derived from JPS's 2007 income statement shown in Exhibit 3.3.

EXHIBIT 3.6

JUNE'S PLANT SHOP
Common Size Income Statement*
For the Year Ended December 31, 2007

Net Sales	$41,550	100.00%
Cost of Goods Sold	(20,160)	(48.52)
Gross Margin	21,390	51.48
Less: Operating Expenses		
Selling and Administrative Expenses	(8,000)	(19.25)
Transportation-out	(450)	(1.08)
Operating Income	12,940	31.14
Nonoperating Items		
Interest Expense	(140)	(.34)
Net Income	$12,800	30.81%

*Percentages do not add exactly because they have been rounded.

Comparisons between Companies

Gross Margin Percentage

Does Wal-Mart sell merchandise at a higher or lower price than Target? The gross margin percentage is useful in answering questions such as this. Specifically, the **gross margin percentage** is defined as:

LO 7

Use ratio analysis to evaluate managerial performance.

$$\frac{\text{Gross margin}}{\text{Net sales}}$$

When comparing two retail companies, all other things being equal, the company with the higher gross margin percentage is pricing its products higher.

CHECK YOURSELF 3.3

The following sales data are from the records of two retail sales companies. All amounts are in thousands.

	Company A	Company B
Sales	$21,234	$43,465
Cost of goods sold	14,864	34,772
Gross margin	$ 6,370	$ 8,693

One company is an upscale department store, and the other is a discount store. Which company is the upscale department store?

Answer

The gross margin percentage for Company A is approximately 30 percent ($6,370 ÷ $21,234). The gross margin percentage for Company B is 20 percent ($8,693 ÷ $43,465). These percentages suggest that Company A is selling goods with a higher markup than Company B, which implies that Company A is the upscale department store.

Net Income Percentage

Another commonly used ratio is the net income percentage. The **net income percentage** (sometimes called **return on sales**) is determined as follows:

$$\frac{\text{Net income}}{\text{Net sales}}$$

Net income expressed as a percentage of sales provides insight as to how much of each sales dollar is left as net income after *all* expenses are paid. When comparing two companies, all other things being equal, the company with the higher return on sales ratio is doing a better job of controlling expenses.

Comparisons within a Particular Company

The previous discussion focused on using common size income data to make comparisons among different companies. Analysts also find it useful to compare a particular company's performance over different periods. To illustrate, assume that June's Plant Shop relocated its store to an upscale shopping mall with a wealthier customer base. June has to pay more for rent but believes she will more than offset the higher rent cost by selling her merchandise at higher prices. June changed locations on January 1, 2008. Exhibit 3.7 contains JPS's 2007 and 2008 income statements. Use the data in this exhibit to determine whether June's strategy was successful.

Analyzing the common size statements suggests that June's strategy did increase the profitability of her business. The increase in the gross margin percentage (51% to 60%) confirms the fact that JPS raised its prices. The increase in the return on sales ratio (31% to 33%) shows that the increase in sales revenue was larger than the increase in total expenses.

EXHIBIT 3.7

JUNE'S PLANT SHOP Common Size Income Statements	2007		2008	
Net Sales	$41,550	100%	$49,860	100%
Cost of Goods Sold	(20,160)	49	(19,944)	(40)
Gross Margin	21,390	51	29,916	60
Less: Operating Expenses				
Selling and Administrative Expenses	(8,000)	(19)	(12,465)	(25)
Transportation-out	(450)	(1)	(500)	(1)
Operating Income	12,940	31	16,951	34
Nonoperating Items				
Interest Expense	(140)	0	(400)	(1)
Net Income	$12,800	31%	$16,551	33%

Real-World Data

Exhibit 3.8 shows the gross margin percentages and return on sales ratios for 10 companies. Three of the companies are manufacturers that produce pharmaceutical products, and the remaining seven companies sell various products at the retail level. These data are for the companies' fiscal years that ended in late 2002 or early 2003.

A review of the data confirms our earlier finding that ratios for companies in the same industry are often more similar than are ratios for companies from different industries. For example, note that the manufacturers have much higher margins, both for gross profit and for net earnings, than do the retailers. Manufacturers are often able to charge higher prices than are retailers because they obtain patents which give them a legal monopoly on the products they create. When a company such as **Pfizer** develops a new drug, no one else can

EXHIBIT 3.8

Industry/Company	Gross Margin %	Return on Sales
Pharmaceutical manufacturers		
Bristol Myers-Squibb	64.7%	11.4%
Johnson & Johnson	71.2	18.2
Pfizer	87.5	28.2
Retail pharmacies		
CVS	25.1	3.0
Rite Aid	23.4	(0.7)
Walgreens	26.5	3.6
Department stores		
Neiman Marcus	32.2	3.4
Wal-Mart	21.5	3.3
Office supplies		
Office Depot	29.6	2.7
Staples	25.4	3.8

produce that drug until the patent expires, giving it lots of control over its price at the wholesale level. Conversely, when Walgreens sells Pfizer's drug at the retail level, it faces price competition from CVS, a company that is trying to sell the same drug to the same consumers. One way CVS can try to get customers to shop at its store is to charge lower prices than its competitors, but this reduces its profit margins, since it must pay the same price to get Pfizer's drug as did Walgreens. As the data in Exhibit 3.8 show, in 2002 CVS had a lower gross margin percentage than did Walgreens, indicating it is charging slightly lower prices for similar goods.

In the examples presented in Exhibit 3.8, the companies with higher gross margin percentages usually had higher return on sales ratios than their competitors, but this was not always the case. In the office supplies business, Office Depot's gross margin percentage was significantly higher than that of its rival, Staples, but its return on sales ratio was considerably lower. Also, while Neiman Marcus had a gross margin percentage that was 50 percent greater than Wal-Mart's [(32.2 − 21.5) ÷ 21.5] their return on sales ratios were almost equal. This is not surprising when you consider how much more luxurious, and costly, the interior of a Neiman Marcus store is compared to a Wal-Mart.

Financing Merchandise Inventory

Suppose a store purchases inventory in October to sell during the holiday season. If the store sells the inventory on account, much of the cash from the sales won't be collected until January or February of the next year. With cash collections from customers lagging three or four months behind when the goods were purchased, how will the store pay for the inventory? One way is to borrow the money. The company could pay for the merchandise in October with money borrowed from a bank. When the cash from fall sales is collected in January and February, the company could repay the bank.

An obvious drawback to obtaining a loan to pay for inventory is the interest expense incurred on the borrowed funds. However, other alternatives for financing inventory purchases are also expensive. If the owner's money is used, it cannot be invested elsewhere, such as in an interest-earning savings account. This failure to earn interest revenue is called an **opportunity cost;** it is effectively a financing cost that is just as real as actual payment of interest expense. Net income falls regardless of whether a business incurs expenses or loses revenue.

A third alternative is to purchase the inventory on account. However, when purchases are made on account, the seller usually charges the buyer an interest fee. This charge may be hidden in the form of higher prices. So although interest costs are lower, the cost of goods sold is higher. As indicated earlier in this chapter, many companies recognize financing costs by offering buyers the opportunity to receive cash discounts by paying for purchases within a short time after the sale. From any perspective, merchandisers incur significant inventory-financing costs.

Accounting information can help companies minimize the cost of financing inventory. As much as possible, businesses should limit how long goods stay in inventory before they are sold. Ratios to help manage inventory turnover are explained in Chapter 4. Companies should also take steps to collect cash as quickly as possible from customers for the goods they purchase. Managing accounts receivable turnover is explained in Chapter 5. The preceding discussion explains the need for such management techniques.

A Look Back <<

Merchandising companies earn profits by selling inventory at prices that are higher than the cost paid for the goods. Merchandising companies include *retail companies* (companies that sell goods to the final consumer) and *wholesale companies* (companies that sell to other merchandising companies). The products sold by merchandising companies are called *inventory.* The costs to purchase inventory, to receive it, and to ready it for sale are *product costs,* which are first accumulated in an inventory account (balance sheet asset account) and then recognized as cost of goods sold (income statement expense account) in the period in which goods are sold. Purchases and sales of inventory can be recorded continually as goods are bought and sold (perpetual system) or at the end of the accounting period (periodic system, discussed in the chapter appendix).

Accounting for inventory includes the treatment of cash discounts, transportation costs, and returns and allowances. The cost of inventory is the list price less any *cash discount* offered by the seller. The cost of freight paid to acquire inventory (*transportation-in*) is considered a product cost. The cost of freight paid to deliver inventory to customers (*transportation-out*) is a selling expense. *Sales returns and allowances* and *sales discounts* are subtracted from sales revenue to determine the amount of *net sales* reported on the income statement. Purchase returns and allowances reduce product cost. Theoretically, the cost of lost, damaged, or stolen inventory is an operating expense. However, because these costs are usually immaterial in amount they are typically included as part of cost of goods sold on the income statement.

Some companies use a *multistep income statement* which reports product costs separately from selling and administrative costs. Cost of goods sold is subtracted from sales revenue to determine *gross margin.* Selling and administrative expenses are subtracted from gross margin to determine income from operations. Other companies report income using a *single-step format* in which the cost of goods sold is listed along with selling and administrative items in a single expense category that is subtracted in total from revenue to determine income from operations.

Managers of merchandising businesses operate in a highly competitive environment. They must manage company operations carefully to remain profitable. *Common size financial statements* (statements presented on a percentage basis) and ratio analysis are useful monitoring tools. Common size financial statements permit ready comparisons among different-size companies. Although a $1 million increase in sales may be good for a small company and bad for a large company, a 10 percent increase can apply to any size company. The two most common ratios used by merchandising companies are the *gross margin percentage* (gross margin ÷ net sales) and the *net income percentage* (net income ÷ net sales). Interpreting these ratios requires an understanding of industry characteristics. For example, a discount store such as **Wal-Mart** would be expected to have a much lower gross margin percentage than an upscale store such as **Neiman Marcus**.

Managers should be aware of the financing cost of carrying inventory. By investing funds in inventory, a firm loses the opportunity to invest them in interest-bearing assets. The cost of financing inventory is an *opportunity cost.* To minimize financing costs, a company should minimize the amount of inventory it carries, the length of time it holds the inventory, and the time it requires to collect accounts receivable after the inventory is sold.

A Look Forward >>

To this point, the text has explained the basic accounting cycle for service and merchandising businesses. Future chapters more closely address specific accounting issues. For example, in Chapter 4 you will learn how to deal with inventory items that are purchased at differing prices. Other chapters will discuss a variety of specific practices that are widely used by real-world companies.

APPENDIX

Identify the primary features of the periodic inventory system.

Periodic Inventory System

Under certain conditions, it is impractical to record inventory sales transactions as they occur. Consider the operations of a fast-food restaurant. To maintain perpetual inventory records, the restaurant would have to transfer from the Inventory account to the Cost of Goods Sold account the *cost* of each hamburger, order of fries, soft drink, or other food items as they were sold. Obviously, recording the cost of each item at the point of sale would be impractical without using highly sophisticated computer equipment (recording the selling price the customer pays is captured by cash registers; the difficulty lies in capturing inventory cost).

The **periodic inventory system** offers a practical solution for recording inventory transactions in a low-technology, high-volume environment. Inventory costs are recorded in a Purchases account at the time of purchase. Purchase returns and allowances and transportation-in are recorded in separate accounts. No entries for the cost of merchandise purchases or sales are recorded in the Inventory account during the period. The cost of goods sold is determined at the end of the period as shown in Exhibit 3.9.

The perpetual and periodic inventory systems represent alternative procedures for recording the same information. The amounts of cost of goods sold and ending inventory reported in the financial statements will be the same regardless of the method used.

The **schedule of cost of goods sold** presented in Exhibit 3.9 is used for internal reporting purposes. It is normally not shown in published financial statements. The amount of cost of goods sold is reported as a single line item on the income statement. The financial statements in Exhibit 3.3 will be the same whether JPS maintains perpetual or periodic inventory records.

EXHIBIT 3.9

Schedule of Cost of Goods Sold for 2007

Beginning Inventory	$ 6,000
Purchases	21,700
Purchase Returns and Allowances	(980)
Transportation-in	300
Cost of Goods Available for Sale	27,020
Ending Inventory	(6,860)
Cost of Goods Sold	$20,160

Advantages and Disadvantages of the Periodic System versus the Perpetual System

The chief advantage of the periodic method is recording efficiency. Recording inventory transactions occasionally (periodically) requires less effort than recording them continually (perpetually). Historically, practical limitations offered businesses like fast-food restaurants or grocery stores no alternative to using the periodic system. The sheer volume of transactions made recording individual decreases to the Inventory account balance as each item was sold impossible. Imagine the number of transactions a grocery store would have to record every business day to maintain perpetual records.

Although the periodic system provides a recordkeeping advantage over the perpetual system, perpetual inventory records provide significant control advantages over periodic records. With perpetual records, the book balance in the Inventory account should agree with the amount of inventory in stock at any given time. By comparing that book balance with the results of a physical inventory count, management can determine the amount of lost, damaged, destroyed, or stolen inventory. Perpetual records also permit more timely and accurate reorder decisions and profitability assessments.

When a company uses the *periodic* inventory system, lost, damaged, or stolen merchandise is automatically included in cost of goods sold. Because such goods are not included in the year-end physical count, they are treated as sold regardless of the reason for their absence. Since the periodic system does not separate the cost of lost, damaged, or stolen merchandise from the cost of goods sold, the amount of any inventory shrinkage is unknown. This feature is a major disadvantage of the periodic system. Without knowing the amount of inventory losses, management cannot weigh the costs of various security systems against the potential benefits.

Advances in such technology as electronic bar code scanning and increased computing power have eliminated most of the practical constraints that once prevented merchandisers with high-volume, low dollar-value inventories from recording inventory transactions on a continual basis. As a result, use of the perpetual inventory system has expanded rapidly in recent years and continued growth can be expected. This text, therefore, concentrates on the perpetual inventory system.

SELF-STUDY REVIEW PROBLEM

Academy Sales Company (ASC) started the 2007 accounting period with the balances given in the following financial statements model. During 2007 ASC experienced the following business events.

1. Purchased $16,000 of merchandise inventory on account, terms 2/10, n/30.
2. The goods that were purchased in Event 1 were delivered FOB shipping point. Freight costs of $600 were paid in cash by the responsible party.
3. Returned $500 of goods purchased in Event 1. The net price of these goods is 500 × .98 = $490.
4. Paid the balance due on the account payable. The payment was made after the discount period had expired.

5a. Recognized $21,000 of cash revenue from the sale of merchandise.

5b. Recognized $15,000 of cost of goods sold.

6. The merchandise in Event 5a was sold to customers FOB destination. Freight costs of $950 were paid in cash by the responsible party.
7. Paid cash of $4,000 for selling and administrative expenses.

Required

a. Record these transactions in a financial statements model like the following one.

Event No.	Cash	+	Inv.	=	Accts. Pay.	+	Com. Stk.	+	Ret. Earn.	Rev.	−	Exp.	=	Net Inc.	Cash Flow
Bal.	25,000	+	3,000	=	0	+	18,000	+	10,000	NA	−	NA	=	NA	NA

b. Calculate the gross margin percentage. Based on ASC's gross margin percentage and the information shown in Exhibit 3.8, classify ASC as an upscale department store, a retail discount store, or an office supplies store.

Solution to Requirement a

Event No.	Cash	+	Inv.	=	Accts. Pay.	+	Com. Stk.	+	Ret. Earn.	Rev.	−	Exp.	=	Net Inc.	Cash Flow
Bal.	25,000	+	3,000	=	0	+	18,000	+	10,000	NA	−	NA	=	NA	NA
1		+	15,680	=	15,680	+		+			−		=		
2	(600)	+	600	=		+		+			−		=		(600) OA
3		+	(490)	=	(490)	+		+			−		=		
4	(15,500)	+		=	(15,190)	+		+	(310)		−	310	=	(310)	(15,500) OA
5a	21,000	+		=		+		+	21,000	21,000	−		=	21,000	21,000 OA
5b		+	(15,000)	=		+		+	(15,000)		−	15,000	=	(15,000)	
6	(950)	+		=		+		+	(950)		−	950	=	(950)	(950) OA
7	(4,000)	+		=		+		+	(4,000)		−	4,000	=	(4,000)	(4,000) OA
Bal.	24,950	+	3,790	=	0	+	18,000	+	10,740	21,000	−	20,260	=	740	(50) NC

Solution to Requirement b

Gross margin equals sales minus cost of goods sold. In this case, the gross margin is $6,000 ($21,000 − $15,000). The gross margin percentage is computed by dividing gross margin by sales. In this case, the gross margin percentage is 28.6 percent ($6,000 ÷ $21,000). Since this percentage is closest to the percentage shown for **Office Depot**, the data suggest ASC may be an office supplies store.

KEY TERMS

allowances 92
cash discount 91
common size financial statements 101
cost of goods available for sale 86
cost of goods sold 86
FOB (free on board) destination 92
FOB (free on board) shipping point 92
gain 99
gross margin 86
gross margin percentage 101
gross profit 86
loss 99
merchandise inventory 85
merchandising businesses 85
multistep income statement 97
net income percentage 102
net method 91
net sales 101
operating income (or loss) 97
opportunity cost 104
period costs 86
periodic inventory system 106
perpetual inventory system 88
product costs 86
purchase discount 91
retail companies 85
return on sales 102
sales discounts 97
schedule of cost of goods sold 106
selling and administrative costs 86
shrinkage 99
single-step income statement 97
transportation-in (freight-in) 92
transportation-out (freight-out) 92
2/10, n/30 91
wholesale companies 85

QUESTIONS

1. Define *merchandise inventory.* What types of costs are included in the Merchandise Inventory account?
2. What is the difference between a product cost and a selling and administrative cost?
3. How is the cost of goods available for sale determined?
4. What portion of cost of goods available for sale is shown on the balance sheet? What portion is shown on the income statement?
5. When are period costs expensed? When are product costs expensed?
6. If PetCo had net sales of $600,000, goods available for sale of $450,000, and cost of goods sold of $375,000, what is its gross margin? What amount of inventory will be shown on its balance sheet?
7. Describe how the perpetual inventory system works. What are some advantages of using the perpetual inventory system? Is it necessary to take a physical inventory when using the perpetual inventory system?
8. What are the effects of the following types of transactions on the accounting equation? Also identify the financial statements that are affected. (Assume that the perpetual inventory system is used.)
   - **a.** Acquisition of cash from the issue of common stock.
   - **b.** Contribution of inventory by an owner of a company.
   - **c.** Purchase of inventory with cash by a company.
   - **d.** Sale of inventory for cash.
9. Northern Merchandising Company sold inventory that cost $12,000 for $20,000 cash. How does this event affect the accounting equation? What financial statements and accounts are affected? (Assume that the perpetual inventory system is used.)
10. If goods are shipped FOB shipping point, which party (buyer or seller) is responsible for the shipping costs?
11. Define *transportation-in.* Is it a product or a period cost?
12. Quality Cellular Co. paid $80 for freight on merchandise that it had purchased for resale to customers (transportation-in) and paid $135 for freight on merchandise delivered to customers (transportation-out). What account is debited for the $80 payment? What account is debited for the $135 payment?
13. Why would a seller grant an allowance to a buyer of the seller's merchandise?
14. Dyer Department Store purchased goods with the terms 2/10, n/30. What do these terms mean?
15. Eastern Discount Stores incurred a $5,000 cash cost. How does the accounting for this cost differ if the cash were paid for inventory versus commissions to sales personnel?
16. What is the purpose of giving a cash discount to charge customers?
17. Define *transportation-out.* Is it a product cost or a period cost for the seller?
18. Ball Co. purchased inventory with a list price of $4,000 with the terms 2/10, n/30. What amount will be debited to the Merchandise Inventory account?

19. Explain the difference between purchase returns and sales returns. How do purchase returns affect the financial statements of both buyer and seller? How do sales returns affect the financial statements of both buyer and seller?
20. Explain the difference between gross margin and a gain.
21. What is the difference between a multistep income statement and a single-step income statement?
22. What is the advantage of using common size income statements to present financial information for several accounting periods?
23. What information is provided by the net income percentage (return on sales ratio)?
24. What is the purpose of preparing a schedule of cost of goods sold?
25. Explain how the periodic inventory system works. What are some advantages of using the periodic inventory system? What are some disadvantages of using the periodic inventory system? Is it necessary to take a physical inventory when using the periodic inventory system?
26. Why does the periodic inventory system impose a major disadvantage for management in accounting for lost, stolen, or damaged goods?

EXERCISES

All Exercises are available with McGraw-Hill's Homework Manager

When the instructions for *any* exercise or problem call for the preparation of an income statement, use the *multistep format* unless otherwise indicated.

Exercise 3-1 *Comparing a merchandising company with a service company*

L.O. 1, 2

The following information is available for two different types of businesses for the 2007 accounting period. Markin Consulting is a service business that provides consulting services to small businesses. College Book Mart is a merchandising business that sells books to college students.

Data for Markin Consulting

1. Received $20,000 from issuing common stock to start the business.
2. Performed services for customers and collected $15,000 cash.
3. Paid salary expense of $9,600.

Data for College Book Mart

1. Received $20,000 from issuing common stock to start the business.
2. Purchased $9,500 of inventory for cash.
3. Inventory costing $8,400 was sold for $15,000 cash.
4. Paid $1,200 cash for operating expenses.

Required

a. Prepare an income statement, balance sheet, and statement of cash flows for each of the companies.
b. What is different about the income statements of the two businesses?
c. What is different about the balance sheets of the two businesses?
d. How are the statements of cash flow different for the two businesses?

Exercise 3-2 *Effect of inventory transactions on financial statements: perpetual system*

L.O. 2

Justin Harris started a small merchandising business in 2006. The business experienced the following events during its first year of operation. Assume that Harris uses the perpetual inventory system.

1. Acquired $30,000 cash from the issue of common stock.
2. Purchased inventory for $25,000 cash.
3. Sold inventory costing $18,000 for $28,000 cash.

Required

a. Record the events in a statements model like the one shown below.

Assets			=	Equity			Rev.	−	Exp.	=	Net Inc.	Cash Flow
Cash	+	Inv.	=	Com. Stk.	+	Ret. Earn.						

b. Prepare an income statement for 2006 (use the multistep format).

c. What is the amount of total assets at the end of the period?

L.O. 2

Exercise 3-3 *Effect of inventory transactions on the income statement and statement of cash flows: perpetual system*

During 2007, Etc. Merchandising Company purchased $40,000 of inventory on account. The company sold inventory on account that cost $30,000 for $45,000. Cash payments on accounts payable were $25,000. There was $40,000 cash collected from accounts receivable. Etc. also paid $8,000 cash for operating expenses. Assume that Etc. started the accounting period with $36,000 in both cash and common stock.

Required

a. Identify the events described in the preceding paragraph and record them in a horizontal statements model like the following one:

Assets					=	Liab.	+	Equity			Rev.	−	Exp.	=	Net Inc.	Cash Flow
Cash	+	Accts. Rec.	+	Inv.	=	Accts. Pay.	+	Com. Stk.	+	Ret. Earn.						
36,000	+	NA	+	NA	=	NA	+	36,000	+	NA	NA	−	NA	=	NA	NA

b. What is the balance of accounts receivable at the end of 2007?

c. What is the balance of accounts payable at the end of 2007?

d. What are the amounts of gross margin and net income for 2007?

e. Determine the amount of net cash flow from operating activities.

f. Explain any differences between net income and net cash flow from operating activities.

L.O. 2

Exercise 3-4 *Recording inventory transactions in a financial statements model*

Tom's Paint Supply experienced the following events during 2006, its first year of operation:

1. Acquired $15,000 cash from the issue of common stock.
2. Purchased inventory for $12,000 cash.
3. Sold inventory costing $6,500 for $11,000 cash.
4. Paid $800 for advertising expense.

Required

Record the events in a statements model like the one shown below.

Assets			=	Equity			Rev.	−	Exp.	=	Net Inc.	Cash Flow
Cash	+	Inv.	=	Com. Stk.	+	Ret. Earn.						

L.O. 3

Exercise 3-5 *Determining which party is responsible for freight cost*

Required

Determine which party, buyer or seller, is responsible for freight charges in each of the following situations:

a. Sold merchandise, freight terms, FOB destination.

b. Sold merchandise, freight terms, FOB shipping point.

c. Purchased merchandise, freight terms, FOB destination.

d. Purchased merchandise, freight terms, FOB shipping point.

Exercise 3-6 ***Effect of purchase returns and allowances and freight costs on financial statements: perpetual system*** **L.O. 2, 3**

The trial balance for The Copy Shop as of January 1, 2006, was as follows:

Account Titles	Debit	Credit
Cash	$12,000	
Inventory	6,000	
Common Stock		$15,000
Retained Earnings		3,000
Total	$18,000	$18,000

The following events affected the company during the 2006 accounting period:

1. Purchased merchandise on account that cost $8,200.
2. Purchased goods FOB shipping point with freight cost of $300 cash.
3. Returned $1,000 of damaged merchandise for credit on account.
4. Agreed to keep other damaged merchandise for which the company received a $500 allowance.
5. Sold merchandise that cost $5,500 for $9,500 cash.
6. Delivered merchandise to customers under terms FOB destination with freight costs amounting to $200 cash.
7. Paid $6,000 on the merchandise purchased in Event 1.

Required

a. Organize appropriate ledger accounts under an accounting equation. Record the beginning balances and the transaction data in the accounts.
b. Prepare an income statement and statement of cash flows for 2006.
c. Explain why a difference does or does not exist between net income and net cash flow from operating activities.

Exercise 3-7 ***Accounting for product costs: perpetual inventory system*** **L.O. 2, 3**

Which of the following would be debited to the Inventory account for a merchandising business using the perpetual inventory system?

Required

a. Transportation-out.
b. Purchase discount.
c. Transportation-in.
d. Purchase of supplies to be used by the business.
e. Purchase of inventory.
f. Allowance received for damaged inventory.

Exercise 3-8 ***Effect of product cost and period cost: horizontal statements model*** **L.O. 1, 2, 3**

Brislin Co. experienced the following events for the 2007 accounting period:

1. Acquired $5,000 cash from the issue of common stock.
2. Purchased $18,000 of inventory on account.
3. Received goods purchased in Event 2 FOB shipping point. Freight cost of $500 paid in cash.
4. Returned $2,000 of goods purchased in Event 2 because of poor quality.
5. Sold inventory on account that cost $14,300 for $22,000.
6. Freight cost on the goods sold in Event 5 was $200. The goods were shipped FOB destination. Cash was paid for the freight cost.
7. Collected $16,500 cash from accounts receivable.
8. Paid $12,000 cash on accounts payable.

9. Paid $1,100 for advertising expense.
10. Paid $2,200 cash for insurance expense.

Required

a. Which of these transactions result in period (selling and administrative) costs? Which result in product costs? If neither, label the transaction NA.

b. Record each event in a horizontal statements model like the following one. The first event is recorded as an example.

Assets			=	Liab.	+	Equity		Rev. − Exp. = Net Inc.	Cash Flow
Cash +	Accts. Rec. +	Inv.	=	Accts. Pay.	+	Com. Stk. +	Ret. Earn.		
5,000 +	NA +	NA	=	NA	+	5,000 +	NA	NA − NA = NA	5,000 FA

L.O. 3

Exercise 3-9 *Cash discounts and purchase returns (net method)*

On March 6, 2006, Lie's Imports purchased merchandise from The Glass Exchange with a list price of $15,500, terms 2/10, n/45. On March 10, Lie's returned merchandise to The Glass Exchange for credit. The list price of the returned merchandise was $3,200. Lie's paid cash to settle the accounts payable on March 15, 2006.

Required

a. What is the amount of the check that Lie's must write to The Glass Exchange on March 15?

b. Record the events in a horizontal statements model like the following one.

Assets		=	Liab.	+	Equity		Rev. − Exp. = Net Inc.	Cash Flow
Cash +	Inv.	=	Accts. Pay.	+	Com. Stk. +	Ret. Earn.		

c. How much would Lie's pay for the merchandise purchased if the payment is not made until March 20, 2006?

d. Record the payment of the merchandise in Event *c* in a horizontal statements model like the one shown above.

e. Why would The Glass Exchange sell merchandise with the terms 2/10, n/45?

L.O. 2, 3

Exercise 3-10 *Effect of sales returns and allowances and freight costs on financial statements: perpetual system*

Cain Company began the 2006 accounting period with $18,000 cash, $50,000 inventory, $40,000 common stock, and $28,000 retained earnings. During the 2006 accounting period, Cain experienced the following events:

1. Sold merchandise costing $38,200 for $66,500 on account to Jones' General Store.
2. Delivered the goods to Jones under terms FOB destination. Freight costs were $600 cash.
3. Received returned damaged goods from Jones. The goods cost Cain $4,000 and were sold to Jones for $7,600.
4. Granted Jones a $2,000 allowance for other damaged goods that Jones agreed to keep.
5. Collected partial payment of $52,000 cash from accounts receivable.

Required

a. Record the events in a statements model like the one shown below.

Assets			=	Equity		Rev. − Exp. = Net Inc.	Cash Flow
Cash +	Accts. Rec. +	Inv.	=	Com. Stk. +	Ret. Earn.		

b. Prepare an income statement, balance sheet, and statement of cash flows.

c. Why would Cain grant the $2,000 allowance to Jones? Who benefits more?

Exercise 3-11 ***Effect of cash discounts on financial statements: perpetual system (net method)*** **L.O. 2, 3**

Lane Sales was started in 2006. The company experienced the following accounting events during its first year of operation:

1. Started business when it acquired $40,000 cash from the issue of common stock.
2. Purchased merchandise with a list price of $42,000 on account, terms 2/10, n/30.
3. Paid off one-half of the accounts payable balance within the discount period.
4. Sold merchandise on account that had a list price of $25,000. Credit terms were 1/20, n/30. The merchandise had cost Lane $18,000.
5. Collected cash from the account receivable within the discount period.
6. Paid $2,600 cash for operating expenses.
7. Paid the balance due on accounts payable. The payment was not made within the discount period.

Required

a. Record the events in a horizontal statements model like the following one.

Assets					=	Liab.	+	Equity			Rev.	−	Exp.	=	Net Inc.	Cash Flow
Cash	+	Accts. Rec.	+	Inv.	=	Accts. Pay.	+	Com. Stk.	+	Ret. Earn.						

b. What is the amount of gross margin for the period? What is the net income for the period?

c. Why would Lane sell merchandise with the terms 1/20, n/30?

d. What do the terms 2/10, n/30 in event 2 mean to Lane?

Exercise 3-12 ***Effect of inventory transactions on the financial statements: comprehensive exercise with sales and purchase returns and discounts*** **L.O. 2, 3**

Boone Sales Company had the following balances in its accounts on January 1, 2005:

Cash	$30,000
Merchandise Inventory	20,000
Land	50,000
Common Stock	40,000
Retained Earnings	60,000

Boone experienced the following events during 2005:

1. Sold merchandise inventory that cost $16,000 for $27,000.
2. Sold land that cost $20,000 for $35,000.

Required

a. Determine the amount of gross margin recognized by Boone.

b. Determine the amount of the gain on the sale of land recognized by Boone.

c. Comment on how the gross margin versus the gain will be recognized on the income statement.

d. Comment on how the gross margin versus the gain will be recognized on the statement of cash flows.

Exercise 3-13 ***Effect of inventory losses: perpetual system*** **L.O. 2, 5**

Mia Sales experienced the following events during 2005, its first year of operation:

1. Started the business when it acquired $50,000 cash from the issue of common stock.
2. Paid $42,000 cash to purchase inventory.

3. Sold inventory costing $25,000 for $53,000 cash.
4. Physically counted inventory showing $15,800 inventory was on hand at the end of the accounting period.

Required

a. Determine the amount of the difference between book balance and the actual amount of inventory as determined by the physical count.

b. Explain how differences between the book balance and the physical count of inventory could arise. Why is being able to determine whether differences exist useful to management?

L.O. 2

Exercise 3-14 ***Determining the effect of inventory transactions on the horizontal statements model: perpetual system***

Lopez Sales Company experienced the following events:

1. Purchased merchandise inventory for cash.
2. Purchased merchandise inventory on account.
3. Sold merchandise inventory for cash. Label the revenue recognition 3a and the expense recognition 3b.
4. Sold merchandise inventory on account. Label the revenue recognition 4a and the expense recognition 4b.
5. Returned merchandise purchased on account.
6. Paid cash for selling and administrative expenses.
7. Paid cash on accounts payable not within the discount period.
8. Paid cash for transportation-in.
9. Collected cash from accounts receivable.
10. Paid cash for transportation-out.

Required

Identify each event as asset source (AS), asset use (AU), asset exchange (AE), or claims exchange (CE). Also explain how each event affects the financial statements by placing a + for increase, − for decrease, or NA for not affected under each of the components in the following statements model. Assume the use of the perpetual inventory system. The first event is recorded as an example.

Event No.	Event Type	Assets	=	Liab.	+	Equity	Rev.	−	Exp.	=	Net Inc.	Cash Flow
1	AE	+ −	=	NA	+	NA	NA	−	NA	=	NA	− OA

L.O. 4

Exercise 3-15 ***Single-step and multistep income statements***

The following information was taken from the accounts of Good Foods Store, a delicatessen. The accounts are listed in alphabetical order, and each has a normal balance.

Accounts Payable	$315
Accounts Receivable	200
Advertising Expense	100
Cash	205
Common Stock	100
Cost of Goods Sold	300
Merchandise Inventory	225
Prepaid Rent	20
Retained Earnings	255
Sales Revenue	500
Salaries Expense	65
Supplies Expense	55

Required

First, prepare an income statement using the single-step approach. Then prepare another income statement using the multistep approach.

Exercise 3-16 *Determining the cost of financing inventory*

L.O. 2

On January 1, 2008, Mel Stark started a small sailboat merchandising business that he named Mel's Sails. The company experienced the following events during the first year of operation:

1. Started the business by issuing common stock for $20,000 cash.
2. Paid $14,000 cash to purchase inventory.
3. Sold a sailboat that cost $9,000 for $16,000 on account.
4. Collected $10,000 cash from accounts receivable.
5. Paid $2,500 for operating expenses.

Required

a. Organize ledger accounts under an accounting equation and record the events in the accounts.
b. Prepare an income statement, balance sheet, and statement of cash flows.
c. Since Mel sold inventory for $16,000, he will be able to recover more than half of the $20,000 he invested in the stock. Do you agree with this statement? Why or why not?

Exercise 3-17 *Financing inventory and cash discounts*

L.O. 3

May Haynes came to you for advice. She has just purchased a large amount of inventory with the terms 2/10, n/60. The amount of the invoice is $260,000. She is currently short on cash but has good credit. She can borrow the money at the appropriate time to take advantage of the discount. The annual interest rate is 7% if she decides to borrow the money. Haynes is sure she will have the necessary cash by the due date of the invoice (but not by the discount date).

Required

a. For how long would Haynes need to borrow the money to take advantage of the discount?
b. How much money would Haynes need to borrow?
c. Write a memo to Haynes outlining the most cost-effective strategy for her to follow. Include in your memo the amount of savings from the alternative you suggest.

Exercise 3-18 *Effect of inventory transactions on the income statement and balance sheet: periodic system (Appendix)*

L.O. 8

Don Moon is the owner of The Clothes Shop. At the beginning of the year, Moon had $1,200 in inventory. During the year, Moon purchased inventory that cost $6,500. At the end of the year, inventory on hand amounted to $1,800.

Required

Calculate the following:

a. Cost of goods available for sale during the year.
b. Cost of goods sold for the year.
c. Inventory amount The Clothes Shop would report on its year-end balance sheet.

Exercise 3-19 *Determining cost of goods sold: periodic system (Appendix)*

L.O. 8

Sunset Retailers uses the periodic inventory system to account for its inventory transactions. The following account titles and balances were drawn from Sunset's records for the year 2007: beginning balance in inventory, $24,900; purchases, $306,400; purchase returns and allowances, $9,600; sales, $680,000; sales returns and allowances, $6,370; transportation-in, $2,160; and operating expenses, $51,400. A physical count indicated that $29,300 of merchandise was on hand at the end of the accounting period.

Required

a. Prepare a schedule of cost of goods sold.
b. Prepare a multistep income statement.

L.O. 7

Exercise 3-20 *Performing ratio analysis using real-world data*

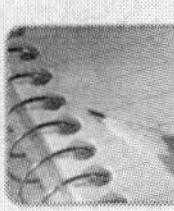

The following data were taken from **Microsoft Corporation's** 2004 annual report. All dollar amounts are in millions.

	Fiscal Years Ending	
	June 30, 2004	June 30, 2003
Revenue	$36,835	$32,187
Cost of Goods Sold	6,716	6,059
Net Income	8,168	7,531

Required

a. Compute Microsoft's gross margin percentage for 2004 and 2003.

b. Compute Microsoft's return on sales percentage for 2004 and 2003.

c. Based on the percentages computed in Requirements *a* and *b*, did Microsoft's performance get better or worse from 2003 to 2004?

d. Compare Microsoft's gross margin percentages and return on sales percentages to those of the other real-world companies discussed in this chapter and discuss whether or not it appears to have better-than-average financial performance or not.

PROBLEMS

All Problems are available with McGraw-Hill's Homework Manager

L.O. 2

CHECK FIGURES
2007 Net Income: $5,300
2009 Total Assets: $45,300

Problem 3-21 *Basic transactions for three accounting cycles: perpetual system*

Ramsey Company was started in 2007 when it acquired $30,000 from the issue of common stock. The following data summarize the company's first three years' operating activities. Assume that all transactions were cash transactions.

	2007	2008	2009
Purchases of Inventory	$24,000	$12,000	$18,500
Sales	26,000	32,000	36,000
Cost of Goods Sold	15,200	18,500	20,000
Selling and Administrative Expenses	5,500	9,400	10,100

Required

Prepare an income statement (use the multistep format) and balance sheet for each fiscal year. (*Hint:* Record the transaction data for each accounting period as an accounting equation before preparing the statements for that year.)

L.O. 1

Problem 3-22 *Identifying product and period costs*

Required

Indicate whether each of the following costs is a product cost or a period cost:

a. Insurance on vans used to deliver goods to customers.
b. Salaries of sales supervisors.
c. Monthly maintenance expense for a leased copier.
d. Goods purchased for resale.
e. Cleaning supplies for the office.
f. Freight on goods purchased for resale.
g. Salary of the marketing director.
h. Freight on goods sold to customer with terms FOB destination.
i. Utilities expense incurred for office building.

Problem 3-23 *Identifying freight cost*

L.O. 3

CHECK FIGURE
Event (b): Freight Costs Paid: $150

Required

For each of the following events, determine the amount of freight paid by Tom's Parts House. Also indicate whether the freight is classified as a product or period cost.

a. Purchased inventory with freight costs of $700, FOB destination.
b. Shipped merchandise to customers with freight costs of $150, FOB destination.
c. Purchased additional merchandise with costs of $250, FOB shipping point.
d. Sold merchandise to a customer. Freight costs were $400, FOB shipping point.

Problem 3-24 *Effect of purchase returns and allowances and purchase discounts on the financial statements: perpetual system (net method)*

L.O. 2, 3

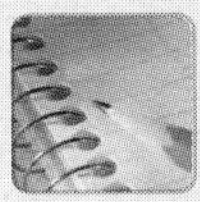

CHECK FIGURES
a. Ending Cash: $16,062
d. Net Income: $2,338

The following events were completed by Chris Toy Shop in September 2009:

Sept.	1	Acquired $30,000 cash from the issue of common stock.
	1	Purchased $22,000 of merchandise on account with terms 2/10, n/30.
	5	Paid $500 cash for freight to obtain merchandise purchased on September 1.
	8	Sold merchandise that cost $5,000 to customers for $9,500 on account, with terms 1/10, n/30.
	8	Returned $800 of defective merchandise from the September 1 purchase to the supplier.
	10	Paid cash for one-half of the balance due on the merchandise purchased on September 1.
	20	Received cash from customers of September 8 sale in settlement of the account balances, but not within the discount period.
	30	Paid the balance due on the merchandise purchased on September 1.
	30	Paid $1,950 cash for selling expenses.

Required

a. Record each event in a statements model like the following one. The first event is recorded as an example.

Assets			=	Liab.	+	Equity		Rev. − Exp. = Net Inc.			Cash Flow
Cash +	Accts. Rec. +	Inv.	=	Accts. Pay.	+	Com. Stk. +	Ret. Earn.				
30,000 +	NA +	NA	=	NA	+	30,000 +	NA	NA −	NA =	NA	30,000 FA

b. Prepare an income statement for the month ending September 30.
c. Prepare a statement of cash flows for the month ending September 30.
d. Explain why there is a difference between net income and cash flow from operating activities.

Problem 3-25 *Comprehensive cycle problem: perpetual system*

L.O. 2, 3, 5

excel
mhhe.com/edmonds2007

At the beginning of 2005, the C. Eaton Company had the following balances in its accounts:

Cash	$ 6,500
Inventory	9,000
Retained Earnings	15,500

During 2005, the company experienced the following events.

1. Purchased inventory with a list price of $3,000 on account from Blue Company under terms 1/10, n/30. The merchandise was delivered FOB shipping point. Freight costs of $150 were paid in cash.
2. Returned $300 of the inventory that it had purchased because the inventory was damaged in transit. The freight company agreed to pay the return freight cost.

3. Paid the amount due on its account payable to Blue Company but not within the cash discount period.
4. Sold inventory with a list price of $6,000 and a cost of $3,500 on account, under terms 2/10, n/45.
5. Received returned merchandise from a customer. The merchandise originally cost $400 and was sold to the customer for $650 cash. The customer was paid $650 cash for the returned merchandise.
6. Delivered goods in Event 4 FOB destination. Freight costs of $80 were paid in cash.
7. Collected the amount due on the account receivable but not within the discount period.
8. Took a physical count indicating that $8,300 of inventory was on hand at the end of the accounting period.

CHECK FIGURES
b. Retained Earnings Ending Balance: $7,220
Net Income: $1,720

Required

a. Identify these events as asset source (AS), asset use (AU), asset exchange (AE), or claims exchange (CE).
b. Record each event in a statements model like the following one.

Event	Balance Sheet					Income Statement			Statement of Cash Flows
	Assets			= Liab.	= Equity	Rev.	− Exp.	= Net Inc.	
	Cash	+ Accts. Rec.	+ Mdse. Inv.	= Accts, Pay.	+ Ret. Earn.				

c. Prepare an income statement, a statement of changes in stockholders' equity, a balance sheet, and a statement of cash flows.

L.O. 6

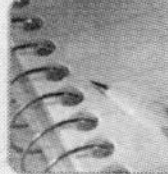

Problem 3-26 ***Using common size income statements to make comparisons***

The following income statements were drawn from the annual reports of Hall Company:

	2005*	2006*
Net Sales	$302,900	$370,500
Cost of Goods Sold	(217,400)	(264,700)
Gross Margin	85,500	105,800
Less: Operating Expense		
Selling and Administrative Expenses	(40,800)	(58,210)
Net Income	$ 44,700	$ 47,590

*All dollar amounts are reported in thousands.

The president's message in the company's annual report stated that the company had implemented a strategy to increase market share by spending more on advertising. The president indicated that prices held steady and sales grew as expected. Write a memo indicating whether you agree with the president's statements. How has the strategy affected profitability? Support your answer by measuring growth in sales and selling expenses. Also prepare common size income statements and make appropriate references to the differences between 2005 and 2006.

Problem 3-27 ***Preparing a schedule of cost of goods sold and multistep and single-step income statements: periodic system (Appendix)***

L.O. 4, 8

mhhe.com/edmonds2007

CHECK FIGURES

a. Cost of Goods Available for Sale: $150,800

b. Net Income: $49,050

The following account titles and balances were taken from the adjusted trial balance of Scoggins Sales Co. at December 31, 2004. The company uses the periodic inventory method.

Account Title	Balance
Advertising Expense	$ 12,800
Supplies Expense	10,700
Interest Expense	150
Merchandise Inventory, January 1	18,000
Merchandise Inventory, December 31	20,100
Miscellaneous Expense	800
Purchases	130,000
Purchase Returns and Allowances	2,700
Rent Expense	14,000
Salaries Expense	53,000
Sales	290,000
Sales Returns and Allowances	8,000
Transportation-in	5,500
Transportation-out	10,800

Required

a. Prepare a schedule to determine the amount of cost of goods sold.
b. Prepare a multistep income statement.
c. Prepare a single-step income statement.

Problem 3-28 ***Comprehensive cycle problem: periodic system (Appendix)***

L.O. 8

mhhe.com/edmonds2007

CHECK FIGURES

a. Ending Cash: $100,640

b. Cost of Goods Sold: $50,810

The following trial balance pertains to Reeves Hardware as of January 1, 2005:

Account Title	Debit	Credit
Cash	$ 74,000	
Accounts Receivable	9,000	
Merchandise Inventory	60,000	
Accounts Payable		$ 5,000
Common Stock		70,000
Retained Earnings		68,000
Total	$143,000	$143,000

The following events occurred in 2005. Assume that Reeves Hardware uses the periodic inventory system.

1. Purchased land for $25,000 cash.
2. Purchased merchandise on account for $23,000, terms 2/10, n/30.
3. The merchandise purchased was shipped FOB shipping point for $230 cash.
4. Returned $2,000 of defective merchandise purchased in Event 2.
5. Sold merchandise for $27,000 cash.
6. Sold merchandise on account for $50,000, terms 1/20, n/30.
7. Paid cash within the discount period on accounts payable due on merchandise purchased in Event 2.
8. Paid $1,200 cash for selling expenses.
9. Collected part of the balance due from accounts receivable in Event 6. Collections were made after the discount period on $12,000 list amount of sales on account. Collections were made during the discount period on $35,000 list amount of sales on account.
10. Performed a physical count indicating that $30,000 of inventory was on hand at the end of the accounting period.

Required

a. Record the above transactions in a horizontal statements model like the following one.

Event	Balance Sheet													Income Statement					Statemt. of Cash Flows
	Assets							=	Equity					Rev.	−	Exp.	=	Net Inc.	
	Cash	+	Accts. Rec.	+	Mdse. Inv.	+	Land	=	Accts. Pay.	+	Com. Stock	+	Ret. Earn.						

b. Prepare a schedule of cost of goods sold and an income statement.

L.O. 7

Problem 3-29 *Performing ratio analysis using real-world data*

Supervalu, Inc., claims to be the largest publicly held food wholesaler in the United States. In addition to being a food wholesaler, it operates "extreme value" retail grocery stores under the name Save-A-Lot. Most of these discount stores are located in inner-city areas not served by others. Whole Food Markets claims to be the world's largest retailer of natural and organic foods. Unlike Save-A-Lot stores that focuses on low-income customers, Whole Foods offers specialty products to customers with sufficient disposal income to spend on such goods. The following data were taken from these companies' 2005 and 2004 annual reports. All dollar amounts are in thousands.

	Supervalu, Inc. February 26, 2005	Whole Foods September 26, 2004
Sales	$19,543,240	$3,864,950
Cost of Goods Sold	16,681,472	2,523,816
Net Income	385,823	129,512

Required

a. Before performing any calculations, speculate as to which company will have the highest gross margin and return on sales percentage. Explain the rationale for your decision.

b. Calculate the gross margin percentages for Supervalu and Whole Foods Market.

c. Calculate the return on sales percentages for Supervalu and Whole Foods Market.

d. Do the calculations from Requirements *b* and *c* confirm your speculations in Requirement *a*?

ANALYZE, THINK, COMMUNICATE

ATC 3-1 Business Applications Case *Understanding real world annual reports*

Required

Use the Topps Company's annual report in Appendix B to answer the following questions.

a. What was Topps' gross margin percentage for 2003 and 2002?

b. What was Topps' return on sales percentage for 2003 and 2002?

c. Topps' Gross Profit on Sales was about $12 million lower in 2003 than in 2002 and this caused its Net Income to be lower as well. However, its gross margin percentage also decreased in 2003. Ignoring taxes, how much higher would its 2003 net income have been if the gross margin percentage in 2003 had been the same as for 2002?

ATC 3-2 Group Exercise *Multistep income statement*

The following quarterly information is given for Raybon for the year ended 2002 (amounts shown are in millions).

	First Quarter	Second Quarter	Third Quarter	Fourth Quarter
Net Sales	$736.0	$717.4	$815.2	$620.1
Gross Margin	461.9	440.3	525.3	252.3
Net Income	37.1	24.6	38.6	31.4

Required

a. Divide the class into groups and organize the groups into four sections. Assign each section financial information for one of the quarters.

(1) Each group should compute the cost of goods sold and operating expenses for the specific quarter assigned to its section and prepare a multistep income statement for the quarter.

(2) Each group should compute the gross margin percentage and cost of goods sold percentage for its specific quarter.

(3) Have a representative of each group put that quarter's sales, cost of goods sold percentage, and gross margin percentage on the board.

Class Discussion

b. Have the class discuss the change in each of these items from quarter to quarter and explain why the change might have occurred. Which was the best quarter and why?

ATC 3-3 Real-World Case *Identifying companies based on financial statement information*

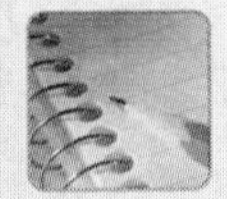

Presented here is selected information from the 2002 fiscal-year reports of four companies. The four companies, in alphabetical order, are **Caterpillar, Inc.**, a manufacturer of heavy machinery; **Oracle Corporation**, a company that develops software; **Peet's Coffee & Tea**, a company that sells coffee products; and **Tiffany & Company**, a company that operates high-end jewelry and department stores. The data for the companies, presented in the order of the amount of their sales in millions of dollars, follow:

	A	B	C	D
Sales	$18,648	$ 9,673	$1,706.6	$104.1
Cost of Goods Sold	14,709	2,406	695.2	48.1
Net Earnings	798	2,224	189.9	4.7
Inventory	2,763	0	732.1	11.0
Accounts Receivable	2,838	2,036	113.1	2.2
Total Assets	32,851	10,800	1,923.6	95.1

Required

Based on these financial data and your knowledge and assumptions about the nature of the businesses that the companies operate, determine which data relate to which companies. Write a memorandum explaining your decisions. Include a discussion of which ratios you used in your analysis, and show the computations of these ratios in your memorandum.

ATC 3-4 Business Applications Case *Using ratios to make comparisons*

The following income statements were drawn from the annual reports of Design Company and Royal Company.

	Design	Royal
Net Sales	$95,700	$52,300
Cost of Goods Sold	68,900	31,400
Gross Margin	26,800	20,900
Less: Selling and Admin. Expenses	22,000	18,800
Net Income	$ 4,800	$ 2,100

Note: All figures are reported in thousands of dollars

Required

a. One of the companies is a high-end retailer that operates in exclusive shopping malls. The other operates discount stores located in low-cost stand-alone buildings. Identify the high-end retailer and the discounter. Support your answer with appropriate ratios.

b. If Design and Royal have equity of $40,000 and $21,000, respectively, which company is the more profitable?

ATC 3-5 Business Applications Case *Using common size statements and ratios to make comparisons*

At the end of 2006, the following information is available for Kinlaw and Parker companies:

	Kinlaw	Parker
Sales	$2,000	$2,000,000
Cost of Goods Sold	1,400	1,200,000
Selling and Administrative Expenses	520	640,000
Total Assets	2,500	2,500,000
Stockholders' Equity	750	730,000

Required

a. Prepare common size income statements for each company.

b. Compute the return on assets and return on equity for each company.

c. Which company is more profitable from the stockholders' perspective?

d. One company is a high-end retailer, and the other operates a discount store. Which is the discounter? Support your selection by referring to appropriate ratios.

ATC 3-6 Written Assignment, Critical Thinking *Effect of sales returns on financial statements*

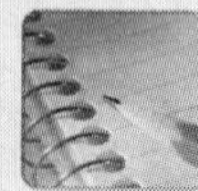

Bell Farm and Garden Equipment reported the following information for 2005:

Net Sales of Equipment	$2,450,567
Other Income	6,786
Cost of Goods Sold	1,425,990
Selling, General, and Administrative Expense	325,965
Net Operating Income	$ 705,398

Selected information from the balance sheet as of December 31, 2005, follows:

Cash and Marketable Securities	$113,545
Inventory	248,600
Accounts Receivable	82,462
Property, Plant, and Equipment—Net	335,890
Other Assets	5,410
Total Assets	$785,907

Assume that a major customer returned a large order to Bell on December 31, 2005. The amount of the sale had been $146,800 with a cost of sales of $94,623. The return was recorded in the books on January 1, 2006. The company president does not want to correct the books. He argues that it makes no difference as to whether the return is recorded in 2005 or 2006. Either way, the return has been duly recognized.

Required

a. Assume that you are the CFO for Bell Farm and Garden Equipment Co. Write a memo to the president explaining how omitting the entry on December 31, 2005, could cause the financial statements to be misleading to investors and creditors. Explain how omitting the return from the customer would affect net income and the balance sheet.

b. Why might the president want to record the return on January 1, 2006, instead of December 31, 2005?

c. Would the failure to record the customer return violate the AICPA Code of Professional Conduct? (See Exhibit 1.4 in Chapter 1.)

d. If the president of the company refuses to correct the financial statements, what action should you take?

ATC 3-7 Ethical Dilemma *Wait until I get mine*

Ada Fontanez is the president of a large company that owns a chain of athletic shoe stores. The company was in dire financial condition when she was hired three years ago. To motivate Fontanez, the board of directors included a bonus plan as part of her compensation package. According to her employment contract, on January 15 of each year, Fontanez is paid a cash bonus equal to 5 percent of the amount of net income reported on the preceding December 31 income statement. Fontanez was sufficiently motivated. Through her leadership, the company prospered. Her efforts were recognized throughout the industry, and she received numerous lucrative offers to leave the company. One offer was so enticing that she decided to change jobs. Her decision was made in late December 2005. However, she decided to resign effective February 1, 2006, to ensure the receipt of her January bonus. On December 31, 2005, the chief accountant, Walter Smith, advised Fontanez that the company had a sizable quantity of damaged inventory. A warehouse fire had resulted in smoke and water damage to approximately $600,000 of inventory. The warehouse was not insured, and the accountant recommended that the loss be recognized immediately. After examining the inventory, Fontanez argued that it could be sold as *damaged goods* to customers at reduced prices. She refused to allow the write-off the accountant recommended. She stated that so long as she is president, the inventory stays on the books at cost. She told the accountant that he could take up the matter with the new president in February.

Required

a. How would an immediate write-off of the damaged inventory affect the December 31, 2005, income statement, balance sheet, and statement of cash flows?

b. How would the write-off affect Fontanez's bonus?

c. If the new president is given the same bonus plan, how will Fontanez's refusal to recognize the loss affect his or her bonus?

d. Assuming that the damaged inventory is truly worthless, comment on the ethical implications of Fontanez's refusal to recognize the loss in the 2005 accounting period.

e. Assume that the damaged inventory is truly worthless and that you are Smith. How would you react to Fontanez's refusal to recognize the loss?

ATC 3-8 Research Assignment *Analyzing Alcoa's profit margins*

Using either Alcoa's most current Form 10-K or the company's annual report, answer the questions below. To obtain the Form 10-K you can use either the EDGAR system following the instructions in Appendix A, or the company's website. The company's annual report is available on its website.

Required

a. What was Alcoa's gross margin percentage for the most current year?

b. What was Alcoa's gross margin percentage for the previous year? Has it changed significantly?

c. What was Alcoa's return on sales percentage for the most current year?

d. What percentage of Alcoa's total sales for the most current year was from operations in the United States?

e. Comment on the appropriateness of comparing Alcoa's gross margin with that of Ford Motor Company. If Ford has a higher/lower margin, does that mean that Ford is a better managed company?

CHAPTER 4

Accounting for Inventories

LEARNING OBJECTIVES

After you have mastered the material in this chapter you will be able to:

1. **Explain how different inventory cost flow methods (specific identification, FIFO, LIFO, and weighted average) affect financial statements.**
2. **Demonstrate the computational procedures for FIFO, LIFO, and weighted average.**
3. **Identify the key elements of a strong system of internal control.**
4. **Identify special internal controls for cash.**
5. **Prepare a bank reconciliation.**
6. **Explain the importance of inventory turnover to a company's profitability.**

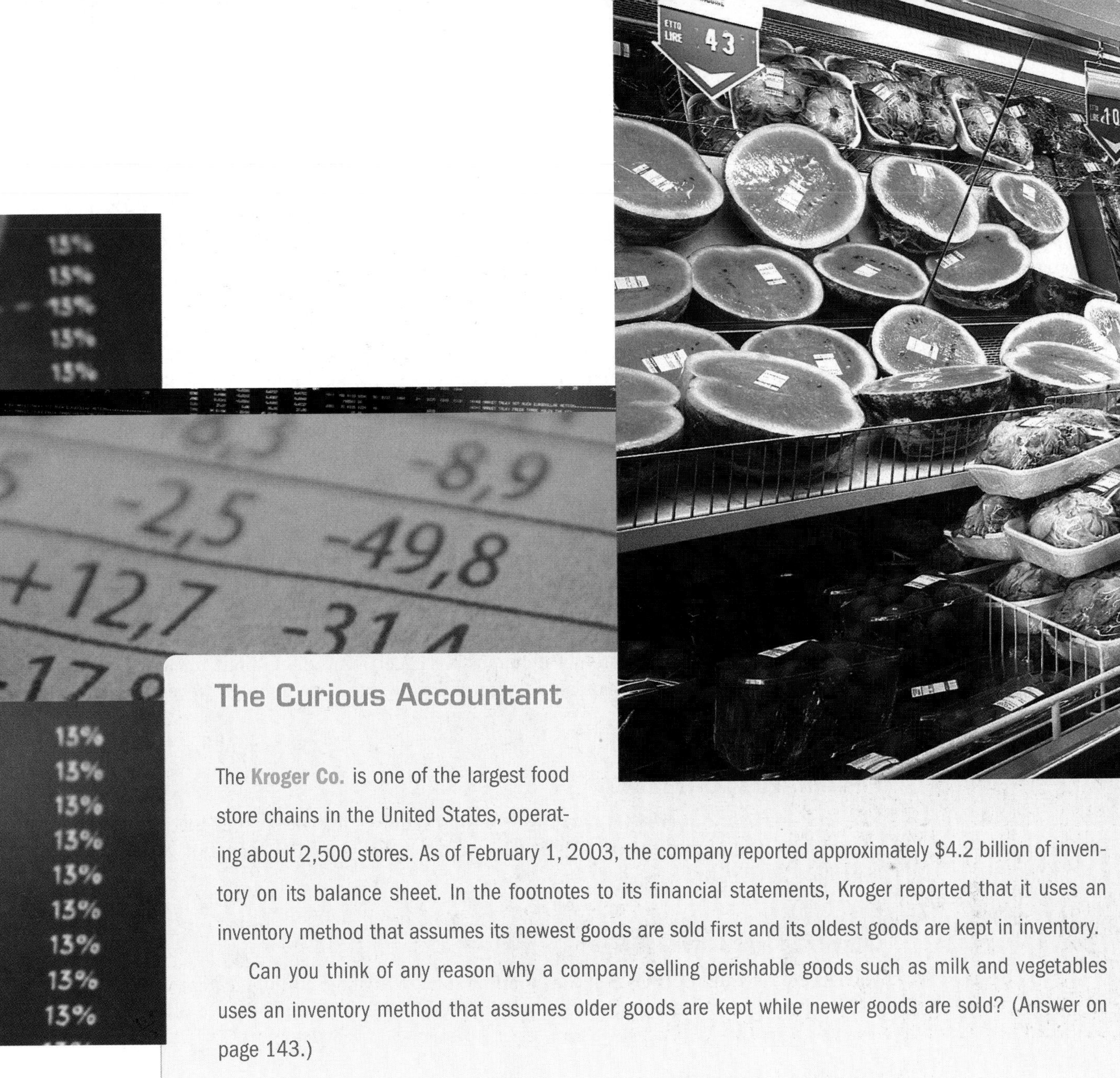

The Curious Accountant

The **Kroger Co.** is one of the largest food store chains in the United States, operating about 2,500 stores. As of February 1, 2003, the company reported approximately $4.2 billion of inventory on its balance sheet. In the footnotes to its financial statements, Kroger reported that it uses an inventory method that assumes its newest goods are sold first and its oldest goods are kept in inventory.

Can you think of any reason why a company selling perishable goods such as milk and vegetables uses an inventory method that assumes older goods are kept while newer goods are sold? (Answer on page 143.)

CHAPTER OPENING

In the previous chapter we used the simplifying assumption that identical inventory items cost the same amount. In practice, businesses often pay different amounts for identical items. Suppose The Mountain Bike Company (TMBC) sells high-end Model 201 helmets. Since all Model 201 helmets are identical, does the helmet supplier charge TMBC the same amount for each helmet? Probably not. You have likely observed that prices change frequently.

Assume TMBC purchases one Model 201 helmet at a cost of $100. Two weeks later TMBC purchases a second Model 201 helmet. Because the supplier has raised prices, the second helmet costs $110. If TMBC sells one of its two helmets, should it record $100 or $110 as cost of goods sold? The following section of this chapter discusses several acceptable alternative methods for determining the amount of cost of goods sold from which companies may choose under generally accepted accounting principles. ■

Inventory Cost Flow Methods

Explain how different inventory cost flow methods (specific identification, FIFO, LIFO, and weighted average) affect financial statements.

Recall that when goods are sold, product costs flow (are transferred) from the Inventory account to the Cost of Goods Sold account. Four acceptable methods for determining the amount of cost to transfer are (1) specific identification; (2) first-in, first-out (FIFO); (3) last-in, first-out (LIFO); and weighted average.

Specific Identification

Suppose TMBC tags inventory items so that it can identify which one is sold at the time of sale. TMBC could then charge the actual cost of the specific item sold to cost of goods sold. Recall that the first inventory item TMBC purchased cost \$100 and the second item cost \$110. Using **specific identification,** cost of goods sold would be \$100 if the first item purchased were sold or \$110 if the second item purchased were sold.

When a company's inventory consists of many low-priced, high-turnover goods the record keeping necessary to use specific identification isn't practical. Imagine the difficulty of recording the cost of each specific food item in a grocery store. Another disadvantage of the specific identification method is the opportunity for managers to manipulate the income statement. For example, TMBC can report a lower cost of goods sold by selling the first instead of the second item. Specific identification is, however, frequently used for high-priced, low-turnover inventory items such as automobiles. For big ticket items like cars, customer demands for specific products limit management's ability to select which merchandise is sold and volume is low enough to manage the recordkeeping.

First-In, First-Out (FIFO)

The **first-in, first-out (FIFO) cost flow method** requires that the cost of the items purchased *first* be assigned to cost of goods sold. Using FIFO, TMBC's cost of goods sold is \$100.

Last-In, First-Out (LIFO)

The **last-in, first-out (LIFO) cost flow method** requires that the cost of the items purchased *last* be charged to cost of goods sold. Using LIFO, TMBC's cost of goods sold is \$110.

Weighted Average

To use the **weighted-average cost flow method,** first calculate the average cost per unit by dividing the *total cost* of the inventory available by the *total number* of units available. In the case of TMBC, the average cost per unit of the inventory is \$105 ([\$100 + \$110] ÷ 2). Cost of goods sold is then calculated by multiplying the average cost per unit by the number of units sold. Using weighted average, TMBC's cost of goods sold is \$105 (\$105 × 1).

Physical Flow

The preceding discussion pertains to the flow of *costs* through the accounting records, *not* the actual **physical flow of goods.** Goods usually move physically on a FIFO basis, which means that the first items of merchandise acquired by a company (first-in) are the first items sold to its customers (first-out). The inventory items on hand at the end of the accounting period are typically the last items in (the most recently acquired goods). If companies did not sell their oldest inventory items first, inventories would include dated, less marketable merchandise. *Cost flow,* however, can differ from *physical flow.* For example, a company may use LIFO or weighted average for financial reporting even if its goods flow physically on a FIFO basis.

Effect of Cost Flow on Financial Statements

Effect on Income Statement

The cost flow method a company uses can significantly affect the gross margin reported in the income statement. To demonstrate, assume that TMBC sold the inventory item discussed previously for $120. The amounts of gross margin using the FIFO, LIFO, and weighted-average cost flow assumptions are shown in the following table:

	FIFO	LIFO	Weighted Average
Sales	$120	$120	$120
Cost of Goods Sold	100	110	105
Gross Margin	$ 20	$ 10	$ 15

Even though the physical flow is assumed to be identical for each method, the gross margin reported under FIFO is double the amount reported under LIFO. Companies experiencing identical economic events (same units of inventory purchased and sold) can report significantly different results in their financial statements. Meaningful financial analysis requires an understanding of financial reporting practices.

Effect on Balance Sheet

Since total product costs are allocated between costs of goods sold and ending inventory, the cost flow method a company uses affects its balance sheet as well as its income statement. Since FIFO transfers the first cost to the income statement, it leaves the last cost on the balance sheet. Similarly, by transferring the last cost to the income statement, LIFO leaves the first cost in ending inventory. The weighted-average method bases both cost of goods sold and ending inventory on the average cost per unit. To illustrate, the ending inventory TMBC would report on the balance sheet using each of the three cost flow methods is shown in the following table:

	FIFO	LIFO	Weighted Average
Ending Inventory	$110	$100	$105

EXHIBIT 4.1

Use of Inventory Cost Flow Methods

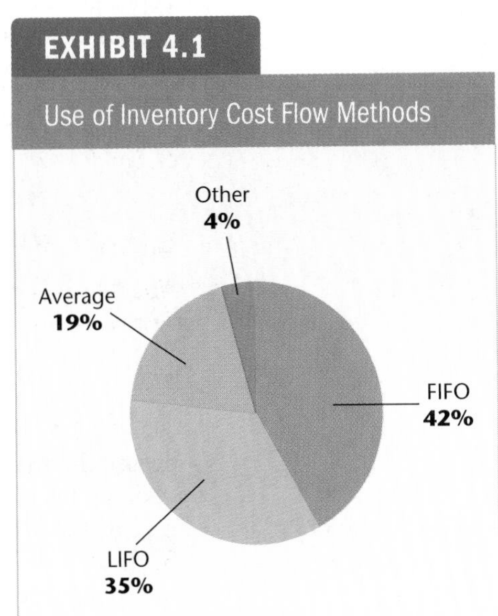

Data source: AICPA, *Accounting Trends and Techniques*, 2000.

The FIFO, LIFO, and weighted-average methods are all used extensively in business practice. The same company may even use one cost flow method for some of its products and different cost flow methods for other products. Exhibit 4.1 illustrates the relative use of the different cost flow methods among U.S. companies.

CHECK YOURSELF 4.1

Nash Office Supply (NOS) purchased two Model 303 copiers at different times. The first copier purchased cost $400 and the second copier purchased cost $450. NOS sold one of the copiers for $600. Determine the gross margin on the sale and the ending inventory balance assuming NOS accounts for inventory using (1) FIFO, (2) LIFO, and (3) weighted average.

Answer

	FIFO	LIFO	Weighted Average
Sales	$600	$600	$600
Cost of Goods Sold	(400)	(450)	(425)
Gross Margin	$200	$150	$175
Ending Inventory	$450	$400	$425

Multiple Layers with Multiple Quantities

Demonstrate the computational procedures for FIFO, LIFO, and weighted average.

The previous example illustrates different **inventory cost flow methods** using only two cost layers ($100 and $110) with only one unit of inventory in each layer. Actual business inventories are considerably more complex. Most real-world inventories are composed of multiple cost layers with different quantities of inventory in each layer. The underlying allocation concepts, however, remain unchanged.

For example, a different inventory item The Mountain Bike Company (TMBC) carries in its stores is a bike called the Eraser. TMBC's beginning inventory and two purchases of Eraser bikes are described below.

Jan. 1	Beginning inventory	10 units @ $200	=	$ 2,000
Mar. 18	First purchase	20 units @ $220	=	4,400
Aug. 21	Second purchase	25 units @ $250	=	6,250
Total cost of the 55 bikes available for sale				$12,650

The accounting records for the period show that TMBC paid cash for all Eraser bike purchases and that it sold 43 bikes at a cash price of $350 each.

Allocating Cost of Goods Available for Sale

The following discussion shows how to determine the cost of goods sold and ending inventory amounts under FIFO, LIFO, and weighted average. We show all three methods to demonstrate how they affect the financial statements differently; TMBC would actually use only one of the methods.

Regardless of the cost flow method chosen, TMBC must allocate the cost of goods available for sale ($12,650) between cost of goods sold and ending inventory. The amounts assigned to each category will differ depending on TMBC's cost flow method. Computations for each method are shown below.

FIFO Inventory Cost Flow

Recall that TMBC sold 43 Eraser bikes during the accounting period. The FIFO method transfers to the Cost of Goods Sold account the *cost of the first 43 bikes* TMBC had available to sell. The first 43 bikes acquired by TMBC were the 10 bikes in the beginning inventory (these were purchased in the prior period) plus the 20 bikes purchased in March and 13 of the bikes purchased in August. The expense recognized for the cost of these bikes ($9,650) is computed as follows:

Jan. 1	Beginning inventory	10 units @ $200	=	$2,000
Mar. 18	First purchase	20 units @ $220	=	4,400
Aug. 21	Second purchase	13 units @ $250	=	3,250
Total cost of the 43 bikes sold				$9,650

Since TMBC had 55 bikes available for sale it would have 12 bikes (55 available − 43 sold) in ending inventory. The cost assigned to these 12 bikes (the ending balance in the Inventory account) equals the cost of goods available for sale minus the cost of goods sold as shown below:

Cost of goods available for sale	$12,650
Cost of goods sold	9,650
Ending inventory balance	$ 3,000

We show the allocation of the cost of goods available for sale between cost of goods sold and ending inventory graphically below.

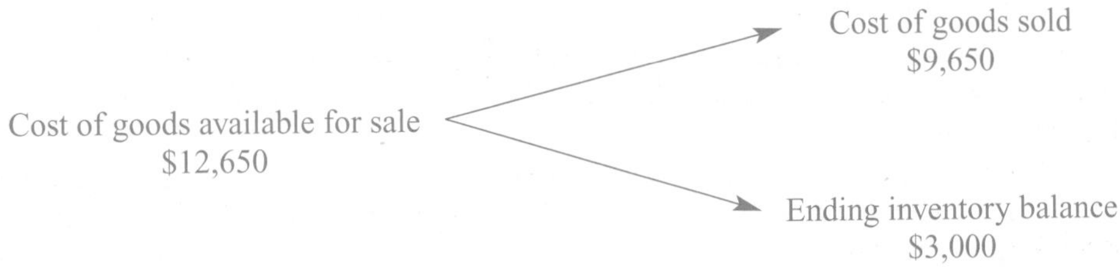

LIFO Inventory Cost Flow

Under LIFO, the cost of goods sold is the cost of the last 43 bikes acquired by TMBC, computed as follows:

Aug. 21	Second purchase	25 units @ $250	=	$ 6,250
Mar. 18	First purchase	18 units @ $220	=	3,960
Total cost of the 43 bikes sold				$10,210

The LIFO cost of the 12 bikes in ending inventory is computed as shown below:

Cost of goods available for sale	$12,650
Cost of goods sold	10,210
Ending inventory balance	$ 2,440

We show the allocation of the cost of goods available for sale between cost of goods sold and ending inventory graphically below.

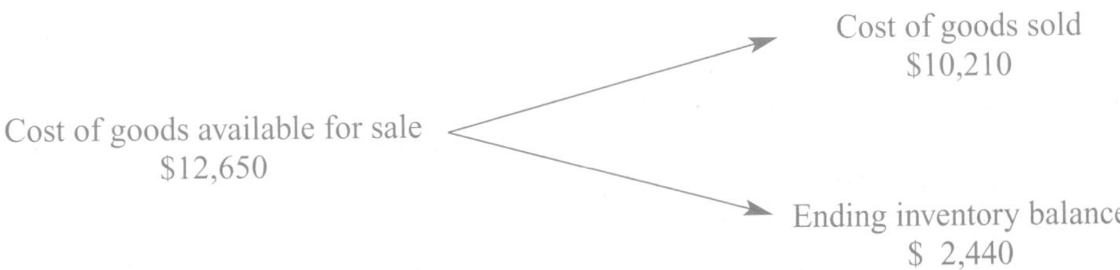

Weighted-Average Cost Flow

The weighted-average cost per unit is determined by dividing the *total cost of goods available for sale* by the *total number of units* available for sale. For TMBC, the weighted-average cost per unit is \$230 (\$12,650 ÷ 55). The weighted-average cost of goods sold is determined by multiplying the average cost per unit by the number of units sold (\$230 × 43 = \$9,890). The cost assigned to the 12 bikes in ending inventory is \$2,760 (12 × \$230).

We show the allocation of the cost of goods available for sale between cost of goods sold and ending inventory graphically below.

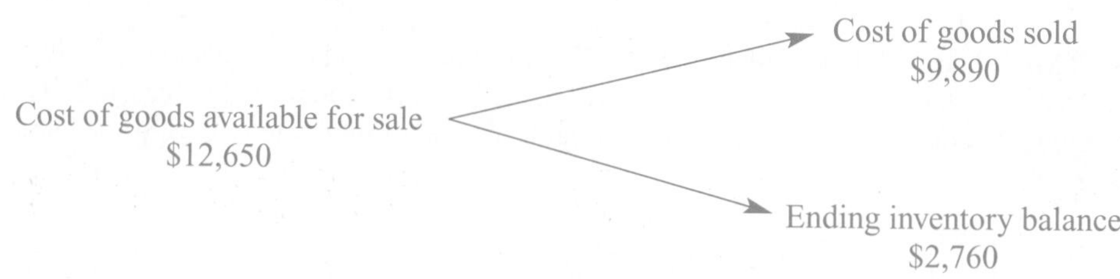

Effect of Cost Flow on Financial Statements

Explain how different inventory cost flow methods (specific identification, FIFO, LIFO, and weighted average) affect financial statements.

Exhibit 4.2 displays partial financial statements for The Mountain Bike Company (TMBC). This exhibit includes only information pertaining to the Eraser bikes inventory item described above. Other financial statement data are omitted.

Recall that assets are reported on the balance sheet in order of liquidity (how quickly they are expected to be converted to cash). Since companies frequently sell inventory on account, inventory is less liquid than accounts receivable. As a result, companies commonly report inventory below accounts receivable on the balance sheet.

Exhibit 4.2 demonstrates that the amounts reported for gross margin on the income statement and inventory on the balance sheet differ significantly. The cash flow from operating activities on the statement of cash flows, however, is identical under all three methods. Regardless of cost flow reporting method, TMBC paid \$10,650 cash (\$4,400 first purchase + \$6,250 second purchase) to purchase inventory and received \$15,050 cash for inventory sold.

The Impact of Income Tax

Based on the financial statement information in Exhibit 4.2, which cost flow method should TMBC use? Most people initially suggest FIFO because FIFO reports the highest gross margin and the largest balance in ending inventory. However, other factors are relevant. FIFO produces the highest gross margin; it also produces the highest net income and the highest income tax expense. In contrast, LIFO results in recognizing the lowest gross margin, lowest net income, and the lowest income tax expense.

Will investors favor a company with more assets and higher net income or one with lower tax expense? Recognize that specific identification, FIFO, LIFO, and weighted average are ***different methods of reporting the same information.*** TMBC experienced only one set of events pertaining to Eraser bikes. Exhibit 4.2 reports those same events three different ways. However, if the FIFO reporting method causes TMBC to pay more taxes than the LIFO method, using FIFO will cause a real reduction in the value of the company. Paying more money in taxes leaves less money in the company. Knowledgeable investors would be more attracted to TMBC if it uses LIFO because the lower tax payments allow the company to keep more value in the business.

Research suggests that, as a group, investors are knowledgeable. They make investment decisions based on economic substance regardless of how information is reported in financial statements.

EXHIBIT 4.2

TMBC COMPANY
Comparative Financial Statements

Partial Income Statements	FIFO	LIFO	Weighted Average
Sales	$15,050	$15,050	$15,050
Cost of Goods Sold	(9,650)	(10,210)	(9,890)
Gross Margin	5,400	4,840	5,160

Partial Balance Sheets	FIFO	LIFO	Weighted Average
Assets			
Cash	$ xx	$ xx	$ xx
Accounts Receivable	xx	xx	xx
Inventory	3,000	2,440	2,760

Partial Statements of Cash Flows	FIFO	LIFO	Weighted Average
Operating Activities			
Cash Inflow from Customers	$15,050	$15,050	$15,050
Cash Outflow for Inventory	(10,650)	(10,650)	(10,650)

The Income Statement versus the Tax Return

In some instances companies may use one accounting method for financial reporting and a different method to compute income taxes (the tax return must explain any differences). With respect to LIFO, however, the Internal Revenue Service requires that companies using LIFO for income tax purposes must also use LIFO for financial reporting. A company could not, therefore, get both the lower tax benefit provided by LIFO and the financial reporting advantage offered under FIFO.

Inflation versus Deflation

Our illustration assumes an inflationary environment (rising inventory prices). In a deflationary environment, the impact of using LIFO versus FIFO is reversed. LIFO produces tax advantages in an inflationary environment, while FIFO produces tax advantages in a deflationary environment. Companies operating in the computer industry where prices are falling would obtain a tax advantage by using FIFO. In contrast, companies that sell medical supplies in an inflationary environment would obtain a tax advantage by using LIFO.

Full Disclosure and Consistency

Generally accepted accounting principles allow each company to choose the inventory cost flow method best suited to its reporting needs. Because results can vary considerably among methods, however, the GAAP principle of **full disclosure** requires that financial statements disclose the method chosen. In addition, so that a company's financial statements are comparable from year to year, the GAAP principle of **consistency** generally requires that companies use the same cost flow method each period. The limited exceptions to the consistency principle are described in more advanced accounting courses.

CHECK YOURSELF 4.2

The following information was drawn from the inventory records of Fields, Inc.

Beginning inventory	200 units @ \$20
First purchase	400 units @ \$22
Second purchase	600 units @ \$24

Assume that Fields sold 900 units of inventory.

1. Determine the amount of cost of goods sold using FIFO.
2. Would using LIFO produce a higher or lower amount of cost of goods sold? Why?

Answer

1. Cost of goods sold using FIFO

Beginning inventory	200 units @ \$20	=	\$ 4,000
First purchase	400 units @ \$22	=	8,800
Second purchase	300 units @ \$24	=	7,200
Total cost of goods sold			\$20,000

2. The inventory records reflect an inflationary environment of steadily rising prices. Since LIFO charges the latest costs (in this case the highest costs) to the income statement, using LIFO would produce a higher amount of cost of goods sold than would using FIFO.

REALITY BYTES

To avoid spoilage or obsolescence, most companies use a first-in, first-out (FIFO) approach for the flow of physical goods. The older goods (first units purchased) are sold before the newer goods are sold. For example, **Kroger** and other food stores stack older merchandise at the front of the shelf where customers are more likely to pick it up first. As a result, merchandise is sold before it becomes dated. However, when timing is not an issue, convenience may dictate the use of the last-in, first-out (LIFO) method. Examples of products that frequently move on a LIFO basis include rock, gravel, dirt, or other nonwasting assets. Indeed, rock, gravel, and dirt are normally stored in piles that are unprotected from weather. New inventory is simply piled on top of the old. Inventory that is sold is taken from the top of the pile because it is convenient to do so. Accordingly, the last inventory purchased is the first inventory sold. Regardless of whether the flow of physical goods occurs on a LIFO or FIFO basis, costs can flow differently. The flow of inventory through the physical facility is a separate issue from the flow of costs through the accounting system.

Key Features of Internal Control Systems

LO 3

Identify the key elements of a strong system of internal control.

Suppose Wal-Mart's corporate-level executives establish a policy to ensure that inventory items have a short shelf life. More specifically, the executives decide to discount the price of any inventory item that is not sold within 30 days. How do the executives know that the store managers around the world will implement this policy? The answer: by establishing an effective set of internal controls.

Internal controls are the policies and procedures used to provide reasonable assurance that the objectives of an enterprise will be accomplished.[1]

Internal controls can be divided into two categories: (1) **accounting controls** are designed to safeguard company assets and ensure reliable accounting records; and (2) **administrative controls** are concerned with evaluating performance and assessing the degree of compliance with company policies and public laws.

Internal control systems vary from company to company. However, most systems include certain basic policies and procedures that have proven effective over time. A discussion of the more common features of a strong system of internal control follows.

Separation of Duties

The likelihood of fraud or theft is reduced if collusion is required to accomplish it. Clear **separation of duties** is frequently used as a deterrent to corruption. When duties are separated, the work of one employee can act as a check on the work of another employee. For example, a person selling seats to a movie may be tempted to steal money received from customers who enter the theater. This temptation is reduced if the person staffing the box office is required to issue tickets that a second employee collects as people enter the theater. If ticket stubs collected by the second employee are compared with the cash receipts from ticket sales, any cash shortages would become apparent. Furthermore, friends and relatives of the ticket agent could not easily enter the theater without paying. Theft or unauthorized entry would require collusion between the ticket agent and the usher who collects the tickets. Both individuals would have to be dishonest enough to steal, yet trustworthy enough to convince each other they would keep the embezzlement secret. Whenever possible, the functions of *authorization, recording,* and *custody of assets* should be performed by separate individuals.

Quality of Employees

A business is only as good as the people it employs. Cheap labor is not a bargain if the employees are incompetent. Employees should be properly trained. In fact, they should be trained to perform a variety of tasks. The ability of employees to substitute for one another prevents disruptions when co-workers are absent because of illnesses, vacations, or other commitments. The capacity to rotate jobs also relieves boredom and increases respect for the contributions of other employees. Every business should strive to maximize the productivity of every employee. Ongoing training programs are essential to a strong system of internal control.

Bonded Employees

The best way to ensure employee honesty is to hire individuals with *high levels of personal integrity.* Employers should screen job applicants using interviews, background checks, and recommendations from prior employers or educators. Even so, screening programs may fail to identify character weaknesses. Further, unusual circumstances may cause honest employees to go astray. Therefore, employees in positions of trust should be bonded. A **fidelity bond** provides insurance that protects a company from losses caused by employee dishonesty.

Required Absences

Employees should be required to take regular vacations and their duties should be rotated periodically. Employees may be able to cover up fraudulent activities if they are always present

[1] *AICPA Professional Standards,* vol. 1, sec. 320, par. 6 (June 1, 1989).

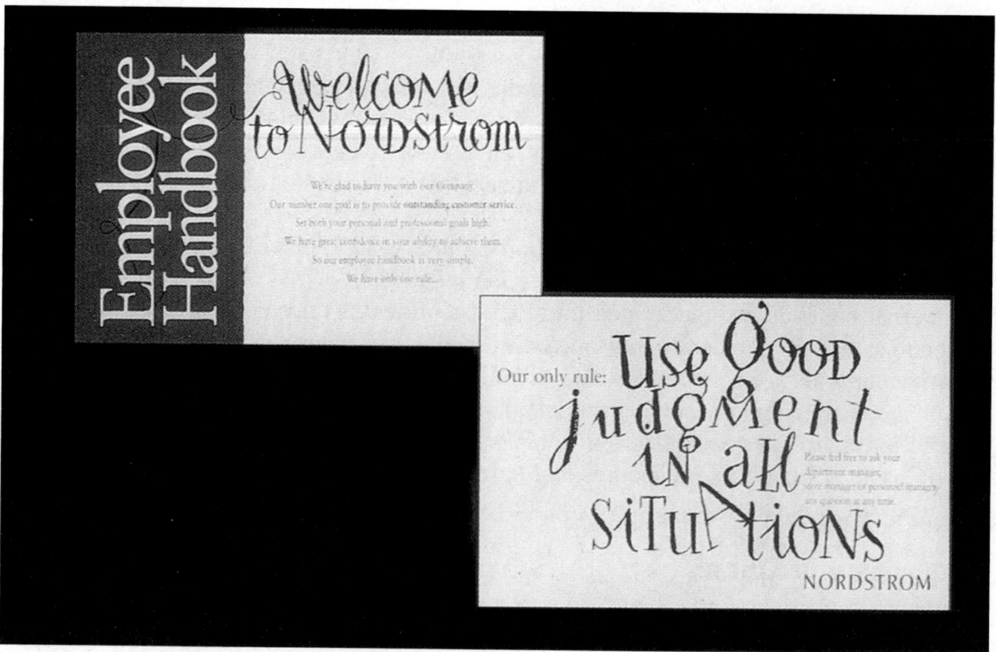

at work. Consider the case of a parking meter collection agent who covered the same route for several years with no vacation. When the agent became sick, a substitute collected more money each day than the regular reader usually reported. Management checked past records and found that the ill meter reader had been understating the cash receipts and pocketing the difference. If management had required vacations or rotated the routes, the embezzlement would have been discovered much earlier.

Procedures Manual

Appropriate accounting procedures should be documented in a **procedures manual.** The manual should be routinely updated. Periodic reviews should be conducted to ensure that employees are following the procedures outlined in the manual.

Authority and Responsibility

Employees are motivated by clear lines of authority and responsibility. They work harder when they have the authority to use their own judgment and they exercise reasonable caution when they are held responsible for their actions. Businesses should prepare an **authority manual** that establishes a definitive *chain of command.* The authority manual should guide both specific and general authorizations. **Specific authorizations** apply to specific positions within the organization. For example, investment decisions are authorized at the division level while hiring decisions are authorized at the departmental level. In contrast, **general authority** applies across different levels of management. For example, employees at all levels may be required to fly coach or to make purchases from specific vendors.

Prenumbered Documents

How would you know if a check were stolen from your check book? If you keep a record of your check numbers, the missing number would tip you off immediately. Businesses also use prenumbered checks to avoid the unauthorized use of their bank accounts. In fact, prenumbered forms are used for all important documents such as purchase orders, receiving reports, invoices, and checks. To reduce errors, prenumbered forms should be as simple and easy to use as possible. Also, the documents should allow for authorized signatures. For example, credit sales slips should be signed by the customer to clearly establish who made the purchase, reducing the likelihood of unauthorized transactions.

Physical Control

Employees walk away with billions of dollars of business assets each year. To limit losses, companies should establish adequate physical control over valuable assets. For example, inventory should be kept in a storeroom and not released without proper authorization. Serial numbers on equipment should be recorded along with the name of the individual who is responsible for the equipment. Unannounced physical counts should be conducted randomly to verify the presence of company-owned equipment. Certificates of deposit and marketable securities should be kept in fireproof vaults. Access to these vaults should be limited to authorized personnel. These procedures protect the documents from fire and limit access to only those individuals who have the appropriate security clearance to handle the documents.

In addition to safeguarding assets, there should be physical control over the accounting records. The accounting journals, ledgers, and supporting documents should be kept in a fireproof safe. Only personnel responsible for recording transactions in the journals should have access to them. With limited access, there is less chance that someone will change the records to conceal fraud or embezzlement.

Performance Evaluations

Because few people can evaluate their own performance objectively, internal controls should include independent verification of employee performance. For example, someone other than the person who has control over inventory should take a physical count of inventory. Internal and external audits serve as independent verification of performance. Auditors should evaluate the effectiveness of the internal control system as well as verify the accuracy of the accounting records. In addition, the external auditors attest to the company's use of generally accepted accounting principles in the financial statements.

Limitations

A system of internal controls is designed to prevent or detect errors and fraud. However, no control system is foolproof. Internal controls can be circumvented by collusion among employees. Two or more employees working together can hide embezzlement by covering for each other. For example, if an embezzler goes on vacation, fraud will not be reported by a replacement who is in collusion with the embezzler. No system can prevent all fraud. However, a good system of internal controls minimizes illegal or unethical activities by reducing temptation and increasing the likelihood of early detection.

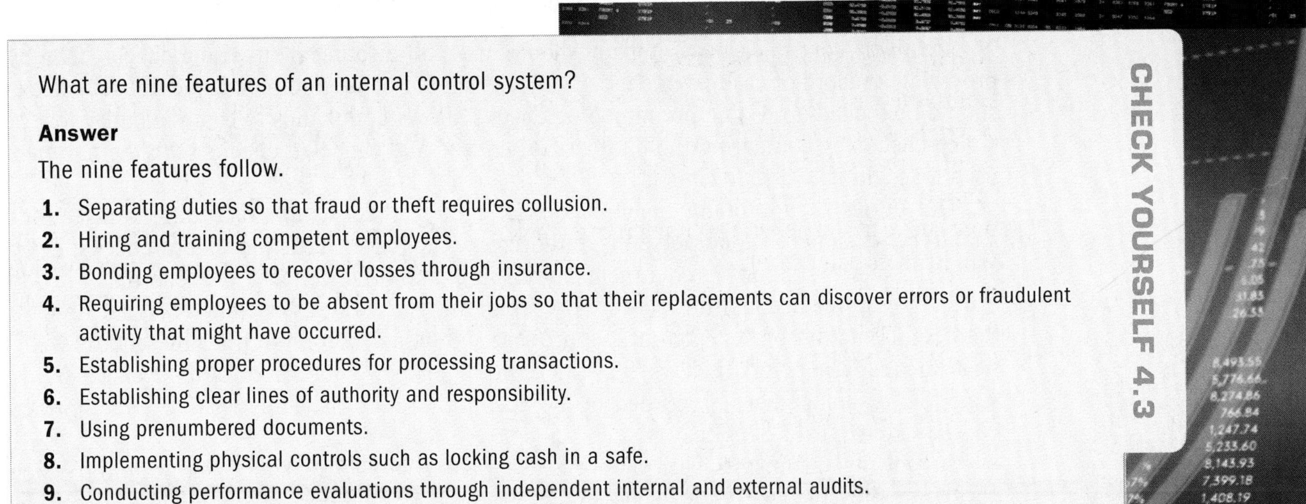

CHECK YOURSELF 4.3

What are nine features of an internal control system?

Answer

The nine features follow.

1. Separating duties so that fraud or theft requires collusion.
2. Hiring and training competent employees.
3. Bonding employees to recover losses through insurance.
4. Requiring employees to be absent from their jobs so that their replacements can discover errors or fraudulent activity that might have occurred.
5. Establishing proper procedures for processing transactions.
6. Establishing clear lines of authority and responsibility.
7. Using prenumbered documents.
8. Implementing physical controls such as locking cash in a safe.
9. Conducting performance evaluations through independent internal and external audits.

Accounting for Cash

LO 4 Identify special internal controls for cash.

For financial reporting purposes, **cash** generally includes currency and other items that are payable *on demand,* such as checks, money orders, bank drafts, and certain savings accounts. Savings accounts that impose substantial penalties for early withdrawal should be classified as *investments* rather than cash. Postdated checks or IOUs represent *receivables* and should not be included in cash. As illustrated in Exhibit 4.3, most companies combine currency and other payable on demand items in a single balance sheet account with varying titles.

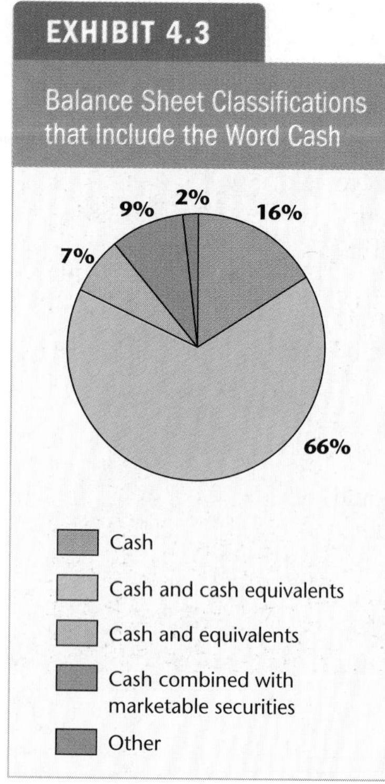

Data Source: AICPA, *Accounting Trends and Techniques*, 2002.

Companies must maintain a sufficient amount of cash to pay employees, suppliers, and other creditors. When a company fails to pay its legal obligations, its creditors can force the company into bankruptcy. Even so, management should avoid accumulating more cash than is needed. The failure to invest excess cash in earning assets reduces profitability. Cash inflows and outflows must be managed to prevent a shortage or surplus of cash.

Controlling Cash

Controlling cash, more than any other asset, requires strict adherence to internal control procedures. Cash has universal appeal. A relatively small suitcase filled with high-denomination currency can represent significant value. Furthermore, the rightful owner of currency is difficult to prove. In most cases, possession constitutes ownership. As a result, cash is highly susceptible to theft and must be carefully protected. Cash is most susceptible to embezzlement when it is received or disbursed. The following controls should be employed to reduce the likelihood of theft.

Cash Receipts

A record of all cash collections should be prepared immediately upon receipt. The amount of cash on hand should be counted regularly. Missing amounts of money can be detected by comparing the actual cash on hand with the book balance. Employees who receive cash should give customers a copy of a written receipt. Customers usually review their receipts to ensure they have gotten credit for the amount paid and call any errors to the receipts clerk's attention. This not only reduces errors but also provides a control on the clerk's honesty. Cash receipts should be deposited in a bank on a timely basis. Cash collected late in the day should be deposited in a night depository. Every effort should be made to minimize the amount of cash on hand. Keeping large amounts of cash on hand not only increases the risk of loss from theft but also places employees in danger of being harmed by criminals who may be tempted to rob the company.

Cash Payments

To effectively control cash, a company should make all disbursements using checks, thereby providing a record of cash payments. All checks should be prenumbered, and unused checks should be locked up. Using prenumbered checks allows companies to easily identify lost or stolen checks by comparing the numbers on unused and canceled checks with the numbers used for legitimate disbursements.

The duties of approving disbursements, signing checks, and recording transactions should be separated. If one person is authorized to approve, sign, and record checks, he or she could falsify supporting documents, write an unauthorized check, and record a cover-up transaction in the accounting records. By separating these duties, the check signer reviews the documentation provided by the approving individual before signing the check. Likewise, the recording clerk reviews the work of both the approving person and the check signer when the disbursement is recorded in the accounting records. Thus writing unauthorized checks requires trilevel collusion.

Supporting documents with authorized approval signatures should be required when checks are presented to the check signer. For example, a warehouse receiving order should be matched with a purchase order before a check is approved to pay a bill from a supplier. Before payments are approved, invoice amounts should be checked and payees verified as valid vendors. Matching supporting documents with proper authorization discourages employees from creating phony documents for a disbursement to a friend or fictitious business. Also, the approval process serves as a check on the accuracy of the work of all employees involved.

Supporting documents should be marked *Paid* when the check is signed. If the documents are not indelibly marked, they could be retrieved from the files and resubmitted for a duplicate, unauthorized payment. A payables clerk could collude with the payee to split extra cash paid out by submitting the same supporting documents for a second payment.

REALITY BYTES

THE COST OF PROTECTING CASH

Could you afford to buy a safe like the one shown here? The vault is only one of many expensive security devices used by banks to safeguard cash. By using checking accounts, companies are able to avoid many of the costs associated with keeping cash safe. In addition to providing physical control, checking accounts enable companies to maintain a written audit trail of cash receipts and payments. Checking accounts represent the most widely used internal control device in modern society. It is difficult to imagine a business operating without the use of checking accounts.

All spoiled and voided checks should be defaced and retained. If defaced checks are not retained, an employee could steal a check and then claim that it was written incorrectly and thrown away. The clerk could then use the stolen check to make an unauthorized payment.

Checking Account Documents

The previous section explained the need for businesses to use checking accounts. A description of four main types of forms associated with a bank checking account follows:

Signature Card

A bank **signature card** shows the bank account number and the signatures of the people authorized to sign checks. The card is retained in the bank's files. If a bank employee is unfamiliar with the signature on a check, he or she can refer to the signature card to verify the signature before cashing the check.

Deposit Ticket

Each deposit of cash or checks is accompanied by a **deposit ticket,** which normally identifies the account number and the name of the account. The depositor lists the individual amounts of currency, coins, and checks, as well as the total deposited, on the deposit ticket.

Bank Check

A written check affects three parties: (1) the person or business writing the check (the *payer*); (2) the bank on which the check is drawn; and (3) the person or business to whom the check is payable (the *payee*). Companies often write **checks** using multicopy, prenumbered forms, with the name of the issuing business preprinted on the face of each check. A remittance notice is usually attached to the check forms. This portion of the form provides the issuer space to record what the check is for (e.g., what invoices are being paid), the amount being disbursed, and the date of payment. When signed by the person whose signature is on the signature card, the check authorizes the bank to transfer the face amount of the check from the payer's account to the payee.

Bank Statement

Periodically, the bank sends the depositor a **bank statement.** The bank statement is presented from the bank's point of view. Checking accounts are liabilities to a bank because the bank is obligated to pay back the money that customers have deposited in their accounts.

Therefore, in the bank's accounting records a customer's checking account has a *credit* balance. As a result, **bank statement debit memos** describe transactions that reduce the customer's account balance (the bank's liability). **Bank statement credit memos** describe activities that increase the customer's account balance (the bank's liability). Since a checking account is an asset (cash) to the depositor, a *bank statement debit memo* requires a *credit entry* to the cash account on the depositor's books. Likewise, when a bank tells you that it has credited your account, you will debit your cash account in response.

Bank statements normally report (a) the balance of the account at the beginning of the period; (b) additions for customer deposits made during the period; (c) other additions described in credit memos (e.g., for interest earned); (d) subtractions for the payment of checks drawn on the account during the period; (e) other subtractions described in debit memos (e.g., for service charges); (f) a running balance of the account; and (g) the balance of the account at the end of the period. The sample bank statement in Exhibit 4.4 illustrates these items with references to the preceding letters in parentheses. Normally, the canceled checks or copies of them are enclosed with the bank statement.

Reconciling the Bank Account

Prepare a bank reconciliation.

Usually the ending balance reported on the bank statement differs from the balance in the depositor's cash account as of the same date. The discrepancy is normally attributable to timing differences. For example, a depositor deducts the amount of a check from its cash account when it writes the check. However, the bank does not deduct the amount of the check from the depositor's account until the payee presents it for payment, which may be

EXHIBIT 4.4

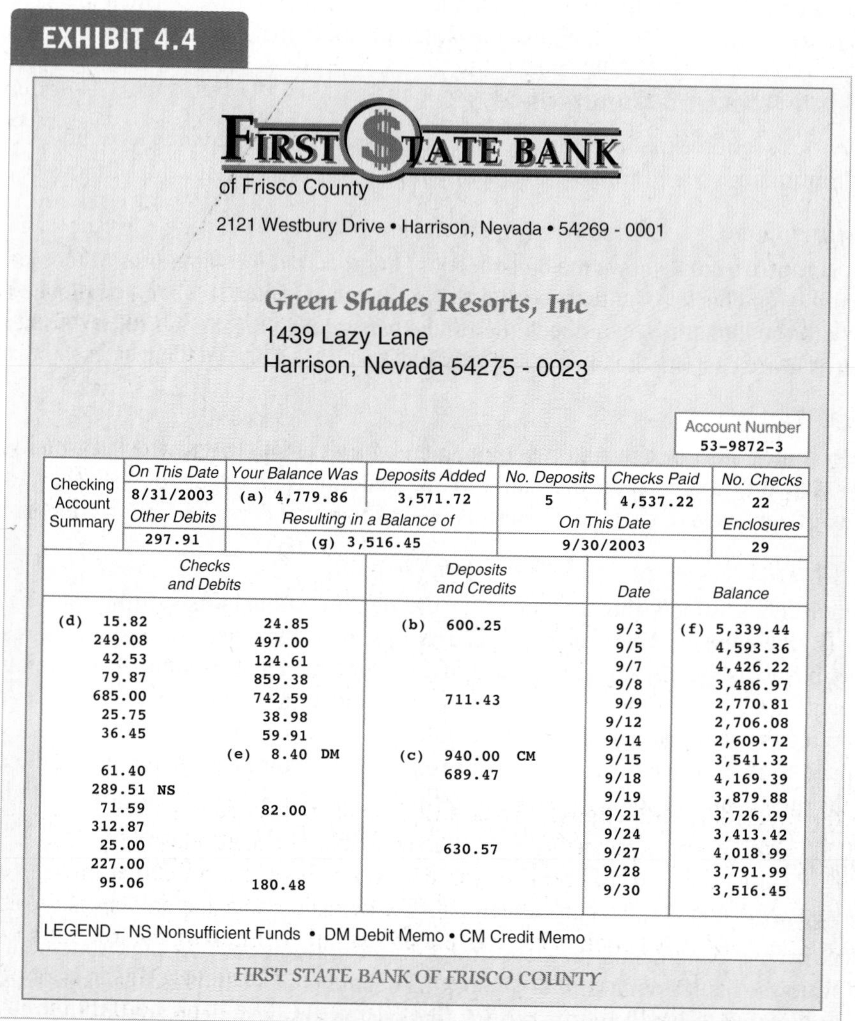

FIRST STATE BANK
of Frisco County
2121 Westbury Drive • Harrison, Nevada • 54269 - 0001

Green Shades Resorts, Inc
1439 Lazy Lane
Harrison, Nevada 54275 - 0023

Account Number
53-9872-3

Checking Account Summary	On This Date	Your Balance Was	Deposits Added	No. Deposits	Checks Paid	No. Checks
	8/31/2003	(a) 4,779.86	3,571.72	5	4,537.22	22
	Other Debits	Resulting in a Balance of		On This Date		Enclosures
	297.91	(g) 3,516.45		9/30/2003		29

Checks and Debits		Deposits and Credits	Date	Balance
(d) 15.82	24.85	(b) 600.25	9/3	(f) 5,339.44
249.08	497.00		9/5	4,593.36
42.53	124.61		9/7	4,426.22
79.87	859.38		9/8	3,486.97
685.00	742.59	711.43	9/9	2,770.81
25.75	38.98		9/12	2,706.08
36.45	59.91		9/14	2,609.72
	(e) 8.40 DM	(c) 940.00 CM	9/15	3,541.32
61.40		689.47	9/18	4,169.39
289.51 NS			9/19	3,879.88
71.59	82.00		9/21	3,726.29
312.87			9/24	3,413.42
25.00		630.57	9/27	4,018.99
227.00			9/28	3,791.99
95.06	180.48		9/30	3,516.45

LEGEND – NS Nonsufficient Funds • DM Debit Memo • CM Credit Memo

FIRST STATE BANK OF FRISCO COUNTY

days, weeks, or even months after the check is written. As a result, the balance on the depositor's books is lower than the balance on the bank's books. Companies prepare a **bank reconciliation** to explain the differences between the cash balance reported on the bank statement and the cash balance recorded in the depositor's accounting records.

Determining True Cash Balance

A bank reconciliation normally begins with the cash balance reported by the bank which is called the **unadjusted bank balance.** The adjustments necessary to determine the amount of cash that the depositor actually owns as of the date of the bank statement are then added to and subtracted from the unadjusted bank balance. The final total is the **true cash balance.** The true cash balance is independently reached a second time by making adjustments to the **unadjusted book balance.** The bank account is reconciled when the true cash balance determined from the perspective of the unadjusted *bank* balance agrees with the true cash balance determined from the perspective of the unadjusted *book* balance. The procedures a company uses to determine the *true cash balance* from the two different perspectives are outlined here.

Adjustments to the Bank Balance

A typical format for determining the true cash balance beginning with the unadjusted bank balance is

Unadjusted bank balance
+ Deposits in transit
− Outstanding checks
= True cash balance

Deposits in transit. Companies frequently leave deposits in the bank's night depository or make them on the day following the receipt of cash. Such deposits are called **deposits in transit.** Since these deposits have been recorded in the depositor's accounting records but have not yet been added to the depositor's account by the bank, they must be added to the unadjusted bank balance.

Outstanding checks. These are disbursements that have been properly recorded as cash deductions on the depositor's books. However, the bank has not deducted the amounts from the depositor's bank account because the checks have not yet been presented by the payee to the bank for payment; that is, the checks have not cleared the bank. **Outstanding checks** must be subtracted from the unadjusted bank balance to determine the true cash balance.

Adjustments to the Book Balance

A typical format for determining the true cash balance beginning with the unadjusted book balance is as follows:

Unadjusted book balance
+ Accounts receivable collections
+ Interest earned
− Bank service charges
− Non-sufficient-funds (NSF) checks
= True cash balance

Accounts receivable collections. To collect cash as quickly as possible, many companies have their customers send payments directly to the bank. The bank adds the collection directly to the depositor's account and notifies the depositor about the collection through a credit memo that is included on the bank statement. The depositor adds the amount of the cash collections to the unadjusted book balance in the process of determining the true cash balance.

Interest earned. Banks pay interest on certain checking accounts. The amount of the interest is added directly to the depositor's bank account. The bank notifies the depositor about the interest through a credit memo that is included on the bank statement. The depositor adds the amount of the interest revenue to the unadjusted book balance in the process of determining the true cash balance.

Service charges. Banks frequently charge depositors fees for services performed. They may also charge a penalty if the depositor fails to maintain a specified minimum cash balance throughout the period. Banks deduct such fees and penalties directly from the depositor's account and advise the depositor of the deduction through a debit memo that is included on the bank statement. The depositor deducts such **service charges** from the unadjusted book balance to determine the true cash balance.

Non-sufficient-funds (NSF) checks. **NSF checks** are checks that a company obtains from its customers and deposits in its checking account. However, when the checks are submitted to the customers' banks for payment, the banks refuse payment because there is insufficient money in the customers' accounts. When such checks are returned, the amounts of the checks are deducted from the company's bank account balance. The company is advised of NSF checks through debit memos that appear on the bank statement. The depositor deducts the amounts of the NSF checks from the unadjusted book balance in the process of determining the true cash balance.

Correction of Errors

In the course of reconciling the bank statement with the cash account, the depositor may discover errors in the bank's records, the depositor's records, or both. If an error is found on the bank statement, an adjustment for it is made to the unadjusted bank balance to determine the true cash balance, and the bank should be notified immediately to correct its records. Errors made by the depositor require adjustments to the book balance to arrive at the true cash balance.

Certified Checks

A **certified check** is guaranteed for payment by a bank. Whereas a regular check is deducted from the customer's account when it is presented for payment, a certified check is deducted from the customer's account when the bank certifies that the check is good. Certified checks, therefore, *have* been deducted by the bank in determining the unadjusted bank balance, whether they have cleared the bank or remain outstanding as of the date of the bank statement. Since certified checks are deducted both from bank and depositor records immediately, they do not cause differences between the depositor and bank balances. As a result, certified checks are not included in a bank reconciliation.

Illustrating a Bank Reconciliation

The following example illustrates preparing the bank reconciliation for Green Shades Resorts, Inc. (GSRI). The bank statement for GSRI is displayed in Exhibit 4.4. Exhibit 4.5 illustrates the completed bank reconciliation. The items on the reconciliation are described below.

Adjustments to the Bank Balance

As of September 30, 2003, the bank statement showed an unadjusted balance of $3,516.45. A review of the bank statement disclosed three adjustments that had to be made to the unadjusted bank balance to determine GSRI's true cash balance.

1. Comparing the deposits on the bank statement with deposits recorded in GSRI's accounting records indicated there was $724.11 of deposits in transit.
2. An examination of the returned checks disclosed that the bank had erroneously deducted a $25 check written by Green Valley Resorts from GSRI's bank account. This

EXHIBIT 4.5

GREEN SHADES RESORTS, INC.
Bank Reconciliation
September 30, 2003

Unadjusted bank balance, September 30, 2003	$3,516.45
Add: Deposits in transit	724.11
Bank error: Check drawn on Green Valley Resorts charged to GSRI	25.00
Less: Outstanding checks	

Check No.	Date	Amount
639	Sept. 18	$ 13.75
646	Sept. 20	29.00
672	Sept. 27	192.50

Total	(235.25)
True cash balance, September 30, 2003	$4,030.31
Unadjusted book balance, September 30, 2003	$3,361.22
Add: Receivable collected by bank	940.00
Error made by accountant (Check no. 633 recorded as $63.45 instead of $36.45)	27.00
Less: Bank service charges	(8.40)
NSF check	(289.51)
True cash balance, September 30, 2003	$4,030.31

amount must be added back to the unadjusted bank balance to determine the true cash balance.

3. The checks returned with the bank statement were sorted and compared to the cash records. Three checks with amounts totaling $235.25 were outstanding.

After these adjustment are made GSRI's true cash balance is determined to be $4,030.31.

Adjustments to the Book Balance

As indicated in Exhibit 4.5, GSRI's unadjusted book balance as of September 30, 2003, was $3,361.22. This balance differs from GSRI's true cash balance because of four unrecorded accounting events:

1. The bank collected a $940 account receivable for GSRI.
2. GSRI's accountant made a $27 recording error.
3. The bank charged GSRI an $8.40 service fee.
4. GSRI had deposited a $289.51 check from a customer who did not have sufficient funds to cover the check.

Two of these four adjustments increase the unadjusted cash balance. The other two decrease the unadjusted cash balance. After the adjustments have been recorded, the cash account reflects the true cash balance of $4,030.31 ($3,361.22 unadjusted cash balance + $940.00 receivable collection + $27.00 recording error − $8.40 service charge − $289.51 NSF check). Since the true balance determined from the perspective of the bank statement agrees with the true balance determined from the perspective of GSRI's books, the bank statement has been successfully reconciled with the accounting records.

Updating GSRI's Accounting Records

Each of the adjustments to the book balance must be recorded in GSRI's financial records. The effects of each adjustment on the financial statements are as follows.

Adjustment 1 ***Recording the $940 receivable collection increases cash and reduces accounts receivable.***

The event is an asset exchange transaction. The effect of the collection on GSRI's financial statements is:

Assets			=	Liab.	+	Equity	Rev.	−	Exp.	=	Net Inc.	Cash Flow
Cash	+	Accts. Rec.										
940	+	(940)	=	NA	+	NA	NA	−	NA	=	NA	940 OA

Adjustment 2 ***Assume the $27 recording error occurred because GSRI's accountant accidentally transposed two numbers when recording check no. 633 for utilities expense.***

The check was written to pay utilities expense of $36.45 but was recorded as a $63.45 disbursement. Since cash payments are overstated by $27.00 ($63.45 − $36.45), this amount must be added back to GSRI's cash balance and deducted from the utilities expense account, which increases net income. The effects on the financial statements are:

Assets	=	Liab.	+	Equity	Rev.	−	Exp.	=	Net Inc.	Cash Flow
Cash	=			Ret. Earn.						
27	=	NA	+	27	NA	−	(27)	=	27	27 OA

Adjustment 3 ***The $8.40 service charge is an expense that reduces assets, stockholders' equity, net income, and cash.***

The effects are:

Assets	=	Liab.	+	Equity	Rev.	−	Exp.	=	Net Inc.	Cash Flow
Cash	=			Ret. Earn.						
(8.40)	=	NA	+	(8.40)	NA	−	8.40	=	(8.40)	(8.40) OA

Adjustment 4 ***The $289.51 NSF check reduces GSRI's cash balance.***

When it originally accepted the customer's check, GSRI increased its cash account. Since there is not enough money in the customer's bank account to pay the check, GSRI didn't actually receive cash so GSRI must reduce its cash account. GSRI will still try to collect the money from the customer. In the meantime, it will show the amount of the NSF check as an account receivable. The adjusting entry to record the NSF check is an asset exchange transaction. Cash decreases and accounts receivable increases. The effect on GSRI's financial statements is:

Assets			=	Liab.	+	Equity	Rev.	−	Exp.	=	Net Inc.	Cash Flow
Cash	+	Accts. Rec.										
(289.51)	+	289.51	=	NA	+	NA	NA	−	NA	=	NA	(289.51) OA

The following information was drawn from Reliance Company's October bank statement. The unadjusted bank balance on October 31 was $2,300. The statement showed that the bank had collected a $200 account receivable for Reliance. The statement also included $20 of bank service charges for October and a $100 check payable to Reliance that was returned NSF. A comparison of the bank statement with company accounting records indicates that there was a $500 deposit in transit and $1,800 of checks outstanding at the end of the month. Based on this information, determine the true cash balance on October 31.

Answer

Since the unadjusted book balance is not given, start with the unadjusted bank balance to determine the true cash balance. The collection of the receivable, the bank service charges, and the NSF check are already recognized in the unadjusted bank balance, so these items are not used to determine the true cash balance. Determine the true cash balance by adding the deposit in transit to and subtracting the outstanding checks from the unadjusted bank balance. The true cash balance is $1,000 ($2,300 unadjusted bank balance + $500 deposit in transit − $1,800 outstanding checks).

Answers to The Curious Accountant

Even though **The Kroger Co.** uses the last-in, first-out *cost flow assumption* for financial reporting purposes, it, like most other companies, actually sells its oldest inventory first. As explained in the text material, GAAP allows a company to report its costs of goods sold in an order that is different from the actual physical flow of its goods. The primary reason some companies use the LIFO assumption is to reduce income taxes. Over the years, Kroger has saved approximately $100 million in taxes by using the LIFO versus the FIFO cost flow assumption when computing its taxable income.

Explain the importance of inventory turnover to a company's profitability.

Assume a grocery store sells two brands of kitchen cleansers, Zjax and Cosmos. Zjax costs $1 and sells for $1.25, resulting in a gross margin of $0.25 ($1.25 − $1.00). Cosmos costs $1.20 and sells for $1.60, resulting in a gross margin of $0.40 ($1.60 − $1.20). Is it more profitable to stock Cosmos than Zjax? Not if the store can sell significantly more cans of Zjax.

Suppose the lower price results in higher customer demand for Zjax. If the store can sell 7,000 units of Zjax but only 3,000 units of Cosmos, Zjax will provide a total gross profit of $1,750 (7,000 units × $0.25 per unit), while Cosmos will provide only $1,200 (3,000 units × $0.40 per unit). How fast inventory sells is as important as the spread between cost and selling price. To determine how fast inventory is selling, financial analysts calculate a ratio that measures the *average number of days it takes to sell inventory.*

Average Number of Days to Sell Inventory

The first step in calculating the average number of days it takes to sell inventory is to compute the **inventory turnover,** as follows:

$$\frac{\text{Cost of goods sold}}{\text{Inventory}}$$

The result of this computation is the number of times the balance in the Inventory account is turned over (sold) each year. To more easily interpret the inventory turnover ratio, analysts often take a further step and determine the **average number of days to sell inventory** (also called the **average days in inventory**), computed as

$$\frac{365}{\text{Inventory turnover}}$$

Is It a Marketing or an Accounting Decision?

As suggested, overall profitability depends upon two elements: gross margin and inventory turnover. The most profitable combination would be to carry high margin inventory that turns over rapidly. To be competitive, however, companies must often concentrate on one or the other of the elements. For example, *discount merchandisers* such as Wal-Mart offer lower prices to stimulate greater sales. In contrast, fashionable stores such as Saks Fifth Avenue charge higher prices to compensate for their slower inventory turnover. These upscale stores justify their higher prices by offering superior style, quality, convenience, service, etc. While decisions about pricing, advertising, service, and so on are often viewed as marketing decisions, effective choices require understanding the interaction between the gross margin percentage and inventory turnover.

Real-World Data

Exhibit 4.6 shows the *average number of days to sell inventory* for eight real-world companies in three different industries. The numbers pertain to fiscal years that ended in late 2002 or early 2003. The data raise several questions.

First, why do Chalone and Mondavi take so long to sell their inventories compared to the other companies? Both of these companies produce and sell wine. Quality wine is aged before it is sold; time spent in inventory is actually a part of the production process. In the wine world, wines produced by Chalone are, on average, considered to be of higher quality than those produced by Mondavi. This higher quality results, in part, from the longer time Chalone's wines spend aging prior to sale.

Why does Starbucks hold its inventory so much longer than the other two fast-food businesses? Starbucks' inventory is mostly coffee. It is more difficult for Starbucks to obtain coffee than it is for McDonald's to obtain beef or Domino's to obtain flour, cheese, and fresh vegetables. Very little coffee is grown in the United States (Hawaii is the only state that produces coffee). Since purchasing coffee requires substantial delivery time, Starbucks cannot order its inventory at the last minute. This problem is further complicated by the fact that coffee harvests are seasonal. Cattle, on the other hand, can be processed into hamburgers year-round. As a result, Starbucks must hold inventory longer than McDonald's or Domino's.

Finally, why do companies in the office supply business take longer to sell inventory than those in the fast-food business? Part of the answer is that food is perishable and stationery is not. But there is also the fact that office supply stores carry many more inventory items than do fast-food restaurants. It is much easier to anticipate customer demand if a company sells only 20 different items than if the company sells 20,000 different items. The problem of anticipating customer demand is solved by holding larger quantities of inventory.

EXHIBIT 4.6

Industry	Company	Average Number of Days to Sell Inventory
Fast Food	Domino's	9
	McDonald's	10
	Starbucks	65
Office Supplies	Office Depot	58
	OfficeMax	92
	Staples	64
Wine	Chalone	642
	Mondavi	548

Effects of Cost Flow on Ratio Analysis

Since the amounts of ending inventory and cost of goods sold are affected by the cost flow method (FIFO, LIFO, etc.) a company uses, the gross margin and inventory turnover ratios are also affected by the cost flow method used. Further, since cost of goods sold affects the amount of net income and retained earnings, many other ratios are also affected by the inventory cost flow method that a company uses. Financial analysts must consider that the ratios they use can be significantly influenced by which accounting methods a company chooses.

A Look Back

This chapter discussed the inventory cost flow methods of first-in, first-out (FIFO), last-in, first-out (LIFO), weighted average, and specific identification. Under *FIFO,* the cost of the items purchased first is reported on the income statement, and the cost of the items purchased last is reported on the balance sheet. Under *LIFO,* the cost of the items purchased last is reported on the income statement, and the cost of the items purchased first is reported on the balance sheet. Under the *weighted-average method,* the average cost of inventory is reported on both the income statement and the balance sheet. Finally, under specific identification the actual cost of the goods is reported on the income statement and the balance sheet.

The policies and procedures used to provide reasonable assurance that the objectives of an enterprise will be accomplished are called *internal controls,* which can be subdivided into two categories: accounting controls and administrative controls. *Accounting controls* are composed of procedures designed to safeguard the assets and ensure that the accounting records contain reliable information. *Administrative controls* are designed to evaluate performance and the degree of compliance with company policies and public laws. While the mechanics of internal control systems vary from company to company, the more prevalent features include the following:

1. *Separation of duties.* Whenever possible, the functions of authorization, recording, and custody should be exercised by different individuals.
2. *Quality of employees.* Employees should be qualified to competently perform the duties that are assigned to them. Companies must establish hiring practices to screen out unqualified candidates. Furthermore, procedures should be established to ensure that employees receive appropriate training to maintain their competence.
3. *Bonded employees.* Employees in sensitive positions should be covered by a fidelity bond that provides insurance to reimburse losses due to illegal actions committed by employees.
4. *Required absences.* Employees should be required to take extended absences from their jobs so that they are not always present to hide unscrupulous or illegal activities.
5. *Procedures manual.* To promote compliance, the procedures for processing transactions should be clearly described in a manual.
6. *Authority and responsibility.* To motivate employees and promote effective control, clear lines of authority and responsibility should be established.
7. *Prenumbered documents.* Prenumbered documents minimize the likelihood of missing or duplicate documents. Prenumbered forms should be used for all important documents such as purchase orders, receiving reports, invoices, and checks.
8. *Physical control.* Locks, fences, security personnel, and other physical devices should be employed to safeguard assets.
9. *Performance evaluations.* Because few people can evaluate their own performance objectively, independent performance evaluations should be performed. Substandard performance will likely persist unless employees are encouraged to take corrective action.

Because cash is such an important business asset and because it is tempting to steal, much of the discussion of internal controls in this chapter focused on cash controls. Special procedures should be employed to control the receipts and payments of cash. One of the most common control policies is to use *checking accounts* for all except petty cash disbursements.

A *bank reconciliation* should be prepared each month to explain differences between the bank statement and a company's internal accounting records. A common reconciliation format determines the true cash balance based on both bank and book records. Items that typically appear on a bank reconciliation include the following:

Unadjusted Bank Balance	XXX	Unadjusted Book Balance	XXX
Add		Add	
Deposits in Transit	XXX	Interest Revenue	XXX
		Collection of Receivables	XXX
Subtract		Subtract	
Outstanding Checks	XXX	Bank Service Charges	XXX
		NSF Checks	XXX
True Cash Balance	XXX	True Cash Balance	XXX

Agreement of the two true cash balances provides evidence that accounting for cash transactions has been accurate.

Finally, this chapter explains how to calculate the time it takes a company to sell its inventory. The measure of how fast inventory sells is called *inventory turnover;* it is computed by dividing cost of goods sold by inventory. The result of this computation is the number of times the balance in the inventory account is turned over each year. The *average number of days to sell inventory* can be determined by dividing the number of days in a year (365) by the inventory turnover ratio.

>> A Look Forward

Accounting for receivables and payables was introduced in Chapter 2 using relatively simple illustrations. For example, we assumed that customers who purchased services on account always paid their bills. In real business practice, some customers do not pay their bills. Among other topics, Chapter 5 examines how companies account for uncollectible accounts receivable.

SELF-STUDY REVIEW PROBLEM 1

Erie Jewelers sells gold earrings. Its beginning inventory of Model 407 gold earrings consisted of 100 pairs of earrings at $50 per pair. Erie purchased two batches of Model 407 earrings during the year. The first batch purchased consisted of 150 pairs at $53 per pair; the second batch consisted of 200 pairs at $56 per pair. During the year, Erie sold 375 pairs of Model 407 earrings.

Required

Determine the amount of product cost Erie would allocate to cost of goods sold and ending inventory assuming that Erie uses (a) FIFO, (b) LIFO, and (c) weighted average.

Solution to Requirements a–c

Goods Available for Sale

Beginning inventory	100	@	$50	=	$ 5,000
First purchase	150	@	53	=	7,950
Second purchase	200	@	56	=	11,200
Goods available for sale	450				$24,150

a. FIFO

Cost of Goods Sold	Pairs		Cost per Pair		Cost of Goods Sold
From beginning inventory	100	@	$50	=	$ 5,000
From first purchase	150	@	53	=	7,950
From second purchase	125	@	56	=	7,000
Total pairs sold	375				$19,950

Ending inventory = Goods available for sale − Cost of goods sold

Ending inventory = $24,150 − $19,950 = $4,200

b. LIFO

Cost of Goods Sold	Pairs		Cost per Pair		Cost of Goods Sold
From second purchase	200	@	$56	=	$11,200
From first purchase	150	@	53	=	7,950
From beginning inventory	25	@	50	=	1,250
Total pairs sold	375				$20,400

Ending inventory = Goods available for sale − Cost of goods sold

Ending inventory = $24,150 − $20,400 = $3,750

c. Weighted average

Goods available for sale ÷ Total pairs = Cost per pair

$24,150 ÷ 450 = $53.6667

Cost of goods sold 375 units @ $53.6667 = $20,125

Ending inventory 75 units @ $53.6667 = $4,025

SELF-STUDY REVIEW PROBLEM 2

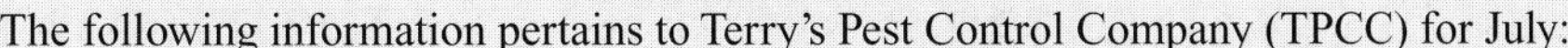

The following information pertains to Terry's Pest Control Company (TPCC) for July:

1. The unadjusted bank balance at July 31 was $870.
2. The bank statement included the following items:
   (a) A $60 credit memo for interest earned by TPCC.
   (b) A $200 NSF check made payable to TPCC.
   (c) A $110 debit memo for bank service charges.
3. The unadjusted book balance at July 31 was $1,400.
4. A comparison of the bank statement with company accounting records disclosed the following:
   (a) A $400 deposit in transit at July 31.
   (b) Outstanding checks totaling $120 at the end of the month.

Required

Prepare a bank reconciliation.

Solution

TERRY'S PEST CONTROL COMPANY Bank Reconciliation July 31	
Unadjusted bank balance	$ 870
Add: Deposits in transit	400
Less: Outstanding checks	(120)
True cash balance	$1,150
Unadjusted book balance	$1,400
Add: Interest revenue	60
Less: NSF check	(200)
Less: Bank service charges	(110)
True cash balance	$1,150

KEY TERMS

accounting controls 133
administrative controls 133
authority manual 134
average number of days to sell inventory (also called the average days in inventory) 144
bank reconciliation 139
bank statement 137
bank statement credit memo 138
bank statement debit memo 138
cash 135
certified check 140
checks 137
consistency 131
deposit ticket 137
deposits in transit 139
fidelity bond 133
first-in, first-out (FIFO) cost flow method 126
full disclosure 131
general authority 134
internal controls 133
inventory cost flow methods 128
inventory turnover 143
last-in, first-out (LIFO) cost flow method 126
non-sufficient-funds (NSF) checks 140
outstanding checks 139
physical flow of goods 126
procedures manual 134
separation of duties 133
service charges 140
signature card 137
specific authorizations 134
specific identification 126
true cash balance 139
unadjusted bank balance 139
unadjusted book balance 139
weighted-average cost flow method 126

QUESTIONS

1. Name and describe the four cost flow methods discussed in this chapter.
2. What are some advantages and disadvantages of the specific identification method of accounting for inventory?
3. What are some advantages and disadvantages of using the FIFO method of inventory valuation?
4. What are some advantages and disadvantages of using the LIFO method of inventory valuation?
5. In an inflationary period, which inventory cost flow method will produce the highest net income? Explain.
6. In an inflationary period, which inventory cost flow method will produce the largest amount of total assets on the balance sheet? Explain.
7. What is the difference between the flow of costs and the physical flow of goods?
8. Does the choice of cost flow method (FIFO, LIFO, or weighted average) affect the statement of cash flows? Explain.
9. Assume that Key Co. purchased 1,000 units of merchandise in its first year of operations for $25 per unit. The company sold 850 units for $40. What is the amount of cost of goods sold using FIFO? LIFO? Weighted average?
10. Assume that Key Co. purchased 1,500 units of merchandise in its second year of operation for $27 per unit. Its beginning inventory was determined in Question 9. Assuming that 1,500 units are sold, what is the amount of cost of goods sold using FIFO? LIFO? Weighted average?

11. Refer to Questions 9 and 10. Which method might be preferable for financial statements? For income tax reporting? Explain.
12. In an inflationary period, which cost flow method, FIFO or LIFO, produces the larger cash flow? Explain.
13. Which inventory cost flow method produces the highest net income in a deflationary period?
14. What are the policies and procedures called that are used to provide reasonable assurance that the objectives of an enterprise will be accomplished?
15. What is the difference between accounting controls and administrative controls?
16. What are several features of an effective internal control system?
17. What is meant by *separation of duties*? Give an illustration.
18. What are the attributes of a high-quality employee?
19. What is a fidelity bond? Explain its purpose.
20. Why is it important that every employee periodically take a leave of absence or vacation?
21. What are the purpose and importance of a procedures manual?
22. What is the difference between specific and general authorizations?
23. Why should documents (checks, invoices, receipts) be prenumbered?
24. What procedures are important in the physical control of assets and accounting records?
25. What is the purpose of independent verification of performance?
26. What items are considered cash?
27. Why is cash more susceptible to theft or embezzlement than other assets?
28. Giving written copies of receipts to customers can help prevent what type of illegal acts?
29. What procedures can help to protect cash receipts?
30. What procedures can help protect cash disbursements?
31. What effect does a debit memo in a bank statement have on the Cash account? What effect does a credit memo in a bank statement have on the Cash account?
32. What information is normally included in a bank statement?
33. Why might a bank statement reflect a balance that is larger than the balance recorded in the depositor's books? What could cause the bank balance to be smaller than the book balance?
34. What is the purpose of a bank reconciliation?
35. What is an outstanding check?
36. What is a deposit in transit?
37. What is a certified check?
38. How is an NSF check accounted for in the accounting records?
39. What information does inventory turnover provide?
40. What is an example of a business that would have a high inventory turnover? A low inventory turnover?

EXERCISES

All Exercises are available with McGraw-Hill's Homework Manager

HM™

Exercise 4-1 *Effect of inventory cost flow assumption on financial statements*

L.O. 1

Required

For each of the following situations, indicate whether FIFO, LIFO, or weighted average applies.

a. In a period of rising prices, net income would be highest.
b. In a period of rising prices, cost of goods sold would be highest.
c. In a period of rising prices, ending inventory would be highest.
d. In a period of falling prices, net income would be highest.
e. In a period of falling prices, the unit cost of goods would be the same for ending inventory and cost of goods sold.

L.O. 1, 2

Exercise 4-2 *Allocating product cost between cost of goods sold and ending inventory*

Mix Co. started the year with no inventory. During the year, it purchased two identical inventory items. The inventory was purchased at different times. The first purchase cost $1,200 and the other, $1,500. One of the items was sold during the year.

Required

Based on this information, how much product cost would be allocated to cost of goods sold and ending inventory on the year-end financial statements, assuming use of

a. FIFO?
b. LIFO?
c. Weighted average?

L.O. 1, 2

Exercise 4-3 *Allocating product cost between cost of goods sold and ending inventory: multiple purchases*

Laird Company sells coffee makers used in business offices. Its beginning inventory of coffee makers was 200 units at $45 per unit. During the year, Laird made two batch purchases of coffee makers. The first was a 300-unit purchase at $50 per unit; the second was a 350-unit purchase at $52 per unit. During the period, Laird sold 800 coffee makers.

Required

Determine the amount of product costs that would be allocated to cost of goods sold and ending inventory, assuming that Laird uses

a. FIFO.
b. LIFO.
c. Weighted average.

L.O. 1, 2

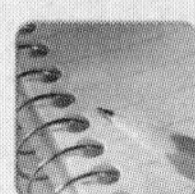

Exercise 4-4 *Effect of inventory cost flow (FIFO, LIFO, and weighted average) on gross margin*

The following information pertains to Porter Company for 2005.

Beginning inventory	70 units @ $13
Units purchased	280 units @ $18

Ending inventory consisted of 30 units. Porter sold 320 units at $30 each. All purchases and sales were made with cash.

Required

a. Compute the gross margin for Porter Company using the following cost flow assumptions: (1) FIFO, (2) LIFO, and (3) weighted average.
b. What is the dollar amount of difference in net income between using FIFO versus LIFO? (Ignore income tax considerations.)
c. Determine the cash flow from operating activities, using each of the three cost flow assumptions listed in Requirement *a*. Ignore the effect of income taxes. Explain why these cash flows have no differences.

L.O. 1, 2

Exercise 4-5 *Effect of inventory cost flow on ending inventory balance and gross margin*

Bristol Sales had the following transactions for DVDs in 2004, its first year of operations.

Jan. 20	Purchased 75 units @ $17	=	$1,275
Apr. 21	Purchased 450 units @ $19	=	8,550
July 25	Purchased 200 units @ $23	=	4,600
Sept. 19	Purchased 100 units @ $29	=	2,900

During the year, Bristol Sales sold 775 DVDs for $60 each.

Required

a. Compute the amount of ending inventory Bristol would report on the balance sheet, assuming the following cost flow assumptions: (1) FIFO, (2) LIFO, and (3) weighted average.

b. Compute the difference in gross margin between the FIFO and LIFO cost flow assumptions.

Exercise 4-6 *Income tax effect of shifting from FIFO to LIFO* — L.O. 1, 2

The following information pertains to the inventory of the La Bonne Company:

Jan. 1	Beginning Inventory	500 units @ $20
Apr. 1	Purchased	2,500 units @ $25
Oct. 1	Purchased	800 units @ $26

During the year, La Bonne sold 3,400 units of inventory at $40 per unit and incurred $17,000 of operating expenses. La Bonne currently uses the FIFO method but is considering a change to LIFO. All transactions are cash transactions. Assume a 30 percent income tax rate. La Bonne started the period with cash of $42,000, inventory of $10,000, common stock of $20,000 and retained earnings of $32,000.

Required

a. Prepare income statements using FIFO and LIFO.

b. Determine the amount of income taxes La Bonne would save if it changed cost flow methods.

c. Determine the cash flow from operating activities under FIFO and LIFO.

d. Explain why cash flow from operating activities is lower under FIFO when that cost flow method produced the higher gross margin.

Exercise 4-7 *Effect of FIFO versus LIFO on income tax expense* — L.O. 1, 2

Holly Hocks Inc. had sales of $225,000 for 2006, its first year of operation. On April 2, the company purchased 200 units of inventory at $190 per unit. On September 1, an additional 150 units were purchased for $210 per unit. The company had 50 units on hand at the end of the year. The company's income tax rate is 40 percent. All transactions are cash transactions.

Required

a. The preceding paragraph describes five accounting events: (1) a sales transaction, (2) the first purchase of inventory, (3) a second purchase of inventory, (4) the recognition of cost of goods sold expense, and (5) the payment of income tax expense. Record the amounts of each event in horizontal statements models like the following ones, assuming first a FIFO and then a LIFO cost flow.

Effect of Events on Financial Statements

Panel 1: FIFO Cost Flow

Event No.	Balance Sheet							Income Statement					Statement of Cash Flows
	Cash	+	Inventory	=	Com. Stk.	+	Ret. Earn.	Rev.	−	Exp.	=	Net Inc.	

Panel 2: LIFO Cost Flow

Event No.	Balance Sheet							Income Statement					Statement of Cash Flows
	Cash	+	Inventory	=	Com. Stk.	+	Ret. Earn.	Rev.	−	Exp.	=	Net Inc.	

b. Compute net income using FIFO.

c. Compute net income using LIFO.

d. Explain the difference, if any, in the amount of income tax expense incurred using the two cost flow assumptions.

e. How does the use of the FIFO versus the LIFO cost flow assumptions affect the statement of cash flows?

L.O. 3

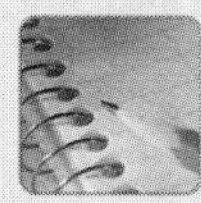

Exercise 4-8 *Features of a strong internal control system*

Required

List and describe nine features of a strong internal control system discussed in this chapter.

L.O. 3, 4

Exercise 4-9 *Internal controls for small businesses*

Required

Assume you are the owner of a small business that has only two employees.

a. Which of the internal control procedures are most important to you?

b. How can you overcome the limited opportunity to use the separation-of-duties control procedure?

L.O. 4

Exercise 4-10 *Internal control for cash*

Required

a. Why are special controls needed for cash?

b. What is included in the definition of *cash*?

L.O. 3

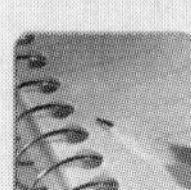

Exercise 4-11 *Internal control procedures to prevent embezzlement*

Bell Gates was in charge of the returns department at The Software Company. She was responsible for evaluating returned merchandise. She sent merchandise that was reusable back to the warehouse, where it was restocked in inventory. Gates was also responsible for taking the merchandise that she determined to be defective to the city dump for disposal. She had agreed to buy a friend a tax planning program at a discount through her contacts at work. That is when the idea came to her. She could simply classify one of the reusable returns as defective and bring it home instead of taking it to the dump. She did so and made a quick $150. She was happy, and her friend was ecstatic; he was able to buy a $400 software package for only $150. He told his friends about the deal, and soon Gates had a regular set of customers. She was caught when a retail store owner complained to the marketing manager that his pricing strategy was being undercut by The Software Company's direct sales to the public. The marketing manager was suspicious because The Software Company had no direct marketing program. When the outside sales were ultimately traced back to Gates, the company discovered that it had lost over $10,000 in sales revenue because of her criminal activity.

Required

Identify an internal control procedure that could have prevented the company's losses. Explain how the procedure would have stopped the embezzlement.

L.O. 3

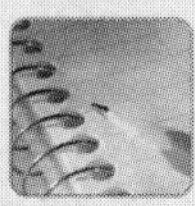

Exercise 4-12 *Internal control procedures to prevent deception*

Emergency Care Medical Centers (ECMC) hired a new physician, Ken Major, who was an immediate success. Everyone loved his bedside manner; he could charm the most cantankerous patient. Indeed, he was a master salesman as well as an expert physician. Unfortunately, Major misdiagnosed a case that resulted in serious consequences to the patient. The patient filed suit against ECMC. In preparation for the defense, ECMC's attorneys discovered that Major was indeed an exceptional salesman. He had worked for several years as district marketing manager for a pharmaceutical company. In fact, he was not a physician at all! He had changed professions without going to medical school. He had lied on his application form. His knowledge of medical terminology had enabled him to fool everyone. ECMC was found negligent and lost a $3 million lawsuit.

Required

Identify the relevant internal control procedures that could have prevented the company's losses. Explain how these procedures would have prevented Major's deception.

Exercise 4-13 *Treatment of NSF check*

L.O. 5

The bank statement of Zone Supplies included a $200 NSF check that one of Zone's customers had written to pay for services that were provided by Zone.

Required

a. Show the effects of recognizing the NSF check on the financial statements by recording the appropriate amounts in a horizontal statements model like the following one.

Assets		= Liab.	+ Equity	Rev.	− Exp.	= Net Inc.	Cash Flow
Cash +	Accts. Rec.						

b. Is the recognition of the NSF check on Zone's books an asset source, use, or exchange transaction?

c. Suppose the customer redeems the check by giving Zone $225 cash in exchange for the bad check. The additional $25 paid a service fee charged by Zone. Show the effects on the financial statements in the horizontal statements model in Requirement *a.*

d. Is the receipt of cash referred to in Requirement *c* an asset source, use, or exchange transaction?

Exercise 4-14 *Adjustments to the balance per books*

L.O. 5

Required

Identify which of the following items are added to or subtracted from the unadjusted *book balance* to arrive at the true cash balance. Distinguish the additions from the subtractions by placing a + beside the items that are added to the unadjusted book balance and a − beside those that are subtracted from it. The first item is recorded as an example.

Reconciling Items	Book Balance Adjusted?	Added or Subtracted?
Outstanding checks	No	N/A
Interest revenue earned on the account		
Deposits in transit		
Service charge		
Automatic debit for utility bill		
Charge for checks		
NSF check from customer		
ATM fee		

Exercise 4-15 *Adjustments to the balance per bank*

L.O. 5

Required

Identify which of the following items are added to or subtracted from the unadjusted *bank balance* to arrive at the true cash balance. Distinguish the additions from the subtractions by placing a + beside the items that are added to the unadjusted bank balance and a − beside those that are subtracted from it. The first item is recorded as an example.

Reconciling Items	Bank Balance Adjusted?	Added or Subtracted?
Bank service charge	No	N/A
Outstanding checks		
Deposits in transit		
Debit memo		
Credit memo		
ATM fee		
Petty cash voucher		
NSF check from customer		
Interest revenue		

L.O. 5

Exercise 4-16 *Adjusting the cash account*

As of May 31, 2004, the bank statement showed an ending balance of $17,250. The unadjusted Cash account balance was $16,450. The following information is available:

1. Deposit in transit, $2,630.
2. Credit memo in bank statement for interest earned in May, $12.
3. Outstanding check, $3,428.
4. Debit memo for service charge, $10.

Required
Determine the true cash balance by preparing a bank reconciliation as of May 31, 2004, using the preceding information.

L.O. 5

Exercise 4-17 *Determining the true cash balance, starting with the unadjusted bank balance*

The following information is available for Stone Company for the month of August:

1. The unadjusted balance per the bank statement on August 31 was $56,300.
2. Deposits in transit on August 31 were $2,600.
3. A debit memo was included with the bank statement for a service charge of $20.
4. A $4,925 check written in August had not been paid by the bank.
5. The bank statement included a $1,000 credit memo for the collection of a note. The principal of the note was $950, and the interest collected was $50.

Required
Determine the true cash balance as of August 31. (*Hint:* It is not necessary to use all of the preceding items to determine the true balance.)

L.O. 5

Exercise 4-18 *Determining the true cash balance, starting with the unadjusted book balance*

Lee Company had an unadjusted cash balance of $7,850 as of April 30. The company's bank statement, also dated April 30, included a $75 NSF check written by one of Lee's customers. There were $920 in outstanding checks and $250 in deposits in transit as of April 30. According to the bank statement, service charges were $50, and the bank collected a $900 note receivable for Lee. The bank statement also showed $12 of interest revenue earned by Lee.

Required
Determine the true cash balance as of April 30. (*Hint:* It is not necessary to use all of the preceding items to determine the true balance.)

Exercise 4-19 *Performing ratio analysis using real-world data*

L.O. 6

Safeway, Inc. operated 1,802 stores as of January 1, 2005. The following data were taken from the company's annual report. All dollar amounts are in thousands.

	Fiscal Years Ending	
	January 1, 2005	January 3, 2004
Revenue	$35,822,900	$35,727,200
Cost of Goods Sold	25,227,600	25,003,000
Net Income	560,200	(169,800)
Merchandise Inventory	2,740,700	2,642,200

Required

a. Compute Safeway's inventory turnover ratio for 2005 and 2004.

b. Compute Safeway's average days to sell inventory for 2005 and 2004.

c. Based on your computations in Requirements *a* and *b*, did Safeway's inventory management get better or worse from 2004 to 2005?

PROBLEMS

All Problems are available with McGraw-Hill's Homework Manager

Problem 4-20 *Effect of different inventory cost flow methods on financial statements*

L.O. 1, 2

mhhe.com/edmonds2007

CHECK FIGURES

a. Cost of Goods Sold–FIFO: $27,540

b. Net Income–LIFO: $6,780

The accounting records of Clear Photography, Inc., reflected the following balances as of January 1, 2007:

Cash	$18,000
Beginning Inventory	13,500 (150 units @ $90)
Common Stock	15,000
Retained Earnings	16,500

The following five transactions occurred in 2007:

1. First purchase (cash) 120 units @ $92
2. Second purchase (cash) 200 units @ $100
3. Sales (all cash) 300 units @ $185
4. Paid $15,000 cash for operating expenses.
5. Paid cash for income tax at the rate of 40 percent of income before taxes.

Required

a. Compute the cost of goods sold and ending inventory, assuming (1) FIFO cost flow, (2) LIFO cost flow, and (3) weighted-average cost flow. Compute income tax expense for each method.

b. Use a vertical model to show the 2007 income statement and statement of cash flows under FIFO, LIFO, and weighted average.

Problem 4-21 *Using internal control to restrict illegal or unethical behavior*

L.O. 3, 4

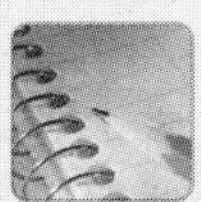

Required

For each of the following fraudulent acts, describe one or more internal control procedures that could have prevented (or helped prevent) the problems.

a. Everyone in the office has noticed what a dedicated employee Jennifer Reidel is. She never misses work, not even for a vacation. Reidel is in charge of the petty cash fund. She transfers funds from the company's bank account to the petty cash account on an as-needed basis. During a surprise audit, the petty cash fund was found to contain fictitious receipts. Over a three-year period, Reidel had used more than $4,000 of petty cash to pay for personal expenses.

b. Bill Bruton was hired as the vice president of the manufacturing division of a corporation. His impressive resume listed a master's degree in business administration from a large state university and numerous collegiate awards and activities, when in fact Bruton had only a high school diploma. In a short time, the company was in poor financial condition because of his inadequate knowledge and bad decisions.

c. Havolene Manufacturing has good internal control over its manufacturing materials inventory. However, office supplies are kept on open shelves in the employee break room. The office supervisor has noticed that he is having to order paper, tape, staplers, and pens with increasing frequency.

L.O. 5

Problem 4-22 *Preparing a bank reconciliation*

CHECK FIGURE
True Cash Balance, October 31, 2006: $9,350

Jim Guidry owns a construction business, Guidry Supply Co. The following cash information is available for the month of October 2006.

As of October 31, the bank statement shows a balance of $12,300. The October 31 unadjusted balance in the Cash account of Guidry Supply Co. is $11,200. A review of the bank statement revealed the following information:

1. A deposit of $1,500 on October 31, 2006, does not appear on the October 31 bank statement.
2. A debit memo for $50 was included in the bank statement for the purchase of a new supply of checks.
3. When checks written during the month were compared with those paid by the bank, three checks amounting to $4,450 were found to be outstanding.
4. It was discovered that a check to pay for repairs was correctly written and paid by the bank for $3,100 but was recorded on the books as $1,300.

Required

Prepare a bank reconciliation at the end of October showing the true cash balance.

L.O. 5

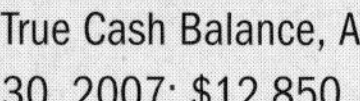

mhhe.com/edmonds2007

Problem 4-23 *Missing information in a bank reconciliation*

The following data apply to Smoot Sports Inc. for April 2007:

1. Balance per the bank on April 30, $12,250.
2. Deposits in transit not recorded by the bank, $2,100.
3. Bank error; check written by Smoot on his personal checking account was drawn on Smoot Sports Inc.'s account, $800.
4. The following checks written and recorded by Smoot Sports Inc. were not included in the bank statement:

CHECK FIGURE
True Cash Balance, April 30, 2007: $12,850

1901	$ 220
1920	580
1921	1,500

5. Credit memo for note collected by the bank, $700.
6. Service charge for collection of note, $10.
7. The bookkeeper recorded a check written for $560 to pay for April's office supplies as $650 in the cash disbursements journal.
8. Bank service charge in addition to the note collection fee, $30.
9. NSF checks returned by the bank, $150.

Required

Determine the amount of the unadjusted cash balance per Smoot Sports Inc.'s books.

L.O. 5

mhhe.com/edmonds2007

Problem 4-24 *Adjustments to the cash account based on the bank reconciliation*

CHECK FIGURE
h. Theft Loss: $800

The following items apply to National Imports' bank reconciliation. Indicate whether each item would be added to, subtracted from, or not included when converting the bank balance to the true cash balance.

a. The bank collected $5,000 of National Imports' accounts receivable. National Imports had instructed its customers to send their payments directly to the bank.

b. The bank mistakenly gave Imports Inc. credit for a $500 deposit made by National Imports.

c. Deposits in transit were $5,600.

d. National Imports' bank statement contained a $525 NSF check. National Imports had received the check from a customer and had included it in one of its bank deposits.

e. The bank statement indicated that National Imports earned $80 of interest revenue.

f. National Imports' accountant mistakenly recorded a $230 check that was written to purchase supplies as $320.

g. Bank service charges for the month were $50.

h. The bank reconciliation disclosed that $800 had been stolen from National Imports' business.

i. Outstanding checks amounted to $1,700.

Problem 4-25 *Bank reconciliation and adjustments to the cash account*

L.O. 5

CHECK FIGURE
a. True Cash Balance, July 31, 2005: $16,234

The following information is available for Mountain Top Hotel for July 2005:

Bank Statement

STATE BANK

Bolta Vista, NV 10001

Mountain Top Hotel
10 Main Street
Bolta Vista, NV 10001

Account number
12-4567
July 31, 2005

Beginning balance 6/30/2005	$ 9,031
Total deposits and other credits	29,800
Total checks and other debits	23,902
Ending balance 7/31/2005	14,929

Checks and Debits		Deposits and Credits		
Check No.	Amount	Date		Amount
2350	$3,761	July	1	$1,102
2351	1,643	July	10	6,498
2352	8,000	July	15	4,929
2354	2,894	July	21	6,174
2355	1,401	July	26	5,963
2357	6,187	July	30	2,084
DM	16	CM		3,050

The following is a list of checks and deposits recorded on the books of the Mountain Top Hotel for July 2005:

Date		Check No.	Amount of Check	Date		Amount of Deposit
July	2	2351	$1,643	July	8	$6,498
July	4	2352	8,000	July	14	4,929
July	10	2353	1,500	July	21	6,174
July	10	2354	2,894	July	26	5,963
July	15	2355	1,401	July	29	2,084
July	20	2356	745	July	30	3,550
July	22	2357	6,187			

Other Information

1. Check no. 2350 was outstanding from June.
2. The credit memo was for collection of notes receivable.
3. All checks were paid at the correct amount.
4. The debit memo was for printed checks.
5. The June 30 bank reconciliation showed a deposit in transit of $1,102.
6. The unadjusted Cash account balance at July 31 was $13,200.

Required

a. Prepare the bank reconciliation for Mountain Top Hotel at the end of July.

b. Identify the adjustments that would be necessary to convert the book balance of the Cash account to the true balance of cash.

L.O. 3, 4, 5

CHECK FIGURE
a. True Cash Balance, May 31, 2006: $22,550

Problem 4-26 *Bank reconciliation and internal control*

Following is a bank reconciliation for Holt's Sandwich Shop for May 31, 2006:

	Cash Account	Bank Statement
Balance as of 5/31/06	$25,000	$22,000
Deposit in transit		4,250
Outstanding checks		(465)
Note collected by bank	1,815	
Bank service charge	(30)	
Automatic payment on loan	(1,000)	
Adjusted cash balance as of 5/31/06	$25,785	$25,785

Because of limited funds, Holt's employed only one accountant who was responsible for receiving cash, recording receipts and disbursements, preparing deposits, and preparing the bank reconciliation. The accountant left the company on June 8, 2006, after preparing the preceding statement. His replacement compared the checks returned with the bank statement to the cash disbursements journal and found the total of outstanding checks to be $3,700.

Required

a. Prepare a corrected bank reconciliation.

b. What is the total amount of cash missing, and how was the difference between the "true cash" per the bank and the "true cash" per the books hidden on the reconciliation prepared by the former employee?

c. What could Holt's do to avoid cash theft in the future?

L.O. 6

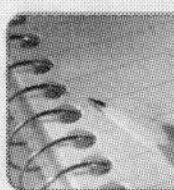

Problem 4-27 *Performing ratio analysis using real-world data*

Ruby Tuesday's, Inc., operated 484 casual dining restaurants across the United States as of June 1, 2004. **Zale Corporation** claims to be "North America's largest specialty retailer of fine jewelry." The following data were taken from these companies' 2004 annual reports. All dollar amounts are in thousands.

	Ruby Tuesday's June 1, 2004	Zale Corporation July 31, 2004
Sales	$1,023,342*	$2,304,440
Cost of Goods Sold	263,033	1,122,946
Net Income	110,009	106,473
Merchandise Inventory	8,068	826,824

*This excludes franchise revenue.

Required

a. Before performing any calculations, speculate as to which company will take the longest to sell its inventory. Explain the rationale for your decision.

b. Calculate the inventory turnover ratios for Ruby Tuesday's and Zale Corporation.

c. Calculate the average days to sell inventory for Ruby Tuesday's and Zale Corporation.

d. Do the calculations from Requirements *b* and *c* confirm your speculations in Requirement *a*?

ANALYZE, THINK, COMMUNICATE

ATC 4-1 Business Applications Case *Understanding real-world annual reports*

Required

Use the **Topps Company**'s annual report in Appendix B to answer the following questions.

The Topps Company, Inc.

a. What was Topps' inventory turnover ratio and average days to sell inventory for the years ended March 1, 2003, and March 2, 2002?

b. Is the company's management of inventory getting better or worse?

c. What cost flow method(s) did Topps use to account for inventory?

ATC 4-2 Group Assignment *Inventory cost flow*

The accounting records of Blue Bird Co. showed the following balances at January 1, 2008:

Cash	$30,000
Beginning inventory (100 units @ $50, 70 units @ $55)	8,850
Common stock	20,000
Retained earnings	18,850

Transactions for 2008 were as follows:

Purchased 100 units @ $54 per unit.
Purchased 250 units @ $58 per unit.
Sold 220 units @ $80 per unit.
Sold 200 units @ $90 per unit.
Paid operating expenses of $3,200.
Paid income tax expense. The income tax rate is 30%.

Required

a. Organize the class into three sections, and divide each section into groups of three to five students. Assign each section one of the cost flow methods, FIFO, LIFO, or weighted average. The company uses the perpetual inventory system.

Group Tasks

Determine the amount of ending inventory, cost of goods sold, gross margin, and net income after income tax for the cost flow method assigned to your section. Also prepare an income statement using that cost flow assumption.

Class Discussion

b. Have a representative of each section put its income statement on the board. Discuss the effect that each cost flow method has on assets (ending inventory), net income, and cash flows. Which method is preferred for tax reporting? For financial reporting? What restrictions are placed on the use of LIFO for tax reporting?

ATC 4-3 Real-World Case *Analyzing inventory management issues at Campbell's Soup*

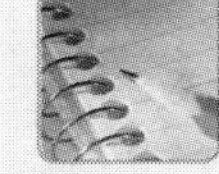

After more than a decade of generally positive economic news, the United States economy began to slow in 2000. At that time, the **Campbell Soup Company** (Campbell's), like many other companies, saw its earnings decline. Campbell's net earnings fell from $714 million in its 2000 fiscal year to $525 million in 2002, but then profits began to improve. By 2004 its earnings were back up to $647 million.

The data below, for Campbell's fiscal years ending on August 3, 2003, and August 1, 2004, pertain to analyzing the company's management of inventory. All dollar amounts are in millions.

	2004	2003
Sales	$7,109	$6,678
Cost of goods sold	4,187	3,805
Ending inventory	795	709
Income before taxes	947	924
Net earnings	647	595*
Income tax rate	32%	32%

*Includes a special charge for a change in accounting principle of ($31). This expense does not affect the requirements below.

Required

a. Compute Campbell's gross margin percentage for 2004 and 2003.
b. Compute Campbell's average days to sell inventory for 2004 and 2003.
c. Did Campbell's earnings improve from 2003 to 2004 due to either better gross margins or better inventory management (turnover)? Explain.
d. How much higher or lower would Campbell's *earnings before taxes* have been in 2004 if its gross margin percentage had been the same as it was in 2003? Show all supporting computations.
e. How much higher or lower would Campbell's *net earnings* have been in 2004 if its gross margin percentage had been the same as it was in 2003? Show all supporting computations.

ATC 4-4 Business Applications Case *Using the average days to sell inventory ratio to make a lending decision*

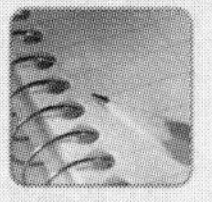

Edna Valley Fruits has applied for a loan and has agreed to use its inventory to collateralize the loan. The company currently has an inventory balance of $206,000. The cost of goods sold for the past year was $5,781,000. The average shelf life for the fruit that Edna Valley sells is 10 days, after which time it begins to spoil and must be sold at drastically reduced prices to dispose of it rapidly. The company maintained steady sales over the past three years and expects to continue at current levels for the foreseeable future.

Required

Based on your knowledge of inventory turnover, write a memo that describes the quality of the inventory as collateral for the loan.

ATC 4-5 Business Applications Case *Using ratios to make comparisons*

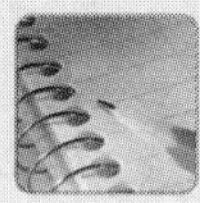

The following accounting information pertains to Java Joint and Coffee Corner at the end of 2008. The only difference between the two companies is that Java uses FIFO while Coffee uses LIFO.

	Java Joint	Coffee Corner
Cash	$ 60,000	$ 60,000
Accounts Receivable	240,000	240,000
Merchandise Inventory	180,000	140,000
Accounts Payable	160,000	160,000
Cost of Goods Sold	900,000	940,000
Building	300,000	300,000
Sales	1,500,000	1,500,000

Required

a. Compute the gross margin percentage for each company, and identify the company that *appears* to be charging the higher prices in relation to its costs.
b. For each company, compute the inventory turnover ratio and the average number of days to sell inventory. Identify the company that *appears* to be incurring the higher inventory financing cost.
c. Explain why the company with the lower gross margin percentage has the higher inventory turnover ratio.

ATC 4-6 Writing Assignment *Internal control procedures*

Alison Marsh was a trusted employee of Small City State Bank. She was involved in everything. She worked as a teller, she accounted for the cash at the other teller windows, and she recorded many of the transactions in the accounting records. She was so loyal that she never would take a day off, even when she was really too sick to work. She routinely worked late to see that all the day's work was posted into the accounting records. She would never take even a day's vacation because they might need her at the bank. Tick and Tack, CPAs, were hired to perform an audit, the first complete audit that had been done in several years. Marsh seemed somewhat upset by the upcoming audit. She said that everything had been properly accounted for and that the audit was a needless expense. When Tick and Tack examined some of the bank's internal control procedures, it discovered problems. In fact, as the audit progressed, it became apparent that a large amount of cash was missing. Numerous adjustments had been made to customer accounts with credit memorandums, and many of the transactions had been posted several days late. In addition, there were numerous cash payments for "office expenses." When the audit was complete, it was determined that more than $200,000 of funds was missing or improperly accounted for. All fingers pointed to Marsh. The bank's president, who was a close friend of Marsh, was bewildered. How could this type of thing happen at this bank?

Required

Prepare a written memo to the bank president, outlining the procedures that should be followed to prevent this type of problem in the future.

ATC 4-7 Ethical Dilemma *I need just a little extra money*

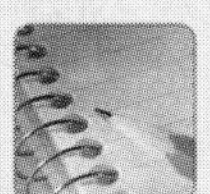

Terry Bailey, an accountant, has worked for the past eight years as a payroll clerk for Fairwell Furniture, a small furniture manufacturing firm in the northeast. Terry recently experienced unfortunate circumstances. Her teenage son required minor surgery and the medical bills not covered by Terry's insurance have financially strained Terry's family.

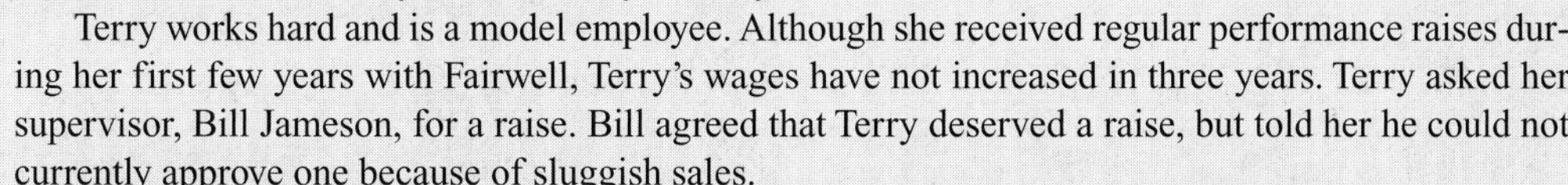

Terry works hard and is a model employee. Although she received regular performance raises during her first few years with Fairwell, Terry's wages have not increased in three years. Terry asked her supervisor, Bill Jameson, for a raise. Bill agreed that Terry deserved a raise, but told her he could not currently approve one because of sluggish sales.

A disappointed Terry returned to her duties while the financial pressures in her life continued. Two weeks later, Larry Tyler, an assembly worker at Fairwell, quit over a dispute with management. Terry conceived an idea. Terry's duties included not only processing employee terminations but also approving time cards before paychecks were issued and then distributing the paychecks to firm personnel. Terry decided to delay processing Mr. Tyler's termination, to forge timecards for Larry Tyler for the next few weeks, and to cash the checks herself. Since she distributed paychecks, no one would find out, and Terry reasoned that she was really entitled to the extra money anyway. In fact, no one did discover her maneuver and Terry stopped the practice after three weeks.

Required

a. Does Terry's scheme affect Fairwell's balance sheet? Explain your answer.

b. Review the AICPA's Articles of Professional Conduct (see Chapter 1) and comment on any of the standards that have been violated.

c. Donald Cressey (see Chapter 1) identified three common features of unethical and criminal conduct. Name these features and explain how they pertain to this case.

ATC 4-8 Research Assignment *Analyzing inventory at Gap Company*

Using either **Gap's** most current Form 10-K or the company's annual report, answer the questions below. To obtain the Form 10-K use either the EDGAR system following the instructions in Appendix A, or the company's website. The company's annual report is available on its website.

Required

a. What was the average amount of inventory per store? Use *all* stores operated by The Gap, Inc., not just those called *The Gap.* (*Hint:* The answer to this question must be computed. The number of stores in operation at the end of the most recent year can be found in the MD&A of the 10-K.)

b. How many *new* stores did Gap open during the year?

c. Using the quarterly financial information in the 10-K, complete the following chart.

Quarter	Sales during Each Quarter
1	$
2	
3	
4	

d. Referring to the chart in Requirement *c*, explain why Gap's sales vary so widely throughout its fiscal year. Do you believe that Gap's inventory level varies throughout the year in relation to sales?

CHAPTER 5

Accounting for Receivables

LEARNING OBJECTIVES

After you have mastered the material in this chapter you will be able to:

1. **Explain the importance of offering credit terms to customers.**
2. **Explain how the allowance method of accounting for uncollectible accounts affects financial statements.**
3. **Show how the direct write-off method of accounting for uncollectible accounts affects financial statements.**
4. **Explain how accounting for notes receivable and accrued interest affects financial statements.**
5. **Explain how accounting for credit card sales affects financial statements.**
6. **Explain the effects of the cost of financing credit sales.**

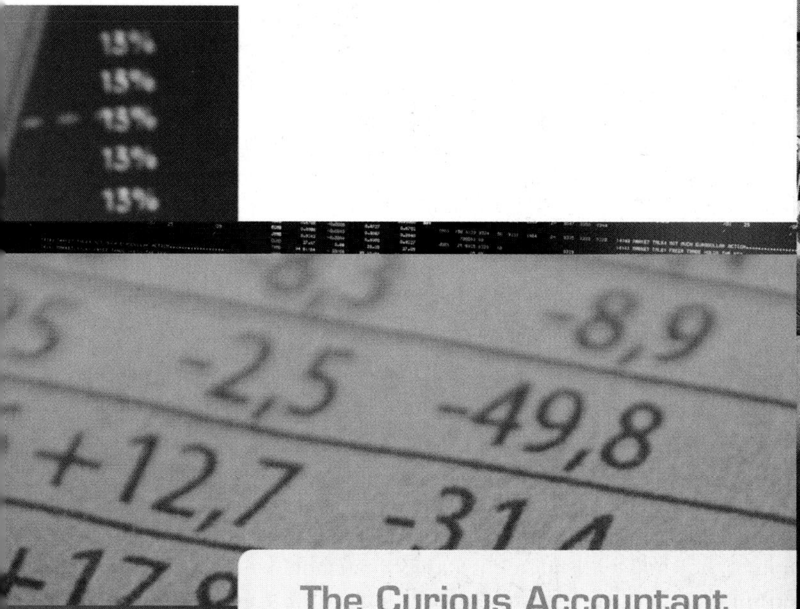

Chapter 5

The Curious Accountant

Suppose **Costco** orders goods from **Procter & Gamble.** Assume that Costco offers to pay for the goods on the day it receives them from Procter & Gamble (a cash purchase) or 30 days later (a purchase on account).

Assume that Procter & Gamble is absolutely sure Costco will pay its account when due. Do you think Procter & Gamble should care whether Costco pays for the goods upon delivery or 30 days later? Why? (Answers on page 165.)

CHAPTER OPENING

LO 1 Explain the importance of offering credit terms to customers.

Many people buy on impulse. If they must wait, the desire to buy wanes. To take advantage of impulse buyers, most merchandising companies offer customers credit because it increases their sales. A disadvantage of this strategy occurs when some customers are unable or unwilling to pay their bills. Nevertheless, the widespread availability of credit suggests that the advantages of increased sales outweigh the disadvantages of some uncollectible accounts.

When a company allows a customer to "buy now and pay later," the company's right to collect cash in the future is called an **account receivable.** *Typically, amounts due from individual accounts receivable are relatively small and the collection period is short. Most accounts receivable are collected within 30 days. When a longer credit term is needed or when a receivable is large, the seller usually requires the buyer to issue a note reflecting a credit agreement between the parties. The note specifies the maturity date, interest rate, and other credit terms. Receivables evidenced by such notes are called* **notes receivable.** *Accounts and notes receivable are reported as assets on the balance sheet.* ■

Allowance Method of Accounting for Uncollectible Accounts

LO 2

Explain how the allowance method of accounting for uncollectible accounts affects financial statements.

Most companies do not expect to collect the full amount (face value) of their accounts receivable. Even carefully screened credit customers sometimes don't pay their bills. The **net realizable value** of accounts receivable represents the amount of receivables a company estimates it will actually collect. The net realizable value is the *face value* less an *allowance for doubtful accounts.*

The **allowance for doubtful accounts** represents a company's estimate of the amount of uncollectible receivables. To illustrate, assume a company with total accounts receivable of $50,000 estimates that $2,000 of its receivables will not be collected. The net realizable value of receivables is computed as follows:

Accounts receivable	$50,000
Less: Allowance for doubtful accounts	(2,000)
Net realizable value of receivables	$48,000

A company cannot know today, of course, the exact amount of the receivables it will not be able to collect in the future. The *allowance for doubtful accounts* and the *net realizable value* are necessarily *estimated amounts.* The net realizable value, however, more closely measures the cash that will ultimately be collected than does the face value. To avoid overstating assets, companies usually report receivables on their balance sheets at the net realizable value.

Reporting accounts receivable in the financial statements at net realizable value is commonly called the **allowance method of accounting for uncollectible accounts.** The following section illustrates using the allowance method for Allen's Tutoring Services (ATS).

Accounting Events Affecting the 2006 Period

Explain how the allowance method of accounting for uncollectible accounts affects financial statements.

Allen's Tutoring Services is a small company that provides tutoring services to college students. Allen's started operations on January 1, 2006. During 2006, Allen's experienced three types of accounting events. These events are discussed below.

Event 1 Revenue Recognition

Allen's Tutoring Services recognized $14,000 of service revenue earned on account during 2006.

This is an asset source transaction. Allen's Tutoring Services obtained assets (accounts receivable) by providing services to customers. Both assets and stockholders' equity (retained earnings) increase. The event increases revenue and net income. Cash flow is not affected. These effects follow:

Event No.	Assets	=	Liab.	+	Equity	Rev.	−	Exp.	=	Net Inc.	Cash Flow
	Accts. Rec.	=			Ret. Earn.						
1	14,000	=	NA	+	14,000	14,000	−	NA	=	14,000	NA

Event 2 Collection of Receivables

Allen's Tutoring Services collected $12,500 cash from accounts receivable in 2006.

This event is an asset exchange transaction. The asset cash increases; the asset accounts receivable decreases. Total assets remains unchanged. Net income is not affected because the revenue was recognized in the previous transaction. The cash inflow is reported in the operating activities section of the statement of cash flows.

Event No.	Assets			=	Liab.	+	Equity	Rev.	−	Exp.	=	Net Inc.	Cash Flow
	Cash	+	Accts. Rec.										
2	12,500	+	(12,500)	=	NA	+	NA	NA	−	NA	=	NA	12,500 OA

Answers to The Curious Accountant

Procter & Gamble would definitely prefer to make the sale to Costco in cash rather than on account. Even though it may be certain to collect its accounts receivable from Costco, the sooner Procter & Gamble gets its cash, the sooner the cash can be reinvested.

The interest cost related to a small account receivable of $50 that takes 30 days to collect may seem immaterial; at 4 percent, the lost interest amounts to less than $.20. However, when one considers that Procter & Gamble had approximately $3.4 billion of accounts receivable on June 30, 2002, the cost of financing receivables for a real-world company becomes apparent. At 4 percent, the cost of waiting 30 days to collect $3.4 billion of cash is $11.2 million ($3.4 billion × 0.04 × [30 ÷ 365]). For one full year, the cost to Procter & Gamble would be more than $136 million ($3.4 billion × 0.04). In 2002 it took Procter & Gamble approximately 31 days to collect its accounts receivable, and the weighted-average interest rate on its debt was approximately 3.7 percent.

Event 3 Recognizing Uncollectible Accounts Expense
Allen's Tutoring Services recognized uncollectible accounts expense for accounts expected to be uncollectible in the future.

The year-end balance in the accounts receivable account is $1,500 ($14,000 of revenue on account − $12,500 of collections). Although Allen's Tutoring Services has the legal right to receive this $1,500 in 2007, the company is not likely to collect the entire amount because some of its customers may not pay the amounts due. Allen's will not know the actual amount of uncollectible accounts until some future time when the customers default (fail to pay). However, the company can *estimate* the amount of receivables that will be uncollectible.

Suppose Allen's Tutoring Services estimates that $75 of the receivables is uncollectible. To improve financial reporting, the company can recognize the estimated expense in 2006. In this way, uncollectible accounts expense and the related revenue will be recognized in the same accounting period (2006). Recognizing an estimated expense is more useful than recognizing no expense. The *matching* of revenues and expenses is improved and the statements are, therefore, more accurate.

The estimated amount of **uncollectible accounts expense** is recognized in a year-end adjusting entry. The adjusting entry reduces the book value of total assets, reduces stockholders' equity (retained earnings), and reduces the amount of reported net income. The statement of cash flows is not affected. The effects of recognizing uncollectible accounts expense are shown here:

Event No.	Assets				=	Liab.	+	Equity	Rev.	−	Exp.	=	Net Inc.	Cash Flow
	Accts. Rec.	−	Allow.	=				Ret. Earn.						
3	NA	−	75	=		NA	+	(75)	NA	−	75	=	(75)	NA

Instead of decreasing the receivables account directly, the asset reduction is recorded in the **contra asset account,** Allowance for Doubtful Accounts. Recall that the contra account is subtracted from the accounts receivable balance to determine the net realizable value of receivables, as follows for ATS:

Accounts receivable	$1,500
Less: Allowance for doubtful accounts	(75)
Net realizable value of receivables	$1,425

Generally accepted accounting principles require disclosure of both the net realizable value and the amount of the allowance account. Many companies disclose these amounts directly in the balance sheet in a manner similar to that shown in the text box above. Other companies disclose this information in the footnotes to the financial statements.

Financial Statements

The financial statements for Allen's Tutoring Services' 2006 accounting period are shown in Exhibit 5.1. As previously indicated, estimating uncollectible accounts improves the usefulness of the 2006 financial statements in two ways. First, the balance sheet reports the amount of cash ($1,500 − $75 = $1,425) the company actually expects to collect (net realizable value of accounts receivable). Second, the income statement provides a clearer picture of managerial performance because it better *matches* the uncollectible accounts expense with the revenue it helped produce. The statements in Exhibit 5.1 show that the cash flow from operating activities ($12,500) differs from net income ($13,925). The statement of cash flows reports only cash collections, whereas the income statement reports revenues earned on account less the estimated amount of uncollectible accounts expense.

EXHIBIT 5.1

Financial Statements for 2006

Income Statement

Service Revenue	$14,000
Uncollectible Accts. Exp.	(75)
Net Income	$13,925

Balance Sheet

Assets		
Cash		$12,500
Accounts Receivable	$1,500	
Less: Allowance	(75)	
Net Realizable Value		1,425
Total Assets		$13,925
Stockholders' Equity		
Retained Earnings		$13,925

Statement of Cash Flows

Operating Activities	
Inflow from Customers	$12,500
Investing Activities	0
Financing Activities	0
Net Change in Cash	12,500
Plus: Beginning Cash Balance	0
Ending Cash Balance	$12,500

CHECK YOURSELF 5.1

Pamlico Inc. began operations on January 1, 2008. During 2008, it earned $400,000 of revenue on account. The company collected $370,000 of accounts receivable. At the end of the year, Pamlico estimates uncollectible accounts expense will be 1 percent of sales. Based on this information alone, what is the net realizable value of accounts receivable as of December 31, 2008?

Answer

Accounts receivable at year end are $30,000 ($400,000 sales on account − $370,000 collection of receivables). The amount in the allowance for doubtful accounts would be $4,000 ($400,000 credit sales × 0.01). The net realizable value of accounts receivable is therefore $26,000 ($30,000 − $4,000).

Accounting Events Affecting the 2007 Period

LO 2

Explain how the allowance method of accounting for uncollectible accounts affects financial statements.

To further illustrate accounting for uncollectible accounts, we discuss six accounting events affecting Allen's Tutoring Services during 2007.

Event 1 **Write-Off of Uncollectible Accounts Receivable**
Allen's Tutoring Services wrote off $70 of uncollectible accounts receivable.

This is an asset exchange transaction. The amount of the uncollectible accounts is removed from the Accounts Receivable account and from the Allowance for Doubtful Accounts account. Since the balances in both the Accounts Receivable and the Allowance accounts decrease, the net realizable value of receivables—and therefore total assets—remains unchanged. The write-off does not affect the income statement. Since the uncollectible accounts expense was recognized in the previous year, the expense would be double counted if it were recognized again at the time an uncollectible account is written off. Finally, the statement of cash flows is not affected by the write-off. These effects are shown in the following statements model:

Event No.	Assets			=	Liab.	+	Equity	Rev.	−	Exp.	=	Net Inc.	Cash Flow
	Accts. Rec.	−	Allow.										
1	(70)	−	(70)	=	NA	+	NA	NA	−	NA	=	NA	NA

The computation of the *net realizable value,* before and after the write-off, is shown below.

	Before Write-Off	After Write-Off
Accounts receivable	$1,500	$1,430
Less: Allowance for doubtful accounts	(75)	(5)
Net realizable value	$1,425	$1,425

Event 2 Revenue Recognition

Allen's Tutoring Services provided $10,000 of tutoring services on account during 2007.

Assets (accounts receivable) and stockholders' equity (retained earnings) increase. Recognizing revenue increases net income. Cash flow is not affected. These effects are illustrated below:

Event No.	Assets	=	Liab.	+	Equity	Rev.	−	Exp.	=	Net Inc.	Cash Flow
	Accts. Rec.	=			Ret. Earn.						
2	10,000	=	NA	+	10,000	10,000	−	NA	=	10,000	NA

Event 3 Collection of Accounts Receivable

Allen's Tutoring Services collected $8,430 cash from accounts receivable.

The balance in the Cash account increases, and the balance in the Accounts Receivable account decreases. Total assets are unaffected. Net income is not affected because revenue was recognized previously. The cash inflow is reported in the operating activities section of the statement of cash flows.

Event No.	Assets			=	Liab.	+	Equity	Rev.	−	Exp.	=	Net Inc.	Cash Flow
	Cash	+	Accts. Rec.										
3	8,430	+	(8,430)	=	NA	+	NA	NA	−	NA	=	NA	8,430 OA

Event 4 Recovery of an Uncollectible Account: Reinstate Receivable

Allen's Tutoring Services recovered a receivable that it had previously written off.

Occasionally, a company receives payment from a customer whose account was previously written off. In such cases, the customer's account should be reinstated and the cash received should be recorded the same way as any other collection on account. The account receivable is reinstated because a complete record of the customer's payment history may be useful if the customer requests credit again at some future date. To illustrate, assume that Allen's Tutoring Services received a $10 cash payment from a customer whose account had previously been written off. The first step is to **reinstate** the account receivable by reversing the previous write-off. The balances in the Accounts Receivable and the Allowance accounts increase. Since the Allowance is a contra asset account, the increase in it offsets the increase in the Accounts Receivable account, and total assets are unchanged. Net income and cash flow are unaffected. These effects are shown here:

Event No.	Assets			=	Liab.	+	Equity	Rev.	−	Exp.	=	Net Inc.	Cash Flow
	Accts. Rec.	−	Allow.										
4	10	−	10	=	NA	+	NA	NA	−	NA	=	NA	NA

Event 5 **Recovery of an Uncollectible Account: Collection of Receivable**
Allen's Tutoring Services recorded collection of the reinstated receivable.

The collection of $10 is recorded like any other collection of a receivable account. Cash increases, and accounts receivable decreases.

Event No.	Assets			=	Liab.	+	Equity	Rev.	−	Exp.	=	Net Inc.	Cash Flow
	Cash	+	Accts. Rec.										
5	10	+	(10)	=	NA	+	NA	NA	−	NA	=	NA	10 OA

Estimating Uncollectible Accounts Expense Using the Percent of Revenue (Sales) Method

Companies recognize the estimated amount of uncollectible accounts expense in a period-end adjusting entry. Since Allen's Tutoring Service began operations in 2006, it had no previous credit history upon which to base its estimate. After consulting trade publications and experienced people in the same industry, ATS made an educated guess as to the amount of expense it should recognize for its first year. In its second year of operation, however, ATS can use its first-year experience as a starting point for estimating the second year (2007) uncollectible accounts expense.

At the end of 2006 ATS estimated uncollectible accounts expense to be $75 on service revenue of $14,000. In 2007 ATS actually wrote off $70 of which $10 was later recovered. ATS therefore experienced actual uncollectible accounts of $60 on service revenue of $14,000 for an uncollectible accounts rate of approximately .43 percent of service revenue. ATS could apply this percentage to the 2007 service revenue to estimate the 2007 uncollectible accounts expense. In practice, many companies determine the percentage estimate of uncollectible accounts on a three- or five-year moving average.

Companies adjust the historical percentage for anticipated future circumstances. For example, they reduce it if they adopt more rigorous approval standards for new credit applicants. Alternatively, they may increase the percentage if economic forecasts signal an economic downturn that would make future defaults more likely. A company will also increase the percentage if it has specific knowledge one or more of its customers is financially distressed. Multiplying the service revenue by the percentage estimate of uncollectible accounts is commonly called the **percent of revenue method** of estimating uncollectible accounts expense.

Event 6 Adjustment for Recognition of Uncollectible Accounts Expense

Using the percent of revenue method, Allen's Tutoring Services recognized uncollectible accounts expense for 2007.

ATS must record this adjustment as of December 31, 2007, to update its accounting records before preparing the 2007 financial statements. After reviewing its credit history, economic forecasts, and correspondence with customers, management estimates uncollectible accounts expense to be 1.35 percent of service revenue, or $135 ($10,000 service revenue × .0135). Recognizing the $135 uncollectible accounts expense decreases both assets (net realizable of receivables) and stockholders' equity (retained earnings). The expense recognition decreases net income. The statement of cash flows is not affected. The financial statements are affected as shown here:

Event No.	Assets			=	Liab.	+	Equity	Rev.	−	Exp.	=	Net Inc.	Cash Flow
	Accts. Rec.	−	Allow.	=			Ret. Earn.						
6	NA	−	135	=	NA	+	(135)	NA	−	135	=	(135)	NA

Analysis of Financial Statements

Exhibit 5.2 displays the 2007 financial statements. The amount of uncollectible accounts expense ($135) differs from the ending balance of the Allowance account ($150). The balance in the Allowance account was $15 before the 2007 adjusting entry for uncollectible accounts expense was recorded. At the end of 2006, Allen's Tutoring Services estimated there would be $75 of uncollectible accounts as a result of 2006 credit sales. Actual write-offs, however, amounted to $70 and $10 of that amount was recovered, indicating the actual uncollectible accounts expense for 2006 was only $60. Hindsight shows the expense for 2006 was overstated by $15. However, if no estimate had been made, the amount of uncollectible accounts expense would have been understated by $60. In some accounting periods estimated uncollectible accounts expense will likely be overstated; in others it may be understated. The allowance method cannot produce perfect results, but it does improve the accuracy of the financial statements.

Since no dividends were paid, retained earnings at the end of 2007 equals the December 31, 2006, retained earnings plus 2007 net income (that is, $13,925 + $9,865 = $23,790). Again, the cash flow from operating activities ($8,440) differs from net income ($9,865) because the statement of cash flows does not include the effects of revenues earned on account or the recognition of uncollectible accounts expense.

EXHIBIT 5.2

Financial Statements for 2007

Income Statement

Service Revenue	$10,000
Uncollectible Accts. Exp.	(135)
Net Income	$ 9,865

Balance Sheet

Assets		
Cash		$20,940
Accounts Receivable	$3,000	
Less: Allowance	(150)	
Net Realizable Value		2,850
Total Assets		$23,790
Stockholders' Equity		
Retained Earnings		$23,790

Statement of Cash Flows

Operating Activities	
Inflow from Customers	$ 8,440
Investing Activities	0
Financing Activities	0
Net Change in Cash	8,440
Plus: Beginning Cash Balance	12,500
Ending Cash Balance	$20,940

CHECK YOURSELF 5.2

Maher Company had beginning balances in Accounts Receivable and Allowance for Doubtful Accounts of $24,200 and $2,000, respectively. During the accounting period Maher earned $230,000 of revenue on account and collected $232,500 of cash from receivables. The company also wrote off $1,950 of uncollectible accounts during the period. Maher estimates uncollectible accounts expense will be 1 percent of credit sales. Based on this information, what is the net realizable value of receivables at the end of the period?

Answer

The balance in the Accounts Receivable account is $19,750 ($24,200 + $230,000 − $232,500 − $1,950). The amount of uncollectible accounts expense for the period is $2,300 ($230,000 × 0.01). The balance in the Allowance for Doubtful Accounts is $2,350 ($2,000 − $1,950 + $2,300). The net realizable value of receivables is therefore $17,400 ($19,750 − $2,350).

Estimating Uncollectible Accounts Expense Using the Percent of Receivables Method

As an alternative to the percent of revenue method, which focuses on estimating the *expense* of uncollectible accounts, companies may estimate the amount of the adjusting entry to record uncollectible accounts expense using the **percent of receivables method.** The percent of receivables method focuses on estimating the most accurate amount for the balance sheet *Allowance for Doubtful Accounts* account.

The longer an account receivable remains outstanding, the less likely it is to be collected. Companies using the percent of receivables method typically determine the age of their individual accounts receivable accounts as part of estimating the allowance for doubtful accounts. An **aging of accounts receivable** schedule classifies all receivables by their due date. Exhibit 5.3 shows an aging schedule for Pyramid Corporation as of December 31, 2007.

A company estimates the required Allowance for Doubtful Accounts balance by applying different percentages to each category in the aging schedule. The percentage for each category is based on a company's previous collection experience for each of the categories. The percentages become progressively higher as the accounts become older. Exhibit 5.4 illustrates computing the allowance balance Pyramid Corporation requires.

EXHIBIT 5.3

PYRAMID CORPORATION
Accounts Receivable Aging Schedule
December 31, 2007

Customer Name	Total Balance	Current	Number of Days Past Due 0–30	31–60	61–90	Over 90
J. Davis	$ 6,700	$ 6,700				
B. Diamond	4,800	2,100	$ 2,700			
K. Eppy	9,400	9,400				
B. Gilman	2,200				$1,000	$1,200
A. Kelly	7,300	7,300				
L. Niel	8,600	1,000	6,000	$ 1,600		
L. Platt	4,600			4,600		
J. Turner	5,500			3,000	2,000	500
H. Zachry	6,900		3,000	3,900		
Total	$56,000	$26,500	$11,700	$13,100	$3,000	$1,700

EXHIBIT 5.4

Balance Required in the Allowance for Doubtful Accounts at December 31, 2007

Number of Days Past Due	Receivables Amount	Percentage Likely to Be Uncollectible	Required Allowance Account Balance
Current	$26,500	.01	$ 265
0–30	11,700	.05	585
31–60	13,100	.10	1,310
61–90	3,000	.25	750
Over 90	1,700	.50	850
Total	$56,000		$3,760

The computations in Exhibit 5.4 mean the *ending balance* in the Allowance for Doubtful Accounts account should be $3,760. This balance represents the amount Pyramid will subtract from total accounts receivable to determine the net realizable value of receivables. To determine the amount of the adjusting entry to recognize uncollectible accounts expense, Pyramid must take into account any existing balance in the allowance account *before* recording the adjustment. For example, if Pyramid Corporation had a $500 balance in the Allowance account before the year-end adjustment, the adjusting entry would need to add $3,260 ($3,760 − $500) to the account. The effects on the financial statements are shown below:

Assets			=	Liab.	+	Equity	Rev.	−	Exp.	=	Net Inc.	Cash Flow
Accts. Rec.	−	Allow.	=			Ret. Earn.						
NA	−	3,260	=	NA	+	(3,260)	NA	−	3,260	=	3,260	NA

Matching Revenues and Expenses versus Asset Measurement

The *percent of revenue* method, with its focus on determining the uncollectible accounts expense, is often called the income statement approach. The *percent of receivables* method, focused on determining the best estimate of the allowance balance, is frequently called the balance sheet approach. Which estimating method is better? In any given year, the results will vary slightly between approaches. In the long run, however, the percentages used in either approach are based on a company's actual history of uncollectible accounts. Accountants routinely revise their estimates as more data become available, using hindsight to determine if the percentages should be increased or decreased. Either approach provides acceptable results.

Recognizing Uncollectible Accounts Expense Using the Direct Write-Off Method

Show how the direct write-off method of accounting for uncollectible accounts affects financial statements.

If uncollectible accounts are not material, generally accepted accounting principles allow companies to account for them using the **direct write-off method.** Under the direct write-off method, a company simply recognizes uncollectible accounts expense *in the period in which it identifies and writes off uncollectible accounts.* No estimates, allowance account, or adjusting entries are needed.

The direct write-off method fails to match revenues with expenses. Revenues are recognized in one period and any related uncollectible accounts expense is recognized in a later period. Also, the direct write-off method overstates assets because receivables are reported at *face value* rather than *net realizable value.* If the amount of uncollectible accounts is immaterial, however, companies accept the minor reporting inaccuracies as a reasonable trade-off for recording convenience.

To illustrate the direct write-off method, return to the first year (2006) that Allen's Tutoring Service (ATS) operated. Assume ATS decided the direct write-off method was appropriate to account for its receivables. Recall that during 2006 ATS recognized $14,000 of revenue on account. The effects on the financial statements are shown below:

Assets	=	Liab.	+	Equity	Rev.	−	Exp.	=	Net Inc.	Cash Flow
Accts. Rec.	=			Ret. Earn.						
14,000	=	NA	+	14,000	14,000	−	NA	=	14,000	NA

ATS believed only an immaterial amount of the $14,000 of accounts receivable would prove uncollectible. It therefore made no year-end adjusting entry for estimated uncollectible accounts. Instead, ATS recognizes uncollectible accounts expense when it determines an account is uncollectible.

In its second accounting period (2007), ATS determined that $70 of accounts receivable were uncollectible. ATS recognized the uncollectible accounts expense in the entry to write off the uncollectible receivables. With the direct write-off method, the write-off reduces the asset account Accounts Receivable and decreases the stockholders' equity account Retained Earnings. On the income statement, expenses increase and net income decreases. The statement of cash flows is not affected by the write-off. The effects on the financial statements are shown below:

Assets	=	Liab.	+	Equity	Rev.	−	Exp.	=	Net Inc.	Cash Flow
Accts. Rec.	=			Ret. Earn.						
(70)	=	NA	+	(70)	NA	−	70	=	(70)	NA

Also in 2007 ATS recovered a $10 account receivable it had previously written off. Recording the recovery of a previously written-off account requires two entries. First, ATS must *reinstate* the receivable (merely reverse the write-off entry above) because it has proved to be collectible after all. Second, ATS must record collecting the reinstated account. With the direct write-off method, reinstating the receivable increases the asset account Accounts Receivable and increases the stockholders' equity account Retained Earnings. On the income statement, expenses decrease and net income increases. The statement of cash flows is not affected. The effects on the financial statements are shown below:

Assets	=	Liab.	+	Equity	Rev.	−	Exp.	=	Net Inc.	Cash Flow
Accts. Rec.	=			Ret. Earn.						
10	=	NA	+	10	NA	−	(10)	=	10	NA

Like the collection of any other receivable, collection of the reinstated account receivable increases the asset account Cash and decreases the asset account Accounts Receivable. The income statement is not affected. The cash inflow is reported in the operating activities section of the statement of cash flows. The effects on the financial statements are shown below:

Assets			=	Liab.	+	Equity	Rev.	−	Exp.	=	Net Inc.	Cash Flow
Cash	−	Accts. Rec.										
10		(10)	=	NA	+	NA	NA	−	NA	=	NA	10 OA

Characteristics of Notes Receivable (Promissory Notes)

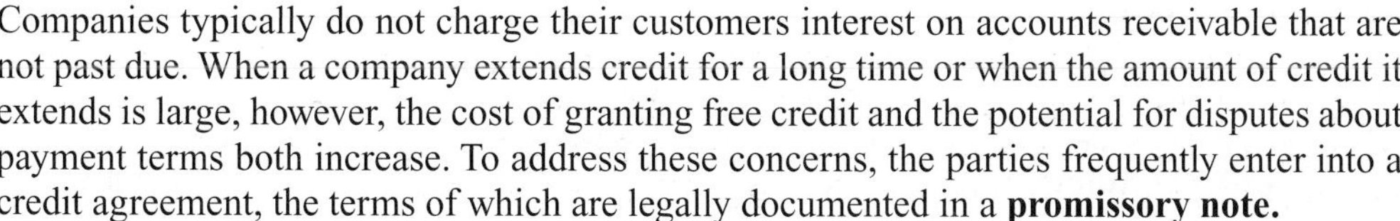

Companies typically do not charge their customers interest on accounts receivable that are not past due. When a company extends credit for a long time or when the amount of credit it extends is large, however, the cost of granting free credit and the potential for disputes about payment terms both increase. To address these concerns, the parties frequently enter into a credit agreement, the terms of which are legally documented in a **promissory note.**

To illustrate, assume Allen's Tutoring Services (ATS) loans some of its idle cash to an individual, Stanford Cummings, so Cummings can buy a car. ATS and Cummings agree that Cummings will repay the money borrowed plus interest at the end of one year. They also agree that ATS will hold the title to the car to secure the debt. Exhibit 5.5 illustrates a promissory note that outlines this credit agreement. For ATS, the credit arrangement represents a *note receivable.*

Features of this note are discussed below. Each feature is cross referenced with a number that corresponds to an item on the promissory note in Exhibit 5.5. Locate each feature in Exhibit 5.5 and read the corresponding description of the feature below.

1. Maker—The person responsible for making payment on the due date is the **maker** of the note. The maker may also be called the *borrower* or *debtor.*
2. Payee—The person to whom the note is made payable is the **payee.** The payee may also be called the *creditor* or *lender.* The payee loans money to the maker and expects the return of the principal and the interest due.
3. Principal—The amount of money loaned by the payee to the maker of the note is the **principal.**
4. Interest—The economic benefit earned by the payee for loaning the principal to the maker is **interest,** which is normally expressed as an annual percentage of the principal amount. For example, a note with a 6 percent interest rate requires interest payments equal to 6 percent of the principal amount every year the loan is outstanding.
5. Maturity Date—The date on which the maker must repay the principal and make the final interest payment to the payee is the **maturity date.**
6. Collateral—Assets belonging to the maker that are assigned as security to ensure that the principal and interest will be paid when due are called **collateral.** In this example, if Cummings fails to pay ATS the amount due, ownership of the car Cummings purchased will be transferred to ATS.

EXHIBIT 5.5

Promissory Note

Promissory Note

$15,000 (3) — *November 1, 2008*

Amount — **Date**

For consideration received, Stanford Cummings **hereby promises to pay to the order of:**

Allen's Tutoring Services (2)

Fifteen thousand and no/100 **Dollars**

payable on October 31, 2009 (5)

plus interest thereon at the rate of 6 **percent per year.** (4)

Collateral Description Automobile title (6)

Signature *Stanford Cummings* (1)

Accounting for Notes Receivable

We illustrate accounting for notes receivable using the credit agreement evidenced by the promissory note in Exhibit 5.5. Allen's Tutoring Services engaged in many transactions during 2008; we discuss here only transactions directly related to the note receivable.

LO 4

Explain how accounting for notes receivable and accrued interest affects financial statements.

Event 1 Loan of Money

The note shows that ATS loaned $15,000 to Stanford Cummings on November 1, 2008. This event is an asset exchange. The asset account Cash decreases and the asset account Notes Receivable increases. The income statement is not affected. The statement of cash flows shows a cash outflow for investing activities. The effects on the financial statements are shown below:

	Assets					=	Liab.	+	Equity	Rev.	−	Exp.	=	Net Inc.	Cash Flow
Date	Cash	+	Notes Rec.	+	Int. Rec.	=			Ret. Earn.						
11/01/08	(15,000)	+	15,000	+	NA	=	NA	+	NA	NA	−	NA	=	NA	(15,000) IA

Event 2 Accrual of Interest

For ATS, loaning money to the maker of the note, Stanford Cummings, represents investing in the note receivable. Cummings will repay the principal ($15,000) plus interest of 6 percent of the principal amount (0.06 × $15,000 = $900), or a total of $15,900, on October 31, 2009, one year from the date he borrowed the money from ATS.

Conceptually, lenders *earn* interest continually even though they do not *collect* cash payment for it every day. Each day, the amount of interest due, called **accrued interest,** is greater than the day before. Companies would find it highly impractical to attempt to record (recognize) accrued interest continually as the amount due increased.

Businesses typically solve the recordkeeping problem by only recording accrued interest when it is time to prepare financial statements or when it is due. At such times, the accounts are *adjusted* to reflect the amount of interest currently due. For example, ATS recorded the asset exchange immediately upon investing in the Note Receivable on November 1, 2008. ATS did not, however, recognize any interest earned on the note until the balance sheet date, December 31, 2008. At year-end ATS made an entry to recognize the interest it had earned during the previous two months (November 1 through December 31). This entry is an **adjusting entry** because it adjusts (updates) the account balances prior to preparing financial statements.

ATS computed the amount of accrued interest by multiplying the principal amount of the note by the annual interest rate and by the length of time for which the note has been outstanding.

Principal ×	Annual interest rate	×	Time outstanding	=	Interest revenue
$15,000 ×	0.06	×	(2/12)	=	$150

ATS recognized the $150 of interest revenue in 2008 although ATS will not collect the cash until 2009. This practice illustrates the **matching concept.** Interest revenue is recognized in (matched with) the period in which it is earned regardless of when the related cash is collected. The adjustment is an asset source transaction. The asset account Interest Receivable increases, and the stockholders' equity account Retained Earnings increases. The income statement reflects an increase in revenue and net income. The statement of cash flows is not affected because ATS will not collect cash until the maturity date (October 31, 2009). The effects on the financial statements are shown below:

	Assets					=	Liab.	+	Equity	Rev.	−	Exp.	=	Net Inc.	Cash Flow
Date	Cash	+	Notes Rec.	+	Int. Rec.	=			Ret. Earn.						
12/31/08	NA	+	NA	+	150	=	NA	+	150	150	−	NA	=	150	NA

Event 3 Collection of Principal and Interest on the Maturity Date

ATS collected $15,900 cash on the maturity date. The collection included $15,000 for the principal plus $900 for the interest. Recall that ATS previously accrued interest in the December 31, 2008, adjusting entry for the two months in 2008 that the note was outstanding. Since year-end, ATS has earned an additional 10 months of interest revenue. ATS must recognize this interest revenue before recording the cash collection. The amount of interest earned in 2009 is computed as follows:

Principal ×	Annual interest rate ×	Time outstanding =	Interest revenue
$15,000 ×	0.06 ×	(10/12) =	$750

The effects on the financial statements are shown below.

	Assets					=	Liab.	+	Equity	Rev.	−	Exp.	=	Net Inc.	Cash Flow
Date	Cash	+	Notes Rec.	+	Int. Rec.	=			Ret. Earn.						
10/31/09	NA	+	NA	+	750	=	NA	+	750	750	−	NA	=	750	NA

The total amount of accrued interest is now $900 ($150 accrued in 2008 plus $750 accrued in 2009). The $15,900 cash collection is an asset exchange transaction. The asset account Cash increases and two asset accounts, Notes Receivable and Interest Receivable, decrease. The income statement is not affected. The statement of cash flows shows a $15,000 inflow from investing activities (recovery of principal) and a $900 inflow from operating activities (interest collection). The effects on the financial statements are shown below.

	Assets					=	Liab.	+	Equity	Rev.	−	Exp.	=	Net Inc.	Cash Flow
Date	Cash	+	Notes Rec.	+	Int. Rec.	=			Ret. Earn.						
10/31/09	15,900	+	(15,000)	+	(900)	=	NA	+	NA	NA	−	NA	=	NA	15,000 IA 900 OA

Financial Statements

The financial statements reveal key differences between the timing of revenue recognition and the exchange of cash. These differences are highlighted below:

	2008	2009	Total
Interest revenue recognized	$150	$750	$900
Cash inflow from operating activities	0	900	900

Accrual accounting calls for recognizing revenue in the period in which it is earned regardless of when cash is collected.

Income statement

Although generally accepted accounting principles require reporting receipts of or payments for interest on the statement of cash flows as operating activities, they do not specify how to classify interest on the income statement. In fact, companies traditionally report interest on the income statement as a nonoperating item. Interest is therefore frequently reported in two different categories within the same set of financial statements.

EXHIBIT 5.6

Typical Balance Sheet Presentation of Receivables

SOUTHERN COMPANY Partial Balance Sheet As of December 31, 2006		
Cash		xxxx
Accounts Receivable	xxxx	
Less: Allowance for Doubtful Accounts	(xxxx)	
Net Realizable Value of Accounts Receivable		xxxx
Interest Receivable		xxxx
Notes Receivable		xxxx

Balance Sheet

As with other assets, companies report interest receivable and notes receivable on the balance sheet in order of their liquidity. **Liquidity** refers to how quickly assets are expected to be converted to cash during normal operations. In the preceding example, ATS expects to convert its accounts receivable to cash before it collects the interest receivable and note receivable. Companies commonly report interest and notes receivable after accounts receivable. Exhibit 5.6 shows a partial balance sheet for Southern Company to illustrate the presentation of receivables.

CHECK YOURSELF 5.3

On October 1, 2006, Mei Company accepted a promissory note for a loan it made to the Asia Pacific Company. The note had a $24,000 principal amount, a four-month term, and an annual interest rate of 4 percent. Determine the amount of interest revenue and the cash inflow from operating activities Mei will report in its 2006 and 2007 financial statements. Also provide in general journal form the year-end adjusting entry needed to recognize 2006 interest revenue.

Answer

The computation of accrued interest revenue is shown below. The interest rate is stated in annual terms even though the term of the note is only four months. Interest rates are commonly expressed as an annual percentage regardless of the term of the note. The *time outstanding* in the following formulas is therefore expressed as a fraction of a year. Mei charged annual interest of 4 percent, but the note was outstanding for only 3/12 of a year in 2006 and 1/12 of a year in 2007.

2006

Principal	×	Annual interest rate	×	Time outstanding	=	Interest revenue
$24,000	×	0.04	×	(3/12)	=	$240

2007

Principal	×	Annual interest rate	×	Time outstanding	=	Interest revenue
$24,000	×	0.04	×	(1/12)	=	$80

In 2006, Mei's cash inflow from interest will be zero.

In 2007, Mei will report a $320 ($240 + $80) cash inflow from operating activities for interest. The adjusting entry to recognize 2006 accrued interest is as follows:

Account	Debit	Credit
Interest Receivable	240	
Interest Revenue		240

Accounting for Credit Card Sales

LO 5

Explain how accounting for credit card sales affects financial statements.

Maintaining accounts and notes receivable is expensive. In addition to uncollectible accounts expense, companies extending credit to their customers incur considerable costs for such clerical tasks as running background checks and maintaining customer records. Many businesses find it more efficient to accept third-party credit cards instead of offering credit directly to their customers. Credit card companies service the merchant's credit sales for a fee that typically ranges between 2 and 8 percent of gross sales.

The credit card company provides customers with plastic cards that permit cardholders to charge purchases at various retail outlets. When a sale takes place, the seller records the transaction on a receipt the customer signs. The receipt is forwarded to the credit card company, which immediately pays the merchant.

The credit card company deducts its service fee from the gross amount of the sale and pays the merchant the net balance (gross amount of sale less credit card fee) in cash. The credit card company collects the gross sale amount directly from the customer. The merchant avoids the risk of uncollectible accounts as well as the cost of maintaining customer credit records. To illustrate, assume that Allen's Tutoring Service experiences the following events.

Event 1 Recognition of Revenue and Expense on Credit Card Sales
ATS accepts a credit card payment for $1,000 of services rendered.

Assume the credit card company charges a 5 percent fee for handling the transaction ($1,000 × 0.05 = $50). ATS's income increases by the amount of revenue ($1,000) and decreases by the amount of the credit card expense ($50). Net income increases by $950. The event increases an asset, accounts receivable, due from the credit card company, and stockholders' equity (retained earnings) by $950 ($1,000 revenue − $50 credit card expense). Cash flow is not affected. These effects are shown here:

Event No.	Assets	=	Liab.	+	Equity	Rev.	−	Exp.	=	Net Inc.	Cash Flow
	Accts. Rec.	=			Ret. Earn.						
1	950	=	NA	+	950	1,000	−	50	=	950	NA

Pawan Kumar

Event 2 Collection of Credit Card Receivable
The collection of the receivable due from the credit card company is recorded like any other receivable collection.

When ATS collects the net amount of $950 ($1,000 − $50) from the credit card company, one asset account (Cash) increases and another asset account (Accounts Receivable) decreases. Total assets are not affected. The income statement is not affected. A $950 cash inflow is reported in the operating activities section of the statement of cash flows. These effects are illustrated below:

Event No.	Assets			=	Liab.	+	Equity	Rev.	−	Exp.	=	Net Inc.	Cash Flow
	Cash	+	Accts. Rec.										
2	950	+	(950)	=	NA	+	NA	NA	−	NA	=	NA	950 OA

Costs of Credit Sales

LO 6

Explain the effects of the cost of financing credit sales.

As mentioned earlier, two costs of extending credit to customers are uncollectible accounts expense and recordkeeping costs. These costs can be significant. Large companies spend literally millions of dollars to buy the equipment and pay the staff necessary to operate entire departments devoted to managing accounts receivable. Further, there is an implicit interest cost associated with extending credit. When a customer is permitted to delay payment, the creditor foregoes the opportunity to invest the amount the customer owes.

Exhibit 5.7 presents part of a footnote from the 2002 annual report of PepsiCo, Inc. This excerpt provides insight into the credit costs real companies incur. First, observe that PepsiCo was owed $2.65 billion of accounts receivable. These receivables represent money that could be in the bank earning interest if all sales had been made in cash. If PepsiCo could have earned interest at 5 percent on that money, the opportunity cost of this lost interest is approximately $132.5 million ($2.65 billion × .05) a year. Next, observe that PepsiCo expects to have uncollectible accounts amounting to $116 million (balance in the allowance account). These are significant costs.

EXHIBIT 5.7

PepsiCo Dec. 28, 2002
PARTIAL FOOTNOTE regarding Receivables
(amounts are shown in millions)

Note 14 Supplemental Financial Information

	2002	**2001**
Accounts receivable:		
Trade receivables	$1,924	$1,663
Other receivables	723	600
	2,647	2,263
Allowance, beginning of year	121	126
Charged to expense	38	41
Other additions (a)	3	2
Deductions (b)	(46)	(48)
Allowance, end of year	116	121
Net receivables	$2,531	$2,142

Average Number of Days to Collect Accounts Receivable

The longer it takes to collect accounts receivable, the greater the opportunity cost of lost income. Also, business experience indicates that the older an account receivable becomes, the less likely it is to be collected. Finally, taking longer to collect an account typically costs more for salaries, equipment, and supplies used in the process of trying to collect it. Businesses are therefore concerned about how long it takes to collect their receivables.

Two ratios help management, or other users, measure a company's collection period. One is the **accounts receivable turnover ratio,** computed as:[1]

$$\frac{\text{Sales}}{\text{Accounts receivable}}$$

Dividing a company's sales by its accounts receivable tells how many times the accounts receivable balance is "turned over" (converted into cash) each year. The higher the turnover, the shorter the collection period. To simplify its interpretation, the accounts receivable turnover ratio is often taken one step further to determine the **average number of days to collect accounts receivable,** sometimes called the *average collection period.* This is computed as:

$$\frac{365}{\text{Accounts receivable turnover ratio}}$$

[1]To be more precise, the ratio could be computed using only credit sales and average accounts receivable. Usually, however, companies do not report credit sales separately from cash sales in published financial statements. Average accounts receivable, if desired, is computed as [(beginning receivables + ending receivables) ÷ 2]. For this course, use the simpler computation shown here (sales ÷ accounts receivable).

This ratio measures how many days, on average, it takes a company to collect its accounts receivable. Since longer collection periods increase costs, shorter periods are obviously more desirable. To illustrate computing the *average number of days to collect accounts receivable* for Allen's Tutoring Services, refer to the 2007 financial statements in Exhibit 5.2. On average, the company takes 104 days to collect its receivables, computed in two steps:

1. The accounts receivable turnover is 3.509 ($10,000 ÷ $2,850) times.
2. The average number of days to collect receivables is 104 (365 ÷ 3.509) days.

In the preceding computations, the net realizable value of accounts receivable was used because that is the amount typically reported in published financial statements. The results would not have been materially different had total accounts receivable been used.

Real-World Data

What is the collection period for real companies? The time required to collect receivables varies among industries and among companies within industries. Column 4 in Exhibit 5.8 displays the average number of days to collect receivables for eight companies in three different industries. These numbers are for the 2002 calendar year.

Since fast-food restaurants require customers to pay cash when they purchase hamburgers or coffee, why do these companies have accounts receivable? The accounts receivable for **Domino's**, **McDonald's**, and **Starbucks** arise because these companies sell goods to restaurants that are independent franchisees. So, for example, Domino's accounts receivable represents future collections from restaurant owners, not customers who purchase pepperoni pizzas.

Are the collection periods for **Mondavi** and **Chalone Wine Group** too long? The answer depends on their credit policies. If they are selling goods to customers on net 30-day terms, there may be reason for concern, but if they allow customers 90 days to pay and the cost of this policy has been built into their pricing structure, the collection periods may not be unreasonable.

Some companies allow their customers extended time to pay their bills because the customers would otherwise have difficulty coming up with the money. For example, Mondavi may sell to a wine retailer that does not have the cash available to pay immediately. If Mondavi allows the retailer sufficient time, the retailer can sell the wine to customers and obtain the cash it needs to pay Mondavi. Many small companies do not have cash available to pay up front. Buying on credit is the only way they can obtain the inventory they need. If a

EXHIBIT 5.8

Industry	Company	Average Days to Sell Inventory	Average Days to Collect Receivables	Length of Operating Cycle
Fast Food	Domino's	9	16	25
	McDonald's	10	21	31
	Starbucks	65	10	75
Office Supplies	Office Depot	58	25	83
	OfficeMax	92	7	99
	Staples	64	11	75
Wine	Chalone	642	74	716
	Mondavi	548	82	630

REALITY BYTES

This chapter explains that, in general, companies want to collect their receivables as quickly as possible. There is a notable exception to this generalization. If a company charges its customers interest on unpaid receivables, the company makes money on the unpaid balance. Many sellers of "big-ticket" goods like furniture, large appliances, and automobiles offer to finance their customers' purchases, allowing customers extended time to pay off their receivables in exchange for the customers' paying additional charges for interest.

For example, most people probably think **General Motors** (GM) makes its profits primarily by selling cars and trucks, but GM often earns more from *financing* vehicle sales than from the sales themselves. In 2003 GM's income from operations, after taxes, was $2,862 million, of which almost all—$2,648—was actually earned from its financing businesses. Only $35 million came from profits directly related to vehicle sales. Even the company's insurance activities produced more profit ($179 million) than selling vehicles.

Should GM therefore stop selling cars and trucks? No. If it did not sell vehicles, GM would have far fewer opportunities to finance the sale of automobiles. For the record, almost half of GM's financing income comes from mortgage activities, not automotive financing. The familiar ditech.com of the "lost another loan to ditech" commercial is a wholly owned subsidiary of GM.

manufacturer or wholesaler wants to sell to such companies, credit sales represent the only option available.

The length of the **operating cycle** is the average time it takes a business to convert inventory to accounts receivable plus the time it takes to convert accounts receivable into cash. The average number of days to collect receivables is one component of the operating cycle for a particular company. The other component is the average number of days to sell inventory ratio that was explained in Chapter 4. The length of the operating cycles for the real-world companies discussed herein is shown in the last column of Exhibit 5.8.

What is the significance of the different operating cycle lengths in Exhibit 5.8? As previously explained, the longer the operating cycle takes, the more it costs the company. Exhibit 5.8 shows it takes **OfficeMax** an average of 24 days longer than Staples to complete an operating cycle. All other things being equal, approximately how much did this longer time reduce OfficeMax's earnings? Assume OfficeMax could invest excess cash at 8 percent (or alternatively, assume it pays 8 percent to finance its inventory and accounts receivable). Using the accounting information reported in OfficeMax's January 25, 2003, financial statements, we can answer the question as follows:

$$\text{OfficeMax's investment in inventory} \times \text{Interest rate} \times \text{Time} = \text{Cost}$$

$$\$906{,}253{,}000 \times 8\% \times 24/365 = \$4{,}767{,}139$$

With 3.69 operating cycles per year (365 ÷ 99), the extended operating cycle costs OfficeMax $17.6 million annually. Based on the assumptions used here, OfficeMax would increase its after-tax net earnings by approximately 15 percent if it could reduce its operating cycle by 24 days. Although this illustration is a rough estimate, it demonstrates that it is important for businesses to minimize the length of their operating cycles.

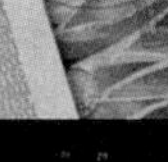

FOCUS ON INTERNATIONAL ISSUES

A ROSE BY ANY OTHER NAME . . .

If a person who studied U.S. GAAP wanted to look at the financial statements of a non-U.S. company, choosing statements of a company from another English-speaking country might seem logical. Presumably, this would eliminate language differences, and only the differences in GAAP would remain. However, this is not true.

When an accountant in the United States uses the term *turnover,* she or he is usually thinking of a financial ratio, such as the accounts receivable turnover ratio. However, in the United Kingdom, the term *turnover* refers to what U.S. accountants call *sales.* U.K. balance sheets do not usually show an account named *Inventory;* rather, they use the term *Stocks.* In the United States, accountants typically use the term *stocks* to refer to certificates representing ownership in a corporation. Finally, if an accountant or banker from the United Kingdom should ever ask you about your *gearing ratio,* he or she probably is not interested in your bicycle but in your debt to assets ratio.

CHECK YOURSELF 5.4

Randolph Corporation had sales for the year of $535,333 and an accounts receivable balance at year end of $22,000. Determine Randolph's average number of days to collect accounts receivable.

Answer

The accounts receivable turnover is 24.33 ($535,333 ÷ $22,000) times per year. The average number of days to collect accounts receivable is 15 (365 ÷ 24.33).

A Look Back <<

We first introduced accounting for receivables in Chapter 2. This chapter presented additional complexities related to accounts receivable, such as the *allowance method of accounting for uncollectible accounts.* The allowance method improves matching of expenses with revenues. It also provides a more accurate measure of the value of accounts receivable on the balance sheet.

Under the allowance method, estimated uncollectible accounts expense is recorded in an adjusting entry at the end of the period in which a company has made credit sales. There are two methods commonly used to estimate the amount of uncollectible accounts expense: the percent of revenue method and the percent of receivables method. With the percent of revenue method, uncollectible accounts expense is measured as a percent of the period's sales. With the percent of receivables method, a company analyzes its accounts receivable at the end of the period, usually classifying them by age, to estimate the amount of the accounts receivable balance that is likely to be uncollectible. The balance in the Allowance for Doubtful Accounts account is then adjusted to equal the estimated amount of uncollectible accounts. Uncollectible accounts expense decreases the net realizable value of receivables (accounts receivable − allowance for doubtful accounts), stockholders' equity, and net income.

The allowance method of accounting for uncollectible accounts is conceptually superior to the *direct write-off method,* in which uncollectible accounts expense is recognized when an account is determined to be uncollectible. The direct write-off method fails to match revenues with expenses and overstates accounts receivable on the balance sheet. It is easier to use, however, and is permitted by generally accepted accounting principles if the amount of uncollectible accounts expense is immaterial.

The chapter also introduced notes receivable and accounting for *accrued interest.* When the term of a promissory note extends over more than one accounting period, companies must record adjusting entries to recognize interest in the appropriate accounting period, even if the cash exchange of interest occurs in a different accounting period.

We also discussed accounting for credit card sales, a vehicle that shifts uncollectible accounts expense to the credit card issuer. Many companies find the benefits of accepting major credit cards to be worth the credit card expense consequently incurred.

Finally, we addressed the costs of making credit sales. In addition to uncollectible accounts expense, interest is a major cost of financing receivables. The length of the collection period provides a measure of the quality of receivables. Short collection periods usually indicate lower amounts of uncollectible accounts and interest cost. Long collection periods imply higher costs. The collection period can be measured in two steps. First, divide sales by the accounts receivable balance to determine the accounts receivable turnover ratio. Then divide the number of days in the year (365) by the accounts receivable turnover ratio.

>> A Look Forward

Chapter 6 discusses accounting for long-term assets such as buildings and equipment. As with inventory cost flow, discussed in Chapter 4, GAAP allows companies to use different accounting methods to report on similar types of business events. Life would be easier for accounting students if all companies used the same accounting methods. However, the business world is complex. For the foreseeable future, people are likely to continue to have diverse views as to the best way to account for a variety of business transactions. To function effectively in today's business environment, it is important for you to be able to recognize differences in reporting practices.

SELF-STUDY REVIEW PROBLEM

During 2007 Calico Company experienced the following accounting events:

1. Provided $120,000 of services on account.
2. Collected $85,000 cash from accounts receivable.
3. Wrote off $1,800 of accounts receivable that were uncollectible.
4. Loaned $3,000 to an individual, Emma Gardner, in exchange for a note receivable.
5. Paid $90,500 cash for operating expenses.
6. Estimated that uncollectible accounts expense would be 2 percent of credit sales. Recorded the year-end adjusting entry.
7. Recorded the year-end adjusting entry for accrued interest on the note receivable (see Event 4). Calico made the loan on August 1. It had a six-month term and a 6 percent rate of interest.

Calico's ledger balances on January 1, 2007, were as follows:

Event No.	Assets									=	Liab.	+	Equity		
	Cash	+	Accts. Rec.	−	Allow.	+	Notes Rec.	+	Int. Rec.	=			Com. Stk.	+	Ret. Earn.
Bal.	12,000		18,000		2,200	+	NA	+	NA	=	NA	+	20,000	+	7,800

Required

a. Record the 2007 events in ledger accounts using the horizontal format shown above.
b. Determine net income for 2007.
c. Determine net cash flow from operating activities for 2007.
d. Determine the net realizable value of accounts receivable at December 31, 2007.
e. What amount of interest revenue will Calico recognize on its note receivable in 2008?

Solution to Requirement *a*.

Event No.	Assets									=	Liab.	+	Equity		
	Cash	+	Accts. Rec.	−	Allow.	+	Notes Rec.	+	Int. Rec.	=			Com. Stk.	+	Ret. Earn.
Bal.	12,000	+	18,000	−	2,200	+	NA	+	NA	=	NA	+	20,000	+	7,800
1	NA	+	120,000	−	NA	+	NA	+	NA	=	NA	+	NA	+	120,000
2	85,000	+	(85,000)	−	NA	+	NA	+	NA	=	NA	+	NA	+	NA
3	NA	+	(1,800)	−	(1,800)	+	NA	+	NA	=	NA	+	NA	+	NA
4	(3,000)	+	NA	−	NA	+	3,000	+	NA	=	NA	+	NA	+	NA
5	(90,500)	+	NA	−	NA	+	NA	+	NA	=	NA	+	NA	+	(90,500)
6	NA	+	NA	−	2,400	+	NA	+	NA	=	NA	+	NA	+	(2,400)
7	NA	+	NA	−	NA	+	NA	+	75*	=	NA	+	NA	+	75
Totals	3,500	+	51,200	−	2,800	+	3,000	+	75	=	NA	+	20,000	+	34,975

*$3,000 × .06 × 5/12 = $75.

Solution to Requirements *b–e*.

b. Net income is $27,175 ($120,000 − $90,500 − $2,400 + $75).
c. Net cash flow from operating activities is an outflow of $5,500 ($85,000 − $90,500).
d. The net realizable value of accounts receivable is $48,400 ($51,200 − $2,800).
e. In 2008, Calico will recognize interest revenue for one month: $3,000 × .06 × 1/12 = $15.

KEY TERMS

QUESTIONS

1. What is the difference between accounts receivable and notes receivable?
2. What is the *net realizable value* of receivables?
3. What type of account is the Allowance for Doubtful Accounts?
4. What are two ways in which estimating uncollectible accounts improves the accuracy of the financial statements?
5. When using the allowance method, why is uncollectible accounts expense an estimated amount?
6. What is the most common format for reporting accounts receivable on the balance sheet? What information does this method provide beyond showing only the net amount?
7. Why is it necessary to reinstate a previously written off account receivable before the collection is recorded?
8. What are some factors considered in estimating the amount of uncollectible accounts receivable?
9. What is the effect on the accounting equation of recognizing uncollectible accounts expense?
10. What is the effect on the accounting equation of writing off an uncollectible account receivable when the allowance method is used? When the direct write-off method is used?
11. How does the recovery of a previously written-off account affect the income statement when the allowance method is used? How does the recovery of a previously written-off account affect the statement of cash flows when the allowance method is used?
12. What is the advantage of using the allowance method of accounting for uncollectible accounts? What is the advantage of using the direct write-off method?
13. How do companies determine the percentage estimate of uncollectible accounts when using the percent of revenue method?
14. What is an advantage of using the percent of receivables method of estimating uncollectible accounts expense?
15. What is "aging of accounts receivable"?
16. What is the difference between the allowance method and the direct write-off method of accounting for uncollectible accounts?
17. When is it acceptable to use the direct write-off method of accounting for uncollectible accounts?
18. What is a promissory note?
19. Define the following terms:
    a. Maker
    b. Payee
    c. Principal
    d. Interest
    e. Maturity date
    f. Collateral
20. What is the formula for computing interest revenue?
21. What is accrued interest?
22. When is an adjusting entry for accrued interest generally recorded?
23. Assume that on July 1, 2006, Big Corp. loaned Little Corp. $12,000 for a period of one year at 6 percent interest. What amount of interest revenue will Big report for 2006? What amount of cash will Big receive upon maturity of the note?
24. In which section of the statement of cash flows will Big report the cash collected in question 23?
25. Why is it generally beneficial for a business to accept major credit cards as payment for goods and services even when the fee charged by the credit card company is substantial?
26. What types of costs do businesses avoid when they accept major credit cards as compared with handling credit sales themselves?
27. How is the accounts receivable turnover ratio computed? What information does the ratio provide?
28. How is the average number of days to collect accounts receivable computed? What information does the ratio provide?

29. Is accounting terminology standard in all countries? What term is used in the United Kingdom to refer to *sales?* What term is used to refer to *inventory?* What is a *gearing ratio?* Is it important to know about these differences?
30. What is the operating cycle of a business?

EXERCISES

All Exercises are available with McGraw-Hill's Homework Manager

Exercise 5-1 *Analysis of financial statement effects of accounting for uncollectible accounts under the allowance method* L.O. 2

Businesses using the allowance method for the recognition of uncollectible accounts expense commonly experience four accounting events:

1. Recognition of revenue on account.
2. Collection of cash from accounts receivable.
3. Recognition of uncollectible accounts expense through a year-end adjusting entry.
4. Write-off of uncollectible accounts.

Required

Show the effect of each event on the elements of the financial statements, using a horizontal statements model like the one shown here. Use the following coding scheme to record your answers: increase is +, decrease is −, not affected is NA. In the cash flow column, indicate whether the item is an operating activity (OA), investing activity (IA), or financing activity (FA). The first transaction is entered as an example.

Event No.	Assets	=	Liab.	+	Equity	Rev.	−	Exp.	=	Net Inc.	Cash Flow
1	+		NA		+	+		NA		+	NA

Exercise 5-2 *Accounting for bad debts: allowance method* L.O. 2

Nina's Accounting Service began operation on January 1, 2007. The company experienced the following events for its first year of operations.

1. Provided $120,000 of accounting services on account.
2. Collected $90,000 cash from accounts receivable.
3. Paid salaries of $24,000 for the year.
4. Adjusted the accounts to reflect management's expectations that uncollectible accounts expense would be $1,200.

Required

a. Organize the transaction data in accounts under on accounting equation.
b. Prepare an income statement, balance sheet, and statement of cash flows for 2007.

Exercise 5-3 *Effect of recognizing uncollectible accounts expense on financial statements: percent of revenue allowance method* L.O. 2

Big A's Auto Service was started on January 1, 2006. The company experienced the following events during its first two years of operation.

Events Affecting 2006

1. Provided $30,000 of repair services on account.
2. Collected $25,000 cash from accounts receivable.
3. Adjusted the accounting records to reflect the estimate that uncollectible accounts expense would be 1 percent of the service revenue on account.

Events Affecting 2007

1. Wrote off a $280 account receivable that was determined to be uncollectible.
2. Provided $35,000 of repair services on account.
3. Collected $31,000 cash from accounts receivable.
4. Adjusted the accounting records to reflect the estimate that uncollectible accounts expense would be 1 percent of the service revenue on account.

Required

a. Organize the transaction data in accounts under an accounting equation.
b. Determine the following amounts:
   (1) Net income for 2006.
   (2) Net cash flow from operating activities for 2006.
   (3) Balance of accounts receivable at the end of 2006.
   (4) Net realizable value of accounts receivable at the end of 2006.
c. Repeat Requirement *b* for the 2007 accounting period.

L.O. 2

Exercise 5-4 *Analyzing financial statement effects of accounting for uncollectible accounts using the percent of revenue allowance method*

Gray Bros. uses the allowance method to account for uncollectible accounts expense. Gray experienced the following four events in 2005:

1. Recognized $48,000 of revenue on account.
2. Collected $42,000 cash from accounts receivable.
3. Determined that $300 of accounts receivable were not collectible and wrote them off.
4. Recognized uncollectible accounts expense for the year. Gray estimates that uncollectible accounts expense will be 2 percent of its sales.

Required

Show the effect of each of these events on the elements of the financial statements, using a horizontal statements model like the following one. Use + for increase, − for decrease, and NA for not affected. In the cash flow column, indicate whether the item is an operating activity (OA), investing activity (IA), or financing activity (FA).

Event No.	Assets					=	Liab.	+	Equity	Rev.	−	Exp.	=	Net Inc.	Cash Flow
	Cash	+	Accts. Rec.	−	Allow.	=			Ret. Earn.						

L.O. 2

Exercise 5-5 *Analyzing account balances for a company using the allowance method of accounting for uncollectible accounts*

The following account balances come from the records of Teton Company.

	Beginning Balance	Ending Balance
Accounts Receivable	$3,000	$3,500
Allowance for Doubtful Accounts	120	200

During the accounting period, Teton recorded $12,000 of service revenue on account. The company also wrote off a $150 account receivable.

Required

a. Determine the amount of cash collected from receivables.
b. Determine the amount of uncollectible accounts expense recognized during the period.

Exercise 5-6 *Effect of recovering a receivable previously written off* L.O. 2

The accounts receivable balance for City Shoe Repair at December 31, 2006, was $84,000. Also on that date, the balance in the Allowance for Doubtful Accounts was $2,400. During 2007, $2,100 of accounts receivable were written off as uncollectible. In addition, City Shoe Repair unexpectedly collected $150 of receivables that had been written off in a previous accounting period. Sales on account during 2007 were $218,000, and cash collections from receivables were $220,000. Uncollectible accounts expense was estimated to be 1 percent of the sales on account for the period.

Required

a. Organize the information in accounts under an accounting equation.

b. Based on the preceding information, compute (after year-end adjustment):

(1) Balance of Allowance for Doubtful Accounts at December 31, 2007.

(2) Balance of Accounts Receivable at December 31, 2007.

(3) Net realizable value of Accounts Receivable at December 31, 2007.

c. What amount of uncollectible accounts expense will City Shoe Repair report for 2007?

d. Explain how the $150 recovery of receivables affected the accounting equation.

Exercise 5-7 *Accounting for uncollectible accounts: percent of receivables allowance method* L.O. 2

King Service Co. experienced the following transactions for 2009, its first year of operations:

1. Provided $66,000 of services on account.
2. Collected $42,000 cash from accounts receivable.
3. Paid $26,000 of salaries expense for the year.
4. King adjusted the accounts using the following information from an accounts receivable aging schedule:

Number of Days Past Due	Amount	Percent Likely to Be Uncollectible	Allowance Balance
Current	$16,000	.01	
0–30	3,000	.05	
31–60	2,000	.10	
61–90	1,000	.30	
Over 90 days	2,000	.50	

Required

a. Organize the information in accounts under an accounting equation.

b. Prepare the income statement for King Service Co. for 2009.

c. What is the net realizable value of the accounts receivable at December 31, 2009?

Exercise 5-8 *Effect of recognizing uncollectible accounts on the financial statements: percent of receivables allowance method* L.O. 2

Bourret Inc. experienced the following events for the first two years of its operations.

2009:

1. Provided $60,000 of services on account.
2. Provided $25,000 of services and received cash.
3. Collected $35,000 cash from accounts receivable.
4. Paid $12,000 of salaries expense for the year.
5. Adjusted the accounting records to reflect uncollectible accounts expense for the year. Bourret estimates that 5 percent of the ending accounts receivable balance will be uncollectible.

2010:

1. Wrote off an uncollectible account of $650.
2. Provided $80,000 of services on account.
3. Provided $15,000 of services and collected cash.
4. Collected $62,000 cash from accounts receivable.

5. Paid $20,000 of salaries expense for the year.
6. Adjusted the accounts to reflect uncollectible accounts expense for the year. Bourret estimates that 5 percent of the ending accounts receivable balance will be uncollectible.

Required

a. Organize the transaction data in accounts under an accounting equation.

b. Prepare the income statement, statement of changes in stockholders' equity, balance sheet, and statement of cash flows for 2009.

c. What is the net realizable value of the accounts receivable at December 31, 2009?

d. Repeat Requirements *a, b,* and *c* for 2010.

L.O. 2, 3

Exercise 5-9 *Accounting for uncollectible accounts: percent of revenue allowance versus direct write-off method*

Classic Auto Parts sells new and used auto parts. Although a majority of its sales are cash sales, it makes a significant amount of credit sales. During 2008, its first year of operations, Classic Auto Parts experienced the following:

Sales on account	$280,000
Cash sales	650,000
Collections of accounts receivable	265,000
Uncollectible accounts charged off during the year	1,200

Required

a. Assume that Classic Auto Parts uses the allowance method of accounting for uncollectible accounts and estimates that 1 percent of its sales on account will not be collected. Answer the following questions:
   (1) What is the Accounts Receivable balance at December 31, 2008?
   (2) What is the ending balance of the Allowance for Doubtful Accounts at December 31, 2008, after all entries and adjusting entries are posted?
   (3) What is the amount of uncollectible accounts expense for 2008?
   (4) What is the net realizable value of accounts receivable at December 31, 2008?

b. Assume that Classic Auto Parts uses the direct write-off method of accounting for uncollectible accounts. Answer the following questions:
   (1) What is the Accounts Receivable balance at December 31, 2008?
   (2) What is the amount of uncollectible accounts expense for 2008?
   (3) What is the net realizable value of accounts receivable at December 31, 2008?

L.O. 3

Exercise 5-10 *Accounting for uncollectible accounts: direct write-off method*

Hogan Business Systems has a small number of sales on account but is mostly a cash business. Consequently, it uses the direct write-off method to account for uncollectible accounts. During 2006 Hogan Business Systems earned $32,000 of cash revenue and $8,000 of revenue on account. Cash operating expenses were $26,500. After numerous attempts to collect a $250 account receivable from Sam Smart, the account was determined to be uncollectible in 2007.

Required

a. Record the effects of (1) cash revenue, (2) revenue on account, (3) cash expenses, and (4) write-off of the uncollectible account on the financial statements using a horizontal statements model like the one shown here. In the Cash Flow column, indicate whether the item is an operating activity (OA), investing activity (IA), or financing activity (FA). Use NA to indicate that an element is not affected by the event.

Assets			=	Liab.	+	Equity	Rev.	−	Exp.	=	Net Inc.	Cash Flow
Cash	+	Accts. Rec.										

b. What amount of net income did Hogan Business Systems report on the 2006 income statement?

Exercise 5-11 *Effect of credit card sales on financial statements*

L.O. 5

Royal Carpet Cleaning provided $90,000 of services during 2006, its first year of operations. All customers paid for the services with major credit cards. Royal submitted the credit card receipts to the credit card company immediately. The credit card company paid Royal cash in the amount of face value less a 3 percent service charge.

Required

a. Record the credit card sales and the subsequent collection of accounts receivable in a horizontal statements model like the one shown here. In the Cash Flow column, indicate whether the item is an operating activity (OA), investing activity (IA), or financing activity (FA). Use NA to indicate that an element is not affected by the event.

Assets	= Liab. + Equity	Rev. − Exp. = Net Inc.	Cash Flow
Cash + Accts. Rec.			

b. Answer the following questions:

(1) What is the amount of total assets at the end of the accounting period?

(2) What is the amount of revenue reported on the income statement?

(3) What is the amount of cash flow from operating activities reported on the statement of cash flows?

(4) Why would Royal Carpet Cleaning accept credit cards instead of providing credit directly to its customers? In other words, why would Royal be willing to pay 3 percent of sales to have the credit card company handle its sales on account?

Exercise 5-12 *Recognizing credit card sales*

L.O. 5

Baucom Company accepted credit cards in payment for $6,850 of services performed during March 2006. The credit card company charged Baucom a 4 percent service fee. The credit card company paid Baucom as soon as it received the invoices.

Required

Based on this information alone, what is the amount of net income earned during the month of March?

Exercise 5-13 *Accounting for notes receivable*

L.O. 4

Babb Enterprises loaned $25,000 to Sneathen Co. on September 1, 2008, for one year at 6 percent interest.

Required

Show the effects of the following transactions in a horizontal statements model like the one shown below.

(1) The loan to Sneathen Co.

(2) The adjusting entry at December 31, 2008.

(3) The adjusting entry and collection of the note on September 1, 2009.

	Assets	= Liab. + Equity	Rev. − Exp. = Net Inc.	Cash Flows
Date	Cash + Notes Rec. + Int. Rec. =	Ret. Earn.		

Exercise 5-14 *Notes receivable—accrued interest*

L.O. 4

On March 1, 2007, Jason's Deli loaned $12,000 to Mark Johnson for one year at 5 percent interest.

Required

Answer the following questions.

a. What is Jason's interest income for 2007?

b. What is Jason's total amount of receivables at December 31, 2007?

c. What amounts will be reported on Jason's 2007 statement of cash flows?
d. What is Jason's interest income for 2008?
e. What is the total amount of cash that Jason's will collect in 2008 from Mark Johnson?
f. What amounts will be reported on Jason's 2008 statement of cash flows?
g. What is the total amount of interest Jason's Deli earned from the loan to Mark Johnson?

L.O. 2, 4

Exercise 5-15 *Comprehensive single-cycle problem*

The following after-closing trial balance was drawn from the accounts of Spruce Timber Co. as of December 31, 2006.

	Debit	Credit
Cash	$ 6,000	
Accounts Receivable	18,000	
Allowance for Doubtful Accounts		$ 2,000
Inventory	24,000	
Accounts Payable		9,200
Common Stock		20,000
Retained Earnings		16,800
Totals	$48,000	$48,000

Transactions for 2007

1. Acquired an additional $10,000 cash from the issue of common stock.
2. Purchased $60,000 of inventory on account.
3. Sold inventory that cost $62,000 for $95,000. Sales were made on account.
4. Wrote off $1,100 of uncollectible accounts.
5. On September 1, Spruce loaned $9,000 to Pine Co. The note had a 7 percent interest rate and a one-year term.
6. Paid $15,800 cash for salaries expense.
7. Collected $80,000 cash from accounts receivable.
8. Paid $52,000 cash on accounts payable.
9. Paid a $5,000 cash dividend to the stockholders.
10. Estimated uncollectible accounts expense to be 1 percent of sales on account.
11. Recorded the accrued interest at December 31, 2007.

Required

a. Organize the transaction data in accounts under an accounting equation.
b. Prepare an income statement, statement of changes in stockholders' equity, balance sheet, and statement of cash flows for 2007.

L.O. 6

Exercise 5-16 *Performing ratio analysis using real-world data*

The following data were taken from **Hershey Foods Corporation's** 2004 annual report. All dollar amounts are in thousands.

	Fiscal Years Ending	
	December 31, 2004	December 31, 2003
Sales	$4,429,248	$4,172,551
Accounts Receivable	408,930	407,612

Required

a. Compute Hershey's accounts receivable ratios for 2004 and 2003.
b. Compute Hershey's average days to collect accounts receivables for 2004 and 2003.
c. Based on the ratios computed in Requirements *a* and *b*, did Hershey's performance get better or worse from 2003 to 2004?

d. In 2004 the average interest rate on Hershey's long-term debt was approximately 7.2 percent. Assume it took Hershey 30 days to collect its receivables. Using an interest rate of 7.2 percent, calculate how much it cost Hershey to finance its receivables for 30 days in 2004.

PROBLEMS

All Problems are available with McGraw-Hill's Homework Manager

Problem 5-17 *Accounting for uncollectible accounts—two cycles using the percent of revenue allowance method*

L.O. 2

CHECK FIGURES
c. Ending Accounts Receivable, 2006: $7,000
d. Net Income, 2007: $23,275

The following transactions apply to Sharp Consulting for 2006, the first year of operation:

1. Recognized $65,000 of service revenue earned on account.
2. Collected $58,000 from accounts receivable.
3. Adjusted accounts to recognize uncollectible accounts expense. Sharp uses the allowance method of accounting for uncollectible accounts and estimates that uncollectible accounts expense will be 2 percent of sales on account.

The following transactions apply to Sharp Consulting for 2007:

1. Recognized $72,500 of service revenue on account.
2. Collected $66,000 from accounts receivable.
3. Determined that $900 of the accounts receivable were uncollectible and wrote them off.
4. Collected $100 of an account that had been previously written off.
5. Paid $48,500 cash for operating expenses.
6. Adjusted accounts to recognize uncollectible accounts expense for 2007. Sharp estimates that uncollectible accounts expense will be 1 percent of sales on account.

Required

Complete all the following requirements for 2006 and 2007. Complete all requirements for 2006 prior to beginning the requirements for 2007.

a. Identify the type of each transaction (asset source, asset use, asset exchange, or claims exchange).

b. Show the effect of each transaction on the elements of the financial statements, using a horizontal statements model like the one shown here. Use + for increase, − for decrease, and NA for not affected. Also, in the Cash Flow column, indicate whether the item is an operating activity (OA), investing activity (IA), or financing activity (FA). The first transaction is entered as an example. (*Hint:* Closing entries do not affect the statements model.)

Event No.	Assets	=	Liab.	+	Equity	Rev.	−	Exp.	=	Net Inc.	Cash Flow
1	+		NA		+	+		NA		+	NA

c. Organize the transaction data in accounts under an accounting equation.

d. Prepare the income statement, statement of changes in stockholders' equity, balance sheet, and statement of cash flows.

Problem 5-18 *Determination of account balances—percent of receivables allowance method of accounting for uncollectible accounts*

L.O. 2

CHECK FIGURE
c. Net Realizable Value $55,104

During the first year of operation, 2006, Martin's Appliance recognized $292,000 of service revenue on account. At the end of 2006, the accounts receivable balance was $57,400. Even though this is his first year in business, the owner believes he will collect all but about 4 percent of the ending balance.

Required

a. What amount of cash was collected by Martin's during 2006?

b. Assuming the use of an allowance system to account for uncollectible accounts, what amount should Martin record as uncollectible accounts expense in 2006?

c. What is the net realizable value of receivables at the end of 2006?

d. Show the effect of the transactions listed in Requirement *c* on the financial statements by recording the appropriate amounts in a horizontal statements model like the one shown here. When you record amounts in the Cash Flow column, indicate whether the item is an operating activity (OA), investing activity (IA), or financing activity (FA). The letters NA indicate that an element is not affected by the event.

Assets					=	Liab.	+	Equity	Rev.	−	Exp.	=	Net Inc.	Cash Flow
Cash	+	Accts. Rec.	−	Allow.										

L.O. 2

CHECK FIGURES

b. Net Income: $62,520
Total Assets: $157,520

Problem 5-19 *Accounting for uncollectible accounts: percent of receivables allowance method*

Hammond Inc. experienced the following transactions for 2007, its first year of operations:

1. Issued common stock for $80,000 cash.
2. Purchased $225,000 of merchandise on account.
3. Sold merchandise that cost $148,000 for $294,000 on account.
4. Collected $242,000 cash from accounts receivable.
5. Paid $210,000 on accounts payable.
6. Paid $46,000 of salaries expense for the year.
7. Paid other operating expenses of $35,000.
8. Hammond adjusted the accounts using the following information from an accounts receivable aging schedule.

Number of Days Past Due	Amount	Percent Likely to Be Uncollectible	Allowance Balance
Current	$33,000	.01	
0–30	12,000	.05	
31–60	3,000	.10	
61–90	2,500	.20	
Over 90 days	1,500	.50	

Required

a. Organize the transaction data in accounts under an accounting equation.

b. Prepare the income statement, statement of changes in stockholders' equity, balance sheet, and statement of cash flows for Hammond Inc. for 2007.

c. What is the net realizable value of the accounts receivable at December 31, 2007?

L.O. 2

CHECK FIGURE

a. Net Realizable Value: $82,775

Problem 5-20 *Determining account balances: percent of revenue allowance method of accounting for uncollectible accounts*

The following information pertains to Bay Cabinet Company's sales on account and accounts receivable:

Accounts Receivable Balance, January 1, 2007	$125,400
Allowance for Doubtful Accounts, January 1, 2007	3,250
Sales on Account, 2007	875,000
Cost of Goods Sold, 2007	620,000
Collections of Accounts Receivable, 2007	910,000

After several collection attempts, Bay Cabinet Company wrote off $2,800 of accounts that could not be collected. Bay estimates that uncollectible accounts expense will be 0.5 percent of sales on account.

Required

a. Compute the following amounts:
   (1) Using the allowance method, the amount of uncollectible accounts expense for 2007.
   (2) Net realizable value of receivables at the end of 2007.

b. Explain why the uncollectible accounts expense amount is different from the amount that was written off as uncollectible.

Problem 5-21 ***Accounting for credit card sales and uncollectible accounts: percent of receivables allowance method***

L.O. 2, 5

excel

mhhe.com/edmonds2007

CHECK FIGURES

b. Net Income: $39,760
Total Assets: $99,760

Bishop Supply Company had the following transactions in 2006:

1. Acquired $60,000 cash from the issue of common stock.
2. Purchased $180,000 of merchandise for cash in 2006.
3. Sold merchandise that cost $110,000 for $200,000 during the year under the following terms:

$ 50,000	Cash Sales
140,000	Credit Card Sales (The credit card company charges a 3 percent service fee.)
10,000	Sales on Account

4. Collected all the amount receivable from the credit card company.
5. Collected $9,200 of accounts receivable.
6. Paid selling and administrative expenses of $46,000.
7. Determined that 5 percent of the ending accounts receivable balance would be uncollectible.

Required

a. Record the above events in a horizontal statements model like the following one. When you record amounts in the Cash Flow column, indicate whether the item is an operating activity (OA), an investing activity (IA), or ą financing activity (FA). The letters NA indicate that an element is not affected by the event.

Event	Balance Sheet											Income Statement					Statemt. of Cash Flows
	Assets							=	Equity			Rev.	–	Exp.	=	Net Inc.	
	Cash	+	Accts. Rec.	–	Allow	+	Mdse. Inv.	=	Com. Stk.	+	Ret. Earn.						

b. Prepare an income statement, statement of changes in stockholders' equity, balance sheet, and statement of cash flows for 2006.

Problem 5-22 ***Accounting for notes receivable and uncollectible accounts using the direct write-off method***

L.O. 3, 4

The following transactions apply to Bialis Co. for 2006, its first year of operations.

1. Issued $100,000 of common stock for cash.
2. Provided $86,000 of services on account.
3. Collected $75,000 cash from accounts receivable.
4. Loaned $10,000 to Horne Co. on October 1, 2006. The note had a one-year term to maturity and an 8 percent interest rate.
5. Paid $32,000 of salaries expense for the year.
6. Paid a $2,000 dividend to the stockholders.
7. Recorded the accrued interest on December 31, 2006 (see item 4).
8. Determined that $560 of accounts receivable were uncollectible.

Required

a. Show the effects of the above transactions in a horizontal statements model like the one shown below.

	Assets				= Liab. +	Equity		Rev. − Exp. = Net Inc.	Cash Flows
Event	Cash +	Accts. Rec. +	Notes Rec. +	Int. Rec.	=	Com. Stk. +	Ret. Earn.		

b. Prepare the income statement, balance sheet, and statement of cash flows for 2006.

L.O. 2, 4, 5

Problem 5-23 *Effect of transactions on the elements of financial statements*

Required

Identify each of the following independent transactions as asset source (AS), asset use (AU), asset exchange (AE), or claims exchange (CE). Also explain how each event affects assets, liabilities, stockholders' equity, net income, and cash flow by placing a + for increase, − for decrease, or NA for not affected under each of the categories. The first event is recorded as an example.

Event	Type of Event	Assets	Liabilities	Common Stock	Retained Earnings	Net Income	Cash Flow
a	AE	+/−	NA	NA	NA	NA	+

a. Collected cash from customers paying their accounts.
b. Recovered an uncollectible account that was previously written off (assume direct write-off method was used).
c. Paid cash for land.
d. Paid cash for other operating expenses.
e. Sold merchandise at a price above cost. Accepted payment by credit card. The credit card company charges a service fee. The receipts have not yet been forwarded to the credit card company.
f. Sold land for cash at its cost.
g. Paid cash to satisfy salaries payable.
h. Submitted receipts to the credit card company (see *e* above) and collected cash.
i. Loaned Carl Maddox cash. The loan had a 5 percent interest rate and a one-year term to maturity.
j. Paid cash to creditors on accounts payable.
k. Accrued three months' interest on the note receivable (see *i* above).
l. Provided services for cash.
m. Paid cash for salaries expense.
n. Provided services on account.
o. Wrote off an uncollectible account (use direct write-off method).

L.O. 2, 4

excel

mhhe.com/edmonds2007

CHECK FIGURES

Total Current Assets: $338,800

Total Current Liabilities: $130,000

Problem 5-24 *Multistep income statement and balance sheet*

Required

Use the following information to prepare a multistep income statement and a balance sheet for Daniels Company for 2006. (*Hint:* Some of the items will *not* appear on either statement, and ending retained earnings must be calculated.)

Operating Expenses	$ 90,000	Allowance for Doubtful Accounts	7,000
Accounts Payable	60,000	Sales Revenue	400,000
Land	77,000	Uncollectible Accounts Expense	14,000
Dividends	12,000	Accounts Receivable	113,000
Beginning Retained Earnings	171,070	Salaries Payable	12,000
Interest Revenue	16,000	Supplies	3,000
Inventory	125,000	Prepaid Rent	14,000
Notes Receivable (short term)	17,000	Common Stock	52,000
Cash	73,000	Cost of Goods Sold	179,000
Interest Receivable (short term)	800	Salaries Expense	58,270
Cash Flow from Investing Activities	102,000	Unearned Revenue	58,000

Problem 5-25 *Missing information*

L.O. 2, 4

CHECK FIGURES
a. Net Realizable Value: $33,600
b. Interest Revenue: $4,000

The following information comes from the accounts of Kemper Company:

Account Title	Beginning Balance	Ending Balance
Accounts Receivable	$30,000	$36,000
Allowance for Doubtful Accounts	1,800	2,400
Notes Receivable	50,000	50,000
Interest Receivable	1,000	5,000

Required

a. There were $180,000 in sales on account during the accounting period. Write-offs of uncollectible accounts were $2,100. What was the amount of cash collected from accounts receivable? What amount of uncollectible accounts expense was reported on the income statement? What was the net realizable value of receivables at the end of the accounting period?

b. The note has an 8 percent interest rate and 24 months to maturity. What amount of interest revenue was recognized during the period? How much cash was collected for interest?

Problem 5-26 *Comprehensive accounting cycle problem (uses percent of revenue allowance method)*

L.O. 2, 4, 5

CHECK FIGURES
Net Income: $113,150
Total Assets: $308,650

The following trial balance was prepared for Lakeview Sales and Service on December 31, 2006, after the closing entries were posted.

Account Title	Debit	Credit
Cash	$ 87,100	
Accounts Receivable	18,760	
Allowance for Doubtful Accounts		$ 960
Inventory	94,600	
Accounts Payable		44,000
Common Stock		90,000
Retained Earnings		65,500
Totals	$200,460	$200,460

Lakeview had the following transactions in 2007:

1. Purchased merchandise on account for $270,000.
2. Sold merchandise that cost $215,000 on account for $350,000.
3. Performed $80,000 of services for cash.
4. Sold merchandise for $76,000 to credit card customers. The merchandise cost $47,500. The credit card company charges a 5 percent fee.
5. Collected $360,000 cash from accounts receivable.
6. Paid $274,000 cash on accounts payable.
7. Paid $126,000 cash for selling and administrative expenses.
8. Collected cash for the full amount due from the credit card company (see item 4).
9. Loaned $60,000 to R. Shell. The note had an 8 percent interest rate and a one-year term to maturity.
10. Wrote off $650 of accounts as uncollectible.
11. Made the following adjusting entries:
    (a) Recorded three months' interest on the note at December 31, 2007 (see item 9).
    (b) Estimated uncollectible accounts expense to be .5 percent of sales on account.

Required

a. Organize the transaction data in accounts under an accounting equation.

b. Prepare an income statement, a statement of changes in stockholders' equity, a balance sheet, and a statement of cash flows for 2007.

L.O. 6

Problem 5-27 *Performing ratio analysis using real-world data*

AutoZone, Inc., claims to be "the nation's leading auto parts retailer." It sells replacement auto parts directly to the consumer. **BorgWarner, Inc.**, has over 17,000 employees and produces automobile parts, such as transmissions and cooling systems, for the world's vehicle manufacturers. The following data were taken from these companies' 2004 annual reports. All dollar amounts are in thousands.

	AutoZone August 28, 2004	BorgWarner December 31, 2004
Sales	$5,637,025	$3,525,300
Accounts Receivable	68,372	499,100

Required

a. Before performing any calculations, speculate as to which company will take the longest to collect its accounts receivables. Explain the rationale for your decision.

b. Calculate the accounts receivable turnover ratios for AutoZone and BorgWarner.

c. Calculate the average days to collect accounts receivables for AutoZone and BorgWarner.

d. Do the calculations from Requirements *b* and *c* confirm your speculations in Requirement *a*?

ANALYZE, THINK, COMMUNICATE

ATC 5-1 Business Applications Case *Understanding real-world annual reports*

Required

Use the **Topps Company**'s annual report in Appendix B to answer the following questions.

a. How long did it take Topps to collect accounts receivable during the year ended March 1, 2003?

b. Approximately what percentage of accounts receivable, as of March 1, 2003, does the company think will not be collected (see Note 3)? Caution, "Reserve for returns," also shown in Note 3, is not related to uncollectible accounts receivable.

c. What do you think the balance in the Reserve for Returns account represents?

ATC 5-2 Group Assignment *Missing information*

The following selected financial information is available for three companies:

	Bell	Card	Zore
Total sales	$125,000	$210,000	?
Cash sales	?	26,000	$120,000
Sales on account	40,000	?	75,000
Accounts receivable, January 1, 2008	6,200	42,000	?
Accounts receivable, December 31, 2008	5,600	48,000	7,500
Allowance for doubtful accounts, January 1, 2008	?	?	405
Allowance for doubtful accounts, December 31, 2008	224	1,680	?
Uncollectible accounts expense, 2008	242	1,200	395
Uncollectible accounts written off	204	1,360	365
Collections of accounts receivable, 2008	?	?	75,235

Required

a. Divide the class into three sections and divide each section into groups of three to five students. Assign one of the companies to each of the sections.

Group Tasks

(1) Determine the missing amounts for your company.
(2) Determine the percentage of accounts receivable estimated to be uncollectible at the end of 2007 and 2008 for your company.
(3) Determine the percentage of total sales that are sales on account for your company.
(4) Determine the accounts receivable turnover for your company.

Class Discussion

b. Have a representative of each section put the missing information on the board and explain how it was determined.
c. Which company has the highest percentage of sales that are on account?
d. Which company is doing the best job of collecting its accounts receivable? What procedures and policies can a company use to better collect its accounts receivable?

ATC 5-3 Real-World Case *Time needed to collect accounts receivable*

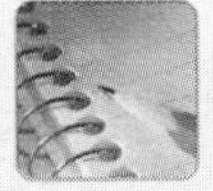

Presented here are the average days to collect accounts receivable for four companies in different industries. The data are for 2002.

Company	Average Days to Collect Accounts Receivable
Boeing (aircraft manufacturer)	34
Ford (automobile manufacturer)	6
Haverty's (furniture retailer)	81
Colgate Palmolive (consumer products manufacturer)	45

Required

Write a brief memorandum that provides possible answers to each of the following questions:

a. Why would a company that manufactures cars (**Ford**) collect its accounts receivable faster than a company that sells furniture (**Haverty's**)? (*Hint:* Ford sells cars to dealerships, not to individual customers.)
b. Why would a company that manufactures and sells large airplanes (**Boeing**) collect its accounts receivable faster than a company that sells toothpaste and soap (**Colgate Palmolive**)?

ATC 5-4 Business Applications Case *Using average number of days to collect accounts receivable to make comparisons*

The following information was drawn from the accounting records of Oakville and Monteray.

Account Title	Oakville	Monteray
Accounts Receivable (year end)	$ 60,000	$ 90,000
Sales on Account	610,000	1,200,000

Required

a. Determine the average number of days to collect accounts receivable for each company.
b. Which company is likely to incur more costs associated with extending credit?
c. Identify and discuss some of the costs associated with extending credit.
d. Explain why a company would be willing to accept the costs of extending credit to its customers.

ATC 5-5 Business Applications Case *Using ratios to make comparisons*

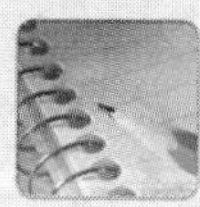

The following accounting information exists for Blackjack and Roulette companies at the end of 2007.

	Blackjack	Roulette
Cash	$ 50,000	$ 60,000
Accounts receivable	190,000	200,000
Allowance for doubtful accounts	5,000	10,000
Merchandise inventory	175,000	165,000
Accounts payable	185,000	175,000
Cost of goods sold	1,125,000	700,000
Sales	1,500,000	1,000,000

Required

a. For each company, compute the gross margin percentage and the average number of days to collect accounts receivable (use the net realizable value of receivables to compute the average days to collect accounts receivable).

b. In relation to cost, which company is charging more for its merchandise?

c. Which company is likely to incur higher financial costs associated with the granting of credit to customers? Explain.

d. Which company appears to have more restrictive credit standards when authorizing credit to its customers? (*Hint:* There is no specific answer to this question. Use your judgment and general knowledge of ratios to answer.)

ATC 5-6 Writing Assignment *Cost of charge sales*

Paul Smith is opening a plumbing supply store in University City. He plans to sell plumbing parts and materials to both wholesale and retail customers. Since contractors (wholesale customers) prefer to charge parts and materials and pay at the end of the month, Paul expects he will have to offer charge accounts. He plans to offer charge sales to the wholesale customers only and to require retail customers to pay with either cash or credit cards. Paul wondered what expenses his business would incur relative to the charge sales and the credit cards.

Required

a. What issues will Paul need to consider if he allows wholesale customers to buy plumbing supplies on account?

b. Write a memo to Paul Smith outlining the potential cost of accepting charge customers. Discuss the difference between the allowance method for uncollectible accounts and the direct write-off method. Also discuss the cost of accepting credit cards.

ATC 5-7 Ethical Dilemma *How bad can it be?*

Alonzo Saunders owns a small training services company that is experiencing growing pains. The company has grown rapidly by offering liberal credit terms to its customers. Although his competitors require payment for services within 30 days, Saunders permits his customers to delay payment for up to 90 days. Saunders' customers thereby have time to fully evaluate the training that employees receive before they must pay for that training. Saunders guarantees satisfaction. If a customer is unhappy, the customer does not have to pay. Saunders works with reputable companies, provides top-quality training, and rarely encounters dissatisfied customers.

The long collection period, however, has created a cash flow problem. Saunders has a $100,000 accounts receivable balance, but needs cash to pay current bills. He has recently negotiated a loan agreement with National Bank of Brighton County that should solve his cash flow problems. The loan agreement requires that Saunders pledge the accounts receivable as collateral for the loan. The bank agreed to loan Saunders 70 percent of the receivables balance, thereby giving him access to $70,000 cash. Saunders is satisfied with this arrangement because he estimates he needs approximately $60,000.

On the day Saunders was to execute the loan agreement, he heard a rumor that his biggest customer was experiencing financial problems and might declare bankruptcy. The customer owed Saunders $45,000. Saunders promptly called the customer's chief accountant and learned "off the record" that the rumor was true. The accountant told Saunders that the company's net worth was negative and most of its assets were pledged as collateral for bank loans. In his opinion, Saunders was unlikely to collect the balance due. Saunders' immediate concern was the impact the circumstances would have on his loan agreement with the bank.

Saunders uses the direct write-off method to recognize uncollectible accounts expense. Removing the $45,000 receivable from the collateral pool would leave only $55,000 of receivables, reducing the available credit to $38,500 ($55,000 × 0.70). Even worse, recognizing the uncollectible accounts expense would so adversely affect his income statement that the bank might further reduce the available credit by reducing the percentage of receivables allowed under the loan agreement. Saunders will have to attest to the quality of the receivables at the date of the loan but reasons that since the information he obtained about the possible bankruptcy was "off the record" he is under no obligation to recognize the uncollectible accounts expense until the receivable is officially uncollectible.

Required

a. How are income and assets affected by the decision not to act on the bankruptcy information?

b. Review the AICPA's Articles of Professional Conduct (see Chapter 1) and comment on any of the standards that would be violated by the actions Saunders is contemplating.

c. Donald Cressey identified three common features of unethical and criminal conduct (see Chapter 1). Identify these features and explain how they apply to this case.

ATC 5-8 Research Assignment ***Comparing Maytag's and Papa John's time to collect accounts receivable***

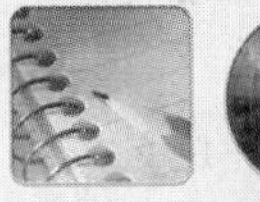

Using the most current annual reports or the Forms 10-K for **Maytag Company** and for **Papa John's International, Inc.**, complete the requirements below. To obtain the Forms 10-K use either the EDGAR system following the instructions in Appendix A or the companies' websites. The annual reports can be found on the companies' websites.

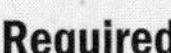

Required

a. What was Maytag's average days to collect accounts receivable? Show your computations.

b. What percentage of accounts receivable did Maytag estimate would not be collected?

c. What was Papa John's average days to collect accounts receivable? Show your computations.

d. What percentage of accounts receivable did Papa John's estimate would not be collected?

e. Briefly explain why Maytag would take longer than Papa John's to collect its accounts receivable.

CHAPTER 6

Accounting for Long-Term Operational Assets

LEARNING OBJECTIVES

After you have mastered the material in this chapter you will be able to:

1. Identify different types of long-term operational assets.
2. Determine the cost of long-term operational assets.
3. Explain how different depreciation methods affect financial statements.
4. Determine how gains and losses on disposals of long-term operational assets affect financial statements.
5. Identify some of the tax issues that affect long-term operational assets.
6. Show how revising estimates affects financial statements.
7. Explain how continuing expenditures for operational assets affect financial statements.
8. Explain how expense recognition for natural resources (depletion) affects financial statements.
9. Explain how expense recognition for intangible assets (amortization) affects financial statements.
10. Understand how expense recognition choices and industry characteristics affect financial performance measures.

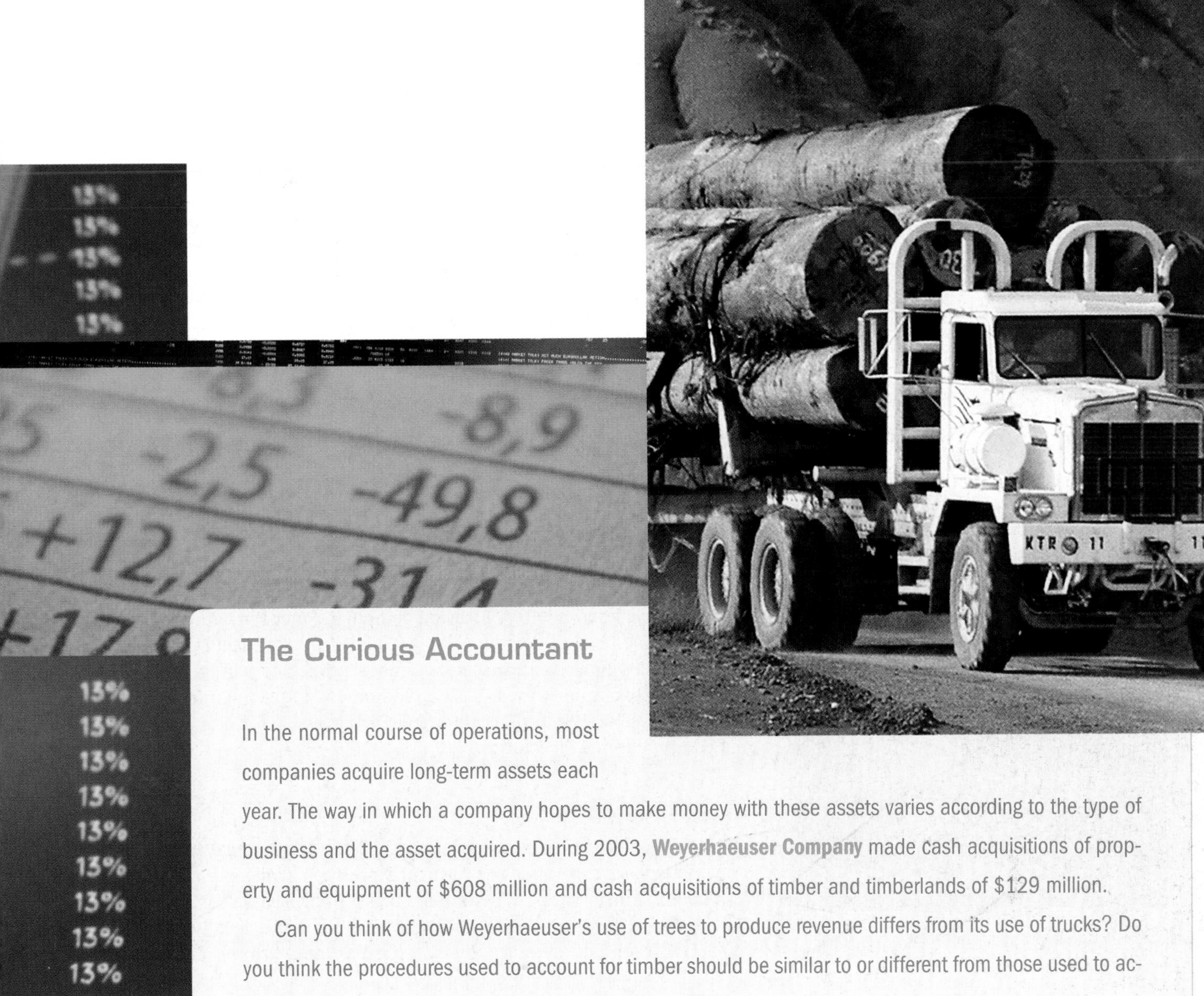

The Curious Accountant

In the normal course of operations, most companies acquire long-term assets each year. The way in which a company hopes to make money with these assets varies according to the type of business and the asset acquired. During 2003, **Weyerhaeuser Company** made cash acquisitions of property and equipment of $608 million and cash acquisitions of timber and timberlands of $129 million.

Can you think of how Weyerhaeuser's use of trees to produce revenue differs from its use of trucks? Do you think the procedures used to account for timber should be similar to or different from those used to account for trucks, and if so, how? (Answers on page 205.)

Chapter 6

CHAPTER OPENING

Companies use assets to produce revenue. Some assets, like inventory or office supplies, are called **current assets** *because they are used relatively quickly (within a single accounting period). Other assets, like equipment or buildings, are used for extended periods of time (two or more accounting periods). These assets are called* **long-term operational assets.**[1] *Accounting for long-term assets raises several questions. For example, what is the cost of the asset? Is it the list price only or should the cost of transportation, transit insurance, setup, and so on be added to the list price? Should the cost of a long-term asset be recognized as expense in the period the asset is purchased or should the cost be expensed over the useful life of the asset? What happens in the accounting records when a long-term asset is retired from use? This chapter answers these questions. It explains accounting for long-term operational assets from the date of purchase through the date of disposal.*

[1] Classifying assets as current versus long term is explained in more detail in Chapter 7.

Tangible versus Intangible Assets

Identify different types of long-term operational assets.

Long-term assets may be tangible or intangible. **Tangible assets** have a physical presence; they can be seen and touched. Tangible assets include equipment, machinery, natural resources, and land. In contrast, intangible assets have no physical form. Although they may be represented by physical documents, **intangible assets** are, in fact, rights or privileges. They cannot be seen or touched. For example, a patent represents an exclusive legal *privilege* to produce and sell a particular product. It protects inventors by making it illegal for others to profit by copying their inventions. Although a patent may be represented by legal documents, the privilege is the actual asset. Since the privilege cannot be seen or touched, the patent is an intangible asset.

Tangible Long-Term Assets

Tangible long-term assets are classified as (1) property, plant, and equipment; (2) natural resources, or (3) land.

Property, Plant, and Equipment

Property, plant, and equipment is sometimes called *plant assets* or *fixed assets*. Examples of property, plant, and equipment include furniture, cash registers, machinery, delivery trucks, computers, mechanical robots, and buildings. The level of detail used to account for these assets varies. One company may include all office equipment in one account, whereas another company might divide office equipment into computers, desks, chairs, and so on. The term used to recognize expense for property, plant, and equipment is **depreciation.**

Natural Resources

Mineral deposits, oil and gas reserves, timber stands, coal mines, and stone quarries are examples of **natural resources.** Conceptually, natural resources are inventories. When sold, the cost of these assets is frequently expensed as *cost of goods sold*. Although inventories are usually classified as short-term assets, natural resources are normally classified as long term because the resource deposits generally have long lives. For example, it may take decades to extract all of the diamonds from a diamond mine. The term used to recognize expense for natural resources is **depletion.**

Land

Land is classified separately from other property because land is not subject to depreciation or depletion. Land has an infinite life. It is not worn out or consumed as it is used. When buildings or natural resources are purchased simultaneously with land, the amount paid must be divided between the land and the other assets because of the nondepreciable nature of the land.

Intangible Assets

Intangible assets fall into two categories, those with *identifiable useful lives* and those with *indefinite useful lives.*

Intangible Assets with Identifiable Useful Lives

Intangible assets with identifiable useful lives include patents and copyrights. These assets may become obsolete (a patent may become worthless if new technology provides a superior product) or may reach the end of their legal lives. The term used when recognizing expense for intangible assets with identifiable useful lives is called **amortization.**

Intangible Assets with Indefinite Useful Lives

The benefits of some intangible assets may extend so far into the future that their useful lives cannot be estimated. For how many years will the **Coca-Cola** trademark attract customers? When will the value of a **McDonald's** franchise end? There are no answers to these questions. Intangible assets such as renewable franchises, trademarks, and goodwill have indefinite useful lives. The costs of such assets are not expensed unless the value of the assets becomes impaired.

Determining the Cost of Long-Term Assets

LO 2

Determine the cost of long-term operational assets.

The **historical cost concept** requires that an asset be recorded at the amount paid for it. This amount includes the purchase price plus any costs necessary to get the asset in the location and condition for its intended use. Common cost components are:

- ***Buildings:*** (1) purchase price, (2) sales taxes, (3) title search and transfer document costs, (4) realtor's and attorney's fees, and (5) remodeling costs.
- ***Land:*** (1) purchase price, (2) sales taxes, (3) title search and transfer document costs, (4) realtor's and attorney's fees, (5) costs for removal of old buildings, and (6) grading costs.
- ***Equipment:*** (1) purchase price (less discounts), (2) sales taxes, (3) delivery costs, (4) installation costs, and (5) costs to adapt for intended use.

The cost of an asset does not include payments for fines, damages, and so on that could have been avoided.

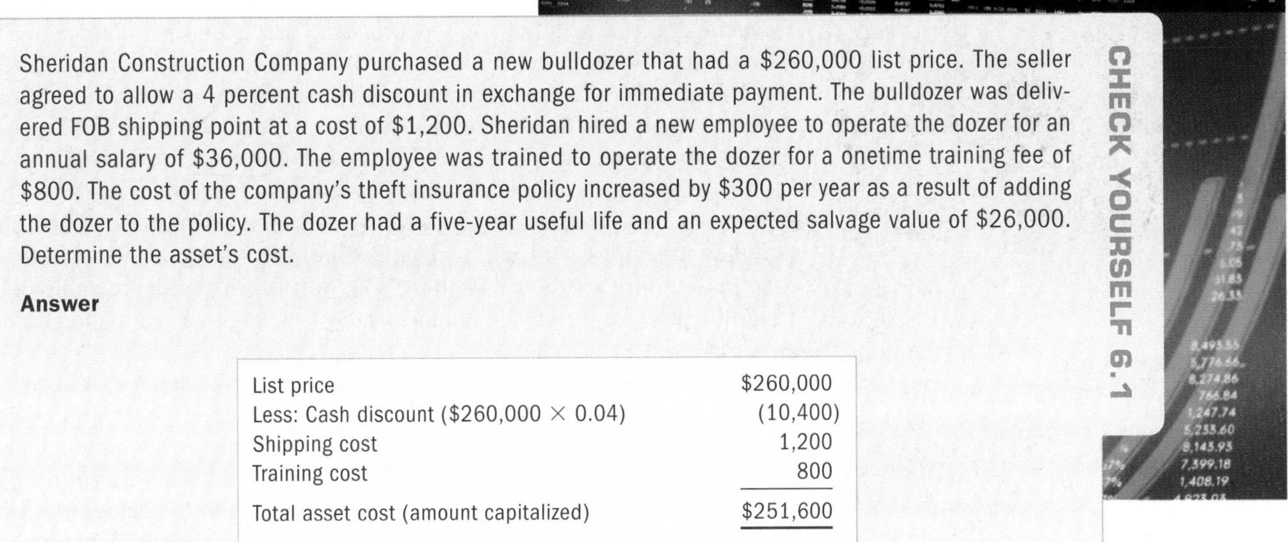

CHECK YOURSELF 6.1

Sheridan Construction Company purchased a new bulldozer that had a $260,000 list price. The seller agreed to allow a 4 percent cash discount in exchange for immediate payment. The bulldozer was delivered FOB shipping point at a cost of $1,200. Sheridan hired a new employee to operate the dozer for an annual salary of $36,000. The employee was trained to operate the dozer for a onetime training fee of $800. The cost of the company's theft insurance policy increased by $300 per year as a result of adding the dozer to the policy. The dozer had a five-year useful life and an expected salvage value of $26,000. Determine the asset's cost.

Answer

List price	$260,000
Less: Cash discount ($260,000 × 0.04)	(10,400)
Shipping cost	1,200
Training cost	800
Total asset cost (amount capitalized)	$251,600

Basket Purchase Allocation

Acquiring a group of assets in a single transaction is known as a **basket purchase.** The total price of a basket purchase must be allocated among the assets acquired. Accountants commonly allocate the purchase price using the **relative fair market value method.** To illustrate, assume that Beatty Company purchased land and a building for $240,000 cash. A real estate appraiser determined the fair market value of each asset to be:

Building	$270,000
Land	90,000
Total	$360,000

The appraisal indicates that the land is worth 25 percent ($90,000 ÷ $360,000) of the total value and the building is worth 75 percent ($270,000 ÷ $360,000). Using these percentages, the actual purchase price is allocated as follows:

Building	0.75 × $240,000 =	$180,000
Land	0.25 × $240,000 =	60,000
Total		$240,000

Methods of Recognizing Depreciation Expense

LO 3

Explain how different depreciation methods affect financial statements.

The life cycle of an operational asset involves (1) acquiring the funds to buy the asset, (2) purchasing the asset, (3) using the asset, and (4) retiring (disposing of) the asset. These stages are illustrated in Exhibit 6.1. The stages involving (1) acquiring funds and (2) purchasing assets have been discussed previously. This section of the chapter describes how accountants recognize the *use* of assets (Stage 3). As they are used, assets suffer from wear and tear called *depreciation.* Ultimately, assets depreciate to the point that they are no longer useful in the process of earning revenue. This process usually takes several years. The amount of an asset's cost that is allocated to expense during an accounting period is called **depreciation expense.**

EXHIBIT 6.1

Life Cycle of an Operational Asset

An asset that is fully depreciated by one company may still be useful to another company. For example, a rental car that is no longer useful to Hertz may still be useful to a local delivery company. As a result, companies are frequently able to sell their fully depreciated assets to other companies or individuals. The expected market value of a fully depreciated asset is called its **salvage value.** The total amount of depreciation a company recognizes for an asset, its **depreciable cost,** is the difference between its original cost and its salvage value.

For example, assume a company purchases an asset for $5,000. The company expects to use the asset for 5 years (the **estimated useful life**) and then to sell it for $1,000 (salvage value). The depreciable cost of the asset is $4,000 ($5,000 − $1,000). The portion of the depreciable cost ($4,000) that represents its annual usage is recognized as depreciation expense.

Accountants must exercise judgment to estimate the amount of depreciation expense to recognize each period. For example, suppose you own a personal computer. You know how much the computer cost, and you know you will eventually need to replace it. How would you determine the amount the computer depreciates each year you use it? Businesses may use any of several acceptable methods to estimate the amount of depreciation expense to recognize each year.

The method used to recognize depreciation expense should match the asset's usage pattern. More expense should be recognized in periods when the asset is used more and less in periods when the asset is used less. Since assets are used to produce revenue, matching expense recognition with asset usage also matches expense recognition with revenue recognition. Three alternative methods for recognizing depreciation expense are (1) straight-line, (2) double-declining-balance, and (3) units-of-production.

EXHIBIT 6.2

Depreciation Methods Used by U.S. Companies

Data source: AICPA Accounting Trends and Techniques, 2002.

The *straight-line* method produces the same amount of depreciation expense each accounting period. *Double-declining-balance,* an accelerated method, produces more depreciation expense in the early years of an asset's life, with a declining amount of expense in later years. *Units-of-production* produces varying amounts of depreciation expense in different accounting periods (more in some accounting periods and less in others). Exhibit 6.2 contrasts the different depreciation methods that U.S. companies use.

Answers to The Curious Accountant

Equipment is a long-term asset used for the purpose of producing revenue. A portion of the equipment's cost is recognized as depreciation expense each accounting period. The expense recognition for the cost of equipment is therefore spread over the useful life of the asset. Timber, however, is not used until the trees are grown. Conceptually, the costs of the trees should be treated as inventories and expensed as cost of goods sold at the time the products made from trees are sold. Even so, some timber companies recognize a periodic charge called *depletion* in a manner similar to that used for depreciation.

Accounting for unusual long-term assets such as timber requires an understanding of specialized "industry practice" accounting rules that are beyond the scope of this course. Many industries have unique accounting problems, and business managers in such industries must understand specialized accounting rules that relate to their companies.

Dryden Enterprises Illustration

To illustrate the different depreciation methods, consider a van purchased by Dryden Enterprises. Dryden plans to use the van as rental property. The van had a list price of $23,500. Dryden obtained a 10 percent cash discount from the dealer. The van was delivered FOB shipping point, and Dryden paid an additional $250 for transportation costs. Dryden also paid $2,600 for a custom accessory package to increase the van's appeal as a rental vehicle. The cost of the van is computed as follows:

List price	$23,500	
Less: Cash discount	(2,350)	$23,500 × 0.10
Plus: Transportation costs	250	
Plus: Cost of customization	2,600	
Total	$24,000	

The van has an estimated *salvage value* of $4,000 and an *estimated useful life* of four years. The following section examines three different patterns of expense recognition for this van.

Straight-Line Depreciation

The first scenario assumes the van is used evenly over its four-year life. The revenue from renting the van is assumed to be $8,000 per year. The matching concept calls for the expense recognition pattern to match the revenue stream. Since the same amount of revenue is recognized in each accounting period, Dryden should use **straight-line depreciation** because it produces equal amounts of depreciation expense each year.

Life Cycle Phase 1

The first phase of the asset life cycle is to acquire funds to purchase the asset. Assume Dryden acquired $25,000 cash on January 1, 2005, by issuing common stock. The effects on the financial statements follow:

Assets						=	Equity			Rev.	−	Exp.	=	Net Inc.	Cash Flow
Cash	+	Van	−	Acc. Dep.		=	Com. Stk.	+	Ret. Earn.						
25,000	+	NA	−	NA		=	25,000	+	NA	NA	−	NA	=	NA	25,000 FA

Life Cycle Phase 2

The second phase of the life cycle is to purchase the van. Assume Dryden bought the van on January 1, 2005, using funds from the stock issue. The cost of the van, previously computed, was $24,000 cash. The effects on the financial statements are:

Assets					=	Equity			Rev. − Exp. = Net Inc.					Cash Flow
Cash	+	Van	−	Acc. Dep.	=	Com. Stk.	+	Ret. Earn.						
(24,000)	+	24,000	−	NA	=	NA	+	NA	NA	−	NA	=	NA	(24,000) IA

Life Cycle Phase 3

Dryden used the van by renting it to customers. The rent revenue each year is $8,000 cash. The effects on the financial statements are shown next:

Assets					=	Equity			Rev. − Exp. = Net Inc.					Cash Flow
Cash	+	Van	−	Acc. Dep.	=	Com. Stk.	+	Ret. Earn.						
8,000	+	NA	−	NA	=	NA	+	8,000	8,000	−	NA	=	8,000	8,000 OA

Although illustrated only once, these effects occur four times—once for each year Dryden earns revenue by renting the van.

At the end of each year, Dryden adjusts its accounts to recognize depreciation expense. The amount of depreciation recognized using the straight-line method is calculated as follows:

$$(\text{Asset cost} - \text{Salvage value}) \div \text{Useful life} = \text{Depreciation expense}$$

$$(\$24{,}000 - \$4{,}000) \div 4 \text{ years} = \$5{,}000 \text{ per year}$$

Recognizing depreciation expense is an asset use transaction that reduces assets and equity. The asset reduction is reported using a **contra asset account** called **Accumulated Depreciation.** Recognizing depreciation expense *does not affect cash flow.* The entire cash outflow for this asset occurred in January 2005 when Dryden purchased the van. Depreciation reflects *using* tangible assets, not spending cash to purchase them. The effects on the financial statements are as follows:

Assets					=	Equity			Rev. − Exp. = Net Inc.					Cash Flow
Cash	+	Van	−	Acc. Dep.	=	Com. Stk.	+	Ret. Earn.						
NA	+	NA	−	5,000	=	NA	+	(5,000)	NA	−	5,000	=	(5,000)	NA

The Depreciation *Expense* account, like other expense accounts, is closed to the Retained Earnings account at the end of each year. The *Accumulated* Depreciation account, in contrast, increases each year, *accumulating* the total amount of depreciation recognized on the asset to date.

Life Cycle Phase 4

Determine how gains and losses on disposals of long-term operational assets affect financial statements.

The final stage in the life cycle of a tangible asset is its disposal and removal from the company's records. Dryden retired the van from service on January 1, 2009, selling it for $4,500 cash. The van's **book value** (cost − accumulated depreciation) when it was sold was $4,000 ($24,000 cost − $20,000 accumulated depreciation), so Dryden recognized a $500 gain ($4,500 − $4,000) on the sale.

Gains are *like* revenues in that they increase assets or decrease liabilities. Gains are *unlike* revenues in that gains result from peripheral (incidental) transactions rather than routine operating activities. Dryden is not in the business of selling vans. Dryden's normal business activity is renting vans. Since selling vans is incidental to Dryden's normal operations, gains are reported separately, after operating income, on the income statement.

If Dryden had sold the asset for less than book value, the company would have recognized a loss on the asset disposal. Losses are similar to expenses in that they decrease assets or increase liabilities. However, like gains, losses result from peripheral transactions. Losses are also reported as nonoperating items on the income statement.

The effects of the asset disposal on the financial statements are shown next:

Assets					=	Equity			Rev. or Gain	−	Exp. or Loss	=	Net Inc.	Cash Flow
Cash	+	Van	−	Acc. Dep.	=	Com. Stk.	+	Ret. Earn.						
4,500	+	(24,000)	−	(20,000)	=	NA	+	500	500	−	NA	=	500	4,500 IA

Although the gain reported on the 2009 income statement is $500, the cash inflow from selling the van is $4,500. Gains and losses are not reported on the statement of cash flows. Instead they are included in the total amount of cash collected from the sale of the asset. In this case, the entire $4,500 is shown in the cash flow from investing activities section of the 2009 statement of cash flows.

Financial Statements

Exhibit 6.3 displays a vertical statements model that shows the financial results for the Dryden illustration from 2005 through 2009. Study the exhibit until you understand how all the figures were derived. The amount of depreciation expense ($5,000) reported on the income statement is constant each year from 2005 through 2008. The amount of accumulated depreciation reported on the balance sheet grows from $5,000 to $10,000, to $15,000, and finally to $20,000. The Accumulated Depreciation account is a *contra asset account* that is subtracted from the Van account in determining total assets.

Study the timing differences between cash flow and net income. Dryden spent $24,000 cash to acquire the van. Over the van's life cycle, Dryden collected $36,500 [($8,000 revenue × 4 years = $32,000) plus ($4,500 from the asset disposal) = $36,500]. The $12,500 difference between the cash collected and the cash paid ($36,500 − $24,000) equals the total net income earned during the van's life cycle.

Although the amounts are the same, the timing of the cash flows and the income recognition are different. For example, in 2005 there was a $24,000 cash outflow to purchase the van and an $8,000 cash inflow from customers. In contrast, the income statement reports net income of $3,000. In 2009, Dryden reported a $500 gain on the asset disposal, but the amount of operating income and the cash flow from operating activities is zero for that year. The gain is only indirectly related to cash flows. The $4,500 of cash received on disposal is reported as a cash inflow from investing activities. Since gains and losses result from peripheral transactions, they do not affect operating income or cash flow from operating activities.

EXHIBIT 6.3 Financial Statements under Straight-Line Depreciation

DRYDEN ENTERPRISES
Financial Statements

	2005	2006	2007	2008	2009
Income Statements					
Rent Revenue	$ 8,000	$ 8,000	$ 8,000	$ 8,000	$ 0
Depreciation Expense	(5,000)	(5,000)	(5,000)	(5,000)	0
Operating Income	3,000	3,000	3,000	3,000	0
Gain on Sale of Van	0	0	0	0	500
Net Income	$ 3,000	$ 3,000	$ 3,000	$ 3,000	$ 500
Balance Sheets					
Assets					
Cash	$ 9,000	$17,000	$25,000	$33,000	$37,500
Van	24,000	24,000	24,000	24,000	0
Accumulated Depreciation	(5,000)	(10,000)	(15,000)	(20,000)	0
Total Assets	$28,000	$31,000	$34,000	$37,000	$37,500
Stockholders' Equity					
Common Stock	$25,000	$25,000	$25,000	$25,000	$25,000
Retained Earnings	3,000	6,000	9,000	12,000	12,500
Total Stockholders' Equity	$28,000	$31,000	$34,000	$37,000	$37,500
Statements of Cash Flows					
Operating Activities					
Inflow from Customers	$ 8,000	$ 8,000	$ 8,000	$ 8,000	$ 0
Investing Activities					
Outflow to Purchase Van	(24,000)				
Inflow from Sale of Van					4,500
Financing Activities					
Inflow from Stock Issue	25,000				
Net Change in Cash	9,000	8,000	8,000	8,000	4,500
Beginning Cash Balance	0	9,000	17,000	25,000	33,000
Ending Cash Balance	$9,000	$17,000	$25,000	$33,000	$37,500

Explain how different depreciation methods affect financial statements.

Double-Declining-Balance Depreciation

For the second scenario, assume demand for the van is strong when it is new, but fewer people rent the van as it ages. As a result, the van produces smaller amounts of revenue as time goes by. To match expenses with revenues, it is reasonable to recognize more depreciation expense in the van's early years and less as it ages.

Double-declining-balance depreciation produces a large amount of depreciation in the first year of an asset's life and progressively smaller levels of expense in each succeeding year. Since the double-declining-balance method recognizes depreciation expense more rapidly than the straight-line method does, it is called an **accelerated depreciation method.** Depreciation expense recognized using double-declining-balance is computed in three steps.

1. *Determine the straight-line rate.* Divide one by the asset's useful life. Since the estimated useful life of Dryden's van is four years, the straight-line rate is 25 percent (1 ÷ 4) per year.
2. *Determine the double-declining-balance rate.* Multiply the straight-line rate by 2 (*double* the rate). The double-declining-balance rate for the van is 50 percent (25 percent × 2).
3. *Determine the depreciation expense.* Multiply the double-declining-balance rate by the book value of the asset *at the beginning of the period* (recall that book value is historical cost minus *accumulated depreciation*). The following table shows the amount of depreciation expense Dryden will recognize over the van's useful life (2005–2008).

Year	Book Value at Beginning of Period	×	Double the Straight-Line Rate	=	Annual Depreciation Expense	
2005	($24,000 − $ 0)	×	0.50	=	$12,000	
2006	(24,000 − 12,000)	×	0.50	=	6,000	
2007	(24,000 − 18,000)	×	0.50	=	~~3,000~~	2,000
2008	(24,000 − 20,000)	×	0.50	=	~~2,000~~	0

Regardless of the depreciation method used, *an asset cannot be depreciated below its salvage value.* This restriction affects depreciation computations for the third and fourth years. Because the van had a cost of $24,000 and a salvage value of $4,000, the total amount of depreciable cost (historical cost − salvage value) is $20,000 ($24,000 − $4,000). Since $18,000 ($12,000 + $6,000) of the depreciable cost is recognized in the first two years, only $2,000 ($20,000 − $18,000) remains to be recognized after the second year. Depreciation expense recognized in the third year is therefore $2,000 even though double-declining-balance computations suggest that $3,000 should be recognized. Similarly, zero depreciation expense is recognized in the fourth year even though the computations indicate a $2,000 charge.

Olds Company purchased an asset that cost $36,000 on January 1, 2005. The asset had an expected useful life of five years and an estimated salvage value of $5,000. Assuming Olds uses the double-declining-balance method, determine the amount of depreciation expense and the amount of accumulated depreciation Olds would report on the 2007 financial statements.

Answer

Year	Book Value at Beginning of Period	×	Double the Straight-Line Rate*	=	Annual Depreciation Expense
2005	($36,000 − $ 0)	×	0.40	=	$14,400
2006	(36,000 − 14,400)	×	0.40	=	8,640
2007	(36,000 − 23,040)	×	0.40	=	5,184
Total accumulated depreciation at December 31, 2007					$28,224

*Double-declining-balance rate = 2 × Straight-line rate = 2 × (1 ÷ 5 years) = 0.40

EXHIBIT 6.4 Financial Statements under Double-Declining-Balance Depreciation

DRYDEN ENTERPRISES Financial Statements					
	2005	**2006**	**2007**	**2008**	**2009**
Income Statements					
Rent Revenue	$15,000	$ 9,000	$ 5,000	$ 3,000	$ 0
Depreciation Expense	(12,000)	(6,000)	(2,000)	0	0
Operating Income	3,000	3,000	3,000	3,000	0
Gain on Sale of Van	0	0	0	0	500
Net Income	$ 3,000	$ 3,000	$ 3,000	$ 3,000	$ 500
Balance Sheets					
Assets					
Cash	$16,000	$25,000	$30,000	$33,000	$37,500
Van	24,000	24,000	24,000	24,000	0
Accumulated Depreciation	(12,000)	(18,000)	(20,000)	(20,000)	0
Total Assets	$28,000	$31,000	$34,000	$37,000	$37,500
Stockholders' Equity					
Common Stock	$25,000	$25,000	$25,000	$25,000	$25,000
Retained Earnings	3,000	6,000	9,000	12,000	12,500
Total Stockholders' Equity	$28,000	$31,000	$34,000	$37,000	$37,500
Statements of Cash Flows					
Operating Activities					
Inflow from Customers	$15,000	$ 9,000	$ 5,000	$ 3,000	$ 0
Investing Activities					
Outflow to Purchase Van	(24,000)				
Inflow from Sale of Van					4,500
Financing Activities					
Inflow from Stock Issue	25,000				
Net Change in Cash	16,000	9,000	5,000	3,000	4,500
Beginning Cash Balance	0	16,000	25,000	30,000	33,000
Ending Cash Balance	$16,000	$25,000	$30,000	$33,000	$37,500

Effects on the Financial Statements

Exhibit 6.4 displays financial statements for the life of the asset assuming Dryden uses double-declining-balance depreciation. The illustration assumes a cash revenue stream of $15,000, $9,000, $5,000, and $3,000 for the years 2005, 2006, 2007, and 2008, respectively. Trace the depreciation expense from the table above to the income statements. Reported depreciation expense is greater in the earlier years and smaller in the later years of the asset's life.

The double-declining-balance method smooths the amount of net income reported over the asset's useful life. In the early years, when heavy asset use produces higher revenue, depreciation expense is also higher. Similarly, in the later years, lower levels of revenue are matched with lower levels of depreciation expense. Net income is constant at $3,000 per year.

The depreciation method a company uses *does not* affect how it acquires the financing, invests the funds, and retires the asset. For Dryden's van, the accounting effects of these life cycle phases are the same as under the straight-line approach. Similarly, the *recording procedures* are not affected by the depreciation method. Different depreciation methods affect only the amounts of depreciation expense recorded each year, not which accounts are used. The general journal entries are therefore not illustrated for the double-declining-balance or the units-of-production depreciation methods.

Units-of-Production Depreciation

Explain how different depreciation methods affect financial statements.

Suppose rental demand for Dryden's van depends on general economic conditions. In a robust economy, travel increases, and demand for renting vans is high. In a stagnant economy, demand for van rentals declines. In such circumstances, revenues fluctuate from year to year. To accomplish the matching objective, depreciation should also fluctuate from year to year. A method of depreciation known as **units-of-production depreciation** accomplishes this goal by basing depreciation expense on actual asset usage.

Computing depreciation expense using units-of-production begins with identifying a measure of the asset's productive capacity. For example, the number of miles Dryden expects its van to be driven may be a reasonable measure of its productive capacity. If the depreciable asset were a saw, an appropriate measure of productive capacity could be the number of board feet the saw was expected to cut during its useful life. In other words, the basis for measuring production depends on the nature of the depreciable asset.

To illustrate computing depreciation using the units-of-production depreciation method, assume that Dryden measures productive capacity based on the total number of miles the van will be driven over its useful life. Assume Dryden estimates this productive capacity to be 100,000 miles. The first step in determining depreciation expense is to compute the cost per unit of production. For Dryden's van, this amount is total depreciable cost (historical cost − salvage value) divided by total units of expected productive capacity (100,000 miles). The depreciation cost per mile is therefore $0.20 ([$24,000 cost − $4,000 salvage] ÷ 100,000 miles). Annual depreciation expense is computed by multiplying the cost per mile by the number of miles driven. Odometer readings indicate the van was driven 40,000 miles, 20,000 miles, 30,000 miles, and 15,000 miles in 2005, 2006, 2007, and 2008, respectively. Dryden developed the following schedule of depreciation charges.

Year	Cost per Mile (a)	Miles Driven (b)	Depreciation Expense (a × b)
2005	$.20	40,000	$8,000
2006	.20	20,000	4,000
2007	.20	30,000	6,000
2008	.20	15,000	~~3,000~~ 2,000

As pointed out in the discussion of the double-declining-balance method, an asset cannot be depreciated below its salvage value. Since $18,000 of the $20,000 ($24,000 cost − $4,000 salvage) depreciable cost is recognized in the first three years of using the van, only $2,000 ($20,000 − $18,000) remains to be charged to depreciation in the fourth year, even though the depreciation computations suggest the charge should be $3,000. As the preceding table indicates, the general formula for computing units-of-production depreciation is:

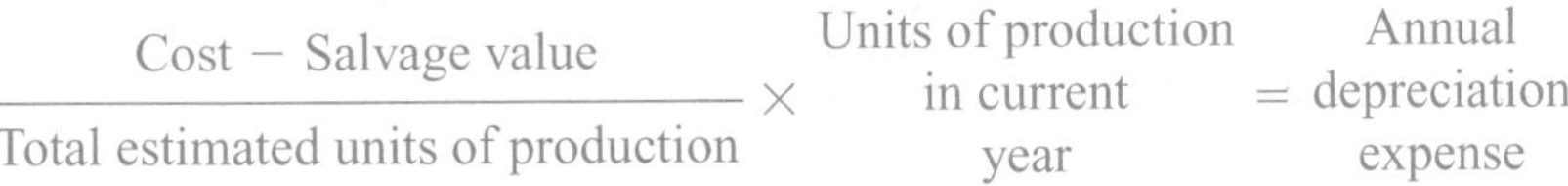

$$\frac{\text{Cost} - \text{Salvage value}}{\text{Total estimated units of production}} \times \begin{array}{c}\text{Units of production}\\ \text{in current}\\ \text{year}\end{array} = \begin{array}{c}\text{Annual}\\ \text{depreciation}\\ \text{expense}\end{array}$$

EXHIBIT 6.5 Financial Statements under Units-of-Production Depreciation

DRYDEN ENTERPRISES Financial Statements					
	2005	**2006**	**2007**	**2008**	**2009**
Income Statements					
Rent Revenue	$11,000	$ 7,000	$ 9,000	$ 5,000	$ 0
Depreciation Expense	(8,000)	(4,000)	(6,000)	(2,000)	0
Operating Income	3,000	3,000	3,000	3,000	0
Gain on Sale of Van	0	0	0	0	500
Net Income	$ 3,000	$ 3,000	$ 3,000	$ 3,000	$ 500
Balance Sheets					
Assets					
Cash	$12,000	$19,000	$28,000	$33,000	$37,500
Van	24,000	24,000	24,000	24,000	0
Accumulated Depreciation	(8,000)	(12,000)	(18,000)	(20,000)	0
Total Assets	$28,000	$31,000	$34,000	$37,000	$37,500
Stockholders' Equity					
Common Stock	$25,000	$25,000	$25,000	$25,000	$25,000
Retained Earnings	3,000	6,000	9,000	12,000	12,500
Total Stockholders' Equity	$28,000	$31,000	$34,000	$37,000	$37,500
Statements of Cash Flows					
Operating Activities					
Inflow from Customers	$11,000	$ 7,000	$ 9,000	$ 5,000	$ 0
Investing Activities					
Outflow to Purchase Van	(24,000)				
Inflow from Sale of Van					4,500
Financing Activities					
Inflow from Stock Issue	25,000				
Net Change in Cash	12,000	7,000	9,000	5,000	4,500
Beginning Cash Balance	0	12,000	19,000	28,000	33,000
Ending Cash Balance	$12,000	$19,000	$28,000	$33,000	$37,500

Exhibit 6.5 displays financial statements that assume Dryden uses units-of-production depreciation. The exhibit assumes a cash revenue stream of $11,000, $7,000, $9,000, and $5,000 for 2005, 2006, 2007, and 2008, respectively. Trace the depreciation expense from the schedule above to the income statements. Depreciation expense is greater in years the van is driven more and smaller in years the van is driven less, providing a reasonable matching of depreciation expense with revenue produced. Net income is again constant at $3,000 per year.

Explain how different depreciation methods affect financial statements.

Comparing the Depreciation Methods

The total amount of depreciation expense Dryden recognized using each of the three methods was $20,000 ($24,000 cost − $4,000 salvage value). The different methods affect the *timing,* but not the *total amount,* of expense recognized. The different methods simply assign

EXHIBIT 6.6

Depreciation Expense under Different Depreciation Methods

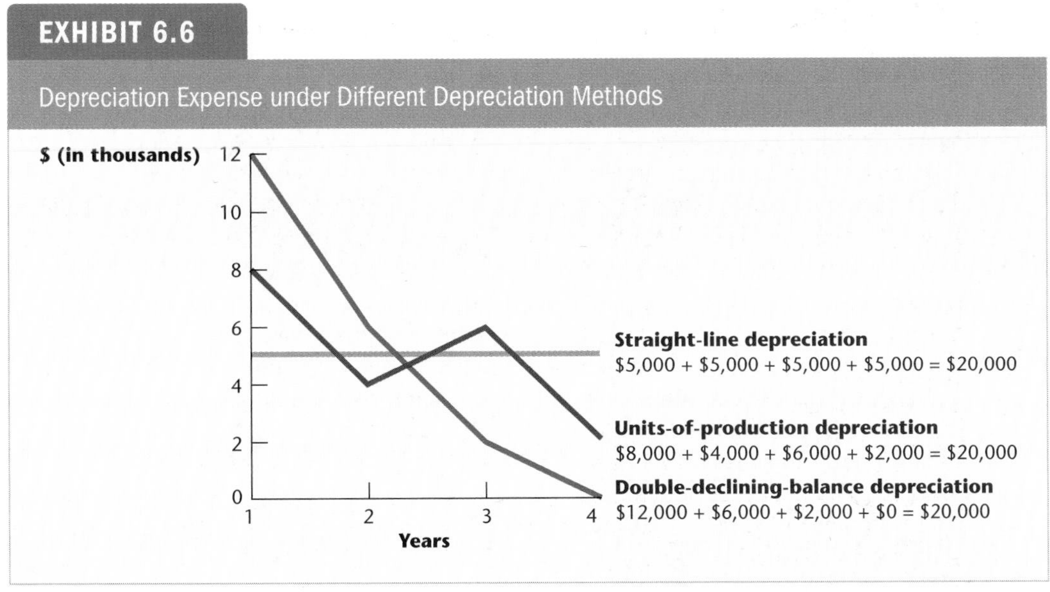

the $20,000 to different accounting periods. Exhibit 6.6 presents graphically the differences among the three depreciation methods discussed above. A company should use the method that most closely matches expenses with revenues.

Income Tax Considerations

LO 5

Identify some of the tax issues that affect long-term operational assets.

The matching principle is not relevant to income tax reporting. The objective of tax reporting is to minimize tax expense. For tax purposes the most desirable depreciation method is the one that produces the highest amount of depreciation expense. Higher expenses mean lower taxes.

The maximum depreciation currently allowed by tax law is computed using an accelerated depreciation method known as the **modified accelerated cost recovery system (MACRS).** MACRS specifies the useful life for designated categories of assets. For example, under the law, companies must base depreciation computations for automobiles, light trucks, technological equipment, and other similar asset types on a 5-year useful life. In contrast, a 7-year life must be used for office furniture, fixtures, and many types of conventional machinery. The law classifies depreciable property, excluding real estate, into one of six categories: 3-year property, 5-year property, 7-year property, 10-year property, 15-year property, and 20-year property. Tables have been established for each category that specify the percentage of cost that can be expensed (deducted) in determining the amount of taxable income. A tax table for 5- and 7-year property is shown here as an example.

Year	5-Year Property, %	7-Year Property, %
1	20.00	14.29
2	32.00	24.49
3	19.20	17.49
4	11.52	12.49
5	11.52	8.93
6	5.76	8.92
7		8.93
8		4.46

The amount of depreciation a company can deduct each year for tax purposes is determined by multiplying the cost of a depreciable asset by the percentage shown in the table. For example, the depreciation expense for year 1 of a 7-year property asset is the cost of the asset multiplied by 14.29 percent. Depreciation for year 2 is the cost multiplied by 24.49 percent.

The tables present some apparent inconsistencies. For example, if MACRS is an accelerated depreciation method, why is less depreciation permitted in year 1 than in years 2 and 3? Also, why is depreciation computed in year 6 for property with a 5-year life and in year 8 for property with a 7-year life? These conditions are the consequence of using the **half-year convention.**

The half-year convention is designed to simplify computing taxable income. Instead of requiring taxpayers to calculate depreciation from the exact date of purchase to the exact date of disposal, the tax code requires one-half year's depreciation to be charged in the year in which an asset is acquired and one-half year's depreciation in the year of disposal. As a result, the percentages shown in the table for the first and last years represent depreciation for one-half year instead of the actual time of usage.

To illustrate computing depreciation using MACRS, assume that Wilson Company purchased furniture (7-year property) for $10,000 cash on July 21. Tax depreciation charges over the useful life of the asset are computed as shown:

Year	Table Factor, %	×	Cost	=	Depreciation Amount
1	14.29		$10,000		$ 1,429
2	24.49		10,000		2,449
3	17.49		10,000		1,749
4	12.49		10,000		1,249
5	8.93		10,000		893
6	8.92		10,000		892
7	8.93		10,000		893
8	4.46		10,000		446
Total over useful life					$10,000

As an alternative to MACRS, the tax code permits using straight-line depreciation. For certain types of assets such as real property (buildings), the tax code requires using straight-line depreciation.

There is no requirement that depreciation methods used for financial reporting be consistent with those used in preparing the income tax return. For example, a company may use straight-line depreciation in its financial statements and MACRS for the tax return. A company making this choice would reduce taxes in the early years of an asset's life because it would report higher depreciation charges on the tax return than in the financial statements. In later years, however, taxes will be higher because under MACRS, the amount of depreciation declines as the asset becomes older. Taxes are delayed but not avoided. The amount of taxes delayed for future payment represent a **deferred tax liability.** Delaying tax payments is advantageous. During the delay period, the money that would have been used to pay taxes can be used instead to make revenue-generating investments.

Revision of Estimates

LO 6

Show how revising estimates affects financial statements.

In order to report useful financial information on a timely basis, accountants must make many estimates of future results, such as the salvage value and useful life of depreciable assets and uncollectible accounts expense. Estimates are frequently revised when new information surfaces. Because revisions of estimates are common, generally accepted accounting principles call for incorporating the revised information into present and future calculations. Prior reports are not corrected.

To illustrate, assume that McGraw Company purchased a machine on January 1, 2003, for $50,000. McGraw estimated the machine would have a useful life of eight years and a salvage value of $3,000. Using the straight-line method, McGraw determined the annual depreciation charge as follows:

($50,000 − $3,000) ÷ 8 years = $5,875 per year

At the beginning of the fifth year, accumulated depreciation on the machine is $23,500 ($5,875 × 4). The machine's book value is $26,500 ($50,000 − $23,500). At this point, what happens if McGraw changes its estimates of useful life or the salvage value? Consider the following revision examples independently of each other.

Revision of Life

Assume McGraw revises the expected life to 14, rather than 8, years. The machine's *remaining* life would then be 10 more years instead of 4 more years. Assume salvage value remains $3,000. Depreciation for each remaining year is:

($26,500 book value − $3,000 salvage) ÷ 10-year remaining life = $2,350

Revision of Salvage

Alternatively, assume the original expected life remained eight years, but McGraw revised its estimate of salvage value to $6,000. Depreciation for each of the remaining four years would be

($26,500 book value − $6,000 salvage) ÷ 4-year remaining life = $5,125

The revised amounts are determined for the full year, regardless of when McGraw revised its estimates. For example, if McGraw decides to change the estimated useful life on October 1, 2008, the change would be effective as of January 1, 2008. The year-end adjusting entry for depreciation would include a full year's depreciation calculated on the basis of the revised estimated useful life.

Continuing Expenditures for Plant Assets

LO 7

Explain how continuing expenditures for operational assets affect financial statements.

Most plant assets require additional expenditures for maintenance or improvement during their useful lives. Accountants must determine if these expenditures should be expensed or capitalized (recorded as assets).

Costs That Are Expensed

The costs of routine maintenance and minor repairs that are incurred to *keep* an asset in good working order are expensed in the period in which they are incurred. Because they reduce net income when incurred, accountants often call repair and maintenance costs **revenue expenditures** (companies subtract them from revenue).

With respect to the previous example, assume McGraw spent $500 for routine lubrication and to replace minor parts. The effects on the financial statements follow:

Assets	=	Equity			Rev.	−	Exp.	=	Net Inc.	Cash Flow
Cash	=	Com. Stk.	+	Ret. Earn.						
(500)	=	NA	+	(500)	NA	−	500	=	(500)	(500) OA

Costs That Are Capitalized

Substantial amounts spent to improve the quality or extend the life of an asset are described as **capital expenditures.** Capital expenditures are accounted for in one of two ways, depending on whether the cost incurred *improves the quality* or *extends the life* of the asset.

Improving Quality

Expenditures such as adding air conditioning to an existing building or installing a trailer hitch on a vehicle improve the quality of service these assets provide. If a capital expenditure improves an asset's quality, the amount is added to the historical cost of the asset. The additional cost is expensed through higher depreciation charges over the asset's remaining useful life.

To demonstrate, return to the McGraw Company example. Recall that the machine originally cost $50,000, had an estimated salvage of $3,000, and had a predicted life of eight years. Recall further that accumulated depreciation at the beginning of the fifth year is $23,500 ($5,875 × 4) so the book value is $26,500 ($50,000 − $23,500). Assume McGraw makes a major expenditure of $4,000 in the machine's fifth year to improve its productive capacity. The effects on the financial statements follow:

Assets					=	Equity			Rev.	−	Exp.	=	Net Inc.	Cash Flow
Cash	+	Mach.	−	Acc. Dep.	=	Com. Stk.	+	Ret. Earn.						
(4,000)	+	4,000	−	NA	=	NA	+	NA	NA	−	NA	=	NA	(4,000) IA

After recording the expenditure, the machine account balance is $54,000 and the asset's book value is $30,500 ($54,000 − $23,500). The depreciation charges for each of the remaining four years are:

($30,500 book value − $3,000 salvage) ÷ 4-year remaining life = $6,875

Extending Life

Expenditures such as replacing the roof of an existing building or putting a new engine in an older vehicle extend the useful life of these assets. If a capital expenditure extends the life of an asset rather than improving the asset's quality of service, accountants view the expenditure as canceling some of the depreciation previously charged to expense. The event is still an asset exchange; cash decreases, and the book value of the machine increases. However, the increase in the book value of the machine results from reducing the balance in the contra asset account, Accumulated Depreciation.

To illustrate, assume that instead of increasing productive capacity, McGraw's $4,000 expenditure had extended the useful life of the machine by two years. The effects of the expenditure on the financial statements follow:

Assets					=	Equity			Rev.	−	Exp.	=	Net Inc.	Cash Flow
Cash	+	Mach.	−	Acc. Dep.	=	Com. Stk.	+	Ret. Earn.						
(4,000)	+	NA	−	(4,000)	=	NA	+	NA	NA	−	NA	=	NA	(4,000) IA

After the expenditure is recognized, the book value is the same as if the $4,000 had been added to the Machine account ($50,000 cost − $19,500 adjusted balance in Accumulated Depreciation = $30,500). Depreciation expense for each of the remaining six years follows:

($30,500 book value − $3,000 salvage) ÷ 6-year remaining life = $4,583

On January 1, 2003, Dager Inc. purchased an asset that cost $18,000. It had a five-year useful life and a $3,000 salvage value. Dager uses straight-line depreciation. On January 1, 2005, it incurred a $1,200 cost related to the asset. With respect to this asset, determine the amount of expense and accumulated depreciation Dager would report in the 2005 financial statements under each of the following assumptions.

1. The $1,200 cost was incurred to repair damage resulting from an accident.
2. The $1,200 cost improved the operating capacity of the asset. The total useful life and salvage value remained unchanged.
3. The $1,200 cost extended the useful life of the asset by one year. The salvage value remained unchanged.

Answer

1. Dager would report the $1,200 repair cost as an expense. Dager would also report depreciation expense of $3,000 ([$18,000 − $3,000] ÷ 5). Total expenses related to this asset in 2005 would be $4,200 ($1,200 repair expense + $3,000 depreciation expense). Accumulated depreciation at the end of 2005 would be $9,000 ($3,000 depreciation expense × 3 years).
2. The $1,200 cost would be capitalized in the asset account, increasing both the book value of the asset and the annual depreciation expense.

	After Effects of Capital Improvement
Amount in asset account ($18,000 + $1,200)	$19,200
Less: Salvage value	(3,000)
Accumulated depreciation on January 1, 2005	(6,000)
Remaining depreciable cost before recording 2005 depreciation	$10,200
Depreciation for 2005 ($10,200 ÷ 3 years)	$ 3,400
Accumulated depreciation at December 31, 2005 ($6,000 + $3,400)	$ 9,400

3. The $1,200 cost would be subtracted from the Accumulated Depreciation account, increasing the book value of the asset. The remaining useful life would increase to four years, which would decrease the depreciation expense.

	After Effects of Capital Improvement
Amount in asset account	$18,000
Less: Salvage value	(3,000)
Accumulated depreciation on January 1, 2005 ($6,000 − $1,200)	(4,800)
Remaining depreciable cost before recording 2005 depreciation	$10,200
Depreciation for 2005 ($10,200 ÷ 4 years)	$ 2,550
Accumulated depreciation at December 31, 2005 ($4,800 + $2,550)	$ 7,350

Natural Resources

The cost of natural resources includes not only the purchase price but also related items such as the cost of exploration, geographic surveys, and estimates. The process of expensing natural resources is commonly called depletion.[2] The most common method used to calculate depletion is units-of-production.

LO 8

Explain how expense recognition for natural resources (depletion) affects financial statements.

[2]In practice, the depletion charge is considered a product cost and allocated between inventory and cost of goods sold. This text uses the simplifying assumption that all resources are sold in the same accounting period in which they are extracted. The full depletion charge is therefore expensed in the period in which the resources are extracted.

To illustrate, assume Apex Coal Mining paid $4,000,000 cash to purchase a mine with an estimated 16,000,000 tons of coal. The unit depletion charge is:

$$\$4,000,000 \div 16,000,000 \text{ tons} = \$0.25 \text{ per ton}$$

If Apex mines 360,000 tons of coal in the first year, the depletion charge is:

$$360,000 \text{ tons} \times \$0.25 \text{ per ton} = \$90,000$$

The depletion of a natural resource has the same effect on the accounting equation as other expense recognition events. Assets (in this case, a *coal mine*) and stockholders' equity decrease. The depletion expense reduces net income. The effects on the financial statements follow:

Assets			=	Equity			Rev.	–	Exp.	=	Net Inc.	Cash Flow
Cash	+	Coal Mine	=	Com. Stk.	+	Ret. Earn.						
(4,000,000)	+	4,000,000	=	NA	+	NA	NA	–	NA	=	NA	(4,000,000) IA
NA	+	(90,000)	=	NA	+	(90,000)	NA	–	90,000	=	(90,000)	NA

Intangible Assets

Explain how expense recognition for intangible assets (amortization) affects financial statements.

Intangible assets provide rights, privileges, and special opportunities to businesses. Common intangible assets include trademarks, patents, copyrights, franchises, and goodwill. Some of the unique characteristics of these intangible assets are described in the following sections.

Trademarks

A **trademark** is a name or symbol that identifies a company or a product. Familiar trademarks include the Polo emblem, the name *Coca-Cola*, and the Nike slogan, "Just do it." Trademarks are registered with the federal government and have an indefinite legal lifetime.

The costs incurred to design, purchase, or defend a trademark are capitalized in an asset account called Trademarks. Companies want their trademarks to become familiar but also face the risk of a trademark being used as the generic name for a product. To protect a trademark, companies in this predicament spend large sums on legal fees and extensive advertising programs to educate consumers. Well-known trademarks that have been subject to this problem include Coke, Xerox, Kleenex, and Vaseline.

Patents

A **patent** grants its owner an exclusive legal right to produce and sell a product that has one or more unique features. Patents issued by the U.S. Patent Office have a legal life of 17 years. Companies may obtain patents through purchase, lease, or internal development. The costs capitalized in the Patent account are usually limited to the purchase price and legal fees to obtain and defend the patent. The research and development costs that are incurred to develop patentable products are usually expensed in the period in which they are incurred.

FOCUS ON INTERNATIONAL ISSUES

U.S. GAAP: A COMPETITIVE DISADVANTAGE?

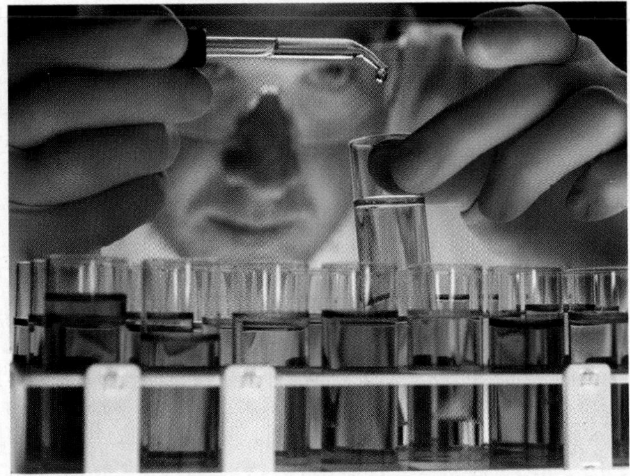

The accounting rules of various countries have many differences, but, over the years, perhaps none have caused as much concern to companies involved in global competition as the rules related to accounting for goodwill and research and development (R&D).

Suppose that Company A paid $300,000 to purchase Company B's assets. Furthermore, suppose Company B's assets have a market value of only $200,000. In the United States, the $100,000 difference is classified as *goodwill.* Before July 2001, this goodwill would have been amortized (expensed) over its useful life. In the United Kingdom, the accounting is very different. A U.K. company is allowed to charge the entire $100,000 *directly against equity* in the year of the purchase. Normally, a cost is first recorded in an asset account and then expensed. When the expense is recognized, net income decreases and retained earnings decreases. Under the U.K. approach, you simply skip the income statement by making a charge directly to Retained Earnings.

In July 2001, the FASB voted to change radically the U.S. GAAP related to accounting for business combinations, which includes accounting for goodwill. Now goodwill is reported on the balance sheet as an asset, but it never has to be written off as an expense, so long as the value of the goodwill does not decrease. The rules governing accounting for business combinations in the United States are now more like those of other industrialized nations.

Suppose Company X is a pharmaceutical company that spends $10 million on the R&D of a new drug. Under U.S. GAAP, the company is required to expense the $10 million immediately. In Japan, the company is allowed to capitalize the cost in an asset account and then to expense it gradually over the useful life of the asset. Therefore, in the year in which R&D costs are incurred, a U.S. company reports more expense and less income than its Japanese counterpart.

Some business people believe that U.S. GAAP can put U.S. companies at a competitive disadvantage in the search for capital. Certainly, the rules pertaining to goodwill and R&D demonstrate how U.S. companies may be forced to report lower earnings. Foreign companies that report higher earnings may be able to attract international investors who would otherwise invest in U.S. companies. Keep in mind that well-informed business professionals know how different accounting rules affect a company's financial statements. If they believe that U.S. GAAP cause a company's earnings to be understated, they take this into consideration when making investment decisions.

Copyrights

A **copyright** protects writings, musical compositions, works of art, and other intellectual property for the exclusive benefit of the creator or persons assigned the right by the creator. The cost of a copyright includes the purchase price and any legal costs associated with obtaining and defending the copyright. Copyrights granted by the federal government extend for the life of the creator plus 70 years. A radio commercial could legally use a Bach composition as background music; it could not, however, use the theme song from the movie, *The Matrix,* without obtaining permission from the copyright owner. The cost of a copyright is often expensed early because future royalties may be uncertain.

Franchises

Franchises grant exclusive rights to sell products or perform services in certain geographic areas. Franchises may be granted by governments or private businesses. Franchises granted by governments include federal broadcasting licenses. Private business franchises include fast-food restaurant chains and brand labels such as **Healthy Choice**. The legal and useful lives of a franchise are frequently difficult to determine. Judgment is often crucial to establishing the estimated useful life for franchises.

REALITY BYTES

In September 2001, **Hewlett-Packard Company (HP)** agreed to pay approximately $24 billion to acquire **Compaq Computer Corporation**. At the time, Compaq's balance sheet showed net assets (assets minus liabilities) of approximately $11.7 billion. Why would HP pay the owners of Compaq twice the value of the assets reported on the company's balance sheet?

HP was likely willing to pay twice the book value of the assets for three reasons. First, the value of the assets on Compaq's balance sheet represented the historical cost of the assets. The current market value of these assets was probably higher than their historical cost, especially for assets such as the Compaq trademark. Second, HP believed that the two companies combined could operate at a lower cost than the two could as separate companies, thus increasing the total income they could generate. Finally, HP probably believed that Compaq had *goodwill,* which enables a company to generate above average earnings from using its assets. In other words, HP was paying for a hidden asset not reported on Compaq's balance sheet.

Just because a company is willing to pay for goodwill does not mean it exists. In February 2005 HP's board of directors fired the company's CEO, Carly Fiorina (pictured here), due in large part to the disappointing performance of HP since its acquisition of Compaq.

Goodwill

Goodwill is the value attributable to favorable factors such as reputation, location, and superior products. Consider the most popular restaurant in your town. If the owner sold the restaurant, do you think the purchase price would be simply the total value of the chairs, tables, kitchen equipment, and building? Certainly not, because much of the restaurant's value lies in its popularity; in other words, its ability to generate a high return is based on the goodwill (reputation) of the business.

Calculating goodwill can be complex; here we present a simple example to illustrate how it is determined. Suppose the accounting records of a restaurant named Bendigo's show:

Assets	=	Liabilities	+	Stockholders' Equity
$200,000	=	$50,000	+	$150,000

Assume a buyer agrees to purchase the restaurant by paying the owner $300,000 cash and assuming the existing liabilities. In other words, the restaurant is purchased at a price of $350,000 ($300,000 cash + $50,000 assumed liabilities). Now assume that the assets of the business (tables, chairs, kitchen equipment, etc.) have a fair market value of only $280,000. Why would the buyer pay $350,000 to purchase assets with a market value of $280,000? Obviously, the buyer is purchasing more than just the assets. The buyer is purchasing the business's goodwill. The amount of the goodwill is the difference between the purchase price and the fair market value of the assets. In this case, the goodwill is $70,000 ($350,000 − $280,000). The effects of the purchase on the financial statements of the buyer follow:

Assets					=	Liab.	+	Equity	Rev.	−	Exp.	=	Net Inc.	Cash Flow
Cash	+	Rest. Assets	+	Goodwill										
(300,000)	+	280,000	+	70,000	=	50,000	+	NA	NA	−	NA	=	NA	(300,000) IA

The fair market value of the restaurant assets represents the historical cost to the new owner. It becomes the basis for future depreciation charges.

Expense Recognition for Intangible Assets

As mentioned earlier, intangible assets fall into two categories, those with *identifiable useful lives* and those with *indefinite useful lives.* Expense recognition for intangible assets depends on which classification applies.

Expensing Intangible Assets with Identifiable Useful Lives

The costs of intangible assets with identifiable useful lives are normally expensed on a straight-line basis using a process called *amortization.* An intangible asset should be amortized over the shorter of two possible time periods: (1) its legal life or (2) its useful life.

To illustrate, assume that Flowers Industries purchased a newly granted patent for $44,000 cash. Although the patent has a legal life of 17 years, Flowers estimates that it will be useful for only 11 years. The annual amortization charge is therefore $4,000 ($44,000 ÷ 11 years). The effects on the financial statements follow:

Assets			=	Equity			Rev.	−	Exp.	=	Net Inc.	Cash Flow
Cash	+	Patent	=	Com. Stk.	+	Ret. Earn.						
(44,000)	+	44,000	=	NA	+	NA	NA	−	NA	=	NA	(44,000) IA
NA	+	(4,000)	=	NA	+	(4,000)	NA	−	4,000	=	(4,000)	NA

Impairment Losses for Intangible Assets with Indefinite Useful Lives

Intangible assets with indefinite useful lives must be tested for impairment annually. The impairment test consists of comparing the fair value of the intangible asset to its carrying value (book value). If the fair value is less than the book value, an impairment loss must be recognized.

To illustrate, return to the example of the Bendigo's restaurant purchase. Recall that the buyer of Bendigo's paid $70,000 for goodwill. Assume the restaurant experiences a significant decline in revenue because many of its former regular customers are dissatisfied with the food prepared by the new chef. Suppose the decline in revenue is so substantial that the new owner believes the Bendigo's name is permanently impaired. The owner decides to hire a different chef and change the name of the restaurant. In this case, the business has suffered a permanent decline in value of goodwill. The company must recognize an impairment loss.

The restaurant's name has lost its value, but the owner believes the location continues to provide the opportunity to produce above-average earnings. Some, but not all, of the goodwill has been lost. Assume the fair value of the remaining goodwill is determined to be $40,000. The impairment loss to recognize is $30,000 ($70,000 − $40,000). The loss reduces the intangible asset (goodwill), stockholder's equity (retained earnings), and net income. The statement of cash flows would not be affected. The effects on the financial statements follow:

Assets	=	Liab.	+	Equity	Rev.	−	Exp./Loss	=	Net Inc.	Cash Flow
Goodwill	=			Ret. Earn.						
(30,000)	=	NA	+	(30,000)	NA	−	30,000	=	(30,000)	NA

Balance Sheet Presentation

This chapter has explained accounting for the acquisition, expense recognition, and disposal of a wide range of long-term assets. Exhibit 6.7 illustrates typical balance sheet presentation of many of the assets discussed.

EXHIBIT 6.7

Balance Sheet Presentation of Operational Assets

Partial Balance Sheet			
Long-Term Assets			
Plant and Equipment			
Buildings	$4,000,000		
Less: Accumulated Depreciation	(2,500,000)	$1,500,000	
Equipment	1,750,000		
Less: Accumulated Depreciation	(1,200,000)	550,000	
Total Plant and Equipment			$2,050,000
Land			850,000
Natural Resources			
Mineral Deposits (Less: Depletion)		2,100,000	
Oil Reserves (Less: Depletion)		890,000	
Total Natural Resources			2,990,000
Intangibles			
Patents (Less: Amortization)		38,000	
Goodwill		175,000	
Total Intangible Assets			213,000
Total Long-Term Assets			$6,103,000

Understand how expense recognition choices and industry characteristics affect financial performance measures.

Managers may have differing opinions about which allocation method (straight-line, accelerated, or units-of-production) best matches expenses with revenues. As a result, one company may use straight-line depreciation while another company in similar circumstances uses double-declining-balance. Since the allocation method a company uses affects the amount of expense it recognizes, analysts reviewing financial statements must consider the accounting procedures companies use in preparing the statements.

Effect of Judgment and Estimation

Assume that two companies, Alpha and Zeta, experience identical economic events in 2005 and 2006. Both generate revenue of $50,000 and incur cost of goods sold of $30,000 during each year. In 2005, each company pays $20,000 for an asset with an expected useful life of five years and no salvage value. How will the companies' financial statements differ if one uses straight-line depreciation and the other uses the double-declining-balance method? To answer this question, first compute the depreciation expense for both companies for 2005 and 2006.

If Alpha Company uses the straight-line method, depreciation for 2005 and 2006 is:

(Cost − Salvage)	÷	Useful life	=	Depreciation expense per year
($20,000 − $0)	÷	5 years	=	$4,000

In contrast, if Zeta Company uses the double-declining-balance method, Zeta recognizes the following amounts of depreciation expense for 2005 and 2006:

	(Cost − Accumulated Depreciation)	×	2 × (Straight-Line Rate)	=	Depreciation Expense
2005	($20,000 − $ 0)	×	[2 × (1 ÷ 5)]	=	$8,000
2006	($20,000 − $8,000)	×	[2 × (1 ÷ 5)]	=	$4,800

Based on these computations, the income statements for the two companies are:

Income Statements	2005		2006	
	Alpha Co.	Zeta Co.	Alpha Co.	Zeta Co.
Sales	$50,000	$50,000	$50,000	$50,000
Cost of Goods Sold	(30,000)	(30,000)	(30,000)	(30,000)
Gross Margin	20,000	20,000	20,000	20,000
Depreciation Expense	(4,000)	(8,000)	(4,000)	(4,800)
Net Income	$16,000	$12,000	$16,000	$15,200

The relevant sections of the balance sheets are:

Plant Assets	2005		2006	
	Alpha Co.	Zeta Co.	Alpha Co.	Zeta Co.
Asset	$20,000	$20,000	$20,000	$20,000
Accumulated Depreciation	(4,000)	(8,000)	(8,000)	(12,800)
Book Value	$16,000	$12,000	$12,000	$ 7,200

The depreciation method is not the only aspect of expense recognition that can vary between companies. Companies may also make different assumptions about the useful lives and salvage values of long-term operational assets. Thus, even if the same depreciation method is used, depreciation expense may still differ.

Since the depreciation method and the underlying assumptions regarding useful life and salvage value affect the determination of depreciation expense, they also affect the amounts of net income, retained earnings, and total assets. Financial statement analysis is affected if it is based on ratios that include these items. Previously defined ratios that are affected include the (1) debt to assets ratio, (2) return on assets ratio, (3) return on equity ratio, and (4) return on sales ratio.

To promote meaningful analysis, public companies are required to disclose all significant accounting policies used to prepare their financial statements. This disclosure is usually provided in the footnotes that accompany the financial statements.

Effect of Industry Characteristics

As indicated in previous chapters, industry characteristics affect financial performance measures. For example, companies in manufacturing industries invest heavily in machinery while insurance companies rely more on human capital. Manufacturing companies therefore

3309 2/6 4637

EXHIBIT 6.8

Industry Data Reflecting the Use of Long-Term Tangible Assets

Industry	Company	Sales ÷ Property, Plant, and Equipment
Cable Companies	Comcast Corp.	0.66
	Cox Communication	0.65
Airlines	Delta	0.80
	United	0.85
Employment Agencies	Kelly Services	21.37
	Manpower, Inc.	56.20

have relatively higher depreciation charges than insurance companies. To illustrate how the type of industry affects financial reporting, examine Exhibit 6.8. This exhibit compares the ratio of sales to property, plant, and equipment for two companies in each of three different industries. These data are for 2002.

The table indicates that for every \$1.00 invested in property, plant, and equipment, **Manpower, Inc.**, produced \$56.20 of sales. In contrast, **Comcast Corp.** and **Delta Airlines** produced only \$0.66 and \$.80, respectively, for each \$1.00 they invested in operational assets. Does this mean the management of Manpower, Inc., is doing a better job than the management of Comcast or Delta? Not necessarily. It means that these companies operate in different economic environments. In other words, it takes significantly more equipment to operate a cable company or an airline than it takes to operate an employment agency.

Effective financial analysis requires careful consideration of industry characteristics, accounting policies, and the reasonableness of assumptions such as useful life and salvage value.

<< A Look Back

This chapter explains that the primary objective of recognizing depreciation is to match the cost of a long-term tangible asset with the revenues the asset is expected to generate. The matching concept also applies to natural resources (depletion) and intangible assets (amortization). The chapter explains how alternative methods can be used to account for the same event (e.g., straight-line versus double-declining-balance depreciation). Companies experiencing exactly the same business events could produce different financial statements. The alternative accounting methods for depreciating, depleting, or amortizing assets include the (1) straight-line, (2) double-declining-balance, and (3) units-of-production methods.

The *straight-line method* produces equal amounts of expense in each accounting period. The amount of the expense recognized is determined using the formula [(cost − salvage) ÷ number of years of useful life]. The *double-declining-balance method* produces proportionately larger amounts of expense in the early years of an asset's useful life and increasingly smaller amounts of expense in the later years of the asset's useful life. The formula for calculating double-declining-balance depreciation is [book value at beginning of period × (2 × the straight-line rate)]. The *units-of-production method* produces expense in direct proportion to the number of units produced during an accounting period. The formula for the amount of expense recognized each period is [(cost − salvage) ÷ total estimated units of production = allocation rate × units of production in current accounting period].

The chapter also discussed *MACRS depreciation,* an accelerated tax reporting method. MACRS is not acceptable under GAAP for public reporting. A company may use MACRS depreciation for tax purposes and straight-line or one of the other methods for public reporting. As a result, differences may exist between the amount of tax expense and the amount of tax liability. Such differences are reported as *deferred income taxes.*

This chapter showed how to account for *changes in estimates* such as the useful life or the salvage value of a depreciable asset. Changes in estimates do not affect the amount of depreciation recognized previously. Instead, the remaining book value of the asset is expensed over its remaining useful life.

After an asset has been placed into service, companies typically incur further costs for maintenance, quality improvement, and extensions of useful life. *Maintenance costs* are expensed in the period in which they are incurred. *Costs that improve the quality* of an asset are added to the cost of the asset, increasing the book value and the amount of future depreciation charges. *Costs that extend the useful life* of an asset are subtracted from the asset's Accumulated Depreciation account, increasing the book value and the amount of future depreciation charges.

A Look Forward >>

In Chapter 7 we move from the assets section of the balance sheet to issues in accounting for liabilities.

SELF-STUDY REVIEW PROBLEM

The following information pertains to a machine purchased by Bakersfield Company on January 1, 2005.

Purchase price	$ 63,000
Delivery cost	$ 2,000
Installation charge	$ 3,000
Estimated useful life	8 years
Estimated units the machine will produce	130,000
Estimated salvage value	$ 3,000

The machine produced 14,400 units during 2005 and 17,000 units during 2006.

Required

Determine the depreciation expense Bakersfield would report for 2005 and 2006 using each of the following methods.

a. Straight-line.

b. Double-declining-balance.

c. Units-of-production.

d. MACRS assuming that the machine is classified as seven-year property.

Solution to Requirements a–d.

a. Straight-line

Purchase price	$63,000	
Delivery cost	2,000	
Installation charge	3,000	
Total cost of machine	68,000	
Less: Salvage value	(3,000)	
	$65,000 ÷ 8 =	$8,125 Depreciation per year
2005	$ 8,125	
2006	$ 8,125	

b. Double-declining-balance

Year	Cost	−	Accumulated Depreciation at Beginning of Year	×	2 × S-L Rate	=	Annual Depreciation
2005	$68,000	−	$ 0	×	(2 × 0.125)	=	$17,000
2006	68,000	−	17,000	×	(2 × 0.125)	=	12,750

c. Units-of-production

(1) (Cost − Salvage value) ÷ Estimated units of production = Depreciation cost per unit produced

$$\frac{\$68,000 - \$3,000}{130,000} = \$0.50 \text{ per unit}$$

(2) Cost per unit × Annual units produced = Annual depreciation expense

2005 $0.50 × 14,400 = $7,200

2006 0.50 × 17,000 = 8,500

d. MACRS

Cost × MACRS percentage = Annual depreciation

2005 $68,000 × 0.1429 = $ 9,717

2006 68,000 × 0.2449 = 16,653

KEY TERMS

accelerated depreciation method 209
accumulated depreciation 206
amortization 202
basket purchase 203
book value 207
capital expenditures 216
contra asset account 206
copyright 219
current assets 201
deferred tax liability 214
depletion 202
depreciable cost 204
depreciation 202
depreciation expense 204
double-declining-balance depreciation 208
estimated useful life 204
franchise 219
goodwill 220
half-year convention 214
historical cost concept 203
intangible assets 202
long-term operational assets 201
modified accelerated cost recovery system (MACRS) 213
natural resources 202
patent 218
property, plant, and equipment 202
relative fair market value method 203
revenue expenditures 215
salvage value 204
straight-line depreciation 205
tangible assets 202
trademark 218
units-of-production depreciation 211

QUESTIONS

1. What is the difference between the functions of long-term operational assets and investments?
2. What is the difference between tangible and intangible assets? Give an example of each.
3. What is the difference between goodwill and specifically identifiable intangible assets?
4. Define *depreciation*. What kind of asset depreciates?
5. Why are natural resources called *wasting assets?*
6. Is land a depreciable asset? Why or why not?
7. Define *amortization*. What kind of assets are amortized?
8. Explain the historical cost concept as it applies to long-term operational assets. Why is the book value of an asset likely to be different from the current market value of the asset?
9. What different kinds of expenditures might be included in the recorded cost of a building?

10. What is a basket purchase of assets? When a basket purchase is made, how is cost assigned to individual assets?
11. What are the stages in the life cycle of a long-term operational asset?
12. Explain straight-line, units-of-production, and double-declining-balance depreciation. When is it appropriate to use each of these depreciation methods?
13. What effect does the recognition of depreciation expense have on total assets? On total equity?
14. Does the recognition of depreciation expense affect cash flows? Why or why not?
15. MalMax purchased a depreciable asset. What would be the difference in total assets at the end of the first year if MalMax chooses straight-line depreciation versus double-declining-balance depreciation?
16. John Smith mistakenly expensed the cost of a long-term tangible fixed asset. Specifically, he charged the cost of a truck to a delivery expense account. How will this error affect the income statement and the balance sheet in the year in which the mistake is made?
17. What is *salvage value?*
18. What type of account (classification) is Accumulated Depreciation?
19. How is the book value of an asset determined?
20. Why is depreciation that has been recognized over the life of an asset shown in a contra account? Why not just reduce the asset account?
21. Assume that a piece of equipment cost $5,000 and had accumulated depreciation recorded of $3,000. What is the book value of the equipment? Is the book value equal to the fair market value of the equipment? Explain.
22. Why would a company choose to depreciate one piece of equipment using the double-declining-balance method and another piece of equipment using straight-line depreciation?
23. Explain MACRS depreciation. When is its use appropriate?
24. Does the method of depreciation required to be used for tax purposes reflect the use of a piece of equipment? Can you use double-declining-balance depreciation for tax purposes?
25. Define *deferred taxes.* Where does the account *Deferred Taxes* appear in the financial statements?
26. Why may it be necessary to revise the estimated life of a plant asset? When the estimated life is revised, does it affect the amount of depreciation per year? Why or why not?
27. How are capital expenditures made to improve the quality of a capital asset accounted for? Would the answer change if the expenditure extended the life of the asset but did not improve quality? Explain.
28. When a long-term operational asset is sold at a gain, how is the balance sheet affected? Is the statement of cash flows affected? If so, how?
29. Define *depletion.* What is the most commonly used method of computing depletion?
30. List several common intangible assets. How is the life determined that is to be used to compute amortization?
31. List some differences between U.S. GAAP and GAAP of other countries.
32. How do differences in expense recognition and industry characteristics affect financial performance measures?

EXERCISES

All Exercises are available with McGraw-Hill's Homework Manager

Unless specifically included, ignore income tax considerations in all exercises and problems.

Exercise 6-1 ***Long-term operational assets used in a business*** **L.O. 1**

Required

Give some examples of long-term operational assets that each of the following companies is likely to own: *(a)* AT&T, *(b)* Caterpillar, *(c)* Amtrak, and *(d)* The Walt Disney Co.

L.O. 1

Exercise 6-2 *Identifying long-term operational assets*

Required

Which of the following items should be classified as long-term operational assets?

a. Cash
b. Buildings
c. Production machinery
d. Accounts receivable
e. Prepaid rent
f. Franchise
g. Inventory
h. Patent
i. Tract of timber
j. Land
k. Computer
l. Goodwill

L.O. 1

Exercise 6-3 *Classifying tangible and intangible assets*

Required

Identify each of the following long-term operational assets as either tangible (T) or intangible (I).

a. Retail store building
b. Shelving for inventory
c. Trademark
d. Gas well
e. Drilling rig
f. FCC license for TV station
g. 18-wheel truck
h. Timber
i. Log loader
j. Dental chair
k. Goodwill
l. Business Web page

L.O. 2

Exercise 6-4 *Determining the cost of an asset*

Northeast Logging Co. purchased an electronic saw to cut various types and sizes of logs. The saw had a list price of $120,000. The seller agreed to allow a 5 percent discount because Northeast paid cash. Delivery terms were FOB shipping point. Freight cost amounted to $2,500. Northeast had to hire an individual to operate the saw. Northeast had to build a special platform to mount the saw. The cost of the platform was $1,000. The saw operator was paid an annual salary of $40,000. The cost of the company's theft insurance policy increased by $2,000 per year as a result of acquiring of the saw. The saw had a four-year useful life and an expected salvage value of $10,000.

Required

Determine the amount to be capitalized in an asset account for the purchase of the saw.

L.O. 2

Exercise 6-5 *Allocating costs on the basis of relative market values*

Midwest Company purchased a building and the land on which the building is situated for a total cost of $900,000 cash. The land was appraised at $200,000 and the building at $800,000.

Required

a. What is the accounting term for this type of acquisition?
b. Determine the amount of the purchase cost to allocate to the land and the amount to allocate to the building.
c. Would the company recognize a gain on the purchase? Why or why not?
d. Record the purchase in a statements model like the following one.

Assets					=	Liab.	+	Equity	Rev.	−	Exp.	=	Net Inc.	Cash Flow
Cash	+	Land	+	Building										

L.O. 2

Exercise 6-6 *Allocating costs for a basket purchase*

Jourdan Company purchased a restaurant building, land, and equipment for $700,000 cash. The appraised value of the assets was as follows:

Land	$160,000
Building	400,000
Equipment	240,000
Total	$800,000

Required

a. Compute the amount to be recorded on the books for each of the assets.

b. Record the purchase in a horizontal statements model like the following one.

Assets				= Liab. + Equity	Rev. − Exp. = Net Inc.	Cash Flow
Cash +	Land +	Building +	Equip.			

Exercise 6-7 *Effect of depreciation on the accounting equation and financial statements* **L.O. 3**

The following events apply to The Pizza Factory for the 2008 fiscal year:

1. The company started when it acquired $18,000 cash from the issue of common stock.
2. Purchased a new pizza oven that cost $15,000 cash.
3. Earned $26,000 in cash revenue.
4. Paid $13,000 cash for salaries expense.
5. Paid $6,000 cash for operating expenses.
6. Adjusted the records to reflect the use of the pizza oven. The oven, purchased on January 1, 2008, has an expected useful life of five years and an estimated salvage value of $3,000. Use straight-line depreciation. The adjusting entry was made as of December 31, 2008.

Required

a. Record the above transactions in a horizontal statements model like the following one.

Event	Balance Sheet							Income Statement			Statemt. of Cash Flows
	Assets				=	Equity		Rev.	− Exp.	= Net Inc.	
	Cash	+ Equip.	− A. Depr.		=	Com. Stock	+ Ret. Earn.				

b. What amount of depreciation expense would The Pizza Factory report on the 2009 income statement?

c. What amount of accumulated depreciation would The Pizza Factory report on the December 31, 2009, balance sheet?

d. Would the cash flow from operating activities be affected by depreciation in 2009?

Exercise 6-8 *Effect of double-declining-balance depreciation on financial statements* **L.O. 3**

Smith Company started operations by acquiring $100,000 cash from the issue of common stock. On January 1, 2005, the company purchased equipment that cost $100,000 cash. The equipment had an expected useful life of five years and an estimated salvage value of $20,000. Smith Company earned $92,000 and $65,000 of cash revenue during 2005 and 2006, respectively. Smith Company uses double-declining-balance depreciation.

Required

a. Record the above transactions in a horizontal statements model like the following one.

Event	Balance Sheet							Income Statement			Statemt. of Cash Flows
	Assets				=	Equity		Rev.	− Exp.	= Net Inc.	
	Cash	+ Equip.	− A. Depr.		=	Com. Stock	+ Ret. Earn.				

b. Prepare income statements, balance sheets, and statements of cash flows for 2005 and 2006. Use a vertical statements format.

L.O. 3, 4

Exercise 6-9 *Events related to the acquisition, use, and disposal of a tangible plant asset: straight-line depreciation*

CJ's Pizza purchased a delivery van on January 1, 2005, for $25,000. In addition, CJ's paid sales tax and title fees of $1,000 for the van. The van is expected to have a four-year life and a salvage value of $6,000.

Required

a. Using the straight-line method, compute the depreciation expense for 2005 and 2006.

b. Assume the van was sold on January 1, 2008, for $12,000. Determine the amount of gain or loss that would be recognized on the asset disposal.

L.O. 3

Exercise 6-10 *Computing and recording straight-line versus double-declining-balance depreciation*

At the beginning of 2006, Precision Manufacturing purchased a new computerized drill press for $50,000. It is expected to have a five-year life and a $5,000 salvage value.

Required

a. Compute the depreciation for each of the five years, assuming that the company uses
   (1) Straight-line depreciation.
   (2) Double-declining-balance depreciation.

b. Record the purchase of the drill press and the depreciation expense for the first year under the straight-line and double-declining-balance methods in a financial statements model like the following one:

Assets					=	Equity	Rev. − Exp. = Net Inc.	Cash Flow
Cash	+	Drill Press	−	Acc. Dep.	=	Ret. Earn		

L.O. 4

Exercise 6-11 *Effect of the disposal of plant assets on the financial statements*

A plant asset with a cost of $40,000 and accumulated depreciation of $36,000 is sold for $6,000.

Required

a. What is the book value of the asset at the time of sale?

b. What is the amount of gain or loss on the disposal?

c. How would the sale affect net income (increase, decrease, no effect) and by how much?

d. How would the sale affect the amount of total assets shown on the balance sheet (increase, decrease, no effect) and by how much?

e. How would the event affect the statement of cash flows (inflow, outflow, no effect) and in what section?

L.O. 8

Exercise 6-12 *Effect of gains and losses on the accounting equation and financial statements*

On January 1, 2008, Gert Enterprises purchased a parcel of land for $12,000 cash. At the time of purchase, the company planned to use the land for future expansion. In 2009, Gert Enterprises changed its plans and sold the land.

Required

a. Assume that the land was sold for $11,200 in 2009.
   (1) Show the effect of the sale on the accounting equation.
   (2) What amount would Gert report on the income statement related to the sale of the land?
   (3) What amount would Gert report on the statement of cash flows related to the sale of the land?

b. Assume that the land was sold for $13,500 in 2009.
   (1) Show the effect of the sale on the accounting equation.
   (2) What amount would Gert report on the income statement related to the sale of the land?
   (3) What amount would Gert report on the statement of cash flows related to the sale of the land?

Exercise 6-13 ***Double-declining-balance and units-of-production depreciation: gain or loss on disposal*** L.O. 3, 4

Print Service Co. purchased a new color copier at the beginning of 2005 for $35,000. The copier is expected to have a five-year useful life and a $5,000 salvage value. The expected copy production was estimated at 2,000,000 copies. Actual copy production for the five years was as follows:

2005	550,000
2006	480,000
2007	380,000
2008	390,000
2009	240,000
Total	2,040,000

The copier was sold at the end of 2009 for $5,200.

Required

a. Compute the depreciation expense for each of the five years, using double-declining-balance depreciation.

b. Compute the depreciation expense for each of the five years, using units-of-production depreciation. (Round cost per unit to three decimal places.)

c. Calculate the amount of gain or loss from the sale of the asset under each of the depreciation methods.

Exercise 6-14 ***Computing depreciation for tax purposes*** L.O. 5

Quality Lumber Company purchased $120,000 of equipment on September 1, 2006.

Required

a. Compute the amount of depreciation expense that is deductible under MACRS for 2006 and 2007, assuming that the equipment is classified as seven-year property.

b. Compute the amount of depreciation expense that is deductible under MACRS for 2006 and 2007, assuming that the equipment is classified as five-year property.

Exercise 6-15 ***Revision of estimated useful life*** L.O. 6

On January 1, 2006, Harris Machining Co. purchased a compressor and related installation equipment for $64,000. The equipment had a three-year estimated life with a $4,000 salvage value. Straight-line depreciation was used. At the beginning of 2008, Harris revised the expected life of the asset to four years rather than three years. The salvage value was revised to $3,000.

Required

Compute the depreciation expense for each of the four years.

Exercise 6-16 ***Distinguishing between revenue expenditures and capital expenditures*** L.O. 7

Zell's Shredding Service has just completed a minor repair on a shredding machine. The repair cost was $900, and the book value prior to the repair was $5,000. In addition, the company spent $8,000 to replace the roof on a building. The new roof extended the life of the building by five years. Prior to the roof replacement, the general ledger reflected the Building account at $90,000 and related Accumulated Depreciation account at $40,000.

Required

After the work was completed, what book value should Zell's report on the balance sheet for the shredding machine and the building?

Exercise 6-17 ***Effect of revenue expenditures versus capital expenditures on financial statements*** L.O. 7

Sequoia Construction Company purchased a forklift for $110,000 cash. It had an estimated useful life of four years and a $10,000 salvage value. At the beginning of the third year of use, the company spent an additional $8,000 that was related to the forklift. The company's financial condition just prior to this expenditure is shown in the following statements model.

Assets					=	Equity			Rev.	−	Exp.	=	Net Inc.	Cash Flow
Cash	+	Forklift	−	Acc. Dep.	=	Com. Stk.	+	Ret. Earn.						
12,000	+	110,000	−	50,000	=	24,000	+	48,000	NA	−	NA	=	NA	NA

Required

Record the $8,000 expenditure in the statements model under each of the following *independent* assumptions:

a. The expenditure was for routine maintenance.
b. The expenditure extended the forklift's life.
c. The expenditure improved the forklift's operating capacity.

L.O. 7

Exercise 6-18 *Effect of revenue expenditures versus capital expenditures on financial statements*

On January 1, 2005, Valley Power Company overhauled four turbine engines that generate power for customers. The overhaul resulted in a slight increase in the capacity of the engines to produce power. Such overhauls occur regularly at two-year intervals and have been treated as maintenance expense in the past. Management is considering whether to capitalize this year's $25,000 cash cost in the engine asset account or to expense it as a maintenance expense. Assume that the engines have a remaining useful life of two years and no expected salvage value. Assume straight-line depreciation.

Required

a. Determine the amount of additional depreciation expense Valley would recognize in 2005 and 2006 if the cost were capitalized in the Engine account.
b. Determine the amount of expense Valley would recognize in 2005 and 2006 if the cost were recognized as maintenance expense.
c. Determine the effect of the overhaul on cash flow from operating activities for 2005 and 2006 if the cost were capitalized and expensed through depreciation charges.
d. Determine the effect of the overhaul on cash flow from operating activities for 2005 and 2006 if the cost were recognized as maintenance expense.

L.O. 8

Exercise 6-19 *Computing and recording depletion expense*

Ecru Sand and Gravel paid $600,000 to acquire 800,000 cubic yards of sand reserves. The following statements model reflects Ecru's financial condition just prior to purchasing the sand reserves. The company extracted 420,000 cubic yards of sand in year 1 and 360,000 cubic yards in year 2.

Assets			=	Equity			Rev.	−	Exp.	=	Net Inc.	Cash Flow
Cash	+	Sand Res.	=	Com. Stk.	+	Ret. Earn.						
700,000	+	NA	=	700,000	+	NA	NA	−	NA	=	NA	NA

Required

a. Compute the depletion charge per unit.
b. Record the acquisition of the sand reserves and the depletion expense for years 1 and 2 in a financial statements model like the preceding one.

L.O. 9

Exercise 6-20 *Computing and recording the amortization of intangibles*

Texas Manufacturing paid cash to purchase the assets of an existing company. Among the assets purchased were the following items:

Patent with 5 remaining years of legal life	$36,000
Goodwill	40,000

Texas's financial condition just prior to the purchase of these assets is shown in the following statements model:

Assets					=	Liab.	+ Equity	Rev.	−	Exp.	=	Net Inc.	Cash Flow
Cash	+	Patent	+	Goodwill									
94,000	+	NA	+	NA	=	NA	+ 94,000	NA	−	NA	+	NA	NA

Required

a. Compute the annual amortization expense for these items if applicable.

b. Record the purchase of the intangible assets and the related amortization expense for year 1 in a horizontal statements model like the preceding one.

Exercise 6-21 *Computing and recording goodwill*

L.O. 9

Mike Wallace purchased the business Magnum Supply Co. for $275,000 cash and assumed all liabilities at the date of purchase. Magnum's books showed tangible assets of $280,000, liabilities of $40,000, and equity of $240,000. An appraiser assessed the fair market value of the tangible assets at $270,000 at the date of purchase. Wallace's financial condition just prior to the purchase is shown in the following statements model:

Assets					=	Liab.	+ Equity	Rev.	−	Exp.	=	Net Inc.	Cash Flow
Cash	+	Tang. Assets	+	Goodwill									
325,000	+	NA	+	NA	=	NA	+ 325,000	NA	−	NA	=	NA	NA

Required

a. Compute the amount of goodwill purchased.

b. Record the purchase in a financial statements model like the preceding one.

Exercise 6-22 *Performing ratio analysis using real-world data*

L.O. 10

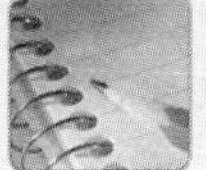

American Greetings Corporation manufactures and sells greeting cards and related items such as gift wrapping paper. **CSX Corporation** is one of the largest railway networks in the nation. The following data were taken from one of the companies' December 31, 2004, annual report and from the other's February 28, 2005, annual report. Revealing which data relate to which company was intentionally omitted. For one company, the dollar amounts are in thousands, while for the other they are in millions.

	Company 1	Company 2
Sales	$8,020	$1,902,727
Depreciation costs	730	57,045
Net earnings	339	95,279
Current assets	2,987	1,281,639
Property, plant, and equipment	19,945	339,792
Total assets	24,581	2,535,628

Required

a. Calculate depreciation costs as a percentage of sales for each company.

b. Calculate property, plant, and equipment as a percentage of total assets for each company.

c. Based on the information now available to you, decide which data relate to which company. Explain the rationale for your decision.

d. Which company appears to be using its assets most efficiently? Explain your answer.

PROBLEMS

All Problems are available with McGraw-Hill's Homework Manager

L.O. 2

Problem 6-23 *Accounting for acquisition of assets including a basket purchase*

CHECK FIGURES
Total cost of equipment: $40,900
Cost allocated to copier: $7,500

Khan Company made several purchases of long-term assets in 2009. The details of each purchase are presented here.

New Office Equipment

1. List price: $40,000; terms: 1/10 n/30; paid within the discount period.
2. Transportation-in: $800.
3. Installation: $500.
4. Cost to repair damage during unloading: $500.
5. Routine maintenance cost after eight months: $120.

Basket Purchase of Office Furniture, Copier, Computers, and Laser Printers for $50,000 with Fair Market Values

1. Office furniture, $24,000.
2. Copier, $9,000.
3. Computers and printers, $27,000.

Land for New Headquarters with Old Barn Torn Down

1. Purchase price, $80,000.
2. Demolition of barn, $5,000.
3. Lumber sold from old barn, $2,000.
4. Grading in preparation for new building, $8,000.
5. Construction of new building, $250,000.

Required

In each of these cases, determine the amount of cost to be capitalized in the asset accounts.

L.O. 3, 4

mhhe.com/edmonds2007

Problem 6-24 *Accounting for depreciation over multiple accounting cycles: straight-line depreciation*

CHECK FIGURES
Net Income, 2005: $1,250
Total Assets, 2009: $35,200

KC Company began operations when it acquired $30,000 cash from the issue of common stock on January 1, 2005. The cash acquired was immediately used to purchase equipment for $30,000 that had a $5,000 salvage value and an expected useful life of four years. The equipment was used to produce the following revenue stream (assume all revenue transactions are for cash). At the beginning of the fifth year, the equipment was sold for $4,500 cash. KC uses straight-line depreciation.

	2005	2006	2007	2008	2009
Revenue	$7,500	$8,000	$8,200	$7,000	$0

Required

Prepare income statements, statements of changes in stockholders' equity, balance sheets, and statements of cash flows for each of the five years.

L.O. 2, 3, 6, 7

Problem 6-25 *Purchase and use of tangible asset: three accounting cycles, double-declining-balance depreciation*

CHECK FIGURES
b. Net Income, 2007: $23,200
Total Assets, 2009: $139,770

The following transactions pertain to Optimal Solutions Inc. Assume the transactions for the purchase of the computer and any capital improvements occur on January 1 each year.

2007

1. Acquired $60,000 cash from the issue of common stock.
2. Purchased a computer system for $25,000. It has an estimated useful life of five years and a $3,000 salvage value.
3. Paid $1,500 sales tax on the computer system.
4. Collected $35,000 in data entry fees from clients.
5. Paid $1,200 in fees to service the computers.
6. Recorded double-declining-balance depreciation on the computer system for 2007.

2008

1. Paid $800 for repairs to the computer system.
2. Bought a case of toner cartridges for the printers that are part of the computer system, $1,200.
3. Collected $38,000 in data entry fees from clients.
4. Paid $900 in fees to service the computers.
5. Recorded double-declining-balance depreciation for 2008.

2009

1. Paid $3,000 to upgrade the computer system, which extended the total life of the system to six years.
2. Paid $900 in fees to service the computers.
3. Collected $35,000 in data entry fees from clients.
4. Recorded double-declining-balance depreciation for 2009.

Required

a. Record the above transactions in a horizontal statements model like the following one.

Event	Balance Sheet									Income Statement					Statemt. of Cash Flows
	Assets					=	Equity			Rev.	−	Exp.	=	Net Inc.	
	Cash	+	Equip.	−	A. Depr.	=	Com. Stock	+	Ret. Earn.						

b. Use a vertical model to present financial statements for 2007, 2008, and 2009.

Problem 6-26 *Calculating depreciation expense using four different methods*

L.O. 3, 5

mhhe.com/edmonds2007

CHECK FIGURES

b. Depreciation Expense, 2008: $4,600

c. Depreciation Expense, 2009: $4,300

O'Brian Service Company purchased a copier on January 1, 2008, for $17,000 and paid an additional $200 for delivery charges. The copier was estimated to have a life of four years or 800,000 copies. Salvage was estimated at $1,200. The copier produced 230,000 copies in 2008 and 250,000 copies in 2009.

Required

Compute the amount of depreciation expense for the copier for calendar years 2008 and 2009, using these methods:

a. Straight-line.
b. Units-of-production.
c. Double-declining-balance.
d. MACRS, assuming that the copier is classified as five-year property.

Problem 6-27 *Effect of straight-line versus double-declining-balance depreciation on the recognition of expense and gains or losses*

L.O. 3, 4

mhhe.com/edmonds2007

CHECK FIGURES

a. Depreciation Expense, Year 2: $6,400

b. Depreciation Expense, Year 2: $8,400

Same Day Laundry Services purchased a new steam press on January 1, for $35,000. It is expected to have a five-year useful life and a $3,000 salvage value. Same Day expects to use the steam press more extensively in the early years of its life.

Required

a. Calculate the depreciation expense for each of the five years, assuming the use of straight-line depreciation.
b. Calculate the depreciation expense for each of the five years, assuming the use of double-declining-balance depreciation.
c. Would the choice of one depreciation method over another produce a different amount of cash flow for any year? Why or why not?
d. Assume that Same Day Laundry Services sold the steam press at the end of the third year for $20,000. Compute the amount of gain or loss using each depreciation method.

L.O. 3, 4

Problem 6-28 *Computing and recording units-of-production depreciation*

McNabb Corporation purchased a delivery van for $25,500 in 2007. The firm's financial condition immediately prior to the purchase is shown in the following horizontal statements model:

Assets							=	Equity			Rev.	−	Exp.	=	Net Inc.	Cash Flow
Cash	+	Van	−	Acc. Dep.			=	Com. Stk.	+	Ret. Earn.						
50,000	+	NA	−	NA			=	50,000	+	NA	NA	−	NA	=	NA	NA

CHECK FIGURES
a. Depreciation Expense, 2007: $7,500
c. Gain on Sale: $1,000

The van was expected to have a useful life of 150,000 miles and a salvage value of $3,000. Actual mileage was as follows:

2007	50,000
2008	70,000
2009	58,000

Required

a. Compute the depreciation for each of the three years, assuming the use of units-of-production depreciation.

b. Assume that McNabb earns $21,000 of cash revenue during 2007. Record the purchase of the van and the recognition of the revenue and the depreciation expense for the first year in a financial statements model like the preceding one.

c. Assume that McNabb sold the van at the end of the third year for $4,000. Show the sale of the van in a statements model like the preceding one.

L.O. 3

Problem 6-29 *Determining the effect of depreciation expense on financial statements*

CHECK FIGURES
a. Company A, Net Income: $20,000
c. Company C, Book Value: $17,750

Three different companies each purchased a machine on January 1, 2005, for $54,000. Each machine was expected to last five years or 200,000 hours. Salvage value was estimated to be $4,000. All three machines were operated for 50,000 hours in 2005, 55,000 hours in 2006, 40,000 hours in 2007, 44,000 hours in 2008, and 31,000 hours in 2009. Each of the three companies earned $30,000 of cash revenue during each of the five years. Company A uses straight-line depreciation, company B uses double-declining-balance depreciation, and company C uses units-of-production depreciation.

Required

Answer each of the following questions. Ignore the effects of income taxes.

a. Which company will report the highest amount of net income for 2005?

b. Which company will report the lowest amount of net income for 2007?

c. Which company will report the highest book value on the December 31, 2007, balance sheet?

d. Which company will report the highest amount of retained earnings on the December 31, 2008, balance sheet?

e. Which company will report the lowest amount of cash flow from operating activities on the 2007 statement of cash flows?

L.O. 6, 8

Problem 6-30 *Accounting for depletion*

CHECK FIGURES
a. Coal Mine Depletion, 2008: $248,000
b. Total Natural Resources: $2,637,000

Favre Exploration Corporation engages in the exploration and development of many types of natural resources. In the last two years, the company has engaged in the following activities:

Jan. 1, 2008	Purchased a coal mine estimated to contain 200,000 tons of coal for $800,000.
July 1, 2008	Purchased for $1,950,000 a tract of timber estimated to yield 3,000,000 board feet of lumber and to have a residual land value of $150,000.
Feb. 1, 2008	Purchased a silver mine estimated to contain 30,000 tons of silver for $750,000.
Aug. 1, 2008	Purchased for $736,000 oil reserves estimated to contain 250,000 barrels of oil, of which 20,000 would be unprofitable to pump.

Required

a. Determine the amount of depletion expense to recognize on the 2008 income statement for each of the four reserves, assuming 62,000 tons of coal, 1,200,000 board feet of lumber, 9,000 tons of silver, and 80,000 barrels of oil are extracted.

b. Prepare the portion of the December 31, 2008, balance sheet that reports natural resources.

Problem 6-31 *Recognizing continuing expenditures for plant assets*

L.O. 3, 4, 6, 7

CHECK FIGURES
b. 2007 Depreciation Expense: $7,000
d. Loss on Sale: $3,250

Big Sky Inc. recorded the following transactions over the life of a piece of equipment purchased in 2005:

Jan. 1, 2005	Purchased the equipment for $36,000 cash. The equipment is estimated to have a five-year life and $6,000 salvage value and was to be depreciated using the straight-line method.
Dec. 31, 2005	Recorded depreciation expense for 2005.
May 5, 2006	Undertook routine repairs costing $750.
Dec. 31, 2006	Recorded depreciation expense for 2006.
Jan. 1, 2007	Made an adjustment costing $3,000 to the equipment. It improved the quality of the output but did not affect the life estimate.
Dec. 31, 2007	Recorded depreciation expense for 2007.
Mar. 1, 2008	Incurred $320 cost to oil and clean the equipment.
Dec. 31, 2008	Recorded depreciation expense for 2008.
Jan. 1, 2009	Had the equipment completely overhauled at a cost of $7,500. The overhaul was estimated to extend the total life to seven years and revised the salvage value to $4,000.
Dec. 31, 2009	Recorded depreciation expense for 2009.
July 1, 2010	Sold the equipment for $9,000 cash.

Required

a. Use a horizontal statements model like the following one to show the effects of these transactions on the elements of the financial statements. Use + for increase, − for decrease, and NA for not affected. The first event is recorded as an example.

Date	Assets	=	Liabilities	+	Equity	Net Inc.	Cash Flow
Jan. 1, 2005	+ −		NA		NA	NA	− IA

b. Determine amount of depreciation expense Big Sky will report on the income statements for the years 2005 through 2009.

c. Determine the book value (cost − accumulated depreciation) Big Sky will report on the balance sheets at the end of the years 2005 through 2009.

d. Determine the amount of the gain or loss Big Sky will report on the disposal of the equipment on July 1, 2010.

Problem 6-32 *Accounting for continuing expenditures*

L.O. 6, 7

Vernon Manufacturing paid $58,000 to purchase a computerized assembly machine on January 1, 2002. The machine had an estimated life of eight years and a $2,000 salvage value. Vernon's financial condition as of January 1, 2005, is shown in the following financial statements model. Vernon uses the straight-line method for depreciation.

Assets					=	Equity			Rev.	−	Exp.	=	Net Inc.	Cash Flow
Cash	+	Mach.	−	Acc. Dep.	=	Com. Stk.	+	Ret. Earn.						
15,000	+	58,000	−	21,000	=	8,000	+	44,000	NA	−	NA	=	NA	NA

CHECK FIGURE
Depreciation Expense: $8,000

Vernon Manufacturing made the following expenditures on the computerized assembly machine in 2005.

Jan. 2	Added an overdrive mechanism for $6,000 that would improve the overall quality of the performance of the machine but would not extend its life. The salvage value was revised to $3,000.
Aug. 1	Performed routine maintenance, $1,150.
Oct. 2	Replaced some computer chips (considered routine), $950.
Dec. 31	Recognized 2005 depreciation expense.

Required

Record the 2005 transactions in a statements model like the preceding one.

L.O. 9

Problem 6-33 *Accounting for intangible assets*

CHECK FIGURE
Goodwill Purchased: $130,000

Mia-Tora Company purchased a fast-food restaurant for $1,400,000. The fair market values of the assets purchased were as follows. No liabilities were assumed.

Equipment	$320,000
Land	200,000
Building	650,000
Franchise (5-year life)	100,000

Required

Calculate the amount of goodwill purchased.

L.O. 9

Problem 6-34 *Accounting for goodwill*

CHECK FIGURE
Impairment Loss: $40,000

Springhill Co. purchased the assets of Canyon Co. for $1,000,000 in 2005. The estimated fair market value of the assets at the purchase date was $920,000. Goodwill of $80,000 was recorded at purchase. In 2007, because of negative publicity, one-half of the goodwill purchased from Canyon Co. was judged to be permanently impaired.

Required

Explain how the recognition of the impairment of the goodwill will affect the 2007 balance sheet, income statement, and statement of cash flows.

L.O. 10

Problem 6-35 *Performing ratio analysis using real-world data*

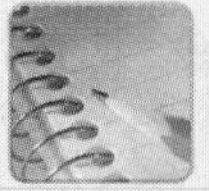

Cooper Tire Rubber Company claims to be the fourth largest tire manufacturer in North America. **Goodyear Tire & Rubber Company** is the largest tire manufacturer in North America. The following information was taken from these companies' December 31, 2004, annual reports. All dollar amounts are in thousands.

	Cooper Tire	Goodyear Tire
Sales	$2,081,609	$18,370,400
Depreciation costs	109,805	628,700
Buildings, machinery, and equipment (net of accumulated depreciation)	694,386	4,629,800
Total assets	2,668,084	16,533,300
Depreciation method	"Straight-line or accelerated"	Straight-line
Estimated life of assets:		
Buildings	10 to 40 years	40 years
Machinery and equipment	4 to 14 years	15 years

Required

a. Calculate depreciation costs as a percentage of sales for each company.

b. Calculate buildings, machinery, and equipment as a percentage of total assets for each company.

c. Which company appears to be using its assets most efficiently? Explain your answer.

d. Identify some of the problems a financial analyst encounters when trying to compare the use of long-term assets of Cooper versus Goodyear.

ANALYZE, THINK, COMMUNICATE

ATC 6-1 Business Applications Case *Understanding real-world annual reports*

Required

Use the Topps Company's annual report in Appendix B to answer the following questions.

a. What method of depreciation does Topps use?

b. What types of intangible assets does Topps have?

c. What are the estimated lives that Topps uses for the various types of long-term assets?

d. As of March 1, 2003, what is the original cost of Topps': Land; Buildings and improvements; and Machinery, equipment and software (see the footnotes)?

e. What was Topps' depreciation expense and amortization expense for 2003 (see the footnotes)?

ATC 6-2 Group Assignment *Different depreciation methods*

Sweet's Bakery makes cakes, pies, and other pastries that it sells to local grocery stores. The company experienced the following transactions during 2008.

1. Started business by acquiring $60,000 cash from the issue of common stock.
2. Purchased bakery equipment for $46,000.
3. Had sales in 2008 amounting to $42,000.
4. Paid $8,200 of cash for supplies which were all used during the year to make baked goods.
5. Incurred other operating expenses of $12,000 for 2008.
6. Recorded depreciation assuming the equipment had a four-year life and a $6,000 salvage value. The MACRS recovery period is five years.
7. Paid income tax. The rate is 30 percent.

Required

a. Organize the class into three sections and divide each section into groups of three to five students. Assign each section a depreciation method: straight-line, double-declining-balance, or MACRS.

Group Task

Prepare an income statement and balance sheet using the preceding information and the depreciation method assigned to your group.

Class Discussion

b. Have a representative of each section put its income statement on the board. Are there differences in net income? In the amount of income tax paid? How will these differences in the amount of depreciation expense change over the life of the equipment?

ATC 6-3 Real-World Case *Different numbers for different industries*

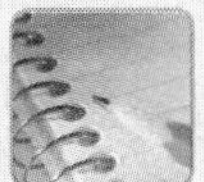

The following ratios are for four companies in different industries. Some of these ratios have been discussed in the textbook; others have not, but their names explain how the ratio was computed. The four sets of ratios, presented randomly, are:

Ratio	Company 1	Company 2	Company 3	Company 4
Operating cycle	39 days	11 days	27 days	234 days
Return on assets	24%	11%	14%	2%
Gross margin	54%	39%	40%	27%
Sales ÷ Property, plant and equipment	64.8 times	2.6 times	1.6 times	2.9 times
Sales ÷ Number of full-time employees	$21,000	$40,000	$585,000	$284,000

The four companies to which these ratios relate, listed in alphabetical order, are:

1. **Anheuser Busch Companies, Inc.**, a company that produces beer and related products. Its fiscal year-end was December 31, 2002.
2. **Caterpillar, Inc.**, a company that manufactures heavy construction equipment. Its fiscal year-end was December 31, 2002.
3. **Outback Steakhouse, Inc.**, which operates over 800 restaurants worldwide, most of them under the name Outback Steakhouse. Its fiscal year-end was December 31, 2002.
4. **Weight Watchers International, Inc.**, a company that provides weight loss services and products. During its fiscal year ending December 28, 2002, 64 percent of its revenues came from meeting fees, and 29 percent came from product sales.

Required

Determine which company should be matched with each set of ratios. Write a memorandum explaining the rationale for your decisions.

ATC 6-4 Business Applications Case *Effect of depreciation on the return on assets ratio*

Organic Bagel Bakery (OBB) was started on January 1, 2005, when it acquired $100,000 cash from the issue of common stock. The company immediately purchased an oven that cost $100,000 cash. The oven had an estimated salvage value of $10,000 and an expected useful life of eight years. OBB used the oven during 2005 to produce $30,000 of cash revenue. Assume that these were the only events affecting OBB during 2005.

Required

(*Hint:* Prepare an income statement and a balance sheet prior to completing the following requirements.)

a. Compute the return on assets ratio as of December 31, 2005, assuming OBB uses the straight-line depreciation method.
b. Recompute the ratio assuming OBB uses the double-declining-balance method.
c. Which depreciation method makes it *appear* that OBB is utilizing its assets more effectively?

ATC 6-5 Business Applications Case *Effect of depreciation on financial statement analysis: straight-line versus double-declining-balance*

Qin Company and Roche Company experienced the exact same set of economic events during 2006. Both companies purchased machines on January 1, 2006. Except for the effects of this purchase, the accounting records of both companies had the following accounts and balances.

As of January 1, 2006	
Total Assets	$200,000
Total Liabilities	80,000
Total Stockholders' Equity	120,000
During 2006	
Total Sales Revenue	100,000
Total Expenses (not including depreciation)	60,000
Liabilities were not affected by transactions in 2006.	

The machines purchased by the companies each cost $40,000 cash. The machines had expected useful lives of five years and estimated salvage values of $4,000. Qin uses straight-line depreciation. Roche uses double-declining-balance depreciation.

Required

a. For both companies, calculate the balances in the preceding accounts on December 31, 2006, after the effects of the purchase and depreciation of the machines have been applied. [*Hint:* The purchases of the machines are asset exchange transactions that do not affect total assets. However, the effect of depreciating the machines changes the amounts in total assets, expense, and equity (retained earnings).]

b. Based on the revised account balances determined in Requirement *a,* calculate the following ratios for both companies:
   (1) Debt to assets ratio.
   (2) Return on assets ratio.
   (3) Return on equity ratio.

c. Disregarding the effects of income taxes, which company produced the higher increase in real economic wealth during 2006?

ATC 6-6 Writing Assignment *Impact of historical cost on asset presentation on the balance sheet*

Assume that you are examining the balance sheets of two companies and note the following information:

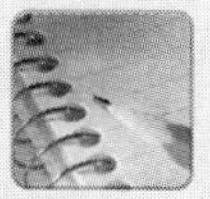

	Company A	Company B
Equipment	$1,130,000	$900,000
Accumulated Depreciation	(730,000)	(500,000)
Book Value	$ 400,000	$400,000

Maxie Smith, a student who has had no accounting courses, remarks that Company A and Company B have the same amount of equipment.

Required

In a short paragraph, explain to Maxie that the two companies do not have equal amounts of equipment. You may want to include in your discussion comments regarding the possible age of each company's equipment, the impact of the historical cost concept on balance sheet information, and the impact of different depreciation methods on book value.

ATC 6-7 Ethical Dilemma *What's an expense?*

Several years ago, Wilson Blowhard founded a communications company. The company became successful and grew by expanding its customer base and acquiring some of its competitors. In fact, most of its growth resulted from acquiring other companies. Mr. Blowhard is adamant about continuing the company's growth and increasing its net worth. To achieve these goals, the business's net income must continue to increase at a rapid pace.

If the company's net worth continues to rise, Mr. Blowhard plans to sell the company and retire. He is, therefore, focused on improving the company's profit any way he can.

In the communications business, companies often use the lines of other communications companies. This line usage is a significant operating expense for Mr. Blowhard's company. Generally accepted accounting principles require operating costs like line use to be expensed as they are incurred each year. Each dollar of line cost reduces net income by a dollar.

After reviewing the company's operations, Mr. Blowhard concluded that the company did not currently need all of the line use it was paying for. It was really paying the owner of the lines now so that the line use would be available in the future for all of Mr. Blowhard's expected new customers. Mr. Blowhard instructed his accountant to capitalize all of the line cost charges and depreciate them over 10 years. The accountant reluctantly followed Mr. Blowhard's instructions and the company's net income for the current year showed a significant increase over the prior year's net income. Mr. Blowhard had found a way to report continued growth in the company's net income and increase the value of the company.

Required

a. How does Mr. Blowhard's scheme affect the amount of income that the company would otherwise report in its financial statements and how does the scheme affect the company's balance sheet? Explain your answer.

b. Review the AICPA's Articles of Professional Conduct (see Chapter 1) and comment on any of the standards that were violated.

c. Review Donald Cressey's identified features of unethical and criminal conduct (see Chapter 1) and comment on which of these features are evident in this case.

ATC 6-8 Research Assignment *Comparing Microsoft's and Intel's operational assets*

This chapter discussed how companies in different industries often use different proportions of current versus long-term assets to accomplish their business objective. The technology revolution resulting from the silicon microchip has often been led by two well-known companies: **Microsoft** and **Intel**. Although often thought of together, these companies are really very different. Using either the most current Forms 10-K or annual reports for Microsoft Corporation and Intel Corporation, complete the requirements below. To obtain the Forms 10-K, use either the EDGAR system following the instructions in Appendix A or the company's website. Microsoft's annual report is available on its website; Intel's annual report is its Form 10-K.

Required

a. Fill in the missing data in the following table. The percentages must be computed; they are not included in the companies 10-Ks. (*Note:* The percentages for current assets and property, plant, and equipment will not sum to 100.)

	Current Assets	Property, Plant, and Equipment	Total Assets
Microsoft			
Dollar Amount	$	$	$
% of Total Assets	%	%	100%
Intel			
Dollar Amount	$	$	$
% of Total Assets	%	%	100%

b. Briefly explain why these two companies have different percentages of their assets in current assets versus property, plant, and equipment.

CHAPTER 7

Accounting for Liabilities

LEARNING OBJECTIVES

After you have mastered the material in this chapter you will be able to:

1. Show how notes payable and related interest expense affect financial statements.
2. Show how sales tax liabilities affect financial statements.
3. Define contingent liabilities and explain how they are reported in financial statements.
4. Explain how warranty obligations affect financial statements.
5. Show how installment notes affect financial statements.
6. Show how a line of credit affects financial statements.
7. Explain how to account for bonds and their related interest costs.
8. Distinguish between current and noncurrent assets and liabilities.
9. Prepare a classified balance sheet.
10. Use the current and debt to assets ratios to assess the level of liquidity.

The Curious Accountant

For its 2002 fiscal year, **AOL Time Warner** (now called Time Warner) reported a net loss of $98.7 billion. That same year, the company had $1.8 billion of interest expense.

With such a huge loss on its income statement, do you think Time Warner was able to make the interest payments on its debt? If so, how? (Answers on page 253.)

Chapter 7

CHAPTER OPENING

Chapter 5 explained the need to estimate the net realizable value of receivables (the amount of receivables a company expects to actually collect). Do companies also estimate the net realizable value of payables (the amount they expect to actually pay)? The answer is no. Unless there is evidence to the contrary, companies are assumed to be going concerns that will continue to operate. Under this **going concern assumption,** *companies expect to pay their obligations in full. Accounts and notes payable are therefore reported at face value. In addition to reporting liabilities for which the amounts due are known, companies report liabilities for which the amounts due are uncertain. Liabilities that are uncertain as to amount are contingent liabilities.*

Chapter 2 discussed several types of liabilities with known amounts due, including accounts payable, salaries payable, and unearned revenue. This chapter introduces other liabilities with known amounts due: notes payable, sales taxes payable, lines of credit, and bond liabilities. We also discuss a contingent liability called warranties payable. We begin with a discussion of **current liabilities,** *those that are payable within one year or the operating cycle, whichever is longer.* ■

Accounting for Current Liabilities

Accounting for Notes Payable

LO 1

Show how notes payable and related interest expense affect financial statements.

Our discussion of promissory notes in Chapter 5 focused on the payee, the company with a note receivable on its books. In this chapter we focus on the maker of the note, the company with a note payable on its books. Since the maker of the note issues (gives) the note to the payee, the maker is sometimes called the **issuer.**

To illustrate, assume that on September 1, 2006, Herrera Supply Company (HSC) borrowed $90,000 from the National Bank. As evidence of the debt, Herrera issued a **note payable** that had a one-year term and an annual interest rate of 9 percent.

Issuing the note is an asset source transaction. The asset account Cash increases and the liability account Notes Payable increases. The income statement is not affected. The statement of cash flows shows a $90,000 cash inflow from financing activities. The effects on the financial statements are as follows:

	Assets	=	Liabilities	+		+	Stockholders' Equity			Rev. − Exp. = Net Inc.	Cash Flow
Date	Cash	=	Notes Pay.	+	Int. Pay.	+	Com. Stk.	+	Ret. Earn.		
09/01/06	90,000	=	90,000	+	NA	+	NA	+	NA	NA − NA = NA	90,000 FA

On December 31, 2006, HSC would record an adjusting entry to recognize four months (September 1 through December 31) of accrued interest expense. The accrued interest is $2,700 [$90,000 × 0.09 × (4 ÷ 12)]. The adjusting entry is a claims exchange. The liability account Interest Payable increases, and the equity account Retained Earnings decreases. The income statement would report interest expense although HSC had not paid any cash for interest in 2006. The effects on the financial statements are as follows:

	Assets	=	Liabilities	+		+	Stockholders' Equity			Rev. − Exp. = Net Inc.	Cash Flow
Date	Cash	=	Notes Pay.	+	Int. Pay.	+	Com. Stk.	+	Ret. Earn.		
12/31/06	NA	=	NA	+	2,700	+	NA	+	(2,700)	NA − 2,700 = (2,700)	NA

HSC would record three journal entries on August 31, 2007 (the maturity date). The first entry recognizes $5,400 of interest expense that accrued in 2007 from January 1 through August 31 [$90,000 × 0.09 × (8 ÷ 12)]. The effects on the financial statements are as follows:

	Assets	=	Liabilities	+		+	Stockholders' Equity			Rev. − Exp. = Net Inc.	Cash Flow
Date	Cash	=	Notes Pay.	+	Int. Pay.	+	Com. Stk.	+	Ret. Earn.		
08/31/07	NA	=	NA	+	5,400	+	NA	+	(5,400)	NA − 5,400 = (5,400)	NA

The second entry records HSC's cash payment for interest on August 31, 2007. This entry is an asset use transaction that reduces both the Cash and Interest Payable accounts for the total amount of interest due, $8,100 [$90,000 × 0.09 × (12 ÷ 12)]. The interest payment includes the four months' interest accrued in 2006 and the eight months accrued in 2007 ($2,700 + $5,400 = $8,100). There is no effect on the income statement because HSC recognized the interest expense in two previous journal entries. The statement of cash flows would report an $8,100 cash outflow from operating activities. The effects on the financial statements follow:

	Assets	=	Liabilities	+		+	Stockholders' Equity			Rev. − Exp. = Net Inc.	Cash Flow
Date	Cash	=	Notes Pay.	+	Int. Pay.	+	Com. Stk.	+	Ret. Earn.		
08/31/07	(8,100)	=	NA	+	(8,100)	+	NA	+	NA	NA − NA = NA	(8,100) OA

The third entry on August 31, 2007, reflects repaying the principal. This entry is an asset use transaction. The Cash account and the Notes Payable account each decrease by $90,000. There is no effect on the income statement. The statement of cash flows would show a $90,000 cash outflow from financing activities. Recall that paying interest is classified as an operating activity even though repaying the principal is a financing activity. The effects on the financial statements are as follows:

	Assets	=	Liabilities	+		+	Stockholders' Equity			Rev. − Exp. = Net Inc.	Cash Flow
Date	Cash	=	Notes Pay.	+	Int. Pay.	+	Com. Stk.	+	Ret. Earn.		
08/31/07	(90,000)	=	(90,000)	+	NA	+	NA	+	NA	NA − NA = NA	(90,000) FA

CHECK YOURSELF 7.1

On October 1, 2006, Mellon Company issued an interest-bearing note payable to Better Banks Inc. The note had a $24,000 principal amount, a four-month term, and an annual interest rate of 4 percent. Determine the amount of interest expense and the cash outflow from operating activities Mellon will report in its 2006 and 2007 financial statements.

Answer

The computation of accrued interest expense is shown below. Unless otherwise specified, the interest rate is stated in annual terms even though the term of the note is only four months. Interest rates are commonly expressed as an annual percentage regardless of the term of the note. The *time outstanding* in the following formulas is therefore expressed as a fraction of a year. Mellon paid interest at an annual rate of 4 percent, but the note was outstanding for only 3/12 of a year in 2006 and 1/12 of a year in 2007.

2006

Principal × Annual interest rate × Time outstanding = Interest expense

$24,000 × 0.04 × (3/12) = $240

2007

Principal × Annual interest rate × Time outstanding = Interest expense

$24,000 × 0.04 × (1/12) = $80

Mellon will report a $320 ($240 + $80) cash outflow from operating activities for interest in 2007.

Accounting for Sales Tax

Show how sales tax liabilities affect financial statements.

Most states require retail companies to collect a sales tax on items sold to their customers. The retailer collects the tax from its customers and remits the tax to the state at regular intervals. The retailer has a current liability for the amount of sales tax collected but not yet paid to the state.

To illustrate, assume Herrera Supply Company (HSC) sells merchandise to a customer for $2,000 cash in a state where the sales tax rate is 6 percent. The effects on the financial statements are shown below.[1]

Assets	=	Liab.	+	Equity			Rev.	−	Exp.	=	Net Inc.	Cash Flow
Cash	=	Sales Tax Pay.	+	Com. Stk.	+	Ret. Earn.						
2,120	=	120	+	NA	+	2,000	2,000	−	NA	=	2,000	2,120 OA

Remitting the tax (paying cash to the tax authority) is an asset use transaction. Both the Cash account and the Sales Tax Payable account decrease. The effects on the financial statements are as follows:

Assets	=	Liab.	+	Equity			Rev.	−	Exp.	=	Net Inc.	Cash Flow
Cash	=	Sales Tax Pay.	+	Com. Stk.	+	Ret. Earn.						
(120)	=	(120)	+	NA	+	NA	NA	−	NA	=	NA	(120) OA

Contingent Liabilities

LO 3

Define contingent liabilities and explain how they are reported in financial statements.

A **contingent liability** is a potential obligation arising from a past event. The amount or existence of the obligation depends on some future event. A pending lawsuit, for example, is a contingent liability. Depending on the outcome, a defendant company could be required to pay a large monetary settlement or could be relieved of any obligation. Generally accepted accounting principles require that companies classify contingent liabilities into three different categories depending on the likelihood of their becoming actual liabilities. The categories and the accounting for each are described below:

1. If the likelihood of a future obligation arising is *probable* (likely) and its amount can be *reasonably estimated,* a liability is recognized in the financial statements. Contingent liabilities in this category include warranties, vacation pay, and sick leave.
2. If the likelihood of a future obligation arising is *reasonably possible* but not likely or if it is probable but *cannot be reasonably estimated,* no liability is reported on the balance sheet. The potential liability is, however, disclosed in the footnotes to the financial statements. Contingent liabilities in this category include legal challenges, environmental damages, and government investigations.
3. If the likelihood of a future obligation arising is *remote,* no liability need be recognized in the financial statements or disclosed in the footnotes to the statements.[2]

Determining whether a contingent liability is probable, reasonably possible, or remote requires professional judgment. Even seasoned accountants seek the advice of attorneys, engineers, insurance agents, and government regulators before classifying significant contingent liabilities. Professional judgment is also required to distinguish between contingent liabilities and **general uncertainties.** All businesses face uncertainties such as competition and damage from floods or storms. Such uncertainties are not contingent liabilities, however, because they do not arise from past events.

[1]The entry to record cost of goods sold for this sale is intentionally omitted.

[2]Companies may, if desired, voluntarily disclose contingent liabilities classified as remote.

EXHIBIT 7.1

Reporting Contingent Liabilities

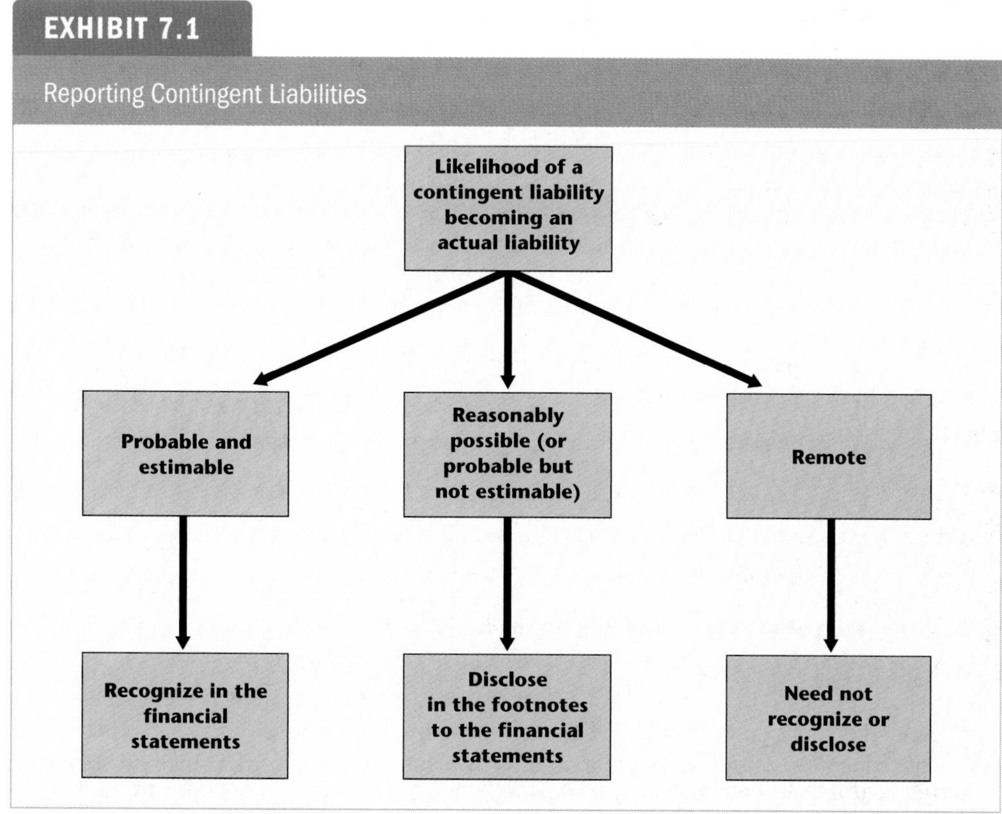

Exhibit 7.1 summarizes the three categories of contingent liabilities and the accounting for each category.

Warranty Obligations

LO 4 Explain how warranty obligations affect financial statements.

To attract customers, many companies guarantee their products or services. Such guarantees are called **warranties.** Warranties take many forms. Usually, they extend for a specified period of time. Within this period, the seller promises to replace or repair defective products without charge. Although the amount and timing of warranty obligations are uncertain, warranties usually represent liabilities that must be reported in the financial statements.

To illustrate accounting for warranty obligations, assume Herrera Supply Company (HSC) had cash of $2,000, inventory of $6,000, common stock of $5,000, and retained earnings of $3,000 on January 1, 2005. The 2005 accounting period is affected by three accounting events: (1) sale of merchandise under warranty; (2) recognition of warranty obligations to customers who purchased the merchandise; and (3) settlement of a customer's warranty claim.

Event 1 Sale of Merchandise

HSC sold for $7,000 cash merchandise that had cost $4,000.

In the following statements model, revenue from the sale is referenced as 1a and the cost of the sale as 1b. The effects of the sales transaction on the financial statements are shown below:

Event No.	Assets			=	Liab.	+	Equity	Rev.	−	Exp.	=	Net Inc.	Cash Flow
	Cash	+	Inventory	=			Ret. Earn.						
1a	7,000	+	NA	=	NA	+	7,000	7,000	−	NA	=	7,000	7,000 OA
1b	NA	+	(4,000)	=	NA	+	(4,000)	NA	−	4,000	=	(4,000)	NA

Event 2 **Recognition of Warranty Expense**

HSC guaranteed the merchandise sold in Event 1 to be free from defects for one year following the date of sale.

Although the exact amount of future warranty claims is unknown, HSC must inform financial statement users of the company's obligation. HSC must estimate the amount of the warranty liability and report the estimate in the 2005 financial statements. Assume the warranty obligation is estimated to be $100. Recognizing this obligation increases liabilities (warranties payable) and reduces stockholders' equity (retained earnings). Recognizing the warranty expense reduces net income. The statement of cash flows is not affected when the obligation and the corresponding expense are recognized. The effects on the financial statements follow:

Event No.	Assets	=	Liab.	+	Equity	Rev. − Exp. = Net Inc.	Cash Flow
			Warr. Pay.	+	Ret. Earn.		
2	NA	=	100	+	(100)	NA − 100 = (100)	NA

Event 3 **Settlement of Warranty Obligation**

HSC paid $40 cash to repair defective merchandise returned by a customer.

The cash payment for the repair is not an expense. Warranty expense was recognized in the period in which the sale was made (when the Warranties Payable account was credited). The payment reduces an asset (cash) and a liability (warranties payable). The income statement is not affected by the repairs payment. However, there is a $40 cash outflow reported in the operating activities section of the statement of cash flows. The effects on the financial statements follow:

Event No.	Assets	=	Liab.	+	Equity	Rev. − Exp. = Net Inc.	Cash Flow
	Cash	=	Warr. Pay.	+	Ret. Earn.		
3	(40)	=	(40)	+	NA	NA − NA = NA	(40) OA

Financial Statements

The financial statements for HSC's 2005 accounting period are shown in Exhibit 7.2.

EXHIBIT 7.2

Financial Statements for 2005

Income Statement

Sales Revenue	$7,000
Cost of Goods Sold	(4,000)
Gross Margin	3,000
Warranty Expense	(100)
Net Income	$2,900

Balance Sheet

Assets	
Cash	$ 8,960
Inventory	2,000
Total Assets	$10,960
Liabilities	
Warranties Payable	$ 60
Stockholders' Equity	
Common Stock	5,000
Retained Earnings	5,900
Total Liab. and Stockholders' Equity	$10,960

Statement of Cash Flows

Operating Activities	
Inflow from Customers	$7,000
Outflow for Warranty	(40)
Net Inflow from Operating Activities	6,960
Investing Activities	0
Financing Activities	0
Net Change in Cash	6,960
Plus: Beginning Cash Balance	2,000
Ending Cash Balance	$8,960

Flotation Systems, Inc. (FSI) began operations in 2006. Its sales were $360,000 in 2006 and $410,000 in 2007. FSI estimates the cost of its one-year product warranty will be 2 percent of sales. Actual cash payments for warranty claims amounted to $5,400 during 2006 and $8,500 during 2007. Determine the amount of warranty expense that FSI would report on its 2006 and 2007 year-end income statements. Also, determine the amount of warranties payable FSI would report on its 2006 and 2007 year-end balance sheet.

Answer

FSI would report Warranty Expense on the December 31, 2006, income statement of $7,200 ($360,000 × .02). Warranty Expense on the December 31, 2007, income statement is $8,200 ($410,000 × .02).

FSI would report Warranties Payable on the December 31, 2006, balance sheet of $1,800 ($7,200 − $5,400). Warranties Payable on the December 31, 2007, balance sheet is $1,500 ($1,800 + $8,200 − $8,500).

REALITY BYTES

Most electrical appliances come with a manufacturer's warranty that obligates the manufacturer to pay for defects that occur during some designated period of time after the point of sale. Why would **Best Buy** issue warranties that obligate it to pay for defects that occur after the manufacturer's warranty has expired? Warranties are in fact insurance policies that generate profits. Best Buy reported that the gross dollar sales from extended warranty programs were 3.6 percent of its total sales in fiscal year 2003. Even more important, Best Buy notes that gross profit margins on products sold with extended warranties are higher than the gross profit margins on products sold without extended warranties. Warranties produce revenues for manufacturers as well as retailers. The only difference is that the revenues generated from manufacturer's warranties are embedded in the sales price. Products with longer, more comprehensive warranties usually sell at higher prices than products with shorter, less extensive warranties.

Accounting for Long-Term Debt

Most businesses finance their investing activities with long-term debt. Recall that current liabilities mature within one year or a company's operating cycle, whichever is longer. Other liabilities are **long-term liabilities.** Long-term debt agreements vary with respect to requirements for paying interest charges and repaying principal (the amount borrowed). Interest payments may be due monthly, annually, at some other interval, or at the maturity date. Interest charges may be based on a **fixed interest rate** that remains constant during the term of the loan or may be based on a **variable interest rate** that fluctuates up or down during the loan period.

Principal repayment is generally required either in one lump sum at the maturity date or in installments that are spread over the life of the loan. For example, each monthly payment on your car loan probably includes both paying interest and repaying some of the principal. Repaying a portion of the principal with regular payments that also include interest is often called loan **amortization.**[3] This section explains accounting for interest and principal with respect to the major forms of long-term debt financing.

Installment Notes Payable

LO 5

Show how installment notes affect financial statements.

Loans that require payments of principal and interest at regular intervals (amortizing loans) are typically represented by **installment notes.** The terms of installment notes usually range from two to five years. To illustrate accounting for installment notes, assume Blair Company was started on January 1, 2005, when it borrowed $100,000 cash from the National Bank. In exchange for the money, Blair issued the bank a five-year installment note with a 9 percent fixed interest rate. The effects on the financial statements are as follows:

	Assets	=	Liab.	+	Equity			Rev.	−	Exp.	=	Net Inc.	Cash Flow
Date	Cash	=	Note Pay.	+	Com. Stk.	+	Ret. Earn.						
2005 Jan. 1	100,000	=	100,000	+	NA	+	NA	NA	−	NA	=	NA	100,000 FA

The loan agreement required Blair to pay five equal installments of $25,709[4] on December 31 of each year from 2005 through 2009. Exhibit 7.3 shows the allocation of each payment between principal and interest. When Blair pays the final installment, both the

EXHIBIT 7.3

Amortization Schedule for Installment Note Payable

Accounting Period Column A	Principal Balance on Jan. 1 Column B	Cash Payment on Dec. 31 Column C	Interest Expense Column D	Principal Repayment Column E	Principal Balance on Dec. 31 Column F
2005	$100,000	$25,709	$9,000	$16,709	$83,291
2006	83,291	25,709	7,496	18,213	65,078
2007	65,078	25,709	5,857	19,852	45,226
2008	45,226	25,709	4,070	21,639	23,587
2009	23,587	25,710*	2,123	23,587	0

*All computations are rounded to the nearest dollar. To fully liquidate the liability, the final payment is one dollar more than the others because of rounding differences.

[3]In Chapter 6 the term *amortization* described the expense recognized when the *cost of an intangible asset* is systematically allocated to expense over the useful life of the asset. This chapter shows that the term amortization refers more broadly to a variety of allocation processes. Here it means the systematic process of allocating the *principal repayment* over the life of a loan.

[4]The amount of the annual payment is determined using the present value concepts presented in a later chapter. Usually the lender (bank or other financial institution) calculates the amount of the payment for the customer. In this chapter we provide the amount of the annual payment.

Answers To The Curious Accountant

Time Warner, Inc., was able to make its interest payments in 2002 for two reasons. (1) Interest is paid with cash, not accrual earnings. Many of the expenses on the company's income statement did not require the use of cash. The company's statement of cash flows shows that net cash flow from operating activities, *after making interest payments*, was a positive $7.0 billion during 2002. (2) The net loss the company incurred was *after* interest expense had been deducted. The capacity of operations to support interest payments is measured by the amount of earnings before interest deductions. For example, look at the 2005 income statement for Blair Company in Exhibit 7.4. This statement shows only $3,000 of net income, but $12,000 of cash revenue was available for the payment of interest. Similarly, Time Warner's 2002 net loss is not an indication of the company's ability to pay interest in the short run.

principal and interest will be paid in full. The amounts shown in Exhibit 7.3 are computed as follows:

1. The Interest Expense (Column D) is computed by multiplying the Principal Balance on Jan. 1 (Column B) by the interest rate. For example, interest expense for 2005 is $100,000 × .09 = $9,000; for 2006 it is $83,291 × .09 = $7,496; and so on.
2. The Principal Repayment (Column E) is computed by subtracting the Interest Expense (Column D) from the Cash Payment on Dec. 31 (Column C). For example, the Principal Repayment for 2005 is $25,709 − $9,000 = $16,709; for 2006 it is $25,709 − $7,496 = $18,213; and so on.
3. The Principal Balance on Dec. 31 (Column F) is computed by subtracting the Principal Repayment (Column E) from the Principal Balance on Jan. 1 (Column B). For example, the Principal Balance on Dec. 31 for 2005 is $100,000 − $16,709 = $83,291; on December 31, 2006, the principal balance is $83,291 − $18,213 = $65,078; and so on. The Principal Balance on Dec. 31 (ending balance) for 2005 ($83,291) is also the Principal Balance on Jan. 1 (beginning balance) for 2006; the principal balance on December 31, 2006, is the principal balance on January 1, 2007; and so on.

Although the amounts for interest expense and principal repayment differ each year, the effects of the annual payment on the financial statements are the same. On the balance sheet, assets (cash) decrease by the total amount of the payment; liabilities (note payable) decrease by the amount of the principal repayment; and stockholders' equity (retained earnings) decreases by the amount of interest expense. Net income decreases from recognizing interest expense. On the statement of cash flows, the portion of the cash payment applied to interest is reported in the operating activities section and the portion applied to principal is reported in the financing activities section. The effects on the financial statements are as follows:

	Assets	=	Liab.	+	Equity			Rev. − Exp. = Net Inc.	Cash Flow
Date	Cash	=	Note Pay.	+	Com. Stk.	+	Ret. Earn.		
2005 Dec. 31	(25,709)	=	(16,709)	+	NA	+	(9,000)	NA − 9,000 = (9,000)	(9,000) OA (16,709) FA

Exhibit 7.4 displays income statements, balance sheets, and statements of cash flows for Blair Company for the accounting periods 2005 through 2009. The illustration assumes that Blair earned $12,000 of rent revenue each year. Since some of the principal is repaid each

EXHIBIT 7.4

BLAIR COMPANY
Financial Statements

	2005	2006	2007	2008	2009
Income Statements					
Rent Revenue	$12,000	$12,000	$12,000	$12,000	$12,000
Interest Expense	(9,000)	(7,496)	(5,857)	(4,070)	(2,123)
Net Income	$ 3,000	$ 4,504	$ 6,143	$ 7,930	$ 9,877
Balance Sheets					
Assets					
Cash	$86,291	$72,582	$58,873	$45,164	$31,454
Liabilities					
Note Payable	$83,291	$65,078	$45,226	$23,587	$ 0
Stockholders' Equity					
Retained Earnings	3,000	7,504	13,647	21,577	31,454
Total Liabilities and Stk. Equity	$86,291	$72,582	$58,873	$45,164	$31,454
Statements of Cash Flows					
Operating Activities					
Inflow from Customers	$ 12,000	$12,000	$12,000	$12,000	$12,000
Outflow for Interest	(9,000)	(7,496)	(5,857)	(4,070)	(2,123)
Investing Activities	0	0	0	0	0
Financing Activities					
Inflow from Note Issue	100,000	0	0	0	0
Outflow to Repay Note	(16,709)	(18,213)	(19,852)	(21,639)	(23,587)
Net Change in Cash	86,291	(13,709)	(13,709)	(13,709)	(13,710)
Plus: Beginning Cash Balance	0	86,291	72,582	58,873	45,164
Ending Cash Balance	$ 86,291	$72,582	$58,873	$45,164	$31,454

year, the note payable amount reported on the balance sheet and the amount of the interest expense on the income statement both decline each year.

CHECK YOURSELF 7.3

On January 1, 2004, Krueger Company issued a $50,000 installment note to State Bank. The note had a 10-year term and an 8 percent interest rate. Krueger agreed to repay the principal and interest in 10 annual payments of $7,451.47 at the end of each year. Determine the amount of principal and interest Krueger paid during the first and second year that the note was outstanding.

Answer

Accounting Period	Principal Balance January 1 A	Cash Payment December 31 B	Applied to Interest C = A × 0.08	Applied to Principal B − C
2004	$50,000.00	$7,451.47	$4,000.00	$3,451.47
2005	46,548.53	7,451.47	3,723.88	3,727.59

Line of Credit

Show how a line of credit affects financial statements.

A **line of credit** enables a company to borrow or repay funds as needed. For example, a business may borrow $50,000 one month and make a partial repayment of $10,000 the next month. Credit agreements usually specify a limit on the amount that can be borrowed. Exhibit 7.5 shows that credit agreements are widely used.

Interest rates on lines of credit normally vary with fluctuations in some designated interest rate benchmark such as the rate paid on U.S. Treasury bills. For example, a company may pay 4 percent interest one month and 4.5 percent the next month, even if the principal balance remains constant.

Lines of credit typically have one-year terms. Although they are classified on the balance sheet as short-term liabilities, lines of credit are frequently extended indefinitely by simply renewing the credit agreement.

To illustrate accounting for a line of credit, assume Lagoon Company owns a wholesale jet-ski distributorship. In the spring, Lagoon borrows money using a line of credit to finance building up its inventory. Lagoon repays the loan over the summer months using cash generated from jet-ski sales. Borrowing or repaying events occur on the first of the month. Interest payments occur at the end of each month. Exhibit 7.6 presents all 2006 line of credit events.

Each borrowing event (March 1, April 1, and May 1) is an asset source transaction. Both cash and the line of credit liability increase. Each repayment (June 1, July 1, and August 1) is an asset use transaction. Both cash and the line of credit liability decrease. Each month's interest expense recognition and payment is an asset use transaction. Assets (cash) and stockholders' equity (retained earnings) decrease, as does net income. The effects of the events on the financial statements are shown in Exhibit 7.7.

EXHIBIT 7.5

Percentage of U.S. Companies Disclosing Credit Agreements

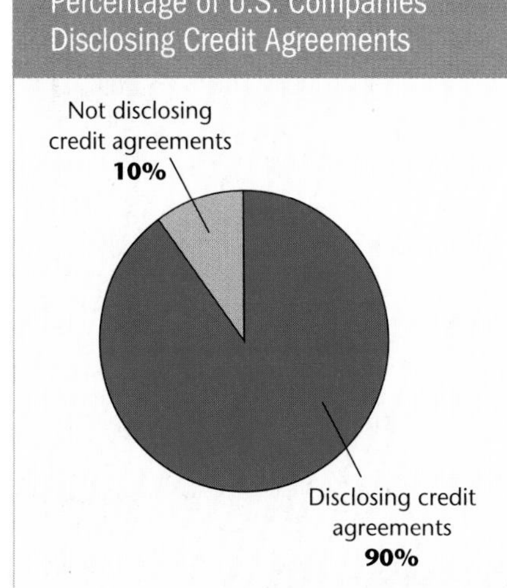

Data source: AICPA, *Accounting Trends and Techniques*, 2002.

EXHIBIT 7.6

Summary of Line of Credit Events

Date	Amount Borrowed (Repaid)	Loan Balance at End of Month	Effective Interest Rate per Month (%)	Interest Expense (rounded to nearest $1)
Mar. 1	$20,000	$ 20,000	0.09 ÷ 12	$150
Apr. 1	30,000	50,000	0.09 ÷ 12	375
May 1	50,000	100,000	0.105 ÷ 12	875
June 1	(10,000)	90,000	0.10 ÷ 12	750
July 1	(40,000)	50,000	0.09 ÷ 12	375
Aug. 1	(50,000)	0	0.09 ÷ 12	0

Bond Liabilities

Many companies borrow money directly from the public by selling **bond certificates,** otherwise called *issuing* bonds. Bond certificates describe a company's obligation to pay interest and to repay the principal. The seller, or **issuer,** of a bond is the borrower; the buyer of a bond, or **bondholder,** is the lender.

From the issuer's point of view, a bond represents an obligation to pay a sum of money to the bondholder on the bond's maturity date. The amount due at maturity is the **face value** of the bond. Most bonds also require the issuer to make cash interest payments based on a

EXHIBIT 7.7

Date	Assets	=	Liabilities	+	Equity	Rev.	−	Exp.	=	Net Inc.	Cash Flow	
Mar. 1	20,000	=	20,000	+	NA	NA	−	NA	=	NA	20,000	FA
31	(150)	=	NA	+	(150)	NA	−	150	=	(150)	(150)	OA
Apr. 1	30,000	=	30,000	+	NA	NA	−	NA	=	NA	30,000	FA
30	(375)	=	NA	+	(375)	NA	−	375	=	(375)	(375)	OA
May 1	50,000	=	50,000	+	NA	NA	−	NA	=	NA	50,000	FA
31	(875)	=	NA	+	(875)	NA	−	875	=	(875)	(875)	OA
June 1	(10,000)	=	(10,000)	+	NA	NA	−	NA	=	NA	(10,000)	FA
30	(750)	=	NA	+	(750)	NA	−	750	=	(750)	(750)	OA
July 1	(40,000)	=	(40,000)	+	NA	NA	−	NA	=	NA	(40,000)	FA
31	(375)	=	NA	+	(375)	NA	−	375	=	(375)	(375)	OA
Aug. 1	(50,000)	=	(50,000)	+	NA	NA	−	NA	=	NA	(50,000)	FA
31	NA	=	NA	+	NA	NA	−	NA	=	NA	NA	

stated interest rate at regular intervals over the life of the bond. Exhibit 7.8 shows a typical bond certificate.

EXHIBIT 7.8

Bond Certificate

Advantages of Issuing Bonds

Bond financing offers companies the following advantages.

1. Bonds usually have longer terms than notes issued to banks. While typical bank loan terms range from 2 to 5 years, bonds normally have 20-year terms to maturity. Longer terms to maturity allow companies to implement long-term strategic plans without having to worry about frequent refinancing arrangements.
2. Bond interest rates may be lower than bank interest rates. Banks earn profits by borrowing money from the public (depositors) at low interest rates, then loaning that money to companies at higher rates. By issuing bonds directly to the public, companies can pay lower interest costs by eliminating the middle man (banks).

Bonds Issued at Face Value

Fixed-Rate, Fixed-Term, Annual Interest Bonds

LO 7

Explain how to account for bonds and their related interest costs.

Assume Marsha Mason needs cash in order to seize a business opportunity. Mason knows of a company seeking a plot of land on which to store its inventory of crushed stone. Mason also knows of a suitable tract of land she could purchase for $100,000. The company has agreed to lease the land it needs from Mason for $12,000 per year. Mason lacks the funds to buy the land.

Some of Mason's friends recently complained about the low interest rates banks were paying on certificates of deposit. Mason suggested that her friends invest in bonds instead of CDs. She offered to sell them bonds with a 9 percent stated interest rate. The terms specified in the bond agreement Mason drafted included making interest payments in cash on December 31 of each year, a five-year term to maturity, and pledging the land as collateral for the

REALITY BYTES

On November 8, 2001, **Enron Corporation** announced that it would have to reduce its stockholders' equity by approximately $1.2 billion. On December 2, 2001, the company filed for Chapter 11 bankruptcy protection.

When covering this story, most of the media's attention focused on the overstatement of earnings that resulted from Enron's improper use of a form of partnerships called "special purpose entities." However, these entities were also used to improperly keep as much as $1 billion of debt off of Enron's balance sheet. Why did this matter to Enron? Enron was a very rapidly growing company and it used lots of debt to finance this growth. From 1999 to 2000 its assets grew from $33.4 billion to $65.5 billion, but its debt grew from $23.8 billion to $54.0 billion. This caused its debt to assets ratio to rise from 71.3 percent to 82.4 percent. The higher debt burden put Enron at risk of having to pay higher interest rates, an unattractive option for a company with this much debt.

bonds.[5] Her friends were favorably impressed, and Mason issued the bonds to them in exchange for cash on January 1, 2001.

Mason used the bond proceeds to purchase the land and immediately contracted to lease it for five years. On December 31, 2005, the maturity date of the bonds, Mason sold the land for its $100,000 book value and used the proceeds from the sale to repay the bond liability.

Mason's business venture involved six distinct accounting events:

1. Received $100,000 cash from issuing five-year bonds at face value.
2. Invested proceeds from the bond issue to purchase land for $100,000 cash.
3. Earned $12,000 cash revenue annually from leasing the land.
4. Paid $9,000 annual interest on December 31 of each year.
5. Sold the land for $100,000 cash.
6. Repaid the bond principal to bondholders.

Effect of Events on Financial Statements

Event 1 Issue Bonds for Cash

Issuing bonds is an asset source transaction.

Assets (cash) and liabilities (bonds payable) increase. Net income is not affected. The $100,000 cash inflow is reported in the financing activities section of the statement of cash flows. These effects are shown here:

Assets	=	Liab.	+	Equity	Rev.	−	Exp.	=	Net Inc.	Cash Flow
Cash	=	Bonds Pay.								
100,000	=	100,000	+	NA	NA	−	NA	=	NA	100,000 FA

[5]In practice, bonds are usually issued for much larger sums of money, often hundreds of millions of dollars. Also, terms to maturity are normally long, with 20 years being common. Using such large amounts for such long terms is unnecessarily cumbersome for instructional purposes. The effects of bond issues can be illustrated efficiently by using smaller amounts of debt with shorter maturities, as assumed in the case of Marsha Mason.

Event 2 **Investment in Land**

Paying $100,000 cash to purchase land is an asset exchange transaction.

The asset cash decreases and the asset land increases. The income statement is not affected. The cash outflow is reported in the investing activities section of the statement of cash flows. These effects are illustrated below:

Assets			=	Liab.	+	Equity	Rev.	−	Exp.	=	Net Inc.	Cash Flow
Cash	+	Land										
(100,000)	+	100,000	=	NA	+	NA	NA	−	NA	=	NA	(100,000) IA

Event 3 **Revenue Recognition**

Recognizing $12,000 cash revenue from renting the property is an asset source transaction.

This event is repeated each year from 2001 through 2005. The event increases assets and stockholders' equity. Recognizing revenue increases net income. The cash inflow is reported in the operating activities section of the statement of cash flows. These effects follow:

Assets	=	Liab.	+	Equity	Rev.	−	Exp.	=	Net Inc.	Cash Flow
Cash	=			Ret. Earn.						
12,000	=	NA	+	12,000	12,000	−	NA	=	12,000	12,000 OA

Event 4 **Expense Recognition**

Mason's $9,000 ($100,000 × 0.09) cash payment represents interest expense.

This event is also repeated each year from 2001 through 2005. The interest payment is an asset use transaction. Cash and stockholders' equity (retained earnings) decrease. The expense recognition decreases net income. The cash outflow is reported in the operating activities section of the statement of cash flows. These effects follow:

Assets	=	Liab.	+	Equity	Rev.	−	Exp.	=	Net Inc.	Cash Flow
Cash	=			Ret. Earn.						
(9,000)	=	NA	+	(9,000)	NA	−	9,000	=	(9,000)	(9,000) OA

Event 5 **Sale of Investment in Land**

Selling the land for cash equal to its $100,000 book value is an asset exchange transaction.

Cash increases and land decreases. Since there was no gain or loss on the sale, the income statement is not affected. The cash inflow is reported in the investing activities section of the statement of cash flows. These effects follow:

Assets			=	Liab.	+	Equity	Rev.	−	Exp.	=	Net Inc.	Cash Flow
Cash	+	Land										
100,000	+	(100,000)	=	NA	+	NA	NA	−	NA	=	NA	100,000 IA

Event 6 **Payoff of Bond Liability**

Repaying the face value of the bond liability is an asset use transaction.

Cash and bonds payable decrease. The income statement is not affected. The cash outflow is reported in the financing activities section of the statement of cash flows:

Assets	=	Liab.	+	Equity	Rev.	−	Exp.	=	Net Inc.	Cash Flow
Cash	=	Bonds Pay.								
(100,000)	=	(100,000)	+	NA	NA	−	NA	=	NA	(100,000) FA

Financial Statements

Explain how to account for bonds and their related interest costs.

Exhibit 7.9 displays Mason Company's financial statements. For simplicity, the income statement does not distinguish between operating and nonoperating items. Rent revenue and interest expense are constant across all accounting periods, so Mason recognizes $3,000 of net income in each accounting period. On the balance sheet, cash increases by $3,000 each year because cash revenue exceeds cash paid for interest. Land remains constant each year

EXHIBIT 7.9

Mason Company Financial Statements

Bonds Issued at Face Value	2001	2002	2003	2004	2005
Income Statements					
Rent Revenue	$ 12,000	$ 12,000	$ 12,000	$ 12,000	$ 12,000
Interest Expense	(9,000)	(9,000)	(9,000)	(9,000)	(9,000)
Net Income	$ 3,000	$ 3,000	$ 3,000	$ 3,000	$ 3,000
Balance Sheets					
Assets					
Cash	$ 3,000	$ 6,000	$ 9,000	$ 12,000	$ 15,000
Land	100,000	100,000	100,000	100,000	0
Total Assets	$103,000	$106,000	$109,000	$112,000	$ 15,000
Liabilities					
Bonds Payable	$100,000	$100,000	$100,000	$100,000	$ 0
Stockholders' Equity					
Retained Earnings	3,000	6,000	9,000	12,000	15,000
Total Liabilities and Stockholders' Equity	$103,000	$106,000	$109,000	$112,000	$ 15,000
Statements of Cash Flows					
Operating Activities					
Inflow from Customers	$ 12,000	$ 12,000	$ 12,000	$ 12,000	$ 12,000
Outflow for Interest	(9,000)	(9,000)	(9,000)	(9,000)	(9,000)
Investing Activities					
Outflow to Purchase Land	(100,000)				
Inflow from Sale of Land					100,000
Financing Activities					
Inflow from Bond Issue	100,000				
Outflow to Repay Bond Liab.					(100,000)
Net Change in Cash	3,000	3,000	3,000	3,000	3,000
Plus: Beginning Cash Balance	0	3,000	6,000	9,000	12,000
Ending Cash Balance	$ 3,000	$ 6,000	$ 9,000	$ 12,000	$ 15,000

at its $100,000 historical cost until it is sold in 2005. Similarly, the bonds payable liability is reported at $100,000 from the date the bonds were issued in 2001 until they are paid off on December 31, 2005.

Compare Blair Company's income statements in Exhibit 7.4 with Mason Company's income statements in Exhibit 7.9. Both Blair and Mason borrowed $100,000 cash at a 9 percent stated interest rate for five-year terms. Blair, however, repaid its liability under the terms of an installment note while Mason did not repay any principal until the end of the five-year bond term. Because Blair repaid part of the principal balance on the installment loan each year, Blair's interest expense declined each year. The interest expense on Mason's bond liability, however, remained constant because the full principal amount was outstanding for the entire five-year bond term.

Security for Loan Agreements

In general, large loans with long terms to maturity pose more risk to lenders (creditors) than small loans with short terms. To reduce the risk that they won't get paid, lenders frequently require borrowers (debtors) to pledge designated assets as **collateral** for loans. For example, when a bank makes a car loan, it usually retains legal title to the car until the loan is fully repaid. If the borrower fails to make the monthly payments, the bank repossesses the car, sells it to someone else, and uses the proceeds to pay the original owner's debt. Similarly, assets like accounts receivable, inventory, equipment, buildings, and land may be pledged as collateral for business loans.

In addition to requiring collateral, creditors often obtain additional protection by including **restrictive covenants** in loan agreements. Such covenants may restrict additional borrowing, limit dividend payments, or restrict salary increases. If the loan restrictions are violated, the borrower is in default and the loan balance is due immediately.

Finally, creditors often ask key personnel to provide copies of their personal tax returns and financial statements. The financial condition of key executives is important because they may be asked to pledge personal property as collateral for business loans, particularly for small businesses.

Current versus Noncurrent

Distinguish between current and noncurrent assets and liabilities.

Because meeting obligations on time is critical to business survival, financial analysts and creditors are interested in whether companies will have enough money available to pay bills when they are due. Most businesses provide information about their bill-paying ability by classifying their assets and liabilities according to liquidity. The more quickly an asset is converted to cash or consumed, the more *liquid* it is. Assets are usually divided into two major classifications: *current* and *noncurrent*. Current items are also referred to as *short term* and noncurrent items as *long term*.

A **current (short-term) asset** is expected to be converted to cash or consumed within one year or an operating cycle, whichever is longer. An **operating cycle** is defined as the average time it takes a business to convert cash to inventory, inventory to accounts receivable, and accounts receivable back to cash. The financial tools used to measure the length of an operating cycle for particular businesses are discussed in Chapter 5. For most businesses, the operating cycle is less than one year. As a result, the one-year rule normally prevails with respect to classifying assets as current. The current assets section of a balance sheet typically includes the following items:

Current Assets
- Cash
- Marketable Securities
- Accounts Receivable
- Short-Term Notes Receivable
- Interest Receivable
- Inventory
- Supplies
- Prepaid Items

Given the definition of current assets, it seems reasonable to assume that **current (short-term) liabilities** would be those due within one year or an operating cycle, whichever is longer. This assumption is usually correct. However, an exception is made for long-term renewable debt. For example, consider a liability that was issued with a 20-year term to maturity. After 19 years, the liability becomes due within one year and is, therefore, a current liability. Even so, the liability will be classified as long term if the company plans to issue new long-term debt and to use the proceeds from that debt to repay the maturing liability. This situation is described as *refinancing short-term debt on a long-term basis.* In general, if a business does not plan to use any of its current assets to repay a debt, that debt is listed as long term even if it is due within one year. The current liabilities section of a balance sheet typically includes the following items:

Current Liabilities
- Accounts Payable
- Short-Term Notes Payable
- Wages Payable
- Taxes Payable
- Interest Payable

Prepare a classified balance sheet.

Balance sheets that distinguish between current and noncurrent items are called **classified balance sheets.** To enhance the usefulness of accounting information, most real-world balance sheets are classified. Exhibit 7.10 displays an example of a classified balance sheet.

Liquidity versus Solvency

Liquidity describes the ability to generate sufficient short-term cash flows to pay obligations as they come due. **Solvency** is the ability to repay liabilities in the long run. Liquidity and solvency are both important to the survival of a business. Financial analysts rely on several ratios to help them evaluate a company's liquidity and solvency. The primary ratio used to evaluate liquidity is the current ratio.

The **current ratio** is defined as:

Use the current and debt to assets ratios to assess the level of liquidity.

$$\frac{\text{Current assets}}{\text{Current liabilities}}$$

Since current assets normally exceed current liabilities, this ratio is usually greater than 100 percent. For example, if a company has \$250 in current assets and \$100 in current liabilities, current assets are 250 percent of current liabilities. The current ratio is traditionally expressed as a decimal rather than as a percentage, however; most analysts would

EXHIBIT 7.10

LIMBAUGH COMPANY
Classified Balance Sheet
As of December 31, 2006

Assets			
Current Assets			
Cash		$ 20,000	
Accounts Receivable		35,000	
Inventory		230,000	
Prepaid Rent		3,600	
Total Current Assets			$288,600
Property, Plant, and Equipment			
Office Equipment	$ 80,000		
Less: Accumulated Depreciation	(25,000)	55,000	
Building	340,000		
Less: Accumulated Depreciation	(40,000)	300,000	
Land		120,000	
Total Property, Plant, and Equipment			475,000
Total Assets			$763,600
Liabilities and Stockholders' Equity			
Current Liabilities			
Accounts Payable		$ 32,000	
Notes Payable		120,000	
Salaries Payable		32,000	
Unearned Revenue		9,800	
Total Current Liabilities			$193,800
Long-Term Liabilities			
Note Payable			100,000
Total Liabilities			293,800
Stockholders' Equity			
Common Stock		200,000	
Retained Earnings		269,800	469,800
Total Liabilities and Stockholders' Equity			$763,600

describe this example as a current ratio of 2.5 to 1 ($250 ÷ $100 = $2.50 in current assets for every $1 in current liabilities). This book uses the traditional format when referring to the current ratio.

The current ratio is among the most widely used ratios in analyzing financial statements. Current ratios can be too high as well as too low. A low ratio suggests that the company may have difficulty paying its short-term obligations. A high ratio suggests that a company is not maximizing its earnings potential because investments in liquid assets usually do not earn as much money as investments in other assets. Companies must try to maintain an effective balance between liquid assets (so they can pay bills on time) and nonliquid assets (so they can earn a good return).

The **debt to assets ratio** is a common measure of solvency. This ratio reveals the percentage of a company's assets that is financed with borrowed money. The higher the ratio, the greater the financial risk. The debt to assets ratio is defined as:

$$\frac{\text{Total debt}}{\text{Total assets}}$$

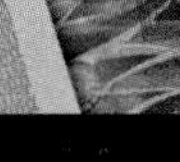

FOCUS ON INTERNATIONAL ISSUES

WHY ARE THESE BALANCE SHEETS BACKWARD?

Many of the differences in accounting rules used around the world would be difficult to detect by merely comparing financial statements of companies in different countries. For example, if a balance sheet for a U.S. company and one for a U.K. company both report an asset called *land,* it might not be clear whether the reported amounts were computed by using the same measurement rules or different measurement rules. Did both companies use historical cost as a basis for measurement? Perhaps not, but this would be difficult to determine by comparing their balance sheets.

However, one difference between financial reporting in the United Kingdom and the United States that is obvious is the arrangement of assets on the balance sheet. In this chapter, we explain that U.S. GAAP requires current assets to be shown first and noncurrent assets second; the same is true of liabilities. In the United Kingdom, noncurrent assets appear first, followed by current assets; however, liabilities are shown in the same order as in the United States. In other countries (e.g., France), both assets and liabilities are shown with noncurrent items first. The accounting rules of some countries require that equity be shown before liabilities; this is the opposite of U.S. GAAP. Therefore, to someone who learned accounting in the United States, the balance sheets of companies from some countries may appear backward or upside down.

No matter in what order the assets, liabilities, and equity accounts are arranged on a company's balance sheet, one accounting concept is true throughout the free world:

Assets = Liabilities + Equity

For a real-world example of the items discussed here, look up the financial statements of ITV, the largest commercial television network in the United Kingdom. Go to www.itvplc.com. Click on "Company Reports" under "FINANCIAL INFORMATION." Next click on "Financial review 2003" or whatever is the most current fiscal year.

While a high debt to assets ratio suggests high risk, it may also signal an opportunity for a high return. Suppose a company earns a 12% return on investment and borrows money at $9%. The 3% spread (12% − 9%) goes into the pockets of the owners. In this case, owners benefit from high levels of debt rather than low levels. So, what is the ideal debt to assets ratio? The best ratio is the one that provides a proper balance between risk and return. Ratios that are excessively high or low suggest poor management.

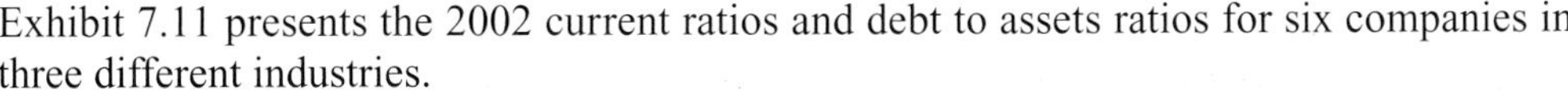

Real-World Data

Exhibit 7.11 presents the 2002 current ratios and debt to assets ratios for six companies in three different industries.

Which of these companies has the highest level of financial risk? Perhaps Safeway because it has the highest debt to assets ratio. The electric utilities have higher debt to assets ratios and lower current ratios than those of the companies in the building supplies business. Does this mean that electric utilities are riskier investments? Not necessarily; since the companies are in different industries, the ratios may not be comparable. Utility companies have

EXHIBIT 7.11

Industry	Company	Current Ratio	Debt to Assets Ratio
Electric utilities	Duke Energy	0.99	0.72
	Dominion Resources	0.81	0.72
Grocery stores	Albertsons	1.24	0.66
	Safeway	1.08	0.77
Building supplies	Home Depot	1.48	0.34
	Lowe's	1.56	0.48

a more stable revenue base than building companies. If the economy turns downward, people are likely to continue to use electricity. However, they are less likely to buy a new home or to add on to their existing home. Because utility companies have a stable source of revenue, creditors are likely to feel comfortable with higher levels of debt for them than they would for building companies. As previously stated, the industry must be considered when interpreting ratios.

Finally, note that the debt to assets ratios, with the exception of the grocery stores, tend to be grouped by industry. Current ratios do vary somewhat among different industries, but they probably do not vary as much as the debt to assets ratios. Why? Because all companies, regardless of how they finance their total assets, must keep sufficient current assets on hand to repay current liabilities.

<< A Look Back

Chapter 7 discussed accounting for current liabilities and long-term debt. Current liabilities are obligations due within one year or the company's operating cycle, whichever is longer. The chapter expanded the discussion of promissory notes begun in Chapter 5. Chapter 5 introduced accounting for the note payee, the lender; Chapter 7 discussed accounting for the note maker (issuer), the borrower. Notes payable and related interest payable are reported as liabilities on the balance sheet. Chapter 7 also discussed accounting for the contingent liability and warranty obligations.

Long-term notes payable mature in two to five years and usually require payments that include a return of principal plus interest. *Lines of credit* enable companies to borrow limited amounts on an as-needed basis. Although lines of credit normally have one-year terms, companies frequently renew them, extending the effective maturity date to the intermediate range of five or more years. Interest on a line of credit is normally paid monthly. Long-term debt financing for more than 10 years usually requires issuing *bonds.*

Finally, Chapter 7 discussed assessing companies' liquidity. The current ratio is current assets divided by current liabilities. The higher the current ratio, the more liquid the business.

>> A Look Forward

A company seeking long-term financing might choose to use debt, such as the types of bonds or term loans that were discussed in this chapter. Owners' equity is another source of long-term financing. Several equity alternatives are available, depending on the type of business organization the owners choose to establish. For example, a company could be organized as a sole proprietorship, partnership, or corporation. Chapter 8 presents accounting issues related to equity transactions for each of these types of business structures.

SELF-STUDY REVIEW PROBLEM

Perfect Picture Inc. (PPI) experienced the following transactions during 2007. The transactions are summarized (transaction data pertain to the full year) and limited to those that affect the company's current liabilities.

1. PPI had cash sales of $820,000. The state requires that PPI charge customers an 8 percent sales tax (ignore cost of goods sold).
2. PPI paid the state sales tax authority $63,000.
3. On March 1, PPI issued a note payable to the County Bank. PPI received $50,000 cash (principal balance). The note had a one-year term and a 6 percent annual interest rate.
4. On December 31, PPI recognized accrued interest on the note issued in Event 3.
5. On December 31, PPI recognized warranty expense at the rate of 3 percent of sales.
6. PPI paid $22,000 cash to settle warranty claims.
7. On January 1, 2006, PPI issued a $100,000 installment note. The note had a 10-year term and an 8 percent interest rate. PPI agreed to repay the principal and interest in 10 annual interest payments of $14,902.94 at the end of each year.

Required

Prepare the liabilities section of the December 31, 2007, balance sheet.

Solution

PERFECT PICTURE INC.
Partial Balance Sheet
December 31, 2007

Current Liabilities	
Sales Tax Payable	$ 2,600
Notes Payable	50,000
Interest Payable	2,500
Warranties Payable	2,600
Installment Note Payable	85,642
Total Liabilities	$143,342

Explanations for amounts shown in the balance sheet:

1. Sales Tax Payable: $820,000 × 0.08 = $65,600 Amount Due − $63,000 Amount Paid = $2,600 Liability as of December 31, 2007.
2. Note Payable: $50,000 Borrowed with no repayment.
3. Interest Payable: $50,000 × 0.06 × 10/12 = $2,500.
4. Warranty Payable: $820,000 × 0.03 = $24,600 Estimated Warranty Liability − $22,000 Cash Paid to Settle Warranty Claims = $2,600 Remaining Liability.
5. Installment Note Payable:

Accounting Period	Principal Bal. January 1 A	Cash Payment December 31 B	Applied to Interest C = A × 0.08	Applied to Principal B − C
2006	$100,000.00	$14,902.94	$8,000.00	$6,902.94
2007	93,097.06	$14,902.94	7,447.76	7,455.18
2008*	$85,641.88			

*The amount due on December 31, 2007, is the same as the amount due on January 1, 2008. The amount shown on the balance sheet has been rounded to the nearest dollar.

KEY TERMS

amortization 252
bond certificates 255
bondholder 255
classified balance sheets 261
collateral 260
contingent liability 248
current (short-term) asset 260
current (short-term) liabilities 245, 261
current ratio 261
debt to assets ratio 262
face value 255
fixed interest rate 251
general uncertainties 248
going concern assumption 245
installment notes 252
issuer 246, 255
line of credit 255
liquidity 261
long-term liabilities 251
note payable 246
operating cycle 260
restrictive covenants 260
solvency 261
stated interest rate 256
variable interest rate 251
warranties 249

QUESTIONS

1. What type of transaction is a cash payment to creditors? How does this type of transaction affect the accounting equation?
2. What is a current liability? Distinguish between a current liability and a long-term debt.
3. What type of entry is the entry to record accrued interest expense? How does it affect the accounting equation?
4. Who is the maker of a note payable?
5. What is the going concern assumption? Does it affect the way liabilities are reported in the financial statements?
6. Why is it necessary to make an adjustment at the end of the accounting period for unpaid interest on a note payable?
7. Assume that on October 1, 2007, Big Company borrowed $10,000 from the local bank at 6 percent interest. The note is due on October 1, 2008. How much interest does Big pay in 2007? How much interest does Big pay in 2008? What amount of cash does Big pay back in 2008?
8. When a business collects sales tax from customers, is it revenue? Why or why not?
9. What is a contingent liability?
10. List the three categories of contingent liabilities.
11. Are contingent liabilities recorded on a company's books? Explain.
12. What is the difference in accounting procedures for a liability that is probable and estimable and one that is reasonably possible but not estimable?
13. What type of liabilities are not recorded on a company's books?
14. What does the term *warranty* mean?
15. What effect does recognizing future warranty obligations have on the balance sheet? On the income statement?
16. When is warranty cost reported on the statement of cash flows?
17. What is the difference between classification of a note as short term or long term?
18. At the beginning of year 1, B Co. has a note payable of $72,000 that calls for an annual payment of $16,246, which includes both principal and interest. If the interest rate is 8 percent, what is the amount of interest expense in year 1 and in year 2? What is the balance of the note at the end of year 2?
19. What is the purpose of a line of credit for a business? Why would a company choose to obtain a line of credit instead of issuing bonds?
20. What are the primary sources of debt financing for most large companies?
21. What are some advantages of issuing bonds versus borrowing from a bank?
22. What are some disadvantages of issuing bonds?
23. Why can a company usually issue bonds at a lower interest rate than the company would pay if the funds were borrowed from a bank?
24. If Roc Co. issued $100,000 of 5 percent, 10-year bonds at the face amount, what is the effect of the issuance of the bonds on the financial statements? What amount of interest expense will Roc Co. recognize each year?

25. What is a classified balance sheet?
26. What is the difference between the liquidity and the solvency of a business?
27. The higher the company's current ratio, the better the company's financial condition. Do you agree with this statement? Explain.

EXERCISES

All Exercises are available with McGraw-Hill's Homework Manager

Exercise 7-1 *Recognizing accrued interest expense* L.O. 1

Classic Corporation borrowed $90,000 from the bank on November 1, 2007. The note had an 8 percent annual rate of interest and matured on April 30, 2008. Interest and principal were paid in cash on the maturity date.

Required

a. What amount of cash did Classic pay for interest in 2007?
b. What amount of interest expense was reported on the 2007 income statement?
c. What amount of total liabilities was reported on the December 31, 2007, balance sheet?
d. What total amount of cash was paid to the bank on April 30, 2008, for principal and interest?
e. What amount of interest expense was reported on the 2008 income statement?

Exercise 7-2 *Effects of recognizing accrued interest on financial statements* L.O. 1

Scott Perkins started Perkins Company on January 1, 2005. The company experienced the following events during its first year of operation.

1. Earned $1,500 of cash revenue for performing services.
2. Borrowed $2,400 cash from the bank.
3. Adjusted the accounting records to recognize accrued interest expense on the bank note. The note, issued on August 1, 2005, had a one-year term and a 7 percent annual interest rate.

Required

a. What is the amount of interest expense in 2005?
b. What amount of cash was paid for interest in 2005?
c. Use a horizontal statements model to show how each event affects the balance sheet, income statement, and statement of cash flows. Indicate whether the event increases (I), decreases (D), or does not affect (NA) each element of the financial statements. In the Cash Flows column, designate the cash flows as operating activities (OA), investing activities (IA), or financing activities (FA). The first transaction has been recorded as an example.

Event No.	Balance Sheet									Income Statement					Statement of Cash Flows
	Cash	=	Notes Pay.	+	Int. Pay.	+	Com. Stk.	+	Ret. Earn.	Rev.	−	Exp.	=	Net Inc.	
1	I	=	NA	+	NA	+	NA	+	I	I	−	NA	=	I	I OA

Exercise 7-3 *Recording sales tax expense* L.O. 2

The University Book Store sells books and other supplies to students in a state where the sales tax rate is 7 percent. The University Book Store engaged in the following transactions for 2008. Sales tax of 7 percent is collected on all sales.

1. Book sales, not including sales tax, for 2008 amounted to $275,000 cash.
2. Cash sales of miscellaneous items in 2008 were $150,000, not including tax.
3. Cost of goods sold amounted to $210,000 for the year.
4. Paid $130,000 in operating expenses for the year.
5. Paid the sales tax collected to the state agency.

Required

a. What is the total amount of sales tax the University Book Store collected and paid for the year?

b. What is the University Book Store's net income for the year?

L.O. 2

Exercise 7-4 *Recognizing sales tax payable*

The following selected transactions apply to Big Stop for November and December 2008. November was the first month of operations. Sales tax is collected at the time of sale but is not paid to the state sales tax agency until the following month.

1. Cash sales for November 2008 were $65,000 plus sales tax of 8 percent.
2. Big Stop paid the November sales tax to the state agency on December 10, 2008.
3. Cash sales for December 2008 were $80,000 plus sales tax of 8 percent.

Required

a. Show the effect of the above transactions on a statements model like the one shown below.

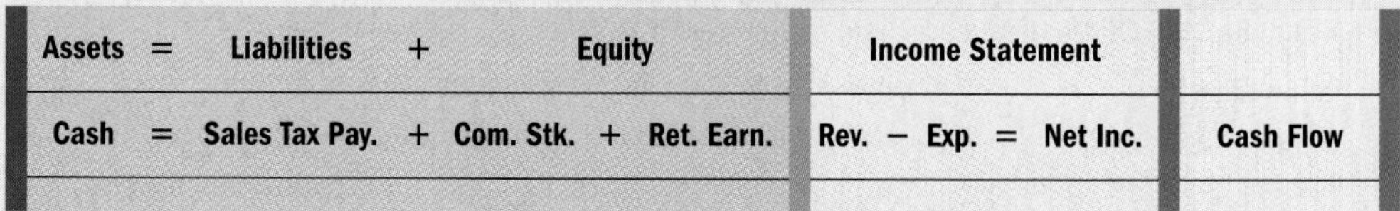

Assets =	Liabilities +		Equity	Income Statement			Cash Flow
Cash =	Sales Tax Pay. +	Com. Stk. +	Ret. Earn.	Rev. −	Exp. =	Net Inc.	Cash Flow

b. What was the total amount of sales tax paid in 2008?

c. What was the total amount of sales tax collected in 2008?

d. What is the amount of the sales tax liability as of December 31, 2008?

e. On what financial statement will the sales tax liability appear?

L.O. 3

Exercise 7-5 *Contingent liabilities*

The following legal situations apply to Stringer Corp. for 2009:

1. A customer slipped and fell on a slick floor while shopping in the retail store. The customer has filed a $5 million lawsuit against the company. Stringer's attorney knows that the company will have to pay some damages but is reasonably certain that the suit can be settled for $500,000.
2. The EPA has assessed a fine against Stringer of $250,000 for hazardous emissions from one of its manufacturing plants. The EPA had previously issued a warning to Stringer and required Stringer to make repairs within six months. Stringer began to make the repairs, but was not able to complete them within the six-month period. Since Stringer has started the repairs, Stringer's attorney thinks the fine will be reduced to $100,000. He is approximately 80 percent certain that he can negotiate the fine reduction because of the repair work that has been completed.
3. One of Stringer's largest manufacturing facilities is located in "tornado alley." Property is routinely damaged by storms. Stringer estimates it may have property damage of as much as $300,000 this coming year.

Required

For each item above, determine the correct accounting treatment.

L.O. 4

Exercise 7-6 *Effect of warranties on income and cash flow*

To support herself while attending school, Ellen Abba sold computers to other students. During her first year of operation, she sold computers that had cost her $120,000 cash for $260,000 cash. She provided her customers with a one-year warranty against defects in parts and labor. Based on industry standards, she estimated that warranty claims would amount to 5 percent of sales. During the year she paid $920 cash to replace a defective hard drive.

Required

a. Prepare an income statement and statement of cash flows for Abba's first year of operation.

b. Explain the difference between net income and the amount of cash flow from operating activities.

Exercise 7-7 *Effect of warranty obligations and payments on financial statements* L.O. 4

The Ja-San Appliance Co. provides a 120-day parts-and-labor warranty on all merchandise it sells. Ja-San estimates the warranty expense for the current period to be $1,250. During the period a customer returned a product that cost $920 to repair.

Required

a. Show the effects of these transactions on the financial statements using a horizontal statements model like the example shown here. Use a + to indicate increase, a − for decrease, and NA for not affected. In the Cash Flow column, indicate whether the item is an operating activity (OA), investing activity (IA), or financing activity (FA).

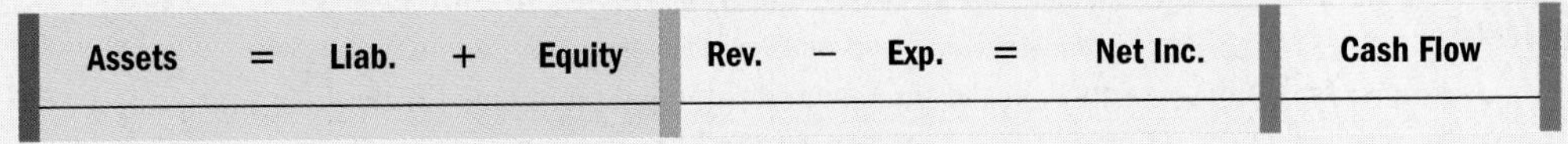

Assets	=	Liab.	+	Equity	Rev.	−	Exp.	=	Net Inc.	Cash Flow

b. Discuss the advantage of estimating the amount of warranty expense.

Exercise 7-8 *Current liabilities* L.O. 2, 4, 8

The following transactions apply to Mabry Equipment Sales Corp. for 2007:

1. The business was started when Mabry Corp. received $50,000 from the issue of common stock.
2. Purchased $175,000 of merchandise on account.
3. Sold merchandise for $200,000 cash (not including sales tax). Sales tax of 8 percent is collected when the merchandise is sold. The merchandise had a cost of $125,000.
4. Provided a six-month warranty on the merchandise sold. Based on industry estimates, the warranty claims would amount to 4 percent of merchandise sales.
5. Paid the sales tax to the state agency on $150,000 of the sales.
6. On September 1, 2007, borrowed $20,000 from the local bank. The note had a 6 percent interest rate and matures on March 1, 2008.
7. Paid $5,600 for warranty repairs during the year.
8. Paid operating expenses of $54,000 for the year.
9. Paid $125,000 of accounts payable.
10. Recorded accrued interest at the end of the year.

Required

a. Record the above transactions in a horizontal statements model like the following one.

Event	Balance Sheet									Income Statement	Statemt. of Cash Flows
	Assets =		Liabilities					+ Equity		Rev. − Exp. = Net Inc.	
	Cash +	Mdse. Inv. =	Acct. Pay. +	Sales Tax Pay. +	War. Pay. +	Int. Pay. +	Notes Pay. +	Com. Stock +	Ret. Earn.		

b. Prepare the income statement, balance sheet, and statement of cash flows for 2007.

c. What is the total amount of current liabilities at December 31, 2007?

Exercise 7-9 *How credit terms affect financial statements* L.O. 5

Marshall Co. is planning to finance an expansion of its operations by borrowing $50,000. City Bank has agreed to loan Marshall the funds. Marshall has two repayment options: (1) to issue a note with the principal due in 10 years and with interest payable annually or (2) to issue a note to repay $5,000 of the principal each year along with the annual interest based on the unpaid principal balance. Assume the interest rate is 9 percent for each option.

Required

a. What amount of interest will Marshall pay in year 1

(1) Under option 1?

(2) Under option 2?

b. What amount of interest will Marshall pay in year 2
   (1) Under option 1?
   (2) Under option 2?

c. Explain the advantage of each option.

L.O. 5

Exercise 7-10 ***Accounting for an installment note payable with annual payments that include interest and principal***

On January 1, 2007, Mooney Co. borrowed $60,000 cash from First Bank by issuing a four-year, 6 percent note. The principal and interest are to be paid by making annual payments in the amount of $17,315. Payments are to be made December 31 of each year, beginning December 31, 2007.

Required

Prepare an amortization schedule for the interest and principal payments for the four-year period.

L.O. 5

Exercise 7-11 ***Long-term installment note payable***

Jim Felix started a business by issuing an $80,000 face value note to State National Bank on January 1, 2008. The note had a 7 percent annual rate of interest and a 10-year term. Payments of $11,390 are to be made each December 31 for 10 years.

Required

a. What portion of the December 31, 2008, payment is applied to
   (1) Interest expense?
   (2) Principal?

b. What is the principal balance on January 1, 2009?

c. What portion of the December 31, 2009, payment is applied to
   (1) Interest expense?
   (2) Principal?

L.O. 5

Exercise 7-12 ***Amortization of a long-term loan***

A partial amortization schedule for a five-year note payable that Chacon Co. issued on January 1, 2008, is shown here:

Accounting Period	Principal Balance January 1	Cash Payment	Applied to Interest	Applied to Principal
2008	$120,000	$30,851	$10,800	$20,051
2009	99,949	30,851	8,995	21,856

Required

a. What rate of interest is Chacon Co. paying on the note?

b. Using a financial statements model like the one shown below, record the appropriate amounts for the following two events:
   (1) January 1, 2008, issue of the note payable.
   (2) December 31, 2009, payment on the note payable.

Event No.	Assets	=	Liab.	+	Equity	Rev.	−	Exp.	=	Net Inc.	Cash Flow
1											

c. If the company earned $90,000 cash revenue and paid $50,000 in cash expenses in addition to the interest in 2008, what is the amount of each of the following? (Disregard income taxes.)
   (1) Net income for 2008.
   (2) Cash flow from operating activities for 2008.
   (3) Cash flow from financing activities for 2008.

d. What is the amount of interest expense on this loan for 2010?

Exercise 7-13 *Accounting for a line of credit* L.O. 6

King Co. uses an approved line of credit not to exceed $200,000 with the local bank to provide short-term financing for its business operations. King either borrows or repays funds on the first day of a month. Interest is payable monthly at the bank's prime interest rate plus .5 percent. The following table shows the amounts borrowed and repaid for 2006 along with the bank's prime interest rate.

Month	Amount Borrowed or (Repaid)	Prime Rate for the Month, %
January	0	4
February	$40,000	4
March	20,000	4.5
April	(10,000)	5
May	(30,000)	4
June	10,000	4.5
July–October	0	4.5
November	50,000	5.5
December	(30,000)	5.25

Required

a. Show the effects of these transactions on the financial statements using a horizontal statements model like the one shown here. Use a + to indicate increase, a − for decrease, and NA for not affected. In the Cash Flow column, indicate whether the item is an operating activity (OA), investing activity (IA), or financing activity (FA).

Assets	=	Liabilities.	+	Equity	Rev.	−	Exp.	=	Net Inc.	Cash Flow

b. What is the total amount of interest expense paid for 2006?

Exercise 7-14 *Two complete accounting cycles: bonds issued at face value with annual interest* L.O. 7

Wyatt Company issued $400,000 of 20-year, 6 percent bonds on January 1, 2007. The bonds were issued at face value. Interest is payable in cash on December 31 of each year. Wyatt immediately invested the proceeds from the bond issue in land. The land was leased for an annual $60,000 of cash revenue, which was collected on December 31 of each year, beginning December 31, 2007.

Required

a. Organize the transaction data in accounts under the accounting equation.

b. Prepare the income statement, balance sheet, and statement of cash flows for 2007 and 2008.

Exercise 7-15 *Preparing a classified balance sheet* L.O. 9

Required

Use the following information to prepare a classified balance sheet for Steller Co. at the end of 2008.

Accounts Receivable	$42,500
Accounts Payable	8,000
Cash	15,260
Common Stock	42,000
Long-Term Notes Payable	23,000
Merchandise Inventory	29,000
Office Equipment	28,500
Retained Earnings	45,460
Prepaid Insurance	3,200

L.O. 10

Exercise 7-16 *Performing ratio analysis using real-world data*

Tupperware Company claims to be "one of the world's leading direct sellers, supplying premium food storage, preparation and serving items to consumers in more than 100 countries through its Tupperware brand." The following data were taken from the company's 2004 annual report. Dollar amounts are in millions.

	Fiscal Years Ending	
	December 31, 2004	**December 31, 2003**
Current assets	$466.0	$411.4
Current liabilities	292.1	290.4
Total assets	983.2	915.9
Total liabilities	692.3	687.7

Required

a. Compute Tupperware's current ratios for 2004 and 2003.

b. Compute Tupperware's debt to assets ratios for 2004 and 2003.

c. Based on the ratios computed in Requirements *a* and *b*, did Tupperware's liquidity get better or worse from 2003 to 2004?

d. Based on the ratios computed in Requirements *a* and *b*, did Tupperware's solvency get better or worse from 2003 to 2004?

PROBLEMS

All Problems are available with McGraw-Hill's Homework Manager

L.O. 1, 2, 3, 4

Problem 7-17 *Accounting for short-term debt and sales tax—two accounting cycles*

The following transactions apply to Artesia Co. for 2009, its first year of operations.

1. Received $40,000 cash from the issue of a short-term note with a 5 percent interest rate and a one-year maturity. The note was made on April 1, 2009.
2. Received $120,000 cash plus applicable sales tax from performing services. The services are subject to a sales tax rate of 6 percent.
3. Paid $72,000 cash for other operating expenses during the year.
4. Paid the sales tax due on $100,000 of the service revenue for the year. Sales tax on the balance of the revenue is not due until 2010.
5. Recognized the accrued interest at December 31, 2009.

The following transactions apply to Artesia Co. for 2010.

1. Paid the balance of the sales tax due for 2009.
2. Received $145,000 cash plus applicable sales tax from performing services. The services are subject to a sales tax rate of 6 percent.
3. Repaid the principal of the note and applicable interest on April 1, 2010.
4. Paid $85,000 of other operating expense during the year.
5. Paid the sales tax due on $120,000 of the service revenue. The sales tax on the balance of the revenue is not due until 2011.

Required

a. Organize the transaction data in accounts under an accounting equation.

b. Prepare an income statement, statement of changes in stockholders' equity, balance sheet, and statement of cash flow for 2009 and 2010.

Problem 7-18 *Effect of accrued interest on financial statements*

L.O. 1

CHECK FIGURES
b. $12,000
i. $38,800

Norman Co. borrowed $15,000 from the local bank on April 1, 2008, when the company was started. The note had an 8 percent annual interest rate and a one-year term to maturity. Norman Co. recognized $42,000 of revenue on account in 2008 and $56,000 of revenue on account in 2009. Cash collections from accounts receivable were $38,000 in 2008 and $58,000 in 2009. Norman Co. paid $26,000 of salaries expense in 2008 and $32,000 of salaries expense in 2009. Repaid loan and interest at maturity date.

Required

a. Organize the information in accounts under an accounting equation.

b. What amount of net cash flow from operating activities would Norman report on the 2008 cash flow statement?

c. What amount of interest expense would Norman report on the 2008 income statement?

d. What amount of total liabilities would Norman report on the December 31, 2008, balance sheet?

e. What amount of retained earnings would Norman report on the December 31, 2008, balance sheet?

f. What amount of cash flow from financing activities would Norman report on the 2008 statement of cash flows?

g. What amount of interest expense would Norman report on the 2009 income statement?

h. What amount of cash flows from operating activities would Norman report on the 2009 cash flow statement?

i. What amount of total assets would Norman report on the December 31, 2009, balance sheet?

Problem 7-19 *Current liabilities*

L.O. 1, 2, 4

The following selected transactions were taken from the books of Caledonia Company for 2008.

1. On March 1, 2008, borrowed $50,000 cash from the local bank. The note had a 6 percent interest rate and was due on September 1, 2008.
2. Cash sales for the year amounted to $225,000 plus sales tax at the rate of 7 percent.
3. Caledonia provides a 90-day warranty on the merchandise sold. The warranty expense is estimated to be 2 percent of sales.
4. Paid the sales tax to the state sales tax agency on $190,000 of the sales.
5. Paid the note due on September 1 and the related interest.
6. On October 1, 2008, borrowed $40,000 cash from the local bank. The note had a 7 percent interest rate and a one-year term to maturity.
7. Paid $3,600 in warranty repairs.
8. A customer has filed a lawsuit against Caledonia for $100,000 for breach of contract. The company attorney does not believe the suit has merit.

Required

a. Answer the following questions:

(1) What amount of cash did Caledonia pay for interest during the year?

(2) What amount of interest expense is reported on Caledonia's income statement for the year?

(3) What is the amount of warranty expense for the year?

b. Prepare the current liabilities section of the balance sheet at December 31, 2008. (*Hint:* first post the liabilities transactions to T-accounts.)

c. Show the effect of these transactions on the financial statements using a horizontal statements model like the one shown here. Use a + to indicate increase, a − for decrease, and NA for not affected. In the Cash Flow column, indicate whether the item is an operating activity (OA), investing activity (IA), or financing activity (FA). The first transaction is recorded as an example.

Assets	=	Liabilities	+	Equity	Rev.	−	Exp.	=	Net Inc.	Cash Flow
+		+		NA	NA		NA		NA	+ FA

L.O. 3

Problem 7-20 *Contingent liabilities*

Required

a. Give an example of a contingent liability that is probable and reasonably estimable. How would this type of liability be shown in the accounting records?

b. Give an example of a contingent liability that is reasonably possible or probable but not reasonably estimable. How would this type of liability be shown in the accounting records?

c. Give an example of a contingent liability that is remote. How is this type of liability shown in the accounting records?

L.O. 9

mhhe.com/edmonds2007

CHECK FIGURES
Total Current Assets: $317,800
Total Current Liabilities: $135,000

Problem 7-21 *Multistep income statement and classified balance sheet*

Required

Use the following information to prepare a multistep income statement and a classified balance sheet for Douglas Company for 2004. (*Hint:* Some of the items will *not* appear on either statement, and ending retained earnings must be calculated.)

Operating Expenses	$ 90,000	Cash	$ 23,000
Land	50,000	Interest Receivable (short term)	800
Accumulated Depreciation	38,000	Cash Flow from Investing Activities	102,000
Accounts Payable	60,000	Allowance for Doubtful Accounts	7,000
Unearned Revenue	58,000	Interest Payable (short term)	3,000
Warranties Payable (short term)	2,000	Sales Revenue	500,000
Equipment	77,000	Uncollectible Accounts Expense	14,000
Notes Payable (long term)	129,000	Interest Expense	32,000
Salvage Value of Equipment	7,000	Accounts Receivable	113,000
Dividends	12,000	Salaries Payable	12,000
Warranty Expense	5,000	Supplies	3,000
Beginning Retained Earnings	28,800	Prepaid Rent	14,000
Interest Revenue	6,000	Common Stock	52,000
Gain on Sale of Equipment	10,000	Cost of Goods Sold	179,000
Inventory	154,000	Salaries Expense	122,000
Notes Receivable (short term)	17,000		

L.O. 5

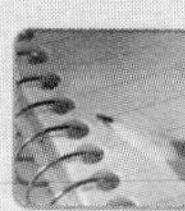

CHECK FIGURES
a. 2006 Ending Principal Balance: $41,337
c. 2008 Net Income: $28,505

Problem 7-22 *Effect of an installment loan on financial statements*

On January 1, 2006, Miller Co. borrowed cash from First City Bank by issuing a $60,000 face value, three-year installment note that had a 7 percent annual interest rate. The note is to be repaid by making annual payments of $22,863 that include both interest and principal on December 31 each year. Miller invested the proceeds from the loan in land that generated lease revenues of $30,000 cash per year.

Required

a. Prepare an amortization schedule for the three-year period.

b. Organize the information in accounts under an accounting equation.

c. Prepare an income statement, balance sheet, and statement of cash flows for each of the three years.

d. Does cash outflow from operating activities remain constant or change each year? Explain.

L.O. 5

Problem 7-23 *Accounting for an installment note payable*

The following transactions apply to Marque Co. for 2008, its first year of operations.

1. Received $30,000 cash in exchange for issuance of common stock.
2. Secured a $100,000, 10-year installment loan from First Bank. The interest rate was 6 percent and annual payments are $13,587.
3. Purchased land for $20,000.
4. Provided services for $85,000 cash.
5. Paid other operating expenses of $34,000.
6. Paid the annual payment on the loan.

Required

a. Organize the transaction data in accounts under an accounting equation.

b. Prepare an income statement and balance sheet for 2008.

c. What is the interest expense for 2009? 2010?

Problem 7-24 *Accounting for a line of credit*

L.O. 6

Quality Sports Equipment uses a line of credit to help finance its inventory purchases. Quality sells ski equipment and uses the line of credit to build inventory for its peak sales months, which tend to be clustered in the winter months. Account balances at the beginning of 2009 were as follows:

Cash	$50,000
Inventory	75,000
Common Stock	60,000
Retained Earnings	65,000

Quality experienced the following transactions for January, February, and March, 2009.

1. January 1, 2009, obtained approval for a line of credit of up to $200,000. Funds are to be obtained or repaid on the first day of each month. The interest rate is the bank prime rate plus 1 percent.
2. January 1, 2009, borrowed $30,000 on the line of credit. The bank's prime interest rate is 5 percent for January.
3. January 15, purchased inventory on account, $68,000.
4. January 31, paid other operating expenses of $8,000.
5. In January, sold inventory for $65,000 on account. The inventory had cost $42,000.
6. January 31, paid the interest due on the line of credit.
7. February 1, borrowed $60,000 on the line of credit. The bank's prime rate is 6 percent for February.
8. February 1, paid the accounts payable from transaction 3.
9. February 10, collected $62,000 of the sales on account.
10. February 20, purchased inventory on account, $72,000.
11. February sales on account were $110,000. The inventory had cost $75,000.
12. February 28, paid the interest due on the line of credit.
13. March 1, repaid $20,000 on the line of credit. The bank's prime rate is 5 percent for March.
14. March 5, paid $50,000 of the accounts payable.
15. March 10, collected $105,000 from accounts receivable.
16. March 20, purchased inventory on account, $72,000.
17. March sales on account were $135,000. The inventory had cost $87,000.
18. March 31, paid the interest due on the line of credit.

Required

a. What is the amount of interest expense for January? February? March?

b. What amount of cash was paid for interest in January? February? March?

Problem 7-25 *Effect of a line of credit on financial statements*

L.O. 6

Shim Company has a line of credit with Bay Bank. Shim can borrow up to $200,000 at any time over the course of the 2006 calendar year. The following table shows the prime rate expressed as an annual percentage along with the amounts borrowed and repaid during 2006. Shim agreed to pay interest at an annual rate equal to 1 percent above the bank's prime rate. Funds are borrowed or repaid on the first day of each month. Interest is payable in cash on the last day of the month. The interest rate is applied to the outstanding monthly balance. For example, Shim pays 5 percent (4 percent + 1 percent) annual interest on $70,000 for the month of January.

CHECK FIGURES
b. Interest Expense: $4,817
Total Assets: $53,183

Month	Amount Borrowed or (Repaid)	Prime Rate for the Month, %
January	$70,000	4
February	40,000	4
March	(20,000)	5
April through October	No change	No change
November	(30,000)	5
December	(20,000)	4

Shim earned $18,000 of cash revenue during 2006.

Required

a. Organize the information in accounts under an accounting equation.
b. Prepare an income statement, balance sheet, and statement of cash flows for 2006.
c. Write a memo discussing the advantages to a business of arranging a line of credit.

L.O. 1, 6, 7

Problem 7-26 *Effect of debt transactions on financial statements*

Required

Show the effect of each of the following independent accounting events on the financial statements using a horizontal statements model like the following one. Use + for increase, − for decrease, and NA for not affected. The first event is recorded as an example.

Event No.	Assets	=	Liab.	+	Equity	Rev.	−	Exp.	=	Net Inc.	Cash Flow
a	+		+		NA	NA		NA		NA	+ FA

a. Borrowed funds using a line of credit.
b. Made an interest payment for funds that had been borrowed against a line of credit.
c. Made a cash payment on a note payable for both interest and principal.
d. Issued a bond at face value.
e. Made an interest payment on a bond that had been issued at face value.

L.O. 10

Problem 7-27 *Performing ratio analysis using real-world data*

Texas Instruments, Inc., claims to be "the world leader in digital signal processing and analog technologies, the semiconductor engines of the Internet age." **Eastman Kodak Company** manufactures Kodak film, cameras and related products. The following data were taken from the companies' December 31, 2004, annual reports. Dollar amounts are in millions.

	Eastman Kodak	Texas Instruments
Current Assets	$ 5,648	$10,190
Current Liabilities	4,990	1,925
Total Assets	14,737	16,299
Total Liabilities	10,926	3,236

Required

a. Compute the current ratio for each company.
b. Compute the debt to assets ratio for each company.
c. Based on the ratios computed in Requirements *a* and *b*, which company had the better liquidity in 2004?
d. Based on the ratios computed in Requirements *a* and *b*, which company had the better solvency in 2004?

ANALYZE, THINK, COMMUNICATE

ATC 7-1 Business Applications Case *Understanding real-world annual reports*

Required

Use the Topps Company's annual report in Appendix B to answer the following questions.

a. What was Topps' current ratio as of March 1, 2003, and March 2, 2002?
b. Did the current ratio get stronger or weaker from 2002 to 2003? Explain briefly why this happened.
c. Topps' balance sheet reports "Accrued expenses and other liabilities." What is included in this category? (See the footnotes.)
d. On its balance sheet Topps shows "Other liabilities" of $22,601,000. Does the company explain what these are? If so, what are they?
e. In the footnotes, Topps reveals that it entered into a credit agreement with two banks in 2000. What amount of credit is available to Topps under this agreement, and when does it expire?
f. What restrictions does the credit agreement place on Topps? Be specific.

ATC 7-2 Group Assignment *Using current ratios to make comparisons*

The following accounting information pertains to Eckert and Ragland companies at the end of 2006:

Account Title	Eckert	Ragland
Cash	$ 22,000	$ 30,000
Wages Payable	30,000	30,000
Merchandise Inventory	45,000	66,000
Building	120,000	95,000
Accounts Receivable	53,000	37,000
Long-term Notes Payable	115,000	145,000
Land	68,000	60,000
Accounts Payable	60,000	54,000
Sales Revenue	330,000	325,000
Expenses	285,000	295,000

Required

a. Organize the class into two sections and divide each section into groups of three to five students. Assign each of the sections one of the companies.

Group Tasks

(1) Identify the current assets and current liabilities, and compute the current ratio for the particular company assigned to the group.
(2) Assuming that all assets and liabilities are listed here, compute the debt to assets ratio for the particular company assigned to the group.

Class Discussion

b. Have a representative from each section report the current ratio and debt to assets ratio for their respective companies.
c. Solicit comments regarding which company has the greater financial risk in both the short and long term.

ATC 7-3 Real-World Case *Unusual types of liabilities*

In the liabilities section of its 2002 balance sheet, Wachovia Corporation reported "noninterest-bearing deposits" of over $44 billion. Wachovia is a very large banking company. In the liabilities section of its 2002 balance sheet, Newmont Mining Corporation reported "reclamation and remediation liabilities" of more than $302 million. Newmont Mining is involved in gold mining and refining activities. In the accrued liabilities reported on its 2002 balance sheet, Conoco Phillips included $1.7 billion for "accrued dismantlement, removal, and environmental costs."

Required

a. For each of the preceding liabilities, write a brief explanation of what you believe the nature of the liability to be and how the company will pay it off. To develop your answers, think about the nature of the industry in which each of the companies operates.

b. Of the three liabilities described, which do you think poses the most risk for the company? In other words, for which liability are actual costs most likely to exceed the liability reported on the balance sheet? Uncertainty creates risk.

ATC 7-4 Business Applications Case *Using the current ratio*

	Hamburger House	Hot Dog Heaven
Current Assets	$90,000	$60,000
Current Liabilities	65,000	33,000

Required

a. Compute the current ratio for each company.

b. Which company has the greater likelihood of being able to pay its bills?

c. Assuming that both companies have the same amount of total assets, which company would produce the higher return on assets ratio?

ATC 7-5 Business Applications Case *Debt versus equity financing*

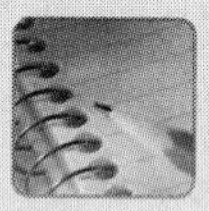

Mack Company plans to invest $50,000 in land that will produce annual rent revenue equal to 15 percent of the investment starting on January 1, 2007. The revenue will be collected in cash at the end of each year, starting December 31, 2007. Mack can obtain the cash necessary to purchase the land from two sources. Funds can be obtained by issuing $50,000 of 10 percent, five-year bonds at their face amount. Interest due on the bonds is payable on December 31 of each year with the first payment due on December 31, 2007. Alternatively, the $50,000 needed to invest in land can be obtained from equity financing. In this case, the stockholders (holders of the equity) will be paid a $5,000 annual distribution. Mack Company is in a 30 percent income tax bracket.

Required

a. Prepare an income statement and statement of cash flows for 2007 under the two alternative financing proposals.

b. Write a short memorandum explaining why one financing alternative provides more net income but less cash flow than the other.

ATC 7-6 Writing Assignment *Definition of elements of financial statements*

Putting "yum" on people's faces around the world is the mission of **YUM Brands, Inc.** Yum was spun off from **PepsiCo** in 1997. A spin-off occurs when a company separates its operations into two or more distinct companies. The company was originally composed of **KFC**, **Pizza Hut**, and **Taco Bell** and was operated as a part of PepsiCo prior to the spin-off. In 2002 YUM acquired **A & W All American Foods** and **Long John Silver's** units. The acquisition pushed YUM's debt to $4.8 billion. YUM's net income before interest and taxes in 2002 was $1.03 million.

Required

a. If YUM's debt remains constant at $4.8 billion for 2003, how much interest will YUM incur in 2003, assuming the average interest rate is 7 percent?

b. Does the debt seem excessive compared with the amount of 2002 net income before interest and taxes? Explain.

c. Assuming YUM pays tax at the rate of 30 percent, what amount of tax will YUM pay in 2002?

d. Assume you are the president of the company. Write a memo to the shareholders explaining how YUM is able to meet its obligations and increase stockholders' equity.

ATC 7-7 Ethical Dilemma *Sometimes debt is not debt*

David Sheridan was a well-respected CPA in his mid-fifties. After spending 10 years at a national accounting firm, he was hired by Global, Inc., a multinational corporation headquartered in the United States. He patiently worked his way up to the top of Global's accounting department and in the early 1990s, took over as chief financial officer for the company. As the Internet began to explode, management at Global, Inc., decided to radically change the nature of its business to one of e-commerce. Two years after the transition, Internet commerce began to slow down, and Global was in dire need of cash in order to continue operations. Management turned to the accounting department.

Global, Inc., needed to borrow a substantial amount of money but couldn't afford to increase the amount of liabilities on the balance sheet for fear of the stock price dropping and banks becoming nervous and demanding repayment of existing loans. David discovered a way that would allow the company to raise the needed cash to continue operations without having to report the long-term notes payable on the balance sheet. Under an obscure rule, companies can set up separate legal organizations that do not have to be reported on the parent company's financial statements, if a third party contributes just 3 percent of the start-up capital. David called a friend, Brian Johnson, and asked him to participate in a business venture with Global. Brian agreed, and created a special purpose entity with Global named BrianCo. For his participation, Brian was awarded a substantial amount of valuable Global stock. Brian then went to a bank and used the stock as collateral to borrow a large sum of money for BrianCo. Then, Global sold some of its poor or underperforming assets to BrianCo for the cash that Brian borrowed. In the end, Global got rid of bad assets, received the proceeds of the long-term note payable, and did not have to show the liability on the balance sheet. Only the top executives and the accountants that worked closely with David knew of the scheme, and they planned to use this method only until the e-commerce portion of Global became profitable again.

Required

a. How did David's scheme affect the overall appearance of Global's financial statements? Why was this important to investors and creditors?

b. Review the AICPA's Articles of Professional Conduct (see Chapter 1) and comment on any of the standards that have been violated.

c. Donald Cressey identified three common features of unethical and criminal conduct (see Chapter 1). Name these features and explain how they materialize in this case.

ATC 7-8 Research Assignment *Analyzing long-term debt at Union Pacific Railroad*

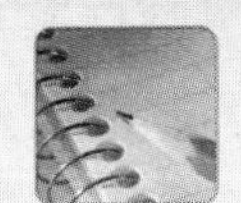

Many companies have a form of debt called *capital leases.* A capital lease is created when a company agrees to rent an asset, such as equipment or a building, for such a long time that GAAP treats the lease as if the asset were purchased using borrowed funds. A capital lease creates a liability for the company that acquired the leased asset because it has promised to make payments to another company for several years in the future. If a company has any capital leases, it must disclose them in the footnotes to the financial statements, and will sometimes disclose them in a separate account in the liabilities section of the balance sheet.

Using the most current Forms 10-K for **Union Pacific Corporation**, complete the requirements below. To obtain the 10-Ks use either the EDGAR system following the instructions in Appendix A, or the company's website.

Required

a. What was Union Pacific's debt to assets ratio? (You will need to compute total liabilities by subtracting "Common shareholders' equity" from total assets.)

b. How much interest expense did Union Pacific incur?

c. What amount of liabilities did Union Pacific have as a result of capital leases? Footnote 5 presents information about Union Pacific's leases.

d. What percentage of Union Pacific's long-term liabilities was the result of capital leases?

e. Many companies try to structure (design) leasing agreements so their leases will *not* be classified as capital leases. Explain why a company such as Union Pacific might want to avoid reporting capital leases.

CHAPTER 8

Proprietorships, Partnerships, and Corporations

LEARNING OBJECTIVES

After you have mastered the material in this chapter you will be able to:

1. Identify the primary characteristics of sole proprietorships, partnerships, and corporations.
2. Analyze financial statements to identify the different types of business organizations.
3. Explain the characteristics of major types of stock issued by corporations.
4. Explain how to account for different types of stock issued by corporations.
5. Show how treasury stock transactions affect a company's financial statements.
6. Explain the effects of declaring and paying cash dividends on a company's financial statements.
7. Explain the effects of stock dividends and stock splits on a company's financial statements.
8. Show how the appropriation of retained earnings affects financial statements.
9. Explain some uses of accounting information in making stock investment decisions.

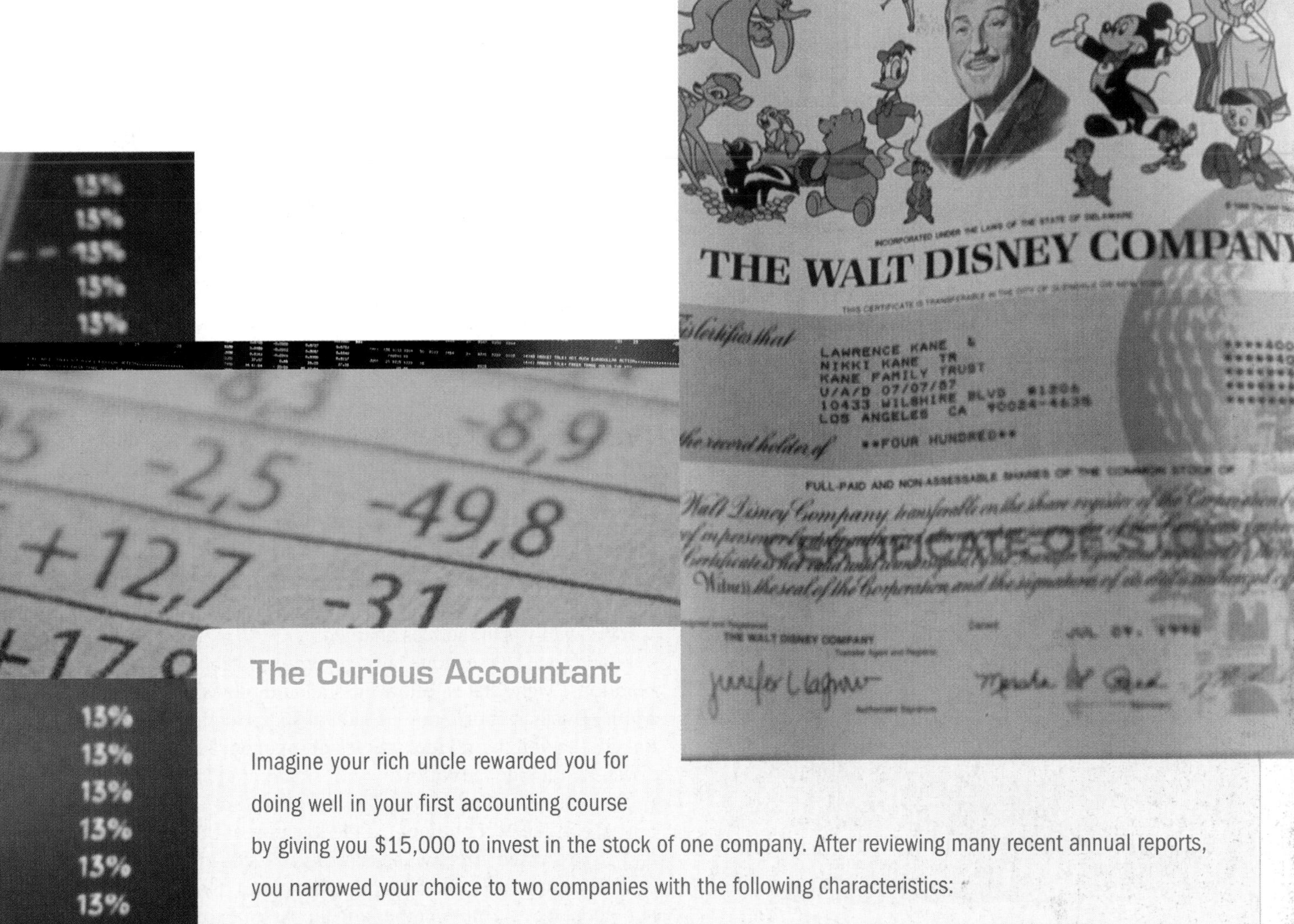

Chapter 8

The Curious Accountant

Imagine your rich uncle rewarded you for doing well in your first accounting course by giving you $15,000 to invest in the stock of one company. After reviewing many recent annual reports, you narrowed your choice to two companies with the following characteristics:

Mystery Company A: This company's stock has only been trading publicly since October 2004. At the time it went public it had net losses totaling about $34 million. This stock is selling for about $26 per share, so you can buy about 577 shares. A friend told you it was a "sure winner," especially at its current price, since it is just starting out and has a lot of growth potential.

Mystery Company B: This company has been in existence since 1923 and has made a profit most years. In the most recent five years, its net earnings totaled over $6 *billion,* and it paid dividends of over $2.1 *billion.* This stock is selling for about $28 per share, so you can buy 535 shares of it. Your friend said "you would have to be goofy to buy this stock."

The names of the real-world companies described above are disclosed later. Based on the information provided, which company's stock would you buy? (Answers on page 284.)

CHAPTER OPENING

You want to start a business. How should you structure it? Should it be a sole proprietorship, partnership, or corporation? Each form of business structure presents advantages and disadvantages. For example, a sole proprietorship allows maximum independence and control while partnerships and corporations allow individuals to pool resources and talents with other people. This chapter discusses these and other features of the three primary forms of business structure. ■

Forms of Business Organizations

LO 1

Identify the primary characteristics of sole proprietorships, partnerships, and corporations.

Sole proprietorships are owned by a single individual who is responsible for making business and profit distribution decisions. If you want to be the absolute master of your destiny, you should organize your business as a proprietorship. Establishing a sole proprietorship is usually as simple as obtaining a business license from local government authorities. Usually no legal ownership agreement is required.

Partnerships allow persons to share their talents, capital, and the risks and rewards of business ownership. Since two or more individuals share ownership, partnerships require clear agreements about how authority, risks, and profits will be shared. Prudent partners minimize misunderstandings by hiring attorneys to prepare a **partnership agreement** which defines the responsibilities of each partner and describes how income or losses will be divided. Since the measurement of income affects the distribution of profits, partnerships frequently hire accountants to ensure that records are maintained in accordance with generally accepted accounting principles (GAAP). Partnerships (and sole proprietorships) also may need professional advice to deal with tax issues.

A **corporation** is a separate legal entity created by the authority of a state government. The paperwork to start a corporation is complex. For most laypersons, engaging professional attorneys and accountants to assist with the paperwork is well worth the fees charged.

Each state has separate laws governing establishing corporations. Many states follow the standard provisions of the Model Business Corporation Act. All states require the initial application to provide **articles of incorporation** which normally include the following information: (1) the corporation's name and proposed date of incorporation; (2) the purpose of the corporation; (3) the location of the business and its expected life (which can be *perpetuity,* meaning *endless*); (4) provisions for capital stock; and (5) the names and addresses of the members of the first board of directors, the individuals with the ultimate authority for operating the business. If the articles are in order, the state establishes the legal existence of the corporation by issuing a charter of incorporation. The charter and the articles are public documents.

Advantages and Disadvantages of Different Forms of Business Organization

Identify the primary characteristics of sole proprietorships, partnerships, and corporations.

Each form of business organization presents a different combination of advantages and disadvantages. Persons wanting to start a business or invest in one should consider the characteristics of each type of business structure.

Regulation

Few laws specifically affect the operations of proprietorships and partnerships. Corporations, however, are usually heavily regulated. The extent of government regulation depends on the size and distribution of a company's ownership interests. Ownership interests in corporations are normally evidenced by **stock certificates.**

Ownership of corporations can be transferred from one individual to another through exchanging stock certificates. As long as the exchanges (buying and selling of shares of stock, often called *trading*) are limited to transactions between individuals, a company is defined as a **closely held corporation.** However, once a corporation reaches a certain size, it may list its stock on a stock exchange such as the **New York Stock Exchange** or the **American Stock Exchange**. Trading on a stock exchange is limited to the stockbrokers who are members of the exchange. These brokers represent buyers and sellers who are willing to pay the brokers commissions for exchanging stock certificates on their behalf. Although closely held corpo-

REALITY BYTES

Edward Nusbaum, CEO of **Grant Thornton**, a Chicago accounting firm, believes that "Sarbanes-Oxley is most likely creating the desired effect of making businesses realize that very strong responsibilities come with being a public company." However, a recent study conducted by Grant Thornton indicates that the cost of regulatory compliance is so significant that many smaller companies are taking their firms' stock off the exchanges. The study found that the number of public companies making the switch to private ownership is up 30 percent since the Sarbanes-Oxley Act went into effect July 30, 2002. A different study by Thomson Financial found similar results. The Thomson study found 60 public companies went private in the first nine months of 2003, up from 49 during the same period in 2002 and nearly double the 32 firms that went private in 2001. Clearly, the expense of regulatory compliance is a distinct disadvantage of the corporate form of business. In contrast, ease of formation and limited regulation are clear advantages of proprietorships and, to a lesser extent, partnerships.

rations are relatively free from government regulation, companies whose stock is publicly traded on the exchanges by brokers are subject to extensive regulation.

The extensive regulation of trading on stock exchanges began in the 1930s. The stock market crash of 1929 and the subsequent Great Depression led Congress to pass the **Securities Act of 1933** and the **Securities Exchange Act of 1934** to regulate issuing stock and to govern the exchanges. The 1934 act also created the Securities and Exchange Commission (SEC) to enforce the securities laws. Congress gave the SEC legal authority to establish accounting principles for corporations that are registered on the exchanges. However, the SEC has generally deferred its rule-making authority to private sector accounting bodies such as the Financial Accounting Standards Board (FASB), effectively allowing the accounting profession to regulate itself.

A number of high-profile business failures around the turn of the century raised questions about the effectiveness of self-regulation and the usefulness of audits to protect the public. The **Sarbanes-Oxley Act of 2002** was adopted to address these concerns. The act creates a five-member Public Company Accounting Oversight Board (PCAOB) with the authority to set and enforce auditing, attestation, quality control, and ethics standards for auditors of public companies. The PCAOB is empowered to impose disciplinary and remedial sanctions for violations of its rules, securities laws, and professional auditing and accounting standards. Public corporations operate in a complex regulatory environment that requires the services of attorneys and professional accountants.

Double Taxation

Corporations pay income taxes on their earnings and then owners pay income taxes on distributions (dividends) received from corporations. As a result, distributed corporate profits are taxed twice—first when income is reported on the corporation's income tax return and a second time when distributions are reported on individual owners' tax returns. This phenomenon is commonly called **double taxation** and is a significant disadvantage of the corporate form of business organization.

To illustrate, assume Glide Corporation earns pretax income of $100,000. Glide is in a 30 percent tax bracket. The corporation itself will pay income tax of $30,000 ($100,000 × 0.30). If the corporation distributes the after-tax income of $70,000 ($100,000 − $30,000) to individual

Answers to The Curious Accountant

Mystery Company A is ***Shopping.com, Ltd.*** (as of December 16, 2004), a company that offers a free, online, comparison shopping service. The origins of the company can be traced back to 1998. On October 25, 2004, Shopping.com's stock was sold to the public in an *initial public offering* (IPO) at $18. The first day its stock traded on NASDAQ it closed at $28.80. During its first month of trading its price ranged from a low of $22.92 per share to a high of $35.62 per share. Obviously, the people trading Shopping.com's stock were not paying much attention to its past profits. Instead, they were focusing on the company's potential.

Mystery Company B is ***Walt Disney Company, Inc.*** (as of December 16, 2004). Of course, only the future will tell which company is the better investment.

stockholders in 15 percent tax brackets,[1] the $70,000 dividend will be reported on the individual tax returns, requiring tax payments of $10,500 ($70,000 × .15). Total income tax of $40,500 ($30,000 + $10,500) is due on $100,000 of earned income. In contrast, consider a proprietorship that is owned by an individual in a 30 percent tax bracket. If the proprietorship earns and distributes $100,000 profit, the total tax would be only $30,000 ($100,000 × .30).

Double taxation can be a burden for small companies. To reduce that burden, tax laws permit small closely held corporations to elect "S Corporation" status. S Corporations are taxed as proprietorships or partnerships. Also, many states have recently enacted laws permitting the formation of **limited liability companies (LLCs)** which offer many of the benefits of corporate ownership yet are in general taxed as partnerships. Since proprietorships and partnerships are not separate legal entities, company earnings are taxable to the owners rather than the company itself.

Limited Liability

Given the disadvantages of increased regulation and double taxation, why would anyone choose the corporate form of business structure over a partnership or proprietorship? A major reason is that the corporate form limits an investor's potential liability as an owner of a business venture. Because a corporation is legally separate from its owners, creditors cannot claim owners' personal assets as payment for the company's debts. Also, plaintiffs must sue the corporation, not its owners. The most that owners of a corporation can lose is the amount they have invested in the company (the value of the company's stock).

Unlike corporate stockholders, the owners of proprietorships and partnerships are *personally liable* for actions they take in the name of their companies. In fact, partners are responsible not only for their own actions but also for those taken by any other partner on behalf of the partnership. The benefit of **limited liability** is one of the most significant reasons the corporate form of business organization is so popular.

Continuity

Unlike partnerships or proprietorships, which terminate with the departure of their owners, a corporation's life continues when a shareholder dies or sells his or her stock. Because of **continuity** of existence, many corporations formed in the 1800s still thrive today.

Transferability of Ownership

The **transferability** of corporate ownership is easy. An investor simply buys or sells stock to acquire or give up an ownership interest in a corporation. Hundreds of millions of shares of stock are bought and sold on the major stock exchanges each day.

[1]As a result of the Jobs and Growth Tax Relief Reconciliation Act (JGTRRA) of 2003, dividends received in tax years after 2002 are taxed at a maximum rate of 15 percent for most taxpayers. Lower income individuals pay a 5 percent tax on dividends received on December 31, 2007, or earlier. This rate falls to zero in 2008. The provisions of JGTRRA are set to expire on December 31, 2008.

Transferring the ownership of proprietorships is much more difficult. To sell an ownership interest in a proprietorship, the proprietor must find someone willing to purchase the entire business. Since most proprietors also run their businesses, transferring ownership also requires transferring management responsibilities. Consider the difference in selling $1 million of Exxon stock versus selling a locally owned gas station. The stock could be sold on the New York Stock Exchange within minutes. In contrast, it could take years to find a buyer who is financially capable of and interested in owning and operating a gas station.

Transferring ownership in partnerships can also be difficult. As with proprietorships, ownership transfers may require a new partner to make a significant investment and accept management responsibilities in the business. Further, a new partner must accept and be accepted by the other partners. Personality conflicts and differences in management style can cause problems in transferring ownership interests in partnerships.

Management Structure

Partnerships and proprietorships are usually managed by their owners. Corporations, in contrast, have three tiers of management authority. The *owners* (**stockholders**) represent the highest level of organizational authority. The stockholders *elect* a **board of directors** to oversee company operations. The directors then *hire* professional executives to manage the company on a daily basis. Since large corporations can offer high salaries and challenging career opportunities, they can often attract superior managerial talent.

While the management structure used by corporations is generally effective, it sometimes complicates dismissing incompetent managers. The chief executive officer (CEO) is usually a member of the board of directors and is frequently influential in choosing other board members. The CEO is also in a position to reward loyal board members. As a result, board members may be reluctant to fire the CEO or other top executives even if the individuals are performing poorly. Corporations operating under such conditions are said to be experiencing **entrenched management.**

Ability to Raise Capital

Because corporations can have millions of owners (shareholders), they have the opportunity to raise huge amounts of capital. Few individuals have the financial means to build and operate a telecommunications network such as AT&T or a marketing distribution system such as Wal-Mart. However, by pooling the resources of millions of owners through public stock and bond offerings, corporations generate the billions of dollars of capital needed for such massive investments. In contrast, the capital resources of proprietorships and partnerships are limited to a relatively small number of private owners. Although proprietorships and partnerships can also obtain resources by borrowing, the amount creditors are willing to lend them is usually limited by the size of the owners' net worth.

Appearance of Capital Structure in Financial Statements

The ownership interest (equity) in a business is composed of two elements: (1) owner/investor contributions and (2) retained earnings. The way these two elements are reported in the financial statements differs for each type of business structure (proprietorship, partnership, or corporation).

LO 2

Analyze financial statements to identify the different types of business organizations.

Presentation of Equity in Proprietorships

Owner contributions and retained earnings are combined in a single Capital account on the balance sheets of proprietorships. To illustrate, assume that Worthington Sole Proprietorship was started on January 1, 2005, when it acquired a $5,000 capital contribution from its owner, Phil Worthington. During the first year of operation, the company generated $4,000 of cash revenues, incurred $2,500 of cash expenses, and distributed $1,000 cash to the owner. Exhibit 8.1 displays 2005 financial statements for Worthington's company. Note on the *capital statement* that distributions are called **withdrawals.** Verify that the $5,500 balance in the Capital account on the balance sheet includes the $5,000 owner contribution and the retained earnings of $500 ($1,500 net income − $1,000 withdrawal).

EXHIBIT 8.1

WORTHINGTON SOLE PROPRIETORSHIP
Financial Statements
As of December 31, 2005

Income Statement	
Revenue	$4,000
Expenses	2,500
Net Income	$1,500

Capital Statement	
Beginning Capital Balance	$ 0
Plus: Investment by Owner	5,000
Plus: Net Income	1,500
Less: Withdrawal by Owner	(1,000)
Ending Capital Balance	$5,500

Balance Sheet	
Assets	
Cash	$5,500
Equity	
Worthington, Capital	$5,500

CHECK YOURSELF 8.1

Weiss Company was started on January 1, 2004, when it acquired $50,000 cash from its owner(s). During 2004 the company earned $72,000 of net income. Explain how the equity section of Weiss's December 31, 2004, balance sheet would differ if the company were a proprietorship versus a corporation.

Answer

Proprietorship records combine capital acquisitions from the owner and earnings from operating the business in a single capital account. In contrast, *corporation* records separate capital acquisitions from the owners and earnings from operating the business. If Weiss were a proprietorship, the equity section of the year-end balance sheet would report a single capital component of $122,000. If Weiss were a corporation, the equity section would report two separate equity components, most likely common stock of $50,000 and retained earnings of $72,000.

Presentation of Equity in Partnerships

The financial statement format for reporting partnership equity is similar to that used for proprietorships. Contributed capital and retained earnings are combined. However, a separate capital account is maintained for each partner in the business to reflect each partner's ownership interest.

To illustrate, assume that Sara Slater and Jill Johnson formed a partnership on January 1, 2006. The partnership acquired $2,000 of capital from Slater and $4,000 from Johnson. The partnership agreement called for each partner to receive an annual distribution equal to 10 percent of her capital contribution. Any further earnings were to be retained in the business and divided equally between the partners. During 2006, the company earned $5,000 of cash revenue and incurred $3,000 of cash expenses, for net income of $2,000 ($5,000 − $3,000). As specified by the partnership agreement, Slater received a $200 ($2,000 × 0.10) cash withdrawal and Johnson received $400 ($4,000 × 0.10). The remaining $1,400 ($2,000 − $200 − $400) of income was retained in the business and divided equally, adding $700 to each partner's capital account.

Exhibit 8.2 displays financial statements for the Slater and Johnson partnership. Again, note that distributions are called *withdrawals.* Also find on the balance sheet a *separate cap-*

EXHIBIT 8.2

SLATER AND JOHNSON PARTNERSHIP
Financial Statements
As of December 31, 2006

Income Statement		Capital Statement		Balance Sheet	
Revenue	$5,000	Beginning Capital Balance	$ 0	Assets	
Expenses	3,000	Plus: Investment by Owners	6,000	Cash	$7,400
Net Income	$2,000	Plus: Net Income	2,000	Equity	
		Less: Withdrawal by Owners	(600)	Slater, Capital	$2,700
		Ending Capital Balance	$7,400	Johnson, Capital	4,700
				Total Capital	$7,400

ital account for each partner. Each capital account includes the amount of the partner's contributed capital plus her proportionate share of the retained earnings.

Presentation of Equity in Corporations

Corporations have more complex capital structures than proprietorships and partnerships. Explanations of some of the more common features of corporate capital structures and transactions follow.

Characteristics of Capital Stock

Explain the characteristics of major types of stock issued by corporations.

Stock issued by corporations may have a variety of different characteristics. For example, a company may issue different classes of stock that grant owners different rights and privileges. Also, the number of shares a corporation can legally issue may differ from the number it actually has issued. Further, a corporation can even buy back its own stock. Finally, a corporation may assign different values to the stock it issues. Accounting for corporate equity transactions is discussed in the next section of the text.

Par Value

Many states require assigning a **par value** to stock. Historically, par value represented the maximum liability of the investors. Par value multiplied by the number of shares of stock issued represents the minimum amount of assets that must be retained in the company as protection for creditors. This amount is known as **legal capital.** To ensure that the amount of legal capital is maintained in a corporation, many states require that purchasers pay at least the par value for a share of stock initially purchased from a corporation. To minimize the amount of assets that owners must maintain in the business, many corporations issue stock with very low par values, often $1 or less. Therefore, *legal capital* as defined by par value has come to have very little relevance to investors or creditors. As a result, many states allow corporations to issue no-par stock.

Stated Value

No-par stock may have a stated value. Like par value, **stated value** is an arbitrary amount assigned by the board of directors to the stock. It also has little relevance to investors and creditors. Stock with a par value and stock with a stated value are accounted for exactly the same way. When stock has no par or stated value, accounting for it is slightly different. These accounting differences are illustrated later in this chapter.

Other Valuation Terminology

The price an investor must pay to purchase a share of stock is the **market value.** The sales price of a share of stock may be more or less than the par value. Another term analysts frequently associate with stock is *book value.* **Book value per share** is calculated by dividing total stockholders' equity (assets − liabilities) by the number of shares of stock owned by investors. Book value per share differs from market value per share because equity is measured in historical dollars and market value reflects investors' estimates of a company's current value.

Stock: Authorized, Issued, and Outstanding

As part of the regulatory function, states approve the maximum number of shares of stock corporations are legally permitted to issue. This maximum number is called **authorized stock.** Authorized stock that has been sold to the public is called **issued stock.** When a corporation buys back some of its issued stock from the public, the repurchased stock is called **treasury stock.** Treasury stock is still considered to be issued stock, but it is no longer outstanding. **Outstanding stock** (total issued stock minus treasury stock) is stock owned by investors outside the corporation. For example, assume a company that is authorized to issue 150 shares of stock issues 100 shares to investors, and then buys back 20 shares of treasury stock. There are 150 shares authorized, 100 shares issued, and 80 shares outstanding.

Classes of Stock

The corporate charter defines the number of shares of stock authorized, the par value or stated value (if any), and the classes of stock that a corporation can issue. Most stock issued is either *common* or *preferred.*

FOCUS ON INTERNATIONAL ISSUES

WHO PROVIDES THE FINANCING?

The accounting rules in a country are affected by who provides financing to businesses in that country. Equity (versus debt) financing is a major source of financing for most businesses in the United States. The stock (equity ownership) of most large U.S. companies is said to be *widely held.* This means that many different institutional investors (e.g., pension funds) and individuals own stock. At the other extreme is a country in which the government owns most industries. In between might be a country in which large banks provide a major portion of business financing, such as Japan or Germany.

It is well beyond the scope of this course to explain specifically how a country's accounting principles are affected by who provides the financing for the country's major industries. Nevertheless, a businessperson should be aware that the source of a company's financing affects its financial reporting. Do not assume that business practices or accounting rules in other countries are like those in the United States.

Common Stock

All corporations issue **common stock.** Common stockholders bear the highest risk of losing their investment if a company is forced to liquidate. On the other hand, they reap the greatest rewards when a corporation prospers. Common stockholders generally enjoy several rights, including: (1) the right to buy and sell stock, (2) the right to share in the distribution of profits, (3) the right to share in the distribution of corporate assets in the case of liquidation, (4) the right to vote on significant matters that affect the corporate charter, and (5) the right to participate in the election of directors.

Preferred Stock

Many corporations issue **preferred stock** in addition to common stock. Holders of preferred stock receive certain privileges relative to holders of common stock. In exchange for special privileges in some areas, preferred stockholders give up rights in other areas. Preferred stockholders usually have no voting rights and the amount of their dividends is usually limited. Preferences granted to preferred stockholders include the following:

1. *Preference as to assets.* Preferred stock often has a liquidation value. In case of bankruptcy, preferred stockholders must be paid the liquidation value before any assets are distributed to common stockholders. However, preferred stockholder claims still fall behind creditor claims.
2. *Preference as to dividends.* Preferred shareholders are frequently guaranteed the right to receive dividends before common stockholders. The amount of the preferred dividend is normally stated on the stock certificate. It may be stated as a dollar value (say, $5) per share or as a percentage of the par value. Most preferred stock has **cumulative dividends,** meaning that if a corporation is unable to pay the preferred dividend in any year, the dividend is not lost but begins to accumulate. Cumulative dividends that have not been paid are called **dividends in arrears.** When a company pays dividends, any preferred stock arrearages must be paid before any other dividends are paid. Noncumulative preferred stock is not often issued because preferred stock is much less attractive if missed dividends do not accumulate.

To illustrate the effects of preferred dividends, consider Dillion, Incorporated, which has the following shares of stock outstanding:

Preferred stock, 4%, $10 par, 10,000 shares
Common stock, $10 par, 20,000 shares

Assume the preferred stock dividend has not been paid for two years. If Dillion pays $22,000 in dividends, how much will each class of stock receive? It depends on whether the preferred stock is cumulative.

Allocation of Distribution for Cumulative Preferred Stock

	To Preferred	To Common
Dividends in arrears	$ 8,000	$ 0
Current year's dividends	4,000	10,000
Total distribution	$12,000	$10,000

Allocation of Distribution for Noncumulative Preferred Stock

	To Preferred	To Common
Dividends in arrears	$ 0	$ 0
Current year's dividends	4,000	18,000
Total distribution	$ 4,000	$18,000

EXHIBIT 8.3

Presence of Preferred Stock in the Capital Structure of U.S. Companies

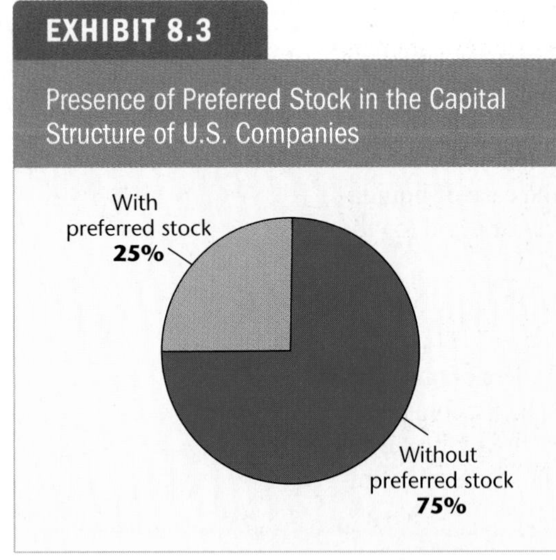

Data source: AICPA, *Accounting Trends and Techniques,* 2002.

The total annual dividend on the preferred stock is $4,000 (0.04 × $10 par × 10,000 shares). If the preferred stock is cumulative, the $8,000 in arrears must be paid first. Then $4,000 for the current year's dividend is paid next. The remaining $10,000 goes to common stockholders. If the preferred stock is noncumulative, the $8,000 of dividends from past periods is ignored. This year's $4,000 preferred dividend is paid first, with the remaining $18,000 going to common.

Other features of preferred stock may include the right to participate in distributions beyond the established amount of the preferred dividend, the right to convert preferred stock to common stock or to bonds, and the potential for having the preferred stock called (repurchased) by the corporation. Detailed discussion of these topics is left to more advanced courses. Exhibit 8.3 indicates that roughly 25 percent of U.S. companies have preferred shares outstanding.

Accounting for Stock Transactions on the Day of Issue

LO 4

Explain how to account for different types of stock issued by corporations.

Issuing stock with a par or stated value is accounted for differently from issuing no-par stock. For stock with either a par or stated value, the total amount acquired from the owners is divided between two separate equity accounts. The amount of the par or stated value is recorded in the stock account. Any amount received above the par or stated value is recorded in an account called **Paid-in Capital in Excess of Par** (or **Stated**) **Value.**

Issuing Par Value Stock

To illustrate the issue of common stock with a par value, assume that Nelson Incorporated is authorized to issue 250 shares of common stock. During 2005, Nelson issued 100 shares of $10 par common stock for $22 per share. The event increases assets and stockholders' equity by $2,200 ($22 × 100 shares). The increase in stockholders' equity is divided into two parts, $1,000 of par value ($10 per share × 100 shares) and $1,200 ($2,200 − $1,000) received in excess of par value. The income statement is not affected. The $2,200 cash inflow is reported in the financing activities section of the statement of cash flows. The effects on the financial statements follow:

Assets	=	Liab.	+	Equity			Rev.	−	Exp.	=	Net Inc.	Cash Flow
Cash	=			Com. Stk.	+	PIC in Excess						
2,200	=	NA	+	1,000	+	1,200	NA	−	NA	=	NA	2,200 FA

The *legal capital* of the corporation is $1,000, the total par value of the issued common stock. The number of shares issued can be easily verified by dividing the total amount in the common stock account by the par value ($1,000 ÷ $10 = 100 shares).

Stock Classification

Assume Nelson Incorporated obtains authorization to issue 400 shares of Class B, $20 par value common stock. The company issues 150 shares of this stock at $25 per share. The event increases assets and stockholders' equity by $3,750 ($25 × 150 shares). The increase in stockholders' equity is divided into two parts, $3,000 of par value ($20 per share × 150 shares) and $750 ($3,750 − $3,000) received in excess of par value. The income statement is not affected. The $3,750 cash inflow is reported in the financing activities section of the statement of cash flows. The effects on the financial statements follow:

Assets	=	Liab.	+	Equity			Rev.	−	Exp.	=	Net Inc.	Cash Flow
Cash	=			Com. Stk.	+	PIC in Excess						
3,750	=	NA	+	3,000	+	750	NA	−	NA	=	NA	3,750 FA

As the preceding event suggests, companies can issue numerous classes of common stock. The specific rights and privileges for each class are described in the individual stock certificates.

Stock Issued at Stated Value

Assume Nelson is authorized to issue 300 shares of a third class of stock, 7 percent cumulative preferred stock with a stated value of $10 per share. Nelson issued 100 shares of the preferred stock at a price of $22 per share. The effects on the financial statements are identical to those described for the issue of the $10 par value common stock.

Assets	=	Liab.	+	Equity			Rev.	−	Exp.	=	Net Inc.	Cash Flow
Cash	=			Pfd. Stk.	+	PIC in Excess						
2,200	=	NA	+	1,000	+	1,200	NA	−	NA	=	NA	2,200 FA

Stock Issued with No Par Value

Assume that Nelson Incorporated is authorized to issue 150 shares of a fourth class of stock. This stock is no-par common stock. Nelson issues 100 shares of this no-par stock at $22 per share. The entire amount received ($22 × 100 = $2,200) is recorded in the stock account. The effects on the financial statements follow:

Assets	=	Liab.	+	Equity			Rev.	−	Exp.	=	Net Inc.	Cash Flow
Cash	=			Com. Stk.	+	PIC in Excess						
2,200	=	NA	+	2,200	+	NA	NA	−	NA	=	NA	2,200 FA

Financial Statement Presentation

Exhibit 8.4 displays Nelson Incorporated's balance sheet after the four stock issuances described above. The exhibit assumes that Nelson earned and retained $5,000 of cash income during 2005. The stock accounts are presented first, followed by the paid-in capital in excess of par (or stated) value accounts. A wide variety of reporting formats is used in practice. For example, another popular format is to group accounts by stock class, with the paid-in capital in excess accounts listed with their associated stock accounts. Alternatively, many companies combine the different classes of stock into a single amount and provide the detailed information in footnotes to the financial statements.

EXHIBIT 8.4

NELSON INCORPORATED Balance Sheet As of December 31, 2005	
Assets	
Cash	$15,350
Stockholders' Equity	
Preferred Stock, $10 Stated Value, 7% cumulative, 300 shares authorized, 100 issued and outstanding	$ 1,000
Common Stock, $10 Par Value, 250 shares authorized, 100 issued and outstanding	1,000
Common Stock, Class B, $20 Par Value, 400 shares authorized, 150 issued and outstanding	3,000
Common Stock, No Par, 150 shares authorized, 100 issued and outstanding	2,200
Paid-in Capital in Excess of Stated Value–Preferred	1,200
Paid-in Capital in Excess of Par Value–Common	1,200
Paid-in Capital in Excess of Par Value–Class B Common	750
Total Paid-in Capital	10,350
Retained Earnings	5,000
Total Stockholders' Equity	$15,350

Stockholders' Equity Transactions after the Day of Issue

LO 5

Show how treasury stock transactions affect a company's financial statements.

Treasury Stock

When a company buys its own stock, the stock purchased is called *treasury stock.* Why would a company buy its own stock? Common reasons include (1) to have stock available to give employees pursuant to stock option plans, (2) to accumulate stock in preparation for a merger or business combination, (3) to reduce the number of shares outstanding in order to increase earnings per share, (4) to keep the price of the stock high when it appears to be falling, and (5) to avoid a hostile takeover (removing shares from the open market reduces the opportunity for outsiders to obtain enough voting shares to gain control of the company).

Conceptually, purchasing treasury stock is the reverse of issuing stock. When a business issues stock, the assets and equity of the business increase. When a business buys treasury stock, the assets and equity of the business decrease. To illustrate, return to the Nelson Incorporated example. Assume that in 2006 Nelson paid $20 per share to buy back 50 shares of the $10 par value common stock that it originally issued at $22 per share. The purchase of treasury stock is an asset use transaction. Assets and stockholders' equity decrease by the cost of the purchase ($20 × 50 shares = $1,000). The income statement is not affected. The cash outflow is reported in the financing activities section of the statement of cash flows. The effects on the financial statements follow:

Assets	=	Liab.	+	Equity			Rev.	−	Exp.	=	Net Inc.	Cash Flow
Cash	=			Other Equity Accts.	−	Treasury Stk.						
(1,000)	=	NA	+	NA	−	1,000	NA	−	NA	=	NA	(1,000) FA

The Treasury Stock account is a contra equity account. It is deducted from the other equity accounts in determining total stockholders' equity. In this example, the Treasury Stock account is debited for the full amount paid ($1,000). The original issue price and the par value of the stock have no effect on the entry. Recording the full amount paid in the treasury stock account is called the **cost method of accounting for treasury stock** transactions. Although other methods could be used, the cost method is the most common.

Assume Nelson reissues 30 shares of treasury stock at a price of $25 per share. As with any other stock issue, the sale of treasury stock is an asset source transaction. In this case, assets and stockholders' equity increase by $750 ($25 × 30 shares). The income statement is not affected. The cash inflow is reported in the financing activities section of the statement of cash flows. The effects on the financial statements follow:

Assets	=	Liab.	+	Equity					Rev.	−	Exp.	=	Net Inc.	Cash Flow
Cash	=			Other Equity Accounts	−	Treasury Stock	+	PIC from Treasury Stk.						
750	=	NA	+	NA	−	(600)	+	150	NA	−	NA	=	NA	750 FA

The decrease in the Treasury Stock account increases stockholders' equity. The $150 difference between the cost of the treasury stock ($20 per share × 30 shares = $600) and the sales price ($750) is *not* reported as a gain. The sale of treasury stock is a capital acquisition, not a revenue transaction. The $150 is additional paid-in capital. *Corporations do not recognize gains or losses on the sale of treasury stock.*

After selling 30 shares of treasury stock, 20 shares remain in Nelson's possession. These shares cost $20 each, so the balance in the Treasury Stock account is now $400 ($20 × 20 shares). Treasury stock is reported on the balance sheet directly below retained earnings. Although this placement suggests that treasury stock reduces retained earnings, the reduction actually applies to the entire stockholders' equity section. Exhibit 8.5 on page 296 shows the presentation of treasury stock in the balance sheet.

CHECK YOURSELF 8.2

On January 1, 2006, Janell Company's Common Stock account balance was $20,000. On April 1, 2006, Janell paid $12,000 cash to purchase some of its own stock. Janell resold this stock on October 1, 2006, for $14,500. What is the effect on the company's cash and stockholders' equity from both the April 1 purchase and the October 1 resale of the stock?

Answer

The April 1 purchase would reduce both cash and stockholders' equity by $12,000. The treasury stock transaction represents a return of invested capital to those owners who sold stock back to the company.

The sale of the treasury stock on October 1 would increase both cash and stockholders' equity by $14,500. The difference between the sales price of the treasury stock and its cost ($14,500 − $12,000) represents additional paid-in capital from treasury stock transactions. The stockholders' equity section of the balance sheet would include Common Stock, $20,000, and Additional Paid-in Capital from Treasury Stock Transactions, $2,500.

Cash Dividend

Explain the effects of declaring and paying cash dividends on a company's financial statements.

Cash dividends are affected by three significant dates: *the declaration date, the date of record,* and *the payment date.* Assume that on October 15, 2006, the board of Nelson Incorporated declared the cash dividend on the 100 outstanding shares of its $10 stated value preferred stock. The dividend will be paid to stockholders of record as of November 15, 2006. The cash payment will be made on December 15, 2006.

Declaration Date

Although corporations are not required to declare dividends, they are legally obligated to pay dividends once they have been declared. They must recognize a liability on the **declaration date** (in this case, October 15, 2006). The increase in liabilities is accompanied by a decrease in retained earnings. The income statement and statement of cash flows are not affected. The effects on the financial statements of *declaring* the $70 (0.07 × $10 × 100 shares) dividend follow:

Assets	=	Liab.	+			Equity			Rev.	−	Exp.	=	Net Inc.	Cash Flow
Cash	=	Div. Pay.	+	Com. Stk.	+	Ret. Earn.								
NA	=	70	+	NA	+	(70)			NA	−	NA	=	NA	NA

Date of Record

Cash dividends are paid to investors who owned the preferred stock on the **date of record** (in this case November 15, 2006). Any stock sold after the date of record but before the payment date (in this case December 15, 2006) is traded **ex-dividend,** meaning the buyer will not receive the upcoming dividend. The date of record is merely a cutoff date. It does not affect the financial statements.

Payment Date

Nelson actually paid the cash dividend on the **payment date.** This event has the same effect as paying any other liability. Assets (cash) and liabilities (dividends payable) both decrease. The income statement is not affected. The cash outflow is reported in the financing activities section of the statement of cash flows. The effects of the cash payment on the financial statements follow:

Assets	=	Liab.	+			Equity	Rev.	−	Exp.	=	Net Inc.	Cash Flow
Cash	=	Div. Pay.	+	Com. Stk.	+	Ret. Earn.						
(70)	=	(70)	+	NA	+	NA	NA	−	NA	=	NA	(70) FA

Stock Dividend

Explain the effects of stock dividends and stock splits on a company's financial statements.

Dividends are not always paid in cash. Companies sometimes choose to issue **stock dividends,** wherein they distribute additional shares of stock to the stockholders. To illustrate, assume that Nelson Incorporated decided to issue a 10 percent stock dividend on its class B, $20 par value common stock. Since dividends apply to outstanding shares only, Nelson will issue 15 (150 outstanding shares × 0.10) additional shares of class B stock.

Assume the new shares are distributed when the market value of the stock is $30 per share. As a result of the stock dividend, Nelson will transfer $450 ($30 × 15 new shares) from retained earnings to paid-in capital.[2] The stock dividend is an equity exchange transaction. The income statement and statement of cash flows are not affected. The effects of the stock dividend on the financial statements follow:

Assets	=	Liab.	+			Equity			Rev.	−	Exp.	=	Net Inc.	Cash Flow
				Com. Stk.	+	PIC in Excess	+	Ret. Earn.						
NA	=	NA	+	300	+	150	+	(450)	NA	−	NA	=	NA	NA

[2]The accounting here applies to small stock dividends. Accounting for large stock dividends is explained in a more advanced course.

Stock dividends have no effect on assets. They merely increase the number of shares of stock outstanding. Since a greater number of shares represents the same ownership interest in the same amount of assets, the market value per share of a company's stock normally declines when a stock dividend is distributed. A lower market price makes the stock more affordable and may increase demand for the stock, which benefits both the company and its stockholders.

Stock Split

A corporation may also reduce the market price of its stock through a **stock split.** A stock split replaces existing shares with a greater number of new shares. Any par or stated value of the stock is proportionately reduced to reflect the new number of shares outstanding. For example, assume Nelson Incorporated declared a 2-for-1 stock split on the 165 outstanding shares (150 originally issued + 15 shares distributed in a stock dividend) of its $20 par value, class B common stock. Nelson notes in the accounting records that the 165 old $20 par shares are replaced with 330 new $10 par shares. Investors who owned the 165 shares of old common stock would now own 330 shares of the new common stock.

Stock splits have no effect on the dollar amounts of assets, liabilities, and stockholders' equity. They only affect the number of shares of stock outstanding. In Nelson's case, the ownership interest that was previously represented by 165 shares of stock is now represented by 330 shares. Since twice as many shares now represent the same ownership interest, the market value per share should be one-half as much as it was prior to the split. However, as with a stock dividend, the lower market price will probably stimulate demand for the stock. As a result, doubling the number of shares will likely reduce the market price to slightly more than one-half of the pre-split value. For example, if the stock were selling for $30 per share before the 2-for-1 split, it might sell for $15.50 after the split.

Appropriation of Retained Earnings

LO 8

Show how the appropriation of retained earnings affects financial statements.

The board of directors may restrict the amount of retained earnings available to distribute as dividends. The restriction may be required by credit agreements, or it may be discretionary. A retained earnings restriction, often called an *appropriation,* is an equity exchange event. It transfers a portion of existing retained earnings to **Appropriated Retained Earnings.** Total retained earnings remains unchanged. To illustrate, assume that Nelson appropriates $1,000 of retained earnings for future expansion. The income statement and the statement of cash flows are not affected. The effects on the financial statements of appropriating $1,000 of retained earnings follow:

Assets	=	Liab.	+	Equity					Rev.	−	Exp.	=	Net Inc.	Cash Flow
				Com. Stk.	+	Ret. Earn.	+	App. Ret. Earn.						
NA	=	NA	+	NA	+	(1,000)	+	1,000	NA	−	NA	=	NA	NA

Financial Statement Presentation

The 2005 and 2006 events for Nelson Incorporated are summarized below. Events 1 through 8 are cash transactions. The results of the 2005 transactions (nos. 1–5) are reflected in Exhibit 8.4. The results of the 2006 transactions (nos. 6–9) are shown in Exhibit 8.5.

1. Issued 100 shares of $10 par value common stock at a market price of $22 per share.

EXHIBIT 8.5

NELSON INCORPORATED Balance Sheet As of December 31, 2006		
Assets		
Cash		$21,030
Stockholders' Equity		
Preferred Stock, $10 Stated Value, 7% cumulative, 300 shares authorized, 100 issued and outstanding	$1,000	
Common Stock, $10 Par Value, 250 shares authorized, 100 issued, and 80 outstanding	1,000	
Common Stock, Class B, $10 Par, 800 shares authorized, 330 issued and outstanding	3,300	
Common Stock, No Par, 150 shares authorized, 100 issued and outstanding	2,200	
Paid-in Capital in Excess of Stated Value–Preferred	1,200	
Paid-in Capital in Excess of Par Value–Common	1,200	
Paid-in Capital in Excess of Par Value–Class B Common	900	
Paid-in Capital in Excess of Cost of Treasury Stock	150	
Total Paid-in Capital		$10,950
Retained Earnings		
Appropriated	1,000	
Unappropriated	9,480	
Total Retained Earnings		10,480
Less: Treasury Stock, 20 shares @ $20 per share		(400)
Total Stockholders' Equity		$21,030

2. Issued 150 shares of class B, $20 par value common stock at a market price of $25 per share.
3. Issued 100 shares of $10 stated value, 7 percent cumulative preferred stock at a market price of $22 per share.
4. Issued 100 shares of no-par common stock at a market price of $22 per share.
5. Earned and retained $5,000 cash from operations.
6. Purchased 50 shares of $10 par value common stock as treasury stock at a market price of $20 per share.
7. Sold 30 shares of treasury stock at a market price of $25 per share.
8. Declared and paid a $70 cash dividend on the preferred stock.
9. Issued a 10 percent stock dividend on the 150 shares of outstanding class B, $20 par value common stock (15 additional shares). The additional shares were issued when the market price of the stock was $30 per share. There are 165 (150 + 15) class B common shares outstanding after the stock dividend.
10. Issued a 2-for-1 stock split on the 165 shares of class B, $20 par value common stock. After this transaction, there are 330 shares outstanding of the class B common stock with a $10 par value.
11. Appropriated $1,000 of retained earnings.

The illustration assumes that Nelson earned net income of $6,000 in 2006. The ending retained earnings balance is determined as follows: Beginning Balance $5,000 − $70 Cash Dividend − $450 Stock Dividend + $6,000 Net Income = $10,480.

THE FINANCIAL ANALYST

Stockholders may benefit in two ways when a company generates earnings. The company may distribute the earnings directly to the stockholders in the form of dividends. Alternatively, the company may retain some or all of the earnings to finance growth and increase its potential for future earnings. If the company retains earnings, the market value of its stock should increase to reflect its greater earnings prospects. How can analysts use financial reporting to help assess the potential for dividend payments or growth in market value?

Explain some uses of accounting information in making stock investment decisions.

Receiving Dividends

Is a company likely to pay dividends in the future? The financial statements can help answer this question. They show if dividends were paid in the past. Companies with a history of paying dividends usually continue to pay dividends. Also, to pay dividends in the future, a company must have sufficient cash and retained earnings. These amounts are reported on the balance sheet and the statement of cash flows.

Increasing the Price of Stock

Is the market value (price) of a company's stock likely to increase? Increases in a company's stock price occur when investors believe the company's earnings will grow. Financial statements provide information that is useful in predicting the prospects for earnings growth. Here also, a company's earnings history is an indicator of its growth potential. However, because published financial statements report historical information, investors must recognize their limitations. Investors want to know about the future. Stock prices are therefore influenced more by forecasts than by history.

For example:

- On May 6, 2003, Cisco Systems, Inc., announced that its profits for the third quarter of the 2003 fiscal year were 35 percent higher than profits in the same quarter of 2002. In reaction to this news, the price of Cisco's stock *fell* 2.6 percent. Why? Because on the same day, Cisco announced that it believed revenue for the fourth quarter of 2003 would be flat compared to the third quarter, and analysts who follow the company were expecting revenues to grow slightly.
- On May 8, 2003, Comcast Corporation announced a first quarter *loss* of $297 million. This loss was over three times greater than its loss had been for the first quarter of the 2002 fiscal year. Yet the stock market's reaction to the news was to *increase* the price of Comcast's stock by 3 percent. In that same announcement the company reported strong revenue growth, which made investors more optimistic about Comcast's future.

In each case, investors reacted to the potential for earnings growth rather than the historical earnings reports. Because investors find forecasted statements more relevant to decision making than historical financial statements, most companies provide forecasts in addition to historical financial statements.

The value of a company's stock is also influenced by nonfinancial information that financial statements cannot provide. For example, suppose ExxonMobil announced in the middle of its fiscal year that it had just discovered substantial oil reserves on property to which it held drilling rights. Consider the following questions:

- What would happen to the price of ExxonMobil's stock on the day of the announcement?
- What would happen to ExxonMobil's financial statements on that day?

The price of ExxonMobil's stock would almost certainly increase as soon as the discovery was made public. However, nothing would happen to its financial statements on that day. There would probably be very little effect on its financial statements for that year. Only after the company began to develop the oil field and sell the oil would its financial statements reflect the discovery. Changes in financial statements tend to lag behind the announcements companies make regarding their earnings potential.

Stock prices are also affected by general economic conditions and consumer confidence as well as the performance measures reported in financial statements. For example, the stock prices of virtually all companies declined sharply immediately after the September 11, 2001, terrorist attacks on the World Trade Center and the Pentagon. Historically based financial statements are of little benefit in predicting general economic conditions or changes in consumer confidence.

Price-earnings Ratio

The most commonly reported measure of a company's value is the price-earnings ratio, frequently called the P/E ratio. The P/E ratio is a company's market price per share of stock divided by the company's annual earnings per share (EPS). In general, high P/E ratios indicate that investors are optimistic about a company's earnings growth potential. For a more detailed discussion of this important ratio refer back to the coverage in Chapter 2.

Exercising Control through Stock Ownership

The more influence an investor has over the operations of a company, the more the investor can benefit from owning stock in the company. For example, consider a power company that needs coal to produce electricity. The power company may purchase some common stock in a coal mining company to ensure a stable supply of coal. What percentage of the mining company's stock must the power company acquire to exercise significant influence over the mining company? The answer depends on how many investors own stock in the mining company and how the number of shares is distributed among the stockholders.

The greater its number of stockholders, the more *widely held* a company is. If stock ownership is concentrated in the hands of a few persons, a company is *closely held.* Widely held companies can generally be controlled with smaller percentages of ownership than closely held companies. Consider a company in which no existing investor owns more than 1 percent of the voting stock. A new investor who acquires a 5 percent interest would immediately become, by far, the largest shareholder and would likely be able to significantly influence board decisions. In contrast, consider a closely held company in which one current shareholder owns 51 percent of the company's stock. Even if another investor acquired the remaining 49 percent of the company, that investor could not control the company.

Financial statements contain some, but not all, of the information needed to help an investor determine ownership levels necessary to permit control. For example, the financial statements disclose the total number of shares of stock outstanding, but they normally contain little information about the number of shareholders and even less information about any relationships between shareholders. Relationships between shareholders are critically important because related shareholders, whether bound by family or business interests, might exercise control by voting as a block. For publicly traded companies, information about the number of shareholders and the identity of some large shareholders is disclosed in reports filed with the Securities and Exchange Commission.

A Look Back 

Starting a business requires obtaining financing; it takes money to make money. Although some money may be borrowed, lenders are unlikely to make loans to businesses that lack some degree of owner financing. Equity financing is therefore critical to virtually all profit-oriented businesses. This chapter has examined some of the issues related to accounting for equity transactions.

The idea that a business must obtain financing from its owners was one of the first events presented in this textbook. This chapter discussed the advantages and disadvantages of organizing a business as a sole proprietorship versus a partnership versus a corporation. These advantages and disadvantages include the following:

1. *Double taxation*—Income of corporations is subject to double taxation, but that of proprietorships and partnerships is not.
2. *Regulation*—Corporations are subject to more regulation than are proprietorships and partnerships.
3. *Limited liability*—An investor's personal assets are not at risk as a result of owning corporate securities. The investor's liability is limited to the amount of the investment. In general proprietorships and partnerships do not offer limited liability. However, laws in some states permit the formation of limited liability companies which operate like proprietorships and partnerships yet place some limits on the personal liability of their owners.
4. *Continuity*—Proprietorships and partnerships dissolve when one of the owners leaves the business. Corporations are separate legal entities that continue to exist regardless of changes in ownership.
5. *Transferability*—Ownership interests in corporations are easier to transfer than those of proprietorships or partnerships.
6. *Management structure*—Corporations are more likely to have independent professional managers than are proprietorships or partnerships.
7. *Ability to raise capital*—Because they can be owned by millions of investors, corporations have the opportunity to raise more capital than proprietorships or partnerships.

Corporations issue different classes of common stock and preferred stock as evidence of ownership interests. In general, *common stock* provides the widest range of privileges including the right to vote and participate in earnings. *Preferred stockholders* usually give up the right to vote in exchange for preferences such as the right to receive dividends or assets upon liquidation before common stockholders. Stock may have a *par value* or *stated value,* which relates to legal requirements governing the amount of capital that must be maintained in the corporation. Corporations may also issue *no-par stock,* avoiding some of the legal requirements that pertain to par or stated value stock.

Stock that a company issues and then repurchases is called *treasury stock.* Purchasing treasury stock reduces total assets and stockholders' equity. Reselling treasury stock represents a capital acquisition. The difference between the reissue price and the cost of the treasury stock is recorded directly in the equity accounts. Treasury stock transactions do not result in gains or losses on the income statement.

Companies may issue *stock splits* or *stock dividends.* These transactions increase the number of shares of stock without changing the net assets of a company. The per share market value usually drops when a company issues stock splits or dividends.

>> A Look Forward

The Financial Analyst sections of the previous chapters have discussed several procedures and ratios used to analyze financial statements. Financial statement analysis is so important that Chapter 9 is devoted solely to a more detailed discussion of this subject. The expanded coverage in Chapter 9 includes new ratios and additional detail about many of the ratios previously introduced. The chapter also covers vertical analysis (analyzing relationships within a specific statement) and horizontal analysis (analyzing relationships across accounting periods). Finally, the chapter discusses limitations associated with financial statement analysis.

SELF-STUDY REVIEW PROBLEM

Edwards Inc. experienced the following events:

1. Issued common stock for cash.
2. Declared a cash dividend.
3. Issued noncumulative preferred stock for cash.
4. Appropriated retained earnings.
5. Distributed a stock dividend.
6. Paid cash to purchase treasury stock.
7. Distributed a 2-for-1 stock split.
8. Issued cumulative preferred stock for cash.
9. Paid a cash dividend that had previously been declared.
10. Sold treasury stock for cash at a higher amount than the cost of the treasury stock.

Required

Show the effect of each event on the elements of the financial statements using a horizontal statements model like the one shown here. Use + for increase, − for decrease, and NA for not affected. In the Cash Flow column, indicate whether the item is an operating activity (OA), investing activity (IA), or a financing activity (FA). The first transaction is entered as an example.

Event	Assets =	Liab. +	Equity	Rev. −	Exp. =	Net Inc.	Cash Flow
1	+	NA	+	NA	NA	NA	+ FA

Solution to Self-Study Review Problem

Event	Assets =	Liab. +	Equity	Rev. −	Exp. =	Net Inc.	Cash Flow
1	+	NA	+	NA	NA	NA	+ FA
2	NA	+	−	NA	NA	NA	NA
3	+	NA	+	NA	NA	NA	+ FA
4	NA	NA	−+	NA	NA	NA	NA
5	NA	NA	−+	NA	NA	NA	NA
6	−	NA	−	NA	NA	NA	− FA
7	NA	NA	NA	NA	NA	NA	NA
8	+	NA	+	NA	NA	NA	+ FA
9	−	−	NA	NA	NA	NA	− FA
10	+	NA	+	NA	NA	NA	+ FA

KEY TERMS

appropriated retained earnings 295
articles of incorporation 282
authorized stock 288
board of directors 285
book value per share 288
closely held corporation 282
common stock 289
continuity 284
corporation 282
cost method of accounting for treasury stock 293
cumulative dividends 289
date of record 294
declaration date 293
dividends in arrears 289
double taxation 283
entrenched management 285
ex-dividend 294
issued stock 288
legal capital 287
limited liability 284
limited liability companies (LLCs) 284
market value 288
outstanding stock 288
Paid-in Capital in Excess of Par Value 290
par value 287
partnerships 282
partnership agreement 282
payment date 294
preferred stock 289
Sarbanes-Oxley Act of 2002 283
Securities Act of 1933 and Securities Exchange Act of 1934 283
sole proprietorships 282
stated value 287
stock certificates 282
stock dividends 294
stockholders 285
stock split 295
transferability 284
treasury stock 288
withdrawals 286

QUESTIONS

1. What are the three major forms of business organizations? Describe each.
2. How are sole proprietorships formed?
3. Discuss the purpose of a partnership agreement. Is such an agreement necessary for partnership formation?
4. What is meant by the phrase *separate legal entity?* To which type of business organization does it apply?
5. What is the purpose of the articles of incorporation? What information do they provide?
6. What is the function of the stock certificate?
7. What prompted Congress to pass the Securities Act of 1933 and the Securities Exchange Act of 1934? What is the purpose of these laws?
8. What are the advantages and disadvantages of the corporate form of business organization?
9. What is a limited liability company? Discuss its advantages and disadvantages.
10. How does the term *double taxation* apply to corporations? Give an example of double taxation.
11. What is the difference between contributed capital and retained earnings for a corporation?
12. What are the similarities and differences in the equity structure of a sole proprietorship, a partnership, and a corporation?
13. Why is it easier for a corporation to raise large amounts of capital than it is for a partnership?
14. What is the meaning of each of the following terms with respect to the corporate form of organization?
    - (a) Legal capital
    - (b) Par value of stock
    - (c) Stated value of stock
    - (d) Market value of stock
    - (e) Book value of stock
    - (f) Authorized shares of stock
    - (g) Issued stock
    - (h) Outstanding stock
    - (i) Treasury stock
    - (j) Common stock
    - (k) Preferred stock
    - (l) Dividends
15. What is the difference between cumulative preferred stock and noncumulative preferred stock?
16. What is no-par stock? How is it recorded in the accounting records?
17. Assume that Best Co. has issued and outstanding 1,000 shares of $100 par value, 10 percent, cumulative preferred stock. What is the dividend per share? If the preferred dividend is two years in arrears, what total amount of dividends must be paid before the common shareholders can receive any dividends?

18. If Best Co. issued 10,000 shares of $20 par value common stock for $30 per share, what amount is credited to the Common Stock account? What amount of cash is received?
19. What is the difference between par value stock and stated value stock?
20. Why might a company repurchase its own stock?
21. What effect does the purchase of treasury stock have on the equity of a company?
22. Assume that Day Company repurchased 1,000 of its own shares for $30 per share and sold the shares two weeks later for $35 per share. What is the amount of gain on the sale? How is it reported on the balance sheet? What type of account is treasury stock?
23. What is the importance of the declaration date, record date, and payment date in conjunction with corporate dividends?
24. What is the difference between a stock dividend and a stock split?
25. Why would a company choose to distribute a stock dividend instead of a cash dividend?
26. What is the primary reason that a company would declare a stock split?
27. If Best Co. had 10,000 shares of $20 par value common stock outstanding and declared a 5-for-1 stock split, how many shares would then be outstanding and what would be their par value after the split?
28. When a company appropriates retained earnings, does the company set aside cash for a specific use? Explain.
29. What is the largest source of financing for most U.S. businesses?
30. What is meant by *equity financing?* What is meant by *debt financing?*
31. What is a widely held corporation? What is a closely held corporation?
32. What are some reasons that a corporation might not pay dividends?

EXERCISES

All Exercises are available with McGraw-Hill's Homework Manager

L.O. 1, 2

Exercise 8-1 *Effect of accounting events on the financial statements of a sole proprietorship*

A sole proprietorship was started on January 1, 2005, when it received $60,000 cash from Mark Pruitt, the owner. During 2005, the company earned $40,000 in cash revenues and paid $19,300 in cash expenses. Pruitt withdrew $5,000 cash from the business during 2005.

Required

Prepare an income statement, capital statement (statement of changes in equity), balance sheet, and statement of cash flows for Pruitt's 2005 fiscal year.

L.O. 1, 2

Exercise 8-2 *Effect of accounting events on the financial statements of a partnership*

Justin Harris and Paul Berryhill started the HB partnership on January 1, 2006. The business acquired $56,000 cash from Harris and $84,000 from Berryhill. During 2006, the partnership earned $65,000 in cash revenues and paid $32,000 for cash expenses. Harris withdrew $2,000 cash from the business, and Berryhill withdrew $3,000 cash. The net income was allocated to the capital accounts of the two partners in proportion to the amounts of their original investments in the business.

Required

Prepare an income statement, capital statement, balance sheet, and statement of cash flows for the HB partnership for the 2006 fiscal year.

L.O. 1, 2

Exercise 8-3 *Effect of accounting events on the financial statements of a corporation*

Morris Corporation was started with the issue of 5,000 shares of $10 par common stock for cash on January 1, 2007. The stock was issued at a market price of $18 per share. During 2007, the company earned $63,000 in cash revenues and paid $41,000 for cash expenses. Also a $4,000 cash dividend was paid to the stockholders.

Required

Prepare an income statement, statement of changes in stockholders' equity, balance sheet, and statement of cash flows for Morris Corporation's 2007 fiscal year.

Exercise 8-4 *Effect of issuing common stock on the balance sheet* L.O. 4

Newly formed Home Medical Corporation has 100,000 shares of $5 par common stock authorized. On March 1, 2006, Home Medical issued 10,000 shares of the stock for $12 per share. On May 2 the company issued an additional 20,000 shares for $20 per share. Home Medical was not affected by other events during 2006.

Required

a. Record the transactions in a horizontal statements model like the following one. In the Cash Flow column, indicate whether the item is an operating activity (OA), investing activity (IA), or financing activity (FA). Use NA to indicate that an element was not affected by the event.

Assets	=	Liab. +	Equity			Rev. − Exp. = Net Inc.	Cash Flow
Cash	=		Com. Stk.	+	PIC in Excess		

b. Determine the amount Home Medical would report for common stock on the December 31, 2006, balance sheet.

c. Determine the amount Home Medical would report for paid-in capital in excess of par.

d. What is the total amount of capital contributed by the owners?

e. What amount of total assets would Home Medical report on the December 31, 2006, balance sheet?

Exercise 8-5 *Reporting common and preferred stock transactions* L.O. 4

Rainey Inc. was organized on June 5, 2007. It was authorized to issue 400,000 shares of $10 par common stock and 50,000 shares of 4 percent cumulative class A preferred stock. The class A stock had a stated value of $25 per share. The following stock transactions pertain to Rainey Inc.:

1. Issued 20,000 shares of common stock for $15 per share.
2. Issued 10,000 shares of the class A preferred stock for $30 per share.
3. Issued 50,000 shares of common stock for $18 per share.

Required

Prepare the stockholders' equity section of the balance sheet immediately after these transactions have been recognized.

Exercise 8-6 *Effect of no-par common and par preferred stock on the horizontal statements model* L.O. 4

Eaton Corporation issued 5,000 shares of no-par common stock for $20 per share. Eaton also issued 2,000 shares of $50 par, 6 percent noncumulative preferred stock at $60 per share.

Required

Record these events in a horizontal statements model like the following one. In the cash flow column, indicate whether the item is an operating activity (OA), investing activity (IA), or financing activity (FA). Use NA to indicate that an element was not affected by the event.

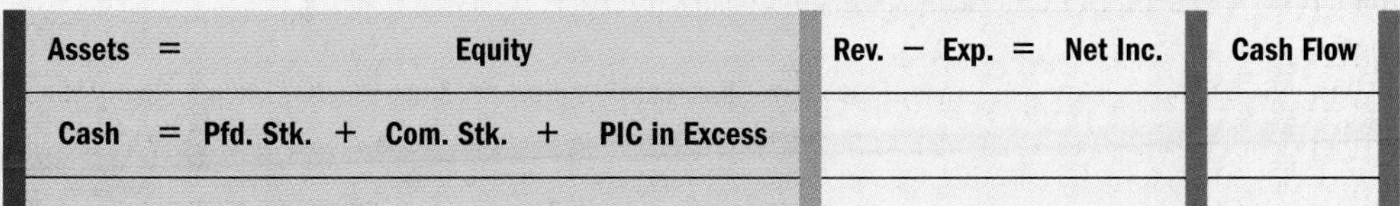

Assets	=	Equity					Rev. − Exp. = Net Inc.	Cash Flow
Cash	=	Pfd. Stk.	+	Com. Stk.	+	PIC in Excess		

Exercise 8-7 *Issuing stock for assets other than cash* L.O. 4

Kaylee Corporation was formed when it issued shares of common stock to two of its shareholders. Kaylee issued 5,000 shares of $10 par common stock to K. Breslin in exchange for $60,000 cash (the issue price was $12 per share). Kaylee also issued 2,500 shares of stock to T. Lindsay in exchange for a one-year-old delivery van on the same day. Lindsay had originally paid $35,000 for the van.

Required

a. What was the market value of the delivery van on the date of the stock issue?

b. Show the effect of the two stock issues on Kaylee's books in a horizontal statements model like the following one. In the Cash Flow column, indicate whether the item is an operating activity (OA), investing activity (IA), or financing activity (FA). Use NA to indicate that an element was not affected by the event.

Assets			=	Equity			Rev. − Exp. = Net Inc.	Cash Flow
Cash	+	Van	=	Com. Stk.	+	PIC in Excess		

L.O. 5

Exercise 8-8 *Treasury stock transactions*

Graves Corporation repurchased 2,000 shares of its own stock for $40 per share. The stock has a par of $10 per share. A month later Graves resold 1,200 shares of the treasury stock for $48 per share.

Required

What is the balance of the treasury stock account after these transactions are recognized?

L.O. 5

Exercise 8-9 *Reporting treasury stock transactions*

The following information pertains to Smoot Corp. at January 1, 2006.

Common stock, $10 par, 10,000 shares authorized, 2,000 shares issued and outstanding	$20,000
Paid-in capital in excess of par, common stock	15,000
Retained earnings	65,000

Smoot Corp. completed the following transactions during 2006:

1. Issued 1,000 shares of $10 par common stock for $28 per share.
2. Repurchased 200 shares of its own common stock for $25 per share.
3. Resold 50 shares of treasury stock for $26 per share.

Required

a. How many shares of common stock were outstanding at the end of the period?
b. How many shares of common stock had been issued at the end of the period?
c. Organize the transactions data in accounts under the accounting equation.
d. Prepare the stockholders' equity section of the balance sheet reflecting these transactions. Include the number of shares authorized, issued, and outstanding in the description of the common stock.

L.O. 6

Exercise 8-10 *Effect of cash dividends on financial statements*

On October 1, 2005, Smart Corporation declared a $60,000 cash dividend to be paid on December 30 to shareholders of record on November 20.

Required

Record the events occurring on October 1, November 20, and December 30 in a horizontal statements model like the following one. In the Cash Flow column, indicate whether the item is an operating activity (OA), investing activity (IA), or financing activity (FA).

Date	Assets	=	Liab.	+	Com. Stock	+	Ret. Earn.	Rev. − Exp. = Net Inc.	Cash Flow

L.O. 6

Exercise 8-11 *Accounting for cumulative preferred dividends*

When Polledo Corporation was organized in January 2007, it immediately issued 5,000 shares of $50 par, 5 percent, cumulative preferred stock and 10,000 shares of $10 par common stock. The company's earnings history is as follows: 2007, net loss of $15,000; 2008, net income of $60,000; 2009, net income of $95,000. The corporation did not pay a dividend in 2007.

Required

a. How much is the dividend arrearage as of January 1, 2008?

b. Assume that the board of directors declares a $40,000 cash dividend at the end of 2008 (remember that the 2007 and 2008 preferred dividends are due). How will the dividend be divided between the preferred and common stockholders?

Exercise 8-12 *Cash dividends for preferred and common shareholders* L.O. 6

B&S Corporation had the following stock issued and outstanding at January 1, 2007:

1. 100,000 shares of $5 par common stock.
2. 5,000 shares of $100 par, 5 percent, noncumulative preferred stock.

On May 10, B&S Corporation declared the annual cash dividend on its 5,000 shares of preferred stock and a $1 per share dividend for the common shareholders. The dividends will be paid on June 15 to the shareholders of record on May 30.

Required

Determine the total amount of dividends to be paid to the preferred shareholders and common shareholders.

Exercise 8-13 *Cash dividends: common and preferred stock* L.O. 6

Wu Corp. had the following stock issued and outstanding at January 1, 2006:

1. 50,000 shares of no-par common stock.
2. 10,000 shares of $100 par, 4 percent, cumulative preferred stock. (Dividends are in arrears for one year, 2005.)

On February 1, 2006, Wu declared a $100,000 cash dividend to be paid March 31 to shareholders of record on March 10.

Required

What amount of dividends will be paid to the preferred shareholders versus the common shareholders?

Exercise 8-14 *Accounting for stock dividends* L.O. 7

Merino Corporation issued a 4 percent stock dividend on 30,000 shares of its $10 par common stock. At the time of the dividend, the market value of the stock was $25 per share.

Required

a. Compute the amount of the stock dividend.
b. Show the effects of the stock dividend on the financial statements using a horizontal statements model like the following one.

Assets	=	Liab.	+	Com. Stk.	+	PIC in Excess	+	Ret. Earn.	Rev.	−	Exp.	=	Net Inc.	Cash Flow

Exercise 8-15 *Determining the effects of stock splits on the accounting records* L.O. 7

The market value of Coe Corporation's common stock had become excessively high. The stock was currently selling for $180 per share. To reduce the market price of the common stock, Coe declared a 2-for-1 stock split for the 300,000 outstanding shares of its $10 par common stock.

Required

a. How will Coe Corporation's books be affected by the stock split?
b. Determine the number of common shares outstanding and the par value after the split.
c. Explain how the market value of the stock will be affected by the stock split.

Exercise 8-16 *Corporate announcements* L.O. 9

Mighty Drugs (one of the three largest drug makers) just reported that its 2004 third quarter profits are essentially the same as the 2003 third quarter profits. In addition to this announcement, the same day, Mighty Drugs also announced that the Food and Drug Administration has just approved a new drug used to treat high blood pressure that Mighty Drugs developed. This new drug has been shown to be extremely effective and has few or no side effects. It will also be less expensive than the other drugs currently on the market.

Required

Using the above information, answer the following questions:

a. What do you think will happen to the stock price of Mighty Drugs on the day these two announcements are made? Explain your answer.
b. How will the balance sheet be affected on that day by the above announcements?
c. How will the income statement be affected on that day by the above announcements?
d. How will the statement of cash flows be affected on that day by the above announcements?

L.O. 9

Exercise 8-17 *Performing ratio analysis using real-world data*

Merck & Company is one of the world's largest pharmaceutical companies. The following data were taken from the company's 2004 annual report.

	Fiscal Years Ending	
	December 31, 2004	**December 31, 2003**
Net earnings (in millions)	$5,813.4	$6,830.9
Earnings per share	$2.62	$2.95

The following data were taken from public stock-price quotes.

Stock price per share on March 1, 2005: $32.13 (Two months after the end of Merck's 2004 fiscal year.)
Stock price per share on March 1, 2004: $48.45 (Two months after the end of Merck's 2003 fiscal year.)

Required

a. Compute Merck's price-earnings ratio for March 1, 2005, and March 1, 2004.
b. Did the financial markets appear to be more optimistic about Merck's future performance on March 1, 2004, or March 1, 2005?
c. Based on the information provided, estimate approximately how many shares of stock Merck had outstanding as of December 31, 2004.

PROBLEMS

All Problems are available with McGraw-Hill's Homework Manager

L.O. 1, 2

mhhe.com/edmonds2007

CHECK FIGURES

a. Net Income: $25,000
b. James Capital: $103,000

Problem 8-18 *Effect of business structure on financial statements*

Ja-San Company was started on January 1, 2007, when the owners invested $160,000 cash in the business. During 2007, the company earned cash revenues of $90,000 and incurred cash expenses of $65,000. The company also paid cash distributions of $10,000.

Required

Prepare a 2007 income statement, capital statement (statement of changes in equity), balance sheet, and statement of cash flows using each of the following assumptions. (Consider each assumption separately.)

a. Ja-San is a sole proprietorship owned by J. Sanford.
b. Ja-San is a partnership with two partners, Kim James and Mary Sanders. James invested $100,000 and Sanders invested $60,000 of the $160,000 cash that was used to start the business. Sanders was expected to assume the vast majority of the responsibility for operating the business. The partnership agreement called for Sanders to receive 60 percent of the profits and James the remaining 40 percent. With regard to the $10,000 distribution, Sanders withdrew $3,000 from the business and James withdrew $7,000.
c. Ja-San is a corporation. The owners were issued 10,000 shares of $10 par common stock when they invested the $160,000 cash in the business.

Problem 8-19 ***Recording and reporting stock transactions and cash dividends across two accounting cycles***

L.O. 4–6

mhhe.com/edmonds2007

CHECK FIGURES

b. Preferred Stock, 2006: $200,000

c. Common Shares Outstanding, 2007: 34,500

Lane Corporation was authorized to issue 100,000 shares of $5 par common stock and 20,000 shares of $100 par, 6 percent, cumulative preferred stock. Lane Corporation completed the following transactions during its first two years of operation:

2006

Jan. 2	Issued 15,000 shares of $5 par common stock for $7 per share.
15	Issued 2,000 shares of $100 par preferred stock for $110 per share.
Feb. 14	Issued 20,000 shares of $5 par common stock for $9 per share.
Dec. 31	During the year, earned $310,000 of cash revenues and paid $240,000 of cash operating expenses.
31	Declared the cash dividend on outstanding shares of preferred stock for 2006. The dividend will be paid on January 31 to stockholders of record on January 15, 2007.

2007

Jan. 31	Paid the cash dividend declared on December 31, 2006.
Mar. 1	Issued 3,000 shares of $100 par preferred stock for $120 per share.
June 1	Purchased 500 shares of common stock as treasury stock at $10 per share.
Dec. 31	During the year, earned $250,000 of cash revenues and paid $175,000 of cash operating expenses.
31	Declared the dividend on the preferred stock and a $0.50 per share dividend on the common stock.

Required

a. Organize the transaction data in accounts under an accounting equation.
b. Prepare the stockholders' equity section of the balance sheet at December 31, 2006.
c. Prepare the balance sheet at December 31, 2007.

Problem 8-20 ***Reporting treasury stock transactions***

L.O. 5, 6, 8

mhhe.com/edmonds2007

CHECK FIGURE

b. Total Paid-In Capital: $264,900

Midwest Corp. completed the following transactions in 2007, the first year of operation:

1. Issued 20,000 shares of $10 par common stock at par.
2. Issued 2,000 shares of $30 stated value preferred stock at $32 per share.
3. Purchased 500 shares of common stock as treasury stock for $15 per share.
4. Declared a 5 percent cash dividend on preferred stock.
5. Sold 300 shares of treasury stock for $18 per share.
6. Paid the cash dividend on preferred stock that was declared in Event 4.
7. Earned revenue of $75,000 and incurred operating expenses of $42,000.
8. Appropriated $6,000 of retained earnings.

Required

a. Organize the transaction in accounts under an accounting equation.
b. Prepare the stockholders' equity section of the balance sheet as of December 31, 2007.

Problem 8-21 ***Reporting treasury stock transactions***

L.O. 5

CHECK FIGURES

Total Paid-In Capital: $451,200

Total Stockholders' Equity: $570,000

Boley Corporation reports the following information in its January 1, 2006, balance sheet:

Stockholders' Equity	
Common Stock, $10 Par Value, 50,000 shares authorized, 30,000 shares issued and outstanding	$300,000
Paid-in Capital in Excess of Par Value	150,000
Retained Earnings	100,000
Total Stockholders' Equity	$550,000

During 2006, Boley was affected by the following accounting events:

1. Purchased 1,000 shares of treasury stock at $18 per share.
2. Reissued 600 shares of treasury stock at $20 per share.
3. Earned $64,000 of cash revenues.
4. Paid $38,000 of cash operating expenses.

Required

Prepare the stockholders' equity section of the year-end balance sheet.

L.O. 4, 6, 7

CHECK FIGURES

b. Total Paid-In Capital: $895,000

b. Retained Earnings: $17,500

Problem 8-22 *Reporting stock dividends*

Chen Corp. completed the following transactions in 2007, the first year of operation:

1. Issued 20,000 shares of $20 par common stock for $30 per share.
2. Issued 5,000 shares of $50 par, 5 percent, preferred stock at $51 per share.
3. Paid the annual cash dividend to preferred shareholders.
4. Issued a 5 percent stock dividend on the common stock. The market value at the dividend declaration date was $40 per share.
5. Later that year, issued a 2-for-1 split on the 21,000 shares of outstanding common stock.
6. Earned $210,000 of cash revenues and paid $140,000 of cash operating expenses.
7. Closed the revenue, expense, and dividend accounts to retained earnings.

Required

a. Record each of these events in a horizontal statements model like the following one. In the Cash Flow column, indicate whether the item is an operating activity (OA), investing activity (IA), or financing activity (FA). Use NA to indicate that an element is not affected by the event.

Assets = Liab. +	Equity	Rev. − Exp. = Net Inc.	Cash Flow
	Pfd. Stk. + Com. Stk. + PIC in Excess PS + PIC in Excess CS + Ret. Earn.		

b. Prepare the stockholders' equity section of the balance sheet at the end of 2007.

L.O. 4, 7

CHECK FIGURES

a. Par value per share: $10

b. Dividend per share: $.60

Problem 8-23 *Analyzing the stockholders' equity section of the balance sheet*

The stockholders' equity section of the balance sheet for Atkins Company at December 31, 2007, is as follows:

Stockholders' Equity

Paid-in Capital		
Preferred Stock, ? Par Value, 6% cumulative, 50,000 shares authorized, 30,000 shares issued and outstanding	$300,000	
Common Stock, $10 Stated Value, 150,000 shares authorized, 50,000 shares issued and ? outstanding	500,000	
Paid-in Capital in Excess of Par–Preferred	30,000	
Paid-in Capital in Excess of Stated Value–Common	200,000	
Total Paid-in Capital		$1,030,000
Retained Earnings		250,000
Treasury Stock, 1,000 shares		(100,000)
Total Stockholders' Equity		$1,180,000

Note: The market value per share of the common stock is $25, and the market value per share of the preferred stock is $12.

Required

a. What is the par value per share of the preferred stock?

b. What is the dividend per share on the preferred stock?

c. What is the number of common stock shares outstanding?

d. What was the average issue price per share (price for which the stock was issued) of the common stock?

e. Explain the difference between the average issue price and the market price of the common stock.

f. If Atkins declared a 2-for-1 stock split on the common stock, how many shares would be outstanding after the split? What amount would be transferred from the retained earnings account because of the stock split? Theoretically, what would be the market price of the common stock immediately after the stock split?

Problem 8-24 *Different forms of business organization*

L.O. 1

Shawn Bates was working to establish a business enterprise with four of his wealthy friends. Each of the five individuals would receive a 20 percent ownership interest in the company. A primary goal of establishing the enterprise was to minimize the amount of income taxes paid. Assume that the five investors are in a 35 percent personal tax bracket and that the corporate tax rate is 25 percent. Also assume that the new company is expected to earn $200,000 of cash income before taxes during its first year of operation. All earnings are expected to be immediately distributed to the owners.

Required

Calculate the amount of after-tax cash flow available to each investor if the business is established as a partnership versus a corporation. Write a memo explaining the advantages and disadvantages of these two forms of business organization. Explain why a limited liability company may be a better choice than either a partnership or a corporation.

Problem 8-25 *Effects of equity transactions on financial statements*

L.O. 4–8

The following events were experienced by Abbot Inc.:

1. Issued cumulative preferred stock for cash.
2. Issued common stock for cash.
3. Distributed a 2-for-1 stock split on the common stock.
4. Issued noncumulative preferred stock for cash.
5. Appropriated retained earnings.
6. Sold treasury stock for an amount of cash that was more than the cost of the treasury stock.
7. Distributed a stock dividend.
8. Paid cash to purchase treasury stock.
9. Declared a cash dividend.
10. Paid the cash dividend declared in Event 9.

Required

Show the effect of each event on the elements of the financial statements using a horizontal statements model like the following one. Use + for increase, − for decrease, and NA for not affected. In the Cash Flow column, indicate whether the item is an operating activity (OA), investing activity (IA), or financing activity (FA). The first transaction is entered as an example.

Event No.	Assets	=	Liab.	+	Equity	Rev.	−	Exp.	=	Net Inc.	Cash Flow
1	+		NA		+	NA		NA		NA	+ FA

L.O. 9

Problem 8-26 ***Performing ratio analysis using real-world data***

Google, Inc., operates the world's largest Internet search engine. International Business Machines Corporation (IBM) is one of the world's largest computer hardware and software companies. The following data were taken from the companies' December 31, 2004, annual reports.

	Google, Inc.	IBM
Net earnings (in thousands)	$399,119	$8,430,000
Earnings per share	$2.07	$5.03

The following data were taken from public stock-price quotes.

Stock price per share on March 1, 2005: (Two months after the end of their 2004 fiscal years.)	$186.06	$93.30

Required

a. Compute the price-earnings ratios for each company as of March 1, 2005.

b. Which company's future performance did the financial markets appear to be more optimistic about as of March 1, 2005?

c. Provide some reasons why the market may view one company's future more optimistically than the other.

ANALYZE, THINK, COMMUNICATE

ATC 8-1 **Business Applications Case** ***Understanding real-world annual reports***

Required

Use the Topps Company's annual report in Appendix B to answer the following questions.

a. Does Topps' common stock have a par value, and if so how much is it?

b. How many shares of Topps' common stock were *outstanding* as of March 1, 2003? Do not forget to consider treasury stock.

c. The dollar-value balance in Topps' Treasury Stock account is larger than the balance in its Common Stock and Additional Paid-In-Capital accounts. How can this be?

d. How many members of Topps' Board of Directors are also officers (employees) of the company as of March 1, 2003?

e. What was the highest and lowest price per share that Topps' common stock sold for during the fiscal year ending on March 1, 2003?

ATC 8-2 **Group Assignment** ***Missing information***

Listed here are the stockholders' equity sections of three public companies for years ending in 2003 and 2002:

	2003	2002
Wendy's (dollar amounts are presented in thousands)		
Stockholders' Equity		
Common stock, ?? Stated Value per share, authorized: 200,000,000; 116,760,000 in 2003 and 114,692,000 in 2002 shares issued, respectively	$ 11,676	$ 10,895
Capital in Excess of Stated Value	54,310	0
Retained Earnings	1,703,488	1,498,607
Acc. Other Comp. Income (Exp.)	46,124	(60,897)
Treasury Stock, at cost: 2,063,000 in 2003	(56,992)	0

	2003	2002
Coca-Cola (dollar amounts are presented in millions)		
Stockholders' Equity		
Common Stock, ?? Par Value per share, authorized: 5,600,000,000; issued: 3,494,799,258 shares in 2003 and 3,490,818,627 shares in 2002	$ 874	$ 873
Capital Surplus	4,395	3,857
Reinvested Earnings	26,687	24,506
Acc. Other Comp. Inc. (loss)	(1,995)	(3,047)
Treasury Stock, at cost: (1,053,267,474 shares in 2003; 1,019,839,490 shares in 2002)	(15,871)	(14,389)
Harley-Davidson (dollar amounts are presented in thousands)		
Stockholders' Equity		
Common stock, ?? Par Value per share, authorized: 800,000,000, issued: 326,489,291 in 2003 and 325,298,404 shares in 2002	3,266	3,254
Additional Paid-in Capital	419,455	386,284
Retained Earnings	3,074,037	2,372,095
Acc. Other Comp. Inc. (loss)	47,174	(46,266)
Treasury Stock, at cost: 24,978,798 for 2003 and 22,636,295 for 2002	(586,240)	(482,360)
Unearned Compensation	0	(92)

Required

a. Divide the class in three sections and divide each section into groups of three to five students. Assign each section one of the companies.

Group Tasks

Based on the company assigned to your group, answer the following questions.

b. What is the per share par or stated value of the common stock in 2003?
c. What was the average issue price of the common stock for each year?
d. How many shares of stock are outstanding at the end of each year?
e. What is the average cost per share of the treasury stock for 2003?
f. Do the data suggest that your company was profitable in 2003?
g. Can you determine the amount of net income from the information given? What is missing?
h. What is the total stockholders' equity of your company for each year?

Class Discussion

i. Have each group select a representative to present the information about its company. Compare the share issue price and the par or stated value of the companies.
j. Compare the average issue price to the current market price for each of the companies. Speculate about what might cause the difference.

ATC 8-3 Real-World Case *Which stock is most valuable?*

Listed here are data for five companies. These data are from companies' annual reports for the fiscal year indicated in the parentheses. The market price per share is the closing price of the companies' stock as of November 17, 2004. Except for market price per share, all amounts are in thousands. The shares outstanding number is the weighted-average number of shares the company used to compute its basic earnings per share.

Company (Fiscal Year-End)	Net Earnings	Shares Outstanding	Stockholders' Equity	Market Price per Share
Amazon.com (12/31/2003)	$ 35,282	395,479	$ (1,036,107)	$39.90
ExxonMobil (12/31/2003)	21,510,000	6,634,000	89,915,000	50.05
Genetech (12/31/2003)	562,527	517,240	6,520,298	49.88
Krispy Kreme (2/01/2004)	57,087	59,188	452,207	12.43
Temple-Inland (1/03/2004)	96,000,000	54,200,000	1,968,000	62.31

Required:

a. Compute the earnings per share (EPS) for each company.

b. Compute the P/E ratio for each company.

c. Using the P/E ratios, rank the companies' stock in the order that the stock market appears to value the companies, from most valuable to least valuable. Identify reasons the ranking based on P/E ratios may not represent the market's optimism about one or two companies.

d. Compute the book value per share for each company.

e. Compare each company's book value per share to its market price per share. Based on the data, rank the companies from most valuable to least valuable. (The higher the ratio of market value to book value, the greater the value the stock market appears to be assigning to a company's stock.)

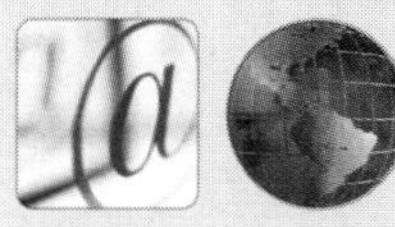

ATC 8-4 Business Applications Case *Finding stock market information*

This problem requires stock price quotations for the New York Stock Exchange, the American Stock Exchange, and NASDAQ. These are available in *The Wall Street Journal* and in the business sections of many daily newspapers as well as on various websites. Stock prices are also available on electronic data services such as CompuServe.

Required

For each company listed here, provide the requested information as of Thursday of last week. (*Hint:* Information about Thursday's stock market is in Friday's newspaper.)

Name of Company	Stock Exchange Where Listed	Closing Price	P/E Ratio
Berkshire Hathaway A			
Devron Energy Corp.			
Intel			
Yahoo			
Xerox			

ATC 8-5 Business Applications Case *Using the P/E ratio*

During 2007, Musicland Corporation and Jazztown Corporation reported net incomes of $62,000 and $54,000, respectively. Each company had 10,000 shares of common stock issued and outstanding. The market price per share of Musicland's stock was $80, while Jazztown's stock sold for $88 per share.

Required

a. Determine the P/E ratio for each company.

b. Based on the P/E ratios computed in Requirement *a*, which company do investors believe has more potential for growth in income?

ATC 8-6 Writing Assignment *Comparison of organizational forms*

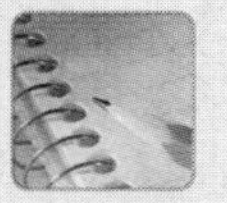

Jim Baku and Scott Hanson are thinking about opening a new restaurant. Baku has extensive marketing experience but does not know that much about food preparation. However, Hanson is an excellent chef. Both will work in the business, but Baku will provide most of the funds necessary to start the business. At this time, they cannot decide whether to operate the business as a partnership or a corporation.

Required

Prepare a written memo to Baku and Hanson describing the advantages and disadvantages of each organizational form. Also, from the limited information provided, recommend the organizational form you think they should use.

ATC 8-7 Ethical Dilemma *Bad news versus very bad news*

Louise Stinson, the chief financial officer of Bostonian Corporation, was on her way to the president's office. She was carrying the latest round of bad news. There would be no executive bonuses this year. Corporate profits were down. Indeed, if the latest projections held true, the company would report a small loss on the year-end income statement. Executive bonuses were tied to corporate profits. The executive compensation plan provided for 10 percent of net earnings to be set aside for bonuses. No profits meant no bonuses. While things looked bleak, Stinson had a plan that might help soften the blow.

After informing the company president of the earnings forecast, Stinson made the following suggestion: Since the company was going to report a loss anyway, why not report a big loss? She reasoned that the directors and stockholders would not be much more angry if the company reported a large loss than if it reported a small one. There were several questionable assets that could be written down in the current year. This would increase the current year's loss but would reduce expenses in subsequent accounting periods. For example, the company was carrying damaged inventory that was estimated to have a value of \$2,500,000. If this estimate were revised to \$500,000, the company would have to recognize a \$2,000,000 loss in the current year. However, next year when the goods were sold, the expense for cost of goods sold would be \$2,000,000 less and profits would be higher by that amount. Although the directors would be angry this year, they would certainly be happy next year. The strategy would also have the benefit of adding \$200,000 to next year's executive bonus pool (\$2,000,000 × 0.10). Furthermore, it could not hurt this year's bonus pool because there would be no pool this year since the company is going to report a loss.

Some of the other items that Stinson is considering include (1) converting from straight-line to accelerated depreciation, (2) increasing the percentage of receivables estimated to be uncollectible in the current year and lowering the percentage in the following year, and (3) raising the percentage of estimated warranty claims in the current period and lowering it in the following period. Finally, Stinson notes that two of the company's department stores have been experiencing losses. The company could sell these stores this year and thereby improve earnings next year. Stinson admits that the sale would result in significant losses this year, but she smiles as she thinks of next year's bonus check.

Required

a. Explain how each of the three numbered strategies for increasing the amount of the current year's loss would affect the stockholders' equity section of the balance sheet in the current year. How would the other elements of the balance sheet be affected?

b. If Stinson's strategy were effectively implemented, how would it affect the stockholders' equity in subsequent accounting periods?

c. Comment on the ethical implications of running the company for the sake of management (maximization of bonuses) versus the maximization of return to stockholders.

d. Formulate a bonus plan that will motivate managers to maximize the value of the firm instead of motivating them to manipulate the reporting process.

e. How would Stinson's strategy of overstating the amount of the reported loss in the current year affect the company's current P/E ratio?

ATC 8-8 Research Assignment *Analyzing PepsiCo's equity structure*

Using either PepsiCo's most current Form 10-K or the company's annual report, answer the questions below. To obtain the Form 10-K use either the EDGAR system following the instructions in Appendix A or the company's website. The company's annual report is available on its website.

Required

a. What is the *book value* of PepsiCo's stockholders' equity that is shown on the company's balance sheet?

b. What is the par value of PepsiCo's common stock?

c. Does PepsiCo have any treasury stock? If so, how many shares of treasury stock does the company hold?

d. Why does the stock of a company such as a PepsiCo have a market value that is higher than its book value?

CHAPTER 9

Financial Statement Analysis

LEARNING OBJECTIVES

After you have mastered the material in this chapter you will be able to:

1. **Describe factors associated with communicating useful information.**
2. **Differentiate between horizontal and vertical analysis.**
3. **Explain ratio analysis.**
4. **Calculate ratios for assessing a company's liquidity.**
5. **Calculate ratios for assessing a company's solvency.**
6. **Calculate ratios for assessing company management's effectiveness.**
7. **Calculate ratios for assessing a company's position in the stock market.**
8. **Identify different forms for presenting analytical data.**
9. **Explain the limitations of financial statement analysis.**

The Curious Accountant

On February 17, 2004, **Cingular Wireless** agreed to pay $41 billion to acquire **AT&T Wireless Services**. Cingular won a bidding war with Vodafone, a European company that also wanted to acquire AT&T Wireless. The winning bid was $11 billion more than Cingular's original offer.

Cingular Wireless is owned by two regional phone companies, **BellSouth** and **SBC Communications**. Shortly after agreeing to buy AT&T Wireless, BellSouth and SBC announced that as a result of the acquisition, their own net earnings would decline by over $2 billion for 2005 through 2007.

Why would Cingular and its parent companies agree to a deal that would reduce their earnings by so much over the next three years? What type of analysis would these companies use to make this decision? (Answers on page 319.)

CHAPTER OPENING

Expressing financial statement information in the form of ratios enhances its usefulness. Ratios permit comparisons over time and among companies, highlighting similarities, differences, and trends. Proficiency with common financial statement analysis techniques benefits both internal and external users. Before beginning detailed explanations of numerous ratios and percentages, however, we consider factors relevant to communicating useful information. ■

Factors in Communicating Useful Information

LO 1

Describe factors associated with communicating useful information.

The primary objective of accounting is to provide information useful for decision making. To provide information that supports this objective, accountants must consider the intended users, the types of decisions users make with financial statement information, and available means of analyzing the information.

The Users

Users of financial statement information include managers, creditors, stockholders, potential investors, and regulatory agencies. These individuals and organizations use financial statements for different purposes and bring varying levels of sophistication to understanding business activities. For example, investors range from private individuals who know little about financial statements to large investment brokers and institutional investors capable of using complex statistical analysis techniques. At what level of user knowledge should financial statements be aimed? Condensing and reporting complex business transactions at a level easily understood by nonprofessional investors is increasingly difficult. Current reporting standards target users that have a reasonably informed knowledge of business, though that level of sophistication is difficult to define.

The Types of Decisions

Just as the knowledge level of potential users varies, the information needs of users varies, depending on the decision at hand. A supplier considering whether or not to sell goods on account to a particular company wants to evaluate the likelihood of getting paid; a potential investor in that company wants to predict the likelihood of increases in the market value of the company's common stock. Financial statements, however, are designed for general purposes; they are not aimed at any specific user group. Some disclosed information, therefore, may be irrelevant to some users but vital to others. Users must employ different forms of analysis to identify information most relevant to a particular decision.

Financial statements can provide only highly summarized economic information. The costs to a company of providing excessively detailed information would be prohibitive. In addition, too much detail leads to **information overload,** the problem of having so much data that important information becomes obscured by trivial information. Users faced with reams of data may become so frustrated attempting to use it that they lose the value of *key* information that is provided.

Information Analysis

Because of the diversity of users, their different levels of knowledge, the varying information needs for particular decisions, and the general nature of financial statements, a variety of analysis techniques has been developed. In the following sections, we explain several common methods of analysis. The choice of method depends on which technique appears to provide the most relevant information in a given situation.

Methods of Analysis

LO 2

Differentiate between horizontal and vertical analysis.

Financial statement analysis should focus primarily on isolating information useful for making a particular decision. The information required can take many forms but usually involves comparisons, such as comparing changes in the same item for the same company over a number of years, comparing key relationships within the same year, or comparing the operations of several different companies in the same industry. This chapter discusses three categories of analysis methods: horizontal, vertical, and ratio. Exhibits 9.1 and 9.2 present comparative financial statements for Milavec Company. We refer to these statements in the examples of analysis techniques.

EXHIBIT 9.1

MILAVEC COMPANY
Income Statements and Statements of Retained Earnings
For the Years Ending December 31

	2008	2007
Sales	$900,000	$800,000
Cost of Goods Sold		
Beginning Inventory	43,000	40,000
Purchases	637,000	483,000
Goods Available for Sale	680,000	523,000
Ending Inventory	70,000	43,000
Cost of Goods Sold	610,000	480,000
Gross Margin	290,000	320,000
Operating Expenses	248,000	280,000
Income before Taxes	42,000	40,000
Income Taxes	17,000	18,000
Net Income	25,000	22,000
Plus: Retained Earnings, Beginning Balance	137,000	130,000
Less: Dividends	0	15,000
Retained Earnings, Ending Balance	$162,000	$137,000

EXHIBIT 9.2

MILAVEC COMPANY
Balance Sheets
As of December 31

	2008	2007
Assets		
Cash	$ 20,000	$ 17,000
Marketable Securities	20,000	22,000
Notes Receivable	4,000	3,000
Accounts Receivable	50,000	56,000
Merchandise Inventory	70,000	43,000
Prepaid Items	4,000	4,000
Property, Plant, and Equipment (net)	340,000	310,000
Total Assets	$508,000	$455,000
Liabilities and Stockholders' Equity		
Accounts Payable	$ 40,000	$ 38,000
Salaries Payable	2,000	3,000
Taxes Payable	4,000	2,000
Bonds Payable, 8%	100,000	100,000
Preferred Stock, 6%, $100 par, cumulative	50,000	50,000
Common Stock, $10 par	150,000	125,000
Retained Earnings	162,000	137,000
Total Liabilities and Stockholders' Equity	$508,000	$455,000

Horizontal Analysis

Horizontal analysis, also called **trend analysis,** refers to studying the behavior of individual financial statement items over several accounting periods. These periods may be several quarters within the same fiscal year or they may be several different years. The analysis of a given item may focus on trends in the absolute dollar amount of the item or trends in percentages. For example, a user may observe that revenue increased from one period to the next by $42 million (an absolute dollar amount) or that it increased by a percentage such as 15 percent.

Absolute Amounts

The **absolute amounts** of particular financial statement items have many uses. Various national economic statistics, such as gross domestic product and the amount spent to replace productive capacity, are derived by combining absolute amounts reported by businesses. Financial statement users with expertise in particular industries might evaluate amounts reported for research and development costs to judge whether a company is spending excessively or conservatively. Users are particularly concerned with how amounts change over time. For example, a user might compare a pharmaceutical company's revenue before and after the patent expired on one of its drugs.

Comparing only absolute amounts has drawbacks, however, because *materiality* levels differ from company to company or even from year to year for a given company. The **materiality** of information refers to its relative importance. An item is considered material if knowledge of it would influence the decision of a reasonably informed user. Generally accepted accounting principles permit companies to account for *immaterial* items in the most convenient way, regardless of technical accounting rules. For example, companies may expense, rather than capitalize and depreciate, relatively inexpensive long-term assets like pencil sharpeners or waste baskets even if the assets have useful lives of many years. The concept of materiality, which has both quantitative and qualitative aspects, underlies all accounting principles.

It is difficult to judge the materiality of an absolute financial statement amount without considering the size of the company reporting it. For reporting purposes, **Exxon Corporation**'s financial statements are rounded to the nearest million dollars. For Exxon, a $400,000 increase in sales is not material. For a small company, however, $400,000 could represent total sales, a highly material amount. Meaningful comparisons between the two companies' operating performance are impossible using only absolute amounts. Users can surmount these difficulties with percentage analysis.

Percentage Analysis

Percentage analysis involves computing the percentage relationship between two amounts. In horizontal percentage analysis, a financial statement item is expressed as a percentage of the previous balance for the same item. Percentage analysis sidesteps the materiality problems of comparing different size companies by measuring changes in percentages rather than absolute amounts. Each change is converted to a percentage of the base year. Exhibit 9.3 presents a condensed version of Milavec's income statement with horizontal percentages for each item.

EXHIBIT 9.3

MILAVEC COMPANY
Comparative Income Statements
For the Years Ending December 31

	2008	2007	Percentage Difference
Sales	$900,000	$800,000	+12.5%*
Cost of Goods Sold	610,000	480,000	+27.1
Gross Margin	290,000	320,000	−9.4
Operating Expenses	248,000	280,000	−11.4
Income before Taxes	42,000	40,000	+5.0
Income Taxes	17,000	18,000	−5.6
Net Income	$ 25,000	$ 22,000	+13.6

*($900,000 − $800,000) ÷ $800,000; all changes expressed as percentages of previous totals.

The percentage changes disclose that, even though Milavec's net income increased slightly more than total sales, products may be underpriced. Cost of goods sold increased much more than sales, resulting in a lower gross margin. Users would also want to investigate why operating expenses decreased substantially despite the increase in sales volume.

Whether basing their analyses on absolute amounts, percentages, or ratios, users must avoid drawing overly simplistic conclusions about the reasons for the results. Numerical relationships flag conditions requiring further study. A change which appears favorable on the surface may not necessarily be a good sign. Users must evaluate the underlying reasons for the change.

CHECK YOURSELF 9.1

The following information was drawn from the annual reports of two retail companies (amounts are shown in millions). One company is an upscale department store; the other is a discount store. Based on this limited information, identify which company is the upscale department store.

	Jenkins Co.	Horn's Inc.
Sales	$325	$680
Cost of Goods Sold	130	408
Gross Margin	$195	$272

Answer

Jenkins' gross margin represents 60 percent ($195 ÷ $325) of sales. Horn's gross margin represents 40 percent ($272 ÷ $680) of sales. Since an upscale department store would have higher margins than a discount store, the data suggest that Jenkins is the upscale department store.

Answers to The Curious Accountant

Although **BellSouth** and **SBC** expect the acquisition of **AT&T Wireless** to depress earnings from 2005 through 2007, they believe the acquisition will significantly increase earnings after 2007. They expect to achieve this benefit by reducing capital expenditures and operating costs; one combined company will need less equipment than two separate companies and will not need to spend as much as two companies for such items as marketing and personnel. They estimate these cost savings will range from $1.4 to $2.1 billion annually.

Not all analysts agree with the two companies' forecasts. After studying the same basic information some analysts think competition from rivals such as **Verizon** may force **Cingular** to spend more on advertising than it expects in order to keep customers from switching providers. These analysts believe the year or so it takes to implement the merger will give rivals the opportunity to steal existing customers from AT&T Wireless. Additionally, some think Verizon currently has a technically superior network, which may cause Cingular to spend more on equipment than it estimated when bidding for AT&T Wireless. These analysts think Cingular paid too much for AT&T Wireless.

Financial analysis techniques can help managers make decisions, but cannot guarantee success. When using such tools as ratios and trend analysis, decision makers must understand the businesses being evaluated, and they must make assumptions about future events. Only the future will tell whether Cingular paid too much for AT&T Wireless, but we can be sure that many ratio and capital budgeting computations were made before Cingular decided how much its winning bid would be.

Source: Companies' filings with the SEC and Roger O. Crockett, "How the Cingular Deal Helps Verizon," *BusinessWeek*, March 1, 2004, pp. 36–37.

When comparing more than two periods, analysts use either of two basic approaches: (1) choosing one base year from which to calculate all increases or decreases or (2) calculating each period's percentage change from the preceding figure. For example, assume Milavec's sales for 2005 and 2006 were $600,000 and $750,000, respectively.

	2008	2007	2006	2005
Sales	$900,000	$800,000	$750,000	$600,000
Increase over 2005 sales	50.0%	33.3%	25.0%	–
Increase over preceding year	12.5%	6.7%	25.0%	–

Analysis discloses that Milavec's 2008 sales represented a 50 percent increase over 2005 sales, and a large increase (25 percent) occurred in 2006. From 2006 to 2007, sales increased only 6.7 percent but in the following year increased much more (12.5 percent).

Vertical Analysis

Vertical analysis uses percentages to compare individual components of financial statements to a key statement figure. Horizontal analysis compares items over many time periods; vertical analysis compares many items within the same time period.

Vertical Analysis of the Income Statement

Vertical analysis of an income statement (also called a *common size* income statement) involves converting each income statement component to a percentage of sales. Although vertical analysis suggests examining only one period, it is useful to compare common size income statements for several years. Exhibit 9.4 presents Milavec's income statements, along with vertical percentages, for 2008 and 2007. This analysis discloses that cost of goods sold increased significantly as a percentage of sales. Operating expenses and income taxes, however, decreased in relation to sales. Each of these observations indicates a need for more analysis regarding possible trends for future profits.

Vertical Analysis of the Balance Sheet

Vertical analysis of the balance sheet involves converting each balance sheet component to a percentage of total assets. The vertical analysis of Milavec's balance sheets in Exhibit 9.5

EXHIBIT 9.4

MILAVEC COMPANY
Vertical Analysis of Comparative Income Statements

	2008		2007	
	Amount	Percentage of Sales	Amount	Percentage of Sales
Sales	$900,000	100.0%	$800,000	100.0%
Cost of Goods Sold	610,000	67.8	480,000	60.0
Gross Margin	290,000	32.2	320,000	40.0
Operating Expenses	248,000	27.6	280,000	35.0
Income before Taxes	42,000	4.7	40,000	5.0
Income Taxes	17,000	1.9	18,000	2.3
Net Income	$ 25,000	2.8%	$ 22,000	2.8%

EXHIBIT 9.5

MILAVEC COMPANY
Vertical Analysis of Comparative Balance Sheets

	2008	Percentage of Total	2007	Percentage of Total
Assets				
Cash	$ 20,000	3.9%	$ 17,000	3.7%
Marketable Securities	20,000	3.9	22,000	4.8
Notes Receivable	4,000	0.8	3,000	0.7
Accounts Receivable	50,000	9.8	56,000	12.3
Merchandise Inventory	70,000	13.8	43,000	9.5
Prepaid Items	4,000	0.8	4,000	0.9
Total Current Assets	168,000	33.1	145,000	31.9
Property, Plant, and Equipment	340,000	67.0	310,000	68.1
Total Assets	$508,000	100.0%	$455,000	100.0%
Liabilities and Stockholders' Equity				
Accounts Payable	$ 40,000	7.9%	$ 38,000	8.4%
Salaries Payable	2,000	0.4	3,000	0.7
Taxes Payable	4,000	0.8	2,000	0.4
Total Current Liabilities	46,000	9.1	43,000	9.5
Bonds Payable, 8%	100,000	19.7	100,000	22.0
Total Liabilities	146,000	28.7	143,000	31.4
Preferred Stock 6%, $100 par	50,000	9.8	50,000	11.0
Common Stock, $10 par	150,000	29.5	125,000	27.5
Retained Earnings	162,000	31.9	137,000	30.1
Total Stockholders' Equity	362,000	71.3	312,000	68.6
Total Liabilities and Stockholders' Equity	$508,000	100.0%	$455,000	100.0%

discloses few large percentage changes from the preceding year. Even small individual percentage changes, however, may represent substantial dollar increases. Inventory, one of the less liquid current assets, has increased 62.8 percent ([$70,000 − $43,000] ÷ $43,000) from 2007 to 2008, which may have unfavorable consequences. Careful analysis requires considering changes in both percentages *and* absolute amounts.

Ratio Analysis

Explain ratio analysis.

Ratio analysis involves studying various relationships between different items reported in a set of financial statements. For example, net earnings (net income) reported on the income statement may be compared to total assets reported on the balance sheet. Analysts calculate many different ratios for a wide variety of purposes. The remainder of this chapter is devoted to discussing some of the more commonly used ratios.

Objectives of Ratio Analysis

As suggested earlier, various users approach financial statement analysis with many different objectives. Creditors are interested in whether a company will be able to pay its debts on time. Both creditors and stockholders are concerned with how the company is financed, whether through debt, equity, or earnings. Stockholders and potential investors analyze past earnings performance and dividend policy for clues to the future value of their investments. In addition to using internally generated data to analyze operations, company managers find much information prepared for external purposes useful for examining past operations and planning future policies. Although many of these objectives are interrelated, it is convenient to group ratios into categories such as measures of debt-paying ability and measures of profitability.

Measures of Debt-Paying Ability

Liquidity Ratios

Calculate ratios for assessing a company's liquidity.

Liquidity ratios indicate a company's ability to pay short-term debts. They focus on current assets and current liabilities. The examples in the following section use the financial statement information reported by Milavec Company.

Working Capital

Working capital is current assets minus current liabilities. Current assets include assets most likely to be converted into cash or consumed in the current operating period. Current liabilities represent debts that must be satisfied in the current period. Working capital therefore measures the excess funds the company will have available for operations, excluding any new funds it generates during the year. Think of working capital as the cushion against short-term debt-paying problems. Working capital at the end of 2008 and 2007 for Milavec Company was as follows.

	2008	2007
Current assets	$168,000	$145,000
− Current liabilities	46,000	43,000
Working capital	$122,000	$102,000

Milavec's working capital increased dramatically from 2007 to 2008, but the numbers themselves say little. Whether $122,000 is sufficient or not depends on such factors as the industry in which Milavec operates, its size, and the maturity dates of its current obligations. We can see, however, that the increase in working capital is primarily due to the increase in inventories.

Current Ratio

Working capital is an absolute amount. Its usefulness is limited by the materiality difficulties discussed earlier. It is hard to draw meaningful conclusions from comparing Milavec's working capital of $122,000 with another company that also has working capital of $122,000. By expressing the relationship between current assets and current liabilities as a ratio, however, we have a more useful measure of the company's debt-paying ability relative to other companies. The **current ratio,** also called the **working capital ratio,** is calculated as follows.

$$\text{Current ratio} = \frac{\text{Current assets}}{\text{Current liabilities}}$$

To illustrate using the current ratio for comparisons, consider Milavec's current position relative to Laroque's, a larger firm with current assets of $500,000 and current liabilities of $378,000.

	Milavec	Laroque
Current assets (a)	$168,000	$500,000
− Current liabilities (b)	46,000	378,000
Working capital	$122,000	$122,000
Current ratio (a ÷ b)	3.65:1	1.32:1

The current ratio is expressed as the number of dollars of current assets for each dollar of current liabilities. In the above example, both companies have the same amount of working capital. Milavec, however, appears to have a much stronger working capital position. Any conclusions from this analysis must take into account the circumstances of the particular companies; there is no single ideal current ratio that suits all companies. In recent years the average current ratio of the 30 companies that constitute the Dow Jones Industrial Average was around 1.35:1; the individual company ratios, however, ranged from .37:1 to 4.22:1. A current ratio can be too high. Money invested in factories and developing new products is usually more profitable than money held as large cash balances or invested in inventory.

Quick Ratio

The **quick ratio,** also known as the **acid-test ratio,** is a conservative variation of the current ratio. The quick ratio measures a company's *immediate* debt-paying ability. Only cash, receivables, and current marketable securities *(quick assets)* are included in the numerator. Less liquid current assets, such as inventories and prepaid items, are omitted. Inventories may take several months to sell; prepaid items reduce otherwise necessary expenditures but do not lead eventually to cash receipts. The quick ratio is computed as follows.

$$\text{Quick ratio} = \frac{\text{Quick assets}}{\text{Current liabilities}}$$

Milavec Company's current ratios and quick ratios for 2008 and 2007 follow.

	2008	2007
Current ratio	$168,000 ÷ $46,000	$145,000 ÷ $43,000
	3.65:1	3.37:1
Quick ratio	$94,000 ÷ $46,000	$98,000 ÷ $43,000
	2.04:1	2.28:1

The decrease in the quick ratio from 2007 to 2008 reflects both a decrease in quick assets and an increase in current liabilities. The result indicates that the company is less liquid (has less ability to pay its short-term debt) in 2008 than it was in 2007.

Accounts Receivable Ratios

Offering customers credit plays an enormous role in generating revenue, but it also increases expenses and delays cash receipts. To minimize uncollectible accounts expense and collect cash for use in current operations, companies want to collect receivables as quickly as possible without losing customers. Two relationships are often examined to assess a company's collection record: *accounts receivable turnover* and *average number of days to collect receivables (average collection period).*

Accounts receivable turnover is calculated as follows.

$$\text{Accounts receivable turnover} = \frac{\text{Net credit sales}}{\text{Average accounts receivable}}$$

Net credit sales refers to total sales on account less sales discounts, allowances, and returns. When most sales are credit sales or when a breakdown of total sales between cash sales and credit sales is not available, the analyst must use total sales in the numerator. The denominator is based on *net accounts receivable* (receivables after subtracting the allowance for doubtful accounts). Since the numerator represents a whole period, it is preferable to use average receivables in the denominator if possible. When comparative statements are available, the average can be based on the beginning and ending balances. Milavec Company's accounts receivable turnover is computed as follows:

	2008	2007
Net sales (assume all on account) (a)	$900,000	$800,000
Beginning receivables (b)	$ 56,000	$ 55,000*
Ending receivables (c)	50,000	56,000
Average receivables (d) = (b + c) ÷ 2	$ 53,000	$ 55,500
Accounts receivable turnover (a ÷ d)	16.98	14.41

*The beginning receivables balance was drawn from the 2006 financial statements, which are not included in the illustration.

The 2008 accounts receivable turnover of 16.98 indicates Milavec collected its average receivables almost 17 times that year. The higher the turnover, the faster the collections. A company can have cash flow problems and lose substantial purchasing power if resources are tied up in receivables for long periods.

Average number of days to collect receivables is calculated as follows.

$$\text{Average number of days to collect receivables} = \frac{\text{365 days}}{\text{Accounts receivable turnover}}$$

This ratio offers another way to look at turnover by showing the number of days, on average, it takes to collect a receivable. If receivables were collected 16.98 times in 2008, the average collection period was 21 days, 365 ÷ 16.98 (the number of days in the year divided by accounts receivable turnover). For 2007, it took an average of 25 days (365 ÷ 14.41) to collect a receivable.

Although the collection period improved, no other conclusions can be reached without considering the industry, Milavec's past performance, and the general economic environment. In recent years the average time to collect accounts receivable for the 25 nonfinancial companies that make up the Dow Jones Industrial Average was around 60 days. (Financial firms are excluded because, by the nature of their business, they have very long collection periods.)

Inventory Ratios

A fine line exists between having too much and too little inventory in stock. Too little inventory can result in lost sales and costly production delays. Too much inventory can use needed space, increase financing and insurance costs, and become obsolete. To help analyze how

efficiently a company manages inventory, we use two ratios similar to those used in analyzing accounts receivable.

Inventory turnover indicates the number of times, on average, that inventory is totally replaced during the year. The relationship is computed as follows.

$$\text{Inventory turnover} = \frac{\text{Cost of goods sold}}{\text{Average inventory}}$$

The average inventory is usually based on the beginning and ending balances that are shown in the financial statements. Inventory turnover for Milavec was as follows.

	2008	2007
Cost of goods sold (a)	$610,000	$480,000
Beginning inventory (b)	43,000	40,000*
Ending inventory (c)	70,000	43,000
Average inventory (d) = (b + c) ÷ 2	$ 56,500	$ 41,500
Inventory turnover (a ÷ d)	10.80	11.57

*The beginning inventory balance was drawn from the company's 2006 financial statements, which are not included in the illustration.

Generally, a higher turnover indicates that merchandise is being handled more efficiently. Trying to compare firms in different industries, however, can be misleading. Inventory turnover for grocery stores and many retail outlets is high. Because of the nature of the goods being sold, inventory turnover is much lower for appliance and jewelry stores. We look at this issue in more detail when we discuss return on investment.

Average number of days to sell inventory is determined by dividing the number of days in the year by the inventory turnover as follows.

$$\text{Average number of days to sell inventory} = \frac{\text{365 days}}{\text{Inventory turnover}}$$

The result approximates the number of days the firm could sell inventory without purchasing more. For Milavec, this figure was 34 days in 2008 (365 ÷ 10.80) and 32 days in 2007 (365 ÷ 11.57). In recent years it took around 30 days, on average, for the companies in the Dow Jones Industrial Average that have inventory to sell their inventory. The time it took individual companies to sell their inventory varied by industry, ranging from 3 days to 55 days.

Solvency Ratios

LO 5

Calculate ratios for assessing a company's solvency.

Solvency ratios are used to analyze a company's long-term debt-paying ability and its financing structure. Creditors are concerned with a company's ability to satisfy outstanding obligations. The larger a company's liability percentage, the greater the risk that the company could fall behind or default on debt payments. Stockholders, too, are concerned about a company's solvency. If a company is unable to pay its debts, the owners could lose their investment. Each user group desires that company financing choices minimize its investment risk, whether their investment is in debt or stockholders' equity.

Debt Ratios

The following ratios represent two different ways to express the same relationship. Both are frequently used.

Debt to assets ratio. This ratio measures the percentage of a company's assets that are financed by debt.

Debt to equity ratio. As used in this ratio, *equity* means stockholders' equity. The debt to equity ratio compares creditor financing to owner financing. It is expressed as the dollar amount of liabilities for each dollar of stockholder's equity.

These ratios are calculated as follows.

$$\text{Debt to assets} = \frac{\text{Total liabilities}}{\text{Total assets}}$$

$$\text{Debt to equity} = \frac{\text{Total liabilities}}{\text{Total stockholders' equity}}$$

Applying these formulas to Milavec Company's results produces the following.

	2008	2007
Total liabilities (a)	$146,000	$143,000
Total stockholders' equity (b)	362,000	312,000
Total assets (liabilities + stockholders' equity) (c)	$508,000	$455,000
Debt to assets (a ÷ c)	29%	31%
Debt to equity ratio (a ÷ b)	0.40:1	0.46:1

Each year less than one-third of the company's assets were financed with debt. The amount of liabilities per dollar of stockholders' equity declined by 0.06. It is difficult to judge whether the reduced percentage of liabilities is favorable. In general, a lower level of liabilities provides greater security because the likelihood of bankruptcy is reduced. Perhaps, however, the company is financially strong enough to incur more liabilities and benefit from financial leverage. The 30 companies that make up the Dow Jones Industrial Average report around 64 percent of their assets, on average, are financed through borrowing.

Number of Times Interest Is Earned

The **times interest earned** ratio measures the burden a company's interest payments represent. Users often consider times interest is earned along with the debt ratios when evaluating financial risk. The numerator of this ratio uses *earnings before interest and taxes (EBIT),* rather than net earnings, because the amount of earnings *before* interest and income taxes is available for paying interest.

$$\text{Times interest earned} = \frac{\text{Earnings before interest expense and taxes}}{\text{Interest expense}}$$

Dividing EBIT by interest expense indicates how many times the company could have made its interest payments. Obviously, interest is paid only once, but the more times it *could* be paid, the bigger the company's safety net. Although interest is paid from cash, not accrual earnings, it is standard practice to base this ratio on accrual-based EBIT, not a cash-based amount. For Milavec, this calculation is as follows.

	2008	2007
Income before taxes	$42,000	$40,000
Interest expense (b)	8,000	8,000*
Earnings before interest and taxes (a)	$50,000	$48,000
Times interest earned (a ÷ b)	6.25 times	6 times

*Interest on bonds: $100,000 × .08 = $8,000.

Any expense or dividend payment can be analyzed this way. Another frequently used calculation is the number of times the preferred dividend is earned. In that case, the numerator is net income (after taxes) and the denominator is the amount of the annual preferred dividend.

CHECK YOURSELF 9.2

Selected data for Riverside Corporation and Academy Company follow (amounts are shown in millions).

	Riverside Corporation	Academy Company
Total liabilities (a)	$650	$450
Stockholders' equity (b)	300	400
Total liabilities + stockholders' equity (c)	$950	$850
Interest expense (d)	$ 65	$ 45
Income before taxes (e)	140	130
Earnings before interest and taxes (f)	$205	$175

Based on this information alone, which company would likely obtain the less favorable interest rate on additional debt financing?

Answer

Interest rates vary with risk levels. Companies with less solvency (long-term debt-paying ability) generally must pay higher interest rates to obtain financing. Two solvency measures for the two companies follow. Recall:

Total assets = Liabilities + Stockholders' equity

	Riverside Corporation	Academy Company
Debt to assets ratio (a ÷ c)	68.4%	52.9%
Times interest earned (f ÷ d)	3.15 times	3.89 times

Since Riverside has a higher percentage of debt and a lower times interest earned ratio, the data suggest that Riverside is less solvent than Academy. Riverside would therefore likely have to pay a higher interest rate to obtain additional financing.

Plant Assets to Long-Term Liabilities

Companies often pledge plant assets as collateral for long-term liabilities. Financial statement users may analyze a firm's ability to obtain long-term financing on the strength of its asset base. Effective financial management principles dictate that asset purchases should be financed over a time span about equal to the expected lives of the assets. Short-term assets should be financed with short-term liabilities; the current ratio, introduced earlier, indicates how well a company manages current debt. Long-lived assets should be financed with long-term liabilities, and the **plant assets to long-term liabilities** ratio suggests how well long-term debt is managed. It is calculated as follows.

$$\text{Plant assets to long-term liabilities} = \frac{\text{Net plant assets}}{\text{Long-term liabilities}}$$

For Milavec Company, these ratios follow.

	2008	2007
Net plant assets (a)	$340,000	$310,000
Bonds payable (b)	100,000	100,000
Plant assets to long-term liabilities (a ÷ b)	3.4:1	3.1:1

Measures of Profitability

Profitability refers to a company's ability to generate earnings. Both management and external users desire information about a company's success in generating profits and how these profits are used to reward investors. Some of the many ratios available to measure different aspects of profitability are discussed in the following two sections.

Measures of Managerial Effectiveness

Calculate ratios for assessing company management's effectiveness.

The most common ratios used to evaluate managerial effectiveness measure what percentage of sales results in earnings and how productive assets are in generating those sales. As mentioned earlier, the *absolute amount* of sales or earnings means little without also considering company size.

Net Margin (or Return on Sales)

Gross margin and *gross profit* are alternate terms for the amount remaining after subtracting the expense cost of goods sold from sales. **Net margin,** sometimes called *operating margin, profit margin,* or the *return on sales ratio,* describes the percent remaining of each sales dollar after subtracting other expenses as well as cost of goods sold. Net margin can be calculated in several ways; some of the more common methods only subtract normal operating expenses or all expenses other than income tax expense. For simplicity, our calculation uses net income (we subtract all expenses). Net income divided by net sales expresses net income (earnings) as a percentage of sales, as follows.

$$\text{Net margin} = \frac{\text{Net income}}{\text{Net sales}}$$

For Milavec Company, the net margins for 2008 and 2007 were as follows.

	2008	2007
Net income (a)	$ 25,000	$ 22,000
Net sales (b)	900,000	800,000
Net margin (a ÷ b)	2.78%	2.75%

Milavec has maintained approximately the same net margin. Obviously, the larger the percentage, the better; a meaningful interpretation, however, requires analyzing the company's history and comparing the net margin to other companies in the same industry. The average net margin for the 30 companies that make up the Dow Jones Industrial Average has been around 10 percent in recent years; some companies, such as Microsoft with 31 percent, have been much higher than the average. Of course, if a company has a net loss, its net margin for that year will be negative.

Asset Turnover Ratio

The **asset turnover ratio** (sometimes called *turnover of assets ratio*) measures how many sales dollars were generated for each dollar of assets invested. As with many ratios used in financial statement analysis, users may define the numerator and denominator of this ratio in different ways. For example, they may use total assets or only include operating assets. Since the numerator represents a whole period, it is preferable to use average assets in the denominator if possible, especially if the amount of assets changed significantly during the year. We use average total assets in our illustration.

$$\text{Asset turnover} = \frac{\text{Net sales}}{\text{Average total assets}}$$

For Milavec, the asset turnover ratios were as follows.

	2008	2007
Net sales (a)	$900,000	$800,000
Beginning assets (b)	$455,000	$420,000*
Ending assets (c)	508,000	455,000
Average assets (d) = (b + c) ÷ 2	$481,500	$437,500
Asset turnover (a ÷ d)	1.87	1.83

*The beginning asset balance was drawn from the 2006 financial statements, which are not included in the illustration.

As with most ratios, the implications of a given asset turnover ratio are affected by other considerations. Asset turnover will be high in an industry that requires only minimal investment to operate, such as real estate sales companies. On the other hand, industries that require large investments in plant and machinery, like the auto industry, are likely to have lower asset turnover ratios. The asset turnover ratios of the companies that make up the Dow Jones Industrial Average have averaged around 0.75 in recent years. This means that annual sales have averaged 75 percent of their assets.

Return on Investment

Return on investment (ROI), also called *return on assets* or *earning power,* is the ratio of wealth generated (net income) to the amount invested (average total assets) to generate the wealth. ROI can be calculated as follows.[1]

$$\text{ROI} = \frac{\text{Net income}}{\text{Average total assets}}$$

For Milavec, ROI was as follows.

2008
$25,000 ÷ $481,500* = 5.19%
2007
$22,000 ÷ $437,500* = 5.03%

*The computation of average assets is shown above.

In general, higher ROIs suggest better performance. The ROI of the large companies that make up the Dow Jones Industrial Average has averaged around 7 percent in recent years. These data suggest that Milavec is performing below average, and therefore signals a need for further evaluation that would lead to improved performance.

Return on Equity

Return on equity (ROE) is often used to measure the profitability of the stockholders' investment. ROE is usually higher than ROI because of financial leverage. Financial leverage refers to using debt financing to increase the assets available to a business beyond the amount of assets financed by owners. As long as a company's ROI exceeds its cost of bor-

[1]Detailed coverage of the return on investment ratio is provided in Chapter 15. As discussed in that chapter, companies frequently manipulate the formula to improve managerial motivation and performance. For example, instead of using net income, companies frequently use operating income because net income may be affected by items that are not controllable by management such as loss on a plant closing, storm damage, and so on.

rowing (interest expense), the owners will earn a higher return on their investment in the company by using borrowed money. For example, if a company borrows money at 8 percent and invests it at 10 percent, the owners will enjoy a return that is higher than 10 percent. ROE is computed as follows.

$$\text{ROE} = \frac{\text{Net income}}{\text{Average total stockholders' equity}}$$

If the amount of stockholders' equity changes significantly during the year, it is desirable to use average equity rather than year-end equity in the denominator. The ROE figures for Milavec Company were as follows.

	2008	2007
Net income (a)	$ 25,000	$ 22,000
Preferred stock, 6%, $100 par, cumulative	50,000	50,000
Common stock, $10 par	150,000	125,000
Retained earnings	162,000	137,000
Total stockholders' equity (b)	$362,000	$312,000
ROE (a ÷ b)	6.9%	7.1%

The slight decrease in ROE is due primarily to the increase in common stock. The effect of the increase in total stockholders' equity offsets the effect of the increase in earnings. This information does not disclose whether Milavec had the use of the additional stockholder investment for all or part of the year. If the data are available, calculating a weighted average amount of stockholders' equity provides more meaningful results.

We mentioned earlier the companies that make up the Dow Jones Industrial Average had an average ROI of 7 percent. The average ROE for the companies in the Dow was 19 percent, indicating effective use of financial leverage.

Stock Market Ratios

Calculate ratios for assessing a company's position in the stock market.

Existing and potential investors in a company's stock use many common ratios to analyze and compare the earnings and dividends of different size companies in different industries. Purchasers of stock can profit in two ways: through receiving dividends and through increases in stock value. Investors consider both dividends and overall earnings performance as indicators of the value of the stock they own.

Earnings per Share

Perhaps the most frequently quoted measure of earnings performance is **earnings per share (EPS).** EPS represents an attempt to express a company's annual earnings in one easily understood figure. Investors may appreciate knowing that a large company's net income increased from $437 million in 2006 to $493 million in 2007. But, if they also learn that the company's EPS increased from $2.19 to $2.47, the increase is easier to understand. When financial analysts cite companies' earnings, they usually speak of EPS, not total net earnings.

EPS differs from *dividends per share.* Rarely would a company distribute all the year's earnings to stockholders. EPS calculations are among the most complex in accounting, and more advanced textbooks devote entire chapters to the subject. At this level, we use the following basic formula.

$$\text{Earnings per share} = \frac{\text{Net earnings available for common stock}}{\text{Average number of outstanding common shares}}$$

EPS pertains to shares of *common stock.* Limiting the numerator to earnings available for common stock eliminates the annual preferred dividend (0.06 × $50,000 = $3,000) from the calculation. Exhibit 9.1 shows that Milavec did not pay the preferred dividends in 2008. Since the preferred stock is cumulative, however, the preferred dividend is in arrears and not available to the common stockholders. The number of common shares outstanding is determined by dividing the book value of the common stock by its par value per share ($150,000 ÷ $10 = 15,000 for 2008 and $125,000 ÷ $10 = 12,500 for 2007). Using these data, Milavec's 2008 EPS is calculated as follows.

$$\frac{\$25{,}000 \text{ (net income)} - \$3{,}000 \text{ (preferred dividend)}}{(15{,}000 + 12{,}500)/2 \text{ (average outstanding common shares)}} = \$1.60 \text{ per share}$$

Investors attribute a great deal of importance to EPS figures. The amounts used in calculating EPS, however, have limitations. Many accounting choices, assumptions, and estimates underlie net income computations, including alternative depreciation methods, different inventory cost flow assumptions, and estimates of future uncollectible accounts or warranty expenses, to name only a few. The denominator is also inexact because various factors (discussed in advanced accounting courses) affect the number of shares to include. Numerous opportunities therefore exist to manipulate EPS figures. Prudent investors consider these variables in deciding how much weight to attach to earnings per share.

Book Value

Book value per share is another frequently quoted measure of a share of stock. It is calculated as follows.

$$\text{Book value per share} = \frac{\text{Stockholders' equity} - \text{Preferred rights}}{\text{Outstanding common shares}}$$

Instead of describing the numerator as stockholders' equity, we could have used assets minus liabilities, the algebraic computation of a company's "net worth." Net worth is a misnomer. A company's accounting records reflect book values, not worth. Because assets are recorded at historical costs and different methods are used to transfer asset costs to expense, the book value of assets after deducting liabilities means little if anything. Nevertheless, investors use the term *book value per share* frequently.

Preferred rights represents the amount of money required to satisfy the claims of preferred stockholders. If the preferred stock has a call premium, the call premium amount is subtracted. In our example, we assume the preferred stock can be retired at par. Book value per share for 2008 was therefore as follows.

$$\frac{\$362{,}000 - \$50{,}000}{15{,}000} = \$20.80 \text{ per share}$$

Price-Earnings Ratio

The **price-earnings ratio,** or *P/E ratio,* compares the earnings per share of a company to the market price for a share of the company's stock. Assume Avalanche Company and Brushfire Company each report earnings per share of $3.60. For the same year, Cyclone Company reports EPS of $4.10. Based on these data alone, Cyclone stock may seem to be the best investment. Suppose, however, that the price for one share of stock in each company is $43.20, $36.00, and $51.25, respectively. Which stock would you buy? Cyclone's stock price is the highest, but so is its EPS. The P/E ratio provides a common base of comparison:

$$\text{Price-earnings ratio} = \frac{\text{Market price per share}}{\text{Earnings per share}}$$

The P/E ratios for the three companies are:

Avalanche	Brushfire	Cyclone
12.0	10.0	12.5

Brushfire might initially seem to be the best buy for your money. Yet there must be some reason that Cyclone's stock is selling at 12½ times earnings. In general, a higher P/E ratio indicates the market is more optimistic about a company's growth potential than it is about a company with a lower P/E ratio. The market price of a company's stock reflects judgments about both the company's current results and expectations about future results. Investors cannot make informed use of these ratios for investment decisions without examining the reasons behind the ratios. In May 2004, the average P/E ratio for the companies in the Dow Jones Industrial Average was around 20.

Dividend Yield

There are two ways to profit from a stock investment. One, investors can sell the stock for more than they paid to purchase it (if the stock price rises). Two, the company that issued the stock can pay cash dividends to the shareholders. Most investors view rising stock prices as the primary reward for investing in stock. The importance of receiving dividends, however, should not be overlooked. Evaluating dividend payments is more complex than simply comparing the dividends per share paid by one company to the dividends per share paid by another company. Receiving a $1 dividend on a share purchased for $10 is a much better return than receiving a $1.50 dividend on stock bought for $100. Computing the **dividend yield** simplifies comparing dividend payments. Dividend yield measures dividends received as a percentage of a stock's market price.

$$\text{Dividend yield} = \frac{\text{Dividends per share}}{\text{Market price per share}}$$

To illustrate, consider Dragonfly Inc. and Elk Company. The information for calculating dividend yield follows:

	Dragonfly	Elk
Dividends per share (a)	$ 1.80	$ 3.00
Market price per share (b)	40.00	75.00
Dividend yield (a ÷ b)	4.5%	4.0%

Even though the dividend per share paid by Elk Company is higher, the yield is lower (4.5 percent versus 4.0 percent) because Elk's stock price is so high. The dividend yields for the companies included in the Dow Jones Industrial Average were averaging around 2 percent in May of 2004.

Other Ratios

Investors can also use a wide array of other ratios to analyze profitability. Most **profitability ratios** use the same reasoning. For example, you can calculate the *yield* of a variety of financial investments. Yield represents the percentage the amount received is of the amount invested. The dividend yield explained above could be calculated for either common or preferred stock. Investors could measure the earnings yield by calculating earnings per share as a percentage of market price. Yield on a bond can be calculated the same way: interest received divided by the price of the bond.

The specific ratios presented in this chapter are summarized in Exhibit 9.6.

Presentation of Analytical Relationships

LO 8

Identify different forms for presenting analytical data.

To communicate with users, companies present analytical information in endless different ways in annual reports. Although providing diagrams and illustrations in annual reports is not usually required, companies often include various forms of graphs and charts along with the underlying numbers to help users interpret financial statement data more easily. Common types presented include bar charts, pie charts, and line graphs. Exhibits 9.7, 9.8, and 9.9 show examples of these forms.

EXHIBIT 9.6

Summary of Key Relationships

Liquidity Ratios	1. Working capital	Current assets − Current liabilities
	2. Current ratio	Current assets ÷ Current liabilities
	3. Quick (acid-test) ratio	(Current assets − Inventory − Prepaid Items) ÷ Current liabilities
	4. Accounts receivable turnover	Net credit sales ÷ Average net receivables
	5. Average number of days to collect receivables	365 ÷ Accounts receivable turnover
	6. Inventory turnover	Cost of goods sold ÷ Average inventory
	7. Average number of days to sell inventory	365 ÷ Inventory turnover
Solvency Ratios	8. Debt to assets ratio	Total liabilities ÷ Total assets
	9. Debt to equity ratio	Total liabilities ÷ Total stockholders' equity
	10. Times interest earned	Earnings before interest expense and taxes ÷ interest expense
	11. Plant assets to long-term liabilities	Net plant assets ÷ Long-term liabilities
Profitability Ratios	12. Net margin	Net income ÷ Net sales
	13. Asset turnover	Net sales ÷ Average total assets
	14. Return on investment (also: return on assets)	Net income ÷ Average total assets
	15. Return on equity	Net income ÷ Average total stockholders' equity
Stock Market Ratios	16. Earnings per share	Net earnings available for common stock ÷ Average outstanding common shares
	17. Book value per share	(Stockholders' equity − Preferred rights) ÷ Outstanding common shares
	18. Price-earnings ratio	Market price per share ÷ Earnings per share
	19. Dividend yield	Dividends per share ÷ Market price per share

EXHIBIT 9.7

Earnings and Dividends on Common Stock

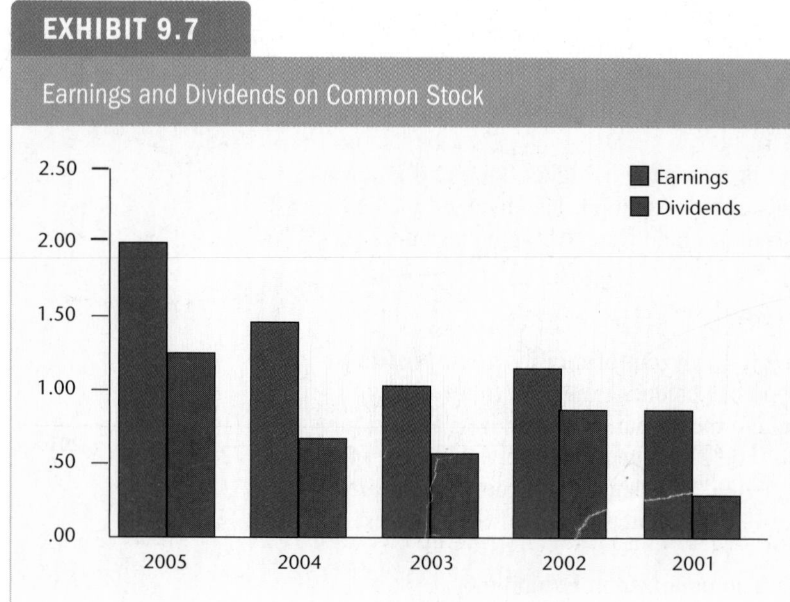

EXHIBIT 9.8

Percentage of Sales Dollar

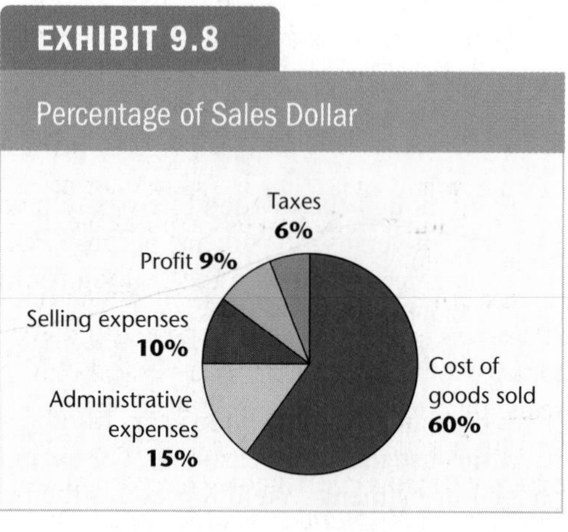

Limitations of Financial Statement Analysis

LO 9

Explain the limitations of financial statement analysis.

Analyzing financial statements is analogous to choosing a new car. Each car is different, and prospective buyers must evaluate and weigh a myriad of features: gas mileage, engine size, manufacturer's reputation, color, accessories, and price, to name a few. Just as it is difficult to compare a Toyota minivan to a Ferrari sports car, so it is difficult to compare a small

REALITY BYTES

The most important source of financial information comes from companies' reports, but decision makers should also consult other sources. Interested persons can access quarterly and annual reports through the SEC's EDGAR database and often from company websites. Many companies will provide printed versions of these reports upon request. Companies also post information on their websites that is not included in their annual reports. For example, some automobile companies provide detailed production data on their websites.

Users can frequently obtain information useful in analyzing a particular company from independent sources as well as from the company itself. For example, the websites of popular news services such as **CNN** (*money.cnn.com*) and **CNBC** (*moneycentral.msn.com*) provide archived news stories and independent financial information about many companies. The websites of brokerage houses like *www.schwab.com* offer free financial information about companies. Finally, libraries often subscribe to independent services that evaluate companies as potential investments. One example worth reviewing is *Value Line Investment Survey*.

textile firm to a giant oil company. To make a meaningful assessment, the potential car buyer must focus on key data that can be comparably expressed for each car, such as gas mileage. The superior gas mileage of the minivan may pale in comparison to the thrill of driving the sports car, but the price of buying and operating the sports car may be the characteristic that determines the ultimate choice.

EXHIBIT 9.9

Profits by Major Industry Segment

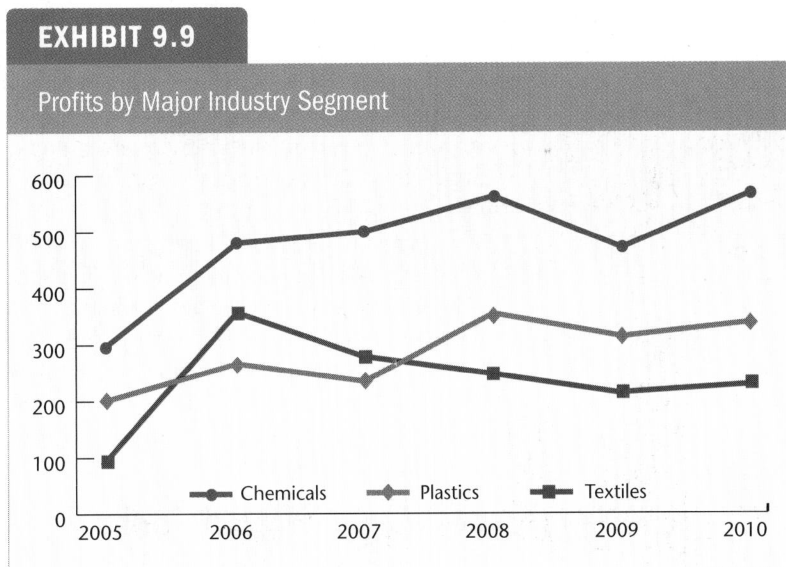

External users can rely on financial statement analysis only as a general guide to the potential of a business. They should resist placing too much weight on any particular figure or trend. Many factors must be considered simultaneously before making any judgments. Furthermore, the analysis techniques discussed in this chapter are all based on historical information. Future events and unanticipated changes in conditions will also influence a company's operating results.

Different Industries

Different industries may be affected by unique social policies, special accounting procedures, or other individual industry attributes. Ratios of companies in different industries are not comparable without considering industry characteristics. A high debt to assets ratio is more acceptable in some industries than others. Even within an industry, a particular business may require more or less working capital than the industry average. If so, the working capital and quick ratios would mean little compared to those of other firms, but may still be useful for trend analysis.

Because of industry-specific factors, most professional analysts specialize in one, or only a few, industries. Financial institutions such as brokerage houses, banks, and insurance companies typically employ financial analysts who specialize in areas such as mineral or oil extraction, chemicals, banking, retail, insurance, bond markets, or automobile manufacturing.

Changing Economic Environment

When comparing firms, analysts must be alert to changes in general economic trends from year to year. Significant changes in fuel costs and interest rates in recent years make old rule-of-thumb guidelines for evaluating these factors obsolete. In addition, the presence or absence of inflation affects business prospects.

Accounting Principles

Financial statement analysis is only as reliable as the data on which it is based. Although most companies follow generally accepted accounting principles, a wide variety of acceptable accounting methods is available from which to choose, including different inventory and depreciation methods, different schedules for recognizing revenue, and different ways to account for oil and gas exploration costs. Analyzing statements of companies that seem identical may produce noncomparable ratios if the companies used different accounting methods. Analysts may seek to improve comparability by trying to recast different companies' financial statements as if the same accounting methods had been applied.

Accrual accounting requires the use of many estimates; uncollectible accounts expense, warranty expense, asset lives, and salvage value are just a few. The reliability of the resulting financial reports depends on the expertise and integrity of the persons who make the estimates.

The quality and usefulness of accounting information are influenced by underlying accounting concepts. Two particular concepts, *conservatism* and *historical cost,* have a tremendous impact on financial reporting. Conservatism dictates recognizing estimated losses as soon as they occur, but gain recognition is almost always deferred until the gains are actually realized. Conservatism produces a negative bias in financial statements. There are persuasive arguments for the conservatism principle, but users should be alert to distortions it may cause in accounting information.

The pervasive use of the historical cost concept is probably the greatest single cause of distorted financial statement analysis results. The historical cost of an asset does not represent its current value. The asset purchased in 1980 for $10,000 is not comparable in value to the asset purchased in 1995 for $10,000 because of changes in the value of the dollar. Using historical cost produces financial statements that report dollars with differing purchasing power in the same statement. Combining these differing dollar values is akin to adding miles to kilometers. To get the most from analyzing financial statements, users should be cognizant of these limitations.

CHECK YOURSELF 9.3

The return on equity for Gup Company is 23.4 percent and for Hunn Company is 17 percent. Does this mean Gup Company is better managed than Hunn Company?

Answer

No single ratio can adequately measure management performance. Even analyzing a wide range of ratios provides only limited insight. Any useful interpretation requires the analyst to recognize the limitations of ratio analysis. For example, ratio norms typically differ between industries and may be affected by changing economic factors. In addition, companies' use of different accounting practices and procedures produces different ratio results even when underlying circumstances are comparable.

A Look Back <<

Financial statement analysis involves many factors, among them user characteristics, information needs for particular types of decisions, and how financial information is analyzed. Analytical techniques include *horizontal, vertical,* and *ratio analysis.* Users commonly calculate ratios to measure a company's liquidity, solvency, and profitability. The specific ratios presented in this chapter are summarized in Exhibit 9.6. Although ratios are easy to calculate and provide useful insights into business operations, when interpreting analytical results, users should consider limitations resulting from differing industry characteristics, differing economic conditions, and the fundamental accounting principles used to produce reported financial information.

A Look Forward

This chapter concludes the *financial* accounting portion of the text. Beginning with chapter 10, we introduce various tools from a branch of the field called *managerial* accounting. Managerial accounting focuses on meeting the accounting information needs of decision makers inside, rather than outside, a company. In addition to financial statement data, inside users require detailed, forward looking information that includes nonfinancial as well as financial components. We begin with a chapter that discusses the value management accounting adds to the decision making process.

SELF-STUDY REVIEW PROBLEM

Financial statements for Stallings Company follow.

INCOME STATEMENTS for the Years Ended December 31	2009	2008
Revenues		
Net Sales	$315,000	$259,000
Expenses		
Cost of Goods Sold	(189,000)	(154,000)
General, Selling, and Administrative Expenses	(54,000)	(46,000)
Interest Expense	(4,000)	(4,500)
Income Before Taxes	68,000	54,500
Income Tax Expense (40%)	(27,200)	(21,800)
Net Earnings	$ 40,800	$ 32,700

Balance Sheets as of December 31	2009	2008
Assets		
Current Assets		
Cash	$ 6,500	$ 11,500
Accounts Receivable	51,000	49,000
Inventories	155,000	147,500
Total Current Assets	212,500	208,000
Plant and Equipment (net)	187,500	177,000
Total Assets	$400,000	$385,000

continued

	2009	2008
Liabilities and Stockholders' Equity		
Liabilities		
Current Liabilities		
Accounts Payable	$ 60,000	$ 81,500
Other	25,000	22,500
Total Current Liabilities	85,000	104,000
Bonds Payable	100,000	100,000
Total Liabilities	185,000	204,000
Stockholders' Equity		
Common Stock (50,000 shares, $3 par)	150,000	150,000
Paid-In Capital in Excess of Par Value	20,000	20,000
Retained Earnings	45,000	11,000
Total Stockholders' Equity	215,000	181,000
Total Liabilities and Stockholders' Equity	$400,000	$385,000

Required

a. Use horizontal analysis to determine which expense item increased by the highest percentage from 2008 to 2009.

b. Use vertical analysis to determine whether the inventory balance is a higher percentage of total assets at the end of 2008 or 2009.

c. Calculate the following ratios for 2008 and 2009. When data limitations prohibit computing averages, use year-end balances in your calculations.

(1) Net margin
(2) Return on investment
(3) Return on equity
(4) Earnings per share
(5) Price-earnings ratio (market price per share at the end of 2009 and 2008 was $12.04 and $8.86, respectively)
(6) Book value per share of common stock
(7) Times interest earned
(8) Working capital
(9) Current ratio
(10) Acid-test ratio
(11) Accounts receivable turnover
(12) Inventory turnover
(13) Debt to equity

Solution to Requirement *a*

Income tax expense increased by the greatest percentage. Computations follow.

Cost of goods sold ($189,000 − $154,000) ÷ $154,000 = 22.73%

General, selling, and administrative ($54,000 − $46,000) ÷ $46,000 = 17.39%

Interest expense decreased.

Income tax expense ($27,200 − $21,800) ÷ $21,800 = 24.77%

Solution to Requirement *b*

2008: $147,500 ÷ $385,000 = 38.31%

2009: $155,000 ÷ $400,000 = 38.75%

Inventory is slightly larger relative to total assets at the end of 2009.

Solution to Requirement *c*

		2009	2008
1.	$\frac{\text{Net income}}{\text{Net sales}}$	$\frac{\$40,800}{\$315,000} = 12.95\%$	$\frac{\$32,700}{\$259,000} = 12.63\%$
2.	$\frac{\text{Net income}}{\text{Average total assets}}$	$\frac{\$40,800}{\$392,500} = 10.39\%$	$\frac{\$32,700}{\$385,000} = 8.49\%$
3.	$\frac{\text{Net income}}{\text{Average total stockholders' equity}}$	$\frac{\$40,800}{\$198,000} = 20.61\%$	$\frac{\$32,700}{\$181,000} = 18.07\%$
4.	$\frac{\text{Net income}}{\text{Average common shares outstanding}}$	$\frac{\$40,800}{50,000} = \$0.816$	$\frac{\$32,700}{50,000} = \$0.654$
5.	$\frac{\text{Market price per share}}{\text{Earnings per share}}$	$\frac{\$12.04}{\$0.816} = 14.75 \text{ times}$	$\frac{\$8.86}{\$0.654} = 13.55 \text{ times}$
6.	$\frac{\text{Stockholders' equity} - \text{Preferred rights}}{\text{Outstanding common shares}}$	$\frac{\$215,000}{50,000} = \$4.30$	$\frac{\$181,000}{50,000} = \$3.62$
7.	$\frac{\text{Net income} + \text{Taxes} + \text{Interest expense}}{\text{Interest expense}}$	$\frac{\$40,800 + \$27,200 + \$4,000}{\$4,000} = 18 \text{ times}$	$\frac{\$32,700 + \$21,800 + \$4,500}{\$4,500} = 13.1 \text{ times}$
8.	Current assets − Current liabilities	$212,500 − $85,000 = $127,500	$208,000 − $104,000 = $104,000
9.	$\frac{\text{Current assets}}{\text{Current liabilities}}$	$\frac{\$212,500}{\$85,000} = 2.5:1$	$\frac{\$208,000}{\$104,000} = 2:1$
10.	$\frac{\text{Quick assets}}{\text{Current liabilities}}$	$\frac{\$57,500}{\$85,000} = 0.68:1$	$\frac{\$60,500}{\$104,000} = 0.58:1$
11.	$\frac{\text{Net credit sales}}{\text{Average net accounts receivable}}$	$\frac{\$315,000}{\$50,000} = 6.3 \text{ times}$	$\frac{\$259,000}{\$49,000} = 5.29 \text{ times}$
12.	$\frac{\text{Cost of goods sold}}{\text{Average inventory}}$	$\frac{\$189,000}{\$151,250} = 1.25 \text{ times}$	$\frac{\$154,000}{\$147,500} = 1.04 \text{ times}$
13.	$\frac{\text{Total liabilities}}{\text{Total stockholders' equity}}$	$\frac{\$185,000}{\$215,000} = 86.05\%$	$\frac{\$204,000}{\$181,000} = 112.71\%$

KEY TERMS

absolute amounts 317
accounts receivable turnover 323
acid-test ratio 322
asset turnover ratio 327
average number of days to collect receivables 323
average number of days to sell inventory 324
book value per share 330
current ratio 322
debt to assets ratio 325
debt to equity ratio 325
dividend yield 331
earnings per share 329
horizontal analysis 317
information overload 316
inventory turnover 324
liquidity ratios 321
materiality 317
net margin 327
percentage analysis 318
plant assets to long-term liabilities 326
price-earnings ratio 330
profitability ratios 331
quick ratio 322
ratio analysis 321
return on equity 328
return on investment 328
solvency ratios 324
times interest earned 325
trend analysis 317
vertical analysis 319
working capital 321
working capital ratio 322

QUESTIONS

1. Why are ratios and trends used in financial analysis?
2. What do the terms *liquidity* and *solvency* mean?
3. What is apparent from a horizontal presentation of financial statement information? A vertical presentation?
4. What is the significance of inventory turnover, and how is it calculated?
5. What is the difference between the current ratio and the quick ratio? What does each measure?
6. Why are absolute amounts of limited use when comparing companies?
7. What is the difference between return on investment and return on equity?
8. Which ratios are used to measure long-term debt-paying ability? How is each calculated?

9. What are some limitations of the earnings per share figure?
10. What is the formula for calculating return on investment (ROI)?
11. What is information overload?
12. What is the price-earnings ratio? Explain the difference between it and the dividend yield.
13. What environmental factors must be considered in analyzing companies?
14. How do accounting principles affect financial statement analysis?

EXERCISES

All Exercises are available with McGraw-Hill's Homework Manager.

L.O. 4

Exercise 9-1 *Inventory turnover*

Selected financial information for Wingo Company for 2007 follows.

Sales	$120,000
Cost of Goods Sold	88,000
Merchandise Inventory	
Beginning of Year	10,000
End of Year	24,000

Required

Assuming that the merchandise inventory buildup was relatively constant, how many times did the merchandise inventory turn over during 2007?

L.O. 5

Exercise 9-2 *Times interest earned*

The following data come from the financial records of Cowser Corporation for 2005.

Sales	$135,000
Interest Expense	4,500
Income Tax Expense	22,500
Net Income	30,000

Required

How many times was interest earned in 2005?

L.O. 4

Exercise 9-3 *Current ratio*

Moran Corporation wrote off a $1,000 uncollectible account receivable against the $8,500 balance in its allowance account.

Required

Explain the effect of the write-off on Moran's current ratio.

L.O. 4

Exercise 9-4 *Working capital and current ratio*

On June 30, 2006, Victor Company's total current assets were $160,000 and its total current liabilities were $100,000. On July 1, 2006, Victor issued a short-term note to a bank for $25,000 cash.

Required

a. Compute Victor's working capital before and after issuing the note.
b. Compute Victor's current ratio before and after issuing the note.

L.O. 4

Exercise 9-5 *Working capital and current ratio*

On June 30, 2006, Victor Company's total current assets were $160,000 and its total current liabilities were $100,000. On July 1, 2006, Victor issued a long-term note to a bank for $25,000 cash.

Required

a. Compute Victor's working capital before and after issuing the note.

b. Compute Victor's current ratio before and after issuing the note.

Exercise 9-6 *Horizontal analysis*

L.O. 2

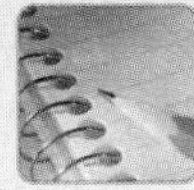

Fredrick Corporation reported the following operating results for two consecutive years.

	2005	2004	Percentage Change
Sales	$1,250,000	$1,000,000	
Cost of Goods Sold	750,000	600,000	
Gross Margin	500,000	400,000	
Operating Expenses	300,000	200,000	
Income before Taxes	200,000	200,000	
Income Taxes	61,000	53,000	
Net Income	$ 139,000	$ 147,000	

Required

a. Compute the percentage changes in Fredrick Corporation's income statement components between the two years.

b. Comment on apparent trends disclosed by the percentage changes computed in Requirement *a*.

Exercise 9-7 *Vertical analysis*

L.O. 2

Sanchez Company reported the following operating results for two consecutive years.

2004	Amount	Percent of Sales
Sales	$500,000	
Cost of Goods Sold	320,000	
Gross Margin	180,000	
Operating Expenses	100,000	
Income before Taxes	80,000	
Income Taxes	24,000	
Net Income	$ 56,000	
2005	**Amount**	**Percent of Sales**
Sales	$480,000	
Cost of Goods Sold	307,000	
Gross Margin	173,000	
Operating Expenses	120,000	
Income before Taxes	53,000	
Income Taxes	16,000	
Net Income	$ 37,000	

Required

Express each income statement component for each of the two years as a percent of sales.

Exercise 9-8 *Ratio analysis*

L.O. 2

Balance sheet data for Embry Corporation follow.

Current Assets	$ 750,000
Long-Term Assets (net)	4,250,000
Total Assets	$5,000,000
Current Liabilities	$ 420,000
Long-Term Liabilities	2,460,000
Total Liabilities	2,880,000
Common Stock and Retained Earnings	2,120,000
Total Liabilities and Stockholders' Equity	$5,000,000

Required

Compute the following:

Working capital	________
Current ratio	________
Debt to assets ratio	________
Debt to equity ratio	________

L.O. 7

Exercise 9-9 *Ratio analysis*

For 2006, Ethridge Corporation reported after-tax net income of $3,600,000. During the year, the number of shares of stock outstanding remained constant at 10,000 of $100 par, 9 percent preferred stock and 400,000 shares of common stock. The company's total stockholders' equity was $20,000,000 at December 31, 2006. Ethridge Corporation's common stock was selling at $52 per share at the end of its fiscal year. All dividends for the year had been paid, including $4.80 per share to common stockholders.

Required

Compute the following:

a. Earnings per share
b. Book value per share of common stock
c. Price-earnings ratio
d. Dividend yield

L.O. 2, 3, 4, 5, 6, 7

Exercise 9-10 *Ratio analysis*

Required

Match each of the following ratios with the formula used to compute it.

________	**1.** Working capital	**a.** Net income ÷ Average total stockholders' equity
________	**2.** Current ratio	**b.** Cost of goods sold ÷ Average inventory
________	**3.** Quick ratio	**c.** Current assets − Current liabilities
________	**4.** Accounts receivable turnover	**d.** 365 ÷ Inventory turnover
________	**5.** Average number of days to collect receivables	**e.** Net income ÷ Average total assets
________	**6.** Inventory turnover	**f.** (Net income − Preferred dividends) ÷ Average outstanding common shares
________	**7.** Average number of days to sell inventory	**g.** (Current assets − Inventory − Prepaid items) ÷ Current liabilities
________	**8.** Debt to assets ratio	**h.** Total liabilities ÷ Total assets
________	**9.** Debt to equity ratio	**i.** 365 ÷ Accounts receivable turnover
________	**10.** Return on investment	**j.** Total liabilities ÷ Total stockholders' equity
________	**11.** Return on equity	**k.** Net credit sales ÷ Average net receivables
________	**12.** Earnings per share	**l.** Current assets ÷ Current liabilities

L.O. 2

Exercise 9-11 *Horizontal and vertical analysis*

Income statements for Shirley Company for 2005 and 2006 follow.

	2006	2005
Sales	$240,000	$200,000
Cost of Goods Sold	147,900	108,000
Selling Expenses	40,100	22,000
Administrative Expenses	24,000	28,000
Interest Expense	6,000	12,000
Total Expenses	218,000	170,000
Income before Taxes	22,000	30,000
Income Taxes Expense	6,000	8,000
Net Income	$ 16,000	$ 22,000

Required

a. Perform a horizontal analysis, showing the percentage change in each income statement component between 2005 and 2006.

b. Perform a vertical analysis, showing each income statement component as a percent of sales for each year.

Exercise 9-12 *Ratio analysis*

L.O. 2, 3, 4, 5, 6, 7

Compute the specified ratios using Kale Company's balance sheet at December 31, 2004.

Assets	
Cash	$ 15,000
Marketable Securities	8,000
Accounts Receivable	13,000
Inventory	11,000
Property and Equipment	170,000
Accumulated Depreciation	(12,500)
Total Assets	$204,500
Equities	
Accounts Payable	$ 8,500
Current Notes Payable	3,500
Mortgage Payable	4,500
Bonds Payable	21,500
Common Stock, $50 Par	110,000
Paid-In Capital in Excess of Par Value	4,000
Retained Earnings	52,500
Total Liabilities and Stockholders' Equity	$204,500

The average number of common stock shares outstanding during 2004 was 880 shares. Net income for the year was $15,000.

Required

Compute each of the following:

a. Current ratio
b. Earnings per share
c. Quick (acid-test) ratio
d. Return on investment
e. Return on equity
f. Debt to equity ratio

L.O. 4, 5, 6, 7

Exercise 9-13 *Comprehensive analysis*

Required

Indicate the effect of each of the following transactions on (1) the current ratio, (2) working capital, (3) stockholders' equity, (4) book value per share of common stock, (5) retained earnings. Assume that the current ratio is greater than 1.0.

a. Collected account receivable.
b. Wrote off account receivable.
c. Purchased treasury stock.
d. Purchased inventory on account.
e. Declared cash dividend.
f. Sold merchandise on account at a profit.
g. Issued stock dividend.
h. Paid account payable.
i. Sold building at a loss.

L.O. 4, 7

Exercise 9-14 *Accounts receivable turnover, inventory turnover, and net margin*

Selected data from Walker Company follow.

Balance Sheet Data As of December 31	2004	2003
Accounts Receivable	$400,000	$376,000
Allowance for Doubtful Accounts	(20,000)	(16,000)
Net Accounts Receivable	$380,000	$360,000
Inventories, Lower of Cost or Market	$480,000	$440,000

Income Statement Data For the Year Ended December 31	2004	2003
Net Credit Sales	$2,000,000	$1,760,000
Net Cash Sales	400,000	320,000
Net Sales	2,400,000	2,080,000
Cost of Goods Sold	1,600,000	1,440,000
Selling, General, & Administrative Expenses	240,000	216,000
Other Expenses	40,000	24,000
Total Operating Expenses	$1,880,000	$1,680,000

Required

Compute the following:

a. The accounts receivable turnover for 2004.
b. The inventory turnover for 2004.
c. The net margin for 2003.

L.O. 4, 5

Exercise 9-15 *Comprehensive analysis*

The December 31, 2005, balance sheet for Ivey Inc. is presented here. These are the only accounts on Ivey's balance sheet. Amounts indicated by question marks (?) can be calculated using the additional information following the balance sheet.

Assets	
Cash	$ 25,000
Accounts Receivable (net)	?
Inventory	?
Property, Plant, and Equipment (net)	294,000
	$432,000
Liabilities and Stockholders' Equity	
Accounts Payable (trade)	$?
Income Taxes Payable (current)	25,000
Long-Term Debt	?
Common Stock	300,000
Retained Earnings	?
	$?
Additional Information	
Current ratio (at year end)	1.5 to 1.0
Total liabilities ÷ Total stockholders' equity	0.8
Gross margin percent	30%
Inventory turnover (Cost of goods sold ÷ Ending inventory)	10.5 times
Gross margin for 2005	$315,000

Required

Determine the following:

a. The balance in trade accounts payable as of December 31, 2005.
b. The balance in retained earnings as of December 31, 2005.
c. The balance in the inventory account as of December 31, 2005.

PROBLEMS

All Problems are available with McGraw-Hill's Homework Manager.

Problem 9-16 *Vertical analysis*

L.O. 2

CHECK FIGURES
NI of 2006: $36,000
Total Expenses of 2005: $135,000

The following percentages apply to Walden Company for 2005 and 2006.

	2006	2005
Sales	100.0%	100.0%
Cost of Goods Sold	61.0	64.0
Gross Margin	39.0	36.0
Selling and Administrative Expenses	26.5	20.5
Interest Expense	2.5	2.0
Total Expenses	29.0	22.5
Income before Taxes	10.0	13.5
Income Tax Expense	5.5	7.0
Net Income	4.5%	6.5%

Required

Assuming that sales were $600,000 in 2005 and $800,000 in 2006, prepare income statements for the two years.

L.O. 5, 6, 7

mhhe.com/edmonds2007

CHECK FIGURES

a. 2004: 12.22 times

c. 2003: 8.5 times

Problem 9-17 *Ratio analysis*

Oxmoore Company's income statement information follows.

	2004	2003
Net Sales	$420,000	$260,000
Income before Interest and Taxes	110,000	85,000
Net Income after Taxes	55,500	63,000
Interest Expense	9,000	8,000
Stockholders' Equity, December 31 (2002: $200,000)	305,000	235,000
Common Stock, par $50, December 31	260,000	230,000

The average number of shares outstanding was 7,800 for 2004 and 6,900 for 2003.

Required

Compute the following ratios for Oxmoore for 2004 and 2003.

a. Times interest earned.
b. Earnings per share based on the average number of shares outstanding.
c. Price-earnings ratio (market prices: 2004, $64 per share; 2003, $78 per share).
d. Return on average equity.
e. Net margin.

L.O. 4

Problem 9-18 *Effect of transactions on current ratio and working capital*

Bellaire Manufacturing has a current ratio of 3:1 on December 31, 2003. Indicate whether each of the following transactions would increase (+), decrease (−), or not affect (NA) Bellaire's current ratio and its working capital.

Required

a. Paid cash for a trademark.
b. Wrote off an uncollectible account receivable.
c. Sold equipment for cash.
d. Sold merchandise at a profit (cash).
e. Declared a cash dividend.
f. Purchased inventory on account.
g. Scrapped a fully depreciated machine (no gain or loss).
h. Issued a stock dividend.
i. Purchased a machine with a long-term note.
j. Paid a previously declared cash dividend.
k. Collected accounts receivable.
l. Invested in current marketable securities.

L.O. 7

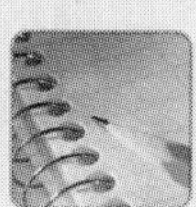

CHECK FIGURE

a. Earnings per share: $4.38

Problem 9-19 *Ratio analysis*

Selected data for Faulkner Company for 2005 and additional information on industry averages follow.

Earnings (net income)		$ 174,000
Preferred Stock (13,200 shares at $50 par, 4%)		$ 660,000
Common Stock (30,000 shares at $1 par, market value $56)		30,000
Paid-in Capital in Excess of Par Value–Common		480,000
Retained Earnings		562,500
		1,732,500
Less: Treasury Stock		
Preferred (1,200 shares)	$54,000	
Common (1,200 shares)	24,000	78,000
Total Stockholders' Equity		$1,654,500

Note: Dividends in arrears on preferred stock: $24,000. The preferred stock can be called for $51 per share.

Industry averages	
Earnings per share	$ 5.20
Price-earnings ratio	9.50
Return on equity	11.20%

Required

a. Calculate and compare Faulkner Company's ratios with the industry averages.
b. Discuss factors you would consider in deciding whether to invest in the company.

Problem 9-20 *Supply missing balance sheet numbers*

L.O. 2

The bookkeeper for Clifford's Country Music Bar went insane and left this incomplete balance sheet. Clifford's working capital is $90,000 and its debt to assets ratio is 40 percent.

CHECK FIGURES
d. $337,500
f. $97,500

Assets	
Current Assets	
Cash	$ 21,000
Accounts Receivable	42,000
Inventory	(A)
Prepaid Items	9,000
Total Current Assets	(B)
Long-Term Assets	
Building	(C)
Less: Accumulated Depreciation	(39,000)
Total Long-Term Assets	210,000
Total Assets	$ (D)
Equities	
Liabilities	
Current Liabilities	
Accounts Payable	$ (E)
Notes Payable	12,000
Income Tax Payable	10,500
Total Current Liabilities	37,500
Long-Term Liabilities	
Mortgage Payable	(F)
Total Liabilities	(G)
Stockholders' Equity	
Common Stock	105,000
Retained Earnings	(H)
Total Stockholders' Equity	(I)
Total Liabilities and Stockholders' Equity	$ (J)

Required

Complete the balance sheet by supplying the missing amounts.

Problem 9-21 *Ratio analysis*

L.O. 2, 3, 4, 5, 6, 7

mhhe.com/edmonds2007

The following financial statements apply to Maronge Company.

CHECK FIGURES
d. 2005: $0.72
k. 2004: 5.47 times

	2005	2004
Revenues		
Net Sales	$210,000	$175,000
Other Revenues	4,000	5,000
Total Revenues	214,000	180,000

continued

	2005	2004
Expenses		
Cost of Goods Sold	126,000	103,000
Selling Expenses	21,000	19,000
General and Administrative Expenses	11,000	10,000
Interest Expense	3,000	3,000
Income Tax Expense	21,000	18,000
Total Expenses	182,000	153,000
Earnings from Continuing Operations before Extraordinary Items	32,000	27,000
Extraordinary Gain (net of $3,000 tax)	4,000	0
Net Earnings	$ 36,000	$ 27,000
Assets		
Current Assets		
Cash	$ 4,000	$ 8,000
Marketable Securities	1,000	1,000
Accounts Receivable	35,000	32,000
Inventories	100,000	96,000
Prepaid Items	3,000	2,000
Total Current Assets	143,000	139,000
Plant and Equipment (net)	105,000	105,000
Intangibles	20,000	0
Total Assets	$268,000	$244,000
Equities		
Liabilities		
Current Liabilities		
Accounts Payable	$ 40,000	$ 54,000
Other	17,000	15,000
Total Current Liabilities	57,000	69,000
Bonds Payable	66,000	67,000
Total Liabilities	123,000	136,000
Stockholders' Equity		
Common Stock ($2 par)	100,000	100,000
Paid-In Capital in Excess of Par Value	15,000	15,000
Retained Earnings	30,000	(7,000)
Total Stockholders' Equity	145,000	108,000
Total Liabilities and Stockholders' Equity	$268,000	$244,000

Required

Calculate the following ratios for 2004 and 2005. When data limitations prohibit computing averages, use year-end balances in your calculations.

a. Net margin
b. Return on investment
c. Return on equity
d. Earnings per share
e. Price-earnings ratio (market prices at the end of 2004 and 2005 were $5.94 and $4.77, respectively)
f. Book value per share of common stock
g. Times interest earned
h. Working capital
i. Current ratio
j. Quick (acid-test) ratio
k. Accounts receivable turnover
l. Inventory turnover
m. Debt to equity ratio
n. Debt to assets ratio

Problem 9-22 *Horizontal analysis*

L.O. 2

CHECK FIGURES
Total Assets: +11.6%
Total Liabilities: +14.4%

Financial statements for Pocca Company follow.

POCCA COMPANY
Balance Sheets
As of December 31

	2006	2005
Assets		
Current Assets		
Cash	$ 16,000	$ 12,000
Marketable Securities	20,000	6,000
Accounts Receivable (net)	54,000	46,000
Inventories	135,000	143,000
Prepaid Items	25,000	10,000
Total Current Assets	250,000	217,000
Investments	27,000	20,000
Plant (net)	270,000	255,000
Land	29,000	24,000
Total Assets	$576,000	$516,000
Equities		
Liabilities		
Current Liabilities		
Notes Payable	$ 17,000	$ 6,000
Accounts Payable	113,800	100,000
Salaries Payable	21,000	15,000
Total Current Liabilities	151,800	121,000
Noncurrent Liabilities		
Bonds Payable	100,000	100,000
Other	32,000	27,000
Total Noncurrent Liabilities	132,000	127,000
Total Liabilities	283,800	248,000
Stockholders' Equity		
Preferred Stock, par value $10, 4% cumulative, non-participating; 7,000 shares authorized and issued; no dividends in arrears	70,000	70,000
Common Stock, $5 par value; 50,000 shares authorized; 10,000 shares issued	50,000	50,000
Paid-In Capital in excess of par value–Preferred	10,000	10,000
Paid-In Capital in excess of par value–Common	30,000	30,000
Retained Earnings	132,200	108,000
Total Stockholders' Equity	292,200	268,000
Total Liabilities and Stockholders' Equity	$576,000	$516,000

POCCA COMPANY
Statements of Income and Retained Earnings
For the Years Ended December 31

	2006	2005
Revenues		
Sales (net)	$230,000	$210,000
Other Revenues	8,000	5,000
Total Revenues	238,000	215,000

continued

	2006	2005
Expenses		
Cost of Goods Sold	120,000	103,000
Selling, General, and Administrative Expenses	55,000	50,000
Interest Expense	8,000	7,200
Income Tax Expense	23,000	22,000
Total Expenses	206,000	182,200
Net Earnings (Net Income)	32,000	32,800
Retained Earnings, January 1	108,000	83,000
Less: Preferred Stock Dividends	2,800	2,800
Common Stock Dividends	5,000	5,000
Retained Earnings, December 31	$132,200	$108,000

Required

Prepare a horizontal analysis of both the balance sheet and income statement.

L.O. 2, 3, 4, 5, 6, 7

mhhe.com/edmonds2007

CHECK FIGURES

k. 2006: 2.05:1

p. 2005: $3.00

Problem 9-23 *Ratio analysis*

Required

Use the financial statements for Pocca Company from Problem 9-22 to calculate the following ratios for 2006 and 2005.

a. Working capital
b. Current ratio
c. Quick ratio
d. Accounts receivable turnover (beginning receivables at January 1, 2005, were $47,000)
e. Average number of days to collect accounts receivable
f. Inventory turnover (beginning inventory at January 1, 2005, was $140,000)
g. Average number of days to sell inventory
h. Debt to assets ratio
i. Debt to equity ratio
j. Times interest earned
k. Plant assets to long-term debt
l. Net margin
m. Asset turnover
n. Return on investment
o. Return on equity
p. Earnings per share
q. Book value per share of common stock
r. Price-earnings ratio (market price per share: 2005, $11.75; 2006, $12.50)
s. Dividend yield on common stock

L.O. 2

mhhe.com/edmonds2007

CHECK FIGURE

2006 Retained Earnings: 23%

Problem 9-24 *Vertical analysis*

Required

Use the financial statements for Pocca Company from Problem 9-22 to perform a vertical analysis of both the balance sheets and income statements for 2006 and 2005.

ANALYZE, THINK, COMMUNICATE

ATC 9-1 Business Applications Case *Analyzing Best Buy Company and Circuit City Stores*

The following information relates to Best Buy and Circuit City Stores, Inc., for their 2003 and 2002 fiscal years.

BEST BUY CO., INC.
Selected Financial Information
(Amounts in millions, except per share amounts)

	March 1, 2003	March 2, 2002
Total current assets	$ 4,867	$ 4,600
Merchandise inventories	2,046	1,875
Property and equipment, net of depreciation	2,062	1,661
Total assets	7,663	7,367
Total current liabilities	3,793	3,705
Total long-term liabilities	1,140	1,141
Total liabilities	4,933	4,846
Total shareholders' equity	2,730	2,521
Total liabilities and shareholders' equity	7,663	7,367
Revenue	20,946	17,711
Cost of goods sold	15,710	13,941
Gross profit	5,236	3,770
Operating income	1,010	908
Interest expense	30	21
Earnings from continuing operations before income tax expense	1,014	926
Income tax expense	392	356
Earnings from continuing operations	622	570
Net earnings	99	570
Basic earnings per share	$ 0.31	$ 1.80

CIRCUIT CITY STORES, INC.
Selected Financial Information
(Amounts in millions except per share data)

	February 28, 2003	February 28, 2002
Total current assets	$3,103	$3,653
Merchandise inventory	1,410	1,234
Property and equipment, net of depreciation	650	733
Total assets	3,799	4,542
Total current liabilities	1,280	1,641
Total long-term liabilities	178	167
Total liabilities	1,458	1,808
Total stockholders' equity	2,342	2,734
Revenues	9,954	9,518
Cost of sales, buying and warehousing	7,603	7,180
Gross profit	2,350	2,328
Interest expense	1	1
Earnings from continuing operations before income taxes	67	206
Provision for income taxes	25	78
Earnings from continuing operations	42	128
Net earnings	106	219
Basic earnings per share:		
Continuing operations	$ 0.20	$ 0.62

Required

a. Compute the following ratios for the companies' 2003 fiscal years:
   (1) Current ratio.
   (2) Average number of days to sell inventory. (Use average inventory.)
   (3) Debt to assets ratio.
   (4) Return on investment. (Use average assets and use "earnings from continuing operations" rather than "net earnings.")
   (5) Gross margin percentage.
   (6) Asset turnover. (Use average assets.)
   (7) Return on sales. (Use "earnings from continuing operations" rather than "net earnings.")
   (8) Plant assets to long-term debt ratio.
b. Which company appears to be more profitable? Explain your answer and identify which of the ratio(s) from Requirement *a* you used to reach your conclusion.
c. Which company appears to have the higher level of financial risk? Explain your answer and identify which of the ratio(s) from Requirement *a* you used to reach your conclusion.
d. Which company appears to be charging higher prices for its goods? Explain your answer and identify which of the ratio(s) from Requirement *a* you used to reach your conclusion.
e. Which company appears to be the more efficient at using its assets? Explain your answer and identify which of the ratio(s) from Requirement *a* you used to reach your conclusion.

ATC 9-2 Group Assignment *Ratio analysis and logic*

Presented here are selected data from the 10-K reports of four companies for the 1997 fiscal year. The four companies, in alphabetical order, are

1. **BellSouth Corporation**, a telephone company that operates in the southeastern United States.
2. **Caterpillar, Inc.**, a manufacturer of heavy machinery.
3. **Dollar General Corporation**, a company that owns Dollar General Stores discount stores.
4. **Tiffany & Company**, a company that operates high-end jewelry stores.

The data, presented in the order of the amount of sales, are as follows. Dollar amounts are in millions.

	A	B	C	D
Sales	$20,561	$18,110	$2,627.3	$1,017.6
Cost of goods sold	6,254	13,374	1,885.2	453.4
Net earnings	3,261	1,665	144.6	72.8
Inventory or NA	2,603	632.0	386.4	
Materials and supplies	398	NA	NA	NA
Accounts receivable	4,750	3,331	0	99.5
Total assets	36,301	20,756	914.8	827.1

Required

a. Divide the class into groups of four or five students per group and then organize the groups into four sections. Assign Task 1 to the first section of groups, Task 2 to the second section, Task 3 to the third section, and Task 4 to the fourth section.

Group Tasks

(1) Assume that you represent BellSouth Corporation. Identify the set of financial data (Column A, B, C, or D) that relates to your company.
(2) Assume that you represent Caterpillar, Inc. Identify the set of financial data (Column A, B, C, or D) that relates to your company.
(3) Assume that you represent Dollar General Corporation. Identify the set of financial data (Column A, B, C, or D) that relates to your company.
(4) Assume that you represent Tiffany & Company. Identify the set of financial data (Column A, B, C, or D) that relates to your company.

Hint: Use a gross margin ratio (gross margin ÷ sales), a net margin ratio (net income ÷ sales), and return on assets (net income ÷ total assets) to facilitate identifying the financial data related to your particular company.

b. Select a representative from each section. Have the representatives explain the rationale for the group's selection. The explanation should include a set of ratios that support the group's conclusion.

ATC 9-3 Research Assignment *Financial analysis information in Dell's annual report*

Dell, Inc., uses its SEC Form 10-K as its official annual report. The company also produces a "Year in Review" summary, which it refers to as an annual report, but that document does not provide sufficient detail to answer the following questions. Using the most current Forms 10-K for Dell, Inc., complete the requirements below. To find the Forms 10-K use either the SEC EDGAR system following the instructions in Appendix A, or the company's website.

Required

a. Find the Management's Discussion and Analysis section (MD&A) of Dell's 10-K. In the first subsection of the MD&A, "Overview," a table summarizes Dell's results of operations for the past three years. Does this table present information in a horizontal or a vertical format?

b. Using the table identified in Requirement *a*, explain how Dell's net income changed over the past three years in absolute amounts and in percentages.

c. Which reflected the greater percentage change, revenue, or net income?

d. Near the middle of the MD&A section there is a subsection called "Liquidity, Capital Commitments, and Contractual Cash Obligations." The second table in this subsection presents data for three items related to Dell's "Cash conversion cycle." Identify these three items and explain what the data related to them tell the reader.

Note: The directions for finding Dell's 10-K were accurate for 2004 and several prior fiscal years. The company may have moved this information in later reports.

ATC 9-4 Writing Assignment *Interpreting ratios*

Following are the debt to assets, return on assets, and return on equity ratios for four companies from two different industries. The range of interest rates each company was paying on its long-term debt is provided. Each of these public companies is a leader in its particular industry, and the data are for the fiscal years ending in 1997. All numbers are percentages.

	Debt to Assets*	Return on Assets	Return on Equity	Interest Rates
Banking Industry				
Wachovia Corporation	92	1.0	11.5	5.7-7.0
Wells Fargo & Co.	87	1.2	9.0	6.1-11.0
Home Construction Industry				
Pulte Corporation	62	2.5	6.5	7.0-10.1
Toll Brothers, Inc.	66	5.8	16.9	7.8-10.5

*Debt to assets ratio is defined as total liabilities divided by total assets.

Required

a. Based only on the debt to assets ratios, the banking companies appear to have the most financial risk. Generally, companies that have more financial risk are charged higher interest rates. Write a brief explanation of why the banking companies can borrow money at lower interest rates than the construction companies.

b. Explain why the return on equity ratio for Wachovia is more than 10 times higher than its return on assets ratio, and Pulte's return on equity ratio is less than 3 times higher than its return on assets ratio.

ATC 9-5 Ethical Dilemma *Making the ratios look good*

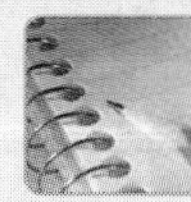

J. Talbot is the accounting manager for Kolla Waste Disposal Corporation. Kolla is having its worst financial year since its inception. The company is expected to report a net loss. In the midst of such bad news, Ms. Talbot surprised the company president, Mr. Winston, by suggesting that the company write off approximately 25 percent of its garbage trucks. Mr. Winston responded by noting that the trucks could still be operated for another two or three years. Ms. Talbot replied, "We may use them for two or three more years, but you couldn't sell them on the street if you had to. Who wants to buy a bunch of old garbage trucks and besides, it will make next year's financials so sweet. No one will care about the additional write-off this year. We are already showing a loss. Who will care if we lose a little bit more?"

Required

a. How will the write-off affect the following year's return on assets ratio?

b. How will the write-off affect the asset and income growth percentages?

c. Would writing off the garbage trucks for the reasons stated present any ethical concerns for Kolla? Explain.

Comprehensive financial statements analysis projects are available at www.mhhe.com/edmonds/survey.

CHAPTER 10

Management Accounting: A Value-Added Discipline

LEARNING OBJECTIVES

After you have mastered the material in this chapter you will be able to:

1. Distinguish between managerial and financial accounting.
2. Identify the cost components of a product made by a manufacturing company: the cost of materials, labor, and overhead.
3. Explain the need for determining the average cost per unit of a product.
4. Distinguish between a cost and an expense.
5. Explain the effects on financial statements of product costs versus general, selling, and administrative costs.
6. Explain how cost classification affects financial statements and managerial decisions.
7. Identify the standards of ethical conduct and the features that motivate misconduct.
8. Distinguish product costs from upstream and downstream costs.
9. Explain how products provided by service companies differ from products made by manufacturing companies.
10. Explain how emerging trends such as activity-based management, value-added assessment, and just-in-time inventory are affecting the managerial accounting discipline.

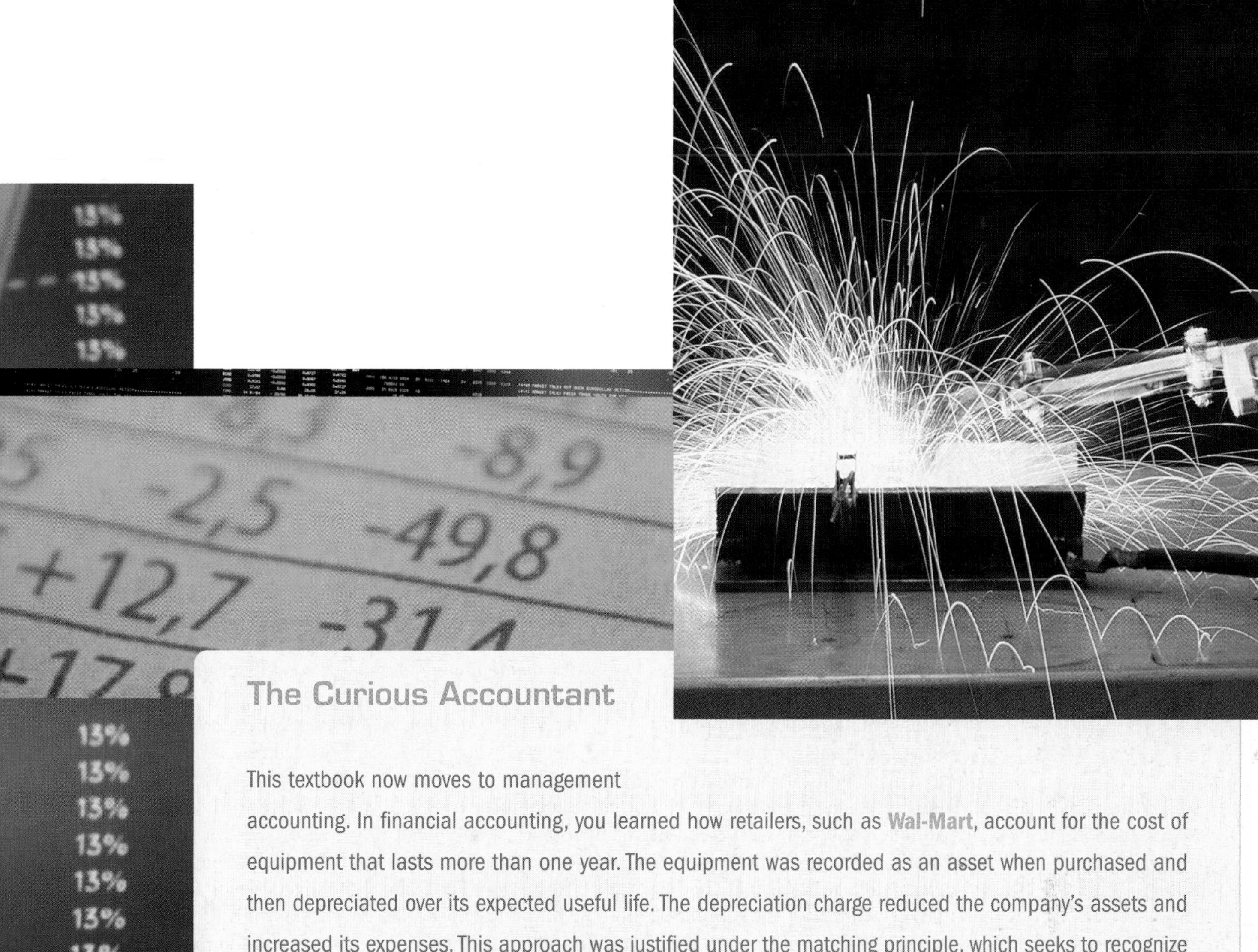

Chapter 10

The Curious Accountant

This textbook now moves to management accounting. In financial accounting, you learned how retailers, such as **Wal-Mart**, account for the cost of equipment that lasts more than one year. The equipment was recorded as an asset when purchased and then depreciated over its expected useful life. The depreciation charge reduced the company's assets and increased its expenses. This approach was justified under the matching principle, which seeks to recognize costs as expenses in the same period that the costs (resources) generate revenue.

In management accounting, the focus will often be on manufacturing entities. Consider the following scenario. **Black & Decker** manufactures cordless hedge trimmers that it sells to Wal-Mart. In order to produce the hedge trimmers, Black & Decker purchased a robotic machine that it expects can be used to produce 1 million hedge trimmers.

Should Black & Decker account for depreciation of its manufacturing equipment the same way Wal-Mart accounts for depreciation of its registers at the checkout counters? If not, how should Black & Decker account for its depreciation? Consider the matching principle when thinking of your answer. (Answers on page 370.)

CHAPTER OPENING

Andy Grove, president and CEO of ***Intel Corporation****, is credited with the motto "Only the paranoid survive." Mr. Grove describes a wide variety of concerns that make him paranoid. He declares:*

> *I worry about products getting screwed up, and I worry about products getting introduced prematurely. I worry about factories not performing well, and I worry about having too many factories. I worry about hiring the right people, and I worry about morale slacking off. And, of course, I worry about competitors. I worry*

about other people figuring out how to do what we do better or cheaper, and displacing us with our customers.

Do Intel's historically based financial statements contain the information Mr. Grove needs? No. **Financial accounting** *is not designed to satisfy all the information needs of business managers. Its scope is limited to the needs of external users such as investors and creditors. The field of accounting designed to meet the needs of internal users is called* **managerial accounting.** ■

Differences between Managerial and Financial Accounting

Distinguish between managerial and financial accounting.

Although the information needs of internal and external users overlap, the needs of managers differ from those of investors or creditors. Some distinguishing characteristics are discussed in the following section.

Users and Types of Information

Financial accounting provides information used primarily by investors, creditors, and others *outside* a business. In contrast, managerial accounting focuses on information used by executives, managers, and employees who work *inside* the business. These two user groups need different types of information.

Internal users need information to *plan*, *direct*, and *control* business operations. The nature of information needed is related to an employee's job level. Lower level employees use nonfinancial information such as work schedules, store hours, and customer service policies. Moving up the organizational ladder, financial information becomes increasingly important. Middle managers use a blend of financial and nonfinancial information. Senior executives concentrate on financial data. To a lesser degree, senior executives also use general economic data and nonfinancial operating information. For example, an executive may consider the growth rate of the economy before deciding to expand the company's workforce.

External users (investors and creditors) have greater needs for general economic information than do internal users. For example, an investor debating whether to purchase stock versus bond securities might be more interested in government tax policy than financial statement data. Exhibit 10.1 summarizes the information needs of different user groups.

Level of Aggregation

External users desire *global information* that reflects the performance of a company as a whole. For example, an investor is not so much interested in the performance of a particular Sears store as she is in the performance of Sears Roebuck Company versus that of JCPenney Company. In contrast, internal users focus on detailed information about specific subunits of the company. To meet the needs of the different user groups financial accounting data are more aggregated than managerial accounting data.

Regulation

Financial accounting is designed to generate information for the general public. In an effort to protect the public interest, Congress established the **Securities and Exchange Commission (SEC)** and gave it authority to regulate public financial reporting practices. The SEC has delegated much of its authority for developing accounting rules to the

EXHIBIT 10.1

Relationship between Type of User and Type of Information

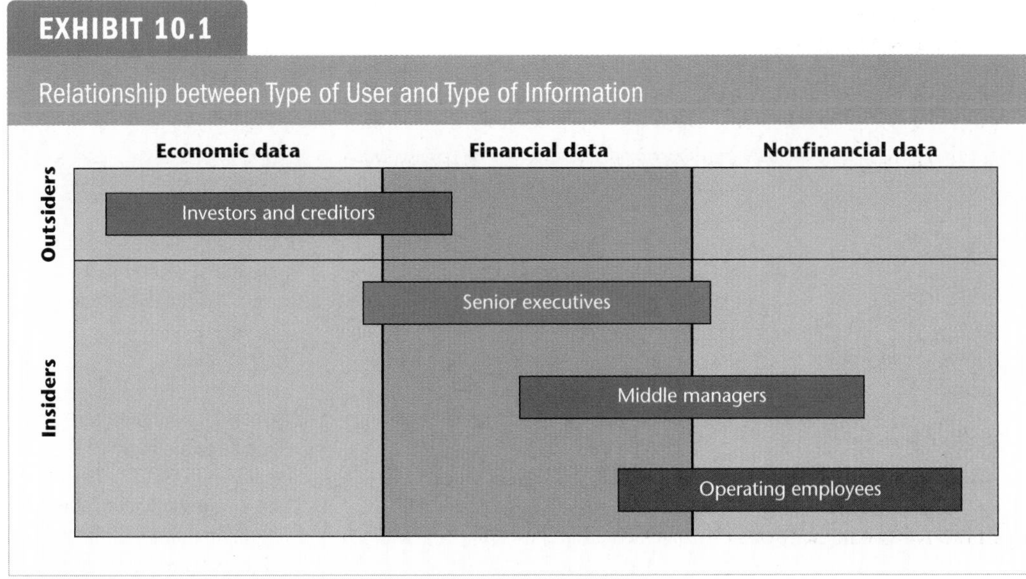

private sector **Financial Accounting Standards Board (FASB),** thereby allowing the accounting profession considerable influence over financial accounting reports. The FASB supports the broad base of pronouncements and practices known as **generally accepted accounting principles (GAAP).** GAAP severely restricts the accounting procedures and practices permitted in published financial statements.

Around the turn of the century, a number of high-profile business failures raised questions about the effectiveness of self-regulation and the usefulness of audits to protect the public. The **Sarbanes-Oxley Act of 2002** was adopted to address these concerns. The act creates a five-member Public Company Accounting Oversight Board (PCAOB) with the authority to set and enforce auditing, attestation, quality control, and ethics standards for auditors of public companies. The PCAOB is empowered to impose disciplinary and remedial sanctions for violations of its rules, securities laws, and professional auditing and accounting standards.

Beyond financial statement data, much of the information generated by management accounting systems is proprietary information not available to the public. Since this information is not distributed to the public, it need not be regulated to protect the public interest. Management accounting is restricted only by the **value-added principle**. Management accountants are free to engage in any information gathering and reporting activity so long as the activity adds value in excess of its cost. For example, management accountants are free to provide forecasted information to internal users. In contrast, financial accounting as prescribed by GAAP does not permit forecasting.

Information Characteristics

While financial accounting is characterized by its objectivity, reliability, consistency, and historical nature, managerial accounting is concerned with relevance and timeliness. Managerial accounting uses more estimates and fewer facts than financial accounting. Financial accounting reports what happened yesterday; managerial accounting reports what is expected to happen tomorrow.

Time Horizon and Reporting Frequency

Financial accounting information is reported periodically, normally at the end of a year. Management cannot wait until the end of the year to discover problems. Planning, controlling, and directing require immediate attention. Managerial accounting information is delivered on a continual basis.

EXHIBIT 10.2

Comparative Features of Managerial versus Financial Accounting Information

Features	Managerial Accounting	Financial Accounting
Users	Insiders including executives, managers, and operators	Outsiders including investors, creditors, government agencies, analysts, and reporters
Information type	Economic and physical data as well as financial data	Financial data
Level of aggregation	Local information on subunits of the organization	Global information on the company as a whole
Regulation	No regulation, limited only by the value-added principle	Regulation by SEC, FASB, and other determinors of GAAP
Information characteristics	Estimates that promote relevance and enable timeliness	Factual information that is characterized by objectivity, reliability, consistency, and accuracy
Time horizon	Past, present, and future	Past only, historically based
Reporting frequency	Continuous reporting	Delayed with emphasis on annual reports

Exhibit 10.2 summarizes significant differences between financial and managerial accounting.

Product Costing

Identify the cost components of a product made by a manufacturing company: the cost of materials, labor, and overhead.

A major focus for managerial accountants is determining **product cost.**[1] Managers need to know the cost of their products for a variety of reasons. For example, **cost-plus pricing** is a common business practice.[2] **Product costing** is also used to control business operations. It is useful in answering questions such as: Are costs higher or lower than expected? Who is responsible for the variances between expected and actual costs? What action can be taken to control the variances?

Product Costs in Manufacturing Companies

The cost of making products includes the cost of materials, labor, and other resources (usually called **overhead**). To understand how these costs affect financial statements, consider the example of Tabor Manufacturing Company.

Tabor Manufacturing Company

Tabor Manufacturing Company makes wooden tables. The company spent $1,000 cash to build four tables: $390 for materials, $470 for a carpenter's labor, and $140 for tools used in making the tables. How much is Tabor's expense? The answer is zero. The $1,000 cash has been converted into products (four tables). The cash payments for materials, labor, and tools were *asset exchange* transactions. One asset (cash) decreased while another asset (tables) increased. Tabor will not recognize any expense until the tables are sold; in the meantime, the cost of the tables is held in an asset account called **Finished Goods Inventory.** Exhibit 10.3 illustrates how cash is transformed into inventory.

[1]This text uses the term *product* in a generic sense to mean both goods and services.

[2]Other pricing strategies will be introduced in subsequent chapters.

EXHIBIT 10.3

Transforming the Asset Cash into the Asset Finished Goods Inventory

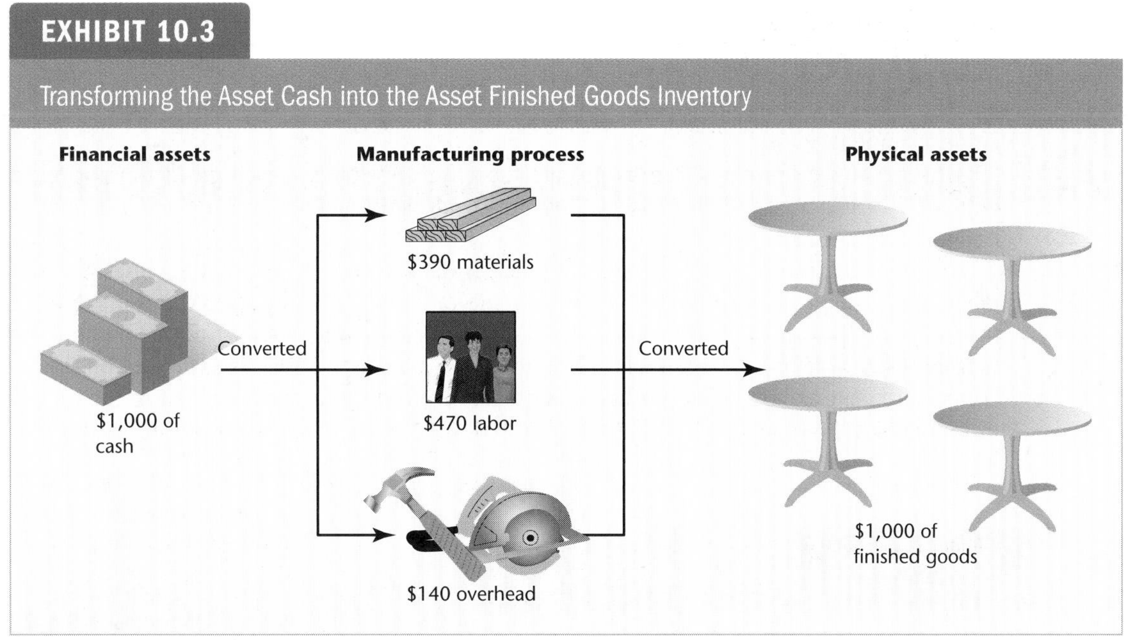

Average Cost per Unit

Explain the need for determining the average cost per unit of a product.

How much did each table made by Tabor cost? The actual cost of each of the four tables likely differs. The carpenter probably spent a little more time on some of the tables than others. Material and tool usage probably varied from table to table. Determining the exact cost of each table is virtually impossible. Minute details such as a second of labor time cannot be effectively measured. Even if Tabor could determine the exact cost of each table, the information would be of little use. Minor differences in the cost per table would make no difference in pricing or other decisions management needs to make. Accountants therefore normally calculate cost per unit as an *average.* In the case of Tabor Manufacturing, the **average cost** per table is $250 ($1,000 ÷ 4 units). Unless otherwise stated, assume *cost per unit* means *average cost per unit.*

CHECK YOURSELF 10.1

All boxes of General Mills' Total Raisin Bran cereal are priced at exactly the same amount in your local grocery store. Does this mean that the actual cost of making each box of cereal was exactly the same?

Answer

No, making each box would not cost exactly the same amount. For example, some boxes contain slightly more or less cereal than other boxes. Accordingly, some boxes cost slightly more or less to make than others do. General Mills uses average cost rather than actual cost to develop its pricing strategy.

Costs Can Be Assets or Expenses

Distinguish between a cost and an expense.

It might seem odd that wages earned by production workers are recorded as inventory instead of being expensed. Remember, however, that expenses are assets used in the process of *earning revenue*. The cash paid to production workers is not used to produce revenue. Instead, the cash is used to produce inventory. Revenue will be earned when the inventory is used (sold). So long as the inventory remains on hand, all product costs (materials, labor, and overhead) remain in an inventory account.

When a table is sold, the average cost of the table is transferred from the Inventory account to the Cost of Goods Sold (expense) account. If some tables remain unsold at the end of the accounting period, part of the *product cost* is reported as an asset (inventory) on the balance sheet while the other part is reported as an expense (cost of goods sold) on the income statement.

Costs that are not classified as product costs are normally expensed in the period in which they are incurred. These costs include *general operating costs, selling and administrative costs, interest costs*, and the *cost of income taxes*.

To illustrate, return to the Tabor Manufacturing example. Recall that Tabor made four tables at an average cost per unit of $250. Assume Tabor pays an employee who sells three of the tables a $200 sales commission. The sales commission is expensed immediately. The total product cost for the three tables (3 tables × $250 each = $750) is expensed on the income statement as cost of goods sold. The portion of the total product cost remaining in inventory is $250 (one table × $250). Exhibit 10.4 shows the relationship between the costs incurred and the expenses recognized for Tabor Manufacturing Company.

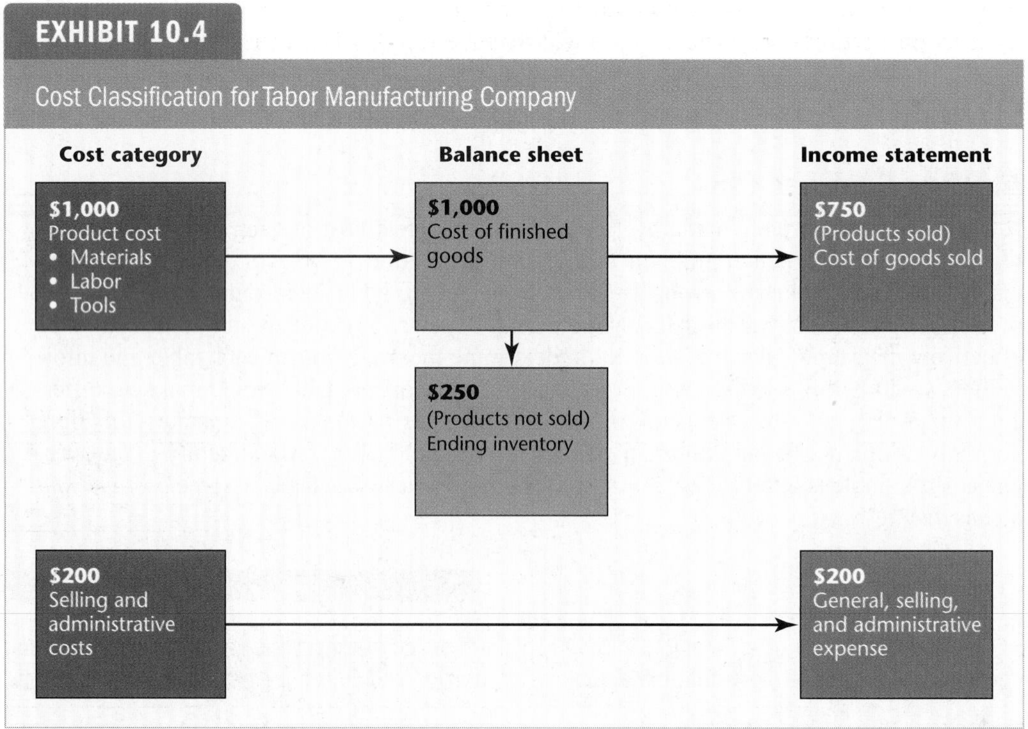

Explain the effects on financial statements of product costs versus general, selling, and administrative costs.

Effect of Product Costs on Financial Statements

We illustrate accounting for product costs in manufacturing companies with Patillo Manufacturing Company, a producer of ceramic pottery. Patillo, started on January 1, 2004, experienced the following accounting events during its first year of operations.[3] *Assume that all transactions except 6, 8, and 10 are cash transactions.*

1. Acquired $15,000 cash by issuing common stock.
2. Paid $2,000 for materials that were used to make products. All products started were completed during the period.

[3]This illustration assumes that all inventory started during the period was completed during the period. Patillo therefore uses only one inventory account, Finished Goods Inventory. Many manufacturing companies normally have three categories of inventory on hand at the end of an accounting period: Raw Materials Inventory, Work in Process Inventory (inventory of partially completed units), and Finished Goods Inventory.

3. Paid $1,200 for salaries of selling and administrative employees.
4. Paid $3,000 for wages of production workers.
5. Paid $2,800 for furniture used in selling and administrative offices.
6. Recognized depreciation on the office furniture purchased in Event 5. The furniture was acquired on January 1, had a $400 estimated salvage value, and a four-year useful life. The annual depreciation charge is $600 [($2,800 − $400) ÷ 4].
7. Paid $4,500 for manufacturing equipment.
8. Recognized depreciation on the equipment purchased in Event 7. The equipment was acquired on January 1, had a $1,500 estimated salvage value, and a three-year useful life. The annual depreciation charge is $1,000 [($4,500 − $1,500) ÷ 3].
9. Sold inventory to customers for $7,500 cash.
10. The inventory sold in Event 9 cost $4,000 to make.

The effects of these transactions on the balance sheet, income statement, and statement of cash flows are shown in Exhibit 10.5. Study each row in this exhibit, paying particular attention to how similar costs such as salaries for selling and administrative personnel and wages for production workers have radically different effects on the financial statements. The example illustrates the three elements of product costs, materials (Event 2), labor (Event 4), and overhead (Event 8). These events are discussed in more detail below.

EXHIBIT 10.5

Effect of Product versus Selling and Administrative Costs on Financial Statements

	Assets								Equity									
Event No.	Cash	+	Inventory	+	Office Furn.*	+	Manuf. Equip.*	=	Com. Stk.	+	Ret. Earn.	Rev.	−	Exp.	=	Net Inc.	Cash Flow	
1	15,000							=	15,000								15,000	FA
2	(2,000)	+	2,000														(2,000)	OA
3	(1,200)							=			(1,200)		−	1,200	=	(1,200)	(1,200)	OA
4	(3,000)	+	3,000														(3,000)	OA
5	(2,800)	+			2,800												(2,800)	IA
6					(600)			=			(600)		−	600	=	(600)		
7	(4,500)	+					4,500										(4,500)	IA
8			1,000	+			(1,000)											
9	7,500							=			7,500	7,500			=	7,500	7,500	OA
10			(4,000)					=			(4,000)		−	4,000	=	(4,000)		
Totals	9,000	+	2,000	+	2,200	+	3,500	=	15,000	+	1,700	7,500	−	5,800	=	1,700	9,000	NC

*Negative amounts in these columns represent accumulated depreciation.

Materials Costs (Event 2)

Materials used to make products are usually called **raw materials**. The cost of raw materials is first recorded in an asset account (Inventory). The cost is then transferred from the Inventory account to the Cost of Goods Sold account at the time the goods are sold. Remember that materials cost is only one component of total manufacturing costs. When inventory is sold, the combined cost of materials, labor, and overhead is expensed as *cost of goods sold*. The costs of materials that can be easily and conveniently traced to products are called **direct raw materials** costs.

Labor Costs (Event 4)

The salaries paid to selling and administrative employees (Event 3) and the wages paid to production workers (Event 4) are accounted for differently. Salaries paid to selling and administrative employees are expensed immediately, but the cost of production wages is added to inventory. Production wages are expensed as part of cost of goods sold at the time the inventory is sold. Labor costs that can be easily and conveniently traced to products are called **direct labor** costs. The cost flow of wages for production employees versus salaries for selling and administrative personnel is shown in Exhibit 10.6.

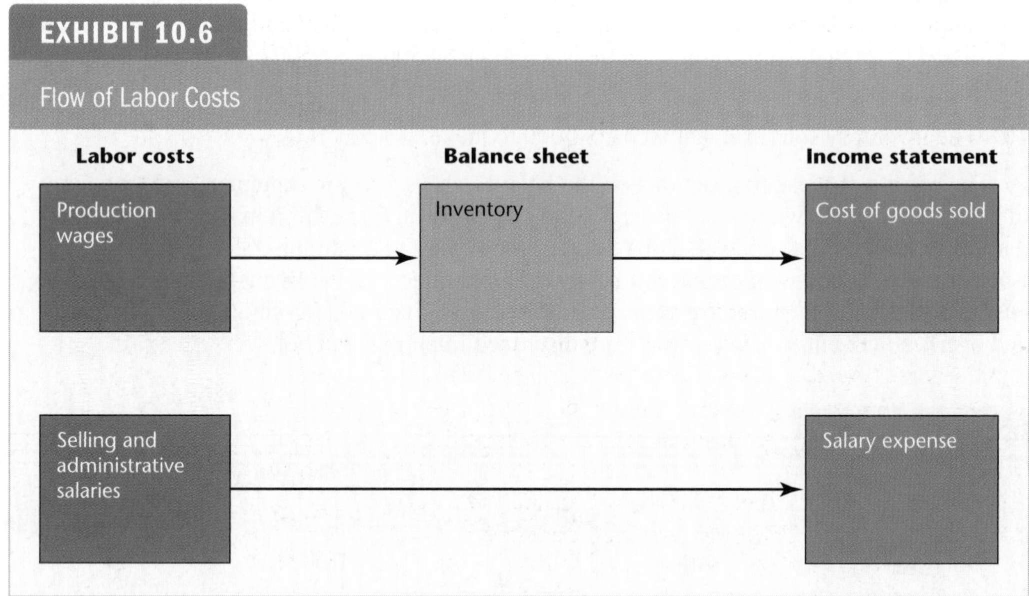

EXHIBIT 10.6
Flow of Labor Costs

Overhead Costs (Event 8)

Although depreciation cost totaled $1,600 ($600 on office furniture and $1,000 on manufacturing equipment), only the $600 of depreciation on the office furniture is expensed directly on the income statement. The depreciation on the manufacturing equipment is split between the income statement (cost of goods sold) and the balance sheet (inventory). The depreciation cost flow for the manufacturing equipment versus the office furniture is shown in Exhibit 10.7.

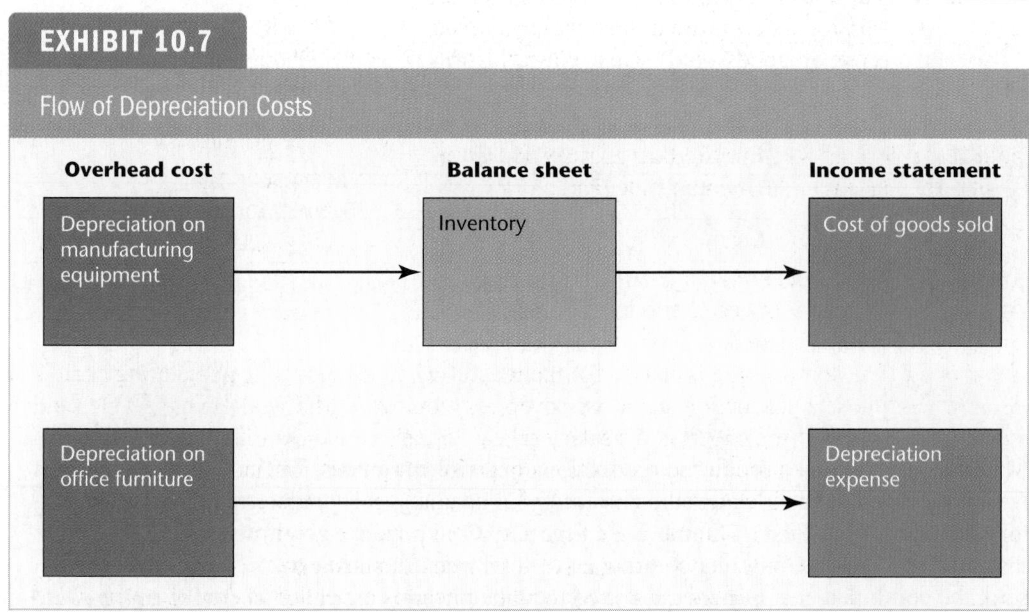

EXHIBIT 10.7
Flow of Depreciation Costs

Total Product Cost. A summary of Patillo Manufacturing's total product cost is shown in Exhibit 10.8.

EXHIBIT 10.8

Schedule of Inventory Costs

Materials	$2,000
Labor	3,000
Manufacturing overhead*	1,000
Total product costs	6,000
Less: Cost of goods sold	(4,000)
Ending inventory balance	$2,000

*Depreciation ([$4,500 − $1,500] ÷ 3)

EXHIBIT 10.9

PATILLO MANUFACTURING COMPANY
Financial Statements

Income Statement for 2004

Sales Revenue		$7,500
Cost of Goods Sold		(4,000)
Gross Margin		3,500
G, S, & A Expenses		
Salaries Expense		(1,200)
Depreciation Expense–Office Furniture		(600)
Net Income		$1,700

Balance Sheet as of December 31, 2004

Cash		$ 9,000
Finished Goods Inventory		2,000
Office Furniture	$2,800	
Accumulated Depreciation	(600)	
Book Value		2,200
Manufacturing Equipment	4,500	
Accumulated Depreciation	(1,000)	
Book Value		3,500
Total Assets		$16,700
Stockholders' Equity		
Common Stock		$15,000
Retained Earnings		1,700
Total Stockholders' Equity		$16,700

Statement of Cash Flows for 2004

Operating Activities	
Inflow from Revenue	$ 7,500
Outflow for Inventory	(5,000)
Outflow for S&A Salaries	(1,200)
Net Inflow from Operating Activities	1,300
Investing Activities	
Outflow for Equipment and Furniture	(7,300)
Financing Activities	
Inflow from Stock Issue	15,000
Net Change in Cash	9,000
Beginning Cash Balance	-0-
Ending Cash Balance	$ 9,000

General, Selling, and Administrative Costs

General, selling, and administrative costs (G,S,&A) are normally expensed *in the period* in which they are incurred. Because of this recognition pattern, nonproduct expenses are sometimes called **period costs.** In Patillo's case, the salary expense for selling and administrative employees and the depreciation on office furniture are period costs reported directly on the income statement.

The income statement, balance sheet, and statement of cash flows for Patillo Manufacturing are displayed in Exhibit 10.9.

The $4,000 cost of goods sold reported on the income statement includes a portion of the materials, labor, and overhead costs incurred by Patillo during the year. Similarly, the $2,000 of finished goods inventory on the balance sheet includes materials, labor, and overhead costs. These product costs will be recognized as expense in the next accounting period when the goods are sold. Initially classifying a cost as a product cost delays, but does not eliminate, its recognition as an expense. All product costs are ultimately recognized as expense (cost of goods sold). Cost classification does not affect cash flow. Cash inflows and outflows are recognized in the period that cash is collected or paid regardless of whether the cost is recorded as an asset or expensed on the income statement.

Overhead Costs: A Closer Look

Costs such as depreciation on manufacturing equipment cannot be easily traced to products. Suppose that Patillo Manufacturing makes both tables and chairs. What part of the depreciation is caused by manufacturing tables versus manufacturing chairs? Similarly, suppose a production supervisor oversees employees who work on both tables and chairs. How much of the supervisor's salary relates to tables and how much to chairs? Likewise, the cost of glue used in the production department would be difficult to trace to tables versus chairs. You could count the drops of glue used on each product, but the information would not be useful enough to merit the time and money spent collecting the data.

Costs that cannot be traced to products and services in a *cost-effective* manner are called **indirect costs**. The indirect costs incurred to make products are called **manufacturing overhead**. Some of the items commonly included in manufacturing overhead are indirect materials, indirect labor, factory utilities, rent of manufacturing facilities, and depreciation on manufacturing assets.

CHECK YOURSELF 10.2

Lawson Manufacturing Company paid production workers wages of $100,000. It incurred materials costs of $120,000 and manufacturing overhead costs of $160,000. Selling and administrative salaries were $80,000. Lawson started and completed 1,000 units of product and sold 800 of these units. The company sets sales prices at $220 above the average per unit production cost. Based on this information alone, determine the amount of gross margin and net income. What is Lawson's pricing strategy called?

Answer

Total product cost is $380,000 ($100,000 labor + $120,000 materials + $160,000 overhead). Cost per unit is $380 ($380,000 ÷ 1,000 units). The sales price per unit is $600 ($380 + $220). Cost of goods sold is $304,000 ($380 × 800 units). Sales revenue is $480,000 ($600 × 800 units). Gross margin is $176,000 ($480,000 revenue − $304,000 cost of goods sold). Net income is $96,000 ($176,000 gross margin − $80,000 selling and administrative salaries). Lawson's pricing strategy is called *cost-plus* pricing.

Since indirect costs cannot be effectively traced to products, they are normally assigned to products using **cost allocation**, a process of dividing a total cost into parts and assigning the parts to relevant cost objects. To illustrate, suppose that production workers spend an eight-hour day making a chair and a table. The chair requires two hours to complete and the table requires six hours. Now suppose that $120 of utilities cost is consumed during the day. How much of the $120 should be assigned to each piece of furniture? The utility cost cannot be directly traced to each specific piece of furniture, but the piece of furniture that required more labor also likely consumed more of the utility cost. Using this line of reasoning, it is rational to allocate the utility cost to the two pieces of furniture based on *direct labor hours* at a rate of $15 per hour ($120 ÷ 8 hours). The chair would be assigned $30 ($15 per hour × 2 hours) of the utility cost and the table would be assigned the remaining $90 ($15 × 6 hours) of utility cost. The allocation of the utility cost is shown in Exhibit 10.10.

We discuss the details of cost allocation in a later chapter. For now, recognize that overhead costs are normally allocated to products rather than traced directly to them.

EXHIBIT 10.10

Cost Allocation

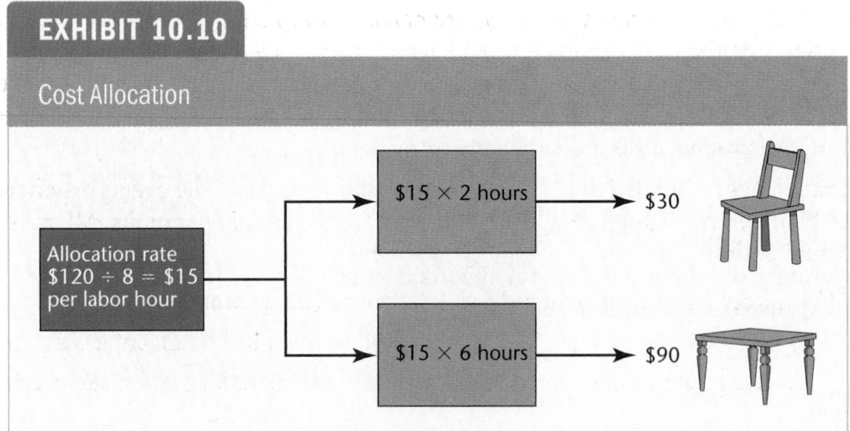

Manufacturing Product Cost Summary

As explained, the cost of a product made by a manufacturing company normally consists of three categories: direct materials, direct labor, and manufacturing overhead. Relevant information about these three cost components is summarized in Exhibit 10.11.

Importance of Cost Classification

What if an expense is misclassified as an asset? Financial statements appear more favorable than the actual condition of the company. Specifically, total assets and net income are overstated. This distortion may have significant consequences for management, investors, and the

EXHIBIT 10.11

Components of Manufacturing Product Costs

Component 1–Direct Materials
Sometimes called *raw materials.* In addition to basic resources such as wood or metals, direct materials can include manufactured parts. For example, engines, glass, and car tires are raw materials for an automotive manufacturer. If the amount of a material in a product is known, it can usually be classified as a direct material. The cost of direct materials can be easily traced to specific products.

Component 2–Direct Labor
The cost of wages paid to factory workers involved in hands-on contact with the products being manufactured. If the amount of time employees worked on a product can be measured, this cost can usually be classified as direct labor. Like direct materials, labor costs must be easily traced to a specific product in order to be classified as direct costs.

Component 3–Manufacturing Overhead
Costs that cannot be easily traced to specific products. These costs are called *indirect costs.* They can include but are not limited to the following:

1. Indirect materials such as glue, nails, paper, and oil. Indirect materials used in the production process may not be part of the finished product. An example is a chemical solvent used to clean products during the production process but not a component material found in the final product.
2. Indirect labor such as the cost of salaries paid to production supervisors, inspectors, and maintenance personnel.
3. Rental cost for manufacturing facilities and equipment.
4. Utility costs.
5. Depreciation on manufacturing facilities and equipment.
6. Security.
7. The cost of preparing equipment for the manufacturing process (setup costs).
8. Maintenance cost for the manufacturing facility and equipment.

government. For example, managers who earn bonuses based on net income will benefit. Similarly, the inflated financial reports may encourage investors to buy stock or lenders to make loans. On the negative side, the inflated earnings will result in the overpayment of income taxes.

LO 6

Explain how cost classification affects financial statements and managerial decisions.

Marion Manufacturing Company

To illustrate practical implications of cost classification, consider the events experienced by Marion Manufacturing Company (MMC) during its first year of operations. All transactions are cash transactions.

1. MMC was started when it acquired $12,000 from issuing common stock.
2. MMC incurred $4,000 of costs to design its product and plan the manufacturing process.
3. MMC incurred specifically identifiable product costs (materials, labor, and overhead) of $8,000.
4. MMC made 1,000 units of product and sold 700 of the units for $18 each.

Exhibit 10.12 displays a set of financial statements prepared under the following two scenarios.

Scenario 1: The $4,000 of design and planning costs are classified as selling and administrative expenses.

Scenario 2: The $4,000 of design and planning costs are classified as product costs, meaning they are first accumulated in the Inventory account and then expensed when the goods are sold. Given that MMC made 1,000 units and sold 700 units of inventory, 70 percent (700 ÷ 1,000) of the design cost has passed through the Inventory account into the Cost of Goods Sold account, leaving 30 percent (300 ÷ 1,000) remaining in the Inventory account.

EXHIBIT 10.12

Financial Statements under Alternative Cost Classification Scenarios

Income Statements	Scenario 1	Scenario 2
Sales Revenue (700 × $18)	$12,600	$12,600
Cost of Goods Sold	(5,600)	(8,400)
Gross Margin	7,000	4,200
Selling and Administrative Expense	(4,000)	0
Net Income	$ 3,000	$ 4,200
Balance Sheets		
Assets		
Cash	$12,600	$12,600
Inventory	2,400	3,600
Total Assets	$15,000	$16,200
Stockholders' Equity		
Common Stock	$12,000	$12,000
Retained Earnings	3,000	4,200
Total Stockholders' Equity	$15,000	$16,200
Statements of Cash Flows		
Operating Activities		
Inflow from Customers	$12,600	$12,600
Outflow for Inventory	(8,000)	(12,000)
Outflow for S&A	(4,000)	0
Net Inflow from Operating Activities	600	600
Investing Activities	0	0
Financing Activities		
Inflow from Stock Issue	12,000	12,000
Net Change in Cash	12,600	12,600
Beginning Cash Balance	0	0
Ending Cash Balance	$12,600	$12,600

Statement Differences

Comparing the financial statements prepared under Scenario 1 with those prepared under Scenario 2 reveals the following.

1. There are no selling and administrative expenses under Scenario 2. The design cost was treated as a product cost and placed into the Inventory account rather than being expensed.
2. Cost of goods sold is $2,800 ($4,000 design cost × .70) higher under Scenario 2.
3. Net income is $1,200 higher under Scenario 2 ($4,000 understated expense − $2,800 overstated cost of goods sold).
4. Ending inventory is $1,200 ($4,000 design cost × .30) higher under Scenario 2.

While the Scenario 2 income statement and balance sheet are overstated, cash flow is not affected by the alternative cost classifications. Regardless of how the design cost is classified, the same amount of cash was collected and paid. This explains why financial analysts consider the statement of cash flows to be a critical source of information.

Practical Implications

The financial statement differences shown in Exhibit 10.12 are *timing differences.* When MMC sells the remaining 300 units of inventory, the $1,200 of design and planning costs included in inventory under Scenario 2 will be expensed through cost of goods sold. In other words, once the entire inventory is sold, total expenses and retained earnings will be the same under both scenarios. Initially recording cost in an inventory account only delays eventual expense recognition. However, the temporary effects on the financial statements can influence the (1) availability of financing, (2) motivations of management, and (3) timing of income tax payments.

Availability of Financing

The willingness of creditors and investors to provide capital to a business is influenced by their expectations of the business's future financial performance. In general, more favorable financial statements enhance a company's ability to obtain financing from creditors or investors.

Management Motivation

Financial statement results might affect executive compensation. For example, assume that Marion Manufacturing adopted a management incentive plan that provides a bonus pool equal to 10 percent of net income. In Scenario 1, managers would receive \$300 (\$3,000 × 0.10). In Scenario 2, however, managers would receive \$420 (\$4,200 × 0.10). Do not be deceived by the small numbers used for convenience in the example. We could illustrate with millions of dollars just as well as with hundreds of dollars. Managers would clearly favor Scenario 2. In fact, managers might be tempted to misclassify costs to manipulate the content of financial statements.

Income Tax Considerations

Since income tax expense is calculated as a designated percentage of taxable income, managers seek to minimize taxes by reporting the minimum amount of taxable income. Scenario 1 in Exhibit 10.12 depicts the most favorable tax condition. In other words, with respect to taxes, managers prefer to classify costs as expenses rather than assets. The Internal Revenue Service is responsible for enforcing the proper classification of costs. Disagreements between the Internal Revenue Service and taxpayers are ultimately settled in federal courts.

Ethical Considerations

Identify the standards of ethical conduct and the features that motivate misconduct.

The preceding discussion provides some insight into conflicts of interest management accountants might face. It is tempting to misclassify a cost if doing so will significantly increase a manager's bonus. Management accountants must be prepared not only to make difficult choices between legitimate alternatives but also to face conflicts of a more troubling nature, such as pressure to:

1. Undertake duties they have not been trained to perform competently.
2. Disclose confidential information.
3. Compromise their integrity through falsification, embezzlement, bribery, and so on.
4. Issue biased, misleading, or incomplete reports.

Yielding to such temptations can have disastrous consequences. The primary job of a management accountant is to provide information useful in making decisions. Information is worthless if its provider cannot be trusted. Accountants have an obligation to themselves, their organizations, and the public to maintain high standards of ethical conduct. In recognition of this obligation, the Institute of Management Accountants (IMA) has issued *Standards of Ethical Conduct for Management Accountants*, which are summarized in Exhibit 10.13. Management accountants are also frequently required to abide by organizational codes of ethics. Failure to adhere to professional and organizational ethical standards can lead to personal disgrace and loss of employment.

EXHIBIT 10.13

Standards of Ethical Conduct for Management Accountants

Competence Management accountants have a responsibility to

- Maintain an appropriate level of professional competence by ongoing development of their knowledge and skills.
- Perform their professional duties in accordance with relevant laws, regulations, and technical standards.
- Prepare complete and clear reports and recommendations after appropriate analysis of relevant and reliable information.

Confidentiality Management accountants have a responsibility to

- Refrain from disclosing confidential information acquired in the course of their work except when authorized, unless legally obligated to do so.
- Inform subordinates as appropriate regarding the confidentiality of information acquired in the course of their work and monitor their activities to ensure the maintenance of the confidentiality.
- Refrain from using or appearing to use confidential information acquired in the course of their work for unethical or illegal advantage either personally or through third parties.

Integrity Management accountants have a responsibility to

- Avoid actual or apparent conflicts of interest and advise all appropriate parties of any potential conflict.
- Refrain from engaging in any activity that would prejudice their ability to carry out their duties ethically.
- Refuse any gift, favor, or hospitality that would influence or would appear to influence their actions.
- Refrain from either actively or passively subverting the attainment of the organization's legitimate and ethical objectives.
- Recognize and communicate professional limitations or other constraints that would preclude responsible judgment or successful performance of an activity.
- Communicate unfavorable as well as favorable information and professional judgments or opinions.
- Refrain from engaging in or supporting any activity that would discredit the profession.

Objectivity Management accountants have a responsibility to

- Communicate information fairly and objectively.
- Disclose fully all relevant information that could reasonably be expected to influence an intended user's understanding of the reports, comments, and recommendations presented.

Upstream and Downstream Costs

LO 8

Distinguish product costs from upstream and downstream costs.

Most companies incur product-related costs before and after, as well as during, the manufacturing process. For example, Ford Motor Company incurs significant research and development costs prior to mass producing a new car model. These **upstream costs** occur before the manufacturing process begins. Similarly, companies normally incur significant costs after the manufacturing process is complete. Examples of **downstream costs** include transportation, advertising, sales commissions, and uncollectible accounts receivable. While upstream and downstream costs are not considered product costs for financial reporting purposes, profitability analysis requires that they be considered in cost-plus pricing decisions. To be profitable, a company must recover the total cost of developing, producing, and delivering its products to customers.

Product Costs in Service Companies

Service businesses, such as doctors' offices, chimney sweeps, and real estate agencies, differ from manufacturing companies in that they provide assistance rather than goods to their customers. *Nevertheless, service companies, like manufacturing companies, incur materials,*

REALITY BYTES

In March 2002, Gene Morse, an accountant employed by WorldCom, discovered accounting fraud at the company. He relayed his findings to his boss, Cynthia Cooper, the company's vice president of internal audit. After further investigation, Ms. Cooper reported her findings to WorldCom's board of directors in June 2002, and the chief financial officer, Scott Sullivan, was fired.

If company management had refused to let Ms. Cooper address the board, would it have been appropriate for her and Mr. Morse to tell the press about the fraud? If they were members of the Institute of Management Accountants (IMA) it would probably have been unethical for them to be "whistleblowers." IMA standards (*SMA Number 1C*, 1983) require a management accountant who is unable to satisfactorily resolve an ethical conflict between himself and his employer to resign from the organization and to submit an informative memorandum to an appropriate representative of the organization. Disclosing such conflicts outside the organization is an inappropriate breach of confidentiality unless required by law. The audit committee of the company's board of directors is an "appropriate representative." In a matter as significant as the WorldCom fraud, the employee would be well advised to seek legal counsel.

For more details on this story, see: "How Three Unlikely Sleuths Discovered Fraud at WorldCom," by Susan Pullman and Deborah Solomon, *The Wall Street Journal*, October 30, 2002, pp. 1 and 16.

labor, and overhead costs in the process of providing services. For example, a hospital providing medical service to a patient incurs costs for medical supplies (materials), salaries of doctors and nurses (labor), and depreciation, utilities, insurance, and so on (overhead).

LO 9 Explain how products provided by service companies differ from products made by manufacturing companies.

The primary difference between manufacturing entities and service companies is that the products provided by service companies are consumed immediately. In contrast, products made by manufacturing companies can be held in the form of inventory until they are sold to customers. Managers of service companies are expected to control costs, improve quality, and increase productivity. Product costing information is useful in achieving these goals regardless of whether a company's product is consumed immediately or later. Although service companies might not report product costs as inventory in their financial statements, they certainly segregate and analyze product costs for internal decision making.

CHECK YOURSELF 10.3

The cost of making a Burger King hamburger includes the cost of materials, labor, and overhead. Does this mean that Burger King is a manufacturing company?

Answer

No, Burger King is not a manufacturing company. It is a service company because its products are consumed immediately. In contrast, there may be a considerable delay between the time the product of a manufacturing company is made and the time it is consumed. For example, it could be several months between the time Ford Motor Company makes an Explorer and the time the Explorer is ultimately sold to a customer. The primary difference between service and manufacturing companies is that manufacturing companies have inventories of products and service companies do not.

Answers to The Curious Accountant

As you have seen, accounting for depreciation related to manufacturing assets is different from accounting for depreciation for nonmanufacturing assets. Depreciation on the checkout equipment at **Wal-Mart** is recorded as depreciation expense. Depreciation on manufacturing equipment at **Black & Decker** is considered a product cost. It is included first as a part of the cost of inventory and eventually as a part of the expense, cost of goods sold. Recording depreciation on manufacturing equipment as an inventory cost is simply another example of the matching principle, because the cost does not become an expense until revenue from the product sale is recognized.

Emerging Trends in Managerial Accounting

LO 10

Explain how emerging trends such as activity-based management, value-added assessment, and just-in-time inventory are affecting the managerial accounting discipline.

Global competition has forced many companies to reengineer their production and delivery systems to eliminate waste, reduce errors, and minimize costs. A key ingredient of successful **reengineering** is benchmarking. **Benchmarking** involves identifying the **best practices** used by world-class competitors. By studying and mimicking these practices, a company uses benchmarking to implement highly effective and efficient operating methods. Best practices employed by world-class companies include total quality management (TQM), activity-based management (ABM), value-added assessment, and just-in-time inventory (JIT).

Total Quality Management

To promote effective and efficient operations, many companies practice **total quality management (TQM)**. TQM is a two-dimensional management philosophy using (1) a systematic problem-solving philosophy that encourages front-line workers to achieve *zero defects* and (2) an organizational commitment to achieving *customer satisfaction.* A key component of TQM is **continuous improvement**, an ongoing process through which employees strive to eliminate waste, reduce response time, minimize defects, and simplify the design and delivery of products and services to customers.

Activity-Based Management

Simple changes in perspective can have dramatic results. For example, imagine how realizing the world is round instead of flat changed the nature of travel. A recent change in perspective developing in management accounting is the realization that an organization cannot manage *costs.* Instead, it manages the *activities* that cause costs to be incurred. **Activities** represent the measures an organization takes to accomplish its goals.

The primary goal of all organizations is to provide products (goods and services) their customers *value.* The sequence of activities used to provide products is called a **value chain. Activity-based management** assesses the value chain to create new or refine existing **value-added activities** and to eliminate or reduce *nonvalue-added activities*. A value-added activity is any unit of work that contributes to a product's ability to satisfy customer needs. For example, cooking is an activity that adds value to food served to a hungry customer. **Nonvalue-added activities** are tasks undertaken that do not contribute to a product's ability to satisfy customer needs. Waiting for the oven to preheat so that food can be cooked does not add value. Most customers value cooked food, but they do not value waiting for it.

To illustrate, consider the value-added activities undertaken by a pizza restaurant. Begin with a customer who is hungry for pizza; certain activities must occur to satisfy that hunger. These activities are pictured in Exhibit 10.14. At a minimum, the restaurant must conduct research and development (devise a recipe), obtain raw materials (acquire the ingredients), manufacture the product (combine and bake the ingredients), market the product (advertise its availability), and deliver the product (transfer the pizza to the customer).

INTERNATIONAL SALES

WHERE IN THE WORLD DO NEW MANAGERIAL ACCOUNTING PRACTICES COME FROM?

Many of the emerging practices in managerial accounting have their foundations in Asian companies. These companies established employee relationships that achieve continuous improvement by encouraging employees to participate in the design as well as the execution of their work. Employee empowerment through the practice known as *kaizen management* recognizes gradual, continuous improvement as the ultimate key to cost reduction and quality control. Employees are encouraged to identify and eliminate nonvalue-added activities, idle time, and waste. The response is overwhelming when employee suggestions are taken seriously. For example, the Toyota Motor Corporation reported the receipt of approximately two million employee suggestions in one year alone.

Source: Takao Tanaka, "Kaizen Budgeting: Toyota's Cost Control System under TQC," *Journal of Cost Management*, Winter 1996, p. 62.

EXHIBIT 10.14

Value Chain

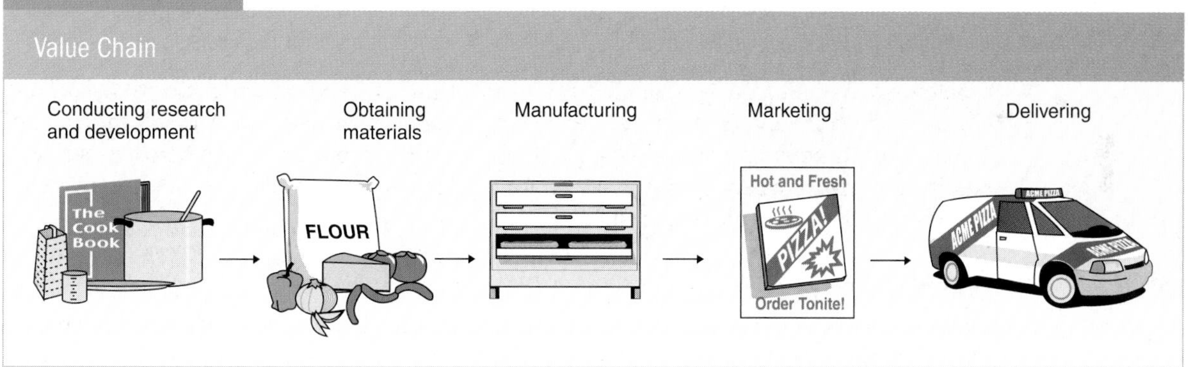

Businesses gain competitive advantages by adding activities that satisfy customer needs. For example, Domino's Pizza grew briskly by recognizing the value customers placed on the convenience of home pizza delivery. Alternatively, Little Caesar's has been highly successful by satisfying customers who value low prices. Other restaurants capitalize on customer values pertaining to taste, ambiance, or location. Businesses can also gain competitive advantages by identifying and eliminating nonvalue-added activities, providing products of comparable quality at lower cost than competitors. Some of the more common nonvalue-added activities and approaches taken to eliminate them are discussed next.

Just-in-Time Inventory

A common nonvalue-added activity found in many business organizations is maintaining excess amounts of inventory. Consumers want products to be available when requested, but they do not benefit when businesses maintain more inventory than necessary to meet demand. In fact, customers could suffer if businesses hold excessive inventory because inventory holding costs must be passed on in the form of higher prices.

Many **inventory holding costs** are obvious: financing, warehouse space, supervision, theft, damage, and obsolescence. Other costs are hidden: diminished motivation, sloppy

■ At Ford Motor Company's plant in Valencia, Spain, suppliers feed parts such as these bumpers just in time and in the right order directly to the assembly line.

work, inattentive attitudes, and increased production time. Many managers work closely with their suppliers to minimize the amount of inventory they carry. They may guarantee the supplier a steady stream of purchases and prompt payment. In exchange, the supplier grants **most-favored customer status** that ensures priority treatment over other customers when shortages exist. Assured priority delivery from a reliable supplier enables a company to minimize the amount of inventory it carries and thereby reduces inventory holding cost.

Many businesses have been able to simultaneously reduce their inventory holding costs and increase customer satisfaction by making products available **just in time (JIT)** for customer consumption. For example, hamburgers that are cooked to order are fresher and more individualized than those that are prepared in advance and stored until a customer orders one. Many fast-food restaurants have discovered that JIT systems lead not only to greater customer satisfaction but also to lower costs through reduced waste.

CHECK YOURSELF 10.4

A strike at a General Motors brake plant caused an almost immediate shutdown of many of the company's assembly plants. What could have caused such a rapid and widespread shutdown?

Answer

A rapid and widespread shutdown could have occurred because General Motors uses a just-in-time inventory system. With a just-in-time inventory system, there is no stockpile of inventory to draw on when strikes or other forces disrupt inventory deliveries. This illustrates a potential negative effect of using a just-in-time inventory system.

Just-in-Time Illustration

To illustrate the benefits of a JIT system, consider Paula Elliot, a student at a large urban university. She helps support herself by selling flowers. Three days each week, Paula drives to a florist, purchases 25 single stem roses, returns to the school, and sells the flowers to individuals from a street corner. She pays $2 per rose and sells each one for $3. Some days she does not have enough flowers to meet customer demand. Other days, she must discard one or two unsold flowers; she believes quality is important and refuses to sell flowers that are not fresh. During May, she purchased 300 roses and sold 280. She calculated her driving cost to be $45. Exhibit 10.15 displays Paula's May income statement.

EXHIBIT 10.15

Income Statement

Sales Revenue (280 units × $3 per unit)	$840
Cost of Goods Sold (300 units × $2 per unit)	(600)
Gross Margin	240
Driving Expense	(45)
Net Income	$195

After studying just-in-time inventory systems in her managerial accounting class, Paula decided to apply the concepts to her small business. She *reengineered* her distribution system by purchasing her flowers from a florist within walking distance of her sales location. She had considered purchasing from this florist earlier but had rejected the idea because the florist's regular selling price of $2.25 per rose was too high. After learning about *most-favored customer status,* she developed a strategy to get a price reduction. By guaranteeing that she would buy at least 30 roses per week, she was able to convince the local florist to match her current cost of $2.00 per rose. The local florist agreed that she could make purchases in batches of any size so long as the total amounted to at least 30 per week. Under this arrangement, Paula was able to buy roses *just in time* to meet customer demand. Each day she purchased a small number of flowers. When she ran out, she simply returned to the florist for additional ones.

The JIT system also enabled Paula to eliminate the cost of the *nonvalue-added activity* of driving to her former florist. Customer satisfaction actually improved because no one was ever turned away because of the lack of inventory. In June, Paula was able to buy and sell 310 roses with no waste and no driving expense. The June income statement is shown in Exhibit 10.16.

EXHIBIT 10.16

Income Statement

Sales Revenue (310 units × $3 per unit)	$930
Cost of Goods Sold (310 units × $2 per unit)	(620)
Gross Margin	310
Driving Expense	0
Net Income	$310

Paula was ecstatic about her $115 increase in profitability ($310 in June − $195 in May = $115 increase), but she was puzzled about the exact reasons for the change. She had saved $40 (20 flowers × $2 each) by avoiding waste and eliminated $45 of driving expenses. These two factors explained only $85 ($40 waste + $45 driving expense) of the $115 increase. What had caused the remaining $30 ($115 − $85) increase in profitability? Paula asked her accounting professor to help her identify the remaining $30 difference.

The professor explained that May sales had suffered from *lost opportunities*. Recall that under the earlier inventory system, Paula had to turn away some prospective customers because she sold out of flowers before all customers were served. Sales increased from 280 roses in May to 310 roses in June. A likely explanation for the 30 unit difference (310 − 280) is that customers who would have purchased flowers in May were unable to do so because of a lack of availability. May's sales suffered from the lost opportunity to earn a gross margin of $1 per flower on 30 roses, a $30 **opportunity cost**. This opportunity cost is the missing link in explaining the profitability difference between May and June. The total $115 difference consists of (1) $40 savings from waste elimination, (2) $45 savings from eliminating driving expense, and (3) opportunity cost of $30. The subject of opportunity cost has widespread application and is discussed in more depth in subsequent chapters of the text.

Value Chain Analysis across Companies

Comprehensive value chain analysis extends from obtaining raw materials to the ultimate disposition of finished products. It encompasses the activities performed not only by a particular organization but also by that organization's suppliers and those who service its finished products. For example, PepsiCo must be concerned with the activities of the company that supplies the containers for its soft drinks as well as the retail companies that sell its products. If cans of Pepsi fail to open properly, the customer is more likely to blame PepsiCo than the supplier of the cans. Comprehensive value chain analysis can lead to identifying and eliminating nonvalue-added activities that occur between companies. For example, container producers could be encouraged to build manufacturing facilities near Pepsi's bottling factories, eliminating the nonvalue-added activity of transporting empty containers from the manufacturer to the bottling facility. The resulting cost savings benefits customers by reducing costs without affecting quality.

A Look Back <<

Managerial accounting focuses on the information needs of *internal users,* while *financial accounting* focuses on the information needs of *external* users. Managerial accounting uses economic, operating, and nonfinancial, as well as financial, data. Managerial accounting information is local (pertains to the company's subunits), is limited by cost/benefit considerations, is more concerned with relevance and timeliness, and is future oriented. Financial accounting information, on the other hand, is more global than managerial accounting information. It supplies information that applies to the whole company. Financial accounting is regulated by numerous authorities, is characterized by objectivity, is focused on reliability and accuracy, and is historical in nature.

Both managerial and financial accounting are concerned with product costing. Financial accountants need product cost information to determine the amount of inventory reported on the balance sheet and the amount of cost of goods sold reported on the income statement. Managerial accountants need to know the cost of products for pricing decisions and for control and evaluation purposes. When determining unit product costs, managers use the average cost per unit. The actual cost of each product requires an unreasonable amount of time and recordkeeping and makes no difference in product pricing and product cost control decisions.

Product costs are the costs incurred to make products: the costs of direct materials, direct labor, and overhead. *Overhead costs* are product costs that cannot be cost effectively traced to a product; therefore, they are assigned to products using *cost allocation*. Overhead costs include indirect materials, indirect labor, depreciation, rent, and utilities for manufacturing facilities. Product costs are first accumulated in an asset account (Inventory). They are expensed as cost of goods sold in the period the inventory is sold. The difference between sales revenue and cost of goods sold is called *gross margin*.

General, selling, and administrative costs are classified separately from product costs. They are subtracted from gross margin to determine net income. General, selling, and administrative costs can be divided into two categories. Costs incurred before the manufacturing process begins (research and development costs) are *upstream costs*. Costs incurred after manufacturing is complete (transportation) are *downstream costs*. Service companies, like manufacturing companies, incur materials, labor, and overhead costs, but the products provided by service companies are consumed immediately. Therefore, service company product costs are not accumulated in an Inventory account. A *code of ethical conduct* is needed in the accounting profession because accountants hold positions of trust and face conflicts of interest. In recognition of the temptations that accountants face, the IMA has issued *Standards of Ethical Conduct for Management Accountants*, which provides accountants guidance in resisting temptations and in making difficult decisions.

Emerging trends such as *just-in-time inventory* and *activity-based management* are methods that many companies have used to reengineer their production and delivery systems to eliminate waste, reduce errors, and minimize costs. Activity-based management seeks to eliminate or reduce *nonvalue-added activities* and to create new *value-added activities*. Just-in-time inventory seeks to reduce inventory holding costs and to lower prices for customers by making inventory available just in time for customer consumption.

>> A Look Forward

In addition to distinguishing costs by product versus G, S, & A classification, other classifications can be used to facilitate managerial decision making. In the next chapter, costs are classified according to the *behavior* they exhibit when the number of units of product increases or decreases (volume of activity changes). You will learn to distinguish between costs that vary with activity volume changes versus costs that remain fixed with activity volume changes. You will learn not only to recognize *cost behavior* but also how to use such recognition to evaluate business risk and opportunity.

SELF-STUDY REVIEW PROBLEM

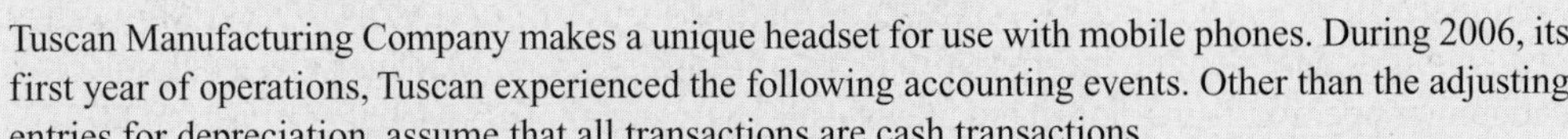

Tuscan Manufacturing Company makes a unique headset for use with mobile phones. During 2006, its first year of operations, Tuscan experienced the following accounting events. Other than the adjusting entries for depreciation, assume that all transactions are cash transactions.

1. Acquired $850,000 cash from the issue of common stock.
2. Paid $50,000 of research and development costs to develop the headset.
3. Paid $140,000 for the materials used to make headsets, all of which were started and completed during the year.
4. Paid salaries of $82,200 to selling and administrative employees.

5. Paid wages of $224,000 to production workers.
6. Paid $48,000 to purchase furniture used in selling and administrative offices.
7. Recognized depreciation on the office furniture. The furniture, acquired January 1, had an $8,000 estimated salvage value and a four-year useful life. The amount of depreciation is computed as ([cost − salvage] ÷ useful life). Specifically, ([$48,000 − $8,000] ÷ 4 = $10,000).
8. Paid $65,000 to purchase manufacturing equipment.
9. Recognized depreciation on the manufacturing equipment. The equipment, acquired January 1, had a $5,000 estimated salvage value and a three-year useful life. The amount of depreciation is computed as ([cost − salvage] ÷ useful life). Specifically, ([$65,000 − $5,000] ÷ 3 = $20,000).
10. Paid $136,000 for rent and utility costs on the manufacturing facility.
11. Paid $41,000 for inventory holding expenses for completed headsets (rental of warehouse space, salaries of warehouse personnel, and other general storage costs).
12. Tuscan started and completed 20,000 headset units during 2006. The company sold 18,400 headsets at a price of $38 per unit.
13. Compute the average product cost per unit and recognize the appropriate amount of cost of goods sold.

Required

a. Show how these events affect the balance sheet, income statement, and statement of cash flows by recording them in a horizontal financial statements model.
b. Explain why Tuscan's recognition of cost of goods sold expense had no impact on cash flow.
c. Prepare a formal income statement for the year.
d. Distinguish between the product costs and the upstream and downstream costs that Tuscan incurred.
e. The company president believes that Tuscan could save money by buying the inventory that it currently makes. The warehouse supervisor said that would not be possible because the purchase price of $27 per unit was above the $26 average cost per unit of making the product. Assuming the purchased inventory would be available on demand, explain how the company president could be correct and why the warehouse supervisor could be biased in his assessment of the option to buy the inventory.

Solution to Requirement *a*

	Assets				=	Equity						
Event No.	Cash +	Inventory +	Office Furn.* +	Manuf. Equip.*	=	Com. Stk. +	Ret. Earn.	Rev.	− Exp.	= Net Inc.	Cash Flow	
1	850,000				=	850,000					850,000	FA
2	(50,000)				=		(50,000)		− 50,000	= (50,000)	(50,000)	OA
3	(140,000) +	140,000									(140,000)	OA
4	(82,200)				=		(82,200)		− 82,200	= (82,200)	(82,200)	OA
5	(224,000) +	224,000									(224,000)	OA
6	(48,000) +		48,000								(48,000)	IA
7			(10,000)		=		(10,000)		− 10,000	= (10,000)		
8	(65,000) +			65,000							(65,000)	IA
9		20,000 +		(20,000)								
10	(136,000) +	136,000									(136,000)	OA
11	(41,000)				=		(41,000)		− 41,000	= (41,000)	(41,000)	OA
12	699,200				=		699,200	699,200		= 699,200	699,200	OA
13		(478,400)			=		(478,400)		− 478,400	= (478,400)		
Totals	763,000 +	41,600 +	38,000 +	45,000	=	850,000 +	37,600	699,200	− 661,600	= 37,600	763,000	NC

*Negative amounts in these columns represent accumulated depreciation.

The average cost per unit of product is determined by dividing the total product cost by the number of headsets produced. Specifically, ($140,000 + $224,000 + $20,000 + $136,000) ÷ 20,000 = $26. Cost of goods sold is $478,400 ($26 × 18,400).

Solution to Requirement *b*

The impact on cash flow occurs when Tuscan pays for various product costs. In this case, cash outflows occurred when Tuscan paid for materials, labor, and overhead. The cash flow consequences of these transactions were recognized before the cost of goods sold expense was recognized.

Solution to Requirement *c*

TUSCAN MANUFACTURING COMPANY Income Statement For the Year Ended December 31, 2006	
Sales Revenue (18,400 units × $38)	$699,200
Cost of Goods Sold (18,400 × $26)	(478,400)
Gross Margin	220,800
R & D Expenses	(50,000)
Selling and Admin. Salary Expense	(82,200)
Admin. Depreciation Expense	(10,000)
Inventory Holding Expense	(41,000)
Net Income	$ 37,600

Solution to Requirement *d*

Inventory product costs for manufacturing companies focus on the costs necessary to make the product. The cost of research and development (Event 2) occurs before the inventory is made and is therefore an upstream cost, not an inventory (product) cost. The inventory holding costs (Event 11) are incurred after the inventory has been made and are therefore downstream costs, not product costs. Selling costs (included in Events 4 and 7) are normally incurred after products have been made and are therefore usually classified as downstream costs. Administrative costs (also included in Events 4 and 7) are not related to making products and are therefore not classified as product costs. Administrative costs may be incurred before, during, or after products are made, so they may be classified as either upstream or downstream costs. Only the costs of materials, labor, and overhead that are actually incurred for the purpose of making goods (Events 3, 5, 9, and 10) are classified as product costs.

Solution to Requirement *e*

Since the merchandise would be available on demand, Tuscan could operate a just-in-time inventory system thereby eliminating the inventory holding expense. Since the additional cost to purchase is $1 per unit ($27 − $26), it would cost Tuscan an additional $20,000 ($1 × 20,000 units) to purchase its product. However, the company would save $41,000 of inventory holding expense. The warehouse supervisor could be biased by the fact that his job would be lost if the company purchased its products and thereby could eliminate the need for warehousing inventory. If Tuscan does not maintain inventory, it would not need a warehouse supervisor.

KEY TERMS

activities 370
activity-based management (ABM) 370
average cost 359
benchmarking 370
best practices 370
continuous improvement 370
cost allocation 364
cost-plus pricing 358
direct labor 362
direct raw materials 361
downstream costs 368
financial accounting 356
Financial Accounting Standards Board (FASB) 357
finished goods inventory 358
general, selling, and administrative costs 363
generally accepted accounting principles (GAAP) 357
indirect costs 363
inventory holding costs 371
just in time (JIT) 372
managerial accounting 356
manufacturing overhead 363
most-favored customer status 372
nonvalue-added activities 370
opportunity cost 373
overhead 358
period costs 363
product costs 358
product costing 358
raw materials 361
reengineering 370
Sarbanes-Oxley Act of 2002 357

Securities and Exchange Commission (SEC) 356
total quality management (TQM) 370
upstream costs 368
value-added activity 370
value-added principle 357
value chain 370

QUESTIONS

1. What are some differences between financial and managerial accounting?
2. What does the value-added principle mean as it applies to managerial accounting information? Give an example of value-added information that may be included in managerial accounting reports but is not shown in publicly reported financial statements.
3. What are the two dimensions of a total quality management (TQM) program? Why is TQM being used in business practice?
4. How does product costing used in financial accounting differ from product costing used in managerial accounting?
5. What does the statement "costs can be assets or expenses" mean?
6. Why are the salaries of production workers accumulated in an inventory account instead of being directly expensed on the income statement?
7. How do product costs affect the financial statements? How does the classification of product cost (as an asset vs. an expense) affect net income?
8. What is an indirect cost? Provide examples of product costs that would be classified as indirect.
9. How does a product cost differ from a general, selling, and administrative cost? Give examples of each.
10. Why is cost classification important to managers?
11. What does the term *reengineering* mean? Name some reengineering practices.
12. What is cost allocation? Give an example of a cost that needs to be allocated.
13. How has the Institute of Management Accountants responded to the need for high standards of ethical conduct in the accounting profession?
14. What are some of the common ethical conflicts that accountants encounter?
15. What costs should be considered in determining the sales price of a product?
16. What does the term *activity-based management* mean?
17. What is a value chain?
18. What do the terms *value-added activity* and *nonvalue-added activity* mean? Provide an example of each type of activity.
19. What is a just-in-time (JIT) inventory system? Name some inventory costs that can be eliminated or reduced by its use.

EXERCISES

All Exercises are available with McGraw-Hill's Homework Manager

Exercise 10-1 ***Identifying financial versus managerial accounting characteristics*** **L.O. 1**

Required

Indicate whether each of the following is representative of managerial or of financial accounting.

a. Information is historically based and usually reported annually.
b. Information is local and pertains to subunits of the organization.
c. Information includes economic and nonfinancial data as well as financial data.
d. Information is global and pertains to the company as a whole.
e. Information is provided to insiders including executives, managers, and operators.
f. Information is factual and is characterized by objectivity, reliability, consistency, and accuracy.
g. Information is reported continuously and has a current or future orientation.

h. Information is provided to outsiders including investors, creditors, government agencies, analysts, and reporters.
i. Information is regulated by the SEC, FASB, and other sources of GAAP.
j. Information is based on estimates that are bounded by relevance and timeliness.

L.O. 5

Exercise 10-2 *Identifying product versus general, selling, and administrative costs*

Required

Indicate whether each of the following costs should be classified as a product cost or as a general, selling, and administrative cost.

a. Indirect labor used to manufacture inventory.
b. Attorney's fees paid to protect the company from frivolous lawsuits.
c. Research and development costs incurred to create new drugs for a pharmaceutical company.
d. The cost of secretarial supplies used in a doctor's office.
e. Depreciation on the office furniture of the company president.
f. Direct materials used in a manufacturing company.
g. Indirect materials used in a manufacturing company.
h. Salaries of employees working in the accounting department.
i. Commissions paid to sales staff.
j. Interest on the mortgage for the company's corporate headquarters.

L.O.. 5

Exercise 10-3 *Classifying costs: product or G, S, & A/asset or expense*

Required

Use the following format to classify each cost as a product cost or a general, selling, and administrative (G, S, & A) cost. Also indicate whether the cost would be recorded as an asset or an expense. The first item is shown as an example.

Cost Category	Product/ G, S, & A	Asset/ Expense
Wages of production workers	Product	Asset
Advertising costs		
Promotion costs		
Production supplies		
Depreciation on administration building		
Depreciation on manufacturing equipment		
Research and development costs		
Cost to set up manufacturing equipment		
Utilities used in factory		
Cars for sales staff		
Distributions to stockholders		
General office supplies		
Raw materials used in the manufacturing process		
Cost to rent office equipment		

L.O. 5

Exercise 10-4 *Identifying effect of product versus general, selling, and administrative costs on financial statements*

Required

Cadeshia Industries recognized accrued compensation cost. Use the following model to show how this event would affect the company's financial statement under the following two assumptions: (1) the compensation is for office personnel and (2) the compensation is for production workers. Use pluses or minuses to show the effect on each element. If an element is not affected, indicate so by placing the letters NA under the appropriate heading.

	Assets = Liab. + Equity	Rev. − Exp. = Net Inc.	Cash Flow
1			
2			

Exercise 10-5 ***Identify effect of product versus general, selling, and administrative costs on financial statements*** L.O. 5

Required

Chappell Industries recognized the annual cost of depreciation on December 31, 2007. Using the following horizontal financial statements model, indicate how this event affected the company's financial statements under the following two assumptions: (1) the depreciation was on office furniture and (2) the depreciation was on manufacturing equipment. Indicate whether the event increases (I), decreases (D), or has no affect (NA) on each element of the financial statements. Also, in the Cash column, indicate whether the cash flow is for operating activities (OA), investing activities (IA), or financing activities (FA). (Note: Show accumulated depreciation as a decrease in the book value of the appropriate asset account.)

	Assets					Equity			
Event No.	Cash +	Inventory +	Manuf. Equip. +	Office Furn.	=	Com. Stk. +	Ret. Earn.	Rev. − Exp. = Net Inc.	Cash Flow
1									
2									

Exercise 10-6 ***Identifying product costs in a manufacturing company*** L.O. 2

Andrea Pomare was talking to another accounting student, Don Cantrell. Upon discovering that the accounting department offered an upper-level course in cost measurement, Andrea remarked to Don, "How difficult can it be? My parents own a toy store. All you have to do to figure out how much something costs is look at the invoice. Surely you don't need an entire course to teach you how to read an invoice."

Required

a. Identify the three main components of product cost for a manufacturing entity.

b. Explain why measuring product cost for a manufacturing entity is more complex than measuring product cost for a retail toy store.

c. Assume that Andrea's parents rent a store for $8,000 per month. Different types of toys use different amounts of store space. For example, displaying a bicycle requires more store space than displaying a deck of cards. Also, some toys remain on the shelf longer than others. Fad toys sell quickly, but traditional toys sell more slowly. Under these circumstances, how would you determine the amount of rental cost required to display each type of toy? Identify two other costs incurred by a toy store that may be difficult to allocate to individual toys.

Exercise 10-7 ***Identifying product versus general, selling, and administrative costs*** L.O. 5

A review of the accounting records of Zammon Manufacturing indicated that the company incurred the following payroll costs during the month of August.

1. Salary of the company president—$75,000.
2. Salary of the vice president of manufacturing—$50,000.
3. Salary of the chief financial officer—$40,000.
4. Salary of the vice president of marketing—$35,000.
5. Salaries of middle managers (department heads, production supervisors) in manufacturing plant—$75,000.

6. Wages of production workers—$540,000.
7. Salaries of administrative secretaries—$78,000.
8. Salaries of engineers and other personnel responsible for maintaining production equipment—$135,000.
9. Commissions paid to sales staff—$128,000.

Required

a. What amount of payroll cost would be classified as general, selling, and administrative expense?
b. Assuming that Zammon made 4,000 units of product and sold 3,600 of them during the month of August, determine the amount of payroll cost that would be included in cost of goods sold.

L.O. 2, 4, 5

Exercise 10-8 *Recording product versus general, selling, and administrative costs in a financial statements model*

Trammell Manufacturing experienced the following events during its first accounting period.

1. Recognized depreciation on manufacturing equipment.
2. Recognized depreciation on office furniture.
3. Recognized revenue from cash sale of products.
4. Recognized cost of goods sold from sale referenced in Event 3.
5. Acquired cash by issuing common stock.
6. Paid cash to purchase raw materials that were used to make products.
7. Paid wages to production workers.
8. Paid salaries to administrative staff.

Required

Use the following horizontal financial statements model to show how each event affects the balance sheet, income statement, and statement of cash flows. Indicate whether the event increases (I), decreases (D), or has no effect (NA) on each element of the financial statements. In the Cash Flow column, indicate whether the cash flow is for operating activities (OA), investing activities (IA), or financing activities (FA). The first transaction has been recorded as an example. (*Note:* Show accumulated depreciation as decrease in the book value of the appropriate asset account.)

	Assets							Equity								
Event No.	Cash	+	Inventory	+	Manuf. Equip.	+	Office Furn.	=	Com. Stk.	+	Ret. Earn.	Rev.	−	Exp.	=	Net Inc.	Cash Flow
1	NA		I		D		NA		NA		NA	NA		NA		NA	NA

L.O. 2, 3, 4

Exercise 10-9 *Allocating product costs between ending inventory and cost of goods sold*

Kasey Manufacturing Company began operations on January 1. During the year, it started and completed 4,000 units of product. The company incurred the following costs.

1. Raw materials purchased and used—$6,000.
2. Wages of production workers—$9,000.
3. Salaries of administrative and sales personnel—$3,600.
4. Depreciation on manufacturing equipment—$10,800.
5. Depreciation on administrative equipment—$4,000.

Kasey sold 3,000 units of product.

Required

a. Determine the total product cost for the year.
b. Determine the total cost of the ending inventory.
c. Determine the total of cost of goods sold.

L.O. 4, 5

Exercise 10-10 *Financial statement effects for manufacturing versus service organizations*

The following financial statements model shows the effects of recognizing depreciation in two different circumstances. One circumstance represents recognizing depreciation on a machine used in a factory. The other circumstance recognizes depreciation on computers used in a consulting firm. The effects of each event have been recorded using the letter (I) to represent increase, (D) for decrease, and (NA) for no effect.

	Assets				Equity						
Event No.	Cash	+ Inventory	+ Equip.	=	Com. Stk.	+ Ret. Earn.	Rev.	− Exp.	=	Net Inc.	Cash Flow
1	NA	NA	D		NA	D	NA	I		D	NA
2	NA	I	D		NA	NA	NA	NA		NA	NA

Required

a. Identify the event that represents depreciation on the computers.

b. Explain why recognizing depreciation on equipment used in a manufacturing company affects financial statements differently from recognizing depreciation on equipment used in a service organization.

Exercise 10-11 ***Identifying the effect of product versus general, selling, and administrative cost on the income statement and statement of cash flows*** L.O. 5

Required

Each of the following events describes acquiring an asset that requires a year-end adjusting entry. Explain how acquiring the asset and making the adjusting entry affect the amount of net income and the cash flow reported on the year-end financial statements. Also, in the Cash Flow column, indicate whether the cash flow is for operating activities (OA), investing activities (IA), or financing activities (FA). Use (NA) for no effect. Assume a December 31 annual closing date. The first event has been recorded as an example. Assume that any products that have been made have not been sold.

	Net Income	Cash Flow
Event No.	Amount of Change	Amount of Change
1. Purchase of printers	NA	(4,000) IA
1. Make adjusting entry	(1,000)	NA

1. Paid $4,000 cash on January 1 to purchase printers to be used for administrative purposes. The printers had an estimated useful life of three years and a $1,000 salvage value.
2. Paid $4,000 cash on January 1 to purchase manufacturing equipment. The equipment had an estimated useful life of three years and a $1,000 salvage value.
3. Paid $5,400 cash in advance on May 1 for a one-year rental contract on administrative offices.
4. Paid $5,400 cash in advance on May 1 for a one-year rental contract on manufacturing facilities.
5. Paid $1,000 cash to purchase supplies to be used by the marketing department. At the end of the year, $50 of supplies was still on hand.
6. Paid $1,000 cash to purchase supplies to be used in the manufacturing process. At the end of the year, $50 of supplies was still on hand.

Exercise 10-12 ***Upstream and downstream costs*** L.O. 8

During 2008, Wake Manufacturing Company incurred $9,000,000 of research and development (R&D) costs to create a long-life battery to use in computers. In accordance with FASB standards, the entire R&D cost was recognized as an expense in 2008. Manufacturing costs (direct materials, direct labor, and overhead) were expected to be $26 per unit. Packaging, shipping, and sales commissions were expected to be $5 per unit. Wake expected to sell 200,000 batteries before new research renders the battery design technologically obsolete. During 2008, Wake made 22,000 batteries and sold 20,000 of them.

Required

a. Identify the upstream and downstream costs.

b. Determine the 2008 amount of cost of goods sold and the ending inventory balance.

c. Determine the sales price assuming that Wake desired to earn a profit margin equal to 25 percent of the *total cost* of developing, making, and distributing the batteries.

d. Prepare an income statement for 2008. Use the sales price developed in Requirement *c*.

e. Why would Wake price the batteries at a level that would generate a loss for the 2008 accounting period?

L.O. 10

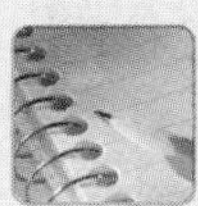

Exercise 10-13 *Value chain analysis*

Autosound Company manufactures and sells high-quality audio speakers. The speakers are encased in solid walnut cabinets supplied by Garrison Cabinet Inc. Garrison packages the speakers in durable moisture-proof boxes and ships them by truck to Autosound's manufacturing facility, which is located 50 miles from the cabinet factory.

Required

Identify the nonvalue-added activities that occur between the companies described in the preceding scenario. Explain how these nonvalue-added activities could be eliminated.

L.O. 10

Exercise 10-14 *Identify the effect of a just-in-time inventory system on financial statements*

After reviewing the financial statements of Baird Company, Tim Hanson concluded that Baird was a service company because its financial statements displayed no inventory accounts.

Required

Explain how Baird's implementation of a 100 percent effective just-in-time inventory system could have led Mr. Hanson to a false conclusion regarding the nature of Baird's business.

L.O. 10

Exercise 10-15 *Using JIT to minimize waste and lost opportunity*

Lucy Quinn, a teacher at Grove Middle School, is in charge of ordering the T-shirts to be sold for the school's annual fund-raising project. The T-shirts are printed with a special Grove School logo. In some years, the supply of T-shirts has been insufficient to satisfy the number of sales orders. In other years, T-shirts have been left over. Excess T-shirts are normally donated to some charitable organization. T-shirts cost the school $4 each and are normally sold for $6 each. Ms. Quinn has decided to order 800 shirts.

Required

a. If the school receives actual sales orders for 750 shirts, what amount of profit will the school earn? What is the cost of waste due to excess inventory?

b. If the school receives actual sales orders for 850 shirts, what amount of profit will the school earn? What amount of opportunity cost will the school incur?

c. Explain how a JIT inventory system could maximize profitability by eliminating waste and opportunity cost.

L.O. 10

Exercise 10-16 *Using JIT to minimize holding costs*

Jay's Pet Supplies purchases its inventory from a variety of suppliers, some of which require a six-week lead time before delivery. To ensure that she has a sufficient supply of goods on hand, Ms. Lane, the owner, must maintain a large supply of inventory. The cost of this inventory averages $40,000. She usually finances the purchase of inventory and pays a 10 percent annual finance charge. Ms. Lane's accountant has suggested that she establish a relationship with a single large distributor who can satisfy all of her orders within a two-week time period. Given this quick turnaround time, she will be able to reduce her average inventory balance to $10,000. Ms. Lane also believes that she could save $6,000 per year by reducing phone bills, insurance, and warehouse rental space costs associated with ordering and maintaining the larger level of inventory.

Required

a. Is the new inventory system available to Ms. Lane a pure or approximate just-in-time system?

b. Based on the information provided, how much of Ms. Lane's inventory holding cost could be eliminated by taking the accountant's advice?

PROBLEMS

All Problems are available with McGraw-Hill's Homework Manager

Problem 10-17 *Product versus general, selling, and administrative costs*

L.O. 2, 3, 4, 5, 6

CHECK FIGURES
a. Average Cost per Unit: $8.40
f. $90,400

Reavis Manufacturing Company was started on January 1, 2006, when it acquired $90,000 cash by issuing common stock. Reavis immediately purchased office furniture and manufacturing equipment costing $10,000 and $28,000, respectively. The office furniture had a five-year useful life and a zero salvage value. The manufacturing equipment had a $4,000 salvage value and an expected useful life of three years. The company paid $12,000 for salaries of administrative personnel and $16,000 for wages to production personnel. Finally, the company paid $18,000 for raw materials that were used to make inventory. All inventory was started and completed during the year. Reavis completed production on 5,000 units of product and sold 4,000 units at a price of $12 each in 2006. (Assume all transactions are cash transactions.)

Required

a. Determine the total product cost and the average cost per unit of the inventory produced in 2006.

b. Determine the amount of cost of goods sold that would appear on the 2006 income statement.

c. Determine the amount of the ending inventory balance that would appear on the December 31, 2006, balance sheet.

d. Determine the amount of net income that would appear on the 2006 income statement.

e. Determine the amount of retained earnings that would appear on the December 31, 2006, balance sheet.

f. Determine the amount of total assets that would appear on the December 31, 2006, balance sheet.

g. Determine the amount of net cash flow from operating activities that would appear on the 2006 statement of cash flows.

h. Determine the amount of net cash flow from investing activities that would appear on the 2006 statement of cash flows.

Problem 10-18 *Effect of product versus period costs on financial statements*

L.O. 2, 4, 5

mhhe.com/edmonds2007

CHECK FIGURES
Cash balance: $47,400
Net income: $10,700

Chateau Manufacturing Company experienced the following accounting events during its first year of operation. With the exception of the adjusting entries for depreciation, all transactions are cash transactions.

1. Acquired $67,000 cash by issuing common stock.
2. Paid $9,500 for the materials used to make products, all of which were started and completed during the year.
3. Paid salaries of $5,300 to selling and administrative employees.
4. Paid wages of $6,200 to production workers.
5. Paid $9,600 for furniture used in selling and administrative offices. The furniture was acquired on January 1. It had a $1,600 estimated salvage value and a four-year useful life.
6. Paid $27,000 for manufacturing equipment. The equipment was acquired on January 1. It had a $3,000 estimated salvage value and a three-year useful life.
7. Sold inventory to customers for $38,000 that had cost $20,000 to make.

Required

Explain how these events would affect the balance sheet, income statement, and statement of cash flows by recording them in a horizontal financial statements model as indicated here. The first event is recorded as an example. In the Cash Flow column, indicate whether the amounts represent financing activities (FA), investing activities (IA), or operating activities (OA).

Event No.	Assets				=	Equity		Rev. − Exp. = Net Inc.	Cash Flow
	Cash	+ Inventory	+ Manuf. Equip.*	+ Office Furn.*	=	Com. Stk.	+ Ret. Earn.	Rev. − Exp. = Net Inc.	Cash Flow
1	67,000					67,000			67,000 FA

*Record accumulated depreciation as negative amounts in these columns.

L.O. 2, 3, 4, 5

Problem 10-19 *Product versus general, selling, and administrative costs*

CHECK FIGURES
Net income: $540
Total assets: $3,540

The following transactions pertain to 2007, the first year operations of Lakeview Company. All inventory was started and completed during 2007. Assume that all transactions are cash transactions.

1. Acquired $3,000 cash by issuing common stock.
2. Paid $600 for materials used to produce inventory.
3. Paid $900 to production workers.
4. Paid $300 rental fee for production equipment.
5. Paid $240 to administrative employees.
6. Paid $120 rental fee for administrative office equipment.
7. Produced 300 units of inventory of which 200 units were sold at a price of $10.50 each.

Required
Prepare an income statement, balance sheet, and statement of cash flows.

L.O. 2, 3, 4, 5

Problem 10-20 *Service versus manufacturing companies*

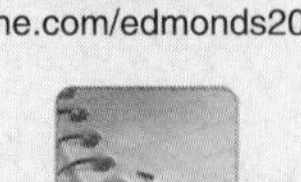
mhhe.com/edmonds2007

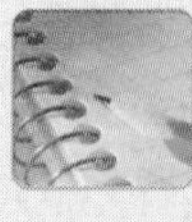

CHECK FIGURES
a. Net loss: $24,000
b. Total assets: $66,000
c. Net income: $13,200

Savoy Company began operations on January 1, 2006, by issuing common stock for $36,000 cash. During 2006, Savoy received $48,000 cash from revenue and incurred costs that required $72,000 of cash payments.

Required
Prepare an income statement, balance sheet, and statement of cash flows for Savoy Company for 2006, under each of the following independent scenarios.

a. Savoy is a promoter of rock concerts. The $72,000 was paid to provide a rock concert that produced the revenue.
b. Savoy is in the car rental business. The $72,000 was paid to purchase automobiles. The automobiles were purchased on January 1, 2006, had four-year useful lives and no expected salvage value. Savoy uses straight-line depreciation. The revenue was generated by leasing the automobiles.
c. Savoy is a manufacturing company. The $72,000 was paid to purchase the following items:
   (1) Paid $9,600 cash to purchase materials that were used to make products during the year.
   (2) Paid $24,000 cash for wages of factory workers who made products during the year.
   (3) Paid $2,400 cash for salaries of sales and administrative employees.
   (4) Paid $36,000 cash to purchase manufacturing equipment. The equipment was used solely to make products. It had a three-year life and a $7,200 salvage value. The company uses straight-line depreciation.
   (5) During 2005, Savoy started and completed 2,000 units of product. The revenue was earned when Savoy sold 1,500 units of product to its customers.
d. Refer to Requirement *c*. Could Savoy determine the actual cost of making the 500th unit of product? How likely is it that the actual cost of the 500th unit of product was exactly the same as the cost of producing the 501st unit of product? Explain why management may be more interested in average cost than in actual cost.

L.O. 2, 3, 4, 5, 6

Problem 10-21 *Importance of cost classification*

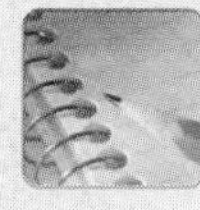

Dextron Manufacturing Company (DMC) was started when it acquired $60,000 by issuing common stock. During the first year of operations, the company incurred specifically identifiable product costs (materials, labor, and overhead) amounting to $30,000. DMC also incurred $20,000 of engineering design and planning costs. There was a debate regarding how the design and planning costs should be classified. Advocates of Option 1 believe that the costs should be classified as general, selling, and administrative costs. Advocates of Option 2 believe it is more appropriate to classify the design and planning costs as product costs. During the year, DMC made 4,000 units of product and sold 3,000 units at a price of $18 each. All transactions were cash transactions.

CHECK FIGURES
a. Option 1: NI = $11,500
Option 2: Total Assets = $76,500

Required

a. Prepare an income statement, balance sheet, and statement of cash flows under each of the two options.
b. Identify the option that results in financial statements more likely to leave a favorable impression on investors and creditors.
c. Assume that DMC provides an incentive bonus to the company president equal to 10 percent of net income. Compute the amount of the bonus under each of the two options. Identify the option that provides the president with the higher bonus.
d. Assume a 35 percent income tax rate. Determine the amount of income tax expense under each of the two options. Identify the option that minimizes the amount of the company's income tax expense.
e. Comment on the conflict of interest between the company president as determined in Requirement *c* and the owners of the company as indicated in Requirement *d*. Describe an incentive compensation plan that would avoid a conflict of interest between the president and the owners.

Problem 10-22 *Value chain analysis*

L.O. 10

Hacienda Company invented a new process for manufacturing ice cream. The ingredients are mixed in high-tech machinery that forms the product into small round beads. Like a bag of balls, the ice cream beads are surrounded by air pockets in packages. This design has numerous advantages. First, each bite of ice cream melts quickly in a person's mouth, creating a more flavorful sensation when compared to ordinary ice cream. Also, the air pockets mean that a typical serving includes a smaller amount of ice cream. This not only reduces materials cost but also provides the consumer with a low-calorie snack. A cup appears full of ice cream, but it is really half full of air. The consumer eats only half the ingredients that are contained in a typical cup of blended ice cream. Finally, the texture of the ice cream makes scooping it out of a large container easy. The frustration of trying to get a spoon into a rock-solid package of blended ice cream has been eliminated. Hacienda Company named the new product Sonic Cream.

Like many other ice cream producers, Hacienda Company purchases its raw materials from a food wholesaler. The ingredients are mixed in Hacienda's manufacturing plant. The packages of finished product are distributed to privately owned franchise ice cream shops that sell Sonic Cream directly to the public.

Hacienda provides national advertising and is responsible for all research and development costs associated with making new flavors of Sonic Cream.

Required

a. Based on the information provided, draw a comprehensive value chain for Hacienda Company that includes its suppliers and customers.
b. Identify the place in the chain where Hacienda Company is exercising its opportunity to create added value beyond that currently being provided by its competitors.

Problem 10-23 *Using JIT to reduce inventory holding costs*

L.O. 10

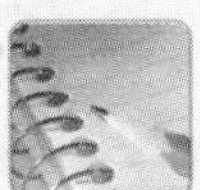

CHECK FIGURE
a. $360,000

Levis Manufacturing Company obtains its raw materials from a variety of suppliers. Levis's strategy is to obtain the best price by letting the suppliers know that it buys from the lowest bidder. Approximately four years ago, unexpected increased demand resulted in materials shortages. Levis was unable to find the materials it needed even though it was willing to pay premium prices. Because of the lack of raw materials, Levis was forced to close its manufacturing facility for two weeks. Its president vowed that her company would never again be at the mercy of its suppliers. She immediately ordered her purchasing agent to perpetually maintain a one-month supply of raw materials. Compliance with the president's orders resulted in a raw materials inventory amounting to approximately $2,000,000. Warehouse rental and personnel costs to maintain the inventory amounted to $10,000 per month. Levis has a line of credit with a local bank that calls for a 12 percent annual rate of interest. Assume that Levis finances the raw materials inventory with the line of credit.

Required

a. Based on the information provided, determine the annual holding cost of the raw materials inventory.

b. Explain how a JIT system could reduce Levis's inventory holding cost.

c. Explain how most-favored customer status could enable Levis to establish a JIT inventory system without risking the raw materials shortages experienced in the past.

L.O. 10

mhhe.com/edmonds2007

CHECK FIGURES
a. $900
b. $3,700

Problem 10-24 *Using JIT to minimize waste and lost opportunity*

Pass CPA Inc. provides review courses for students studying to take the CPA exam. The cost of textbooks is included in the registration fee. Text material requires constant updating and is useful for only one course. To minimize printing costs and ensure availability of books on the first day of class, Pass CPA has books printed and delivered to its offices two weeks in advance of the first class. To ensure that enough books are available, Pass CPA normally orders 10 percent more than expected enrollment. Usually there is an oversupply of books that is thrown away. However, demand occasionally exceeds expectations by more than 10 percent and there are too few books available for student use. Pass CPA had been forced to turn away students because of a lack of textbooks. Pass CPA expects to enroll approximately 100 students per course. The tuition fee is $800 per student. The cost of teachers is $25,000 per course, textbooks cost $60 each, and other operating expenses are estimated to be $35,000 per course.

Required

a. Prepare an income statement, assuming that 95 students enroll in a course. Determine the cost of waste associated with unused books.

b. Prepare an income statement, assuming that 115 students attempt to enroll in the course. Note that five students are turned away because of too few textbooks. Determine the amount of lost profit resulting from the inability to serve the five additional students.

c. Suppose that textbooks can be produced through a high-speed copying process that permits delivery *just in time* for class to start. The cost of books made using this process, however, is $65 each. Assume that all books must be made using the same production process. In other words, Pass CPA cannot order some of the books using the regular copy process and the rest using the high-speed process. Prepare an income statement under the JIT system assuming that 95 students enroll in a course. Compare the income statement under JIT with the income statement prepared in Requirement *a*. Comment on how the JIT system would affect profitability.

d. Assume the same facts as in Requirement *c* with respect to a JIT system that enables immediate delivery of books at a cost of $65 each. Prepare an income statement under the JIT system, assuming that 115 students enroll in a course. Compare the income statement under JIT with the income statement prepared in Requirement *b*. Comment on how the JIT system would affect profitability.

e. Discuss the possible effect of the JIT system on the level of customer satisfaction.

ANALYZE, THINK, COMMUNICATE

ATC 10-1 Business Applications Case *Financial versus managerial accounting*

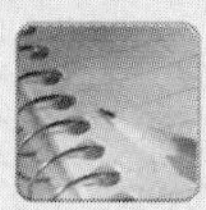

An article in the April 12, 2004, edition of *BusinessWeek,* "The Costco Way—Higher Wages Mean Higher Profits," compared **Costco Wholesale Corporation** data with **Wal-Mart's Sam's Club** data. The tables below present some of the data used to support this claim.

How Costco Spends More on Employees

	Costco	Sam's Club
Average hourly wage rate	$15.97	$11.53
Employees covered by a health-care plan	82%	47%
Average annual health-care costs per employee	$5,735	$3,500
Employees covered by a retirement plan	91%	64%
Average annual retirement costs per employee	$1,330	$747

Benefits to Costco from Spending More on Employees		
	Costco	**Sam's Club**
Annual employee turnover	6%	21%
Labor and overhead cost as a percent of sales	9.8%	17%
Annual sales per square foot	$795	$516
Annual profit per employee	$13,647	$11,039

Required

a. Is the information in the tables above best described as primarily financial accounting data or managerial accounting data in nature? Explain.

b. Provide additional examples of managerial and financial accounting information that could apply to Costco.

c. Explain why a manager of an individual Costco store needs different kinds of information than someone who is considering lending the company money or investing in its common stock.

ATC 10-2 Group Assignment *Product versus upstream and downstream costs*

Victor Holt, the accounting manager of Sexton Inc., gathered the following information for 2006. Some of it can be used to construct an income statement for 2006. Ignore items that do not appear on an income statement. Some computations may be required. For example, the cost of manufacturing equipment would not appear on the income statement. However, the cost of manufacturing equipment is needed to compute the amount of depreciation. All units of product were started and completed in 2006.

1. Issued $864,000 of common stock.
2. Paid engineers in the product design department $10,000 for salaries that were accrued at the end of the previous year.
3. Incurred advertising expenses of $70,000.
4. Paid $720,000 for materials used to manufacture the company's product.
5. Incurred utility costs of $160,000. These costs were allocated to different departments on the basis of square footage of floor space. Mr. Holt identified three departments and determined the square footage of floor space for each department to be as shown in the table below:

Department	Square Footage
Research and development	10,000
Manufacturing	60,000
Selling and administrative	30,000
Total	100,000

6. Paid $880,000 for wages of production workers.
7. Paid cash of $658,000 for salaries of administrative personnel. There was $16,000 of accrued salaries owed to administrative personnel at the end of 2006. There was no beginning balance in the Salaries Payable account for administrative personnel.
8. Purchased manufacturing equipment two years ago at a cost of $10,000,000. The equipment had an eight-year useful life and a $2,000,000 salvage value.
9. Paid $390,000 cash to engineers in the product design department.
10. Paid a $258,000 cash dividend to owners.
11. Paid $80,000 to set up manufacturing equipment for production.
12. Paid a one-time $186,000 restructuring cost to redesign the production process to implement a just-in-time inventory system.
13. Prepaid the premium on a new insurance policy covering nonmanufacturing employees. The policy cost $72,000 and had a one-year term with an effective starting date of May 1. Four

employees work in the research and development department and eight employees in the selling and administrative department. Assume a December 31 closing date.

14. Made 69,400 units of product and sold 60,000 units at a price of $70 each.

Required

a. Divide the class into groups of four or five students per group, and then organize the groups into three sections. Assign Task 1 to the first section of groups, Task 2 to the second section of groups, and Task 3 to the third section of groups.

Group Tasks

(1) Identify the items that are classified as product costs and determine the amount of cost of goods sold reported on the 2006 income statement.

(2) Identify the items that are classified as upstream costs and determine the amount of upstream cost expensed on the 2006 income statement.

(3) Identify the items that are classified as downstream costs and determine the amount of downstream cost expensed on the 2006 income statement.

b. Have the class construct an income statement in the following manner. Select a member of one of the groups assigned the first group task identifying the product costs. Have that person go to the board and list the costs included in the determination of cost of goods sold. Anyone in the other groups who disagrees with one of the classifications provided by the person at the board should voice an objection and explain why the item should be classified differently. The instructor should lead the class to a consensus on the disputed items. After the amount of cost of goods sold is determined, the student at the board constructs the part of the income statement showing the determination of gross margin. The exercise continues in a similar fashion with representatives from the other sections explaining the composition of the upstream and downstream costs. These items are added to the income statement started by the first group representative. The final result is a completed income statement.

ATC 10-3 Research Assignment *Skills needed by managerial accountants*

The September 1999 issue of *Strategic Finance* contains the article "Counting More, Counting Less: Transformations in the Management Accounting Profession," written by Keith Russell, Gary Siegel, and C. S. Kuleszo. It appears on pages 38 to 44. This article reviews findings from a survey of managerial accountants conducted by the Institute of Management Accountants (IMA). Read this article and complete the following requirements.

Required

a. What skills did the management accountants identify as being most important for their success?

b. Did the respondents see their work as being more closely associated with the accounting or finance function?

c. Like all business professionals, management accountants must continuously update their skills. What were the five most important skills the respondents said they had acquired in the five years prior to the survey?

d. Nonaccountants often view accountants as persons who work alone sitting at a desk. What percentage of the respondents to the IMA survey said they work on cross-functional teams?

ATC 10-4 Writing Assignment *Emerging practices in managerial accounting*

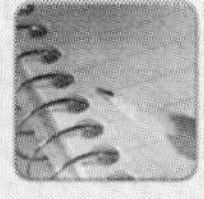

The 1998 annual report of the **Maytag Corporation** contained the following excerpt:

> *During the first quarter of 1996, the Company announced the restructuring of its major appliance operations in an effort to strengthen its position in the industry and to deliver improved performance to both customers and shareowners. This included the consolidation of two separate organizational units into a single operation responsible for all activities associated with the manufacture and distribution of the Company's brands of major appliances and the closing of a cooking products plant in Indianapolis, Indiana, with transfer of that production to an existing plant in Cleveland, Tennessee.*

The restructuring cost Maytag $40 million and disrupted the lives of many of the company's employees.

Required

Assume that you are Maytag's vice president of human relations. Write a letter to the employees who are affected by the restructuring. The letter should explain why it was necessary for the company to undertake the restructuring. Your explanation should refer to the ideas discussed in the section "Emerging Trends in Managerial Accounting" of this chapter.

ATC 10-5 Ethical Dilemma *Product cost versus selling and administrative expense*

Eddie Emerson is a proud woman with a problem. Her daughter has been accepted into a prestigious law school. While Ms. Emerson beams with pride, she is worried sick about how to pay for the school; she is a single parent who has to support herself and her three children. She had to go heavily into debt to finance her own education. Even though she now has a good job, family needs have continued to outpace her income and her debt burden is staggering. She knows she will be unable to borrow the money needed for her daughter's law school.

Ms. Emerson is the controller of a small manufacturing company. She has just accepted a new job offer. She has not yet told her employer that she will be leaving in a month. She is concerned that her year-end incentive bonus may be affected if her boss learns of her plans to leave. She plans to inform the company immediately after receiving the bonus. She knows her behavior is less than honorable, but she believes that she has been underpaid for a long time. Her boss, a relative of the company's owner, makes twice what she makes and does half the work. Why should she care about leaving with a little extra cash? Indeed, she is considering an opportunity to boost the bonus.

Ms. Emerson's bonus is based on a percentage of net income. Her company recently introduced a new product line that required substantial production start-up costs. Ms. Emerson is fully aware that GAAP requires these costs to be expensed in the current accounting period, but no one else in the company has the technical expertise to know exactly how the costs should be treated. She is considering misclassifying the start-up costs as product costs. If the costs are misclassified, net income will be significantly higher, resulting in a nice boost in her incentive bonus. By the time the auditors discover the misclassification, Ms. Emerson will have moved on to her new job. If the matter is brought to the attention of her new employer, she will simply plead ignorance. Considering her daughter's needs, Ms. Emerson decides to classify the start-up costs as product costs.

Required

a. Based on this information, indicate whether Ms. Emerson believes the number of units of product sold will be equal to, less than, or greater than the number of units made. Write a brief paragraph explaining the logic that supports your answer.

b. Explain how the misclassification could mislead an investor or creditor regarding the company's financial condition.

c. Explain how the misclassification could affect income taxes.

d. Identify the factors that contributed to the breach of ethical conduct. When constructing your answer, you may want to refer to the section "Common Features of Ethical Misconduct" in Chapter 1 of this text.

e. Review the standards of ethical conduct shown in Exhibit 10.13 and identify at least two standards that Ms. Emerson's misclassification of the start-up costs violated.

CHAPTER 11

Cost Behavior, Operating Leverage, and Profitability Analysis

LEARNING OBJECTIVES

After you have mastered the material in this chapter you will be able to:

1. **Distinguish between fixed and variable cost behavior.**
2. **Demonstrate the effects of operating leverage on profitability.**
3. **Prepare an income statement using the contribution margin approach.**
4. **Calculate the magnitude of operating leverage.**
5. **Demonstrate how the relevant range and the decision-making context affect cost behavior.**
6. **Determine the sales price of a product using a cost-plus pricing approach.**
7. **Calculate the break-even point.**
8. **Calculate the sales volume required to realize a target profit.**
9. **Calculate the margin of safety in units, dollars, and percentage.**

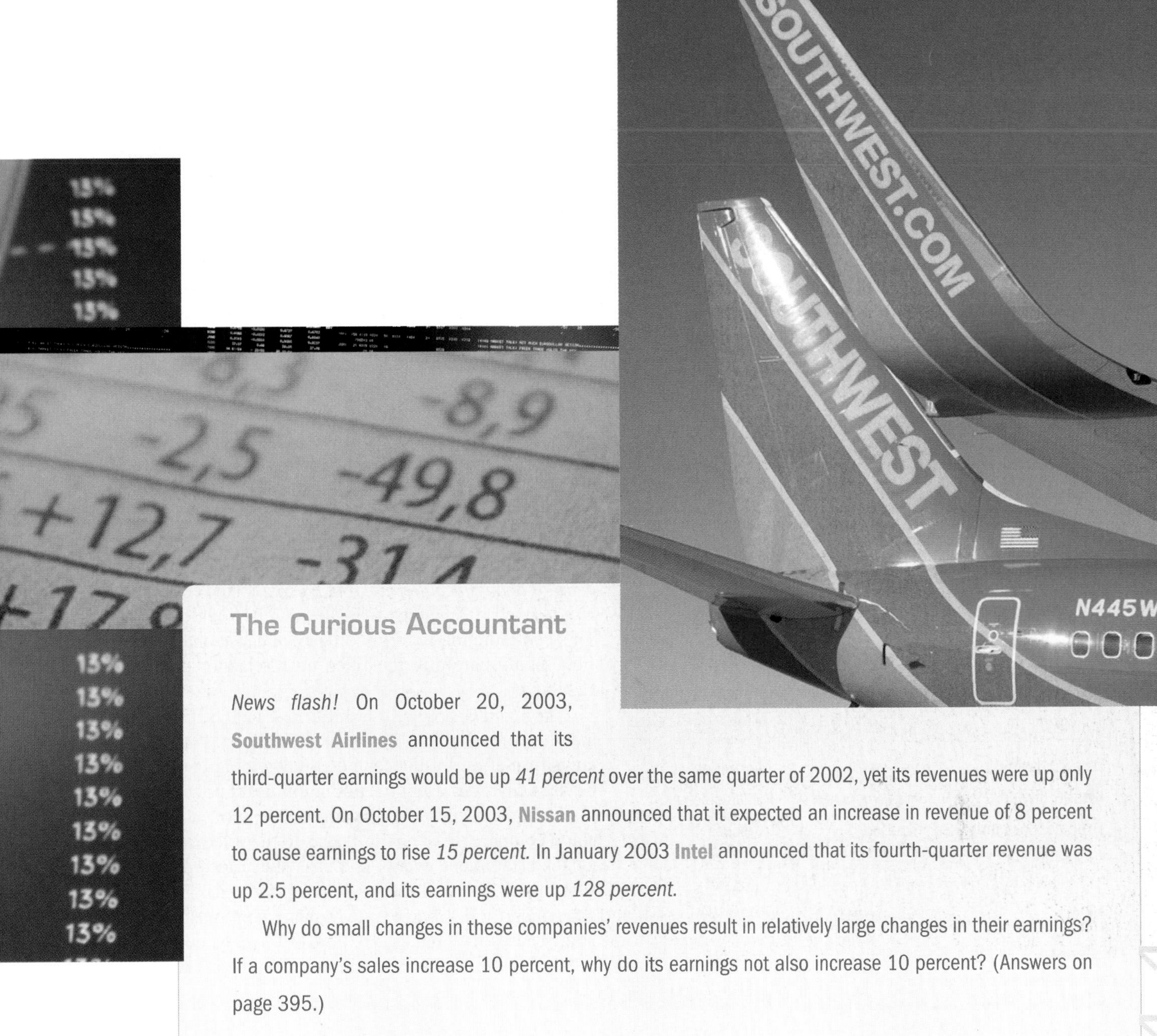

The Curious Accountant

News flash! On October 20, 2003, **Southwest Airlines** announced that its third-quarter earnings would be up *41 percent* over the same quarter of 2002, yet its revenues were up only 12 percent. On October 15, 2003, **Nissan** announced that it expected an increase in revenue of 8 percent to cause earnings to rise *15 percent.* In January 2003 **Intel** announced that its fourth-quarter revenue was up 2.5 percent, and its earnings were up *128 percent.*

Why do small changes in these companies' revenues result in relatively large changes in their earnings? If a company's sales increase 10 percent, why do its earnings not also increase 10 percent? (Answers on page 395.)

CHAPTER OPENING

Three college students are planning a vacation. One of them suggests inviting a fourth person along, remarking that four can travel for the same cost as three. Certainly, some costs will be the same whether three or four people go on the trip. For example, the hotel room costs $800 per week, regardless of whether three or four people stay in the room. In accounting terms, the cost of the hotel room is a **fixed cost.** *The total amount of a fixed cost does not change when volume changes. The total hotel room cost is $800 whether 1, 2, 3, or 4 people use the room. In contrast, some costs vary in direct proportion with changes in volume. When volume increases, total variable cost increases; when volume decreases, total variable cost decreases. For example, the cost of tickets to a theme park is a* **variable cost.** *The total cost of tickets increases proportionately with each vacationer who goes to the theme park.* **Cost behavior** *(fixed versus variable) can significantly impact profitability. This chapter explains cost behavior and ways it can be used to increase profitability.* ■

Fixed Cost Behavior

LO 1

Distinguish between fixed and variable cost behavior.

How much more will it cost to send one additional employee to a sales meeting? If more people buy our products, can we charge less? If sales increase by 10 percent, how will profits be affected? Managers seeking answers to such questions must understand cost behavior. Knowing how costs behave relative to the level of business activity enables managers to more effectively plan and control costs. To illustrate, consider the entertainment company Star Productions Inc. (SPI).

SPI specializes in promoting rock concerts. It is considering paying a band $48,000 to play a concert. Obviously, SPI must sell enough tickets to cover this cost. In this example, the relevant activity base is the number of tickets sold. The cost of the band is a *fixed cost* because it does not change regardless of the number of tickets sold. Exhibit 11.1 illustrates the fixed cost behavior pattern, showing the *total cost* and the *cost per unit* at three different levels of activity.

EXHIBIT 11.1

Fixed Cost Behavior

Number of tickets sold (a)	2,700	3,000	3,300
Total cost of band (b)	$48,000	$48,000	$48,000
Cost per ticket sold (b ÷ a)	$17.78	$16.00	$14.55

Total versus *per unit* fixed costs behave differently. The total cost for the band remains constant (fixed) at $48,000. In contrast, fixed cost per unit decreases as volume (number of tickets sold) increases. The term *fixed cost* is consistent with the behavior of *total cost.* Total fixed cost remains constant (fixed) when activity changes. However, there is a contradiction between the term *fixed cost per unit* and the *per unit behavior pattern of a fixed cost.* Fixed cost per unit is *not* fixed. It changes with the number of tickets sold. This contradiction in terminology can cause untold confusion. Study carefully the fixed cost behavior patterns in Exhibit 11.2.

EXHIBIT 11.2

Fixed Cost Behavior

When Activity	Increases	Decreases
Total fixed cost	Remains constant	Remains constant
Fixed cost **per unit**	Decreases	Increases

The fixed cost data in Exhibit 11.1 help SPI's management decide whether to sponsor the concert. For example, the information influences potential pricing choices. The per unit costs represent the minimum ticket prices required to cover the fixed cost at various levels of activity. SPI could compare these per unit costs to the prices of competing entertainment events (such as the prices of movies, sporting events, or theater tickets). If the price is not competitive, tickets will not sell and the concert will lose money. Management must also consider the number of tickets to be sold. The volume data in Exhibit 11.1 can be compared to the band's track record of ticket sales at previous concerts. Analyzing these data can reduce the risk of undertaking an unprofitable venture.

Demonstrate the effects of operating leverage on profitability.

Operating Leverage

EXHIBIT 11.3

Operating Leverage

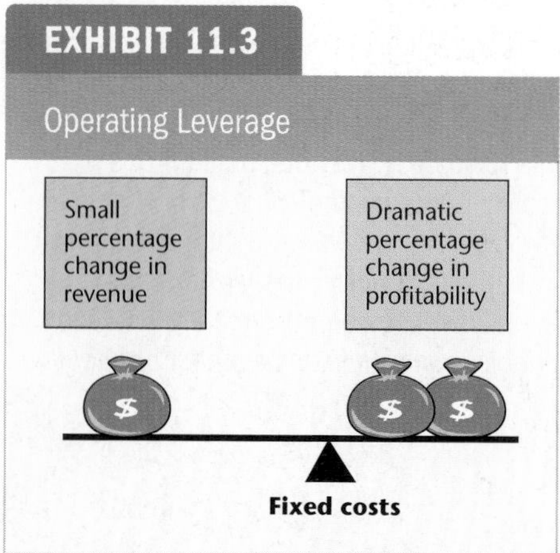

Heavy objects can be moved with little effort using *physical* leverage. Business managers apply **operating leverage** to magnify small changes in revenue into dramatic changes in profitability. The *lever* managers use to achieve disproportionate changes between revenue and profitability is fixed costs. The leverage relationships between revenue, fixed costs, and profitability are displayed in Exhibit 11.3.

When all costs are fixed, every sales dollar contributes one dollar toward the potential profitability of a project. Once sales dollars cover fixed costs, each additional sales dollar represents pure profit. As a result, a small change in sales volume can significantly affect profitability. To illustrate, assume SPI estimates it will sell 3,000 tickets for $18 each. A 10 percent difference in actual sales volume will produce a 90 percent difference in profitability. Examine the data in Exhibit 11.4 to verify this result.

FOCUS ON INTERNATIONAL ISSUES

FIXED COSTS BRING INTERNATIONAL INTRIGUE INTO THE AUTOMOBILE INDUSTRY

In 2000, amidst great fanfare, **General Motors (GM)** and **Fiat S.p.A.** of Italy announced that GM had purchased a 20 percent equity stake in Fiat for $2.4 billion. The two automakers planned to combine some operations that had been separate, reducing the operating costs for both companies. In some cases these savings were achieved. A special clause in the contract, however, became problematic for GM in 2005.

As part of the financial agreement, Fiat insisted on the right to require GM to purchase all of Fiat between 2005 and 2010. This arrangement is called a *put option.* When the deal was struck neither company thought Fiat would ever exercise the option, but if it did, the two companies would have to negotiate a purchase price. By late 2004, circumstances had changed.

Fiat's CEO suggested he might force GM to purchase Fiat unless GM paid a significant price to void the put option. GM did not want to make such a payment, and the two sides entered difficult negotiations with legal action looking likely. What caused this drastic change in conditions? As *The Wall Street Journal* put it, "Fiat Auto ... is caught in a trap of high fixed costs and shrinking market share." The same could be said of GM and the automobile manufacturing business in general. Manufacturing vehicles requires high fixed costs. By 2005 automakers' worldwide *excess* capacity was 24 million units. In 2004, GM, the largest company in the auto industry, produced only 9.1 million vehicles worldwide. GM was already at risk of experiencing a downgrade in its debt rating and did not need the added burden of Fiat's unprofitable operations and high debt. Facing high fixed costs and the inability to raise prices due to the glut of cars on the market, Fiat was at risk of bankruptcy without a new source of cash.

Both companies faced difficult choices. The heavily fixed-cost structure of the auto industry, coupled with excess capacity, is a major source of their problems. If a company had only variable costs, it would have no excess capacity, but it would have no economies of scale either. When times are good and sales are expanding, fixed costs can cause profits to soar. In recent years, however, the auto industry has not experienced great sales growth, so its high fixed costs have created problems for many manufacturers.

In March of 2005, GM agreed to pay Fiat $2 billion to cancel the deal described above.

Source: Company data and "Separation Anxiety: For GM and Fiat, a Messy Breakup Could Be in the Works," *The Wall Street Journal,* January 24, 2005, pp. A-1 and A-13.

EXHIBIT 11.4

Effect of Operating Leverage on Profitability

Number of tickets sold	2,700	⇐−10% ⇐	3,000	⇒+10% ⇒	3,300
Sales revenue ($18 per ticket)	$48,600		$54,000		$59,400
Cost of band (fixed cost)	(48,000)		(48,000)		(48,000)
Gross margin	$ 600	⇐−90% ⇐	$ 6,000	⇒+90% ⇒	$11,400

Calculating Percentage Change

The percentages in Exhibit 11.4 are computed as follows:

$$[(\text{Alternative measure} - \text{Base measure}) \div \text{Base measure}] \times 100 = \%\ \text{change}$$

The *base measure is the starting point.* To illustrate, compute the percentage change in gross margin when moving from 3,000 units (base measure) to 3,300 units (the alternative measure).

$$[(\text{Alternative measure} - \text{Base measure}) \div \text{Base measure}] \times 100 = \%\ \text{change}$$

$$[(\$11{,}400 - \$6{,}000) \div \$6{,}000] \times 100 = 90\%$$

The percentage *decline* in profitability is similarly computed:

[(Alternative measure − Base measure) ÷ Base measure] × 100 = % change

[($600 − $6,000) ÷ $6,000] × 100 = (90%)

Risk and Reward Assessment

Risk refers to the possibility that sacrifices may exceed benefits. A fixed cost represents a commitment to an economic sacrifice. It represents the ultimate risk of undertaking a particular business project. If SPI pays the band but nobody buys a ticket, the company will lose $48,000. SPI can avoid this risk by substituting *variable costs* for the *fixed cost.*

Variable Cost Behavior

LO 2

Demonstrate the effects of operating leverage on profitability.

To illustrate variable cost behavior, assume SPI arranges to pay the band $16 per ticket sold instead of a fixed $48,000. Exhibit 11.5 shows the total cost of the band and the cost per ticket sold at three different levels of activity.

Since SPI will pay the band $16 for each ticket sold, the *total* variable cost increases in direct proportion to the number of tickets sold. If SPI sells one ticket, total band cost will be $16 (1 × $16); if SPI sells two tickets, total band cost will be $32 (2 × $16); and so on. The total cost of the band increases proportionately as ticket sales move from 2,700 to 3,000 to 3,300. The variable cost *per ticket* remains $16, however, regardless of whether the number of tickets sold is 1, 2, 3, or 3,000. The behavior of variable cost *per unit* is contradictory to the word *variable.* Variable cost per unit remains *constant* regardless of how many tickets are sold. Study carefully the variable cost behavior patterns in Exhibit 11.6.

EXHIBIT 11.5

Variable Cost Behavior

Number of tickets sold (a)	2,700	3,000	3,300
Total cost of band (b)	$43,200	$48,000	$52,800
Cost per ticket sold (b ÷ a)	$16	$16	$16

EXHIBIT 11.6

Variable Cost Behavior

When Activity	**Increases**	**Decreases**
Total variable cost	Increases proportionately	Decreases proportionately
Variable cost **per unit**	Remains constant	Remains constant

Shifting the cost structure from fixed to variable enables SPI to avoid the fixed cost risk. If no one buys a ticket, SPI loses nothing because it incurs no cost. If only one person buys a ticket at an $18 ticket price, SPI earns a $2 profit ($18 sales revenue − $16 cost of band). Should managers therefore avoid fixed costs whenever possible? Not necessarily.

Shifting the cost structure from fixed to variable reduces not only the level of risk but also the potential for profits. Managers cannot avoid the risk of fixed costs without also sacrificing the benefits. Variable costs do not offer operating leverage. Exhibit 11.7 shows that

EXHIBIT 11.7

Variable Cost Eliminates Operating Leverage

Number of tickets sold	2,700	⇐−10% ⇐	3,000	⇒+10% ⇒	3,300
Sales revenue ($18 per ticket)	$48,600		$54,000		$59,400
Cost of band (variable cost)	(43,200)		(48,000)		(52,800)
Gross margin	$ 5,400	⇐−10% ⇐	$ 6,000	⇒+10% ⇒	$ 6,600

a variable cost structure produces a proportional relationship between sales and profitability. A 10 percent increase or decrease in sales results in a corresponding 10 percent increase or decrease in profitability.

What cost structure is best? Should a manager use fixed or variable costs? The answer depends on sales volume expectations. A manager who expects revenues to increase should use a fixed cost structure. On the other hand, if future sales growth is uncertain or if the manager believes sales volume is likely to decline, a variable cost structure makes more sense.

CHECK YOURSELF 11.1

Suppose you are sponsoring a political rally at which Ralph Nader will speak. You estimate that approximately 2,000 people will buy tickets to hear Mr. Nader's speech. The tickets are expected to be priced at $12 each. Would you prefer a contract that agrees to pay Mr. Nader $10,000 or one that agrees to pay him $5 per ticket purchased?

Answer

Your answer would depend on how certain you are that 2,000 people will purchase tickets. If it were likely that many more than 2,000 tickets would be sold, you would be better off with a fixed cost structure, agreeing to pay Mr. Nader a flat fee of $10,000. If attendance numbers are highly uncertain, you would be better off with a variable cost structure thereby guaranteeing a lower cost if fewer people buy tickets.

Answers to The Curious Accountant

The explanation for how a company's earnings can rise faster, as a percentage, than its revenue rises is operating leverage, and operating leverage is due entirely to fixed costs. When a company's output increases, its fixed cost per unit decreases. As long as it can keep prices about the same, this lower unit cost will result in higher profit per unit sold. In real world companies, the relationship between changing sales levels and changing earnings levels can be very complex, but the existence of fixed costs helps to explain why an 8 percent rise in revenue can cause a 15 percent rise in net earnings.

CHECK YOURSELF 11.2

If both **Kroger Food Stores** and **Delta Airlines** were to experience a 5 percent increase in revenues, which company would be more likely to experience a higher percentage increase in net income?

Answer

Delta would be more likely to experience a higher percentage increase in net income because a large portion of its cost (e.g., employee salaries and depreciation) is fixed cost, while a large portion of Kroger's cost is variable (e.g., cost of goods sold).

An Income Statement under the Contribution Margin Approach

Prepare an income statement using the contribution margin approach.

The impact of cost structure on profitability is so significant that managerial accountants frequently construct income statements that classify costs according to their behavior patterns. Such income statements first subtract variable costs from revenue; the resulting subtotal is called the **contribution margin.** The contribution margin represents the amount available to cover fixed expenses and thereafter to provide company profits. Net income is computed by subtracting the fixed costs from the contribution margin. A contribution margin style income statement cannot be used for public reporting (GAAP prohibits its use in external financial reports), but it is widely used for internal reporting purposes. Exhibit 11.8 illustrates income statements prepared using the contribution margin approach.

EXHIBIT 11.8

Income Statements

	Company	
	Bragg Co.	**Biltmore Co.**
Variable Cost per Unit (a)	$ 6	$ 12
Sales Revenue (10 units × $20)	$200	$200
Variable Cost (10 units × a)	(60)	(120)
Contribution Margin	140	80
Fixed Cost	(120)	(60)
Net Income	$ 20	$ 20

Measuring Operating Leverage Using Contribution Margin

Calculate the magnitude of operating leverage.

A contribution margin income statement allows managers to easily measure operating leverage. The magnitude of operating leverage can be determined as follows:

$$\text{Magnitude of operating leverage} = \frac{\text{Contribution margin}}{\text{Net income}}$$

Applying this formula to the income statement data reported for Bragg Company and Biltmore Company in Exhibit 11.8 produces the following measures.

Bragg Company:

$$\text{Magnitude of operating leverage} = \frac{\$140}{\$20} = 7$$

Biltmore Company:

$$\text{Magnitude of operating leverage} = \frac{\$80}{\$20} = 4$$

The computations show that Bragg is more highly leveraged than Biltmore. Bragg's change in profitability will be seven times greater than a given percentage change in revenue. In contrast, Biltmore's profits change by only four times the percentage change in revenue. For example, a 10 percent increase in revenue produces a 70 percent increase (10 percent × 7) in profitability for Bragg Company and a 40 percent increase (10 percent × 4) in profitability for Biltmore Company. The income statements in Exhibits 11.9 and 11.10 confirm these expectations.

Operating leverage itself is neither good nor bad; it represents a strategy that can work to a company's advantage or disadvantage, depending on how it is used. The next section explains how managers can use operating leverage to create a competitive business advantage.

EXHIBIT 11.9

Comparative Income Statements for Bragg Company

Units (a)	10		11
Sales Revenue ($20 × a)	$200	⇒+10% ⇒	$220
Variable Cost ($6 × a)	(60)		(66)
Contribution Margin	140		154
Fixed Cost	(120)		(120)
Net Income	$ 20	⇒+70% ⇒	$ 34

EXHIBIT 11.10

Comparative Income Statements for Biltmore Company

Units (a)	10		11
Sales Revenue ($20 × a)	$200	⇒+10% ⇒	$220
Variable Cost ($12 × a)	(120)		(132)
Contribution Margin	80		88
Fixed Cost	(60)		(60)
Net Income	$ 20	⇒+40% ⇒	$ 28

CHECK YOURSELF 11.3

Boeing Company's 2001 10K annual report filed with the Securities and Exchange Commission refers to "higher commercial airlines segment margins." Is Boeing referring to gross margins or contribution margins?

Answer

Since the data come from the company's external annual report, the reference must be to gross margins (revenue − cost of goods sold), a product cost measure. The contribution margin (revenue − variable cost) is a measure used in internal reporting.

Cost Behavior Summarized

LO 1

Distinguish between fixed and variable cost behavior.

The term *fixed* refers to the behavior of *total* fixed cost. The cost *per unit* of a fixed cost *varies inversely* with changes in the level of activity. As activity increases, fixed cost per unit decreases. As activity decreases, fixed cost per unit increases. These relationships are graphed in Exhibit 11.11.

The term *variable* refers to the behavior of *total* variable cost. Total variable cost increases or decreases proportionately with changes in the volume of activity. In contrast, variable cost *per unit* remains *fixed* at all levels of activity. These relationships are graphed in Exhibit 11.12.

The relationships between fixed and variable costs are summarized in the chart in Exhibit 11.13. Study these relationships thoroughly.

The Relevant Range

LO 5

Demonstrate how the relevant range and the decision-making context affect cost behavior.

Suppose SPI, the rock concert promoter mentioned earlier, must pay $5,000 to rent a concert hall with a seating capacity of 4,000 people. Is the cost of the concert hall fixed or variable? Since total cost remains unchanged regardless of whether one ticket, 4,000 tickets, or any number in between is sold, the cost is fixed relative to ticket sales. However, what if demand for tickets is significantly more than 4,000? In that case, SPI might rent a larger

EXHIBIT 11.11

Graphical Presentation of Fixed Cost Behavior

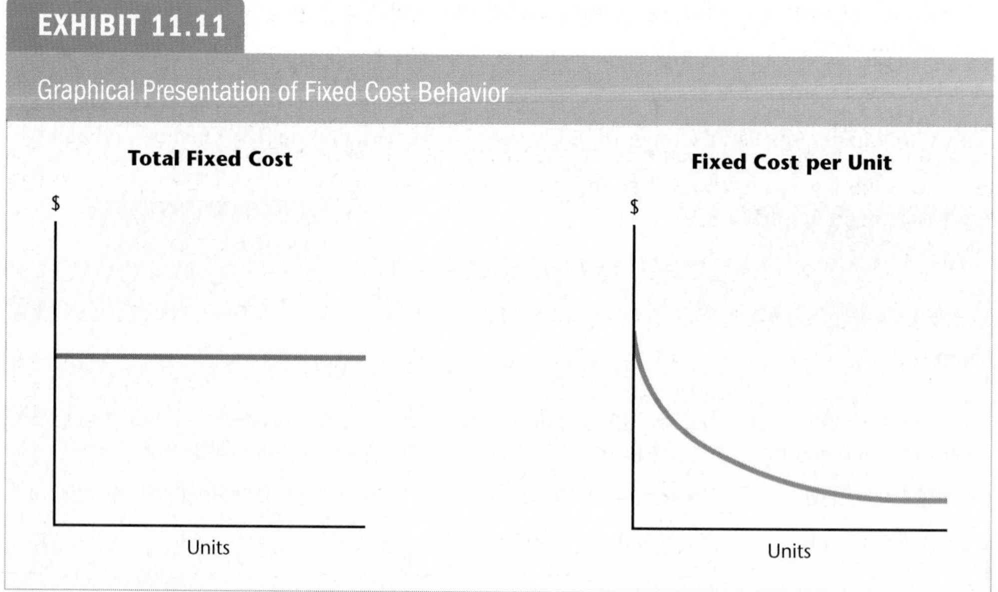

EXHIBIT 11.12

Graphical Presentation of Variable Cost Behavior

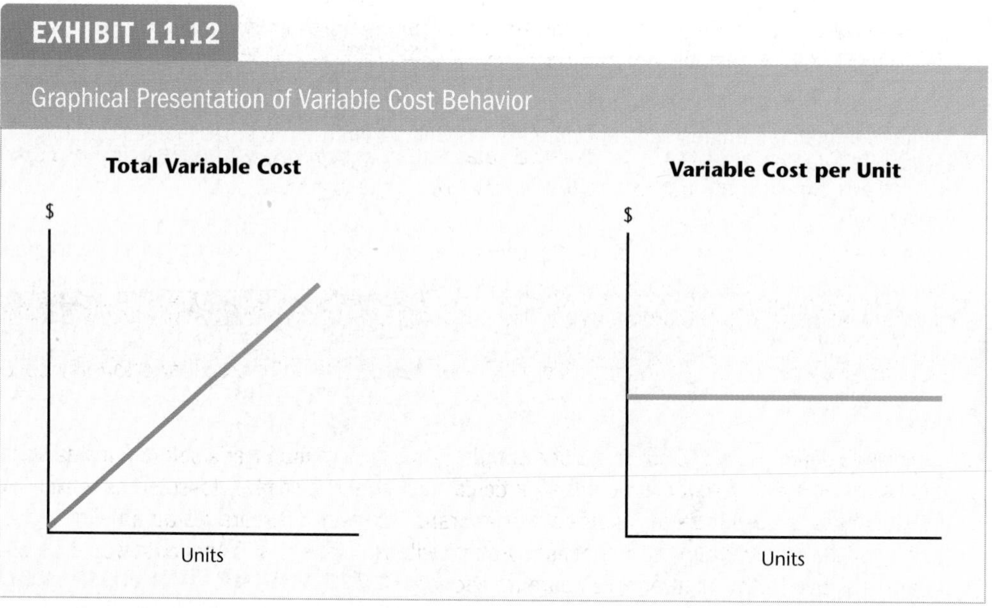

EXHIBIT 11.13

Fixed and Variable Cost Behavior

When Activity Level Changes	Total Cost	Cost per Unit
Fixed cost	Remains constant	Changes *inversely*
Variable cost	Changes in direct proportion	Remains constant

concert hall at a higher cost. In other words, *the cost is fixed only for a designated range of activity (1 to 4,000).*

A similar circumstance affects many variable costs. For example, a supplier may offer a volume discount to buyers who purchase more than a specified number of products. Descriptions of cost behavior pertain to a specified range of activity. The range of activity over which the definitions of fixed and variable costs are valid is commonly called the **relevant range.**

Context-Sensitive Definitions of Fixed and Variable

The behavior pattern of a particular cost may be either fixed or variable, depending on the context. For example, the cost of the band was fixed at $48,000 when SPI was considering hiring it to play a single concert. Regardless of how many tickets SPI sold, the total band cost was $48,000. However, the band cost becomes variable if SPI decides to hire it to perform at a series of concerts. The total cost and the cost per concert for one, two, three, four, or five concerts are shown in Exhibit 11.14.

EXHIBIT 11.14

Cost Behavior Relative to Number of Concerts

Number of concerts (a)	1	2	3	4	5
Cost per concert (b)	$48,000	$48,000	$ 48,000	$ 48,000	$ 48,000
Total cost (a × b)	$48,000	$96,000	$144,000	$192,000	$240,000

In this context, the total cost of hiring the band increases proportionately with the number of concerts while cost per concert remains constant. The band cost is therefore variable. The same cost can behave as either a fixed cost or a variable cost, depending on the **activity base.** When identifying a cost as fixed or variable, first ask, fixed or variable *relative to what activity base?* The cost of the band is fixed relative to *the number of tickets sold for a specific concert;* it is variable relative to *the number of concerts produced.*

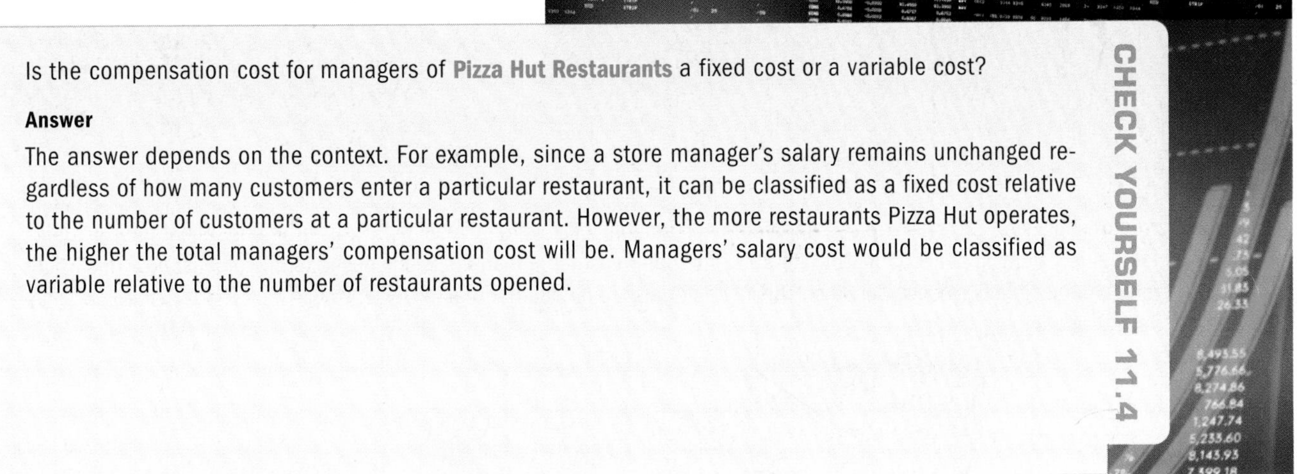

Is the compensation cost for managers of **Pizza Hut Restaurants** a fixed cost or a variable cost?

Answer

The answer depends on the context. For example, since a store manager's salary remains unchanged regardless of how many customers enter a particular restaurant, it can be classified as a fixed cost relative to the number of customers at a particular restaurant. However, the more restaurants Pizza Hut operates, the higher the total managers' compensation cost will be. Managers' salary cost would be classified as variable relative to the number of restaurants opened.

Mixed Costs

Some costs have both fixed and variable components. Consider the cost Delta Airlines incurs to use airport facilities. An airport may charge Delta a flat annual rental fee for terminal space plus a charge each time a plane takes off or lands. The flat rental fee is a fixed cost while the charge per flight is variable. The total facilities cost is mixed. Such costs are called **mixed costs** or **semivariable costs.**

To minimize the recordkeeping difficulties involved in identifying actual fixed and variable costs, many companies make decisions using estimated rather than actual costs. Several techniques exist to divide total cost into estimated fixed and variable components.

REALITY BYTES

Stella, a business student, works part time at **Costco Wholesale, Inc.**, to help pay her college expenses. She is currently taking a managerial accounting course, and has heard her instructor refer to depreciation as a fixed cost. However, as a requirement for her first accounting course, Stella reviewed Costco's financial statements for 2000, 2001, and 2002. The depreciation expense increased about 34 percent over these three years. She is not sure why depreciation expense would be considered a fixed cost.

Stella's accounting instructor reminded her that when an accountant says a cost is fixed, he or she means the cost is fixed in relation to one particular factor. A cost that is fixed in relation to one factor can be variable when compared to some other factor. For example, the depreciation for a retailer may be fixed relative to the number of customers who visit a particular store, but variable relative to the number of stores the company opens. In fact, Costco's depreciation increased from 2000 to 2002 mainly because the company built and opened additional stores.

Stella's instructor suggested Costco's depreciation expense would be more stable if analyzed on a per store basis, rather than in total. Being curious, Stella prepared the following table, where costs are in thousands. Over the three years, she noted that total depreciation expense increased 34.3 percent, while depreciation per store increased only 12.4 percent. Although the costs on a per store basis were more stable than the total depreciation costs, they still were not fixed, so she asked her instructor for further explanation.

Fiscal year	Total Depreciation Expense	Average Depreciation Expense per Store
2000	$254,397	$812.8
2001	301,297	873.3
2002	341,781	913.9

The instructor suggested Costco's average per store depreciation costs were increasing because the equipment and buildings purchased for the new stores (opened from 2000 to 2002) probably cost more than those purchased for the older stores. This would raise the average depreciation expense per store. The instructor also reminded her that in the real world very few costs are perfectly fixed or perfectly variable.

Determining the Contribution Margin per Unit

LO 6

Determine the sales price of a product using a cost-plus pricing approach.

Recall that the *contribution margin* is the difference between sales revenue and variable costs. It measures the amount available to cover fixed costs and thereafter to provide enterprise profits. Consider the following illustration.

Bright Day Distributors sells nonprescription health food supplements including vitamins, herbs, and natural hormones in the northwestern United States. Bright Day recently obtained the rights to distribute the new herb mixture Delatine. Recent scientific research found that Delatine delayed aging in laboratory animals. The researchers hypothesized that the substance would have a similar effect on humans. Their theory could not be confirmed because of the relatively long human life span. The news media reported the research findings; as stories turned up on television and radio news, talk shows, and in magazines, demand for Delatine increased.

Delatine costs $24 per bottle. Bright Day uses a **cost-plus pricing** strategy; it sets prices at cost plus a markup equal to 50 percent of cost. A bottle of Delatine is priced at $36 ($24 + [0.50 × $24]). The **contribution margin per unit** is:

Sales revenue per unit	$36
Variable cost per unit	24
Contribution margin per unit	$12

For every bottle of Delatine it sells, Bright Day earns a $12 contribution margin. Bright Day's first concern is whether it can sell enough units for total contribution margin to cover fixed costs. The president made this position clear when he said, "We don't want to lose money on this product. We have to sell enough units to pay our fixed costs." Bright Day can use the per unit contribution margin to determine the quantity of sales required to break even.

Determining the Break-Even Point

LO 7 Calculate the break-even point.

Bright Day's management team suspects that enthusiasm for Delatine will abate quickly as the news media shift to other subjects. To attract customers immediately, the product managers consider television advertising. The marketing manager suggests running a campaign of cable channel ads at an estimated cost of $60,000. The company president asks, "How many bottles of Delatine would we have to sell to *break even?*"

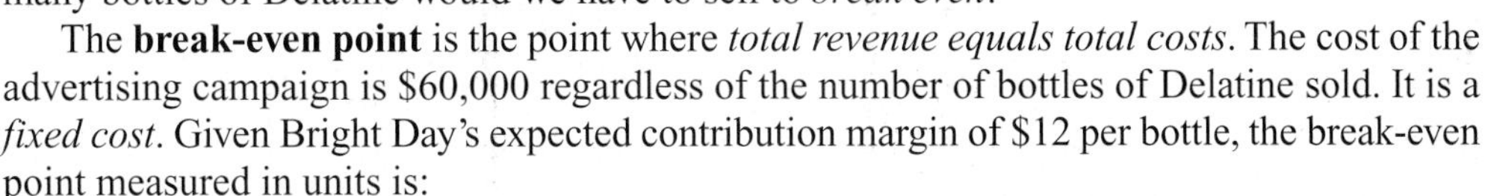

The **break-even point** is the point where *total revenue equals total costs*. The cost of the advertising campaign is $60,000 regardless of the number of bottles of Delatine sold. It is a *fixed cost*. Given Bright Day's expected contribution margin of $12 per bottle, the break-even point measured in units is:

$$\text{Break-even volume in units} = \frac{\text{Fixed costs}}{\text{Contribution margin per unit}}$$

$$= \frac{\$60{,}000}{\$12} = 5{,}000 \text{ units}$$

The break-even point measured in *sales dollars* is the number of units that must be sold to break even multiplied by the sales price per unit. For Delatine, the break-even point in sales dollars is $180,000 (5,000 units × $36). The following income statement confirms these results.

Sales Revenue (5,000 units × $36)	$180,000
Total Variable Expenses (5,000 units × $24)	(120,000)
Total Contribution Margin (5,000 units × $12)	60,000
Fixed Expenses	(60,000)
Net Income	$ 0

Using the Contribution Approach to Estimate the Sales Volume Necessary to Reach a Target Profit

LO 8 Calculate the sales volume required to realize a target profit.

Bright Day's president decides the ad campaign should produce a $40,000 profit. He asks the accountant to determine the sales volume that is required to achieve this level of profitability. For this result, the contribution margin must be sufficient to cover the fixed costs and to provide the desired profit. The required sales volume in units can be computed as shown here:

$$\text{Sales volume in units} = \frac{\text{Fixed costs} + \text{Desired profit}}{\text{Contribution margin per unit}}$$

$$= \frac{\$60{,}000 + \$40{,}000}{\$12} = 8{,}333.33 \text{ units}$$

The required volume in sales dollars is this number of units multiplied by the sales price per unit (8,333.33 units × \$36 = \$300,000). The following income statement confirms this result; all amounts are rounded to the nearest whole dollar.

Sales Revenue (8,333.33 units × \$36)	\$300,000
Total Variable Expenses (8,333.33 units × \$24)	(200,000)
Total Contribution Margin (8,333.33 units × \$12)	100,000
Fixed Expenses	(60,000)
Net Income	\$ 40,000

In practice, the company will not sell partial bottles of Delatine. The accountant rounds 8,333.33 bottles to whole units. For planning and decision making, managers frequently make decisions using approximate data. Accuracy is desirable, but it is not as important as relevance. Do not be concerned when computations do not produce whole numbers. Rounding and approximation are common characteristics of managerial accounting data.

Calculating the Margin of Safety

LO 9

Calculate the margin of safety in units, dollars, and percentage.

Based on the sales records of other products, Bright Day's marketing department believes that budgeted sales of 8,333 units is an attainable goal. Even so, the company president is concerned because Delatine is a new product and no one can be certain about how the public will react to it. He is willing to take the risk of introducing a new product that fails to produce a profit, but he does not want to take a loss on the product. He therefore focuses on the gap between the budgeted sales and the sales required to break even. The amount of this gap, called the *margin of safety,* can be measured in units or in sales dollars as shown here:

	In Units	In Dollars
Budgeted sales	8,333	\$299,988
Break-even sales	(5,000)	(180,000)
Margin of safety	3,333	\$119,988

The **margin of safety** measures the cushion between budgeted sales and the break-even point. It quantifies the amount by which actual sales can fall short of expectations before the company will begin to incur losses.

To help compare diverse products or companies of different sizes, the margin of safety can be expressed as a percentage. Divide the margin of safety by the budgeted sales volume[1] as shown here:

$$\text{Margin of safety} = \frac{\text{Budgeted sales} - \text{Break-even sales}}{\text{Budgeted sales}}$$

$$\text{Margin of safety} = \frac{\$299{,}988 - \$180{,}000}{\$299{,}988} \times 100 = 40\%$$

This analysis suggests actual sales would have to fall short of expected sales by 40 percent before Bright Day would experience a loss on Delatine. The large margin of safety suggests the proposed advertising program to market Delatine has minimal risk.

[1]The margin of safety percentage can be based on actual as well as budgeted sales. For example, an analyst could compare the margins of safety of two companies under current operating conditions by substituting actual sales for budgeted sales in the computation, as follows: ([Actual sales − Break-even sales] ÷ Actual sales).

Suppose that Bright Day is considering the possibility of selling a protein supplement that will cost Bright Day $5 per bottle. Bright Day believes that it can sell 4,000 bottles of the supplement for $25 per bottle. Fixed costs associated with selling the supplement are expected to be $42,000. Does the supplement have a wider margin of safety than Delatine?

Answer

Calculate the break-even point for the protein supplement.

$$\text{Break-even volume in units} = \frac{\text{Fixed costs}}{\text{Contribution margin per unit}} = \frac{\$42{,}000}{\$25 - \$5} = 2{,}100 \text{ units}$$

Calculate the margin of safety. Note that the margin of safety expressed as a percentage can be calculated using the number of units or sales dollars. Using either units or dollars yields the same percentage.

$$\text{Margin of safety} = \frac{\text{Budgeted sales} - \text{Break-even sales}}{\text{Budgeted sales}} = \frac{4{,}000 - 2{,}100}{4{,}000} = 47.5\%$$

The margin of safety for Delatine (40.0 percent) is below that for the protein supplement (47.5 percent). This suggests that Bright Day is more likely to incur losses selling Delatine than selling the supplement.

A Look Back 

To plan and control business operations effectively, managers need to understand how different costs behave in relation to changes in the volume of activity. Total *fixed cost* remains constant when activity changes. Fixed cost per unit decreases with increases in activity and increases with decreases in activity. In contrast, total *variable cost* increases proportionately with increases in activity and decreases proportionately with decreases in activity. Variable cost per unit remains constant regardless of activity levels. The definitions of fixed and variable costs have meaning only within the context of a specified range of activity (the relevant range) for a defined period of time. In addition, cost behavior depends on the relevant volume measure (a store manager's salary is fixed relative to the number of customers visiting a particular store but is variable relative to the number of stores operated). A mixed cost has both fixed and variable cost components.

Fixed costs allow companies to take advantage of *operating leverage.* With operating leverage, each additional sale decreases the cost per unit. This principle allows a small percentage change in volume of revenue to cause a significantly larger percentage change in profits. The *magnitude of operating leverage* can be determined by dividing the contribution margin by net income. When all costs are fixed and revenues have covered fixed costs, each additional dollar of revenue represents pure profit. Having a fixed cost structure (employing operating leverage) offers a company both risks and rewards. If sales volume increases, costs do not increase, allowing profits to soar. Alternatively, if sales volume decreases, costs do not decrease and profits decline significantly more than revenues. Companies with high variable costs in relation to fixed costs do not experience as great a level of operating leverage. Their costs increase or decrease in proportion to changes in revenue. These companies face less risk but fail to reap disproportionately higher profits when volume soars.

Under the contribution margin approach, variable costs are subtracted from revenue to determine the *contribution margin.* Fixed costs are then subtracted from the contribution margin to determine net income. The contribution margin represents the amount available to pay fixed costs and provide a profit. Although not permitted by GAAP for external reporting, many companies use the contribution margin format for internal reporting purposes.

The *break-even point* (the point where total revenue equals total cost) in units can be determined by dividing fixed costs by the contribution margin per unit. The break-even point in sales dollars can be determined by multiplying the number of break-even units by the sales price per unit. To determine sales in units to obtain a designated profit, the sum of fixed costs and desired profit is divided by the contribution margin per unit.

The *margin of safety* is the number of units or the amount of sales dollars by which actual sales can fall below expected sales before a loss is incurred. The margin of safety can also be expressed as a percentage to permit comparing different size companies. The margin of safety can be computed as a percentage by dividing the difference between budgeted sales and break-even sales by the amount of budgeted sales.

>> A Look Forward

The next chapter begins investigating cost measurement. Accountants seek to determine the cost of certain objects. A cost object may be a product, a service, a department, a customer, or any other thing for which the cost is being determined. Some costs can be directly traced to a cost object, while others are difficult to trace. Costs that are difficult to trace to cost objects are called *indirect costs,* or *overhead.* Indirect costs are assigned to cost objects through *cost allocation.* The next chapter introduces the basic concepts and procedures of cost allocation.

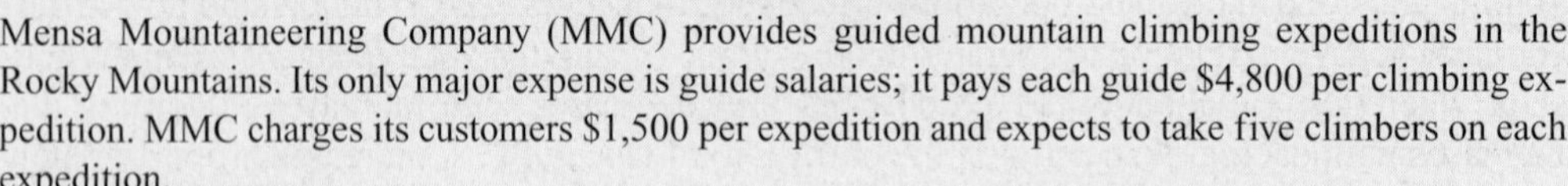

SELF-STUDY REVIEW PROBLEM 1

Mensa Mountaineering Company (MMC) provides guided mountain climbing expeditions in the Rocky Mountains. Its only major expense is guide salaries; it pays each guide $4,800 per climbing expedition. MMC charges its customers $1,500 per expedition and expects to take five climbers on each expedition.

Part 1

Base your answers on the preceding information.

Required

a. Determine the total cost of guide salaries and the cost of guide salaries per climber assuming that four, five, or six climbers are included in a trip. Relative to the number of climbers in a single expedition, is the cost of guides a fixed or a variable cost?

b. Relative to the number of expeditions, is the cost of guides a fixed or a variable cost?

c. Determine the profit of an expedition assuming that five climbers are included in the trip.

d. Determine the profit assuming a 20 percent increase (six climbers total) in expedition revenue. What is the percentage change in profitability?

e. Determine the profit assuming a 20 percent decrease (four climbers total) in expedition revenue. What is the percentage change in profitability?

f. Explain why a 20 percent shift in revenue produces more than a 20 percent shift in profitability. What term describes this phenomenon?

Part 2

Assume that the guides offer to make the climbs for a percentage of expedition fees. Specifically, MMC will pay guides $960 per climber on the expedition. Assume also that the expedition fee charged to climbers remains at $1,500 per climber.

Required

g. Determine the total cost of guide salaries and the cost of guide salaries per climber assuming that four, five, or six climbers are included in a trip. Relative to the number of climbers in a single expedition, is the cost of guides a fixed or a variable cost?

h. Relative to the number of expeditions, is the cost of guides a fixed or a variable cost?

i. Determine the profit of an expedition assuming that five climbers are included in the trip.

j. Determine the profit assuming a 20 percent increase (six climbers total) in expedition revenue. What is the percentage change in profitability?

k. Determine the profit assuming a 20 percent decrease (four climbers total) in expedition revenue. What is the percentage change in profitability?

l. Explain why a 20 percent shift in revenue does not produce more than a 20 percent shift in profitability.

Solution to Part 1, Requirement *a*

Number of climbers (a)	4	5	6
Total cost of guide salaries (b)	$4,800	$4,800	$4,800
Cost per climber (b ÷ a)	1,200	960	800

Since the total cost remains constant (fixed) regardless of the number of climbers on a particular expedition, the cost is classified as fixed. Note that the cost per climber decreases as the number of climbers increases. This is the *per unit* behavior pattern of a fixed cost.

Solution to Part 1, Requirement *b*

Since the total cost of guide salaries changes proportionately each time the number of expeditions increases or decreases, the cost of salaries is variable relative to the number of expeditions.

Solution to Part 1, Requirements *c, d,* and *e*

Number of Climbers	4	Percentage Change	5	Percentage Change	6
Revenue ($1,500 per climber)	$6,000	⇐(20%) ⇐	$7,500	⇒+20% ⇒	$9,000
Cost of guide salaries (fixed)	4,800		4,800		4,800
Profit	$1,200	⇐(55.6%) ⇐	$2,700	⇒+55.6% ⇒	$4,200

Percentage change in revenue: ±$1,500 ÷ $7,500 = ±20%

Percentage change in profit: ±$1,500 ÷ $2,700 = ±55.6%

Solution to Part 1, Requirement *f*

Since the cost of guide salaries remains fixed while volume (number of climbers) changes, the change in net income, measured in absolute dollars, exactly matches the change in revenue. More specifically, each time MMC increases the number of climbers by one, revenue and net income increase by $1,500. Since the base figure for net income ($2,700) is lower than the base figure for revenue ($7,500), the percentage change in net income ($1,500 ÷ $2,700 = 55.6%) is higher than percentage change in revenue ($1,500 ÷ $7,500). This phenomenon is called *operating leverage.*

Solution for Part 2, Requirement *g*

Number of climbers (a)	4	5	6
Per climber cost of guide salaries (b)	$ 960	$ 960	$ 960
Cost per climber (b × a)	3,840	4,800	5,760

Since the total cost changes in proportion to changes in the number of climbers, the cost is classified as variable. Note that the cost per climber remains constant (stays the same) as the number of climbers increases or decreases. This is the *per unit* behavior pattern of a variable cost.

Solution for Part 2, Requirement *h*

Since the total cost of guide salaries changes proportionately with changes in the number of expeditions, the cost of salaries is also variable relative to the number of expeditions.

Solution for Part 2, Requirements *i, j,* and *k*

Number of Climbers	4	Percentage Change	5	Percentage Change	6
Revenue ($1,500 per climber)	$6,000	⇐(20%) ⇐	$7,500	⇒+20% ⇒	$9,000
Cost of guide salaries (variable)	3,840		4,800		5,760
Profit	$2,160	⇐(20%) ⇐	$2,700	⇒+20% ⇒	$3,240

Percentage change in revenue: ±$1,500 ÷ $7,500 = ±20%
Percentage change in profit: ±$540 ÷ $2,700 = ±20%

Solution for Part 2, Requirement *l*

Since the cost of guide salaries changes when volume (number of climbers) changes, the change in net income is proportionate to the change in revenue. More specifically, each time the number of climbers increases by one, revenue increases by $1,500 and net income increases by $540 ($1,500 − $960). Accordingly, the percentage change in net income will always equal the percentage change in revenue. This means that there is no operating leverage when all costs are variable.

SELF-STUDY REVIEW PROBLEM 2

Sharp Company makes and sells pencil sharpeners. The variable cost of each sharpener is $20. The sharpeners are sold for $30 each. Fixed operating expenses amount to $40,000.

Required

a. Determine the break-even point in units and sales dollars.

b. Determine the sales volume in units and dollars that is required to attain a profit of $12,000. Verify your answer by preparing an income statement using the contribution margin format.

c. Determine the margin of safety between sales required to attain a profit of $12,000 and break-even sales.

Solution to Requirement *a*

Formula for Computing Break-even Point in Units

$$\frac{\text{Fixed cost + Target profit}}{\text{Contribution margin per unit}} = \frac{\$40{,}000 + \$0}{\$30 - \$20} = 4{,}000 \text{ Units}$$

Break-even Point in Sales Dollars

Sales price	$ 30
Times number of units	4,000
Sales volume in dollars	$120,000

Solution to Requirement *b*

Formula for Computing Unit Sales Required to Attain Desired Profit

$$\frac{\text{Fixed cost + Target profit}}{\text{Contribution margin per unit}} = \frac{\$40{,}000 + \$12{,}000}{\$30 - \$20} = 5{,}200 \text{ units}$$

Sales Dollars Required to Attain Desired Profit	
Sales price	$ 30
Times number of units	5,200
Sales volume in dollars	$156,000

Income Statement	
Sales Volume in Units (a)	5,200
Sales Revenue (a × $30)	$156,000
Variable Costs (a × $20)	(104,000)
Contribution Margin	52,000
Fixed Costs	(40,000)
Net Income	$ 12,000

Solution to Requirement *c*

Margin of Safety Computations	Units	Dollars
Budgeted sales	5,200	$156,000
Break-even sales	(4,000)	(120,000)
Margin of safety	1,200	$ 36,000

Percentage Computation

$$\frac{\text{Margin of safety in \$}}{\text{Budgeted sales}} = \frac{\$36,000}{\$156,000} = 23.08\%$$

KEY TERMS

activity base 399
break-even point 401
contribution margin 396
contribution margin per unit 401
cost-plus pricing 401
cost behavior 391
fixed cost 391
margin of safety 402
mixed costs (semivariable costs) 399
operating leverage 392
relevant range 398
variable cost 391

QUESTIONS

1. Define *fixed cost* and *variable cost* and give an example of each.
2. How can knowing cost behavior relative to volume fluctuations affect decision making?
3. Define the term *operating leverage* and explain how it affects profits.
4. How is operating leverage calculated?

5. Explain the limitations of using operating leverage to predict profitability.
6. If volume is increasing, would a company benefit more from a pure variable or a pure fixed cost structure? Which cost structure would be advantageous if volume is decreasing?
7. Explain the risk and rewards to a company that result from having fixed costs.
8. Are companies with predominately fixed cost structures likely to be most profitable?
9. How is the relevant range of activity related to fixed and variable cost? Give an example of how the definitions of these costs become invalid when volume is outside the relevant range.
10. Which cost structure has the greater risk? Explain.
11. The president of Bright Corporation tells you that he sees a dim future for his company. He feels that his hands are tied because fixed costs are too high. He says that fixed costs do not change and therefore the situation is hopeless. Do you agree? Explain.
12. All costs are variable because if a business ceases operations, its costs fall to zero. Do you agree with the statement? Explain.
13. Verna Salsbury tells you that she thinks the terms fixed cost and variable cost are confusing. She notes that fixed cost per unit changes when the number of units changes. Furthermore, variable cost per unit remains fixed regardless of how many units are produced. She concludes that the terminology seems to be backward. Explain why the terminology appears to be contradictory.
14. What does the term *break-even point* mean? Name the two ways it can be measured.
15. How does a contribution margin income statement differ from the income statement used in financial reporting?
16. If Company A has a projected margin of safety of 22 percent while Company B has a margin of safety of 52 percent, which company is at greater risk when actual sales are less than budgeted?
17. Mary Hartwell and Jane Jamail, college roommates, are considering the joint purchase of a computer that they can share to prepare class assignments. Ms. Hartwell wants a particular model that costs $2,000; Ms. Jamail prefers a more economical model that costs $1,500. In fact, Ms. Jamail is adamant about her position, refusing to contribute more than $750 toward the purchase. If Ms. Hartwell is also adamant about her position, should she accept Ms. Jamail's $750 offer and apply that amount toward the purchase of the more expensive computer?

EXERCISES

All Exercises are available with McGraw-Hill's Homework Manager

L.O. 1

Exercise 11-1 *Identifying cost behavior*

Hoover's Kitchen, a fast-food restaurant company, operates a chain of restaurants across the nation. Each restaurant employs eight people; one is a manager paid a salary plus a bonus equal to 3 percent of sales. Other employees, two cooks, one dishwasher, and four waitresses, are paid salaries. Each manager is budgeted $3,000 per month for advertising cost.

Required

Classify each of the following costs incurred by Hoover's Kitchen as fixed, variable, or mixed.

a. Manager's compensation relative to the number of customers.
b. Waitresses' salaries relative to the number of restaurants.
c. Advertising costs relative to the number of customers for a particular restaurant.
d. Rental costs relative to the number of restaurants.
e. Cooks' salaries at a particular location relative to the number of customers.
f. Cost of supplies (cups, plates, spoons, etc.) relative to the number of customers.

Exercise 11-2 *Identifying cost behavior* L.O. 1

At the various activity levels shown, Taylor Company incurred the following costs.

	Units sold	20	40	60	80	100
a.	Total salary cost	$1,200.00	$1,600.00	$2,000.00	$2,400.00	$2,800.00
b.	Total cost of goods sold	1,800.00	3,600.00	5,400.00	7,200.00	9,000.00
c.	Depreciation cost per unit	240.00	120.00	80.00	60.00	48.00
d.	Total rent cost	3,200.00	3,200.00	3,200.00	3,200.00	3,200.00
e.	Total cost of shopping bags	2.00	4.00	6.00	8.00	10.00
f.	Cost per unit of merchandise sold	90.00	90.00	90.00	90.00	90.00
g.	Rental cost per unit of merchandise sold	36.00	18.00	12.00	9.00	7.20
h.	Total phone expense	80.00	100.00	120.00	140.00	160.00
i.	Cost per unit of supplies	1.00	1.00	1.00	1.00	1.00
j.	Total insurance cost	480.00	480.00	480.00	480.00	480.00

Required

Identify each of these costs as fixed, variable, or mixed.

Exercise 11-3 *Determining fixed cost per unit* L.O. 1

Simon Corporation incurs the following annual fixed costs:

Item	Cost
Depreciation	$ 30,000
Officers' salaries	100,000
Long-term lease	40,000
Property taxes	10,000

Required

Determine the total fixed cost per unit of production, assuming that Simon produces 4,000, 4,500, or 5,000 units.

Exercise 11-4 *Determining total variable cost* L.O. 1

The following variable production costs apply to goods made by Keller Manufacturing Corporation.

Item	Cost per Unit
Materials	$5.00
Labor	2.80
Variable overhead	0.40
Total	$8.20

Required

Determine the total variable production cost, assuming that Keller makes 10,000, 15,000, or 20,000 units.

L.O. 1

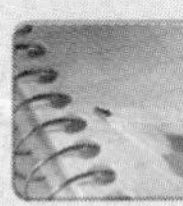

Exercise 11-5 *Fixed versus variable cost behavior*

Whaley Company's cost and production data for two recent months included the following:

	January	February
Production (units)	100	200
Rent	$2,000	$2,000
Utilities	$ 500	$1,000

Required

a. Separately calculate the rental cost per unit and the utilities cost per unit for both January and February.

b. Based on both total and per unit amounts, identify which cost is variable and which is fixed. Explain your answer.

L.O. 1

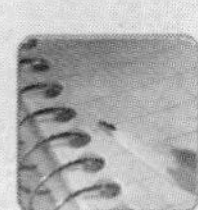

Exercise 11-6 *Fixed versus variable cost behavior*

Hernadez Trophies makes and sells trophies it distributes to little league ballplayers. The company normally produces and sells between 10,000 and 13,000 trophies per year. The following cost data apply to various activity levels.

Number of Trophies	10,000	11,000	12,000	13,000
Total costs incurred				
Fixed	$ 60,000			
Variable	50,000			
Total costs	$110,000			
Cost per unit				
Fixed	$ 6.00			
Variable	5.00			
Total cost per trophy	$11.00			

Required

a. Complete the preceding table by filling in the missing amounts for the levels of activity shown in the first row of the table. Round all cost per unit figures to the nearest whole penny.

b. Explain why the total cost per trophy decreases as the number of trophies increases.

L.O. 1

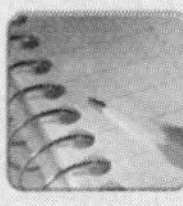

Exercise 11-7 *Fixed versus variable cost behavior*

Barlow Entertainment sponsors rock concerts. The company is considering a contract to hire a band at a cost of $50,000 per concert.

Required

a. What are the total band cost and the cost per person if concert attendance is 2,000, 2,500, 3,000, 3,500, or 4,000?

b. Is the cost of hiring the band a fixed or a variable cost?

c. Draw a graph and plot total cost and cost per unit if attendance is 2,000, 2,500, 3,000, 3,500, or 4,000.

d. Identify Barlow's major business risks and explain how they can be minimized.

Exercise 11-8 *Fixed versus variable cost behavior* L.O. 1

Barlow Entertainment sells souvenir T-shirts at each rock concert that it sponsors. The shirts cost $8 each. Any excess shirts can be returned to the manufacturer for a full refund of the purchase price. The sales price is $12 per shirt.

Required

a. What are the total cost of shirts and cost per shirt if sales amount to 2,000, 2,500, 3,000, 3,500, or 4,000?

b. Is the cost of T-shirts a fixed or a variable cost?

c. Draw a graph and plot total cost and cost per shirt if sales amount to 2,000, 2,500, 3,000, 3,500, or 4,000.

d. Comment on Barlow's likelihood of incurring a loss due to its operating activities.

Exercise 11-9 *Graphing fixed cost behavior* L.O. 1

The following graphs depict the dollar amount of fixed cost on the vertical axes and the level of activity on the horizontal axes.

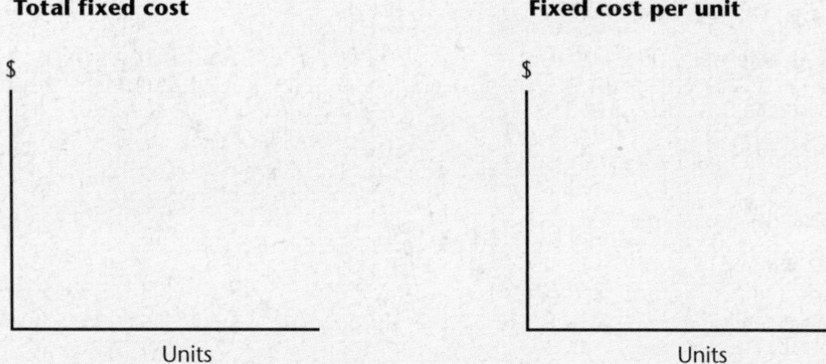

Required

a. Draw a line that depicts the relationship between total fixed cost and the level of activity.

b. Draw a line that depicts the relationship between fixed cost per unit and the level of activity.

Exercise 11-10 *Graphing variable cost behavior* L.O. 1

The following graphs depict the dollar amount of variable cost on the vertical axes and the level of activity on the horizontal axes.

Total variable cost | **Variable cost per unit**

$ | $

Units | Units

Required

a. Draw a line that depicts the relationship between total variable cost and the level of activity.

b. Draw a line that depicts the relationship between variable cost per unit and the level of activity.

Exercise 11-11 *Mixed cost at different levels of activity* L.O. 1

Damon Corporation paid one of its sales representatives $5,000 during the month of March. The rep is paid a base salary plus $15 per unit of product sold. During March, the rep sold 200 units.

Required

Calculate the total monthly cost of the sales representative's salary for each of the following months.

Month	April	May	June	July
Number of units sold	240	160	250	160
Total variable cost				
Total fixed cost				
Total salary cost				

L.O. 1, 2

Exercise 11-12 *Using fixed cost as a competitive business strategy*

The following income statements illustrate different cost structures for two competing companies.

Income Statements		
	Company Name	
	Keef	Reef
Number of Customers (a)	80	80
Sales Revenue (a × $250)	$20,000	$20,000
Variable Cost (a × $200)	N/A	(16,000)
Variable Cost (a × $0)	0	N/A
Contribution Margin	20,000	4,000
Fixed Cost	(16,000)	0
Net Income	$ 4,000	$ 4,000

Required

a. Reconstruct Keef's income statement, assuming that it serves 160 customers when it lures 80 customers away from Reef by lowering the sales price to $150 per customer.

b. Reconstruct Reef's income statement, assuming that it serves 160 customers when it lures 80 customers away from Keef by lowering the sales price to $150 per customer.

c. Explain why the price-cutting strategy increased Keef Company's profits but caused a net loss for Reef Company.

L.O. 3, 4

Exercise 11-13 *Using contribution margin format income statement to measure the magnitude of operating leverage*

The following income statement was drawn from the records of Mantooth Company, a merchandising firm.

MANTOOTH COMPANY Income Statement For the Year Ended December 31, 2006	
Sales Revenue (3,500 units × $120)	$420,000
Cost of Goods Sold (3,500 units × $64)	(224,000)
Gross Margin	196,000
Sales Commissions (10% of sales)	(42,000)
Administrative Salaries Expense	(60,000)
Advertising Expense	(20,000)
Depreciation Expense	(25,000)
Shipping and Handling Expenses (3,500 units × $4.00)	(14,000)
Net Income	$ 35,000

Required

a. Reconstruct the income statement using the contribution margin format.

b. Calculate the magnitude of operating leverage.

c. Use the measure of operating leverage to determine the amount of net income Mantooth will earn if sales increase by 10 percent.

Exercise 11-14 *Assessing the magnitude of operating leverage* L.O. 4

The following income statement applies to Lyons Company for the current year:

Income Statement	
Sales Revenue (400 units × $25)	$10,000
Variable Cost (400 units × $10)	(4,000)
Contribution Margin	6,000
Fixed Costs	(3,500)
Net Income	$ 2,500

Required

a. Use the contribution margin approach to calculate the magnitude of operating leverage.

b. Use the operating leverage measure computed in Requirement *a* to determine the amount of net income that Lyons Company will earn if it experiences a 20 percent increase in revenue. The sales price per unit is not affected.

c. Verify your answer to Requirement *b* by constructing an income statement based on a 20 percent increase in sales revenue. The sales price is not affected. Calculate the percentage change in net income for the two income statements.

Exercise 11-15 *Break-even point* L.O. 7

Thorpe Corporation sells products for $15 each that have variable costs of $10 per unit. Thorpe's annual fixed cost is $300,000.

Required

Determine the break-even point in units and dollars.

Exercise 11-16 *Desired profit* L.O. 8

Jaffe Company incurs annual fixed costs of $60,000. Variable costs for Jaffe's product are $7.50 per unit, and the sales price is $12.50 per unit. Jaffe desires to earn an annual profit of $40,000.

Required

Determine the sales volume in dollars and units required to earn the desired profit.

Exercise 11-17 *Determining fixed and variable cost per unit* L.O. 1

Vidal Corporation produced and sold 24,000 units of product during October. It earned a contribution margin of $96,000 on sales of $336,000 and determined that cost per unit of product was $12.50.

Required

Based on this information, determine the variable and fixed cost per unit of product.

Exercise 11-18 *Determining variable cost from incomplete cost data* L.O. 1

Amaya Corporation produced 150,000 watches that it sold for $24 each during 2006. The company determined that fixed manufacturing cost per unit was $6 per watch. The company reported a $600,000 gross margin on its 2006 financial statements.

Required

Determine the total variable cost, the variable cost per unit, and the total contribution margin.

L.O. 7, 8, 9

Exercise 11-19 *Margin of safety*

Information concerning a product produced by Cheung Company appears here.

Sales price per unit	$160
Variable cost per unit	$35
Total annual fixed manufacturing and operating costs	$900,000

Required

Determine the following:

a. Contribution margin per unit.
b. Number of units that Cheung must sell to break even.
c. Sales level in units that Cheung must reach to earn a profit of $360,000.
d. Determine the margin of safety in units, sales dollars, and as a percentage.

L.O. 9

Exercise 11-20 *Margin of safety*

Bates Company makes a product that sells for $18 per unit. The company pays $8 per unit for the variable costs of the product and incurs annual fixed costs of $150,000. Bates expects to sell 24,000 units of product.

Required

Determine Bates' margin of safety in units, sales dollars, and as a percentage.

PROBLEMS

All Problems are available with McGraw-Hill's Homework Manager

L.O. 1

Problem 11-21 *Identifying cost behavior*

Required

Identify the following costs as fixed or variable.
Costs related to plane trips between San Diego, California, and Orlando, Florida, follow. Pilots are paid on a per trip basis.

a. Pilots' salaries relative to the number of trips flown.
b. Depreciation relative to the number of planes in service.
c. Cost of refreshments relative to the number of passengers.
d. Pilots' salaries relative to the number of passengers on a particular trip.
e. Cost of a maintenance check relative to the number of passengers on a particular trip.
f. Fuel costs relative to the number of trips.

National Union Bank operates several branch offices in grocery stores. Each branch employs a supervisor and two tellers.

g. Tellers' salaries relative to the number of tellers in a particular district.
h. Supplies cost relative to the number of transactions processed in a particular branch.
i. Tellers' salaries relative to the number of customers served at a particular branch.
j. Supervisors' salaries relative to the number of branches operated.
k. Supervisors' salaries relative to the number of customers served in a particular branch.
l. Facility rental costs relative to the size of customer deposits.

Costs related to operating a fast-food restaurant follow.

m. Depreciation of equipment relative to the number of restaurants.
n. Building rental cost relative to the number of customers served in a particular restaurant.
o. Manager's salary of a particular restaurant relative to the number of employees.
p. Food cost relative to the number of customers.
q. Utility cost relative to the number of restaurants in operation.
r. Company president's salary relative to the number of restaurants in operation.
s. Land costs relative to the number of hamburgers sold at a particular restaurant.
t. Depreciation of equipment relative to the number of customers served at a particular restaurant.

Problem 11-22 *Cost behavior and averaging*

L.O. 1

mhhe.com/edmonds2007

Jenny Tang has decided to start Tang Cleaning, a residential housecleaning service company. She is able to rent cleaning equipment at a cost of $600 per month. Labor costs are expected to be $50 per house cleaned and supplies are expected to cost $5 per house.

CHECK FIGURES
c. Total supplies cost for cleaning 30 houses: $150
d. Total cost for 20 houses: $1,700

Required

a. Determine the total expected cost of equipment rental and the expected cost of equipment rental per house cleaned, assuming that Tang Cleaning cleans 10, 20, or 30 houses during one month. Is the cost of equipment a fixed or a variable cost?
b. Determine the total expected cost of labor and the expected cost of labor per house cleaned, assuming that Tang Cleaning cleans 10, 20, or 30 houses during one month. Is the cost of labor a fixed or a variable cost?
c. Determine the total expected cost of supplies and the expected cost of supplies per house cleaned, assuming that Tang Cleaning cleans 10, 20, or 30 houses during one month. Is the cost of supplies a fixed or a variable cost?
d. Determine the total expected cost of cleaning houses, assuming that Tang Cleaning cleans 10, 20, or 30 houses during one month.
e. Determine the expected cost per house, assuming that Tang Cleaning cleans 10, 20, or 30 houses during one month. Why does the cost per unit decrease as the number of houses increases?

Problem 11-23 *Context-sensitive nature of cost behavior classifications*

L.O. 1

Citizens Bank's start-up division establishes new branch banks. Each branch opens with three tellers. Total teller cost per branch is $80,000 per year. The three tellers combined can process up to 80,000 customer transactions per year. If a branch does not attain a volume of at least 50,000 transactions during its first year of operations, it is closed. If the demand for services exceeds 80,000 transactions, an additional teller is hired, and the branch is transferred from the start-up division to regular operations.

CHECK FIGURE
b. Average teller cost for 60,000 transactions: $1.33

Required

a. What is the relevant range of activity for new branch banks?
b. Determine the amount of teller cost in total and the teller cost per transaction for a branch that processes 50,000, 60,000, 70,000, or 80,000 transactions. In this case (the activity base is the number of transactions for a specific branch), is the teller cost a fixed or a variable cost?
c. Determine the amount of teller cost in total and the teller cost per branch for Citizens Bank, assuming that the start-up division operates 10, 15, 20, or 25 branches. In this case (the activity base is the number of branches), is the teller cost a fixed or a variable cost?

Problem 11-24 *Context-sensitive nature of cost behavior classifications*

L.O. 1

mhhe.com/edmonds2007

Adriane Dawkins operates a sales booth in computer software trade shows, selling an accounting software package, *Accountech*. She purchases the package from a software manufacturer for $200 each. Booth space at the convention hall costs $7,500 per show.

CHECK FIGURES
a. Average cost at 300 units: $225
b. Average price at 150 units: $310

Required

a. Sales at past trade shows have ranged between 100 and 300 software packages per show. Determine the average cost of sales per unit if Ms. Dawkins sells 100, 150, 200, 250, or 300 units of *Accountech* at a trade show. Use the following chart to organize your answer. Is the cost of booth space fixed or variable?

	Sales Volume in Units (a)				
	100	150	200	250	300
Total cost of software (a × $200)	$20,000				
Total cost of booth rental	7,500				
Total cost of sales (b)	$27,500				
Average cost per unit (b ÷ a)	$275.00				

b. If Ms. Dawkins wants to earn a $60 profit on each package of software she sells at a trade show, what price must she charge at sales volumes of 100, 150, 200, 250, or 300 units?

c. Record the total cost of booth space if Ms. Dawkins attends one, two, three, four, or five trade shows. Record your answers in the following chart. Is the cost of booth space fixed or variable relative to the number of shows attended?

	Number of Trade Shows Attended				
	1	2	3	4	5
Total cost of booth rental	$7,500				

d. Ms. Dawkins provides decorative shopping bags to customers who purchase software packages. Some customers take the bags; others do not. Some customers stuff more than one software package into a single bag. The number of bags varies in relation to the number of units sold, but the relationship is not proportional. Assume that Ms. Dawkins uses $40 of bags for every 50 software packages sold. What is the additional cost per unit sold? Is the cost fixed or variable?

L.O. 2

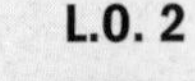

mhhe.com/edmonds2007

CHECK FIGURES

Part 1, b: $3,200

Part 2, h: 10%

Part 3, k: cost per student for 22 students: $20

Problem 11-25 *Effects of operating leverage on profitability*

Smartt Training Services (STS) provides instruction on the use of computer software for the employees of its corporate clients. It offers courses in the clients' offices on the clients' equipment. The only major expense STS incurs is instructor salaries; it pays instructors $4,000 per course taught. STS recently agreed to offer a course of instruction to the employees of Cartee Incorporated at a price of $360 per student. Cartee estimated that 20 students would attend the course.

Base your answer on the preceding information.

Part 1:

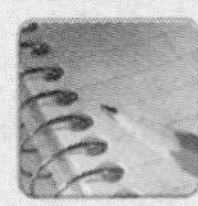

Required

a. Relative to the number of students in a single course, is the cost of instruction a fixed or a variable cost?

b. Determine the profit, assuming that 20 students attend the course.

c. Determine the profit, assuming a 10 percent increase in enrollment (i.e., enrollment increases to 22 students). What is the percentage change in profitability?

d. Determine the profit, assuming a 10 percent decrease in enrollment (i.e., enrollment decreases to 18 students). What is the percentage change in profitability?

e. Explain why a 10 percent shift in enrollment produces more than a 10 percent shift in profitability. Use the term that identifies this phenomenon.

Part 2:

The instructor has offered to teach the course for a percentage of tuition fees. Specifically, she wants $200 per person attending the class. Assume that the tuition fee remains at $360 per student.

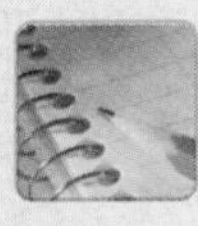

Required

f. Is the cost of instruction a fixed or a variable cost?

g. Determine the profit, assuming that 20 students take the course.

h. Determine the profit, assuming a 10 percent increase in enrollment (i.e., enrollment increases to 22 students). What is the percentage change in profitability?

i. Determine the profit, assuming a 10 percent decrease in enrollment (i.e., enrollment decreases to 18 students). What is the percentage change in profitability?

j. Explain why a 10 percent shift in enrollment produces a proportional 10 percent shift in profitability.

Part 3:

STS sells a workbook with printed material unique to each course to each student who attends the course. Any workbooks that are not sold must be destroyed. Prior to the first class, STS printed 20 copies of the books based on the client's estimate of the number of people who would attend the course. Each workbook costs $20 and is sold to course participants for $32. This cost includes a royalty fee paid to the author and the cost of duplication.

Required

k. Calculate the workbook cost in total and per student, assuming that 18, 20, or 22 students attempt to attend the course.

l. Classify the cost of workbooks as fixed or variable relative to the number of students attending the course.

m. Discuss the risk of holding inventory as it applies to the workbooks.

n. Explain how a just-in-time inventory system can reduce the cost and risk of holding inventory.

Problem 11-26 ***Effects of fixed and variable cost behavior on the risk and rewards of business opportunities***

L.O. 1, 2

Autumn and Zogby Universities offer executive training courses to corporate clients. Autumn pays its instructors $6,000 per course taught. Zogby pays its instructors $300 per student enrolled in the class. Both universities charge executives a $360 tuition fee per course attended.

CHECK FIGURES
a. Zogby NI: $1,200
b. NI: $2,000

Required

a. Prepare income statements for Autumn and Zogby, assuming that 20 students attend a course.

b. Autumn University embarks on a strategy to entice students from Zogby University by lowering its tuition to $200 per course. Prepare an income statement for Autumn, assuming that the university is successful and enrolls 40 students in its course.

c. Zogby University embarks on a strategy to entice students from Autumn University by lowering its tuition to $200 per course. Prepare an income statement for Zogby, assuming that the university is successful and enrolls 40 students in its course.

d. Explain why the strategy described in Requirement *b* produced a profit but the same strategy described in Requirement *c* produced a loss.

e. Prepare income statements for Autumn and Zogby Universities, assuming that 15 students attend a course, assuming that both universities charge executives a $360 tuition fee per course attended.

f. It is always better to have fixed than variable cost. Explain why this statement is false.

g. It is always better to have variable than fixed cost. Explain why this statement is false.

Problem 11-27 ***Analyzing operating leverage***

L.O. 4

Norm Champion is a venture capitalist facing two alternative investment opportunities. He intends to invest $500,000 in a start-up firm. He is nervous, however, about future economic volatility. He asks you to analyze the following financial data for the past year's operations of the two firms he is considering and give him some business advice.

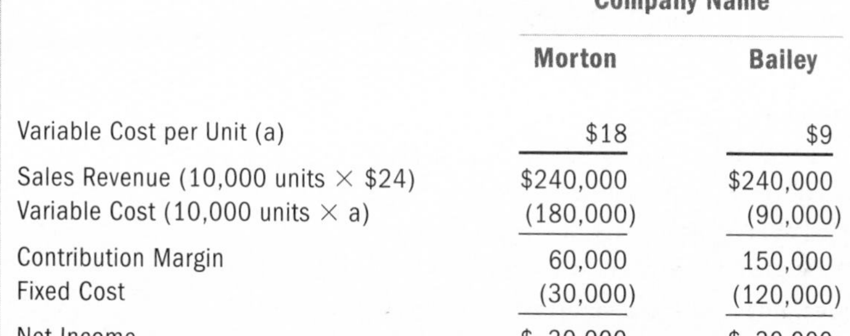

	Company Name	
	Morton	**Bailey**
Variable Cost per Unit (a)	$18	$9
Sales Revenue (10,000 units × $24)	$240,000	$240,000
Variable Cost (10,000 units × a)	(180,000)	(90,000)
Contribution Margin	60,000	150,000
Fixed Cost	(30,000)	(120,000)
Net Income	$ 30,000	$ 30,000

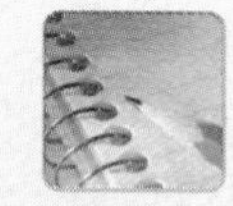

CHECK FIGURES
b. % of change for Bailey: 50
c. % of change for Morton: (20)

Required

a. Use the contribution margin approach to compute the operating leverage for each firm.
b. If the economy expands in coming years, Morton and Bailey will both enjoy a 10 percent per year increase in sales, assuming that the selling price remains unchanged. Compute the change in net income for each firm in dollar amount and in percentage. (*Note:* Since the number of units increases, both revenue and variable cost will increase.)
c. If the economy contracts in coming years, Morton and Bailey will both suffer a 10 percent decrease in sales volume, assuming that the selling price remains unchanged. Compute the change in net income for each firm in dollar amount and in percentage. (*Note:* Since the number of units decreases, both total revenue and total variable cost will decrease.)
d. Write a memo to Norm Champion with your analyses and advice.

L.O. 3, 7

mhhe.com/edmonds2007

CHECK FIGURE
a. 12,000 units

Problem 11-28 *Determining the break-even point and preparing a contribution margin income statement*

Dester Manufacturing Company makes a product that it sells for $50 per unit. The company incurs variable manufacturing costs of $20 per unit. Variable selling expenses are $5 per unit, annual fixed manufacturing costs are $187,000, and fixed selling and administrative costs are $113,000 per year.

Required

a. Determine the break-even point in units and dollars.
b. Confirm your results by preparing a contribution margin income statement for the break-even sales volume.

L.O. 9

CHECK FIGURES
b. NI:
Skin Cream $102,000
Bath Oil $88,000
Color Gel $90,000

Problem 11-29 *Margin of safety and operating leverage*

Musso Company is considering the addition of a new product to its cosmetics line. The company has three distinctly different options: a skin cream, a bath oil, or a hair coloring gel. Relevant information and budgeted annual income statements for each of the products follow.

	Relevant Information		
	Skin Cream	Bath Oil	Color Gel
Budgeted Sales in Units (a)	70,000	120,000	40,000
Expected Sales Price (b)	$8	$3	$12
Variable Costs Per Unit (c)	$5	$1	$ 7
Income Statements			
Sales Revenue (a × b)	$560,000	$360,000	$480,000
Variable Costs (a × c)	(350,000)	(120,000)	(280,000)
Contribution Margin	210,000	240,000	200,000
Fixed Costs	(150,000)	(200,000)	(150,000)
Net Income	$ 60,000	$ 40,000	$ 50,000

Required

a. Determine the margin of safety as a percentage for each product.
b. Prepare revised income statements for each product, assuming a 20 percent increase in the budgeted sales volume.
c. For each product, determine the percentage change in net income that results from the 20 percent increase in sales. Which product has the highest operating leverage?
d. Assuming that management is pessimistic and risk averse, which product should the company add to its cosmetic line? Explain your answer.
e. Assuming that management is optimistic and risk aggressive, which product should the company add to its cosmetics line? Explain your answer.

ANALYZE, THINK, COMMUNICATE

ATC 11-1 Business Applications *Operating leverage*

The following information was taken from the Form 10-K SEC filings for **CSX Corporation** and **Starbucks Corporation**. It is from the 2002 fiscal year reports, and all dollar amounts are in millions.

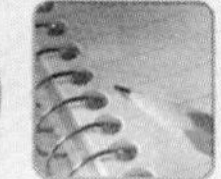

Description of Business for CSX Corporation

CSX Corporation (CSX or the Company) operates one of the largest rail networks in the United States and also provides intermodal transportation services across the United States and key markets in Canada and Mexico. Its marine operations include an international terminal services company and a domestic container-shipping company.

CSX Corporation	2002	2001
Operating revenues	$8,172	$8,110
Operating earnings	424	293

Description of Business for Starbucks Corporation

Starbucks Corporation (together with its subsidiaries, Starbucks or the Company) purchases and roasts high-quality whole bean coffees and sells them, along with fresh, rich-brewed coffees, Italian-style espresso beverages, cold blended beverages, a variety of pastries and confections, coffee-related accessories and equipment, a selection of premium teas, and a line of compact discs primarily through Company-operated retail stores.

At fiscal year-end, Starbucks had 3,496 Company-operated stores in 43 states, the District of Columbia, and five Canadian provinces (which comprise the Company's North American Retail operating segment), as well as 322 stores in the United Kingdom, 33 stores in Australia, and 29 stores in Thailand.

Starbucks	2002	2001
Operating revenues	$3,289	$2,649
Operating earnings	319	281

Required

a. Determine which company appears to have the higher operating leverage.

b. Write a paragraph or two explaining why the company you identified in Requirement *a* might be expected to have the higher operating leverage.

c. If revenues for both companies declined, which company do you think would likely experience the greatest decline in operating earnings? Explain your answer.

ATC 11-2 Group Assignment *Operating leverage*

The Parent Teacher Association (PTA) of Meadow High School is planning a fund-raising campaign. The PTA is considering the possibility of hiring Eric Logan, a world-renowned investment counselor, to address the public. Tickets would sell for $28 each. The school has agreed to let the PTA use Harville Auditorium at no cost. Mr. Logan is willing to accept one of two compensation arrangements. He will sign an agreement to receive a fixed fee of $10,000 regardless of the number of tickets sold. Alternatively, he will accept payment of $20 per ticket sold. In communities similar to that in which Meadow is located, Mr. Logan has drawn an audience of approximately 500 people.

Required

a. In front of the class, present a statement showing the expected net income assuming 500 people buy tickets.

b. Divide the class into groups and then organize the groups into four sections. Assign one of the following tasks to each section of groups.

Group Tasks

(1) Assume the PTA pays Mr. Logan a fixed fee of $10,000. Determine the amount of net income that the PTA will earn if ticket sales are 10 percent higher than expected. Calculate the percentage change in net income.

(2) Assume that the PTA pays Mr. Logan a fixed fee of $10,000. Determine the amount of net income that the PTA will earn if ticket sales are 10 percent lower than expected. Calculate the percentage change in net income.

(3) Assume that the PTA pays Mr. Logan $20 per ticket sold. Determine the amount of net income that the PTA will earn if ticket sales are 10 percent higher than expected. Calculate the percentage change in net income.

(4) Assume that the PTA pays Mr. Logan $20 per ticket sold. Determine the amount of net income that the PTA will earn if ticket sales are 10 percent lower than expected. Calculate the percentage change in net income.

c. Have each group select a spokesperson. Have one of the spokespersons in each section of groups go to the board and present the results of the analysis conducted in Requirement *b.* Resolve any discrepancies in the computations presented at the board and those developed by the other groups.

d. Draw conclusions regarding the risks and rewards associated with operating leverage. At a minimum, answer the following questions.

(1) Which type of cost structure (fixed or variable) produces the higher growth potential in profitability for a company?

(2) Which type of cost structure (fixed or variable) produces the higher risk of declining profitability for a company?

(3) Under what circumstances should a company seek to establish a fixed cost structure?

(4) Under what circumstances should a company seek to establish a variable cost structure?

ATC 11-3 Research Assignment *Fixed versus variable cost*

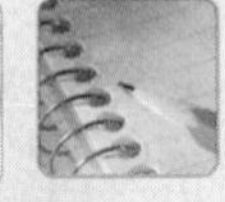

The March 8, 2004, edition of *BusinessWeek* contained an article titled "Courting the Mass Affluent" (see page 68). The article discusses the efforts of **Charles Schwab Corp.** to attract a bigger share of investors who have $100,000 to $1 million to invest. Read this article and complete the following requirements.

Required

a. Schwab increased its marketing budget during the first quarter of 2004. What was the amount of the increase? Is this cost fixed or variable relative to the number of new customers that the company attracts?

b. Assume that Schwab acquires a significant number of new customers. Name several costs that are likely to remain fixed as revenue increases.

c. Assume that Schwab acquires a significant number of new customers. Name several costs that are likely to vary with increasing revenue.

d. Consider the cost of establishing a new customer account. Describe a set of circumstances under which this would be a fixed cost and a different set of circumstances under which this would be a variable cost.

ATC 11-4 Writing Assignment *Operating leverage, margin of safety, and cost behavior*

The article "Up Front: More Condensing at the Digest?" in the October 19, 1998, issue of *BusinessWeek* reported that Thomas Ryder, CEO of **Reader's Digest Association**, was considering a spin-off of Reader's Digest's direct-marketing operations into a joint venture with **Time Warner**. The article's author, Robert McNatt, noted that the direct marketing of books, music, and videos is a far larger part of the Reader's Digest business than is its namesake magazine. Furthermore, the article stated that 1998 direct-marketing sales of $1.6 billion were down 11 percent from 1997. The decline in revenue caused the division's operating profits to decline 58 percent. The article stated that the contemplated alliance with Time Warner could provide some fast help. Gerald Levin, Time Warner chairman, has said that his company's operations provide customer service and product fulfillment far better than other Web sellers do because of Time Warner's established 250 websites.

Required

a. Write a memo explaining how an 11 percent decrease in sales could result in a 58 percent decline in operating profits.

b. Explain briefly how the decline in revenue will affect the company's margin of safety.

c. Explain why a joint venture between Reader's Digest's direct-marketing division and Time Warner could work to the advantage of both companies. (*Hint:* Consider the effects of fixed cost behavior in formulating your response.)

ATC 11-5 Ethical Dilemma *Profitability versus social conscience (effects of cost behavior)*

Advances in biological technology have enabled two research companies, Bio Labs Inc. and Scientific Associates, to develop an insect-resistant corn seed. Neither company is financially strong enough to develop the distribution channels necessary to bring the product to world markets. World Agra Distributors Inc. has negotiated contracts with both companies for the exclusive right to market their seed. Bio Labs signed an agreement to receive an annual royalty of $1,000,000. In contrast, Scientific Associates chose an agreement that provides for a royalty of $0.50 per pound of seed sold. Both agreements have a 10-year term. During 2004, World Agra sold approximately 1,600,000 pounds of the Bio Labs Inc. seed and 2,400,000 pounds of the Scientific Associates seed. Both types of seed were sold for $1.25 per pound. By the end of 2004, it was apparent that the seed developed by Scientific Associates was superior. Although insect infestation was virtually nonexistent for both types of seed, the seed developed by Scientific Associates produced corn that was sweeter and had consistently higher yields.

World Agra Distributors' chief financial officer, Roger Weatherstone, recently retired. To the astonishment of the annual planning committee, Mr. Weatherstone's replacement, Ray Borrough, adamantly recommended that the marketing department develop a major advertising campaign to promote the seed developed by Bio Labs Inc. The planning committee reluctantly approved the recommendation. A $100,000 ad campaign was launched; the ads emphasized the ability of the Bio Labs seed to avoid insect infestation. The campaign was silent with respect to taste or crop yield. It did not mention the seed developed by Scientific Associates. World Agra's sales staff was instructed to push the Bio Labs seed and to sell the Scientific Associates seed only on customer demand. Although total sales remained relatively constant during 2005, sales of the Scientific Associates seed fell to approximately 1,300,000 pounds while sales of the Bio Labs Inc. seed rose to 2,700,000 pounds.

Required

a. Determine the amount of increase or decrease in profitability experienced by World Agra in 2005 as a result of promoting Bio Labs seed. Support your answer with appropriate commentary.

b. Did World Agra's customers in particular and society in general benefit or suffer from the decision to promote the Bio Labs seed?

c. Review the standards of ethical conduct in Exhibit 10.13 of Chapter 10 and comment on whether Mr. Borrough's recommendation violated any of the standards in the code of ethical conduct.

d. Comment on your belief regarding the adequacy of the Standards of Ethical Conduct for Managerial Accountants to direct the conduct of management accountants.

CHAPTER 12

Cost Accumulation, Tracing, and Allocation

LEARNING OBJECTIVES

After you have mastered the material in this chapter you will be able to:

1. **Describe the relationships among cost objects, cost drivers, and cost accumulation.**
2. **Distinguish direct costs from indirect costs.**
3. **Use basic mathematics to compute indirect cost allocations.**
4. **Select appropriate cost drivers for allocating indirect costs in a variety of different circumstances.**
5. **Use allocation to solve problems that emerge in the process of making cost-plus pricing decisions.**
6. **Explain why companies establish indirect cost pools.**
7. **Recognize human motivation as a key variable in the allocation process.**

The Curious Accountant

A former patient of a California hospital complained about being charged $7 for a single aspirin tablet. After all, an entire bottle of 100 aspirins can be purchased at the local grocery store for around $2.

Can you think of any reasons, other than shameless profiteering, that a hospital would need to charge $7 for an aspirin? Remember that the hospital is not just selling the aspirin; it is also delivering it to the patient. (Answers on page 431.)

Chapter 12

CHAPTER OPENING

What does it cost? This is one of the questions most frequently asked by business managers. Managers must have reliable cost estimates to price products, evaluate performance, control operations, and prepare financial statements. As this discussion implies, managers need to know the cost of many different things. The things we are trying to determine the cost of are commonly called **cost objects.** *For example, if we are trying to determine the cost of operating a department, that department is the cost object. Cost objects may be products, processes, departments, services, activities, and so on. This chapter explains techniques managerial accountants use to determine the cost of a variety of cost objects.*

Use of Cost Drivers to Accumulate Costs

LO 1

Describe the relationships among cost objects, cost drivers, and cost accumulation.

Accountants use **cost accumulation** to determine the cost of a particular object. Suppose the Atlanta Braves advertising manager wants to promote a Tuesday night ball game by offering free baseball caps to all children who attend. What would the promotion cost? The team's accountant must *accumulate* many individual costs and add them together. For simplicity consider only three cost components: (1) the cost of the caps, (2) the cost of advertising the promotion, and (3) the cost of an employee to work on the promotion.

Cost accumulation begins with identifying the cost objects. The primary cost object is the cost of the promotion. Three secondary cost objects are (1) the cost of caps, (2) the cost of advertising, and (3) the cost of labor. The costs of the secondary cost objects are combined to determine the cost of the primary cost object.

Determining the costs of the secondary cost objects requires identifying what *drives* those costs. A **cost driver** has a *cause-and-effect* relationship with a cost object. For example, the *number of caps* (cost driver) has an effect on the *cost of caps* (cost object). The *number of advertisements* is a cost driver for the *advertising cost* (cost object); the *number of labor hours* worked is a cost driver for the *labor cost* (cost object). Using the following assumptions about unit costs and cost drivers, the accumulated cost of the primary cost object (cost of the cap promotion) is:

Cost Object	Cost per Unit	×	Cost Driver	=	Total Cost of Object
Cost of caps	$2.50	×	4,000 Caps	=	$10,000
Cost of advertising	$100.00	×	50 Advertisements	=	5,000
Cost of labor	$8.00	×	100 Hours	=	800
Cost of cap promotion					$15,800

The Atlanta Braves should run the promotion if management expects it to produce additional revenues exceeding $15,800.

Estimated versus Actual Cost

The accumulated cost of the promotion—$15,800—is an *estimate.* Management cannot know *actual* costs and revenues until after running the promotion. While actual information is more accurate, it is not relevant for deciding whether to run the promotion because the decision must be made before the actual cost is known. Managers must accept a degree of inaccuracy in exchange for the relevance of timely information. Many business decisions are based on estimated rather than actual costs.

Managers use cost estimates to set prices, bid on contracts, evaluate proposals, distribute resources, plan production, and set goals. Certain circumstances, however, require actual cost data. For example, published financial reports and managerial performance evaluations use actual cost data. Managers frequently accumulate both estimated and actual cost data for the same cost object. For example, companies use cost estimates to establish goals and use actual costs to evaluate management performance in meeting those goals. The following discussion provides a number of business examples that use estimated data, actual data, or a combination of both.

Assignment of Cost to Objects in a Retail Business

Exhibit 12.1 displays the January income statement for In Style, Inc. (ISI), a retail clothing store. ISI subdivides its operations into women's, men's, and children's departments. To encourage the departmental managers to maximize sales, ISI began paying the manager of each department a bonus based on a percentage of departmental sales revenue.

Although the bonus incentive increased sales revenue, it also provoked negative consequences. The departmental managers began to argue over floor space; each manager wanted more space to display merchandise. The managers reduced prices; they increased sales commissions. In the drive to maximize sales, the managers ignored the need to control costs. To improve the situation, the store manager decided to base future bonuses on each department's contribution to profitability rather than its sales revenue.

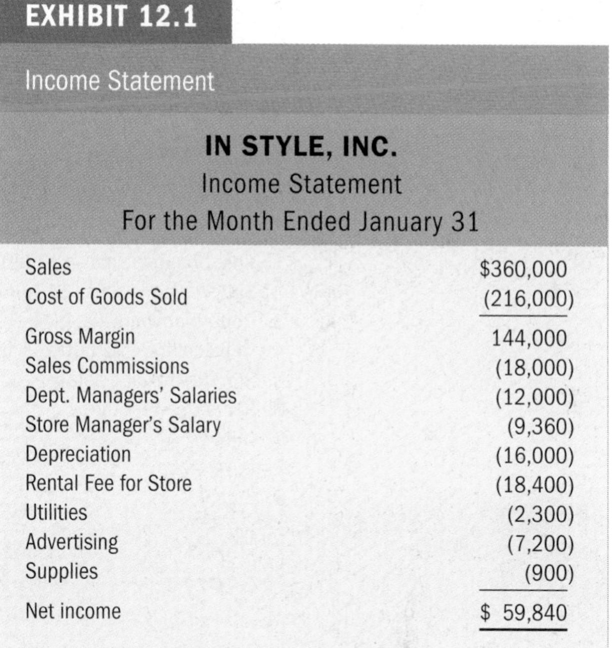

EXHIBIT 12.1

Income Statement

IN STYLE, INC.
Income Statement
For the Month Ended January 31

Sales	$360,000
Cost of Goods Sold	(216,000)
Gross Margin	144,000
Sales Commissions	(18,000)
Dept. Managers' Salaries	(12,000)
Store Manager's Salary	(9,360)
Depreciation	(16,000)
Rental Fee for Store	(18,400)
Utilities	(2,300)
Advertising	(7,200)
Supplies	(900)
Net income	$ 59,840

Identifying Direct versus Indirect Costs

The new bonus strategy requires determining the cost of operating each department. Each department is a separate *cost object*. Assigning costs to the departments (cost objects) requires **cost tracing** and cost allocation. **Direct costs** can be easily traced to a cost object. **Indirect costs** cannot be easily traced to a cost object. Whether or not a cost is easily traceable requires *cost/benefit analysis*.

Some of ISI's costs can be easily traced to the cost objects (specific departments). The cost of goods sold is an example of an easily traced cost. Price tags on merchandise can be coded so cash register scanners capture the departmental code for each sale. The cost of goods sold is not only easily traceable but also useful information. Companies need cost of goods sold information for financial reporting (income statement) and for management decisions (determining inventory reorder points, pricing strategies, and cost control). Because the cost of tracing *cost of goods sold* is small relative to the benefits obtained, cost of goods sold is a *direct cost.*

Distinguish direct costs from indirect costs.

In contrast, the cost of supplies (shopping bags, sales slips, pens, staples, price tags) used by each department is much more difficult to trace. How could the number of staples used to seal shopping bags be traced to any particular department? The sales staff could count the number of staples used, but doing so would be silly for the benefits obtained. Although tracing the cost of supplies to each department may be possible, it is not worth the effort of doing so. The cost of supplies is therefore an *indirect cost*. Indirect costs are also called **overhead costs.**

Direct and indirect costs can be described as follows:

> **Direct costs** can be traced to cost objects in a *cost-effective* manner.
> **Indirect costs** cannot be traced to objects in a *cost-effective* manner.

By analyzing the accounting records, ISI's accountant classified the costs from the income statement in Exhibit 12.1 as direct or indirect, as shown in Exhibit 12.2. The next paragraph explains the classifications.

All figures represent January costs. Items 1 though 4 are direct costs, traceable to the cost objects in a cost-effective manner. Cost of goods sold is traced to departments at the point of sale using cash register scanners. Sales commissions are based on a percentage of departmental sales and are therefore easy to trace to the departments. Departmental managers' salaries are also easily traceable to the departments. Equipment, furniture, and fixtures are tagged with department codes that permit tracing depreciation charges directly to specific departments. Items 5 through 8 are incurred on behalf of the company as a whole and are therefore not directly traceable to a specific department. Although Item 9 could be traced to specific departments, the cost of doing so would exceed the benefits. The cost of supplies is therefore also classified as indirect.

Cost Classifications—Independent and Context Sensitive

Whether a cost is direct or indirect is independent of whether it is fixed or variable. In the ISI example, both cost of goods sold and the cost of supplies vary relative to sales volume (both

EXHIBIT 12.2

Classification of Income Statement Costs

Cost Item	Direct Costs Women's	Men's	Children's	Indirect Costs
1. Cost of goods sold–$216,000	$120,000	$58,000	$38,000	
2. Sales commissions–$18,000	9,500	5,500	3,000	
3. Dept. managers' salaries–$12,000	5,000	4,200	2,800	
4. Depreciation–$16,000	7,000	5,000	4,000	
5. Store manager's salary				$ 9,360
6. Rental fee for store				18,400
7. Utilities				2,300
8. Advertising				7,200
9. Supplies				900
Totals	$141,500	$72,700	$47,800	$38,160

are variable costs), but cost of goods sold is direct and the cost of supplies is indirect. Furthermore, the cost of rent and the cost of depreciation are both fixed relative to sales volume, but the cost of rent is indirect and the cost of depreciation is direct. In fact, the very same cost can be classified as direct or indirect, depending on the cost object. The store manager's salary is not directly traceable to a specific department, but it is traceable to a particular store.

Similarly, identifying costs as direct or indirect is independent of whether the costs are relevant to a given decision. ISI could avoid both cost of goods sold and the cost of supplies for a particular department if that department were eliminated. Both costs are relevant to a segment elimination decision, yet one is direct, and the other is indirect. You cannot memorize costs as direct or indirect, fixed or variable, relevant or not relevant. When trying to identify costs as to type or behavior, you must consider the context in which the costs occur.

Allocating Indirect Costs to Objects

Use basic mathematics to compute indirect cost allocations.

Cost allocation involves dividing a total cost into parts and assigning the parts to designated cost objects. How should ISI allocate the $38,160 of indirect costs to each of the three departments? First, identify a cost driver for each cost to be allocated. For example, there is a cause and effect relationship between store size and rent cost; the larger the building, the higher the rent cost. This relationship suggests that the more floor space a department occupies, the more rent cost that department should bear. To illustrate, assume ISI's store capacity is 23,000 square feet and the women's, men's, and children's departments occupy 12,000, 7,000, and 4,000 square feet, respectively. ISI can achieve a rational allocation of the rent cost using the following two-step process.[1]

Step 1. Compute the *allocation rate* by dividing the *total cost to be allocated* ($18,400 rental fee) by the *cost driver* (23,000 square feet of store space). The *cost driver is also called the* **allocation base.** This computation produces the **allocation rate,** as follows:

Total cost to be allocated	÷	Cost driver (allocation base)	=	Allocation rate
$18,400 rental fee	÷	23,000 square feet	=	$0.80 per square foot

[1]Other mathematical approaches achieve the same result. This text consistently uses the two-step method described here. Specifically, the text determines allocations by (1) computing a *rate* and (2) multiplying the *rate* by the *weight of the base* (cost driver).

REALITY BYTES

How does **Southwest Airlines** know the cost of flying a passenger from Houston, Texas, to Los Angeles, California? The fact is that Southwest does not know the actual cost of flying particular passengers anywhere. There are many indirect costs associated with flying passengers. Some of these include the cost of planes, fuel, pilots, office buildings, and ground personnel. Indeed, besides insignificant food and beverage costs, there are few costs that could be traced directly to customers. Southwest and other airlines must use allocation and averaging to determine the estimated cost of providing transportation services to customers. Estimated rather than actual cost is used for decision-making purposes.

Step 2. Multiply the *allocation rate* by the *weight of the cost driver* (weight of the base) to determine the allocation per *cost object,* as follows:

Cost Object	Allocation Rate	×	Number of Square Feet	=	Allocation per Cost Object
Women's department	$0.80	×	12,000	=	$ 9,600
Men's department	0.80	×	7,000	=	5,600
Children's department	0.80	×	4,000	=	3,200
Total			23,000		$18,400

It is also plausible to presume utilities cost is related to the amount of floor space a department occupies. Larger departments will consume more heating, lighting, air conditioning, and so on than smaller departments. Floor space is a reasonable cost driver for utility cost. Based on square footage, ISI can allocate utility cost to each department as follows:

Step 1. Compute the allocation rate by dividing the total cost to be allocated ($2,300 utility cost) by the cost driver (23,000 square feet of store space):

Total cost to be allocated	÷	Cost driver	=	Allocation rate
$2,300 utility cost	÷	23,000 square feet	=	$0.10 per square foot

Step 2. Multiply the *allocation rate* by the weight of the *cost driver* to determine the allocation per *cost object*:

Cost Object	Allocation Rate	×	Number of Square Feet	=	Allocation per Cost Object
Women's department	$0.10	×	12,000	=	$1,200
Men's department	0.10	×	7,000	=	700
Children's department	0.10	×	4,000	=	400
Total			23,000		$2,300

CHECK YOURSELF 12.1

HealthCare Inc. wants to estimate the cost of operating the three departments (Dermatology, Gynecology, and Pediatrics) that serve patients in its Health Center. Each department performed the following number of patient treatments during the most recent year of operation: Dermatology, 2,600; Gynecology, 3,500; and Pediatrics, 6,200. The annual salary of the Health Center's program administrator is $172,200. How much of the salary cost should HealthCare allocate to the Pediatrics Department?

Answer

Step 1 Compute the *allocation rate.*

Total cost to be allocated	÷	Cost driver (patient treatments)	=	Allocation rate
$172,200 salary cost	÷	(2,600 + 3,500 + 6,200)	=	$14 per patient treatment

Step 2 Multiply the *allocation rate* by the *weight of the cost driver* (weight of the base) to determine the allocation per *cost object.*

Cost Object	Allocation Rate	×	No. of Treatments	=	Allocation per Cost Object
Pediatrics department	$14	×	6,200	=	$86,800

Selecting a Cost Driver

LO 4

Select appropriate cost drivers for allocating indirect costs in a variety of different circumstances.

Companies can frequently identify more than one cost driver for a particular indirect cost. For example, ISI's shopping bag cost is related to both the *number of sales transactions* and the *volume of sales dollars.* As either of these potential cost drivers increases, shopping bag usage also increases. The most useful cost driver is the one with the strongest cause and effect relationship.

Consider shopping bag usage for T-shirts sold in the children's department versus T-shirts sold in the men's department. Assume ISI studied T-shirt sales during the first week of June and found the following:

Department	Children's	Men's
Number of sales transactions	120	92
Volume of sales dollars	$1,440	$1,612

Given that every sales transaction uses a shopping bag, the children's department uses far more shopping bags than the men's department even though it has a lower volume of sales dollars. A reasonable explanation for this circumstance is that children's T-shirts sell for less than men's T-shirts. The number of sales transactions is the better cost driver because it has a stronger cause and effect relationship with shopping bag usage than does the volume of sales dollars. Should ISI therefore use the number of sales transactions to allocate supply cost to the departments? Not necessarily.

The *availability of information* also influences cost driver selection. Although the number of sales transactions is the more accurate cost driver, ISI could not use this allocation base unless it maintains records of the number of sales transactions per department. If the store tracks the volume of sales dollars but not the number of transactions, it must use dollar volume even if the number of transactions is the better cost driver. For ISI, sales volume in dollars appears to be the best *available* cost driver for allocating supply cost.

Assuming that sales volume for the women's, men's, and children's departments was $190,000, $110,000, and $60,000, respectively, ISI can allocate the supplies cost as follows:

Step 1. Compute the allocation rate by dividing the total cost to be allocated ($900 supplies cost) by the cost driver ($360,000 total sales volume):

Total cost to be allocated	÷	Cost driver	=	Allocation rate
$900 supplies cost	÷	$360,000 sales volume	=	$0.0025 per sales dollar

Step 2. Multiply the allocation rate by the weight of the cost driver to determine the allocation per cost object:

Cost Object	Allocation Rate	×	Sales Volume	=	Allocation per Cost Object
Women's department	$0.0025	×	$190,000	=	$475
Men's department	0.0025	×	110,000	=	275
Children's department	0.0025	×	60,000	=	150
Total			$360,000		$900

ISI believes sales volume is also the appropriate allocation base for advertising cost. The sales generated in each department were likely influenced by the general advertising campaign. ISI can allocate advertising cost as follows:

Step 1. Compute the allocation rate by dividing the total cost to be allocated ($7,200 advertising cost) by the cost driver ($360,000 total sales volume):

Total cost to be allocated	÷	Cost driver	=	Allocation rate
$7,200 advertising cost	÷	$360,000 sales volume	=	$0.02 per sales dollar

Step 2. Multiply the allocation rate by the weight of the cost driver to determine the allocation per cost object:

Cost Object	Allocation Rate	×	Sales Volume	=	Allocation per Cost Object
Women's department	$0.02	×	$190,000	=	$3,800
Men's department	0.02	×	110,000	=	2,200
Children's department	0.02	×	60,000	=	1,200
Total			$360,000		$7,200

There is no strong cause and effect relationship between the store manager's salary and the departments. ISI pays the store manager the same salary regardless of sales level, square footage of store space, number of labor hours, or any other identifiable variable. Because no plausible cost driver exists, ISI must allocate the store manager's salary arbitrarily. Here the manager's salary is simply divided equally among the departments as follows:

Step 1. Compute the allocation rate by dividing the total cost to be allocated ($9,360 manager's monthly salary) by the allocation base (number of departments):

Total cost to be allocated	÷	Cost driver	=	Allocation rate
$9,360 store manager's salary	÷	3 departments	=	$3,120 per department

Step 2. Multiply the allocation rate by the weight of the cost driver to determine the allocation per cost object:

Cost Object	Allocation Rate	×	Number of Departments	=	Allocation per Cost Object
Women's department	$3,120	×	1	=	$3,120
Men's department	3,120	×	1	=	3,120
Children's department	3,120	×	1	=	3,120
Total			3		$9,360

As the allocation of the store manager's salary demonstrates, many allocations are arbitrary or based on a weak relationship between the allocated cost and the allocation base (cost driver). Managers must use care when making decisions using allocated costs.

Behavioral Implications

Using the indirect cost allocations just discussed, Exhibit 12.3 shows the profit each department generated in January. ISI paid the three departmental managers bonuses based on each department's contribution to profitability. The store manager noticed an immediate change in the behavior of the departmental managers. For example, the manager of the women's department offered to give up 1,000 square feet of floor space because she believed reducing the selection of available products would not reduce sales significantly. Customers would simply buy different brands. Although sales would not decline dramatically, rent and utility cost allocations to the women's department would decline, increasing the profitability of the department.

In contrast, the manager of the children's department wanted the extra space. He believed the children's department was losing sales because it did not have enough floor space to display a competitive variety of merchandise. Customers came to the store to shop at the women's department, but they did not come specifically for children's wear. With additional space, the children's department could carry items that would draw customers to the store specifically to buy children's clothing. He believed the extra space would increase sales enough to cover the additional rent and utility cost allocations.

The store manager was pleased with the emphasis on profitability that resulted from tracing and assigning costs to specific departments.

EXHIBIT 12.3

Profit Analysis by Department

	Department			
	Women's	Men's	Children's	Total
Sales	$190,000	$110,000	$60,000	$360,000
Cost of goods sold	(120,000)	(58,000)	(38,000)	(216,000)
Sales commissions	(9,500)	(5,500)	(3,000)	(18,000)
Dept. managers' salary	(5,000)	(4,200)	(2,800)	(12,000)
Depreciation	(7,000)	(5,000)	(4,000)	(16,000)
Store manager's salary	(3,120)	(3,120)	(3,120)	(9,360)
Rental fee for store	(9,600)	(5,600)	(3,200)	(18,400)
Utilities	(1,200)	(700)	(400)	(2,300)
Advertising	(3,800)	(2,200)	(1,200)	(7,200)
Supplies	(475)	(275)	(150)	(900)
Departmental profit	$ 30,305	$ 25,405	$ 4,130	$ 59,840

Answers to The Curious Accountant

When we compare the cost that a hospital charges for an aspirin to the price we pay for an aspirin, we are probably not considering the full cost that we incur to purchase aspirin. If someone asks you what you pay for an aspirin, you would probably take the price of a bottle, say $2, and divide it by the number of pills in the bottle, say 100. This would suggest their cost is $.02 each. What does it cost to buy the aspirins when all costs are considered? First, there is your time to drive to the store; what do you get paid per hour? Then, there is the cost of operating your automobile. You get the idea; in reality, the cost of an aspirin, from a business perspective, is much more than just the cost of the pills themselves.

Exhibit 12.4 shows the income statement of Tenent Healthcare Corporation for three recent years. Tenent Healthcare claims to be ". . . the second largest investor-owned health care services company in the United States." In 2002 it operated 114 hospitals with 27,870 beds in 16 states. As you can see, while it generated almost $14 billion in revenue, it also incurred a lot of expenses. Look at its first two expense categories. Although it incurred $2 billion in supplies expenses, it incurred almost three times this amount in compensation expense. In other words, it cost a lot more to have someone deliver the aspirin to your bed than the aspirin itself costs.

In 2002 Tenent earned $785 million from its $13.9 billion in sales. This is a return on sales percentage of 5.6 percent ($785 ÷ $13,913). Therefore, on a $7 aspirin, Tenent would earn 39 cents of profit, which is still not a bad profit for selling one aspirin. As a comparison, in 2002, Kroger's return on sales was 2.3 percent.

EXHIBIT 12.4

TENENT HEALTHCARE CORPORATION
Consolidated Statements of Income
(Dollars in Millions)

	Years ended May 31		
	2000	**2001**	**2002**
Net operating revenues	$11,414	$12,053	$13,913
Operating expenses:			
Salaries and benefits	4,508	4,680	5,346
Supplies	1,595	1,677	1,960
Provision for doubtful accounts	851	849	986
Other operating expenses	2,525	2,603	2,824
Depreciation	411	428	472
Goodwill amortization	94	99	101
Other amortization	28	27	31
Impairment of goodwill and long-lived assets and restructuring charges	355	143	99
Loss from early extinguishment of debt	–	56	383
Operating income	1,047	1,491	1,711
Interest expense	(479)	(456)	(327)
Investment earnings	22	37	32
Minority interests	(21)	(14)	(38)
Net gains on sales of facilities and long-term investments	49	28	–
Income before income taxes	618	1,086	1,378
Income taxes	(278)	(443)	(593)
Income from continuing operations, before discontinued operations and cumulative effect of accounting change	340	643	785
Discontinued operations, net of taxes	(19)	–	–
Cumulative effect of accounting change, net of taxes	(19)	–	–
Net income	$ 302	$ 643	$ 785

Effects of Cost Behavior on Selecting the Most Appropriate Cost Driver

LO 4

Select appropriate cost drivers for allocating indirect costs in a variety of different circumstances.

As previously mentioned, indirect costs may exhibit variable or fixed cost behavior patterns. Failing to consider the effects of cost behavior when allocating indirect costs can lead to significant distortions in product cost measurement. We examine the critical relationships between cost behavior and cost allocation in the next section of the text.

Using Volume Measures to Allocate Variable Overhead Costs

A *causal relationship* exists between variable overhead product costs (indirect materials, indirect labor, inspection costs, utilities, etc.) and the volume of production. For example, the cost of indirect materials such as glue, staples, screws, nails, and varnish will increase or decrease in proportion to the number of desks a furniture manufacturing company makes. *Volume measures are good cost drivers* for allocating variable overhead costs.

Volume can be expressed by such measures as the number of units produced, the number of labor hours worked, or the amount of *direct* materials used in production. Given the variety of possible volume measures, how does management identify the most appropriate cost driver (allocation base) for assigning particular overhead costs? Consider the case of Filmier Furniture Company.

Using Units as the Cost Driver

During the most recent year, Filmier Furniture Company produced 4,000 chairs and 1,000 desks. It incurred $60,000 of *indirect materials* cost during the period. How much of this cost should Filmier allocate to chairs versus desks? Using number of units as the cost driver produces the following allocation.

Step 1. Compute the allocation rate.

Total cost to be allocated	÷ Cost driver	=	Allocation rate
$60,000 indirect materials cost	÷ 5,000 units	=	$12 per unit

Step 2. Multiply the allocation rate by the weight of the cost driver to determine the allocation per cost object.

Product	Allocation Rate	×	Number of Units Produced	=	Allocated Cost
Desks	$12	×	1,000	=	$12,000
Chairs	12	×	4,000	=	48,000
Total			5,000	=	$60,000

Using Direct Labor Hours as the Cost Driver

Using the number of units as the cost driver assigns an *equal amount* ($12) of indirect materials cost to each piece of furniture. However, if Filmier uses more indirect materials to make a desk than to make a chair, assigning the same amount of indirect materials cost to each is inaccurate. Assume Filmier incurs the following direct costs to make chairs and desks:

	Desks	Chairs	Total
Direct labor hours	3,500 hrs.	2,500 hrs.	6,000 hrs.
Direct materials cost	$1,000,000	$500,000	$1,500,000

Both direct labor hours and direct materials cost are volume measures that indicate Filmier uses more indirect materials to make a desk than a chair. It makes sense that the amount of direct labor used is related to the amount of indirect materials used. Because production workers use materials to make furniture, it is plausible to assume that the more hours they work, the more materials they use. Using this reasoning, Filmier could assign the indirect materials cost to the chairs and desks as follows:

Step 1. Compute the allocation rate.

Total cost to be allocated	÷	Cost driver	=	Allocation rate
$60,000 indirect materials cost	÷	6,000 hours	=	$10 per hour

Step 2. Multiply the allocation rate by the weight of the cost driver.

Product	Allocation Rate	×	Number of Labor Hours	=	Allocated Cost
Desks	$10.00	×	3,500	=	$35,000
Chairs	10.00	×	2,500	=	25,000
Total			6,000	=	$60,000

Basing the allocation on labor hours rather than number of units assigns a significantly larger portion of the indirect materials cost to desks ($35,000 versus $12,000). Is this allocation more accurate? Suppose the desks, but not the chairs, require elaborate, labor-intensive carvings. A significant portion of the labor is then not related to consuming indirect materials (glue, staples, screws, nails, and varnish). It would therefore be inappropriate to allocate the indirect materials cost based on direct labor hours.

Using Direct Material Dollars as the Cost Driver

If labor hours is an inappropriate allocation base, Filmier can consider direct material usage, measured in material dollars, as the allocation base. It is likely that the more lumber (direct material) Filmier uses, the more glue, nails, and so forth (indirect materials) it uses. It is reasonable to presume direct materials usage drives indirect materials usage. Using direct materials dollars as the cost driver for indirect materials produces the following allocation:

Step 1. Compute the allocation rate.

Total cost to be allocated	÷	Cost driver	=	Allocation rate
$60,000 indirect materials cost	÷	$1,500,000 direct material dollars	=	$0.04 per direct material dollar

Step 2. Multiply the allocation rate by the weight of the cost driver.

Product	Allocation Rate	×	Number of Direct Material Dollars	=	Allocated Cost
Desks	$0.04	×	$1,000,000	=	$40,000
Chairs	0.04	×	500,000	=	20,000
Total			$1,500,000	=	$60,000

Selecting the Best Cost Driver

Which of the three volume-based cost drivers (units, labor hours, or direct material dollars) results in the most accurate allocation of the overhead cost? Management must use judgment to decide. In this case, direct material dollars appears to have the most convincing relationship to indirect materials usage. If the cost Filmier was allocating were fringe benefits, however, direct labor hours would be a more appropriate cost driver. If the cost Filmier was allocating were machine maintenance cost, a different volume-based cost driver, machine hours, would be an appropriate base. The most accurate allocations of indirect costs may actually require using multiple cost drivers.

CHECK YOURSELF 12.2

Boston Boat Company builds custom sailboats for customers. During the current accounting period, the company built five different size boats that ranged in cost from $35,000 to $185,000. The company's manufacturing overhead cost for the period was $118,000. Would you recommend using the number of units (boats) or direct labor hours as the base for allocating the overhead cost to the five boats? Why?

Answer

Using the number of units as the allocation base would assign the same amount of overhead cost to each boat. Since larger boats require more overhead cost (supplies, utilities, equipment, etc.) than smaller boats, there is no logical link between the number of boats and the amount of overhead cost required to build a particular boat. In contrast, there is a logical link between direct labor hours used and overhead cost incurred. The more labor used, the more supplies, utilities, equipment, and so on used. Since larger boats require more direct labor than smaller boats, using direct labor hours as the allocation base would allocate more overhead cost to larger boats and less overhead cost to smaller boats, producing a logical overhead allocation. Therefore, Boston should use direct labor hours as the allocation base.

Allocating Fixed Overhead Costs

Fixed costs present a different cost allocation problem. By definition, the volume of production does not drive fixed costs. Suppose Lednicky Bottling Company rents its manufacturing facility for $28,000 per year. The rental cost is fixed regardless of how much product Lednicky bottles. However, Lednicky may still use a volume-based cost driver as the allocation base. The purpose of allocating fixed costs to products is to distribute a *rational share* of the overhead cost to each product. Selecting an allocation base that spreads total overhead cost equally over total production often produces a rational distribution. For example, assume Lednicky produced 2,000,000 bottles of apple juice during 2006. If it sold 1,800,000 bottles of the juice during 2006, how much of the $28,000 of rental cost should Lednicky allocate to ending inventory and how much to cost of goods sold? A rational allocation follows:

Step 1. Compute the allocation rate.

Total cost to be allocated	÷	Allocation base (cost driver)	=	Allocation rate
$28,000 rental cost	÷	2,000,000 bottles	=	$0.014 per bottle of juice

Because the base (number of units) used to allocate the cost does not drive the cost, it is sometimes called an *allocation base* instead of a *cost driver*. However, many managers use the term *cost driver* in conjunction with fixed cost even though that usage is technically inaccurate. The terms *allocation base* and *cost driver* are frequently used interchangeably.

Step 2. Multiply the allocation rate by the weight of the cost driver.

Financial Statement Item	Allocation Rate	×	Number of Bottles	=	Allocated Cost
Inventory	$0.014	×	200,000	=	$ 2,800
Cost of goods sold	0.014	×	1,800,000	=	25,200

Using number of units as the allocation base assigns equal amounts of the rental cost to each unit of product. Equal allocation is appropriate so long as the units are homogeneous. If the units are not identical, however, Lednicky may need to choose a different allocation base to rationally distribute the rental cost. For example, if some of the bottles are significantly larger than others, Lednicky may find using some physical measure, like liters of direct material used, to be a more appropriate allocation base. Whether an indirect cost is fixed or variable, selecting the most appropriate allocation base requires sound reasoning and judgment.

Allocating Costs to Solve Timing Problems

LO 5

Use allocation to solve problems that emerge in the process of making cost-plus pricing decisions.

Monthly fluctuations in production volume complicate fixed cost allocations. To illustrate, assume Grave Manufacturing pays its production supervisor a monthly salary of $3,000. Furthermore, assume Grave makes 800 units of product in January and 1,875 in February. How much salary cost should Grave assign to the products made in January and February, respectively? The allocation seems simple. Just divide the $3,000 monthly salary cost by the number of units of product made each month as follows:

January	$3,000	÷	800 units	=	$3.75 cost per unit
February	$3,000	÷	1,875 units	=	$1.60 cost per unit

If Grave Manufacturing based a cost-plus pricing decision on these results, it would price products made in January significantly higher than products made in February. It is likely such price fluctuations would puzzle and drive away customers. Grave needs an allocation base that will spread the annual salary cost evenly over annual production. A timing problem exists, however, because Grave must allocate the salary cost before the end of the year. In order to price its products, Grave needs to know the allocated amount before the actual cost information is available. Grave can manage the timing problem by using estimated rather than actual costs.

Grave Manufacturing can *estimate* the annual cost of the supervisor's salary (indirect labor) as $36,000 ($3,000 × 12 months). The *actual* cost of indirect labor may differ because the supervisor might receive a pay raise or be replaced with a person who earns less. Based on current information, however, $36,000 is a reasonable estimate of the annual indirect labor cost. Grave must also estimate total annual production volume. Suppose Grave produced 18,000 units last year and expects no significant change in the current year. It can allocate indirect labor cost for January and February as follows:

Step 1. Compute the allocation rate.

Total cost to be allocated	÷	Allocation base (cost driver)	=	Allocation rate
$36,000	÷	18,000 units	=	$2.00 per unit

Step 2. Multiply the rate by the weight of the base (number of units per month) to determine how much of the salary cost to allocate to each month's production.

Month	Allocation Rate	×	Number of Units Produced	=	Allocation per Month
January	$2.00	×	800	=	$1,600
February	2.00	×	1,875	=	3,750

Grave Manufacturing will add these indirect cost allocations to other product costs to determine the total estimated product cost to use in cost-plus pricing or other managerial decisions.

Because the overhead allocation rate is determined *before* actual cost and volume data are available, it is called the **predetermined overhead rate.** Companies use predetermined overhead rates for product costing estimates and pricing decisions during a year, but they must use actual costs in published year-end financial statements. If necessary, companies adjust their accounting records at year-end when they have used estimated data on an interim basis. The procedures for making such adjustments are discussed in a later chapter.

Establishing Cost Pools

LO 6

Explain why companies establish indirect cost pools.

Allocating *individually* every single indirect cost a company incurs would be tedious and not particularly useful relative to the benefit obtained. Instead, companies frequently accumulate many individual costs into a single **cost pool.** The *total* of the pooled costs is then allocated to the cost objects. For example, a company may accumulate costs for gas, water, electricity, and telephone service into a single *utilities* cost pool. It would then allocate the total cost in the utilities cost pool to the cost objects rather than individually allocating each of the four types of utility cost.

How far should pooling costs go? Why not pool utility costs with fringe benefit costs? The most accurate cost information comes from pooling costs with common cost drivers. To obtain rational allocations of various indirect costs to cost objects, companies must use different allocation bases (cost drivers). They should therefore limit pooling to costs with common cost drivers.

Cost Allocation: The Human Factor

LO 7

Recognize human motivation as a key variable in the allocation process.

Cost allocations significantly affect individuals. They may influence managers' performance evaluations and compensation. They may dictate the amount of resources various departments, divisions, and other organizational subunits receive. Control over resources usually offers managers prestige and influence over organization operations. The following scenario illustrates the emotional impact and perceptions of fairness of cost allocation decisions.

Using Cost Allocations in a Budgeting Decision

Sharon Southport, dean of the School of Business at a major state university, is in dire need of a budgeting plan. Because of cuts in state funding, the money available to the School of Business for copying costs next year will be reduced substantially. Dean Southport supervises four departments: management, marketing, finance, and accounting. The Dean knows the individual department chairpersons will be unhappy and frustrated with the deep cuts they face.

Using Cost Drivers to Make Allocations

To address the allocation of copying resources, Dean Southport decided to meet with the department chairs. She explained that the total budgeted for copying costs will be $36,000. Based on past usage, department allocations would be as follows: $12,000 for management, $10,000 for accounting, $8,000 for finance, and $6,000 for marketing.

Dr. Bill Thompson, the management department chair, immediately protested that his department could not operate on a $12,000 budget for copy costs. Management has more faculty members than any other department. Dr. Thompson argued that copy costs are directly related to the number of faculty members, so copy funds should be allocated based on the number of faculty members. Dr. Thompson suggested that number of faculty members rather than past usage should be the allocation base.

Since the School of Business has 72 faculty members (29 in management, 16 in accounting, 12 in finance, and 15 in marketing), the allocation should be as follows:

Step 1. Compute the allocation rate.

Total cost to be allocated	÷	Cost driver	=	Allocation rate
$36,000	÷	72	=	$500 per faculty member

Step 2. Multiply the rate by the weight of the driver (the number of faculty per department) to determine the allocation per cost object (department).

Department	Allocation Rate	×	Number of Faculty	=	Allocation per Department	Allocation Based on Past Usage
Management	$500	×	29		$14,500	$12,000
Accounting	500	×	16		8,000	10,000
Finance	500	×	12		6,000	8,000
Marketing	500	×	15		7,500	6,000
Total					$36,000	$36,000

Seeing these figures, Dr. Bob Smethers, chair of the accounting department, questioned the accuracy of using the number of faculty members as the cost driver. Dr. Smethers suggested the number of *students* rather than the number of *faculty* members drives the cost of copying. He argued that most copying results from duplicating syllabi, exams, and handouts. The accounting department teaches mass sections of introductory accounting that have extremely high student/teacher ratios. Because his department teaches more students, it spends more on copying costs even though it has fewer faculty members. Dr. Smethers recomputed the copy cost allocation as follows.

Step 1. Compute the allocation rate based on number of students. University records indicate that the School of Business taught 1,200 students during the most recent academic year. The allocation rate (copy cost per student) follows.

Total cost to be allocated	÷	Cost driver	=	Allocation rate
$36,000	÷	1,200	=	$30 per student

Step 2. Multiply the rate by the weight of the driver (number of students taught by each department) to determine the allocation per cost object (department).

Department	Allocation Rate	×	Number of Students	=	Allocation per Department	Allocation Based on Past Usage
Management	$30	×	330		$ 9,900	$12,000
Accounting	30	×	360		10,800	10,000
Finance	30	×	290		8,700	8,000
Marketing	30	×	220		6,600	6,000
Total					$36,000	$36,000

Choosing the Best Cost Driver

Dr. Thompson objected vigorously to using the number of students as the cost driver. He continued to argue that the size of the faculty is a more appropriate allocation base. The chair of the finance department sided with Dr. Smethers, the chair of the marketing department kept quiet, and the dean had to settle the dispute.

Dean Southport recognized that the views of the chairpersons were influenced by self-interest. The allocation base affects the amount of resources available to each department. Furthermore, the dean recognized that the size of the faculty does drive some of the copying costs. For example, the cost of copying manuscripts that faculty submit for publication relates to faculty size. The more articles faculty submit, the higher the copying cost. Nevertheless, the dean decided the number of students has the most significant impact on copying costs. She also wanted to encourage faculty members to minimize the impact of funding cuts on student services. Dean Southport therefore decided to allocate copying costs based on the number of students taught by each department. Dr. Thompson stormed angrily out of the meeting. The dean developed a budget by assigning the available funds to each department using the number of students as the allocation base.

Controlling Emotions

Dr. Thompson's behavior may relieve his frustration but it doesn't indicate clear thinking. Dean Southport recognized that Dr. Thompson's contention that copy costs were related to faculty size had some merit. Had Dr. Thompson offered a compromise rather than an emotional outburst, he might have increased his department's share of the funds. Perhaps a portion of the allocation could have been based on the number of faculty members with the balance allocated based on the number of students. Had Dr. Thompson controlled his anger, the others might have agreed to compromise. Technical expertise in computing numbers is of little use without the interpersonal skills to persuade others. Accountants may provide numerical measurements, but they should never forget the impact of their reports on the people in the organization.

<< A Look Back

Managers need to know the costs of products, processes, departments, activities, and so on. The target for which accountants attempt to determine cost is a *cost object*. Knowing the cost of specific objects enables management to control costs, evaluate performance, and price products. *Direct costs* can be cost-effectively traced to a cost object. *Indirect costs* cannot be easily traced to designated cost objects.

The same cost can be direct or indirect, depending on the cost object to which it relates. For example, the salary of a **Burger King** restaurant manager can be directly traced to a particular store but cannot be traced to particular food items made and sold in the store. Classifying a cost as direct or indirect is independent of whether the cost behaves as fixed or variable; it is also independent of whether the cost is relevant to a given decision. A direct cost could be either fixed or variable or either relevant or irrelevant, depending on the context and the designated cost object.

Indirect costs are assigned to cost objects using *cost allocation*. Allocation divides an indirect cost into parts and distributes the parts among the relevant cost objects. Companies frequently allocate costs to cost objects in proportion to the *cost drivers* that cause the costs to be incurred. The first step in allocating an indirect cost is to determine the allocation rate by dividing the total cost to be allocated by the chosen cost driver. The next step is to multiply the allocation rate by the amount of the cost driver for a particular object. The result is the amount of indirect cost to assign to the cost object.

A particular indirect cost may be related to more than one driver. The best cost driver is the one that most accurately reflects the amount of the resource used by the cost object. Objects that consume the most resources should be allocated a proportionately greater share of the costs. If no suitable cost driver exists, companies may use arbitrary allocations such as dividing a total cost equally among cost objects.

Cost allocations have behavioral implications. Using inappropriate cost drivers can distort allocations and lead managers to make choices that are detrimental to the company's profitability.

To avoid the inefficiency of allocating every individual indirect cost, managers accumulate many indirect costs into *cost pools*. The costs combined in a pool should have a common cost driver. A single allocation can then be made of the cost pool total.

A Look Forward >>

The next chapter introduces the concept of *relevance*. Applying the concepts you have learned to real-world business problems can be challenging. Frequently, so much data is available that it is difficult to distinguish important from useless information. The next chapter will help you learn to identify information that is relevant in a variety of short-term decision-making scenarios including special orders, outsourcing, segment elimination, and asset replacement.

SELF-STUDY REVIEW PROBLEM

New budget constraints have pressured Body Perfect Gym to control costs. The owner of the gym, Mr. Ripple, has notified division managers that their job performance evaluations will be highly influenced by their ability to minimize costs. The gym has three divisions, weight lifting, aerobics, and spinning. The owner has formulated a report showing how much it cost to operate each of the three divisions last year. In preparing the report, Mr. Ripple identified several indirect costs that must be allocated among the divisions. These indirect costs are $4,200 of laundry expense, $48,000 of gym supplies, $350,000 of office rent, $50,000 of janitorial services, and $120,000 for administrative salaries. To provide a reasonably accurate cost allocation, Mr. Ripple has identified several potential cost drivers. These drivers and their association with each division follow.

Cost Driver	Weight Lifting	Aerobics	Spinning	Total
Number of participants	26	16	14	56
Number of instructors	10	8	6	24
Square feet of gym space	12,000	6,000	7,000	25,000
Number of staff	2	2	1	5

Required

a. Identify the appropriate cost objects.

b. Identify the most appropriate cost driver for each indirect cost, and compute the allocation rate for assigning each indirect cost to the cost objects.

c. Determine the amount of supplies expense that should be allocated to each of the three divisions.

d. The spinning manager wants to use the number of staff rather than the number of instructors as the allocation base for the supplies expense. Explain why the spinning manager would take this position.

e. Identify two cost drivers other than your choice for Requirement *b* that could be used to allocate the cost of the administrative salaries to the three divisions.

Solution to Requirement *a*

The objective is to determine the cost of operating each division. Therefore, the cost objects are the three divisions (weight lifting, aerobics, and spinning).

Solution to Requirement *b*

The costs, appropriate cost drivers, and allocation rates for assigning the costs to the departments follow:

Cost	Base	Computation	Allocation Rate
Laundry expense	Number of participants	$ 4,200 ÷ 56	$75 per participant
Supplies expense	Number of instructors	48,000 ÷ 24	$2,000 per instructor
Office rent	Square feet	350,000 ÷ 25,000	$14 per square foot
Janitorial service	Square feet	50,000 ÷ 25,000	$2 per square foot
Administrative salaries	Number of divisions	120,000 ÷ 3	$40,000 per division

There are other logical cost drivers. For example, supplies expense could be allocated based on the number of staff. It is also logical to use a combination of cost drivers. For example, the allocation of supplies expense could be based on the combined number of instructors and staff. For this problem, we assumed that Mr. Ripple chose the number of instructors as the base for allocating supplies expense.

Solution to Requirement *c*

Department	Cost to Be Allocated	Allocation Rate	×	Weight of Base	=	Amount Allocated
Weight lifting	Supplies expense	$2,000	×	10	=	$20,000
Aerobics	Supplies expense	2,000	×	8	=	16,000
Spinning	Supplies expense	2,000	×	6	=	12,000
Total						$48,000

Solution to Requirement *d*

If the number of staff were used as the allocation base, the allocation rate for supplies expense would be as follows:

$48,000 ÷ 5 staff = $9,600 per staff member

Using this rate, the total supplies expense would be allocated among the three divisions as follows:

Department	Cost to Be Allocated	Allocation Rate	×	Weight of Base	=	Amount Allocated
Weight lifting	Supplies expense	$9,600	×	2	=	$19,200
Aerobics	Supplies expense	9,600	×	2	=	19,200
Spinning	Supplies expense	9,600	×	1	=	9,600
Total						$48,000

By using the number of staff as the allocation base instead of the number of instructors, the amount of overhead cost allocated to the spinning division falls from $12,000 to $9,600. Since managers are evaluated based on minimizing costs, it is clearly in the spinning manager's self-interest to use the number of staff as the allocation base.

Solution to Requirement *e*

Among other possibilities, bases for allocating the administrative salaries include the number of participants, the number of lessons, or the number of instructors.

KEY TERMS

allocation base 426
allocation rate 426
cost accumulation 424
cost allocation 426, 435
cost driver 424
cost objects 423
cost pool 436
cost tracing 425
direct cost 425
indirect cost 425
overhead costs 425
predetermined overhead rate 436

QUESTIONS

1. What is a cost object? Identify four different cost objects in which an accountant would be interested.
2. Why is cost accumulation imprecise?
3. If the cost object is a manufactured product, what are the three major cost categories to accumulate?
4. What is a direct cost? What criteria are used to determine whether a cost is a direct cost?
5. Why are the terms *direct cost* and *indirect cost* independent of the terms *fixed cost* and *variable cost*? Give an example to illustrate.
6. Give an example of why the statement, "All direct costs are avoidable," is incorrect.
7. What are the important factors in determining the appropriate cost driver to use in allocating a cost?
8. How is an allocation rate determined? How is an allocation made?
9. In a manufacturing environment, which costs are direct and which are indirect in product costing?
10. Why are some manufacturing costs not directly traceable to products?
11. What is the objective of allocating indirect manufacturing overhead costs to the product?
12. On January 31, the managers of Integra Inc. seek to determine the cost of producing their product during January for product pricing and control purposes. The company can easily determine the costs of direct materials and direct labor used in January production, but many fixed indirect costs are not affected by the level of production activity and have not yet been incurred. The managers can reasonably estimate the overhead costs for the year based on the fixed indirect costs incurred in past periods. Assume the managers decide to allocate an equal amount of these estimated costs to the products produced each month. Explain why this practice may not provide a reasonable estimate of product costs in January.
13. Respond to the following statement: "The allocation base chosen is unimportant. What is important in product costing is that overhead costs be assigned to production in a specific period by an allocation process."
14. Larry Kwang insists that the costs of his school's fund-raising project should be determined after the project is complete. He argues that only after the project is complete can its costs be determined accurately and that it is a waste of time to try to estimate future costs. Georgia Sundum counters that waiting until the project is complete will not provide timely information for planning expenditures. How would you arbitrate this discussion? Explain the trade-offs between accuracy and timeliness.
15. Define the term *cost pool*. How are cost pools important in allocating costs?

EXERCISES

All Exercises are available with McGraw-Hill's Homework Manager

L.O. 1, 3

Exercise 12-1 *Allocating costs between divisions*

Loftis Services Company (LSC) has 50 employees, 36 of whom are assigned to Division A and 14 to Division B. LSC incurred $360,000 of fringe benefits cost during 2006.

Required

Determine the amount of the fringe benefits cost to be allocated to Division A and to Division B.

L.O. 2

Exercise 12-2 *Direct versus indirect costs*

Burr Ridge Construction Company is composed of two divisions: (1) Home Construction and (2) Commercial Construction. The Home Construction Division is in the process of building 12 houses and the Commercial Construction Division is working on 3 projects. Cost items of the company follow:

Labor on a particular house
Salary of the supervisor of commercial construction projects
Supplies, such as glue and nails, used by the Home Construction Division
Cost of building permits
Materials used in commercial construction projects
Depreciation on home building equipment (small tools such as hammers or saws)
Company president's salary
Depreciation on crane used in commercial construction
Depreciation on home office building
Salary of corporate office manager
Wages of workers assigned to a specific construction project
Supplies used by the Commercial Construction Division

Required

a. Identify each cost as being a direct or indirect cost assuming the cost objects are the individual products (houses or projects).

b. Identify each cost as being a direct or indirect cost, assuming the cost objects are the two divisions.

c. Identify each cost as being a direct or indirect cost assuming the cost object is Burr Ridge Construction Company as a whole.

L.O. 3, 4

Exercise 12-3 *Allocating overhead cost among products*

Donna Hats Inc. manufactures three different styles of hats: Vogue, Beauty, and Deluxe. Donna expects to incur $600,000 of overhead cost during the next fiscal year. Other budget information follows.

	Vogue	Beauty	Deluxe	Total
Direct labor hours	3,000	5,000	4,500	12,500
Machine hours	1,000	1,000	1,000	3,000

Required

a. Use direct labor hours as the cost driver to compute the allocation rate and the budgeted overhead cost for each product.

b. Use machine hours as the cost driver to compute the allocation rate and the budgeted overhead cost for each product.

c. Describe a set of circumstances where it would be more appropriate to use direct labor hours as the allocation base.

d. Describe a set of circumstances where it would be more appropriate to use machine hours as the allocation base.

Exercise 12-4 *Allocating overhead costs among products*

L.O. 3, 4

Ritchey Company makes three products in its factory: plastic cups, plastic tablecloths, and plastic bottles. The expected overhead costs for the next fiscal year include the following.

Factory manager's salary	$150,000
Factory utility cost	70,000
Factory supplies	30,000
Total overhead costs	$250,000

Ritchey uses machine hours as the cost driver to allocate overhead costs. Budgeted machine hours for the products are as follows.

Cups	500 Hours
Tablecloths	800
Bottles	1,200
Total machine hours	2,500

Required

a. Allocate the budgeted overhead costs to the products.

b. Provide a possible explanation as to why Ritchey chose machine hours, instead of labor hours, as the allocation base.

Exercise 12-5 *Allocating costs among products*

L.O. 3, 4

Sudderth Construction Company expects to build three new homes during a specific accounting period. The estimated direct materials and labor costs are as follows.

Expected Costs	Home 1	Home 2	Home 3
Direct labor	$120,000	$180,000	$340,000
Direct materials	180,000	260,000	360,000

Assume Sudderth needs to allocate two major overhead costs ($80,000 of employee fringe benefits and $40,000 of indirect materials costs) among the three jobs.

Required

Choose an appropriate cost driver for each of the overhead costs and determine the total cost of each house.

Exercise 12-6 *Allocating to smooth cost over varying levels of production*

L.O. 3, 5

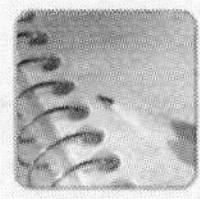

Production workers for Bakari Manufacturing Company provided 320 hours of labor in January and 480 hours in February. Bakari expects to use 4,000 hours of labor during the year. The rental fee for the manufacturing facility is $7,200 per month.

Required

Explain why allocation is needed. Based on this information, how much of the rental cost should be allocated to the products made in January and to those made in February?

Exercise 12-7 *Allocating to solve a timing problem*

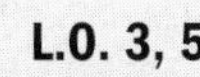

L.O. 3, 5

Production workers for Poole Manufacturing Company provided 2,700 hours of labor in January and 1,800 hours in February. The company, whose operation is labor intensive, expects to use 36,000 hours of labor during the year. Poole paid a $45,000 annual premium on July 1 of the prior year for an insurance policy that covers the manufacturing facility for the following 12 months.

Required

Explain why allocation is needed. Based on this information, how much of the insurance cost should be allocated to the products made in January and to those made in February?

L.O. 3, 5

Exercise 12-8 *Allocating a fixed cost*

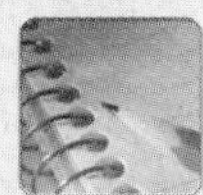

Coastal Air is a large airline company that pays a customer relations representative $4,000 per month. The representative, who processed 1,000 customer complaints in January and 1,300 complaints in February, is expected to process 16,000 customer complaints during 2007.

Required

a. Determine the total cost of processing customer complaints in January and in February.

b. Explain why allocating the cost of the customer relations representative would or would not be relevant to decision making.

L.O. 3, 5

Exercise 12-9 *Allocating overhead cost to accomplish smoothing*

Mimosa Corporation expects to incur indirect overhead costs of $72,000 per month and direct manufacturing costs of $11 per unit. The expected production activity for the first four months of 2007 is as follows.

	January	February	March	April
Estimated production in units	4,000	7,000	3,000	6,000

Required

a. Calculate a predetermined overhead rate based on the number of units of product expected to be made during the first four months of the year.

b. Allocate overhead costs to each month using the overhead rate computed in Requirement *a*.

c. Calculate the total cost per unit for each month using the overhead allocated in Requirement *b*.

L.O. 3, 5

Exercise 12-10 *Allocating overhead for product costing*

Seiko Manufacturing Company produced 1,200 units of inventory in January 2007. It expects to produce an additional 8,400 units during the remaining 11 months of the year. In other words, total production for 2007 is estimated to be 9,600 units. Direct materials and direct labor costs are $64 and $52 per unit, respectively. Seiko Company expects to incur the following manufacturing overhead costs during 2007:

Production supplies	$ 4,800
Supervisor salary	192,000
Depreciation on equipment	144,000
Utilities	36,000
Rental fee on manufacturing facilities	96,000
Total	$472,800

Required

a. Determine the cost of the 1,200 units of product made in January.

b. Is the cost computed in Requirement *a* actual or estimated? Could Seiko improve accuracy by waiting until December to determine the cost of products?

L.O. 3, 5

Exercise 12-11 *How fixed cost allocation affects a pricing decision*

Barnhart Manufacturing Co. expects to make 48,000 chairs during 2006. The company made 8,000 chairs in January. Materials and labor costs for January were $32,000 and $48,000, respectively. Barnhart produced 3,000 chairs in February. Materials and labor costs for February were $12,000 and $18,000, respectively. The company paid the $240,000 annual rental fee on its manufacturing facility on January 1, 2006. Ignore other manufacturing overhead costs.

Required

Assuming that Barnhart desires to sell its chairs for cost plus 30 percent of cost, what price should be charged for the chairs produced in January and February?

Exercise 12-12 *Cost pools* L.O. 6

McLaurin Department Stores Inc. has three departments: women's, men's, and children's. The following are the indirect costs related to its operations:

Payroll taxes
Paper rolls for cash registers
Medical insurance
Salaries of secretaries
Water bill
Vacation pay
Sewer bill
Staples
Natural gas bill
Pens
Ink cartridges

Required

a. Organize the costs in the following three pools: indirect materials, indirect labor, and indirect utilities, assuming that each department is a cost object.
b. Identify an appropriate cost driver for each pool.
c. Explain why accountants use cost pools.

Exercise 12-13 *Human factor* L.O. 7

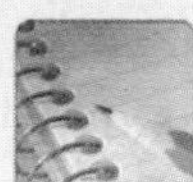

Brentwood Clinics provides medical care in three departments: internal medicine (IM), pediatrics (PD), and obstetrics gynecology (OB). The estimated costs to run each department follow:

	IM	PD	OB
Physicians	$400,000	$300,000	$200,000
Nurses	80,000	120,000	160,000

Brentwood expects to incur $360,000 of indirect (overhead) costs in the next fiscal year.

Required

a. Based on the information provided, name four allocation bases that could be used to assign the overhead cost to each department.
b. Assume the manager of each department is permitted to recommend how the overhead cost should be allocated to the departments. Which of the allocation bases named in Requirement *a* is the manager of OB most likely to recommend? Explain why. What argument may the manager of OB use to justify his choice of the allocation base?
c. Which of the allocation bases would result in the fairest allocation of the overhead cost from the perspective of the company president?
d. Explain how classifying overhead costs into separate pools could improve the fairness of the allocation of the overhead costs.

PROBLEMS

All Problems are available with McGraw-Hill's Homework Manager

L.O. 1, 2, 3, 4, 5

mhhe.com/edmonds2007

CHECK FIGURE
a. (2) $590,000

Problem 12-14 *Cost accumulation and allocation*

Belcher Manufacturing Company makes two different products, M and N. The company's two departments are named after the products; for example, Product M is made in Department M. Belcher's accountant has identified the following annual costs associated with these two products.

Financial data	
Salary of vice president of production division	$ 90,000
Salary of supervisor Department M	38,000
Salary of supervisor Department N	28,000
Direct materials cost Department M	150,000
Direct materials cost Department N	210,000
Direct labor cost Department M	120,000
Direct labor cost Department N	340,000
Direct utilities cost Department M	60,000
Direct utilities cost Department N	12,000
General factorywide utilities	18,000
Production supplies	18,000
Fringe benefits	69,000
Depreciation	360,000
Nonfinancial data	
Machine hours Department M	5,000
Machine hours Department N	1,000

Required

a. Identify the costs that are (1) direct costs of Department M, (2) direct costs of Department N, and (3) indirect costs.

b. Select the appropriate cost drivers for the indirect costs and allocate these costs to Departments M and N.

c. Determine the total estimated cost of the products made in Departments M and N. Assume that Belcher produced 2,000 units of Product M and 4,000 units of Product N during the year. If Belcher prices its products at cost plus 30 percent of cost, what price per unit must it charge for Product M and for Product N?

L.O. 1, 3, 4

Problem 12-15 *Selecting an appropriate cost driver (What is the base?)*

The Newman School of Vocational Technology has organized the school training programs into three departments. Each department provides training in a different area as follows: nursing assistant, dental hygiene, and office technology. The school's owner, Lucy Newman, wants to know how much it costs to operate each of the three departments. To accumulate the total cost for each department, the accountant has identified several indirect costs that must be allocated to each. These costs are $15,750 of phone expense, $3,360 of office supplies, $864,000 of office rent, $96,000 of janitorial services, and $72,000 of salary paid to the dean of students. To provide a reasonably accurate allocation of costs, the accountant has identified several possible cost drivers. These drivers and their association with each department follow.

Cost Driver	Department 1	Department 2	Department 3
Number of telephones	28	16	19
Number of faculty members	20	16	12
Square footage of office space	24,000	14,000	10,000
Number of secretaries	2	2	2

Required

a. Identify the appropriate cost objects.
b. Identify the appropriate cost driver for each indirect cost and compute the allocation rate for assigning each indirect cost to the cost objects.
c. Determine the amount of telephone expense that should be allocated to each of the three departments.
d. Determine the amount of supplies expense that should be allocated to Department 3.
e. Determine the amount of office rent that should be allocated to Department 2.
f. Determine the amount of janitorial services cost that should be allocated to Department 1.
g. Identify two cost drivers not listed here that could be used to allocate the cost of the dean's salary to the three departments.

Problem 12-16 *Cost allocation in a service industry*

L.O. 1, 2

CHECK FIGURES
b. To SF: $1,114;
To NY: $546

Eagle Airlines is a small airline that occasionally carries overload shipments for the overnight delivery company Never-Fail Inc. Never-Fail is a multimillion-dollar company started by Peter Never immediately after he failed to finish his first accounting course. The company's motto is "We Never-Fail to Deliver Your Package on Time." When Never-Fail has more freight than it can deliver, it pays Eagle to carry the excess. Eagle contracts with independent pilots to fly its planes on a per trip basis. Eagle recently purchased an airplane that cost the company $6,000,000. The plane has an estimated useful life of 100,000,000 miles and a zero salvage value. During the first week in January, Eagle flew two trips. The first trip was a round trip flight from Chicago to San Francisco, for which Eagle paid $500 for the pilot and $350 for fuel. The second flight was a round trip from Chicago to New York. For this trip, it paid $300 for the pilot and $150 for fuel. The round trip between Chicago and San Francisco is approximately 4,400 miles and the round trip between Chicago and New York is 1,600 miles.

Required

a. Identify the direct and indirect costs that Eagle incurs for each trip.
b. Determine the total cost of each trip.
c. In addition to depreciation, identify three other indirect costs that may need to be allocated to determine the cost of each trip.

Problem 12-17 *Cost allocation in a manufacturing company*

L.O. 1, 3, 4

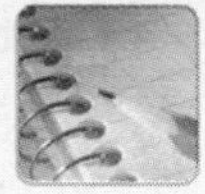

CHECK FIGURES
d. Jan.: $8,000
Feb.: $6,000

McCord Manufacturing Company makes tents that it sells directly to camping enthusiasts through a mail-order marketing program. The company pays a quality control expert $75,000 per year to inspect completed tents before they are shipped to customers. Assume that the company completed 1,600 tents in January and 1,200 tents in February. For the entire year, the company expects to produce 15,000 tents.

Required

a. Explain how changes in the cost driver (number of tents inspected) affect the total amount of fixed inspection cost.
b. Explain how changes in the cost driver (number of tents inspected) affect the amount of fixed inspection cost per unit.
c. If the cost objective is to determine the cost per tent, is the expert's salary a direct or an indirect cost?
d. How much of the expert's salary should be allocated to tents produced in January and February?

Problem 12-18 *Fairness in the allocation process*

L.O. 1, 4, 7

excel
mhhe.com/edmonds2007

Foreman Manufacturing Company uses two departments to make its products. Department I is a cutting department that is machine intensive and uses very few employees. Machines cut and form parts and then place the finished parts on a conveyor belt that carries them to Department II where they are assembled into finished goods. The assembly department is labor intensive and requires many workers to assemble parts into finished goods. The company's manufacturing facility incurs two significant overhead costs, employee fringe benefits and utility costs. The annual costs of fringe benefits are $504,000 and utility costs are $360,000. The typical consumption patterns for the two departments are as follows.

	Department I	Department II	Total
Machine hours used	16,000	4,000	20,000
Direct labor hours used	5,000	13,000	18,000

The supervisor of each department receives a bonus based on how well the department controls costs. The company's current policy requires using a single activity base (machine hours or labor hours) to allocate the total overhead cost of $864,000.

Required

a. Assume that you are the supervisor of Department I. Choose the allocation base that would minimize your department's share of the total overhead cost. Calculate the amount of overhead that would be allocated to both departments using the base that you selected.

b. Assume that you are the supervisor of Department II. Choose the allocation base that would minimize your department's share of the total overhead cost. Calculate the amount of overhead that would be allocated to both departments using the base that you selected.

c. Assume that you are the plant manager and have the authority to change the company's overhead allocation policy. Formulate an overhead allocation policy that would be fair to the supervisors of both Department I and Department II. Compute the overhead allocations for each department using your policy.

L.O. 1, 3, 5

Problem 12-19 *Allocation to accomplish smoothing*

CHECK FIGURES
a. $5.60
c. March: $59.20

Roddick Corporation estimated its overhead costs would be $36,000 per month except for January when it pays the $72,000 annual insurance premium on the manufacturing facility. Accordingly, the January overhead costs were expected to be $108,000 ($72,000 + $36,000). The company expected to use 7,000 direct labor hours per month except during July, August, and September when the company expected 9,000 hours of direct labor each month to build inventories for high demand that normally occurs during the holiday season. The company's actual direct labor hours were the same as the estimated hours. The company made 3,500 units of product in each month except July, August, and September in which it produced 4,500 units each month. Direct labor costs were $29 per unit, and direct materials costs were $19 per unit.

Required

a. Calculate a predetermined overhead rate based on direct labor hours.

b. Determine the total allocated overhead cost for January, March, and August.

c. Determine the cost per unit of product for January, March, and August.

d. Determine the selling price for the product, assuming that the company desires to earn a gross margin of $20 per unit.

L.O. 1, 3, 5

Problem 12-20 *Allocating indirect costs between products*

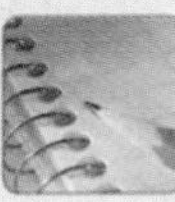

CHECK FIGURES
a. Cost/unit for EZRecords: $225
b. Cost/unit for ProOffice: $230

Dana Helton is considering expanding her business. She plans to hire a salesperson to cover trade shows. Because of compensation, travel expenses, and booth rental, fixed costs for a trade show are expected to be $15,000. The booth will be open 30 hours during the trade show. Ms. Helton also plans to add a new product line, ProOffice, which will cost $180 per package. She will continue to sell the existing product, EZRecords, which costs $100 per package. Ms. Helton believes that the salesperson will spend approximately 20 hours selling EZRecords and 10 hours marketing ProOffice.

Required

a. Determine the estimated total cost and cost per unit of each product, assuming that the salesperson is able to sell 80 units of EZRecords and 50 units of ProOffice.

b. Determine the estimated total cost and cost per unit of each product, assuming that the salesperson is able to sell 200 units of EZRecords and 100 units of ProOffice.

c. Explain why the cost per unit figures calculated in Requirement *a* are different from the amounts calculated in Requirement *b*. Also explain how the differences in estimated cost per unit will affect pricing decisions.

ANALYZE, THINK, COMMUNICATE

ATC 12-1 Business Applications Case *Allocating fixed costs at Porsche*

During its fiscal year ending on July 31, 2004, the Dr. Ing. h.c. F. **Porsche AG**, commonly known as "Porsche," manufactured 81,531 vehicles. During that same year Porsche recorded depreciation of €186,302,000. (Porsche's financial information is reported in euros. The symbol € represents the euro.) For this case, assume all depreciation relates to manufacturing activities.

Required

a. Indicate whether the depreciation charge is a:

(1) Product cost, or general, selling, and administrative cost.

(2) Fixed or variable cost relative to the volume of production.

(3) Direct or indirect cost if the cost object is the cost of vehicles made in the 2004 fiscal year.

b. Assume that Porsche incurred depreciation of €15,500,000 in each month of the 2004 fiscal year. It produced 6,000 vehicles during February and 7,000 during March. What was the average amount of depreciation cost per vehicle produced during each of these two months?

c. If Porsche had expected to produce 80,000 vehicles during 2004, what would its predetermined overhead charge per vehicle for depreciation have been? Explain the advantage of using this amount to determine the cost of manufacturing a car in February and March versus the amounts you computed in Requirement *b*.

d. If Porsche's management had estimated the profit per vehicle based on its budgeted production of 80,000 units, would you expect its actual profit per vehicle to be higher or lower than expected? Explain.

ATC 12-2 Group Assignment *Selection of the cost driver*

Vulcan College School of Business is divided into three departments, accounting, marketing, and management. Relevant information for each of the departments follows.

Cost Driver	Accounting	Marketing	Management
Number of students	1,400	800	400
Number of classes per semester	64	36	28
Number of professors	20	24	10

Vulcan is a private school that expects each department to generate a profit. It rewards departments for profitability by assigning 20 percent of each department's profits back to that department. Departments have free rein as to how to use these funds. Some departments have used them to supply professors with computer technology. Others have expanded their travel budgets. The practice has been highly successful in motivating the faculty to control costs. The revenues and direct costs for the year 2004 follow.

	Accounting	Marketing	Management
Revenue	$29,600,000	$16,600,000	$8,300,000
Direct costs	24,600,000	13,800,000	6,600,000

Vulcan allocates to the School of Business $4,492,800 of indirect overhead costs such as administrative salaries and costs of operating the registrar's office and the bookstore.

Required

a. Divide the class into groups and organize the groups into three sections. Assign each section a department. Assume that the dean of the school is planning to assign an equal amount of the college overhead to each department. Have the students in each group prepare a response to the dean's plan. Each group should select a spokesperson who is prepared to answer the following questions.

(1) Is your group in favor of or opposed to the allocation plan suggested by the dean?

(2) Does the plan suggested by the dean provide a fair allocation? Why?

The instructor should lead a discussion designed to assess the appropriateness of the dean's proposed allocation plan.

b. Have each group select the cost driver (allocation base) that best serves the self-interest of the department it represents.

c. Consensus on Requirement *c* should be achieved before completing Requirement *d.* Each group should determine the amount of the indirect cost to be allocated to each department using the cost driver that best serves the self-interest of the department it represents. Have a spokesperson from each section go to the board and show the income statement that would result for each department.

d. Discuss the development of a cost driver(s) that would promote fairness rather than self-interest in allocating the indirect costs.

ATC 12-3 Research Assignment *Cost accounting issues at real-world companies*

The July 2003 issue of *Strategic Finance* contains the article "Roles and Practices in Management Accounting Today: Results from the 2003 IMA-E&Y Survey" written by Ashish Garg, Debashis Ghosh, James Hudick, and Chwen Nowacki. This article reviews findings from a survey of managerial accountants conducted by the Institute of Management Accountants (IMA). Read this article and complete the following requirements.

Required

a. The article notes that cost management is an important element for strategic decision making. Why did respondents to the survey believe this was the case?

b. The authors noted that decision makers were most interested in "actionable" cost information. What are the attributes of actionable cost information?

c. Ninety-eight percent of respondents to the survey said that factors exist that cause distortions of cost information. What factors were identified that are responsible for these distortions?

d. Considering the proliferation of "off the shelf" software that is available, many people believe only a minority of companies develop their own cost management systems. According to the article, what percentage of companies actually do develop their systems "in house," and what do you think are the implications of the in-house development for managerial accountants?

ATC 12-4 Writing Assignment *Selection of the appropriate cost driver*

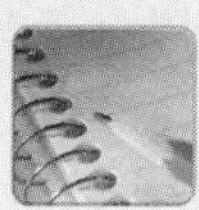

Bullions Enterprises, Inc. (BEI), makes gold, silver, and bronze medals used to recognize outstanding athletic performance in regional and national sporting events. The per unit direct costs of producing the medals follows.

	Gold	Silver	Bronze
Direct materials	$300	$130	$ 35
Labor	120	120	120

During 2002, BEI made 1,200 units of each type of medal for a total of 3,600 (1,200 × 3) medals. All medals are created through the same production process, and they are packaged and shipped in identical containers. Indirect overhead costs amounted to $324,000. BEI currently uses the number of units as the cost driver for the allocation of overhead cost. As a result, BEI allocated $90 ($324,000 ÷ 3,600 units) of overhead cost to each medal produced.

Required

The president of the company has questioned the wisdom of assigning the same amount of overhead to each type of medal. He believes that overhead should be assigned on the basis of the cost to produce the medals. In other words, more overhead should be charged to expensive gold medals, less to silver, and even less to bronze. Assume that you are BEI's chief financial officer. Write a memo responding to the president's suggestion.

ATC 12-5 Ethical Dilemma *Allocation to achieve fairness*

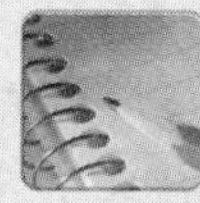

The American Acupuncture Association offers continuing professional education courses for its members at its annual meeting. Instructors are paid a fee for each student attending their courses but are charged a fee for overhead costs that is deducted from their compensation. Overhead costs include fees paid to rent instructional equipment such as overhead projectors, provide supplies to participants, and offer refreshments during coffee breaks. The number of courses offered is used as the allocation base for determining the overhead charge. For example, if overhead costs amount to $5,000 and 25 courses are offered, each course is allocated an overhead charge of $200 ($5,000 ÷ 25 courses). Heidi McCarl, who taught one of the courses, received the following statement with her check in payment for her instructional services.

Instructional fees (20 students × $50 per student)	$1,000
Less: Overhead charge	(200)
Less: Charge for sign language assistant	(240)
Amount due instructor	$ 560

Although Ms. McCarl was well aware that one of her students was deaf and required a sign language assistant, she was surprised to find that she was required to absorb the cost of this service.

Required

a. Given that the Americans with Disabilities Act stipulates that the deaf student cannot be charged for the cost of providing sign language, who should be required to pay the cost of sign language services?

b. Explain how allocation can be used to promote fairness in distributing service costs to the disabled. Describe two ways to treat the $240 cost of providing sign language services that improve fairness.

CHAPTER 13

Relevant Information for Special Decisions

LEARNING OBJECTIVES

After you have mastered the material in this chapter you will be able to:

1. **Identify the characteristics of relevant information.**
2. **Recognize sunk costs and explain why they are not relevant in decision making.**
3. **Distinguish between unit-level, batch-level, product-level, and facility-level costs and understand how these costs affect decision making.**
4. **Identify opportunity costs and explain why they are relevant in decision making.**
5. **Distinguish between quantitative and qualitative characteristics of decision making.**
6. **Make appropriate special order decisions by analyzing relevant information.**
7. **Make appropriate outsourcing decisions by analyzing relevant information.**
8. **Make appropriate segment elimination decisions by analyzing relevant information.**
9. **Make appropriate asset replacement decisions by analyzing relevant information.**

Chapter 13

The Curious Accountant

In February 2003 *The Wall Street Journal* ran an article about the difference between prescription drug prices in the United States and Canada. The article showed the Canadian prices for 10 popular prescription drugs, such as **Celebrex** and **Zocor**, were only 38 percent of prices charged in the United States.

Major pharmaceutical companies have *earnings before tax* that average around 25 percent of sales, indicating that their costs average around 75 percent of the prices they charge. In other words, it cost approximately 75 cents to generate one dollar of revenue. Given that drugs are sold in Canada for 38 percent of the U.S. sales price, a drug that is sold in the U.S. for a dollar would be sold in Canada for only 38 cents.

How can drugs be sold in Canada for less (38 cents) than cost (75 cents)? (Answer on page 460.)

CHAPTER OPENING

Mary Daniels is a partner in a small investment company. Her research indicates that Secor Inc. is a likely takeover target of a multinational corporation. Ms. Daniels wants to buy some Secor stock because she is certain its price will appreciate significantly in the immediate future. She is, however, short of cash. She wishes she had known about Secor last week when she bought 1,000 shares of Telstar Communications Inc. at $24 per share. Telstar had recently launched a series of satellites designed to make worldwide phone service feasible and convenient. With a small device not much larger than a thick credit card, customers could send and receive phone calls anywhere in the world. The day after Ms. Daniels bought the stock, Telstar announced technical difficulties with the satellites, and its stock price dropped to $20 per share. She told herself that Telstar stock is going nowhere, but if she sold it now, she'd take a $4,000 loss [($24 cost − $20 market) × 1,000 shares]. Ms. Daniels decided to hold the Telstar stock instead of selling it and buying Secor. The Secor stock seemed like a sure thing, but she didn't want to incur a loss. Did Ms. Daniels make the right decision? ■

The Decision Environment

Business decision makers cope with enormous challenges. They frequently must make decisions with incomplete information, yet are also faced with an overabundance of useless information. Highly successful executives may seem to have an uncanny knack for distinguishing between relevant and irrelevant data. Success, however, is not a matter of luck. The keys to effective decision making are discussed in the following pages.

Relevant Information

Identify the characteristics of relevant information.

Two primary characteristics distinguish relevant from useless information. First, **relevant information** *differs among the alternatives under consideration*. Suppose you are deciding between two job offers. Both jobs offer the same salary. Salary, therefore, is not *relevant* to the decision-making process. Although salary is important in choosing a job, it is not relevant in choosing between these two job offers. If you receive a third job offer that pays a different salary, salary then becomes relevant because you could differentiate the third offer from the other two.

A second characteristic of relevant information is that it is *future oriented*. "Don't cry over spilled milk." "It's water over the dam." These aphorisms remind people they cannot change the past. With regard to business decisions, the principle means *you cannot avoid a cost that has already been incurred*.

To illustrate, return to the opening of this chapter. Recall that Mary Daniels had purchased 1,000 shares of Telstar stock at $24 per share. She had an opportunity to sell the Telstar stock at $20 per share and invest the proceeds in Secor shares, which were expected to increase in value because Secor was rumored to be the target of a takeover attempt. Ms. Daniels decided to keep her investment in Telstar because she did not want to incur a loss. Did she make the right choice?

Whether Ms. Daniels will make more money by holding the Telstar stock instead of selling it and buying Secor is unknown. The stock price of either company could go up or down. However, she based the decision on *irrelevant* data. Ms. Daniels incurred a loss *when the price of Telstar dropped*. She cannot *avoid* a loss that already exists. Past mistakes should not affect current decisions. Owning the Telstar stock is equivalent to having $20,000 cash today. The relevant question is whether to invest the $20,000 in Telstar or Secor. If Secor is the better alternative, Ms. Daniels should sell the Telstar stock and buy Secor stock.

Sunk Cost

Recognize sunk costs and explain why they are not relevant in decision making.

Ms. Daniels' Telstar stock investment is an example of a *sunk cost*. A **sunk cost** has been incurred in a past transaction. *Since* sunk costs *have been incurred in past transactions and cannot be changed, they are not relevant for making current decisions*.

Why even bother to collect historical information if it is not relevant? Historical information may be useful in predicting the future. A company that earned $5,000,000 last year is more likely to earn $5,000,000 this year than a company that earned $5,000 last year. The predictive capacity is relevant because it provides insight into the future.

Relevant (Differential) Revenues

LO 1

Identify the characteristics of relevant information.

As indicated, relevant revenues must (1) be future oriented and (2) differ for the alternatives under consideration. Since relevant revenues differ between the alternatives, they are sometimes called **differential revenues.** For example, suppose that Pecks Department Stores sells

men's, women's, and children's clothing and is considering eliminating the children's line. The revenue generated by the children's department is *differential (relevant) revenue* because Pecks' total revenue would be different if the department were eliminated.

Relevant (Avoidable) Costs

Identify the characteristics of relevant information.

Businesses seek to minimize cost. Managers *avoid* costs whenever possible. In fact, **relevant costs** are frequently called **avoidable costs.** Avoidable (relevant) costs are the costs managers can eliminate by making specific choices. Return to the Pecks Department Stores example. Costs management could avoid by eliminating the children's department include: merchandise cost; the salaries of buyers and sales staff; interest on debt used to finance the inventory; packaging and transportation; insurance; lost, damaged, and stolen merchandise; uncollectible accounts; shopping bags; sales slips; price tags; and other supplies. Many other costs could *not* be avoided. For example, the company president's salary cannot be avoided by closing down the children's line. Pecks will pay the president her salary whether or not it closes the children's department. Other costs that cannot be avoided include depreciation on the buildings, rent, property taxes, general advertising, and storewide utilities. If a cost is the same (does not *differ*) for two alternatives, it cannot be avoided by selecting one of the alternatives. In other words, *avoidable costs differ between the alternatives.*

Relationship of Cost Avoidance to a Cost Hierarchy

Classifying costs into one of four hierarchical levels helps identify avoidable costs.[1]

Distinguish between unit-level, batch-level, product-level, and facility-level costs and understand how these costs affect decision making.

1. *Unit-level costs.* Costs incurred each time a company generates one unit of product are **unit-level costs.**[2] Examples include the cost of direct materials, direct labor, inspections, packaging, shipping, and handling. Incremental (additional) unit-level costs increase *with each additional unit of product generated. Unit-level costs can be avoided by eliminating the production of a single unit of product.*

[1]R. Cooper and R. S. Kaplan, *The Design of Cost Management Systems* (Englewood Cliffs, NJ: Prentice Hall, 1991). Our classifications are broader than those typically presented. They encompass service and merchandising companies as well as manufacturing businesses. The original cost hierarchy was developed as a platform for activity-based costing. These classifications are equally useful as a tool for identifying avoidable costs.

[2]Recall that we use the term *product* in a generic sense to represent producing goods or services.

2. *Batch-level costs.* Many products are generated in batches rather than individual units. For example, a heating and air conditioning technician may service a batch of air conditioners in an apartment complex. Some of the job costs apply only to individual units, and other costs relate to the entire batch. For instance, the labor to service each air conditioner is a unit-level cost, but the cost of driving to the site is a **batch-level cost.**

   Classifying costs as unit- versus batch-level frequently depends on the context rather than the type of cost. For example, shipping and handling costs to send 200 computers to a university are batch-level costs. In contrast, the shipping and handling cost to deliver a single computer to each of a number of individual customers is a unit-level cost. Eliminating a batch of work avoids both batch-level and unit-level costs. Similarly, adding a batch of work increases batch-level and unit-level costs. Increasing the number of units in a particular batch increases unit-level but not batch-level costs. Decreasing the number of units in a batch reduces unit-level costs but not batch-level costs.

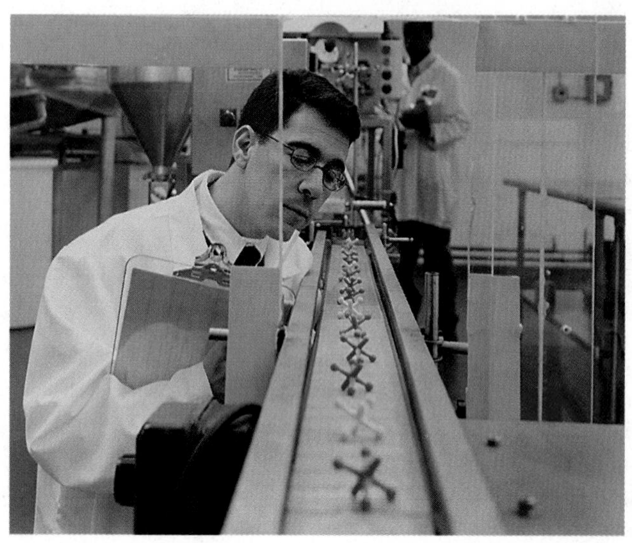

3. *Product-level costs.* Costs incurred to support specific products or services are called **product-level costs.** Product-level costs include quality inspection costs, engineering design costs, the costs of obtaining and defending patents, the costs of regulatory compliance, and inventory holding costs such as interest, insurance, maintenance, and storage. *Product-level costs can be avoided by discontinuing a product line.* For example, suppose the Snapper Company makes the engines used in its lawn mowers. Buying engines from an outside supplier instead of making them would allow Snapper to avoid the product-level costs such as legal fees for patents, manufacturing supervisory costs of producing the engines, and the maintenance and inventory costs of holding engine parts.
4. *Facility-level costs.* **Facility-level costs** are incurred to support the entire company. They are not related to any specific product, batch, or unit of product. Because these costs maintain the facility as a whole, they are frequently called *facility-sustaining costs*. Facility-level costs include building rent or depreciation, personnel administration and training, property and real estate taxes, insurance, maintenance, administrative salaries, general selling costs, landscaping, utilities, and security. Total facility-level costs cannot be avoided unless the entire company is dissolved. However, eliminating a business segment (such as a division, department, or office) may enable a company to avoid some facility-level costs. For example, if a bank eliminates one of its branches, it can avoid the costs of renting, maintaining, and insuring that particular branch building. In general, *segment-level* facility costs can be avoided when a segment is eliminated. In contrast, *corporate-level* facility costs cannot be avoided unless the corporation is eliminated.

Precise distinctions between the various categories are often difficult to draw. One company may incur sales staff salaries as a facility-level cost while another company may pay sales commissions traceable to product lines or even specific units of a product line. Cost classifications cannot be memorized. Classifying specific cost items into the appropriate categories requires thoughtful judgment.

Relevance Is an Independent Concept

The concept of relevance is independent from the concept of cost behavior. In a given circumstance, relevant costs could be either fixed or variable. Consider the following illustration. Executives of Better Bakery Products are debating whether to add a new product, either cakes or pies, to the company's line. Projected costs for the two options follow.

Cost of Cakes		Cost of Pies	
Materials (per unit)	$ 1.50	Materials (per unit)	$ 2.00
Direct labor (per unit)	1.00	Direct labor (per unit)	1.00
Supervisor's salary*	25,000.00	Supervisor's salary*	25,000.00
Franchise fee†	50,000.00	Advertising‡	40,000.00

*It will be necessary to hire a new production supervisor at a cost of $25,000 per year.

†Cakes will be distributed under a nationally advertised label. Better Bakery pays an annual franchise fee for the right to use the product label. Because of the established brand name, Better Bakery will not be required to advertise the product.

‡Better Bakery will market the pies under its own name and will advertise the product in the local market in which the product sells.

Identify the characteristics of relevant information.

Which costs are relevant? Fifty cents per unit of the materials can be avoided by choosing cakes instead of pies. A portion of the materials cost is therefore relevant. Labor costs will be one dollar per unit whether Better Bakery makes cakes or pies. Labor cost is therefore not relevant. Although both materials and direct labor are variable costs, one is relevant but the other is not.

Since Better Bakery must hire a supervisor under either alternative, the supervisor's salary is not relevant. The franchise fee can be avoided if Better Bakery makes pies and advertising costs can be avoided if it makes cakes. All three of these costs are fixed, but only two are relevant. Finally, all the costs (whether fixed or variable) could be avoided if Better Bakery rejects both products. Whether a cost is fixed or variable has no bearing on its relevance.

Relevance of Opportunity Costs

Identify opportunity costs and explain why they are relevant in decision making.

Suppose you pay $50 for a highly sought-after ticket to an Olympic event. Just outside the stadium, someone offers to buy your ticket for $500. If you decline the offer, how much does attending the event cost you? From a decision-making perspective, the cost is $500. If you enter the stadium, you give up the *opportunity* to obtain $500 cash. The relevant cost is $500. The $50 original purchase price is an irrelevant *sunk cost.* The sacrifice represented by a lost opportunity is an **opportunity cost.** Opportunity costs that are (1) future oriented and (2) differ between the alternatives are relevant for decision-making purposes.

Suppose a few minutes after you turn down the offer to sell your ticket for $500, another person offers you $600 for the ticket. If you decline the second offer, has your opportunity cost risen to $1,100 (the first $500 offer plus the second $600 offer)? No; opportunity costs are not cumulative. If you had accepted the first offer, you could not have accepted the second. You may have many opportunities, but accepting one alternative eliminates the possibility of accepting any others. Accountants normally measure opportunity cost as the highest value of the available alternative courses of action. In this case, the opportunity cost of attending the Olympic event is $600.

Opportunity costs are not recorded in financial accounting records and are not reported in financial statements. You would not report the above described $600 opportunity cost as an expense on the income statement, but it will certainly affect your decision about whether to attend the Olympic event. *Opportunity costs are relevant costs.*

CHECK YOURSELF 13.1

Aqua Inc. makes statues for use in fountains. On January 1, 2003, the company paid $13,500 for a mold to make a particular type of statue. The mold had an expected useful life of four years and a salvage value of $1,500. On January 1, 2005, the mold had a market value of $3,000 and a salvage value of $1,200. The expected useful life did not change. What is the relevant cost of using the mold during 2005?

Answer

The relevant cost of using the mold in 2005 is the opportunity cost ([market value − salvage value] ÷ remaining useful life), in this case, ($3,000 − $1,200) ÷ 2 = $900. The book value of the asset and associated depreciation is based on a sunk cost that cannot be avoided because it has already been incurred and therefore is not relevant to current decisions. In contrast, Aqua could avoid the opportunity cost (market value) by selling the mold.

REALITY BYTES

Determining what price to charge for their company's goods or services is one of the most difficult decisions that business managers make. Charge too much and customers will go elsewhere. Charge less than customers are willing to pay and lose the opportunity to earn profits. This problem is especially difficult when managers are deciding if they should reduce (mark down) the price of aging inventory—for example, flowers that are beginning to wilt, fruit that is beginning to overripen, or clothing that is going out of season.

At first managers may be reluctant to mark down the inventory below its cost because this would cause the company to take a loss on the aging inventory. However, the concept of sunk cost applies here. Since the existing inventory has already been paid for, its cost is sunk. Since the cost is sunk it is not relevant to the decision. Does this mean the merchandise should be sold for any price? Not necessarily. The concept of opportunity cost must also be considered.

If the goods are marked down too far, too quickly, they may be sold for less than is possible. The lost potential revenue is an opportunity cost. To minimize the opportunity cost, the amount of a markdown must be the smallest amount necessary to sell the merchandise. The decision is further complicated by qualitative considerations. If a business develops a reputation for repeated markdowns, customers may hesitate to buy goods, thinking that the price will fall further if they only wait a while. The result is a dilemma as to when and how much to mark down aging inventories.

How do managers address this dilemma? Part of the answer has been the use of technology. For years airlines have used computerized mathematical models to help them decide how many seats on a particular flight should be sold at a discount. More recently, retailers have used this same type of modeling software. Such software allows retailers to take fewer markdowns at more appropriate times, thereby resulting in higher overall gross profit margins.

(For a more complete discussion of this topic, see *The Wall Street Journal,* August 7, 2001, pp. A-1, A-6.)

Relevance Is Context-Sensitive

Identify the characteristics of relevant information.

A particular cost that is relevant in one context may be irrelevant in another. Consider a store that carries men's, women's, and children's clothing. The store manager's salary could not be avoided by eliminating the children's department, but it could be avoided if the entire store were closed. The salary is not relevant to deciding whether to eliminate the children's department but is relevant with respect to deciding to close a store. In one context, the salary is not relevant. In the other context, it is relevant.

Relationship between Relevance and Accuracy

Information need not be exact to be relevant. You may decide to delay purchasing a laptop computer you want if you know its price is going to drop even if you don't know exactly how much the price decrease will be. You know part of the cost can be avoided by waiting; you are just not sure of the amount.

The most useful information is both relevant and precise. Totally inaccurate information is useless. Likewise, irrelevant information is useless regardless of its accuracy.

Quantitative versus Qualitative Characteristics of Decision Making

Distinguish between quantitative and qualitative characteristics of decision making.

Relevant information can have both **quantitative** and **qualitative characteristics.** The previous examples focused on quantitative data. Now consider qualitative issues. Suppose you are deciding which of two laptop computers to purchase. Computer A costs $300 more than Computer B. Both computers satisfy your technical requirements; however, Computer A has a more attractive appearance. From a quantitative standpoint, you would select Computer B because you could avoid $300 of cost. However, if the laptop will be used in circumstances when clients need to be impressed, appearance—a qualitative characteristic—may be more important than minimizing cost. You might purchase Computer A even though quantitative factors favor Computer B. Both qualitative and quantitative data are relevant to decision making.

As with quantitative data, qualitative features must *differ* between the alternatives to be relevant. If the two computers were identical in appearance, attractiveness would not be relevant to making the decision.

Relevant Information and Special Decisions

Make appropriate special order decisions by analyzing relevant information.

Four types of special decisions are frequently encountered in business practice: (1) special order, (2) outsourcing, (3) segment elimination, and (4) asset replacement.

Special Order Decisions

Occasionally, a company receives an offer to sell its goods at a price significantly below its normal selling price. The company must make a **special order decision** to accept or reject the offer.

Quantitative Analysis

Assume Premier Office Products manufactures printers. Premier expects to make and sell 2,000 printers in 10 batches of 200 units per batch during the coming year. Expected production costs are summarized in Exhibit 13.1.

Adding its normal markup to the total cost per unit, Premier set the selling price at $360 per printer.

Suppose Premier receives a *special order* from a new customer for 200 printers. If Premier accepts the order, its expected sales would increase from 2,000 units to 2,200 units. But the special order customer is willing to pay only $250 per printer. This price is well below not only Premier's normal selling price of $360 but also the company's expected per unit cost of $329.25. Should Premier accept or reject the special order? At first glance, it seems Premier should reject the special order because the customer's offer is below the expected cost per unit. Analyzing relevant costs and revenue leads, however, to a different conclusion.

EXHIBIT 13.1

Budgeted Cost for Expected Production of 2,000 Printers

Unit-level costs		
Materials costs (2,000 units × $90)	$180,000	
Labor costs (2,000 units × $82.50)	165,000	
Overhead (2,000 units × $7.50)	15,000	
Total unit-level costs (2,000 × $180)		$360,000
Batch-level costs		
Assembly setup (10 batches × $1,700)	17,000	
Materials handling (10 batches × $500)	5,000	
Total batch-level costs (10 batches × $2,200)		22,000
Product-level costs		
Engineering design	14,000	
Production manager salary	63,300	
Total product-level costs		77,300
Facility-level costs		
Segment-level costs		
Division manager's salary	85,000	
Administrative costs	12,700	
Corporate-level costs		
Company president's salary	43,200	
Depreciation	27,300	
General expenses	31,000	
Total facility-level costs		199,200
Total expected cost		$658,500
Cost per unit: $658,500 ÷ 2,000 = $329.25		

Answers to The Curious Accountant

There are several factors that enable drug companies to reduce their prices to certain customers. One significant factor is the issue of relevant cost. Pharmaceutical manufacturers have a substantial amount of fixed cost, such as research and development. For example, in 2002 **Pfizer, Inc.**, had research and development expenses that were 16 percent of sales, while its cost of goods sold expense was only 12.5 percent of sales. With respect to a special order decision, the research and development costs would not change and therefore would not be relevant. In contrast, the unit-level cost of goods sold would increase and therefore would be relevant. Clearly, relevant costs are significantly less than the total cost. If Canadian prices are based on relevant costs, that is, if drug companies view Canadian sales as a special order opportunity, the lower prices may provide a contribution to profitability even though they are significantly less than the prices charged in the United States.

The quantitative analysis follows in three steps.

Step 1 **Determine the amount of the relevant (differential) revenue Premier will earn by accepting the special order.** Premier's alternatives are (1) to accept or (2) to reject the special order. If Premier accepts the special order, additional revenue will be \$50,000 (\$250 × 200 units). If Premier rejects the special order, additional revenue will be zero. Since the amount of revenue differs between the alternatives, the \$50,000 is relevant.

Step 2 **Determine the amount of the relevant (differential) cost Premier will incur by accepting the special order.** Examine the costs in Exhibit 13.1. If Premier accepts the special order, it will incur additional unit-level costs (materials, labor, and overhead). It will also incur the cost of one additional 200-unit batch. The unit- and batch-level costs are relevant because Premier could avoid them by rejecting the special order. The other costs in Exhibit 13.1 are not relevant because Premier will incur them whether it accepts or rejects the special order.

Step 3 **Accept the special order if the relevant revenue exceeds the relevant (avoidable) cost. Reject the order if relevant cost exceeds relevant revenue.** Exhibit 13.2 summarizes the relevant figures. Since the relevant revenue exceeds the relevant cost, Premier should accept the special order because profitability will increase by \$11,800.

EXHIBIT 13.2

Relevant Information for Special Order of 200 Printers

Differential revenue (\$250 × 200 units)	\$50,000
Avoidable unit-level costs (\$180 × 200 units)	(36,000)
Avoidable batch-level costs (\$2,200 × 1 batch)	(2,200)
Contribution to income	\$11,800

Opportunity Costs

Premier can consider the special order because it has enough excess productive capacity to make the additional units. Suppose Premier has the opportunity to lease its excess capacity (currently unused building and equipment) for \$15,000. If Premier uses the excess capacity to make the additional printers, it must forgo the opportunity to lease the excess capacity to a third party. Sacrificing the potential leasing income represents an opportunity cost of accepting the special order. Adding this opportunity cost to the other relevant costs increases the cost of accepting the special order to \$53,200 (\$38,200 unit-level and batch-level costs + \$15,000 opportunity cost). The avoidable costs would then exceed the differential revenue, resulting in a projected loss of $3,200 ($50,000 differential revenue − $53,200 avoidable costs). Under these circumstances Premier would be better off rejecting the special order and leasing the excess capacity.

Relevance and the Decision Context

Assume Premier does not have the opportunity to lease its excess capacity. Recall the original analysis indicated the company could earn an $11,800 contribution to profit by accepting a special order to sell 200 printers at $250 per unit (see Exhibit 13.2). Because Premier can earn a contribution to profit by selling printers for $250 each, can the company reduce its normal selling price (price charged to existing customers) to $250? The answer is no, as illustrated in Exhibit 13.3.

EXHIBIT 13.3

Projections Based on 2,200 Printers at a Sales Price of $250 per Unit

Revenue ($250 × 2,200 units)		$ 550,000
Unit-level costs ($180 × 2,200 units)	$396,000	
Batch-level costs ($2,200 × 11 batches)	24,200	
Product-level costs	77,300	
Facility-level costs	199,200	
Total cost		(696,700)
Projected loss		$(146,700)

If a company is to be profitable, it must ultimately generate revenue in excess of total costs. Although the facility-level and product-level costs are not relevant to the special order decision, they are relevant to the operation of the business as a whole.

Make appropriate outsourcing decisions by analyzing relevant information.

Qualitative Characteristics

Should a company ever reject a special order if the relevant revenues exceed the relevant costs? Qualitative characteristics may be even more important than quantitative ones. If Premier's regular customers learn the company sold printers to another buyer at $250 per unit, they may demand reduced prices on future purchases. Exhibit 13.3 shows Premier cannot reduce the price for all customers. Special order customers should therefore come from outside Premier's normal sales territory. In addition, special order customers should be advised that the special price does not apply to repeat business. Cutting off a special order customer who has been permitted to establish a continuing relationship is likely to lead to ill-feelings and harsh words. A business's reputation can depend on how management handles such relationships. Finally, at full capacity, Premier should reject any special orders at reduced prices because filling those orders reduces its ability to satisfy customers who pay full price.

Outsourcing Decisions

Companies can sometimes purchase products they need for less than it would cost to make them. This circumstance explains why automobile manufacturers purchase rather than make many of the parts in their cars or why a caterer might buy gourmet desserts from a specialty company. Buying goods and services from other companies rather than producing them internally is commonly called **outsourcing.**

Quantitative Analysis

Assume Premier Office Products is considering whether to outsource production of the printers it currently makes. A supplier has offered to sell an unlimited supply of printers to Premier for $240 each. The estimated cost of making the printers is $329.25 per unit (see Exhibit 13.1). The data suggest that Premier could save money by outsourcing. Analyzing relevant costs proves this presumption wrong.

A two-step quantitative analysis for the outsourcing decision follows:

Step 1 **Determine the production costs Premier can avoid if it outsources printer production.** A review of Exhibit 13.1 discloses the costs Premier could avoid by outsourcing. If Premier purchases the printers, it can avoid the unit-level costs (materials, labor, overhead), assembly setup costs, and materials handling costs. It can also avoid the product-level costs (engineering design costs and production manager salary). Deciding to outsource will not, however, affect the facility-level costs. Because Premier will incur them whether or not it outsources printer production, the facility-level costs are not relevant to the outsourcing decision. Exhibit 13.4 shows the avoidable (relevant) costs of outsourcing.

EXHIBIT 13.4

Relevant Cost of Expected Production for Outsourcing 2,000 Printers

Unit-level costs ($180 × 2,000 units)	$360,000
Batch-level costs ($2,200 × 10 batches)	22,000
Product-level costs	77,300
Total relevant cost	$459,300
Cost per unit: $459,300 ÷ 2,000 = $229.65	

Step 2 **Compare the avoidable (relevant) production costs with the cost of buying the product and select the lower-cost option.** Because the relevant production cost is less than the purchase price of the printers ($229.65 per unit versus $240.00), the quantitative analysis suggests that Premier should continue to make the printers. Profitability would decline by $20,700 [$459,300 − ($240 × 2,000)] if printer production were outsourced.

Opportunity Costs

Suppose Premier's accountant determines that the space Premier currently uses to manufacture printers could be converted to warehouse space for storing finished goods. Using this space for warehouse storage would save Premier the $40,000 per year it currently spends to rent warehouse space. By using the space to manufacture printers, Premier is *forgoing the opportunity* to save $40,000 in warehouse costs. Because this *opportunity cost* can be avoided by purchasing the printers, it is relevant to the outsourcing decision. After adding the opportunity cost to the other relevant costs, the total relevant cost increases to $499,300 ($459,300 + $40,000) and the relevant cost per unit becomes $249.65 ($499,300 ÷ 2,000). Since Premier can purchase printers for $240, it should outsource printer production. It would be better off buying the printers and using the warehouse space to store finished goods than to continue producing the printers.

Evaluating the Effect of Growth on the Level of Production

The decision to outsource would change if expected production increased from 2,000 to 3,000 units. Because some of the avoidable costs are fixed relative to the level of production, cost per unit decreases as volume increases. For example, the product-level costs (engineering design, production manager's salary, and opportunity cost) are fixed relative to the level of production. Exhibit 13.5 shows the relevant cost per unit if Premier expects to produce 3,000 printers.

EXHIBIT 13.5

Relevant Cost of Expected Production for Outsourcing 3,000 Printers

Unit-level costs ($180 × 3,000 units)	$540,000
Batch-level costs ($2,200 × 15 batches)	33,000
Product-level costs	77,300
Opportunity cost	40,000
Total relevant cost	$690,300
Cost per unit: $690,300 ÷ 3,000 units = $230.10	

At 3,000 units of production, the relevant cost of making printers is less than the cost of outsourcing ($230.10 versus $240.00). If management believes

FOCUS ON INTERNATIONAL ISSUES

OUTSOURCING—HOW DO THEY DO IT IN JAPAN?

Many outsourcing opportunities suffer from a lack of long-term commitment. For example, a supplier may be able to attain economic efficiencies by redesigning its facilities to produce a product needed by a special order customer. Unfortunately, the redesign cost cannot be recovered on a small order quantity. The supplier needs assurances of a long-term relationship to justify a significant investment in the supply relationship. Japanese businesses have resolved this problem through what are sometimes called *obligational contract relationships*. While these contracts are renewable annually, most suppliers expect to form a supply relationship that will last more than five years. Indeed, Japanese custom establishes a commitment between the supplier and the buyer that includes the exchange of sensitive cost information. If deficiencies in price, delivery, or quality conformance occur, the buyer is likely to send production engineers to the offices of the supplier. The buyer's engineers will study the facilities of the supplier and give detailed advice as to how to achieve improved results. In the process of analyzing the supplier's operations, the buyer obtains detailed information regarding the supplier's costs. This information is used to negotiate prices that ensure reasonable rather than excessive profits for the supplier. Costs are controlled for not only the supplier but also the buyer.

Source: Miles B. Gietzmann, "Emerging Practices in Cost Accounting," *Management Accounting* (UK), January 1995, pp. 24–25.

the company is likely to experience growth in the near future, it should reject the outsourcing option. Managers must consider potential growth when making outsourcing decisions.

Qualitative Features

A company that uses **vertical integration** controls the full range of activities from acquiring raw materials to distributing goods and services. Outsourcing reduces the level of vertical integration, passing some of a company's control over its products to outside suppliers. The reliability of the supplier is critical to an outsourcing decision. An unscrupulous supplier may lure an unsuspecting manufacturer into an outsourcing decision using **low-ball pricing.** Once the manufacturer is dependent on the supplier, the supplier raises prices. If a price sounds too good to be true, it probably is too good to be true. Other potential problems include product quality and delivery commitments. If the printers do not work properly or are not delivered on time, Premier's customers will be dissatisfied with Premier, not the supplier. Outsourcing requires that Premier depend on the supplier to deliver quality products at designated prices according to a specified schedule. Any supplier failures will become Premier's failures.

To protect themselves from unscrupulous or incompetent suppliers, many companies establish a select list of reliable **certified suppliers.** These companies seek to become the preferred customers of the suppliers by offering incentives such as guaranteed volume purchases with prompt payments. These incentives motivate the suppliers to ship high-quality products on a timely basis. The purchasing companies recognize that prices ultimately depend on the suppliers' ability to control costs, so the buyers and suppliers work together to minimize costs. For example, buyers may share confidential information about their production plans with suppliers if such information would enable the suppliers to more effectively control costs.

Companies must approach outsourcing decisions cautiously even when relationships with reliable suppliers are ensured. Outsourcing has both internal and external effects. It usually displaces employees. If the supplier experiences difficulties, reestablishing internal production capacity is expensive once a trained workforce has been released. Loyalty and trust are difficult to build but easy to destroy. In fact, companies must consider not only the employees who will be discharged but also the morale of those who remain. Cost reductions achieved through outsourcing are of little benefit if they are acquired at the expense of low morale and reduced productivity.

In spite of potential pitfalls outsourcing entails, the vast majority of U.S. businesses engage in some form of it. Such widespread acceptance suggests that most companies believe the benefits achieved through outsourcing exceed the potential shortcomings.

CHECK YOURSELF 13.2

Addison Manufacturing Company pays a production supervisor a salary of $48,000 per year. The supervisor manages the production of sprinkler heads that are used in water irrigation systems. Should the production supervisor's salary be considered a relevant cost to a special order decision? Should the production supervisor's salary be considered a relevant cost to an outsourcing decision?

Answer

The production supervisor's salary is not a relevant cost to a special order decision because Addison would pay the salary regardless of whether it accepts or rejects a special order. Since the cost does not differ for the alternatives, it is not relevant. In contrast, the supervisor's salary would be relevant to an outsourcing decision. Addison could dismiss the supervisor if it purchased the sprinkler heads instead of making them. Since the salary could be avoided by purchasing heads instead of making them, the salary is relevant to an outsourcing decision.

Segment Elimination Decisions

LO 8

Make appropriate segment elimination decisions by analyzing relevant information.

Businesses frequently organize operating results into subcomponents called **segments.** Segment data are used to make comparisons among different products, departments, or divisions. For example, in addition to the companywide income statement provided for external users, JCPenney may prepare separate income statements for each retail store for internal users. Executives can then evaluate managerial performance by comparing profitability measures among stores. *Segment reports* can be prepared for products, services, departments, branches, centers, offices, or divisions. These reports normally show segment revenues and costs. The primary objective of segment analysis is to determine whether relevant revenues exceed relevant costs.

Quantitative Analysis

Assume Premier Office Products makes copy equipment and computers as well as printers. Each product line is made in a separate division of the company. Division (segment) operating results for the most recent year are shown in Exhibit 13.6. Initial review of the results suggests the copier division should be eliminated because it is operating at a loss. However, analyzing the relevant revenues and expenses leads to a different conclusion.

A three-step quantitative analysis for the segment elimination decision follows:

Step 1 **Determine the amount of relevant (differential) revenue that pertains to eliminating the copier division.** The alternatives are (1) to eliminate or (2) to continue to operate the copier division. If Premier eliminates the copier line it will lose the $550,000 of revenue the copier division currently produces. If the division continues to operate Premier will earn the revenue. Since the revenue differs between the alternatives, it is relevant.

Step 2 **Determine the amount of cost Premier can avoid if it eliminates the copier division.** If it eliminates copiers, Premier can avoid the unit-level, batch-level, product-level, and segment-level facility-sustaining costs. The relevant revenue and the avoidable costs are shown in Exhibit 13.7.

EXHIBIT 13.6

Projected Revenues and Costs by Segment

	Copiers	Computers	Printers	Total
Projected revenue	$550,000	$850,000	$780,000	$2,180,000
Projected costs				
Unit-level costs				
Materials costs	(120,000)	(178,000)	(180,000)	(478,000)
Labor costs	(160,000)	(202,000)	(165,000)	(527,000)
Overhead	(30,800)	(20,000)	(15,000)	(65,800)
Batch-level costs				
Assembly setup	(15,000)	(26,000)	(17,000)	(58,000)
Materials handling	(6,000)	(8,000)	(5,000)	(19,000)
Product-level costs				
Engineering design	(10,000)	(12,000)	(14,000)	(36,000)
Production manager salary	(52,000)	(55,800)	(63,300)	(171,100)
Facility-level costs				
Segment level				
Division manager salary	(82,000)	(92,000)	(85,000)	(259,000)
Administrative costs	(12,200)	(13,200)	(12,700)	(38,100)
Allocated—corporate level				
Company president salary	(34,000)	(46,000)	(43,200)	(123,200)
Building rental	(19,250)	(29,750)	(27,300)	(76,300)
General facility expenses	(31,000)	(31,000)	(31,000)	(93,000)
Projected profit (loss)	$ (22,250)	$136,250	$121,500	$ 235,500

Premier will incur the corporate-level facility-sustaining costs whether it eliminates the copier segment or continues to operate it. Since these costs do not differ between the alternatives, they are not relevant to the elimination decision. These indirect costs have been *allocated* to the three segments. In this case the total $93,000 of general corporate-level facility expenses has been allocated equally among the three segments, $31,000 to each. The other two corporate-level facility costs (president's salary and building rental) have not been allocated equally among the three segments. A total cost can be allocated among segments in many ways. Regardless of the allocation, the total cost is unchanged before and after the segment elimination. These and other allocated costs are not relevant.

EXHIBIT 13.7

Relevant Revenue and Cost Data for Copier Segment

Projected revenue	$550,000
Projected costs	
Unit-level costs	
Materials costs	(120,000)
Labor costs	(160,000)
Overhead	(30,800)
Batch-level costs	
Assembly setup	(15,000)
Materials handling	(6,000)
Product-level costs	
Engineering design	(10,000)
Production manager salary	(52,000)
Facility-level costs	
Segment level	
Division manager salary	(82,000)
Administrative costs	(12,200)
Projected profit (loss)	$ 62,000

Step 3 **If the relevant revenue is less than the avoidable cost, eliminate the segment (division). If not, continue to operate it.** Because operating the segment is contributing $62,000 per year to company profitability (see Exhibit 13.7), Premier should not eliminate the copier division. Exhibit 13.8 shows Premier's estimated revenues and costs if the computer and printer divisions were operated without the copier division. Projected company profit declines by $62,000 ($235,500 − $173,500) without

EXHIBIT 13.8

Projected Revenues and Costs without Copier Division

	Computers	Printers	Total
Projected revenue	$850,000	$780,000	$1,630,000
Projected costs			
Unit-level costs			
Materials costs	(178,000)	(180,000)	(358,000)
Labor costs	(202,000)	(165,000)	(367,000)
Overhead	(20,000)	(15,000)	(35,000)
Batch-level costs			
Assembly setup	(26,000)	(17,000)	(43,000)
Materials handling	(8,000)	(5,000)	(13,000)
Product-level costs			
Engineering design	(12,000)	(14,000)	(26,000)
Production manager salary	(55,800)	(63,300)	(119,100)
Facility-level costs			
Segment level			
Division manager salary	(92,000)	(85,000)	(177,000)
Administrative costs	(13,200)	(12,700)	(25,900)
Allocated–corporate level*			
Company president salary	(63,000)	(60,200)	(123,200)
Depreciation	(39,375)	(36,925)	(76,300)
General facility expenses	(46,500)	(46,500)	(93,000)
Projected profit (loss)	$ 94,125	$ 79,375	$ 173,500

*The general corporate-level facility costs that were previously *allocated* to the copier division have been reassigned on the basis of one-half to the computer division and one-half to the printer division.

the copier segment, confirming that eliminating it would be detrimental to Premier's profitability.

Qualitative Considerations in Decisions to Eliminate Segments

As with other special decisions, management should consider qualitative factors when determining whether to eliminate segments. Employee lives will be disrupted; some employees may be reassigned elsewhere in the company, but others will be discharged. As with outsourcing decisions, reestablishing internal production capacity is difficult once a trained workforce has been released. Furthermore, employees in other segments, suppliers, customers, and investors may believe that the elimination of a segment implies the company as a whole is experiencing financial difficulty. These individuals may lose confidence in the company and seek business contacts with other companies they perceive to be more stable.

Management must also consider the fact that sales of different product lines are frequently interdependent. Some customers prefer one-stop shopping; they want to buy all their office equipment from one supplier. If Premier no longer sells copiers, customers may stop buying its computers and printers. Eliminating one segment may reduce sales of other segments.

What will happen to the space Premier used to make the copiers? Suppose Premier decides to make telephone systems in the space it previously used for copiers. The contribution to profit of the telephone business would be an *opportunity cost* of operating the copier segment. As demonstrated in previous examples, adding the opportunity cost to the avoidable costs of operating the copier segment could change the decision.

As with outsourcing, volume changes can affect elimination decisions. Because many costs of operating a segment are fixed, the cost per unit decreases as production increases. Growth can transform a segment that is currently producing real losses into a segment that produces real profits. Managers must consider growth potential when making elimination decisions.

CHECK YOURSELF 13.3

Capital Corporation is considering eliminating one of its operating segments. Capital employed a real estate broker to determine the marketability of the building that houses the segment. The broker obtained three bids for the building: $250,000, $262,000, and $264,000. The book value of the building is $275,000. Based on this information alone, what is the relevant cost of the building?

Answer

The book value of the building is a sunk cost that is not relevant. There are three bids for the building, but only one is relevant because Capital could sell the building only once. The relevant cost of the building is the highest opportunity cost, which in this case is $264,000.

Summary of Relationships between Avoidable Costs and the Hierarchy of Business Activity

Distinguish between unit-level, batch-level, product-level, and facility-level costs and understand how these costs affect decision making.

A relationship exists between the cost hierarchy and the different types of special decisions just discussed. A special order involves making additional units of an existing product. Deciding to accept a special order affects unit-level and possibly batch-level costs. In contrast, outsourcing a product stops the production of that product. Outsourcing can avoid many product-level as well as unit- and batch-level costs. Finally, if a company eliminates an entire business segment, it can avoid some of the facility-level costs. The more complex the decision level, the more opportunities there are to avoid costs. Moving to a higher category does not mean, however, that all costs at the higher level of activity are avoidable. For example, all product-level costs may not be avoidable if a company chooses to outsource a product. The company may still incur inventory holding costs or advertising costs whether it makes or buys the product. Understanding the relationship between decision type and level of cost hierarchy helps when identifying avoidable costs. The relationships are summarized in Exhibit 13.9. For each type of decision, look for avoidable costs in the categories marked with an X. Remember also that sunk costs cannot be avoided.

EXHIBIT 13.9

Relationship between Decision Type and Level of Cost Hierarchy

Decision Type	Unit level	Batch level	Product level	Facility level
Special order	X	X		
Outsourcing	X	X	X	
Segment elimination	X	X	X	X

Equipment Replacement Decisions

Make appropriate asset replacement decisions by analyzing relevant information.

Equipment may become technologically obsolete long before it fails physically. Managers should base **equipment replacement decisions** on profitability analysis rather than physical deterioration. Assume Premier Office Products is considering replacing an existing machine with a new one. The following table summarizes pertinent information about the two machines:

Old Machine		New Machine	
Original cost	$ 90,000	Cost of the new machine	$29,000
Accumulated depreciation	(33,000)	Salvage value (in 5 years)	4,000
Book value	$ 57,000	Operating expenses ($4,500 × 5 years)	22,500
Market value (now)	$ 14,000		
Salvage value (in 5 years)	2,000		
Annual depreciation expense	11,000		
Operating expenses ($9,000 × 5 years)	45,000		

Quantitative Analysis

First determine what relevant costs Premier will incur if it keeps the *old machine.*

1. The *original cost* ($90,000), *current book value* ($57,000), *accumulated depreciation* ($33,000), and *annual depreciation expense* ($11,000) are different measures of a cost that was incurred in a prior period. They represent irrelevant sunk costs.
2. The $14,000 market value represents the current sacrifice Premier must make if it keeps using the existing machine. In other words, if Premier does not keep the machine, it can sell it for $14,000. In economic terms, *forgoing the opportunity* to sell the machine costs as much as buying it. The *opportunity cost* is therefore relevant to the replacement decision.
3. The salvage value of the old machine reduces the opportunity cost. Premier can sell the old machine now for $14,000 or use it for five more years and then sell it for $2,000. The opportunity cost of using the old machine for five more years is therefore $12,000 ($14,000 − $2,000).
4. Because the $45,000 ($9,000 × 5) of operating expenses will be incurred if the old machine is used but can be avoided if it is replaced, the operating expenses are relevant costs.

Next, determine what relevant costs will be incurred if Premier purchases and uses the *new machine.*

1. The cost of the new machine represents a future economic sacrifice Premier must incur if it buys the new machine. It is a relevant cost.
2. The salvage value reduces the cost of purchasing the new machine. Part ($4,000) of the $29,000 cost of the new machine will be recovered at the end of five years. The relevant cost of purchasing the new machine is $25,000 ($29,000 − $4,000).
3. The $22,500 ($4,500 × 5) of operating expenses will be incurred if the new machine is purchased; it can be avoided if the new machine is not purchased. The operating expenses are relevant costs.

The relevant costs for the two machines are summarized here:

Old Machine		New Machine	
Opportunity cost	$14,000	Cost of the new machine	$29,000
Salvage value	(2,000)	Salvage value	(4,000)
Operating expenses	45,000	Operating expenses	22,500
Total	$57,000	Total	$47,500

The analysis suggests that Premier should acquire the new machine because buying it produces the lower relevant cost. The $57,000 cost of using the old machine can be *avoided* by incurring the $47,500 cost of acquiring and using the new machine. Over the five-year period, Premier would save $9,500 ($57,000 − $47,500) by purchasing the new machine.

One caution: this analysis ignores income tax effects and the time value of money, which are explained in a later chapter. The discussion in this chapter focuses on identifying and using relevant costs in decision making.

A Look Back 

Decision making requires managers to choose from alternative courses of action. Successful decision making depends on a manager's ability to identify *relevant information*. Information that is relevant for decision making differs among the alternatives and is future oriented. Relevant revenues are sometimes called *differential revenues* because they differ among the alternatives. Relevant costs are sometimes called *avoidable costs* because they can be eliminated or avoided by choosing a specific course of action.

Costs that do not differ among the alternatives are not avoidable and therefore not relevant. *Sunk costs* are not relevant in decision making because they have been incurred in past transactions and therefore cannot be avoided. *Opportunity costs* are relevant because they represent potential benefits that may or may not be realized, depending on the decision maker's choice. In other words, future benefits that differ among the alternatives are relevant. Opportunity costs are not recorded in the financial accounting records.

Classifying costs into one of four hierarchical levels facilitates identifying relevant costs. *Unit-level costs* such as materials and labor are incurred each time a single unit of product is made. These costs can be avoided by eliminating the production of a single unit of product. *Batch-level costs* are associated with producing a group of products. Examples include setup costs and inspection costs related to a batch (group) of work rather than a single unit. Eliminating a batch would avoid both batch-level costs and unit-level costs. *Product-level costs* are incurred to support specific products or services (design and regulatory compliance costs). Product-level costs can be avoided by discontinuing a product line. *Facility-level costs*, like the president's salary, are incurred on behalf of the whole company or a segment of the company. In segment elimination decisions, the facility-level costs related to a particular segment being considered for elimination are relevant and avoidable. Those applying to the company as a whole are not avoidable.

Cost behavior (fixed or variable) is independent from the concept of relevance. Furthermore, a cost that is relevant in one decision context may be irrelevant in another context. Decision making depends on qualitative as well as quantitative information. *Quantitative information refers to information that can be measured using numbers. Qualitative information* is nonquantitative information such as personal preferences or opportunities.

Four types of special decisions that are frequently encountered in business are (1) *special orders*, (2) *outsourcing*, (3) *elimination decisions*, and (4) *asset replacement*. The relevant costs in a special order decision are the unit-level and batch-level costs that will be incurred if the special order is accepted. If the differential revenues from the special order exceed the relevant costs, the order should be accepted. Outsourcing decisions determine whether goods and services should be purchased from other companies. The relevant costs are the unit-level, batch-level, and product-level costs that could be avoided if the company outsources the product or service. If these costs are more than the cost to buy and the qualitative characteristics are satisfactory, the company should outsource. Segment-related unit-level, batch-level, product-level, and facility-level costs that can be avoided when a segment is eliminated are relevant. If the segment's avoidable costs exceed its differential revenues, it should be eliminated, assuming favorable qualitative factors. Asset replacement decisions compare the relevant costs of existing equipment with the relevant costs of new equipment to determine whether replacing the old equipment would be profitable.

A Look Forward 

The next chapter introduces the topics of planning and cost control. You will learn how to prepare budgets and projected (pro forma) financial statements. Finally, you will learn the importance of considering human factors as well as the quantitative aspects of the budgeting process.

SELF-STUDY REVIEW PROBLEM

Flying High Inc. (FHI) is a division of The Master Toy Company. FHI makes remote-controlled airplanes. During 2004, FHI incurred the following costs in the process of making 5,000 planes.

Unit-level materials costs (5,000 units @ $80)	$ 400,000
Unit-level labor costs (5,000 units @ $90)	450,000
Unit-level overhead costs (5,000 @ $70)	350,000
Depreciation cost on manufacturing equipment*	50,000
Other manufacturing overhead†	140,000
Inventory holding costs	240,000
Allocated portion of The Master Toy Company's facility-level costs	600,000
Total costs	$2,230,000

*The manufacturing equipment, which originally cost $250,000, has a book value of $200,000, a remaining useful life of four years, and a zero salvage value. If the equipment is not used in the production process, it can be leased for $30,000 per year.

†Includes supervisors' salaries and rent for the manufacturing building.

Required

a. FHI uses a cost-plus pricing strategy. FHI sets its price at product cost plus $100. Determine the price that FHI should charge for its remote-controlled airplanes.

b. Assume that a potential customer that operates a chain of high-end toy stores has approached FHI. A buyer for this chain has offered to purchase 1,000 planes from FHI at a price of $275 each. Ignoring qualitative considerations, should FHI accept or reject the order?

c. FHI has the opportunity to purchase the planes from Arland Manufacturing Company for $325 each. Arland maintains adequate inventories so that it can supply its customers with planes on demand. Should FHI accept the opportunity to outsource the making of its planes?

d. Use the contribution margin format to prepare an income statement based on historical cost data. Prepare a second income statement that reflects the relevant cost data that Master Toy should consider in a segment elimination decision. Based on a comparison of these two statements, indicate whether Master Toy should eliminate the FHI division.

e. FHI is considering replacing the equipment it currently uses to manufacture its planes. It could purchase replacement equipment for $480,000 that has an expected useful life of four years and a salvage value of $40,000. The new equipment would increase productivity substantially, reducing unit-level labor costs by 20 percent. Assume that FHI would maintain its production and sales at 5,000 planes per year. Prepare a schedule that shows the relevant costs of operating the old equipment versus the costs of operating the new equipment. Should FHI replace the equipment?

Solution to Requirement *a*

Product Cost for Remote-Controlled Airplanes

Unit-level materials costs (5,000 units × $80)	$ 400,000
Unit-level labor costs (5,000 units × $90)	450,000
Unit-level overhead costs (5,000 units × $70)	350,000
Depreciation cost on manufacturing equipment	50,000
Other manufacturing overhead	140,000
Total product cost	$1,390,000

The cost per unit is $278 ($1,390,000 ÷ 5,000 units). The sales price per unit is $378 ($278 + $100). Depreciation expense is included because cost-plus pricing is usually based on historical cost rather than relevant cost. To be profitable in the long run, a company must ultimately recover the amount it paid for the equipment (the historical cost of the equipment).

Solution to Requirement *b*

The incremental (relevant) cost of making 1,000 additional airplanes follows. The depreciation expense is not relevant because it represents a sunk cost. The other manufacturing overhead costs are not relevant because they will be incurred regardless of whether FHI makes the additional planes.

Per Unit Relevant Product Cost for Airplanes	
Unit-level materials costs	$ 80
Unit-level labor costs	90
Unit-level overhead costs	70
Total relevant product cost	$240

Since the relevant (incremental) cost of making the planes is less than the incremental revenue, FHI should accept the special order. Accepting the order will increase profits by $35,000 [($275 incremental revenue − $240 incremental cost) × 1,000 units].

Solution to Requirement *c*

Distinguish this decision from the special order opportunity discussed in Requirement *b*. That special order (Requirement *b*) decision hinged on the cost of making additional units with the existing production process. In contrast, a make-or-buy decision compares current production with the possibility of making zero units (closing down the entire manufacturing process). If the manufacturing process were shut down, FHI could avoid the unit-level costs, the cost of the lost opportunity to lease the equipment, the other manufacturing overhead costs, and the inventory holding costs. Since the planes can be purchased on demand, there is no need to maintain any inventory. The allocated portion of the facility-level costs is not relevant because it would be incurred regardless of whether FHI manufactured the planes. The relevant cost of making the planes follows.

Relevant Manufacturing Cost for Airplanes	
Unit-level materials costs (5,000 units × $80)	$ 400,000
Unit-level labor costs (5,000 units × $90)	450,000
Unit-level overhead costs (5,000 units × $70)	350,000
Opportunity cost of leasing the equipment	30,000
Other manufacturing overhead costs	140,000
Inventory holding cost	240,000
Total product cost	$1,610,000

The relevant cost per unit is $322 ($1,610,000 ÷ 5,000 units). Since the relevant cost of making the planes ($322) is less than the cost of purchasing them ($325), FHI should continue to make the planes.

Solution to Requirement *d*

Income Statements	Historical Cost Data	Relevant Cost Data
Revenue (5,000 units × $378)	$1,890,000	$1,890,000
Less variable costs:		
Unit-level materials costs (5,000 units × $80)	(400,000)	(400,000)
Unit-level labor costs (5,000 units × $90)	(450,000)	(450,000)
Unit-level overhead costs (5,000 units × $70)	(350,000)	(350,000)
Contribution Margin	690,000	690,000
Depreciation cost on manufacturing equipment	(50,000)	

continued

	Historical Cost Data	Relevant Cost Data
Opportunity cost of leasing manufacturing equipment		(30,000)
Other manufacturing overhead costs	(140,000)	(140,000)
Inventory holding costs	(240,000)	(240,000)
Allocated facility-level administrative costs	(600,000)	
Net Loss	$ (340,000)	
Contribution to Master Toy's Profitability		$ 280,000

Master Toy should not eliminate the segment (FHI). Although it appears to be incurring a loss, the allocated facility-level administrative costs are not relevant because Master Toy would incur these costs regardless of whether it eliminated FHI. Also, the depreciation cost on the manufacturing equipment is not relevant because it is a sunk cost. However, since the company could lease the equipment if the segment were eliminated, the $30,000 potential rental fee represents a relevant opportunity cost. The relevant revenue and cost data show that FHI is contributing $280,000 to the profitability of The Master Toy Company.

Solution to Requirement e

The relevant costs of using the old equipment versus the new equipment are the costs that differ for the two alternatives. In this case relevant costs include the purchase price of the new equipment, the opportunity cost of the old equipment, and the labor costs. These items are summarized in the following table. The data show the total cost over the four-year useful life of the replacement equipment.

Relevant Cost Comparison

	Old Equipment	New Equipment
Opportunity to lease the old equipment ($30,000 × 4 years)	$ 120,000	
Cost of new equipment ($480,000 − $40,000)		$ 440,000
Unit-level labor costs (5,000 units × $90 × 4 years)	1,800,000	
Unit-level labor costs (5,000 units × $90 × 4 years × .80)		1,440,000
Total relevant costs	$1,920,000	$1,880,000

Since the relevant cost of operating the new equipment is less than the cost of operating the old equipment, FHI should replace the equipment.

KEY TERMS

avoidable costs 455
batch-level costs 456
certified suppliers 463
differential revenues 454
equipment replacement decisions 467
facility-level costs 456
low-ball pricing 463
opportunity costs 457
outsourcing 461
product-level costs 456
qualitative characteristics 459
quantitative characteristics 459
relevant costs 455
relevant information 454
segment 464
special order decision 459
sunk costs 454
unit-level costs 455
vertical integration 463

QUESTIONS

1. Identify the primary qualities of revenues and costs that are relevant for decision making.
2. Are variable costs always relevant? Explain.
3. Identify the four hierarchical levels used to classify costs. When can each of these levels of costs be avoided?

4. Describe the relationship between relevance and accuracy.
5. "It all comes down to the bottom line. The numbers never lie." Do you agree with this conclusion? Explain your position.
6. Carmon Company invested $300,000 in the equity securities of Mann Corporation. The current market value of Carmon's investment in Mann is $250,000. Carmon currently needs funds for operating purposes. Although interest rates are high, Carmon's president has decided to borrow the needed funds instead of selling the investment in Mann. He explains that his company cannot afford to take a $50,000 loss on the Mann stock. Evaluate the president's decision based on this information.
7. What is an opportunity cost? How does it differ from a sunk cost?
8. A local bank advertises that it offers a free noninterest-bearing checking account if the depositor maintains a $500 minimum balance in the account. Is the checking account truly free?
9. A manager is faced with deciding whether to replace machine A or machine B. The original cost of machine A was $20,000 and that of machine B was $30,000. Because the two cost figures differ, they are relevant to the manager's decision. Do you agree? Explain your position.
10. Are all fixed costs unavoidable?
11. Identify two qualitative considerations that could be associated with special order decisions.
12. Which of the following would not be relevant to a make-or-buy decision?
    - **(a)** Allocated portion of depreciation expense on existing facilities.
    - **(b)** Variable cost of labor used to produce products currently purchased from suppliers.
    - **(c)** Warehousing costs for inventory of completed products (inventory levels will be constant regardless of whether products are purchased or produced).
    - **(d)** Cost of materials used to produce the items currently purchased from suppliers.
    - **(e)** Property taxes on the factory building.
13. What two factors should be considered in deciding how to allocate shelf space in a retail establishment?
14. What level(s) of costs is (are) relevant in special order decisions?
15. Why would a company consider outsourcing products or services?
16. Chris Sutter, the production manager of Satellite Computers, insists that the floppy drives used in the company's upper-end computers be outsourced since they can be purchased from a supplier at a lower cost per unit than the company is presently incurring to produce the drives. Jane Meyers, his assistant, insists that if sales growth continues at the current levels, the company will be able to produce the drives in the near future at a lower cost because of the company's predominately fixed cost structure. Does Ms. Meyers have a legitimate argument? Explain.
17. Identify some qualitative factors that should be considered in addition to quantitative costs in deciding whether to outsource.
18. The managers of Wilcox Inc. are suggesting that the company president eliminate one of the company's segments that is operating at a loss. Why may this be a hasty decision?
19. Why would a supervisor choose to continue using a more costly old machine instead of replacing it with a less costly new machine?

EXERCISES

All Exercises are available with McGraw-Hill's Homework Manager

Exercise 13-1 *Distinction between relevance and cost behavior* L.O. 1

Lucy Taylor is trying to decide which of two different kinds of candy to sell in her retail candy store. One type is a name-brand candy that will practically sell itself. The other candy is cheaper to purchase but does not carry an identifiable brand name. Ms. Taylor believes that she will have to incur significant advertising costs to sell this candy. Several cost items for the two types of candy are as follows:

Brandless Candy		Name-Brand Candy	
Cost per box	$ 4.00	Cost per box	$ 6.00
Sales commissions per box	0.50	Sales commissions per box	1.00
Rent of display space	1,500.00	Rent of display space	1,500.00
Advertising	3,000.00	Advertising	2,000.00

Required

Identify each cost as being relevant or irrelevant to Ms. Taylor's decision and indicate whether it is fixed or variable relative to the number of boxes sold.

L.O. 1, 2

Exercise 13-2 *Distinction between relevance and cost behavior*

Bron Company makes and sells a single product. Bron incurred the following costs in its most recent fiscal year.

Cost Items Appearing on the Income Statement	
Materials Cost ($7 per unit)	Sales Commissions (2% of sales)
Company President's Salary	Salaries of Administrative Personnel
Depreciation on Manufacturing Equipment	Shipping and Handling ($0.25 per unit)
Customer Billing Costs (1% of sales)	Depreciation on Office Furniture
Rental Cost of Manufacturing Facility	Manufacturing Supplies ($0.25 per unit)
Advertising Costs ($250,000 per year)	Production Supervisor's Salary
Labor Cost ($5 per unit)	

Bron could purchase the products that it currently makes. If it purchased the items, the company would continue to sell them using its own logo, advertising program, and sales staff.

Required

Identify each cost as relevant or irrelevant to the outsourcing decision and indicate whether the cost is fixed or variable relative to the number of products manufactured and sold.

L.O. 1

Exercise 13-3 *Distinction between avoidable costs and cost behavior*

Elegance Company makes fine jewelry that it sells to department stores throughout the United States. Elegance is trying to decide which of two bracelets to manufacture. Elegance has a labor contract that prohibits the company from laying off workers freely. Cost data pertaining to the two choices follow.

	Bracelet A	Bracelet B
Cost of materials per unit	$ 30	$ 50
Cost of labor per unit	40	40
Advertising cost per year	8,000	6,000
Annual depreciation on existing equip.	5,000	4,000

Required

a. Identify the fixed costs and determine the amount of fixed cost for each product.

b. Identify the variable costs and determine the amount of variable cost per unit for each product.

c. Identify the avoidable costs and determine the amount of avoidable cost for each product.

L.O. 1, 2, 6

Exercise 13-4 *Special order decision*

Solid Concrete Company pours concrete slabs for single-family dwellings. Russell Construction Company, which operates outside Solid's normal sales territory, asks Solid to pour 40 slabs for Russell's new development of homes. Solid has the capacity to build 300 slabs and is presently working on 250 of them. Russell is willing to pay only $3,000 per slab. Solid estimates the cost of a typical job to include unit-level materials, $1,500; unit-level labor, $1,000; and an allocated portion of facility-level overhead, $700.

Required

Should Solid accept or reject the special order to pour 40 slabs for $3,000 each? Support your answer with appropriate computations.

Exercise 13-5 ***Special order decision*** **L.O. 1, 2, 6**

Lance Company manufactures a personal computer designed for use in schools and markets it under its own label. Lance has the capacity to produce 20,000 units a year but is currently producing and selling only 15,000 units a year. The computer's normal selling price is $1,600 per unit with no volume discounts. The unit-level costs of the computer's production are $600 for direct materials, $200 for direct labor, and $250 for indirect unit-level manufacturing costs. The total product- and facility-level costs incurred by Lance during the year are expected to be $2,000,000 and $800,000, respectively. Assume that Lance receives a special order to produce and sell 4,000 computers at $1,200 each.

Required

Should Lance accept or reject the special order? Support your answer with appropriate computations.

Exercise 13-6 ***Identifying qualitative factors for a special order decision*** **L.O. 5**

Required

Describe the qualitative factors that Lance should consider before accepting the special order described in Exercise 13-5.

Exercise 13-7 ***Using the contribution margin approach for a special order decision*** **L.O. 6**

Shane Company, which produces and sells a small digital clock, bases its pricing strategy on a 30 percent markup on total cost. Based on annual production costs for 15,000 units of product, computations for the sales price per clock follow.

Unit-level costs	$180,000
Fixed costs	60,000
Total cost (a)	240,000
Markup (a × 0.30)	72,000
Total sales (b)	$312,000
Sales price per unit (b ÷ 15,000)	$20.80

Required

a. Shane has excess capacity and receives a special order for 6,000 clocks for $15 each. Calculate the contribution margin per unit; based on it, should Shane accept the special order?

b. Support your answer by preparing a contribution margin income statement for the special order.

Exercise 13-8 ***Outsourcing decision*** **L.O. 7**

Rider Bicycle Manufacturing Company currently produces the handlebars used in manufacturing its bicycles, which are high-quality racing bikes with limited sales. Rider produces and sells only 5,000 bikes each year. Due to the low volume of activity, Rider is unable to obtain the economies of scale that larger producers achieve. For example, Rider could buy the handlebars for $30 each; they cost $34 each to make. The following is a detailed breakdown of current production costs.

Item	Unit Cost	Total
Unit-level costs		
Materials	$14	$ 70,000
Labor	11	55,000
Overhead	4	20,000
Allocated facility-level costs	5	25,000
Total	$34	$170,000

After seeing these figures, Rider's president remarked that it would be foolish for the company to continue to produce the handlebars at $34 each when it can buy them for $30 each.

Required

Do you agree with the president's conclusion? Support your answer with appropriate computations.

L.O. 7

Exercise 13-9 *Establishing price for an outsourcing decision*

Easy Cut Inc. makes and sells lawn mowers for which it currently makes the engines. It has an opportunity to purchase the engines from a reliable manufacturer. The annual costs of making the engines are shown here.

Cost of materials (20,000 units × $20)	$ 400,000
Labor (20,000 units × $25)	500,000
Depreciation on manufacturing equipment*	45,000
Salary of supervisor of engine production	180,000
Rental cost of equipment used to make engines	120,000
Allocated portion of corporate-level facility-sustaining costs	45,000
Total cost to make 20,000 engines	$1,290,000

*The equipment has a book value of $72,000 but its market value is zero.

Required

a. Determine the maximum price per unit that Easy Cut would be willing to pay for the engines.
b. Would the price computed in Requirement *a* change if production increased to 25,000 units? Support your answer with appropriate computations.

L.O. 5, 7

Exercise 13-10 *Outsourcing decision with qualitative factors*

Surround Sound Inc. (SSI), which makes and sells 80,000 radios annually, currently purchases the radio speakers it uses for $8 each. Each radio uses one speaker. The company has idle capacity and is considering the possibility of making the speakers that it needs. SSI estimates that the cost of materials and labor needed to make speakers would be a total of $7 for each speaker. In addition, the costs of supervisory salaries, rent, and other manufacturing costs would be $160,000. Allocated facility-level costs would be $96,000.

Required

a. Determine the change in net income SSI would experience if it decides to make the speakers.
b. Discuss the qualitative factors that SSI should consider.

L.O. 4, 7

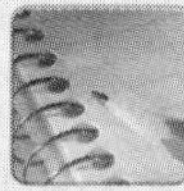

Exercise 13-11 *Outsourcing decision affected by opportunity costs*

Sertoma Electronics currently produces the shipping containers it uses to deliver the electronics products it sells. The monthly cost of producing 9,000 containers follows.

Unit-level materials	$ 4,500
Unit-level labor	6,000
Unit-level overhead	3,900
Product-level costs*	9,000
Allocated facility-level costs	22,500

*One-third of these costs can be avoided by purchasing the containers.

Loehman Container Company has offered to sell comparable containers to Sertoma for $2.25 each.

Required

a. Should Sertoma continue to make the containers? Support your answer with appropriate computations.
b. Sertoma could lease the space it currently uses in the manufacturing process. If leasing would produce $9,000 per month, would your answer to Requirement *a* be different? Explain.

L.O. 4

Exercise 13-12 *Opportunity cost*

Swift Truck Lines Inc. owns a truck that cost $80,000. Currently, the truck's book value is $48,000, and its expected remaining useful life is four years. Swift has the opportunity to purchase for $60,000 a replacement truck that is extremely fuel efficient. Fuel cost for the old truck is expected to be $8,000 per year more than fuel cost for the new truck. The old truck is paid for but, in spite of being in good condition, can be sold for only $32,000.

Required

Should Swift Truck Lines replace the old truck with the new fuel-efficient model, or should it continue to use the old truck until it wears out? Explain.

Exercise 13-13 *Opportunity costs*

L.O. 4, 5

Tim Kozlowski owns his own taxi, for which he bought a $20,000 permit to operate two years ago. Mr. Kozlowski earns $37,000 a year operating as an independent but has the opportunity to sell the taxi and permit for $75,000 and take a position as dispatcher for Trenton Taxi Co. The dispatcher position pays $31,000 a year for a 40-hour week. Driving his own taxi, Mr. Kozlowski works approximately 55 hours per week. If he sells his business, he will invest the $75,000 and can earn a 10 percent return.

Required

a. Determine the opportunity cost of owning and operating the independent business.
b. Based solely on financial considerations, should Mr. Kozlowski sell the taxi and accept the position as dispatcher?
c. Discuss the qualitative as well as quantitative factors that Mr. Kozlowski should consider.

Exercise 13-14 *Segment elimination decision*

L.O. 8

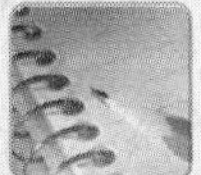

Quell Company operates three segments. Income statements for the segments imply that profitability could be improved if Segment A were eliminated.

QUELL COMPANY
Income Statements for the Year 2009

Segment	A	B	C
Sales	$196,000	$260,000	$345,000
Cost of Goods Sold	(143,000)	(98,000)	(190,000)
Sales Commissions	(20,000)	(38,000)	(22,000)
Contribution Margin	33,000	124,000	133,000
General Fixed Oper. Exp. (allocation of president's salary)	(44,000)	(52,000)	(44,000)
Advertising Expense (specific to individual divisions)	(3,000)	(10,000)	0
Net Income	$ (14,000)	$ 62,000	$ 89,000

Required

a. Explain the effect on profitability if Segment A is eliminated.
b. Prepare comparative income statements for the company as a whole under two alternatives: (1) the retention of Segment A and (2) the elimination of Segment A.

Exercise 13-15 *Segment elimination decision*

L.O. 8

Moreno Transport Company divides its operations into four divisions. A recent income statement for Hess Division follows.

MORENO TRANSPORT COMPANY
Hess Division
Income Statement for the Year 2005

Revenue	$650,000
Salaries for Drivers	(420,000)
Fuel Expenses	(80,000)
Insurance	(110,000)
Division-Level Facility-Sustaining Costs	(60,000)
Companywide Facility-Sustaining Costs	(130,000)
Net Loss	$(150,000)

Required

a. Should Hess Division be eliminated? Support your answer by explaining how the division's elimination would affect the net income of the company as a whole. By how much would companywide income increase or decrease?

b. Assume that Hess Division is able to increase its revenue to $700,000 by raising its prices. Would this change the decision you made in Requirement *a*? Determine the amount of the increase or decrease that would occur in companywide net income if the segment were eliminated if revenue were $700,000.

c. What is the minimum amount of revenue required to justify continuing the operation of Hess Division?

L.O. 8

Exercise 13-16 *Identifying avoidable cost of a segment*

Howell Corporation is considering the elimination of one of its segments. The segment incurs the following fixed costs. If the segment is eliminated, the building it uses will be sold.

Advertising expense	$ 97,000
Supervisory salaries	159,000
Allocation of companywide facility-level costs	45,000
Original cost of building	100,000
Book value of building	60,000
Market value of building	70,000
Maintenance costs on equipment	50,000
Real estate taxes on building	7,000

Required

Based on this information, determine the amount of avoidable cost associated with the segment.

L.O. 9

Exercise 13-17 *Asset replacement decision*

A machine purchased three years ago for $200,000 has a current book value using straight-line depreciation of $120,000; its operating expenses are $30,000 per year. A replacement machine would cost $250,000, have a useful life of nine years, and would require $14,000 per year in operating expenses. It has an expected salvage value of $66,000 after nine years. The current disposal value of the old machine is $60,000; if it is kept nine more years, its residual value would be $10,000.

Required

Based on this information, should the old machine be replaced? Support your answer.

L.O. 9

Exercise 13-18 *Asset replacement decision*

McKee Company is considering replacement of some of its manufacturing equipment. Information regarding the existing equipment and the potential replacement equipment follows.

Existing Equipment		Replacement Equipment	
Cost	$ 90,000	Cost	$95,000
Operating expenses*	105,000	Operating expenses*	20,000
Salvage value	10,000	Salvage value	14,000
Market value	60,000	Useful life	8 years
Book value	32,000		
Remaining useful life	8 years		

*The amounts shown for operating expenses are the cumulative total of all such expected expenses to be incurred over the useful life of the equipment.

Required

Based on this information, recommend whether to replace the equipment. Support your recommendation with appropriate computations.

Exercise 13-19 ***Asset replacement decision*** L.O. 9

Pendorric Company paid $72,000 to purchase a machine on January 1, 2006. During 2008, a technological breakthrough resulted in the development of a new machine that costs $125,000. The old machine costs $40,000 per year to operate, but the new machine could be operated for only $12,000 per year. The new machine, which will be available for delivery on January 1, 2009, has an expected useful life of four years. The old machine is more durable and is expected to have a remaining useful life of four years. The current market value of the old machine is $20,000. The expected salvage value of both machines is zero.

Required

Based on this information, recommend whether to replace the machine. Support your recommendation with appropriate computations.

Exercise 13-20 ***Annual versus cumulative data for replacement decision*** L.O. 4, 9

Because of rapidly advancing technology, Sayre Publications Inc. is considering replacing its existing typesetting machine with leased equipment. The old machine, purchased two years ago, has an expected useful life of six years and is in good condition. Apparently, it will continue to perform as expected for the remaining four years of its expected useful life. A four-year lease for equipment with comparable productivity can be obtained for $15,000 per year. The following data apply to the old machine.

Original cost	$180,000
Accumulated depreciation	60,000
Current market value	77,500
Estimated salvage value	7,500

Required

a. Determine the annual opportunity cost of using the old machine. Based on your computations, recommend whether to replace it.

b. Determine the total cost of the lease over the four-year contract. Based on your computations, recommend whether to replace the old machine.

PROBLEMS

All Problems are available with McGraw-Hill's Homework Manager

Problem 13-21 ***Context-sensitive relevance*** L.O. 1

Required

Respond to each requirement independently.

a. Describe two decision-making contexts, one in which unit-level materials costs are avoidable, and the other in which they are unavoidable.

b. Describe two decision-making contexts, one in which batch-level setup costs are avoidable, and the other in which they are unavoidable.

c. Describe two decision-making contexts, one in which advertising costs are avoidable, and the other in which they are unavoidable.

d. Describe two decision-making contexts, one in which rent paid for a building is avoidable, and the other in which it is unavoidable.

e. Describe two decision-making contexts, one in which depreciation on manufacturing equipment is avoidable, and the other in which it is unavoidable.

L.O. 1

CHECK FIGURES

a. Contribution to profit for Job A: $168,000

b. Contribution to profit: $(1,000)

Problem 13-22 *Context-sensitive relevance*

Myl Construction Company is a building contractor specializing in small commercial buildings. The company has the opportunity to accept one of two jobs; it cannot accept both because they must be performed at the same time and Myl does not have the necessary labor force for both jobs. Indeed, it will be necessary to hire a new supervisor if either job is accepted. Furthermore, additional insurance will be required if either job is accepted. The revenue and costs associated with each job follow.

Cost Category	Job A	Job B
Contract price	$700,000	$600,000
Unit-level materials	250,000	220,000
Unit-level labor	240,000	243,000
Unit-level overhead	17,000	14,000
Supervisor's salary	80,000	80,000
Rental equipment costs	25,000	28,000
Depreciation on tools (zero market value)	20,000	20,000
Allocated portion of companywide facility-sustaining costs	9,000	8,000
Insurance cost for job	16,000	16,000

Required

a. Assume that Myl has decided to accept one of the two jobs. Identify the information relevant to selecting one job versus the other. Recommend which job to accept and support your answer with appropriate computations.

b. Assume that Job A is no longer available. Myl's choice is to accept or reject Job B alone. Identify the information relevant to this decision. Recommend whether to accept or reject Job B. Support your answer with appropriate computations.

L.O. 3, 5, 6

CHECK FIGURE

a. Relevant cost per unit: $56

Problem 13-23 *Effect of order quantity on special order decision*

Bogati Quilting Company makes blankets that it markets through a variety of department stores. It makes the blankets in batches of 1,000 units. Bogati made 20,000 blankets during the prior accounting period. The cost of producing the blankets is summarized here.

Materials cost ($20 per unit × 20,000)	$ 400,000
Labor cost ($25 per unit × 20,000)	500,000
Manufacturing supplies ($3 × 20,000)	60,000
Batch-level costs (20 batches at $4,000 per batch)	80,000
Product-level costs	140,000
Facility-level costs	300,000
Total costs	$1,480,000
Cost per unit = $1,480,000 ÷ 20,000 = $74	

Required

a. Quality Motels has offered to buy a batch of 500 blankets for $55 each. Bogati's normal selling price is $90 per unit. Based on the preceding quantitative data, should Bogati accept the special order? Support your answer with appropriate computations.

b. Would your answer to Requirement *a* change if Quality offered to buy a batch of 1,000 blankets for $55 per unit? Support your answer with appropriate computations.

c. Describe the qualitative factors that Bogati Quilting Company should consider before accepting a special order to sell blankets to Quality Motels.

Problem 13-24 ***Effects of the level of production on an outsourcing decision*** **L.O. 5, 6**

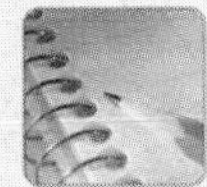

CHECK FIGURE
a. Total relevant cost: $75,000

Vaida Chemical Company makes a variety of cosmetic products, one of which is a skin cream designed to reduce the signs of aging. Vaida produces a relatively small amount (15,000 units) of the cream and is considering the purchase of the product from an outside supplier for $4.50 each. If Vaida purchases from the outside supplier, it would continue to sell and distribute the cream under its own brand name. Vaida's accountant constructed the following profitability analysis.

Revenue (15,000 units × $10)	$150,000
Unit-level materials costs (15,000 units × $1.40)	(21,000)
Unit-level labor costs (15,000 units × $0.50)	(7,500)
Unit-level overhead costs (15,000 × $0.10)	(1,500)
Unit-level selling expenses (15,000 × $0.25)	(3,750)
Contribution margin	116,250
Skin cream production supervisor's salary	(45,000)
Allocated portion of facility-level costs	(11,250)
Product-level advertising cost	(36,000)
Contribution to companywide income	$ 24,000

Required

a. Identify the cost items relevant to the make-or-outsource decision.
b. Should Vaida continue to make the product or buy it from the supplier? Support your answer by determining the change in net income if Vaida buys the cream instead of making it.
c. Suppose that Vaida is able to increase sales by 10,000 units (sales will increase to 25,000 units). At this level of production, should Vaida make or buy the cream? Support your answer by explaining how the increase in production affects the cost per unit.
d. Discuss the qualitative factors that Vaida should consider before deciding to outsource the skin cream. How can Vaida minimize the risk of establishing a relationship with an unreliable supplier?

Problem 13-25 ***Outsourcing decision affected by equipment replacement*** **L.O. 5, 7, 9**

CHECK FIGURES
a. Avoidable cost per unit: $119
b. Avoidable cost per unit with new equipment: $31

Grant Bike Company (GBC) makes the frames used to build its bicycles. During 2006, GBC made 20,000 frames; the costs incurred follow.

Unit-level materials costs (20,000 units × $40)	$ 800,000
Unit-level labor costs (20,000 units × $50)	1,000,000
Unit-level overhead costs (20,000 × $10)	200,000
Depreciation on manufacturing equipment	100,000
Bike frame production supervisor's salary	80,000
Inventory holding costs	300,000
Allocated portion of facility-level costs	500,000
Total costs	$2,980,000

GBC has an opportunity to purchase frames for $102 each.

Additional Information

1. The manufacturing equipment, which originally cost $500,000, has a book value of $400,000, a remaining useful life of four years, and a zero salvage value. If the equipment is not used to produce bicycle frames, it can be leased for $60,000 per year.
2. GBC has the opportunity to purchase for $960,000 new manufacturing equipment that will have an expected useful life of four years and a salvage value of $80,000. This equipment will increase productivity substantially, reducing unit-level labor costs by 60 percent. Assume that GBC will continue to produce and sell 20,000 frames per year in the future.
3. If GBC outsources the frames, the company can eliminate 80 percent of the inventory holding costs.

Required

a. Determine the avoidable cost per unit of making the bike frames, assuming that GBC is considering the alternatives between making the product using the existing equipment and outsourcing the product to the independent contractor. Based on the quantitative data, should GBC outsource the bike frames? Support your answer with appropriate computations.
b. Assuming that GBC is considering whether to replace the old equipment with the new equipment, determine the avoidable cost per unit to produce the bike frames using the new equipment and the avoidable cost per unit to produce the bike frames using the old equipment. Calculate the impact on profitability if the bike frames were made using the old equipment versus the new equipment.
c. Assuming that GBC is considering to either purchase the new equipment or outsource the bike frame, calculate the impact on profitability between the two alternatives.
d. Discuss the qualitative factors that GBC should consider before making a decision to outsource the bike frame. How can GBC minimize the risk of establishing a relationship with an unreliable supplier?

L.O. 8

mhhe.com/edmonds2007

CHECK FIGURE
a. Contribution to profit: $12,000

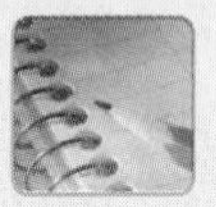

Problem 13-26 ***Eliminating a segment***

Lackey Boot Co. sells men's, women's, and children's boots. For each type of boot sold, it operates a separate department that has its own manager. The manager of the men's department has a sales staff of nine employees, the manager of the women's department has six employees, and the manager of the children's department has three employees. All departments are housed in a single store. In recent years, the children's department has operated at a net loss and is expected to continue doing so. Last year's income statements follow.

	Men's Department	Women's Department	Children's Department
Sales	$580,000	$430,000	$165,000
Cost of Goods Sold	(260,000)	(180,000)	(103,000)
Gross Margin	320,000	250,000	62,000
Department Manager's Salary	(50,000)	(40,000)	(20,000)
Sales Commissions	(106,000)	(82,000)	(30,000)
Rent on Store Lease	(20,000)	(20,000)	(20,000)
Store Utilities	(5,000)	(5,000)	(5,000)
Net Income (loss)	$139,000	$103,000	$ (13,000)

Required

a. Determine whether to eliminate the children's department.
b. Confirm the conclusion you reached in Requirement *a* by preparing income statements for the company as a whole with and without the children's department.
c. Eliminating the children's department would increase space available to display men's and women's boots. Suppose management estimates that a wider selection of adult boots would increase the store's net earnings by $32,000. Would this information affect the decision that you made in Requirement *a*? Explain your answer.

L.O. 4, 8

CHECK FIGURE
a. Contribution to profit: $(40,000)

Problem 13-27 ***Effect of activity level and opportunity cost on segment elimination decision***

Partlow Manufacturing Co. produces and sells specialized equipment used in the petroleum industry. The company is organized into three separate operating branches: Division A, which manufactures and sells heavy equipment; Division B, which manufactures and sells hand tools; and

Division C, which makes and sells electric motors. Each division is housed in a separate manufacturing facility. Company headquarters is located in a separate building. In recent years, Division B has been operating at a net loss and is expected to continue doing so. Income statements for the three divisions for 2008 follow.

	Division A	Division B	Division C
Sales	$3,200,000	$ 750,000	$4,000,000
Less: Cost of Goods Sold			
Unit-Level Manufacturing Costs	(1,900,000)	(450,000)	(2,400,000)
Rent on Manufacturing Facility	(400,000)	(220,000)	(300,000)
Gross Margin	900,000	80,000	1,300,000
Less: Operating Expenses			
Unit-Level Selling and Admin. Expenses	(200,000)	(35,000)	(250,000)
Division-Level Fixed Selling and Admin. Expenses	(250,000)	(85,000)	(300,000)
Headquarters Facility-Level Costs	(150,000)	(150,000)	(150,000)
Net Income (loss)	$ 300,000	$(190,000)	$ 600,000

Required

a. Based on the preceding information, recommend whether to eliminate Division B. Support your answer by preparing companywide income statements before and after eliminating Division B.

b. During 2008, Division B produced and sold 20,000 units of hand tools. Would your recommendation in response to Requirement *a* change if sales and production increase to 30,000 units in 2009? Support your answer by comparing differential revenue and avoidable cost for Division B, assuming that it sells 30,000 units.

c. Suppose that Partlow could sublease Division B's manufacturing facility for $320,000. Would you operate the division at a production and sales volume of 30,000 units, or would you close it? Support your answer with appropriate computations.

Problem 13-28 ***Comprehensive problem including special order, outsourcing, and segment elimination decisions***

L.O. 6, 7, 8

excel

mhhe.com/edmonds2007

CHECK FIGURE

a. CM: $7,500

Weems Inc. makes and sells state-of-the-art electronics products. One of its segments produces The Math Machine, an inexpensive four-function calculator. The company's chief accountant recently prepared the following income statement showing annual revenues and expenses associated with the segment's operating activities. The relevant range for the production and sale of the calculators is between 30,000 and 60,000 units per year.

Revenue (40,000 units × $16)	$ 640,000
Unit-Level Variable Costs	
Materials Cost (40,000 × $4)	(160,000)
Labor Cost (40,000 × $2)	(80,000)
Manufacturing Overhead (40,000 × $1)	(40,000)
Shipping and Handling (40,000 × $0.50)	(20,000)
Sales Commissions (40,000 × $2)	(80,000)
Contribution Margin	260,000
Fixed Expenses	
Advertising Costs	(40,000)
Salary of Production Supervisor	(120,000)
Allocated Companywide Facility-Level Expenses	(160,000)
Net Loss	$ (60,000)

Required (Consider each of the requirements independently.)

a. A large discount store has approached the owner of Weems about buying 5,000 calculators. It would replace The Math Machine's label with its own logo to avoid affecting Weems' existing customers. Because the offer was made directly to the owner, no sales commissions on the transaction would be involved, but the discount store is willing to pay only $9.00 per calculator. Based on quantitative factors alone, should Weems accept the special order? Support your answer with appropriate computations. Specifically, by what amount would the special order increase or decrease profitability?

b. Weems has an opportunity to buy the 40,000 calculators it currently makes from a reliable competing manufacturer for $9.80 each. The product meets Weems' quality standards. Weems could continue to use its own logo, advertising program, and sales force to distribute the products. Should Weems buy the calculators or continue to make them? Support your answer with appropriate computations. Specifically, how much more or less would it cost to buy the calculators than to make them? Would your answer change if the volume of sales were increased to 60,000 units?

c. Because the calculator division is currently operating at a loss, should it be eliminated from the company's operations? Support your answer with appropriate computations. Specifically, by what amount would the segment's elimination increase or decrease profitability?

ANALYZE, THINK, COMMUNICATE

ATC 13-1 Business Application Case *Elimination of a product line*

The following excerpts were drawn from the article entitled "The Scottish Shogun," published in *U.S. News & World Report,* May 19, 1997, on pages 44 and 45.

The Japanese car maker [**Mazda Motor Company**] has accumulated nearly a billion dollars in operating losses in three years. Its market share in Japan fell from nearly 8 percent to below 5 percent in the first half of the decade, and its overall car production dropped by a stunning 46 percent. In fact, Mazda has been fighting for its life. To salvage the company, **Ford Motor Co.**, Mazda's biggest shareholder, gambled $430 million [in 1996] and raised its equity stake in Mazda to 33.4 percent, which in practice gave it operating control. The U.S. car maker chose Henry Wallace, a Ford man for 25 years, to spearhead a turnaround. Mr. Wallace is the first foreigner to lead a big Japanese company. In this case, Mr. Wallace has been warmly embraced by the Japanese—both inside and outside Mazda. Wallace's first move was to retrench—cut product lines, consolidate sales channels, reduce inventory, and in the United States, halt unprofitable fleet and car-rental sales. Wallace also took action to instill a profit motive among the board of directors. Wallace observed, "I don't think previously there was a strong profit motive within the company." Instead, Mazda was a club of engineers who turned out wonderful niche cars—some with exotic styling, others with superb performance—that few consumers wanted to buy. When drivers developed a taste for sport utility vehicles, Mazda's beautiful sedans collected dust on the lots.

Required

a. The article indicated that one action Mr. Wallace took was to cut product lines. Explain which levels (unit, batch, product, and/or facility) of costs could be avoided by eliminating product lines. What sacrifices will Mazda likely have to make to obtain the cost savings associated with eliminating product lines?

b. Suppose that the cost data in the table below apply to three sales channels that were eliminated through the consolidation program.

Additional Information

(1) Sales are expected to drop by 10 percent because of the consolidation program. The remaining sales volume was absorbed by other sales channels.

(2) Half of the sales staff accepted transfers that placed them in positions in other sales channels. The other half left the company.

(3) The supervisor of Channel 1 accepted a job transfer. The other two supervisors left the company.

Annual Costs of Operating Each Sales Channel	Channel 1	Channel 2	Channel 3
Unit-level selling costs:			
Selling supplies	$ 32,000	$ 22,000	$ 40,000
Sales commissions	355,000	225,000	425,000
Shipping and handling	40,000	24,000	49,000
Miscellaneous	20,000	17,000	29,000
Facility-level selling costs:			
Rent	245,000	236,000	240,000
Utilities	40,000	48,000	50,000
Staff salaries	900,000	855,000	1,088,000
Supervisory salaries	150,000	100,000	170,000
Depreciation on equipment	300,000	307,000	303,000
Allocated companywide expenses	100,000	100,000	100,000

(4) The combined equipment, with an expected remaining useful life of four years and a $700,000 salvage value, had a market value of $625,000.

(5) The offices operated by the eliminated channels were closed.

Determine the amount of annual costs saved by consolidating the sales channels.

c. How will reducing inventory save costs?

d. Although the cost-cutting measures are impressive, Mr. Wallace was quoted as saying, "Obviously no one is going to succeed in our business just by reducing costs." Speculate as to some other measures that Mr. Wallace could take to improve Mazda's profitability.

ATC 13-2 Group Assignment *Relevance and cost behavior*

Maccoa Soft, a division of Zayer Software Company, produces and distributes an automated payroll software system. A contribution margin format income statement for Maccoa Soft for the past year follows.

Revenue (12,000 units × $1,200)	$14,400,000
Unit-Level Variable Costs	
Product Materials Cost (12,000 × $60)	(720,000)
Installation Labor Cost (12,000 × $200)	(2,400,000)
Manufacturing Overhead (12,000 × $2)	(24,000)
Shipping and Handling (12,000 × $25)	(300,000)
Sales Commissions (12,000 × $300)	(3,600,000)
Nonmanufacturing Miscellaneous Costs (12,000 × $5)	(60,000)
Contribution Margin (12,000 × $608)	7,296,000
Fixed Costs	
Research and Development	(2,700,000)
Legal Fees to Ensure Product Protection	(780,000)
Advertising Costs	(1,200,000)
Rental Cost of Manufacturing Facility	(600,000)
Depreciation on Production Equipment (zero market value)	(300,000)
Other Manufacturing Costs (salaries, utilities, etc.)	(744,000)
Division-Level Facility Sustaining Costs	(1,730,000)
Allocated Companywide Facility-Level Costs	(1,650,000)
Net Loss	$(2,408,000)

Required

a. Divide the class into groups and then organize the groups into three sections. Assign Task 1 to the first section, Task 2 to the second section, and Task 3 to the third section. Each task should be considered independently of the others.

Group Tasks

(1) Assume that Maccoa has excess capacity. The sales staff has identified a large franchise company with 200 outlets that is interested in Maccoa's software system but is willing to pay only $800 for each system. Ignoring qualitative considerations, should Maccoa accept the special order?

(2) Maccoa has the opportunity to purchase a comparable payroll system from a competing vendor for $600 per system. Ignoring qualitative considerations, should Maccoa outsource producing the software? Maccoa would continue to sell and install the software if the manufacturing activities were outsourced.

(3) Given that Maccoa is generating a loss, should Zayer eliminate it? Would your answer change if Maccoa could increase sales by 1,000 units?

b. Have a representative from each section explain its respective conclusions. Discuss the following:

(1) Representatives from Section 1 should respond to the following: The analysis related to the special order (Task 1) suggests that all variable costs are always relevant. Is this conclusion valid? Explain your answer.

(2) Representatives from Section 2 should respond to the following: With respect to the outsourcing decision, identify a relevant fixed cost and a nonrelevant fixed cost. Discuss the criteria for determining whether a cost is or is not relevant.

(3) Representatives from Section 3 should respond to the following: Why did the segment elimination decision change when the volume of production and sales increased?

ATC 13-3 Research Assignment *Systems replacement decision*

The April 2003 issue of *Strategic Finance* contains an article "Why Automate Payables and Receivables? Electronic Are More Accurate and Less Costly," written by Suzanne Hurt. It appears on pages 33 to 35. This article notes that while financial resource management (FRM) software is available to automate processing transactions such as receivables and payables, 86 percent of these transactions are still paper based. In the article, the author explains some of the reasons companies should consider switching to an Internet-based FRM system and gives some examples of the cost savings that companies such as **General Electric** have realized by adopting such software. Read this article and complete the following requirements.

Required

a. Identify the relevant costs a company should consider when considering the switch from a manual system to an Internet-based FRM system of accounting for receivables and payables. Think carefully. The article does not specify all of these costs.

b. The article notes that one advantage of an Internet-based FRM system is that it allows companies to get money from receivables collected and deposited into the bank more quickly. What type of cost does this represent for a company that continues to use a manual system rather than adopt an automated system?

c. The author identifies what she thinks is the biggest challenge facing a company trying to switch to an Internet-based FRM system. What is this challenge?

ATC 13-4 Writing Assignment *Relevant versus full cost*

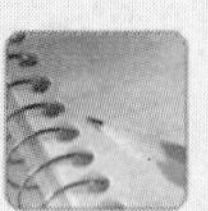

State law permits the State Department of Revenue to collect taxes for municipal governments that operate within the state's jurisdiction and allows private companies to collect taxes for municipalities. To promote fairness and to ensure the financial well-being of the state, the law dictates that the Department of Revenue must charge municipalities a fee for collection services that is above the cost of providing such services but does not define the term *cost.* Until recently, Department of Revenue officials have included a proportionate share of all departmental costs such as depreciation on buildings and equipment, supervisory salaries, and other facility-level overhead costs when determining the cost of providing collection services, a measurement approach known as full costing. The full costing approach has led to a pricing structure that places the Department of Revenue at a competitive disadvantage relative to private collection companies. Indeed, highly efficient private companies have been able to consistently underbid the Revenue Department for municipal customers. As a result, it has lost 30 percent of its municipal collection business over the last two years. The inability to be price competitive led the revenue commissioner to hire a consulting firm to evaluate the current practice of determining the cost to provide collection services.

The consulting firm concluded that the cost to provide collection services should be limited to the relevant costs associated with providing those services, defined as the difference between the costs that would be incurred if the services were provided and the costs that would be incurred if the services were not provided. According to this definition, the costs of depreciation, supervisory salaries, and other facility-level overhead costs are not included because they are the same regardless of whether the Department of Revenue provides collection services to municipalities. The Revenue Department adopted the relevant cost approach and immediately reduced the price it charges municipalities to collect their taxes and rapidly recovered the collection business it had lost. Indeed, several of the private collection companies were forced into bankruptcy. The private companies joined together and filed suit against the Revenue Department, charging that the new definition of cost violates the intent of the law.

Required

a. Assume that you are an accountant hired as a consultant for the private companies. Write a brief memo explaining why it is inappropriate to limit the definition of the costs of providing collection services to relevant costs.

b. Assume that you are an accountant hired as a consultant for the Department of Revenue. Write a brief memo explaining why it is appropriate to limit the definition of the costs of providing collection services to relevant costs.

c. Speculate on how the matter will be resolved.

ATC 13-5 Ethical Dilemma *Asset replacement clouded by self-interest*

John Dillworth is in charge of buying property used as building sites for branch offices of the National Bank of Commerce. Mr. Dillworth recently paid $110,000 for a site located in a growing section of the city. Shortly after purchasing this lot, Mr. Dillworth had the opportunity to purchase a more desirable lot at a significantly lower price. The traffic count at the new site is virtually twice that of the old site, but the price of the lot is only $80,000. It was immediately apparent that he had overpaid for the previous purchase. The current market value of the purchased property is only $75,000. Mr. Dillworth believes that it would be in the bank's best interest to buy the new lot, but he does not want to report a loss to his boss, Kelly Fullerton. He knows that Ms. Fullerton will severely reprimand him, even though she has made her share of mistakes. In fact, he is aware of a significant bad loan that Ms. Fullerton recently approved. When confronted with the bad debt by the senior vice president in charge of commercial lending, Ms. Fullerton blamed the decision on one of her former subordinates, Ira Sacks. Ms. Fullerton implied that Mr. Sacks had been dismissed for reckless lending decisions when, in fact, he had been an excellent loan officer with an uncanny ability to assess the creditworthiness of his customers. Indeed, Mr. Sacks had voluntarily resigned to accept a better position.

Required

a. Determine the amount of the loss that would be recognized on the sale of the existing branch site.

b. Identify the type of cost represented by the $110,000 original purchase price of the land. Also identify the type of cost represented by its current market value of $75,000. Indicate which cost is relevant to a decision as to whether the original site should be replaced with the new site.

c. Is Mr. Dillworth's conclusion that the old site should be replaced supported by quantitative analysis? If not, what facts do justify his conclusion?

d. Assuming that Mr. Dillworth is a certified management accountant (CMA), do you believe the failure to replace the land violates any of the standards of ethical conduct in Exhibit 10.13 in Chapter 10? If so, which standards would be violated?

e. Discuss the ethical dilemma that Mr. Dillworth faces within the context of Donald Cressey's common features of ethical misconduct that were outlined in Chapter 1.

CHAPTER 14

Planning for Profit and Cost Control

LEARNING OBJECTIVES

After you have mastered the material in this chapter you will be able to:

1. **Describe the budgeting process and the benefits it provides.**
2. **Explain the relationship between budgeting and human behavior.**
3. **Prepare a sales budget and related schedule of cash receipts.**
4. **Prepare an inventory purchases budget and related schedule of cash payments.**
5. **Prepare a selling and administrative expense budget and related schedule of cash payments.**
6. **Prepare a cash budget.**
7. **Prepare a pro forma income statement, balance sheet, and statement of cash flows.**

Chapter 14

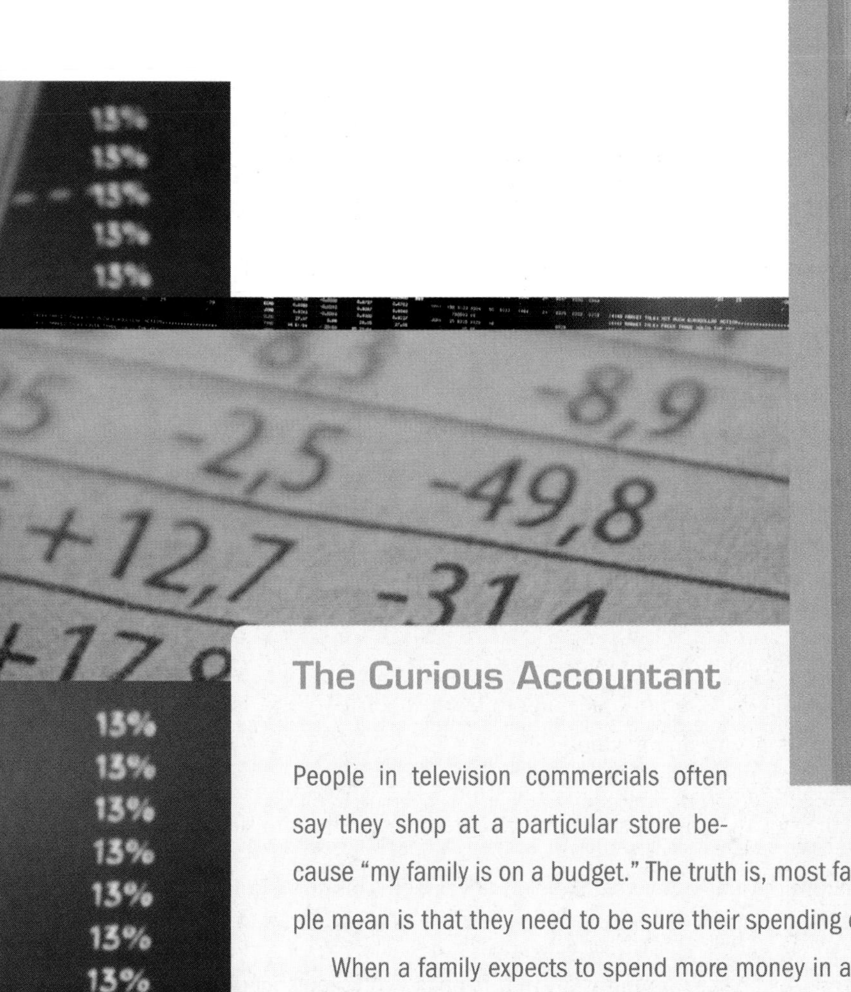

The Curious Accountant

People in television commercials often say they shop at a particular store because "my family is on a budget." The truth is, most families do not have a formal budget. What these people mean is that they need to be sure their spending does not exceed their available cash.

When a family expects to spend more money in a given year than it will earn, it must plan on borrowing funds needed to make up the difference. However, even if a family's income for a year will exceed its spending, it may still need to borrow money because the timing of its cash inflows may not match the timing of its cash outflows. Whether a budget pertains to a family or a business, its preparers must recognize the issues facing that entity to anticipate potential financial problems. There is no "one size fits all" budget.

The **United States Olympic Committee (USOC)**, like all large organizations, devotes considerable effort to budget planning.

Think about the Olympic Games and how the USOC generates revenues and incurs expenditures. Can you identify any unusual circumstances facing the USOC that complicate its budgeting efforts? (Answers on page 503.)

CHAPTER OPENING

Planning is crucial to operating a profitable business. Expressing business plans in financial terms is commonly called **budgeting.** *The budgeting process involves coordinating the financial plans of all areas of the business. For example, the production department cannot prepare a manufacturing plan until it knows how many units of product to produce. The number of units to produce depends on the marketing department's sales projection.*

The marketing department cannot project sales volume until it knows what products the company will sell. Product information comes from the research and development department. The point should be clear: a company's master budget results from combining numerous specific plans prepared by different departments.

Master budget preparation is normally supervised by a committee. The budget committee is responsible for settling disputes among various departments over budget matters. The committee also monitors reports on how various segments are progressing toward achieving their budget goals. The budgeting committee is not an accounting committee. It is a high-level committee that normally includes the company president, vice presidents of marketing, purchasing, production, and finance, and the controller. ■

The Planning Process

Describe the budgeting process and the benefits it provides.

Planning normally addresses short, intermediate, and long-range time horizons. Short-term plans are more specific than long-term plans. Consider, for example, your decision to attend college. Long-term planning requires considering general questions such as:

- Do I want to go to college?
- How do I expect to benefit from the experience?
- Do I want a broad knowledge base, or am I seeking to learn specific job skills?
- In what field do I want to concentrate my studies?

Many students go to college before answering these questions. They discover the disadvantages of poor planning the hard way. While their friends are graduating, they are starting over in a new major.

Intermediate-range planning usually covers three to five years. In this stage, you consider which college to attend, how to support yourself while in school, and whether to live on or off campus.

Short-term planning focuses on the coming year. In this phase you plan specific courses to take, decide which instructors to choose, schedule part-time work, and join a study group. Short-term plans are specific and detailed. Their preparation may seem tedious, but careful planning generally leads to efficient resource use and high levels of productivity.

Three Levels of Planning for Business Activity

Businesses describe the three levels of planning as *strategic planning, capital budgeting,* and *operations budgeting.* **Strategic planning** involves making long-term decisions such as defining the scope of the business, determining which products to develop or discontinue, and identifying the most profitable market niche. Upper-level management is responsible for these decisions. Strategic plans are descriptive rather than quantitative. Objectives such as "to have the largest share of the market" or "to be the best-quality producer" result from strategic planning. Although strategic planning is an integral component of managing a business, an in-depth discussion of it is beyond the scope of this text.

Capital budgeting focuses on intermediate range planning. It involves such decisions as whether to buy or lease equipment, whether to stimulate sales, or whether to increase the company's asset base. Capital budgeting is discussed in detail in a later chapter.

The central focus of this chapter is the *master budget* which describes short-term objectives in specific amounts of sales targets, production goals, and financing plans. The master budget describes how management intends to achieve its objectives and directs the company's short-term activities.

The master budget normally covers one year. It is frequently divided into quarterly projections and often subdivides quarterly data by month. Effective managers cannot wait until year-end to know whether operations conform to budget targets. Monthly data provide feedback to permit making necessary corrections promptly.

Many companies use **perpetual,** or **continuous, budgeting** covering a 12-month reporting period. As the current month draws to a close, an additional month is added at the end of the budget period, resulting in a continuous 12-month budget. A perpetual budget offers the advantage of keeping management constantly focused on thinking ahead to the next 12 months. The more traditional annual approach to budgeting invites a frenzied stop-and-go mentality, with managers preparing the budget in a year-end rush that is soon forgotten. Changing conditions may not be discussed until the next year-end budget is due. A perpetual budget overcomes these disadvantages.

Advantages of Budgeting

Budgeting is costly and time-consuming. The sacrifices, however, are more than offset by the benefits. Budgeting promotes planning and coordination; it enhances performance measurement and corrective action.

Planning

Almost everyone makes plans. Each morning, people think about what they will do during the day. Thinking ahead is planning. Most business managers think ahead about how they will direct operations. Unfortunately, planning is frequently as informal as making a few mental notes. Informal planning cannot be effectively communicated. The business manager might know what her objectives are, but neither her superiors nor her subordinates know. Because it serves as a communication tool, budgeting can solve these problems. The budget formalizes and documents managerial plans, clearly communicating objectives to both superiors and subordinates.

Coordination

Sometimes a choice benefits one department at the expense of another. For example, a purchasing agent may order large quantities of raw materials to obtain discounts from suppliers. But excessive quantities of materials pose a storage problem for the inventory supervisor who must manage warehouse costs. The budgeting process forces coordination among departments to promote decisions in the best interests of the company as a whole.

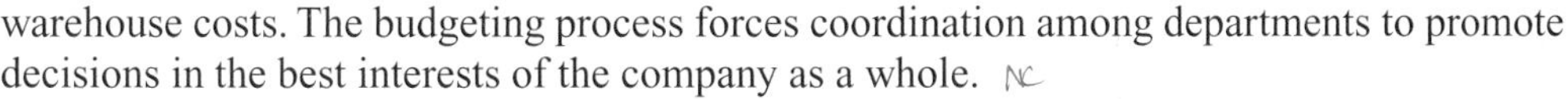
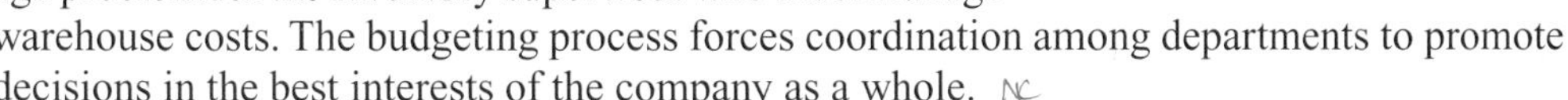

Performance Measurement

Budgets are specific, quantitative representations of management's objectives. Comparing actual results to budget expectations provides a way to evaluate performance. For example, if a company budgets sales of $10 million, it can judge the performance of the sales department against that level. If actual sales exceed $10 million, the company should reward the sales department; if actual sales fall below $10 million, the company should seek an explanation for the shortfall from the sales manager.

Corrective Action

Budgeting provides advance notice of potential shortages, bottlenecks, or other weaknesses in operating plans. For example, a cash budget alerts management to when the company can expect cash shortages during the coming year. The company can make borrowing arrangements before it needs the money. Without knowing ahead of time, management might be unable to secure necessary financing on short notice, or it may have to pay excessively high interest rates to obtain funds. Budgeting advises managers of potential problems in time for them to devise effective solutions.

Budgeting and Human Behavior

LO 2

Explain the relationship between budgeting and human behavior.

Effective budgeting requires sensitivity on the part of upper management to the effect on employees of budget expectations. People are often uncomfortable with budgets. Budgets are constraining. They limit individual freedom in favor of an established plan. Many people find evaluation based on budget expectations stressful. Most students experience a similar fear about testing. Like examinations, budgets represent standards by which performance is evaluated. Employees worry about whether their performance will meet expectations.

The attitudes of high-level managers significantly impact budget effectiveness. Subordinates are keenly aware of management's expectations. If upper-level managers degrade, make fun of, or ignore the budget, subordinates will follow suit. If management uses budgets to humiliate, embarrass, or punish subordinates, employees will resent the treatment and the budgeting process. Upper-level managers must demonstrate that they view the budget as a sincere effort to express realistic goals employees are expected to meet. An honest, open, respectful atmosphere is essential to budgeting success.

Participative budgeting has frequently proved successful in creating a healthy atmosphere. This technique invites participation in the budget process by personnel at all levels of the organization, not just upper-level managers. Information flows from the bottom up as well as from the top down during budget preparation. Because they are directly responsible for meeting budget goals, subordinates can offer more realistic targets. Including them in budget preparation fosters development of a team effort. Participation fosters more cooperation and motivation, and less fear. With participative budgeting, subordinates cannot complain that the budget is management's plan. The budget is instead a self-imposed constraint. Employees can hold no one responsible but themselves if they fail to accomplish the budget objectives they established.

Upper management participates in the process to ensure that employee-generated objectives are consistent with company objectives. Furthermore, if subordinates were granted complete freedom to establish budget standards, they might be tempted to adopt lax standards to ensure they will meet them. Both managers and subordinates must cooperate if the participatory process is to produce an effective budget. If developed carefully, budgets can motivate employees to achieve superior performance. Normal human fears must be overcome, and management must create an honest budget atmosphere.

The Master Budget

LO 1

Describe the budgeting process and the benefits it provides.

The **master budget** is a group of detailed budgets and schedules representing the company's operating and financial plans for a future accounting period. The master budget usually includes (1) *operating budgets,* (2) *capital budgets,* and (3) *pro forma financial statements.* The budgeting process normally begins with preparing the **operating budgets** which focus on detailed operating activities. This chapter illustrates operating budgets for Hampton Hams, a retail sales company that uses (1) a sales budget, (2) an inventory purchases budget, (3) a selling and administrative (S&A) expense budget, and (4) a cash budget.

The sales budget includes a schedule of cash receipts from customers. The inventory purchases and S&A expense budgets include schedules of cash payments for inventory and expenses. Preparing the master budget begins with the sales forecast. Based on the sales forecast, the detailed budgets for inventory purchases and operating expenses are developed. The schedules of cash receipts and cash payments provide the foundation for preparing the cash budget.

The **capital budget** describes the company's intermediate-range plans for investments in facilities, equipment, new products, store outlets, and lines of business. The capital budget affects several operating budgets. For example, equipment acquisitions result in additional depreciation expense on the S&A expense budget. The cash flow effects of capital investments influence the cash budget.

The operating budgets are used to prepare *pro forma statements.* **Pro forma financial statements** are based on projected (budgeted) rather than historical information. Hampton Hams prepares a pro forma income statement, balance sheet, and statement of cash flows.

Exhibit 14.1 shows how information flows in a master budget.

EXHIBIT 14.1

Information Flows in the Master Budget

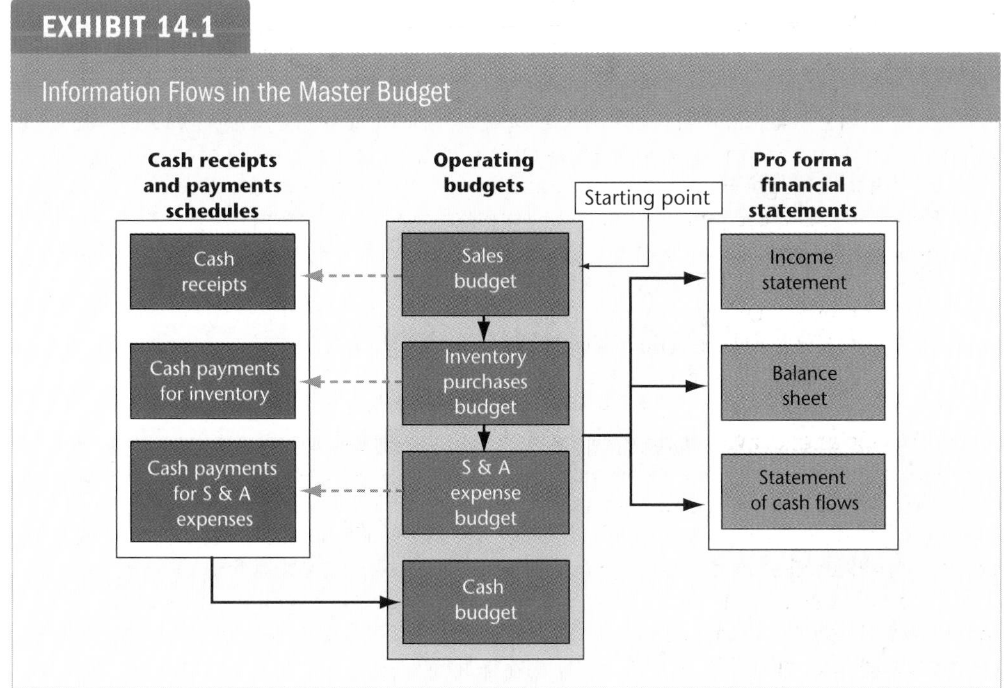

Hampton Hams Budgeting Illustration

Hampton Hams (HH), a major corporation, sells cured hams nationwide through retail outlets in shopping malls. By focusing on a single product and standardized operations, the company controls costs stringently. As a result, it offers high-quality hams at competitive prices.

Hampton Hams has experienced phenomenal growth during the past five years. It opened two new stores in Indianapolis, Indiana, last month and plans to open a third new store in October. Hampton Hams finances new stores by borrowing on a line of credit arranged with National Bank. National's loan officer has requested monthly budgets for each of the first three months of the new store's operations. The accounting department is preparing the new store's master budget for October, November, and December. The first step is developing a sales budget.

Sales Budget

Prepare a sales budget and related schedule of cash receipts.

Preparing the master budget begins with the sales forecast. The accuracy of the sales forecast is critical because all the other budgets are derived from the sales budget. Normally, the marketing department coordinates the development of the sales forecast. Sales estimates frequently flow from the bottom up to the higher management levels. Sales personnel prepare sales projections for their products and territories and pass them up the line where they are combined with the estimates of other sales personnel to develop regional and national estimates. Using various information sources, upper-level sales managers adjust the estimates generated by sales personnel. Adjustment information comes from industry periodicals and trade journals, economic analysis, marketing surveys, historical sales figures, and changes in competition. Companies assimilate this data using sophisticated computer programs, statistical techniques, and quantitative methods, or, simply, professional judgment. Regardless of the technique, the senior vice president of sales ultimately develops a sales forecast for which she is held responsible.

To develop the sales forecast for HH's new store, the sales manager studied the sales history of existing stores operating in similar locations. He then adjusted for start-up conditions. October is an opportune time to open a new store because customers will learn the store's location before the holiday season. The sales manager expects significant sales growth in November and December as customers choose the company's hams as the centerpiece for many Thanksgiving and winter holiday dinner tables.

The new store's sales are expected to be \$160,000 in October (\$40,000 in cash and \$120,000 on account). Sales are expected to increase 20 percent per month during November and December. Based on these estimates, the sales manager prepared the sales budget in Exhibit 14.2.

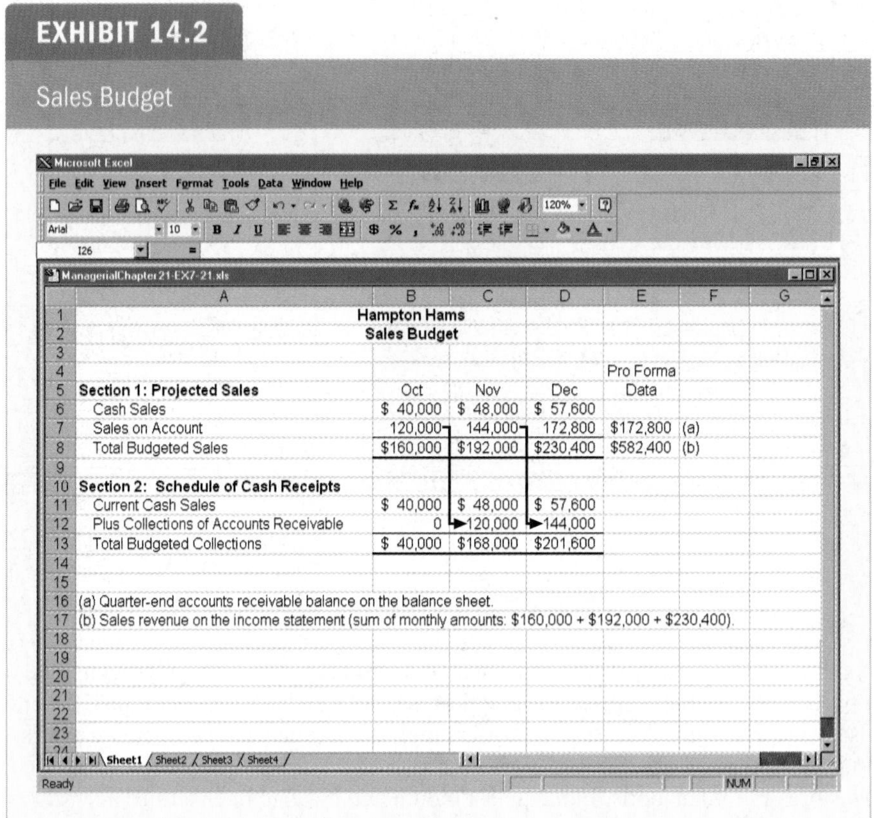

EXHIBIT 14.2

Sales Budget

Hampton Hams
Sales Budget

	Oct	Nov	Dec	Pro Forma Data	
Section 1: Projected Sales					
Cash Sales	\$ 40,000	\$ 48,000	\$ 57,600		
Sales on Account	120,000	144,000	172,800	\$172,800	(a)
Total Budgeted Sales	\$160,000	\$192,000	\$230,400	\$582,400	(b)
Section 2: Schedule of Cash Receipts					
Current Cash Sales	\$ 40,000	\$ 48,000	\$ 57,600		
Plus Collections of Accounts Receivable	0	120,000	144,000		
Total Budgeted Collections	\$ 40,000	\$168,000	\$201,600		

(a) Quarter-end accounts receivable balance on the balance sheet.
(b) Sales revenue on the income statement (sum of monthly amounts: \$160,000 + \$192,000 + \$230,400).

Projected Sales

The sales budget has two sections. Section 1 shows the projected sales for each month. The November sales forecast reflects a 20 percent increase over October sales. For example, November *cash sales* are calculated as \$48,000 [\$40,000 + (\$40,000 × 0.20)] and December *cash sales* as \$57,600 [\$48,000 + (\$48,000 × 0.20)]. *Sales on account* are similarly computed.

Schedule of Cash Receipts

Section 2 is a schedule of the cash receipts for the projected sales. This schedule is used later to prepare the cash budget. The accountant has assumed in this schedule that Hampton Hams will collect accounts receivable from credit sales *in full* in the month following the sale. In practice, collections may be spread over several months, and some receivables may become uncollectible accounts. Regardless of additional complexities, the objective is to estimate the amount and timing of expected cash receipts.

In the HH case, *total cash receipts* are determined by adding the current month's *cash sales* to the cash collected from the previous month's *credit sales* (accounts receivable balance). Cash receipts for each month are determined as follows:

- October receipts are projected to be \$40,000. Because the store opens in October, no accounts receivable from September exist to be collected in October. Cash receipts for October equal the amount of October's cash sales.
- November receipts are projected to be \$168,000 (\$48,000 November cash sales + \$120,000 cash collected from October sales on account).

FOCUS ON INTERNATIONAL ISSUES

CASH FLOW PLANNING IN BORDEAUX

The year 2000 was considered the greatest year for wine in the Bordeaux region of France since at least 1982, and the winemakers could look forward to selling their wines for record prices, but there was one catch: these wines would not be released to consumers until late in 2003. The winemakers had incurred most of their costs in 2000 when the vines were being tended and the grapes were being processed into wine. In many industries this would mean the companies would have to finance their inventories for almost four years—not an insignificant cost. A company must finance its inventory by either borrowing the money, which results in out-of-pocket interest expense, or using its own funds. The second option generates an opportunity cost resulting from the interest revenue that could have been earned if these funds were not being used to finance the inventory.

To address this potential cash flow problem, many of the winemakers in Bordeaux offer some of their wines for sale as "futures." That means the wines are purchased and paid for while they are still aging in barrels in France. Selling wine as futures reduces the time inventory must be financed from four years to only one to two years. Of course there are other types of costs in such deals. For one, the wines must be offered at lower prices than they are expected to sell for upon release. The winemakers have obviously decided this cost is less than the cost of financing inventory through borrowed money, or they would not do it.

Companies in other industries use similar techniques to speed up cash flow, such as factoring of accounts receivable. A major reason entities prepare cash budgets is to be sure they will have enough cash on hand to pay bills as they come due. If the budget indicates a temporary cash flow deficit, action must be taken to avoid the problem, and revised budgets must be prepared. Budgeting is not a static process.

- December receipts are projected to be $201,600 ($57,600 December cash sales + $144,000 cash collected from November sales on account).

Pro Forma Financial Statement Data

The Pro Forma Data column in the sales budget displays two figures HH will report on the quarter-end (December 31) budgeted financial statements. Since HH expects to collect December credit sales in January, the *accounts receivable balance* will be $172,800 on the December 31, 2006, pro forma balance sheet (shown later in Exhibit 14.7).

The $582,400 of *sales revenue* in the Pro Forma Data column will be reported on the budgeted income statement for the quarter (shown later in Exhibit 14.6). The sales revenue represents the sum of October, November, and December sales ($160,000 + $192,000 + $230,400 = $582,400).

Inventory Purchases Budget

LO 4

Prepare an inventory purchases budget and related schedule of cash payments.

The inventory purchases budget shows the amount of inventory HH must purchase each month to satisfy the demand projected in the sales budget. The *total inventory needed* each month equals the amount of inventory HH plans to sell that month plus the amount of inventory HH wants on hand at month-end. To the extent that total inventory needed exceeds the inventory on hand at the beginning of the month, HH will need to purchase additional inventory. The amount of inventory to purchase is computed as follows:

Cost of budgeted sales	XXX
Plus: Desired ending inventory	XXX
Total inventory needed	XXX
Less: Beginning inventory	(XXX)
Required purchases	XXX

It is HH's policy to maintain an ending inventory equal to 25 percent of the next month's *projected cost of goods sold.* HH's cost of goods sold normally equals 70 percent of *sales.* Using this information and the sales budget, the accounting department prepared the inventory purchases budget shown in Exhibit 14.3.

Projected Purchases

Section 1 of the inventory purchases budget shows required purchases for each month. HH determined *budgeted cost of goods sold* for October by multiplying October *budgeted sales* by 70 percent ($160,000 × 0.70 = $112,000). Budgeted cost of goods sold for November and December were similarly computed. The October *desired ending inventory* was computed by multiplying November *budgeted cost of goods sold* by 25 percent ($134,400 × 0.25 = $33,600). Desired ending inventory for November is $40,320 ($161,280 × .25). Desired ending inventory for December is based on January projected cost of goods sold (not shown in the exhibit). HH expects ham sales to decline after the winter holidays. Because January projected cost of goods sold is only $140,000, the December desired ending inventory falls to $35,000 ($140,000 × .25).

Schedule of Cash Payments for Inventory Purchases

Section 2 is the schedule of cash payments for inventory purchases. HH makes all inventory purchases on account. The supplier requires that HH pay for 60 percent of inventory purchases in the month goods are purchased. HH pays the remaining 40 percent the month after purchase.

Cash payments are projected as follows (amounts are rounded to the nearest whole dollar):

EXHIBIT 14.3

Inventory Purchases Budget

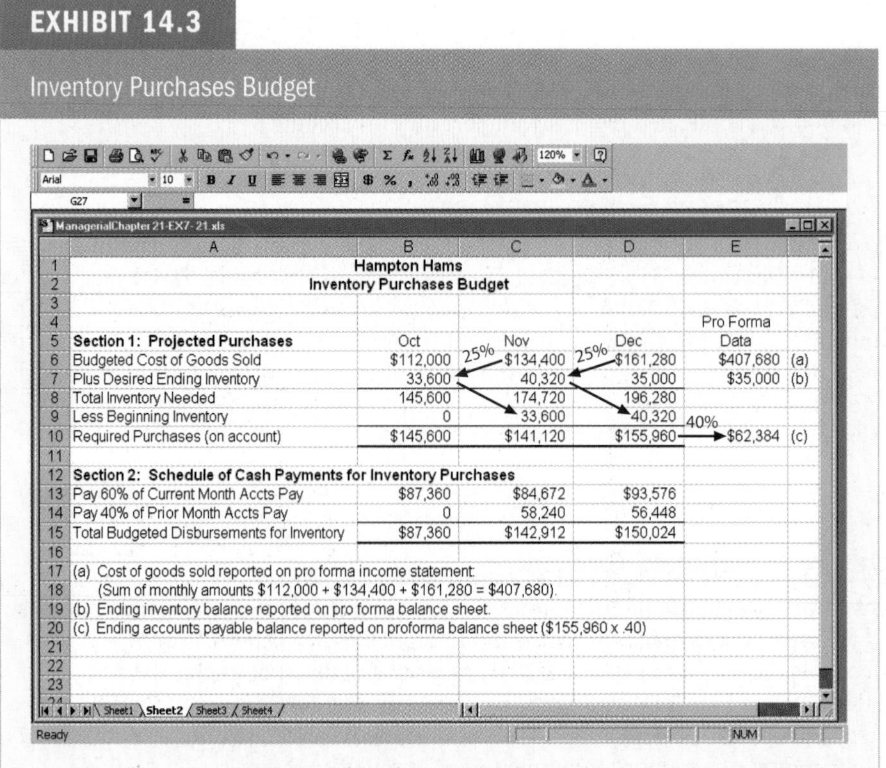

Hampton Hams
Inventory Purchases Budget

	Oct	Nov	Dec	Pro Forma Data	
Section 1: Projected Purchases					
Budgeted Cost of Goods Sold	$112,000	$134,400	$161,280	$407,680	(a)
Plus Desired Ending Inventory	33,600	40,320	35,000	$35,000	(b)
Total Inventory Needed	145,600	174,720	196,280		
Less Beginning Inventory	0	33,600	40,320		
Required Purchases (on account)	$145,600	$141,120	$155,960	$62,384	(c)
Section 2: Schedule of Cash Payments for Inventory Purchases					
Pay 60% of Current Month Accts Pay	$87,360	$84,672	$93,576		
Pay 40% of Prior Month Accts Pay	0	58,240	56,448		
Total Budgeted Disbursements for Inventory	$87,360	$142,912	$150,024		

(a) Cost of goods sold reported on pro forma income statement.
(Sum of monthly amounts $112,000 + $134,400 + $161,280 = $407,680).
(b) Ending inventory balance reported on pro forma balance sheet.
(c) Ending accounts payable balance reported on proforma balance sheet ($155,960 x .40)

- October cash payments for inventory are $87,360. Because the new store opens in October, no accounts payable balance from September remains to be paid in October. Cash payments for October equal 60 percent of October inventory purchases.
- November cash payments for inventory are $142,912 (40 percent of October purchases + 60 percent of November purchases).
- December cash payments for inventory are $150,024 (40 percent of November purchases + 60 percent of December purchases).

Pro Forma Financial Statement Data

The Pro Forma Data column in the inventory purchases budget displays three figures HH will report on the quarter-end budgeted financial statements. The $407,680 *cost of goods sold* reported on the pro forma income statement (shown later in Exhibit 14.6) is the sum of the monthly cost of goods sold amounts ($112,000 + $134,400 + $161,280 = $407,680).

The $35,000 *ending inventory* as of December 31, 2006, is reported on the pro forma balance sheet (shown later in Exhibit 14.7). December 31 is the last day of both the month of December and the three-month quarter represented by October, November, and December.

The $62,384 of *accounts payable* reported on the pro forma balance sheet (shown later in Exhibit 14.7) represents the 40 percent of December inventory purchases HH will pay for in January ($155,960 × .40).

Main Street Sales Company purchased $80,000 of inventory during June. Purchases are expected to increase by 2 percent per month in each of the next three months. Main Street makes all purchases on account. It normally pays cash to settle 70 percent of its accounts payable during the month of purchase and settles the remaining 30 percent in the month following purchase. Based on this information, determine the accounts payable balance Main Street would report on its July 31 balance sheet.

Answer

Purchases for the month of July are expected to be $81,600 ($80,000 × 1.02). Main Street will pay 70 percent of the resulting accounts payable in cash during July. The remaining 30 percent represents the expected balance in accounts payable as of July 31. Therefore, the balance would be $24,480 ($81,600 × 0.3).

Selling and Administrative Expense Budget

Projected S&A Expenses

Prepare a selling and administrative expense budget and related schedule of cash payments.

Section 1 of Exhibit 14.4 shows the selling and administrative (S&A) expense budget for Hampton Hams' new store. Most of the projected expenses are self-explanatory; depreciation and interest, however, merit comment. The depreciation expense is based on projections in the *capital expenditures budget.* Although not presented in this chapter, the capital budget calls for the cash purchase of $130,000 of store fixtures on October 1. The supplier allows a thirty-day inspection period. As a result, payment for the fixtures is budgeted for the end of October. The fixtures are expected to have a useful life of 10 years and a $10,000 salvage value. Using the straight-line method, HH estimates annual depreciation expense at $12,000 [($130,000 − $10,000) ÷ 10]. Monthly depreciation expense is $1,000 ($12,000 annual charge ÷ 12 months).

Interest expense is missing from the S&A expense budget. HH cannot estimate interest expense until it completes its borrowing projections. Expected borrowing (financing activities) and related interest expense are shown in the *cash budget.*

Schedule of Cash Payments for Selling and Administrative Expenses

Section 2 of the S&A expense budget shows the schedule of cash payments. There are several differences between the S&A expenses recognized on the pro forma income statement

EXHIBIT 14.4

Selling and Administrative Expense Budget

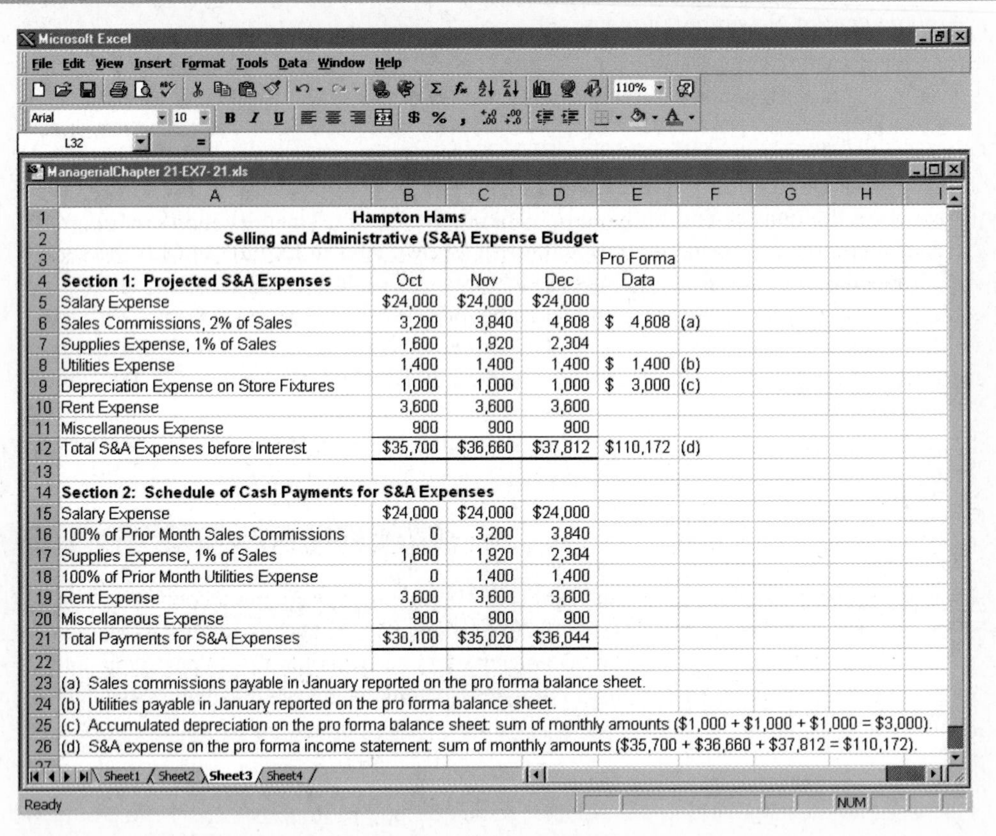

	Hampton Hams				
	Selling and Administrative (S&A) Expense Budget				
				Pro Forma	
Section 1: Projected S&A Expenses	Oct	Nov	Dec	Data	
Salary Expense	$24,000	$24,000	$24,000		
Sales Commissions, 2% of Sales	3,200	3,840	4,608	$ 4,608	(a)
Supplies Expense, 1% of Sales	1,600	1,920	2,304		
Utilities Expense	1,400	1,400	1,400	$ 1,400	(b)
Depreciation Expense on Store Fixtures	1,000	1,000	1,000	$ 3,000	(c)
Rent Expense	3,600	3,600	3,600		
Miscellaneous Expense	900	900	900		
Total S&A Expenses before Interest	$35,700	$36,660	$37,812	$110,172	(d)
Section 2: Schedule of Cash Payments for S&A Expenses					
Salary Expense	$24,000	$24,000	$24,000		
100% of Prior Month Sales Commissions	0	3,200	3,840		
Supplies Expense, 1% of Sales	1,600	1,920	2,304		
100% of Prior Month Utilities Expense	0	1,400	1,400		
Rent Expense	3,600	3,600	3,600		
Miscellaneous Expense	900	900	900		
Total Payments for S&A Expenses	$30,100	$35,020	$36,044		

(a) Sales commissions payable in January reported on the pro forma balance sheet.
(b) Utilities payable in January reported on the pro forma balance sheet.
(c) Accumulated depreciation on the pro forma balance sheet: sum of monthly amounts ($1,000 + $1,000 + $1,000 = $3,000).
(d) S&A expense on the pro forma income statement: sum of monthly amounts ($35,700 + $36,660 + $37,812 = $110,172).

and the cash payments for S&A expenses. First, Hampton Hams pays sales commissions and utilities expense the month following their incurrence. Since the store opens in October there are no payments due from September. Cash payments for sales commissions and utilities in October are zero. In November, HH will pay the October expenses for these items and in December it will pay the November sales commissions and utility expenses. Depreciation expense does not affect the cash payments schedule. The cash outflow for the store fixtures occurs when the assets are purchased, not when they are depreciated. The cost of the investment in store fixtures is in the cash budget, not in the cash outflow for S&A expenses.

Pro Forma Financial Statement Data

The Pro Forma Data column of the S&A expense budget displays four figures HH will report on the quarter-end budgeted financial statements. The first and second figures are the sales commissions payable ($4,608) and utilities payable ($1,400) on the pro forma balance sheet in Exhibit 14.7. Because December sales commissions and utilities expense are not paid until January, these amounts represent liabilities as of December 31. The third figure in the column ($3,000) is the amount of accumulated depreciation on the pro forma balance sheet in Exhibit 14.7. Since depreciation accumulates, the $3,000 balance is the sum of the monthly depreciation amounts ($1,000 + $1,000 + $1,000 = $3,000). The final figure in the Pro Forma Data column ($110,172) is the total S&A expenses reported on the pro forma income statement in Exhibit 14.6. The total S&A expense is the sum of the monthly amounts ($35,700 + $36,660 + $37,812 = $110,172).

Cash Budget

Prepare a cash budget.

Little is more important to business success than effective cash management. If a company experiences cash shortages, it will be unable to pay its debts and may be forced into bankruptcy. If excess cash accumulates, a business loses the opportunity to earn investment income or reduce interest costs by repaying debt. Preparing a **cash budget** alerts management to anticipated cash shortages or excess cash balances. Management can plan financing activities, making advance arrangements to cover anticipated shortages by borrowing and planning to repay past borrowings and make appropriate investments when excess cash is expected.

The cash budget is divided into three major sections: (1) a cash receipts section, (2) a cash payments section, and (3) a financing section. Much of the data needed to prepare the cash budget are included in the cash receipts and payments schedules previously discussed; however, further refinements to project financing needs and interest costs are sometimes necessary. The completed cash budget is shown in Exhibit 14.5.

EXHIBIT 14.5

Cash Budget

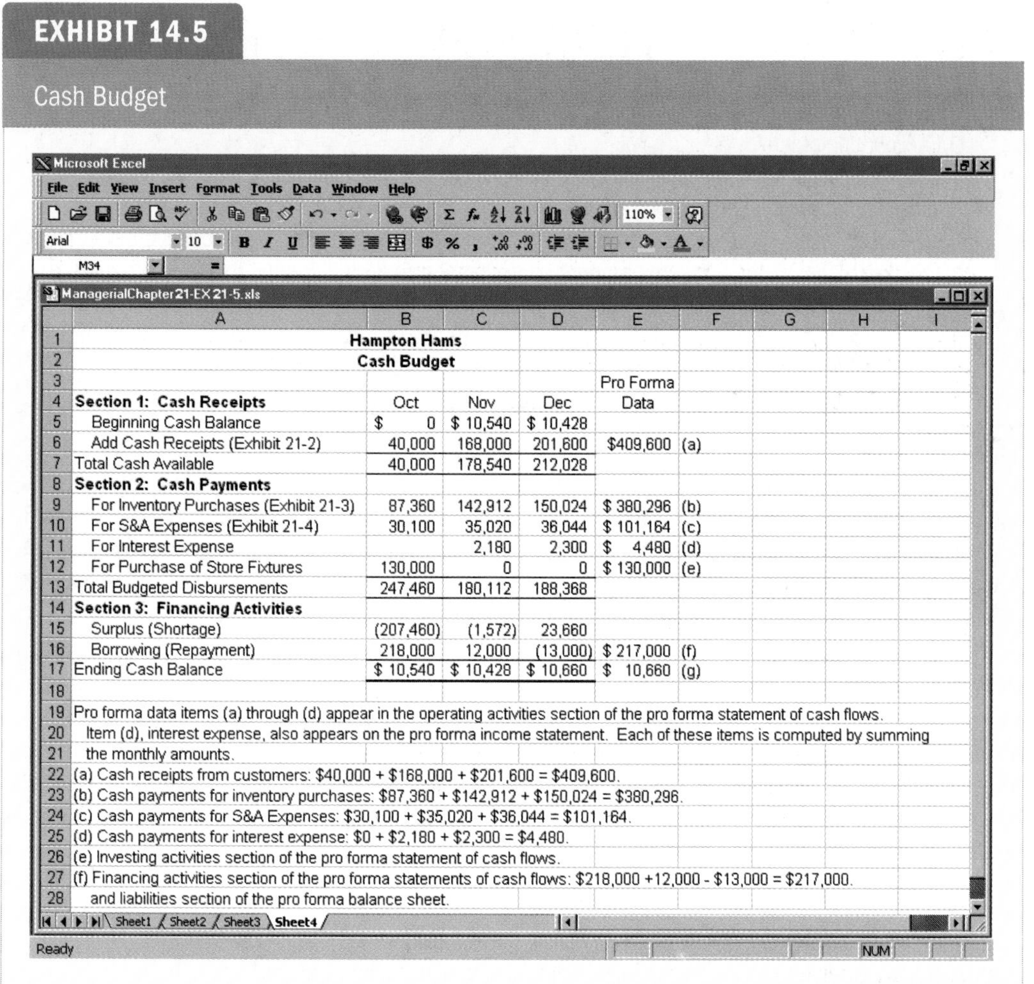

Hampton Hams
Cash Budget

	Oct	Nov	Dec	Pro Forma Data	
Section 1: Cash Receipts					
Beginning Cash Balance	$ 0	$ 10,540	$ 10,428		
Add Cash Receipts (Exhibit 21-2)	40,000	168,000	201,600	$409,600	(a)
Total Cash Available	40,000	178,540	212,028		
Section 2: Cash Payments					
For Inventory Purchases (Exhibit 21-3)	87,360	142,912	150,024	$ 380,296	(b)
For S&A Expenses (Exhibit 21-4)	30,100	35,020	36,044	$ 101,164	(c)
For Interest Expense		2,180	2,300	$ 4,480	(d)
For Purchase of Store Fixtures	130,000	0	0	$ 130,000	(e)
Total Budgeted Disbursements	247,460	180,112	188,368		
Section 3: Financing Activities					
Surplus (Shortage)	(207,460)	(1,572)	23,660		
Borrowing (Repayment)	218,000	12,000	(13,000)	$ 217,000	(f)
Ending Cash Balance	$ 10,540	$ 10,428	$ 10,660	$ 10,660	(g)

Pro forma data items (a) through (d) appear in the operating activities section of the pro forma statement of cash flows. Item (d), interest expense, also appears on the pro forma income statement. Each of these items is computed by summing the monthly amounts.
(a) Cash receipts from customers: $40,000 + $168,000 + $201,600 = $409,600.
(b) Cash payments for inventory purchases: $87,360 + $142,912 + $150,024 = $380,296.
(c) Cash payments for S&A Expenses: $30,100 + $35,020 + $36,044 = $101,164.
(d) Cash payments for interest expense: $0 + $2,180 + $2,300 = $4,480.
(e) Investing activities section of the pro forma statement of cash flows.
(f) Financing activities section of the pro forma statements of cash flows: $218,000 +12,000 - $13,000 = $217,000.
and liabilities section of the pro forma balance sheet.

Cash Receipts Section

The total cash available (Exhibit 14.5, row 7) is determined by adding the beginning cash balance to the cash receipts from customers. There is no beginning cash balance in October because the new store is opening that month. The November beginning cash balance is the October ending cash balance. The December beginning cash balance is the November ending cash balance. Cash receipts from customers comes from the *schedule of cash receipts* in the sales budget (Exhibit 14.2, section 2, row 13).

REALITY BYTES

Budgeting in Governmental Entities

This chapter has presented several reasons organizations should prepare budgets, but for governmental entities, budgets are not simply good planning tools—law requires them. If a manager at a commercial enterprise does not accomplish the budget objectives established for his or her part of the business, the manager may receive a poor performance evaluation. At worst, they may be fired. If managers of governmental agencies spend more than their budgets allow, they may have broken the law. In some cases the manager could be required to personally repay the amount by which the budget was exceeded. Since governmental budgets are enacted by the relevant elected bodies, to violate the budget is to break the law.

Because budgets are so important for governments and are not to be exceeded, government accounting practices require that budgeted amounts be formally entered into the bookkeeping system. As you have learned, companies do not make formal accounting entries when they order goods; they only make an entry when the goods are received. Governmental accounting systems are different. Each time goods or services are ordered by a government, an "encumbrance" is recorded against the budgeted amount so that agencies do not commit to spend more money than their budgets allow.

Cash Payments Section

Cash payments include expected cash outflows for inventory purchases, S&A expenses, interest expense, and investments. The cash payments for inventory purchases comes from the *schedule of cash payments for inventory purchases* (Exhibit 14.3, section 2, row 15). The cash payments for S&A expenses comes from the *schedule of cash payments for S&A expenses* (Exhibit 14.4, section 2, row 21).

HH borrows or repays principal and pays interest on the last day of each month. The cash payments for interest are determined by multiplying the loan balance for the month by the monthly interest rate. Since there is no outstanding debt during October, there is no interest payment at the end of October. HH expects outstanding debt of $218,000 during the month of November. The bank charges interest at the rate of 12% per year, or 1% per month. The November interest expense and cash payment for interest is $2,180 ($218,000 × .01). The outstanding loan balance during December is $230,000. The December interest expense and cash payment for interest is $2,300 ($230,000 × .01). Determining the amount to borrow or repay at the end of each month is discussed in more detail in the next section of the text.

Finally, the cash payment for the store fixtures comes from the *capital expenditures budget* (not shown in this chapter).

Financing Section

HH has a line of credit under which it can borrow or repay principal in increments of $1,000 at the end of each month as needed. HH desires to maintain an ending cash balance of at least $10,000 each month. With the $207,460 projected cash shortage in row 15 of the cash budget ($40,000 cash balance in row 7 less $247,460 budgeted cash payments in row 13), HH must borrow $218,000 on October 31 to maintain an ending cash balance of at least $10,000. This $218,000 balance is outstanding during November. On November 30, HH must borrow an additional $12,000 to cover the November projected cash shortage of $1,572 plus the $10,000 desired ending cash balance. HH projects a surplus of $23,660 for the month of December. This surplus will allow HH to repay $13,000 of debt and still maintain the desired $10,000 cash balance.

Pro Forma Financial Statement Data

Figures in the Pro Forma Data column of the cash budget (Exhibit 14.5) are alphabetically referenced. The cash receipts from customers, item (a), and the cash payment items (b), (c), and (d) are reported in the operating activities section of the pro forma statement of cash flows (Exhibit 14.8). The interest expense, item (d), is also reported on the pro forma income statement (Exhibit 14.6). The figures are determined by summing the monthly amounts. The $130,000 purchase of store fixtures, item (e), is reported in the investing activities section of the pro forma statement of cash flows. The $217,000 net borrowings, item (f), is reported in the financing activities section of the pro forma statement of cash flows (Exhibit 14.8) and also as a liability on the pro forma balance sheet (Exhibit 14.7). The $10,660 ending cash balance, item (g), is reported as the ending balance on the pro forma statement of cash flows and as an asset on the pro forma balance sheet.

CHECK YOURSELF 14.2

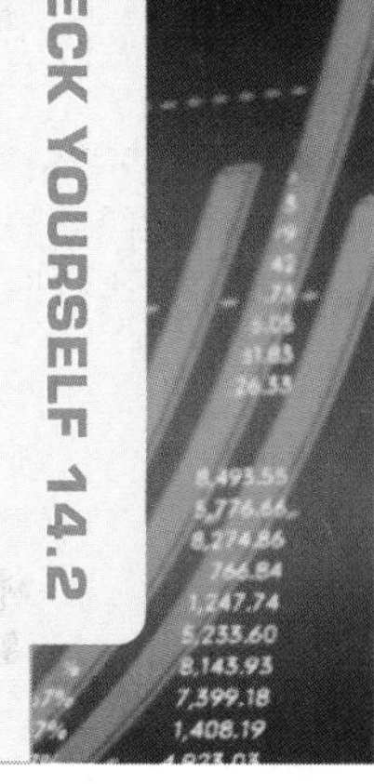

Astor Company expects to incur the following operating expenses during September: salary expense, $25,000; utility expense, $1,200; depreciation expense, $5,400; and selling expense, $14,000. In general, it pays operating expenses in cash in the month in which it incurs them. Based on this information alone, determine the total amount of cash outflow Astor would report in the operating activities section of the pro forma statement of cash flows.

Answer

Depreciation is not included in cash outflows because companies do not pay cash when they recognize depreciation expense. The total cash outflow is $40,200 ($25,000 + $1,200 + $14,000).

Pro Forma Income Statement

LO 7

Prepare a pro forma income statement, balance sheet, and statement of cash flows.

Exhibit 14.6 shows the budgeted income statement for Hampton Hams' new store. The figures for this statement come from Exhibits 14.2, 14.3, 14.4, and 14.5. The budgeted income statement provides an advance estimate of the new store's expected profitability. If expected profitability is unsatisfactory, management could decide to abandon the project or modify planned activity. Perhaps HH could lease less costly store space, pay employees a lower rate, or reduce the number of employees hired. The pricing strategy could also be examined for possible changes.

Budgets are usually prepared using spreadsheets or computerized mathematical models that allow managers to easily undertake "what-if" analysis. What if the growth rate differs from expectations? What if interest rates increase or decrease? Exhibits 14.2 through 14.5 in this chapter were prepared using Microsoft Excel. When variables such as growth rate, collection assumptions, or interest rates are changed, the spreadsheet software instantly recalculates the budgets. Although managers remain responsible for data analysis and decision making, computer technology offers powerful tools to assist in those tasks.

EXHIBIT 14.6

HAMPTON HAMS
Pro Forma Income Statement
For the Quarter Ended December 31, 2006

		Data Source
Sales Revenue	$582,400	Exhibit 14.2
Cost of Goods Sold	(407,680)	Exhibit 14.3
Gross Margin	174,720	
Selling and Administrative Expenses	(110,172)	Exhibit 14.4
Operating Income	64,548	
Interest Expense	(4,480)	Exhibit 14.5
Net Income	$ 60,068	

Pro Forma Balance Sheet

Most of the figures on the pro forma balance sheet in Exhibit 14.7 have been explained. The new store has no contributed capital because its operations will be financed through debt and retained earnings. The amount of retained earnings equals the amount of net income because no earnings from prior periods exist and no distributions are planned.

EXHIBIT 14.7

HAMPTON HAMS
Pro Forma Balance Sheet
As of the Quarter Ended December 31, 2006

			Data Source
Assets			
Cash		$ 10,660	Exhibit 14.5
Accounts Receivable		172,800	Exhibit 14.2
Inventory		35,000	Exhibit 14.3
Store Fixtures	$130,000		Exhibit 14.4 Discussion
Accumulated Depreciation	(3,000)		Exhibit 14.4 Discussion
Book Value of Store Fixtures		127,000	
Total Assets		$345,460	
Liabilities			
Accounts Payable		$ 62,384	Exhibit 14.3
Sales Commissions Payable		4,608	Exhibit 14.4
Utilities Payable		1,400	Exhibit 14.4
Line of Credit Borrowings		217,000	Exhibit 14.5
Equity			
Retained Earnings		60,068	
Total Liabilities and Equity		$345,460	

Pro Forma Statement of Cash Flows

Exhibit 14.8 shows the pro forma statement of cash flows. All information for this statement comes from the cash budget in Exhibit 14.5.

EXHIBIT 14.8

HAMPTON HAMS
Pro Forma Statement of Cash Flows
For the Quarter Ended December 31, 2006

Cash Flow from Operating Activities		
Cash Receipts from Customers	$409,600	
Cash Payments for Inventory	(380,296)	
Cash Payments for S&A Expenses	(101,164)	
Cash Payments for Interest Expense	(4,480)	
Net Cash Flow for Operating Activities		$ (76,340)
Cash Flow from Investing Activities		
Cash Outflow to Purchase Fixtures		(130,000)
Cash Flow from Financing Activities		
Inflow from Borrowing on Line of Credit		217,000
Net Change in Cash		10,660
Plus Beginning Cash Balance		0
Ending Cash Balance		$ 10,660

Answers to The Curious Accountant

Budget preparation at the USOC is complicated by the fact that the timing of its revenues does not match the timing of its expenditures. The USOC spends a lot of money helping to train athletes for the United States Olympic team. Training takes place year-round, every year, for many athletes. The USOC's training facilities in Colorado must also be maintained continuously.

Conversely, much of the USOC's revenues are earned in big batches, received every two years. This money comes from fees the USOC receives for the rights to broadcast the Olympic games on television in the United States. Most companies have a one-year budget cycle during which they attempt to anticipate the coming year's revenues and expenses. This model would not work well for the USOC.

Every business, like every family, faces its own set of circumstances. Those individuals responsible for preparing an entity's budget must have a thorough understanding of the environment in which the entity operates. This is the reason the budget process must be participatory if it is to be successful. No one person, or small group, can anticipate all the issues that will face a large organization in the coming budget period; they need input from employees at all levels.

CHECK YOURSELF 14.3

How do pro forma financial statements differ from the financial statements presented in a company's annual report to stockholders?

Answer

Pro forma financial statements are based on estimates and projections about business events that a company expects to occur in the future. The financial statements presented in a company's annual report to stockholders are based on historical events that occurred prior to the preparation of the statements.

A Look Back <<

The planning of financial matters is called *budgeting.* The degree of detail in a company's budget depends on the budget period. Generally, the shorter the time period, the more specific the plans. *Strategic planning* involves long-term plans, such as the overall objectives of the business. Examples of strategic planning include which products to manufacture and sell and which market niches to pursue. Strategic plans are stated in broad, descriptive terms. Capital budgeting deals with intermediate investment planning. *Operations budgeting* focuses on short-term plans and is used to create the master budget.

A budgeting committee is responsible for consolidating numerous departmental budgets into a master budget for the whole company. The *master budget* has detailed objectives stated in specific amounts; it describes how management intends to achieve its objectives. The master budget usually covers one year. Budgeting supports planning, coordination, performance measurement, and corrective action.

Employees may be uncomfortable with budgets, which can be constraining. Budgets set standards by which performance is evaluated. To establish an effective budget system, management should recognize the effect on human behavior of budgeting. Upper-level management must set a positive atmosphere by taking budgets seriously and avoiding using them to humiliate subordinates. One way to create the proper atmosphere is to encourage subordinates' participation in the budgeting process; *participative budgeting* can lead to goals that are more realistic about what can be accomplished and to establish a team effort in trying to reach those goals.

The primary components of the master budget are the *operating budgets,* the *capital budget,* and the *pro forma financial statements.* The budgeting process begins with preparing the operating budgets, which consist of detailed schedules and budgets prepared by various company departments. The first operating budget to be prepared is the sales budget. The detailed operating budgets for inventory purchases and S&A expenses are based on the projected sales from the sales budget. The information in the schedules of cash receipts (prepared in conjunction with the sales budget) and cash payments (prepared in conjunction with the inventory purchases and S&A expense budgets) is used in preparing the cash budget. The cash budget subtracts cash payments from cash receipts; the resulting cash surplus or shortage determines the company's financing activities.

The capital budget describes the company's long-term plans regarding investments in facilities, equipment, new products, or other lines of business. The information from the capital budget is used as input to several of the operating budgets.

The pro forma financial statements are prepared from information in the operating budgets. The operating budgets for sales, inventory purchases, and S&A expenses contain information that is used to prepare the income statement and balance sheet. The cash budget includes the amount of interest expense reported on the income statement, the ending cash balance, the capital acquisitions reported on the balance sheet, and most of the information included in the statement of cash flows.

>> A Look Forward

Once a company has completed its budget, it has defined its plans. Then the plans must be followed. The next chapter investigates the techniques used to evaluate performance. You will learn to compare actual results to budgets, to calculate variances, and to identify the parties who are normally accountable for deviations from expectations. Finally, you will learn about the human impact management must consider in taking corrective action when employees fail to accomplish budget goals.

SELF-STUDY REVIEW PROBLEM

The Getaway Gift Company operates a chain of small gift shops that are located in prime vacation towns. Getaway is considering opening a new store on January 1, 2007. Getaway's president recently attended a business seminar that explained how formal budgets could be useful in judging the new store's likelihood of succeeding. Assume you are the company's accountant. The president has asked you to explain the budgeting process and to provide sample reports that show the new store's operating expectations for the first three months (January, February, and March). Respond to the following specific requirements:

Required

a. List the operating budgets and schedules included in a master budget.

b. Explain the difference between pro forma financial statements and the financial statements presented in a company's annual reports to shareholders.

c. Prepare a sample sales budget and a schedule of expected cash receipts using the following assumptions. Getaway estimates January sales will be $400,000 of which $100,000 will be cash and $300,000 will be credit. The ratio of cash sales to sales on account is expected to remain constant over the three-month period. The company expects sales to increase 10 percent per month. The company expects to collect 100 percent of the accounts receivable generated by credit sales in the month following the sale. Use this information to determine the amount of accounts receivable that Getaway would report on the March 31 pro forma balance sheet and the amount of sales it would report on the first quarter pro forma income statement.

d. Prepare a sample inventory purchases budget using the following assumptions. Cost of goods sold is 60 percent of sales. The company desires to maintain a minimum ending inventory equal to 25 percent of the following month's cost of goods sold. Getaway makes all inventory purchases on account. The company pays 70 percent of accounts payable in the month of purchase. It pays the remaining 30 percent in the following month. Prepare a schedule of expected cash payments for inventory purchases. Use this information to determine the amount of cost of goods sold Getaway would report on the first quarter pro forma income statement and the amounts of ending inventory and accounts payable it would report on the March 31 pro forma balance sheet.

Solution to Requirement *a*

A master budget would include (1) a sales budget and schedule of cash receipts, (2) an inventory purchases budget and schedule of cash payments for inventory, (3) a general, selling, and administrative expenses budget and a schedule of cash payments related to these expenses, and (4) a cash budget.

Solution to Requirement *b*

Pro forma statements result from the operating budgets listed in the response to Requirement *a.* Pro forma statements describe the results of expected future events. In contrast, the financial statements presented in a company's annual report reflect the results of events that have actually occurred in the past.

Solution to Requirement *c*

General Information				
Sales growth rate		**10%**		**Pro Forma Statement Data**
Sales Budget	**January**	**February**	**March**	
Sales				
Cash sales	$100,000	$110,000	$121,000	
Sales on account	300,000	330,000	363,000	$ 363,000*
Total sales	$400,000	$440,000	$484,000	$1,324,000†
Schedule of Cash Receipts				
Current cash sales	$100,000	$110,000	$121,000	
Plus 100% of previous month's credit sales	0	300,000	330,000	
Total budgeted collections	$100,000	$410,000	$451,000	

*Ending accounts receivable balance reported on March 31 pro forma balance sheet.

†Sales revenue reported on first quarter pro forma income statement (sum of monthly sales).

Solution to Requirement *d*

General Information				
Cost of goods sold percentage		**60%**		**Pro Forma Statement Data**
Desired ending inventory percentage of CGS		**25%**		
Inventory Purchases Budget	**January**	**February**	**March**	
Budgeted cost of goods sold	$240,000	$264,000	$290,400	$794,400*
Plus: Desired ending inventory	66,000	72,600	79,860	79,860†
Inventory needed	306,000	336,600	370,260	
Less: Beginning inventory	0	(66,000)	(72,600)	
Required purchases	$306,000	$270,600	$297,660	89,298‡
Schedule of Cash Payments for Inventory Purchases				
70% of current purchases	$214,200	$189,420	$208,362	
30% of prior month's purchases	0	91,800	81,180	
Total budgeted payments for inventory	$214,200	$281,220	$289,542	

*Cost of goods sold reported on first quarter pro forma income statement (sum of monthly amounts).

†Ending inventory balance reported on March 31 pro forma balance sheet.

‡Ending accounts payable balance reported on pro forma balance sheet ($297,660 × 0.3).

KEY TERMS

budgeting 489
capital budget 492
capital budgeting 490
cash budget 499
master budget 492
operating budgets 492
participative budgeting 492
perpetual (continuous) budgeting 491
pro forma financial statements 492
strategic planning 490

QUESTIONS

1. Budgets are useful only for small companies that can estimate sales with accuracy. Do you agree with this statement?
2. Why does preparing the master budget require a committee?
3. What are the three levels of planning? Explain each briefly.
4. What is the primary factor that distinguishes the three different levels of planning from each other?
5. What is the advantage of using a perpetual budget instead of the traditional annual budget?
6. What are the advantages of budgeting?
7. How may budgets be used as a measure of performance?
8. Ken Shilov, manager of the marketing department, tells you that "budgeting simply does not work." He says that he made budgets for his employees and when he reprimanded them for failing to accomplish budget goals, he got unfounded excuses. Suggest how Mr. Shilov could encourage employee cooperation.
9. What is a master budget?
10. What is the normal starting point in developing the master budget?
11. How does the level of inventory affect the production budget? Why is it important to manage the level of inventory?
12. What are the components of the cash budget? Describe each.
13. The primary reason for preparing a cash budget is to determine the amount of cash to include on the budgeted balance sheet. Do you agree or disagree with this statement? Explain.
14. What information does the pro forma income statement provide? How does its preparation depend on the operating budgets?
15. How does the pro forma statement of cash flows differ from the cash budget?

EXERCISES

All Exercises are available with McGraw-Hill's Homework Manager

L.O. 1, 2

Exercise 14-1 *Budget responsibility*

Janet Pace, the accountant, is a perfectionist. No one can do the job as well as she can. Indeed, she has found budget information provided by the various departments to be worthless. She must change everything they give her. She has to admit that her estimates have not always been accurate, but she shudders to think of what would happen if she used the information supplied by the marketing and operating departments. No one seems to care about accuracy. Indeed, some of the marketing staff have even become insulting. When Ms. Pace confronted one of the salesmen with the fact that he was behind in meeting his budgeted sales forecast, he responded by saying, "They're your numbers. Why don't you go out and make the sales? It's a heck of a lot easier to sit there in your office and make up numbers than it is to get out and get the real work done." Ms. Pace reported the incident, but, of course, nothing was done about it.

Required

Write a short report suggesting how the budgeting process could be improved.

Exercise 14-2 *Preparing the sales budget* L.O. 3, 7

Digital Flash, which expects to start operations on January 1, 2007, will sell digital cameras in shopping malls. Digital Flash has budgeted sales as indicated in the following table. The company expects a 10 percent increase in sales per month for February and March. The ratio of cash sales to sales on account will remain stable from January through March.

Sales	January	February	March
Cash sales	$ 40,000	?	?
Sales on account	60,000	?	?
Total budgeted sales	$100,000	?	?

Required

a. Complete the sales budget by filling in the missing amounts.

b. Determine the amount of sales revenue Digital Flash will report on its second quarter pro forma income statement.

Exercise 14-3 *Preparing a schedule of cash receipts* L.O. 3, 7

The budget director of Amy's Florist has prepared the following sales budget. The company had $200,000 in accounts receivable on July 1. Amy's Florist normally collects 100 percent of accounts receivable in the month following the month of sale.

Sales	July	August	September
Sales Budget			
Cash sales	$ 60,000	$ 66,000	$ 72,600
Sales on account	150,000	165,000	181,500
Total budgeted sales	$210,000	$231,000	$254,100
Schedule of Cash Receipts			
Current cash sales	?	?	?
Plus collections from accounts receivable	?	?	?
Total budgeted collections	$260,000	$216,000	$237,600

Required

a. Complete the schedule of cash receipts by filling in the missing amounts.

b. Determine the amount of accounts receivable the company will report on its third quarter pro forma balance sheet.

Exercise 14-4 *Preparing sales budgets with different assumptions* L.O. 3

Stenton Corporation, which has three divisions, is preparing its sales budget. Each division expects a different growth rate because economic conditions vary in different regions of the country. The growth expectations per quarter are 2 percent for East Division, 3 percent for West Division, and 5 percent for South Division.

Division	First Quarter	Second Quarter	Third Quarter	Fourth Quarter
East Division	$300,000	?	?	?
West Division	400,000	?	?	?
South Division	100,000	?	?	?

Required

a. Complete the sales budget by filling in the missing amounts. (Round figures to the nearest dollar.)

b. Determine the amount of sales revenue that the company will report on its quarterly pro forma income statements.

L.O. 3

Exercise 14-5 *Determining cash receipts from accounts receivable*

Special Delivery operates a mail-order business that sells clothes designed for frequent travelers. It had sales of $400,000 in December. Because Special Delivery is in the mail-order business, all sales are made on account. The company expects a 25 percent drop in sales for January. The balance in the Accounts Receivable account on December 31 was $80,000 and is budgeted to be $60,000 as of January 31. Special Delivery normally collects accounts receivable in the month following the month of sale.

Required

a. Determine the amount of cash Special Delivery expects to collect from accounts receivable during January.

b. Is it reasonable to assume that sales will decline in January for this type of business? Why or why not?

L.O. 3

Exercise 14-6 *Using judgment in making a sales forecast*

Kandy Inc. is a candy store located in a large shopping mall.

Required

Write a brief memo describing the sales pattern that you would expect Kandy to experience during the year. In which months will sales likely be high? In which months will sales likely be low? Explain why.

L.O. 4

Exercise 14-7 *Preparing an inventory purchases budget*

Designer Lighting Company sells lamps and other lighting fixtures. The purchasing department manager prepared the following inventory purchases budget. Designer Lighting's policy is to maintain an ending inventory balance equal to 10 percent of the following month's cost of goods sold. April's budgeted cost of goods sold is $90,000.

	January	February	March
Budgeted cost of goods sold	$75,000	$80,000	$86,000
Plus: Desired ending inventory	8,000	?	?
Inventory needed	83,000	?	?
Less: Beginning inventory	16,000	?	?
Required purchases (on account)	$67,000	$80,600	$86,400

Required

a. Complete the inventory purchases budget by filling in the missing amounts.

b. Determine the amount of cost of goods sold the company will report on its first quarter pro forma income statement.

c. Determine the amount of ending inventory the company will report on its pro forma balance sheet at the end of the first quarter.

L.O. 4

Exercise 14-8 *Preparing a schedule of cash payments for inventory purchases*

Book Warehouse buys books and magazines directly from publishers and distributes them to grocery stores. The wholesaler expects to purchase the following inventory.

	April	May	June
Required purchases (on account)	$60,000	$80,000	$100,000

Book Warehouse's accountant prepared the following schedule of cash payments for inventory purchases. Book Warehouse's suppliers require that 90 percent of purchases on account be paid in the month of purchase; the remaining 10 percent are paid in the month following the month of purchase.

Schedule of Cash Payments for Inventory Purchases			
	April	May	June
Payment for current accounts payable	$54,000	?	?
Payment for previous accounts payable	4,000	?	?
Total budgeted payments for inventory	$58,000	$78,000	$98,000

Required

a. Complete the schedule of cash payments for inventory purchases by filling in the missing amounts.
b. Determine the amount of accounts payable the company will report on its pro forma balance sheet at the end of the second quarter.

Exercise 14-9 *Determining the amount of expected inventory purchases and cash payments* L.O. 4

Jakal Company, which sells electric razors, had $280,000 of cost of goods sold during the month of June. The company projects a 5 percent increase in cost of goods sold during July. The inventory balance as of June 30 is $30,000, and the desired ending inventory balance for July is $25,000. Jakal pays cash to settle 80 percent of its purchases on account during the month of purchase and pays the remaining 20 percent in the month following the purchase. The accounts payable balance as of June 30 was $32,000.

Required

a. Determine the amount of purchases budgeted for July.
b. Determine the amount of cash payments budgeted for inventory purchases in July.

Exercise 14-10 *Preparing a schedule of cash payments for selling and administrative expenses* L.O. 5

The budget director for Shining Window Cleaning Services prepared the following list of expected operating expenses. All expenses requiring cash payments are paid for in the month incurred except salary expense and insurance. Salary is paid in the month following the month in which it is incurred. The insurance premium for six months is paid on October 1. October is the first month of operations; accordingly, there are no beginning account balances.

	October	November	December
Budgeted Operating Expenses			
Equipment lease expense	$ 7,000	$ 7,000	$ 7,000
Salary expense	6,400	6,800	6,900
Cleaning supplies	2,600	2,860	3,146
Insurance expense	1,000	1,000	1,000
Depreciation on computer	1,600	1,600	1,600
Rent	1,800	1,800	1,800
Miscellaneous expenses	600	600	600
Total operating expenses	$21,000	$21,660	$22,046
Schedule of Cash Payments for Operating Expenses			
Equipment lease expense	?	?	?
Prior month's salary expense, 100%	?	?	?
Cleaning supplies	?	?	?
Insurance premium	?	?	?
Depreciation on computer	?	?	?
Rent	?	?	?
Miscellaneous expenses	?	?	?
Total disbursements for operating expenses	$18,000	$18,660	$19,346

Required

a. Complete the schedule of cash payments for operating expenses by filling in the missing amounts.
b. Determine the amount of salaries payable the company will report on its pro forma balance sheet at the end of the fourth quarter.
c. Determine the amount of prepaid insurance the company will report on its pro forma balance sheet at the end of the fourth quarter.

L.O. 4

Exercise 14-11 *Preparing inventory purchases budgets with different assumptions*

Executive officers of Cary Company are wrestling with their budget for the next year. The following are two different sales estimates provided by two difference sources.

Source of Estimate	First Quarter	Second Quarter	Third Quarter	Fourth Quarter
Sales manager	$400,000	$320,000	$300,000	$480,000
Marketing consultant	500,000	450,000	420,000	630,000

Cary's past experience indicates that cost of goods sold is about 70 percent of sales revenue. The company tries to maintain 10 percent of the next quarter's expected cost of goods sold as the current quarter's ending inventory. This year's ending inventory is $30,000. Next year's ending inventory is budgeted to be $32,000.

Required

a. Prepare an inventory purchases budget using the sales manager's estimate.

b. Prepare an inventory purchases budget using the marketing consultant's estimate.

L.O. 5, 7

Exercise 14-12 *Determining the amount of cash payments and pro forma statement data for selling and administrative expenses*

January budgeted selling and administrative expenses for the retail shoe store that Nell Walker plans to open on January 1, 2006, are as follows: sales commissions, $20,000; rent, $15,000; utilities, $5,000; depreciation, $4,000; and miscellaneous, $2,000. Utilities are paid in the month following their incursion. Other expenses are expected to be paid in cash in the month in which they are incurred.

Required

a. Determine the amount of budgeted cash payments for January selling and administrative expenses.

b. Determine the amount of utilities payable the store will report on the January 31st pro forma balance sheet.

c. Determine the amount of depreciation expense the store will report on the income statement for the year 2006, assuming that monthly depreciation remains the same for the entire year.

L.O. 6, 7

Exercise 14-13 *Preparing a cash budget*

The accountant for Tricia's Dress Shop prepared the following cash budget. Tricia's desires to maintain a cash cushion of $14,000 at the end of each month. Funds are assumed to be borrowed and repaid on the last day of each month. Interest is charged at the rate of 2 percent per month.

Cash Budget	July	August	September
Section 1: Cash Receipts			
Beginning cash balance	$ 42,500	$?	$?
Add cash receipts	180,000	200,000	240,600
Total cash available (a)	222,500	?	?
Section 2: Cash Payments			
For inventory purchases	165,526	140,230	174,152
For S&A expenses	54,500	60,560	61,432
For interest expense	0	?	?
Total budgeted disbursements (b)	220,026	?	?
Section 3: Financing Activities			
Surplus (shortage)	2,474	?	?
Borrowing (repayments) (c)	11,526	?	?
Ending Cash Balance (a − b + c)	$ 14,000	$ 14,000	$ 14,000

Required

a. Complete the cash budget by filling in the missing amounts. Round all computations to the nearest whole dollar.

b. Determine the amount of net cash flows from operating activities Tricia's will report on the third quarter pro forma statement of cash flows.

c. Determine the amount of net cash flows from financing activities Tricia's will report on the third quarter pro forma statement of cash flows.

Exercise 14-14 *Determining amount to borrow and pro forma statement balances*

L.O. 6, 7

Jane Hesline owns a small restaurant in New York City. Ms. Hesline provided her accountant with the following summary information regarding expectations for the month of June. The balance in accounts receivable as of May 31 is $50,000. Budgeted cash and credit sales for June are $100,000 and $500,000, respectively. Credit sales are made through Visa and MasterCard and are collected rapidly. Ninety percent of credit sales is collected in the month of sale, and the remainder is collected in the following month. Ms. Hesline's suppliers do not extend credit. Consequently, she pays suppliers on the last day of the month. Cash payments for June are expected to be $620,000. Ms. Hesline has a line of credit that enables the restaurant to borrow funds on demand; however, they must be borrowed on the last day of the month. Interest is paid in cash also on the last day of the month. Ms. Hesline desires to maintain a $20,000 cash balance before the interest payment. Her annual interest rate is 9 percent. Disregard any credit card fees.

Required

a. Compute the amount of funds Ms. Hesline needs to borrow for June, assuming that the beginning cash balance is zero.

b. Determine the amount of interest expense the restaurant will report on the June pro forma income statement.

c. What amount will the restaurant report as interest expense on the July pro forma income statement?

Exercise 14-15 *Preparing pro forma income statements with different assumptions*

L.O. 7

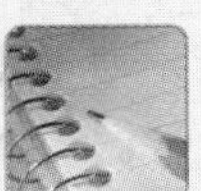

Andy Collum, the controller of Grime Corporation, is trying to prepare a sales budget for the coming year. The income statements for the last four quarters follow.

	First Quarter	Second Quarter	Third Quarter	Fourth Quarter	Total
Sales revenue	$160,000	$180,000	$200,000	$260,000	$800,000
Cost of goods sold	96,000	108,000	120,000	156,000	480,000
Gross profit	64,000	72,000	80,000	104,000	320,000
Selling & admin. expense	16,000	18,000	20,000	26,000	80,000
Net income	$ 48,000	$ 54,000	$ 60,000	$ 78,000	$240,000

Historically, cost of goods sold is about 60 percent of sales revenue. Selling and administrative expenses are about 10 percent of sales revenue.

Tim Grime, the chief executive officer, told Mr. Collum that he expected sales next year to be 10 percent above last year's level. However, Sara Lund, the vice president of sales, told Mr. Collum that she believed sales growth would be only 5 percent.

Required

a. Prepare a pro forma income statement including quarterly budgets for the coming year using Mr. Grime's estimate.

b. Prepare a pro forma income statement including quarterly budgets for the coming year using Ms. Lund's estimate.

c. Explain why two executive officers in the same company could have different estimates of future growth.

PROBLEMS

All Problems are available with McGraw-Hill's Homework Manager

L.O. 3

mhhe.com/edmonds2007

CHECK FIGURES
c. Feb.: $96,000
March: $115,600

Problem 14-16 *Preparing a sales budget and schedule of cash receipts*

Bedimo Pointers Inc. expects to begin operations on January 1, 2007; it will operate as a specialty sales company that sells laser pointers over the Internet. Bedimo expects sales in January 2007 to total $100,000 and to increase 10 percent per month in February and March. All sales are on account. Bedimo expects to collect 60 percent of accounts receivable in the month of sale, 30 percent in the month following the sale, and 10 percent in the second month following the sale.

Required

a. Prepare a sales budget for the first quarter of 2007.

b. Determine the amount of sales revenue Bedimo will report on the first 2007 quarterly pro forma income statement.

c. Prepare a cash receipts schedule for the first quarter of 2007.

d. Determine the amount of accounts receivable as of March 31, 2007.

L.O. 4, 7

CHECK FIGURES
a. May: $71,000
c. June: $76,760

Problem 14-17 *Preparing the inventory purchases budget and schedule of cash payments*

Stine Inc. sells fireworks. The company's marketing director developed the following cost of goods sold budget for April, May, June, and July.

	April	May	June	July
Budgeted cost of goods sold	$60,000	$70,000	$80,000	$86,000

Stine had a beginning inventory balance of $3,600 on April 1 and a beginning balance in accounts payable of $14,800. The company desires to maintain an ending inventory balance equal to 10 percent of the next period's cost of goods sold. Stine makes all purchases on account. The company pays 60 percent of accounts payable in the month of purchase and the remaining 40 percent in the month following purchase.

Required

a. Prepare an inventory purchases budget for April, May, and June.

b. Determine the amount of ending inventory Stine will report on the end-of-quarter pro forma balance sheet.

c. Prepare a schedule of cash payments for inventory for April, May, and June.

d. Determine the balance in accounts payable Stine will report on the end-of-quarter pro forma balance sheet.

L.O. 7

CHECK FIGURE
a. 12.75%

Problem 14-18 *Preparing pro forma income statements with different assumptions*

Top executive officers of Chesnokov Company, a merchandising firm, are preparing the next year's budget. The controller has provided everyone with the current year's projected income statement.

	Current Year
Sales revenue	$2,000,000
Cost of goods sold	1,400,000
Gross profit	600,000
Selling & admin. expenses	260,000
Net income	$ 340,000

Cost of goods sold is usually 70 percent of sales revenue, and selling and administrative expenses are usually 10 percent of sales plus a fixed cost of $60,000. The president has announced that the company's goal is to increase net income by 15 percent.

Required

The following items are independent of each other.

a. What percentage increase in sales would enable the company to reach its goal? Support your answer with a pro forma income statement.

b. The market may become stagnant next year, and the company does not expect an increase in sales revenue. The production manager believes that an improved production procedure can cut cost of goods sold by 2 percent. What else can the company do to reach its goal? Prepare a pro forma income statement illustrating your proposal.

c. The company decides to escalate its advertising campaign to boost consumer recognition, which will increase selling and administrative expenses to $340,000. With the increased advertising, the company expects sales revenue to increase by 15 percent. Assume that cost of goods sold remains a constant proportion of sales. Can the company reach its goal?

Problem 14-19 *Preparing a schedule of cash payments for selling and administrative expenses*

L.O. 5, 6

CHECK FIGURE
a. Sept.: $22,460

Shah is a retail company specializing in men's hats. Its budget director prepared the list of expected operating expenses that follows. All items are paid when the expenses are incurred except sales commissions and utilities, which are paid in the month after they are incurred. July is the first month of operations, so there are no beginning account balances.

	July	August	September
Salary expense	$12,000	$12,000	$12,000
Sales commissions (4 percent of sales)	1,600	1,500	1,800
Supplies expense	360	400	440
Utilities	1,200	1,200	1,200
Depreciation on store equipment	2,600	2,600	2,600
Rent	6,600	6,600	6,600
Miscellaneous	720	720	720
Total S&A expenses before interest	$25,080	$25,020	$25,360

Required

a. Prepare a schedule of cash payments for selling and administrative expenses.

b. Determine the amount of utilities payable as of September 30.

c. Determine the amount of sales commissions payable as of September 30.

Problem 14-20 *Preparing a cash budget*

L.O. 6

CHECK FIGURE
Feb. cash surplus before financing activities: $7,010

Hoyt Medical Clinic has budgeted the following cash flows.

	January	February	March
Cash receipts	$100,000	$106,000	$126,000
Cash payments			
For inventory purchases	90,000	72,000	85,000
For S&A expenses	31,000	32,000	27,000

Hoyt Medical had a cash balance of $8,000 on January 1. The company desires to maintain a cash cushion of $5,000. Funds are assumed to be borrowed, in increments of $1,000, and repaid on the last day of each month; the interest rate is 1 percent per month. Hoyt pays its vendor on the last day of the month also. The company had a $40,000 beginning balance in its line of credit liability account.

Required

Prepare a cash budget. (Round all computations to the nearest whole dollar.)

L.O. 3, 4, 5

mhhe.com/edmonds2007

CHECK FIGURES

c. 1st QTR purchases for peaches: $141,120
2nd QTR purchases for oranges: $312,840

Problem 14-21 *Preparing budgets with multiple products*

Fresh Fruits Corporation wholesales peaches and oranges. Beth Fresh is working with the company's accountant to prepare next year's budget. Ms. Fresh estimates that sales will increase 5 percent annually for peaches and 10 percent for oranges. The current year's sales revenue data follow.

	First Quarter	Second Quarter	Third Quarter	Fourth Quarter	Total
Peaches	$220,000	$240,000	$300,000	$240,000	$1,000,000
Oranges	400,000	450,000	570,000	380,000	1,800,000
Total	$620,000	$690,000	$870,000	$620,000	$2,800,000

Based on the company's past experience, cost of goods sold is usually 60 percent of sales revenue. Company policy is to keep 20 percent of the next period's estimated cost of goods sold as the current period's ending inventory. (*Hint:* Use the cost of goods sold for the first quarter to determine the beginning inventory for the first quarter.)

Required

a. Prepare the company's sales budget for the next year for each quarter by individual product.

b. If the selling and administrative expenses are estimated to be $700,000, prepare the company's budgeted annual income statement.

c. Ms. Fresh estimates next year's ending inventory will be $34,000 for peaches and $56,000 for oranges. Prepare the company's inventory purchases budgets for the next year showing quarterly figures by product.

L.O. 3, 4, 5

mhhe.com/edmonds2007

CHECK FIGURES

c. Dec. purchases: $113,250
g. Nov. surplus before financing activities: $19,505

Problem 14-22 *Preparing a master budget for a retail company with no beginning account balances*

Unici Company is a retail company that specializes in selling outdoor camping equipment. The company is considering opening a new store on October 1, 2006. The company president formed a planning committee to prepare a master budget for the first three months of operation. He assigned you, the budget coordinator, the following tasks.

Required

a. October sales are estimated to be $120,000 of which 40 percent will be cash and 60 percent will be credit. The company expects sales to increase at the rate of 25 percent per month. Prepare a sales budget.

b. The company expects to collect 100 percent of the accounts receivable generated by credit sales in the month following the sale. Prepare a schedule of cash receipts.

c. The cost of goods sold is 60 percent of sales. The company desires to maintain a minimum ending inventory equal to 10 percent of the next month's cost of goods sold. Ending inventory at December 31 is expected to be $12,000. Assume that all purchases are made on account. Prepare an inventory purchases budget.

d. The company pays 70 percent of accounts payable in the month of purchase and the remaining 30 percent in the following month. Prepare a cash payments budget for inventory purchases.

e. Budgeted selling and administrative expenses per month follow.

Salary expense (fixed)	$18,000
Sales commissions	5 percent of Sales
Supplies expense	2 percent of Sales
Utilities (fixed)	$1,400
Depreciation on store equipment (fixed)*	$4,000
Rent (fixed)	$4,800
Miscellaneous (fixed)	$1,200

*The capital expenditures budget indicates that Unici will spend $164,000 on October 1 for store fixtures, which are expected to have a $20,000 salvage value and a three-year (36-month) useful life.

Use this information to prepare a selling and administrative expenses budget.

f. Utilities and sales commissions are paid the month after they are incurred; all other expenses are paid in the month in which they are incurred. Prepare a cash payments budget for selling and administrative expenses.
g. Unici borrows funds, in increments of $1,000, and repays them on the last day of the month. The company also pays its vendors on the last day of the month. It pays interest of 1 percent per month in cash on the last day of the month. To be prudent, the company desires to maintain a $12,000 cash cushion. Prepare a cash budget.
h. Prepare a pro forma income statement for the quarter.
i. Prepare a pro forma balance sheet at the end of the quarter.
j. Prepare a pro forma statement of cash flows for the quarter.

Problem 14-23 *Behavioral impact of budgeting*

L.O. 2

CHECK FIGURE
a. NI: $945,000
c. NI: $1,035,000

Vanhorn Corporation has three divisions, each operating as a responsibility center. To provide an incentive for divisional executive officers, the company gives divisional management a bonus equal to 20 percent of the excess of actual net income over budgeted net income. The following is Dancy Division's current year's performance.

	Current Year
Sales revenue	$4,500,000
Cost of goods sold	2,700,000
Gross profit	1,800,000
Selling & admin. expenses	900,000
Net income	$ 900,000

The president has just received next year's budget proposal from the vice president in charge of Dancy Division. The proposal budgets a 5 percent increase in sales revenue with an extensive explanation about stiff market competition. The president is puzzled. Dancy has enjoyed revenue growth of around 10 percent for each of the past five years. The president had consistently approved the division's budget proposals based on 5 percent growth in the past. This time, the president wants to show that he is not a fool. "I will impose a 15 percent revenue increase to teach them a lesson!" the president says to himself smugly.

Assume that cost of goods sold and selling and administrative expenses remain stable in proportion to sales.

Required

a. Prepare the budgeted income statement based on Dancy Division's proposal of a 5 percent increase.
b. If growth is actually 10 percent as usual, how much bonus would Dancy Division's executive officers receive if the president had approved the division's proposal?
c. Prepare the budgeted income statement based on the 15 percent increase the president imposed.
d. If the actual results turn out to be a 10 percent increase as usual, how much bonus would Dancy Division's executive officers receive since the president imposed a 15 percent increase?
e. Propose a better budgeting procedure for Vanhorn.

ANALYZE, THINK, COMMUNICATE

ATC 14-1 Business Applications Case *Preparing and using pro forma statements*

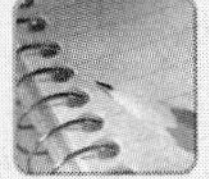

Nancy Chen and Tim Hoffer recently graduated from the same university. After graduation they decided not to seek jobs in established organizations but to start their own small business. They hoped this would provide more flexibility in their personal lives for a few years. Since both of them enjoyed cooking, they decided on a business selling vegetarian wraps and fruit juices from a street cart near their alma mater.

They bought a small enclosed cart for $3,500 that was set up for selling food. This cost, along with the cost for supplies to get started, a business license, and street vendor license, brought their initial expenditures to $4,500. They used $500 of their personal savings, and they borrowed $4,000 from Nancy's parents. They agreed to pay interest on the outstanding loan balance each month based on an annual rate of 6 percent. They will repay the principal over the next two years as cash becomes available.

After two months in business, September and October, they had average monthly revenues of $5,800 and out-of-pocket costs of $3,600 for ingredients, paper supplies, and so on, but not interest. Tim thinks they should repay some of the money they borrowed, but Nancy thinks they should prepare a set of forecasted financial statements for their first year in business before deciding whether or not to repay any principal on the loan. She remembers a bit about budgeting from a survey of accounting course she took and thinks the results from their first two months in business can be extended over the next 10 months to prepare the budget they need. They estimate the cart will last at least three years, after which they expect to sell it for $500 and move on to something else in their lives. Nancy agrees to prepare a forecasted (pro forma) income statement, balance sheet, and statement of cash flows for their first year in business, which includes the two months already passed.

Required

a. Prepare the annual pro forma financial statements that you would expect Nancy to prepare based on her comments about her expectations for the business. Assume no principal will be repaid on the loan.

b. Review the statements you prepared for the first requirement and prepare a list of reasons why Tim and Nancy's business results probably will not agree with their budgeted statements.

ATC 14-2 Group Assignment *Master budget and pro forma statements*

The following trial balance was drawn from the records of Havel Company as of October 1, 2005.

Cash	$ 16,000	
Accounts receivable	60,000	
Inventory	40,000	
Store equipment	200,000	
Accumulated depreciation		$ 76,800
Accounts payable		72,000
Line of credit loan		100,000
Common stock		50,000
Retained earnings		17,200
Totals	$316,000	$316,000

Required

a. Divide the class into groups, each with four or five students. Organize the groups into three sections. Assign Task 1 to the first section, Task 2 to the second section, and Task 3 to the third section.

Group Tasks

(1) Based on the following information, prepare a sales budget and a schedule of cash receipts for October, November, and December. Sales for October are expected to be $180,000, consisting of $40,000 in cash and $140,000 on credit. The company expects sales to increase at the rate of 10 percent per month. All of accounts receivable is collected in the month following the sale.

(2) Based on the following information, prepare a purchases budget and a schedule of cash payments for inventory purchases for October, November, and December. Cost of goods sold for October is expected to be $72,000. Cost of goods sold is expected to increase by 10 percent per month in November and December. Havel expects January cost of goods sold to be $89,000. The company desires to maintain a minimum ending inventory equal to 20 percent of the next month's cost of goods sold. Seventy-five percent of accounts payable is paid in the month that the purchase occurs; the remaining 25 percent is paid in the following month.

(3) Based on the following selling and administrative expenses budgeted for October, prepare a selling and administrative expenses budget for October, November, and December.

Cash payments for sales commissions and utilities are made in the month following the one in which the expense is incurred. Supplies and other operating expenses are paid in cash in the month in which they are incurred. As of October 1, no amounts were payable for either commissions or utilities from the previous month.

Sales commissions (10% increase per month)	$ 7,200
Supplies expense (10% increase per month)	1,800
Utilities (fixed)	2,200
Depreciation on store equipment (fixed)	1,600
Salary expense (fixed)	34,000
Rent (fixed)	6,000
Miscellaneous (fixed)	1,000

b. Select a representative from each section. Have the representatives supply the missing information in the following pro forma income statement and balance sheet for the fourth quarter of 2005. The statements are prepared as of December 31, 2005.

Income Statement		
Sales Revenue		$?
Cost of Goods Sold		?
Gross Margin		357,480
Operating Expenses		?
Operating Income		193,290
Interest Expense		(2,530)
Net Income		$190,760
Balance Sheet		
Assets		
Cash		$ 9,082
Accounts Receivable		?
Inventory		?
Store Equipment	$200,000	
Accumulated Depreciation Store Equipment	?	
Book Value of Equipment		118,400
Total Assets		$314,682
Liabilities		
Accounts Payable		?
Utilities Payable		?
Sales Commissions Payable		?
Line of Credit		23,936
Equity		
Common Stock		50,000
Retained Earnings		?
Total Liabilities and Equity		$314,682

c. Indicate whether Havel will need to borrow money during October.

ATC 14-3 Research Assignment ***Simplifying the budget process***

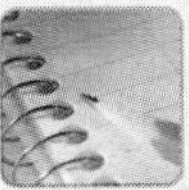

By their nature, large entities often generate big, complex budgets. There is a danger, however, that budgets can become so detailed and complex that they do not get used after being prepared. In the article, "Streamline Budgeting in the new Millennium: Concentrate on Simplicity and Usefulness, Not Unrealistic Numbers," *Strategic Finance,* December 2001, pp. 45–50, Bruce Neumann provides suggestions for improving the budgeting process. Read this article and complete the following requirements.

Required

a. What are the five steps of budgeting that the author identifies?

b. Briefly explain what the article means by "the Three C's" of motivation for those preparing a budget.

c. The article describes "activity budgeting" as one method for streamlining an entity's budget. Explain the basic concept of activity budgeting.

d. The article describes "global budgeting" as one method for streamlining an entity's budget. Explain the basic concept of global budgeting.

e. Does the author suggest that more budget categories be devoted to fixed-cost categories or variable-cost categories?

ATC 14-4 Writing Assignment *Continuous budgeting*

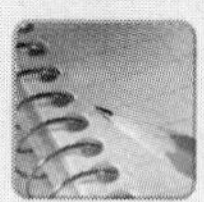

HON Company is the largest maker of mid-priced office furniture in the United States and Canada. Its management has expressed dissatisfaction with its *annual* budget system. Fierce competition requires businesses to be flexible and innovative. Building the effects of innovation into an annual budget is difficult because actions and outcomes often are evolutionary. Innovation unfolds as the year progresses. Consequently, HON's management team reached the conclusion that "when production processes undergo continuous change, standards developed annually for static conditions no longer offer meaningful targets for gauging their success."

Required

Assume that you are HON Company's budget director. Write a memo to the management team explaining how the practice of continuous budgeting could overcome the shortcomings of an annual budget process. (For insight, read the article "Continuous Budgeting at the HON Company," *Management Accounting,* January 1996. This article describes HON's real-world experience with a continuous budget system.)

ATC 14-5 Ethical Dilemma *Bad budget system or unethical behavior?*

Clarence Cleaver is the budget director for the Harris County School District. Mr. Cleaver recently sent an urgent e-mail message to Sally Simmons, principal of West Harris County High. The message severely reprimanded Ms. Simmons for failing to spend the funds allocated to her to purchase computer equipment. Ms. Simmons responded that her school already has a sufficient supply of computers; the computer lab is never filled to capacity and usually is less than half filled. Ms. Simmons suggested that she would rather use the funds for teacher training. She argued that the reason the existing computers are not fully utilized is that the teachers lack sufficient computer literacy necessary to make assignments for their students.

Mr. Cleaver responded that it is not Ms. Simmons's job to decide how the money is to be spent; that is the school board's job. It is the principal's job to spend the money as the board directed. He informed Ms. Simmons that if the money is not spent by the fiscal closing date, the school board would likely reduce next year's budget allotment. To avoid a potential budget cut, Mr. Cleaver reallocated Ms. Simmons's computer funds to Jules Carrington, principal of East Harris County High. Mr. Carrington knows how to buy computers regardless of whether they are needed. Mr. Cleaver's final words were, "Don't blame me if parents of West High students complain that East High has more equipment. If anybody comes to me, I'm telling them that you turned down the money."

Required

a. Do Mr. Cleaver's actions violate the standards of ethical conduct shown in Exhibit 10.13 of Chapter 10?

b. Explain how participative budgeting could improve the allocation of resources for the Harris County School District.

CHAPTER 15

Performance Evaluation

LEARNING OBJECTIVES

After you have mastered the material in this chapter you will be able to:

1. **Describe the concept of decentralization.**
2. **Describe the differences among cost, profit, and investment centers.**
3. **Explain the controllability concept.**
4. **Distinguish between flexible and static budgets.**
5. **Compute revenue and cost variances and interpret whether the variances signal favorable or unfavorable performance.**
6. **Compute sales volume variances (differences between static and flexible budgets) and explain how volume variances affect fixed and variable costs.**
7. **Compute and interpret flexible budget variances (differences between flexible budget and actual results).**
8. **Evaluate investment opportunities using the return on investment technique.**
9. **Evaluate investment opportunities using the residual income technique.**

The Curious Accountant

In 1978 Bernie Marcus and Arthur Blank founded **The Home Depot, Inc.**, and their first store opened in 1979. One year later they had four stores, 300 employees, and sales of $22 million. By 2000 there were 1,123 Home Depot stores with 226,000 employees and annual sales of $45.7 billion. Mr. Marcus was the company's CEO during these 20 years of tremendous growth, and he ran the company with a decentralized management style. He wanted store managers to operate individual stores as if they were their owners. Using this strategy, he saw the company's stock price rise from less than $1 per share to over $45 per share (when adjusted for stock splits). In December 2000, Mr. Marcus stepped down as Home Depot's CEO and an outsider, Bob Nardelli, was appointed as his replacement.

Two significant things happened during the first two years of Mr. Nardelli's tenure. First, he began implementing a much more centralized management system, and second, the stock price fell by 51 percent. A few examples of his management changes are: he required stores to hire more part-time employees and fewer full-time employees whether the local manager wanted to or not; he implemented a centralized purchasing system; he required local stores to carry new product lines, such as small appliances, even if the store manager objected. As a result of the change in management style, several long-time store managers left the company, and others complained. Despite these problems, Mr. Marcus, who still yielded considerable influence as a major stockholder and member of the board of directors, stood behind Mr. Nardelli and the changes he was implementing.

What could explain why a company that had enjoyed so much success under a decentralized management system would switch to a more centralized system? Why would the architect of the decentralized system that had been so successful support the man who replaced his system? (Answers on page 529.)

CHAPTER OPENING

Walter Keller, a production manager, complained to the accountant, Kelly Oberson, that the budget system failed to control his department's labor cost. Ms. Oberson responded, "people, not budgets, control costs." Budgeting is one of many tools management uses to control business operations. Managers are responsible for using control tools effectively. **Responsibility accounting** *focuses on evaluating the performance of individual managers. For example, expenses controlled by a production department manager are presented in one report and expenses controlled by a marketing department manager are presented in a different report. This chapter discusses the development and use of a responsibility accounting system.* ■

Decentralization Concept

Describe the concept of decentralization.

Effective responsibility accounting requires clear lines of authority and responsibility. Divisions of authority and responsibility normally occur as a natural consequence of managing business operations. In a small business, one person can control everything: marketing, production, management, accounting. In contrast, large companies are so complex that authority and control must be divided among many people.

Consider the hiring of employees. A small business usually operates in a limited geographic area. The owner works directly with employees. She knows the job requirements, local wage rates, and the available labor pool. She is in a position to make informed hiring decisions. In contrast, a major corporation may employ thousands of employees throughout the world. The employees may speak different languages and have different social customs. Their jobs may require many different skills and pay a vast array of wage rates. The president of the corporation cannot make informed hiring decisions for the entire company. Instead, he delegates *authority* to a professional personnel manager and holds that manager *responsible* for hiring practices.

Decision-making authority is similarly delegated to individuals responsible for managing specific organization functions such as production, marketing, and accounting. Delegating authority and responsibility is referred to as **decentralization.**

Responsibility Centers

Describe the differences among cost, profit, and investment centers.

Decentralized businesses are usually subdivided into distinct reporting units called responsibility centers. A **responsibility center** is an organizational unit that controls identifiable revenue or expense items. The unit may be a division, a department, a subdepartment, or even a single machine. For example, a transportation company may identify a semitrailer truck as a responsibility center. The company holds the truck driver responsible for the revenues and expenses associated with operating the truck. Responsibility centers may be divided into three categories: cost, profit, and investment.

A **cost center** is an organizational unit that incurs expenses but does not generate revenue. Cost centers normally fall on the lower levels of an organization chart. The manager of a cost center is judged on his ability to keep costs within budget parameters.

A **profit center** differs from a cost center in that it not only incurs costs but also generates revenue. The manager of a profit center is judged on his ability to produce revenue in excess of expenses.

Investment center managers are responsible for revenues, expenses, and the investment of capital. Investment centers normally appear at the upper levels of an organization chart.

Controllability Concept

Explain the controllability concept.

The **controllability concept** is crucial to an effective responsibility accounting system. Managers should only be evaluated based on revenues or costs they control. Holding individuals responsible for things they cannot control is demotivating. Isolating control, however, may be difficult, as illustrated in the following case.

Dorothy Pasewark, a buyer for a large department store chain, was criticized when stores could not resell the merchandise she bought at the expected price. Ms. Pasewark countered that the sales staff caused the sluggish sales by not displaying the merchandise properly. The sales staff charged that the merchandise had too little sales potential to justify setting up more enticing displays. The division of influence between the buyer and the sales staff clouds the assignment of responsibility.

Since the exercise of control may be clouded, managers are usually held responsible for items over which they have *predominant* rather than *absolute* control. At times responsibility accounting may be imperfect. Management must strive to ensure that praise or criticism is administered as fairly as possible.

Preparing Flexible Budgets

Distinguish between flexible and static budgets.

A **flexible budget** is an extension of the *master budget* discussed in Chapter 14. The master budget is based solely on the planned volume of activity. The master budget is frequently called a **static budget** because it remains unchanged even if the actual volume of activity differs from the planned volume. Flexible budgets differ from static budgets in that they show expected revenues and costs at a *variety* of volume levels.

To illustrate the differences between static and flexible budgets, consider Melrose Manufacturing Company, a producer of small, high-quality trophies used in award ceremonies. Melrose plans to make and sell 18,000 trophies during 2006. Management's best estimates of the expected sales price and per unit costs for the trophies are called *standard* prices and costs. The standard price and costs for the 18,000 trophies follow.

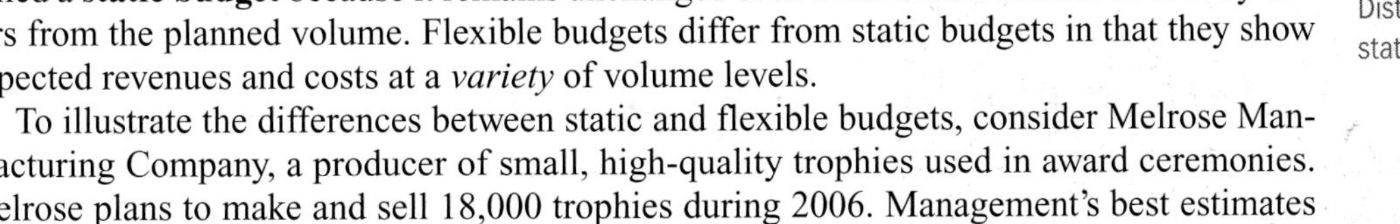

Per unit sales price and variable costs	
Expected sales price	$80.00
Standard materials cost	12.00
Standard labor cost	16.80
Standard overhead cost	5.60
Standard general, selling, and administrative cost	15.00
Fixed costs	
Manufacturing cost	$201,600
General, selling, and administrative cost	90,000

Static and flexible budgets use the same per unit *standard* amounts and the same fixed costs. Exhibit 15.1 shows Melrose Manufacturing's static budget in column D of the Excel spreadsheet. The amounts of sales revenue and variable costs in column D come from multiplying the per unit standards in column C by the number of units in cell D4 (planned volume). For example, the sales revenue in cell D7 comes from multiplying the per unit sales price in cell C7 by the number of units in cell D4 ($80 × 18,000 units = $1,440,000). The variable costs are similarly computed; the cost per unit amount in column C is multiplied by the planned volume in cell D4.

What if management wants to know the amount net income would be if volume were 16,000, 17,000, 18,000, 19,000, or 20,000 units? Management needs a series of *flexible budgets*. With little effort, an accountant can provide *what-if* information on the Excel spreadsheet. By copying to columns F through J the formulas used to determine the static budget amounts in column D, then changing the volume variables in row 4 to the desired levels, the spreadsheet instantly calculates the alternative flexible budgets in columns F through J.

EXHIBIT 15.1

Static and Flexible Budgets in Excel Spreadsheet

	Per Unit Standards	Static Budget	Flexible Budgets				
Number of Units		18,000	16,000	17,000	18,000	19,000	20,000
Sales Revenue	$80.00	$1,440,000	$1,280,000	$1,360,000	$1,440,000	$1,520,000	$1,600,000
Variable Manuf. Costs							
Materials	$12.00	216,000	192,000	204,000	216,000	228,000	240,000
Labor	16.80	302,400	268,800	285,600	302,400	319,200	336,000
Overhead	5.60	100,800	89,600	95,200	100,800	106,400	112,000
Variable G,S,&A	15.00	270,000	240,000	255,000	270,000	285,000	300,000
Contribution Margin		550,800	489,600	520,200	550,800	581,400	612,000
Fixed Costs							
Manufacturing		201,600	201,600	201,600	201,600	201,600	201,600
G,S,&A		90,000	90,000	90,000	90,000	90,000	90,000
Net Income		$ 259,200	$ 198,000	$ 228,600	$ 259,200	$ 289,800	$ 320,400

Management can use the flexible budgets for both planning and performance evaluation. For example, managers may assess whether the company's cash position is adequate by assuming different levels of volume. They may judge if the number of employees, amounts of materials, and equipment and storage facilities are appropriate for a variety of different potential levels of volume. In addition to helping plan, flexible budgets are critical to implementing an effective performance evaluation system.

CHECK YOURSELF 15.1

The static (master) budget of Parcel Inc. called for a production and sales volume of 25,000 units. At that volume, total budgeted fixed costs were $150,000 and total budgeted variable costs were $200,000. Prepare a flexible budget for an expected volume of 26,000 units.

Answer

Budgeted fixed costs would remain unchanged at $150,000 because changes in the volume of activity do not affect budgeted fixed costs. Budgeted variable costs would increase to $208,000, computed as follows: calculate the budgeted variable cost per unit ($200,000 ÷ 25,000 units = $8) and then multiply that variable cost per unit by the expected volume ($8 × 26,000 units = $208,000).

Determining Variances for Performance Evaluation

Compute revenue and cost variances and interpret whether the variances signal favorable or unfavorable performance.

One means of evaluating managerial performance is to compare *standard* amounts with *actual* results. The differences between the standard and actual amounts are called **variances;** variances can be either **favorable** or **unfavorable.** When actual sales revenue is greater than expected (planned) revenue, a company has a favorable sales variance because maximizing revenue is desirable. When actual sales are less than expected, an unfavorable sales variance exists. Because managers try to minimize costs, favorable cost variances exist when actual costs are *less* than standard costs. Unfavorable cost variances exist when actual costs are *more* than standard costs. These relationships are summarized below.

- When actual sales exceed expected sales, variances are favorable.
- When actual sales are less than expected sales, variances are unfavorable.
- When actual costs exceed standard costs, variances are unfavorable.
- When actual costs are less than standard costs, variances are favorable.

Compute sales volume variances (differences between static and flexible budgets) and explain how volume variances affect fixed and variable costs.

Sales Volume Variances

The amount of a **sales volume variance** is the difference between the static budget (which is based on planned volume) and a flexible budget based on actual volume. This variance measures management effectiveness in attaining the planned volume of activity. To illustrate, assume Melrose Manufacturing Company actually makes and sells 19,000 trophies during 2006. The planned volume of activity was 18,000 trophies. Exhibit 15.2 shows Melrose's static budget, flexible budget, and volume variances.

Interpreting the Sales and Variable Cost Volume Variances

Because the static and flexible budgets are based on the same standard sales price and per unit variable costs, the variances are solely attributable to the difference between the planned and actual volume of activity. Marketing managers are usually responsible for the volume variance. Because the sales volume drives production levels, production

EXHIBIT 15.2

Melrose Manufacturing Company's Volume Variances

	Static Budget	Flexible Budget	Volume Variances	
Number of units	18,000	19,000	1,000	Favorable
Sales revenue	$1,440,000	$1,520,000	$80,000	Favorable
Variable manufacturing costs				
Materials	216,000	228,000	12,000	Unfavorable
Labor	302,400	319,200	16,800	Unfavorable
Overhead	100,800	106,400	5,600	Unfavorable
Variable G, S, & A	270,000	285,000	15,000	Unfavorable
Contribution margin	550,800	581,400	30,600	Favorable
Fixed costs				
Manufacturing	201,600	201,600	0	
G, S, & A	90,000	90,000	0	
Net income	$ 259,200	$ 289,800	$30,600	Favorable

managers have little control over volume. Exceptions occur; for example, if poor production quality control leads to inferior goods that are difficult to sell, the production manager is responsible. The production manager is responsible for production delays that affect product availability, which may restrict sales volume. Under normal circumstances, however, the marketing campaign determines the volume of sales. Upper-level marketing managers develop the promotional program and create the sales plan; they are in the best position to explain why sales goals are or are not met. When marketing managers refer to **making the numbers,** they usually mean reaching the sales volume in the static (master) budget.

In the case of Melrose Manufacturing Company, the marketing manager not only achieved but also exceeded by 1,000 units the planned volume of sales. Exhibit 15.2 shows the activity variances resulting from the extra volume. At the standard price, the additional volume produces a favorable revenue variance of $80,000 (1,000 units × $80 per unit). The increase in volume also produces unfavorable variable cost variances. The net effect of producing and selling the additional 1,000 units is an increase of $30,600 in the contribution margin, a positive result. These preliminary results suggest that the marketing manager is to be commended. The analysis, however, is incomplete. For example, examining market share could reveal whether the manager won customers from competitors or whether the manager simply reaped the benefit of an unexpected industrywide increase in demand. The increase in sales volume could have been attained by reducing the sales price; the success of that strategy will be analyzed further in a later section of this chapter.

The unfavorable variable cost variances in Exhibit 15.2 are somewhat misleading because variable costs are, by definition, expected to increase as volume increases. In this case the unfavorable cost variances are more than offset by the favorable revenue variance, resulting in a higher contribution margin. The variable cost volume variances could be more appropriately labeled "expected" rather than unfavorable. However, the cost volume variances are described as unfavorable because actual cost is greater than planned cost.

Fixed Cost Considerations

The fixed costs are the same in both the static and flexible budgets. By definition, the budgeted amount of fixed costs remains unchanged regardless of the volume of activity. What insights can management gain by analyzing costs that don't change? Consider the *operating leverage* fixed costs provide. A small increase in sales volume can have a dramatic impact on profitability. Although the 1,000 unit volume variance represents only a 5.6 percent increase in revenue ($80,000 variance ÷ $1,440,000 static budget sales base), it produces an 11.8 percent increase in profitability ($30,600 variance ÷ $259,200 static budget net income base). To understand why profitability increased so dramatically, management should analyze the effect of fixed costs on the higher than expected sales volume.

Companies using a cost-plus pricing strategy must be concerned with differences between the planned and actual volume of activity. Because actual volume is unknown until the end of the year, selling prices must be based on planned volume. At the *planned volume* of activity of 18,000 units, Melrose's fixed cost per unit is expected to be as follows:

Fixed manufacturing cost	$201,600
Fixed G, S, & A cost	90,000
Total fixed cost	$291,600 ÷ 18,000 units = $16.20 per trophy

Based on the *actual volume* of 19,000 units, the fixed cost per unit is actually $15.35 per trophy ($291,600 ÷ 19,000 units). Because Melrose's prices were established using the $16.20 budgeted cost rather than the $15.35 actual cost, the trophies were overpriced, giving competitors a price advantage. Although Melrose sold more trophies than expected, sales volume might have been even greater if the trophies had been competitively priced.

Underpricing (not encountered by Melrose in this example) can also be detrimental. If planned volume is overstated, the estimated fixed cost per unit will be understated and prices will be set too low. When the higher amount of actual costs is subtracted from revenues, actual profits will be lower than expected. To avoid these negative consequences, companies that consider unit cost in pricing decisions must monitor volume variances closely.

The volume variance is *unfavorable* if actual volume is less than planned because cost per unit is higher than expected. Conversely, if actual volume is greater than planned, cost per unit is less than expected, resulting in a *favorable* variance. Both favorable and unfavorable variances can have negative consequences. Managers should strive for the greatest possible degree of accuracy.

Flexible Budget Variances

Compute and interpret flexible budget variances (differences between flexible budget and actual results).

For performance evaluation, management compares actual results to a flexible budget based on the *actual* volume of activity. Because the actual results and the flexible budget reflect the same volume of activity, any variances result from differences between standard and actual per unit amounts. To illustrate computing and analyzing flexible budget variances, we assume that Melrose's *actual* per unit amounts during 2006 were those shown in the following table. The 2006 per unit *standard* amounts are repeated here for your convenience.

	Standard	Actual
Sales price	$80.00	$78.00
Variable materials cost	12.00	11.78
Variable labor cost	16.80	17.25
Variable overhead cost	5.60	5.75

Actual and budgeted fixed costs are shown in Exhibit 15.3.

Exhibit 15.3 shows Melrose's 2006 flexible budget, actual results, and flexible budget variances. The flexible budget is the same one compared to the static budget in Exhibit 15.2. Recall the flexible budget amounts come from multiplying the standard per unit amounts by the actual volume of production. For example, the sales revenue in the flexible budget comes from multiplying the standard sales price by the actual volume ($80 × 19,000). The variable costs are similarly computed. The *actual results* are calculated by multiplying the actual per unit sales price and cost figures from the preceding table by the actual volume of activity. For example, the sales revenue in the Actual Results column comes from multiplying the actual sales price by the actual volume ($78 × 19,000 = $1,482,000). The actual cost figures are similarly computed. The differences between the flexible budget figures and the actual results are the **flexible budget variances.**

EXHIBIT 15.3

Flexible Budget Variances for Melrose Manufacturing Company

	Flexible Budget	Actual Results	Flexible Budget Variances	
Number of units	19,000	19,000	0	
Sales revenue	$1,520,000	$1,482,000	$38,000	Unfavorable
Variable manufacturing costs				
Materials	228,000	223,820	4,180	Favorable
Labor	319,200	327,750	8,550	Unfavorable
Overhead	106,400	109,250	2,850	Unfavorable
Variable G, S, & A	285,000	283,100	1,900	Favorable
Contribution margin	581,400	538,080	43,320	Unfavorable
Fixed costs				
Manufacturing	201,600	210,000	8,400	Unfavorable
G, S, & A	90,000	85,000	5,000	Favorable
Net income	$ 289,800	$ 243,080	$46,720	Unfavorable

Calculating the Sales Price Variance

Because both the flexible budget and actual results are based on the actual volume of activity, the flexible budget variance is attributable to sales price, not sales volume. In this case, the actual sales price of $78 per unit is less than the standard price of $80 per unit. Because Melrose sold its product for less than the standard sales price, the **sales price variance** is *unfavorable.* Even though the price variance is unfavorable, however, sales volume was 1,000 units more than expected. It is possible the marketing manager generated the additional volume by reducing the sales price. Whether the combination of lower sales price and higher sales volume is favorable or unfavorable depends on the amount of the unfavorable sales price variance versus the amount of the favorable sales volume variance. The *total* sales variance (price and volume) follows:

Actual sales (19,000 units × $78 per unit)	$1,482,000	
Expected sales (18,000 units × $80 per unit)	1,440,000	
Total sales variance	$ 42,000	Favorable

Alternatively,

Activity variance (i.e., sales volume)	$ 80,000	Favorable
Sales price variance	(38,000)	Unfavorable
Total sales variance	$ 42,000	Favorable

This analysis indicates that reducing the sales price had a favorable impact on *total* revenue. Use caution when interpreting variances as good or bad; in this instance, the unfavorable sales price variance was more than offset by the favorable volume variance. All unfavorable variances are not bad; all favorable variances are not good. Variances signal the need to investigate.

CHECK YOURSELF 15.2

Scott Company's master budget called for a planned sales volume of 30,000 units. Budgeted direct materials cost was $4 per unit. Scott actually produced and sold 32,000 units with an actual materials cost of $3.90 per unit. Determine the volume variance for materials cost and identify the organizational unit most likely responsible for this variance. Determine the flexible budget variance for materials cost and identify the organizational unit most likely responsible for this variance.

Answer

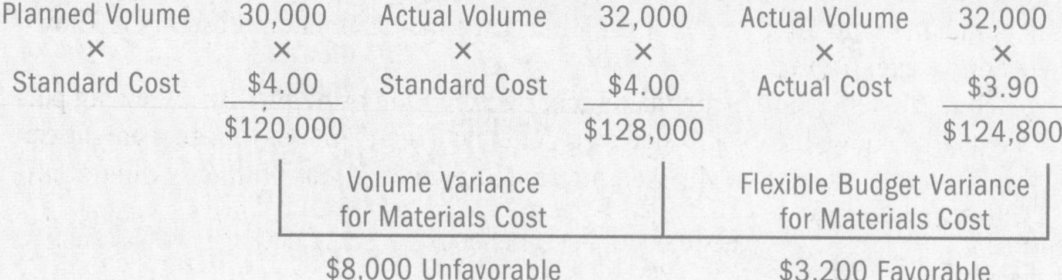

The materials volume variance is unfavorable because the materials cost ($128,000) is higher than was expected ($120,000). However, this could actually be positive because higher volume was probably caused by increasing sales. Further analysis would be necessary to determine whether the overall effect on the company's profitability was positive or negative. The marketing department is most likely to be responsible for the volume variance.

The flexible budget materials cost variance is favorable because the cost of materials was less than expected at the actual volume of activity. Either the production department (used less than the expected amount of materials) or the purchasing department (obtained materials at a favorable price) is most likely to be responsible for this variance.

Answers to The Curious Accountant

The management at **The Home Depot**, along with former CEO Bernie Marcus, understands that the environment in which a business operates changes and successful companies are willing to alter the way they do business to keep up with those changes. For example, in 2000, Home Depot had nine regional purchasing offices that operated independently. Mr. Nardelli consolidated these into one central office. This reduced the cost of ordering inventory—one purchase order is cheaper to process than nine—and it gave the company more power to negotiate lower prices from its suppliers.

One of Mr. Nardelli's changes was to implement a more detailed performance measurement system for each store. Among other things, this system allowed the company to reduce the amount of inventory it carries, thus saving the company the cost of financing that inventory.

The new CEO was willing to admit if a change did not work and to quickly make another change. His requirement to use more part-time employees led to some customer dissatisfaction, so it was revised.

To be fair, the drop in Home Depot's stock price had many causes. The stock price had grown rapidly over the years because the company had grown rapidly. However, the larger a company becomes, the harder it is to maintain a given growth rate. For example, if a company has only ten stores, it can open one new one and realize a ten percent growth rate. If the company has 1,000 stores, it must open 100 new stores to realize a ten percent growth rate. Furthermore, the economy in general was much weaker during 2001 and 2002 than it had been during the 1990s.

Even though Home Depot's stock price fell during Mr. Nardelli's first two years as CEO, its profit margins were up and its cash balance was up. Also, its sales increased by 27 percent from 2000 to 2002, and its earnings were up 42 percent.

Sources: Company disclosures, stock-market data, and Dan Morse, "A Hardware Chain Struggles to Adjust to a New Blueprint," *The Wall Street Journal*, January 17, 2003, pp. A-1 and A-6.

Need for Standards

As the previous discussion suggests, standards are the building blocks for preparing the static and flexible budgets. Standard costs help managers plan and also establish benchmarks against which actual performance can be judged. Highlighting differences between standard (expected) and actual performance focuses management attention on the areas of greatest need. Because management talent is a valuable and expensive resource, businesses cannot afford to have managers spend large amounts of time on operations that are functioning normally. Instead, managers should concentrate on areas not performing as expected. In other words, management should attend to the exceptions; this management philosophy is known as **management by exception.**

Standard setting fosters using the management by exception principle. By reviewing performance reports that show differences between actual and standard costs, management can focus its attention on the items that show significant variances. Areas with only minor variances need little or no review.

Managerial Performance Measurement

As previously discussed, managers are assigned responsibility for certain cost, profit, or investment centers. They are then evaluated based on how their centers perform relative to specific goals and objectives. The measurement techniques (variance analysis and contribution margin format income reporting) used for cost and profit centers have been discussed in this and previous chapters. The remainder of this chapter discusses performance measures for investment centers.

Return on Investment

Evaluate investment opportunities using the return on investment technique.

Society confers wealth, prestige, and power upon those who have control of assets. Unsurprisingly, managers are motivated to increase the amount of assets employed by the investment centers they control. When companies have additional assets available to invest, how do upper-level managers decide which centers should get them? The additional assets are frequently allotted to the managers who demonstrate the greatest potential for increasing the company's wealth. Companies often assess managerial potential by comparing the return on investment ratios of various investment centers. The **return on investment (ROI)** is the ratio of wealth generated (operating income) to the amount invested (operating assets) to generate the wealth. ROI is commonly expressed with the following equation.

$$\text{ROI} = \frac{\text{Operating income}}{\text{Operating assets}}$$

To illustrate using ROI for comparative evaluations, assume Panther Holding Company is a large corporation with three operating divisions. The following accounting data is from the records of each division:

	Lumber Manufacturing Division	Home Building Division	Furniture Manufacturing Division
Operating income	$ 60,000	$ 46,080	$ 81,940
Operating assets	300,000	256,000	482,000

The ROI for each division is:

$$\text{Lumber manufacturing:} \quad \frac{\text{Operating income}}{\text{Operating assets}} = \$60{,}000 \div \$300{,}000 = 20\%$$

$$\text{Home building:} \quad \frac{\text{Operating income}}{\text{Operating assets}} = \$46{,}080 \div \$256{,}000 = 18\%$$

$$\text{Furniture manufacturing:} \quad \frac{\text{Operating income}}{\text{Operating assets}} = \$81{,}940 \div \$482{,}000 = 17\%$$

All other things being equal, higher ROIs indicate better performance. In this case the Lumber Manufacturing Division manager is the best performer. Assume Panther obtains additional funding for expanding the company's operations. Which investment center is most likely to receive the additional funds?

If the manager of the Lumber Manufacturing Division convinces the upper level management team that his division would continue to outperform the other two divisions, the Lumber Manufacturing Division would most likely get the additional funding. The manager of the lumber division would then invest the funds in additional operating assets which would in turn increase the division's operating income. As the division prospers, Panther would reward the manager for exceptional performance. Rewarding the manager of the lumber division would likely motivate the other managers to improve their divisional ROIs. Internal competition would improve the performance of the company as a whole.

CHECK YOURSELF 15.3

Green View is a lawn services company whose operations are divided into two districts. The District 1 manager controls $12,600,000 of operating assets. District 1 produced $1,512,000 of operating income during the year. The District 2 manager controls $14,200,000 of operating assets. District 2 reported $1,988,000 of operating income for the same period. Use return on investment to determine which manager is performing better.

Answer

District 1

ROI = Operating income ÷ Operating assets = $1,512,000 ÷ $12,600,000 = 12%

District 2

ROI = Operating income ÷ Operating assets = $1,988,000 ÷ $14,200,000 = 14%

Because the higher ROI indicates the better performance, the District 2 manager is the superior performer. This conclusion is based solely on quantitative results. In real-world practice, companies also consider qualitative factors.

Qualitative Considerations

Why do companies compute ROI using operating income and operating assets instead of using net income and total assets? Suppose Panther's corporate headquarters closes a furniture manufacturing plant because an economic downturn temporarily reduces the demand for furniture. It would be inappropriate to include these nonoperating plant assets in the denominator of the ROI computation. Similarly, if Panther sells the furniture plant and realizes a large gain on the sale, including the gain in the numerator of the ROI formula would distort the result. Since the manager of the Furniture Manufacturing Division does not control closing the plant or selling it, it is unreasonable to include the effects of these decisions in computing the ROI. These items would, however, be included in computing net income and total assets. Most companies use operating income and operating assets to compute ROI because those variables measure performance more accurately.

Factors Affecting Return on Investment

Management can gain insight into performance by dividing the ROI formula into two separate ratios as follows:

$$\text{ROI} = \frac{\text{Operating income}}{\text{Sales}} \times \frac{\text{Sales}}{\text{Operating assets}}$$

The first ratio on the right side of the equation is called the margin. The **margin** is a measure of management's ability to control operating expenses relative to the level of sales. In general, high margins indicate superior performance. Management can increase the margin by reducing the level of operating expenses necessary to generate sales. Decreasing operating expenses increases profitability.

The second ratio in the expanded ROI formula is called turnover. **Turnover** is a measure of the amount of operating assets employed to support the achieved level of sales. Operating assets are scarce resources. To maximize profitability, they must be used wisely. Just as excessive expenses decrease profitability, excessive investments in operating assets also limit profitability.

Both the short and expanded versions of the ROI formula produce the same end result. To illustrate, we will use the ROI for the Lumber Manufacturing Division of Panther Holding Company. Recall that the division employed $300,000 of operating assets to produce $60,000 of operating income, resulting in the following ROI:

$$\text{ROI} = \frac{\text{Operating income}}{\text{Operating assets}} = \frac{\$60{,}000}{\$300{,}000} = 20\%$$

Further analysis of the accounting records indicates the Lumber Manufacturing Division had sales of \$600,000. The following computation demonstrates that the expanded ROI formula produces the same result as the short formula:

$$\begin{aligned} \text{ROI} &= \text{Margin} \times \text{Turnover} \\ &= \frac{\text{Operating income}}{\text{Sales}} \times \frac{\text{Sales}}{\text{Operating assets}} \\ &= \frac{\$60{,}000}{\$600{,}000} \times \frac{\$600{,}000}{\$300{,}000} \\ &= .10 \times 2 \\ &= 20\% \end{aligned}$$

The \$60,000 of funds released by reducing the operating assets can be returned to headquarters or be reinvested by LMD depending on the opportunities available.

The benefits of increasing the *margin* by increasing sales or reducing expenses are intuitive. They are so obvious that, in their zeal to increase margins, managers for many years overlooked the effect of *turnover*. Growing use of the ROI ratio has alerted managers to the benefits of controlling operating assets as well as expenses. Because ROI blends many aspects of managerial performance into a single ratio that enables comparisons between companies, comparisons between investment centers within companies, and comparisons between different investment opportunities within an investment center, ROI has gained widespread acceptance as a performance measure.

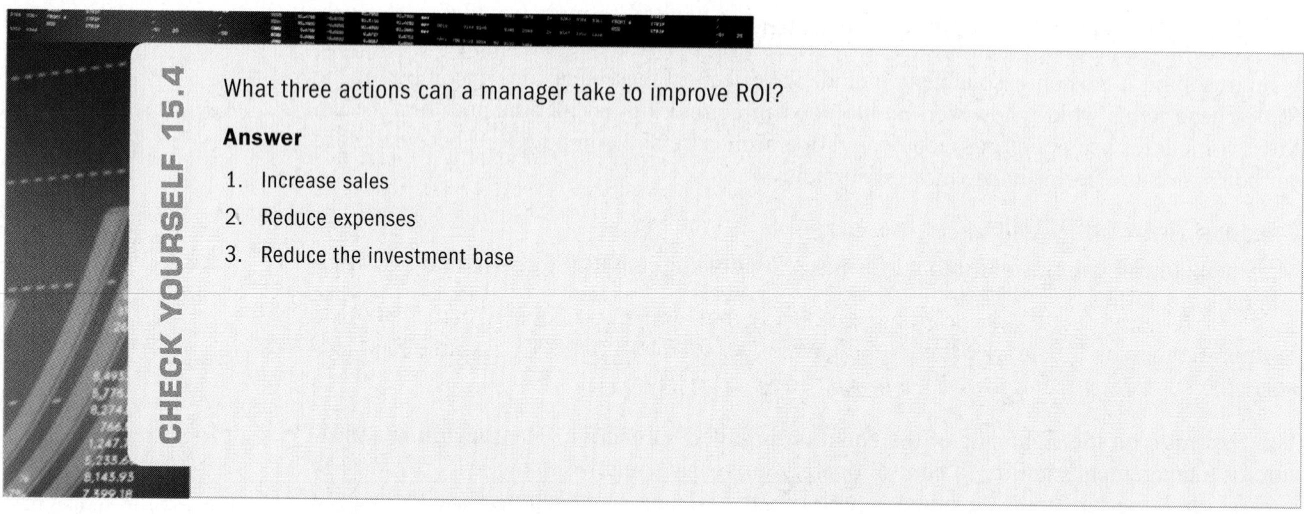

CHECK YOURSELF 15.4

What three actions can a manager take to improve ROI?

Answer

1. Increase sales
2. Reduce expenses
3. Reduce the investment base

Residual Income

LO 9

Evaluate investment opportunities using the residual income technique.

Suppose Panther Holding Company evaluates the manager of the Lumber Manufacturing Division (LMD) based on his ability to maximize ROI. The corporation's overall ROI is approximately 18 percent. LMD, however, has consistently outperformed the other investment centers. Its ROI is currently 20 percent. Now suppose the manager has an opportunity to invest additional funds in a project likely to earn a 19 percent ROI. Would the manager accept the investment opportunity?

These circumstances place the manager in an awkward position. The corporation would benefit from the project because the expected ROI of 19 percent is higher than the corporate average ROI of 18 percent. Personally, however, the manager would suffer from accepting the project because it would reduce the division ROI to less than the current 20 percent. The

FOCUS ON INTERNATIONAL ISSUES

DO MANAGERS IN DIFFERENT COUNTRIES STRESS THE SAME PERFORMANCE MEASURES?

Companies operating in different countries frequently choose different performance measures to evaluate their managers. For example, although U.S. companies tend to favor some form of return on investment (ROI), Japanese companies tend to emphasize return on sales (ROS) as a primary measure of financial performance.* In general, the Japanese assume a constant sales price, thereby requiring a reduction in cost or an increase in volume to generate an increase in ROS. This approach is consistent with the Japanese orientation toward long-term growth and profitability. In contrast, the majority of U.S. companies focus on ROI, which encourages and emphasizes short-term profitability. U.S. firms were at one time criticized for their emphasis on short-term profitability, but the more entrenched style of Japanese companies has hindered their ability to adapt to changing times. As a result, many Japanese companies have begun to reevaluate their management philosophy and the corresponding measures of performance. Even so, in a world filled with diversity, managers will likely continue to stress performance measures that reflect a variety of social customs.

*Robert S. Kaplan, "Measures for Manufacturing Excellence," *Emerging Practices in Cost Management* in WG&L Corporate Finance Network Database, 1998.

manager is forced to choose between his personal best interests and the best interests of the corporation. When faced with decisions such as these, many managers choose to benefit themselves at the expense of their corporations, a condition described as **suboptimization.**

To avoid *suboptimization*, many businesses base managerial evaluation on **residual income.** This approach measures a manager's ability to maximize earnings above some targeted level. The targeted level of earnings is based on a minimum desired ROI. Residual income is calculated as follows:

$$\text{Residual income} = \text{Operating income} - (\text{Operating assets} \times \text{Desired ROI})$$

To illustrate, recall that LMD currently earns $60,000 of operating income with the $300,000 of operating assets it controls. ROI is 20 percent ($60,000 ÷ $300,000). Assume Panther's desired ROI is 18 percent. LMD's residual income is therefore:

$$\begin{aligned}\text{Residual income} &= \text{Operating income} - (\text{Operating assets} \times \text{Desired ROI})\\ &= \$60{,}000 - (\$300{,}000 \times .18)\\ &= \$60{,}000 - \$54{,}000\\ &= \$6{,}000\end{aligned}$$

Now assume that Panther Holding Company has $50,000 of additional funds available to invest. Because LMD consistently performs at a high level, Panther's corporate management team offers the funds to the LMD manager. The manager believes he could invest the additional $50,000 at a 19 percent rate of return.

If the LMD manager's evaluation is based solely on ROI, he is likely to reject the additional funding because investing the funds at 19 percent would lower his overall ROI. If the LMD manager's evaluation is based on residual income, however, he is likely to accept the funds because an additional investment at 19 percent would increase his residual income as follows:

$$\begin{aligned}\text{Operating income} &= \$50{,}000 \times .19\\ &= \$9{,}500\end{aligned}$$

REALITY BYTES

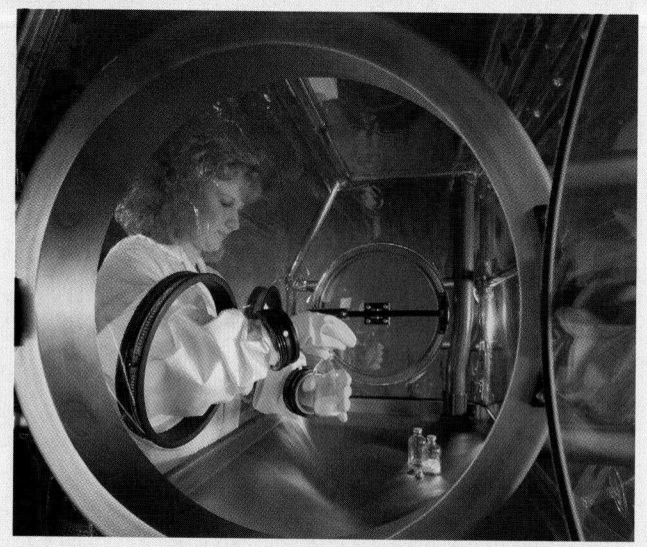

In recent years the residual income approach has been refined to produce a new technique called economic value added (EVA). EVA was developed and trademarked by the consulting firm Stern Stewart & Co. EVA uses the basic formula behind residual income [Operating income − (Operating assets × Desired ROI)]. EVA, however, uses different definitions of operating income and operating assets. For example, research and development (R&D) costs are classified as operating assets under EVA. In contrast, R&D costs are classified as expenses under traditional accounting. As a result, operating assets and operating income are higher under EVA than they are under the residual income approach. There are more than 100 such differences between EVA and residual income. However, most companies make only a few adjustments when converting from the residual income approach to EVA. Even so, these refinements seem to have had significant benefits. In a recent article in *Fortune* magazine, Shawn Tully concluded, "Managers who run their businesses according to the precepts of EVA have hugely increased the value of their companies. Investors who know about EVA, and know which companies are employing it, have grown rich."

$$\begin{aligned}\text{Residual income} &= \text{Operating income} - (\text{Operating assets} \times \text{Desired ROI})\\ &= \$9{,}500 - (\$50{,}000 \times .18)\\ &= \$9{,}500 - \$9{,}000\\ &= \$500\end{aligned}$$

Accepting the new project would add $500 to LMD's residual income. If the manager of LMD is evaluated based on his ability to maximize residual income, he would benefit by investing in any project that returns an ROI in excess of the desired 18 percent. The reduction in LMD's overall ROI does not enter into the decision. The residual income approach solves the problem of suboptomization.

The primary disadvantage of the residual income approach is that it measures performance in absolute dollars. As a result, a manager's residual income may be larger simply because her investment base is larger rather than because her performance is superior.

To illustrate, return to the example where Panther Holding Company has $50,000 of additional funds to invest. Assume the manager of the Lumber Manufacturing Division (LMD) and the manager of the Furniture Manufacturing Division (FMD) each have investment opportunities expected to earn a 19 percent return. Recall that Panther's desired ROI is 18 percent. If corporate headquarters allots $40,000 of the funds to the manager of LMD and $10,000 to the manager of FMD, the increase in residual income earned by each division is as follows:

$$\text{LMD's Residual income} = (\$40{,}000 \times .19) - (\$40{,}000 \times .18) = \$400$$

$$\text{FMD's Residual income} = (\$10{,}000 \times .19) - (\$10{,}000 \times .18) = \$100$$

Does LMD's higher residual income mean LMD's manager is outperforming FMD's manager? No. It means LMD's manager received more operating assets than FMD's manager received.

CHECK YOURSELF 15.5

Young Company's desired rate of return is 14 percent. Christina Fallin, manager of Young's northeastern investment center, controls $12,600,000 of operating assets. During the most recent year, Fallin's district produced operating income of $1,839,600. Determine the amount of the northeastern investment center's residual income.

Answer

Residual income = Operating income − (Operating assets × Desired ROI)

Residual income = $1,839,600 − ($12,600,000 × 0.14) = $75,600

Responsibility Accounting and the Balanced Scorecard

Throughout the text we have discussed many financial measures companies use to evaluate managerial performance. Examples include standard cost systems to evaluate cost center managers; the contribution margin income statement to evaluate profit center managers; and ROI/residual income to evaluate the performance of investment center managers. Many companies may have goals and objectives such as "satisfaction guaranteed" or "we try harder" that are more suitably evaluated using nonfinancial measures. To assess how well they accomplish the full range of their missions, many companies use a *balanced scorecard.*

A **balanced scorecard** includes financial and nonfinancial performance measures. Standard costs, income measures, ROI, and residual income are common financial measures used in a balanced scorecard. Nonfinancial measures include defect rates, cycle time, on-time deliveries, number of new products or innovations, safety measures, and customer satisfaction surveys. Many companies compose their scorecards to highlight leading versus lagging measures. For example, customer satisfaction survey data is a leading indicator of the sales growth which is a lagging measure. The balanced scorecard is a holistic approach to evaluating managerial performance. It is gaining widespread acceptance among world-class companies.

A Look Back <<

The practice of delegating authority and responsibility is referred to as *decentralization.* Clear lines of authority and responsibility are essential in establishing a responsibility accounting system. In a responsibility accounting system, segment managers are held accountable for profits based on the amount of control they have over the profits in their segment.

Responsibility reports are used to compare actual results with budgets. The reports should be simple with variances highlighted to promote the *management by exception* doctrine. Individual managers should be held responsible only for those revenues or costs they control. Each manager should receive only summary information about the performance of the responsibility centers under her supervision.

A *responsibility center* is the point in an organization where control over revenue or expense is located. *Cost centers* are segments that incur costs but do not generate revenues. *Profit centers* incur costs and also generate revenues, producing a measurable profit. *Investment centers* incur costs, generate revenues, and use identifiable capital investments.

One of the primary purposes of responsibility accounting is to evaluate managerial performance. Comparing actual results with standards and budgets and calculating *return on investment* are used for this purpose. Because return on investment uses revenues, expenses, and investment, problems with measuring these parameters must be considered. The return on investment can be analyzed in terms of the margin earned on sales as well as the turnover (asset utilization) during the period. The *residual income approach* is sometimes used to avoid *suboptimization*, which occurs when managers choose to reject investment projects that would benefit their company's ROI but would reduce their investment center's ROI. The residual income approach evaluates managers based on their ability to generate earnings above some targeted level of earnings.

>> A Look Forward

The next chapter expands on the concepts in this chapter. You will see how managers select investment opportunities that will affect their future ROIs. You will learn to apply present value techniques to compute the net present value and the internal rate of return for potential investment opportunities. You will also learn to use less sophisticated analytical techniques such as payback and the unadjusted rate of return.

SELF-STUDY REVIEW PROBLEM 1

Bugout Pesticides Inc. established the following standard price and costs for a termite control product that it sells to exterminators.

Variable price and cost data (per unit)	Standard	Actual
Sales price	$52.00	$49.00
Materials cost	10.00	10.66
Labor cost	12.00	11.90
Overhead cost	7.00	7.05
General, selling, and administrative (G, S, & A) cost	8.00	7.92
Expected fixed costs (in total)		
Manufacturing	$150,000	$140,000
General, selling, and administrative	60,000	64,000

The 2006 master budget was established at an expected volume of 25,000 units. Actual production and sales volume for the year was 26,000 units.

Required

a. Prepare the pro forma income statement for Bugout's 2006 master budget.
b. Prepare a flexible budget income statement at the actual volume.
c. Determine the sales activity (volume) variances and indicate whether they are favorable or unfavorable. Comment on how Bugout would use the variances to evaluate performance.
d. Determine the flexible budget variances and indicate whether they are favorable or unfavorable.
e. Identify the two variances Bugout is most likely to analyze further. Explain why you chose these two variances. Who is normally responsible for the variances you chose to investigate?

Solution to Requirements *a, b,* and *c*

Number of units		25,000	26,000	
	Per Unit Standards	Master Budget	Flexible Budget	Volume Variances
Sales revenue	$52	$1,300,000	$1,352,000	$52,000 F
Variable manufacturing costs				
Materials	10	(250,000)	(260,000)	10,000 U
Labor	12	(300,000)	(312,000)	12,000 U
Overhead	7	(175,000)	(182,000)	7,000 U
Variable G, S, & A	8	(200,000)	(208,000)	8,000 U
Contribution margin		375,000	390,000	15,000 F
Fixed costs				
Manufacturing		(150,000)	(150,000)	0
G, S, & A		(60,000)	(60,000)	0
Net income		$ 165,000	$ 180,000	$15,000 F

The sales activity variances are useful in determining how changes in sales volume affect revenues and costs. Since the flexible budget is based on standard prices and costs, the variances do not provide insight into differences between standard prices and costs versus actual prices and costs.

Solution to Requirement *d*

Number of units		26,000	26,000	
	Actual Unit Price/Cost	Flexible Budget*	Actual Results	Flexible Budget Variances
Sales revenue	$49.00	$1,352,000	$1,274,000	$78,000 U
Variable manufacturing costs				
Materials	10.66	(260,000)	(277,160)	17,160 U
Labor	11.90	(312,000)	(309,400)	2,600 F
Overhead	7.05	(182,000)	(183,300)	1,300 U
Variable G, S, & A	7.92	(208,000)	(205,920)	2,080 F
Contribution margin		390,000	298,220	91,780 U
Fixed costs				
Manufacturing		(150,000)	(140,000)	10,000 F
G, S, & A		(60,000)	(64,000)	4,000 U
Net income		$ 180,000	$ 94,220	$85,780 U

*The price and cost data for the flexible budget come from the previous table.

Solution to Requirement *e*

The management by exception doctrine focuses attention on the sales price variance and the materials variance. The two variances are material in size and are generally under the control of management. Upper-level marketing managers are responsible for the sales price variance. These managers are normally responsible for establishing the sales price. In this case, the actual sales price is less than the planned sales price, resulting in an unfavorable flexible budget variance. Mid-level production supervisors and purchasing agents are normally responsible for the materials cost variance. This variance could have been caused by waste or by paying more for materials than the standard price.

SELF-STUDY REVIEW PROBLEM 2

The following financial statements apply to Hola Division, one of three investment centers operated by Costa Corporation. Costa Corporation has a desired rate of return of 15 percent. Costa Corporation Headquarters has $80,000 of additional operating assets to assign to the investment centers.

HOLA DIVISION Income Statement For the Year Ended December 31, 2006	
Sales Revenue	$78,695
Cost of Goods Sold	(50,810)
Gross Margin	27,885
Operating Expenses	
Selling Expenses	(1,200)
Depreciation Expense	(1,125)
Operating Income	25,560
Nonoperating Expense	
Loss on Sale of Land	(3,200)
Net Income	$22,360

HOLA DIVISION Balance Sheet As of December 31, 2006	
Assets	
Cash	$ 8,089
Accounts Receivable	22,870
Merchandise Inventory	33,460
Equipment Less Acc. Dep.	77,581
Nonoperating Assets	8,250
Total Assets	$150,250
Liabilities	
Accounts Payable	$ 5,000
Notes Payable	58,000
Stockholders' Equity	
Common Stock	55,000
Retained Earnings	32,250
Total Liab. and Stk. Equity	$150,250

Required

a. Should Costa use operating income or net income to determine the rate of return (ROI) for the Hola investment center? Explain.

b. Should Costa use operating assets or total assets to determine the ROI for the Hola investment center? Explain.

c. Calculate the ROI for Hola.

d. The manager of the Hola division has an opportunity to invest the funds at an ROI of 17 percent. The other two divisions have investment opportunities that yield only 16 percent. The manager of Hola rejects the additional funding. Why would the manager of Hola reject the funds under these circumstances?

e. Calculate the residual income from the investment opportunity available to Hola and explain how residual income could be used to encourage the manager to accept the additional funds.

Solution to Requirement *a*

Costa should use operating income because net income frequently includes items over which management has no control, such as the loss on sale of land.

Solution to Requirement *b*

Costa should use operating assets because total assets frequently includes items over which management has no control, such as assets not currently in use.

Solution to Requirement *c*

ROI = Operating Income/Operating Assets = $25,560/$142,000 = 18%

Solution to Requirement *d*

Since the rate of return on the investment opportunity (17 percent) is below Hola's current ROI (18 percent), accepting the opportunity would decrease Hola's average ROI, which would have a negative effect on the manager's performance evaluation. While it is to the advantage of the company as a whole for Hola to accept the investment opportunity, it will reflect negatively on the manager to do so. This phenomenon is called *suboptimization.*

Solution to Requirement *e*

Operating income from the investment opportunity is $13,600 ($80,000 × .17)

Residual income = Operating income − (Operating assets × Desired ROI)

Residual income = $13,600 − ($80,000 × .15)

Residual income = $13,600 − $12,000

Residual income = $1,600

Since the investment opportunity would increase Hola's residual income, the acceptance of the opportunity would improve the manager's performance evaluation, thereby motivating the manager to accept it.

KEY TERMS

balanced scorecard 535
controllability concept 523
cost center 522
decentralization 522
favorable variance 525
flexible budget 523
flexible budget variance 527
investment center 523
making the numbers 526
management by exception 529
margin 531
profit center 522
residual income 533
responsibility accounting 522
responsibility center 522
return on investment 530
sales price variance 528
sales volume variance 525
static budget 523
suboptimization 533
turnover 531
unfavorable variance 525
variances 525

QUESTIONS

1. Pam Kelly says she has no faith in budgets. Her company, Kelly Manufacturing Corporation, spent thousands of dollars to install a sophisticated budget system. One year later the company's expenses are still out of control. She believes budgets simply do not work. How would you respond to Ms. Kelly's beliefs?
2. What is a responsibility center?
3. What are the three types of responsibility centers? Explain how each differs from the others.
4. What is the difference between a static budget and a flexible budget? When is each used?
5. When the operating costs for Bill Smith's production department were released, he was sure that he would be getting a raise. His costs were $20,000 less than the planned cost in the master budget. His supervisor informed him that the results look good but that a more in-depth analysis is necessary before raises can be assigned. What other considerations could Mr. Smith's supervisor be interested in before she rates his performance?
6. When are sales and cost variances favorable and unfavorable?
7. Joan Mason, the marketing manager for a large manufacturing company, believes her unfavorable sales volume variance is the responsibility of the production department. What production circumstances that she does not control could have been responsible for her poor performance?

8. When would variable cost volume variances be expected to be unfavorable? How should unfavorable variable cost volume variances be interpreted?
9. What factors could lead to an increase in sales revenues that would not merit congratulations to the marketing manager?
10. With respect to fixed costs, what are the consequences of the actual volume of activity exceeding the planned volume?
11. How are flexible budget variances determined? What causes these variances?
12. Minnie Divers, the manager of the marketing department for one of the industry's leading retail businesses, has been notified by the accounting department that her department experienced an unfavorable sales volume variance in the preceding period but a favorable sales price variance. Based on these contradictory results, how would you interpret her overall performance as suggested by her variances?
13. How do variance reports promote the management by exception doctrine?
14. Carmen Douglas claims that her company's performance evaluation system is unfair. Her company uses return on investment (ROI) to evaluate performance. Ms. Douglas says that even though her ROI is lower than another manager's, her performance is far superior. Is it possible that Ms. Douglas is correct? Explain your position.
15. What two factors affect the computation of return on investment?
16. What three ways can a manager increase the return on investment?
17. How can a residual income approach to performance evaluation reduce the likelihood of sub-optimization?
18. Is it true that the manager with the highest residual income is always the best performer?

EXERCISES

All Exercises are available with McGraw-Hill's Homework Manager

L.O. 5

Exercise 15-1 *Classifying variances as favorable or unfavorable*

Required

Indicate whether each of the following variances is favorable or unfavorable. The first one has been done as an example.

Item to Classify	Standard	Actual	Type of Variance
Sales volume	40,000 units	42,000 units	Favorable
Sales price	$3.60 per unit	$3.63 per unit	
Materials cost	$2.90 per pound	$3.00 per pound	
Materials usage	91,000 pounds	90,000 pounds	
Labor cost	$10.00 per hour	$9.60 per hour	
Labor usage	61,000 hours	61,800 hours	
Fixed cost spending	$400,000	$390,000	
Fixed cost per unit (volume)	$3.20 per unit	$3.16 per unit	

L.O. 5

Exercise 15-2 *Determining amount and type (favorable vs. unfavorable) of variance*

Required

Compute variances for the following items and indicate whether each variance is favorable (F) or unfavorable (U).

Item	Budget	Actual	Variance	F or U
Sales revenue	$490,000	$506,000		
Cost of goods sold	$385,000	$360,000		
Material purchases at 5,000 pounds	$275,000	$280,000		
Materials usage	$180,000	$178,000		
Sales price	$500	$489		
Production volume	950 units	900 units		
Wages at 4,000 hours	$60,000	$58,700		
Labor usage at $16 per hour	$96,000	$97,000		
Research and development expense	$22,000	$25,000		
Selling and administrative expenses	$49,000	$40,000		

Exercise 15-3 ***Preparing master and flexible budgets*** L.O. 4

Burrel Manufacturing Company established the following standard price and cost data.

Sales price	$7.50 per unit
Variable manufacturing cost	3.00 per unit
Fixed manufacturing cost	3,000 total
Fixed selling and administrative cost	1,200 total

Burrel planned to produce and sell 1,100 units. Actual production and sales amounted to 1,200 units.

Required

a. Prepare the pro forma income statement in contribution format that would appear in a master budget.

b. Prepare the pro forma income statement in contribution format that would appear in a flexible budget.

Exercise 15-4 ***Determining sales volume variances*** L.O. 6

Required

Use the information provided in Exercise 15-3.

a. Determine the sales volume variances.

b. Classify the variances as favorable (F) or unfavorable (U).

c. Comment on the usefulness of the variances with respect to performance evaluation and identify the member of the management team most likely to be responsible for these variances.

d. Explain why the fixed cost variances are zero.

e. Determine the fixed cost per unit based on planned activity and the fixed cost per unit based on actual activity. Assuming Burrel uses information in the master budget to price the company's product, comment on how the volume variance could affect the company's profitability.

Exercise 15-5 ***Determining flexible budget variances*** L.O. 7

Use the standard price and cost data provided in Exercise 15-3. Assume that the actual sales price is $7.20 per unit and that the actual variable cost is $3.10 per unit. The actual fixed manufacturing cost is $2,850, and the actual selling and administrative expenses are $1,275.

Required

a. Determine the flexible budget variances.

b. Classify the variances as favorable (F) or unfavorable (U).

c. Comment on the usefulness of the variances with respect to performance evaluation and identify the member(s) of the management team who is (are) most likely to be responsible for these variances.

Exercise 15-6 ***Using a flexible budget to accommodate market uncertainty*** L.O. 7

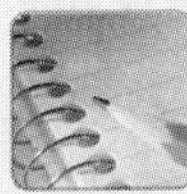

According to its original plan, Katta Consulting Services Company would charge its customers for service at $200 per hour in 2006. The company president expects consulting services provided to customers to reach 40,000 hours at that rate. The marketing manager, however, argues that actual results may range from 35,000 hours to 45,000 hours because of market uncertainty. Katta's standard variable cost is $90 per hour, and its standard fixed cost is $3,000,000.

Required

Develop flexible budgets based on the assumptions of service levels at 35,000 hours, 40,000 hours, and 45,000 hours.

L.O. 6, 7

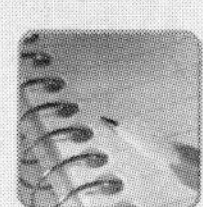

Exercise 15-7 *Evaluating a decision to increase sales volume by lowering sales price*

Rauch Educational Services had budgeted its training service charge at $80 per hour. The company planned to provide 40,000 hours of training services during 2007. By reducing the service charge to $70 per hour, the company was able to increase the actual number of hours to 42,000.

Required

a. Determine the sales volume variance, and indicate whether it is favorable (F) or unfavorable (U).

b. Determine the flexible budget variance, and indicate whether it is favorable (F) or unfavorable (U).

c. Did reducing the price of training services increase profitability? Explain.

L.O. 6

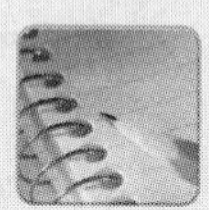

Exercise 15-8 *Responsibility for sales volume variance*

Holbrook Company expected to sell 400,000 of its pagers during 2006. It set the standard sales price for the pager at $30 each. During June, it became obvious that the company would be unable to attain the expected volume of sales. Holbrook's chief competitor, Coker, Inc., had lowered prices and was pulling market share from Holbrook. To be competitive, Holbrook matched Coker's price, lowering its sales price to $28 per pager. Coker responded by lowering its price even further to $24 per pager. In an emergency meeting of key personnel, Holbrook's accountant, Vickie Dees, stated, "Our cost structure simply won't support a sales price in the $24 range." The production manager, Jean Volker, said, "I don't understand why I'm here. The only unfavorable variance on my report is a fixed cost volume variance and that one is not my fault. We can't be making the product if the marketing department isn't selling it."

Required

a. Describe a scenario in which the production manager is responsible for the fixed cost volume variance.

b. Describe a scenario in which the marketing manager is responsible for the fixed cost volume variance.

c. Explain how a decline in sales volume would affect Holbrook's ability to lower its sales price.

L.O. 4

Exercise 15-9 *Income statement for internal use*

Geis Company has provided the following 2005 data.

Budget	
Sales	$408,000
Variable product costs	164,000
Variable selling expense	48,000
Other variable expenses	4,000
Fixed product costs	16,800
Fixed selling expense	25,200
Other fixed expenses	2,400
Interest expense	900
Variances	
Sales	8,800 U
Variable product costs	4,000 F
Variable selling expense	2,400 U
Other variable expenses	1,200 U
Fixed product costs	240 F
Fixed selling expense	400 F
Other fixed expenses	160 U
Interest expense	100 F

Required

Prepare in good form a budgeted and actual income statement for internal use. Separate operating income from net income in the statements.

Exercise 15-10 *Evaluating a cost center including flexible budgeting concepts*

L.O. 4

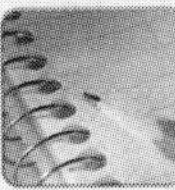

Herrera Medical Equipment Company makes a blood pressure measuring kit. Cedric Major is the production manager. The production department's static budget and actual results for 2005 follow.

	Static Budget	Actual Results
	20,000 kits	*21,000 kits*
Direct materials	$150,000	$161,700
Direct labor	135,000	138,600
Variable manufacturing overhead	35,000	44,600
Total variable costs	320,000	344,900
Fixed manufacturing cost	180,000	178,000
Total manufacturing cost	$500,000	$522,900

Required

a. Convert the static budget into a flexible budget.

b. Use the flexible budget to evaluate Mr. Major's performance.

c. Explain why Mr. Major's performance evaluation does not include sales revenue and net income.

Exercise 15-11 *Evaluating a profit center*

L.O. 2, 3

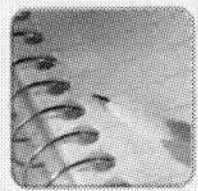

Shelia Parham, the president of Best Toys Corporation, is trying to determine this year's pay raises for the store managers. Best Toys has seven stores in the southwestern United States. Corporate headquarters purchases all toys from different manufacturers globally and distributes them to individual stores. Additionally, headquarters makes decisions regarding location and size of stores. These practices allow Best Toys to receive volume discounts from vendors and to implement coherent marketing strategies. Within a set of general guidelines, store managers have the flexibility to adjust product prices and hire local employees. Ms. Parham is considering three possible performance measures for evaluating the individual stores: cost of goods sold, return on sales (net income divided by sales), and return on investment.

Required

a. Using the concept of controllability, advise Ms. Parham about the best performance measure.

b. Explain how a balanced scorecard can be used to help Ms. Parham.

Exercise 15-12 *Return on investment*

L.O. 8

An investment center of Milton Corporation shows an operating income of $7,200 on total operating assets of $30,000.

Required

Compute the return on investment.

Exercise 15-13 *Return on investment*

L.O. 8

Giddens Company calculated its return on investment as 15 percent. Sales are now $180,000, and the amount of total operating assets is $300,000.

Required

a. If expenses are reduced by $18,000 and sales remain unchanged, what return on investment will result?

b. If both sales and expenses cannot be changed, what change in the amount of operating assets is required to achieve the same result?

L.O. 9

Exercise 15-14 *Residual income*

Tyler Corporation has a desired rate of return of 10 percent. Andy Tan is in charge of one of Tyler's three investment centers. His center controlled operating assets of $3,000,000 that were used to earn $390,000 of operating income.

Required

Compute Mr. Tan's residual income.

L.O. 9

Exercise 15-15 *Residual income*

Brannon Cough Drops operates two divisions. The following information pertains to each division for 2005.

	Division A	Division B
Sales	$180,000	$60,000
Operating income	$ 18,000	$ 9,600
Average operating assets	$ 72,000	$48,000
Company's desired rate of return	20%	20%

Required

a. Compute each division's residual income.

b. Which division increased the company's profitability more?

L.O. 8, 9

Exercise 15-16 *Return on investment and residual income*

Required

Supply the missing information in the following table for Haley Company.

Sales	$300,000
ROI	?
Operating assets	?
Operating income	?
Turnover	2
Residual income	?
Margin	0.10
Desired rate of return	18%

L.O. 8, 9

Exercise 15-17 *Comparing return on investment with residual income*

The Spokane Division of Cascade Inc. has a current ROI of 20 percent. The company target ROI is 15 percent. The Spokane Division has an opportunity to invest $4,000,000 at 18 percent but is reluctant to do so because its ROI will fall to 19.2 percent. The present investment base for the division is $6,000,000.

Required

Demonstrate how Cascade can motivate the Spokane Division to make the investment by using the residual income method.

PROBLEMS

All Problems are available with McGraw-Hill's Homework Manager

L.O. 4, 6

CHECK FIGURES

a. NI = $81,000

b. NI at 29,000 units: $72,000

Problem 15-18 *Determining sales volume variances*

Tolbert Publications established the following standard price and costs for a hardcover picture book that the company produces.

Standard price and variable costs	
Sales price	$36.00
Materials cost	9.00
Labor cost	4.50
Overhead cost	6.30
General, selling, and administrative costs	7.20
Planned fixed costs	
Manufacturing	$135,000
General, selling, and administrative	54,000

Tolbert planned to make and sell 30,000 copies of the book.

Required

a. Prepare the pro forma income statement that would appear in the master budget.

b. Prepare flexible budget income statements, assuming production volumes of 29,000 and 31,000 units.

c. Determine the sales volume variances, assuming production and sales volume are actually 31,000 units.

d. Indicate whether the variances are favorable (F) or unfavorable (U).

e. Comment on how Tolbert could use the variances to evaluate performance.

Problem 15-19 *Determining and interpreting flexible budget variances*

L.O. 7

CHECK FIGURE
Flexible budget variance of NI: $20,450 U

Use the standard price and cost data supplied in Problem 15-18. Assume that Tolbert actually produced and sold 31,000 books. The actual sales price and costs incurred follow.

Actual price and variable costs	
Sales price	$35.00
Materials cost	9.20
Labor cost	4.40
Overhead cost	6.35
General, selling, and administrative costs	7.00
Actual fixed costs	
Manufacturing	$120,000
General, selling, and administrative	60,000

Required

a. Determine the flexible budget variances.

b. Indicate whether each variance is favorable (F) or unfavorable (U).

c. Identify the management position responsible for each variance. Explain what could have caused the variance.

Problem 15-20 *Flexible budget planning*

L.O. 4

mhhe.com/edmonds2007

CHECK FIGURES
a. NI = $180,000
c. NI = $162,500

Tommie Okes, the president of Star Computer Services, needs your help. He wonders about the potential effects on the firm's net income if he changes the service rate that the firm charges its customers. The following basic data pertain to fiscal year 2007.

Standard rate and variable costs	
Service rate per hour	$80.00
Labor cost	40.00
Overhead cost	7.20
General, selling, and administrative cost	4.30
Expected fixed costs	
Facility repair	$525,000.00
General, selling, and administrative	150,000.00

Required

a. Prepare the pro forma income statement that would appear in the master budget if the firm expects to provide 30,000 hours of services in 2007.

b. A marketing consultant suggests to Mr. Okes that the service rate may affect the number of service hours that the firm can achieve. According to the consultant's analysis, if Star charges customers $75 per hour, the firm can achieve 38,000 hours of services. Prepare a flexible budget using the consultant's assumption.

c. The same consultant also suggests that if the firm raises its rate to $85 per hour, the number of service hours will decline to 25,000. Prepare a flexible budget using the new assumption.

d. Evaluate the three possible outcomes you determined in Requirements *a, b,* and *c* and recommend a pricing strategy.

L.O. 2

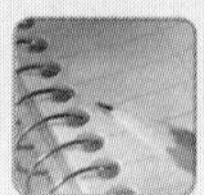

Problem 15-21 *Different types of responsibility centers*

First National Bank is a large municipal bank with several branch offices. The bank's computer department handles all data processing for bank operations. In addition, the bank sells the computer department's expertise in systems development and excess machine time to several small business firms, serving them as a service bureau.

The bank currently treats the computer department as a cost center. The manager of the computer department prepares a cost budget annually for senior bank officials to approve. Monthly operating reports compare actual and budgeted expenses. Revenues from the department's service bureau activities are treated as other income by the bank and are not reflected on the computer department's operating reports. The costs of serving these clients are included in the computer department reports, however.

The manager of the computer department has proposed that bank management convert the computer department to a profit or investment center.

Required

a. Describe the characteristics that differentiate a cost center, a profit center, and an investment center from each other.

b. Would the manager of the computer department be likely to conduct the operations of the department differently if the department were classified as a profit center or an investment center rather than as a cost center? Explain.

L.O. 8, 9

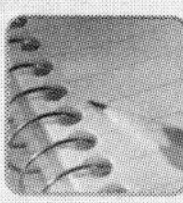

CHECK FIGURE
c. 16.60%

Problem 15-22 *Comparing return on investment and residual income*

Hannant Corporation operates three investment centers. The following financial statements apply to the investment center named Abacon Division.

ABACON DIVISION Income Statement For the Year Ended December 31, 2006	
Sales Revenue	$91,285
Cost of Goods Sold	(59,620)
Gross Margin	31,665
Operating Expenses	
Selling Expenses	(1,445)
Depreciation Expense	(1,200)
Operating Income	29,020
Nonoperating Expense	
Gain on Sale of Land	4,180
Net Income	$33,200

ABACON DIVISION Balance Sheet As of December 31, 2006	
Assets	
Cash	$ 19,103
Accounts Receivable	37,432
Merchandise Inventory	38,255
Equipment Less Accum. Dep.	80,000
Non-Operating Assets	9,000
Total Assets	$183,790
Liabilities	
Accounts Payable	$ 7,000
Notes Payable	65,700
Stockholders' Equity	
Common Stock	70,000
Retained Earnings	41,090
Total Liab. and Stk. Equity	$183,790

Required

a. Should operating income or net income be used to determine the rate of return (ROI) for the Abacon investment center? Explain your answer.

b. Should operating assets or total assets be used to determine the ROI for the Abacon investment center? Explain your answer.

c. Calculate the ROI for Abacon.

d. Hannant has a desired ROI of 12 percent. Headquarters has $100,000 of funds to assign its investment centers. The manager of the Abacon division has an opportunity to invest the funds at an ROI of 15 percent. The other two divisions have investment opportunities that yield only 14 percent. Even so, the manager of Abacon rejects the additional funding. Explain why the manager of Abacon would reject the funds under these circumstances.

e. Explain how residual income could be used to encourage the manager to accept the additional funds.

Problem 15-23 *Return on investment*

L.O. 8

mhhe.com/edmonds2007

CHECK FIGURES

c. 15%

d. (3) 18.75%

Tipton Corporation's balance sheet indicates that the company has $300,000 invested in operating assets. During 2006, Tipton earned operating income of $45,000 on $600,000 of sales.

Required

a. Compute Tipton's margin for 2006.

b. Compute Tipton's turnover for 2006.

c. Compute Tipton's return on investment for 2006.

d. Recompute Tipton's ROI under each of the following independent assumptions.

(1) Sales increase from $600,000 to $750,000, thereby resulting in an increase in operating income from $45,000 to $60,000.

(2) Sales remain constant, but Tipton reduces expenses resulting in an increase in operating income from $45,000 to $48,000.

(3) Tipton is able to reduce its invested capital from $300,000 to $240,000 without affecting operating income.

Problem 15-24 *Comparing return on investment and residual income*

L.O. 8, 9

The manager of the Cranston Division of Wynn Manufacturing Corporation is currently producing a 20 percent return on invested capital. Wynn's desired rate of return is 16 percent. The Cranston Division has $6,000,000 of capital invested in operating assets and access to additional funds as needed. The manager is considering a new investment in operating assets that will require a $1,500,000 capital commitment and promises an 18 percent return.

CHECK FIGURES

b. The ROI would decline to 19.60%.

c. RI would increase by $30,000.

Required

a. Would it be advantageous for Wynn Manufacturing Corporation if the Cranston Division makes the investment under consideration?
b. What effect would the proposed investment have on the Cranston Division's return on investment? Show computations.
c. What effect would the proposed investment have on the Cranston Division's residual income? Show computations.
d. Would return on investment or residual income be the better performance measure for the Cranston Division's manager? Explain.

ANALYZE, THINK, COMMUNICATE

ATC 15-1 Business Applications Case *Static versus flexible budget variances*

Vince Jacobs is the manufacturing production supervisor for High-Five Inline Skates Company. Trying to explain why he did not get the year-end bonus he had expected, he told his wife, "This is the dumbest place I ever worked. Last year the company set up this budget assuming it would sell 200,000 skates. Well, it sold only 190,000. The company lost money and gave me a bonus for not using as much materials and labor as was called for in the budget. This year, the company has the same 200,000 goal and it sells 210,000. The company's making all kinds of money. You'd think I'd get this big fat bonus. Instead, management tells me I used more materials and labor than was budgeted. They say the company would have made a lot more money if I'd stayed within my budget. I guess I gotta wait for another bad year before I get a bonus. Like I said, this is the dumbest place I ever worked."

High-Five Company's master budget and the actual results for the most recent year of operating activity follow.

	Master Budget	Actual Results	Variances	F or U
Number of units	200,000	210,000	10,000	
Sales revenue	$40,000,000	$42,630,000	$2,630,000	F
Variable manufacturing costs				
Materials	(6,000,000)	(6,115,200)	115,200	U
Labor	(5,600,000)	(5,974,500)	374,500	U
Overhead	(2,400,000)	(2,471,700)	71,700	U
Variable general, selling, and admin. costs	(7,600,000)	(8,110,200)	510,200	U
Contribution margin	18,400,000	19,958,400	1,558,400	F
Fixed costs				
Manufacturing overhead	(8,150,000)	(8,205,000)	55,000	U
General, selling, and admin. costs	(7,200,000)	(7,176,000)	24,000	F
Net income	$ 3,050,000	$ 4,577,400	$1,527,400	F

Required

a. Did High-Five increase unit sales by cutting prices or by using some other strategy?
b. Is Mr. Jacobs correct in his conclusion that something is wrong with the company's performance evaluation process? If so, what do you suggest be done to improve the system?
c. Prepare a flexible budget and recompute the budget variances.
d. Explain what might have caused the fixed costs to be different from the amount budgeted.
e. Assume that the company's material price variance was favorable and its material usage variance was unfavorable. Explain why Mr. Jacobs may not be responsible for these variances. Now, explain why he may have been responsible for the material usage variance.
f. Assume the labor price variance is favorable. Was the labor usage variance favorable or unfavorable?

ATC 15-2 Group Assignment *Return on investment versus residual income*

Bellco, a division of Becker International Corporation, is operated under the direction of Antoin Sedatt. Bellco is an independent investment center with approximately $72,000,000 of assets that generate approximately $8,640,000 in annual net income. Becker International has additional investment capital of $12,000,000 that is available for the division managers to invest. Mr. Sedatt is aware of an investment opportunity that will provide an 11 percent annual net return. Becker International's desired rate of return is 10 percent.

Required

Divide the class into groups of four or five students and then organize the groups into two sections. Assign Task 1 to the first section and Task 2 to the second section.

Group Tasks

1. Assume that Mr. Sedatt's performance is evaluated based on his ability to maximize return on investment (ROI). Compute ROI using the following two assumptions: Bellco retains its current asset size and Bellco accepts and invests the additional $12,000,000 of assets. Determine whether Mr. Sedatt should accept the opportunity to invest additional funds. Select a spokesperson to present the decision made by the group.
2. Assume that Mr. Sedatt's performance is evaluated based on his ability to maximize residual income. Compute residual income using the following two assumptions: Bellco retains its current asset base and Bellco accepts and invests the additional $12,000,000 of assets. Determine whether Mr. Sedatt should accept the opportunity to invest additional funds. Select a spokesperson to present the decision made by the group.
3. Have a spokesperson from one of the groups in the first section report the two ROIs and the group's recommendation for Mr. Sedatt. Have the groups in this section reach consensus on the ROI and the recommendation.
4. Have a spokesperson from the second section report the two amounts of residual income and disclose the group's recommendation for Mr. Sedatt. Have this section reach consensus on amounts of residual income.
5. Which technique (ROI or residual income) is more likely to result in suboptimization?

ATC 15-3 Research Assignment *Centralized or decentralized management*

The Curious Accountant story in this chapter related how one company, **The Home Depot**, grew from a small business into a large business in about 20 years. Another company that has experienced explosive growth since its founding in 1971 is **Bed Bath & Beyond, Inc.** Read the article "What's Beyond for Bed Bath & Beyond?" by Nanette Byrnes that appears on pages 46 and 50 of the January 19, 2004, issue of *BusinessWeek* and answer the following questions.

Required

a. Does the management at Bed Bath & Beyond operate using a centralized or decentralized organizational style?
b. Give specific examples from the article to support your conclusion in Requirement *a*.
c. Some analysts think Bed Bath & Beyond may not be able to maintain its historic growth rate into the future. What are some of their concerns, and how might a centralized or decentralized management style affect these issues?
d. Based on the related article, "Like Father Like Son," that appears next to the Bed Bath & Beyond story, what role do the children of the founders of Bed Bath & Beyond play at the company, and what are the reasons for this?

ATC 15-4 Writing Assignment *Nonfinancial performance measures*

The article "How Nonfinancial Performance Measures Are Used" (*Management Accounting*, February 1998) describes several emerging performance measures that do not rely on financial data. Read this article and complete the following requirements.

Required

a. What are nonfinancial performance measures? Provide several examples.
b. The article describes five categories of nonfinancial performance measures. Identify these categories. Which category do executives consider most important?

c. Can you compute variances for nonfinancial performance measures? Explain.

d. Comment on the extent to which executives use nonfinancial measures.

e. The authors indicate that their study identified three red flags that executives need to address to use nonfinancial performance measures more effectively. Identify and briefly discuss these three red flags.

ATC 15-5 Ethical Dilemma *Manipulating return on investment and residual income*

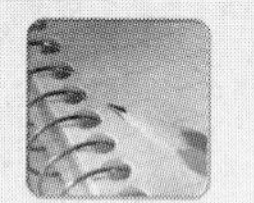

The October 5, 1998, issue of *BusinessWeek* includes the article "Who Can You Trust?" authored by Sarah Bartlett. Among other dubious accounting practices, the article describes a trick known as the "big bath," which occurs when a company makes huge unwarranted asset write-offs that drastically overstate expenses. Outside auditors (CPAs) permit companies to engage in the practice because the assets being written off are of questionable value. Because the true value of the assets cannot be validated, auditors have little recourse but to accept the valuations suggested by management. Recent examples of questionable write-offs include **Motorola's** $1.8 billion restructuring charge and the multibillion-dollar write-offs for "in-process" research taken by high-tech companies such as **Compaq Computer Corp.** and **WorldCom, Inc.**

Required

a. Why would managers want their companies to take a big bath? (*Hint:* Consider how a big bath affects return on investment and residual income in the years following the write-off.)

b. Annual reports are financial reports issued to the public. The reports are the responsibility of auditors who are CPAs who operate under the ethical standards promulgated by the American Institute of Certified Public Accountants. As a result, attempts to manipulate annual report data are not restricted by the Institute of Management Accountants Standards of Ethical Conduct shown in Exhibit 10.13 of Chapter 10. Do you agree or disagree with this conclusion? Explain your position.

CHAPTER 16

Planning for Capital Investments

LEARNING OBJECTIVES

After you have mastered the material in this chapter you will be able to:

1. Explain the time value of money concept and apply it to capital investment decisions.
2. Use present value tables to determine the present value of future cash flows.
3. Use computer software in determining present values.
4. Determine and interpret the net present value of an investment opportunity.
5. Determine the internal rate of return of an investment opportunity.
6. Determine the payback period for an investment opportunity.
7. Determine the unadjusted rate of return for an investment opportunity.
8. Conduct a postaudit of a completed investment.

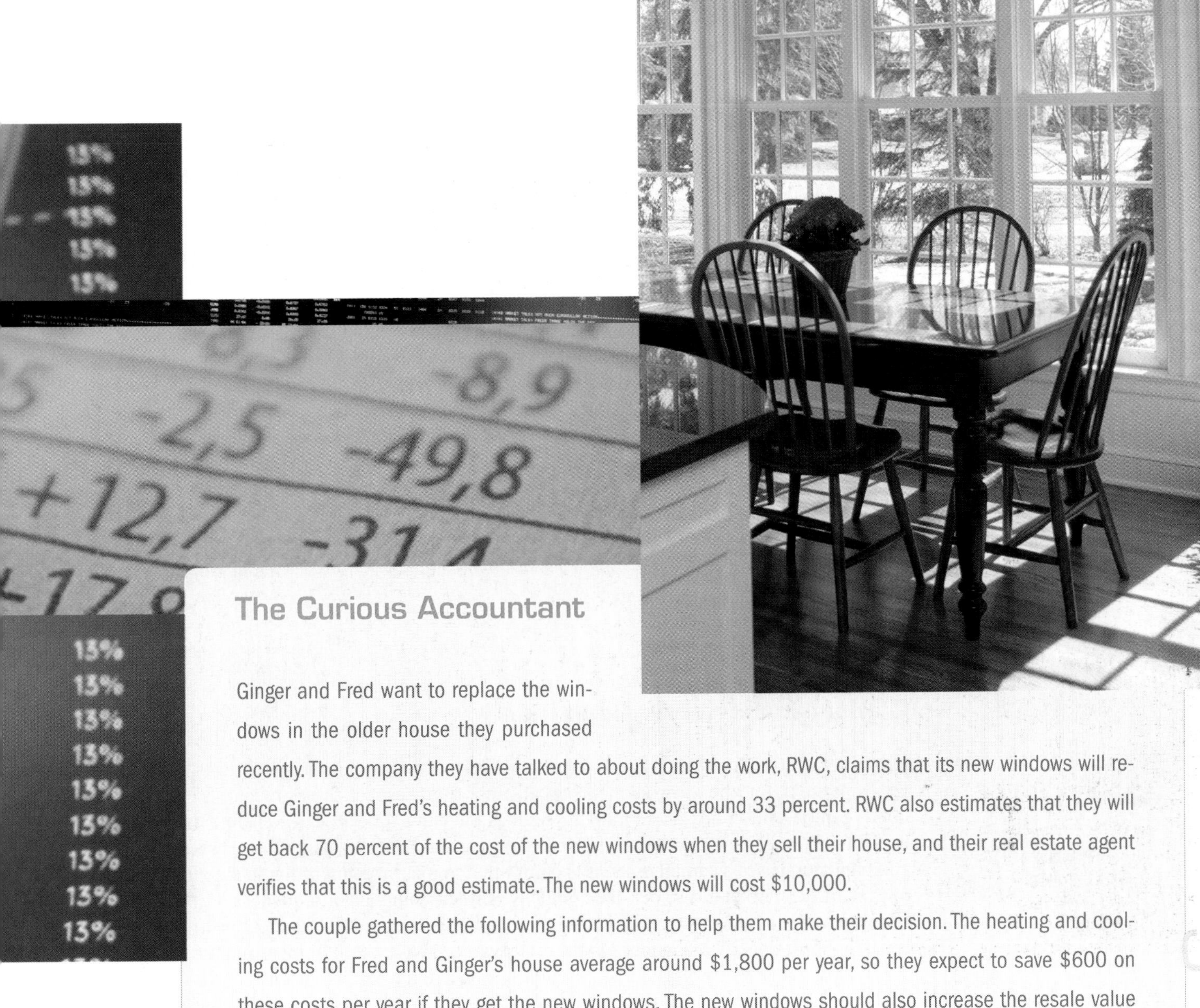

The Curious Accountant

Ginger and Fred want to replace the windows in the older house they purchased recently. The company they have talked to about doing the work, RWC, claims that its new windows will reduce Ginger and Fred's heating and cooling costs by around 33 percent. RWC also estimates that they will get back 70 percent of the cost of the new windows when they sell their house, and their real estate agent verifies that this is a good estimate. The new windows will cost $10,000.

The couple gathered the following information to help them make their decision. The heating and cooling costs for Fred and Ginger's house average around $1,800 per year, so they expect to save $600 on these costs per year if they get the new windows. The new windows should also increase the resale value by $7,000 (.70 × $10,000) when they decide to move. They expect to stay in this house for 10 years, so the total savings in energy costs are estimated at $6,000 (10 × $600). These savings, along with the higher resale value, bring the total return on their investment to $13,000 ($6,000 + $7,000).

To pay for the windows they would have to withdraw the money from a mutual fund that has earned an average annual return of only 4 percent over the past few years. They are hesitant about liquidating the mutual fund, but think that spending $10,000 today in order to receive future savings and income of $13,000 seems like a good deal.

Can Fred and Ginger simply compare the $13,000 future cash inflows to the $10,000 cost of the windows in order to decide if replacing them is a good idea? If not, what analysis should they perform in order to make their decision? (Answers on page 567.)

Chapter 16

CHAPTER OPENING

The president of EZ Rentals (EZ) is considering expanding the company's rental service business to include LCD projectors that can be used with notebook computers. A marketing study forecasts that renting projectors could generate revenue of $200,000 per year. The possibility of increasing revenue is alluring, but EZ's president has a number of unanswered questions. How much do the projectors cost? What is their expected useful life? Will they have a salvage value? Does EZ have the money to buy them? Does EZ have the technical expertise to support the product? How much will training cost? How long will customer demand last? What if EZ buys the projectors and they become technologically obsolete? How quickly will EZ be able to recover the investment? Are there more profitable ways to invest EZ's funds?

Spending large sums of money that will have long-term effects on company profits makes most managers anxious. What if a cell phone manufacturer spends millions of dollars to build a factory in the United States and its competitors locate their manufacturing facilities in countries that provide cheap labor? The manufacturer's cell phones will be overpriced, but it cannot move overseas because it cannot find a buyer for the factory. What if a pharmaceutical company spends millions of dollars to develop a drug which then fails to receive FDA approval? What if a communications company installs underground cable but satellite transmission steals its market? What if a company buys computer equipment that rapidly becomes technologically obsolete? Although these possibilities may be remote, they can be expensive when they do occur. For example, Wachovia Bank's 1997 annual report discloses a $70 million dollar write-off of computer equipment. This chapter discusses some of the analytical techniques companies use to evaluate major investment opportunities. ■

Capital Investment Decisions

Explain the time value of money concept and apply it to capital investment decisions.

Purchases of long-term operational assets are **capital investments.** Capital investments differ from stock and bond investments in an important respect. Investments in stocks and bonds can be sold in organized markets such as the New York Stock Exchange. In contrast, investments in capital assets normally can be recovered only by using those assets. Once a company purchases a capital asset, it is committed to that investment for an extended period of time. If the market turns sour, the company is stuck with the consequences. It may also be unable to seize new opportunities because its capital is committed. Business profitability ultimately hinges, to a large extent, on the quality of a few key capital investment decisions.

A capital investment decision is essentially a decision to exchange current cash outflows for the expectation of receiving future cash inflows. For EZ Rentals, purchasing LCD projectors, cash outflows today, provides the opportunity to collect $200,000 per year in rental revenue, cash inflows in the future. Assuming the projectors have useful lives of four years and no salvage value, how much should EZ be willing to pay for the future cash inflows? If you were EZ's president, would you spend $700,000 today to receive $200,000 each year for the next four years? You would give up $700,000 today for the opportunity to receive $800,000 (4 × $200,000) in the future. What if you collect less than $200,000 per year? If revenue is only $160,000 per year, you would lose $60,000 [$700,000 − (4 × $160,000)]. Is $700,000 too much to pay for the opportunity to receive $200,000 per year for four years? If $700,000 is too much, would you spend $600,000? If not, how about $500,000? There is no one right answer to these questions. However, understanding the *time value of money* concept can help you develop a rational response.

Time Value of Money

The **time value of money** concept recognizes that *the present value of a dollar received in the future is less than a dollar.* For example, you may be willing to pay only $0.90 today for a promise to receive $1.00 one year from today. The further into the future the receipt is expected to occur, the smaller is its present value. In other words, one dollar to be received two years from today is worth less than one dollar to be received one year from today. Likewise, one dollar to be received three years from today is less valuable than one dollar to be received two years from today, and so on.

The present value of cash inflows decreases as the time until expected receipt increases for several reasons. First, you could deposit today's dollar in a savings account to earn *interest* that increases its total value. If you wait for your money, you lose the opportunity to earn interest. Second, the expectation of receiving a future dollar carries an element of risk. Changed conditions may result in the failure to collect. Finally, *inflation* diminishes the buying power of the dollar. In other words, the longer you must wait to receive a dollar, the less you will be able to buy with it.

When a company invests in capital assets, it sacrifices present dollars in exchange for the opportunity to receive future dollars. Since trading current dollars for future dollars is risky, companies expect compensation before they invest in capital assets. The compensation a company expects is called *return on investment (ROI)*. As discussed in Chapter 23, ROI is expressed as a percentage of the investment. For example, the ROI for a $1,000 investment that earns annual income of $100 is 10 percent ($100 ÷ $1,000 = 10%).

Determining the Minimum Rate of Return

To establish the minimum expected *return on investment* before accepting an investment opportunity, most companies consider their cost of capital. To attract capital, companies must provide benefits to their creditors and owners. Creditors expect interest payments; owners expect dividends and increased stock value. Companies that earn lower returns than their cost of capital eventually go bankrupt; they cannot continually pay out more than they collect. *The* **cost of capital** *represents the* **minimum rate of return** *on investments.* Calculating the cost of capital is a complex exercise which is beyond the scope of this text. It is addressed in finance courses. We discuss how management accountants *use* the cost of capital to evaluate investment opportunities. Companies describe the cost of capital in a variety of ways: the *minimum rate of return*, the *desired rate of return*, the *required rate of return*, the *hurdle rate*, the *cutoff rate*, or the *discount rate*. These terms are used interchangeably throughout this chapter.

CHECK YOURSELF 16.1

Study the following cash inflow streams expected from two different potential investments.

	Year 1	Year 2	Year 3	Total
Alternative 1	$2,000	$3,000	$4,000	$9,000
Alternative 2	4,000	3,000	2,000	9,000

Based on visual observation alone, which alternative has the higher present value? Why?

Answer

Alternative 2 has the higher present value. The size of the discount increases as the length of the time period increases. In other words, a dollar received in year 3 has a lower present value than a dollar received in year 1. Since most of the expected cash inflows from Alternative 2 are received earlier than those from Alternative 1, Alternative 2 has a higher present value even though the total expected cash inflows are the same.

Converting Future Cash Inflows to Their Equivalent Present Values

Given a desired rate of return and the amount of a future cash flow, present value can be determined using algebra. To illustrate, refer to the $200,000 EZ expects to earn the first year it leases LCD projectors.[1] Assuming EZ desires a 12 percent rate of return, what amount of cash would EZ be willing to invest today (present value outflow) to obtain a $200,000 cash inflow at the end of the year (future value)? The answer follows:[2]

$$\text{Investment} + (0.12 \times \text{Investment}) = \text{Future cash inflow}$$
$$1.12\ \text{Investment} = \$200{,}000$$
$$\text{Investment} = \$200{,}000 \div 1.12$$
$$\text{Investment} = \$178{,}571$$

If EZ invests $178,571 cash on January 1 and earns a 12 percent return on the investment, EZ will have $200,000 on December 31. An investor who is able to earn a 12 percent return on investment is indifferent between having $178,571 now or receiving $200,000 one year from now. The two options are equal, as shown in the following mathematical proof:

$$\text{Investment} + (0.12 \times \text{Investment}) = \$200{,}000$$
$$\$178{,}571 + (0.12 \times \$178{,}571) = \$200{,}000$$
$$\$178{,}571 + \$21{,}429 = \$200{,}000$$
$$\$200{,}000 = \$200{,}000$$

Use present value tables to determine the present value of future cash flows.

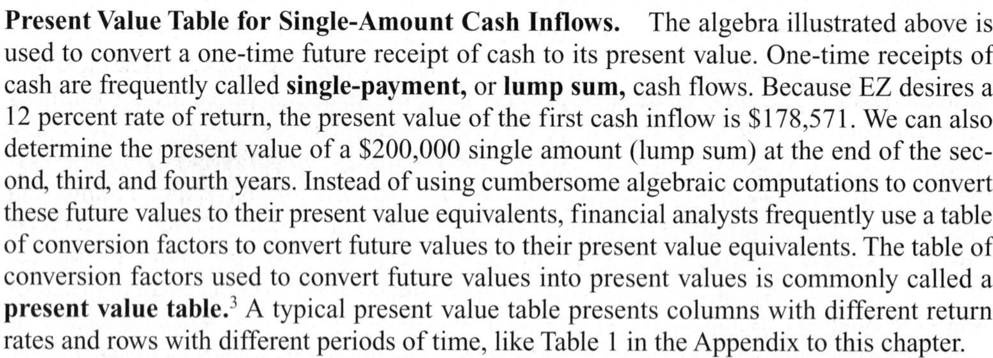

Present Value Table for Single-Amount Cash Inflows. The algebra illustrated above is used to convert a one-time future receipt of cash to its present value. One-time receipts of cash are frequently called **single-payment,** or **lump sum,** cash flows. Because EZ desires a 12 percent rate of return, the present value of the first cash inflow is $178,571. We can also determine the present value of a $200,000 single amount (lump sum) at the end of the second, third, and fourth years. Instead of using cumbersome algebraic computations to convert these future values to their present value equivalents, financial analysts frequently use a table of conversion factors to convert future values to their present value equivalents. The table of conversion factors used to convert future values into present values is commonly called a **present value table.**[3] A typical present value table presents columns with different return rates and rows with different periods of time, like Table 1 in the Appendix to this chapter.

To illustrate using the present value table, locate the conversion factor in Table 1 at the intersection of the 12% column and the one period row. The conversion factor is 0.892857. Multiplying this factor by the $200,000 expected cash inflow yields $178,571 ($200,000 × 0.892857). This is the same value determined algebraically in the previous section of this chapter. The conversion factors in the present value tables simplify converting future values to present values.

The conversion factors for the second, third, and fourth periods are 0.797194, 0.711780, and 0.635518, respectively. These factors are in the 12% column at rows 2, 3, and 4, respectively. Locate these factors in Table 1 of the Appendix. Multiplying the conversion factors by the future cash inflow for each period produces their present value equivalents, shown in Exhibit 16.1. Exhibit 16.1 indicates that investing $607,470 today at a 12 percent rate of return is equivalent to receiving $200,000 per year for four years. Because EZ Rentals desires to earn (at least) a 12 percent rate of return, the company should be willing to pay up to $607,470 to purchase the LCD projectors.

Present Value Table for Annuities. The algebra described previously for converting equal lump-sum cash inflows to present value equivalents can be further simplified by adding the present value table factors together before multiplying them by the cash inflows. The total of the present value table factors in Exhibit 16.1 is 3.037349 (0.892857 + 0.797194 + 0.711780 + 0.635518). Multiplying this **accumulated conversion factor** by the expected annual cash inflow results in the same present value equivalent of $607,470 ($200,000 ×

[1] The following computations assume the $200,000 cash inflow is received on the last day of each year. In actual practice the timing of cash inflows is less precise and present value computations are recognized to be approximate, not exact.

[2] All computations in this chapter are rounded to the nearest whole dollar.

[3] The present value table is based on the formula $[1 \div (1 + r)^n]$ where r equals the rate of return and n equals the number of periods.

EXHIBIT 16.1

Present Value of a $200,000 Cash Inflow to Be Received for Four Years

PV	=	FV	×	Present Value Table Factor	=	Present Value Equivalent
Period 1 PV	=	$200,000	×	0.892857	=	$178,571
Period 2 PV	=	200,000	×	0.797194	=	159,439
Period 3 PV	=	200,000	×	0.711780	=	142,356
Period 4 PV	=	200,000	×	0.635518	=	127,104
Total						$607,470

3.037349). As with lump-sum conversion factors, accumulated conversion factors can be calculated and organized in a table with *columns* for different rates of return and *rows* for different periods of time. Table 2 in the Appendix is a present value table of accumulated conversion factors. Locate the conversion factor at the intersection of the 12% column and the fourth time period row. The factor at this intersection is 3.037349, confirming that the accumulated conversion factors represent the sum of the single-payment conversion factors.

The conversion factors in Table 2 apply to annuities. An **annuity** is a series of cash flows that meets three criteria: (1) equal payment amounts; (2) equal time intervals between payments; and (3) a constant rate of return. For EZ Rentals, the expected cash inflows from renting LCD projectors are all for equivalent amounts ($200,000); the expected intervals between cash inflows are equal lengths of time (one year); and the rate of return for each inflow is constant at 12 percent. The series of expected cash inflows from renting the projectors is therefore an annuity. The present value of an annuity table can be used only if all of these conditions are satisfied.

The present value of an annuity table (Table 2) simplifies converting future cash inflows to their present value equivalents. EZ Rentals can convert the cash inflows as shown in Exhibit 16.1, using four conversion factors, multiplying each conversion factor by the annual cash inflow (four multiplications), and adding the resulting products. In contrast, EZ can recognize that the series of payments is an annuity, which requires multiplying a single conversion factor from Table 2 by the amount of the annuity payment. Regardless of the conversion method, the result is the same (a present value of $607,470). Recall that EZ can also make the conversion using algebra. The table values are derived from algebraic formulas. The present value tables reduce the computations needed to convert future values to present values.

Use computer software in determining present values.

Software Programs That Calculate Present Values. Software programs offer an even more efficient means of converting future values into present value equivalents. These programs are frequently built into handheld financial calculators and computer spreadsheet programs. As an example, we demonstrate the procedures used in a Microsoft Excel spreadsheet.

An Excel spreadsheet offers a variety of financial functions, one of which converts a future value annuity into its present value equivalent. This present value function uses the syntax PV(*rate,nper,pmt*) in which *rate* is the desired rate of return, *nper* is the number of periods, and *pmt* is the amount of the payment (periodic cash inflow). To convert a future value annuity into its present value equivalent, provide the function with the appropriate amounts for the rate, number of periods, and amount of the annuity (cash inflows) into a spreadsheet cell. Press the Enter key and the present value equivalent appears in the spreadsheet cell.

The power of the spreadsheet to perform computations instantly is extremely useful for answering what-if questions. Exhibit 16.2 demonstrates this power by providing spreadsheet conversions for three different scenarios. The first scenario demonstrates the annuity assumptions for EZ Rentals, providing the present value equivalent ($607,470) of a four-year cash inflow of $200,000 per year at a 12 percent rate of interest. The present value is a *negative* number. This format indicates that an initial $607,470 *cash outflow* is required to

EXHIBIT 16.2

Microsoft Excel Spreadsheet Present Value Function

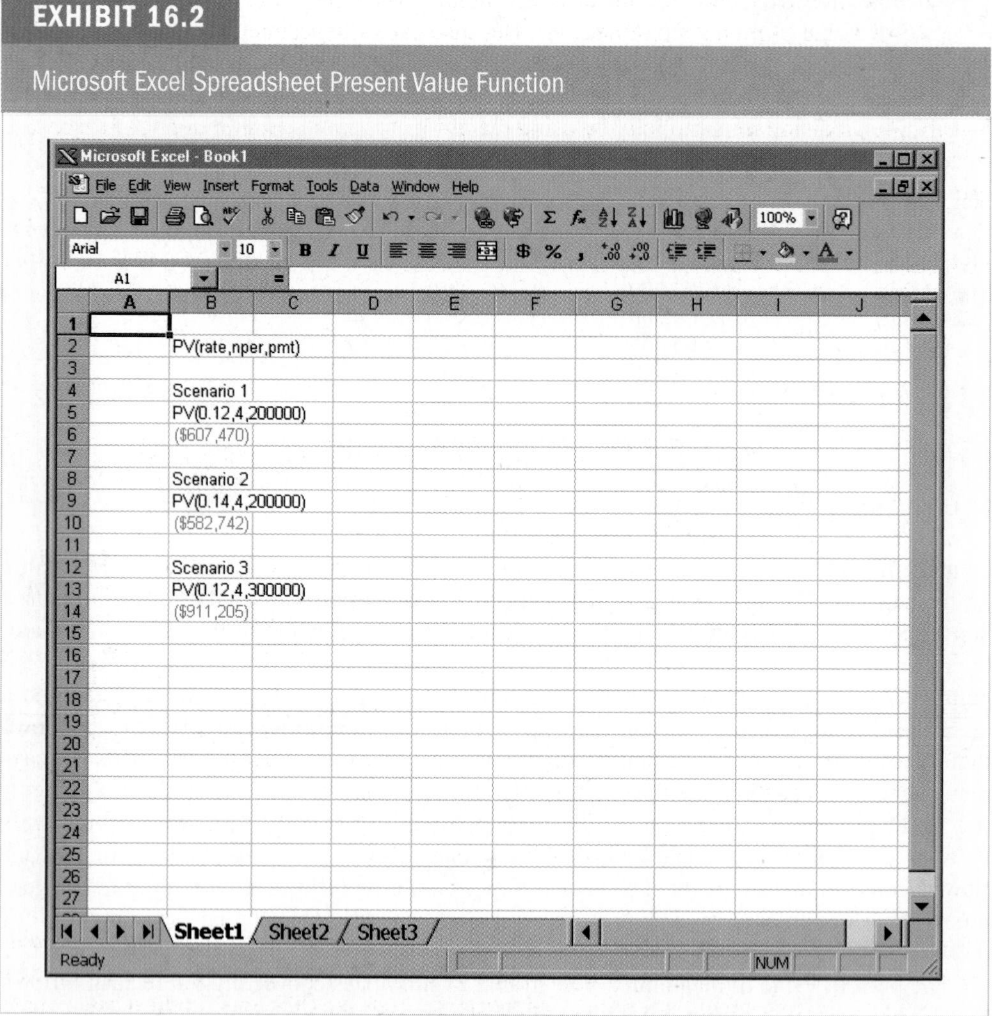

obtain the four-year series of cash inflows. The present value equivalent in Scenario 2 shows the present value if the annuity assumptions reflect a 14 percent, rather than 12 percent, desired rate of return. The present value equivalent in Scenario 3 shows the present value if the annuity assumptions under Scenario 1 are changed to reflect annual cash inflows of $300,000, rather than $200,000. A wide range of scenarios could be readily considered by changing any or all the variables in the spreadsheet function. In each case, the computer does the calculations, giving the manager more time to analyze the data rather than compute it.

Although software is widely used in business practice, the diversity of interfaces used by different calculators and spreadsheet programs makes it unsuitable for textbook presentations. This chapter uses the present value tables in the Appendix to this chapter in the text illustrations and the end-of-chapter exercises and problems. If you use software to solve these problems, your answers will be the same. All these tools—formulas, conversion tables, software—are based on the same mathematical principles and will produce the same results.

Ordinary Annuity Assumption. All the conversion methods described above assume the cash inflows occur at the *end* of each accounting period. This distribution pattern is called an **ordinary annuity.**[4] In practice, cash inflows are likely to be received throughout the period, not just at the end. For example, EZ Rentals is likely to collect cash revenue from renting projectors each month rather than in a single lump-sum receipt at the end of each of the four

[4] When equal cash inflows occur at the beginning of each accounting period, the distribution is called an *annuity due*. Although some business transactions are structured as annuities due, they are less common than ordinary annuities. This text uses the ordinary annuity assumption.

years. Companies frequently use the ordinary annuity assumption in practice because it simplifies time value of money computations. Because capital investment decisions are necessarily based on uncertain projections about future cash inflows, the lives of investment opportunities, and the appropriate rates of return, achieving pinpoint accuracy is impossible. Sacrificing precision for simplicity by using the ordinary annuity assumption is a reasonable trade-off in the decision-making process.

Reinvestment Assumption. The present value computations in the previous sections show that investing $607,470 today at a 12 percent rate of return is equivalent to receiving four individual $200,000 payments at the end of four successive years. Exhibit 16.3 illustrates that a cash inflow of $200,000 per year is equivalent to earning a 12 percent rate of return on a $607,470 investment.[5]

EXHIBIT 16.3

Cash Flow Classifications for EZ's Investment in Projectors

Time Period	(a) Investment Balance During the Year	(b) Annual Cash Inflow	(c) Return on Investment (a × 0.12)	(d) Recovered Investment (b − c)	(e) Year-End Investment Balance (a − d)
1	$607,470	$200,000	$ 72,896	$127,104	$480,366
2	480,366	200,000	57,644	142,356	338,010
3	338,010	200,000	40,561	159,439	178,571
4	178,571	200,000	21,429	178,571	0
Totals		$800,000	$192,530	$607,470	

It is customary to assume that the desired rate of return includes the effects of *compounding*.[6] Saying an investment is "earning the desired rate of return" assumes the cash inflows generated by the investment are reinvested at the desired rate of return. In this case, we are assuming that EZ will reinvest the $200,000 annual cash inflows in other investments that will earn a 12 percent return.

Techniques for Analyzing Capital Investment Proposals

Determine and interpret the net present value of an investment opportunity.

Managers can choose from among numerous analytical techniques to help them make capital investment decisions. Each technique has advantages and disadvantages. A manager may apply more than one technique to a particular proposal to take advantage of more information. Since most companies have computer capabilities that include a variety of standard capital budgeting programs, applying different techniques to the same proposal normally requires little extra effort. Limiting analysis to only one tool could produce biased results. Obtaining more than one perspective offers substantial benefit.

Net Present Value

By using the present value conversion techniques described earlier, EZ Rentals' management determined it would be willing to invest $607,470 today (present value) to obtain a four-year,

[5] Exhibit 16.3 is analogous to an amortization table for a long-term note with equal payments of principal and interest.

[6] *Compounding* refers to reinvesting investment proceeds so the total amount of invested capital increases, resulting in even higher returns. For example, assume $100 is invested at a 10 percent compounded annual rate of return. At the end of the first year, the investment yields a $10 return ($100 × 0.10). The $10 return plus any recovered investment is reinvested so that the total amount of invested capital at the beginning of the second year is $110. The return for the second year is $11 ($110 × 0.10). All funds are reinvested so that the return for the third year is $12.10 [($110 + $11) × 0.10].

$200,000 future value annuity cash inflow. The $607,470 investment is *not* the cost of the LCD projectors, it is the amount EZ is willing to pay for them. The projectors may cost EZ Rentals more or less than their present value. To determine whether EZ should invest in the projectors, management must compare the present value of the future cash inflows ($607,470) to the cost of the projectors (the current cash outflow required to purchase them). Subtracting the cost of the investment from the present value of the future cash inflows determines the **net present value** of the investment opportunity. A positive net present value indicates the investment will yield a rate of return higher than 12 percent. A negative net present value means the return is less than 12 percent.

To illustrate, assume EZ can purchase the projectors for $582,742. Assuming the desired rate of return is 12 percent, EZ should buy them. The net present value of the investment opportunity is computed as follows.

Present value of future cash inflows	$607,470
Cost of investment (required cash outflow)	(582,742)
Net present value	$ 24,728

The positive net present value suggests the investment will earn a rate of return in excess of 12 percent (if cash flows are indeed $200,000 each year). Because the projected rate of return is higher than the desired rate of return, this analysis suggests EZ should accept the investment opportunity.

CHECK YOURSELF 16.2

To increase productivity, Wald Corporation is considering the purchase of a new machine that costs $50,000. Wald expects using the machine to increase annual net cash inflows by $12,500 for each of the next five years. Wald desires a minimum annual rate of return of 10 percent on the investment. Determine the net present value of the investment opportunity and recommend whether Wald should acquire the machine.

Answer

Present value of future cash flows = Future cash flow × Table 2 factor (n = 5, r = 10%)

Present value of future cash flows = $12,500 × 3.790787 = $47,385

Net present value = PV of future cash flows − Cost of machine

Net present value = $47,385 − $50,000 = ($2,615)

The negative net present value indicates the investment will yield a rate of return below the desired rate of return. Wald should not acquire the new machine.

Internal Rate of Return

LO 5

Determine the internal rate of return of an investment opportunity.

The net present value method indicates EZ's investment in the projectors will provide a return in excess of the desired rate, but it does not provide the actual rate of return to expect from the investment. If EZ's management team wants to know the rate of return to expect from investing in the projectors, it must use the *internal rate of return method.* The **internal rate of return** is the rate at which the present value of cash inflows equals the cash outflows. It is the rate that will produce a zero net present value. For EZ Rentals, the internal rate of return can be determined as follows. First, compute the *present value table factor* for a $200,000 annuity that would yield a $582,742 present value cash outflow (cost of investment).

Present value table factor × $200,000 = $582,742

Present value table factor = $582,742 ÷ $200,000

Present value table factor = 2.91371

Second, since the expected annual cash inflows represent a four-year annuity, scan Table 2 in the Appendix at period n = 4. Try to locate the table factor 2.91371. The rate listed at the top of the column in which the factor is located is the internal rate of return. Turn to Table 2 and determine the internal rate of return for EZ Rentals before you read further. The above factor is in the 14 percent column. The difference in the table value (2.913712) and the value computed here (2.91371) is due to truncation. If EZ invests $582,742 in the projectors and they produce a $200,000 annual cash flow for four years, EZ will earn a 14 percent rate of return on the investment.

The *internal rate of return* may be compared with a *desired rate of return* to determine whether to accept or reject a particular investment project. Assuming EZ desires to earn a minimum rate of return of 12 percent, the preceding analysis suggests it should accept the investment opportunity because the internal rate of return (14 percent) is higher than the desired rate of return (12 percent). An internal rate of return below the desired rate suggests management should reject a particular proposal. The desired rate of return is sometimes called the *cutoff rate* or the *hurdle rate.* To be accepted, an investment proposal must provide an internal rate of return higher than the hurdle rate, cutoff rate, or desired rate of return. These terms are merely alternatives for the *cost of capital*. Ultimately, to be accepted, an investment must provide an internal rate of return higher than a company's cost of capital.

Techniques for Measuring Investment Cash Flows

The EZ Rentals example represents a simple capital investment analysis. The investment option involved only one cash outflow and a single annuity inflow. Investment opportunities often involve a greater variety of cash outflows and inflows. The following section of this chapter discusses different types of cash flows encountered in business practice.

Cash Inflows

Cash inflows generated from capital investments come from *four basic sources*. As in the case of EZ Rentals, the most common source of cash inflows is incremental revenue. **Incremental revenue** refers to the *additional* cash inflows from operating activities generated by using additional capital assets. For example, a taxi company expects revenues from taxi fares to increase if it purchases additional taxicabs. Similarly, investing in new apartments should increase rent revenue; opening a new store should result in additional sales revenue.

A second type of cash inflow results from *cost savings*. Decreases in cash outflows have the same beneficial effect as increases in cash inflows. Either way, a firm's cash position improves. For example, purchasing an automated computer system may enable a company to reduce cash outflows for salaries. Similarly, relocating a manufacturing facility closer to its raw materials source can reduce cash outflows for transportation costs.

An investment's *salvage value* provides a third source of cash inflows. Even when one company has finished using an asset, the asset may still be useful to another company. Many assets are sold after a company no longer wishes to use them. The salvage value represents a one-time cash inflow obtained when a company terminates an investment.

Companies can also experience a cash inflow through a *reduction in the amount* of **working capital** needed to support an investment. A certain level of working capital is required to support most business investments. For example, a new retail store outlet requires cash, receivables, and inventory to operate. When an investment is terminated, the decrease in the working capital commitment associated with the investment normally results in a cash inflow.

Cash Outflows

Cash outflows fall into *three primary categories*. One category consists of outflows for the *initial investment*. Managers must be alert to all the cash outflows connected with purchasing a capital asset. The purchase price, transportation costs, installation costs, and training costs are examples of typical cash outflows related to an initial investment.

A second category of cash outflows may result from *increases in operating expenses*. If a company increases output capacity by investing in additional equipment, it may experience higher utility bills, labor costs, and maintenance expenses when it places the equipment into service. These expenditures increase cash outflows.

Third, *increases in working capital* commitments result in cash outflows. Frequently, investments in new assets must be supported by a certain level of working capital. For example, investing in a copy machine requires spending cash to maintain a supply of paper and toner. Managers should treat an increased working capital commitment as a cash outflow in the period the commitment occurs.

Exhibit 16.4 lists the cash inflows and outflows discussed. The list is not exhaustive but does summarize the most common cash flows businesses experience.

EXHIBIT 16.4

Typical Cash Flows Associated With Capital Investments

Inflows	Outflows
1. Incremental revenue	1. Initial investment
2. Cost savings	2. Incremental expenses
3. Salvage values	3. Working capital commitments
4. Recovery of working capital	

Techniques for Comparing Alternative Capital Investment Opportunities

The management of Torres Transfer Company is considering two investment opportunities. One alternative, involving the purchase of new equipment for $80,000, would enable Torres to modernize its maintenance facility. The equipment has an expected useful life of five years and a $4,000 salvage value. It would replace existing equipment that had originally cost $45,000. The existing equipment has a current book value of $15,000 and a trade-in value of $5,000. The old equipment is technologically obsolete but can operate for an additional five years. On the day Torres purchases the new equipment, it would also pay the equipment manufacturer $3,000 for training costs to teach employees to operate the new equipment. The modernization has two primary advantages. One, it will improve management of the small parts inventory. The company's accountant believes that by the end of the first year, the carrying value of the small parts inventory could be reduced by $12,000. Second, the modernization is expected to increase efficiency, resulting in a $21,500 reduction in annual operating expenses.

The other investment alternative available to Torres is purchasing a truck. Adding another truck would enable Torres to expand its delivery area and increase revenue. The truck costs $115,000. It has a useful life of five years and a $30,000 salvage value. Operating the truck will require the company to increase its inventory of supplies, its petty cash account, and its accounts receivable and payable balances. These changes would add $5,000 to the company's working capital base immediately upon buying the truck. The working capital cash outflow is expected to be recovered at the end of the truck's useful life. The truck is expected to produce $69,000 per year in additional revenues. The driver's salary and other operating expenses are expected to be $32,000 per year. A major overhaul costing $20,000 is expected to be required at the end of the third year of operation. Assuming Torres desires to earn a rate of return of 14 percent, which of the two investment alternatives should it choose?

Net Present Value

Determine and interpret the net present value of an investment opportunity.

Begin the analysis by calculating the net present value of the two investment alternatives. Exhibit 16.5 shows the computations. Study this exhibit. Each alternative is analyzed using three steps. Step 1 requires identifying all cash inflows; some may be annuities, and others may be lump-sum receipts. In the case of Alternative 1, the cost saving is an annuity, and the inflow from the salvage value is a lump-sum receipt. Once the cash inflows have been identified, the appropriate conversion factors are identified and the cash inflows are converted to their equivalent present values. Step 2 follows the same process to determine the present value of the cash outflows. Step 3 subtracts the present value of the outflows from the present value of the inflows to determine the net present value. The same three-step approach is used to determine the net present value of Alternative 2.

EXHIBIT 16.5

Net Present Value Analysis

	Amount	×	Conversion Factor	=	Present Value
Alternative 1: Modernize Maintenance Facility					
Step 1: Cash inflows					
1. Cost savings	$21,500	×	3.433081*	=	$73,811
2. Salvage value	4,000	×	0.519369†	=	2,077
3. Working capital recovery	12,000	×	0.877193‡	=	10,526
Total					$86,414
Step 2: Cash outflows					
1. Cost of equipment ($80,000 cost–$5,000 trade-in)	$75,000	×	1.000000§	=	$75,000
2. Training costs	3,000	×	1.000000§	=	3,000
Total					$78,000
Step 3: Net present value					
Total present value of cash inflows					$86,414
Total present value of cash outflows					(78,000)
Net present value					$ 8,414
Alternative 2: Purchase Delivery Truck					
Step 1: Cash inflows					
1. Incremental revenue	$69,000	×	3.433081*	=	$236,883
2. Salvage value	30,000	×	0.519369†	=	15,581
3. Working capital recovery	5,000	×	0.519369†	=	2,597
Total					$255,061
Step 2: Cash outflows					
1. Cost of truck	$115,000	×	1.000000§	=	$115,000
2. Working capital increase	5,000	×	1.000000§	=	5,000
3. Increased operating expense	32,000	×	3.433081*	=	109,859
4. Major overhaul	20,000	×	0.674972⁺	=	13,499
Total					$243,358
Step 3: Net present value					
Total present value of cash inflows					$255,061
Total present value of cash outflows					(243,358)
Net present value					$ 11,703

*Present value of annuity table 2, $n = 5$, $r = 14\%$.

†Present value of single payment table 1, $n = 5$, $r = 14\%$.

‡Present value of single payment table 1, $n = 1$, $r = 14\%$.

§Present value at beginning of period 1.

⁺Present value of single payment table 1, $n = 3$, $r = 14\%$.

With respect to Alternative 1, the original cost and the book value of the existing equipment are ignored. As indicated in a previous chapter, these measures represent *sunk costs*; they are not relevant to the decision. The concept of relevance applies to long-term capital investment decisions just as it applies to the short-term special decisions that were discussed in Chapter 13. To be relevant to a capital investment decision, costs or revenues must involve different present and future cash flows for each alternative. Since the historical cost of the old equipment does not differ between the alternatives, it is not relevant.

Since the *net present value* of each investment alternative is *positive*, either investment will generate a return in excess of 14 percent. Which investment is the more favorable? The data could mislead a careless manager. Alternative 2 might seem the better choice because it

REALITY BYTES

Developing proficiency with present value mathematics is usually the most difficult aspect of capital budgeting for students taking their first managerial accounting course. In real-world companies, the most difficult aspect of capital budgeting is forecasting cash flows for several years into the future. Consider the following capital budgeting project.

In 1965 representatives from the **Georgia Power Company** visited Ms. Taylor's fifth grade class to tell her students about the Edwin I. Hatch Nuclear Plant that was going to be built nearby. One of the authors of this text was a student in that class.

In 1966 construction began on the first unit of the plant, and the plant started producing electricity in 1975. The next year, 10 years after hearing the presentation in his fifth grade class, the author worked on construction of the second unit of the plant during the summer before his senior year of college. This second unit began operations in 1978.

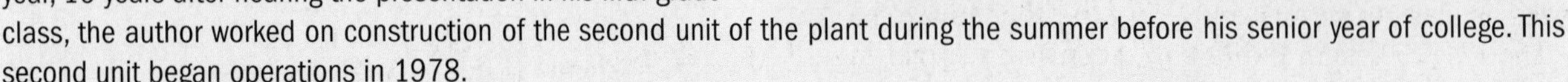

In its 2002 annual report, the **Southern Company,** which is now the major owner of the plant, stated that the Hatch plant is expected to operate until 2038, and that decommissioning of the plant will continue until 2042. The cost to construct both units of the plant was $934 million. The estimated cost to dismantle and decommission the plant is over $1 billion.

It seems safe to assume that the students in Ms. Taylor's fifth grade class were not among the first to hear about the power company's plans for the Hatch plant. Thus, we can reasonably conclude that the life of this capital project will be at least 85 years, from around 1960 until 2042.

Try to imagine that you were assigned the task of predicting the cash inflows and outflows for a project that was expected to last 85 years. Clearly, mastering present value mathematics would not be your biggest worry.

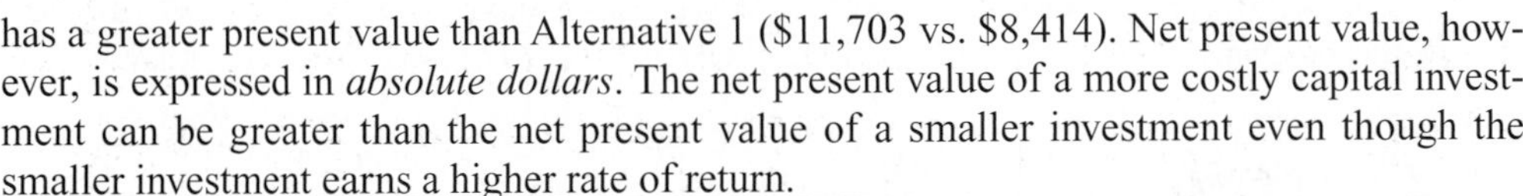

has a greater present value than Alternative 1 ($11,703 vs. $8,414). Net present value, however, is expressed in *absolute dollars*. The net present value of a more costly capital investment can be greater than the net present value of a smaller investment even though the smaller investment earns a higher rate of return.

To compare different size investment alternatives, management can compute a **present value index** by dividing the present value of cash inflows by the present value of cash outflows. *The higher the ratio, the higher the rate of return per dollar invested in the proposed project.* The present value indices for the two alternatives Torres Transfer Company is considering are as follows.

$$\text{Present value index for Alternative 1} = \frac{\text{Present value of cash inflows}}{\text{Present value of cash outflows}} = \frac{\$86{,}414}{\$78{,}000} = 1.108$$

$$\text{Present value index for Alternative 2} = \frac{\text{Present value of cash inflows}}{\text{Present value of cash outflows}} = \frac{\$255{,}061}{\$243{,}358} = 1.048$$

Management can use the present value indices to rank the investment alternatives. In this case, Alternative 1 yields a higher return than Alternative 2.

Internal Rate of Return

LO 5 Determine the internal rate of return of an investment opportunity.

Management can also rank investment alternatives using the internal rate of return for each investment. Generally, *the higher the internal rate of return, the more profitable the investment.* We previously demonstrated how to calculate the internal rate of return for an investment that generates a simple cash inflow annuity. The computations are significantly more complex for investments with uneven cash flows. Recall that the internal rate of return is the rate that produces a zero net present value. Manually computing the rate that produces a zero net present value is a tedious trial-and-error process. You must first estimate the rate of return for a particular investment, then calculate the net present value. If the calculation produces a negative net present value, you try a lower estimated rate of return and recalculate. If this calculation produces a positive net present value, the actual internal rate of return lies between the first and second estimates. Make a third estimate and once again recalculate the net present value, and so on. Eventually you will determine the rate of return that produces a net present value of zero.

Many calculators and spreadsheet programs are designed to make these computations. We illustrate the process with a Microsoft Excel spreadsheet. Excel uses the syntax *IRR* (*values, guess*) in which *values* refers to cells that specify the cash flows for which you want to calculate the internal rate of return and *guess* is a number you estimate is close to the actual internal rate of return (IRR). The IRRs for the two investment alternatives available to Torres Transfer Company are shown in Exhibit 16.6. Study this exhibit. Excel requires netting cash outflows against cash inflows for each period in which both outflows and inflows are expected. For your convenience, we have labeled the net cash flows in the spreadsheet. Labeling is not necessary to execute the IRR function. The entire function, including values and guess, can be entered into a single cell of the spreadsheet. Persons familiar with spreadsheet programs learn to significantly simplify the input required.

The IRR results in Exhibit 16.6 confirm the ranking determined using the present value index. Alternative 1 (modernize maintenance facility), with an internal rate of return of 18.69 percent, ranks above Alternative 2 (purchase a truck) with an internal rate of return of 17.61 percent, even though Alternative 2 has a higher net present value (see Exhibit 16.5). Alternative 2, however, still may be the better investment option, depending on the amount available to invest. Suppose Torres has $120,000 of available funds to invest. Because Alternative 1 requires an initial investment of only $78,000, $42,000 ($120,000 − $78,000) of capital will not be invested. If Torres has no other investment opportunities for this $42,000, the

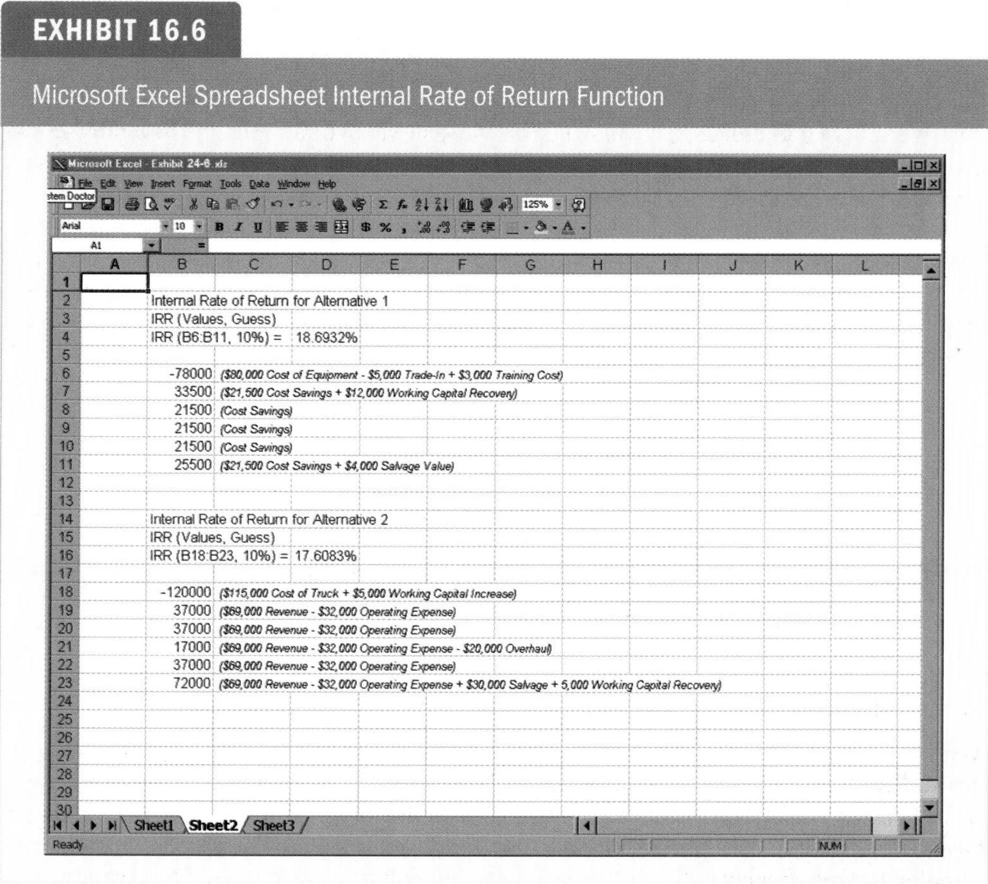

EXHIBIT 16.6

Microsoft Excel Spreadsheet Internal Rate of Return Function

Row	B	C
2	Internal Rate of Return for Alternative 1	
3	IRR (Values, Guess)	
4	IRR (B6:B11, 10%) = 18.6932%	
6	-78000	($80,000 Cost of Equipment - $5,000 Trade-In + $3,000 Training Cost)
7	33500	($21,500 Cost Savings + $12,000 Working Capital Recovery)
8	21500	(Cost Savings)
9	21500	(Cost Savings)
10	21500	(Cost Savings)
11	25500	($21,500 Cost Savings + $4,000 Salvage Value)
14	Internal Rate of Return for Alternative 2	
15	IRR (Values, Guess)	
16	IRR (B18:B23, 10%) = 17.6083%	
18	-120000	($115,000 Cost of Truck + $5,000 Working Capital Increase)
19	37000	($69,000 Revenue - $32,000 Operating Expense)
20	37000	($69,000 Revenue - $32,000 Operating Expense)
21	17000	($69,000 Revenue - $32,000 Operating Expense - $20,000 Overhaul)
22	37000	($69,000 Revenue - $32,000 Operating Expense)
23	72000	($69,000 Revenue - $32,000 Operating Expense + $30,000 Salvage + 5,000 Working Capital Recovery)

company would be better off investing the entire $120,000 in Alternative 2 ($115,000 cost of truck + $5,000 working capital increase). Earning 17.61 percent on a $120,000 investment is better than earning 18.69 percent on a $78,000 investment with no return on the remaining $42,000. Management accounting requires exercising judgment when making decisions.

Relevance and the Time Value of Money

Suppose you have the opportunity to invest in one of two capital projects. Both projects require an immediate cash outflow of $6,000 and will produce future cash inflows of $8,000. The only difference between the two projects is the timing of the inflows. The receipt schedule for both projects follows.

	Project 1	Project 2
2007	$3,500	$2,000
2008	3,000	2,000
2009	1,000	2,000
2010	500	2,000
Total	$8,000	$8,000

Because both projects cost the same and produce the same total cash inflows, they may appear to be equal. Whether you select Project 1 or Project 2, you pay $6,000 and receive $8,000. Because of the time value of money, however, Project 1 is preferable to Project 2. To see why, determine the net present value of both projects, assuming a 10 percent desired rate of return.

Computation of Net Present Value for Project 1 and Project 2

Net Present Value for Project 1

Period	Cash Inflow	×	Conversion Factor Table 1, r = 10%	=	Present Value
1	$3,500	×	0.909091	=	$3,182
2	3,000	×	0.826446	=	2,479
3	1,000	×	0.751315	=	751
4	500	×	0.683013	=	342
Present value of future cash inflows					6,754
Present value of cash outflow					(6,000)
Net present value Project 1					$ 754

Net Present Value for Project 2

	Cash Inflow Annuity	×	Conversion Factor Table 2, r = 10%, n = 4	
Present value of cash inflow	$2,000	×	3.169865	$6,340
Present value of cash outflow				(6,000)
Net present value Project 2				$ 340

The net present value of Project 1 ($754) exceeds the net present value of Project 2 ($340). The timing as well as the amount of cash flows has a significant impact on capital investment returns. Recall that to be relevant, costs or revenues must differ between alternatives. Differences in the timing of cash flow payments or receipts are also relevant for decision-making purposes.

Answers to The Curious Accountant

Ginger and Fred should not simply compare $10,000 spent today with $13,000 in energy savings and higher resale value that are to be received in the future. A dollar received in the future is worth less than a dollar spent today because of the time value of money. In order to decide if the replacement windows are worth their cost, today's $10,000 must be compared in common values with the $13,000 that they estimate will be received in the future.

This problem can be solved using the net present value approach that is explained in this chapter. This method calculates the present value of all dollars spent and received, and chooses the option with the highest present value. These computations are shown below. Note that a discount rate of 4 percent is used, because this is the rate that will be lost if the mutual fund is liquidated. This 4 percent is an opportunity cost.

The windows cost more than the present value of their future benefits, so this opportunity has a negative net present value of $404.51 ($10,000.00 − $9,595.49). Therefore, from a strictly financial point of view, Fred and Ginger should not buy the windows. Of course there may be nonquantitative factors in favor of buying the windows that the analysis above did not consider. Perhaps Ginger and Fred believe their new neighbors will like them more if they improve the looks of their house. If Fred and Ginger believe that being liked by their neighbors is worth $404.51, they should go ahead and purchase the windows.

Annual savings in heating and cooling costs	$ 600	
× Present value factor of a 10-year annuity, at 4%	8.110896	
Present value of the annual energy savings		$ 4,866.54
Increase in resale value of the house	$ 7,000	
× Present value factor of $1 in 10 years, at 4%	0.675564	
Present value of the increase in resale value		4,728.95
Total present value of buying the windows		$ 9,595.49
Cost of the new windows, today		$10,000.00

Tax Considerations

The previous examples have ignored the effect of income taxes on capital investment decisions. Taxes affect the amount of cash flows generated by investments. To illustrate, assume Wu Company purchases an asset that costs $240,000. The asset has a four-year useful life, no salvage value, and is depreciated on a straight-line basis. The asset generates cash revenue of $90,000 per year. Assume Wu's income tax rate is 40 percent. What is the net present value of the asset, assuming Wu's management desires to earn a 10 percent rate of return after taxes? The first step in answering this question is to calculate the annual cash flow generated by the asset, as shown in Exhibit 16.7.

Because recognizing depreciation expense does not require a cash payment (cash is paid when assets are purchased, not when depreciation is recognized), depreciation expense must be added back to after-tax income to determine the annual cash inflow. Once the cash flow is determined, the net present value is computed as shown here.

Cash flow annuity	×	Conversion factor Table 2, $r = 10\%$, $n = 4$	=	Present value cash inflows	−	Present value cash outflows	=	Net present value
$78,000	×	3.169865	=	$247,249	−	$240,000	=	$7,249

The depreciation sheltered some of the income from taxation. Income taxes apply to income after deducting depreciation expense. Without depreciation expense, income taxes each year would have been $36,000 ($90,000 × 0.40) instead of $12,000 ($30,000 × 0.40).

EXHIBIT 16.7

Determining Cash Flow from Investment

	Period 1	Period 2	Period 3	Period 4
Cash revenue	$90,000	$90,000	$90,000	$90,000
Depreciation expense (noncash)	(60,000)	(60,000)	(60,000)	(60,000)
Income before taxes	30,000	30,000	30,000	30,000
Income tax at 40%	(12,000)	(12,000)	(12,000)	(12,000)
Income after tax	18,000	18,000	18,000	18,000
Depreciation add back	60,000	60,000	60,000	60,000
Annual cash inflow	$78,000	$78,000	$78,000	$78,000

The $24,000 difference ($36,000 − $12,000) is known as a *depreciation tax shield.* The amount of the depreciation tax shield can also be computed by multiplying the depreciation expense by the tax rate ($60,000 × 0.40 = $24,000).

Because of the time value of money, companies benefit by maximizing the depreciation tax shield early in the life of an asset. For this reason, most companies calculate depreciation expense for tax purposes using the *modified accelerated cost recovery system (MACRS)* permitted by tax law rather than using straight-line depreciation. MACRS recognizes depreciation on an accelerated basis, assigning larger amounts of depreciation in the early years of an asset's useful life. The higher depreciation charges result in lower amounts of taxable income and lower income taxes. In the later years of an asset's useful life, the reverse is true, and lower depreciation charges result in higher taxes. Accelerated depreciation does not allow companies to avoid paying taxes but to delay them. The longer companies can delay paying taxes, the more cash they have available to invest.

Techniques That Ignore the Time Value of Money

Several techniques for evaluating capital investment proposals ignore the time value of money. Although these techniques are less accurate, they are quick and simple. When investments are small or the returns are expected within a short time, these techniques are likely to result in the same decisions that more sophisticated techniques produce.

Payback Method

Determine the payback period for an investment opportunity.

The **payback method** is simple to apply and easy to understand. It shows how long it will take to recover the initial cash outflow (the cost) of an investment. The formula for computing the payback period, measured in years, is as follows.

Payback period = Net cost of investment ÷ Annual net cash inflow

To illustrate, assume Winston Cleaners can purchase a new ironing machine that will press shirts in half the time of the one currently used. The new machine costs $100,000 and will reduce labor cost by $40,000 per year over a four-year useful life. The payback period is computed as follows.

Payback period = $100,000 ÷ $40,000 = 2.5 years

Interpreting Payback. Generally, investments with shorter payback periods are considered better. Because the payback method measures only investment recovery, not profitability, however, this conclusion can be invalid when considering investment alternatives. To illustrate, assume Winston Cleaners also has the opportunity to purchase a different machine that costs $100,000 and provides an annual labor savings of $40,000. However, the second machine will last for five instead of four years. The payback period is still 2.5 years ($100,000 ÷ $40,000), but the second machine is a better investment because it improves profitability by providing an additional year of cost savings. The payback analysis does not measure this difference between the alternatives.

Unequal Cash Flows. The preceding illustration assumed Winston's labor cost reduction saved the same amount of cash each year for the life of the new machine. The payback method requires adjustment when cash flow benefits are unequal. Suppose a company purchases a machine for $6,000. The machine will be used erratically and is expected to provide incremental revenue over the next five years as follows.

2007	2008	2009	2010	2011
$3,000	$1,000	$2,000	$1,000	$500

Based on this cash inflow pattern, what is the payback period? There are two acceptable solutions. One accumulates the incremental revenue until the sum equals the amount of the original investment.

Year	Annual Amount	Cumulative Total
2007	$3,000	$3,000
2008	1,000	4,000
2009	2,000	6,000

This approach indicates the payback period is three years.

A second solution uses an averaging concept. The average annual cash inflow is determined. This figure is then used in the denominator of the payback equation. Using the preceding data, the payback period is computed as follows.

1. Compute the average annual cash inflow.

$$\begin{array}{l} 2007 + 2008 + 2009 + 2010 + 2011 = \text{Total} \div 5 = \text{Average} \\ \$3{,}000 + \$1{,}000 + \$2{,}000 + \$1{,}000 + \$500 = \$7{,}500 \div 5 = \$1{,}500 \end{array}$$

2. Compute the payback period.

$$\begin{array}{c}\text{Net cost of} \\ \text{investment}\end{array} \div \begin{array}{c}\text{Average annual} \\ \text{net cash inflow}\end{array} = \$6{,}000 \div \$1{,}500 = 4 \text{ years}$$

The average method is useful when a company purchases a number of similar assets with differing cash return patterns.

Unadjusted Rate of Return

The **unadjusted rate of return** method is another common evaluation technique. Investment cash flows are not adjusted to reflect the time value of money. The unadjusted rate of return is sometimes called the *simple rate of return.* It is computed as follows.

LO 7

Determine the unadjusted rate of return for an investment opportunity.

$$\begin{array}{c}\text{Unadjusted} \\ \text{rate of return}\end{array} = \frac{\text{Average incremental increase in annual net income}}{\text{Net cost of original investment}}$$

To illustrate computing the unadjusted rate of return, assume The Dining Table Inc. is considering establishing a new restaurant that will require a $2,000,000 original investment. Management anticipates operating the restaurant for 10 years before significant renovations will be required. The restaurant is expected to provide an average after-tax return of $280,000 per year. The unadjusted rate of return is computed as follows.

$$\text{Unadjusted rate of return} = \$280{,}000 \div \$2{,}000{,}000 = 14\% \text{ per year}$$

The accuracy of the unadjusted rate of return suffers from the failure to recognize the recovery of invested capital. With respect to a depreciable asset, the capital investment is normally recovered through revenue over the life of the asset. To illustrate, assume we purchase a $1,000 asset with a two-year life and a zero salvage value. For simplicity, ignore income taxes. Assume the asset produces $600 of cash revenue per year. The income statement for the first year of operation appears as follows.

Revenue	$600
Depreciation Expense	(500)
Net Income	$100

What is the amount of invested capital during the first year? First, a $1,000 cash outflow was used to purchase the asset (the original investment). Next, we collected $600 of cash revenue of which $100 was a *return on investment* (net income) and $500 was a **recovery of investment.** As a result, $1,000 was invested in the asset at the beginning of the year and $500 was invested at the end of the year. Similarly, we will recover an additional $500 of capital during the second year of operation, leaving zero invested capital at the end of the second year. Given that the cash inflows from revenue are collected somewhat evenly over the life of the investment, the amount of invested capital will range from a beginning balance of $1,000 to an ending balance of zero. On average, we will have $500 invested in the asset (the midpoint between $1,000 and zero). The average investment can be determined by dividing the total original investment by 2 ($1,000 ÷ 2 = $500). The unadjusted rate of return based on average invested capital can be calculated as follows.

$$\begin{array}{c}\text{Unadjusted rate of return}\\ \text{(Based on average investment)}\end{array} = \frac{\text{Average incremental increase in annual net income}}{\text{Net cost of original investment} \div 2}$$

$$= \frac{\$100}{\$1{,}000 \div 2} = 20\%$$

To avoid distortions caused by the failure to recognize the recovery of invested capital, the unadjusted rate of return should be based on the *average investment* when working with investments in depreciable assets.

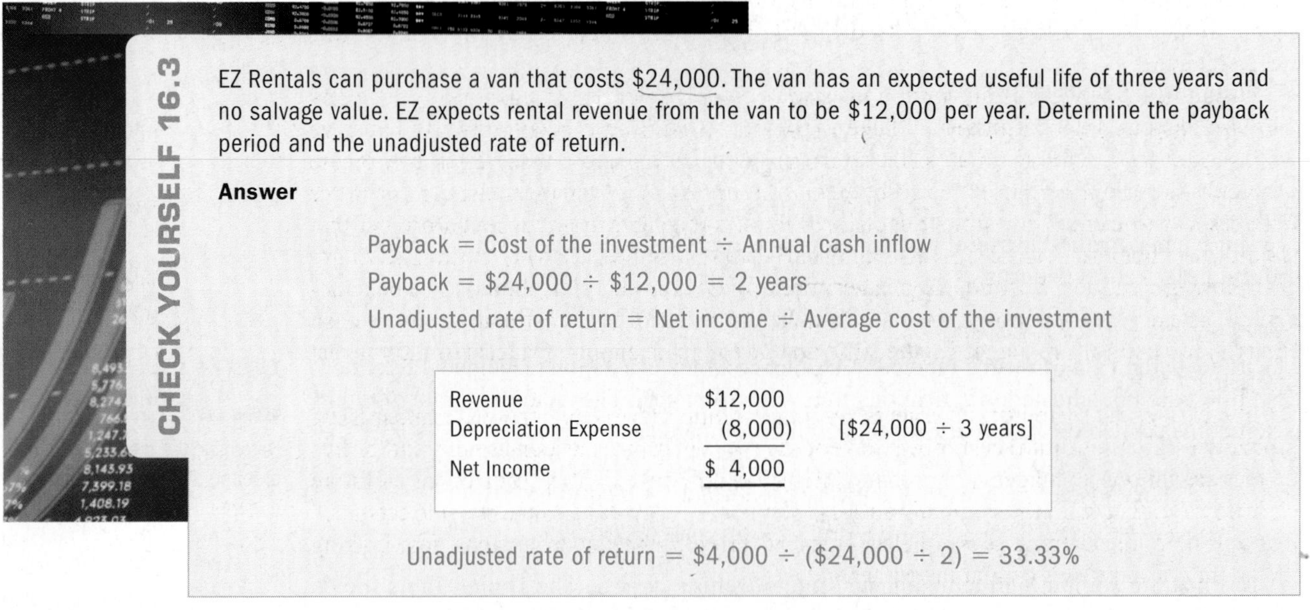

CHECK YOURSELF 16.3

EZ Rentals can purchase a van that costs $24,000. The van has an expected useful life of three years and no salvage value. EZ expects rental revenue from the van to be $12,000 per year. Determine the payback period and the unadjusted rate of return.

Answer

Payback = Cost of the investment ÷ Annual cash inflow
Payback = $24,000 ÷ $12,000 = 2 years
Unadjusted rate of return = Net income ÷ Average cost of the investment

Revenue	$12,000	
Depreciation Expense	(8,000)	[$24,000 ÷ 3 years]
Net Income	$ 4,000	

Unadjusted rate of return = $4,000 ÷ ($24,000 ÷ 2) = 33.33%

Real-World Reporting Practices

In a recent study, researchers found that companies in the forest products industry use discounted cash flow techniques more frequently when the capital project being considered is a long-term timber investment. The use of techniques that ignore the time value of money increased when other shorter-term capital investment projects were being considered. Exhibit 16.8 shows the researchers' findings.

EXHIBIT 16.8

Forestry Industry Investments

Long-term investments in timber

Net present value **38%**
9% Unadjusted rate of return
Internal rate of return **38%**
15% Payback period

Investments in other assets

Net present value **22%**
13% Unadjusted rate of return
Internal rate of return **33%**
32% Payback period

Data Source: J. Bailes, J. Nielsen, and S. Lawton, "How Forest Product Companies Analyze Capital Budgets," *Management Accounting,* October 1998, pp. 24–30.

Postaudits

Conduct a postaudit of a completed investment.

The analytical techniques for evaluating capital investment proposals depend highly on estimates of future cash flows. Although predictions cannot be perfectly accurate, gross miscalculations can threaten the existence of an organization. For example, optimistic projections of future cash inflows that do not materialize will lead to investments that do not return the cost of capital. Managers must take their projections seriously. A postaudit policy can encourage managers to carefully consider their capital investment decisions. A **postaudit** is conducted at the completion of a capital investment project, using the same analytical technique that was used to justify the original investment. For example, if an internal rate of return was used to justify approving an investment project, the internal rate of return should be computed in the postaudit. In the postaudit computation, *actual* rather than estimated cash flows are used. Postaudits determine whether the expected results were achieved.

Postaudits should focus on continuous improvement rather than punishment. Managers who are chastised for failing to achieve expected results might become overly cautious when asked to provide estimates for future projects. Being too conservative can create problems as serious as those caused by being too optimistic. Managers can err two ways with respect to capital investment decisions. First, a manager might accept a project that should have been rejected. This mistake usually stems from excessively optimistic future cash flow projections. Second, a manager might reject a project that should have been accepted. These missed opportunities are usually the result of underestimating future cash flows. A too cautious manager can become unable to locate enough projects to fully invest the firm's funds.

Idle cash earns no return. If projects continue to outperform expectations, managers are probably estimating future cash flows too conservatively. If projects consistently fail to live up to expectations, managers are probably being too optimistic in their projections of future cash flows. Either way, the company suffers. The goal of a postaudit is to provide feedback that will help managers improve the accuracy of future cash flow projections, maximizing the quality of the firm's capital investments.

A Look Back <<

Capital expenditures have a significant, long-term effect on profitability. They usually involve major cash outflows that are recovered through future cash inflows. The most common cash inflows include incremental revenue, operating cost savings, salvage value, and working capital releases. The most common outflows are the initial investment, increases in operating expenses, and working capital commitments.

Several techniques for analyzing the cash flows associated with capital investments are available. The techniques can be divided into two categories: (1) techniques that use time value of money concepts and (2) techniques that ignore the time value of money. Generally, techniques that ignore the time value of money are less accurate but simpler and easier to understand. These techniques include the *payback method* and the *unadjusted rate of return method.*

The techniques that use time value of money concepts are the *net present value method* and the *internal rate of return method.* These methods offer significant improvements in accuracy but are more difficult to understand. They may involve tedious computations and require using experienced judgment. Computer software and programmed calculators that ease the tedious computational burden are readily available to most managers. Furthermore, the superiority of the techniques justifies learning how to use them. These methods should be used when investment expenditures are larger or when cash flows extend over a prolonged time period.

>> A Look Forward

This chapter probably completes your introduction to accounting. We sincerely hope that this text has provided you a meaningful learning experience that will serve you well as you progress through your academic training and, ultimately, your career. Good luck and best wishes!

APPENDIX

TABLE 1 Present Value of $1

n	4%	5%	6%	7%	8%	9%	10%	12%	14%	16%	20%
1	0.961538	0.952381	0.943396	0.934579	0.925926	0.917431	0.909091	0.892857	0.877193	0.862069	0.833333
2	0.924556	0.907029	0.889996	0.873439	0.857339	0.841680	0.826446	0.797194	0.769468	0.743163	0.694444
3	0.888996	0.863838	0.839619	0.816298	0.793832	0.772183	0.751315	0.711780	0.674972	0.640658	0.578704
4	0.854804	0.822702	0.792094	0.762895	0.735030	0.708425	0.683013	0.635518	0.592080	0.552291	0.482253
5	0.821927	0.783526	0.747258	0.712986	0.680583	0.649931	0.620921	0.567427	0.519369	0.476113	0.401878
6	0.790315	0.746215	0.704961	0.666342	0.630170	0.596267	0.564474	0.506631	0.455587	0.410442	0.334898
7	0.759918	0.710681	0.665057	0.622750	0.583490	0.547034	0.513158	0.452349	0.399637	0.353830	0.279082
8	0.730690	0.676839	0.627412	0.582009	0.540269	0.501866	0.466507	0.403883	0.350559	0.305025	0.232568
9	0.702587	0.644609	0.591898	0.543934	0.500249	0.460428	0.424098	0.360610	0.307508	0.262953	0.193807
10	0.675564	0.613913	0.558395	0.508349	0.463193	0.422411	0.385543	0.321973	0.269744	0.226684	0.161506
11	0.649581	0.584679	0.526788	0.475093	0.428883	0.387533	0.350494	0.287476	0.236617	0.195417	0.134588
12	0.624597	0.556837	0.496969	0.444012	0.397114	0.355535	0.318631	0.256675	0.207559	0.168463	0.112157
13	0.600574	0.530321	0.468839	0.414964	0.367698	0.326179	0.289664	0.229174	0.182069	0.145227	0.093464
14	0.577475	0.505068	0.442301	0.387817	0.340461	0.299246	0.263331	0.204620	0.159710	0.125195	0.077887
15	0.555265	0.481017	0.417265	0.362446	0.315242	0.274538	0.239392	0.182696	0.140096	0.107927	0.064905
16	0.533908	0.458112	0.393646	0.338735	0.291890	0.251870	0.217629	0.163122	0.122892	0.093041	0.054088
17	0.513373	0.436297	0.371364	0.316574	0.270269	0.231073	0.197845	0.145644	0.107800	0.080207	0.045073
18	0.493628	0.415521	0.350344	0.295864	0.250249	0.211994	0.179859	0.130040	0.094561	0.069144	0.037561
19	0.474642	0.395734	0.330513	0.276508	0.231712	0.194490	0.163508	0.116107	0.082948	0.059607	0.031301
20	0.456387	0.376889	0.311805	0.258419	0.214548	0.178431	0.148644	0.103667	0.072762	0.051385	0.026084

TABLE 2 Present Value of an Annuity of $1

n	4%	5%	6%	7%	8%	9%	10%	12%	14%	16%	20%
1	0.961538	0.952381	0.943396	0.934579	0.925926	0.917431	0.909091	0.892857	0.877193	0.862069	0.833333
2	1.886095	1.859410	1.83393	1.808018	1.783265	1.759111	1.735537	1.690051	1.646661	1.605232	1.527778
3	2.775091	2.723248	2.673012	2.624316	2.577097	2.531295	2.486852	2.401831	2.321632	2.245890	2.106481
4	3.629895	3.545951	3.465106	3.387211	3.312127	3.239720	3.169865	3.037349	2.913712	2.798181	2.588735
5	4.451822	4.329477	4.212364	4.100197	3.992710	3.889651	3.790787	3.604776	3.433081	3.274294	2.990612
6	5.242137	5.075692	4.917324	4.766540	4.622880	4.485919	4.355261	4.111407	3.888668	3.684736	3.325510
7	6.002055	5.786373	5.582381	5.389289	5.206370	5.032953	4.868419	4.563757	4.288305	4.038565	3.604592
8	6.732745	6.463213	6.209794	5.971299	5.746639	5.534819	5.334926	4.967640	4.638864	4.343591	3.837160
9	7.435332	7.107822	6.801692	6.515232	6.246888	5.995247	5.759024	5.328250	4.946372	4.606544	4.030967
10	8.110896	7.721735	7.360087	7.023582	6.710081	6.417658	6.144567	5.650223	5.216116	4.833227	4.192472
11	8.760477	8.306414	7.886875	7.498674	7.138964	6.805191	6.495061	5.937699	5.452733	5.028644	4.327060
12	9.385074	8.863252	8.383844	7.942686	7.536078	7.160725	6.813692	6.194374	5.660292	5.197107	4.439217
13	9.985648	9.393573	8.852683	8.357651	7.903776	7.486904	7.103356	6.423548	5.842362	5.342334	4.532681
14	10.563123	9.898641	9.294984	8.745468	8.244237	7.786150	7.366687	6.628168	6.002072	5.467529	4.610567
15	11.118387	10.379658	9.712249	9.107914	8.559479	8.060688	7.606080	6.810864	6.142168	5.575456	4.675473
16	11.652296	10.837770	10.105895	9.446649	8.851369	8.312558	7.823709	6.973986	6.265060	5.668497	4.729561
17	12.165669	11.274066	10.477260	9.763223	9.121638	8.543631	8.021553	7.119630	6.372859	5.748704	4.774634
18	12.659297	11.689587	10.827603	10.059087	9.371887	8.755625	8.201412	7.249670	6.467420	5.817848	4.812195
19	13.133939	12.085321	11.158116	10.335595	9.603599	8.905115	8.364920	7.365777	6.550369	5.877455	4.843496
20	13.590326	12.462210	11.469921	10.594014	9.818147	9.128546	8.513564	7.469444	6.623131	5.928841	4.869580

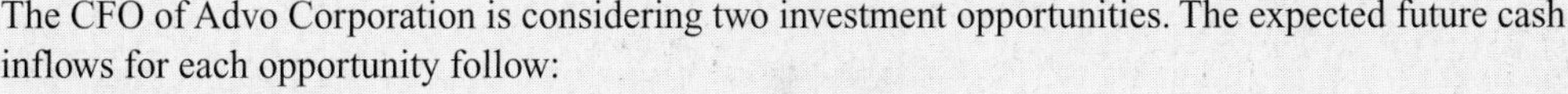

SELF-STUDY REVIEW PROBLEM

The CFO of Advo Corporation is considering two investment opportunities. The expected future cash inflows for each opportunity follow:

	Year 1	Year 2	Year 3	Year 4
Project 1	$144,000	$147,000	$160,000	$178,000
Project 2	204,000	199,000	114,000	112,000

Both investments require an initial payment of $400,000. Advo's desired rate of return is 16 percent.

Required

a. Compute the net present value of each project. Which project should Advo adopt based on the net present value approach?

b. Use the summation method to compute the payback period for each project. Which project should Advo adopt based on the payback approach?

Solution to Requirement *a*

Project 1					
	Cash Inflows		Table Factor*		Present Value
Year 1	$144,000	×	0.862069	=	$124,138
Year 2	147,000	×	0.743163	=	109,245
Year 3	160,000	×	0.640658	=	102,505
Year 4	178,000	×	0.552291	=	98,308
PV of cash inflows					434,196
Cost of investment					(400,000)
Net present value					$ 34,196

*Table 1, n = 1 through 4, r = 16%

Project 2						
	Cash Inflows		Table Factor*		Present Value
Year 1	$204,000	×	0.862069	=	$175,862
Year 2	199,000	×	0.743163	=	147,889
Year 3	114,000	×	0.640658	=	73,035
Year 4	112,000	×	0.552291	=	61,857
PV of cash inflows					458,643
Cost of investment					(400,000)
Net present value					$ 58,643

*Table 1, n = 1 through 4, r = 16%

Advo should adopt Project 2 since it has a greater net present value.

Solution to Requirement *b*

Cash Inflows	Project 1	Project 2
Year 1	$144,000	$204,000
Year 2	147,000	199,000
Total	$291,000	$403,000

By the end of the second year, Project 2's cash inflows have more than paid for the cost of the investment. In contrast, Project 1 still falls short of investment recovery by $109,000 ($400,000 − $291,000). Advo should adopt Project 2 since it has a shorter payback period.

KEY TERMS

accumulated conversion factor 556
annuity 557
capital investments 554
cost of capital 555
incremental revenue 561
internal rate of return 560
minimum rate of return 555
net present value 560
ordinary annuity 558
payback method 568
postaudit 571
present value index 564
present value table 556
recovery of investment 570
single-payment (lump-sum) 556
time value of money 554
unadjusted rate of return 569
working capital 561

QUESTIONS

1. What is a capital investment? How does it differ from an investment in stocks or bonds?
2. What are three reasons that cash is worth more today than cash to be received in the future?
3. "A dollar today is worth more than a dollar in the future." "The present value of a future dollar is worth less than one dollar." Are these two statements synonymous? Explain.
4. Define the term *return on investment.* How is the return normally expressed? Give an example of a capital investment return.
5. How does a company establish its minimum acceptable rate of return on investments?
6. If you wanted to have $500,000 one year from today and desired to earn a 10 percent return, what amount would you need to invest today? Which amount has more value, the amount today or the $500,000 a year from today?
7. Why are present value tables frequently used to convert future values to present values?
8. Define the term *annuity.* What is one example of an annuity receipt?

9. How can present value "what-if " analysis be enhanced by using software programs?
10. Receiving $100,000 per year for five years is equivalent to investing what amount today at 14 percent? Provide a mathematical formula to solve this problem, assuming use of a present value annuity table to convert the future cash flows to their present value equivalents. Provide the expression for the Excel spreadsheet function that would perform the present value conversion.
11. Maria Espinosa borrowed $15,000 from the bank and agreed to repay the loan at 8 percent annual interest over four years, making payments of $4,529 per year. Because part of the bank's payment from Ms. Espinosa is a recovery of the original investment, what assumption must the bank make to earn its desired 8 percent compounded annual return?
12. Two investment opportunities have positive net present values. Investment A's net present value amounts to $40,000 while B's is only $30,000. Does this mean that A is the better investment opportunity? Explain.
13. What criteria determine whether a project is acceptable under the net present value method?
14. Does the net present value method provide a measure of the rate of return on capital investments?
15. Which is the best capital investment evaluation technique for ranking investment opportunities?
16. Paul Henderson is a manager for Spark Company. He tells you that his company always maximizes profitability by accepting the investment opportunity with the highest internal rate of return. Explain to Mr. Henderson how his company may improve profitability by sometimes selecting investment opportunities with lower internal rates of return.
17. What is the relationship between desired rate of return and internal rate of return?
18. What typical cash inflow and outflow items are associated with capital investments?
19. "I always go for the investment with the shortest payback period." Is this a sound strategy? Why or why not?
20. "The payback method cannot be used if the cash inflows occur in unequal patterns." Do you agree or disagree? Explain.
21. What are the advantages and disadvantages associated with the unadjusted rate of return method for evaluating capital investments?
22. How do capital investments affect profitability?
23. What is a postaudit? How is it useful in capital budgeting?

EXERCISES

All Exercises are available with McGraw-Hill's Homework Manager

Exercise 16-1 *Identifying cash inflows and outflows* — L.O. 1

Required

Indicate which of the following items will result in cash inflows and which will result in cash outflows. The first one is shown as an example.

Item	Type of Cash Flow
a. Incremental revenue	Inflow
b. Initial investment	
c. Salvage values	
d. Recovery of working capital	
e. Incremental expenses	
f. Working capital commitments	
g. Cost savings	

Exercise 16-2 *Determining the present value of a lump-sum future cash receipt* — L.O. 1, 2

Mark Nelson turned 20 years old today. His grandfather established a trust fund that will pay Mr. Nelson $50,000 on his next birthday. However, Mr. Nelson needs money today to start his college education. His father is willing to help and has agreed to give Mr. Nelson the present value of the future cash inflow, assuming a 10 percent rate of return.

Required

a. Use a present value table to determine the amount of cash that Mr. Nelson's father should give him.

b. Use an algebraic formula to prove that the present value of the trust fund (the amount of cash computed in Requirement *a*) is equal to its $50,000 future value.

L.O. 1, 2

Exercise 16-3 *Determining the present value of a lump-sum future cash receipt*

Ginger Smalley expects to receive a $300,000 cash benefit when she retires five years from today. Ms. Smalley's employer has offered an early retirement incentive by agreeing to pay her $180,000 today if she agrees to retire immediately. Ms. Smalley desires to earn a rate of return of 12 percent.

Required

a. Assuming that the retirement benefit is the only consideration in making the retirement decision, should Ms. Smalley accept her employer's offer?

b. Identify the factors that cause the present value of the retirement benefit to be less than $300,000.

L.O. 1, 2

Exercise 16-4 *Determining the present value of an annuity*

The dean of the School of Social Science is trying to decide whether to purchase a copy machine to place in the lobby of the building. The machine would add to student convenience, but the dean feels compelled to earn an 8 percent return on the investment of funds. Estimates of cash inflows from copy machines that have been placed in other university buildings indicate that the copy machine would probably produce incremental cash inflows of approximately $8,000 per year. The machine is expected to have a three-year useful life with a zero salvage value.

Required

a. Use Present Value Table 1 in the chapter's Appendix to determine the maximum amount of cash the dean should be willing to pay for a copy machine.

b. Use Present Value Table 2 in the chapter's Appendix to determine the maximum amount of cash the dean should be willing to pay for a copy machine.

c. Explain the consistency or lack of consistency in the answers to Requirements *a* and *b*.

L.O. 4

Exercise 16-5 *Determining net present value*

Transit Shuttle Inc. is considering investing in two new vans that are expected to generate combined cash inflows of $20,000 per year. The vans' combined purchase price is $65,000. The expected life and salvage value of each are four years and $15,000, respectively. Transit Shuttle has an average cost of capital of 14 percent.

Required

a. Calculate the net present value of the investment opportunity.

b. Indicate whether the investment opportunity is expected to earn a return that is above or below the cost of capital and whether it should be accepted.

L.O. 4

Exercise 16-6 *Determining net present value*

Travis Vintor is seeking part-time employment while he attends school. He is considering purchasing technical equipment that will enable him to start a small training services company that will offer tutorial services over the Internet. Travis expects demand for the service to grow rapidly in the first two years of operation as customers learn about the availability of the Internet assistance. Thereafter, he expects demand to stabilize. The following table presents the expected cash flows.

Year of Operation	Cash Inflow	Cash Outflow
2006	$5,400	$3,600
2007	7,800	4,800
2008	8,400	5,040
2009	8,400	5,040

In addition to these cash flows, Mr. Vintor expects to pay $8,400 for the equipment. He also expects to pay $1,440 for a major overhaul and updating of the equipment at the end of the second year of operation. The equipment is expected to have a $600 salvage value and a four-year useful life. Mr. Vintor desires to earn a rate of return of 8 percent.

Required

(Round computations to the nearest whole penny.)

a. Calculate the net present value of the investment opportunity.

b. Indicate whether the investment opportunity is expected to earn a return that is above or below the desired rate of return and whether it should be accepted.

Exercise 16-7 *Using present value index* L.O. 4

Wrencher Company has a choice of two investment alternatives. The present value of cash inflows and outflows for the first alternative is $60,000 and $56,000, respectively. The present value of cash inflows and outflows for the second alternative is $146,000 and $142,000, respectively.

Required

a. Calculate the net present value of each investment opportunity.

b. Calculate the present value index for each investment opportunity.

c. Indicate which investment will produce the higher rate of return.

Exercise 16-8 *Determining the internal rate of return* L.O. 5

Medina Manufacturing Company has an opportunity to purchase some technologically advanced equipment that will reduce the company's cash outflow for operating expenses by $1,280,000 per year. The cost of the equipment is $6,186,530.56. Medina expects it to have a 10-year useful life and a zero salvage value. The company has established an investment opportunity hurdle rate of 15 percent and uses the straight-line method for depreciation.

Required

a. Calculate the internal rate of return of the investment opportunity.

b. Indicate whether the investment opportunity should be accepted.

Exercise 16-9 *Using the internal rate of return to compare investment opportunities* L.O. 5

Smith and Hough (S&H) is a partnership that owns a small company. It is considering two alternative investment opportunities. The first investment opportunity will have a five-year useful life, will cost $9,335.16, and will generate expected cash inflows of $2,400 per year. The second investment is expected to have a useful life of three years, will cost $6,217.13, and will generate expected cash inflows of $2,500 per year. Assume that S&H has the funds available to accept only one of the opportunities.

Required

a. Calculate the internal rate of return of each investment opportunity.

b. Based on the internal rates of return, which opportunity should S&H select?

c. Discuss other factors that S&H should consider in the investment decision.

Exercise 16-10 *Determining the cash flow annuity with income tax considerations* L.O. 1, 2

To open a new store, Ross Tire Company plans to invest $640,000 in equipment expected to have a four-year useful life and no salvage value. Ross expects the new store to generate annual cash revenues of $840,000 and to incur annual cash operating expenses of $520,000. Ross's average income tax rate is 30 percent. The company uses straight-line depreciation.

Required

Determine the expected annual net cash inflow from operations for each of the first four years after Ross opens the new store.

Exercise 16-11 *Evaluating discounted cash flow techniques* L.O. 8

Kay Vickery is angry with Gene Libby. He is behind schedule developing supporting material for tomorrow's capital budget committee meeting. When she approached him about his apparent

lackadaisical attitude in general and his tardiness in particular, he responded, "I don't see why we do this stuff in the first place. It's all a bunch of estimates. Who knows what future cash flows will really be? I certainly don't. I've been doing this job for five years, and no one has ever checked to see if I even came close at these guesses. I've been waiting for marketing to provide the estimated cash inflows on the projects being considered tomorrow. But, if you want my report now, I'll have it in a couple of hours. I can make up the marketing data as well as they can."

Required

Does Mr. Libby have a point? Is there something wrong with the company's capital budgeting system? Write a brief response explaining how to improve the investment evaluation system.

L.O. 6

Exercise 16-12 *Determining the payback period*

Cascade Airline Company is considering expanding its territory. The company has the opportunity to purchase one of two different used airplanes. The first airplane is expected to cost $1,800,000; it will enable the company to increase its annual cash inflow by $600,000 per year. The plane is expected to have a useful life of five years and no salvage value. The second plane costs $3,600,000; it will enable the company to increase annual cash flow by $900,000 per year. This plane has an eight-year useful life and a zero salvage value.

Required

a. Determine the payback period for each investment alternative and identify the alternative Cascade should accept if the decision is based on the payback approach.

b. Discuss the shortcomings of using the payback method to evaluate investment opportunities.

L.O. 6

Exercise 16-13 *Determining the payback period with uneven cash flows*

Shaw Company has an opportunity to purchase a forklift to use in its heavy equipment rental business. The forklift would be leased on an annual basis during its first two years of operation. Thereafter, it would be leased to the general public on demand. Shaw would sell it at the end of the fifth year of its useful life. The expected cash inflows and outflows follow.

Year	Nature of Item	Cash Inflow	Cash Outflow
2008	Purchase price		$48,000
2008	Revenue	$20,000	
2009	Revenue	20,000	
2010	Revenue	14,000	
2010	Major overhaul		6,000
2011	Revenue	12,000	
2012	Revenue	9,600	
2012	Salvage value	6,400	

Required

a. Determine the payback period using the accumulated cash flows approach.

b. Determine the payback period using the average cash flows approach.

L.O. 7

Exercise 16-14 *Determining the unadjusted rate of return*

Tharpe Painting Company is considering whether to purchase a new spray paint machine that costs $3,000. The machine is expected to save labor, increasing net income by $450 per year. The effective life of the machine is 15 years according to the manufacturer's estimate.

Required

a. Determine the unadjusted rate of return based on the average cost of the investment.

b. Discuss the shortcomings of using the unadjusted rate of return to evaluate investment opportunities.

L.O. 6, 7

Exercise 16-15 *Computing the payback period and unadjusted rate of return for one investment opportunity*

Padgett Rentals can purchase a van that costs $48,000; it has an expected useful life of three years and no salvage value. Padgett uses straight-line depreciation. Expected revenue is $24,000 per year.

Required

a. Determine the payback period.

b. Determine the unadjusted rate of return based on the average cost of the investment.

PROBLEMS

All Problems are available with McGraw-Hill's Homework Manager

Problem 16-16 ***Using present value techniques to evaluate alternative investment opportunities***

L.O. 4

excel

mhhe.com/edmonds2007

CHECK FIGURES

a. NPV of the vans investment: $100,811.42

b. NPV index of the trucks investment: 1.126

Parcel Delivery is a small company that transports business packages between Boston and Philadelphia. It operates a fleet of small vans that moves packages to and from a central depot within each city and uses a common carrier to deliver the packages between the depots in the two cities. Parcel recently acquired approximately $4 million of cash capital from its owners, and its president, Roger Makris, is trying to identify the most profitable way to invest these funds.

Nick Wells, the company's operations manager, believes that the money should be used to expand the fleet of city vans at a cost of $720,000. He argues that more vans would enable the company to expand its services into new markets, thereby increasing the revenue base. More specifically, he expects cash inflows to increase by $280,000 per year. The additional vans are expected to have an average useful life of four years and a combined salvage value of $100,000. Operating the vans will require additional working capital of $40,000, which will be recovered at the end of the fourth year.

In contrast, Leigh Young, the company's chief accountant, believes that the funds should be used to purchase large trucks to deliver the packages between the depots in the two cities. The conversion process would produce continuing improvement in operating savings with reductions in cash outflows as the following:

Year 1	Year 2	Year 3	Year 4
$160,000	$320,000	$400,000	$440,000

The large trucks are expected to cost $800,000 and to have a four-year useful life and a $80,000 salvage value. In addition to the purchase price of the trucks, up-front training costs are expected to amount to $16,000. Parcel Delivery's management has established a 16 percent desired rate of return.

Required

a. Determine the net present value of the two investment alternatives.

b. Calculate the present value index for each alternative.

c. Indicate which investment alternative you would recommend. Explain your choice.

Problem 16-17 ***Using the payback period and unadjusted rate of return to evaluate alternative investment opportunities***

L.O. 6, 7

CHECK FIGURES

a. Payback period of the yogurt investment: 1.77 years
Unadjusted rate of return of the cappuccino investment: 52.86%

Brice Looney owns a small retail ice cream parlor. He is considering expanding the business and has identified two attractive alternatives. One involves purchasing a machine that would enable Mr. Looney to offer frozen yogurt to customers. The machine would cost $2,700 and has an expected useful life of three years with no salvage value. Additional annual cash revenues and cash operating expenses associated with selling yogurt are expected to be $1,980 and $300, respectively.

Alternatively, Mr. Looney could purchase for $3,360 the equipment necessary to serve cappuccino. That equipment has an expected useful life of four years and no salvage value. Additional annual cash revenues and cash operating expenses associated with selling cappuccino are expected to be $2,760 and $810, respectively.

Income before taxes earned by the ice cream parlor is taxed at an effective rate of 20 percent.

Required

a. Determine the payback period and unadjusted rate of return (use average investment) for each alternative.

b. Indicate which investment alternative you would recommend. Explain your choice.

L.O. 4, 5

CHECK FIGURES

a. NPV of A: $17,950.68

b. Rate of return of B: 12%

Problem 16-18 *Using net present value and internal rate of return to evaluate investment opportunities*

Jane Crawford, the president of Crawford Enterprises, is considering two investment opportunities. Because of limited resources, she will be able to invest in only one of them. Project A is to purchase a machine that will enable factory automation; the machine is expected to have a useful life of four years and no salvage value. Project B supports a training program that will improve the skills of employees operating the current equipment. Initial cash expenditures for Project A are $400,000 and for Project B are $160,000. The annual expected cash inflows are $126,188 for Project A and $52,676 for Project B. Both investments are expected to provide cash flow benefits for the next four years. Crawford Enterprise's cost of capital is 8 percent.

Required

a. Compute the net present value of each project. Which project should be adopted based on the net present value approach?

b. Compute the approximate internal rate of return of each project. Which one should be adopted based on the internal rate of return approach?

c. Compare the net present value approach with the internal rate of return approach. Which method is better in the given circumstances? Why?

L.O. 4, 6

CHECK FIGURES

a. NPV of #1: $164,189.94

b. Payback period of #2: less than 2 years.

Problem 16-19 *Using net present value and payback period to evaluate investment opportunities*

Lowell Cox saved $800,000 during the 25 years that he worked for a major corporation. Now he has retired at the age of 50 and has begun to draw a comfortable pension check every month. He wants to ensure the financial security of his retirement by investing his savings wisely and is currently considering two investment opportunities. Both investments require an initial payment of $600,000. The following table presents the estimated cash inflows for the two alternatives.

	Year 1	Year 2	Year 3	Year 4
Opportunity #1	$178,000	$188,000	$252,000	$324,000
Opportunity #2	328,000	348,000	56,000	48,000

Mr. Cox decides to use his past average return on mutual fund investments as the discount rate; it is 8 percent.

Required

a. Compute the net present value of each opportunity. Which should Mr. Cox adopt based on the net present value approach?

b. Compute the payback period for each project. Which should Mr. Cox adopt based on the payback approach?

c. Compare the net present value approach with the payback approach. Which method is better in the given circumstances?

L.O. 4, 6, 7

mhhe.com/edmonds2007

CHECK FIGURES

a. NPV = $71,810

d. Payback period: 2.32 years

Problem 16-20 *Effects of straight-line versus accelerated depreciation on an investment decision*

Hilyer Electronics is considering investing in manufacturing equipment expected to cost $184,000. The equipment has an estimated useful life of four years and a salvage value of $24,000. It is expected to produce incremental cash revenues of $96,000 per year. Hilyer has an effective income tax rate of 30 percent and a desired rate of return of 12 percent.

Required

a. Determine the net present value and the present value index of the investment, assuming that Hilyer uses straight-line depreciation for financial and income tax reporting.

b. Determine the net present value and the present value index of the investment, assuming that Hilyer uses double-declining-balance depreciation for financial and income tax reporting.

c. Why do the net present values computed in Requirements *a* and *b* differ?

d. Determine the payback period and unadjusted rate of return (use average investment), assuming that Hilyer uses straight-line depreciation.

e. Determine the payback period and unadjusted rate of return (use average investment), assuming that Hilyer uses double-declining-balance depreciation. (Note: Use average annual cash flow when computing the payback period and average annual income when determining the unadjusted rate of return.)

f. Why are there no differences in the payback periods or unadjusted rates of return computed in Requirements *d* and *e*?

Problem 16-21 *Applying the net present value approach with and without tax considerations*

L.O. 4

mhhe.com/edmonds2007

CHECK FIGURE
a. $(46,120.48)

Buck Novak, the chief executive officer of Novak Corporation, has assembled his top advisers to evaluate an investment opportunity. The advisers expect the company to pay $400,000 cash at the beginning of the investment and the cash inflow for each of the following four years to be the following.

Year 1	Year 2	Year 3	Year 4
$84,000	$96,000	$120,000	$184,000

Mr. Novak agrees with his advisers that the company should use the discount rate (required rate of return) of 12 percent to compute net present value to evaluate the viability of the proposed project.

Required

a. Compute the net present value of the proposed project. Should Mr. Novak approve the project?

b. Lydia Hollman, one of the advisers, is wary of the cash flow forecast and she points out that the advisers failed to consider that the depreciation on equipment used in this project will be tax deductible. The depreciation is expected to be $80,000 per year for the four-year period. The company's income tax rate is 30 percent per year. Use this information to revise the company's expected cash flow from this project.

c. Compute the net present value of the project based on the revised cash flow forecast. Should Mr. Novak approve the project?

Problem 16-22 *Comparing internal rate of return with unadjusted rate of return*

L.O. 5, 7

CHECK FIGURE
b. Internal rate of return: 12%

Masters Auto Repair Inc. is evaluating a project to purchase equipment that will not only expand the company's capacity but also improve the quality of its repair services. The board of directors requires all capital investments to meet or exceed the minimum requirement of a 10 percent rate of return. However, the board has not clearly defined the rate of return. The president and controller are pondering two different rates of return: unadjusted rate of return and internal rate of return. The equipment, which costs $400,000, has a life expectancy of five years. The increased net profit per year will be approximately $28,000, and the increased cash inflow per year will be approximately $110,800.

Required

a. If it uses the unadjusted rate of return (use average investment) to evaluate this project, should the company invest in the equipment?

b. If it uses the internal rate of return to evaluate this project, should the company invest in the equipment?

c. Which method is better for this capital investment decision?

Problem 16-23 *Postaudit evaluation*

L.O. 8

CHECK FIGURE
b. NPV: $(654,174)

Sean Roberts is reviewing his company's investment in a cement plant. The company paid $15,000,000 five years ago to acquire the plant. Now top management is considering an opportunity to sell it. The president wants to know whether the plant has met original expectations before he decides its fate. The company's discount rate for present value computations is 8 percent. Expected and actual cash flows follow.

	Year 1	Year 2	Year 3	Year 4	Year 5
Expected	$3,300,000	$4,920,000	$4,560,000	$4,980,000	$4,200,000
Actual	2,700,000	3,060,000	4,920,000	3,900,000	3,600,000

Required

a. Compute the net present value of the expected cash flows as of the beginning of the investment.
b. Compute the net present value of the actual cash flows as of the beginning of the investment.
c. What do you conclude from this postaudit?

ANALYZE, THINK, COMMUNICATE

ATC 16-1 Business Applications Case *Lottery winnings consulting job*

The February 20, 2004, drawing for the Mergmillions multistate lottery produced one winning ticket. More than a month after the drawing no one had come forward to claim the $239 million prize. Perhaps the winner was simply confused about whether to take the winnings as a lump-sum, immediate payment, or annual payments over the next 26 years.

Assume that you work as a personal financial planner, and that one of your clients held the winning lottery ticket. He faces the choice of (1) taking annual payments of $9,192,308 over the next 26 years ($239 million ÷ 26), or (2) taking an immediate one-time payment of $136 million.

Required

a. Assume you believe you can invest your client's winnings and safely earn an average annual return of 7 percent. Should he take the immediate cash payment or should he take the 26 annual payments? Ignore tax considerations and show the supporting computations used to reach your answer.
b. Assume your client is not convinced you can safely earn an annual rate of 7 percent on his money. What is the minimum annual rate of return you would need to earn for him before he would be better off taking the immediate cash payout of $136 million rather than the 26 annual payments of $9,192,308? Ignore tax considerations and show the supporting computations used to reach your answer.

(The tables in the chapter's Appendix end at 20 periods, so the factors for 26 periods are provided below.)

Present Value of $1

n	4%	5%	6%	7%	8%	9%	10%	12%	14%
26	0.3607	0.2812	0.2198	0.1722	0.1352	0.1064	0.0839	0.0525	0.0331

Present Value of an Annuity of $1

n	4%	5%	6%	7%	8%	9%	10%	12%	14%
26	15.9828	14.3752	13.0032	11.8258	10.8100	9.9290	9.1609	7.8957	6.9061

ATC 16-2 Group Assignment *Net present value*

Espada Real Estate Investment Company (EREIC) purchases new apartment complexes, establishes a stable group of residents, and then sells the complexes to apartment management companies. The average holding time is three years. EREIC is currently investigating two alternatives.

1. EREIC can purchase Harding Properties for $4,500,000. The complex is expected to produce net cash inflows of $360,000, $502,500, and $865,000 for the first, second, and third years of operation, respectively. The market value of the complex at the end of the third year is expected to be $5,175,000.
2. EREIC can purchase Summit Apartments for $3,450,000. The complex is expected to produce net cash inflows of $290,000, $435,000, and $600,000 for the first, second, and third years of

operation, respectively. The market value of the complex at the end of the third year is expected to be $4,050,000.

EREIC has a desired rate of return of 12 percent.

Required

a. Divide the class into groups of four or five students per group and then divide the groups into two sections. Assign Task 1 to the first section and Task 2 to the second section.

Group Tasks

(1) Calculate the net present value and the present value index for Harding Properties.

(2) Calculate the net present value and the present value index for Summit Apartments.

b. Have a spokesperson from one group in the first section report the amounts calculated by the group. Make sure that all groups in the section have the same result. Repeat the process for the second section. Have the class as a whole select the investment opportunity that EREIC should accept given that the objective is to produce the higher rate of return.

c. Assume that EREIC has $4,500,000 to invest and that any funds not invested in real estate properties must be invested in a certificate of deposit earning a 5 percent return. Would this information alter the decision made in Requirement *b*?

d. This requirement is independent of Requirement *c*. Assume there is a 10 percent chance that the Harding project will be annexed by the city of Hoover, which has an outstanding school district. The annexation would likely increase net cash flows by $37,500 per year and would increase the market value at the end of year 3 by $300,000. Would this information change the decision reached in Requirement *b*?

ATC 16-3 Research Assignment *Real world capital budgeting issues*

In recent years companies have devoted considerable time trying to decide if new software systems should be purchased. Vendors trying to sell the systems in question are happy to provide their own analysis to the prospective buyer showing how profitable their system will be. Not surprisingly, buyers are often skeptical of the objectivity of such analysis, and prefer to do their own. "Sizing Up Your Payoff," *BusinessWeek,* October 29, 2001, presents anecdotal evidence about problems companies have encountered when evaluating the profitability of proposed software systems. Read this article and complete the following requirements.

Required

a. The focus of the article is on "return on investment" (ROI) analysis. Of the four techniques presented in this chapter for analyzing capital projects, which do you think is most closely related to the ROI analysis discussed by the article?

b. Give an example from the article of a company that appears to be using the payback method, at least in part, for capital budgeting decisions.

c. Give an example from the article of a company that appears to be using the internal rate of return method, at least in part, for capital budgeting decisions.

d. Give an example from the article of a company that used a postaudit to evaluate a capital budgeting decision it had made. What were the results of this postaudit?

e. The article discusses a capital project study that Metreo, Inc., undertook before buying a software system. How long did this study take? How many employees were asked to provide input into the analysis?

ATC 16-4 Writing Assignment *Limitations of capital investment techniques*

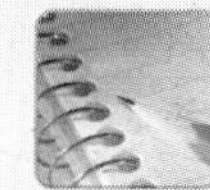

Webb Publishing Company is evaluating two investment opportunities. One is to purchase an Internet company with the capacity to open new marketing channels through which Webb can sell its books. This opportunity offers a high potential for growth but involves significant risk. Indeed, losses are projected for the first three years of operation. The second opportunity is to purchase a printing company that would enable Webb to better control costs by printing its own books. The potential savings are clearly predictable but would make a significant change in the company's long-term profitability.

Required

Write a response discussing the usefulness of capital investment techniques (net present value, internal rate of return, payback, and unadjusted rate of return) in making a choice between these two alternative investment opportunities. Your response should discuss the strengths and weaknesses of capital budgeting techniques in general. Furthermore, it should include a comparison between techniques based on the time value of money versus those that are not.

ATC 16-5 Ethical Dilemma *Postaudit*

Gaines Company recently initiated a postaudit program. To motivate employees to take the program seriously, Gaines established a bonus program. Managers receive a bonus equal to 10 percent of the amount by which actual net present value exceeds the projected net present value. Victor Holt, manager of the North Western Division, had an investment proposal on his desk when the new system was implemented. The investment opportunity required a $250,000 initial cash outflow and was expected to return cash inflows of $90,000 per year for the next five years. Gaines' desired rate of return is 10 percent. Mr. Holt immediately reduced the estimated cash inflows to $70,000 per year and recommended accepting the project.

Required

a. Assume that actual cash inflows turn out to be $91,000 per year. Determine the amount of Mr. Holt's bonus if the original computation of net present value were based on $90,000 versus $70,000.

b. Is Mr. Holt's behavior in violation of any of the standards of ethical conduct in Exhibit 10.13 of Chapter 10?

c. Speculate about the long-term effect the bonus plan is likely to have on the company.

d. Recommend how to compensate managers in a way that discourages gamesmanship.

Accessing the EDGAR Database Through the Internet

Successful business managers need many different skills, including communication, interpersonal, computer, and analytical. Most business students become very aware of the data analysis skills used in accounting, but they may not be as aware of the importance of "data-finding" skills. There are many sources of accounting and financial data. The more sources you are able to use, the better.

One very important source of accounting information is the EDGAR database. Others are probably available at your school through the library or business school network. Your accounting instructor will be able to identify these for you and make suggestions regarding their use. By making the effort to learn to use electronic databases, you will enhance your abilities as a future manager and your marketability as a business graduate.

These instructions assume that you know how to access and use an Internet navigator, such as Netscape. After you activate the Navigator program on your computer, follow the instructions to retrieve data from the Securities and Exchange Commission's EDGAR database. Be aware that the SEC may have changed its interface since this appendix was written. Accordingly, be prepared for slight differences between the following instructions and what appears on your computer screen. Take comfort in the fact that changes are normally designed to simplify user access. If you encounter a conflict between the following instructions and the instructions provided in the SEC interface, remember that the SEC interface is more current and should take precedence over the following instructions.

1. To connect to EDGAR, type in the following address: **http://www.sec.gov/**.
2. After the SEC home page appears, under the heading **Filings & Forms (EDGAR),** click on **Search for Company Filings.**
3. From the screen that appears, click on **Companies & Other Filers.**
4. On the screen that appears, enter the name of the company whose file you wish to retrieve and click on the **Find Companies** button.
5. The following screen will present a list of companies that have the same, or similar, names to the one you entered. Identify the company you want and click on the CIK number beside it.
6. Enter the SEC form number that you want to retrieve in the window titled **Form Type** that appears in the upper right portion of the screen that appears. For example, if you want Form 10-K, which will usually be the case, enter **10-K,** and click on the **Retrieve Filings** button.
7. A list of the forms you requested will be presented, along with the date they were filed with the SEC. You may be given a choice of **[text]** or **[html]** file format. The **[text]** format will present one large file for the form you requested. The **[html]** format will probably present several separate files from which you must choose. These will be named Document 1 . . ., Document 2 . . ., etc. Usually, you should choose the file whose name ends in **10k.txt.** Form 10-K/A is an amended Form 10-K and it sometimes contains more timely information, but usually, the most recent Form 10-K will contain the information you need.
8. Once the 10-K has been retrieved, you can search it online or save it on your hard drive or diskette. If you want to save it, do so by using the **Save As** command from the pull-down menu at the top of the screen named **File.**
9. The financial statements are seldom located near the beginning of a company's 10-K, so it is necessary to scroll down the file until you find them. Typically, they are located about one-half to three-fourths of the way through the report.

Topps Annual Report 2003

Stockholders' Letter

Dear Stockholders:

Fiscal 2003, ended March 1, 2003, marked the beginning of a Company-wide program devoted to building for future growth. In last year's Annual Report, we characterized the upcoming year as one of strategic investment. It was all of that and more as the Company made meaningful progress against targeted initiatives, in a difficult business environment.

Overall, we aimed to strengthen Topps position as a global marketer of branded confectionery and entertainment products. In fact, we recently announced that we will be reporting the sports and entertainment segments as one business—Entertainment—due to their similarities and the way we are now organized to manage them.

Here is a sampling of Topps strategies that guided our activities last year along with some specific achievements against them to date. For financial details see Management's Discussion beginning on page 7.

Confectionery

In fiscal 2003, we set out to grow the core brand franchises of Ring Pop, Push Pop and Baby Bottle Pop, as measured by heightened consumer awareness, greater retail distribution, and increased sales.

Ring Pop and Push Pop brands both delivered strong performances with impressive sales gains in the United States. The impetus for progress was execution against our three-pronged strategy—providing children with compelling high quality products, expanding product availability (distribution and in-store location) and advertising on kids' television programs. Overseas, we also aimed to secure confectionery listings in several key retailers and were on the mark in virtually every instance.

Baby Bottle Pop presented a particular challenge, coming off a year-long special retail promotion at Wal-Mart, as well as our expectation of lower sales in Japan after the product's rollout there last year. Still, we had reason to envision that much, if not all, of that lost ground could be made up by a highly anticipated brand extension. "Baby Bottle Pop with Candy Juice," was originally scheduled to reach market early enough in the fiscal year to impact financial results. Technical difficulties, however, delayed its introduction until this past January when first shipments were made, at last.

Fast-forwarding to today, we are very encouraged by early reports of consumer response to the new entry as well as solid trade acceptance. "Candy Juice" may well turn out to have been worth the wait. Further, a new brand, "Juicy Drop Pop," is making its initial appearance overseas as we speak.

Another goal for us in fiscal 2003 was to begin branching out into other kids' confectionery segments by creating one or more brands outside the lollipop category, for marketing in fiscal 2004. We analyzed the candy universe to identify areas of opportunity based on a variety of factors such as segment size and growth, price points, trade channel development and competitive framework. Qualitative and quantitative research was conducted to gain consumer insights about targeted segments. That data was used to guide internal and external new product development activities.

At present, there are several candidates in development, at least one of which is expected to see light of day this fiscal year. Work on these and other new confectionery products continues apace.

Entertainment

In fiscal 2003, the principal focus was on leveraging our strengths (brands and know-how) against current products and new formats. As mentioned earlier, this segment is now comprised of sports and non-sports products, including trading cards, stickers, albums, internet, and other entertainment offerings.

Our traditional sports card products performed relatively well during the period, winning an enviable number of industry awards and, as best one can tell, gaining market share.

Nonetheless, the consumer base for traditional cards declined yet again and there is little protection for sales and margins in such a lengthy down cycle. Simply too many competitors vie for bits of too small a pie. Accordingly, in the fourth quarter, we significantly modified our expectations regarding next year's traditional card sales and took the steps necessary to bring staffing, costs and marketing plans more in line with reality.

That said, we are as resolved as ever to advance the market leadership position Topps has held for decades, by continuing to create innovative products with purpose and appeal. After all, the Topps brand itself is and can continue to be a powerful sponsor for traditional and non-traditional offerings alike. Take "etopps" for instance, a relatively new brand of cards we sell exclusively on the internet via Initial Player Offerings (IPOs). Last year the number of registered etopps users and buyers expanded and we will continue to invest in its future. If you haven't already done so, we invite you to go to the site (www.etopps.com) and see for yourself what etopps is all about.

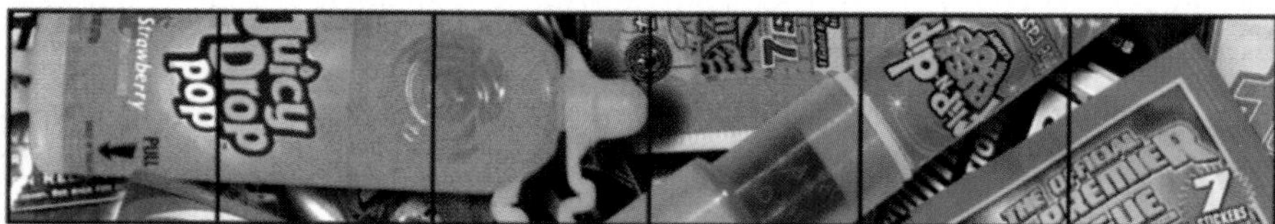

Another major strategy in fiscal 2003 was to improve the performance of our European football sticker album products. Results were outstanding, even excluding World Cup sales which occur only once every four years. We offered consumers compelling product innovations, utilized considerably more in-store merchandising than before and increased album sampling which appears to have brought more sticker buyers into the fold.

By way of example, Topps Italy successfully introduced a brand new concept marketed through our confectionery distribution system – Bubble Gum with Mini Stickers – featuring Calcio football players. This product was a significant success, making the case that combining creativity with brand equity is more than a good idea. It is an imperative going forward. Additional efforts along this line can be anticipated.

Last but not least, other Entertainment opportunities continue to dot our radar screen such as Simpsons Sticker Gum, released late last year. Presently scheduled for marketing this year are Yu-Gi-Oh! Stickers and Albums, The Incredible Hulk cards and punch-out cards featuring Beyblade, a popular Japanese animation property. We remain highly selective as to which licenses are pursued.

Conclusion

We hope the foregoing is helpful in providing perspective on last year's performance. No doubt, attention to strategic goals will continue to play a key role in shaping the Company's future.

We would like to express our appreciation to the entire Topps family of employees, both here and abroad, for their tireless efforts. These are the people in every discipline of the business that make the trains go on time, so to speak, and not bump into one another. And Happy Anniversary Bazooka Joe—50 years young is worth celebrating!

On behalf of the Organization, we also thank our fans, collectors, customers, licensors, stockholders and suppliers for their valued support.

Chairman, Chief Executive Officer and President

OFFICERS OF THE TOPPS COMPANY, INC.

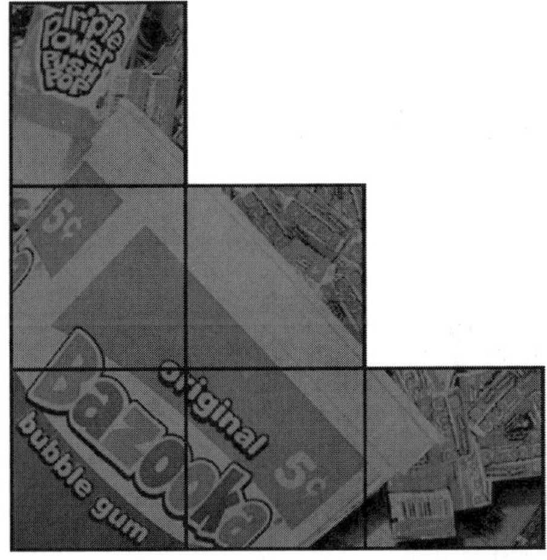

Triple Power Push Pop
5¢
original
Bazooka
bubble gum
5¢

financial highlights

	Year Ended		
	March 1, 2003	March 2, 2002	March 3, 2001
	(In thousands of dollars, except share data)		
Net sales	**$ 290,079**	$ 300,180	$ 437,440
Income from operations	**20,782**	36,564	121,917
Net income	**16,936**	28,462	88,489
Cash provided by operations	**6,200**	1,619	104,120
Working capital	**141,484**	136,389	140,487
Stockholders' equity	**196,768**	194,054	196,542
Net income per share - basic	**$ 0.41**	$ 0.66	$ 1.97
- diluted	**$ 0.40**	$ 0.64	$ 1.91
Weighted average shares outstanding - basic	**41,353,000**	43,073,000	45,011,000
- diluted	**42,065,000**	44,276,000	46,366,000

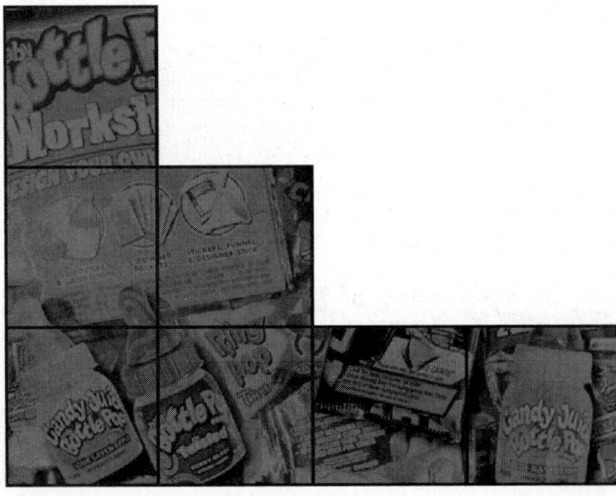

The Company has two reportable business segments: Confectionery and Entertainment. Consistent with Topps organizational structure and product line similarities, Entertainment now combines the former Sports and Entertainment segments into one.

The following table sets forth, for the periods indicated, net sales by key business segment:

	Year Ended		
	March 1, 2003	March 2, 2002	March 3, 2001
	(In thousands of dollars)		
Confectionery	**$146,865**	$152,127	$170,700
Entertainment	**143,214**	148,053	266,740
Total	**$290,079**	$300,180	$437,440

Fiscal 2003 Versus 2002*

In fiscal 2003, the Company's consolidated net sales decreased 3.4% to $290.1 million from $300.2 million in fiscal 2002. This decrease was primarily a function of a reduction in the popularity of products featuring Pokémon, which generated $6.0 million in sales in fiscal 2003 versus $24.1 million in fiscal 2002. Stronger European currencies served to increase fiscal 2003 sales by $3.9 million.

Net sales of the Confectionery segment, which includes Ring Pop, Push Pop, Baby Bottle Pop and Bazooka brand bubble gum, decreased 3.5% in 2003 to $146.9 million from $152.1 million in 2002. Excluding sales of Pokémon products, confectionery sales decreased 0.7%. Sales results reflect growth in the U.S. of Ring Pop and Push Pop, the successful roll out of Pro Flip Pop in Japan and the introduction of Yu-Gi-Oh! sticker pops in the U.S. and Canada. These gains were offset by lower sales of Baby Bottle Pop. Confectionery products accounted for 51% of the Company's consolidated net sales in both 2003 and 2002.

Net sales of the Entertainment segment, which includes cards, sticker albums and Internet activities, decreased 3.3% in fiscal 2003 to $143.2 million. Excluding sales of Pokémon products which decreased to $4.5 million in fiscal 2003 from $18.2 million, Entertainment sales increased 6.9%. Sales of European sports sticker albums increased significantly, driven by the World Cup soccer tour which occurs once every four years, substantial increases in sales of U.K. Premier League soccer products and the successful introduction of a new concept — bubble gum with mini stickers — in Italy. Internet activities, which include etopps (cards sold online via an IPO format) and thePit.com (an online sports card exchange), generated $11.9 million in sales and $0.7 million in contributed margin losses (before overhead) in 2003 versus $5.8 million in sales and $1.4 million in contributed margin losses in the prior year. Sales of traditional U.S. sports cards were lower in fiscal 2003, reflecting continued industry declines. In February 2003, the Company restructured its U.S. sports operations, reducing headcount and the number of products it expects to release going forward. In fiscal 2003, the Company also marketed products featuring the Star Wars, Spider-Man, Yu-Gi-Oh! and Hamtaro properties, among others. Entertainment products represented 49% of the Company's consolidated net sales in both 2003 and 2002.

Consolidated gross profit as a percentage of net sales decreased to 35.1% in 2003 from 37.9% in 2002. Margins this year were negatively impacted by the reduction in sales of high-margin Pokémon products, an increase in sales of lower margin products and the absence of rebates received last year from a foreign distributor.

Other income (expense) was $184,000 this year versus an expense of $215,000 last year, in part the result of government cash incentives to maintain our New York office location received in 2003, versus non-cash foreign exchange losses in 2002 on dollar-denominated cash balances held in Europe.

Selling, general & administrative expenses ("SG&A") increased as a percentage of net sales to 28.0% in 2003 from 25.7% a year ago. SG&A dollar spending increased to $81.1 million from $77.1 million due to the absence of a $2.4 million favorable Internet-related legal settlement received in 2002, a $1.6 million unfavorable legal settlement recorded in 2003 and an increase in marketing costs primarily related to etopps. Partially offsetting these increases was the elimination of goodwill amortization in 2003 in accordance with FAS 142, which totaled $1.6 million, and lower costs associated with the employee incentive compensation program.

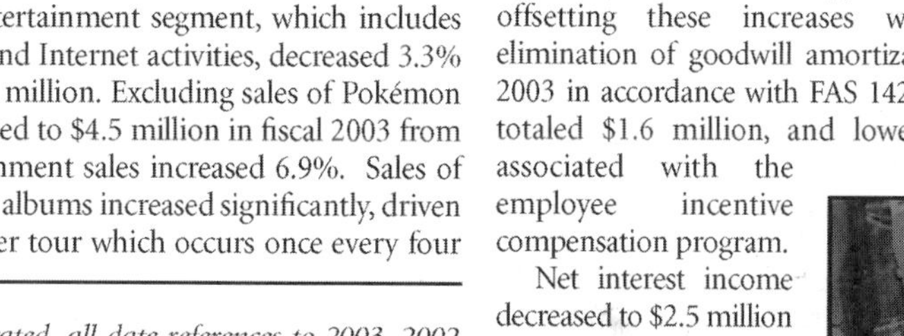

Net interest income decreased to $2.5 million in fiscal 2003 from $4.9 million in fiscal 2002

* *Unless otherwise indicated, all date references to 2003, 2002 and 2001 refer to the fiscal years ended March 1, 2003, March 2, 2002 and March 3, 2001, respectively.*

reflecting less favorable interest rates and a lower average cash balance.

The effective tax rate in 2003 of 27.3% reflects provisions for federal, state and local income taxes in accordance with statutory income tax rates. The decrease versus the 2002 rate of 31.3% was a function of certain one-time R&D and foreign tax benefits received this year.

Net income in fiscal 2003 was $16.9 million, or $0.40 per diluted share, versus $28.5 million, or $0.64 per diluted share in 2002.

Fiscal 2002 Versus 2001

In fiscal 2002, the Company's consolidated net sales decreased $137.2 million or 31.4% to $300.2 million from $437.4 million in fiscal 2001. This decrease was primarily a function of a $155.5 million decline in Pokémon sales to $24.1 million in fiscal 2002 from $179.6 million in fiscal 2001.

Net sales of the Confectionery segment decreased $18.6 million or 10.9% in 2002 to $152.1 million from $170.7 million in 2001. Sales of Pokémon confectionery products decreased $33.0 million to $5.9 million in 2002 from $38.9 million in 2001. Topps branded (non-Pokémon) confectionery sales increased 10.9%, reflecting strong domestic growth of Ring Pop and Push Pop, worldwide growth of Baby Bottle Pop and the introduction of seasonal candy products. Confectionery products accounted for 51% of the Company's consolidated net sales in 2002, compared with 39% in 2001.

Net sales of the Entertainment segment decreased $118.7 million or 44.5% in fiscal 2002 to $148.1 million, reflecting a $122.4 million decrease in sales of Pokémon products to $18.2 million. Sales of traditional sports products decreased 8.4% due to lower sales of football and basketball products, partially offset by higher sales of baseball and European soccer products. Internet activities, which include etopps and thePit.com, generated $5.8 million in sales and $1.4 million in contributed margin losses (before overhead) in the year versus $0.1 million in sales and $0.5 million in contributed margin losses in the prior year. Non-sports card and sticker album releases in 2002 included Lord of the Rings, Monsters, Inc., Planet of the Apes and Enduring Freedom. Entertainment products represented 49% of the Company's consolidated net sales in 2002, compared with 61% in 2001.

Consolidated gross profit as a percentage of net sales decreased to 37.9% in 2002 from 45.7% in 2001. Margins in 2002 were impacted by the reduction in sales of high-margin Pokémon products as well as an increase in sports autograph and relic costs and lower gross profit margins at thePit.com.

Other income (expense) was an expense of $215,000 in 2002 versus income of $3.0 million in 2001 primarily as a result of non-cash foreign exchange losses in 2002 on dollar-denominated cash balances held in Europe, as well as lower levels of prompt payment discounts on European inventory purchases.

Selling, general & administrative expenses increased as a percentage of net sales to 25.7% in 2002 from 18.5% in 2001 as a result of lower sales. SG&A dollar spending decreased to $77.1 million from $81.0 million due to a $2.4 million favorable Internet-related legal settlement, a reduction in etopps overhead expenses and lower marketing expenditures overseas.

Net interest income decreased to $4.9 million in fiscal 2002 from $5.7 million in fiscal 2001 reflecting lower interest rates and a lower average cash balance than in 2001.

The effective tax rate in 2002 of 31.3% reflects provisions for federal, state and local income taxes in accordance with statutory income tax rates. The increase versus the 2001 rate of 30.7% was a function of the lower mix of international earnings and the lower effective rates on those earnings as well as the absence of certain one-time tax benefits present in 2001.

Net income in fiscal 2002 was $28.5 million, or $0.64 per diluted share, versus $88.5 million, or $1.91 per diluted share in 2001.

Quarterly Comparisons

Management believes that quarter-to-quarter comparisons of sales and operating results are affected by a number of factors, including but not limited to new product introductions, the scheduling of product releases, seasonal products and the timing of various expenses such as advertising. Thus, quarterly results vary. See Note 17 of Notes to Consolidated Financial Statements.

Inflation

In the opinion of management, inflation has not had a material effect on the operations of the Company.

Liquidity and Capital Resources

Management believes that the Company has adequate means to meet its liquidity and capital resource needs over the foreseeable future as a result of the combination of cash on hand, anticipated cash from operations and credit line availability.

As of March 1, 2003, the Company had $114.3 million in cash and cash equivalents.

On June 26, 2000, the Company entered into a credit agreement with Chase Manhattan Bank and LaSalle Bank National Association. The agreement provides for a $35.0 million unsecured facility to cover revolver and letter of credit needs and expires on June 26, 2004. Interest rates are variable and a function of the Company's EBITDA. The credit agreement contains restrictions and prohibitions of a nature generally found in loan agreements of this type and requires the Company, among other things, to comply with certain financial covenants, limits the Company's ability to repurchase its shares, sell or acquire assets or borrow additional money and prohibits the payment of dividends. The credit agreement may be terminated by the Company at any point over the four-year term (provided the Company repays all outstanding amounts thereunder) without penalty. The full $35.0 million credit line was available as of March 1, 2003.

In October 1999, the Board of Directors authorized the Company to purchase up to 5 million shares of the Company's common stock. In October 2001, purchases against this authorization were completed, and the Board of Directors authorized the purchase of up to an additional 5 million shares of stock. As of March 2003, the Company had purchased 2.6 million shares against this new authorization. During fiscal 2003, the Company purchased a total of 1.6 million shares at an average price per share of $9.01.

During 2003, the Company's net decrease in cash and cash equivalents was $6.8 million versus a decrease of $37.7 million in 2002. Cash flow from operating activities in 2003 was $6.2 million versus $1.6 million last year, primarily as a result of European tax payments in 2002 on the prior year's Pokémon product sales, partially offset by lower net income in 2003. Cash flow from investing activities this year reflects $3.8 million in capital expenditures, principally on computer software and systems and Ring Pop production equipment, versus the $5.7 million acquisition of thePit.com and $5.1 million in capital expenditures last year. Cash flow from financing activities was driven by treasury stock purchases net of cash received from options exercised of $12.9 million this year versus $24.3 million last year.

Stockholders' equity of $196.8 million in fiscal 2003 was $2.7 million above fiscal 2002 levels, as net income of $16.9 million was partially offset by $12.9 million in net treasury stock purchases.

Future minimum payments under non-cancelable leases which extend into the year 2014 are $1,531,000 (2004), $1,531,000 (2005), $1,531,000 (2006), $1,454,000 (2007), $1,400,000 (2008) and $2,980,000 thereafter.

Future minimum payments required under the Company's existing sports and entertainment contracts, with various expiration dates extending into the year 2004, are estimated to be $12,162,000.

Critical Accounting Policies

The preparation of financial statements in conformity with accounting principles generally accepted in the United States of America requires Topps management to make estimates and assumptions that affect the reported amounts of revenue, expenses, assets, liabilities and the disclosure of contingent assets and liabilities.

On an on-going basis, Topps management evaluates its estimates and judgments, including those related to revenue recognition, intangible assets and reserves, based on historical experience and on various other factors that are believed to be reasonable under the circumstances. Actual results may differ from these estimates. Note 1 to the Company's consolidated financial statements, "Summary of Significant Accounting Policies," summarizes each of its significant accounting policies. Additionally, Topps management believes the following critical accounting policies, among others, affect its more significant judgments and estimates used in the preparation of its consolidated financial statements.

Revenue Recognition: Revenue related to sales of the Company's products is generally recognized when products are shipped, the title and risk of loss has passed to the customer, the sales price is fixed or determinable and collectibility is reasonably assured. Sales made on a returnable basis are recorded net of a provision for estimated returns. These estimates are revised, as necessary, to reflect actual experience and market conditions.

Intangible Assets: Intangible assets include trademarks and the value of sports, entertainment and proprietary product rights. Amortization is by the straight-line method over estimated lives of up to twenty years. Management evaluates the recoverability of intangible assets under the provisions of SFAS 144, based on undiscounted projections of future cash flows attributable to the individual assets.

Estimates: The preparation of financial statements in conformity with generally accepted accounting principles requires management to make estimates and assumptions which affect the reporting of assets and liabilities as of the dates of the financial statements and revenues and expenses during the reporting period. These estimates primarily relate to the provision for sales returns, allowance for doubtful accounts, inventory obsolescence and asset valuations. Actual results could differ from these estimates.

Disclosures About Market Risk

The Company's exposure to market risk associated with activities in derivative financial instruments (e.g., hedging or currency swap agreements), other financial instruments and derivative commodity instruments is confined to the impact of mark-to-market changes in foreign currency rates on the Company's forward contracts and options. The Company has no long-term debt and does not engage in any commodity-related derivative transactions. As of March 1, 2003, the Company had $27.3 million in forward contracts which were entered into for the purpose of hedging foreign exchange risk associated with forecasted receipts and disbursements.

New Accounting Pronouncements

In June 2001, the FASB issued SFAS 141 "Business Combinations." SFAS 141 applies prospectively to all business combinations initiated after June 30, 2001 and to all business combinations accounted for using the purchase method for which the date of acquisition is July 1, 2001, or later. The Company adopted SFAS 141 during fiscal 2002. The adoption of this standard did not have a material impact on the Company's financial condition or results of operations.

In June 2001, the FASB issued SFAS 142 "Goodwill and Other Intangible Assets." SFAS 142 addresses financial accounting and reporting for acquired goodwill and other intangible assets. Under SFAS 142, goodwill and some intangible assets are no longer amortized, but rather are reviewed for impairment on a periodic basis. In addition, the standard includes provisions for the reclassification of certain intangibles as goodwill, reassessment of the useful lives of intangibles and the identification of reporting units for purposes of assessing potential future impairment of goodwill. The standard also required the Company to complete a transitional impairment test within six months of the date of adoption. The Company adopted the provisions of this Statement effective March 3, 2002. Amortization of existing goodwill, which was $1.6 million for each of the years ended March 2, 2002, March 3, 2001 and February 26, 2000, respectively, ceased upon adoption. The Company completed an impairment test of goodwill on August 31, 2002 and concluded that no impairment exists.

In August 2001, the FASB issued SFAS 143 "Accounting for Asset Retirement Obligations." SFAS 143 addresses financial accounting and reporting for obligations associated with the retirement of tangible long-lived assets and the associated retirement costs. The adoption of SFAS 143 was effective March 3, 2002. The adoption of this standard did not have a material impact on the Company's financial condition or results of operations.

In October 2001, the FASB issued SFAS 144 "Accounting for the Impairment or Disposal of Long-Lived Assets." SFAS 144 superseded previous guidance for financial accounting and reporting for the impairment or disposal of long-lived assets and for segments of a business to be disposed of. The Company adopted SFAS 144 during fiscal 2002. The adoption of this standard did not have a material impact on the Company's financial condition or results of operations.

In April 2002, the FASB issued SFAS 145 "Rescission of FASB Statements No. 4, 44, and 64, Amendment of FASB Statement No. 13, and Technical Corrections." Among other changes, SFAS 145 rescinded SFAS 4 "Reporting Gains and Losses from Extinguishment of Debt," which required all gains and losses from the extinguishment of debt to be aggregated and, if material, to be classified as an extraordinary item, net of related income tax effects. The rescission of SFAS 4 is effective for fiscal years beginning after May 15, 2002. The primary impact of SFAS 145 on the Company is that future gains and losses from the extinguishment of debt will be subject to the criteria of APB Opinion 30 "Reporting the Results of Operations – Reporting the Effects of Disposal of a Segment of a Business, and Extraordinary Unusual and Infrequently Occurring Events and Transactions." Therefore, debt extinguishments in future periods may not be classified as an extraordinary item, net of related income tax effects, but instead as a component of income from continuing operations. The adoption of this standard did not have a material impact on the Company's financial condition or results of operations.

In June 2002, the FASB issued SFAS 146 "Accounting for Costs Associated with Exit or Disposal Activities" which is effective for exit or disposal activities initiated after December 31, 2002. SFAS 146 addresses financial accounting and reporting for costs incurred in connection with exit or disposal activities, including restructurings, and supersedes Emerging Issues Task Force (EITF) Issue No. 94-3 "Liability Recognition for Certain Employee Termination Benefits and Other Costs to Exit an Activity (including Certain Costs Incurred in a Restructuring)." Under SFAS 146, a liability related to an exit or disposal activity is not recognized until such liability has actually been incurred, as opposed to a liability being recognized at the time of a commitment to an exit plan, which was the standard for liability recognition under EITF Issue 94-3. As a result of adopting SFAS 146, the Company did not record $570,000 in restructuring expenses in fiscal 2003 and will recognize them in fiscal 2004.

In December 2002, the FASB issued SFAS 148 "Accounting for Stock-Based Compensation - Transition and Disclosure" which is effective for fiscal years ending after December 15, 2002. SFAS 148 provides alternative methods of transition for any entity that voluntarily changes to the fair value based method of accounting for stock-based employee compensation. The Company does not expect the adoption of SFAS 148 to have a material effect on its financial condition or results of operations.

FIN 45 "Guarantor's Accounting and Disclosure Requirements for Guarantees, Including Indirect Guarantees of Indebtedness of Others" was issued in November 2002. FIN 45 elaborates on certain disclosure requirements and clarifies certain recognition criteria related to guarantees. The disclosure requirements of FIN 45 are effective for periods ending after December 15, 2002, and the recognition criteria of FIN 45 are effective on a prospective basis for guarantees issued or modified after December 31, 2002. The impact of FIN 45 on the Company's financial condition or results of operations is not determinable since FIN 45 primarily impacts guarantees issued or modified in future periods.

consolidated statements of operations

The Topps Company, Inc. and Subsidiaries
(In thousands of dollars, except share data)

	Year Ended		
	March 1, 2003	March 2, 2002	March 3, 2001
Net sales	**$ 290,079**	$ 300,180	$ 437,440
Cost of sales	**188,345**	186,339	237,529
Gross profit on sales	**101,734**	113,841	199,911
Other income (expense)	**184**	(215)	2,964
Selling, general and administrative expenses	**81,136**	77,062	80,958
Income from operations	**20,782**	36,564	121,917
Interest income, net	**2,516**	4,894	5,717
Income before provision for income taxes	**23,298**	41,458	127,634
Provision for income taxes	**6,362**	12,996	39,145
Net income	**$ 16,936**	$ 28,462	$ 88,489
Net income per share - basic	**$ 0.41**	$ 0.66	$ 1.97
- diluted	**$ 0.40**	$ 0.64	$ 1.91
Weighted average shares outstanding - basic	**41,353,000**	43,073,000	45,011,000
- diluted	**42,065,000**	44,276,000	46,366,000

See Notes to Consolidated Financial Statements.

consolidated balance sheets

The Topps Company, Inc. and Subsidiaries
(In thousands of dollars, except share data)

	March 1, 2003	March 2, 2002
ASSETS		
Current assets:		
Cash and cash equivalents	**$ 114,259**	$ 121,057
Accounts receivable, net	**25,205**	20,039
Inventories	**28,681**	23,096
Income tax receivable	**2,029**	3,230
Deferred tax assets	**3,267**	4,343
Prepaid expenses and other current assets	**10,302**	11,807
Total current assets	**183,743**	183,572
Property, plant and equipment, net	**14,606**	14,606
Goodwill	**48,839**	46,773
Intangible assets, net	**6,041**	7,251
Other assets	**8,399**	5,748
Total assets	**$ 261,628**	$ 257,950
LIABILITIES AND STOCKHOLDERS' EQUITY		
Current liabilities:		
Accounts payable	**$ 9,074**	$ 10,966
Accrued expenses and other liabilities	**29,243**	30,274
Income taxes payable	**3,942**	5,943
Total current liabilities	**42,259**	47,183
Deferred income taxes	**-**	-
Other liabilities	**22,601**	16,713
Total liabilities	**64,860**	63,896
Commitments and contingencies	**-**	-
Stockholders' equity:		
Preferred stock, *par value $.01 per share, authorized 10,000,000 shares, none issued*	**-**	-
Common stock, *par value $.01 per share, authorized 100,000,000 shares, issued 49,244,000 in 2003 and 49,189,000 in 2002*	**492**	492
Additional paid-in capital	**27,344**	26,824
Treasury stock, *8,564,000 shares in 2003 and 7,143,000 shares in 2002*	**(80,791)**	(67,415)
Retained earnings	**262,877**	245,941
Accumulated other comprehensive loss	**(13,154)**	(11,788)
Total stockholders' equity	**196,768**	194,054
Total liabilities and stockholders' equity	**$ 261,628**	$ 257,950

See Notes to Consolidated Financial Statements.

consolidated statements of cash flows

The Topps Company, Inc. and Subsidiaries
(In thousands of dollars, except share data)

	Year Ended		
	March 1, 2003	March 2, 2002	March 3, 2001
Operating Activities			
Net income	**$ 16,936**	$ 28,462	$ 88,489
Add (subtract) non-cash items included in net income:			
Depreciation and amortization	**5,038**	5,525	4,345
Deferred taxes on income	**1,076**	(3,242)	2,007
Net effect of changes in:			
Receivables	**(5,166)**	(9,176)	14,960
Inventories	**(5,585)**	789	(2,188)
Income tax receivable	**1,201**	8,339	(11,317)
Prepaid expenses and other current assets	**1,505**	(7,446)	1,029
Payables and other current liabilities	**(4,924)**	(26,439)	7,752
Other	**(3,881)**	4,807	(957)
Cash provided by operating activities	**6,200**	1,619	104,120
Investing Activities			
Purchase of subsidiary	**-**	(5,680)	-
Net additions to property, plant and equipment	**(3,807)**	(5,108)	(3,360)
Cash used in investing activities	**(3,807)**	(10,788)	(3,360)
Financing Activities			
Exercise of employee stock options	**1,449**	5,074	3,266
Purchase of treasury stock	**(14,305)**	(29,364)	(21,374)
Cash used in financing activities	**(12,856)**	(24,290)	(18,108)
Effect of exchange rate changes on cash and cash equivalents	**3,665**	(4,225)	236
Net (decrease) increase in cash and cash equivalents	**(6,798)**	(37,684)	82,888
Cash and cash equivalents at beginning of year	**121,057**	158,741	75,853
Cash and cash equivalents at end of year	**$ 114,259**	$ 121,057	$ 158,741
Supplemental disclosure of cash flow information:			
Interest paid	**$ 91**	$ 83	$ 119
Income taxes paid	**$ 12,578**	$ 24,024	$ 30,854

See Notes to Consolidated Financial Statements.

consolidated statements of stockholders' equity and comprehensive income

The Topps Company, Inc. and Subsidiaries
(In thousands of dollars)

	Total	Common Stock	Additional Paid-in Capital	Treasury Stock	Retained Earnings	Other Comprehensive Income (Loss)
Stockholders' equity as of 2/26/2000	$ 129,175	$ 478	$ 18,498	$ (16,677)	$ 128,990	$ (2,114)
Net income	88,489	-	-	-	88,489	-
Translation adjustment	(1,430)	-	-	-	-	(1,430)
Minimum pension liability	(1,584)	-	-	-	-	(1,584)
Total comprehensive income	85,475	-	-	-	88,489	(3,014)
Purchase of treasury stock	(21,374)	-	-	(21,374)	-	-
Exercise of employee stock options	3,266	6	3,260	-	-	-
Stockholders' equity as of 3/3/2001	$ 196,542	$ 484	$ 21,758	$ (38,051)	$ 217,479	$ (5,128)
Net income	28,462	-	-	-	28,462	-
Translation adjustment	(3,304)	-	-	-	-	(3,304)
Minimum pension liability	(3,356)	-	-	-	-	(3,356)
Total comprehensive income	21,802	-	-	-	28,462	(6,660)
Purchase of treasury stock	(29,364)	-	-	(29,364)	-	-
Exercise of employee stock options	5,074	8	5,066	-	-	-
Stockholders' equity as of 3/2/2002	$ 194,054	$ 492	$ 26,824	$ (67,415)	$ 245,941	$ (11,788)
Net income	16,936	-	-	-	16,936	-
Translation adjustment	3,399	-	-	-	-	3,399
Minimum pension liability	(4,765)	-	-	-	-	(4,765)
Total comprehensive income	15,570	-	-	-	16,936	(1,366)
Purchase of treasury stock	(14,305)	-	-	(14,305)	-	-
Exercise of employee stock options	1,449	-	520	929	-	-
Stockholders' equity as of 3/1/2003	**$ 196,768**	**$ 492**	**$ 27,344**	**$ (80,791)**	**$ 262,877**	**$ (13,154)**

See Notes to Consolidated Financial Statements.

notes to consolidated financial statements

NOTE 1

Summary of Significant Accounting Policies

Principles of Consolidation: The consolidated financial statements include the accounts of The Topps Company, Inc. and its subsidiaries ("the Company"). All intercompany items and transactions have been eliminated in consolidation.

The Company and its subsidiaries operate and report financial results on a fiscal year of 52 or 53 weeks which ends on the Saturday closest to the end of February. Fiscal 2001 was comprised of 53 weeks versus 52 weeks in both fiscal 2002 and fiscal 2003.

Foreign Currency Translation: The financial statements of subsidiaries outside the United States, except those subsidiaries located in highly inflationary economies or where costs are primarily U.S. dollar-based, are generally measured using the local currency as the functional currency. Assets and liabilities of these subsidiaries are translated at the rates of exchange as of the balance sheet date. The resultant translation adjustments are included in accumulated other comprehensive income. Income and expense items are translated at the average exchange rate for the month. Gains and losses from foreign currency transactions of these subsidiaries are included in net income. For subsidiaries operating in highly inflationary economies or where inventory costs are U.S. dollar-based, the financial statements are measured using the U.S. dollar as the functional currency. Gains and losses from balance sheet translation adjustments are also included in net income.

Derivative Financial Instruments: Derivative financial instruments are used for hedging purposes by the Company in the management of its foreign currency exposures. The Company does not hold or issue derivative financial instruments for trading purposes.

Gains or losses arising from the derivative financial instruments are recorded in earnings. On March 4, 2001, the Company adopted the provisions of SFAS 133 "Accounting for Derivative Instruments and Hedging Activities" and related standards, as amended. SFAS 133 provides a comprehensive standard for the recognition and measurement of derivatives and hedging activities.

Cash Equivalents: The Company considers investments in highly liquid debt instruments with a maturity of three months or less to be cash equivalents.

Inventories: Inventories are stated at lower of cost or market. Cost is determined on the first-in, first-out basis.

Property, Plant and Equipment ("PP&E"): PP&E is stated at cost. Depreciation is computed using the straight-line method. Estimated useful lives used in computing depreciation are twenty-five years for buildings, three to twelve years for machinery, equipment and software and the remaining lease period for leasehold improvements. In accordance with SFAS 144, the Company periodically evaluates the carrying value of its PP&E for circumstances which may indicate impairment.

Intangible Assets: Intangible assets include trademarks and the value of sports, entertainment and proprietary product rights. Amortization is by the straight-line method over estimated lives of up to twenty years. Management evaluates the recoverability of intangible assets under the provisions of SFAS 144, based on undiscounted projections of future cash flows attributable to the individual assets.

Revenue Recognition: Revenue related to sales of the Company's products is generally recognized when products are shipped, the title and risk of loss has passed to the customer, the sales price is fixed or determinable and collectibility is reasonably assured. Sales made on a returnable basis are recorded net of a provision for estimated returns. These estimates are revised, as necessary, to reflect actual experience and market conditions.

Estimates: The preparation of financial statements in conformity with generally accepted accounting principles requires management to make estimates and assumptions which affect the reporting of assets and liabilities as of the dates of the financial statements and revenues and expenses during the reporting period. These estimates primarily relate to the provision for sales returns, allowance for doubtful accounts, inventory obsolescence and asset valuations. Actual results could differ from these estimates.

Reclassifications: Certain items in the prior years' financial statements have been reclassified to conform with the current year's presentation. Beginning in the first quarter of fiscal 2002, prepress, autograph and relic costs related to future period releases, which previously had been included in prepaid expenses and other current assets, were reclassified to inventory. Autograph, relic and freight costs related to merchandise sold in the period, which previously were included in selling, general and administrative expenses, were reclassified to cost of goods sold.

The Company has adopted the EITF Issue 01-9 accounting standards that require certain trade promotion expenses, such as slotting fees, to be reported as a reduction of net sales rather than as marketing expense. This presentation has been reflected on the Consolidated Statements of Operations for the fiscal years ended March 1, 2003, March 2, 2002 and March 3, 2001.

Income Taxes: The Company provides for deferred income taxes resulting from temporary differences between the valuation of assets and liabilities in the financial statements and the carrying amounts for tax purposes. Such differences are measured using the enacted tax rates and laws that will be in effect when the differences are expected to reverse.

Employee Stock Options: The Company accounts for stock-based employee compensation based on the intrinsic value of stock options granted in accordance with the provisions of APB 25 "Accounting for Stock Issued to Employees." Information relating to stock-based employee compensation, including the pro forma effects had the Company accounted for stock-based employee compensation based on the fair value of stock options granted in accordance with SFAS 123 "Accounting for Stock-Based Compensation," is as follows:

	2003		2002		2001	
	(In thousands of dollars, except share data)					
	As reported	**Pro forma**	As reported	Pro forma	As reported	Pro forma
Net income	**$ 16,936**	**$ 15,586**	$ 28,462	$ 26,721	$ 88,489	$ 87,279
Earnings per share	**$ 0.40**	**$ 0.37**	$ 0.64	$ 0.60	$ 1.91	$ 1.88

In determining the preceding pro forma amounts under SFAS 123, the fair value of each option grant is estimated as of the date of grant using the Black-Scholes option-pricing model with the following assumptions: no dividend yield in any year; risk free interest rate, estimated volatility and expected life, as follows: fiscal 2003 - 4.5%, 35% and 6.5 years respectively; fiscal 2002 - 5.7%, 59% and 6.7 years respectively; and fiscal 2001 - 6.5%, 56% and 6.6 years respectively

NOTE 2

Earnings Per Share

Earnings per share is computed in accordance with SFAS 128. Basic EPS is computed using weighted average shares outstanding, while diluted EPS is computed using weighted average shares outstanding plus shares representing stock distributable under stock-based plans computed using the treasury stock method.

The following table represents the computation of weighted average shares outstanding - diluted:

	Year Ended		
	March 1, 2003	March 2, 2002	March 3, 2001
Weighted average shares outstanding:			
Basic	**41,353,000**	43,073,000	45,011,000
Effect of dilutive stock options	**712,000**	1,203,000	1,355,000
Diluted	**42,065,000**	44,276,000	46,366,000

In the above calculation, the following shares were not included in the effect of dilutive stock options because they had an anti-dilutive effect: 1,532,000 (2003), 469,000 (2002) and 918,000 (2001).

NOTE 3

Accounts Receivable

	March 1, 2003	March 2, 2002
	(In thousands of dollars)	
Gross receivables	**$ 43,250**	$ 37,565
Reserve for returns	**(16,443)**	(15,877)
Allowance for discounts and doubtful accounts	**(1,602)**	(1,649)
Net	**$ 25,205**	$ 20,039

NOTE 4

Inventories

	March 1, 2003	March 2, 2002
	(In thousands of dollars)	
Raw materials	$ 6,162	$ 6,395
Work in process	2,229	1,274
Finished products	20,290	15,427
Total	$ 28,681	$ 23,096

NOTE 5

Property, Plant and Equipment, Net

	March 1, 2003	March 2, 2002
	(In thousands of dollars)	
Land	$ 42	$ 42
Buildings and improvements	2,278	2,291
Machinery, equipment and software	26,621	22,801
Total PP&E	$ 28,941	$ 25,134
Accumulated depreciation and amortization	(14,335)	(10,528)
Net	$ 14,606	$ 14,606

NOTE 6

Intangible Assets

On March 3, 2002, the Company adopted SFAS 141 "Business Combinations" and SFAS 142 "Goodwill and Other Intangible Assets" which require the Company to prospectively cease amortization of goodwill and instead conduct periodic tests of goodwill for impairment. The table below compares reported earnings and earnings per share for the year ended March 1, 2003, with earnings and earnings per share assuming pro forma application of the new accounting standards for the year ended March 2, 2002.

	March 1, 2003	March 2, 2002
	(In thousands of dollars)	
Net income	$ 16,936	$ 28,462
Add back:		
Goodwill amortization	-	1,568
Adjusted net income	$ 16,936	$ 30,030
Adjusted basic net income per share	$ 0.41	$ 0.70
Adjusted diluted net income per share	$ 0.40	$ 0.68

The Company has evaluated its goodwill and intangible assets acquired prior to June 30, 2002 using the criteria of SFAS 141, and has determined that no intangible assets should be reclassified to goodwill. The Company has also evaluated its intangible assets and determined that all such assets have determinable lives. Furthermore, the Company has reassessed the useful lives and residual values of all intangible assets to review for any necessary amortization period adjustments. Based on that assessment, no adjustments were made to the amortization period or residual values of the intangible assets. In order to conform with the definitions contained in SFAS 142, the Company reclassified $1.5 million in deferred financing fees from intangible assets to other assets and $0.8 million in software development costs from intangible assets to property, plant and equipment. Additionally, $1.9 million of deferred tax assets related to thePit.com acquisition were reclassified to goodwill.

SFAS 142 prescribes a two-phase process for impairment testing of goodwill. The first phase, completed on August 31, 2002, screens for impairment; while the second phase (if necessary), required to be completed by March 1, 2003, measures the impairment. The Company has completed the first phase and has concluded that no impairment of goodwill exists. Therefore, completion of phase two of the transitional impairment test was not necessary.

For the year ended March 1, 2003, no goodwill or other intangibles were acquired, impaired or disposed. Intangible assets consisted of the following as of March 1, 2003 and March 2, 2002:

March 1, 2003

	Gross Carrying Value	Accumulated Amortization	Net
	(In thousands of dollars)		
Licenses & contracts	$ 21,879	$ (16,594)	$ 5,285
Intellectual property	12,584	(12,473)	111
Software & other	2,953	(2,602)	351
FAS 132 pension	294	-	294
Total intangibles	$ 37,710	$ (31,669)	$ 6,041

March 2, 2002

	Gross Carrying Value	Accumulated Amortization	Net
	(In thousands of dollars)		
Licenses & contracts	$ 21,879	$ (15,717)	$ 6,162
Intellectual property	12,584	(12,315)	269
Software & other	2,953	(2,477)	476
FAS 132 pension	344	-	344
Total intangibles	$ 37,760	$ (30,509)	$ 7,251

Over the next five years the Company expects the annual amortization of the intangible assets detailed above to be as follows:

Fiscal Year	Amount (in thousands)
2004	$ 1,060
2005	$ 826
2006	$ 826
2007	$ 748
2008	$ 670

NOTE 7

Accrued Expenses and Other Liabilities

	March 1, 2003	March 2, 2002
	(In thousands of dollars)	
Royalties	**$ 6,407**	$ 9,009
Employee compensation	**5,563**	7,136
Payments received in advance	**3,700**	1,391
Advertising and marketing expenses	**2,271**	2,908
Legal settlement	**1,612**	-
Other	**9,690**	9,830
Total	**$ 29,243**	$ 30,274

NOTE 8

Depreciation and Amortization

	Year Ended March 1, 2003	March 2, 2002	March 3, 2001
	(In thousands of dollars)		
Depreciation expense	**$ 3,756**	$ 2,601	$ 1,685
Amortization of intangible assets	**1,160**	1,237	1,004
Amortization of goodwill	**-**	1,568	1,568
Amortization of deferred financing fees	**122**	119	88
Total	**$ 5,038**	$ 5,525	$ 4,345

NOTE 9

Long-Term Debt

On June 26, 2000, the Company entered into a credit agreement with Chase Manhattan Bank and LaSalle Bank National Association. The agreement provides for a $35.0 million unsecured facility to cover revolver and letter of credit needs and expires on June 26, 2004. Interest rates are variable and a function of the Company's EBITDA. The credit agreement contains restrictions and prohibitions of a nature generally found in loan agreements of this type and requires the Company, among other things, to comply with certain financial covenants, limits the Company's ability to repurchase its shares, sell or acquire assets or borrow additional money and prohibits the payment of dividends. The credit agreement may be terminated by the Company at any point over the four-year term (provided the Company repays all outstanding amounts thereunder) without penalty. The full $35.0 million credit line was available as of March 1, 2003.

NOTE 10

Income Taxes

The Company provides for deferred income taxes resulting from temporary differences between the valuation of assets and liabilities in the financial statements and the carrying amounts for tax purposes. Such differences are measured using the enacted tax rates and laws that will be in effect when the differences are expected to reverse.

U.S. and foreign operations contributed to income before provision for income taxes as follows:

	Year Ended		
	March 1, 2003	March 2, 2002	March 3, 2001
	(In thousands of dollars)		
United States	**$ 14,157**	$ 25,275	$ 36,359
Europe	**7,861**	15,744	89,201
Canada	**992**	739	1,762
Latin America	**288**	(300)	312
Total income before provision for income taxes	**$ 23,298**	$ 41,458	$ 127,634

Provision for income taxes consists of:

	Year Ended		
	March 1, 2003	March 2, 2002	March 3, 2001
	(In thousands of dollars)		
Current income taxes:			
Federal	**$ 3,899**	$ 8,609	$ 6,467
Foreign	**3,301**	3,889	27,323
State and local	**146**	614	2,459
Total current	**$ 7,346**	$ 13,112	$ 36,249
Deferred income taxes (benefit):			
Federal	**$ (434)**	$ (719)	$ 1,554
Foreign	**(330)**	262	1,020
State and local	**(220)**	341	322
Total deferred	**$ (984)**	$ (116)	$ 2,896
Total provision for income taxes	**$ 6,362**	$ 12,996	$ 39,145

The reasons for the difference between the provision for income taxes and the amount computed by applying the statutory federal income tax rate to income before provision for income taxes are as follows:

	Year Ended		
	March 1, 2003	March 2, 2002	March 3, 2001
	(In thousands of dollars)		
Computed expected tax provision	**$ 8,154**	$ 14,510	$ 44,672
Increase (decrease) in taxes resulting from:			
State and local taxes, net of federal tax benefit	**617**	900	2,327
Foreign and U.S. tax effects attributable to foreign operations	**(1,387)**	(2,274)	(7,080)
Amortization of intangibles	**-**	549	549
R&D	**(502)**	-	-
Other permanent differences	**(520)**	(689)	(1,323)
Provision for income taxes	**$ 6,362**	$ 12,996	$ 39,145

Deferred U.S. income taxes have not been provided on undistributed earnings of foreign subsidiaries as the Company considers such earnings to be permanently reinvested in the businesses as of March 1, 2003. These undistributed foreign earnings could become subject to U.S. income tax if remitted, or deemed remitted, as a dividend. Determination of the deferred U.S. income tax liability on these unremitted earnings is not practical, since such liability, if any, is dependent on circumstances existing at the time of the remittance. The cumulative amount of unremitted earnings from foreign subsidiaries that is expected to be permanently reinvested was approximately $27.8 million on March 1, 2003.

During the year the Company received a refund in the amount of $1.3 million from a foreign tax credit carryback claim that was filed with the Internal Revenue Service and reduced the provision for income taxes. The successful claim resulted from a favorable ruling in a prior tax year.

Taxing authorities periodically challenge positions taken by the Company on its tax returns. On the basis of present information, it is the opinion of the Company's management that any assessments resulting from current tax audits will not have a material adverse effect on the Company's consolidated results of operations or its consolidated financial position.

The components of deferred income tax assets and liabilities are as follows:

	Year Ended	
	March 1, 2003	March 2, 2002
	(In thousands of dollars)	
Deferred income tax assets:		
Provision for estimated losses on sales returns	**$ 1,290**	$ 929
Provision for inventory obsolescence	**852**	1,075
Tax assets of thePit.com	**581**	1,937
Total deferred income tax assets*	**$ 2,723**	$ 3,941
Deferred income tax liabilities:		
Amortization	**$ 1,224**	$ 2,786
Depreciation	**625**	383
Post-retirement benefits	**(1,889)**	(1,593)
Other	**(504)**	(1,978)
Total deferred income tax liabilities*	**$ (544)**	$ (402)

* *Net deferred tax assets of $3,267 and $4,343 are presented on the Consolidated Balance Sheet in fiscal 2003 and 2002 respectively.*

NOTE 11

Employee Benefit Plans

The Company maintains qualified and non-qualified defined benefit pensions in the U.S. and Ireland as well as a postretirement healthcare plan in the U.S. for all eligible non-bargaining unit personnel. The Company has previously not included information on the Irish pension in this footnote. The Company is also a participant in a multi-employer defined contribution pension plan covering domestic bargaining unit employees.

In addition, the Company sponsors a defined contribution plan, which qualifies under Sections 401(a) and 401(k) of the Internal Revenue Code (the "401(k) Plan"). While all non-bargaining unit employees are eligible to participate in the 401(k) Plan, participation is optional. The Company does not contribute to the 401(k) Plan.

The following tables summarize benefit costs, as well as the benefit obligations, plan assets and funded status associated with the Company's U.S. and Irish pension and U.S. postretirement healthcare benefit plans.

	Pension Benefits		Postretirement Healthcare Benefits	
	March 1, 2003	March 2, 2002	**March 1, 2003**	March 2, 2002
	(In thousands of dollars)			
Reconciliation of change in benefit obligation				
Benefit obligation at beginning of year	**$ 31,662**	$ 27,691	**$ 6,981**	$ 6,836
Service cost	**1,184**	1,003	**225**	217
Interest cost	**2,316**	1,984	**514**	479
Benefits paid	**(1,120)**	(1,200)	**(546)**	(546)
Actuarial (gains) losses	**3,376**	1,467	**2,390**	(5)
Plan amendments/Effect of foreign currency	**440**	717	**(46)**	-
Benefit obligation at end of year	**$ 37,858**	$ 31,662	**$ 9,518**	$ 6,981
Reconciliation of change in the fair value of plan assets				
Fair value of plan assets at beginning of year	**$ 20,329**	$ 17,101	**$ -**	$ -
Actual return on plan assets	**(2,445)**	20	**-**	-
Employer contributions	**689**	4,639	**546**	546
Benefits paid	**(1,120)**	(1,200)	**(546)**	(546)
Participant's contributions/Effect of foreign currency	**738**	(231)	**-**	-
Fair value of plan assets at end of year	**$ 18,191**	$ 20,329	**$ -**	$ -

	Pension Benefits		Postretirement Healthcare Benefits	
	March 1, 2003	March 2, 2002	**March 1, 2003**	March 2, 2002
	(In thousands of dollars)			
Funded status				
Funded status	**$ (19,667)**	$ (11,332)	**$ (9,518)**	$ (6,981)
Unrecognized actuarial (gains) losses	**15,995**	9,486	**1,347**	(915)
Unrecognized prior service cost	**539**	697	**-**	-
Unrecognized initial transition obligation	**(707)**	(608)	**2,298**	2,774
Net amount recognized in the consolidated balance sheets	**$ (3,840)**	$ (1,757)	**$ (5,873)**	$ (5,122)
Components of amounts recognized in the consolidated balance sheets				
Prepaid benefit cost	**$ 1,890**	$ 3,474	**$ -**	$ -
Accrued benefit liability	**(16,879)**	(11,686)	**(5,873)**	(5,122)
Intangible asset	**539**	691	**-**	-
Accumulated other comprehensive expense	**10,610**	5,764	**-**	-
Net amount recognized in the consolidated balance sheets	**$ (3,840)**	$ (1,757)	**$ (5,873)**	$ (5,122)

	Pension Benefits			Postretirement Healthcare Benefits		
	March 1, 2003	March 2, 2002	March 3, 2001	**March 1, 2003**	March 2, 2002	March 3, 2001
	(In thousands of dollars)					
Components of net periodic benefit cost						
Service cost	**$ 1,184**	$ 1,003	$ 817	**$ 225**	$ 217	$ 175
Interest cost	**2,316**	1,984	1,896	**514**	479	474
Expected return on plan assets	**(1,643)**	(1,457)	(1,451)	**-**	-	-
Amortization of initial transition obligation	**(51)**	180	152	**221**	221	221
Prior service cost	**133**	66	(15)	**-**	-	-
Actuarial (gains) losses/Special charges	**875**	491	192	**337**	(22)	(82)
Net periodic benefit cost	**$ 2,814**	$ 2,267	$ 1,591	**$ 1,297**	$ 895	$ 788

As of March 1, 2003 and March 2, 2002, both the qualified and non-qualified pension plans had accumulated benefit obligations in excess of plan assets. Information is as follows:

	Pension Benefits	
	March 1, 2003	March 2, 2002
	(In thousands of dollars)	
Projected benefit obligation	**$ 33,990**	$ 29,150
Accumulated benefit obligation	**$ 30,495**	$ 25,802
Fair value of plan assets	**$ 15,280**	$ 17,420

The weighted-average actuarial assumptions used for the U.S. pension and postretirement healthcare plans are as follows:

	Pension and Postretirement Healthcare Benefits	
	March 1, 2003	March 2, 2002
Discount rate	**6.3%**	7.0%
Expected return on plan assets	**8.0%**	8.5%
Rate of compensation increase	**4.5%**	5.0%

Assumptions for healthcare cost increases are as follows: 10% in fiscal 2003, trending down to a 5.0% increase in fiscal 2008. Increases in healthcare costs could significantly affect the reported postretirement benefits cost and benefit obligations. A one percentage point change in assumed healthcare benefit cost trends would have the following effect:

	1-Percentage Point (In thousands of dollars)	
	Increase	Decrease
On total service and interest cost component	$ 118	$ (97)
On postretirement benefit obligation (APBO)	$ 1,066	$ (914)

NOTE 12

Stock Option Plans

The Company has Stock Option Plans that provide for the granting of non-qualified stock options, incentive stock options and stock appreciation rights (SARs) to employees, non-employee directors and consultants within the meaning of Section 422A of the Internal Revenue Code. Options granted generally vest over two or three years and expire ten years after the grant date. The following table summarizes information about the Plans.

	March 1, 2003		March 2, 2002		March 3, 2001	
Stock Options	**Shares**	**Weighted Average Exercise Price**	Shares	Weighted Average Exercise Price	Shares	Weighted Average Exercise Price
Outstanding at beginning of year	**3,956,127**	**$ 6.88**	4,309,369	$ 6.34	4,684,052	$ 5.81
Granted	**166,000**	**$ 10.12**	599,306	$ 10.55	569,550	$ 9.35
Exercised	**(220,750)**	**$ 6.21**	(768,335)	$ 4.93	(587,058)	$ 3.57
Forfeited	**(143,400)**	**$ 15.68**	(184,213)	$ 14.24	(357,175)	$ 11.25
Outstanding at end of year	**3,757,977**	**$ 6.73**	3,956,127	$ 6.88	4,309,369	$ 6.34
Options exercisable at end of year	**3,383,854**	**$ 6.32**	3,181,109	$ 6.08	3,491,735	$ 5.97
Weighted average fair value of options granted during the year	**$4.12**		$6.86		$5.84	

Summarized information about stock options outstanding and exercisable at March 1, 2003 is as follows:

	Options Outstanding			Options Exercisable	
Exercise Price Ranges	Outstanding as of 3/1/03	Weighted Average Remaining Contractual Life	Weighted Average Exercise Price	Exercisable as of 3/1/03	Weighted Average Exercise Price
$1.76 - $3.53	939,984	4.9	$ 2.60	939,984	$ 2.60
$3.54 - $5.29	612,250	5.5	$ 4.55	612,250	$ 4.55
$5.30 - $7.05	246,500	3.6	$ 6.20	246,500	$ 6.20
$7.06 - $8.81	603,500	3.2	$ 7.81	603,500	$ 7.81
$8.82 - $10.57	1,020,493	7.2	$ 9.90	704,495	$ 9.76
$10.58 - $12.34	335,250	5.6	$ 11.10	277,125	$ 11.00
	3,757,977	5.3	$ 6.73	3,383,854	$ 6.32

NOTE 13

Capital Stock

In October 1999, the Board of Directors authorized the Company to purchase up to 5 million shares of stock. In October 2001, purchases against this authorization were completed, and the Board of Directors authorized the purchase of up to an additional 5 million shares of stock. As of March 1, 2003, the Company had purchased 2.6 million shares against this new authorization. During fiscal 2003, the Company purchased a total of 1.6 million shares at an average price per share of $9.01.

NOTE 14

Segment and Geographic Information

Following is the breakdown of industry segments as required by SFAS 131. The Company has two reportable business segments: Confectionery and Entertainment. Consistent with Topps organizational structure and product line similarities, Entertainment now combines the former Sports and Entertainment segments into one.

The Confectionery segment consists of a variety of lollipop products including Ring Pop, Push Pop and Baby Bottle Pop, the Bazooka bubble gum line and other novelty confectioneries including Pokémon products.

The Entertainment segment primarily consists of cards and sticker album products featuring sports and non-sports licenses, including Pokémon.

The Company's management regularly evaluates the performance of each segment based upon its contributed margin, which is profit after cost of goods, product development, advertising and promotional costs and obsolescence, but before unallocated general and administrative expenses and manufacturing overhead, depreciation and amortization, other income, net interest income and income taxes.

The Company does not allocate assets among its business segments and therefore does not include a breakdown of assets or depreciation and amortization by segment.

Business Segments

	Year Ended		
	March 1, 2003	March 2, 2002	March 3, 2001
	(In thousands of dollars)		
Net Sales			
Confectionery	**$ 146,865**	$ 152,127	$ 170,700
Entertainment	**143,214**	148,053	266,740
Total Net Sales	**$ 290,079**	$ 300,180	$ 437,440
Contributed Margin			
Confectionery	**$ 52,101**	$ 54,880	$ 64,390
Entertainment	**39,313**	47,464	119,653
Total Contributed Margin	**$ 91,414**	$ 102,344	$ 184,043
Reconciliation of contributed margin to income before provision for income taxes			
Total contributed margin	**$ 91,414**	$ 102,344	$ 184,043
Unallocated general and administrative expenses and manufacturing overhead	**(65,778)**	(60,040)	(58,917)
Depreciation & amortization	**(5,038)**	(5,525)	(4,345)
Other income	**184**	(215)	2,964
Income from operations	**20,782**	36,564	121,917
Interest income, net	**2,516**	4,894	5,717
Income before provision for income taxes	**$ 23,298**	$ 41,458	$ 127,634

Net sales to unaffiliated customers and income from operations, as presented below, are based on the location of the ultimate customer. Income from operations is defined as contributed margin less unallocated general and administrative expenses and manufacturing overhead, depreciation and amortization, and other income. Identifiable assets, as presented below, are those assets located in each geographic area.

Geographic Areas

	Year Ended		
	March 1, 2003	March 2, 2002	March 3, 2001
	(In thousands of dollars)		
Net Sales			
United States	**$ 212,464**	$ 220,368	$ 216,780
Europe	**48,555**	48,387	180,419
Other	**29,060**	31,425	40,241
Total Net Sales	**$ 290,079**	$ 300,180	$ 437,440
Income from Operations			
United States	**$ 12,306**	$ 22,579	$ 32,591
Europe	**5,406**	11,216	80,132
Other	**3,070**	2,769	9,194
Total Income from Operations	**$ 20,782**	$ 36,564	$ 121,917
Identifiable Assets			
United States	**$ 213,840**	$ 216,170	$ 171,385
Europe	**41,020**	35,271	101,819
Other	**6,768**	6,509	7,068
Total Identifiable Assets	**$ 261,628**	$ 257,950	$ 280,272

NOTE 15

Acquisition of thePit.com, Inc.

On August 26, 2001, the Company acquired all of the outstanding common stock of thePit.com, Inc., which operates a sports card exchange, for a net $5.7 million in cash. The acquisition was accounted for using the purchase method of accounting. The financial statements of thePit.com, Inc. have been consolidated into the financial statements of the Company. As part of the purchase price allocation, $780,000 ($470,000 for technology and $310,000 for marketing agreements) was reclassified from goodwill to intangibles and is being amortized over 5 years. The amount of goodwill remaining after the reclassification was $4.1 million.

NOTE 16

Fair Value of Financial Instruments

The carrying value of cash, accounts receivable, accounts payable and accrued liabilities approximates fair value due to their short-term nature.

The Company enters into foreign currency forward contracts to hedge its foreign currency exposure. As of March 1, 2003, the Company had outstanding foreign currency forward contracts, which will mature at various dates, in the amount of $27,286,000, with over 60% of the contracts maturing within six months, as compared to $12,504,000 as of March 2, 2002. The fair value of these forward contracts is the amount the Company would receive or pay to terminate the contracts. The approximate pre-tax impact on earnings to the Company to terminate these agreements as of March 1, 2003 and March 2, 2002 was $(400,000) and $519,000, respectively. The Company believes there is no significant credit risk of non-performance by counter parties of the foreign currency forward contracts.

NOTE 17

Quarterly Results of Operations (Unaudited)

	2003				2002			
	1st	**2nd**	**3rd**	**4th**	1st	2nd	3rd	4th
	(In thousands of dollars, except share data)							
Net sales	**$ 87,739**	**$ 69,999**	**$ 66,656**	**$ 65,685**	$ 86,892	$ 81,214	$ 72,052	$ 60,022
Gross profit on sales	**32,635**	**25,296**	**21,649**	**22,154**	37,702	36,207	22,259	17,673
Income from operations	**10,665**	**6,311**	**813**	**2,993**	16,993	12,295	5,917	1,359
Net income	**7,341**	**4,692**	**2,910**	**1,993**	11,629	8,852	6,532	1,449
Net income per share								
- basic	**$ 0.17**	**$ 0.11**	**$ 0.07**	**$ 0.05**	$ 0.27	$ 0.20	$ 0.15	$ 0.03
- diluted	**$ 0.17**	**$ 0.11**	**$ 0.07**	**$ 0.05**	$ 0.26	$ 0.20	$ 0.15	$ 0.03

NOTE 18

Commitments and Contingencies

Future minimum payments under non-cancelable leases which extend into the year 2014 are $1,531,000 (2004), $1,531,000 (2005), $1,531,000 (2006), $1,454,000 (2007), $1,400,000 (2008) and $2,980,000 thereafter.

Future minimum payments required under the Company's existing sports and entertainment contracts, with various expiration dates extending into the year 2004, are estimated to be $12,162,000.

Total royalty expense under the Company's sports and entertainment licensing contracts was $25,344,000 (2003), $25,669,000 (2002) and $46,727,000 (2001).

Advertising and marketing expenses (which encompass media spending and consumer promotions costs) included in selling, general and administrative expenses amounted to $20,145,000 (2003), $18,790,000 (2002) and $21,514,000 (2001).

The Company transacts business in many countries, utilizing many different currencies. It is thus exposed to the effect of exchange rate fluctuations on sales and purchase transactions. The Company enters into both foreign currency forward contracts and options on currency forward contracts to manage these exposures and to minimize the effects of foreign currency transactions on cash flow. Such contracts are entered into primarily to hedge against future commitments. The Company does not engage in foreign currency speculation. The Company may be exposed to credit losses in the event of non-performance by counterparties to these instruments. Management believes, however, the risk of incurring such losses is remote as the contracts are entered into with major financial institutions.

Report of Independent Public Accountants

Board of Directors and Stockholders
The Topps Company, Inc.:

We have audited the accompanying consolidated balance sheets of The Topps Company, Inc. and Subsidiaries as of March 1, 2003 and March 2, 2002, and the related consolidated statements of operations, stockholders' equity and cash flows for each of the three years in the period ended March 1, 2003. These financial statements are the responsibility of the Company's management. Our responsibility is to express an opinion on these financial statements based on our audits.

We conducted our audits in accordance with auditing standards generally accepted in the United States of America. Those standards require that we plan and perform the audit to obtain reasonable assurance about whether the financial statements are free of material misstatement. An audit includes examining, on a test basis, evidence supporting the amounts and disclosures in the financial statements. An audit also includes assessing the accounting principles used and significant estimates made by management, as well as evaluating the overall financial statement presentation. We believe that our audits provide a reasonable basis for our opinion.

In our opinion, such financial statements present fairly, in all material respects, the financial position of The Topps Company, Inc. and Subsidiaries as of March 1, 2003 and March 2, 2002 and the results of their operations and cash flows for each of the three years in the period ended March 1, 2003 in conformity with accounting principles generally accepted in the United States of America.

As discussed in Note 6 of the notes to the consolidated financial statements, in 2003 the Company changed its method of accounting for goodwill and other intangible assets to conform to Statement of Financial Accounting Standards ("SFAS") No. 142.

Deloitte & Touche LLP

DELOITTE & TOUCHE LLP
New York, New York
April 4, 2003

Market and Dividend Information

The Company's common stock is traded on the Nasdaq National Market under the symbol TOPP. The following table sets forth, for the periods indicated, the high and low sales price for the common stock during the last two fiscal years as reported on the Nasdaq National Market. As of March 1, 2003, there were approximately 4,500 holders of record.

	Fiscal year ended March 1, 2003		Fiscal year ended March 2, 2002	
	High Price	**Low Price**	High Price	Low Price
First quarter	**$ 11.06**	**$ 9.35**	$ 10.40	$ 8.78
Second quarter	**$ 10.57**	**$ 8.20**	$ 12.29	$ 9.60
Third quarter	**$ 9.93**	**$ 7.36**	$ 12.16	$ 9.05
Fourth quarter	**$ 9.97**	**$ 7.79**	$ 12.49	$ 9.06

The Company did not pay a dividend in fiscal 2003, and any future dividend payments, should they occur, would require an amendment of the Company's Credit Agreement. See "Management's Discussion and Analysis of Financial Condition and Results of Operations - Liquidity and Capital Resources" and "Notes to Consolidated Financial Statements - Note 9."

selected consolidated financial data

	2003	2002	2001	2000	1999
		(In thousands of dollars, except share data, unaudited)			
OPERATING DATA:					
Net sales	**$ 290,079**	$ 300,180	$ 437,440	$ 374,193	$ 229,414
Gross profit on sales	**101,734**	113,841	199,911	166,895	93,037
Selling, general and administrative expenses	**81,136**	77,062	80,958	72,798	70,534
Income from operations	**20,782**	36,564	121,917	94,852	26,658
Interest income (expense), net	**2,516**	4,894	5,717	1,712	(454)
Net income	**16,936**	28,462	88,489	59,215	15,571
Income from operations per share					
- basic	**$ 0.50**	$ 0.85	$ 2.71	$ 2.04	$ 0.57
- diluted	**$ 0.49**	$ 0.83	$ 2.63	$ 2.00	$ 0.57
Net income per share					
- basic	**$ 0.41**	$ 0.66	$ 1.97	$ 1.28	$ 0.34
- diluted	**$ 0.40**	$ 0.64	$ 1.91	$ 1.25	$ 0.33
Cash dividends	**-**	-	-	-	-
Wtd. avg. shares outstanding					
- basic	**41,353,000**	43,073,000	45,011,000	46,398,000	46,415,000
- diluted	**42,065,000**	44,276,000	46,366,000	47,463,000	46,678,000
BALANCE SHEET DATA:					
Cash and equivalents	**$ 114,259**	$ 121,057	$ 158,741	$ 75,853	$ 41,728
Working capital	**141,484**	136,389	140,487	71,952	24,919
Net property, plant and equipment	**14,606**	14,606	11,181	9,181	7,429
Long-term debt, less current portion	**-**	-	-	-	5,158
Total assets	**261,628**	257,950	280,272	203,313	151,453
Stockholders' equity	**$ 196,768**	**$ 194,054**	$ 196,542	$ 129,175	$ 77,224

Certain items in the prior years' financial statements have been reclassified to conform with the current year's presentation.

Fiscal 2000 and 1999 Net sales and SG&A do not reflect the reclassification of slotting expenses included in the figures for fiscal 2001, 2002 and 2003.

Fiscal 1999 Income from operations includes non-recurring income of $3.5 million related to the sale of the Company's manufacturing facility in Cork, Ireland and of equipment in Cork, Ireland and Duryea, Pennsylvania.

Board of Directors

Arthur T. Shorin*
Chairman, Chief Executive Officer and President

Allan A. Feder
Independent Business Consultant

Stephen D. Greenberg
Managing Director
Allen & Company, LLC

Ann Kirschner
President, Comma International

David Mauer
Chief Executive Officer
E & B Giftware, LLC

Edward D. Miller*
Senior Advisor
Former President and CEO
AXA Financial, Inc.

Jack H. Nusbaum
Senior Partner and Chairman
Willkie Farr & Gallagher

Richard Tarlow
Chairman
Carlson & Partners

Stanley Tulchin*
Chairman
Stanley Tulchin Associates, Inc.

*Nominated to stand for re-election to the Company's Board of Directors at the 2003 Annual Meeting of Stockholders.

Officers

Arthur T. Shorin
Chairman, Chief Executive Officer and President

Scott Silverstein
Executive Vice President

Ronald L. Boyum
Vice President - Marketing and Sales and General Manager Confectionery

Edward P. Camp
Vice President and President -Hobby Division

Michael P. Clancy
Vice President - International and Managing Director, Topps International Limited

Michael J. Drewniak
Vice President - Manufacturing

Ira Friedman
Vice President - Publishing and New Product Development

Warren Friss
Vice President - Internet Business and General Counsel

Leon J. Gutmann
Assistant Treasurer and Assistant Secretary

Catherine K. Jessup
Vice President - Chief Financial Officer

William G. O'Connor
Vice President - Administration

John Perillo
Vice President - Operations

Subsidiaries

Topps Argentina, SRL
Managing Director - Juan P. Georgalos

Topps UK Limited
Managing Director - Jeremy Charter

Topps Italia, SRL
Managing Director - Furio Cicogna

Topps Canada, Inc.
General Manager - Michael Pearl

Topps International Limited
Managing Director - Michael P. Clancy

Topps Europe Limited
Managing Director - Christopher Rodman

Topps Enterprises, Inc.

Topps Finance, Inc.

Corporate Information

Annual Meeting
Thursday, June 26, 2003
10:30 A.M.
J.P. Morgan Chase & Co.
270 Park Avenue
New York, NY 10017

Investor Relations
Brod Group LLC
445 Park Avenue
New York, NY 10036

Corporate Counsel
Willkie Farr & Gallagher
787 Seventh Avenue
New York, NY 10019

Independent Auditors
Deloitte & Touche LLP
Two World Financial Center
New York, NY 10281

Registrar and Transfer Agent
American Stock Transfer & Trust Company
59 Maiden Lane
New York, NY 10038
877-777-0800 ext 6820

Form 10-K — A copy of the Company's Annual Report on Form 10-K as filed with the Securities and Exchange Commission will be available at the Topps website www.topps.com or upon written request to the Assistant Treasurer.

The Double-Entry Accounting System

INTRODUCTION

*To prepare financial statements, a company must have a system that captures the vast numbers of business transactions in which it engages each year. The most widely used system, **double-entry accounting,** is so effective it has been in use for hundreds of years! This Appendix explains the rules for recording transactions using double-entry accounting.*

DEBIT/CREDIT TERMINOLOGY

An account form known as a **T-account** is a good starting point for learning double-entry recording procedures. A T-account looks like the letter "T" drawn on a piece of paper. The account title is written across the top of the horizontal bar of the T. The left side of the vertical bar is the **debit** side, and the right side is the **credit** side. An account has been *debited* when an amount is written on the left side and *credited* when an amount is written on the right side. For any given account, the difference between the total debit and credit amounts is the **account balance.**

The rules for using debits and credits to record transactions in T-accounts are as follows:

					Claims			
Assets		=	Liabilities		+	Equity		
Debit	Credit		Debit	Credit		Debit	Credit	
+	−		−	+		−	+	

Notice that a debit can represent an increase or a decrease. Likewise, a credit can represent an increase or a decrease. Whether a debit or credit is an increase or a decrease depends on the type of account (asset, liability, or stockholders' equity) in question. The rules of debits and credits are summarized as follows:

1. Debits increase asset accounts; credits decrease asset accounts.
2. Debits decrease liability and stockholders' equity accounts; credits increase liability and stockholders' equity accounts.

We now demonstrate the use of debits and credits in the double-entry accounting system.

The General Journal

Businesses find it impractical to record every individual transaction directly into accounts. Imagine the number of cash transactions a grocery store has each day. To simplify record-keeping, businesses rely on **source documents** such as cash register tapes as the basis for entering transaction data into the accounting system. Other source documents include invoices, time cards, check stubs, and deposit tickets.

Accountants further simplify recordkeeping by initially recording data from source documents into **journals.** Journals provide a chronological record of business transactions. *Transactions are recorded in journals before they are entered into ledger accounts.* Journals are therefore **books of original entry.** Companies may use different **special journals** to record specific types of recurring transactions. For example, a company may use one special journal to record sales on account, another to record purchases on account, a third to record cash receipts, and a fourth to record cash payments. Transactions that do not fall into any of these categories are recorded in the **general journal.** Although special journals can be useful, companies can keep records without them by recording all transactions in the general journal. For simplicity, this appendix illustrates a general journal only.

At a minimum, the general journal shows the dates, the account titles, and the amounts of each transaction. The date is recorded in the first column, followed by the title of the account to be debited. The title of the account to be credited is indented and written on the line directly below the account to be debited. The dollar amount of the transaction is recorded in the Debit and Credit columns. For example, providing services for $1,000 cash on August 1 would be recorded in general journal format as follows:

Date	Account Title	Debit	Credit
Aug. 1	Cash	1,000	
	Service Revenue		1,000

THE GENERAL LEDGER

The collection of all the accounts used by a particular business is called the **general ledger.** In a manual system, the ledger could be a book with pages for each account where entries are recorded by hand. In more sophisticated systems, the general ledger is maintained in electronic form. Data is entered into electronic ledgers using computer keyboards or scanners. Companies typically assign each ledger account a name and a number. A list of all ledger accounts and their account numbers is called the **chart of accounts.** A previously stated, accounting data are first recorded in journals. The data are then transferred to the ledger accounts through a process called **posting.** The posting process for the August 1, $1,000 revenue transaction is shown below.

Date	Account Title	Debit	Credit
Aug. 1	Cash	1,000	
	Service Revenue		1,000

Case			
Aug. 1	1,000		

Service Revenue			
		Aug. 1	1,000

ILLUSTRATION OF RECORDING PROCEDURES

We use the following transactions data to illustrate the process of recording transactions into a general journal and then posting them into a general ledger. The transactions data applies to the Mestro Financial Services Company. The journal entries are shown in Exhibit A.1. The general ledger after posting is shown in Exhibit A.2.

1. Acquired $28,000 cash by issuing common stock on January 1, 2007.
2. Purchased $1,100 of supplies on account.

EXHIBIT A.1

Event No.	Account Title	Debit	Credit
1	Cash	28,000	
	Common Stock		28,000
2	Supplies	1,100	
	Accounts Payable		1,100
3	Prepaid Rent	12,000	
	Cash		12,000
4	Accounts Receivable	23,000	
	Consulting Revenue		23,000
5	General Operating Expenses	16,000	
	Accounts Payable		16,000
6	Cash	20,000	
	Accounts Receivable		20,000
7	Accounts Payable	13,000	
	Cash		13,000
8	Dividends	1,000	
	Cash		1,000
9	Supplies Expense	900	
	Supplies		900
10	Rent Expense	3,000	
	Prepaid Rent		3,000
11	Salaries Expense	1,200	
	Salaries Payable		1,200

3. Paid $12,000 cash in advance for a one-year lease on office space.
4. Earned $23,000 of consulting revenue on account.
5. Incurred $16,000 of general operating expenses on account.
6. Collected $20,000 cash from receivables.
7. Paid $13,000 cash on accounts payable.
8. Paid a $1,000 cash dividend to stockholders.

Information for Adjusting Entries

9. There was $200 of supplies on hand at the end of the accounting period.
10. The one-year lease on the office space was effective beginning on October 1, 2007.
11. There was $1,200 of accrued salaries at the end of 2007.

Trial Balance

To test accuracy, accountants regularly prepare an internal accounting schedule called a **trial balance**. A trial balance lists every ledger account and its balance. Debit balances

EXHIBIT A.2

MESTRO FINANCIAL SERVICES COMPANY
T-Accounts, 2007

Assets = Liabilities + Equity

Assets

Cash

	Debit		Credit
1.	28,000	3.	12,000
6.	20,000	7.	13,000
		8.	1,000
Bal.	22,000		

Accounts Receivable

	Debit		Credit
4.	23,000	6.	20,000
Bal.	3,000		

Supplies

	Debit		Credit
2.	1,100	9.	900
Bal.	200		

Prepaid Rent

	Debit		Credit
3.	12,000	10.	3,000
Bal.	9,000		

Liabilities

Accounts Payable

	Debit		Credit
7.	13,000	2.	1,100
		5.	16,000
		Bal.	4,100

Salaries Payable

	Debit		Credit
		11.	1,200
		Bal.	1,200

Equity

Common Stock

	Debit		Credit
		1.	28,000
		Bal.	28,000

Dividends

	Debit		Credit
8.	1,000		

Consulting Revenue

	Debit		Credit
		4.	23,000

General Operating Expenses

	Debit		Credit
5.	16,000		

Salaries Expense

	Debit		Credit
11.	1,200		

Supplies Expense

	Debit		Credit
9.	900		

Rent Expense

	Debit		Credit
10.	3,000		

are listed in one column and credit balances are listed in an adjacent column. The columns are totaled and the totals are compared. Exhibit A.3 displays the trial balance for Mestro Financial Services Company after the adjusting entries have been posted to the ledger.

If the debit total does not equal the credit total, the accountant knows to search for an error. Even if the totals are equal, however, there may be errors in the accounting records. For example, equal trial balance totals would not disclose errors like the following: failure to record transactions; misclassifications, such as debiting the wrong account; or incorrectly recording the amount of a transaction, such as recording a $200 transaction as $2,000. Equal debits and credits in a trial balance provide evidence rather than proof of accuracy.

Financial Statements

Supplemented with details from the Cash and Common Stock ledger accounts, the trial balance (Exhibit A.3) provides the information to prepare the financial statements shown in Exhibit A.4.

EXHIBIT A.3

MESTRO FINANCIAL SERVICES COMPANY
Trial Balance
December 31, 2007

Account Titles	Debit	Credit
Cash	$22,000	
Accounts Receivable	3,000	
Supplies	200	
Prepaid Rent	9,000	
Accounts Payable		$ 4,100
Salaries Payable		1,200
Common Stock		28,000
Dividends	1,000	
Consulting Revenue		23,000
General Operating Expenses	16,000	
Salaries Expense	1,200	
Supplies Expense	900	
Rent Expense	3,000	
Totals	$56,300	$56,300

EXHIBIT A.4

MESTRO FINANCIAL SERVICES COMPANY
Financial Statements
For 2007

Income Statement
For the Year Ended December 31, 2007

Consulting Revenue		$23,000
Expenses		
General Operating Expenses	$16,000	
Salaries Expense	1,200	
Supplies Expense	900	
Rent Expense	3,000	
Total Expenses		(21,100)
Net Income		$ 1,900

continued

Statement of Changes in Stockholders' Equity
For the Year Ended December 31, 2007

Beginning Common Stock	$ 0	
Plus: Common Stock Issued	28,000	
Ending Common Stock		$28,000
Beginning Retained Earnings	0	
Plus: Net Income	1,900	
Less: Dividends	(1,000)	
Ending Retained Earnings		900
Total Stockholders' Equity		$28,900

Balance Sheet
As of December 31, 2007

Assets		
Cash	$22,000	
Accounts Receivable	3,000	
Supplies	200	
Prepaid Rent	9,000	
Total Assets		$34,200
Liabilities		
Accounts Payable	$ 4,100	
Salaries Payable	1,200	
Total Liabilities		$ 5,300
Stockholders' Equity		
Common Stock	28,000	
Retained Earnings	900	
Total Stockholders' Equity		28,900
Total Liabilities and Stockholders' Equity		$34,200

Statement of Cash Flows
For the Year Ended December 31, 2007

Cash Flows from Operating Activities		
Inflow from Customers	$20,000	
Outflow for Expenses	(25,000)	
Net Cash Flow for Operating Activities		$(5,000)
Cash Flows from Investing Activities		0
Cash Flows from Financing Activities		
Inflow from Issue of Common Stock	28,000	
Outflow for Dividends	(1,000)	
Net Cash Flow from Financing Activities		27,000
Net Change in Cash		22,000
Plus: Beginning Cash Balance		0
Ending Cash Balance		$22,000

KEY TERMS

account balance 620
books of original entry 620
chart of accounts 621
credit 620
debit 620
double-entry accounting 620
general journal 621
general ledger 621
journals 620
posting 621
source documents 620
special journals 620
T-account 620
trial balance 622

EXERCISES

Appendix 1-1 *Debit/credit terminology*

Required

For each of the following independent events, identify the account that would be debited and the account that would be credited. The accounts for the first event are identified as an example.

Event	Account Debited	Account Credited
a	Cash	Common Stock

a. Received cash by issuing common stock.
b. Received cash for services to be performed in the future.
c. Provided services on account.
d. Paid accounts payable.
e. Paid cash in advance for one year's rent.
f. Paid cash for operating expenses.
g. Paid salaries payable.
h. Purchased supplies on account.
i. Paid cash dividends to the stockholders.
j. Recognized revenue for services completed; previously collected the cash in Event *b*.
k. Received cash in payment of accounts receivable.
l. Paid salaries expense.
m. Recognized expense for prepaid rent that had been used up by the end of the accounting period.

Appendix 1-2 *Recording transactions in general journal and T-accounts*

The following events apply to Pearson Service Co. for 2006, its first year of operation.

1. Received cash of $50,000 from the issue of common stock.
2. Performed $90,000 worth of services on account.
3. Paid $64,000 cash for salaries expense.
4. Purchased supplies for $12,000 on account.
5. Collected $78,000 of accounts receivable.
6. Paid $8,500 of the accounts payable.
7. Paid a $5,000 dividend to the stockholders.
8. Had $1,500 of supplies on hand at the end of the period.

Required

a. Record these events in general journal form.
b. Post the entries to T-accounts and determine the ending balance in each account.

c. Determine the amount of total assets at the end of 2006.

d. Determine the amount of net income for 2006.

Appendix 1-3 ***Recording events in the general journal, posting to T-accounts, and preparing a trial balance***

The following events apply to Complete Business Service in 2007, its first year of operations.

1. Received $30,000 cash from the issue of common stock.
2. Earned $25,000 of service revenue on account.
3. Incurred $10,000 of operating expenses on account.
4. Received $20,000 cash for performing services.
5. Paid $8,000 cash to purchase land.
6. Collected $22,000 of cash from accounts receivable.
7. Received a $6,000 cash advance for services to be provided in the future.
8. Purchased $900 of supplies on account.
9. Made a $7,500 payment on accounts payable.
10. Paid a $5,000 cash dividend to the stockholders.
11. Recognized $500 of supplies expense.
12. Recognized $5,000 of revenue for services provided to the customer in Event 7.

Required

a. Record the events in the general journal.

b. Post the events to T-accounts and determine the ending account balances.

c. Test the equality of the debit and credit balances of the T-accounts by preparing a trial balance.

Appendix 1-4 ***One complete accounting cycle***

The following events apply to Paradise Vacations' first year of operations:

1. Acquired $20,000 cash from the issue of common stock on January 1, 2005.
2. Purchased $800 of supplies on account.
3. Paid $4,200 cash in advance for a one-year lease on office space.
4. Earned $28,000 of revenue on account.
5. Incurred $12,500 of other operating expenses on account.
6. Collected $24,000 cash from accounts receivable.
7. Paid $9,000 cash on accounts payable.
8. Paid a $3,000 cash dividend to the stockholders.

Information for Adjusting Entries

9. There was $150 of supplies on hand at the end of the accounting period.
10. The lease on the office space covered a one-year period beginning November 1.
11. There was $3,600 of accrued salaries at the end of the period.

Required

a. Record these transactions in general journal form.

b. Post the transaction data from the journal to ledger T-accounts.

c. Prepare a trial balance.

d. Prepare an income statement, statement of changes in stockholders' equity, a balance sheet, and a statement of cash flows.

GLOSSARY

absolute amounts Dollar totals reported in accounts on financial reports that can be misleading because they make no reference to the relative size of the company being analyzed. *p. 317*

accelerated depreciation methods Depreciation methods that recognize depreciation expense more rapidly in the early stages of an asset's life than in the later stages of its life. *p. 209*

account balance Difference between total debits and total credits in an account. *p. 620*

accounting Service-based profession that provides reliable and relevant financial information useful in making decisions. *p. 3*

accounting controls Procedures designed to safeguard assets and to ensure accuracy and reliability of the accounting records and reports. *p. 133*

accounting cycle A cycle consisting of these stages: recording accounting data, adjusting the accounts, preparing the financial statements, and closing the nominal accounts; when one accounting cycle ends, a new one begins. *p. 48*

accounting equation Expression of the relationship between the assets and the claims on those assets. *p. 5*

accounting event Economic occurrence that causes changes in an enterprise's assets, liabilities, or equity. *p. 6*

accounting period Span of time covered by the financial statements, normally one year, but may be a quarter, a month or some other time span. *p. 12*

account receivable Expected future cash receipt arising from permitting a customer to *buy now and pay later;* typically a relatively small balance due within a short time period. *pp. 42, 163*

accounts Records used for classifying and summarizing transaction data; subclassifications of financial statement elements.

accounts receivable turnover ratio Financial ratio that measures how fast accounts receivable are turned into cash; computed by dividing sales by accounts receivable. *pp. 178, 323*

accrual Recognition of events before exchanging cash. *p. 42*

accrual accounting Accounting system that recognizes expenses or revenues when they occur regardless of when cash is exchanged. *p. 41*

accrued expenses Expenses that are recognized before cash is paid. An example is accrued salaries expense. *p. 44*

accrued interest Interest revenue or expense that is recognized before cash has been exchanged. *p. 174*

accumulated conversion factors Factors used to convert a series of future cash inflows into their present value equivalent and that are applicable to cash inflows of equal amounts spread over equal interval time periods and that can be determined by computing the sum of the individual single factors used for each period. *p. 556*

accumulated depreciation Contra asset account that indicates the sum of all depreciation expense recognized for an asset since the date of acquisition. *p. 206*

acid-test ratio (quick ratio) Measure of immediate debt-paying ability; calculated by dividing very liquid assets (cash, receivables, and marketable securities) by current liabilities.

activities The actions taken by an organization to accomplish its mission. *p. 370*

activity base Factor that causes changes in variable cost; is usually some measure of volume when used to define cost behavior. *p. 399*

activity-based management (ABM) Management of the activities of an organization to add the greatest value by developing products that satisfy the needs of that organization's customers. *p. 370*

adjusting entry Entry that updates account balances prior to preparing financial statements. *pp. 44, 174*

administrative controls Procedures designed to evaluate performance and the degree of compliance with a firm's policies and public laws. *p. 133*

aging of accounts receivable Classifying each account receivable by the number of days it has been outstanding. The aging schedule is used to develop an estimate of the amount of the allowance for doubtful accounts. *p. 170*

allocation Process of dividing a total cost into parts and apportioning the parts among the relevant cost objects. *p. 426*

allocation base Cost driver used as the basis for the allocation process. *p. 426*

allocation rate Factor used to allocate or assign costs to a cost object; determined by taking the total cost to be allocated and dividing it by the appropriate cost driver. *p. 426*

allowance for doubtful accounts Contra asset account that contains an amount equal to the accounts receivable that are expected to be uncollectible. *p. 164*

allowance method of accounting for uncollectible accounts Method of accounting for bad debts in which bad debts are estimated and expensed in the same period in which the corresponding sales are recognized. The receivables are reported in the financial statements at net realizable value (the amount expected to be collected in cash). *p. 164*

allowances Reductions in the selling price of goods extended to buyers because the goods are defective or of lower quality than the buyer ordered to encourage a buyer to keep merchandise that would otherwise be returned. *p. 92*

amortization Method of systematically allocating the costs of intangible assets to expense over their useful lives; also term for converting the discount on a note or a bond to interest expense over a designated period. *pp. 202, 252*

amortizing See *amortization.*

annual report Document in which an organization provides information to stockholders, usually on an annual basis. *p. 20*

annuity Series of equal payments made over a specified number of periods. *p. 557*

appropriated retained earnings Retained earnings restricted by the board of directors for a specific purpose (e.g., to repay debt or for future expansion); although a part of total retained earnings, not available for distribution as dividends. *p. 295*

articles of incorporation Items on an application filed with a state agency for the formation of a corporation; contains such information as the corporation's name, its purpose, its location, its expected life, provisions for its capital stock, and a list of the members of its board of directors. *p. 282*

articulation A term used to describe interrelationships among the financial statements. For example, the amount of net income reported on the income statement is added to beginning retained earnings as a component in calculating the ending retained earnings balance reported on the statement of changes in stockholders' equity. *p. 12*

asset exchange transaction A transaction that decreases one asset while increasing another asset so that total assets do not change; for example, the purchase of land with cash. *p. 43*

assets Economic resources used by a business to produce revenue. *p. 4*

asset source transaction Transaction that increases an asset and a claim on assets; three types of asset source transactions are acquisitions from owners (equity), borrowings from creditors (liabilities), or earnings from operations (revenues). *pp. 7, 42*

asset turnover ratio The amount of net income divided by average total assets.

asset use transaction Transaction that decreases an asset and a claim on assets; the three types are distributions (transfers to owners), liability payments (to creditors), or expenses (used to operate the business). *p. 43*

authority manual A document that outlines the chain of command for authority and responsibility. The authority manual provides guidelines for specific positions such as personnel officer as well as general authority such as all vice presidents are authorized to spend up to a designated limit. *p. 134*

authorized stock Number of shares that the corporation is approved by the state to issue. *p. 288*

average cost The total cost of making products divided by the total number of products made. *p. 359*

average number of days to collect accounts receivable Length of the average collection period for accounts receivable; computed by dividing 365 by the accounts receivable turnover ratio. *pp. 178, 323*

average number of days to sell inventory Financial ratio that measures the average number of days that inventory stays in stock before being sold. *pp. 144, 324*

avoidable costs Future costs that can be avoided by taking a specified course of action. To be avoidable in a decision-making context, costs must differ among the alternatives. For example, if the cost of material used to make two different products is the same for both products, that cost could not be avoided by choosing to produce one product over the other. Therefore, the material's cost would not be an avoidable cost. *p. 455*

balanced score card A management evaluation tool that includes financial and nonfinancial measures. *p. 535*

balance sheet Statement that lists the assets of a business and the corresponding claims (liabilities and equity) on those assets. *p. 14*

bank reconciliation Schedule that identifies and explains differences between the cash balance reported by the bank and the cash balance in the firm's accounting records. *p. 139*

bank statement Statement issued by a bank (usually monthly) that denotes all activity in the bank account for that period. *p. 137*

bank statement credit memo Memorandum that describes an increase in the account balance. *p. 138*

bank statement debit memo Memorandum that describes a decrease in the account balance. *p. 138*

basket purchase Acquisition of several assets in a single transaction with no specific cost attributed to each asset. *p. 203*

batch-level costs The costs associated with producing a batch of products. For example, the cost of setting up machinery to produce 1,000 products is a batch-level cost. The classification of batch-level costs is context sensitive. Postage for one product would be classified as a unit-level cost. In contrast, postage for a large number of products delivered in a single shipment would be classified as a batch-level cost. *p. 456*

benchmarking Identifying the best practices used by world-class competitors. *p. 370*

best practices Practices used by world-class companies. *p. 370*

board of directors Group of individuals elected by the stockholders of a corporation to oversee its operations. *p. 285*

bond certificates Debt securities used to obtain long-term financing in which a company borrows funds from a number of lenders, called *bondholders;* usually issued in denominations of $1,000. *p. 255*

bondholder The party buying a bond (the lender or creditor). *p. 255*

book of original entry A journal in which transactions are first recorded. *p. 620*

book value Historical (original) cost of an asset minus the accumulated depreciation; alternatively, undepreciated amount to date. *p. 207*

book value per share Value of stock determined by dividing the total stockholders' equity by the number of shares of stock. *pp. 288, 330*

break-even point Point where total revenue equals total cost; can be expressed in units or sales dollars. *p. 401*

budgeting Form of planning that formalizes a company's goals and objectives in financial terms. *p. 489*

capital budget Budget that describes the company's plans regarding investments, new products, or lines of business for the coming year; is used as input to prepare many of the operating budgets and becomes a formal part of the master budget. *p. 492*

capital budgeting Financial planning activities that cover the intermediate range of time such as whether to buy or lease equipment, whether to purchase a particular investment, or whether to increase operating expenses to stimulate sales. *p. 490*

capital expenditures (on an existing asset) Substantial amounts of funds spent to improve an asset's quality or to extend its life. *p. 216*

capital investments Expenditures for the purchase of operational assets that involve a long-term commitment of funds that can be critically important to the company's ultimate success; normally recovered through the use of the assets. *p. 554*

cash Coins, currency, checks, balances in checking and certain savings accounts, money orders, bank drafts, certificates of deposit, and other items that are payable on demand. *p. 135*

cash budget A budget that focuses on cash receipts and payments that are expected to occur in the future. *p. 499*

cash discount Discount offered on merchandise sold to encourage prompt payment; offered by sellers of merchandise and represent sales discounts to the seller when they are used and purchase discounts to the purchaser of the merchandise. *p. 91*

certified check Check guaranteed by a bank to be drawn on an account having funds sufficient to pay the check. *p. 140*

certified suppliers Suppliers who have gained the confidence of the buyer by providing quality goods and services at desirable prices and usually in accordance with strict delivery specifications; frequently provide the buyer with preferred customer status in exchange for guaranteed purchase quantities and prompt payment schedules. *p. 463*

chart of accounts List of all ledger accounts and their corresponding account numbers. *p. 621*

checks Prenumbered forms, sometimes multicopy, with the name of the business issuing them preprinted on the face, indicating to whom they are paid, the amount of the payment, and the transaction date. *p. 137*

claims Owners' and creditors' interests in a business's assets. *p. 5*

claims exchange transaction Transaction that decreases one claim and increases another so that total claims do not change. For example, the accrual of interest expense is a claims exchange transaction; liabilities increase, and the recognition of the expense causes retained earnings to decrease. *p. 44*

classified balance sheet Balance sheet that distinguishes between current and noncurrent items. *p. 261*

closely held corporation Corporation whose stock is exchanged between a limited number of individuals. *p. 282*

closing See *closing the books.*

closing the books Process of transferring balances from temporary accounts (Revenue, Expense, and Dividends) to the permanent account (Retained Earnings). *p. 48*

Code of Professional Conduct A set of guidelines established by the American Institute of Certified Public Accountants (AICPA) to promote high ethical conduct among its membership. *p. 17*

collateral Assets pledged as security for a loan. *pp. 173, 260*

common size financial statements Financial statements in which amounts are converted to percentages to allow a better comparison of period-to-period and company-to-company financial data since all information is placed on a common basis. *p. 101*

common stock Basic class of corporate stock that carries no preferences as to claims on assets or dividends; certificates that evidence ownership in a company. *pp. 6, 289*

conservatism A principle that guides accountants in uncertain circumstances to select the alternative that produces the lowest amount of net income. *p. 49*

consistency A principle that encourages the continuing use of the same accounting method(s) so that financial statements are comparable across time. *p. 131*

contingent liability A potential obligation, the amount of which depends on the outcome of future events. *p. 248*

continuity Concept that describes the fact that a corporation's life may extend well beyond the time at which any particular shareholder decides to retire or to sell his or her stock. *p. 284*

continuous improvement Total quality management (TQM) feature that refers to an ongoing process through which employees learn to eliminate waste, reduce response time, minimize defects, and simplify the design and delivery of products and services to customers. *p. 370*

contra asset account Account subtracted from another account with which it is associated; has the effect of reducing the asset account with which it is associated. *pp. 165, 206*

contribution margin Difference between a company's sales revenue and total variable cost; represents the amount available to cover fixed cost and thereafter to provide a profit. *p. 396*

contribution margin per unit The contribution margin per unit is equal to the sales price per unit minus the variable cost per unit. *p. 401*

copyright Legal protection of writings, musical compositions, and other intellectual property for the exclusive use of the creator or persons assigned the right by the creator. *p. 219*

corporation Legal entity separate from its owners; formed when a group of individuals with a common purpose join together in an organization according to state laws. *p. 282*

cost accumulation Process of determining the cost of a particular object by accumulating many individual costs into a single total cost. *p. 424*

cost allocation Process of dividing a total cost into parts and assigning the parts to relevant objects. *pp. 364, 426, 435*

cost behavior How a cost reacts (goes up, down, or remains the same) relative to changes in some measure of activity (e.g., the behavior pattern of the cost of raw materials is to increase as the number of units of product made increases). *p. 391*

cost center Type of responsibility center which incurs costs but does not generate revenue. *p. 522*

cost driver Any factor, usually some measure of activity, that causes cost to be incurred, sometimes referred to as *activity base* or *allocation base*. Examples are labor hours, machine hours, or some other measure of activity whose change causes corresponding changes in the cost object. *p. 424*

cost method of accounting for treasury stock Method of accounting for treasury stock in which the purchase of treasury stock is recorded at its cost to the firm but does not consider the original issue price or par value. *p. 293*

cost objects Objects for which managers need to know the cost; can be products, processes, departments, services, activities, and so on. *p. 423*

cost of capital Return paid to investors and creditors for the use of their assets (capital); usually represents a company's minimum rate of return. *p. 555*

cost of goods available for sale Total costs paid to obtain goods and to make them ready for sale, including the cost of beginning inventory plus purchases and transportation-in costs, less purchase returns and allowances and purchase discounts. *p. 86*

cost of goods sold Total cost incurred for the goods sold during a specific accounting period. *p. 86*

cost-plus pricing Pricing strategy that sets the price at cost plus a markup equal to a percentage of the cost. *pp. 358, 401*

cost pool Many individual costs that have been accumulated into a single total for the purposes of allocation.

cost tracing Relating specific costs to the objects that cause their incurrence. *p. 425*

credit Entry that increases liability and equity accounts or decreases asset accounts. *pp. 4, 620*

creditors Individuals or institutions that have loaned goods or services to a business.

cumulative dividends Preferred dividends that accumulate from year to year until paid. *p. 289*

current (short-term) assets Assets that will be converted to cash or consumed within one year or an operating cycle, whichever is longer. *pp. 201, 260*

current (short-term) liability Obligation due within one year or an operating cycle, whichever is longer. *pp. 245, 261*

current ratio Measure of liquidity (short-term debt-paying ability); calculated by dividing current assets by current liabilities. *pp. 261, 322*

date of record Date that establishes who will receive the dividend payment: shareholders who actually own the stock on the record date will be paid the dividend even if the stock is sold before the dividend is paid. *p. 294*

debit Entry that increases asset accounts or decreases liability and equity accounts. *p. 620*

debt to assets ratio Financial ratio that measures a company's level of risk. *pp. 262, 325*

debt to equity ratio Financial ratio that compares creditor financing to owner financing, expressed as the dollar amount of liabilities for each dollar of stockholder's equity. *p. 325*

decentralization Practice of delegating authority and responsibility for the operation of business segments. *p. 522*

declaration date Date on which the board of directors actually declares a dividend. *p. 293*

deferral Recognition of revenue or expense in a period after the cash is exchanged. *p. 42*

deferred tax liability Taxes not paid until future years because of the difference in accounting methods selected for financial statements and methods required for tax purposes (e.g., a company may select straight-line depreciation for financial statement reporting but will be required to use MACRS for tax reporting). *p. 214*

depletion Method of systematically allocating the costs of natural resources to expense as the resources are removed from the land. *p. 202*

deposits in transit Deposits recorded in a depositor's books but not received and recorded by the bank. *p. 139*

deposit ticket Bank form that accompanies checks and cash deposited into a bank account; normally specifies the account number, name of the account, and a record of the checks and cash being deposited. *p. 137*

depreciable cost Original cost minus salvage value (of a long-term depreciable asset). *p. 204*

depreciation Decline in value of long-term tangible assets such as buildings, furniture, or equipment. It is systematically recognized by accountants as depreciation expense over the useful lives of the affected assets. *p. 202*

depreciation expense Portion of the original cost of a long-term tangible asset systematically allocated to an expense account in a given period. *p. 204*

differential revenues Future-oriented revenues that differ among the alternatives under consideration. *p. 454*

direct cost Cost that is easily traceable to a cost object and for which the sacrifice to trace is small in relation to the information benefits attained. *p. 425*

direct labor Wages paid to production workers whose efforts can be easily and conveniently traced to products. *p. 362*

direct raw materials Costs of raw materials used to make products that can be easily and conveniently traced to those products. *p. 361*

direct write-off method Method of recognizing bad debts expense only when accounts are determined to be uncollectible. *p. 171*

dividend Transfer of wealth from a business to its owners. *p. 9*

dividends in arrears Cumulative dividends on preferred stock that have not been paid; must be paid prior to paying dividends to common stockholders. *p. 289*

dividend yield Ratio for comparing stock dividends paid in relation to the market price; calculated as dividends per share divided by market price per share. *p. 331*

double-declining-balance depreciation Depreciation method that recognizes larger amounts of depreciation in the early stages of an asset's life and progressively smaller amounts as the asset ages.

double-entry accounting (bookkeeping) Method of keeping records that provides a system of checks and balances by recording transactions in a dual format. *pp. 7, 620*

double taxation Policy to tax corporate profits distributed to owners twice, once when the income is reported on the corporation's income tax return and again when the dividends are reported on the individual's return. *p. 283*

downstream costs Costs, such as delivery costs and sales commissions, incurred after the manufacturing process is complete. *p. 368*

earnings The difference between revenues and expenses. Same as net income or profit. *p. 4*

earnings per share Measure of the value of a share of common stock in terms of company earnings; calculated as net income available to common stockholders divided by the average number of outstanding common shares. *p. 329*

elements Primary components of financial statements including assets, liabilities, equity, contributions, revenue, expenses, distributions, and net income. *p. 4*

entity See *reporting entities.*

entrenched management Management that may have become ineffective but because of political implications may be difficult to remove. *p. 285*

equipment replacement decisions Decisions regarding whether existing equipment should be replaced with newer equipment based on identification and comparison of the avoidable costs of the old and new equipment to determine which equipment is more profitable to operate. *p. 467*

equity Portion of assets remaining after the creditors' claims have been satisfied (i.e., Assets Liabilities Equity); also called *residual interest* or *net assets. p. 5*

estimated useful life Time for which an asset is expected to be used by a business. *p. 204*

ex-dividend Stock traded after the date of record but before the payment date; does not receive the benefit of the upcoming dividend. *p. 294*

expenses Economic sacrifices (decreases in assets or increase in liabilities) that are incurred in the process of generating revenue. *pp. 9, 12, 47, 63*

face value Amount of the bond to be paid back (to the bondholders) at maturity. *p. 255*

facility-level costs Costs incurred on behalf of the whole company or a segment of the company; not related to any specific product, batch, or unit of production or service and unavoidable unless the entire company or segment is eliminated. *p. 456*

favorable variance Variance that occurs when actual costs are less than standard costs or when actual sales are higher than standard sales. *p. 525*

fidelity bond Insurance policy that a company buys to insure itself against loss due to employee dishonesty. *p. 133*

financial accounting Field of accounting designed to meet the information needs of external users of business information (creditors, investors, governmental agencies, financial analysts, etc.); its objective is to classify and record business events and transactions to facilitate the production of external financial reports (income statement, balance sheet, statement of cash flows, and statement of changes in equity). *pp. 15, 356*

Financial Accounting Standards Board (FASB) Privately funded organization with the primary authority for the establishment of accounting standards in the United States. *pp. 18, 357*

financial statements Primary means of communicating the financial information of an organization to the external users. The four general-purpose financial statements are the income statement, statement of changes in equity, balance sheet, and statement of cash flows. *p. 4*

financing activities Cash inflows and outflows from transactions with investors and creditors (except interest). These cash flows include cash receipts from the issue of stock, borrowing activities, and cash disbursements associated with dividends. *p. 14*

finished goods inventory Asset account used to accumulate the product costs (direct materials, direct labor, and overhead) associated with completed products that have not yet been sold. *p. 358*

first-in, first-out (FIFO) cost flow method Inventory cost flow method that treats the first items purchased as the first items sold for the purpose of computing cost of goods sold. *p. 126*

fixed cost Cost that in total remains constant when activity volume changes; varies per unit inversely with changes in the volume of activity. *p. 391*

fixed interest rate Interest rate (charge for the use of money) that does not change over the life of the loan. *p. 251*

flexible budgets Budgets that show expected revenues and costs at a variety of different activity levels. *p. 523*

flexible budget variances Differences between budgets based on standard amounts at the actual level of activity and actual results; caused by differences in standard and actual unit cost since the volume of activity is the same. *p. 527*

FOB (free on board) destination Term that designates the seller as the responsible party for freight costs (transportation-in costs). *p. 92*

FOB (free on board) shipping point Term that designates the buyer as the responsible party for freight costs (transportation-in costs). *p. 92*

franchise Exclusive right to sell products or perform services in certain geographic areas. *p. 219*

full disclosure A principle that requires financial statements to include all relevant information about an entity's operations and financial condition. Full disclosure is frequently accomplished by adding footnotes to the financial statements. *p. 131*

gains Increases in assets or decreases in liabilities that result from peripheral or incidental transactions. *p. 99*

general authority Policies and procedures that apply across different levels of a company's management, such as everyone flies coach class. *p. 134*

general journal Journal in which all types of accounting transactions can be entered but which is commonly used to record adjusting and closing entries and unusual types of transactions.

general ledger Complete set of accounts used in accounting systems. *pp. 11, 621*

generally accepted accounting principles (GAAP) Rules and regulations that accountants agree to follow when preparing financial reports for public distribution. *pp. 10, 357*

general, selling, and administrative costs All costs not associated with obtaining or manufacturing a product; in practice are sometimes referred to as *period costs* because they are normally expensed in the period in which the economic sacrifice is incurred. *p. 363*

general uncertainties Uncertainties inherent in operating a business, such as competition and damage from storms. Unlike contingent liabilities, these uncertainties arise from future rather than past events. *p. 248*

going concern assumption Assumption that a company will continue to operate indefinitely, will pay its obligations and should therefore report those obligations at their full face value in the financial statements. *p. 245*

goodwill Added value of a successful business that is attributable to factors—reputation, location, and superior products—that enable the business to earn above-average profits; stated differently, the excess paid for an existing business over the appraised value of the net assets. *p. 220*

gross margin (gross profit) Difference between sales revenue and cost of goods sold; the amount a company makes from selling goods before subtracting operating expenses. *p. 86*

gross margin percentage Expression of gross margin as a percentage of sales computed by dividing gross margin by net sales; the amount of each dollar of sales that is profit before deducting any operating expenses. *p. 101*

gross profit See *gross margin.*

half-year convention Tax rule that requires six months of depreciation expense to be taken in the year of purchase of the asset and the year of disposal regardless of the purchase date. *p. 214*

historical cost concept Actual price paid for an asset when it was purchased. *pp. 10, 203*

horizontal analysis Analysis technique that compares amounts of the same item over several time periods. *p. 317*

horizontal statements model Arrangement of a set of financial statements horizontally across a sheet of paper. *p. 16*

income Added value created in transforming resources into more desirable states. *p. 4*

income statement Statement that measures the difference between the asset increases and the asset decreases associated with running a business. This definition is expanded in subsequent chapters as additional relationships among the elements of the financial statements are introduced. *p. 12*

incremental revenue Additional cash inflows from operations generated by using an additional capital asset. *p. 561*

indirect cost Cost that cannot be easily traced to a cost object and for which the economic sacrifice to trace is not worth the informational benefits. *pp. 363, 425*

information overload Situation in which presentation of too much information confuses the user of the information. *p. 316*

installment notes Obligations requiring principal repayments at regular intervals over the life of the loan. *p. 252*

intangible assets Assets that may be represented by pieces of paper or contracts that appear tangible; however, the true value of an intangible asset lies in the rights and privileges extended to its owners. *p. 202*

interest Fee paid for the use of borrowed funds; also refers to revenue from debt securities. *pp. 4, 173*

internal controls A company's policies and procedures designed to reduce the opportunity for fraud and to provide reasonable assurance that its objectives will be accomplished. *pp. 18, 133*

internal rate of return Rate that will produce a present value of an investment's future cash inflows that equals cash outflows required to acquire the investment; alternatively, the rate that produces in a net present value of zero. *p. 560*

inventory cost flow methods Methods used to allocate the cost of goods available for sale between cost of goods sold and inventory. *p. 128*

inventory holding costs Costs associated with acquiring and retaining inventory including cost of storage space; lost, stolen, or damaged merchandise; insurance; personnel and management costs; and interest. *p. 371*

inventory turnover Ratio of cost of goods sold to inventory that indicates how many times a year the average inventory is sold (turned over). *pp. 143, 324*

investing activities One of the three categories of cash inflows and outflows shown on the statement of cash flows; includes cash received and spent by the business on productive assets and investments in the debt and equity of other companies. *p. 15*

investment center Type of responsibility center for which revenue, expense and capital investments can be measured. *p. 523*

issued stock Stock sold to the public. *p. 288*

issuer Individual or business that issues a note payable, bonds payable, or stock (the party receiving cash). See also *maker. pp. 246, 255*

journals Books of original entry in which accounting data are entered chronologically before posting to the ledger accounts. *p. 620*

just in time (JIT) Inventory flow system that minimizes the amount of inventory on hand by making inventory available for customer consumption on demand, therefore eliminating the need to store inventory. The system reduces explicit holding costs including financing, warehouse storage, supervision, theft, damage, and obsolescence. It also eliminates hidden opportunity costs such as lost revenue due to the lack of availability of inventory. *p. 372*

last-in, first-out (LIFO) cost flow method Inventory cost flow method that treats the last items purchased as the first items sold for the purpose of computing cost of goods sold. *p. 126*

legal capital Amount of assets that should be maintained as protection for creditors; the number of shares multiplied by the par value. *p. 287*

liabilities Obligations of a business to relinquish assets, provide services, or accept other obligations. *p. 5*

limited liability Concept that investors in a corporation may not be held personally liable for the actions of the corporation (the creditors cannot lay claim to the owners' personal assets as payment for the corporation's debts). *p. 284*

limited liability companies (LLC) Organizations offering many of the best features of corporations and partnerships and with many legal benefits of corporations (e.g., limited liability and centralized management) but permitted by the Internal Revenue Service to be taxed as a partnership, thereby avoiding double taxation of profits. *p. 284*

line of credit Preapproved credit arrangement with a lending institution in which a business can borrow money by simply writing a check up to the approved limit. *p. 255*

liquidation Process of dividing up the assets and returning them to the resource providers. Creditors normally receive first priority in business liquidations; in other words, assets are distributed to creditors first. After creditor claims have been satisfied, the remaining assets are distributed to the investors (owners) of the business. *p. 4*

liquidity Ability to convert assets to cash quickly and meet short-term obligations. *pp. 14, 176, 261*

liquidity ratios Measures of short-term debt-paying ability. *p. 321*

long-term liabilities Liabilities with maturity dates beyond one year or the company's operating cycle, whichever is longer; noncurrent liabilities. *p. 251*

long-term operational assets Assets used by a business to generate revenue; condition of being used distinguishes them from assets that are sold (inventory) and assets that are held (investments). *p. 201*

losses Decreases in assets or increases in liabilities that result from peripheral or incidental transactions. *p. 99*

low-ball pricing Pricing a product below competitors' price to lure customers away and then raising the price once customers depend on the supplier for the product. *p. 463*

maker The party issuing a note (the borrower). *p. 173*

managerial accounting Branch of accounting that provides information useful to internal decision makers and managers in operating an organization. *pp. 16, 356*

manufacturing overhead Production costs that cannot be traced directly to products. *p. 363*

margin Component in the determination of the return on investment. Computed by dividing operating income by sales. *p. 531*

margin of safety Difference between break-even sales and budgeted sales expressed in units, dollars, or as a percentage; the amount by which actual sales can fall below budgeted sales before a loss is incurred. *p. 402*

market interest rate Current interest rate available on a wide range of alternative investments.

master budget Composition of the numerous separate but interdependent departmental budgets that cover a wide range of operating and financial factors such as sales, production, manufacturing expenses, and administrative expenses. *p. 492*

matching concept Process of matching expenses with the revenues they produce; three ways to match expenses with revenues include matching expenses directly to revenues, matching expenses to the period in which they are incurred, and matching expenses systematically with revenues. *pp. 49, 174*

materiality Concept that recognizes practical limits in financial reporting by allowing flexible handling of matters not considered material; information is considered material if the decisions of a reasonable person would be influenced by its omission or misstatement; can be measured in absolute, percentage, quantitative, or qualitative terms. *p. 317*

maturity date The date a liability is due to be settled (the date the borrower is expected to repay a debt). *p. 173*

merchandise inventory Supply of finished goods held for resale to customers. *p. 85*

minimum rate of return Minimum amount of profitability required to persuade a company to accept an investment opportunity; also known as *desired rate of return, required rate of return, hurdle rate, cutoff rate,* and *discount rate. p. 555*

mixed costs (semivariable costs) Costs composed of a mixture of fixed and variable components. *p. 399*

modified accelerated cost recovery system (MACRS) Prescribed method of depreciation for tax purposes that provides the maximum depreciation expense deduction permitted under tax law. *p. 213*

most-favored customer status Arrangement by which a supplier and customer achieve mutual benefit by providing each other with favorable treatment that is not extended to other associates. *p. 372*

multistep income statement Income statement format that matches particular revenue items with related expense items and distinguishes between recurring operating activities and nonoperating items such as gains and losses. *p. 97*

natural resources Mineral deposits, oil and gas reserves, and reserves of timber, mines, and quarries are examples; sometimes called *wasting assets* because their value wastes away as the resources are removed. *p. 202*

net income Increase in net assets resulting from operating the business. *p. 12*

net income percentage Another term for *return on sales.* Refer to *return on sales* for the definition. *p. 102*

net loss Decrease in net assets resulting from operating the business. *p. 12*

net margin Profitability measurement that indicates the percentage of each sales dollar resulting in profit; calculated as net income divided by net sales. *p. 327*

net method A method of accounting for cash discounts that records inventory purchases at the net price (the list price minus the purchase discount). *p. 91*

net present value Evaluation technique that uses a desired rate of return to discount future cash flows back to their present value equivalents and then subtracts the cost of the investment from the present value equivalents to determine the net present value. A zero or positive net present value (present value of cash inflows equals or exceeds the present value of cash outflows) implies that the investment opportunity provides an acceptable rate of return. *p. 560*

net realizable value Face amount of receivables less an allowance for accounts whose collection is doubtful (amount actually expected to be collected). *p. 164*

net sales Sales less returns from customers and allowances or cash discounts given to customers. *p. 101*

non-sufficient-funds (NSF) check Customer's check deposited but returned by the bank on which it was drawn because the customer did not have enough funds in its account to pay the check. *p. 140*

nonvalue-added activities Tasks undertaken that do not contribute to a product's ability to satisfy customer needs. *p. 370*

note payable A liability that results from executing a legal document called a *promissory note* which describes the interest rate, maturity date, collateral, and so on. *p. 246*

notes receivable Notes that evidence rights to receive cash in the future from the maker of a *promissory note*; usually specify the maturity date, interest rate, and other credit terms. *p. 163*

operating activities Cash inflows and outflows associated with operating the business. These cash flows normally result from revenue and expense transactions including interest. *p. 15*

operating budgets Budgets prepared by different departments within a company that will become a part of the company's master budget; typically include a sales budget, an inventory purchases budget, a selling and administrative budget, and a cash budget. *p. 492*

operating cycle Time required to turn cash into inventory, inventory into receivables, and receivables back to cash. *pp. 180, 260*

operating income (or loss) Income statement subtotal representing the difference between operating revenues and operating expenses, but before recognizing gains and losses from peripheral activities which are added to or subtracted from operating income to determine net income or loss. *p. 97*

operating leverage Operating condition in which a percentage change in revenue produces a proportionately larger percentage change in net income; measured by dividing the contribution margin by net income. The higher the proportion of fixed cost to total costs, the greater the operating leverage. *p. 392*

opportunity cost Cost of lost opportunities such as the failure to make sales due to an insufficient supply of inventory or the wage a working student forgoes to attend class. *pp. 104, 373, 457*

ordinary annuity Annuity whose cash inflows occur at the end of each accounting period. *p. 558*

outsourcing The practice of buying goods and services from another company rather than producing them internally. *p. 461*

outstanding checks Checks deducted from the depositor's cash account balance but not yet presented to the bank for payment. *p. 139*

outstanding stock Stock owned by outside parties; normally the amount of stock issued less the amount of treasury stock. *p. 288*

overhead Costs associated with producing products that cannot be cost effectively traced to products including indirect costs such as indirect materials, indirect labor, utilities, rent, and depreciation. *p. 358*

overhead costs Indirect costs of doing business that cannot be directly traced to a product, department, or process, such as depreciation. *p. 425*

paid-in capital in excess of par (or stated) value Any amount received above the par or stated value of stock when stock is issued. *p. 290*

participative budgeting Budget technique that allows subordinates to participate with upper-level managers in setting budget objectives, thereby encouraging cooperation and support in the attainment of the company's goals. *p. 492*

partnership agreement Legal document that defines the responsibilities of each partner and describes the division of income and losses. *p. 282*

partnerships Business entities owned by at least two people who share talents, capital, and the risks of the business. *p. 282*

par value Arbitrary value assigned to stock by the board of directors. *p. 287*

patent Legal right granted by the U.S. Patent Office ensuring a company or an individual the exclusive right to a product or process. *p. 218*

payback method Technique that evaluates investment opportunities by determining the length of time necessary to recover the initial net investment through incremental revenue or cost savings; the shorter the period, the better the investment opportunity. *p. 568*

payee The party collecting cash. *p. 173*

payment date Date on which a dividend is actually paid. *p. 294*

percentage analysis Analysis of relationships between two different items to draw conclusions or make decisions. *p. 318*

percent of receivables method Estimating the amount of the allowance for doubtful accounts as a percentage of the outstanding receivables balance. The percentage is typically based on a combination of factors such as historical experience, economic conditions, and the company's credit policies. *p. 170*

percent of revenue method Estimating the amount of uncollectible accounts expense as a percentage of the revenue earned on account during the accounting period. The percentage is typically based on a combination of factors such as historical experience, economic conditions, and the company's credit policies. *p. 169*

period costs General, selling, and administrative costs that are expensed in the period in which the economic sacrifice is made. *pp. 49, 86, 363*

periodic inventory system Method of accounting for changes in the Inventory account only at the end of the accounting period. *p. 106*

permanent accounts Accounts that contain information transferred from one accounting period to the next. *p. 48*

perpetual (continuous) budgeting Continuous budgeting activity normally covering a 12-month time span by replacing the current month's budget at the end of each month with a new budget; keeps management constantly involved in the budget process so that changing conditions are incorporated on a timely bases. *p. 491*

perpetual inventory system Method of accounting for inventories that increases the Inventory account each time merchandise is purchased and decreases it each time merchandise is sold. *p. 88*

physical flow of goods Physical movement of goods through the business; normally a FIFO flow so that the first goods purchased are the first goods delivered to customers, thereby reducing the likelihood of obsolete inventory. *p. 126*

plant assets to long-term liabilities Financial ratio that suggests how well a company manages its long-term debt. *p. 326*

postaudit Repeat calculation using the techniques originally employed to analyze an investment project; accomplished with the use of actual data available at the completion of the investment project so that the actual results can be compared with expected results based on estimated data at the beginning of the project. Its purpose is to provide feedback as to whether the expected results were actually accomplished in improving the accuracy of future analysis. *p. 571*

posting Process of copying information from journals to ledgers. *p. 621*

preferred stock Stock that receives some form of preferential treatment (usually as to dividends) over common stock; normally has no voting rights.

prepaid items Deferred expenses. An example is prepaid insurance. *p. 50*

present value index Present value of cash inflows divided by the present value of cash outflows. Higher index numbers indicate higher rates of return. *p. 564*

present value table Table that consists of a list of factors to use in converting future values into their present value equivalents; composed of columns that represent different return rates and rows that depict different periods of time. *p. 556*

price-earnings (P/E) ratio Measurement used to compare the values of different stocks in terms of earnings; calculated as market price per share divided by earnings per share. *pp. 59, 330*

principal Amount of cash actually borrowed. *p. 173*

procedures manual Manual that sets forth the accounting procedures to be followed. *p. 134*

product costing Classification and accumulation of individual inputs (materials, labor, and overhead) for determining the cost of making a good or providing a service. *pp. 86, 358*

product costs All costs related to obtaining or manufacturing a product intended for sale to customers; are accumulated in inventory accounts and expensed as cost of goods sold at the point of sale. For a manufacturing company, product costs include direct materials, direct labor, and manufacturing overhead. *p. 363*

productive assets Assets used to operate the business; frequently called *long-term assets*. *p. 15*

product-level costs Costs incurred to support different kinds of products or services; can be avoided by the elimination of a product line or a type of service. *p. 456*

profitability ratios Measurements of a firm's ability to generate earnings. *p. 331*

profit center Type of responsibility center for which both revenues and costs can be indentified. *p. 522*

pro forma financial statements Budgeted financial statements prepared from the information in the master budget. *p. 492*

promissory note A legal document representing a credit agreement between a lender and a borrower. The note specifies technical details such as the maker, payee, interest rate, maturity date, payment terms, and any collateral. *p. 173*

property, plant, and equipment Category of assets, sometimes called *plant assets*, used to produce products or to carry on the administrative and selling functions of a business; includes machinery and equipment, buildings, and land. *p. 202*

purchase discount Reduction in the gross price of merchandise extended under the condition that the purchaser pay cash for the merchandise within a stated time (usually within 10 days of the date of the sale). *p. 91*

qualitative characteristics Nonquantifiable features such as company reputation, welfare of employees, and customer satisfaction that can be affected by certain decisions. *p. 459*

quantitative characteristics Numbers in decision making subject to mathematical manipulation, such as the dollar amounts of revenues and expenses. *p. 459*

quick ratio See *acid-test ratio. p. 322*

ratio analysis See *percentage analysis. p. 321*

raw materials Physical commodities (e.g., wood, metal, paint) used in the manufacturing process. *p. 361*

realization A term that usually refers to actually collecting cash. *p. 41*

recognition Reporting an accounting event in the financial statements. *p. 41*

recovery of investment Recovery of the funds used to acquire the original investment. *p. 570*

reengineering Business practices designed by companies to make production and delivery systems more competitive in world markets by eliminating or minimizing waste, errors, and costs. *p. 370*

reinstate Recording an account receivable previously written off back into the accounting records, generally when cash is collected long after the original due date. *p. 168*

relative fair market value method Method of assigning value to individual assets acquired in a basket purchase in which each asset is assigned a percentage of the total price paid for all assets. The percentage assigned equals the market value of a particular asset divided by the total of the market values of all assets acquired in the basket purchase. *p. 203*

relevant costs Future-oriented costs that differ between business alternatives; also known as *avoidable costs. p. 455*

relevant information Decision-making information about costs, costs savings, or revenues that have these features: (1) future-oriented information and (2) the information differs between the alternatives; decision specific (information that is relevant in one decision may not be relevant in another decision). *p. 454*

relevant range Range of activity over which the definitions of fixed and variable costs are valid. *p. 398*

reliability concept Information is reliable if it can be independently verified. Reliable information is factual rather than subjective. *p. 10*

reporting entities Particular businesses or other organizations for which financial statements are prepared. *p. 7*

residual income Approach that evaluates managers on their ability to maximize the dollar value of earnings above some targeted level of earnings. *p. 533*

responsibility center Point in an organization where the control over revenue or expense items is located. *p. 522*

restrictive covenants Special provisions specified in the loan contract that are designed to prohibit management from taking certain actions that place creditors at risk. *p. 260*

retail companies Companies that sell goods to consumers. *p. 85*

retained earnings Portion of stockholders' equity that includes all earnings retained in the business since inception (revenues minus expenses and distributions for all accounting periods). *p. 6*

return on equity Measure of the profitability of a firm based on earnings generated in relation to stockholders' equity; calculated as net income divided by stockholders' equity. *p. 328*

return on investment Measure of profitability based on the asset base of the firm. It is calculated as net income divided by average total assets. ROI is a product of net margin and asset turnover. *pp. 328, 530*

return on sales Percent of net income generated by each $1 of sales; computed by dividing net income by net sales. *p. 102*

revenue The economic benefit (increase in assets or decrease in liabilities) gained by providing goods or services to customers. *pp. 8, 12, 55, 63*

revenue expenditures Costs incurred for repair or maintenance of long-term operational assets; recorded as expenses and subtracted from revenue in the accounting period in which incurred. *p. 215*

salaries payable Amounts of future cash payments owed to employees for services that have already been performed. *p. 44*

sales discount Cash discount extended by the seller of goods to encourage prompt payment. When the buyer of the goods takes advantage of the discount to pay less than the original selling price, the difference between the selling price and the cash collected is the sales discount. *p. 97*

sales price variance Difference between actual sales and expected sales based on the standard sales price per unit times the actual level of activity. *p. 528*

sales volume variance Difference between sales based on a static budget (standard sales price times standard level of activity) and sales based on a flexible budget (standard sales price times actual level of activity). *p. 525*

salvage value Expected selling price of an asset at the end of its useful life. *p. 204*

Sarbanes-Oxley Act of 2002 Federal law established to promote ethical behavior in corporate governance and fairness in financial reporting. Key provisions of the act include a requirement that a company's chief executive officer (CEO) and chief financial officer (CFO) must certify in writing that they have reviewed the financial reports being issued, and that the reports present fairly the company's financial status. An executive who falsely certifies the company's financial reports is subject to significant fines and imprisonment. The act also establishes the Public Company Accounting Oversight Board (PCAOB). This Board assumes the primary responsibility for developing and enforcing auditing standards for CPAs who audit SEC companies. The Sarbanes-Oxley Act also prohibits auditors from providing most types of nonaudit services to companies they audit. *pp. 283, 357*

schedule of cost of goods sold Schedule that reflects the computation of the amount of the cost of goods sold under the periodic inventory system; an internal report not shown in the formal financial statements. *p. 106*

Securities Act of 1933 and Securities Exchange Act of 1934 Acts passed after the stock market crash of 1929 designed to regulate the issuance of stock and govern the stock exchanges; created the Securities and Exchange Commission (SEC), which has the authority to establish accounting policies for companies registered on the stock exchanges. *p. 283*

Securities and Exchange Commission (SEC) Government agency responsible for overseeing the accounting rules to be followed by companies required to be registered with it. *p. 356*

segment Component part of an organization that is designated as a reporting entity. *p. 464*

selling and administrative costs Costs that cannot be directly traced to products that are recognized as expenses in the period in which they are incurred. Examples include advertising expense and rent expense. *p. 86*

separation of duties Internal control feature of, whenever possible, assigning the functions of authorization, recording, and custody to different individuals. *p. 133*

service charges Fees charged by a bank for services performed or a penalty for the depositor's failing to maintain a specified minimum cash balance throughout the period. *p. 140*

shrinkage A term that reflects decreases in inventory for reasons other than sales to customers. *p. 99*

signature card Bank form that records the bank account number and the signatures of the people authorized to write checks on an account. *p. 137*

single-payment (lump-sum) A one-time receipt of cash which can be converted to its present value using a conversion factor. *p. 556*

single-step income statement Single comparison between total revenues and total expenses. *p. 97*

sole proprietorships Businesses (usually small) owned by one person. *p. 282*

solvency Ability of a business to pay liabilities in the long run. *p. 261*

solvency ratios Measures of a firm's long-term debt-paying ability. *p. 324*

source documents Documents such as a cash register tape, invoice, time card, or check stub that provide accounting information to be recorded in the accounting journals and ledgers. *p. 620*

special journals Journals designed to improve the efficiency of recording specific types of repetitive transactions. *p. 620*

special order decisions Decisions of whether to accept orders from nonregular customers who want to buy goods or services significantly below the normal selling price. If the order's relevant revenues exceed its avoidable costs, the order should be accepted. Qualitative features such as the order's effect on the existing customer base if accepted must also be considered. *p. 459*

specific authorizations Policies and procedures that apply to designated levels of management, such as the policy that the right to approve overtime pay may apply only to the plant manager. *p. 134*

specific identification Inventory method that allocates costs between cost of goods sold and ending inventory using the cost of the specific goods sold or retained in the business. *p. 126*

stakeholders Parties interested in the operations of a business, including owners, lenders, employees, suppliers, customers, and government agencies. *p. 4*

stated interest rate Rate of interest specified in the bond contract that will be paid at specified intervals over the life of the bond. *p. 256*

stated value Arbitrary value assigned to stock by the board of directors. *p. 287*

statement of cash flows Statement that explains how a business obtained and used cash during an accounting period. *p. 14*

statement of changes in stockholders' equity Statement that summarizes the transactions occurring during the accounting period that affected the owners' equity *p. 14*

static budgets Budgets such as the master budget based solely on the level of planned activity; remain constant even when volume of activity changes. *p. 523*

stock certificate Evidence of ownership interest issued when an investor contributes assets to a corporation; describes the rights and privileges that accompany ownership. p. *282*

stock dividend Proportionate distribution of additional shares of the declaring corporation's stock. *p. 294*

stockholders Owners of a corporation. *pp. 6, 285*

stockholders' equity Stockholders' equity represents the portion of the assets that is owned by the stockholders. *p. 6*

stock split Proportionate increase in the number of outstanding shares; designed to reduce the market value of the stock and its par value. *p. 295*

straight-line depreciation Method of computing depreciation that allocates the cost of an asset to expense in equal amounts over its life. The formula for calculating straight line depreciation is [(Cost − Salvage)/Useful Life]. *p. 205*

strategic planning Planning activities associated with long-range decisions such as defining the scope of the business, determining which products to develop, deciding whether to discontinue a business segment, and determining which market niche would be most profitable. *p. 490*

suboptimization Situation in which managers act in their own self-interests even though the organization as a whole suffers. *p. 533*

sunk costs Costs that have been incurred in past transactions and therefore are not relevant for decision making. *p. 454*

T-account Simplified account form, named for its shape, with the account title placed at the top of a horizontal bar, debit entries listed on the left side of the vertical bar, and credit entries shown on the right side. *p. 620*

tangible assets Assets that can be touched, such as equipment, machinery, natural resources, and land. *p. 202*

temporary accounts Accounts used to collect information for a single accounting period (usually revenue, expense, and distribution accounts). *p. 48*

times interest earned ratio Ratio that computes how many times a company would be able to pay its interest by using the amount of earnings available to make interest payments; amount of earnings is net income before interest and income taxes. *p. 325*

time value of money Recognition that the present value of a promise to receive a dollar some time in the future is worth less than a dollar because of interest, risk, and inflation factors. For example, a person may be willing to pay $0.90 today for the right to receive $1.00 one year from today. *p. 554*

total quality management (TQM) Management philosophy that includes: (1) a continuous systematic problem-solving philosophy that engages personnel at all levels of the organization to eliminate waste, defects, and nonvalue-added activities; and (2) to manage quality costs in a manner that leads to the highest level of customer satisfaction. *p. 370*

trademark Name or symbol that identifies a company or an individual product. *p. 218*

transaction Particular event that involves the transfer of something of value between two entities. *p. 6*

transferability Concept referring to the practice of dividing the ownership of corporations into small units that are represented by shares of stock, which permits the easy exchange of ownership interests. *p. 284*

transportation-in (freight-in) Cost of freight on goods purchased under terms FOB shipping point that is usually added to the cost of inventory and is a product cost. *p. 92*

transportation-out (freight-out) Freight cost for goods delivered to customers under terms FOB destination; a period cost expensed when it is incurred. *p. 92*

treasury stock Stock first issued to the public and then bought back by the corporation. *p. 288*

trend analysis Study of the performance of a business over a period of time. *p. 317*

trial balance List of ledger accounts and their balances that provides a check on the mathematical accuracy of the recording process. *p. 622*

true cash balance Actual balance of cash owned by a company at the close of business on the date of the bank statement. *p. 139*

turnover Component in the determination of the return on investment. Computed by dividing sales by operating assets. *p. 531*

2/10, n/30 Expression meaning the seller will allow the purchaser a 2 percent discount off the gross invoice price if the purchaser pays cash for the merchandise within 10 days from the date of purchase. *p. 91*

unadjusted bank balance Ending cash balance reported by the bank as of the date of the bank statement. *p. 139*

unadjusted book balance Balance of the Cash account as of the date of the reconciliation before making any adjustments. *p. 139*

unadjusted rate of return Measure of profitability computed by dividing the average incremental increase in annual net income by the average cost of the original investment (original cost ÷ 2). *p. 569*

uncollectible accounts expense Expense associated with uncollectible accounts receivable; the amount recognized may be estimated using the percent of revenue or the percent of receivables method, or actual losses may be recorded using the direct write-off method. *p. 165*

unearned revenue Revenue for which cash has been collected but the service has not yet been performed. *p. 51*

unfavorable variance Variance that occurs when actual costs exceed standard costs or when actual sales are less than standard sales. *p. 525*

unit-level costs Costs incurred each time a company makes a single product or performs a single service and that can be avoided by eliminating a unit of product or service. Likewise, unit-level costs increase with each additional product produced or service provided. *p. 455*

units-of-production depreciation Depreciation method based on a measure of production rather than a measure of time; for example, an automobile may be depreciated based on the expected miles to be driven rather than on a specific number of years. *p. 211*

upstream costs Costs incurred before the manufacturing process begins, for example, research and development costs. *p. 368*

value-added activity Any unit of work that contributes to a product's ability to satisfy customer needs. *p. 370*

value-added principle The benefits attained (value added) from the process should exceed the cost of the process. *p. 357*

value chain Linked sequence of activities that create value for the customer. *p. 370*

variable cost Cost that in total changes in direct proportion to changes in volume of activity; remains constant per unit when volume of activity changes. *p. 391*

variable interest rate Interest rate that fluctuates (may change) from period to period over the life of the loan. *p. 251*

variances Differences between standard and actual amounts. *p. 525*

vertical analysis Analysis technique that compares items on financial statements to significant totals.

vertical integration Attainment of control over the entire spectrum of business activity from production to sales; as an example a grocery store that owns farms. *p. 463*

vertical statements model Arrangement of a full set of financial statements on a single page with account titles arranged from the top to the bottom of the page. *p. 57*

warranties Promises to correct deficiencies or dissatisfactions in quality, quantity, or performance of products or services sold. *p. 249*

weighted-average cost flow method Inventory cost flow method in which the cost allocated between inventory and cost of goods sold is based on the average cost per unit, which is determined by dividing total costs of goods available for sale during the accounting period by total units available for sale during the period. If the average is recomputed each time a purchase is made, the result is called a *moving average*. *p. 126*

wholesale companies Companies that sell goods to other businesses. *p. 85*

withdrawals Distributions to the owners of proprietorships and partnerships. *p. 286*

working capital Current assets minus current liabilities. *pp. 321, 561*

working capital ratio Another term for the current ratio; calculated by dividing current assets by current liabilities. *p. 322*

PHOTO CREDITS

Chapter 1
p. 3 Corbis, p. 6 Don Farrall/Getty Images, p. 19 Reuters/Corbis, p. 20 Royalty Free/Corbis

Chapter 2
p. 41 © 2005 by Reader's Digest, p. 49 AP/Wide World Photos

Chapter 3
p. 85 Spencer Grant/PhotoEdit, Inc., p. 86 StockTrek/Getty Images, p. 106 John S. Reid

Chapter 4
p. 125 Royalty Free/Corbis, p. 130 Corbis, p. 132 Martial Colomb/Getty Images, p. 134 Courtesy of Nordstrom, p. 137 Keith Brofsky/Getty Images, p. 140 Kieth Brofsky/Getty Images

Chapter 5
p. 163 France Freeman/Costco Wholesale, p. 177 Janis Christie/Getty Images, p. 180 Jack Star/Photolink/Getty Images

Chapter 6
p. 201 Photodisc/Getty Images, p. 208 Ryan McVay/Getty Images, p. 219 Photodisc/Getty Images, p. 220 AP/Wide World Photos

Chapter 7
p. 245 Mario Tama/Getty Images, p. 251 Ryan McVay/Getty Images, p. 257 AP/Wide World Photos, p. 263 Royalty Free/Corbis, p. 260 Keith Brofsky/Getty Images

Chapter 8
p. 281 Amy Etra/PhotoEdit, Inc., p. 282 Royalty Free/Corbis, p. 285 Courtesy AT&T, p. 288 Jeff Smith/Getty Images, p. 298 Royalty Free/Corbis

Chapter 9
p. 315 Brian Marcus/Bloomberg News/Landov, p. 316 Don Farrall/Getty Images, p. 324 Photolink/Getty Images, p. 327 John Rizzo/Bloomberg News/Landov

Chapter 10
p. 355 Photolink/Getty Images, p. 356 Image reprinted by arrangement with Sears Roebuck & Co., p. 369 Win Mcnamee/Reuters/Landov, p. 372 Courtesy of Ford Motor Company

Chapter 11
p. 391 Courtesy Southwest Airlines, p. 393 Corbis Sygma, p. 400 Costco Wholesale

Chapter 12
p. 423 Royalty Free/Corbis, p. 424 Cele Seldon, p. 427 Courtesy Southwest Airlines, p. 434 Corbis

Chapter 13
p. 453 Corbis, p. 454 Corbis, p. 456 Getty Images, p. 458 Janis Christie/Getty Images, p. 463 Getty Images

Chapter 14
p. 489 Landov, p. 491 Getty Images, p. 495 Getty Images, p. 500 Getty Images

Chapter 15
p. 521 Photo Courtesy Home Depot, p. 522 Corbis, p. 525 Corbis, p. 533 Corbis, p. 534 Digital Vision

Chapter 16
p. 553 Getty Images, p. 555 Getty Images, p. 561 Corbis, p. 564 Getty Images

INDEX

A

D

E

F

G

H

J

K

L

M

N

O

P

Q

R

S

T

U

V

W

X

Z